Handbook of
LABOR ECONOMICS

VOLUME

4B

INTRODUCTION TO THE SERIES

The aim of the *Handbooks in Economics* series is to produce Handbooks for various branches of economics, each of which is a definitive source, reference, and teaching supplement for use by professional researchers and advanced graduate students. Each Handbook provides self-contained surveys of the current state of a branch of economics in the form of chapters prepared by leading specialists on various aspects of this branch of economics. These surveys summarize not only received results but also newer developments, from recent journal articles and discussion papers. Some original material is also included, but the main goal is to provide comprehensive and accessible surveys.

The Handbooks are intended to provide not only useful reference volumes for professional collections but also possible supplementary readings for advanced courses for graduate students in economics.

KENNETH J. ARROW and **MICHAEL D. INTRILIGATOR**

Handbook of
LABOR ECONOMICS

VOLUME *4B*

Edited by

DAVID CARD

ORLEY ASHENFELTER

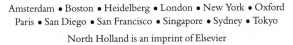

Amsterdam • Boston • Heidelberg • London • New York • Oxford
Paris • San Diego • San Francisco • Singapore • Sydney • Tokyo
North Holland is an imprint of Elsevier

ELSEVIER

North Holland is an imprint of Elsevier
525 B Street, Suite 1800, San Diego, CA 92101-4495, USA
Radarweg 29, 1000 AE Amsterdam, The Netherlands

First edition 2011
Reprinted 2011

Library of Congress Cataloging-in-Publication Data
A catalog record for this book is available from the Library of Congress

British Library Cataloguing in Publication Data
A catalogue record for this book is available from the British Library

ISBN 4A: 978-0-44-453450-7
ISBN 4B: 978-0-44-453452-1
Set ISBN: 978-0-44-453468-2

For information on all North Holland publications
visit our web site at elsevierdirect.com

Printed and bound in Great Britain
11 12 13 14 10 9 8 7 6 5 4 3 2

CONTENTS OF VOLUME 4B

CONTENTS OF VOLUME 4A

Costas Meghir
Yale University, University College London, IFS and IZA

Luigi Pistaferri
Stanford University, NBER, CEPR and IZA

Roland G. Fryer Jr.
Harvard University, EdLabs, NBER

Alan Manning
Centre for Economic Performance, London School of Economics,
Houghton Street, London WC2A 2AE

Daron Acemoglu
MIT, NBER and CIFAR

David Autor
MIT, NBER and IZA

Tito Boeri
Università Bocconi and Fondazione Rodolfo Debenedetti

Enrico Moretti
UC Berkeley, NBER, CEPR and IZA

Douglas Almond
Columbia University

Janet Currie
Columbia University

Sandra E. Black
Department of Economics, University of Texas at Austin, IZA and NBER

Paul J. Devereux
School of Economics and Geary Institute, University College Dublin, CEPR and IZA

Marianne Bertrand
Booth School of Business, University of Chicago, NBER, CEPR and IZA

W. Bentley MacLeod
Columbia University, Department of Economics, 420 West 118th, MC 3308,
New York, NY 10027-7296, USA

Nicholas Bloom
Stanford, Centre for Economic Performance and NBER

John Van Reenen
London School of Economics, Centre for Economic Performance, NBER and CEPR

Paul Oyer
Stanford GSB and NBER

Scott Schaefer
David Eccles School of Business and Institute for Public and International Affairs, University of Utah

CHAPTER 9

Earnings, Consumption and Life Cycle Choices [☆]

Costas Meghir [*], Luigi Pistaferri [**]

[*] Yale University, University College London, IFS and IZA

[**] Stanford University, NBER, CEPR and IZA

Contents

[☆] Thanks to Misha Dworsky and Itay Saporta for excellent research assistance, and to Giacomo De Giorgi, Mario Padula and Gianluca Violante for comments. Pistaferri's work on this chapter was partly funded from NIH/NIA under grant 1R01AG032029-01 and NSF under grant SES-0921689. Costas Meghir thanks the ESRC for funding under the Professorial Fellowship Scheme grant RES-051-27-0204 and under the ESRC centre at the IFS.

Handbook of Labor Economics, Volume 4b

ISSN 0169-7218, DOI 10.1016/S0169-7218(11)02407-5

Abstract

We discuss recent developments in the literature that studies how the dynamics of earnings and wages affect consumption choices over the life cycle. We start by analyzing the theoretical impact of income changes on consumption—highlighting the role of persistence, information, size and insurability of changes in economic resources. We next examine the empirical contributions, distinguishing between papers that use only income data and those that use both income and consumption data. The latter do this for two purposes. First, one can make explicit assumptions about the structure of credit and insurance markets and identify the income process or the information set of the individuals. Second, one can assume that the income process or the amount of information that consumers have are known and test the implications of the theory. In general there is an identification issue that has only recently being addressed with better data or better "experiments". We conclude with a discussion of the literature that endogenizes people's earnings and therefore change the nature of risk faced by households.

JEL classification: E21; D91; J31

Keywords: Consumption; Risk; Income dynamics; Life cycle

1. INTRODUCTION

The objective of this chapter is to discuss recent developments in the literature that studies how the dynamics of earnings and wages affect consumption choices over the life cycle. Labor economists and macroeconomists are the main contributors to this area of research. A theme of interest for both labor economics and macroeconomics is to understand how much risk households face, to what extent risk affects basic household choices such as consumption, labor supply and human capital investments, and what types of risks matter in explaining behavior.[1] These are questions that have a long history in economics.

A fruitful distinction is between *ex-ante* and *ex-post* household responses to risk. *Ex-ante* responses answer the question: "What do people do in the anticipation of shocks to their economic resources?". *Ex-post* responses answer the question: "What do people do when they are actually hit by shocks to their economic resources?". A classical example of *ex-ante* response is precautionary saving induced by uncertainty about future household income (see Kimball, 1990, for a modern theoretical treatment, and Carroll and Samwick, 1998, and Guiso et al., 1992, for empirical tests).[2] An example of *ex-post*

---

[1] In this chapter we will be primarily interested in labor market risks. Nevertheless, it is worth stressing that households face other types of risks that may play an important role in understanding behavior at different points of the life cycle. An example is mortality risk, which may be fairly negligible for working-age individuals but becomes increasingly important for people past their retirement age. Another example is interest rate risk, which may influence portfolio choice and optimal asset allocation decisions. In recent years, there has been a renewed interest in studying the so-called "wealth effect", i.e., how shocks to the value of assets (primarily stocks and real estate) influence consumption. Another branch of the literature has studied the interaction between interest rate risk and labor market risk. Davis and Willen (2000) study if households use portfolio decisions optimally to hedge against labor market risk.

[2] The precautionary motive for saving was also discussed in passing by Keynes (1936), and analyzed more formally by Sandmo (1970), and Modigliani and Sterling (1983). Kimball (1990) shows that to generate a precautionary motive for

response is downward revision of consumption as a result of a negative income shock (see Hall and Mishkin, 1982; Heathcote et al., 2007). More broadly, *ex-ante* responses to risk may include:[3] (a) precautionary labor supply, i.e., cutting the consumption of leisure rather than the consumption of goods (Low, 2005) (b) delaying the adjustment to the optimal stock of durable goods in models with fixed adjustment costs of the (S,s) variety (Bertola et al., 2005); (c) shifting the optimal asset allocation towards safer assets in asset pricing models with incomplete markets (Davis and Willen, 2000); (d) increasing the amount of insurance against formally insurable events (such as a fire in the home) when the risk of facing an independent, uninsurable event (such as a negative productivity shock) increases (known as "background risk" effects, see Gollier and Pratt, 1996, for theory and Guiso et al., 1996, for an empirical test); (e) and various forms of income smoothing activities, such as signing implicit contracts with employers that promise to keep wages constant in the face of variable labor productivity (see Azariadis, 1975 and Baily (1977), for a theoretical discussion and Guiso et al., 2005, for a recent test using matched employer–employee data), or even making occupational or educational choices that are associated with less volatile earnings profiles. *Ex-post* responses include: (a) running down assets or borrowing at high(er) cost (Sullivan, 2008); (b) selling durables (Browning and Crossley, 2003);[4] (c) change (family) labor supply (at the intensive and extensive margin), including changing investment in the human capital of children (Attanasio et al., 2008; Beegle et al., 2004; Ginja, 2010); (d) using family networks, loans from friends, etc. (Hayashi et al., 1996; Angelucci et al., 2010); (e) relocating or migrating (presumably for lack of local job opportunities) or changing job (presumably because of increased firm risk) (Blanchard and Katz, 1992); (f) applying for government-provided insurance (see Gruber, 1997; Gruber and Yelowitz, 1999; Blundell and Pistaferri, 2003; Kniesner and Ziliak, 2002); (g) using charities (Dehejia et al., 2007).

Ex-ante and *ex-post* responses are clearly governed by the same underlying forces. The *ex-post* impact of an income shock on consumption is much attenuated if consumers have access to sources of insurance (both self-insurance and outside insurance) allowing them to smooth intertemporally their marginal utility. Similarly, *ex-ante* responses may be amplified by the expectation of borrowing constraints (which limit the ability to smooth *ex-post* temporary fluctuations in income). Thus, the structure of credit and insurance

---

saving, individuals must have preferences characterized by prudence (convex marginal utility). Besley (1995) and Carroll and Kimball (2005) discuss a case in which precautionary saving may emerge even for non-prudent consumers facing binding liquidity constraints.

[3] We will use the terms "risk" and "uncertainty" interchangeably. In reality, there is a technical difference between the two, dating back to Knight (1921). A risky event has an unknown outcome, but the underlying outcome distribution is known (a "known unknown"). An uncertain event also involves an unknown outcome, but the underlying distribution is unknown as well (an "unknown unknown"). According to Knight, the difference between risk and uncertainty is akin to the difference between objective and subjective probability.

[4] Frictions may make this channel excessively costly, although in recent times efficiency has increased due to the positive effect exerted by the Internet revolution (i.e., selling items on *ebay*).

markets and the nature of the income process, including the persistence and the volatility of shocks as well as the sources of risk, underlie both the *ex-ante* and the *ex-post* responses.

Understanding how much risk and what types of risks people face is important for a number of reasons. First, the list of possible behavioral responses given above suggests that fluctuations in microeconomic uncertainty can generate important fluctuations in aggregate savings, consumption, and growth.[5] The importance of risk and of its measurement is well captured in the following quote from Browning et al. (1999):

> *"In order to...quantify the impact of the precautionary motive for savings on both the aggregate capital stock and the equilibrium interest rate...analysts require a measure of the magnitude of microeconomic uncertainty, and how that uncertainty evolves over the business cycle".*

Another reason to care about risk is for its policy implications. Most of the labor market risks we will study (such as risk of unemployment, of becoming disabled, and generally of low productivity on the job due to health, employer mismatch, etc.) have negative effects on people's welfare and hence there would in principle be a demand for insurance against them. However, these risks are subject to important adverse selection and moral hazard issues. For example, individuals who were fully insured against the event of unemployment would have little incentive to exert effort on the job. Moreover, even if informational asymmetries could be overcome, enforcement of insurance contracts would be at best limited. For these reasons, we typically do not observe the emergence of a private market for insuring productivity or unemployment risks. As in many cases of market failure, the burden of insuring individuals against these risks is taken on (at least in part) by the government. A classical normative question is: How should government insurance programs be optimally designed? The answer depends partly on the amount and characteristics of risks being insured. To give an example, welfare reform that make admission into social insurance programs more stringent (as heavily discussed in the Disability Insurance literature) reduce disincentives to work or apply when not eligible, but also curtails insurance to the truly eligible (Low and Pistaferri, 2010). To be able to assess the importance of the latter problem is crucial to know how much smoothing is achieved by individuals on their own and how large disability risk is. A broader issue is whether the government should step in to provide insurance against "initial conditions", such as the risk of being born to bad parents or that of growing up in bad neighborhoods.

Finally, the impact of shocks on behavior also matters for the purposes of understanding the likely effectiveness of stabilization or "stimulus" policies, another classical question in economics. As we shall see, the modern theory of intertemporal consumption draws a sharp distinction between income changes that are anticipated and those that are not (i.e., shocks); it also highlights that consumption should respond more strongly to persistent shocks vis-à-vis shocks that do not last long. Hence, the standard

---

[5] If risk is countercyclical, it may also provide an explanation for the equity premium puzzle, see Mankiw (1986).

model predicts that consumption may be affected *immediately* by the announcement of persistent tax reforms to occur at some point in the future. Consumption will not change at the time the reform is actually implemented because there are no news in a plan that is implemented as expected. The model also predicts that consumption is substantially affected by a surprise permanent tax reform that happens today. What allows people to disconnect their consumption from the vagaries of their incomes is the ability to transfer resources across periods by borrowing or putting money aside. Naturally, the possibility of liquidity constraints makes these predictions much less sharp. For example, consumers who are liquidity constrained will not be able to change their consumption at the time of the announcement of a permanent tax change, but only at the time of the actual passing of the reform (this is sometimes termed *excess sensitivity of consumption to predicted income changes*). Moreover, even an unexpected tax reform that is transitory in nature may induce large consumption responses.

These are all *ex-post* response considerations. As far as *ex-ante* responses are concerned, uncertainty about future income realizations or policy uncertainty itself will also impact consumption. The response of consumers to an increase in risk is to reduce consumption—or increase savings. This opens up another path for stabilization policies. For example, if the policy objective is to stimulate consumption, one way of achieving this would be to reduce the amount of risk that people face (such as making firing more costly to firms, etc.) or credibly committing to policy stability. All these issues are further complicated when viewed from a General Equilibrium perspective: a usual example is that stabilization policies are accompanied by increases in future taxation, which consumers may anticipate.

Knowing the stochastic structure of income has relevance besides its role for explaining consumption fluctuations, as important as they may be. Consider the rise in wage and earnings inequality that has taken place in many economies over the last 30 years (especially in the US and in the UK). This poses a number of questions: Does the rise in inequality translate into an increase in the extent of risk that people face? There is much discussion in the press and policy circles about the possibility that idiosyncratic risk has been increasing and that it has been progressively shifted from firms and governments onto workers (one oft-cited example is the move from defined benefit pensions, where firms bear the risk of underperforming stock markets, to defined contribution pensions, where workers do).[6] This shift has happened despite the "great moderation" taking place at the aggregate level. Another important issue to consider is whether the rise in inequality is a permanent or a more temporary phenomenon, because a policy intervention aimed at reducing the latter (such as income maintenance policies) differs radically from a policy intervention aimed at reducing the former (training programs, etc.). A permanent rise in income inequality is a change in the wage *structure* due to,

---

[6] One example is the debate in the popular press on the so-called "great risk shift" (Hacker, 2006; The Economist, 2007).

for example, skill-biased technological change that permanently increases the returns to observed (schooling) and unobserved (ability) skills. A transitory rise in inequality is sometimes termed "wage instability".[7]

The rest of the chapter is organized as follows. We start off in Section 2 with a discussion of what the theory predicts regarding the impact of changes in economic resources on consumption. As we shall see, the theory distinguishes quite sharply between persistent and transient changes, anticipated and unanticipated changes, insurable and uninsurable changes, and—if consumption is subject to adjustment costs— between small and large changes.

Given the importance of the nature of income changes for predicting consumption behavior, we then move in Section 3 to a review of the literature that has tried to come up with measures of wage or earnings risk using univariate data on wages, earnings or income. The objective of these papers has been that of identifying the most appropriate characterization of the income process in a parsimonious way. We discuss the modeling procedure and the evidence supporting the various models. Most papers make no distinction between unconditional and conditional variance of shocks.[8] Others assume that earnings are exogenous. More recent papers have relaxed both assumptions. We also discuss in this section papers that have taken a more statistical path, while retaining the exogeneity assumption, and modeled in various way the dynamics and heterogeneity of risk faced by individuals. We later discuss papers that have explored the possibility of endogenizing risk by including labor supply decisions, human capital (or health) investment decisions, or job-to-job mobility decisions. We confine this discussion to the end of the chapter (Section 5) because this approach is considerably more challenging and in our view represents the most promising development of the literature to date.

In Section 4 we discuss papers that use consumption and income data jointly. Our reading is that they do so with two different (and contrasting) objectives. Some papers assume that the life cycle-permanent income hypothesis provides a correct description of consumer behavior and use the extra information available to either identify the "correct" income process faced by individuals (which is valuable given the difficulty of doing so statistically using just income data) or identify the amount of information people have about their future income changes. The idea is that even if the correct income process could be identified, there would be no guarantee that the estimated "unexplained" variability in earnings represents "true" risk as seen from the individual standpoint (the excess variability represented by measurement error being the most trivial example). Since risk "is in the eye of the beholder", some researchers have

---

[7] What may generate such an increase? Candidates include an increase in turnover rates, or a decline in unionization or controlled prices. Increased wage instability was first studied by Moffitt and Gottschalk (1994), who challenge the conventional view that the rise in inequality has been mainly permanent. They show that up to half of the wage inequality increase we observe in the US is due to a rise in the "transitory" component.

[8] The conditional variance is closer to the concept of risk emphasized by the theory (as in the Euler equation framework, see Blanchard and Mankiw, 1988).

noticed that consumption would reflect whatever amount of information (and, in the first case, whatever income process) people face. We discuss papers that have taken the route of using consumption and income data to extract information about risk faced (or perceived) by individuals, such as Blundell and Preston (1998), Guvenen (2007), Guvenen and Smith (2009), Heathcote et al. (2007), Cunha et al. (2005), and Primiceri and van Rens (2009). Other papers in this literature use consumption and income data jointly in a more traditional way: they assume that the income process is correct and that the individual has no better information than the econometrician and proceed to test the empirical implications of the theory, e.g., how smooth is consumption relative to income. Hall and Mishkin (1982) and Blundell et al. (2008b) are two examples. In general there is an identification issue: one cannot separately identify insurance and information. We discuss two possible solutions proposed in the literature. First, identification of episodes in which shocks are unanticipated and of known duration (e.g., unexpected transitory tax refunds or other payments from the government, or weather shocks). If the assumptions about information and duration hold, all that remains is "insurability". Second, we discuss the use of subjective expectations to extract information about future income. These need to be combined with consumption and realized income data to identify insurance and durability of shocks.[9] The chapter concludes with a discussion of future research directions in Section 6.

2. THE IMPACT OF INCOME CHANGES ON CONSUMPTION: SOME THEORY

In this section we discuss what theory has to say regarding the impact of income changes on consumption.

2.1. The life cycle-permanent income hypothesis

To see how the degree of persistence of income shocks and the nature of income changes affect consumption, consider a simple example in which income is the only source of uncertainty of the model.[10] Preferences are quadratic, consumers discount the future at rate $\frac{1-\beta}{\beta}$ and save on a single risk-free asset with deterministic real return r, $\beta(1+r) = 1$ (this precludes saving due to returns outweighing impatience), the horizon is finite (the consumer dies with certainty at age A and has no bequest motive for saving), and credit markets are perfect. As we shall see, quadratic preferences are in some ways quite restrictive. Nevertheless, this simple characterization is very useful because it provides the correct qualitative intuition for most of the effects of interest; this intuition carries over with minor modifications to the more sophisticated cases. In the quadratic preferences

---

[9] Another possible solution is to envision using multiple response (consumption, labor supply, etc.), where the information set is identical but insurability of shocks may differ.

[10] The definition of income used here includes earnings and transfers (public and private) received by all family members. It excludes financial income.

case, the change in household consumption can be written as

$$\Delta C_{i,a,t} = \pi_a \sum_{j=0}^{A} \frac{E\left(Y_{i,a+j,t+j}|\Omega_{i,a,t}\right) - E\left(Y_{i,a+j,t+j}|\Omega_{i,a-1,t-1}\right)}{(1+r)^j} \qquad (1)$$

where a indexes age and t time, $\pi_a = \frac{r}{1+r}[1 - \frac{1}{(1+r)^{A-a+1}}]^{-1}$ is an "annuity" parameter that increases with age and $\Omega_{i,a,t}$ is the consumer's information set at age a. Despite its simplicity, this expression is rich enough to identify three key issues regarding the response of consumption to changes in the economic resources of the household.

First, consumption responds to news in the income process, but not to expected changes. Only innovations to (current and future) income that arrive at age a (the term $E(Y_{i,a+j,t+j}|\Omega_{i,a,t}) - E(Y_{i,a+j,t+j}|\Omega_{i,a-1,t-1})$) have the potential to change consumption between age $a - 1$ and age a. Anticipated changes in income (for which there is no innovation) do not affect consumption. Assistant Professors promoted in February may rent a larger apartment immediately, in the anticipation of the higher salary starting in September. We will record an increase in consumption in February (when the income change is announced), but not in September (when the income change actually occurs). This is predicated on the assumption that consumers can transfer resources from the future to the present by, e.g., borrowing. In the example above, a liquidity constrained Assistant Professor will not change her (rent) consumption at the time of the announcement of a promotion, but only at the time of the actual salary increase. With perfect credit markets, however, the model predicts that anticipated changes *do* affect consumption when they are announced. In terms of stabilization policies, this means that two types of income changes will affect consumption. First, consumption may be affected immediately by the announcement of tax reforms to occur at some point in the future. Consumption will not change at the time the reform is actually implemented. Second, consumption may be affected by a surprise tax reform that happens today.

The second key issue emerging from Eq. (1) is that the life cycle horizon also plays an important role (the term π_a). A transitory innovation smoothed over 40 years has a smaller impact on consumption than the same transitory innovation to be smoothed over 10 years. For example, if one assumes that the income process is i.i.d., the marginal propensity to consume with respect to an income change from (1) is simply π_a. Assuming $r = 0.02$, the marginal propensity to consume out of income shock increases from 0.04 (when $A - a = 40$) to 0.17 (when $A - a = 5$), and it is 1 in the last period of life. Intuitively, at the end of the life cycle transitory shocks would look, effectively, like permanent shocks. With liquidity constraints, however, shocks may have similar effects on consumption independently of the age at which they are received.

The last key feature of Eq. (1) is the persistence of innovations. More persistent innovations have a larger impact than short-lived innovations. To give a more formal

Table 1 The response of consumption to income shocks under quadratic preferences.

ρ	θ	$A - a$	κ
1	−0.2	40	0.81
1	0	10	1
0.99	−0.2	40	0.68
0.95	−0.2	40	0.39
0.8	−0.2	40	0.13
0.95	−0.2	30	0.45
0.95	−0.2	20	0.53
0.95	−0.2	10	0.65
0.95	−0.1	40	0.44
0.95	−0.01	40	0.48
1	0	∞	1
0	−0.2	40	0.03

characterization of the importance of persistence, suppose that income follows an ARMA(1,1) process:

$$Y_{i,a,t} = \rho Y_{i,a-1,t-1} + \varepsilon_{i,a,t} + \theta \varepsilon_{i,a-1,t-1}. \tag{2}$$

In this case, substituting (2) in (1), the consumption response is given by

$$\Delta C_{i,a,t} = \left(\frac{r}{1+r}\right)\left[1 - \frac{1}{(1+r)^{A-a+1}}\right]^{-1}\left[1 + \frac{\rho+\theta}{1+r-\rho}\left(1 - \left(\frac{\rho}{1+r}\right)^{A-a}\right)\right]\varepsilon_{i,a,t}$$

$$= \kappa\,(r, \rho, \theta, A - a)\,\varepsilon_{i,a,t}.$$

Table 1 below shows the value of the marginal propensity to consume κ for various combinations of ρ, θ, and $A - a$ (setting $r = 0.02$). A number of facts emerge. If the income shock represents an innovation to a random walk process ($\rho = 1, \theta = 0$), consumption responds one-to-one to it regardless of the horizon (the response is attenuated only if shocks end after some period, say $L < A$).[11] A decrease in the persistence of the shock lowers the value of κ. When $\rho = 0.8$ (and $\theta = -0.2$), for example, the value of κ is a modest 0.13. A decrease in the persistence of the MA component acts in the same direction (but the magnitude of the response is much attenuated). In this case as well, the presence of liquidity constraints may invalidate the

---

[11] This could be the case if y is labor income and L is retirement. However, if y is household income, it is implausible to assume that shocks (permanent or transitory) end at retirement. Events like death of a spouse, fluctuations in the value of assets, intergenerational transfers towards children or relatives, etc., all conjure to create some income risk even after formal retirement from the labor force.

sharp prediction of the model. For example, more and less persistent shocks may have a similar effect on consumption. When the consumer is hit by a short-lived negative shock, she can smooth the consumption response over the entire horizon by borrowing today (and repaying in the future when income reverts to the mean). If borrowing is precluded, short-lived or long-lived shocks have similar impacts on consumption.

The income process (2) considered above is restrictive, because there is a single error component which follows an ARMA(1,1) process. As we discuss in Section 3, a very popular characterization in calibrated macroeconomic models is to assume that income is the sum of a random walk process and a transitory i.i.d. component:

$$Y_{i,a,t} = p_{i,a,t} + \varepsilon_{i,a,t} \tag{3}$$

$$p_{i,a,t} = p_{i,a-1,t-1} + \zeta_{i,a,t}. \tag{4}$$

The appeal of this income process is that it is close to the notion of a Friedman's permanent income hypothesis income process.[12] In this case, the response of consumption to the two types of shocks is:

$$\Delta C_{i,a,t} = \pi_a \varepsilon_{i,a,t} + \zeta_{i,a,t} \tag{5}$$

which shows that consumption responds one-to-one to permanent shocks but the response of consumption to a transitory shock depends on the time horizon. For young consumers (with a long time horizon), the response should be small. The response should increase as consumers age. Figure 1 plots the value of the response for a consumer who lives until age 75. Clearly, it is only in the last 10 years of life or so that there is a substantial response of consumption to a transitory shock. The graph also plots for the purpose of comparison the expected response in the infinite horizon case. An interesting implication of this graph is that a transitory unanticipated stabilization policy is likely to affect substantially only the behavior of older consumers (unless liquidity constraints are important—which may well be the case for younger consumers).[13]

Note finally that if the permanent component were literally permanent ($p_{i,a,t} = p_i$), it would affect the level of consumption but not its change (unless consumers were learning about p_i, see Guvenen, 2007).

In the classical version of the LC-PIH the *size* of income changes does not matter. One reason why the size of income changes may matter is because of adjustment costs:

[12] See Friedman (1957). Meghir (2004) provides an analysis of how the PIH has influenced modern theory of consumption.

[13] However, liquidity constraints have asymmetric effects. A transitory tax cut, which raises consumers' disposable income temporarily, invites savings not borrowing (unless the consumer is already consuming sub-optimally). In contrast, temporary tax hikes may have strong effects if borrowing is not available. On the other hand unanticipated stabilization interpretation may increase uncertainty and hence precautionary savings.

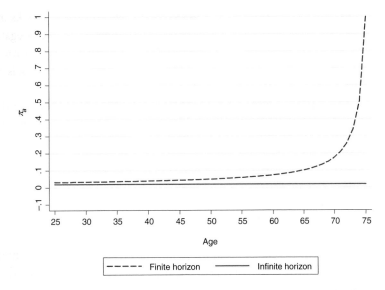

Figure 1   *The response of consumption to a transitory income shock.*

Consumers tend to smooth consumption and follow the theory when expected income changes are large, but are less likely to do so when the changes are small and the costs of adjusting consumption are not trivial. Suppose for example that consumers who want to adjust their consumption upwards in response to an expected income increase need to face the cost of negotiating a loan with a bank. It is likely that the utility loss from not adjusting fully to the new equilibrium is relatively small when the expected income increase is small, which suggests that no adjustment would take place if the transaction cost associated with negotiating a loan is high enough.[14] This "magnitude hypothesis" has been formally tested by Scholnick (2010), who use a large data set provided by a Canadian bank that includes information on both credit cards spending as well as mortgage payment records. As in Stephens (2008) he argues that the final mortgage payment represent an expected shock to disposable income (that is, income net of pre-committed debt service payments). His test of the magnitude hypothesis looks at whether the response of consumption to expected income increases depends on the relative amount of mortgage payments. See also Chetty and Szeidl (2007).[15]

Outside the quadratic preference world, uncertainty about future income realizations will also impact consumption. The response of consumers to an increase in risk is to

[14] The magnitude argument could also explain Hsieh's (2003) puzzling findings that consumption is excessively sensitive to tax refunds but not payments from the Alaska Permanent Fund. In fact, tax refunds are typically smaller than payments from the Alaska Permanent fund (although the actual amount of the latter is somewhat more uncertain).

[15] Another element that may matter, but that has been neglected in the literature, is the time distance that separates the announcement of the income change from its actual occurrence. The smaller the time distance, the lower the utility loss from inaction.

reduce consumption—or increase savings. This opens up another path for stabilization policies. If the policy objective is to stimulate consumption, one way of achieving this would be to reduce the risk that people face. We consider more realistic preference specifications in the following section.

2.2. Beyond the PIH

The beauty of the model with quadratic preferences is that it gives very sharp predictions regarding the impact on consumption of various types of income shocks. For example, there is the sharp prediction that permanent shocks are entirely consumed (an MPC of 1). Unfortunately, quadratic preferences have well known undesirable features, such as increasing risk aversion and lack of a precautionary motive for saving. Do the predictions of this model survive under more realistic assumptions about preferences? The answer is: only qualitatively. The problem with more realistic preferences, such as CRRA, is that they deliver no closed form solution for consumption—that is, there is no analytical expression for the "consumption function" and hence the value of the propensity to consume in response to risk (income shocks) is not easily derivable. This is also the reason why the literature moved on to estimating Euler equations after Hall (1978). The advantage of the Euler equation approach is that one can be silent about the sources of uncertainty faced by the consumer (including, crucially, the stochastic structure of the income process). However, in the Euler equation context only a limited set of parameters (preference parameters such as the elasticity of intertemporal substitution or the intertemporal discount rate) can be estimated.[16] Our reading is that there is some dissatisfaction in the literature regarding the evidence coming from Euler equation estimates (see Browning and Lusardi, 1996; Attanasio and Weber, 2010).

Recently there has been an attempt to go back to the concept of a "consumption function". Two approaches have been followed. First, the Euler equation that describe the expected dynamics of the growth in the marginal utility can be approximated to describe the dynamics of consumption growth. Blundell et al. (2008b), extending Blundell and Preston (1998) (see also Blundell and Stoker, 1994), derive an approximation of the mapping between the expectation error of the Euler equation and the income shock. Carroll (2001) and Kaplan and Violante (2009) discuss numerical simulations in the buffer-stock and Bewley model, respectively. We discuss the results of these two approaches in turn.

2.2.1. Approximation of the Euler equation
Blundell et al. (2008b) consider the consumption problem faced by household i of age a in period t. Assuming that preferences are of the CRRA form, the objective is to choose

---

[16] And even that limited objective has proved difficult to achieve, due to limited cross-sectional variability in interest rates and short panels. See Attanasio and Low (2004).

a path for consumption C so as to:

$$\max_{C} E_a \sum_{j=0}^{A-a} \beta^j \frac{C_{i,a+j,t+j}^{1-\gamma} - 1}{1 - \gamma} e^{Z_{i,a+j,t+j}' \vartheta_{a+j}}, \tag{6}$$

where $Z_{i,a+j,t+j}$ incorporates taste shifters (such as age, household composition, etc.), and we denote with $E_a\left(.\right) = E(.|\Omega_{i,a,t})$. Maximization of (6) is subject to the budget constraint, which in the self-insurance model assumes individuals have access to a risk free bond with real return r

$$A_{i,a+j+1,t+j+1} = (1+r)\left(A_{i,a+j,t+j} + Y_{i,a+j,t+j} - C_{i,a+j,t+j}\right) \tag{7}$$

$$A_{i,A} = 0 \tag{8}$$

with $A_{i,a,t}$ given. Blundell et al. (2008b) set the retirement age after which labor income falls to zero at L, assumed known and certain, and the end of the life cycle at age A. They assume that there is no uncertainty about the date of death. With budget constraint (7), optimal consumption choices can be described by the Euler equation (assuming for simplicity that there is no preference heterogeneity, or $\vartheta_a = 0$):

$$C_{i,a-1,t-1}^{-\gamma} = \beta(1+r) E_{a-1} C_{i,a,t}^{-\gamma}. \tag{9}$$

As it is, Eq. (9) is not useful for empirical purposes. Blundell et al. (2008b) show that the Euler equation can be approximated as follows:

$$\Delta \log C_{i,a,t} \simeq \eta_{i,a,t} + f_{i,a,t}^C$$

where $\eta_{i,a,t}$ is a consumption shock with $E_{a-1}(\eta_{i,a,t}) = 0$, $f_{i,a,t}^c$ captures any slope in the consumption path due to interest rates, impatience or precautionary savings and the error in the approximation is $O(E_a \eta_{i,a,t}^2)$.[17] Suppose that any idiosyncratic component to this gradient to the consumption path can be adequately picked up by a vector of deterministic characteristics $\Gamma_{i,a,t}^c$ and a stochastic individual element $\xi_{i,a}$

$$\Delta \log C_{i,a,t} - \Gamma_{i,a,t}^c = \Delta c_{i,a,t} \simeq \eta_{i,a,t} + \xi_{i,a,t}.$$

Assume log income is

$$\log Y_{i,a,t} = p_{i,a,t} + \varepsilon_{i,a,t} \tag{10}$$

---

[17] This is an approximation for the logarithm of the sum of an arbitrary series of variables.

$$p_{i,a,t} = \Gamma^y_{i,a,t} + p_{i,a-1,t-1} + \zeta_{i,a,t} \tag{11}$$

where $\Gamma^y_{i,a,t}$ represent observable characteristics influencing the growth of income. Income growth can be written as:

$$\Delta \log Y_{i,a,t} - \Gamma^y_{i,a,t} = \Delta y_{i,a,t} = \zeta_{i,a,t} + \Delta \varepsilon_{i,a,t}.$$

The (*ex-post*) intertemporal budget constraint is

$$\sum_{j=0}^{A-a} \frac{C_{i,a+j,t+j}}{(1+r)^j} = \sum_{j=0}^{L-a} \frac{Y_{i,a+j,t+j}}{(1+r)^j} + A_{i,a,t}$$

where A is the age of death and L is the retirement age. Applying the approximation above and taking differences in expectations gives

$$\eta_{i,a,t} \simeq \Xi_{i,a,t} \left[\zeta_{i,a,t} + \pi_a \varepsilon_{i,a,t} \right]$$

where π_a is an annuitization factor, $\Xi_{i,a,t} = \dfrac{\sum_{j=0}^{A-a} \frac{Y_{i,a+j,t+j}}{(1+r)^j}}{\sum_{j=0}^{A-a} \frac{Y_{i,a+j,t+j}}{(1+r)^j} + A_{i,a,t}}$ is the share of future labor income in current human and financial wealth, and the error of the approximation is $O([\zeta_{i,a,t} + \pi_a \varepsilon_{i,a,t}]^2 + E_{a-1}[\zeta_{i,a,t} + \pi_a \varepsilon_{i,a,t}]^2)$. Then[18]

$$\Delta c_{i,a,t} \simeq \xi_{i,a,t} + \Xi_{i,a,t} \zeta_{i,a,t} + \pi_a \Xi_{i,a,t} \varepsilon_{i,a,t} \tag{12}$$

with a similar order of approximation error.[19] The random term $\xi_{i,a,t}$ can be interpreted as the innovation to higher moments of the income process.[20] As we shall see, Meghir and Pistaferri (2004) find evidence of this using PSID data.

---

[18] Blundell et al. (2008a) contains a lengthier derivation of such an expression, including discussion of the order of magnitude of the approximation error involved.

[19] Results from a simulation of a stochastic economy presented in Blundell et al. (2008a) show that the approximation (12) can be used to accurately detect changes in the time series pattern of permanent and transitory variances to income shocks.

[20] This characterization follows Caballero (1990), who presents a model with stochastic higher moments of the income distribution. He shows that there are two types of innovation affecting consumption growth: innovation to the mean (the term $\Xi_{i,a,t}(\zeta_{i,a,t} + \pi_a \varepsilon_{i,a,t})$), and "a term that takes into account revisions in variance forecast" ($\xi_{i,a,t}$). Note that this term is not capturing precautionary savings *per se*, but the innovation to the consumption component that generates it (i.e., consumption growth due to precautionary savings will change to accommodate changes in the forecast of the amount of uncertainty one expects in the future).

The interpretation of the impact of income shocks on consumption growth in the PIH model with CRRA preferences is straightforward. For individuals a long time from the end of their life with the value of current financial assets small relative to remaining future labor income, $\Xi_{i,a,t} \simeq 1$, and permanent shocks pass through more or less completely into consumption whereas transitory shocks are (almost) completely insured against through saving. Precautionary saving can provide effective self-insurance against permanent shocks only if the stock of assets built up is large relative to future labor income, which is to say $\Xi_{i,a,t}$ is appreciably smaller than unity, in which case there will also be some smoothing of permanent shocks through self insurance.

The most important feature of the approximation approach is to show that the effect of an income shock on consumption depends not only on the persistence of the shock and the planning horizon (as in the LC-PIH case with quadratic preferences), but also on preference parameters. *Ceteris paribus*, the consumption of more prudent households will respond less to income shocks. The reason is that they can use their accumulated stock of precautionary wealth to smooth the impact of the shocks (for which they were saving precautiously against in the first place). Simulation results (below) confirm this basic intuition.

2.2.2. Kaplan and Violante

Kaplan and Violante (2009) investigate the amount of consumption insurance present in a life cycle version of the standard incomplete markets model with heterogenous agents (e.g., Rios-Rull, 1996; Huggett, 1996). Kaplan and Violante's setup differs from that in Blundell et al. (2008b; BPP) by adding the uncertainty component μ_a to life expectancy, and by omitting the taste shifters from the utility function. μ_a is the probability of dying at age a. It is set to 0 for all $a < L$ (the known retirement age) and it is greater than 0 for $L \leq a \leq A$. Their model also differs from BPP by specifying a realistic social security system. Two baseline setups are investigated—a natural borrowing constraint setup (henceforth NBC), in which consumers are only constrained by their budget constraint, and a zero borrowing constraint setup (henceforth ZBC), in which consumers have to maintain non-negative assets at all ages. The income process is similar to BPP.[21] Part of Kaplan and Violante's analysis is designed to check whether the amount of insurance predicted by the Bewley model can be consistently estimated using the identification strategy proposed by BPP and whether BPP's estimates using PSID and CEX data conform to values obtained from calibrating their theoretical model.

Kaplan and Violante (2009) calibrate their model to match the US data. Survival rates are obtained from the NCHS, the intertemporal discount rate is calibrated to match a wealth-income ratio of 2.5, the permanent shock parameters (σ_ζ^2 and the variance of the

---

[21] There are two differences though: Blundell et al. (2008b) allow for an MA(1) transitory component (while in Kaplan and Violante this is an i.i.d. component), and for time-varying variance (while Kaplan and Violante assume stationarity).

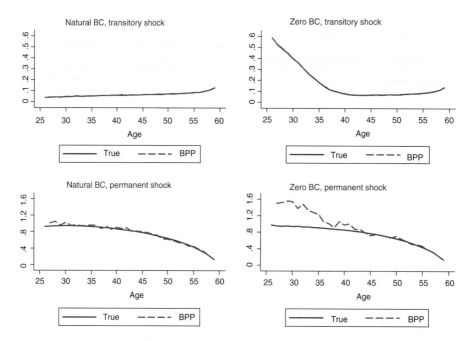

Figure 2   *Age profile of MPC coefficients for transitory and permanent income shocks. (Source: Kaplan and Violante (2009))*

initial draw of the process) are calibrated to match PSID data and the variance of the transitory shock (σ_ε^2) is set to the 1990-1992 BPP point estimate (0.05). The Kaplan and Violante (2009) model is solved numerically. This allows for the calculation of both the "true"[22] and the BPP estimators of the "partial insurance parameters" (the response of consumption to permanent and transitory income shocks).

Figure 2 is reproduced from Kaplan and Violante (2009).[23] It plots the theoretical marginal propensity to consume for the transitory shocks (upper panels) and the permanent shocks (lower panels) against age (continuous line) and those obtained using BPP's identification methodology (dashed line). The left panels refer to the NBC environment; the right panels to the ZBC environment. A number of interesting findings emerge. First, in the NBC environment the MPC with respect to transitory shocks is fairly low throughout the life cycle, and similarly to what is shown in Fig. 1, increases over the life cycle due to reduced planning horizon effect. The life cycle average MPC is 0.06. Second, there is considerable insurance also against permanent shock, which increases over the life cycle due to the ability to use the accumulated wealth to smooth these shocks. The life cycle average MPC is 0.77, well below the MPC of 1 predicted

---

[22] "True" in this context is in the sense of the actual insurance parameters given the model data generating process.

[23] We thank Gianluca Violante for providing the data.

by the infinite horizon PIH model.[24] Third, the ZBC environment affects only the ability to insure transitory shocks (which depend on having access to loans), but not the ability to insure permanent shocks (which depend on having access to a storage technology, and hence it is not affected by credit restrictions). Fourth, the performance of the BPP estimators is remarkably good. Only in the case of the ZBC environment and a permanent shock does the BPP estimator display an upward bias, and even in that case only very early in the life cycle. According to KV the source of the bias is the failure of the orthogonality condition used by BPP for agents close to the borrowing constraint. It is worth noting that the ZBC environment is somewhat extreme as it assumes no unsecured borrowing. Finally, KV compare the average MPCs obtained in their model (0.06 and 0.77) with the actual estimates obtained by BPP using actual data. As we shall see, BPP find an estimate of the MPC with respect to permanent shocks of 0.64 (s.e. 0.09) and an estimate of the MPC with respect to transitory shocks of 0.05 (s.e. 0.04). Clearly, the "theoretical" MPCs found by KV lie well in the confidence interval of BPP's estimates. One thing that seems not to be borne out in the data is that theoretically the degree of smoothing of permanent shocks should be strictly increasing and convex with age, while BPP report an increasing amount of insurance with age as a non-significant finding.[25] As discussed by Kaplan and Violante (2009), the theoretical pattern of the smoothing coefficients is the result of two forces: a wealth composition effect and a horizon effect. The increase in wealth over the life cycle due to precautionary and retirement motives means that agents are better insured against shocks. As the horizon shortens, the effect of permanent shock resembles increasingly that of a transitory shock.

Given that the response of consumption to shocks of various nature is so different (and so relevant for policy in theory and practice), it is natural to turn to studies that analyze the nature and persistence of the income process.

3. MODELING THE INCOME PROCESS

In this section we discuss the specification and estimation of the income process. Two main approaches will be discussed. The first looks at earnings as a whole, and interprets risk as the year-to-year volatility that cannot be explained by certain observables (with various degrees of sophistication). The second approach assumes that part of the variability in earnings is endogenous (induced by choices). In the first approach, researchers assume that consumers receive an uncertain but *exogenous* flow of earnings in each period. This literature has two objectives: (a) identification of the correct process

---

[24] Blundell et al. (2008a) simulate the model described in the Appendix of Blundell et al. (2008b) using their estimates of the income process and find a value of $\Xi_{i,a,t}$ of 0.8 or a little lower for individuals aged twenty years before retirement. Carroll (2001) presents simulations that show for a buffer stock model in which consumers face both transitory and permanent income shocks, the steady state value of $\Xi_{i,a,t}$ is between 0.75 and 0.92 for a wide range of plausible parameter values.

[25] Hall and Mishkin (1982) reported similar findings for their MPC out of transitory shocks (the factor π_a in Eq. (5)).

for earnings, (b) identification of the information set—which defines the concept of an "innovation". In the second approach, the concept of risk needs revisiting, because one first needs to identify the "primitive" risk factors. For example, if endogenous fluctuations in earnings were to come exclusively from people freely choosing their hours, the "primitive" risk factor would be the hourly wage. We will discuss this second approach at the end of the chapter, in Section 5.

There are various models proposed in the literature aimed at addressing the issue of how to model risk in exogenous earnings. They typically model earnings as the sum of a number of random components. These components differ in a number of respects, primarily their persistence, whether there are time- (or age- or experience-) varying loading factors attached to them, and whether they are economically relevant or just measurement error. We discuss these various models in Section 3.1. As said in the Introduction, to have an idea about the correct income process is key to understanding the response of consumption to income shocks.[26] As for the issue of information set, the question that is being asked is whether the consumer knows more than the econometrician.[27] This is sometimes known as the *superior information* issue. The individual may have advance information about events such as a promotion, that the econometrician may never hope to predict on the basis of observables (unless, of course, promotions are perfectly predictable on the basis of things like seniority within a firm, education, etc.).[28]

In general, a researcher's identification strategy for the correct DGP for income, earnings or wages will be affected by data availability. While the ideal data set is a long, large panel of individuals, this is somewhat a rare event and can be plagued by problems such as attrition (see Baker and Solon, 2003, for an exception). More frequently, researchers have available panel data on individuals, but the sample size is limited, especially if one restricts the attention to a balanced sample (for example, Baker, 1997; MaCurdy, 1982). Alternatively, one could use an unbalanced panel (as in

---

[26] Another reason why having an idea of the right earnings process is important emerges in the treatment effect literature. Whether the TTE (treatment-on-the-treated effect) can be estimated from simple comparison of means for treated and untreated individuals depends (among other things) on the persistence of earnings.

[27] Other papers have considered the consequences of the opposite assumption, i..e, cases in which consumers know *less* than the econometrician (Pischke, 1995). To consider a simple example, assume a standard transitory/permanent income process. Individuals who are unable to distinguish the two components will record a (non-stationary) MA(1) process. The interesting issue is how much consumers lose from ignoring (or failing to investigate) the correct income process they face. The cost of investing in collecting information may depend on size of the income changes, inattention costs, salience considerations, etc.

[28] A possible way to assess the discrepancy of information between the household and the econometrician is to compare measures of uncertainty obtained *via* estimation of dynamic income processes with measures of risk recovered from subjective expectations data. Data on the subjective distribution of future incomes or the probability of future unemployment are now becoming available for many countries, including the US (in particular, the Survey of Economic Expectations and the Health and Retirement Survey), and have been used, among others, by Dominitz and Manski (1997) and Barsky et al. (1997). This is an interesting avenue for future empirical research which we discuss further in Section 4.

Meghir and Pistaferri, 2004; Heathcote et al., 2007). An important exception is the case where countries have available administrative data sources with reports on earnings or income from tax returns or social security records. The important advantage of such data sets is the accuracy of the information provided and the lack of attrition, other than what is due to migration and death. The important disadvantage is the lack of other information that is pertinent to modeling, such as hours of work and in some cases education or occupation, depending on the source of the data. Even less frequently, one may have available employer–employee matched data sets, with which it may be possible to identify the role of firm heterogeneity separately from that of individual heterogeneity, either in a descriptive way such as in Abowd et al. (1999), or allowing also for shocks, such as in Guiso et al. (2005), or in a more structural fashion as in Postel-Vinay and Robin (2002), Cahuc et al. (2006), Postel-Vinay and Turon (2010) and Lise et al. (2009). Less frequent and more limited in scope is the use of pseudo-panel data, which misses the variability induced by genuine idiosyncratic shocks, but at least allows for some results to be established where long panel data is not available (see Banks et al., 2001; Moffitt, 1993).

3.1. Specifications

The typical specification of income processes found in the literature is implicitly or explicitly motivated by Friedman's permanent income hypothesis, which has led to an emphasis on the distinction between permanent and transitory shocks to income. Of course things are never as simple as that: permanent shocks may not be as permanent and transitory shocks may be reasonably persistent. Finally, what may pass as a permanent shock may sometimes be heterogeneity in disguise. Indeed these issues fuel a lively debate in this field, which may not be possible to resolve without identifying assumptions. In this section we present a reasonably general specification that encompasses a number of views in the literature and then discuss estimation of this model.

We denote by $Y_{i,a,t}$ a measure of income (such as earnings) for individual i of age a in period t. This is typically taken to be annual earnings and individuals not working over a whole year are usually dropped.[29] Issues having to do with selection and endogenous labor supply decisions will be dealt with in a separate section. Many of the specifications for the income process take the form

$$\ln Y_{i,a,t}^e = d_t^e + \beta^{e\prime} X_{i,a,t} + u_{i,a,t}. \tag{13}$$

[29] In the literature the focus is mainly on employed workers and self-employed workers are typically also dropped. This is a particularly important selection for the purpose of measuring risk given that the self-employed face much higher earnings risk than the employed. On the other hand, this avoids accounting for endogenous selection into self-employment based on risk preferences (see Skinner, 1988; Guiso et al., 2002; Fuchs-Schundeln and Schundeln, 2005).

In the above e denotes a particular group (such as education and sex) and $X_{i,a,t}$ will typically include a polynomial in age as well as other characteristics including region, race and sometimes marital status. From now on we omit the superscript "e" to simplify notation. In (13) the error term $u_{i,a,t}$ is defined such that $E(u_{i,a,t}|X_{i,a,t}) = 0$. This allows us to work with residual log income $\widehat{y_{i,a,t}} = \ln Y_{i,a,t} - \hat{d}_t - \hat{\beta}' X_{i,a,t}$, where $\hat{\beta}$ and the aggregate time effects $\hat{d}_t$ can be estimated using OLS. Henceforth we will ignore this first step and we will work directly with residual log income $y_{i,a,t}$, where the effect of observable characteristics and common aggregate time trends have been eliminated.

The key element of the specification in (13) is the time series properties of $u_{i,a,t}$. A specification that encompasses many of the ideas in the literature is

$$u_{i,a,t} = a \times f_i + v_{i,a,t} + p_{i,a,t} + m_{i,a,t}$$
$$v_{i,a,t} = \Theta_q(L)\varepsilon_{i,a,t} \qquad \text{Transitory process} \qquad (14)$$
$$P_p(L)p_{i,a,t} = \zeta_{i,a,t} \qquad \text{Permanent process}$$

where L is a lag operator such that $Lz_{i,a,t} = z_{i,a-1,t-1}$. In (14) the stochastic process consists of an individual specific life cycle trend ($a \times f_i$); a transitory shock $v_{i,a,t}$, which is modeled as an MA process whose lag polynomial of order q is denoted $\Theta_q(L)$; a permanent shock $P_p(L)p_{i,a,t} = \zeta_{i,a,t}$, which is an autoregressive process with high levels of persistence possibly including a unit root, also expressed in the lag polynomial of order p, $P_p(L)$; and measurement error $m_{i,a,t}$ which may be taken as classical i.i.d. or not.

3.1.1. A simple model of earnings dynamics

We start with the relatively simpler representation where the term $a \times f_i$ is excluded. Moreover we restrict the lag polynomials $\Theta(L)$ and $P(L)$: it is not generally possible to identify $\Theta(L)$ and $P(L)$ without any further restrictions. Thus we start with the typical specification used for example in MaCurdy (1982) and Abowd and Card (1989):

$$u_{i,a,t} = v_{i,a,t} + p_{i,a,t} + m_{i,a,t}$$
$$v_{i,a,t} = \varepsilon_{i,a,t} - \theta\varepsilon_{i,a-1,t-1} \qquad \text{Transitory process}$$
$$p_{i,a,t} = p_{i,a-1,t-1} + \zeta_{i,a,t} \qquad \text{Permanent process} \qquad (15)$$
$$p_{i,0,t-a} = h_i$$

with $m_{i,a,t}$, $\zeta_{i,a,t}$ and $\varepsilon_{i,a,t}$ all being independently and identically distributed and where h_i reflects initial heterogeneity, which here persists forever through the random walk ($a = 0$ is the age of entry in the labor market, which may differ across groups due to different school leaving ages). Generally, as we will show, the existence of classical measurement error causes problems in the identification of the transitory shock process.

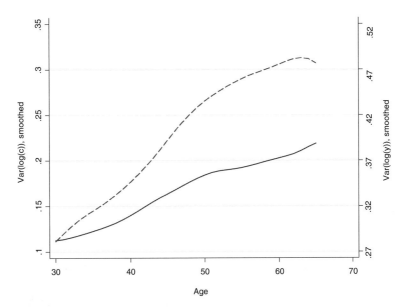

Figure 3   *The variance of log income (from the PSID, dashed line) and log consumption (from the CEX, continuous line) over the life cycle.*

There are two principal motivations for the permanent/transitory decompositions: the first motivation draws from economics: the decomposition reflects well the original insights of Friedman (1957) by distinguishing how consumption can react to different types of income shock, while introducing uncertainty into the model.[30] The second is statistical: At least for the US and for the UK the variance of income increases over the life cycle (see Fig. 3, which uses consumption data from the CEX and income data from the PSID). This, together with the increasing life cycle variance of consumption points to a unit root in income, as we shall see below. Moreover, income growth ($\Delta y_{i,a,t}$) has limited serial correlation and behaves very much like an MA process of order 2 or three: this property is delivered by the fact that all shocks above are assumed i.i.d. In our example growth in income has been restricted to an $MA(2)$.[31]

Even in such a tight specification identification is not straightforward: as we will illustrate we cannot separately identify the parameter θ, the variance of the measurement error and the variance of the transitory shock. But first consider the identification of the variance of the permanent shock. Define unexplained earnings growth as:

$$g_{i,a,t} \equiv \Delta y_{i,a,t} = \Delta m_{i,a,t} + (1 + \theta L)\Delta \varepsilon_{i,a,t} + \zeta_{i,a,t}. \tag{16}$$

[30] See Meghir (2004) for a description and interpretation of Friedman's contribution.
[31] See below for some empirical evidence on this.

Then the key moment condition for identifying the variance of the permanent shock is

$$E\left(\zeta_{i,a,t}^2\right) = E\left[g_{i,a,t}\left(\sum_{j=-(1+q)}^{(1+q)} g_{i,a+j,t+j}\right)\right] \tag{17}$$

where q is the order of the moving average process in the original levels equation; in our example $q = 1$. Hence, if we know the order of serial correlation of log income we can identify the variance of the permanent shock without any need to identify the variance of the measurement error or the parameters of the MA process. Indeed, in the absence of a permanent shock the moment in (17) will be zero, which offers a way of testing for the presence of a permanent component *conditional* on knowing the order of the MA process. If the order of the MA process is one in the levels, then to implement this we will need at least six individual-level observations to construct this moment. The moment is then averaged over individuals and the relevant asymptotic theory for inference is one that relies on a large number of individuals N.

At this point we need to mention two potential complications with the econometrics. First, when carrying out inference we have to take into account that $y_{i,a,t}$ has been constructed using the pre-estimated parameters d_t and β in Eq. (13). Correcting the standard errors for this generated regressor problem is relatively simple to do and can be done either analytically, based on the delta method, or just by using the bootstrap. Second, as said above, to estimate such a model we may have to rely on panel data where individuals have been followed for the necessary minimum number of periods/years (6 in our example); this means that our results may be biased due to endogenous attrition. In practice any adjustment for this is going to be extremely hard to do because we usually do not observe variables that can adequately explain attrition and at the same time do not explain earnings. Administrative data may offer a promising alternative to relying on attrition-prone panel data.

The order of the MA process for $v_{i,a,t}$ will not be known in practice and it has to be estimated. This can be done by estimating the autocovariance structure of $g_{i,a,t}$ and deciding *a priori* on the suitable criterion for judging whether they should be taken as zero. One approach followed in practice is to use the t-statistic or the F-statistics for higher order autocovariances. However, we need to recognize that given an estimate of q the analysis that follows is conditional on that estimate of q, which in turn can affect inference, particularly for the importance of the variance of the permanent effect $\sigma_\zeta^2 = E(\zeta_{i,a,t}^2)$.

3.1.2. Estimating and identifying the properties of the transitory shock

The next issue is the identification of the parameters of the moving average process of the transitory shock and those of measurement error. It turns out that the model is underidentified, which is not surprising: in our example we need to estimate three parameters, namely the variance of the transitory shock $\sigma_\varepsilon^2 = E(\varepsilon_{i,a,t}^2)$, the MA coefficient θ and the variance of the measurement error $\sigma_m^2 = E(m_{i,a,t}^2)$.[32] To illustrate the underidentification point suppose that $|\theta| < 1$ and assume that the measurement error is independently and identically distributed. We take as given that $q = 1$. Then the autocovariances of order higher than three will be zero, whatever the value of our unknown parameters, which is the root of the identification problem. The first and second order autocovariances imply

$$\sigma_\varepsilon^2 = \frac{E\left(g_{i,a,t}g_{i,a-2,t-2}\right)}{\theta} \qquad \text{I}$$

$$\sigma_m^2 = -E\left(g_{i,a,t}g_{i,a-1,t-1}\right) - \frac{(1+\theta)^2}{\theta}E\left(g_{i,a,t}g_{i,a-2,t-2}\right) \quad \text{II.}$$

(18)

The sign of $E(g_{i,a,t}g_{i,a-2,t-2})$ defines the sign of θ. Taking the two variances as functions of the MA coefficient we note two points. First, $\sigma_m^2(\theta)$ declines and $\sigma_\varepsilon^2(\theta)$ increases when θ declines in absolute value. Second, for sufficiently low values of $|\theta|$ the estimated variance of the measurement error $\sigma_m^2(\theta)$ may become negative. Given the sign of θ (defined by I in Eq. (18)) this fact defines a bound for the MA coefficient. Suppose for example that $\theta < 0$, we have that $\theta \in [-1, \tilde{\theta}]$, where $\tilde{\theta}$ is the negative value of θ that sets σ_m^2 in (18) to zero. If θ was found to be positive the bounds would be in a positive range. The bounds on θ in turn define bounds on σ_ε^2 and σ_m^2.

An alternative empirical strategy is to rely on an external estimate of the variance of the measurement error, $\overline{\sigma_m^2}$. Define the moments, adjusted for measurement error as:

$$E\left[g_{i,a,t}^2 - 2\overline{\sigma_m^2}\right] = \sigma_\zeta^2 + 2\left(1 + \theta + \theta^2\right)\sigma_\varepsilon^2$$

$$E\left(g_{i,a,t}g_{i,a-1,t-1} + \overline{\sigma_m^2}\right) = -\left(1+\theta\right)^2\sigma_\varepsilon^2$$

$$E\left(g_{i,a,t}g_{i,a-2,t-2}\right) = \theta\sigma_\varepsilon^2$$

where $\overline{\sigma_m^2}$ is available externally. The three moments above depend only on θ, σ_ζ^2 and σ_m^2. We can then estimate these parameters using a Minimum Distance procedure.

Such external measures can sometimes be obtained through validation studies. For example, Bound and Krueger (1991) conduct a validation study of the CPS data on earnings and conclude that measurement error explains 35 percent of the overall variance of the rate of growth of earnings of males in the CPS. Bound et al. (1994) find a value of 26 percent using the PSID-Validation Study.[33]

---

[32] Assuming as we do below that the measurement error is i.i.d.

[33] See Bound et al. (2001) for a recent survey of the growing literature on measurement error in micro data.

3.1.3. Estimating alternative income processes

Time varying impacts An alternative specification with very different implications is one where

$$\ln Y_{i,a,t} = \rho \ln Y_{i,a-1,t-1} + d_t(X'_{i,a,t}\beta + h_i + v_{i,a,t}) + m_{i,a,t} \tag{19}$$

where h_i is a fixed effect while $v_{i,a,t}$ follows some MA process and $m_{i,a,t}$ is measurement error (see Holtz-Eakin et al., 1988). This process can be estimated by method of moments following a suitable transformation of the model. Define $\theta_t = d_t/d_{t-1}$ and quasi-difference to obtain:

$$\ln Y_{i,a,t} = (\rho + \theta_t) \ln Y_{i,a-1,t-1} - \theta_t \rho \ln Y_{i,a-2,t-2} + d_t(\Delta X'_{i,a,t}\beta + \Delta v_{i,a,t})$$
$$+ m_{i,a,t} - \theta_t m_{i,a-1,t-1}. \tag{20}$$

In this model the persistence of the shocks is captured by the autoregressive component of $\ln Y$, which means that the effects of time varying characteristics are persistent to an extent. Given estimates of the levels equation in (20) the autocovariance structure of the residuals can be used to identify the properties of the error term $d_t \Delta v_{i,a,t} + m_{i,a,t} - \theta_t m_{i,a-1,t-1}$.

Alternatively, the fixed effect with the autoregressive component can be replaced by a random walk in a similar type of model. This could take the form

$$\ln Y_{i,a,t} = d_t(X'_{i,a,t}\beta + p_{i,a,t} + v_{i,a,t}) + m_{i,a,t}. \tag{21}$$

In this model $p_{i,a,t} = p_{i,a-1,t-1} + \zeta_{i,a,t}$ as before, but the shocks have a different effect depending on aggregate conditions. Given fixed T a linear regression in levels can provide estimates for d_t, which can now be treated as known.

Now define $\theta_t = d_t/d_{t-1}$ and consider the following transformation

$$\ln Y_{i,a,t} - \theta_t \ln Y_{i,a-1,t-1} = d_t(\zeta_{i,a,t} + \Delta v_{i,a,t}) + m_{i,a,t} - \theta_t m_{i,a-1,t-1}. \tag{22}$$

The autocovariance structure of $\ln Y_{i,a,t} - \theta_t \ln Y_{i,a-1,t-1}$ can be used to estimate the variances of the shocks, very much like in the previous examples. We will not be able to identify separately the variance of the transitory shock from that of measurement error, just like before. In general, one can construct a number of variants of the above model but we will move on to another important specification, keeping from now on any macroeconomic effects additive.

It should be noted that (22) is a popular model among labor economists but not among macroeconomists. One reason is that it is hard to use in macro models—one needs to know the entire sequence of prices, address general equilibrium issues, etc.

Stochastic growth in earnings Now consider generalizing in a different way the income process and allow the residual income growth (16) to become

$$g_{i,a,t} = f_i + \Delta m_{i,a,t} + (1 + \theta L)\Delta \varepsilon_{i,a,t} + \zeta_{i,a,t} \tag{23}$$

where the f_i is a fixed effect. The fundamental difference of this specification from the one presented before is that the income growth of a particular individual will be correlated over time. In the particular specification above, all theoretical autocovariances of order three or above will be equal to the variance of the fixed effect f_i. Consider starting with the null hypothesis that the model is of the form presented in (15) but with an unknown order for the MA process governing the transitory shock $v_{i,a,t} = \Theta_q(L)\varepsilon_{i,a,t}$. In practice we will have a panel data set containing some finite number of time series observations but a large number of individuals, which defines the maximum order of autocovariance that can be estimated. In the PSID these can be about 30 (using annual data). The pattern of empirical autocovariances consistent with (16) is one where they decline abruptly and become all insignificantly different from zero beyond that point. The pattern consistent with (23) is one where the autocovariances are never zero but after a point become all equal to each other, which is an estimate of the variance of f_i.

Evidence reported in MaCurdy (1982), Abowd and Card (1989), Topel and Ward (1992), Moffitt and Gottschalk (1994) and Meghir and Pistaferri (2004) and others all find similar results: Autocovariances decline in absolute value, they are statistically insignificant after the 1st or 2nd order, and have no clear tendency to be positive. They interpret this as evidence that there is no random growth term. Figure 4 uses PSID data and plot the second, third and fourth order autocovariances of earnings growth (with 95% confidence intervals) against calendar time. They confirm the findings in the literature: After the second lag no autocovariance is statistically significant for any of the years considered, and there are as many positive estimates as negative ones. In fact, there is no clear pattern in these estimates.

With a long enough panel and a large number of cross sectional observations we should be able to detect the difference between the two alternatives. However, there are a number of practical and theoretical difficulties. First, with the usual panel data, the higher order autocovariances are likely to be estimated based on a relatively low number of individuals. This, together with the fact that the residuals already contain noise from removing the estimated effects of characteristics such as age and even time effects will mean that higher order autocovariances are likely to be imprecisely estimated, even if the variance of f_i is indeed non-zero. Perhaps administrative data is one way round this, because we will be observing long run data on a large number of individuals. However, such data is not always available either because it is not organized in a usable way or because of confidentiality issues.

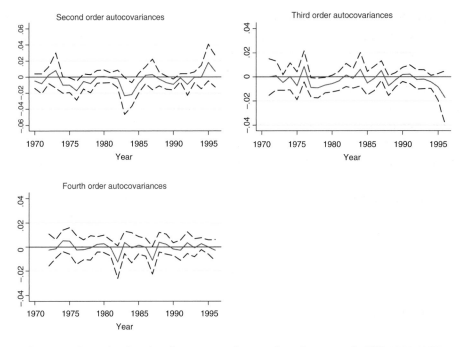

Figure 4   Second to fourth order autocovariances of earnings growth, PSID 1967-1997.

The other issue is that without a clearly articulated hypothesis we may not be able to distinguish among many possible alternatives, because we do not know the order of the MA process, q, or even if we should be using an MA or AR representation, or if the "permanent component" has a unit root or less. If we did, we could formulate a method of moments estimator and, subject to the constraints from the amount of years we observe, we could estimate our model and test our null hypothesis.

The practical identification problem is well illustrated by an argument in Guvenen (2009). Consider the possibility that the component we have been referring to as permanent, $p_{i,a,t}$, does not follow a random walk, but follows some stationary autoregressive process. In this case the increase in the variance over the life cycle will be captured by the term $a \times f_i$. The theoretical autocovariances of $g_{i,a,t}$ will never become exactly zero; they will start negative and gradually increase asymptotically to a positive number which will be the variance of f_i, say σ_f^2. Specifically if $p_{i,a,t} = \rho p_{i,a-1,t-1} + \zeta_{i,a,t}$ with $|\rho| < 1$, there is no other transitory stochastic component, and the variance of the initial draw of the permanent component is zero, the autocovariances of order k have the form

$$E\left(g_{i,a,t}g_{i,a-k,t-k}\right) = \sigma_f^2 + \rho^{k-1}\left[\frac{\rho-1}{\rho+1}\right]\sigma_\zeta^2 \quad \text{for } k > 0. \tag{24}$$

As ρ approaches one the autocovariances will approach σ_f^2. However, the autocovariance in (24) is the sum of a positive and a negative component. Guvenen (2009) has shown, based on simulations, that it is almost impossible in practice with the usual sample sizes to distinguish the implied pattern of the autocovariances from (24) from the one estimated from PSID data. The key problem with this is that the usual panel data that is available either follows individuals for a limited number of time periods, or suffers from severe attrition, which is probably not random, introducing biases. Thus, in practice it is very difficult to identify the nature of the income process without some prior assumptions and without combining information with another process, such as consumption or labor supply.

Haider and Solon (2006) provide a further illustration of how difficult it is to distinguish one model from the other. They are interested in the association between current and lifetime income. They write current log earnings as

$$y_{i,a,t} = h_i + a f_i$$

and lifetime earnings as (approximately)

$$\log V_i = r - \log r + h_i + r^{-1} f_i.$$

The slope of a regression of $y_{i,a,t}$ onto $\log V_i$ is:

$$\lambda_a = \frac{\sigma_h^2 + r^{-1} a \sigma_f^2}{\sigma_h^2 + r^{-1} \sigma_f^2}.$$

Hence, the model predicts that λ_a should increase linearly with age. In the absence of a random growth term ($\sigma_f^2 = 0$), $\lambda_a = 1$ at all ages. Figure 5, reproduced from Haider and Solon (2006) shows that there is evidence of a linear growth in λ_a only early in the life cycle (up until age 35); however, between age 35 and age 50 there is no evidence of a linear growth in λ_a (if anything, there is evidence that λ_a declines and one fails to reject the hypothesis $\lambda_a = 1$); finally, after age 50, there is evidence of a decline in λ_a that does not square well with any random growth term in earnings.

Other enrichments/issues The literature has addressed many other interesting issues having to do with wage dynamics, which here we only mention in passing. First, the importance of firm or match effects. Matched employer–employee data could be used to address these issues, and indeed some papers have taken important steps in this direction (see Abowd et al., 1999; Postel-Vinay and Robin, 2002; Guiso et al., 2005).

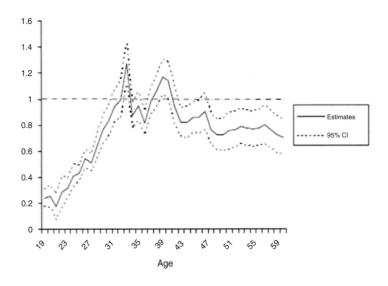

Figure 5   *Estimates of λ_a from Haider and Solon (2006).*

A number of papers have remarked that wages fall dramatically at job displacement, generating so-called "scarring" effects (Jacobson et al., 1993; von Wachter et al., 2007). The nature of these scarring effects is still not very well understood. On the one hand, people may be paid lower wages after a spell of unemployment due to fast depreciation of their skills (Ljunqvist and Sargent, 1998). Another explanation could be loss of specific human capital that may be hard to immediately replace at a random firm upon re-entry (see Low et al., forthcoming).

3.1.4. The conditional variance of earnings

The typical empirical strategy followed in the precautionary savings literature, in the attempt to understand the role of risk in shaping household asset accumulation choices, typically proceeds in two steps. In the first step, risk is estimated from a univariate ARMA process for earnings (similar to one of those described earlier). Usually the variance of the residual is the assumed measure of risk. There are some variants of this typical strategy—for example, allowing for transitory and permanent income shocks. In the second step, the outcome of interest (assets, savings, or consumption growth) is regressed onto the measure of risk obtained in the first stage, or simulations are used to infer the importance of the precautionary motive for saving. Examples include Banks et al. (2001) and Zeldes (1989). In one of the earlier attempts to quantify the importance of the precautionary motive for saving, Caballero (1990) concluded —using estimates of risk from MaCurdy (1982)—that precautionary savings could explain about 60% of asset accumulation in the US.

A few recent papers have taken up the issue of risk measurement (i.e., modeling the conditional variance of earnings) in a more complex way. Here we comment primarily on Meghir and Pistaferri (2004).[34]

Meghir and Pistaferri (2004) Returning to the model presented in Section 3.1.1 we can extend this by allowing the variances of the shocks to follow a dynamic structure with heterogeneity. A relatively simple possibility is to use ARCH(1) structures of the form

$$
\begin{aligned}
E_{t-1}(\varepsilon_{i,a,t}^2) &= \gamma_t + \gamma \varepsilon_{i,a-1,t-1}^2 + v_i \quad \text{Transitory} \\
E_{t-1}(\zeta_{i,a,t}^2) &= \varphi_t + \varphi \zeta_{i,a-1,t-1}^2 + \xi_i \quad \text{Permanent}
\end{aligned}
\tag{25}
$$

where $E_{t-1}(.)$ denotes an expectation conditional on information available at time $t-1$. The parameters are all education-specific. Meghir and Pistaferri (2004) test whether they vary across education. The terms γ_t and φ_t are year effects which capture the way that the variance of the transitory and permanent shocks change over time, respectively. In the empirical analysis they also allow for life cycle effects. In this specification we can interpret the lagged shocks ($\varepsilon_{i,a-1,t-1}$, $\zeta_{i,a-1,t-1}$) as reflecting the way current information is used to form revisions in expected risk. Hence it is a natural specification when thinking of consumption models which emphasize the role of the *conditional* variance in determining savings and consumption decisions.

The terms v_i and ξ_i are fixed effects that capture all those elements that are invariant over time and reflect long term occupational choices, etc. The latter reflects permanent variability of income due to factors unobserved by the econometrician. Such variability may in part have to do with the particular occupation or job that the individual has chosen. This variability will be known by the individuals when they make their occupational choices and hence it also reflects preferences. Whether this variability reflects permanent risk or not is of course another issue which is difficult to answer without explicitly modeling behavior.[35]

As far as estimating the mean and variance process of earnings is concerned, this model does not require the explicit specification of the distribution of the shocks; moreover the possibility that higher order moments are heterogeneous and/or follow some kind of dynamic process is not excluded. In this sense it is very well suited for investigating some key properties of the income process. Indeed this is important,

---

[34] See also Jensen and Shore (2008) for a similar approach.

[35] An interesting possibility allowed in ARCH models for time-series data is that of asymmetry of response to shocks. In other words, the conditional variance function is allowed to respond asymmetrically to positive and negative past shocks. This could be interesting here as well, for a considerable amount of asymmetry in the distribution of earnings is related to unemployment. Caballero (1990) shows that asymmetric distributions enhance the need for precautionary savings. In the case discussed here, however, models embedding the notion of asymmetry are not identifiable. The reason is that the transitory and permanent shocks are not separately observable.

because as discussed earlier the properties of the variance of income have implications for consumption and savings.

However, this comes at a price: first, Meghir and Pistaferri (2004) need to impose linear separability of heterogeneity and dynamics in both the mean and the variance. This allows them to deal with the initial conditions problem without any instruments. Second, they do not have a complete model that would allow them to simulate consumption profiles. Hence the model must be completed by specifying the entire distribution.

Identification of the ARCH process If the shocks ε and ζ were observable it would be straightforward to estimate the parameters of the ARCH process in (25). However they are not. What we do observe (or can estimate) is $g_{i,a,t} = \Delta m_{i,a,t} + (1+\theta L)\Delta\varepsilon_{i,a,t} + \zeta_{i,a,t}$. To add to the complication we have already argued that θ is not point identified. Nevertheless the following two key moment conditions identify the parameters of the ARCH process, conditional on the unobserved heterogeneity (ν and ξ):

$$E_{t-2}\left(g_{i,a+q+1,t+q+1}g_{i,a,t} - \theta\gamma_t - \gamma g_{i,a+q,t+q}g_{i,a-1,t-1} - \theta\nu_i\right) = 0 \quad \text{Transitory}$$

$$E_{t-q-3}\left[g_{i,a,t}\left(\sum_{j=-(1+q)}^{(1+q)} g_{i,a+j,t+j}\right)\right. \tag{26}$$

$$\left. -\varphi_t - \varphi g_{i,a-1,t-1}\left(\sum_{j=-(1+q)}^{(1+q)} g_{i,a+j-1,t+j-1}\right) - \xi_i\right] = 0 \qquad \text{Permanent.}$$

The important point here is that it is sufficient to know the order of the MA process q.[36] We do not need to know the parameters themselves. The parameter θ that appears in (26) for the transitory shock is just absorbed by the time effects on the variance or the heterogeneity parameter. Hence measurement error, which prevents the identification of the MA process does not prevent identification of the properties of the variance, so long as such error is classical.

The moments above are conditional on unobserved heterogeneity; to complete identification we need to control for that. As the moment conditions demonstrate, estimating the parameters of the variances is akin to estimating a dynamic panel data model with additive fixed effects. Typically we should be guided in estimation by asymptotic arguments that rely on the number of individuals tending to infinity and the number of time periods being fixed and relatively short.

One consistent approach to estimation would be to use first differences to eliminate the heterogeneity and then use instruments dated $t-3$ for the transitory shock and dated

---

[36] In cases where the order of the MA process is greater than 1 the parameter θ that appears in (26) is the parameter on the longest MA lag.

$t - q - 4$ for the permanent one. In this case the moment conditions become

$$E_{t-3}\left(\Delta g_{i,a+q+1,t+q+1}g_{i,a,t} - d_t^T - \gamma \Delta g_{i,a+q,t+q}g_{i,a-1,t-1}\right) = 0 \quad \text{Transitory}$$

$$E_{t-q-4}\left[\Delta g_{i,a,t}\left(\sum_{j=-(1+q)}^{(1+q)} g_{i,a+j,t+j}\right) - d_t^P\right.$$

$$\left. -\varphi \Delta g_{i,a-1,t-1}\left(\sum_{j=-(1+q)}^{(1+q)} g_{i,a+j-1,t+j-1}\right)\right] = 0 \qquad \text{Permanent}$$

(27)

where $\Delta x_t = x_t - x_{t-1}$. In practice, however, as Meghir and Pistaferri (2004) found out, lagged instruments suggested above may be only very weakly correlated with the entities in the expectations above. This means that the rank condition for identification is not satisfied and consequently the ARCH parameters may not be identifiable through this approach. An alternative may be to use a likelihood approach, which will exploit all the moments implied by the specification and the distributional assumption; this however may be particularly complicated. A convenient approximation may be to use a within group estimator on (26). This involves subtracting the individual mean of each expression on the right hand side, i.e. just replace all expressions in (26) by quantities where the individual mean has been removed. For example $g_{i,a+q+1,t+q+1}g_{i,a,t}$ is replaced by $g_{i,a+q+1,t+q+1}g_{i,a,t} - \frac{1}{T-q-1}\Sigma_{t=1}^{T-q-1}g_{i,a+q+1,t+q+1}g_{i,a,t}$. Nickell (1981) and Nerlove (1971) have shown that this estimator is inconsistent for fixed T. Effectively this implies that the estimates may be biased when T is short because the individual specific mean may not satisfy the moment conditions for short T. In practice this estimator will work well with long panel data. Meghir and Pistaferri use individuals observed for at least 16 periods. Effectively, while ARCH effects are likely to be very important for understanding behavior, there is no doubt that they are difficult to identify. A likelihood based approach, although very complex, may ultimately prove the best way forward.

Other approaches

3.1.5. A summary of existing studies

In this section we provide a summary of the key studies in the literature.[37] Most of the information is summarized in Table 2, but we also offer a brief description of the key results of the papers in the text. Some of the earliest studies are those of Hause (1980), who was investigating the importance of on-the-job training, and Lillard and Willis (1978), who were interested in earnings mobility. Both find an important role for

---

[37] In the discussion of the literature we make primarily reference to US studies on males. See among others Dickens (2000) for the UK, Cappellari (2004) for Italy, and Alvarez (2004) for Spain. There is little evidence on female earnings dynamics, most likely because of the difficulty of modeling labor market participation (see Hyslop, 2001; Voena, 2010).

Table 2 Income process studies.

Authors	Year publ.	Data	Measure of income	Specification	Results
Lillard & Willis	1978	1967-73 PSID males	Annual earnings in levels	$u_{i,a,t} = h_i + p_{i,a,t}$ $p_{i,a,t} = \rho p_{i,a-1,t-1} + \zeta_{i,a,t}$	Individual fixed effects explain 73% of cross-sectional variance with no covariates (i.e., $\frac{\sigma_h^2}{\sigma_u^2} = 0.73$). Controls for standard wage equation covariates reduce this share to 60.6%; with additional controls for labor market conditions, the figure is 47.1%. AR shock has little persistence ($\rho = 0.35$ with full covariates, $\rho = 0.406$ with time effects only).[a]
Hause	1980	1964-69 Swedish males aged 21-26	Annual earnings in levels	$y_{i,a,t} = h_i + f_i a + u_{i,a,t}$ $u_{i,a,t} = \rho u_{i,a-1,t-1} + \varepsilon_{i,a,t}$ $\varepsilon_{i,a,t} \sim \text{niid}(0, \sigma_\varepsilon^2)$	Individual heterogeneity in slope and intercept of early-career earnings profile is substantial. Variance of AR innovations declines rapidly with time. In model with stationary process for $u_{i,a,t}$, $\sigma_{hf} < 0$, consistent with tradeoff between initial earnings and wage growth predicted by a human capital model.[b]

Table 2 (continued)

Authors	Year publ.	Data	Measure of income	Specification	Results
MaCurdy	1982	1967–76 PSID continuously married white males	Annual earnings in first-differences and levels, Average hourly wages in first-differences and levels	$u_{i,a,t} = h_i + e_{i,a,t}$ $e_{i,a,t} \sim \text{ARMA}(p,q)$	Estimated variance of individual fixed effect h_i is negative and insignificant, so individual heterogeneity is dropped in main specification. Both measures of income are stationary in first-differences and non-stationary in levels (i.e., the author finds a random walk component in levels). MA(2) or ARMA(1,1) is preferred for first-differences. ARMA(1,2) with a unit root ($\rho = 0.975$ for wages, $\rho = 0.974$ for earnings, not significantly different from 1) is preferred for levels.
Abowd & Card	1989	1969–79 PSID males 1969–79 PSID males excluding SEO 1966–75 NLS males 1971–75 SIME/DIME control group	Annual earnings in first-differences Annual hours in first-differences	$g_{i,a,t}^{\text{earnings}} = \mu v_{i,a,t} + \Delta m_{i,a,t}^{\text{earnings}}$ $+ e_{i,a,t}^{\text{earnings}}$ $g_{it}^{\text{hours}} = v_{i,a,t} + \Delta m_{i,a,t}^{\text{hours}} + e_{i,a,t}^{\text{hours}}$ $v \sim \text{MA}(2)$, e, m serially uncorrelated. $m^{\text{earnings}} \perp\!\!\!\perp m^{\text{hours}}$, e have unrestricted within period VCV. v, m, e mutually independent	Extensive fitting procedure supports MA(2) for persistent shock v. Loading factor μ would capture behavioral responses to changes in the wage rate ($\mu = 1$ implies proportional changes in hours and earnings at a constant wage). However, changes in earnings do not seem to reflect behavioral responses to wage changes: $\mu = 1.09$ in PSID, 1.35 in PSID excluding SEO, 1.56 in NLS, 1.01 in SIME/DIME: $\mu = 1$ is not rejected in any sample.

(continued on next page)

Table 2 (continued)

Authors	Year publ.	Data	Measure of income	Specification	Results
Topel & Ward	1992	1957–72 LEED file, males only (matched firm–worker administrative records)	Quarterly SS earnings from a single employer, in annual first-differences[c]	$g_{i,a,t} = \Delta\eta_{i,a,t}$ where $\eta_{i,a,t} = p_{i,a,t} + e_{i,a,t}$ contains an AR(1) $(p_{i,a,t}) +$ a white noise $(e_{i,a,t})$.	Raw autocovariance of earnings growth is strongly negative at one lag, then is small (insignificant) and negative at higher lags. AR coefficient $\rho = 0.970$ is insignificantly different from 1. Authors conclude on-the-job wage growth is a random walk, and so current wage is a sufficient statistic for the value of a job for early-career workers.
Gottschalk & Moffitt	1995	1969–87 PSID white males	Annual earnings in levels	$u_{iat} = \mu_t p_{i,a,t} + v_{i,a,t}$ $p_{ia} = p_{i,a-1,t-1} + \zeta_{i,a,t}$ $v_{ia} = \rho_t v_{i,a-1,t-1} + e_{i,a,t}$ $\quad + \lambda_t \theta e_{i,a-1,t-1}$ Legend: Loading of persistent shock (μ_t), AR coefficient (ρ_t), MA coefficient (λ_t), persistent earnings shock $(\zeta_{i,a,t})$, and transitory earnings shock $(e_{a,t})$.	Half the increase in cross-sectional variance is due to increase in the transitory innovation variance, and half is due to increase in the permanent innovation variance. Increase in transitory variance dominated in the second half of the 1980s.

Table 2 (continued)

Authors	Year publ.	Data	Measure of income	Specification	Results
Farber & Gibbons	1996	1979-91 NLSY males and females after 1st transition to work	Hourly wage rate in levels	$u_{i,a,t} = p_{i,a,t} + m_{i,a,t}$ $p_{i,a,t} = p_{i,a-1,t-1} + \zeta_{i,a,t}$	Authors reject hypothesis of martingale with classical measurement error or with AR(1) measurement error. Also run specification with stationary AR(1) in v_{it} and rejects it.
Baker	1997	1967-86 PSID males	Annual earnings in first-differences and levels	Model 1 (HIP): $u_{i,a,t} = h_i + f_i a + p_{i,a,t}$ $g_{i,a,t} = f_i + \Delta p_{i,a,t}$ where $p_{i,a,t} = \rho p_{i,a-1,t-1} + \zeta_{i,a,t}$ (AR(1)). Model 2 (RIP with RW): $u_{i,a,t} = h_i + e_{i,a,t}$ $g_{i,a,t} = \Delta e_{i,a,t}$ $e_{i,a,t} \sim$ ARMA(1,1) or ARMA(1,2), time-varying variances for innovations to $e_{i,a,t}$ are estimated in both models.	Tests and rejects restrictions of no heterogeneity in growth rates and levels (in OLS estimates of HIP model). RIP specification does not reject RW. Nested model yields $\rho = 0.665$; first-differenced estimates of nested model yield much smaller AR coefficient. Monte Carlo evidence is presented suggesting that joint tests for zero higher-order autocovariances overreject with small samples or a large number of restrictions (as is the case here).

(continued on next page)

Table 2 (continued)

Authors	Year publ.	Data	Measure of income	Specification	Results
Chamberlain & Hirano	1999	1967-1991 PSID males aged 24-33	Annual earnings	$y_{i,a,t} = g_t(x(i,\beta)) + h_i + P_{i,a,t} + v_{i,a,t}$ $P_{i,a,t} = \rho P_{i,a-1,t-1} + \zeta_{i,a,t}$ Transitory shock $v_{i,a,t}$ heteroskedastic across individuals: $v_{i,a,t} \sim N(0, \frac{1}{h_i})$ $h_{i,a,t} \sim$ Gamma.	Substantial heteroskedasticity in $v_{i,a,t}$. AR coefficient point estimate $= 0.98$.
Geweke & Keane	2000	1968-89 PSID males	Annual earnings	$y_{i,a,t} = \lambda y_{i,a-1,t-1} + (1-\lambda)$ $[X_{i,a,t}\beta + h_i + \mu P_{i,0,t-a}] + P_{i,a,t}$ $P_{i,a,t} = \rho P_{i,a-1,t-1} + \zeta_{i,a,t}$ Initial conditions $y_{i,0,t-a} = X^0_{i,0,t-a}\beta^0 + \zeta_{i,0,t-a}$ Innovations $\zeta_{i,a,t}$ and initial conditions draw $\zeta_{i,0,t-a}$ drawn from mixtures of 3 normals, allowing for non-normality of shocks. Initial conditions depend on different observables (X^0) than do current-period earnings (X). Marital status jointly modeled.	AR coefficient ρ on shock is 0.665, but not directly comparable to other AR coefficients because model includes lagged earnings. 60% to 70% of cross-section variance due to transitory shocks. Strong evidence of non-normality for initial conditions draw $\zeta_{i,0,t-a}$ and innovations $\zeta_{i,a,t}$: both shocks are left skewed and leptokurtic (density at mode about 3 times larger than predicted by normality). Non-normal shocks greatly improve fit to cross-sectional distribution and predictions of economic mobility. Non-normal model has less serial correlation.

Table 2 (continued)

Authors	Year publ.	Data	Measure of income	Specification	Results
Baker & Solon	2003	1975–83 Canadian males (administrative income tax records)	Annual earnings	$u_{i,a,t} = \mu_t[h_i + f_i a + p_{i,a,t}] + e_{i,a,t}$ $p_{i,a,t} = p_{i,a-1,t-1} + \zeta_{i,a,t}$ (random walk in permanent income) $e_{i,a,t} = \rho e_{i,a-1,t-1} + \lambda_t \epsilon_{i,a,t}$ (AR(1) with time-varying variance in transitory income) $\epsilon_{i,a,t} \sim \text{niid}(0, \sigma_{\text{age}}^2)$ (age-varying heteroskedasticity in transitory earnings innovation).	Estimated separately for two-year birth cohorts, both random walk component and profile heterogeneity (HIP and RIP) are important. Restricted specifications ($\sigma_\zeta = 0$, or $\sigma_f = 0$) inflate ρ and attribute more of the variance to transitory shocks (instability) than in the unrestricted model. Transitory innovation variance is U-shaped over the life cycle.
Meghir & Pistaferri	2004	PSID males 1968–1993	Annual earnings in first differences	Three education groups: High School Dropout (D), High School Graduate (H) and College (C). For each education group: $\ln y_{i,a,t} = f(a,t) + p_{i,a,t} + e_{i,a,t} + m_{i,a,t} \, p_{i,a,t} =$ $p_{i,a-1,t-1} + \epsilon_{i,a,t} \, e_{i,a,t} =$ $\xi_{i,a,t} + \theta\xi_{i,a-1,t-1} m_{i,a,t}$ is i.i.d. measurement error $\epsilon_{i,a,t}$ and $\xi_{i,a,t}$ are serially uncorrelated model conditional variance of shocks as: $E_{t-1}(\epsilon_{i,a,t}) =$ $d_{1t} + \zeta_{1i} + g_1(\text{age}) +$ $\rho\epsilon_{i,a-1,t-1}^2 \, E_{t-1}(\xi_{i,a,t}) =$ $d_{2t} + \zeta_{2i} + g_2(\text{age}) + \rho_\xi \xi_{i,a-1,t-1}^2$	Tested for absence of unit root using autocovariance structure and reject. Error process set to random walk plus MA(1) transitory shock plus measurement error. Variances of shocks (permanent, transitory) D:(0.033, 0.055), H:(0.028, 0.027), C:(0.044, 0.005) pooled: (0.031, 0.030); ARCH effects (permanent, transitory): D:(0.33, 0.19), H:(0.89, 067), C:(0.028, 0.39), pooled: (0.56, 0.40)

(continued on next page)

Table 2 (continued)

Authors	Year publ.	Data	Measure of income	Specification	Results
Haider & Solon	2006	1951–91 HRS-SSA matched panel males[d]	Annual earnings (observe SS-taxable earnings)	Assume panel distribution of log yearly earnings $y_{i,a,t}$ is MVN, i.e., log earnings normal in each year, jointly distributed MVN. The authors can then impute censored earnings with a Tobit in each year. Pairwise ACVs across all years in panel are estimated with separate bivariate Tobits.	Measurement error and transitory shocks imply that annual earnings in any given year are a poor proxy for lifetime earnings in that it is subject to non-classical measurement error that varies over the life cycle.[e]
Browning, Alvarez, & Ejrnaes	2006	1968–93 PSID white males	Annual after-tax earnings	For each individual/age: $y_t = \delta(1 - \omega^t) + \alpha t + \beta^t y_0 + \sum_{s=0}^{t-1} \beta^s (\epsilon_{t-s} + \theta \epsilon_{t-s-1})^f$ $y_t^{obs} = y_t + m_t$ (classical measurement error), ϵ ARCH(1) and m i.i.d. Individual heterogeneity allowed in $(\nu, \theta, \alpha, \beta, \delta, \omega)$. Distributions are parametrized as linear or logistic (for restricted parameters) functions of 6 independent normal latent factors.	The model is estimated under different assumptions regarding AR coefficient β: (1) β is a unit root for everyone, (2) $\beta < 1$ for everyone, and (3) β is a mixture of a unit root and a stable AR. Of these, a model where $\beta < 1$ for all agents is the only one not conclusively rejected by χ^2 tests. The median AR coefficient is 0.79.

Table 2 (continued)

Authors	Year publ.	Data	Measure of income	Specification	Results
Hryshko	2008	1968–97 PSID males excluding SEO	Annual earnings, first–differences and levels	$u_{i,a,t} = h_i + f_i a + p_{i,a,t} + v_{i,a,t} + m_{i,a,t}$ $p_{i,a,t} = p_{i,a-1,t-1} + \zeta_{i,a,t}$ $v_{i,a,t} = \theta(L)\epsilon_{i,a,t}$, i.e., heterogeneous intercept and slope, measurement error, RW in permanent income, and MA in transitory component.	Estimates in first–differences with σ_m^2 fixed at point estimate from another specification yield no heterogeneity in growth rates.
Altonji, Smith & Vidangos	2009	1978–96 PSID males	Annual earnings. Hours, wages, job transitions also used	$y_{i,a,t} = \gamma_0 + \gamma_X X_{i,a,t} +$ $\gamma_w(w^{\text{latent}} - \gamma_0 - \gamma_X X_{i,a,t}) +$ $\gamma_h(h_{i,a,t} - \gamma_0 - \gamma_X X_{i,a,t}) + e_{i,a,t}$ $e_{i,a,t} = \rho_e e_{i,a-1,t-1} + \epsilon_{i,a,t} y_{i,a,t}$ is log wages (not the residual): wage w and hours h are endogenous, with their own dynamic error structure. This is a joint statistical model of employment transitions, wages, hours worked, and earnings.[h] Discrete outcomes (employment transitions) are probit (usually with multiple error components): all shocks are independent normals. Wages, hours, and earnings are log–linear. Other important aspects: wage and hours include two individual fixed effects: μ_i ("ability") appears in all structural equations; n_i ("mobility") appears in all but the wage equation.	Authors present some simulated variance decompositions for lifetime and cross–sectional log earnings (not residuals) among white males. Earnings shocks and hours shocks contribute more than twice as much to cross–sectional variance than they do to lifetime variance (25% vs. 9% for both shocks combined). Search frictions (job–specific wage/hours shocks, job destruction, and job–to–job changes) generate 37% of variance in lifetime earnings, with job–specific wage shocks most important. Ability (μ) generates 11% of lifetime earnings variance, and education generates 31.4% of variance.[g]

(continued on next page)

Table 2 (continued)

Authors	Year publ.	Data	Measure of income	Specification	Results
Guvenen	2009	1968–93 PSID males	Annual earnings in levels	$u_{i,a,t} = h_i + f_i a + p_{i,a,t} + \mu_t v_{i,a,t} + \lambda_t \xi_{i,a,t}$ $p_{i,a,t} = \rho p_{i,a-1,t-1} + v_{i,a,t}$ $v_{i,a,t} \sim$ i.i.d.	Estimates of the process with slope heterogeneity yield estimates of AR coefficient ρ significantly below 1 (0.821 in the full sample), while estimates without heterogeneity ($\sigma_f = 0$) indicate a random walk in permanent income. MaCurdy's (1982) test for heterogeneity is criticized for low power regarding higher-order autocovariances.
Low, Meghir & Pistaferri	2010	SIPP	Hourly rate in first differences	$w_{i,j(t_0),a,t} = p_{i,a,t} + \epsilon_{i,a,t} + v_{i,j(t_0),a,t}$ $p_{i,a,t} = p_{i,a-1,t-1} + \zeta_{i,a,t}$ where $v_{i,j(t_0),a,t}$ is a match fixed effect. Allow for job mobility and participation. Estimates parameters using wage growth moments and allows for endogenous selection due to job mobility and employment.	Estimated standard deviation of permanent shocks is 0.10, of the match effect 0.23 and of the measurement error 0.09. Ignoring mobility increases st. dev of permanent shock to 0.15.

a Authors cut sample by race (black/white).

b No covariates, so profile heterogeneity captures differences across education groups (focus is on low education workers).

c I.e., $g_{i,a,t} = y_{i,a,t} - y_{i,a-4,t-4}$ where t indexes quarters.

d 1931–33 birth cohort only.

e Sample average estimated ACVs pooled over full earnings history (from bivariate Tobit procedures) are very close to results from uncensored data in other studies (Baker and Solon, 2003, Böhlmark and Lindquist, 2006): ACV1 = 0.89, ACV2 = 0.82, ACV3 = 0.78, ACV4 = 0.75, ACV5 = 0.72, ACV6 = 0.69.

f $[\delta]$ = "long-run" average earnings; $[\omega]$ = inverse speed of convergence to "long-run" average earnings; $[\alpha]$ = linear time trend; $[\beta]$ = AR(1) coefficient; $[\theta]$ = MA(1) coefficient; $[\epsilon]$ = ARCH WN, with constant v, ARCH coefficient $\frac{\exp(\phi)}{1+\exp(\phi)}$.

g Parametrization of the model makes it difficult to compare point estimates to other results from the literature. Results for impulse-response to particular shocks are interesting results, but the less detailed models in the income-process literature reviewed here typically present unconditional dynamic behavior rather than distinguishing particular shocks.

h "Joint" in the sense that it is more complex than the univariate earnings processes presented here, but still based only on labor market behavior; "statistical" in the sense that the model's structural equations are not derived from utility maximization.

unobserved heterogeneity and conclude that the process of income is stationary. Hause used the idea of heterogeneous income profiles, which later played a central role in the debate in this literature.

Following these papers are two of the most important works in this literature, namely MaCurdy (1982) and Abowd and Card (1989). Both use PSID data for ten years, but covering different time periods. Abowd and Card also use NLS data and data from an income maintenance experiment. The emphasis on these papers is precisely to understand the time series properties of earnings and extract information relating to the variance of the shocks. They both conclude that the best representation of earnings is one with a unit root in levels and MA(2) in first differences. Abowd and Card go further and also model the time series properties of hours of work jointly with earnings, potentially extracting the extent to which earnings fluctuations are due to hours fluctuations. The papers by Low et al. (forthcoming) and Altonji et al. (2009), which explicitly make the distinction between shocks and endogenous responses to shocks, can be seen as related to this work. Similar conclusions are reached by Topel and Ward (1992) using matched firm-worker administrative records spanning 16 years. They conclude that earnings are best described by a random walk plus an i.i.d. error.

In an important paper Gottschalk and Moffitt (1995) use the permanent-transitory decomposition to fit data on earnings and to try to understand the relative importance of the change in the permanent and transitory variance in explaining the changes in US inequality over the 1980s and 1990s. Their permanent component is defined to be a random walk with a time varying variance. The transitory component is an AR(1), also with time varying variance. Both variances were shown to increase over time. They also consider a variety of other models including most importantly the random growth model, where age is interacted with a fixed effect. As we have already explained, this is an important alternative to the random walk model because they both explain the increase in variance of earnings with age, but have fundamentally different economic implications. In their results the two models fit equally well the data[38]. Based on earlier results by Abowd and Card (1989), Gottschalk and Moffitt choose the random walk model as their vehicle for analysis of inequality and mobility patterns in the data.

Farber and Gibbons (1996) provide a structural interpretation of wage dynamics. The key idea here is that firms publicly learn the worker's ability and at each point in time the wage is set equal to the conditional expectation of workers' productivity. Among other results this implies that wage *levels* follow a martingale. The result is however fragile; for example, if heterogeneous returns to experience are allowed for, the martingale result no longer holds. Their results indeed reject the martingale hypothesis. The model is quite restrictive, because it does not allow for the incumbent firm to have superior information

---

[38] The χ^2 for the random growth model is slightly larger than the one based on the model with the random walk. However, the models are not nested and such a comparison is not directly valid without suitable adjustments.

as in Acemoglu and Pischke (1998). Moreover, given the specification in levels (rather than in logs), the relevance of this paper to the literature we are discussing here is mainly because of its important attempt to offer a structural interpretation to wage dynamics rather than for its actual results.

Baker (1997) compares results of fitting the profile heterogeneity model[39] to the one where a unit root is allowed for. He fits the levels model to the level of autocovariances of log earnings. When no profile heterogeneity is allowed for, the model displays a unit root. However, when profile heterogeneity is allowed for, the unit root becomes an autoregressive coefficient of about 0.6. Thus, clearly, the unit root is required, when heterogeneity is not allowed for to explain the long term persistence and presumably the increasing variance over the life cycle. However, this can be captured equally well by the profile heterogeneity. As remarked by Gottschalk and Moffitt, and Baker himself, the profile heterogeneity model, as specified by Baker, will imply autocovariances that are increasing with the square of experience/age.[40] However, Baker does not seem to exploit this pattern because he fits the autocovariance structure without conditioning on age or potential experience. This may reduce the ability to reject the profile heterogeneity model in favor of the unit root one. Nevertheless, with his approach he finds that both the unit root model and the profile heterogeneity model fit the data similarly. However, when estimating the encompassing model, $u_{i,a,t} = h_i + a \times f_i + p_{i,a,t}$ with $p_{i,a,t} = \rho p_{i,a-1,t-1} + \zeta_{i,a,t}$, ρ, the coefficient on the AR component is significantly lower than 1, rejecting the unit root hypothesis; moreover the variance of f_i is significantly different from zero. On the basis of this, the best fitting model would be heterogeneous income profiles with a reasonably persistent transitory shock. Nevertheless, there still is a puzzle: the autocovariances of residual income growth of order higher than two are all very small and individually insignificant. Baker directly tests that these are indeed *jointly* zero and despite the apparent insignificance of all of them individually he rejects this hypothesis and concludes that the evidence against the unit root and in favor of the profile heterogeneity model is strong. We suspect that his may be due to the way inference was carried out: Meghir and Pistaferri (2004) also test that all autocovariances of order 3 or more are zero (in the PSID) and they fail to reject this with a *p*-value of 12%.[41] Perhaps the reason for this difference with Baker is that Meghir and Pistaferri use the block bootstrap, thus bypassing the problem of estimating the covariance matrix of the second order moments using the fourth order ones and allowing for more general serial correlation.

The unit root model is particularly attractive for understanding such phenomena as the increase in the variance of consumption over the life cycle, as originally documented by Deaton and Paxson (1994); the fact that mobility in income exceeds mobility in

---

[39] By profile heterogeneity he means that the residual in the earnings equation is $h_i + a \times f_i + v_{i,a,t}$, where $v_{i,a,t}$ may follow an MA or a stationary AR model. This model is also known as Heterogeneous Income Profiles (HIP).

[40] He used $a \times f_i$. Other functional forms would imply different patterns. Consider for example $\sqrt{a} \times f_i$.

[41] See note to Table II in Meghir and Pistaferri (2004).

consumption (Jappelli and Pistaferri, 2006); and the fact that the consumption distribution is more lognormal than the income distribution (Battistin et al., 2009). However, the heterogeneous income profiles model is also attractive from the point of view of labor economics. It is well documented that returns to education and experience tend to increase with ability indicators. Such ability indicators are either unobserved in data sets used for studying earnings dynamics or are simply inadequate and not used. There is no real reason why the two hypotheses should be competing and they are definitely not logically inconsistent with each other. Indeed a model with a unit root process and a transitory component as well as a heterogeneous income profile is identifiable.

Specifically, Baker and Solon (2003) estimate a model along the lines of the specification in (21), which allows both for profile heterogeneity and imposes a random walk on the permanent component, as well as an AR(1) transitory one. Their rich model is estimated with a large Canadian administrative data set. There is enough in their model to allow for the possibility that individual components are unimportant. For example the variance of the permanent shock could be estimated to be zero, in which case the model would be one of profile heterogeneity with an autoregressive component, very much like in Baker (1997). Yet the variance of the permanent shock is very precisely estimated and indeed quite large (0.007). Thus these authors find clear evidence (on Canadian data) of both a permanent shock and of long run heterogeneity in the growth profiles. Thinking of the permanent shocks as uncertainty and profile heterogeneity as information known by the individual at the start of life, their estimation provides an interesting balance between the amount of wage variance due to uncertainty and that due to heterogeneity: on the one hand their estimate is a quarter that of Meghir and Pistaferri (2004); on the other hand it is still substantial from a welfare perspective and in terms of its implications for precautionary savings.

Meghir and Pistaferri (2004) adopt the unit root model with MA transitory shocks and measurement error, after testing the specification and finding it acceptable. With their approach they do not find evidence of profile heterogeneity. They also allow for the variances of the shocks to depend on age, time and unobserved heterogeneity as well as ARCH effects. The latter are important because they reflect the volatility of uncertainty. In their model they thus allow heteroskedasticity due to permanent heterogeneity to compete with the impact of volatility shocks. They find very large ARCH effects both for the permanent and the transitory shock, implying large effects on precautionary savings, over and above the effects due to the average variance of the shocks. They also find strong evidence of permanent heterogeneity in variances. One interpretation is that there is considerable uncertainty in income profiles, as expressed by the random walk, but there is also widespread heterogeneity in the distributions from which the permanent and transitory income shocks are drawn. Indeed this idea of heterogeneity was taken up by Browning et al. (2006) who estimate an income process with almost all aspects being individual-specific. They conclude that the nature of the income process varies across individuals, with some being best characterized by a unit root in the process, while others by a stationary one.

Clearly the presence of a random walk in earnings is controversial and has led to a voluminous amount of work. This is not because of some nerdy or pedantic fixation with the exact time series specification of income but is due to the importance of this issue for asset accumulation and welfare.[42]

Guvenen (2009) compares what he calls a HIP (heterogeneous income profiles) income process and a RIP (restricted income profiles) income process and their empirical implications. The (log) income process (in a simplified form) is as follows:

$$y_{i,a,t} = X'_{i,a,t}\beta_t + h_i + a \times f_i + p_{i,a,t} + d_t\varepsilon_{i,a,t}$$
$$p_{i,a,t} = \rho p_{i,a-1,t-1} + \varphi_t\zeta_{i,a,t}$$

with an initial condition equal to 0.

The estimation strategy is based on minimizing the "distance" between the elements of the $(T \times T)$ empirical covariance matrix of income residuals in levels and its counterpart implied by the model described above (where income residuals $\hat{y}_{i,a,t}$ are obtained regressing $y_{i,a,t}$ on $X'_{i,a,t}$).[43] The main findings are as follows. First, mis-specification of a HIP process as a RIP process results in a biased estimation of the persistence parameter ρ and an overestimation of σ_ε^2. The estimates of ρ are much smaller for HIP ($\rho = 0.82$) compared to RIP ($\rho = 0.99$—insignificantly different from 1). When estimating HIP models, the dispersion of income profiles (σ_f^2) is significant. This dispersion is higher for more educated groups. Finally, 65 to 80 percent of income inequality at the age of retirement is due to heterogeneous profiles.

Hryshko (2009), in an important paper, sets out to resolve the random walk vs. stochastic growth process controversy by carrying out Monte Carlo simulations and empirical analysis on PSID data. First, he generates data based on a process with a random walk and persistent transitory shocks. He then fits a (misspecified) model assuming heterogenous age profiles and an AR(1) component and finds that the estimated persistence of the AR component is biased downwards and that there is evidence for heterogeneous age profile. In the empirical data he finds that the model with the random walk cannot be rejected, while he finds little evidence in support of the model with heterogeneous growth rates. While these results are probably not going to be viewed as conclusive, what is clear is that the encompassing model of, say, Baker (1997) may not be

---

[42] For example, if the income process were written as $y_{ia,,t} = h_i + a \times f_i + \varepsilon_{i,a,t}$, with $\varepsilon_{i,a,t}$ being an i.i.d. error term, consumption would respond very little to changes in income (unless consumers had to learn about f_i and/or h_i, see Guvenen (2007).

[43] The main problem when using the autocovariances is that because of sample attrition, fewer and fewer individuals contribute to the higher autocovariances, raising concerns about potential selectivity bias. Using also consumption data would help to overcome this problem since consumption is forward looking by nature, see Guvenen and Smith (2009).

a reliable way of testing the competing hypotheses. It also shows that the evidence for the random walk is indeed very strong and reinforces the results by Baker and Solon (2003), which support the presence of a unit root as well as heterogeneous income profiles.

Most approaches described above have been based on quite parsimonious time series representations. However three papers stand out for their attempt to model the process in a richer fashion: Geweke and Keane (2000) and Chamberlain and Hirano (1999) use a Bayesian approach and allow for more complex dynamics and (in the latter) for heterogeneity in the dynamics of income; Browning et al. (2006) emphasize the importance of heterogeneity even more. Specifically, Geweke and Keane (2000) follow a Bayesian approach to model life cycle earnings based on the PSID, with the primary motivation of understanding income mobility and to improve the fit *vis-à-vis* earlier mobility studies, such as the one by Lillard and Willis (1978). Their modeling approach is very flexible, allowing for lagged income, serially correlated shocks and permanent unobserved characteristics. They find that at any point in time about 60-70% of the variance in earnings is accounted for by transitory shocks that average out over the life cycle. But the result they emphasize most is the fact that the shocks are not normal and that allowing for departure from normal heteroskedastic shocks is crucial for fitting the data. In this respect their results are similar to those of Meghir and Pistaferri (2004), who allow for ARCH effects. Nevertheless, the interpretation of the two models is different, because of the dynamics in the variance allowed by the latter.

Similar to Geweke and Keane, Chamberlain and Hirano (1999) also use a Bayesian approach to estimate predictive distributions of earnings, given past histories; they also use data from the PSID. They motivate their paper explicitly by thinking of an individual who has to predict future income when making consumption plans. The main difference of their approach from that of Geweke and Keane is that they allow for heteroskedastic innovations to income and heterogeneity in the dynamics of earnings. They find that the shock process has a unit root when the serial correlation coefficient is constrained to be one for all individuals. When it is allowed to be heterogeneous it is centered around 0.97 with a population standard deviation of 0.07, which implies about half individuals having a unit root in their process.

Browning et al. (2006) extend this idea further by allowing the entire income process to be heterogeneous. Their model allows for all parameters of the income process to be different across individuals, including a heterogeneous income profile and a heterogeneous serial correlation coefficient restricted to be in the open interval (0, 1). This stable model is then mixed with a unit root model, with some mixing probability estimated from the data. This then implies that with some probability an individual faces an income process with a unit root; alternatively the process is stationary with heterogenous coefficients. They estimate their model using the same PSID data as Meghir and Pistaferri (2004) and find that the median AR(1) coefficient is 0.8, with a proportion of individuals (about 30%) having an AR(1) coefficient over 0.9. They attribute their result to the fact that they have decoupled the serial correlation properties of the shocks from the speed of convergence to some long run mean, which is governed by a different coefficient.

Beyond the controversy on the nature of the income process (but not unrelated), a newer literature has emerged, where the sources of uncertainty are distinguished in a more structural fashion. We discuss these papers and other related contributions in Section 5.

4. USING CHOICES TO LEARN ABOUT RISK

In this section we discuss papers that use consumption and income data jointly. Traditionally, this was done for testing the implications of the life cycle permanent income hypothesis, for example the main proposition that consumption responds strongly to permanent income and very little to transitory income. In this traditional view, the income process was taken as given and it was assumed that the individual had the same amount of information as the econometrician. In this approach, the issue of interest was insurance (or more properly "smoothing") not information. More recently, a number of papers have argued that consumption and income data can be used jointly to measure the extent of risk faced by households and understand its nature. This approach starts from the consideration that the use of income data alone is unlikely to be conclusive about the extent of risk that people face. The idea is to use actual individual choices (such as consumption, labor supply, human capital investment decisions) to infer the amount of risk that people face. This is because, assuming consumers behave rationally, their actual choices will reflect the amount of risk that they face. Among the papers pursuing this idea, Blundell and Preston (1998), and Cunha et al. (2005) deserve a special mention. As correctly put by Cunha and Heckman (2007), "purely statistical decompositions cannot distinguish uncertainty from other sources of variability. Transitory components as measured by a statistical decomposition may be perfectly predictable by agents, partially predictable or totally unpredictable". Another reason why using forward looking "choices" allows us to learn about features of the earnings process is that consumption choices should reflect the nature of income changes. For example, if we were to observe a large consumption response to a given income change, we could infer that the income change is unanticipated and persistent (Blundell and Preston, 1998; Guvenen and Smith, 2009). We discuss these two approaches, together with notable contributions, in turn.

4.1. Approach 1: identifying insurance for a given information set

Using joint data on consumption and income to estimate the impact of income on consumption has a long tradition in economics. Following Friedman (1957), many researchers have used consumption and income data (both aggregate data and household data) to test the main implication of the theory, namely that consumption is strongly related to permanent income and not much related to current or transitory income. Papers that do this include Liviatan (1963), Bhalla (1979), Musgrove (1979),

Attfield (1976, 1980), Mayer (1972), Klein and Liviatan (1957), and Kreinin (1961). Later contributions include Sargent (1978), Wolpin (1982) and Paxson (1992).

Most papers propose a statistical representation of the following type:

$$Y = Y^P + Y^T$$
$$C = C^P + C^T$$
$$Y^P = X^P \beta^P + \zeta$$
$$Y^T = X^T \beta^T + \varepsilon$$
$$C^P = \kappa^P Y^P$$
$$C^T = \kappa^T Y^T + \eta$$

in which $Y(C)$ is current income (consumption), divided into permanent $Y^P(C^P)$ and transitory $Y^T(C^T)$. The main objective of most papers is to estimate κ_P, test whether $\kappa_P > \kappa_T$, and or/test whether $\kappa_P = 1$ (the income proportionality hypothesis). The earlier contributions (Bhalla, 1979; Musgrove, 1979) write a model for Y^P directly as a function of observables (such as education, occupation, industry, etc.). In contrast, Sargent (1978) and Wolpin (1982) use the restrictions on the theory imposed by the rational expectations framework. An important paper in this respect is Hall and Mishkin (1982).

4.1.1. Hall and Mishkin (1982)

The authors in the papers above do not write explicitly the stochastic structure of income. For example, in the statistical characterization above, permanent income is literally permanent (a fixed effect). The first paper to use micro panel data to decompose income shocks into permanent and transitory components writing an explicit stochastic income process is Hall and Mishkin (1982), who investigate whether households follow the rational expectations formulation of the permanent income hypothesis using PSID data on income and food consumption. Their setup assumes quadratic preferences (and hence looks at consumption and income changes), imposes that the marginal propensity to consume with respect to permanent shocks is 1, and leaves only the MPC with respect to transitory shocks free for estimation.

The income process is described by Eqs (3) and (4) (enriched to allow for some serial correlation of the MA type in the transitory component), so that the change in consumption is given by Eq. (5):

$$\Delta C_{i,a,t} = \zeta_{i,a,t} + \pi_a \varepsilon_{i,a,t}.$$

Since the PSID has information only on food consumption, this equation is recast in terms of food spending (implicitly assuming separability between food and other non-durable goods):

$$\Delta C^F_{i,a,t} = \alpha(\zeta_{i,a,t} + \pi_a \varepsilon_{i,a,t}) + \Delta m^F_{i,a,t}$$

where α is the proportion of income spent of food, and m^F is a stochastic element added to food consumption (measurement error), not correlated with the random elements of income ($\zeta_{i,a,t}$ and $\varepsilon_{i,a,t}$). The model is estimated using maximum likelihood assuming that all the random elements are normally distributed.

Hall and Mishkin (1982) also allow for the possibility that the consumer has some "advance information" (relative to the econometrician) about the income process.[44] Calling Υ the degree of advance information, they rewrite their model as:

$$\Delta C^F_{i,a,t} = \alpha \Upsilon (\zeta_{i,a+1,t+1} + \pi_{a+1} \varepsilon_{i,a+1,t+1})$$
$$+ \alpha (1 - \Upsilon)(\zeta_{i,a,t} + \pi_a \varepsilon_{i,a,t}) + \Delta m^F_{i,a,t}. \tag{28}$$

Their estimates of (28) only partly confirm the PIH. Their estimate of Υ is 0.25 and their estimate of π (which they assume to be constant over the life cycle) is 0.29, too high to be consistent with plausible interest rates. They reconcile this result with the possibility of excess sensitivity. They note that, contrary to the theory's prediction, $\text{cov}(\Delta C_a, \Delta Y_{a-1}) \neq 0$. Hall and Mishkin suggest a set up where a fraction μ of the households overreact to changes in transitory income rather than follow the permanent income. Estimating this model, the authors find that approximately 20 percent of consumers do not follow the permanent income hypothesis.[45]

4.2. Approach 2: identifying an information set for a given insurance configuration

Why can consumption and income data be useful in identifying an information set or learning more about the nature of the income process? To see this point very clearly, consider a simple extension of an example used by Browning et al. (1999). Certain features of the income process are not identifiable using income data alone. However, we might learn about them using jointly income and consumption data (or even labor supply, or more generally any choice that is affected by income). Assume that the income process is given by the sum of a random walk ($p_{i,a,t}$), a transitory shock ($\varepsilon_{i,a,t}$) and a measurement error ($m_{i,a,t}$, which may even reflect "superior information", i.e., information that is

---

[44] There are two possible interpretation for $\Upsilon > 0$. First, the consumer has better information than the econometrician regarding future income. Second, the timing of income and consumption information in the PSID is not synchronized. Interviews typically are conducted at the end of the first quarter. Income refers to the previous calendar, while consumption may possibly refer to the time of the interview, which may mean that the consumer chooses his consumption at age a after having observed at least 1/4 of his income at age $a + 1$.

[45] Altonji et al. (2002) extend Hall and Mishkin's model in a number of directions.

observed by the individual but not by an econometrician):

$$Y_{i,a,t} = p_{i,a,t} + \varepsilon_{i,a,t} + m_{i,a,t}$$
$$p_{i,a,t} = p_{i,a-1,t-1} + \zeta_{i,a,t}.$$

Written in first differences, this becomes

$$\Delta Y_{i,a,t} = \zeta_{i,a,t} + \Delta \varepsilon_{i,a,t} + \Delta m_{i,a,t}.$$

As discussed in Section 3, one cannot separately identify transitory shocks and measurement error (unless access to validation data gives us an estimate of the amount of variability explained by measurement error, as in Meghir and Pistaferri, 2004; or higher order restrictions are invoked, as in Cragg, 1997; or assumptions about separate serial correlation of the two components are imposed). Assume as usual that preferences are quadratic, $\beta (1 + r) = 1$ and that the consumer's horizon is infinite for simplicity. The change in consumption is given by Eq. (5) adapted to the infinite horizon case:

$$\Delta C_{i,a,t} = \zeta_{i,a,t} + \frac{r}{1+r} \varepsilon_{i,a,t}. \tag{29}$$

The component $m_{i,a,t}$ does not enter (29) because consumption does not respond to measurement error in income. However, note that if $m_{i,a,t}$ represented "superior information", then this assumption would have behavioral content: it would be violated if liquidity constraints were binding—and hence $m_{i,a,t}$ would belong in (29).

Suppose a researcher has access to panel data on consumption and income (a very stringent requirement, as it turns out).[46] Then one can use the following covariance restrictions:

$$\text{var}(\Delta Y_{i,a,t}) = \sigma_\zeta^2 + 2(\sigma_\varepsilon^2 + \sigma_m^2)$$
$$\text{cov}(\Delta Y_{i,a,t}, \Delta Y_{i,a-1,t-1}) = -(\sigma_\varepsilon^2 + \sigma_m^2)$$

---

[46] Surprisingly, neither the US nor the UK have a data set with panel data on both income and a comprehensive measure of consumption. In the US, for example, the Panel Study of Income Dynamics (PSID) contains longitudinal income data, but the information on consumption is scanty (limited to food and few more items, although since 1999 the amount of information on consumption has increased substantially). The Consumer Expenditure Survey (CEX) is a rotating panel that follows households for at most four quarters. Leaving aside the complicated details of the sampling frame, there are basically only one observation on annual consumption and two (overlapping) observations on income. Blundell et al. (2008b) have used an imputation procedure to create panel data on income and consumption in the PSID. As far as we know, only the Italian SHIW and the Russian LMS provide panel data on both income and consumption (although the panel samples are not large). The SHIW panel data have been used by Pistaferri (2001), Jappelli and Pistaferri (2006), and recently by Krueger and Perri (2009) and Kaufmann and Pistaferri (2009) to study some of the issues discussed in this chapter. See Gorodnichenko et al. (2010) for details on the RLMS.

$$\text{var}(\Delta C_{i,a,t}) = \sigma_\zeta^2 + \left(\frac{r}{1+r}\right)^2 \sigma_\varepsilon^2.$$

As is clear from the first two moments, σ_ε^2 and σ_m^2 cannot be told apart from income data alone (although the variance of permanent shocks can actually be identified using $\sigma_\zeta^2 = \text{var}(\Delta Y_{i,a,t}) + 2\text{cov}(\Delta Y_{i,a,t}, \Delta Y_{i,a-1,t-1})$, the stationary version of Eq. (17) above). However, the availability of consumption data solves the identification problem. In particular, one could identify the variance of transitory shocks from

$$\sigma_\varepsilon^2 = \left(\frac{r}{1+r}\right)^{-2} \left[\text{var}\left(\Delta C_{i,a,t}\right) - \text{var}\left(\Delta Y_{i,a,t}\right) - 2\text{cov}\left(\Delta Y_{i,a,t}, \Delta Y_{i,a-1,t-1}\right)\right]. \quad (30)$$

Note also that if one is willing to use the covariance between changes in consumption and changes in income ($\text{cov}(\Delta C_{i,a,t}, \Delta Y_{i,a,t}) = \sigma_\zeta^2 + (\frac{r}{1+r})\sigma_\varepsilon^2$), then there is even an overidentifying restriction that can be used to test the model.

It is useful at this point to separate the literature into two sub-branches—the papers devoted to learning features of the income process, and those devoted to identifying information set.

4.2.1. Is the increase in income inequality permanent or transitory?

Blundell and Preston (1998) use the link between the income process and consumption inequality to understand the nature and causes of the increase in inequality of consumption and the relative importance of changes in the variance of transitory and permanent shocks. Their motivation is that for the UK they have only repeated cross-section data, and the variances of income shocks are changing over time due to, for example, rising inequality. Hence for a given cohort, say, and even ignoring measurement error, one has:

$$\text{var}(y_{i,a,t}) = \text{var}(p_{i,0,t-a}) + \sum_{j=0}^{a} \text{var}(\zeta_{i,j,t-a+j}) + \text{var}(\varepsilon_{i,a,t})$$

where $j = 0$ corresponds to the age of entry of this cohort in the labor market. With repeated cross-sections one can write the change in the variance of income for a given cohort as

$$\Delta\text{var}(y_{i,a,t}) = \text{var}(\zeta_{i,a,t}) + \Delta\text{var}(\varepsilon_{i,a,t}).$$

Hence, a rise in inequality (the left-hand side of this equation) may be due to a rise in "volatility" $\Delta\text{var}(\varepsilon_{i,a,t}) > 0$ or the presence of a persistent income shock, $\text{var}(\zeta_{i,a,t})$. In repeated cross-sections the problem of distinguishing between the two sources is unsolvable if one focuses just on income data. Suppose instead one has access to repeated cross-section data on consumption (which, conveniently, may or may not come from the same data set—the use of multiple data sets is possible as long as samples are drawn randomly from the same underlying population). Then we can see that the change in consumption inequality for a given cohort is:

$$\Delta \mathrm{var}\left(c_{i,a,t}\right) = \mathrm{var}\left(\zeta_{i,a,t}\right) + \left(\frac{r}{1+r}\right)^2 \mathrm{var}\left(\varepsilon_{i,a,t}\right)$$

assuming one can approximate the variance of the change by the change of the variances (see Deaton and Paxson, 1994, for a discussion of the conditions under which this approximation is acceptable). Here one can see that the growth in consumption inequality is dominated by the permanent component (for small r the second term on the right hand side vanishes). Indeed, assuming $r \approx 0$, we can see that the change in consumption inequality identifies the variance of the permanent component and that the difference between the change in income inequality and the change in consumption inequality identifies the change in the variance of the transitory shock.[47] However, the possibility of partial insurance, serially correlated shocks, measurement error, or lack of cross-sectional orthogonality may generate underidentification.

Related to Blundell and Preston (1998) is a paper by Hryshko (2008). He estimates jointly a consumption function (based on the CRRA specification) and an income process. Based on the evidence from Hryshko (2009) and the literature, as well as the need to match the increasing inequality of consumption over the life cycle, he assumes that the income process is the sum of a random walk and a transitory shock. However, he also allows the structural shocks (i.e. the transitory shock and the innovation to the permanent component) to be correlated. In simulations he shows that such a correlation can be very important for interpreting life cycle consumption. This additional feature cannot be identified without its implications for consumption and thus provides an excellent example of the joint identifying power of the two processes (income and consumption). He then estimates jointly the income and consumption process using simulated methods of moment. In addition, just like Blundell et al. (2008b) he estimates the proportion of the permanent and the transitory shock that are insured, finding that 37% of permanent shocks are insured via channels other than savings; transitory shocks are only insured via savings.

4.2.2. Identifying an information set
Now we discuss three examples where the idea of jointly using consumption and income data has been used to identify an individual's information set.

Cunha et al. (2005) The authors estimate what components of measured lifetime income variability are due to uncertainty realized after their college decision time, and

---

[47] Using information on the change in the covariance between consumption and income one gets an overidentifying restriction that as before can be used to test the model.

what components are due to heterogeneity (known at the time the decision is made). The identification strategy depends on the specification of preferences and on the assumptions made about the structure of markets. In their paper markets are complete. The goal is to identify the distributions of predictable heterogeneity and uncertainty separately. The authors find that about half of the variance of unobservable components in the returns to schooling are known and acted on by the agents when making schooling choices. The framework of their paper has been extended in Cunha and Heckman (2007), where the authors show that a large fraction of the increase in inequality in recent years is due to the increase in the variance of the unforecastable components. In particular, they estimate the fraction of future earnings that is forecastable and how this fraction has changed over time using college decision choices. For less skilled workers, roughly 60% of the increase in wage variability is due to uncertainty. For more skilled workers, only 8% of the increase in wage variability is due to uncertainty.

The following simplified example demonstrates their identification strategy in the context of consumption choices. Suppose as usual that preferences are quadratic, $\beta(1+r) = 1$, initial assets are zero, the horizon is infinite, but the consumer receives income only in two periods, t and $t+1$. Consumption is therefore

$$C_{i,a,t} = \frac{r}{1+r} Y_{i,a,t} + \frac{r}{(1+r)^2} E\left(Y_{i,a+1,t+1} | \Omega_{i,a,t}\right).$$

Write income in $t+1$ as

$$Y_{i,a+1,t+1} = X'_{i,a+1,t+1}\beta + \zeta^A_{i,a+1,t+1} + \zeta^U_{i,a+1,t+1}$$

where $X'_{i,a+1,t+1}\beta$ is observed by both the individual and the econometrician, $\zeta^A_{i,a+1,t+1}$ is potentially observed only by the individual, and $\zeta^U_{i,a+1,t+1}$ is unobserved by both. The idea is that one can form the following "deviation" variables

$$z^C_{i,a,t} = C_{i,a,t} - \frac{r}{1+r} Y_{i,a,t} - \frac{r}{(1+r)^2} X'_{i,a+1,t+1}\beta$$

$$z^Y_{i,a+1,t+1} = Y_{i,a+1,t+1} - X'_{i,a+1,t+1}\beta.$$

If $\text{cov}(z^C_{i,a,t}, z^Y_{i,a+1,t+1}) \neq 0$, there is evidence of "superior information", i.e., the consumer used more than just $X'_{i,a+1,t+1}\beta$ to decide how much to consume in period t.

Primiceri and van Rens (2009) Primiceri and van Rens (2009) assume that consumers are unable to smooth permanent shocks, and that any attenuated response measures the amount of advance information that they have about developments in their (permanent) income. Using CEX data, they find that all of the increase in income inequality over the 1980-2000 period can be attributed to an increase in the variance of permanent shocks but that most of the permanent income shocks are anticipated by individuals; hence consumption inequality remains flat even though income inequality increases. While their results challenge the common view that permanent shocks were important only in the early 1980s (see Card and Di Nardo, 2002; Moffitt and Gottschalk, 1994), they could be explained by the poor quality of income data in the CEX (see Heathcote, 2009).

The authors decompose idiosyncratic changes in income into predictable and unpredictable permanent income shocks and to transitory shocks. They estimate the contribution of each element to total income inequality using CEX data. The log income process is specified as follows

$$y_{i,a,t} = p_{i,a,t} + \varepsilon_{i,a,t} \tag{31}$$
$$p_{i,a,t} = p_{i,a-1,t-1} + \zeta^U_{i,a,t} + \zeta^A_{i,a,t} \tag{32}$$

where $\varepsilon_{i,a,t}$ and $\zeta^U_{i,a,t}$ are unpredictable to the individual and $\zeta^A_{i,a,t}$ is predictable to the individual but unobservable to the econometrician. Using CRRA utility with incomplete markets (there is only a risk free bond) log consumption can be shown to follow (approximately):

$$c_{i,a,t} = c_{i,a-1,t-1} + \zeta^U_{i,a,t}. \tag{33}$$

From Eqs (31)–(33), the following cohort-specific moment conditions are implied:

$$\Delta\mathrm{var}\left(y_{i,a,t}\right) = \mathrm{var}(\zeta^U_{i,a,t}) + \mathrm{var}(\zeta^A_{i,a,t}) + \Delta\mathrm{var}(\varepsilon_{i,a,t})$$
$$\Delta\mathrm{var}(c_{i,a,t}) = \mathrm{var}(\zeta^U_{i,a,t})$$
$$\Delta\mathrm{cov}(y_{i,a,t}, c_{i,a,t}) = \mathrm{var}(\zeta^U_{i,a,t})$$
$$\mathrm{cov}(\Delta y_{i,a,t}, y_{-1 i,a-1,t-1}) = -\mathrm{var}(\varepsilon_{i,a,t}).$$

where $\mathrm{var}(\cdot)$ and $\mathrm{cov}(\cdot)$ denote cross-sectional variances and covariances, respectively. Using these moment conditions, it is possible to (over)identify $\mathrm{var}(\zeta^U_t)$ and $\mathrm{var}(\zeta^A_t)$ for $t = 1, \ldots, T$ and $\mathrm{var}(\varepsilon_t)$ for $t = 0, \ldots, T$. The authors estimate the model using a Bayesian likelihood based approach evaluating the posterior using the MCMC algorithm. They find that predictable permanent income shocks are the main source of income inequality.

The model above cannot distinguish between predictable permanent shocks and risk sharing. To address this issue, the authors argue that if consumption does not respond to income shocks because of risk sharing, we would expect part of that risk sharing to happen through taxes and transfers and part through markets for financial assets. They show that re-estimating the model for income before taxes, income before taxes excluding financial income and for earned income before tax and transfers yields very close estimates to the baseline model (see Heathcote, 2009, for a discussion of their testing strategy).

Guvenen (2009) and Guvenen and Smith (2009) In Guvenen's (2007) model, income data are generated by the heterogeneous income profile specification. However, individuals do not know the parameters of their own profile. In particular, they ignore the slope of life cycle profile f_i and the value of the persistent component. They need to learn about these parameters using Bayesian updating by observing successive income realizations, which are noisy because of the mean reverting transitory shock. He shows that this model can be made to fit the consumption data very well (both in terms of levels and variance over the life cycle) and in some ways better than the process that includes a unit root. By introducing learning, Guveven relaxes the restriction linking the income process to consumption and as a result weakens the identifying information implied by this link. This allows the income process to be stationary and consumption to behave as if income is not stationary. Thus, from a welfare point of view the individual is facing essentially as much uncertainty as they would under the random walk model, which is why the model can fit the increasing inequality over the life cycle. In Guvenen's model it is just the interpretation of the nature of uncertainty that has changed. The fact that the income process conditional on the individual is basically deterministic (except for the small transitory shock) has lost its key welfare implications. Thus whether the income is highly uncertain or deterministic becomes irrelevant for issues that have to do with insurance and precautionary savings: individuals perceive it as highly uncertain and this is all that matters.[48]

While Guvenen (2007) calibrates the consumption profile, Guvenen and Smith (2009) use consumption data jointly with income data to estimate the structural parameters of the model. They extend the consumption imputation procedure of Blundell et al. (2008b) to create a panel of income and consumption data in the PSID. As in Guvenen (2007), they assume that the income process is the sum of a random trend that consumers must learn about in Bayesian fashion, an AR(1) process with AR coefficient below 1, and a serially uncorrelated component.

The authors estimate the structural parameters of their model by applying an indirect inference approach—a simulation based approach suitable for models in which it is very difficult to specify the criterion function.[49] The authors define an auxiliary model in

---

[48] Guvenen's characterization of the stochastic income process is appealing because it is consistent, in a "reduced form" sense, with the human capital model (Ben-Porath, 1967). We say in a "reduced form" sense because in his framework age or potential experience are used in lieu of actual experience, thus sidestepping the thorny issue of endogenous employment decisions (see Huggett et al., 2009).

[49] The main difference from Guvenen (2009) is that the present paper estimates all the structural parameters jointly using income and consumption data (whereas in the 2007 paper income process parameters were estimated using only income data and preference parameters were taken from other studies in the literature).

which consumption and income depend on lags and leads of consumption and income, as well as growth rates of income at various lags and leads. For their estimation, the authors construct the panel of imputed household consumption by combining data from the PSID and CEX. As in Guvenen (2009) the authors find that income shocks are less persistent in the HIP case ($\rho = 0.76$) than in the RIP case (ρ close to one), and that there is a significant evidence for heterogeneity in income growth. In addition, they find that prior uncertainty is quite small ($\Lambda = 0.19$, meaning that about 80 percent of the uncertainty about the random trend component is resolved in the first period of life). They therefore argue that the amount of uninsurable lifetime income risk that households perceive is smaller than what is typically assumed in calibrated macroeconomic models. Statistically speaking, the estimate is very imprecise and one could conclude that everything about the random trend term is known early on in the life cycle.

4.3. Information or insurance?

In the three examples above it is possible to solve the identification problem by making the following assumptions. First, consumption responds to signal but not to noise. Similarly, consumption responds to unanticipated income changes, but not to forecastable ones. While the orthogonality of consumption to measurement error in income is not implausible, orthogonality to anticipated changes in income has behavioral content. Households will respond to anticipated changes in income, causing the theory to fail, if there are intertemporal distortions induced by, e.g. liquidity constraints.[50]

Second, the structure of markets is such that the econometrician can predict response of consumption to income shocks on the basis of a model of individual behavior. For example, in the strict version of the PIH with infinite horizon, the marginal propensity to consume out of a permanent shock is 1 and the marginal propensity to consume out of transitory shock is equal to the annuity value $\frac{r}{1+r}$.[51] That is, one identifies the variances of interest only under the assumption that the chosen model of behavior describes the data accurately.

But what if there is more insurance than predicted by, for example, the simple PIH version of the theory? There are alternative theories that predict that consumers may insure their income shocks to a larger extent than predicted by a simple model with just self-insurance through a risk-free bond. One example is the full insurance model. Clearly, it is hard to believe full insurance is literally true. The model has obvious theoretical problems, such as private information and limited enforcement. Moreover, there are serious empirical problems: The full insurance hypothesis is soundly rejected by the data (Cochrane, 1991; Attanasio and Davis, 1996; Hayashi et al., 1996).

---

[50] The effect is asymmetric: Liquidity constraints should matter only for anticipated income increases (where the optimal response would be to borrow), but not for anticipated income declines (where the optimal response would be to save, which is not limited—unless storage technologies are missing).

[51] Another implicit assumption, of course, is that the theory is correct.

But outside the extreme case of the full insurance model, there is perhaps more insurance than predicted by the strict PIH version with just a risk-free bond. In Section 2.2.2, we saw that standard Bewley-type models can generate some insurance against permanent shocks as long as people accumulate some precautionary wealth. To achieve this result, one does not require sophisticated contingent Arrow-Debreu markets. All is needed is a simple storage technology (such as a saving account).

A recent macroeconomic literature has explored a number of theoretical alternatives to the insurance configurations described above. These alternative models fall under two broad groups: those that assume public information but limited enforcement of contracts, and those that assume full commitment but private information. These models prove that the self-insurance case is Pareto-inefficient even conditioning on limited enforcement and private information issues. In both types of models, agents typically achieve more insurance than under a model with a single non-contingent bond, but less than under a complete markets environment. These models show that the relationship between income shocks and consumption depends on the degree of persistence of income shocks. Alvarez and Jermann (2000), for example, explore the nature of income insurance schemes in economies where agents cannot be prevented from withdrawing participation if the loss from the accumulated future income gains they are asked to forgo becomes greater than the gains from continuing participation. Such schemes, if feasible, allow individuals to keep some of the positive shocks to their income and therefore offer only partial income insurance. If income shocks are persistent enough and agents are infinitely lived, then participation constraints become so severe that no insurance scheme is feasible. With finite lived agents, the future benefits from a positive permanent shock exceed those from a comparable transitory shock. This suggests that the degree of insurance should be allowed to differ between transitory and permanent shocks and should also be allowed to change over time and across different groups. Krueger and Perri (2006) provide an empirical review of income and consumption inequality in the 80's and 90's. They then suggest a theoretical macro model based on self insurance with limited commitment trying to explain the moderate expansion in consumption inequality compared to income inequality. Their hypothesis is that an increase in the volatility of idiosyncratic labor income has not only been an important factor in the increase in income inequality, but has also caused a change in the development of financial markets, allowing individual households to better insure against the bigger idiosyncratic income fluctuations.

Another reason for partial insurance is moral hazard. This is the direction taken in Attanasio and Pavoni (2007). Here the economic environment is characterized by moral hazard and hidden asset accumulation, e.g., individuals have hidden access to a simple credit market. The authors show that, depending on the cost of shirking and the persistence of the income shock, some partial insurance is possible and a linear insurance rule can be obtained as an exact (closed form) solution in a dynamic Mirrlees model with CRRA utility. In particular, the response of consumption to permanent income shocks can be interpreted as a measure of the severity of informational problems. Their empirical analysis finds evidence for "excess smoothness" of consumption with respect to permanent shocks. However, they show that the Euler equation for consumption is still valid and that the empirical content of the model lies in how consumption reacts to unexpected income shocks.

We now want to provide a simple example of the identification issue: does the attenuated response of consumption to income shocks reflect "insurance/smoothing" or "information"? Assume that log income and log consumption changes are given by the following equations:[52]

$$\Delta y_{i,a,t} = \Delta \varepsilon_{i,a,t} + \zeta_{i,a,t}^{A} + \zeta_{i,a,t}^{U}$$
$$\Delta c_{i,a,t} = \zeta_{i,a,t}^{U} + \pi_a \varepsilon_{i,a,t}.$$

In this case, income shifts because of anticipated permanent changes in income (e.g., a pre-announced promotion) and unanticipated permanent changes in income. In theory, consumption changes only in response to the unanticipated component. Suppose that our objective is to estimate the extent of "information", i.e., how large are permanent changes in income that are unanticipated:

$$\Upsilon = \frac{\sigma_{\zeta^U}^2}{\sigma_{\zeta^U}^2 + \sigma_{\zeta^A}^2}.$$

A possible way of identifying this parameter is to run a simple IV regression of $\Delta c_{i,a,t}$ onto $\Delta y_{i,a,t}$ using $(\Delta y_{i,a-1,t-1} + \Delta y_{i,a,t} + \Delta y_{i,a+1,t+1})$ as an instrument (see Guiso et al., 2005). This yields indeed:

$$\frac{\mathrm{cov}\left(\Delta c_{i,a,t}, \Delta y_{i,a-1,t-1} + \Delta y_{i,a,t} + \Delta y_{i,a+1,t+1}\right)}{\mathrm{cov}\left(\Delta y_{i,a,t}, \Delta y_{i,a-1,t-1} + \Delta y_{i,a,t} + \Delta y_{i,a+1,t+1}\right)} = \frac{\sigma_{\zeta^U}^2}{\sigma_{\zeta^U}^2 + \sigma_{\zeta^A}^2} = \Upsilon.$$

In contrast to this case, suppose now that $\sigma_{\zeta^A}^2 = 0$ (no advance or superior information), but there is some insurance against permanent and transitory shocks, measured by the partial insurance parameters Φ and Ψ. What is the IV regression above identifying? The model now is

$$\Delta y_{i,a,t} = \zeta_{i,a,t}^{U} + \Delta \varepsilon_{i,a,t} \tag{34}$$
$$\Delta c_{i,a,t} = \Phi \zeta_{i,a,t}^{U} + \Psi \varepsilon_{i,a,t} \tag{35}$$

---

[52] Assuming for simplicity no news between period $t-1$ and period t about the path of $\zeta_{i,a+j,t+j}^{A}$ $(j \geq 0)$.

and the IV parameter takes the form

$$\frac{\text{cov}\left(\Delta c_{i,a,t},\, \Delta y_{i,a-1,t-1} + \Delta y_{i,a,t} + \Delta y_{i,a+1,t+1}\right)}{\text{cov}\left(\Delta y_{i,a,t},\, \Delta y_{i,a-1,t-1} + \Delta y_{i,a,t} + \Delta y_{i,a+1,t+1}\right)} = \frac{\Phi \sigma^2_{\zeta U}}{\sigma^2_{\zeta U}} = \Phi,$$

which is what Blundell et al. (2008b) assume.

Hence, the same moment $\frac{\text{cov}(\Delta c_{i,a,t},\Delta y_{i,a-1,t-1}+\Delta y_{i,a,t}+\Delta y_{i,a+1,t+1})}{\text{cov}(\Delta y_{i,a,t},\Delta y_{i,a-1,t-1}+\Delta y_{i,a,t}+\Delta y_{i,a+1,t+1})}$ has two entirely different interpretations depending on what assumptions one makes about information and insurance. What if we have both an anticipated component and partial insurance? It's easy to show that in this case

$$\frac{\text{cov}\left(\Delta c_{i,a,t},\, \Delta y_{i,a-1,t-1} + \Delta y_{i,a,t} + \Delta y_{i,a+1,t+1}\right)}{\text{cov}\left(\Delta y_{i,a,t},\, \Delta y_{i,a-1,t-1} + \Delta y_{i,a,t} + \Delta y_{i,a+1,t+1}\right)} = \Phi \Upsilon$$

a combination of information and insurance.

In sum, suppose that a researcher finds that consumption responds very little to what the econometrician defines to be a shock to economic resources (for the moment, neglect the distinction between transitory and permanent shocks). There are at least two economically interesting reasons why this might be the case. First, it is possible that what the econometrician defines to be a shock is not, in fact, a shock at all when seen from the point of view of the individual. In other words, the change in economic resources identified by the econometrician as an innovation might be predicted in advance (at least partly) by the consumer. Hence if the consumer is rational and not subject to borrowing constraints, her consumption will not respond to changes in income that are anticipated. It follows that the "extent of attenuation" of consumption in response to income shocks measures the extent of "superior information" that the consumers possess.

The other possibility is that what the econometrician defines to be a shock is correctly a shock when seen from the point of view of the individual. However, suppose that the consumer has access to insurance mechanisms over and above self-insurance (for example, government insurance, intergenerational transfers, etc.). Hence, consumption will react little to the shock (or less than predicted by a model with just self-insurance). In this case, the "extent of attenuation" of consumption in response to income shocks measures the extent of "partial insurance" that the consumer has available against income shocks.[53]

More broadly, identification of information sets requires taking a stand on the structure of (formal and informal) credit and insurance markets. What looks like lack of information may be liquidity constraints in disguise (consumer responds too much to

---

[53] A confounding issue is the possibility that the availability of public insurance displaces self-insurance or creates disincentives to save because of asset testing (see Hubbard et al., 1995).

Table 3 Partial insurance estimates from Blundell et al. (2008b).

	Whole sample	Born 1940s	Born 1930s	No College	Low wealth
Φ (Partial insurance perm. shock)	0.6423 (0.0945)	0.7928 (0.1848)	0.6889 (0.2393)	0.9439 (0.1783)	0.8489 (0.2848)
Ψ (Partial insurance trans. shock)	0.0533 (0.0435)	0.0675 (0.0705)	−0.0381 (0.0737)	0.0768 (0.0602)	0.2877 (0.1143)

Note: Standard errors in parenthesis.

negative transitory shock, and what looks like superior information may be insurance in disguise (consumer responds too little to permanent shocks).

4.4. Approaching the information/insurance conundrum

The literature has considered two approaches to solve the information/insurance identification issue. A first method attempts to identify episodes in which income changes unexpectedly, and to evaluate in a quasi-experimental setting how consumption reacts to such changes. A second approach estimates the impact of shocks combining realizations and expectations of income or consumption in surveys where data on subjective expectations are available (see Hayashi (1985) and Pistaferri (2001), for means, and Kaufmann and Pistaferri (2009), for covariance restrictions).

Each of these approaches has pros and cons, as we shall discuss below. Before discussing these approaches, we discuss Blundell et al. (2008b), which does impose assumptions about the information set(s) of the agents and estimates insurance, but provides a test of "superior information".

4.4.1. Blundell et al. (2008b)

The consumption model considered in Blundell et al. (2008b) is given by Eq. (12), while their income process is given by (10) and (11). In their study they create panel data on a comprehensive consumption measure for the PSID using an imputation procedure based on food demand estimates from the CEX. Table 3 reproduces their main results. They find that consumption is nearly insensitive to transitory shocks (the estimated coefficient is around 5 percent, but higher among poor households), while their estimate of the response of consumption to permanent shocks is significantly lower than 1 (around 0.65, but higher for poor or less educated households), suggesting that households are able to insure at least part of the permanent shocks.

These results show (a) that the estimates of the insurance coefficients in the baseline case are statistically consistent with the values predicted by the calibrated Kaplan-Violante model of Section 2.2.2; (b) that younger cohorts have harder time smoothing their shocks, presumably because of the lack of sufficient wealth; (c) groups with actual or presumed low wealth are not able to insure permanent shocks (as expected from the

Table 4 Test of Superior Information, from Blundell et al. (2008b).

Test cov $(\Delta y_{a+1}, \Delta c_a) = 0$ for all a	p-value 0.25
Test cov $(\Delta y_{a+2}, \Delta c_a) = 0$ for all a	p-value 0.27
Test cov $(\Delta y_{a+3}, \Delta c_a) = 0$ for all a	p-value 0.74
Test cov $(\Delta y_{a+4}, \Delta c_a) = 0$ for all a	p-value 0.68

model) and even have difficulties smoothing transitory shocks (credit markets can be unavailable for people with little or no collateral).

While the setting of Blundell et al. (2008b) cannot be used to distinguish between insurance and information, their paper provides a test of their assumption about richness of the information set. In particular, they follow Cunha et al. (2005) and test whether unexpected consumption growth (defined as the residual of a regression of consumption growth on observable household characteristics) is correlated with future income changes (defined also as the residual of a regression of income growth on observable household characteristics). If this was the case, then consumption contains more information than used by the econometrician. Their test of superior information reported in Table 4 shows that consumption is not correlated with future income changes.

Blundell et al. (2008b) find little evidence of anticipation. This suggests the persistent labor income shocks that were experienced in the 1980s were not anticipated. These were largely changes in the returns to skills, shifts in government transfers and the shift of risk from firms to workers.

Finally, the results of Blundell et al. (2008b) can be used to understand why consumption inequality in the US has grown less than income inequality during the past two decades. Their findings suggest that the widening gap between consumption and income inequality is due to the change in the durability of income shocks. In particular, a growth in the variance of permanent shocks in the early eighties was replaced by a continued growth in the variance of transitory income shocks in the late eighties. Since they find little evidence that the degree of insurance with respect to shocks of different durability changes over this period, it is the relative increase in the variability of more insurable shocks rather than greater insurance opportunities that explains the disjuncture between income and consumption inequality.

4.4.2. Solution 1: the quasi-experimental approach

The approach we discuss in this section does not require estimation of an income process, or even observing the individual shocks.[54] Rather, it compares households that are exposed to shocks with households that are not (or the same households before and after

---

[54] This section draws on Jappelli and Pistaferri (2010).

the shock), and assumes that the difference in consumption arises from the realization of the shocks. The idea here is to identify episodes in which changes in income are unanticipated, easy to characterize (i.e., persistent or transient), and (possibly) large.

The first of such attempts dates back to a study by Bodkin (1959), who laid down fifty years ago all the ingredients of the quasi-experimental approach.[55] In this pioneering study, the experiment consists of looking at the consumption behavior of WWII veterans after the receipt of unexpected dividend payments from the National Service Life Insurance. Bodkin assumes that the dividend payments are unanticipated and represent a windfall source of income, and finds a point estimate of the marginal propensity to consume non-durables out of this windfall income is as high as 0.72, a strong violation of the permanent income model.[56]

The subsequent literature has looked at the economic consequences of illness (Gertler and Gruber, 2002), disability (Stephens, 2001; Meyer and Mok, 2006), unemployment (Gruber, 1997; Browning and Crossley, 2001), and, in the context of developing countries, weather shocks (Wolpin, 1982; Paxson, 1992) and crop losses (Cameron and Worswick, 2003). Some of these shocks are transitory (i.e. temporary job loss), and others are permanent (disability); some are positive (dividend pay-outs), others negative (illness). The framework in Section 2 suggests that it is important to distinguish between the effects of these various types of shocks because, according to the theory, consumption should change almost one-for-one in response to permanent shocks (positive or negative), but may react asymmetrically if shocks are transitory. Indeed, if households are credit constrained (can save but not borrow) they will cut consumption strongly when hit by a negative transitory shock, but will not react much to a positive one.

Recent papers in the quasi-experimental framework look at the effect of unemployment shocks on consumption, and the smoothing benefits provided by unemployment insurance (UI) schemes. As pointed out by Browning and Crossley (2001) unemployment insurance provides two benefits to consumers. First, it provides "consumption smoothing benefits" for consumers who are liquidity constrained. In the absence of credit constraints, individuals who faced a negative transitory shock such as unemployment would borrow to smooth their consumption. If they are unable to borrow they would need to adjust their consumption downward considerably. Unemployment insurance provides some liquidity and hence it has positive welfare effects. Second, unemployment insurance reduces the conditional variance of consumption growth and hence the need to accumulate precautionary savings.

---

[55] As reported by Chao (2003), it was Friedman himself, in his *Theory of the Consumption Function* (1957, p. 215), who suggested using this quasi-experimental variation to test the main predictions of the PIH. In the words of Friedman, it provided a "controlled experiment" of consumption behavior.

[56] According to Friedman (as reported by Chao, 2003), people were told more payments were coming, so the NSLI dividends were actually a measure of permanent shocks to income, which would provide support for the PIH. He also noticed that the payments were partly expected.

One of the earlier attempts to estimate the welfare effects of unemployment insurance is Gruber (1997). Using the PSID, he constructs a sample of workers who lose their job between period $t-1$ and period t, and regresses the change in food spending over the same time span against the UI replacement rate an individual is eligible for (i.e., potential benefits). Gruber finds a large smoothing effect of UI, in particular that a 10 percentage point rise in the replacement rate reduces the fall in consumption upon unemployment by about 3 percent. He also finds that the fall in consumption at zero replacement rates is about 20 percent, suggesting that consumers face liquidity constraints.

Browning and Crossley (2001) extend Gruber's idea to a different country (Canada instead of the US), using a more comprehensive measure of consumption (instead of just food) and legislated changes in UI (instead of state-time variation). Moreover, their data are rich enough to allow them to identify presumably liquidity constrained households (in particular, their data set provide information on assets at the time of job loss). Browning and Crossley estimate a small elasticity of expenditures with respect to UI benefit (5 percent). But this small effect masks substantial heterogeneity, with low-assets households at time of job loss exhibiting elasticities as high as 20 percent. This is consistent with the presence of liquidity constraints.

A critique of this approach is that the response of consumption to unemployment shocks is confounded by three sets of issues (similar arguments apply to papers that look at unpredictable income changes due to illness or disability, as in Stephens, 2001). First, some of these shocks may not come as a surprise, and individuals may have saved in their anticipation. For example, being laid off by Chrysler in 2009 should hardly come as a surprise. Ideally, one would overcome this problem by, say, matching job accident data or firm closure data with consumption data. Second, the theory predicts that consumers smooth marginal utility, not consumption per se. If an unemployment shock brings more leisure and if consumption is a substitute for leisure, an excess response of consumption to the transitory shock induced by losing one's job does not necessarily represent a violation of the theory. Finally, even if unemployment shocks are truly fully unanticipated, they may be partially insured through government programs such as unemployment insurance (and disability insurance in case of disability shocks). An attenuated consumption response to a permanent income shock due to disability may be explained by the availability of government-provided insurance, rather than representing a failure of the theory. Therefore a complete analysis of the impact of unemployment or disability shocks requires explicit modeling of the type of insurance available to individuals as well as of the possible interactions between public and private insurance.

The above discussion suggests that it might be easier to test the theory in contexts in which insurance over and above self-insurance is not available, such as in developing countries. Gertler and Gruber (2002) look at the effect of income shocks arising from major illness on consumption in Indonesia. They find that while people are able to smooth the effect of minor illnesses (which could be interpreted as transitory shocks, or anticipated events), they experience considerably more difficulty in smoothing the impact of major illnesses (which could be interpreted as permanent shocks).

Wolpin (1982) and Paxson (1992) study the effect of weather shocks in India and Thailand, respectively. In agricultural economies, weather shocks affect income directly through the production function and deviations from normal weather conditions are truly unanticipated events. Wolpin (1982) uses Indian regional time series data on rainfall to construct long run moments as instruments for current income (which is assumed to measure permanent income with error). The estimated permanent income elasticity ranges from 0.91 to 1.02 depending on the measure of consumption, thus supporting strongly the permanent income model. Paxson (1992) uses regional Thai data on weather to measure transitory shocks and finds that Thai consumers have a high propensity to save out of transitory weather shocks, in support of the theory. However, she also finds that they have a propensity to save out of permanent shocks above zero, which rejects a strong version of the permanent income hypothesis.

Studies using quasi-experimental variation to identify shocks to household income have the obvious advantage that the identification strategy is clear and easy to explain and understand. However, these studies' obvious limitation is that they capture only one type of shock at a time, for instance illness, job loss, rainfall, extreme temperatures, or crop loss. One may wonder, for example, whether the Gruber (1997) and Browning and Crossley (2001) estimates obtained in a sample of job losers have external validity for examining the effect of other types of shocks (especially those that are much harder to insure, such as shocks to one's productivity).

A second limitation of the approach is that some of the income shocks (in particular, unemployment and disability shocks), cannot be considered as truly exogenous events. For instance, for some people unemployment is a voluntary choice, and for others disability could be reported just to obtain benefits (a moral hazard issue). For this reason, not all income variability is necessarily unanticipated, or exogenous to the agent (Low et al., forthcoming). The lesson of the literature is that identifying episodes of genuine exogenous and unanticipated income changes is very difficult. One such case is weather conditions, to the extent at least to which people don't move to different regions to offset bad weather conditions.

4.4.3. Solution 2: subjective expectations

As pointed out in Sections 4.1 and 4.2, identifying income shocks is difficult because people may have information that is not observed by the econometrician. For instance, they may know in advance that they will face a temporary change in their income (such as a seasonal lay-off). When the news is realized, the econometrician will measure as a shock what is in fact an expected event. The literature based on subjective expectations attempts to circumvent the problem by asking people to report quantitative information on their expectations, an approach forcefully endorsed by Manski (2004). This literature relies therefore on survey questions, rather than retrospective data (as in Section 4.2), to elicit information on the conditional distribution of future income, and measures shocks as deviations of actual realizations from elicited expectations.

Hayashi (1985) is the first study to adopt this approach. He uses a four-quarter panel of Japanese households containing respondents' expectations about expenditure and income in the following quarter. Hayashi works with disaggregate consumers' expenditure, allowing each component to have a different degree of durability. He specifies a consumption rule and, allowing for measurement error in expenditures, estimates the covariances between expected and unexpected changes in consumption and expected and unexpected changes in income. His results are in line with Hall and Mishkin (1982), suggesting a relatively high sensitivity of consumption to income shocks.

Pistaferri (2001) combines income realizations and quantitative subjective income expectations contained in the 1989-93 Italian Survey of Household Income and Wealth (SHIW) to point identify separately the transitory and the permanent income shocks. To see how subjective income expectations allow the estimation of transitory and income shocks for each household, consider the income process of Eqs (3) and (4). Define $E(x_{i,a,t}|\Omega_{i,a-1,t-1})$ as the subjective expectation of $x_{i,a,t}$ given the individual's information set at age $a - 1$. It is worth pointing out that $\Omega_{i,a-1,t-1}$ is the set of information possessed at the individual level; the econometrician's information set is generally less rich. The assumption of rational expectations implies that the transitory shock at time t can be point identified by:

$$\varepsilon_{i,a,t} = -E\left(\Delta Y_{i,a,t}|\Omega_{i,a-1,t-1}\right). \tag{36}$$

Using Eqs (3), (4) and (36), the permanent shock at time t is identified by the expression:

$$\zeta_{i,a,t} = \Delta Y_{i,a,t} - E\left(\Delta Y_{i,a,t}|\Omega_{i,a-1,t-1}\right) + E\left(\Delta Y_{i,a+1,t+1}|\Omega_{i,a,t}\right)$$

i.e., the income innovation at age a adjusted by a factor that takes into account the arrival of new information concerning the change in income between a and $a + 1$. Thus, the transitory and permanent shocks can be identified if one observes, for at least two consecutive time periods, the conditional expectation and the realization of income, a requirement satisfied by the 1989-93 SHIW. Pistaferri estimates the saving for a rainy day equation of Campbell (1987) and finds that consumers save most of the transitory shocks and very little of the permanent shocks, supporting the saving for a rainy day model.

Kaufmann and Pistaferri (2009) use the same Italian survey used by Pistaferri (2001), but different years (1995-2001) to distinguish the superior information issue from the

Table 5 EWMD Results, from Kaufmann and Pistaferri (2009).

Parameter	(1)	(2)	(3)
$\sigma^2_{\varepsilon U}$	0.1056 (0.0191)	0.1172 (0.0175)	0.0197 (0.0208)
$\sigma^2_{\varepsilon A}$	0	0	0.0541 (0.0163)
σ^2_y	0	0	0.0342 (0.0215)
$\sigma^2_{\zeta U}$	0.0301 (0.0131)	0.0253 (0.0113)	0.0208 (0.0133)
$\sigma^2_{\zeta A}$	0	0	0.0127 (0.0251)
σ^2_c		0.0537 (0.0062)	0.0474 (0.0097)
σ^2_e			0.1699 (0.0225)
Ψ		0.1442 (0.0535)	0.3120 (0.4274)
Φ		0.6890 (0.2699)	0.9341 (0.5103)
χ^2 (df; p-value)	3.2440 (1; 7%)	16.4171 (5; 0.6%)	36.4001 (12; 0.03%)

insurance issue mentioned in Section 4.2. Their empirical strategy is to consider the covariance restrictions implied by the theory on the joint behavior of consumption, income realizations, *and* subjective quantitative income expectations.

Their results are reproduced in Table 5. Their most general model separates transitory changes in log income into anticipated (with variance $\sigma^2_{\varepsilon A}$), unanticipated ($\sigma^2_{\varepsilon U}$), and measurement error (σ^2_y); separates permanent changes in income in anticipated ($\sigma^2_{\zeta A}$) and unanticipated ($\sigma^2_{\zeta U}$); allows for measurement error in consumption and subjective income expectations (σ^2_c and σ^2_e, respectively), and allows for partial insurance with respect to transitory shocks (Ψ) and permanent shocks (Φ).

In column (1) they put themselves in the shoes of a researcher with access to just income data. This researcher cannot separate anticipated from unanticipated changes in income or transitory changes from measurement error, so she assumes that measurement error is absent and all changes are unforecastable, resulting in upward biased estimates of $\sigma^2_{\zeta U}$ and $\sigma^2_{\varepsilon U}$. In column (2) they add consumption data. The researcher is still unable to separate anticipated from unanticipated, so any "superior information" is loaded onto the insurance coefficients Ψ and Φ. In particular, the data provide evidence of some insurance with respect to permanent and transitory shocks. Note that unlike what is predicted by the traditional version of the PIH, the transitory shock is not fully insured, perhaps because of binding borrowing constraints (see Jappelli and Pistaferri (2006)). In column (3) one adds data on subjective income expectations and the model is now overidentified. A number of interesting facts emerge. First, the transitory variation in income is split between the anticipated component (about 50%), the unanticipated component (20%) and measurement error (30%). This lowers the estimated degree of insurance with respect to transitory shocks. Similarly, a good fraction of the permanent variation (about 1/3) appears anticipated, and this now pushes the estimated insurance coefficient towards 1—i.e., these results show evidence that there is no insurance whatsoever with respect to permanent shocks.

There are a few notes of caution to add to the commentary on these results. First, the overidentifying restrictions are rejected. Second, while the economic significance of the results is in accordance with the idea that part of the estimated smoothing effects reflect information, the standard errors are high, preventing reliable inference.

Subjective expectations: data problems

There is considerable promise in the use of subjective expectations to evaluate the validity of various consumption models. However, it is fair to say that studies that use subjective expectations are subject to various criticisms. In particular, issues are raised about their reliability and informational content; moreover, it is still the case that subjective expectations are seldom available alongside consumption and income data or are confined to special survey modules. We are aware of only four data sets containing quantitative subjective expectations of future income in developed countries: the Italian SHIW, the Dutch DHS, the Japan SFC, and the US SEE.[57] See Attanasio (2009) for a survey of quantitative subjective expectation collection efforts currently undergoing in developing countries.

The Italian SHIW offers the opportunity to test some simple hypotheses regarding the validity of subjective data. In 1989 and 1991 people were asked to assign probability weights summing to 100 to various classes of income growth. In 1995 and 1998 they were asked instead to provide the minimum and maximum expected income, plus the probability that their income was going to be below the mid-point of the distribution. A first issue one may address is whether the wording of the subjective expectation questions affects reliability. The response rates for 1989, 1991, 1995 and 1998 are 57%, 96%, 87%, and 94%, respectively. The big jump in response rates between 1989 and 1991 (and somehow also between 1995 and 1998) may be due to interviewers being instructed to improve at eliciting data rather than bearing any meaningful relation with the question format. The fact that the SHIW has a panel component allows us to test for individual learning. The response rate in 1991 for people who were asked the same question format in the previous wave is 97% vs. 96% for people with no previous experience (95% vs. 95% in 1998). Hence, there is no evidence that having been asked the question before

---

[57] Many surveys also contain *qualitative* subjective expectations (such as those used to construct the Consumer Confidence index).

makes a difference in terms of response rates. Finally, we compute the proportions of people who are "confused". In 1989-91 people were also asked more qualitative questions, such as whether they were expecting their income to be "rather variable" in the future. We define an individual to be "confused" if she reports income as being "rather variable" but reports a degenerate distribution of expectations. For 1995-98, we assume that an individual is confused if she reports different minimum and maximum expected incomes, but then reports a probability of income below the midpoint of zero or 100%. Although the two definitions are not strictly comparable, it is interesting that the proportion of "confused" is higher in 1989-91 (17%) than in 1995-98 (11%), suggesting that people have more difficulty understanding the first type of question (which is trying to elicit the individual p.d.f.) than the second type of question (where the goal is to elicit the individual c.d.f).

5. INCOME PROCESSES, LABOR SUPPLY AND MOBILITY

The type of income processes discussed in Section 3 do not distinguish between fluctuations in income caused by exogenous shocks and those caused by endogenous responses to shocks. This is particularly important when the income process is used to assess and simulate the amount of risk faced by individuals.

For example in all the papers considered earlier, labor supply is assumed exogenous; no attention is paid to mobility across firms; no attempt is made to understand whether a shock to productivity comes from bad health, firm re-organization, learning, changes in skill prices, etc.. In sum, this is a black box approach in which the various sources of earnings fluctuations are aggregated to form a sort of "sufficient statistic" (often due to data availability). However, one may want to analyze the economic forces behind the degree of persistence and the amount of variability we observe in earnings. One reason is that different types of shock may be differently insurable, raising important policy implications. Moreover, it may allow us to better characterize behavior.

In a key contribution in this direction Abowd and Card (1989) extended the earlier literature to consider joint movements of hours and wages. Having established that both hours and earnings growth can be represented by an MA(2) process, they then link the two based on the life cycle model. Their approach can reveal how much of the variation in earnings comes from genuine shocks to wages and how much is due to responses to these shocks through hours of work. Their conclusion was that the common components in the variation of earnings and hours could not be explained by variation in productivity. With their approach they opened up the idea of considering the stochastic properties of different related quantities jointly and using this framework to assess how much of the fluctuations can be attributed to risk, as opposed to endogenous response, such as changing hours. Of course, to the extent that hours may be driven by short term demand for labor in the workplace, rather than voluntary adjustments, such fluctuations may also represent risk.

Extending the income process to allow for endogenous fluctuations

The key issue highlighted by the Abowd and Card approach is the distinction between shocks and responses to shocks. While Abowd and Card do not go all the way in that direction, they do relate the fluctuations in earnings and hours.

Low et al. (forthcoming) develop this direction by taking a much more structural approach and explicitly modeling labor supply and job mobility in a search and matching framework.[58] Not only is this approach explicit about distinguishing between shocks and responses to shocks, but it also distinguishes different types of uncertainty, loosely associated with employment risk and productivity risk.

The first important modification is Low et al. (forthcoming) they are now explicit about modeling wages per unit of time. In the specific application the unit of time is a quarter and the individual may either be working over this period or not. Extending the framework to a richer labor supply framework (the intensive margin) is relatively straightforward. The second modification is allowing for match effects; this implies that one source of fluctuations is obtaining a different job; what job one samples is a separate source of risk, to the extent that match effects are important. However, individuals can accept or reject job offers, a fact that needs to be recognized when combining such a process with a model of life cycle consumption and labor supply.

In what follows we use the notation w for (hourly) wages. Hence we specify

$$\ln w_{i,a,t} = d_t + X'_{i,a,t}\psi + p_{i,a,t} + v_{i,a,t} + a_{ij(t_0)} \tag{37}$$

where $w_{i,a,t}$ is the real hourly wage, d_t represents the log price of human capital at time t, $X_{i,a,t}$ a vector of regressors including age, $p_{i,a,t}$ the permanent component of wages, and $v_{i,a,t}$ the transitory error component. All parameters of the wage process are education specific (subscripts omitted for simplicity).

In principle, the term $e_{i,a,t}$ might be thought of as representing a mix between a transitory shock and measurement error. In the usual decomposition of shocks into transitory and permanent components, researchers work with annual earnings data where transitory shocks may well be important because of unemployment spells. In this framework, what is probably the most important source of transitory shocks is modeled explicitly through the employment and job mobility.

The term $a_{ij(t_0)}$ denotes a firm–worker match-specific component where $j(t_0)$ indexes the firm that the worker joined in period $t_0 \le t$.[59] It is drawn from a normal distribution with mean zero and variance σ_a^2. Low et al. (forthcoming) model the match

---

[58] Heathcote et al. (2007) show that it is possible to derive a linear latent factor structure for log wages, hours, and consumption in a rich framework with heterogeneous agents and incomplete markets under some assumptions.

[59] We should formally have a j subscript on wages but since it does not add clarity we have dropped it. Note also that in the absence of firm data one cannot distinguish between a pure firm effect and a pure match effect. In the latter case, one can imagine $\alpha_{ij(t_0)}$ as being the part of the matching rent that accrues to the worker. Low, Meghir and Pistaferri take the bargaining process that produces this sharing outcome as given.

effect as constant over the life of the worker-employer relationship. If the worker switches to a different employer between t and $t + 1$, however, there will be some resulting wage growth which we can term a mobility premium denoted as $\xi_{i,a+1,t+1} = a_{ij(t+1)} - a_{ij(t_0)}$. The match effect is assumed normally distributed and successive draws of $a_{ij(t)}$ are assumed independent; however, because of the endogenous mobility decisions successive *realizations* of the match effect will be correlated. Since offers can be rejected when received, only a censored distribution of $\xi_{i,a+1,t+1}$ is observed. The match effect $a_{ij(.)}$ is complementary to individual productivity.[60] Both the match effect and the idiosyncratic shock can have education-specific distributions. To keep things relatively simple, suppose the information structure is such that workers and firms are completely informed about $u_{i,a,t}$ and $a_{ij(.)}$ when they meet (jobs are "search goods").[61]

Assume that the permanent component of wages follows a random walk process:

$$u_{i,a,t} = u_{i,a-1,t-1} + \zeta_{i,a,t}. \tag{38}$$

The random shock to the permanent process, $\zeta_{i,a,t}$ is normally distributed with mean zero and variance σ_ζ^2 and is independent over time. Assume this shock reflects uncertainty.[62]

Given a particular level of unobserved productivity, the worker will be willing to work for some firms but not for others, depending on the value of the match. The measurement error $e_{i,a,t}$ is normally distributed with variance σ_e^2 and independent over time. As far as the policy implications of the model are concerned, we are interested in estimating σ_a^2 and σ_ζ^2. We describe later how these are estimated.

In order to make sense of such a process, we need to make further assumptions relating to firm behavior. Thus it is simpler to assume that there are constant returns to scale in labor implying that the firm is willing to hire anyone who can produce non-negative rents. In this context, receiving an outside offer is akin to a wage shock; however, a worker need not accept such an outside offer. This means that some wage rises, that are due to such offers are attributed to pure risk. In practice they are the result of a shock and a response to that shock. The implicit assumption is that the firm does not respond to outside offers.[63]

---

[60] Ideally one would like to allow also for shocks to the match effect. These will act as within-firm aggregate shocks. Restricting match effects to be constant is forced by the lack of matched firm and individual data.

[61] The importance of match effects in explaining wages has been stressed by Topel and Ward (1992) and Abowd et al. (1999). Postel-Vinay and Robin (2002) show in an equilibrium setting how firm and individual heterogeneity translate into a match effect.

[62] As discussed in earlier sections, an important issue is how much of the period-to-period variability of wages reflects uncertainty. A large component of this variability is measurement error, which here is allowed for.

[63] The fact that returns to tenure tend to be very low is evidence that responses to outside offers are not of first order importance in understanding wage fluctuations. Altonji and Williams (2005) assess this literature and conclude that their preferred estimate for the US is a return to tenure of 1.1 percent a year.

The above structure describes both the sources of shocks and the reactions to them. First, we have the shocks to productivity $\zeta_{i,a,t}$; second, there are shocks to job opportunities: these are reflected in the job arrival rate when employed and when unemployed, as well as by the possibility of a lay off (job destruction). Finally, there is the draw of a match specific effect. Individuals can respond to these by quitting into unemployment and accepting or rejecting a job offer. This model clarifies what aspect of earnings fluctuations reflects risk and what reflects an endogenous reaction to risk. The discussion also highlights the distinction between just describing the fluctuations of income vis-à-vis estimating a model of income fluctuations whose intention is to understand the welfare implications of risk.

Estimating the model Once we recognize that earnings fluctuations are also due to endogenous reactions to shocks, we need to take this into account in estimation in an internally consistent way. In the Low et al. (forthcoming) model the two ways that individuals can react is by deciding whether to work or not and deciding whether to accept alternative job offers. These decisions are a function of the offers received by the worker, which means that the distribution of wages is truncated both by the decision to work or not and by the decision to move firms. Thus estimating the components of risk involves correcting for selection both into work and for job mobility.

The effect of the modifications that Low et al. (forthcoming) allow for relative to the standard approach, and in particular that of accounting for the effect of job mobility, is to reduce substantially the estimated variance of permanent shocks from the one reported in, for example, Meghir and Pistaferri (2004). However, this does not necessarily mean that overall uncertainty declined: these modifications have changed the balance between permanent and transitory factors and have allowed for a better understanding of the sources of uncertainty and its welfare implications. Job destruction for example is a transitory, albeit persistent shock, because after a while it is expected that the individual will obtain a job and climb again the ladder of job quality. Persistence will be governed by the rate of arrival of job offers. On the other hand shocks to wages are literally permanent because of the random walk structure. The authors show that data simulated from the model can indeed replicate very well the earnings dynamics estimated with the less structural approaches in the literature. The differences in modeling are however very important because they have implications for consumption, savings and welfare.

The second recent paper along the lines of understanding the sources of shocks is that of Altonji et al. (2009). They estimate a complex stochastic model of wages, hours of work, transitions between employment and unemployment, and between jobs. Each of these events is governed by a reduced form model depending on exogenous characteristics, endogenous states and on exogenous shocks, which are the underlying source of fluctuations. Importantly, the model allows for selection into work and selection induced by transitions between jobs. The stochastic process of *wages* includes a match specific effect, an individual fixed effect and an AR(1) process; the AR coefficient is estimated to be 0.92 in various specifications, which is short of a random walk. Persistence is further reinforced by an AR(1) transitory shock and a further independent shock to *earnings*, which follows an AR process with an estimated coefficient of about 0.55. The lack of a random walk and the overall structure of the model does mean that the fit of the standard deviation of log earnings is not very good. In particular, the model predicts a flatter life cycle profile in the cross sectional variance of log-earnings than what is seen in the data. Nevertheless, both these papers make it clear that in order to understand uncertainty and its impact we need to account for the origin of the shocks. This should help further in identifying the nature of uncertainty and the persistence of shocks.

Other approaches to endogenizing volatility

Here we discuss other approaches to endogenizing wage or earnings volatility.

Postel-Vinay and Turon (2010) test whether the observed covariance structure of earnings in the UK may be generated by a structural job search model with on-the-job search. Individuals who are currently unemployed can move back into employment conditional on receiving an offer and finding this offer acceptable; people with jobs can stay with their current employer (if the job is not destroyed), move to another firm (conditional on receiving an outside offer) or move into unemployment. In each period, offered wages are subject to i.i.d. productivity shocks. These may induce renegotiations (by mutual consent) of the bargained wage, resulting occasionally in wage cuts or wage raises. However, mutual consent means that there are cases in which productivity shocks are insufficient to generate wage changes, and so wages are fixed at the previous period's level. This is the primary source of persistence observed in the data—an analyst may find evidence of a random walk in earnings even though the underlying productivity shock to wages is a pure i.i.d.

Low and Pistaferri (2010) use data on subjective reports of work limitations available from the PSID to identify health shocks separately from other shocks to productivity. Their framework is similar to that of Low et al. (forthcoming). It is simpler in certain dimensions (there are no firm specific effects and hence no job-to-job decisions), but richer in others (the modeling of health risk, the disability insurance institutional framework and the behavior of the social security system in the screening process). They use their model to assess quantitatively how large are the screening errors made by the disability evaluators and to examine the welfare consequences of changes in the features of the disability insurance program that affect the insurance-incentive trade-off, such as increasing the strictness of the screening test, reducing benefits, or increasing the probability of re-assessment.

Huggett et al. (2009) study human capital accumulation. In their model individuals may choose to divert some of their working time to the production of human capital. People differ in initial human capital (schooling, parents' teachings, etc.), initial financial wealth, and the innate ability to learn. Among other things, their framework generalizes Ben-Porath (1967) to allow for risk, i.e., shocks to the existing stock of human capital.

Their questions of interest are: (a) How much of lifetime inequality is determined before entry in the labor market (initial conditions)? and (b) How much is due to episodes of good or bad luck over the life cycle (shocks)? The answers to these two questions have clear policy relevance. If the answer to (a) is "a lot", one would want early intervention policies (e.g., public education). If the answer to (b) is "a lot", one would want to expand income maintenance programs (UI, means-tested welfare, etc.). In Huggett et al. (2009) wages grow because of shocks to existing human capital, or systematic fanning out due to differences in learning abilities. Old people do not invest, hence only the first force is present at the end of the life cycle. This provides an important idea for identification: Data on old workers can be used to identify the distribution of shocks to human capital. They next construct an age profile for the first, second, and third moment of earnings. Age, time, and cohort effects are not separately identifiable, so need to impose some restrictions, such as: (a) No time effects, or (b) No cohort effects. Finally, they calibrate the distribution of initial conditions (initial human capital and learning ability) and the shape of the human capital production function to match the age profile of the first three moments of earnings, while fixing the remaining parameters to realistic values taken from the literature. Huggett et al. (2009) use their model to do two things: (1) compute how much lifetime inequality is due to initial conditions and how much is due to shocks, and (2) run counterfactual experiments (shutting down risk to human capital or learning ability differences). Their results are that between 60% and 70% of the variability in lifetime utility (or earnings) is due to variability in initial conditions. Among initial conditions, the lion's share is taken by heterogeneity in initial human capital (rather than initial wealth or innate ability). Eliminating learning ability heterogeneity makes the age profile of inequality flat (even declining over a good fraction of the working life, 35-55). Eliminating shocks to human capital generates a more moderate U-shape age profile of inequality. For our purposes, one of the main points of the paper is that the standard incomplete markets model (for example, Heathcote (2009))—which assumes an exogenous income process—may exaggerate the weight played by shocks as opposed to initial conditions in determining lifetime inequality. Hence, it may overestimate the welfare gain of government insurance programs and underestimate the welfare gain of providing insurance against "bad initial conditions" (bad schools, bad parents, bad friends, etc.). Note however that the "exaggeration" effect of incomplete markets models only holds under the assumption that initial conditions are fully known to the agents at the beginning of the life cycle. If people have to "learn" their initial conditions, then they will face unpredictable innovations to these processes. Recent work by Guvenen (2007) estimates that people can forecast only about 60% of their "learning ability"—the remaining 40% is uncertainty revealed (quite slowly) over the life cycle. Similar conclusions are reached in work by Cunha et al. (2005).

Shocks and labor market equilibrium

We have moved from the standard reduced form models of income fluctuations to the more structural approach of Low et al. (forthcoming). However, there is further to go.

What is missing from this framework is an explicit treatment of equilibrium pay policies. More specifically, in Low et al. (forthcoming) the wage shocks are specified as shocks to the match specific effect, without specifying how these shocks arise. If we think about the match specific effect as being produced by a combination of the qualities of the worker and of the firm, then as in Postel-Vinay and Robin (2002), we can work out the pay policy of the firm under different assumptions on the strategies that individuals and firms follow. In that framework income/earnings, but only because individuals either receive alternative job offers, to which the incumbent firm responds, or because they move to an alternative firm.

Lise et al. (2009) generalize this framework to allow for shocks to the firm's productivity. In this context, the observed wage shocks are further decomposed into fluctuations originating in shocks to the productivity of the firm, responses to alternative offers or to moving to new jobs, either via unemployment or directly by firm to firm transition. In this context, the shocks are specified as changes in basic underlying characteristics of the firm as well as due to search frictions. This model thus comes closest to providing a full structural interpretation of income shocks, allowing also for the behavior of firms and strategies that lead to wages not being always responsive to the underlying shocks.[64] While this offers a way forward in understanding the source of fluctuations, the approach is not complete because it assumes that both individuals and firms are risk neutral. In this sense individuals have no interest in insurance and do not save for precautionary reasons. Extending such models to allow for risk aversion, wage contracts that partially insure the worker and for savings, is the natural direction for obtaining an integrated approach of earnings fluctuations and an analysis of the effects of risk.[65]

To provide an idea of how these more structural approaches work, we give a brief overview of the Lise et al. (2009) model. Individuals are characterized by a type denoted by x. These are individual characteristics that are possibly observed or unobserved. The key restriction here is that all characteristics contribute to one productivity index. Individual utility is the income they receive from work, as in a standard search model. This linearity is technically very important but as said above it precludes any consideration of risk aversion. A key ingredient in the Lise et al. (2009) paper is that firms or jobs employ one worker in a particular position, which is an extreme form of decreasing returns to scale and leads to an option value of waiting for a good worker under certain circumstances. The job is also characterized by a type y; this can be thought of as representing prior investments in technology and market conditions. However, this productivity level is subject to shocks, which can be conceived of as product market shocks. A key ingredient of the model is that the individual characteristics and the firm type may be complementary, in such a way that total output in the economy can be increased by

---

[64] See Guiso et al. (2005) for a more reduced form approach decomposing wage shocks onto a component related to (transitory and permanent) firm shocks, and one related to idiosyncratic shocks (including measurement error).

[65] Lise et al. (2009) are working in this direction.

allocating good worker types to high productivity firms and lower worker types to lower productivity ones (log-super modularity), very much like in a Becker marriage market.

At the heart of the model is pay determination in response to the quality of the worker and the firm, and in response to outside offers that result from on-the-job search. Very much like Low et al. (forthcoming), the following shocks are embedded in the model: random changes in productivity y, individuals receiving an outside offer from an alternative job, and exogenous job destruction. However, the important difference is that Lise et al. (2009) derive the impact of these shocks to both employment and wages explicitly accounting for the incentive structure both from the side of the worker and the firm making persistence endogenous. Specifically, when the productivity of the firm changes, this translates to a wage change only if the relationship remains profitable *and* one of the two partners can make a credible threat to leave the partnership; if the relationship ceases to be feasible there is separation; and if there is no common agreement to renegotiate, wages remain at their previous level. The model leads to a number of interesting implications about the stochastic evolution of wages and about pay policy: wages are smoother than productivity; the effect of worker and firm heterogeneity cannot be decomposed in a log-linear fashion as in Abowd et al. (1999); and wages grow with time, due to on the job search. It is possible that the combination of the relatively smooth pay policy within the firm and the nature of job mobility combine to give a time series process of wages that looks like a random walk, as discussed by Postel-Vinay and Turon (2010): In their model the combination of i.i.d. shocks and wage renegotiations in an environment with search frictions leads to wages with a unit root. Interestingly they also show that the implied variance of the shocks can have an ARCH structure, as identified by Meghir and Pistaferri (2004).

6. CONCLUSIONS

We started this chapter by discussing the importance of measuring and understanding labor market risks. In particular, what is the impact of risk on behavior? What types of risks matter? Answering these questions has proved to be quite difficult. One banal problem that hinders analysis is that for the countries most studied in the literature, the US and the UK, long panel data with regular observations on consumption, income and wealth are not available. Moreover, in most cases data are of debatable quality. Take the issue of answering the question whether the rise in inequality is due to phenomena like skill-biased technical change or wage instability. One proposal (as argued in Blundell and Preston, 1998) is to study consumption inequality. The papers that have done so include Cutler and Katz (1992), Dynarski and Gruber (1997), Krueger and Perri (2006), Blundell et al. (2008b), and Attanasio et al. (2004). Most papers find that consumption inequality rises less than income inequality. In the US the difference is substantial, and some papers go so far as to claim that consumption inequality has not changed at all

(Krueger and Perri). Given that all these analyses use the CEX, and given that the CEX suffers from severe problems of detachment from National Accounts, it is worth wondering whether this evidence is spurious and due to data problems.[66] Some recent papers (Attanasio et al., 2004; Battistin and Padula, 2010), have combined Diary and Interview CEX data in an ingenious way to revise upward the estimates of the trends in consumption inequality. Nevertheless, the finding that consumption inequality rises less rapidly than income inequality is confirmed.

We have discussed how empirical researchers have come up with ingenious ways of remedying data difficulties. A separate problem is that identification of the "correct" income process from income data is not straightforward. Yet, the income process is key for interpreting and predicting consumption responses. For example, the theory predicts that consumption responds strongly to permanent shocks and very little to transitory shocks. But we do not observe these components separately, so we have to come up with methods (typically, statistical methods) to extract them from observed income data. These methods may suffer from bias or statistical power problems. Furthermore, even if repeated observations of income realizations were able to provide information on the "correct" income process (in terms of its persistence, number of components, etc.), it would still not solve the problem of how much of the measured variability is anticipated and how much is unanticipated by the consumer, which is another key distinction for predicting consumption responses to changes in income. As said earlier, the theory predicts that consumption responds to unanticipated changes but not to anticipated ones (unless there are liquidity constraints or adjustment costs). In the literature, authors have suggested that some of these problems can be solved by the joint use of consumption and income data (or labor supply and income data). While this is an important development, it does not necessarily solve the problem. There is a third distinction (besides "permanent vs. transitory" and "anticipated vs. unanticipated") that is necessary to understand how consumption reacts to shocks; the distinction between "insurable" and "uninsurable" (or partially insurable) shocks, which requires taking some stand on such complicated issues as structure of credit and insurance markets, other decision margins within the household (spousal labor supply, family networks, etc.), and the modeling of government transfers (which may sometimes displace private transfers and self-insurance). This is an identification problem that has so far found only partial and unsatisfactory solutions.

Finally, on the data front one has to point out that large progress has been achieved through the use of administrative data available now in many countries. This of course does not solve the problems with consumption data, but it does allow us to understand potentially much better the dynamics of income and of wage determination. Much can be achieved by further theoretical developments and the systematic collection of excellent data.

---

[66] However, a recent special issue of the Review of Economic Dynamics (2010) has confirmed that for many other countries (in which data are better) consumption inequality also rises less than income inequality.

REFERENCES

Abowd, John, Card, David, 1989. On the covariance structure of earnings and hours changes. Econometrica 57 (2), 411–445.

Abowd, John, Kramarz, Francis, Margolis, David, 1999. High wage workers and high wage firms. Econometrica 67 (2), 251–333.

Acemoglu, Daron, Pischke, Jorn-Steffen, 1998. Why do firms train? Theory and evidence. Quarterly Journal of Economics 113 (1), 79–118.

Altonji, Joseph, Paula Martins, Ana, Siow, Aloysious, 2002. Dynamic factor models of consumption, hours, and income. Research in Economics 56 (1), 3–59.

Altonji, Joseph, Williams, Nicholas, 2005. Do wages rise with job seniority? A reassessment. Industrial and Labor Relations Review 58 (3), 370–397.

Altonji, Joseph, Smith, Anthony, Vidangos, Ivan, 2009. modeling earnings dynamics. Finance and economics dicussion series. Federal Reserve Board, Divisions of Research & Statistics and Monetary Affairs, Washington, DC.

Alvarez, Fernando, Jermann, Urban, 2000. Efficiency, equilibrium and asset pricing with risk of default. Econometrica 68 (4), 775–797.

Alvarez, J., 2004. Dynamics and seasonality in quarterly panel data: an analysis of earnings mobility in Spain. Journal of Business and Economic Statistics 22 (4), 443–456.

Angelucci, Manuela, De Giorgi, Giacomo, Rangel, Marcos, Rasul, Imran, 2010. Insurance and investment within family networks.

Attanasio, Orazio, 2009. Expectations and perceptions in developing countries: Their measurement and their use. American Economic Review 99 (2), 87–92.

Attanasio, Davis, Steven J., 1996. Relative wage movements and the distribution of consumption. Journal of Political Economy 104 (6), 1227–1262.

Attanasio, Orazio, Low, Hamish, 2004. Estimating Euler equations. Review of Economic Dynamics 7 (2), 406–435.

Attanasio, O.P., Pavoni, N., 2007. Risk sharing in private information models with asset accumulation: explaining the excess smoothness of consumption. NBER Working Paper 12994.

Attanasio, O.P., Weber, G., 2010. Consumption and saving: models of intertemporal allocation and their implications for public policy. Mimeo, University College London.

Attanasio, Orazio, Battistin, Erich, Ichimura, Hidehiko, 2004. What really happened to consumption inequality in the US? NBER Working Paper 10338.

Attanasio, Orazio, Low, Hamish, Sanchez-Marcos, Virginia, 2008. Explaining changes in female labor supply in a life-cycle model. American Economic Review 98 (4), 1517–1552.

Attfield, Clifford L.F., 1976. Estimation of the structural parameters in a permanent income model. Economica 43 (171), 247–254.

Attfield, Clifford L.F., 1980. Testing the assumptions of the permanent-income model. Journal of the American Statistical Association 75 (369), 32–38.

Azariadis, Costas, 1975. Implicit contracts and underemployment equilibria. Journal of Political Economy 83 (6), 1183–1202.

Baily, Martin N., 1977. On the theory of layoffs and unemployment. Econometrica 45 (5), 1043–1063.

Baker, Michael., 1997. Growth-rate heterogeneity and the covariance structure of life-cycle earnings. Journal of Labor Economics 15 (2), 338–375.

Baker, Michael, Solon, Gary, 2003. Earnings dynamics and inequality among Canadian Men, 1976-1992: evidence from longitudinal income tax records. Journal of Labor Economics 21 (2), 267–288.

Banks, James, Blundell, Richard, Brugiavini, Agar, 2001. Risk pooling, precautionary saving and consumption growth. Review of Economic Studies 68 (4), 757–779.

Barsky, Robert, Thomas Juster, F., Kimball, Miles S., Shapiro, Matthew D., 1997. Preference parameters and behavioral heterogeneity: an experimental approach in the health and retirement study. Quarterly Journal of Economics 112 (2), 537–579.

Battistin, Erich, Blundell, Richard, Lewbel, Arthur, 2009. Why is consumption more log normal than income? Gibrat's law revisited. Journal of Political Economy 117 (6), 1140–1154.

Battistin, Erich, Padula, Mario, 2010. Errors in survey reports of consumption expenditures. Unpublished manuscript.

Beegle, Kathleen, Thomas, Duncan, Frankenberg, Elizabeth, Sikoki, Bondan, Strauss, John, Teruel, Graciela, 2004. Education during a crisis. Journal of Development Economics 74 (1), 53–86.

Besley, Timothy, 1995. Savings, credit and insurance. In: Chenery, Hollis, Srinivasan, T.N. (Eds.), Handbook of Development Economics, vol. 3. Elsevier, pp. 2123–2207 (Chapter 36).

Ben-Porath, Yoram, 1967. The production of human capital and the life cycle of earnings. Journal of Political Economy 75 (4), 352–365.

Bertola, Giuseppe, Guiso, Luigi, Pistaferri, Luigi, 2005. Uncertainty and consumer durables adjustment. Review of Economic Studies 72 (4), 973–1007.

Bhalla, Surjit S., 1979. Measurement errors and the permanent income hypothesis: evidence from rural India. American Economic Review 69 (3), 295–307.

Blanchard, Olivier J., Katz, Lawrence F., 1992. Regional evolutions. Brookings papers on Economic Activity 1, 1–61.

Blanchard, Olivier Jean, Mankiw, N., Gregory, 1988. Consumption: beyond certainty equivalence. American Economic Review 78 (2), 173–177.

Blundell, Richard, Pistaferri, Luigi, 2003. Income volatility and household consumption: the impact of food assistance programs. Journal of Human Resources 38 (Supplement), 1032–1050.

Blundell, Richard, Preston, Ian, 1998. Consumption inequality and income uncertainty. Quarterly Journal of Economics 113 (2), 603–640.

Blundell, Richard, Stoker, Thomas, 1994. Consumption and the timing of income risk. IFS Working Papers: W94/09, Institute for Fiscal Studies, London.

Blundell, Richard, Low, Hamish, Preston, Ian, 2008a. Decomposing changes in income risk using consumption data. IFS Working Papers: W08/13, Institute for Fiscal Studies, London.

Blundell, Richard, Pistaferri, Luigi, Preston, Ian, 2008b. Consumption inequality and partial insurance. American Economic Review 98 (5), 1887–1921.

Bodkin, R., 1959. Windfall income and consumption. American Economic Review 49 (4), 602–614.

Böhlmark, Anders, Lindquist, Matthew J., 2006. Life-cycle variations in the association between current and lifetime income: replication and extension for Sweden. Journal of Labor Economics 24 (4), 879–896.

Bound, John, Krueger, Alan, 1991. The extent of measurement error in longitudinal earnings data: do two wrongs make a right? Journal of Labor Economics 9 (1), 1–24.

Bound, John, Brown, Charles, Duncan, Greg, Rodgers, Wilalrd, 1994. Evidence on the validity of cross-sectional and longitudinal labor market data. Journal of Labor Economics 12 (3), 345–368.

Bound, John, Brown, Charles, Mathiowetz, Nancy, 2001. Measurement error in survey data. In: Handbook of Econometrics, vol. 5. Elsevier Science, North-Holland, Amsterdam, New York, Oxford (Chapter 59).

Browning, Martin, Crossley, Thomas, 2001. Unemployment insurance benefit levels and consumption changes. Journal of Public Economics 80 (1), 1–23.

Browning, Martin, Crossley, Thomas, 2003 Shocks, stocks and socks: consumption smoothing and the replacement of durables. Working Paper 2003-07, McMaster University Department of Economics.

Browning, Martin, Lusardi, Annamaria, 1996. Household saving: micro theories and micro facts. Journal of Economic Literature 34 (4), 1797–1855.

Browning, Martin, Ejrnaes, Mette, Alvarez, Javier, 2006. Modelling income processes with lots of heterogeneity. Discussion Paper 285, University of Oxford Department of Economics, Oxford, UK.

Browning, Martin, Peter Hansen, Lars, Heckman, James, 1999. Micro data and general equilibrium models. In: Handbook of Macroeconomics, vol. 1A. Elsevier Science, North-Holland, Amsterdam, New York, Oxford, pp. 543–633.

Caballero, Ricardo, 1990. Consumption puzzles and precautionary savings. Journal of Monetary Economics 25 (1), 113–136.

Cahuc, Pierre, Postel-Vinay, Fabien, Robin, Jean-Marc, 2006. Wage bargaining with on-the-job search: theory and evidence. Econometrica 74 (2), 323–364.

Cameron, Lisa, Worswick, Christopher, 2003. The labor market as a smoothing device: labor supply responses to crop loss. Review of Development Economics 7 (2), 327–341.

Campbell, J.Y., 1987. Does saving anticipate declining labor income? An alternative test of the permanent income hypothesis. Econometrica 55, 1249–1273.

Cappellari, L., 2004. The dynamics and inequality of Italian men's earnings: long-term changes or transitory fluctuations? Journal of Human Resources XXXIX (2), 475–499.

Card, D., Di Nardo, J.E., 2002. Skill-biased technological change and rising wage inequality: some problems and puzzles. Journal of Labor Economics 20 (4), 733–783.

Carroll, Christopher, 2001. Precautionary saving and the marginal propensity to consume out of permanent income. NBER Working Paper 8233.

Carroll, Christopher D., Kimball, Miles S., 2005. Liquidity constraints and precautionary saving. Manuscript, Johns Hopkins University.

Carroll, Christopher, Samwick, Andrew, 1998. How important is precautionary saving? Review of Economics and Statistics 80 (3), 410–419.

Chamberlain, Gary, Hirano, Keisuke, 1999. Predictive distributions based on longitudinal earnings data. Annales d'Economie et de Statistique 55-56, 211–242.

Chao, H.K., 2003. Milton Friedman and the emergence of the permanent income hypothesis. History of Political Economy 35 (1), 77–104.

Chetty, Raj, Szeidl, Adam, 2007. Consumption commitments and risk preferences. The Quarterly Journal of Economics 122 (2), 831–877.

Cochrane, John., 1991. A simple test of consumption insurance. Journal of Political Economy 99 (5), 957–976.

Cragg, J.G., 1997. Using higher moments to estimate the simple errors-in-variables model. Rand Journal of Economics 28 (0), S71–S91.

Cunha, Flavio, Heckman, James, 2007. The evolution of inequality, heterogeneity and uncertainty in labor earnings in the US Economy. IZA Discussion Paper No. 3115.

Cunha, Flavio, Heckman, James, Navarro, Salvador, 2005. Separating uncertainty from heterogeneity in life cycle earnings. Oxford Economic Papers 57 (2), 191–261.

Cutler, David, Katz, Lawrence, 1992. Rising inequality? Changes in the distribution of income and consumption in the 1980's. American Economic Review, Papers and Proceedings 82 (2), 546–551.

Davis, Steven, Willen, Paul, 2000. Occupation-level income shocks and asset returns: their covariance and implications for portfolio choice. CRSP Working Paper No. 523.

Deaton, Angus, Paxson, Christina, 1994. Intertemporal choice and inequality. Journal of Political Economy 102 (3), 384–394.

Dehejia, Rajeev, DeLeire, Thomas, Luttmer, Erzo, 2007. Insuring consumption and happiness through religious organizations. Journal of Public Economics 91 (1–2), 259–279.

Dickens, Richard., 2000. The evolution of individual male earnings in Great Britain: 1975-95. The Economic Journal 110 (460), 27–49.

Dominitz, Jeff, Manski, Charles, 1997. Using expectations data to study subjective income expectations. Journal of the American Statistical Association 92 (439), 855–867.

Dynarski, Susan, Gruber, Jonathan, 1997. Can families smooth variable earnings? Brooking Papers on Economic Activity 1, 229–305.

The Economist, 2007. Shifting Sand. January 6: 63.

Farber, Henry, Gibbons, Robert, 1996. Learning and wage dynamics. Quarterly Journal of Economics 111 (4), 1007–1047.

Friedman, M., 1957. A Theory of the Consumption Function. Princeton University Press, Princeton.

Fuchs-Schundeln, Nicola, Schundeln, Matthias, 2005. Precautionary savings and self-selection: evidence from the German reunification 'experiment'. Quarterly Journal of Economics 120 (3), 1085–1120.

Gertler, P, Gruber, J., 2002. Insuring consumption against illness. American Economic Review 92 (1), 51–70.

Geweke, John, Keane, Michael, 2000. An empirical analysis of earnings dynamics among men in the PSID: 1968-1989. Journal of Econometrics 96 (2), 293–356.

Ginja, Rita, 2010. Income shocks and investments in human capital. Mimeo, University College London Department of Economics.

Gollier, C., Pratt, J.W., 1996. Risk vulnerability and the tempering effect of background risk. Econometrica 64 (5), 1109–1123.

Gorodnichenko, Yuriy, Stolyarov, Dmitriy, Sabirianova, Klara, 2010. Inequality and volatility moderation in Russia: evidence from micro-level panel data on consumption and income. Review of Economic Dynamics 13, 209–237.

Gottschalk, Peter, Moffitt, Robert, 1995. Trends in the covariance structure of earnings in the US: 1969-1987. Working Paper, Boston College Department of Economics.

Gruber, J., 1997. The consumption smoothing benefits of unemployment insurance. American Economic Review 87 (1), 192–205.

Gruber, Jonathan, Yelowitz, Aaron, 1999. Public health insurance and private savings. Journal of Political Economy 107 (6), 1249–1274.

Guiso, Luigi, Jappelli, Tullio, Pistaferri, Luigi, 2002. An empirical analysis of earnings and employment risk. Journal of Business and Economic Statistics 20 (2), 241–253.

Guiso, Luigi, Jappelli, Tullio, Terlizzese, Daniele, 1992. Earnings uncertainty and precautionary saving. Journal of Monetary Economics 30 (2), 307–337.

Guiso, Luigi, Jappelli, Tullio, Terlizzese, Daniele, 1996. Income risk, borrowing constraints, and portfolio choice. American Economic Review 86 (1), 158–172.

Guiso, Luigi, Pistaferri, Luigi, Schivardi, Fabiano, 2005. Insurance within the firm. Journal of Political Economy 113 (5), 1054–1087.

Guvenen, Fatih, 2007. Learning your earning: are labor income shocks really very persistent? American Economic Review 97 (3), 687–712.

Guvenen, Fatih., 2009. An empirical investigation of labor income processes. Review of Economic Dynamics 12, 58–79.

Guvenen, Fatih, Smith, Anthony, 2009. Inferring labor income risk from economic choices: an indirect inference approach. Mimeo, University of Minnesota.

Hacker, Jacob., 2006. The Great Risk Shift: the Assault on American Jobs, Families, Health Care, and Retirement and How You Can Fight Back. Oxford University Press US, New York.

Haider, Stephen, Solon, Gary, 2006. Life-cycle variation in the association between current and lifetime earnings. American Economic Review 96 (4), 1308–1320.

Hall, R.E., 1978. Stochastic implications of the life-cycle permanent income hypothesis: theory and evidence. Journal of Political Economy 86, 971–987.

Hall, R.E., Mishkin, F.S., 1982. The sensitivity of consumption to transitory income: estimates from panel data on households. Econometrica 50, 461–481.

Hause, John, 1980. The fine structure of earnings and the on-the-job training hypothesis. Econometrica 48 (4), 1013–1029.

Hayashi, F., 1985. The permanent income hypothesis and consumption durability: analysis based on Japanese panel data. Quarterly Journal of Economics 100, 1083–1113.

Hayashi, Fumio, Altonji, Joseph, Kotlikoff, Lawrence, 1996. Risk sharing between and within families. Econometrica 64 (2), 261–294.

Heathcote, Jonathan, 2009. Discussion of Heterogeneous Life-Cycle Profiles, Income Risk and Consumption Inequality by Giorgio Primiceri and Thijs van Rens. Journal of Monetary Economics 56 (1), 40–42.

Heathcote, Jonathan, Storesletten, Kjetil, Violante, Giovanni L., 2007 Consumption and labour supply with partial insurance: an analytical framework. CEPR Discussion Paper 6280.

Holtz-Eakin, Douglas, Whitney, Newey, Harvey, Rosen, 1988. Estimating vector autoregressions with panel data. Econometrica 56 (6), 1371–1395.

Hryshko, Dmytro, 2008. Identifying household income processes using a life cycle model of consumption. Mimeo, University of Alberta.

Hryshko, Dmytro, 2009. RIP to HIP: The data reject heterogeneous labor income profiles. Mimeo, University of Alberta.

Hsieh, C.T., 2003. Do consumers react to anticipated income shocks? Evidence from the Alaska permanent fund. American Economic Review 93, 397–405.

Hubbard, Ronald G., Skinner, Jonathan, Zeldes, Stephen, 1995. Precautionary saving and social insurance. Journal of Political Economy 103 (2), 360–399.

Huggett, Mark., 1996. Wealth distribution in life-cycle economies. Journal of Monetary Economics 38, 469–494.

Huggett, Mark, Ventura, Gustavo, Yaron, Amir, 2009. Sources of Lifetime Inequality. NBER Working Paper 13224.

Hyslop, Dean R., 2001. Rising US earnings inequality and family labor supply: the covariance structure of intrafamily earnings. American Economic Review 91 (4), 755–777.

Jacobson, Louis, LaLonde, Robert, Sullivan, Daniel, 1993. Earnings losses of displaced workers. American Economic Review 83 (4).

Jappelli, Tullio, Pistaferri, Luigi, 2006. Intertemporal choice and consumption mobility. Journal of the European Economic Association 4 (1), 75–115.

Jappelli, Tullio, Pistaferri, Luigi, 2010. The consumption response to income changes. Annual Review of Economics 2, 479–506.

Jensen, Shane T., Shore, Stephen H., 2008. Changes in the distribution of income volatility. Unpublished manuscript.

Kaplan, Greg, Violante, Giovanni, 2009. How much consumption insurance beyond self-insurance? NBER Working Paper 15553.

Kaufmann, K., Pistaferri, L., 2009. Disentangling insurance and information in intertemporal consumption choices. American Economic Review, Papers and Proceedings 99 (2), 387–392.

Keynes, J.M., 1936. The General Theory of Employment, Interest, and Money. Harcourt, Brace, New York.

Kimball, Miles, 1990. Precautionary saving in the small and in the large. Econometrica 58 (1), 53–73.

Klein, L., Liviatan, N., 1957. The significance of income variability on savings behavior. Bulletin of the Oxford Institute of Statistics 19, 151–160.

Kniesner, Thomas J., Ziliak, James P., 2002. Tax reform and automatic stabilization. The American Economic Review 92 (3), 590–612.

Knight, Frank, 1921. Risk, Uncertainty, and Profit. Hart, Schaffner & Marx, Boston, MA.

Kreinin, Mordechai, 1961. Windfall income and consumption–additional evidence. American Economic Review 388–390.

Krueger, Dirk, Perri, Fabrizio, 2006. Does income inequality lead to consumption inequality? Evidence and theory. Review of Economic Studies 73 (1), 163–193.

Krueger, Dirk, Perri, Fabrizio, 2009. How do households respond to income shocks? Mimeo, University of Pennsylvania.

Lillard, Lee, Willis, Robert, 1978. Dynamic aspects of earning mobility. Econometrica 46 (5), 985–1012.

Lise, Jeremy, Meghir, Costas, Robin, Jean-Marc, 2009. Matching, sorting, and wages. Mimeo, University College London.

Liviatan, N., 1963. Tests of the permanent income hypothesis based on a reinterview savings survey. In: Christ, C.F., et al. (Eds.), Measurements and Economics: Studies in Mathematical Economics and Econometrics. Stanford University Press, Palo Alto.

Ljunqvist, Lars, Sargent, Thomas J., 1998. The European unemployment dilemma. Journal of Political Economy 106, 514–550.

Low, Hamish., 2005. Self-insurance in a life-cycle model of labour supply and savings. Review of Economic Dynamics 8 (4), 945–975.

Low, Hamish, Pistaferri, Luigi, 2010. Disability risk, disability insurance and life cycle behavior. Mimeo, Stanford University.

Low, H., Meghir, C., Pistaferri, L., 2010. Wage risk and employment risk over the life cycle. American Economic Review (September) (forthcoming).

MaCurdy, Thomas, 1982. The use of time series processes to model the error structure of earnings in a longitudinal data analysis. Journal of Econometrics 18 (1), 82–114.

Mankiw, Nicholas G., 1986. The equity premium and the concentration of aggregate shocks. Journal of Financial Economics 17, 211–219.

Manski, C.F., 2004. Measuring expectations. Econometrica 72, 1329–1376.

Mayer, T., 1972. Permanent Income, Wealth, and Consumption. University of California Press, Berkeley.

Meghir, Costas, 2004. A retrospective of Friedman's theory of permanent income. Economic Journal 114 (496), F293-F306(1).

Meghir, Costas, Pistaferri, Luigi, 2004. Income variance dynamics and heterogeneity. Econometrica 72 (1), 1–32.

Meyer, Bruce, Mok, Wallace, 2006. Disability, earnings, income and consumption. Harris School Working Paper Series 06.10.

Modigliani, F., Sterling, A., 1983. Determinants of private saving with special reference to the role of social security-cross-country tests. In: The Determinants of National Saving and Wealth. MacMillian, London, pp. 24–55.

Moffitt, Robert, 1993. Identification and estimation of dynamic models with a time series of repeated cross-sections. Journal of Econometrics 59, 99–123.

Moffitt, Robert, Gottschalk, Peter, 1994. Trends in the autocovariance structure of earnings in the US: 1969-1987. Unpublished.

Musgrove, P., 1979. Permanent household income and consumption in urban South America. American Economic Review 69 (3), 355–368.

Nerlove, Marc, 1971. Further evidence on the estimation of dynamic economic relations from a time series of cross sections. Econometrica 39 (2), 359–382.

Nickell, S., 1981. Biases in dynamic models with fixed effects. Econometrica 49 (6), 1417–1426.

Paxson, C.H., 1992. Using weather variability to estimate the response of savings to transitory income in Thailand. American Economic Review 82 (1), 15–33.

Pischke, Jorn-Steffen, 1995. Individual income, incomplete information, and aggregate consumption. Econometrica 63 (4), 805–840.

Pistaferri, Luigi, 2001. Superior information, income shocks and the permanent income hypothesis. Review of Economics and Statistics 83, 465–476.

Postel-Vinay, Fabien, Robin, Jean-Marc, 2002. Equilibrium wage dispersion with worker and employer heterogeneity. Econometrica 70 (6), 2295–2350.

Postel-Vinay, Fabien, Turon, Hélène, 2010. On-the-job search, productivity shocks, and the individual earnings process. International Economic Review 51 (3), 599–629.

Primiceri, G.E., van Rens, T., 2009. Heterogeneous life-cycle profiles, income risk and consumption inequality. Journal of Monetary Economics 56 (1), 20–39.

Review of Economic Dynamics, 2010. Cross-sectional facts for macroeconomists. Review of Economic Dynamics 13 (1).

Rios-Rull, Victor, 1996. Life-cycle economies and aggregate fluctuations. Review of Economic Studies 63, 465–490.

Sandmo, A., 1970. The effect of uncertainty on saving decisions. Review of Economic Studies 37 (3), 353–360.

Sargent, Thomas, 1978. Rational expectations, econometric exogeneity, and consumption. Journal of Political Economy 86 (4), 673–700.

Scholnick, Barry, 2010. Credit card use after the final mortgage payment: does the magnitude of income shocks matter? Mimeo, University of Alberta.

Skinner, J.S., 1988. Risky income, life cycle consumption, and precautionary savings. Journal of Monetary Economics 22, 237–255.

Stephens, Melvin, 2001. The long-run consumption effects of earnings shocks. Review of Economics and Statistics 83 (1), 28–36.

Stephens, Melvin, 2008. The consumption response to predictable changes in discretionary income: evidence from the repayment of vehicle loans. Review of Economics and Statistics 90 (2), 241–252.

Sullivan, J.X., 2008. Borrowing during unemployment: unsecured debt as a safety net. Journal of Human Resources 43 (2), 383–412.

Topel, Robert, Ward, Michael, 1992. Job mobility and the careers of young men. Quarterly Journal of Economics 107 (2), 439–479.

Voena, Alessandra, 2010. Yours, mine and ours: do divorce laws affect the intertemporal behavior of married couples? Mimeo, Stanford University.

von Wachter, Till, Song, Jae, Manchester, Joyce, 2007. Long-term earnings losses due to job separation during the 1982 recession: an analysis using longitudinal administrative data from 1974 to 2004. Discussion Paper No.: 0708-16, Columbia University.

Wolpin, K.I., 1982. A new test of the permanent income hypothesis: the impact of weather on the income and consumption of farm households in India. Int. Econ. Rev 23 (3), 583–594.

Zeldes, S.P., 1989. Consumption and liquidity constraints: an empirical investigation. Journal of Political Economy 97, 305–346.

CHAPTER 10

Racial Inequality in the 21st Century: The Declining Significance of Discrimination

Roland G. Fryer Jr.[1]

Harvard University, EdLabs, NBER

Contents

[1] I am enormously grateful to Lawrence Katz, Steven Levitt, Derek Neal, William Julius Wilson and numerous other colleagues whose ideas and collaborative work fill this chapter. Vilsa E. Curto and Meghan L. Howard provided truly exceptional research assistance. Support from the Education Innovation Laboratory at Harvard University (EdLabs), is gratefully acknowledged.

Handbook of Labor Economics, Volume 4b
© 2011 Elsevier B.V.

ISSN 0169-7218, DOI 10.1016/S0169-7218(11)02408-7

Abstract

There are large and important differences between blacks in whites in nearly every facet of life—earnings, unemployment, incarceration, health, and so on. This chapter contains three themes. First, relative to the 20th century, the significance of discrimination as an explanation for racial inequality across economic and social indicators has declined. Racial differences in social and economic outcomes are greatly reduced when one accounts for educational achievement; therefore, the new challenge is to understand the obstacles undermining the development of skill in black and Hispanic children in primary and secondary school. Second, analyzing ten large datasets that include children ranging in age from eight months old seventeen years old, we demonstrate that the racial achievement gap is remarkably robust across time, samples, and particular assessments used. The gap does not exist in the first year of life, but black students fall behind quickly thereafter and observables cannot explain differences between racial groups after kindergarten. Third, we provide a brief history of efforts to close the achievement gap.

There are several programs—various early childhood interventions, more flexibility and stricter accountability for schools, data-driven instruction, smaller class sizes, certain student incentives, and bonuses for effective teachers to teach in high-need schools, which have a positive return on investment, but they cannot close the achievement gap in isolation. More promising are results from a handful of high-performing charter schools, which combine many of the investments above in a comprehensive framework and provide an "existence proof"—demonstrating that a few simple investments can dramatically increase the achievement of even the poorest minority students. The challenge for the future is to take these examples to scale.

JEL classification: I0; J0; J15

Keywords: Racial achievement gap; Charter schools; Racial inequality

> *"In the 21st Century, the best anti-poverty program around is a world-class education."*
>
> **President Barack Obama,**
> **State of the Union Address (January 27, 2010)**

1. INTRODUCTION

Racial inequality is an American tradition. Relative to whites, blacks earn twenty-four percent less, live five fewer years, and are six times more likely to be incarcerated on a given day. Hispanics earn twenty-five percent less than whites and are three times more likely to be incarcerated.[2] At the end of the 1990s, there were one-third more black men under the jurisdiction of the corrections system than there were enrolled in colleges or universities (Ziedenberg and Schiraldi, 2002). While the majority of barometers of economic and social progress have increased substantially since the passing of the civil rights act, large disparities between racial groups have been and continue to be an everyday part of American life.

---

[2] The Hispanic-white life expectancy gap actually favors Hispanics in the United States. This is often referred to as the "Hispanic Paradox" (Franzini et al., 2001).

Understanding the causes of current racial inequality is a subject of intense debate. A wide variety of explanations—which range from genetics (Jensen, 1973; Rushton, 1995) to personal and institutional discrimination (Darity and Mason, 1998; Pager, 2007; Krieger and Sidney, 1996) to the cultural backwardness of minority groups (Reuter, 1945; Shukla, 1971)—have been put forth. Renowned sociologist William Julius Wilson argues that a potent interaction between poverty and racial discrimination can explain current disparities (Wilson, 2010).

Decomposing the share of inequality attributable to these explanations is exceedingly difficult, as experiments (field, quasi-, or natural) or other means of credible identification are rarely available.[3] Even in cases where experiments are used (i.e., audit studies), it is unclear precisely what is being measured (Heckman, 1998). The lack of success in convincingly identifying root causes of racial inequality has often reduced the debate to a competition of "name that residual"—arbitrarily assigning identity to unexplained differences between racial groups in economic outcomes after accounting for a set of confounding factors. The residuals are often interpreted as "discrimination," "culture," "genetics," and so on. Gaining a better understanding of the root causes of racial inequality is of tremendous importance for social policy, and the purpose of this chapter.

This chapter contains three themes. First, relative to the 20th century, the significance of discrimination as an explanation for racial inequality across economic and social indicators has declined. Racial differences in social and economic outcomes are greatly reduced when one accounts for educational achievement; therefore, the new challenge is to understand the obstacles undermining the achievement of black and Hispanic children in primary and secondary school. Second, analyzing ten large datasets that include children ranging in age from eight months old to seventeen years old, we demonstrate that the racial achievement gap is remarkably robust across time, samples, and particular assessments used. The gap does not exist in the first year of life, but black students fall behind quickly thereafter and observables cannot explain differences between racial groups after kindergarten.

Third, we provide a brief history of efforts to close the achievement gap. There are several programs—various early childhood interventions, more flexibility and stricter accountability for schools, data-driven instruction, smaller class sizes, certain student incentives, and bonuses for effective teachers to teach in high-need schools, which have a positive return on investment, but they cannot close the achievement gap in isolation.[4] More promising are results from a handful of high-performing charter schools, which combine many of the investments above in a comprehensive model and provide a powerful "existence proof"—demonstrating that a few simple investments can dramatically increase the achievement of even the poorest minority students.

---

[3] List (2005), which examines whether social preferences impact outcomes in the actual market through field experiments in the sportscard market, is a notable exception.

[4] For details on the treatment effects of these programs, see Jacob and Ludwig (2008), Guskey and Gates (1985), and Fryer (2010).

An important set of questions is: (1) whether one can boil the success of these charter schools down to a form that can be taken to scale in traditional public schools; (2) whether we can create a competitive market in which only high-quality schools can thrive; and (3) whether alternative reforms can be developed to eliminate achievement gaps. Closing the racial achievement gap has the potential to substantially reduce or eliminate many of the social ills that have plagued minority communities for centuries.

2. THE DECLINING SIGNIFICANCE OF DISCRIMINATION

One of the most important developments in the study of racial inequality has been the quantification of the importance of pre-market skills in explaining differences in labor market outcomes between blacks and whites (Neal and Johnson, 1996; O'Neill, 1990). Using the National Longitudinal Survey of Youth 1979 (NLSY79), a nationally representative sample of 12,686 individuals aged 14 to 22 in 1979, Neal and Johnson (1996) find that educational achievement among 15- to 18-year-olds explains all of the black-white gap in wages among young women and 70% of the gap among men. Accounting for pre-market skills also eliminates the Hispanic-white gap. Important critiques such as racial bias in the achievement measure (Darity and Mason, 1998; Jencks, 1998), labor market dropouts, or the potential that forward-looking minorities underinvest in human capital because they anticipate discrimination in the market cannot explain the stark results.[5]

We begin by replicating the seminal work of Neal and Johnson (1996) and extending their work in four directions. First, the most recent cohort of NLSY79 is between 42 and 44 years old (15 years older than in the original analysis), which provides a better representation of the lifetime gap. Second, we perform a similar analysis with the National Longitudinal Survey of Youth 1997 cohort (NLSY97). Third, we extend the set of outcomes to include unemployment, incarceration, and measures of physical health. Fourth, we investigate the importance of pre-market skills among graduates of thirty-four elite colleges and universities in the College and Beyond database, 1976 cohort.

To understand the importance of academic achievement in explaining life outcomes, we follow the lead of Neal and Johnson (1996) and estimate least squares models of the form:

$$\text{outcome}_i = \sum_R \beta_R R_i + \Gamma X_i + \varepsilon_i, \tag{1}$$

where i indexes individuals, X_i denotes a set of control variables, and R_i is a full set of racial identifiers.

[5] Lang and Manove (2006) show that including years of schooling in the Neal and Johnson (1996) specification causes the gap to increase—arguing that when one controls for AFQT performance, blacks have higher educational attainment than whites and that the labor market discriminates against blacks by not financially rewarding them for their greater education.

Table 1   The importance of educational achievement on racial differences in labor market outcomes (NLSY79).

	Wage				Unemployment			
	Men		Women		Men		Women	
Black	−0.394	−0.109	−0.131	0.127	2.312	1.332	3.779	2.901
	(0.043)	(0.046)	(0.043)	(0.046)	(0.642)	(0.384)	(1.160)	(1.042)
Hispanic	−0.148	0.039	−0.060	0.161	2.170	1.529	2.759	2.181
	(0.049)	(0.047)	(0.051)	(0.051)	(0.691)	(0.485)	(0.973)	(0.871)
Age	0.027	0.012	−0.011	0.016	1.191	1.202	0.956	0.941
	(0.023)	(0.022)	(0.024)	(0.022)	(0.175)	(0.178)	(0.131)	(0.133)
AFQT		0.270		0.288		0.561		0.735
		(0.021)		(0.023)		(0.082)		(0.123)
$AFQT^2$		0.039		−0.009		1.005		1.276
		(0.019)		(0.020)		(0.151)		(0.161)
Obs.	1167	1167	1044	1044	1315	1315	1229	1229
R^2	0.068	0.206	0.009	0.135	0.022	0.050	0.040	0.058
% Reduction		72		197		75		32

The dependent variable in columns 1 through 4 is the log of hourly wages of workers. The wage observations come from 2006. All wages are measured in 2006 dollars. The wage measure is created by multiplying the hourly wage at each job by the number of hours worked at each job that the person reported as a current job and then dividing that number by the total number of hours worked during a week at all current jobs. Wage observations below $1 per hour or above $115 per hour are eliminated from the data. The dependent variable in columns 5 through 8 is a binary variable indicating whether the individual is unemployed. The unemployment variable is taken from the individual's reported employment status in the raw data. In both sets of regressions, the sample consists of the NLSY79 cross-section sample plus the supplemental samples of blacks and Hispanics. Respondents who did not take the ASVAB test are included in the sample and a dummy variable is included in the regressions that include AFQT variables to indicate if a person did not have a valid AFQT score. This includes 134 respondents who had a problem with their test according to the records. All included individuals were born after 1961. The percent reduction reported in even-numbered columns represents the reduction in the coefficient on black when controls for AFQT are added. Standard errors are in parentheses.

Table 1 presents racial disparities in wage and unemployment for men and women, separately.[6] The odd-numbered columns present racial differences on our set of outcomes controlling only for age. The even-numbered columns add controls for the Armed Forces Qualifying Test (AFQT)—a measure of educational achievement that has been shown to be racially unbiased (Wigdor and Green, 1991)—and its square. Black men earn 39.4% less than white men; black women earn 13.1% less than white women. Accounting for educational achievement drastically reduces these inequalities—39.4% to 10.9% for black men and 13.1% *lower* than whites to 12.7% *higher* for black women.[7] An eleven percent difference between white and black men with similar educational achievement is a large and important number, but a small fraction of the original gap. Hispanic men earn 14.8% less than whites in the raw data—62% less than the raw black-white gap—which reduces

[6] Summary statistics for NLSY79 are displayed, by race, in Table A.1.

[7] This may be due, in part, to differential selection out of the labor market between black and white women. See Neal (2005) for a detailed account of this.

to 3.9% more than whites when we account for AFQT. The latter is not statistically significant. Hispanic women earn six percent less than white women (not significant) without accounting for achievement. Adding controls for AFQT, Hispanic women earn sixteen percent *more* than comparable white women and these differences are statistically significant.

Labor force participation follows a similar pattern. Black men are more than twice as likely to be unemployed in the raw data and thirty percent more likely after controlling for AFQT. For women, these differences are 3.8 and 2.9 times more likely, respectively. Hispanic-white differences in unemployment with and without controlling for AFQT are strikingly similar to black-white gaps.

Table 2 replicates Table 1 using the NLSY97.[8] The NLSY97 includes 8984 youths between the ages of 12 and 16 at the beginning of 1997; these individuals are 21 to 27 years old in 2006-2007, the most recent years for which wage measures are available. In this sample, black men earn 17.9% less than white men and black women earn 15.3% less than white women. When we account for educational achievement, racial differences in wages measured in the NLSY97 are strikingly similar to those measured in NLSY79— 10.9% for black men and 4.4% for black women. The raw gaps, however, are much smaller in the NLSY97, which could be due either to the younger age of the workers and a steeper trajectory for white males (Farber and Gibbons, 1996) or to real gains made by blacks in recent years. After adjusting for age, Hispanic men earn 6.5% less than white men and Hispanic women earn 5.7% less than white women, but accounting for AFQT eliminates the Hispanic-white gap for both men and women.

Black men in the NLSY97 are almost three times as likely to be unemployed, which reduces to twice as likely when we account for educational achievement. Black women are roughly two and a half times more likely to be unemployed than white women, but controlling for AFQT reduces this gap to seventy-five percent more likely. Hispanic men are twenty-five percent more likely to be unemployed in the raw data, but when we control for AFQT, this difference is eliminated. Hispanic women are fifty percent more likely than white women to be unemployed and this too is eliminated by controlling for AFQT. Similar to the NLSY79, controlling for AFQT has less of an impact on racial differences in unemployment than on wages.

Table 3 employs a Neal and Johnson specification on two social outcomes: incarceration and physical health. The NLSY79 asks the "type of residence" in which the respondent is living during each administration of the survey, which allows us to construct a measure of whether the individual was ever incarcerated when the survey was administered across all years of the sample.[9] The NLSY97 asks individuals if they have been sentenced to jail, an adult corrections institution, or a juvenile corrections

---

[8] Summary statistics for NLSY97 are displayed, by race, in Table A.2.

[9] Lochner and Moretti (2004) use a similar approach to determine incarceration rates, using type of residence in Census data and in the NLSY79.

Table 2 The importance of educational achievement on racial differences in labor market outcomes (NLSY97).

	Wage				Unemployment			
	Men		Women		Men		Women	
Black	−0.179	−0.109	−0.153	−0.044	2.848	2.085	2.596	1.759
	(0.023)	(0.024)	(0.020)	(0.021)	(0.377)	(0.298)	(0.380)	(0.278)
Hispanic	−0.065	−0.014	−0.057	0.035	1.250	0.994	1.507	1.065
	(0.023)	(0.024)	(0.023)	(0.023)	(0.205)	(0.170)	(0.267)	(0.202)
Mixed race	0.007	0.009	−0.090	−0.057	3.268	3.216	1.317	1.278
	(0.143)	(0.145)	(0.072)	(0.065)	(1.661)	(1.618)	(0.975)	(0.911)
Age	0.064	0.062	0.039	0.039	0.934	0.937	1.084	1.081
	(0.006)	(0.006)	(0.006)	(0.006)	(0.038)	(0.038)	(0.048)	(0.048)
AFQT		0.089		0.148		0.664		0.595
		(0.011)		(0.012)		(0.049)		(0.052)
$AFQT^2$		−0.022		−0.035		1.248		1.140
		(0.012)		(0.012)		(0.095)		(0.107)
Obs.	3278	3278	3204	3204	3294	3294	3053	3053
R^2	0.047	0.065	0.029	0.081	0.032	0.051	0.026	0.049
% Reduction		39		71		41		52

The dependent variable in columns 1 through 4 is the log of hourly wages of workers. The wage observations come from 2006 and 2007. All wages are measured in 2006 dollars. The wage measure for each year is created by multiplying the hourly wage at each job by the number of hours worked at each job that the person reported as a current job and then dividing that number by the total number hours worked during a week at all current jobs. If a person worked in both years, the wage is the average of the two wage observations. Otherwise the reported wage is from the year for which the individual has valid wage data. Wage observations below $1 per hour or above $115 per hour are eliminated from the data. The dependent variable in columns 5 through 8 is a binary variable indicating whether the individual is unemployed. The unemployment variable is taken from the individual's reported employment status in the raw data. The employment status from 2006 is used for determining unemployment. The coefficients in columns 5 through 8 are odds ratios from logistic regressions. Respondents who did not take the ASVAB test are included in the sample and a dummy variable is included to indicate if a person did not have a valid AFQT score in the regressions that include AFQT variables. The percent reduction reported in even-numbered columns represents the reduction in the coefficient on black when controls for AFQT are added. Standard errors are in parentheses.

institution in the past year for each yearly follow-up survey of participants. In 2006, the NLSY79 included a 12-Item Short Form Health Survey (SF-12) for all individuals over age 40. The SF-12 consists of twelve self-reported health questions ranging from whether the respondent's health limits him from climbing several flights of stairs to how often the respondent has felt calm and peaceful in the past four weeks. The responses to these questions are combined to create physical and mental component summary scores.

Adjusting for age, black males are about three and a half times and Hispanics are about two and a half times more likely to have ever been incarcerated when surveyed.[10] Controlling for AFQT, this is reduced to about eighty percent more likely

[10] We focus on the estimates from NLSY79 because we have many more years of observations for these individuals than for those in the NLSY97, which gives us a more accurate picture of incarceration.

Table 3 The importance of educational achievement on racial differences in incarceration and health outcomes.

	Incarceration								Physical health			
	NLSY79				NLSY97				NLSY79			
	Men		Women		Men		Women		Men		Women	
Black	3.494	1.777	1.054	0.418	2.325	1.417	1.218	0.710	−0.151	0.011	−0.230	−0.111
	(0.549)	(0.304)	(0.484)	(0.226)	(0.245)	(0.159)	(0.244)	(0.148)	(0.053)	(0.061)	(0.068)	(0.076)
Hispanic	2.599	1.549	1.135	0.497	1.641	1.120	0.908	0.591	−0.140	−0.035	0.030	0.125
	(0.476)	(0.300)	(0.573)	(0.275)	(0.196)	(0.136)	(0.216)	(0.146)	(0.061)	(0.063)	(0.065)	(0.071)
Mixed race					0.851	0.887	5.306	4.760				
					(0.511)	(0.557)	(2.428)	(2.207)				
Age	1.044	1.077	1.424	1.341	1.070	1.072	1.012	1.002	−0.035	−0.038	0.064	0.068
	(0.087)	(0.092)	(0.400)	(0.387)	(0.034)	(0.035)	(0.062)	(0.062)	(0.028)	(0.027)	(0.035)	(0.035)
AFQT		0.352		0.346		0.447		0.458		0.164		0.127
		(0.052)		(0.138)		(0.033)		(0.057)		(0.028)		(0.036)
AFQT^2		0.746		1.187		0.905		1.166		−0.023		−0.035
		(0.089)		(0.291)		(0.063)		(0.158)		(0.023)		(0.030)
Obs.	1989	1989	1894	1894	4599	4599	4385	4385	1588	1588	1576	1576
R^2	0.046	0.114	0.007	0.078	0.021	0.066	0.009	0.050	0.008	0.033	0.012	0.020
% Reduction	69		1178		69		233		107		52	

The dependent variable in columns 1 through 8 is a measure of whether the individual was ever incarcerated. In the NLSY79 data, this variable is equal to one if the individual reported their residence as jail during any of the yearly follow-up surveys or if they reported having been sentenced to a corrective institution before the baseline survey and is equal to zero otherwise. In the NLSY97 data, this variable is equal to one if the person reports having been sentenced to jail, an adult corrections institution, or a juvenile corrections institution in the past year during any of the yearly administrations of the survey and is equal to zero otherwise. The coefficients in columns 1 through 8 are odds ratios from logistic regressions. The dependent variable in columns 9 through 12 is the physical component score (PCS) reported in the NLSY79 derived from the 12-Item Short Form Health Survey of individuals over age 40. The PCS is standardized to have a mean of zero and a standard deviation of one. Individuals who do not have valid PCS data are not included in these regressions. In the NLSY79 regressions, included individuals were born after 1961. Respondents who did not take the ASVAB test are included in the sample and a dummy variable is included in the regressions that include AFQT variables to indicate if a person did not have a valid AFQT score. For NLSY79, this includes 134 respondent that had a problem with their test according to the records. The percent reduction reported in even-numbered columns represents the reduction in the coefficient on black when controls for AFQT are added. Standard errors are in parentheses.

for blacks and fifty percent more likely for Hispanics. Again, the racial differences in incarceration after controlling for achievement is a large and important number that deserves considerable attention in current discussions of racial inequality in the United States. Yet, the importance of educational achievement in the teenage years in explaining racial differences is no less striking.

The final two columns of Table 3 display estimates from similar regression equations for the SF-12 physical health measure, which has been standardized to have a mean of zero and standard deviation of one for ease of interpretation. Without accounting for achievement, there is a black-white disparity of 0.15 standard deviations in self-reported physical health for men and 0.23 standard deviations for women. For Hispanics, the differences are −0.140 for men and 0.030 for women. Accounting for educational achievement eliminates the gap for men and cuts the gap in half for black women [−0.111 (0.076)]. The remaining difference for black women is not statistically significant. Hispanic women report better health than white women with or without accounting for AFQT.

Extending Neal and Johnson (1996) further, we turn our attention to the College and Beyond (C&B) Database, which contains data on 93,660 full-time students who entered thirty-four elite colleges and universities in the fall of 1951, 1976, or 1989. We focus on the cohort from 1976.[11] The C&B data contain information drawn from students' applications and transcripts, Scholastic Aptitude Test (SAT) and the American College Test (ACT) scores, standardized college admissions exams that are designed to assess a student's readiness for college, as well as information on family demographics and socioeconomic status in their teenage years.[12] The C&B database also includes responses to a survey administered in 1995 or 1996 to all three cohorts that provides detailed information on post-college labor market outcomes. Wage data were collected when the respondents were approximately 38 years old, and reported as a series of ranges. We assigned individuals the midpoint value of their reported income range as their annual income.[13] The response rate to the 1996 survey was approximately 80%. Table A.3 contains summary statistics used in our analysis.

---

[11] There are two reasons for this. First, the 1976 College & Beyond cohort can be reasonably compared to the NLSY79 cohort because they are all born within a seven-year period. Second, there are issues with using either the 1951 or the 1989 data. The 1951 cohort presents issues of selection bias—black students who entered top colleges in this year were too few in number and those who did were likely to be incredibly motivated and intelligent students, in comparison to both their non-college-going black peers and their white classmates. The 1989 cohort is problematic because the available wage data for that cohort was obtained when that cohort was still quite young. Wage variance is likely to increase a great deal beyond the levels observed in the available wage data. Additionally, some individuals who have high expected earnings were pursuing graduate degrees at the time wage data were gathered, artificially depressing their observed wages.

[12] Ninety-two percent of the sample has valid SAT scores.

[13] Individuals in the wage range "less than $1000" are excluded from the analysis as they cannot have made this wage as full-time workers and therefore should not be compared to the rest of the sample.

Table 4 The importance of educational achievement on racial differences in labor market outcomes (C&B 76).

	Men		Women	
Black	−0.273	−0.152	0.186	0.286
	(0.042)	(0.047)	(0.035)	(0.031)
Hispanic	−0.038	−0.007	0.005	0.059
	(0.081)	(0.077)	(0.094)	(0.088)
Other race	0.153	0.147	0.271	0.270
	(0.066)	(0.062)	(0.048)	(0.049)
SAT		0.003		0.001
		(0.001)		(0.001)
SAT^2		−0.000		−0.000
		(0.000)		(0.000)
Obs.	11,088	11,088	8976	8976
R^2	0.007	0.015	0.004	0.012
% Reduction		44		53

The dependent variable is the log of annual income. Annual income is reported as a series of ranges; each individual is assigned the midpoint of their reported income range as their annual income. Income data were collected for either 1994 or 1995. Individuals who report earning less than $1000 annually or who were students at the time of data collection are excluded from these regressions. Those individuals with missing SAT scores are included in the sample and a dummy variable is included in the regressions that include SAT variables to indicate that a person did not have a valid AFQT score. All regressions use institution weights and standard errors are clustered at the institution level. Standard errors are in parentheses.

Table 4 presents racial disparities in income for men and women from the 1976 cohort of the C&B Database.[14] The odd-numbered columns present raw racial differences. The even-numbered columns add controls for performance on the SAT and its square.[15] Black men from this sample earn 27.3% less than white men, but when we account for educational achievement, the gap shrinks to 15.2%. Black women earn more than white women by 18.6%, which increases to an advantage of 28.6% when accounting for SAT scores. There are no differences in income between Hispanics and whites with or without accounting for achievement.

In developing countries, eradicating poverty takes a large and diverse set of strategies: battling disease, fighting corruption, building schools, providing clean water, and so on (Schultz and Strauss, 2008). In the United States, important progress toward racial

[14] A measure of current unemployment for the individuals surveyed was also created. However, only 39 out of 19,257 with valid answers as to employment status could be classified as unemployed, making an analysis of unemployment by race infeasible. Although 1876 reported that they were not currently working for reasons other than retirement, the vast majority of these individuals were out of the labor force rather than unemployed. More details on this variable can be found in the data appendix.

[15] The SAT is presently called the SAT Reasoning Test and the letters "SAT" no longer stand for anything. At the time these SAT scores were gathered, however, the test was officially called the "Scholastic Aptitude Test" and was believed to function as a valid intelligence test. The test also had a substantially different format and included a different range of question types.

equality can be made if one ensures that black and white children obtain the same skills. This is an enormous improvement over the battles for basic access and equality that were fought in the 20th century, but we must now work to close the racial achievement gaps in education—high-quality education is the new civil rights battleground.[16]

3. BASIC FACTS ABOUT RACIAL DIFFERENCES IN ACHIEVEMENT BEFORE KIDS ENTER SCHOOL

We begin our exploration of the racial achievement gap with data on mental function in the first year of life. This approach has two virtues. First, nine months is one of the earliest ages at which one can reliably test cognitive achievement in infants. Second, data on the first year of life provide us with a rare opportunity to potentially understand whether genetics is an important factor in explaining racial differences later in life.[17]

There are only two datasets that both are nationally representative and contain assessments of mental function before the first year of life. The first is the US Collaborative Perinatal Project (CPP) (Bayley, 1965), which includes over 31,000 women who gave birth in twelve medical centers between 1959 and 1965. The second dataset is the Early Childhood Longitudinal Study, Birth Cohort (ECLS-B), a nationally representative sample with measures of mental functioning (a shortened version of the Bayley Scale of Infant Development) for over 10,000 children aged one and under. Summary statistics for the variables we use in our core specifications are displayed by race in Table A.4 (CPP) and Table A.5 (ECLS-B).

Figures 1 and 2 plot the density of mental test scores by race at various ages in the ECLS-B and CPP data sets, respectively.[18] In Fig. 1, the test score distributions on the Bayley Scale at age nine months for children of different races are visually indistinguishable. By age two, the white distribution has demonstrably shifted to the right. At age four, the cognitive score is separated into two components: literacy (which measures early language and literacy skills) and math (which measures early mathematics skills and math readiness). Gaps in literacy are similar to disparities at age two; early math skills differences are more pronounced. Figure 2 shows a similar pattern using the CPP data. At age eight months, all races look similar. By age four, whites are far ahead of blacks and Hispanics and these differences continue to grow over time. Figures 1 and 2 make

---

[16] This argument requires an important leap of faith. We have demonstrated that educational achievement is correlated with better economic and social outcomes, but we have not proven that this relationship is causal. We will come back to this in the conclusion.

[17] Some scholars have argued that the combination of high heritability of innate ability (typically above 0.6 for adults, but somewhat lower for children, e.g., Neisser et al. (1996) or Plomin et al. (2000), and persistent racial gaps in test scores is evidence of genetic differences across races (Jensen, 1973, 1998; Rushton and Jensen, 2005). As Nisbett (1998) and Phillips et al. (1998a,b) argue, however, the fact that blacks, whites, and Asians grow up in systematically different physical and social environments makes it difficult to draw strong, causal, genetically-based conclusions.

[18] This analysis is a replication and extension of Bayley (1965) and Fryer and Levitt (2004).

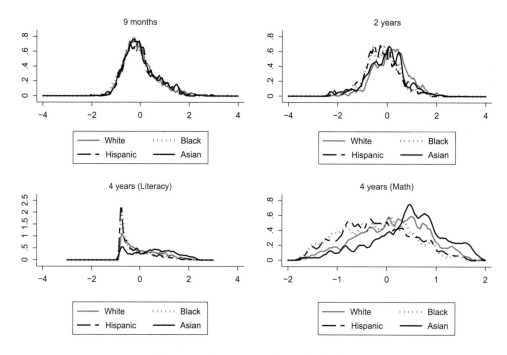

Figure 1   *Emergence of gaps in ECLS-B.*

one of the key points of this section: the commonly observed racial achievement gap only emerges after the first year of life.

To get a better sense of the magnitude (and standard errors) of the change from nine months to seven years old, we estimate least squares models of the following form:

$$\text{outcome}_{i,a} = \sum_R \beta_R R_i + \Gamma X_i + \varepsilon_{i,a} \tag{2}$$

where i indexes individuals, a indexes age in years, and R_i corresponds to the racial group to which an individual belongs. The vector X_i captures a wide range of possible control variables including demographics, home and prenatal environment; $\varepsilon_{i,a}$ is an error term. The variables in the ECLS-B and CPP datasets are similar, but with some important differences.[19] In the ECLS-B dataset, demographic variables include the gender of the child, the age of the child at the time of assessment (in months), and the region of the country in which the child lives. Home environment variables include a single socioeconomic status measure (by quintile), the mother's age, the number of siblings, and the family structure (child lives with: "two biological parents," "one biological parent," and so on). There is also a "parent as teacher" variable included

---

[19] For more information on the coding of these variables, see the data appendix.

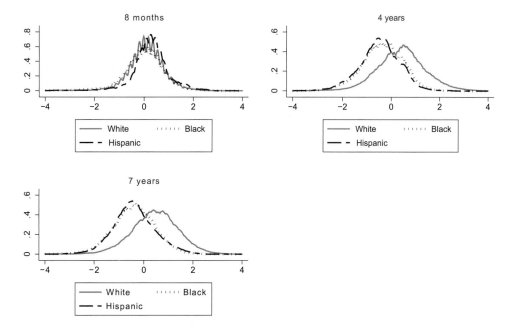

Figure 2   *Emergence of gaps in CPP.*

in the home environment variables. The "parent as teacher" score is coded based on interviewer observations of parent-child interactions in a structured problem-solving environment and is based on the Nursing Child Assessment Teaching Scale (NCATS). Our set of prenatal environment controls include: the birthweight of the child (in 1000-gram ranges), the amount premature that the child was born (in 7-day ranges), and a set of dummy variables representing whether the child was a single birth, a twin, or one in a birth of three or more.

In the CPP dataset, demographic variables include the age of the child at the time of assessment (in months) and the gender of the child. Our set of home environment variables provides rich proxies of the environment in which children were reared. The set of home variables includes: parental education (both mother's and father's, which have been transformed to dichotomous variables ranging from "high school dropout" to "college degree or more"), parental occupation (a set of mutually exclusive and collectively exhaustive dummy variables: "no occupation," "professional occupation," or "non-professional occupation"), household income during the first three months of pregnancy (in $500 ranges), mother's age, number of siblings, and each mother's reaction to and interactions with the child, which are assessed by the interviewer (we indicate whether a mother is indifferent, accepting, attentive, over-caring, or if she behaves in another manner). The set of prenatal environment controls for the CPP is the same as the set of prenatal environment controls in the ECLS-B dataset. Also included in the analysis of both datasets is interviewer fixed effects, which adjust for any mean differences in scoring of the test across interviewers.[20] It is important to stress that a causal interpretation of the coefficients on the covariates is likely to be inappropriate; we view these particular variables as proxies for a broader set of environmental and behavioral factors.

The coefficients on the race variables across the first three waves of ECLS-B and CPP datasets are presented in Table 5. The omitted race category is non–Hispanic white, so the other race coefficients are relative to that omitted group. Each column reflects a different regression and potentially a different dataset. The odd-numbered columns have no controls. The even-numbered columns control for interviewer fixed effects, age at which the test was administered, the gender of the child, region, socioeconomic status, variables to proxy for a child's home environment (family structure, mother's age, number of siblings, and parent-as-teacher measure) and prenatal condition (birth weight, premature birth, and multiple births).[21] Even-numbered columns for CPP data omit region and the parent-as-teacher measure, which are unique to ECLS-B.[22]

In infancy, blacks lag whites by 0.077 (0.031) standard deviations in the raw ECLS-B data. Hispanics and Asians also slightly trail whites by 0.025 (0.029) and 0.027 (0.040), respectively. Adding our set of controls eliminates these trivial differences. The patterns in the CPP data are strikingly similar. Yet, raw gaps of almost 0.4 standard deviations between blacks and whites are present on the test of mental function in the ECLS-B at age two. Even after including extensive controls, a black-white gap of 0.219 (0.036) standard deviations remains. Hispanics look similar to blacks. Asians lag whites by a smaller margin than blacks or Hispanics in the raw data but after including controls they are the worst-performing ethnic group. By age four, a large test score gap has emerged for blacks and Hispanics in both datasets—but especially in the CPP. In the raw CPP data, blacks lag whites by almost 0.8 standard deviations and Hispanics fare even worse. The inclusion of controls reduces the gap to roughly 0.3 standard deviations for blacks and 0.5 standard deviations for Hispanics. In the ECLS-B, black math scores trail white scores by 0.337 (0.032) in the raw data and trail by 0.130 (0.036) with controls. Black-white differences in literacy are −0.195 (0.031) without controls and 0.020 (0.035) with controls. The identical estimates for Hispanics are −0.311 (0.029) and −0.174 (0.034) in math; −0.293 (0.028) and −0.103 (0.033) in literacy. Asians are the highest-performing ethnic group in

[20] In ECLS, each of the 13 regions was staffed by one field supervisor and between 14 and 19 interviewers, for a total of 256 field staff (243 interviewers), who conducted an average of 42 child assessments each. The number of interviews per interviewer ranges from 1 to 156. Almost all interviewers assessed children from different races (Bethel et al., 2004). There are 184 interviewers in CPP for eight-month-olds, 305 for four-year-olds, and 217 for seven-year-olds. In the CPP, there are many interviewers for whom virtually all of the children assessed were of the same race.

[21] Because the age at which the test is taken is such an important determinant of test performance, we include separate indicators for months of age in our specification.

[22] It should also be noted that in the CPP dataset, there is not a single SES measure, but the set of variables including parental education, parental occupation, and family income provides a rich proxy for socioeconomic status.

Table 5 Racial differences in the mental function composite score, ECLS-B and CPP.

	Less than 1 year				2 years		4 years						7 years	
	CPP		ECLS-B		ECLS-B		CPP		ECLS-B, Math		ECLS-B, Literacy		CPP	
Black	−0.096	0.024	−0.077	0.006	−0.393	−0.219	−0.296	−0.785	−0.337	−0.130	−0.195	0.020	−0.854	−0.348
	(0.012)	(0.017)	(0.031)	(0.021)	(0.031)	(0.036)	(0.016)	(0.011)	(0.032)	(0.036)	(0.031)	(0.035)	(0.010)	(0.016)
Hispanic	0.183	−0.039	−0.025	−0.021	−0.401	−0.262	−0.542	−0.895	−0.311	−0.174	−0.293	−0.103	−0.846	−0.545
	(0.034)	(0.040)	(0.029)	(0.018)	(0.028)	(0.032)	(0.039)	(0.032)	(0.029)	(0.034)	(0.028)	(0.033)	(0.031)	(0.038)
Asian	—	—	−0.027	−0.017	−0.237	−0.324	—	—	0.298	0.086	0.443	0.218	—	—
	—	—	(0.040)	(0.023)	(0.041)	(0.043)	—	—	(0.038)	(0.038)	(0.044)	(0.040)	—	—
Other race	−0.171	−0.107	−0.023	0	−0.229	−0.135	−0.271	−0.443	−0.213	−0.066	−0.103	0.050	−0.345	−0.208
	(0.067)	(0.060)	(0.041)	(0.025)	(0.045)	(0.043)	(0.057)	(0.062)	(0.050)	(0.044)	(0.048)	(0.046)	(0.061)	(0.057)
Obs.	31,116	31,116	7468	7468	7468	7468	31,116	31,116	7468	7468	7468	7468	31,116	31,116
R^2	0.000	0.240	0.001	0.766	0.066	0.306	0.000	0.320	0.051	0.425	0.040	0.380	0.180	0.320
Controls	N	Y	N	Y	N	Y	N	Y	N	Y	N	Y	N	Y

The dependent variable is the mental composite score, which is normalized to have a mean of zero and a standard deviation of one in each wave for the full, unweighted sample in CPP and the full sample with wave 3 weights in ECLS-B. Non-Hispanic whites are the omitted race category in each regression and all race coefficients are relative to that group. The unit of observation is a child. Estimation is done using weighted least squares for the ECLS-B sample (columns 3–6 and 9–12) using sample weights provided in the third wave of the data set. Estimation is done using ordinary least squares for the CPP sample (columns 1–2, 7–8, and 13–14). In addition to the variables included in the table, indicator variables for children with missing values on each covariate are also included in the regressions. Standard errors are in parentheses. Columns 1 through 4 present results for children under one year; Columns 5 and 6 present results for 2-year-olds; Columns 7 through 12 present results for 4-year-olds; Columns 13 and 14 present results for 7-year-olds.

both subjects on the age four tests. Racial disparities at age seven, available only in CPP, are generally similar to those at age four.

There are at least three possible explanations for the emergence of racial differences with age. The first is that the skills tested in one-year-olds are not the same as those required of older children, and there are innate racial differences only in the skills that are acquired later. For instance, an infant scores high if she babbles expressively or looks around to find the source of the noise when a bell rings, while older children are tested directly on verbal skills and puzzle-solving ability. Despite these clear differences in the particular tasks undertaken, the outcomes of these early and subsequent tests are correlated by about 0.30, suggesting that they are, to some degree, measuring a persistent aspect of a child's ability.[23] Also relevant is the fact that the Bayley Scales of Infant Development (BSID) score is nearly as highly correlated with measures of parental IQ as childhood aptitude tests.

Racial differences in rates of development are a second possible explanation for the patterns in our data. If black infants mature earlier than whites, then black performance on early tests may be artificially inflated relative to their long-term levels. On the other hand, if blacks are less likely to be cognitively stimulated at home or more likely to be reared in environments that Shonkoff (2006) would label as characterized by "toxic stress," disruptions in brain development may occur, which may significantly retard cognitive growth.

A third possible explanation for the emerging pattern of racial gaps is that the relative importance of genes and environmental factors in determining test outcomes varies over time. In contrast to the first two explanations mentioned above, under this interpretation, the measured differences in test scores are real, and the challenge is to construct a model that can explain the racial divergence in test scores with age.

To better understand the third explanation, Fryer and Levitt (forthcoming) provide two statistical models that are consistent with the data presented above. Here we provide a brief overview of the models and their predictions.

The first parameter of interest is the correlation between test scores early on and later in life. Fryer and Levitt (forthcoming) assign a value of 0.30 to that correlation. The measured correlation between test scores early and late in life and parental test scores is also necessary for the analysis. Based on prior research (e.g., Yeates et al., 1983), we take these two correlations as 0.36 and 0.39, respectively.[24] The estimated black–white test score gap at young ages is taken as 0.077 based on our findings in ECLS-B, compared to a gap of 0.78 at later ages based on our findings in CPP.

---

[23] Nonetheless, Lewis and McGurk (1972) are pessimistic about the generalizability of these infant test scores. Work focusing on infant attention and habituation is also predictive of future test scores (e.g., Bornstein and Sigman, 1986; McCall and Carriger, 1993), but unfortunately our data do not include such information.

[24] It is important to note that substantial uncertainty underlies these correlations, which are based on a small number of studies carried out on a non-representative sample.

The primary puzzle raised by our results is the following: how does one explain small racial gaps on the BSID test scores administered at ages 8 to 12 months and large racial gaps in tests of mental ability later in life, despite the fact that these two test scores are reasonably highly correlated with one another ($\rho = 0.3$), and both test scores are similarly correlated with parental test scores ($\rho \geq 0.3$)?

The basic building blocks

Let θ_a denote the measured test score of an individual at age a. We assume that test scores are influenced by an individual's genetic make-up (G) and his environment (E_a) at age a. The simplest version of the canonical model of genes and environment takes the following form:

$$\theta_a = \alpha_a G + \beta_a E_a + \varepsilon_a. \tag{3}$$

In this model, the individual's genetic endowment is fixed over time, but environmental factors vary and their influence may vary. θ_a, G, and E_a are all normalized into standard deviation units. Initially we will assume that G, E_a, and ϵ_a are uncorrelated for an individual at any point in time (this assumption will be relaxed below), and that E_a and the error terms for an individual at different ages are also uncorrelated.[25] There will, however, be a positive correlation between an individual's genetic endowment G and the genetic endowment of his or her mother (which we denote G_m). We will further assume, in accord with the simplest models of genetic transmission, that the correlation between G and G_m is 0.50.[26]

We are interested in matching two different aspects of the data: (1) correlations between test scores, and (2) racial test score gaps at different ages. The test score correlations of interest are those of an individual at the age of one (for which we use the subscript b for baby) and later in childhood (denoted with subscript c).

Under the assumptions above, these correlations are as follows:

$$\text{corr}(\theta_b, \theta_m) = 0.5\alpha_b\alpha_m = 0.36 \tag{4}$$

$$\text{corr}(\theta_c, \theta_m) = 0.5\alpha_c\alpha_m = 0.39 \tag{5}$$

$$\text{corr}(\theta_b, \theta_c) = \alpha_b\alpha_c = 0.30 \tag{6}$$

where the 0.5 in the first two equations reflects the assumed genetic correlation between mother and child, and the values 0.36, 0.39, and 0.30 are our best estimates of the empirical values of these correlations based on past research cited above.

---

[25] Allowing for an individual's environment to be positively correlated at different points in time causes this simple model to show even greater divergence from what is observed in the data. We relax the assumption that environment is not correlated across ages for an individual when we introduce a correlation between parental test scores and the child's environment below.

[26] As noted below, factors such as assortative mating can cause that correlation to be higher.

The racial test score gaps in this model are given by:

$$\Delta\theta_b = \alpha_b \Delta G + \beta_b \Delta E_b = 0.077 \qquad (7)$$
$$\Delta\theta_c = \alpha_c \Delta G + \beta_c \Delta E_c = 0.854 \qquad (8)$$

where the symbol Δ in front of a variable signifies the mean racial gap between blacks and whites for that variable. The values 0.077 and 0.854 represent our estimates of the black-white test score gap at ages nine months and seven years from Table 5.[27] For Hispanics, these differences are 0.025 and 0.846, respectively.

Solving Eqs (4)–(6), this simple model yields a value of 1.87 for α_m^2. Under the assumptions of the model, however, the squared value of the coefficients α and β represent the share of the variance in the measured test score explained by genetic and environmental factors, respectively, meaning that α_m^2 is bounded at one. Thus, this simple model is not consistent with the observed correlations in the data. The correlation between child and mother test scores observed in the data is too large relative to the correlation between the child's own test scores at different ages.

Consequently, we consider two extensions to this simple model that can reproduce these correlations in the data: assortative mating and allowing for a mother's test score to influence the child's environment.[28]

Assortative mating

If women with high G mate with men who also have high G, then the parent child $\text{corr}(G, G_m)$ is likely to exceed 0.50. Assuming a value of $\alpha_m^2 = 0.80$, which is consistent with prior research, the necessary $\text{corr}(G, G_m)$ to solve the system of equations above is roughly 0.76, which requires the correlation between parents on G to be around 0.50, not far from the 0.45 value reported for that coefficient in a literature review (Jensen, 1978).[29] With that degree of assortative mating, the other parameters that emerge from the model are $\alpha_b = 0.53$ and $\alpha_c = 0.57$. Using these values of α_b and α_c, it is possible to generate the observed racial gaps in (7) and (8). If we assume as an upper bound that environments for black and Hispanic babies are the same as those for white babies

---

[27] Note that the racial gap at age seven is based on earlier CPP data. The evidence suggests that racial gaps have diminished over time (Dickens and Flynn, 2006). Thus, a value of 0.854 in Eq. (7) may be too large. The only implication this has for solving our model is to reduce the black-white differences in environment that are necessary to close the model. We use the raw racial gaps in this analysis, rather than the estimates controlling for covariates, because our goal in this section is to decompose the differences into those driven by genes versus environments. Many of the covariates included in our specifications could be operating through either of those channels.

[28] A third class of models that we explored has multiple dimensions of intelligence (e.g., lower-order and higher-order thinking) that are weighted differently by tests administered to babies versus older children. We have not been able to make such a model consistent with the observed correlations without introducing either assortative mating or allowing the mother's test score to influence the child's environment.

[29] The correlation of 0.5 can be derived as follows. Let $G = 0.5G(M) + 0.5G(F)$. Taking the correlation of both sides with respect to $G(M)$ and assuming unit variance, $\text{corr}(G, G(M)) = 0.76$ only if $\text{corr}(G(M), G(F)) = 0.5$.

(i.e., $\Delta E_b = 0$) in Eq. (7), then the implied racial gap in G is a modest 0.145 standard deviations for blacks and 0.04 for Hispanics.[30]

To fit Eq. (8) requires $\beta_c \Delta E_c = 0.77$. If $\beta_c = 0.77$ (implying that environmental factors explain about half of the variance in test scores), then a one standard deviation gap in environment between black and white children and a 1.14 standard deviation gap between Hispanic and white children would be needed to generate the observed childhood racial test score gap[31]. If environmental factors explain less of the variance, a larger racial gap in environment would be needed. Taking a simple non-weighted average across environmental proxies available in the ECLS yields a 1.2 standard deviation gap between blacks and whites[32].

Allowing parental test scores to influence the child's environment

A second class of model consistent with our empirical findings is one in which the child's environment is influenced by the parent's test score, as in Dickens and Flynn (2001). One example of such a model would be

$$\theta_a = \alpha_a G + \beta_a E_a(\theta_m, \tilde{E}_a) + \varepsilon_a \tag{9}$$

where Eq. (9) differs from the original Eq. (3) by allowing the child's environment to be a function of the mother's test score, as well as factors $\tilde{E}_a$ that are uncorrelated with the mother's test score. In addition, we relax the earlier assumption that the environments an individual experiences as a baby and as a child are uncorrelated. We do not, however, allow for assortative mating in this model. Under these assumptions, Eq. (9) produces the following three equations for our three key test score correlations

$$\text{corr}(\theta_b, \theta_m) = 0.5\alpha_b\alpha_m + \beta_b\text{cov}(E_b, \theta_m) = 0.36 \tag{10}$$

$$\text{corr}(\theta_c, \theta_m) = 0.5\alpha_c\alpha_m + \beta_c\text{cov}(E_c, \theta_m) = 0.39 \tag{11}$$

$$\text{corr}(\theta_b, \theta_c) = \alpha_b\alpha_c + \beta_b\beta_c\text{cov}(E_b, E_c) = 0.30. \tag{12}$$

Allowing parental ability to influence the child's environment introduces extra degrees of freedom; indeed, this model is so flexible that it can match the data both under

---

[30] Allowing black babies to have worse environments makes the implied racial gap in G even smaller.

[31] Estimates from Fryer and Levitt (2004) on racial differences in achievement when black, white, Asian, and Hispanic students enter kindergarten, along with the assortative mating model above, imply that even smaller differences in environment explain later test scores.

[32] Fryer and Levitt (2004) find a 0.75 standard deviation difference between blacks and whites in socioeconomic status, a 0.83 standard deviation gap in the number of children's books in the home, a 1.30 standard deviation difference in female-headed households, a 1.51 standard deviation difference in whether or not one feels safe in their neighborhood, a 1.5 standard deviation difference in the percentage of kids in their school who participate in the free lunch program, and a 1.31 difference in the amount of loitering reported around the school by non-students. All estimates are derived by taking the difference in the mean of a variable between blacks and whites and dividing by the standard deviation for whites. The socioeconomic composite measure contains parental income, education, and occupation.

the assumption of very small and large racial differences in G (e.g., $\Delta G \leq 1$ standard deviation). In order for our findings to be consistent with small racial differences in G, the importance of environmental factors must start low and grow sharply with age. In the most extreme case (where environment has no influence early in life: $\beta_b = 0$), solving Eqs (10) and (12) implies $\alpha_b = 0.80$ and $\alpha_c = 0.37$. If $\beta_c = 0.77$ (as in the assortative mating model discussed above), then a correlation of 0.29 between the mother's test score and the child's environment is necessary to solve Eq. (11). The mean racial gap in G implied by Eq. (7) is 0.096 standard deviations. To match the test score gap for children requires a mean racial difference in environmental factors of approximately one standard deviation.

A model in which parents' scores influence their offspring's environment is, however, equally consistent with mean racial gaps in G of one standard deviation. For this to occur, G must exert little influence on the baby's test score, but be an important determinant of the test scores of children. Take the most extreme case in which G has no influence on the baby's score (i.e., $\alpha_b = 0$). If genetic factors are not directly determining the baby's test outcomes, then environmental factors must be important. Assuming $\beta_b = 0.80$, Eq. (10) implies a correlation between the mother's test score and the baby's environment of 0.45. If we assume that the correlation between the baby's environment and the child's environment is 0.70, then Eq. (12) implies a value of $\beta_c = 0.54$. If we maintain the earlier assumption of $\alpha_m^2 = 0.80$, as well as a correlation between the mother's test score and the child's environment of 0.32, then a value of $\alpha_c = 0.49$ is required to close the model. If there is a racial gap of one standard deviation in G, then Eqs (7) and (8) imply 0.096 and 0.67 standard deviation racial gaps in environment factors for babies and children, respectively, to fit our data.

Putting the pieces together, the above analysis shows that the simplest genetic models are not consistent with the evidence presented on racial differences in the cognitive ability of infants. These inconsistencies can be resolved in two ways: incorporating assortative mating or allowing parental ability to affect the offspring's environment. With assortative mating, our data imply a minimal racial gap in intelligence (0.11 standard deviations as an upper bound), but a large racial gap in environmental factors. When parent's ability influences the child's environment, our results can be made consistent with almost any value for a racial gap in G (from roughly zero to a full standard deviation), depending on the other assumptions that are made. Thus, despite stark empirical findings, our data cannot resolve these difficult questions—much depends on the underlying model.

4. INTERVENTIONS TO FOSTER HUMAN CAPITAL BEFORE CHILDREN ENTER SCHOOL

In the past five decades there have been many attempts to close the racial achievement gap before kids enter school.[33] Table 6 provides an overview of twenty well-known programs,

---

[33] See Carneiro and Heckman (2003) for a nice review of policies to foster human capital.

Table 6 Early childhood interventions to increase achievement.

Early childhood interventions	Ages treated	Impact	Study
Abecedarian project	Birth–5 years	5 points on Wechsler Intelligence Scale at age 12; 5–7 points on various subscales of WJ-R	Campbell and Ramey (1994)
Baby college (HCZ)	Prenatal–3 years		
Early Head Start	Prenatal–3 years		
Early training project	4–6 years	2–5 points on Stanford-Binet IQ scores at the end of 4th grade	Gray and Klaus (1970)
Educare	Birth–5 years		
Harlem gems	4–5 years		
Harlem study	2–3 years		
Head Start	3–5 years	0.09 standard deviations on PPVT receptive vocabulary after 1st grade; 0.08 standard deviations on WJ-III oral comprehension after 1st grade	Puma et al. (2010)
Houston parent-child development centers	1–2 years		
Infant Health and Development Program	Birth–3 years	0.19 standard deviations on PPVT; 0.21 standard deviations on receptive language; 0.20 standard deviations on vocabulary, 0.16 standard deviations on reasoning, 0.22 standard deviations on visual-motor and spatial; 0.09 standard deviations on visual motor integration	Brooks-Gunn et al. (1992)

(continued on next page)

Table 6 (continued)

Early childhood interventions	Ages treated	Impact	Study
Milwaukee Project	Birth–6 years	23 points on Stanford–Binet IQ scores at age 6	Garber (1988)
Mother–child home program	3–4 years		
Nurse family partnership	Prenatal–2 years	4 points on Mental Development Index scores at age 2	Olds et al. (2002)
Parents as teachers	Prenatal–5 years		
Perry Preschool	3–4 years	Heckman et al. (2009) report 7%–10% rate of return on program investment	Schweinhart et al. (1993)
Prenatal/early infancy project	Prenatal–2 years		
Syracuse University Family Development	Prenatal–5 years		Lally et al. (1987)
The three year old journey	3 years		
Tulsa Pre–K Program	4 years	Ranging from 0.38 to 0.79 standard deviations on WJ-R	Gormley et al. (2005)
Yale experiment	Birth–2 years		

The set of interventions included in this table was generated in two ways. First, we used Heckman (1999) and Heckman et al. (2009) as the basis for a thorough literature review on early childhood intervention programs. We investigated all of the programs included in these papers, and then examined the papers written on this list of programs for additional programs. Second, we examined all of the relevant reports available through the IES What Works Clearinghouse. From this original list, we included twenty of the most credibly evaluated, largest scale programs in our final list.

the ages they serve, and their treatment effects (in the cases in which they have been credibly evaluated).

Perhaps the most famous early intervention program for children involved 64 students in Ypsilanti, Michigan, who attended the Perry Preschool program in 1962. The program consisted of a 2.5-hour daily preschool program and weekly home visits by teachers, and targeted children from disadvantaged socioeconomic backgrounds with IQ scores in the range of 70-85. An active learning curriculum—High/Scope—was used in the preschool program in order to support both the cognitive and non-cognitive development of the children over the course of two years beginning when the children were three years old. Schweinhart et al. (1993) find that students in the Perry Preschool program had higher test scores between the ages of 5 and 27, 21% less grade retention or special services required, 21% higher graduation rates, and half the number of lifetime arrests in comparison to children in the control group. Considering the financial benefits that are associated with the positive outcomes of the Perry Preschool, Heckman et al. (2009) estimated that the rate of return on the program is between 7 and 10%, passing a cost-benefit analysis.

Another important intervention, which was initiated three years after the Perry Preschool program is Head Start. Head Start is a preschool program funded by federal matching grants that is designed to serve 3- to 5-year-old children living at or below the federal poverty level.[34] The program varies across states in terms of the scope of services provided, with some centers providing full-day programs and others only half-day. In 2007, Head Start served over 900,000 children at an average annual cost of about $7300 per child.

Evaluations of Head Start have often been difficult to perform due to the non-random nature of enrollment in the program. Currie and Thomas (1995) use a national sample of children and compare children who attended a Head Start program with siblings who did not attend Head Start, based on the assumption that examining effects within the family unit will reduce selection bias. They find that those children who attended Head Start scored higher on preschool vocabulary tests but that for black students, these gains were lost by age ten. Using the same analysis method with updated data, Garces et al. (2002) find several positive outcomes associated with Head Start attendance. They conclude that there is a positive effect from Head Start on the probability of attending college and—for whites—the probability of graduating from high school. For black children, Head Start led to a lower likelihood of being arrested or charged with a crime later in life.

Puma et al. (2005), in response to the 1998 reauthorization of Head Start, conduct an evaluation using randomized admission into Head Start.[35] The impact of being offered

[34] Local Head Start agencies are able to extend coverage to those meeting other eligibility criteria, such as those with disabilities and those whose families report income between 100 and 130% of the federal poverty level.

[35] Students not chosen by lottery to participate in Head Start were not precluded from attending other high-quality early childhood centers. Roughly ninety percent of the treatment sample and forty-three percent of the control sample attended center-based care.

admission into Head Start for three and four year olds is 0.10 to 0.34 standard deviations in the areas of early language and literacy. For 3-year-olds, there were also small positive effects in the social-emotional domain (0.13 to 0.18 standard deviations) and on overall health status (0.12 standard deviations). Yet, by the time the children who received Head Start services have completed first grade, almost all of the positive impact on initial school readiness has faded. The only remaining impacts in the cognitive domain are a 0.08 standard deviation increase in oral comprehension for 3-year-old participants and a 0.09 standard deviation increase in receptive vocabulary for the 4-year-old cohort (Puma et al., 2010).[36]

A third, and categorically different, program is the Nurse Family Partnership. Through this program, low-income first-time mothers receive home visits from a registered nurse beginning early in the pregnancy that continue until the child is two years old—a total of fifty visits over the first two years. The program aims to encourage preventive health practices, reduce risky health behaviors, foster positive parenting practices, and improve the economic self-sufficiency of the family. In a study of the program in Denver in 1994-95, Olds et al. (2002) find that those children whose mothers had received home visits from nurses (but not those who received home visits from paraprofessionals) were less likely to display language delays and had superior mental development at age two. In a long-term evaluation of the program, Olds et al. (1998) find that children born to women who received nurse home visits during their pregnancy between 1978 and 1980 have fewer juvenile arrests, convictions, and violations of probation by age fifteen than those whose mothers did not receive treatment.

Other early childhood interventions—many based on the early success of the Perry Preschool, Head Start, and the Nurse Family Partnership—include the Abecedarian Project, the Early Training Project, the Infant Health and Development Program, the Milwaukee Project, and Tulsa's universal pre-kindergarten program. The Abecedarian Project provided full-time, high-quality center-based childcare services for four cohorts of children from low-income families from infancy through age five between 1971 and 1977. Campbell and Ramey (1994) find that at age twelve, those children who were randomly assigned to the project scored 5 points higher on the Wechsler Intelligence Scale and 5-7 points higher on various subscales of the Woodcock-Johnson Psycho-Educational Battery achievement test. The Early Training Project provided children from low-income homes with summertime experiences and weekly home visits during the three summers before entering first grade in an attempt to improve the children's school readiness. Gray and Klaus (1970) report that children who received these intervention services maintained higher Stanford-Binet IQ scores (2-5 points) at the end of fourth grade. The Infant Health and Development Program specifically targeted families with low birthweight, preterm infants and provided them with weekly home visits during

---

[36] The Early Head Start program, established in 1995 to provide community-based supplemental services to low-income families with infants and toddlers, has similar effects (Administration for Children and Families, 2006).

the child's first year and biweekly visits through age three, as well as enhanced early childhood educational care and bimonthly parent group meetings. Brooks-Gunn et al. (1992) report that this program had positive effects on language development at the end of first grade, with participant children scoring 0.09 standard deviations higher on receptive vocabulary and 0.08 standard deviations higher on oral comprehension. The Milwaukee Project targeted newborns born to women with IQs lower than 80; mothers received education, vocational rehabilitation, and child care training while their children received high-quality educational programming and three balanced meals daily at "infant stimulation centers" for seven hours a day, five days a week until the children were six years old. Garber (1988) finds that this program resulted in an increase of 23 points on the Stanford-Binet IQ test at age six for treatment children compared to control children.

Unlike the other programs described, Tulsa's preschool program is open to all 4-year-old children. It is a basic preschool program that has high standards for teacher qualification (a college degree and early childhood certification are both required) and a comparatively high rate of penetration (63% of eligible children are served). Gormley et al. (2005) use a birthday cutoff regression discontinuity design to evaluate the program and find that participation improves scores on the Woodcock-Johnson achievement test significantly (from 0.38 to 0.79 standard deviations).

Beyond these highly effective programs, Table 6 demonstrates that there is large variance in the effectiveness of well-known early childhood programs. The Parents as Teachers Program, for instance, shows mixed and generally insignificant effects on initial measures of cognitive development (Wagner and Clayton, 1999). In an evaluation of the Houston Parent-Child Development Centers, Andrews et al. (1982) find no significant impact on children's cognitive skills at age one and mixed impacts on cognitive development at age two. Even so, the typical early childhood intervention passes a simple cost-benefit analysis.[37]

There are two potentially important caveats going forward. First, most of the programs are built on the insights gained from Perry and Head Start, yet what we know about infant development in the past five decades has increased dramatically. For example, psychologists used to assume that there was a relatively equal degree of early attachment across children but they now acknowledge that there is a great deal of variance in the stability of early attachment (Thompson, 2000). Tying new programs to the lessons learned from previously successful programs while incorporating new insights from biology and developmental psychology is both the challenge and opportunity going forward.

---

[37] Researchers consider a variety of outcomes in determining the monetary value of the benefits of such programs, including the program's impact on need for special education services, grade retention, incarceration rates, and wages. Heckman et al. (2009) estimate that the long-term return on investment of the Perry Preschool program is between seven and ten percent.

Second, and more important for our purposes here, even the most successful early interventions cannot close the achievement gap in isolation. If we truly want to eliminate the racial achievement gap, early interventions may or may not be necessary but the evidence forces one to conclude that they are not sufficient.

5. THE RACIAL ACHIEVEMENT GAP IN KINDERGARTEN THROUGH 12TH GRADE

As we have seen, children begin life on equal footing, but important differences emerge by age two and their paths quickly diverge. In this section, we describe basic facts about the racial achievement gap from the time children enter kindergarten to the time they exit high school. Horace Mann famously argued that schools were "the great equalizer," designed to eliminate differences between children that are present when they enter school because of different background characteristics. As this section will show, if anything, schools currently tend to exacerbate group differences.

Basic facts about racial differences in educational achievement using ECLS-K

The Early Childhood Longitudinal Study, Kindergarten Cohort (ECLS-K) is a nationally representative sample of over 20,000 children entering kindergarten in 1998. Information on these children has been gathered at six separate points in time. The full sample was interviewed in the fall and spring of kindergarten, and the spring of first, third, fifth, and eighth grades. Roughly 1000 schools are included in the sample, with an average of more than twenty children per school in the study. As a consequence, it is possible to conduct within-school or even within-teacher analyses.

A wide range of data is gathered on the children in the study, which is described in detail at the ECLS website http://nces.ed.gov/ecls. We utilize just a small subset of the available information in our baseline specifications, the most important of which are cognitive assessments administered in kindergarten, first, third, fifth, and eighth grades. The tests were developed especially for the ECLS, but are based on existing instruments including Children's Cognitive Battery (CCB); Peabody Individual Assessment Test—Revised (PIAT-R); Peabody Picture Vocabulary Test-3 (PPVT-3); Primary Test of Cognitive Skills (PTCS); and Woodcock-Johnson Psycho-Educational Battery—Revised (WJ-R). The questions are administered orally through spring of first grade, as it is not assumed that students know how to read until then. Students who are missing data on test scores, race, or gender are dropped from our sample. Summary statistics for the variables we use in our core specifications are displayed by race in Table A.6.

Table 7 presents a series of estimates of the racial test score gap in math (Panel A) and reading (Panel B) for the tests taken over the first nine years of school. Similar to our analysis of younger children in the previous section, the specifications estimated are least

Table 7 The evolution of the achievement gap (ECLS), K-8.

	Fall K		Spring 1st		Spring 3rd		Spring 5th		Spring 8th		Spring 8th (adjusted)	
A. Math												
Black	−0.393	−0.100	−0.440	−0.179	−0.498	−0.284	−0.539	−0.304	−0.522	−0.256	−0.961	−0.422
	(0.029)	(0.035)	(0.034)	(0.042)	(0.033)	(0.040)	(0.033)	(0.048)	(0.034)	(0.058)	(0.055)	(0.093)
Hispanic	−0.427	−0.104	−0.314	−0.086	−0.292	−0.074	−0.253	−0.062	−0.240	−0.014	−0.475	−0.030
	(0.024)	(0.030)	(0.025)	(0.027)	(0.025)	(0.029)	(0.025)	(0.032)	(0.025)	(0.042)	(0.045)	(0.078)
Asian	0.106	0.171	0.016	0.120	0.044	0.104	0.141	0.161	0.138	0.186	0.363	0.392
	(0.064)	(0.046)	(0.057)	(0.055)	(0.062)	(0.053)	(0.052)	(0.041)	(0.059)	(0.054)	(0.115)	(0.117)
Other race	−0.232	−0.016	−0.215	0.015	−0.237	−0.000	−0.215	−0.048	−0.206	0.012	−0.358	0.084
	(0.052)	(0.049)	(0.047)	(0.042)	(0.044)	(0.051)	(0.047)	(0.068)	(0.050)	(0.076)	(0.093)	(0.150)
Controls	N	Y	N	Y	N	Y	N	Y	N	Y	N	Y
School FEs	N	Y	N	Y	N	Y	N	Y	N	Y	N	Y
Obs.	7576	7576	7576	7576	7576	7576	7576	7576	7576	7576	7576	7576
R^2	0.116	0.533	0.106	0.564	0.127	0.627	0.141	0.682	0.136	0.667	0.135	0.665

(continued on next page)

Table 7 (continued)

	Fall K		Spring 1st		Spring 3rd		Spring 5th		Spring 8th		Spring 8th (adjusted)	
B. Reading												
Black	−0.246	0.009	−0.270	−0.022	−0.391	−0.160	−0.453	−0.246	−0.503	−0.168	−0.918	−0.284
	(0.031)	(0.037)	(0.034)	(0.037)	(0.035)	(0.044)	(0.034)	(0.045)	(0.036)	(0.051)	(0.060)	(0.090)
Hispanic	−0.267	−0.073	−0.160	0.003	−0.199	−0.028	−0.189	−0.007	−0.183	−0.000	−0.382	−0.004
	(0.028)	(0.033)	(0.033)	(0.029)	(0.033)	(0.035)	(0.031)	(0.032)	(0.030)	(0.035)	(0.055)	(0.065)
Asian	0.194	0.218	0.199	0.273	0.041	0.068	0.061	0.096	0.082	0.071	0.197	0.182
	(0.059)	(0.050)	(0.042)	(0.043)	(0.042)	(0.043)	(0.036)	(0.043)	(0.040)	(0.046)	(0.088)	(0.100)
Other race	−0.175	−0.002	−0.164	0.058	−0.217	0.003	−0.188	−0.046	−0.169	0.036	−0.345	0.065
	(0.063)	(0.056)	(0.050)	(0.043)	(0.048)	(0.043)	(0.049)	(0.044)	(0.043)	(0.053)	(0.082)	(0.097)
Controls	N	Y	N	Y	N	Y	N	Y	N	Y	N	Y
School FEs	N	Y	N	Y	N	Y	N	Y	N	Y	N	Y
Obs.	7091	7091	7091	7091	7091	7091	7091	7091	7091	7091	7091	7091
R^2	0.050	0.501	0.047	0.589	0.085	0.637	0.108	0.680	0.129	0.687	0.121	0.679

The dependent variable in each column is test score from the designated subject and grade. Odd-numbered columns estimate the raw racial test score gaps and do not include any other controls. Specifications in the even-numbered columns include controls for socioeconomic status, number of books in the home (linear and quadratic terms), gender, age, birth weight, dummies for mother's age at first birth (less than twenty years old and at least thirty years old), a dummy for being a Women, Infants, Children (WIC) participant, missing dummies for all variables with missing data, and school fixed effects. Test scores are IRT scores, normalized to have mean zero and standard deviation one in the full, weighted sample. Non-Hispanic whites are the omitted race category, so all of the race coefficients are gaps relative to that group. The sample is restricted to students from whom data were collected in every wave from fall kindergarten through spring eighth grade, as well as students who have non-missing race and non-missing gender. Panel weights are used. The unit of observation is a student. Robust standard errors are located in parentheses.

squares regressions of the form:

$$\text{outcome}_{i,g} = \sum_R \beta_R R_i + \Gamma X_i + \varepsilon_{i,g} \qquad (13)$$

where $\text{outcome}_{i,g}$ denotes an individual i's test score in grade g and X_i represents an array of student-level social and economic variables describing each student's environment. The variable R_i is a full set of race dummies included in the regression, with non-Hispanic white as the omitted category. In all instances, we use sampling weights provided in the dataset.

The vector X_i contains a parsimonious set of controls—the most important of which is a composite measure of socio-economic status constructed by the researchers conducting the ECLS survey. The components used in the SES measure are parental education, parental occupational status, and household income. Other variables included as controls are gender, child's age at the time of enrollment in kindergarten, WIC participation (a nutrition program aimed at relatively low income mothers and children), mother's age at first birth, birth weight, and the number of children's books in the home.[38] When there are multiple observations of social and economic variables (SES, number of books in the home, and so on), for all specifications, we only include the value recorded in the fall kindergarten survey.[39] While this particular set of covariates might seem idiosyncratic, Fryer and Levitt (2004) have shown that results one obtains with this small set of variables mirror the findings when they include an exhaustive set of over 100 controls. Again, we stress that a causal interpretation is unwarranted; we view these variables as proxies for a broader set of environmental and behavioral factors. The odd-numbered columns of Table 7 present the differences in means, not including any covariates. The even-numbered columns mirror the main specification in Fryer and Levitt (2004).

The raw black-white gap in math when kids enter school is 0.393 (0.029), shown in column one of Panel A. Adding our set of controls decreases this difference to 0.100 (0.035). By fifth grade, Asians outperform other racial groups and Hispanics have gained ground relative to whites, but blacks have lost significant ground. The black-white achievement gap in fifth grade is 0.539 (0.033) standard deviations without controls and 0.304 (0.048) with controls. Disparities in eighth grade look similar, but a peculiar aspect of ECLS-K (very similar tests from kindergarten through eighth grade with different weights on the components of the test) masks potentially important differences between groups. If one restricts attention on the eighth grade exam to subsections of the test which are not mastered by everyone (eliminating the counting and shapes subsection, for example), a large racial gap emerges. Specifically, blacks are trailing whites by 0.961 (0.055) in the raw data and 0.422 (0.093) with the inclusion of controls.

---

[38] A more detailed description of each of the variables used is provided in the data appendix.

[39] Including all the values of these variables from each survey or only those in the relevant years does not alter the results.

The black-white test score gap grows, on average, roughly 0.60 standard deviations in the raw data and 0.30 when we include controls between the fall of kindergarten and spring of eighth grade. The table also illustrates that the control variables included in the specification shrink the gap a roughly constant amount of approximately 0.30 standard deviations regardless of the year of testing. In other words, although blacks systematically differ from whites on these background characteristics, the impact of these variables on test scores is remarkably stable over time. Whatever factor is causing blacks to lose ground is likely operating through a different channel.[40]

In contrast to blacks, Hispanics gain substantial ground relative to whites, despite the fact that they are plagued with many of the social problems that exist among blacks—low socioeconomic status, inferior schools, and so on. One explanation for Hispanic convergence is an increase in English proficiency, though we have little direct evidence on this question.[41] Calling into question that hypothesis is the fact that after controlling for other factors Hispanics do not test particularly poorly on reading, even upon school entry. Controlling for whether or not English is spoken in the home does little to affect the initial gap or the trajectory of Hispanics.[42] The large advantage enjoyed by Asians in the first two years of school is maintained. We also observe striking losses by girls relative to boys in math—over two-tenths of a standard deviation over the four-year period—which is consistent with other research (Becker and Forsyth, 1994; Fryer and Levitt, forthcoming).

Panel B of Table 7 is identical to Panel A, but estimates racial differences in reading scores rather than math achievement. After adding our controls, black children score very similarly to whites in reading in the fall of kindergarten. As in math, however, blacks lose substantial ground relative to other racial groups over the first nine years of school. The coefficient on the indicator variable black is 0.009 standard deviations above whites in the fall of kindergarten and 0.246 standard deviations below whites in the spring of fifth grade, or a loss of over 0.25 standard deviations for the typical black child relative to the typical white child. In eighth grade, the gap seems to shrink to 0.168 (0.051), but accounting for the fact that a large fraction of students master the most basic parts of the exam left over from the early elementary years gives a raw gap of 0.918 (0.060) and 0.284 (0.090) with controls. The impact of covariates—explaining about 0.2 to 0.25 of a standard deviation gap between blacks and whites across most grades—is slightly smaller than in the math regressions. Hispanics experience a much smaller gap relative to whites,

[40] The results above are not likely a consequence of the particular testing instrument used. If one substitutes the teachers' assessment of the student's ability as the dependent variable, virtually identical results emerge. Results are available from the author upon request.

[41] Hispanics seem to increase their position relative to whites in states where English proficiency is known to be a problem (Arizona, California, and Texas).

[42] One interesting caveat: Hispanics are also less likely to participate in preschool, which could explain their poor initial scores and positive trajectory. However, including controls for the type of program/care children have prior to entering kindergarten does nothing to explain why Hispanics gain ground.

and it does not grow over time. The early edge enjoyed by Asians diminishes by third grade.

One potential explanation for such large racial achievement gaps, even after accounting for differences in the schools that racial minorities attend, is the possibility that they are assigned inferior teachers within schools. If whites and Asians are more likely to be in advanced classes with more skilled teachers then this sorting could exacerbate differences and explain the divergence over time. Moreover, with such an intense focus on teacher quality as a remedy for racial achievement gaps, it useful to understand whether and the extent to which gaps exist when minorities and non-minorities have the same teacher. This analysis is possible in ECLS-K—the data contain, on average, 3.3 students per teacher within each year of data collection (note that because the ECLS surveys subsamples within each classroom, this does not reflect the true student-teacher ratios in these classrooms).

Table 8 estimates the racial achievement gap in math and reading over the first nine years of school including teacher fixed effects. For each grade, there are two columns. The first column estimates racial differences with school fixed effects on a sample of students for whom we have valid information on their teacher. This restriction reduces the sample approximately one percent from the original sample in Table 7. Across all grades and both subjects, accounting for sorting into classrooms has very little marginal impact on the racial achievement gap beyond including school fixed effects. The average gain in standard deviations from including teacher fixed effects is only about 0.014. The minimum marginal gain from including the teacher controls is 0.006 and the maximum difference is 0.072; however, in several cases the gap is not actually reduced by including teacher fixed effects. There are two important takeaways. First, differential sorting within schools does not seem to be an important contributor to the racial achievement gap. Second, although much has been made of the importance of teacher quality in eliminating racial disparities (Levin and Quinn, 2003; Barton, 2003), the above analysis suggests that racial gaps among students with the same teacher are stark.

In an effort to uncover the factors that are associated with the divergent trajectories of blacks and whites, Table 9 explores the sensitivity of these "losing ground" estimates across a wide variety of subsamples of the data. We report only the coefficients on the black indicator variable and associated standard errors in the table. The top row of the table presents the baseline results using a full sample and our parsimonious set of controls (the full set of controls used in Tables 7 and 8, but omitting fixed effects). For the eighth grade scores, we restrict the test to components that are not mastered by all students.[43] In that specification, blacks lose an average of 0.356 (0.047) standard deviations in math and 0.483 (0.060) in reading relative to whites over the first nine years of school.

---

[43] Using the full eighth grade test reduces the magnitude of losing ground by roughly half, but the general patterns are the same.

Table 8 The evolution of the achievement gap (ECLS), K-8: accounting for teachers.

	Fall K		Spring 1st		Spring 3rd		Spring 5th		Spring 8th		Spring 8th (adjusted)	
A. Math												
Black	−0.100	−0.085	−0.183	−0.111	−0.284	−0.309	−0.324	−0.261	−0.258	−0.239	−0.428	−0.449
	(0.035)	(0.043)	(0.042)	(0.059)	(0.040)	(0.059)	(0.046)	(0.055)	(0.058)	(0.088)	(0.093)	(0.153)
Hispanic	−0.104	−0.049	−0.087	−0.067	−0.074	−0.050	−0.067	−0.088	−0.015	−0.064	−0.030	−0.118
	(0.030)	(0.036)	(0.027)	(0.035)	(0.029)	(0.042)	(0.032)	(0.037)	(0.042)	(0.044)	(0.078)	(0.084)
Asian	0.171	0.198	0.092	0.076	0.104	0.120	0.151	0.100	0.184	0.108	0.385	0.240
	(0.046)	(0.052)	(0.050)	(0.061)	(0.053)	(0.057)	(0.041)	(0.047)	(0.054)	(0.060)	(0.118)	(0.125)
Other race	−0.016	0.063	0.012	−0.014	0.000	0.037	−0.051	−0.041	0.009	−0.014	0.080	−0.008
	(0.049)	(0.055)	(0.042)	(0.049)	(0.051)	(0.057)	(0.068)	(0.052)	(0.076)	(0.100)	(0.150)	(0.177)
Controls	Y	Y	Y	Y	Y	Y	Y	Y	Y	Y	Y	Y
School FEs	N	Y	Y	Y	Y	Y	Y	Y	Y	Y	Y	N
Teacher FEs	N	N	N	Y	N	Y	N	Y	N	Y	N	Y
Obs.	7576	7576	7514	7514	7526	7526	7484	7484	7511	7511	7511	7511
R^2	0.533	0.688	0.546	0.763	0.619	0.812	0.671	0.842	0.663	0.873	0.662	0.858

Table 8 (continued)

	Fall K		Spring 1st		Spring 3rd		Spring 5th		Spring 8th		Spring 8th (adjusted)	
B. Reading												
Black	0.009	0.015	−0.025	−0.011	−0.160	−0.294	−0.245	−0.178	−0.169	−0.126	−0.285	−0.233
	(0.037)	(0.042)	(0.037)	(0.051)	(0.044)	(0.050)	(0.045)	(0.048)	(0.051)	(0.050)	(0.090)	(0.091)
Hispanic	−0.073	−0.052	−0.002	−0.026	−0.028	−0.050	−0.004	−0.019	−0.002	−0.046	−0.008	−0.081
	(0.033)	(0.042)	(0.029)	(0.036)	(0.035)	(0.050)	(0.032)	(0.038)	(0.035)	(0.037)	(0.065)	(0.075)
Asian	0.218	0.239	0.257	0.208	0.068	0.022	0.094	0.017	0.069	0.031	0.180	0.093
	(0.050)	(0.056)	(0.042)	(0.061)	(0.043)	(0.050)	(0.043)	(0.057)	(0.046)	(0.057)	(0.100)	(0.121)
Other race	−0.002	−0.010	0.055	0.077	0.003	0.010	−0.045	−0.032	0.036	0.021	0.065	0.041
	(0.056)	(0.050)	(0.043)	(0.056)	(0.043)	(0.049)	(0.044)	(0.046)	(0.052)	(0.061)	(0.097)	(0.119)
Controls	Y	Y	Y	Y	Y	Y	Y	Y	Y	Y	Y	Y
School FEs	Y	N	Y	N	Y	N	Y	N	Y	N	Y	N
Teacher FEs	N	Y	N	Y	N	Y	N	Y	N	Y	N	Y
Obs.	7091	7091	7032	7032	7044	7044	7009	7009	7035	7035	7035	7035
R^2	0.501	0.671	0.568	0.767	0.629	0.814	0.665	0.832	0.683	0.832	0.675	0.809

The dependent variable in each column is test score from the designated subject and grade. All specifications include controls for race, socioeconomic status, number of books in the home (linear and quadratic terms), gender, age, birth weight, dummies for mother's age at first birth (less than twenty years old and at least thirty years old), a dummy for being a Women, Infants, Children (WIC) participant, and missing dummies for all variables with missing data. Odd-numbered columns include school fixed effects, whereas even-numbered columns include teacher fixed effects. Test scores are IRT scores, normalized to have mean zero and standard deviation one in the full, weighted sample. Non-Hispanic whites are the omitted race category, so all of the race coefficients are gaps relative to that group. The sample is restricted to students from whom data were collected in every wave from fall kindergarten through spring eighth grade and students for whom teacher data was available in the relevant grade, as well as students who have non-missing race and non-missing gender. Panel weights are used. The unit of observation is a student. Robust standard errors are located in parentheses.

Table 9 Sensitivity analysis for losing ground, ECLS (Fall K vs. Spring 8th).

	Math			Reading		
	Fall K	Spring 8th (adjusted)	Lost ground	Fall K	Spring 8th (adjusted)	Lost ground
Baseline	−0.063 (0.030)	−0.419 (0.057)	−0.356 (0.047)	0.076 (0.028)	−0.407 (0.064)	−0.483 (0.060)
Unweighted	−0.056 (0.019)	−0.407 (0.037)	−0.351 (0.032)	0.070 (0.020)	−0.457 (0.039)	−0.527 (0.037)
By gender:						
Males	−0.047 (0.046)	−0.446 (0.082)	−0.399 (0.066)	0.092 (0.040)	−0.374 (0.087)	−0.466 (0.085)
Females	−0.077 (0.038)	−0.385 (0.079)	−0.307 (0.068)	0.058 (0.039)	−0.430 (0.093)	−0.488 (0.083)
By SES quintile:						
Bottom	0.037 (0.049)	−0.209 (0.112)	−0.246 (0.094)	0.018 (0.051)	−0.346 (0.151)	−0.364 (0.138)
Second	−0.085 (0.059)	−0.320 (0.115)	−0.236 (0.103)	−0.006 (0.042)	−0.227 (0.124)	−0.221 (0.116)
Third	−0.113 (0.057)	−0.547 (0.110)	−0.433 (0.099)	0.079 (0.057)	−0.511 (0.132)	−0.590 (0.128)
Fourth	−0.075 (0.079)	−0.465 (0.137)	−0.390 (0.106)	0.237 (0.080)	−0.392 (0.154)	−0.629 (0.141)
Top	0.035 (0.093)	−0.348 (0.179)	−0.383 (0.135)	0.125 (0.094)	−0.517 (0.192)	−0.643 (0.186)
By family structure:						
Two biological parents	−0.091 (0.054)	−0.504 (0.094)	−0.413 (0.069)	0.079 (0.049)	−0.471 (0.092)	−0.551 (0.096)
Single mother	0.035 (0.046)	−0.264 (0.113)	−0.299 (0.102)	0.126 (0.047)	−0.154 (0.132)	−0.280 (0.122)
Teen mother at birth	−0.061 (0.050)	−0.361 (0.094)	−0.300 (0.079)	−0.021 (0.040)	−0.364 (0.121)	−0.343 (0.111)
Mother in her 20s at birth	−0.066 (0.044)	−0.463 (0.087)	−0.397 (0.072)	0.127 (0.042)	−0.440 (0.090)	−0.567 (0.086)
Mother over 30 at birth	−0.038 (0.063)	−0.335 (0.199)	−0.297 (0.165)	0.235 (0.076)	−0.201 (0.218)	−0.436 (0.234)
By region:						
Northeast	0.056 (0.057)	−0.058 (0.139)	−0.113 (0.122)	0.124 (0.057)	−0.320 (0.132)	−0.444 (0.129)
Midwest	−0.148 (0.072)	−0.604 (0.106)	−0.457 (0.097)	0.003 (0.068)	−0.422 (0.156)	−0.425 (0.156)
South	−0.065 (0.043)	−0.403 (0.081)	−0.338 (0.066)	0.044 (0.039)	−0.410 (0.086)	−0.454 (0.081)
West	0.007 (0.072)	−0.513 (0.200)	−0.520 (0.164)	0.227 (0.095)	−0.122 (0.268)	−0.349 (0.236)

Table 9 (continued)

	Math			Reading		
	Fall K	Spring 8th (adjusted)	Lost ground	Fall K	Spring 8th (adjusted)	Lost ground
By location type:						
Central city	−0.070 (0.049)	−0.466 (0.089)	−0.396 (0.072)	0.063 (0.045)	−0.439 (0.105)	−0.502 (0.097)
Suburban	−0.070 (0.054)	−0.369 (0.099)	−0.299 (0.081)	0.115 (0.053)	−0.338 (0.113)	−0.454 (0.109)
Rural	−0.101 (0.050)	−0.526 (0.163)	−0.425 (0.161)	−0.052 (0.046)	−0.566 (0.149)	−0.514 (0.155)
By school type:						
Public school	−0.073 (0.031)	−0.418 (0.061)	−0.345 (0.051)	0.071 (0.029)	−0.397 (0.067)	−0.468 (0.062)
Private school	0.006 (0.114)	−0.369 (0.172)	−0.376 (0.118)	0.075 (0.112)	−0.420 (0.228)	−0.495 (0.216)
School >50% black	−0.261 (0.154)	−0.887 (0.318)	−0.626 (0.235)	−0.084 (0.119)	−0.550 (0.267)	−0.467 (0.287)
School >50% white	−0.123 (0.060)	−0.409 (0.145)	−0.286 (0.135)	0.027 (0.082)	−0.423 (0.117)	−0.449 (0.140)

Specifications in this table include controls for race, socioeconomic status, number of books in the home (linear and quadratic terms), gender, age, birth weight, dummies for mother's age at first birth (less than twenty years old and at least thirty years old), a dummy for being a Women, Infants, Children (WIC) participant, and missing dummies for all variables with missing data. Only the coefficients on black are reported. The sample is restricted to students from whom data were collected in every wave from fall kindergarten through spring eighth grade, as well as students who have non-missing race and non-missing gender. Panel weights are used (except in the specification). The top row shows results from the baseline specification across the entire sample, the second row shows the results when panel weights are omitted, and the remaining rows correspond to the baseline specification restricted to particular subsets of the data.

Surprisingly, blacks lose similar amounts of ground across many subsets of the data, including by sex, location type, and whether or not a student attends private schools. The results vary quite a bit across the racial composition of schools, quintiles of the socioeconomic status distribution, and by family structure. Blacks in schools with greater than fifty percent blacks lose substantially more ground in math than do blacks in greater than fifty percent white schools. In reading, their divergence follows similar paths. The top three SES quintiles lose more ground than the lower two quintiles in both math and reading, but the differences are particularly stark in reading. The two largest losing ground coefficients in the table are for the fourth and fifth quintile of SES in reading. Black students in these categories lose ground at an alarming rate—roughly 0.6 standard deviations over 9 years. This latter result could be related to the fact that, in the ECLS-K, a host of variables which are broad proxies for parenting practices differ between blacks and whites. For instance, black college graduates have the same number of children's books for their kids as white high school graduates. A similar phenomenon emerges with respect to family structure; the most ground is lost, relative to whites, by black students who have both biological parents. Investigating within-race regressions, Fryer and Levitt (2004) show that the partial correlation between SES and test scores are about half the magnitude for blacks relative to whites. In other words, there is something that higher income buys whites that is not fully realized among blacks. The limitation of this argument is that including these variables as controls does not substantially alter the divergence in black-white achievement over the first nine years of school. This issue is beyond the scope of this chapter but deserves further exploration.

We conclude our analysis of ECLS-K by investigating racial achievement gaps on questions assessing specific skills in kindergarten and eighth grade. Table 10 contains unadjusted means on questions tested in each subsample of the test. The entries in the table are means of probabilities that students have mastered the material in that subtest. Math sections include: counting, numbers, and shapes; relative size; ordinality and sequence; adding and subtracting; multiplying and dividing; place value; rate and measurement; fractions; and area and volume. Reading sections include: letter recognition, beginning sounds, ending sounds, sight words, words in context, literal inference, extrapolation, evaluation, nonfiction evaluation, and complex syntax evaluation. In kindergarten, the test excluded fractions and area and volume (in math) as well as nonfiction evaluation and complex syntax evaluation (in reading).

All students enter kindergarten with a basic understanding of counting, numbers, and shapes. Black students have a probability of 0.896 (0.184) of having mastered this material and the corresponding probability for whites is 0.964 (0.102). Whites outpace blacks on all other dimensions. Hispanics are also outpaced by whites on all dimensions, while Asians actually fare better than whites on all dimensions. By eighth grade, students have essentially mastered six out of the nine areas tested in math, and six out of the ten in reading. Interestingly, on every dimension where there is room for growth, whites

Table 10 Unadjusted means on questions assessing specific sets of skills, ECLS.

	Fall K				Spring 8th			
	White	Black	Hispanic	Asian	White	Black	Hispanic	Asian
Math								
Count, number, shapes	0.964	0.896	0.851	0.965	1.000	1.000	1.000	1.000
	(0.102)	(0.184)	(0.242)	(0.103)	(0.000)	(0.000)	(0.000)	(0.000)
Relative size	0.660	0.400	0.398	0.668	1.000	1.000	1.000	1.000
	(0.314)	(0.313)	(0.339)	(0.325)	(0.000)	(0.000)	(0.000)	(0.000)
Ordinality, sequence	0.271	0.088	0.102	0.333	1.000	1.000	1.000	1.000
	(0.334)	(0.201)	(0.218)	(0.385)	(0.000)	(0.000)	(0.000)	(0.000)
Add/subtract	0.051	0.009	0.011	0.088	1.000	0.998	0.999	1.000
	(0.139)	(0.047)	(0.050)	(0.191)	(0.003)	(0.006)	(0.004)	(0.002)
Multiply/divide	0.003	0.000	0.000	0.006	0.990	0.955	0.977	0.989
	(0.028)	(0.006)	(0.012)	(0.049)	(0.055)	(0.121)	(0.087)	(0.050)
Place value	0.000	0.000	0.000	0.000	0.940	0.769	0.877	0.947
	(0.002)	(0.000)	(0.000)	(0.003)	(0.187)	(0.324)	(0.259)	(0.189)
Rate and measurement	0.000	0.000	0.000	0.000	0.762	0.405	0.606	0.822
	(0.000)	(0.000)	(0.000)	(0.000)	(0.324)	(0.364)	(0.372)	(0.307)
Fractions	—	—	—	—	0.460	0.124	0.279	0.609
					(0.415)	(0.268)	(0.371)	(0.426)
Area and volume	—	—	—	—	0.204	0.040	0.094	0.376
					(0.323)	(0.163)	(0.223)	(0.404)

(continued on next page)

Table 10 (continued)

	Fall K				Spring 8th			
	White	Black	Hispanic	Asian	White	Black	Hispanic	Asian
Reading								
Letter recognition	0.758	0.591	0.570	0.782	1.000	1.000	1.000	1.000
	(0.279)	(0.330)	(0.346)	(0.298)	(0.000)	(0.000)	(0.000)	(0.000)
Beginning sounds	0.366	0.217	0.214	0.450	1.000	1.000	1.000	1.000
	(0.340)	(0.293)	(0.287)	(0.377)	(0.000)	(0.000)	(0.000)	(0.000)
Ending sounds	0.210	0.113	0.108	0.298	1.000	1.000	1.000	1.000
	(0.279)	(0.209)	(0.202)	(0.342)	(0.000)	(0.000)	(0.000)	(0.000)
Sight words	0.039	0.012	0.015	0.094	1.000	0.999	1.000	1.000
	(0.139)	(0.063)	(0.089)	(0.242)	(0.001)	(0.003)	(0.001)	(0.001)
Words in context	0.018	0.004	0.007	0.051	0.992	0.970	0.987	0.995
	(0.090)	(0.029)	(0.055)	(0.167)	(0.023)	(0.046)	(0.029)	(0.016)
Literal inference	0.004	0.000	0.001	0.013	0.955	0.851	0.926	0.969
	(0.043)	(0.006)	(0.022)	(0.062)	(0.104)	(0.187)	(0.136)	(0.074)
Extrapolation	0.001	0.000	0.000	0.001	0.887	0.671	0.824	0.914
	(0.014)	(0.000)	(0.007)	(0.009)	(0.202)	(0.303)	(0.249)	(0.161)
Evaluation	0.001	0.000	0.000	0.002	0.737	0.462	0.639	0.776
	(0.009)	(0.001)	(0.005)	(0.010)	(0.261)	(0.298)	(0.282)	(0.243)
Evaluating nonfiction	—	—	—	—	0.363	0.113	0.227	0.441
					(0.367)	(0.244)	(0.316)	(0.398)
Evaluating complex syntax	—	—	—	—	0.079	0.020	0.043	0.107
					(0.141)	(0.063)	(0.097)	(0.155)

Entries are unadjusted mean scores on specific areas of questions in kindergarten fall and eighth grade spring. They are proficient probability scores, which are constructed using IRT scores and provide the probability of mastery of a specific set of skills. Dashes indicate areas that were not included in kindergarten fall exams. Standard deviations are located in parentheses.

outpace blacks—and by roughly a constant amount. Blacks only begin to close the gap after white students have demonstrated mastery of a specific area and therefore can improve no more. While it is possible that this implies that blacks will master the same material as whites but on a longer timeline, there is a more disconcerting possibility—as skills become more difficult, a non-trivial fraction of black students may never master the skills. If these skills are inputs into future subject matter, then this could lead to an increasing black-white achievement gap. The same may apply to Hispanic children, although they are closer to closing the gap with white students than blacks are.

In summary, using the ECLS-K—a recent and remarkably rich nationally representative dataset of students from the beginning of kindergarten through their eighth grade year—we demonstrate an important and remarkably robust racial achievement gap that seems to grow as children age. Blacks underperform whites in the same schools, the same classrooms, and on every aspect of each cognitive assessment. Hispanics follow a similar, though less stark, pattern.

Basic facts about racial differences in educational achievement using CNLSY79

Having exhausted possibilities in the ECLS-K, we now turn to the Children of the National Longitudinal Survey of Youth 1979 (CNLSY79). The CNLSY79 is a survey of children born to NLSY79 female respondents that began in 1986. The children of these female respondents are estimated to represent over 90% of all the children ever to be born to this cohort of women. As of 2006, a total of 11,466 children have been identified as having been born to the original 6283 NLSY79 female respondents, mostly during years in which they were interviewed. In addition to all the mother's information from the NLSY79, the child survey includes assessments of each child as well as additional demographic and development information collected from either the mother or child. The CNLSY79 includes the Home Observation for Measurement of Environment (HOME), an inventory of measures related to the quality of the home environment, as well as three subtests from the full Peabody Individual Achievement Test (PIAT) battery: the Mathematics, Reading Recognition, and Reading Comprehension assessments. We use the Mathematics and Reading Recognition assessments for our analysis.[44]

Most children for whom these assessments are available are between the ages of five and fourteen. Administration of the PIAT Mathematics assessment is relatively straightforward. Children enter the assessment at an age-appropriate item (although this is not essential to the scoring) and establish a "basal" by attaining five consecutive correct responses. If no basal is achieved then a basal of "1" is assigned. A "ceiling" is reached when five of seven items are answered incorrectly. The non-normalized raw score is equivalent to the ceiling item minus the number of incorrect responses between the basal and the ceiling scores. The PIAT Reading Recognition subtest measures word

---

[44] Results from analysis of the Reading Comprehension assessment are qualitatively very similar to results from using the Reading Recognition assessment and are available from the author upon request.

recognition and pronunciation ability, essential components of reading achievement. Children read a word silently, then say it aloud. PIAT Reading Recognition contains 84 items, each with four options, which increase in difficulty from preschool to high school levels. Skills assessed include matching letters, naming names, and reading single words aloud. Table A.7 contains summary statistics for variables used in our analysis.

To our knowledge, the CNLSY is the only large nationally representative sample that contains achievement tests both for mothers and their children, allowing one to control for maternal academic achievement in investigating racial disparities in achievement. Beyond the simple transmission of any genetic component of achievement, more educated mothers are more likely to spend time with their children engaging in achievement-enhancing activities such as reading, using academically stimulating toys, encouraging young children to learn the alphabet and numbers, and so on (Klebanov, 1994).

Tables 11 and 12 provide estimates of the racial achievement gap, by age, for children between the ages of five and fourteen.[45] Table 11 provides estimates for elementary school ages and Table 12 provides similar estimates for middle school aged children. Both tables contain two panels: Panel A presents results for math achievement and Panel B presents results for reading achievement. The first column under each age presents raw racial differences (and includes dummies for the child's age in months and for the year in which the assessment was administered). The second column adds controls for race, gender, free lunch status, special education status, whether the child attends a private school, family income, the HOME inventory, mother's standardized AFQT score, and dummies for the mother's birth year. Most important of these controls, and unique relative to other datasets, is maternal AFQT.

Two interesting observations emerge. First, gaps in reading are large and positive for blacks relative to whites for children under the age of seven. At age five, blacks are 0.174 (0.042) standard deviations behind whites. Controlling for maternal IQ, blacks are 0.395 (0.045) standard deviations *ahead* of whites. The black advantage, after controlling for maternal AFQT, tends to decrease as children age. At age fourteen, blacks are one-quarter standard deviation behind whites even after controlling for maternal achievement—a loss of roughly 0.650 standard deviations in ten years.

A second potentially important observation is that, in general, the importance of maternal achievement is remarkably constant over time. Independent of the raw data, maternal achievement demonstrably shifts the black coefficient roughly 0.4 to 0.5 standard deviations relative to whites. At age five, the raw difference between blacks and whites is −0.579 (0.040) in math and −0.174 (0.042) in reading. Accounting for maternal AFQT, these differences are −0.147 (0.046) and 0.395 (0.045)—a 0.432 standard deviation shift in math and 0.569 shift in reading. At age fourteen, maternal

---

[45] This corresponds, roughly, to kindergarten entry through ninth grade. To avoid complications due to potential differences in grade retention by race, we analyze CNLSY data by age.

Table 11 Determinants of PIAT math and reading recognition scores, elementary school (CNLSY79).

	Age 5		Age 6		Age 7		Age 8		Age 9		Age 10	
A. Math												
Black	−0.579	−0.147	−0.622	−0.137	−0.651	−0.129	−0.661	−0.197	−0.639	−0.132	−0.649	−0.146
	(0.040)	(0.046)	(0.039)	(0.044)	(0.039)	(0.044)	(0.038)	(0.044)	(0.038)	(0.042)	(0.039)	(0.044)
Hispanic	−0.466	−0.147	−0.598	−0.193	−0.503	−0.074	−0.527	−0.127	−0.417	−0.026	−0.555	−0.135
	(0.045)	(0.047)	(0.044)	(0.046)	(0.045)	(0.046)	(0.044)	(0.046)	(0.045)	(0.045)	(0.044)	(0.046)
Mother's AFQT score		0.234		0.269		0.354		0.289		0.332		0.312
		(0.022)		(0.021)		(0.021)		(0.021)		(0.020)		(0.021)
Controls	N	Y	N	Y	N	Y	N	Y	N	Y	N	Y
Obs.	3118	3118	3208	3208	3228	3228	3217	3217	3199	3199	3107	3107
R^2	0.101	0.193	0.125	0.248	0.124	0.265	0.155	0.254	0.146	0.286	0.157	0.284
B. Reading recognition												
Black	−0.174	0.395	−0.207	0.246	−0.331	0.193	−0.557	−0.083	−0.525	0.012	−0.590	−0.093
	(0.042)	(0.045)	(0.039)	(0.044)	(0.040)	(0.043)	(0.040)	(0.044)	(0.040)	(0.043)	(0.040)	(0.046)
Hispanic	−0.402	0.017	−0.349	0.037	−0.273	0.158	−0.442	−0.025	−0.290	0.124	−0.435	−0.001
	(0.047)	(0.047)	(0.045)	(0.046)	(0.046)	(0.047)	(0.045)	(0.048)	(0.047)	(0.046)	(0.046)	(0.049)
Mother's AFQT score		0.314		0.276		0.329		0.308		0.337		0.337
		(0.021)		(0.022)		(0.021)		(0.021)		(0.021)		(0.021)
Controls	N	Y	N	Y	N	Y	N	Y	N	Y	N	Y
Obs.	3052	3052	3174	3174	3224	3224	3216	3216	3195	3195	3106	3106
R^2	0.069	0.234	0.110	0.229	0.078	0.246	0.092	0.224	0.083	0.266	0.093	0.235

The dependent variable in each column is the Peabody Individual Achievement Test (PIAT) score for the designated subject and age. All specifications include dummies for the child's age in months and dummies for the year in which the assessment was administered. Odd-numbered columns estimate the raw racial test score gaps and also include a dummy for missing race. Non-black, non-Hispanic respondents are the omitted race category, so all of the race coefficients are gaps relative to that group. Specifications in the even-numbered columns include controls for gender, free lunch status, special education status, a dummy for attending a private school, parents' income, the Home Observation for Measurement of Environment (HOME) inventory, which is an inventory of measures related to the quality of the home environment, mother's AFQT score (standardized across the entire sample of mothers in our dataset), and dummies for the mother's birth year. Also included are missing dummies for all variables with missing data. Robust standard errors are located in parentheses. See data appendix for details of the sample construction.

Table 12 Determinants of PIAT math and reading recognition scores, middle school (CNLSY79).

	Age 11		Age 12		Age 13		Age 14	
A. Math								
Black	−0.681	−0.193	−0.729	−0.253	−0.685	−0.192	−0.781	−0.250
	(0.039)	(0.044)	(0.040)	(0.046)	(0.040)	(0.043)	(0.056)	(0.060)
Hispanic	−0.520	−0.112	−0.558	−0.148	−0.489	−0.084	−0.577	−0.111
	(0.047)	(0.049)	(0.046)	(0.049)	(0.049)	(0.049)	(0.066)	(0.068)
Mother's AFQT score		0.318		0.325		0.350		0.351
		(0.022)		(0.022)		(0.021)		(0.031)
Controls	N	Y	N	Y	N	Y	N	Y
Obs.	3022	3022	2824	2824	2738	2738	1443	1443
R^2	0.160	0.292	0.163	0.288	0.151	0.302	0.173	0.328
B. Reading recognition								
Black	−0.583	−0.069	−0.600	−0.119	−0.579	−0.067	−0.697	−0.251
	(0.040)	(0.045)	(0.043)	(0.046)	(0.042)	(0.045)	(0.058)	(0.063)
Hispanic	−0.332	0.106	−0.350	0.064	−0.275	0.153	−0.408	−0.013
	(0.048)	(0.049)	(0.048)	(0.050)	(0.051)	(0.051)	(0.066)	(0.069)
Mother's AFQT score		0.343		0.329		0.362		0.324
		(0.022)		(0.022)		(0.022)		(0.031)
Controls	N	Y	N	Y	N	Y	N	Y
Obs.	3012	3012	2830	2830	2740	2740	1452	1452
R^2	0.105	0.266	0.093	0.236	0.093	0.270	0.135	0.271

The dependent variable in each column is the Peabody Individual Achievement Test (PIAT) score for the designated subject and age. All specifications include dummies for the child's age in months and dummies for the year in which the assessment was administered. Odd-numbered columns estimate the raw racial test score gaps and also include a dummy for missing race. Non-black, non-Hispanic respondents are the omitted race category, so all of the race coefficients are gaps relative to that group. Specifications in the even-numbered columns include controls for gender, free lunch status, special education status, a dummy for attending a private school, parents' income, the Home Observation for Measurement of Environment (HOME) inventory, which is an inventory of measures related to the quality of the home environment, mother's AFQT score (standardized across the entire sample of mothers in our dataset), and dummies for the mother's birth year. Also included are missing dummies for all variables with missing data. Robust standard errors are located in parentheses. See data appendix for details regarding sample construction.

achievement explains 0.531 standard deviations in math and 0.446 in reading despite the fact that the raw gaps on both tests increased substantially. The stability of the magnitudes in the shift of the gap once one controls for maternal AFQT suggests that whatever is causing blacks to lose ground relative to whites is operating through a different channel.

Basic facts about racial differences in achievement using district administrative files

Thus far we have concentrated on nationally representative samples because of their obvious advantages. Yet, using the restricted-use version of ECLS-K, we discovered that some large urban areas with significant numbers of chronically underperforming schools may not be adequately represented. For instance, New York City contains roughly 3.84% of black school children, but is only 1.46% of the ECLS-K Sample. Chicago has 2.42% of the population of black students and is only 1.13% of the ECLS-K sample. Ideally, sample weights would correct for this imbalance, but if schools with particular characteristics (i.e., predominantly minority and chronically poor performing) are not sampled or refuse to participate for any reason, weights will not necessarily compensate for this imbalance.

To understand the impact of this potential sampling problem, we collected administrative data from four representative urban school districts: Chicago, Dallas, New York City, and Washington, DC. The richness of the data varies by city, but all data sets include information on student race, gender, free lunch eligibility, behavioral incidents, attendance, matriculation with course grades, whether a student is an English Language Learner (ELL), and special education status. The data also include a student's first and last names, birth date, and address. We use address data to link every student to their census block group and impute the average income of that block group to every student who lives there. In Dallas and New York we are able to link students to their classroom teachers. New York City administrative files also contain teacher value-added data for teachers in grades four through eight and question-level data for each student's state assessment.

The main outcome variable in these data is an achievement assessment unique to each city. In May of every school year, students in Dallas public elementary schools take the Texas Assessment of Knowledge and Skills (TAKS) if they are in grades three through eight. New York City administers mathematics and English Language Arts tests, developed by McGraw-Hill, in the winter for students in third through eighth grade. In Washington, DC, the DC Comprehensive Assessment System (DC-CAS) is administered each April to students in grades three through eight and ten. All Chicago students in grades three through eight take the Illinois Standards Achievement Test (ISAT). See the data appendix for more details on each assessment.

One drawback of using school district administrative files is that individual-level controls only include a mutually exclusive and collectively exhaustive set of race dummies, indicators for free lunch eligibility, special education status, and whether a student is an ELL student. A student is income-eligible for free lunch if her family income is below 130% of the federal poverty guidelines, or categorically eligible if (1) the student's household receives assistance under the Food Stamp Program, the Food Distribution Program on Indian Reservations (FDPIR), or the Temporary Assistance for Needy Families Program (TANF); (2) the student was enrolled in Head Start on the basis of meeting that program's low-income criteria; (3) the student is homeless; (4) the student is a migrant child; or (5) the student is a runaway child receiving assistance from a program under the Runaway and Homeless Youth Act and is identified by the local educational liaison. Determination of special education and ELL status varies by district. For example, in Washington, DC, special education status is determined through a series of observations, interviews, reviews of report cards and administration of tests. In Dallas, any student who reports that his or her home language is not English is administered a test and ELL status is based on the student's score. Tables A.8–A.11 provide summary statistics used in our analysis in Chicago, Dallas, New York, and Washington, DC, respectively.

Table 13 presents estimates of the racial achievement gap in math (Panel A) and reading (Panel B) for New York City, Washington, DC, Dallas, and Chicago using the standard least squares specification employed thus far. Each city contains three columns. The first column reports the raw racial gap with no controls. The second column adds a small set of individual controls available in the administrative files in each district and the final column under each city includes school fixed effects.

In NYC, blacks trail whites by 0.696 (0.024) standard deviations, Hispanics trail whites by 0.615 (0.023), and Asians outpace whites by 0.266 (0.022) in the raw data. Adding sex, free lunch status, ELL status, special education status, age (including quadratic and cubic terms), and income quintiles reduces these gaps to 0.536 (0.020) for blacks and 0.335 (0.018) for Hispanics. Asians continue to outperform other racial groups. Including school fixed effects further suppresses racial differences for blacks and Hispanics—yielding gaps of 0.346 (0.005) and 0.197 (0.005), respectively. The Asian gap increases modestly with the inclusion of school fixed effects.

Dallas follows a pattern similar to NYC—there is a black-white gap of 0.690 (0.124) in the raw data which decreases to 0.678 (0.108) with the inclusion of controls, and 0.528 (0.031) with school fixed effects. Asians and Hispanics in Dallas follow a similar pattern to that documented in NYC. Both Chicago and Washington, DC, have raw racial gaps that hover around one standard deviation for blacks and 0.75 for Hispanics. Accounting for differences in school assignment reduces the black-white gaps to 0.657 (0.029) in DC and 0.522 (0.011) in Chicago—roughly half of the original gaps. Asians continue to outpace all racial groups in Chicago and are on par with whites in Washington, DC.

Panel B of Table 13 estimates racial differences in reading achievement across our four cities. Similar to the results presented earlier using nationally representative samples, racial gaps on reading assessments are smaller than those on math assessments. In NYC, the raw gap is 0.634 (0.025) and the gap is 0.285 (0.005) with controls and school fixed effects. Dallas contains gaps of similar magnitude to those in NYC and adding school fixed effects

Table 13 Racial achievement gap in urban districts.

	New York City			Washington, DC			Dallas			Chicago		
A. Math												
Black	−0.696	−0.536	−0.346	−1.162	−0.747	−0.657	−0.690	−0.678	−0.528	−0.978	−0.740	−0.522
	(0.024)	(0.020)	(0.005)	(0.089)	(0.049)	(0.029)	(0.124)	(0.108)	(0.031)	(0.049)	(0.032)	(0.011)
Hispanic	−0.615	−0.335	−0.197	−0.830	−0.401	−0.461	−0.392	−0.230	−0.079	−0.687	−0.435	−0.254
	(0.023)	(0.018)	(0.005)	(0.114)	(0.053)	(0.034)	(0.121)	(0.104)	(0.030)	(0.046)	(0.028)	(0.010)
Asian	0.266	0.335	0.345	−0.056	0.105	0.058	0.216	0.270	0.348	0.270	0.423	0.337
	(0.022)	(0.021)	(0.005)	(0.100)	(0.053)	(0.046)	(0.131)	(0.118)	(0.063)	(0.053)	(0.050)	(0.015)
Other race	−0.566	−0.420	−0.247	−0.155	−0.015	0.021	−0.407	−0.405	−0.226	−0.256	−0.194	−0.251
	(0.032)	(0.028)	(0.018)	(0.188)	(0.153)	(0.164)	(0.180)	(0.177)	(0.122)	(0.084)	(0.072)	(0.051)
Controls	N	Y	Y	N	Y	Y	N	Y	Y	N	Y	Y
School FEs	N	N	Y	N	N	Y	N	N	Y	N	N	Y
Obs.	434,593	434,593	434,593	20,331	20,331	20,331	33,561	33,561	33,561	177,787	177,787	177,787
R^2	0.131	0.283	0.362	0.111	0.285	0.405	0.030	0.084	0.149	0.108	0.145	0.240
% Reduction		22.9	35.6		35.7	12.1		1.8	22.2		24.3	29.5

(continued on next page)

Table 13 (continued)

B. Reading

	New York City			Washington, DC			Dallas			Chicago		
Black	−0.634	−0.455	−0.285	−1.163	−0.708	−0.599	−0.782	−0.761	−0.561	−0.846	−0.587	−0.381
	(0.025)	(0.020)	(0.005)	(0.073)	(0.044)	(0.030)	(0.137)	(0.119)	(0.031)	(0.046)	(0.029)	(0.012)
Hispanic	−0.670	−0.328	−0.194	−1.004	−0.410	−0.444	−0.680	−0.473	−0.278	−0.714	−0.433	−0.253
	(0.024)	(0.019)	(0.005)	(0.097)	(0.049)	(0.035)	(0.133)	(0.114)	(0.029)	(0.045)	(0.027)	(0.010)
Asian	0.007	0.103	0.121	−0.410	−0.172	−0.204	−0.195	−0.104	0.002	0.029	0.194	0.151
	(0.023)	(0.019)	(0.005)	(0.101)	(0.052)	(0.048)	(0.133)	(0.114)	(0.062)	(0.051)	(0.035)	(0.015)
Other race	−0.559	−0.395	−0.249	−0.251	−0.063	−0.052	−0.497	−0.496	−0.290	−0.105	−0.034	−0.091
	(0.031)	(0.027)	(0.019)	(0.161)	(0.102)	(0.167)	(0.187)	(0.188)	(0.121)	(0.081)	(0.067)	(0.053)
Controls	N	Y	Y	N	Y	Y	N	Y	Y	N	Y	Y
School FEs	N	N	Y	N	N	Y	N	N	Y	N	N	Y
Obs.	426,806	426,806	426,806	20,243	20,243	20,243	28,126	28,126	28,126	176,767	176,767	176,767
R^2	0.087	0.273	0.335	0.095	0.282	0.380	0.030	0.115	0.180	0.069	0.126	0.205
% Reduction		28.4	37.3		39.1	15.4		2.6	26.2		30.6	35.1

The dependent variable in each column is the state assessment in that subject taken during the 2008–09 school year. For New York City, these are the New York State mathematics and English Language Arts (ELA) exams. For Washington, DC, these are the District of Columbia Comprehensive Assessment System (DC-CAS) mathematics and reading exams. For Dallas, these are the Texas Assessment of Knowledge and Skills (TAKS) mathematics and reading exams (English versions). For Chicago, these are the Illinois Standards Achievement Test (ISAT) mathematics and reading exams. All test scores are standardized to have mean zero and standard deviation one within each grade. Non-Hispanic whites are the omitted race category, so all of the race coefficients are gaps relative to that group. The New York City and Chicago specifications include students in grades three through eight. Washington, DC, includes students in grades three through eight and ten. Dallas includes students in grades three through five. The first specification for each city estimates the raw racial test score gap in each city and does not include any other controls. The second specification for each city includes controls for gender, free lunch status, English language learner (ELL) status, special education status, age in years (linear, quadratic, and cubic terms), census block group income quintile dummies, and missing dummies for all variables with missing data. The third specification includes the same set of controls as well as school fixed effects. Age, special education status, and income data are not available in the Chicago data. Standard errors, located in parentheses, are clustered at the school level. Percent reduction refers to the percent by which the magnitude of the coefficient on black is reduced relative to the coefficient on black in the preceding column. See data appendix for details regarding sample and variable construction.

has little effect on racial disparities. Chicago and Washington, DC, trail the other cities in the raw gaps—0.846 (0.046) and 1.163 (0.073) respectively—but these differences are drastically reduced after accounting for the fact that blacks and whites attend different schools. The Chicago gap, with school fixed effects, is 0.381 (0.012) (45% of the original gap) and the corresponding gap in DC is 0.599 (0.030). These gaps are strikingly similar in magnitude to racial differences in national samples such as ELCS-K and CNLSY79, suggesting that biased sampling is not a first-order problem.

Thus far, we have concentrated on average achievement across grades three through eight in NYC, Chicago, and DC, and grades three through five in Dallas. Our analysis of ECLS suggests that racial gaps increase over time. Krueger and Whitmore (2001) and Phillips et al. (1998b) also find that the black-white achievement gap widens as children get older, which they attribute to the differential quality of schools attended by black and white students. Figure 3 plots the raw black-white achievement gap in math (Panel A) and reading (Panel B) for all grades available in each city. In math, DC shows a remarkable increase in the gap as children age—increasing from 0.990 (0.077) in third grade to 1.424 (0.174) in eighth grade. The gap in NYC also increased with age, but much less dramatically. Racial disparities in Chicago are essentially flat across grade levels, and, if anything, racial differences decrease in Dallas. A similar pattern is observed in reading: the gap in DC is increasing over time whereas the gap in other cites is relatively flat. The racial achievement gap in reading in DC is roughly double that in any other city. Figure 4 provides similar data for Hispanics. Hispanics follow a similar, but less consistent, pattern as blacks.

In NYC and Dallas, we were able to obtain data on classroom assignments that allow us to estimate models with teacher fixed effects. In elementary school, we assign the student's main classroom teacher. In middle schools we assign teachers according to subject: for math (resp. ELA) assessment scores, we compare students with the same math (resp. ELA) teacher. In Dallas, there are 1950 distinct teachers in the sample, with an average of 14 students per teacher. In New York City, there are 16,398 ELA teachers and 16,069 math teachers, with an average of about 25 students per teacher (note that in grades three through five, the vast majority of students have the same teacher for both ELA and math, so the actual number of distinct teachers in the dataset is 20,064.)

Table 14 supplements our analysis by including teacher fixed effects in NYC (Panel A) and Dallas (Panel B) for both math and reading. Each city contains four columns, two for math and two for reading. For comparison, the odd-numbered columns are identical to the school fixed effects specifications in Table 13, but estimated on a sample of students for which we have valid information on their classroom teacher. This restricted sample is 92% of the original for NYC and 99% of the original for Dallas. The even-numbered columns contain teacher fixed effects. Consistent with the analysis in ECLS-K, accounting for sorting into classrooms has a modest marginal effect on the racial achievement gap beyond the inclusion of school fixed effects. The percent reduction

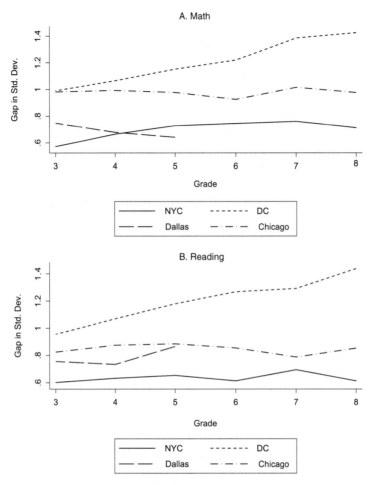

Figure 3   *Black-white achievement gap (raw) by grade.*

in the black coefficient in NYC is 20.0% in math and 25.0% in reading. In Dallas, these reductions are 0.9% and 3.0%, respectively.

Table 15 concludes our analysis of our school district administrative files by investigating the source of the racial achievement gap in NYC across particular skills tested. The math section of the NYC state assessment is divided into five strands: number sense and operations, algebra, geometry, measurement, and statistics and probability. ELA exams are divided into three standards for grades three through eight: (1) information and understanding; (2) literary response and expression; and (3) critical analysis and evaluation. The information and understanding questions measure a student's ability to gather information from spoken language and written text and to transmit knowledge orally and textually. Literary response and expression refers to a student's ability to make connections to a diverse set of texts and to speak and write for creative expression.

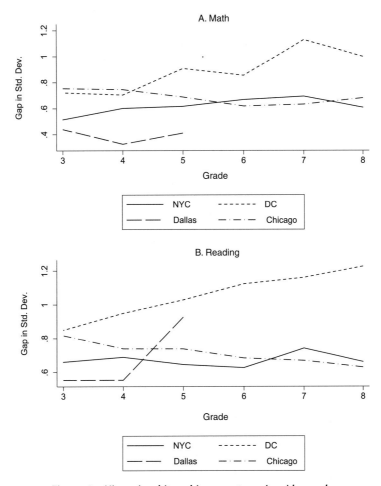

Figure 4 *Hispanic-white achievement gap (raw) by grade.*

Critical analysis and evaluation measures how well a student can examine an idea or argument and create a coherent opinion in response. There is no clear pattern in the emphasizing or deemphasizing of particular topics between third and eighth grades. The ELA exams focus more heavily on information and understanding and literary response and expression than on critical analysis and evaluation across all years tested. The math exams focus heavily on number sense until eighth grade, when the focus shifts to algebra and geometry. There are also segments of geometry in fifth grade and statistics and probability in seventh grade.

The most striking observation about Table 15 is how remarkably robust the racial achievement gap in NYC is across grade levels and sets of skills tested. There are substantial racial gaps on every skill at every grade level. The disparities in reading achievement are roughly half as large as the disparities in math.

Table 14 Racial achievement gap in urban districts: accounting for teachers.

	Math		Reading	
A. NYC				
Black	−0.350	−0.280	−0.286	−0.214
	(0.005)	(0.005)	(0.006)	(0.005)
Hispanic	−0.198	−0.149	−0.193	−0.139
	(0.005)	(0.005)	(0.005)	(0.005)
Asian	0.350	0.331	0.124	0.110
	(0.005)	(0.005)	(0.006)	(0.005)
Other race	−0.246	−0.195	−0.251	−0.204
	(0.019)	(0.018)	(0.020)	(0.019)
Controls	Y	Y	Y	Y
School FEs	Y	N	Y	N
Teacher FEs	N	Y	N	Y
Obs.	398,062	398,062	391,854	391,854
R^2	0.359	0.477	0.332	0.445
% Reduction		20.0		25.0
B. Dallas				
Black	−0.530	−0.525	−0.563	−0.546
	(0.031)	(0.032)	(0.031)	(0.031)
Hispanic	−0.079	−0.099	−0.278	−0.270
	(0.030)	(0.030)	(0.029)	(0.030)
Asian	0.347	0.313	−0.004	−0.025
	(0.063)	(0.063)	(0.063)	(0.063)
Other race	−0.227	−0.155	−0.289	−0.244
	(0.122)	(0.121)	(0.121)	(0.121)
Controls	Y	Y	Y	Y
School FEs	Y	N	Y	N
Teacher FEs	N	Y	N	Y
Obs.	33,507	33,507	27,949	27,949
R^2	0.149	0.255	0.181	0.274
% Reduction		0.9		3.0

The dependent variable in each column is the state assessment in that subject taken during the 2008-09 school year. For New York City, these are the New York State mathematics and English Language Arts (ELA) exams. For Dallas, these are the Texas Assessment of Knowledge and Skills (TAKS) mathematics and reading exams (English versions). All test scores are standardized to have mean zero and standard deviation one within each grade. Non-Hispanic whites are the omitted race category, so all of the race coefficients are gaps relative to that group. The New York City specifications include students in grades three through eight. The Dallas specifications include students in grades three through five. All specifications include controls for gender, free lunch status, English language learner (ELL) status, special education status, age in years (linear, quadratic, and cubic terms), census block group income quintile dummies, and missing dummies for all variables with missing data. Odd-numbered columns include school fixed effects, whereas even-numbered columns include teacher fixed effects. The samples are restricted to students for whom teacher data in the relevant subject are available. Standard errors are located in parentheses. Percent reduction refers to the percent by which the magnitude of the coefficient on black is reduced relative to the coefficient on black in the preceding column. See data appendix for details regarding sample and variable construction.

Table 15 Unadjusted means on questions assessing specific sets of skills, NYC.

A. Elementary school

	3rd Grade		4th Grade		5th Grade	
	Black	White	Black	White	Black	White
Math						
Math st. 1: number sense/operations	−0.192	0.338	−0.233	0.393	−0.229	0.378
	(1.053)	(0.812)	(1.032)	(0.801)	(1.006)	(0.836)
Math st. 2: algebra	−0.196	0.274	−0.172	0.294	−0.221	0.306
	(1.088)	(0.777)	(1.079)	(0.769)	(1.081)	(0.790)
Math st. 3: geometry	−0.130	0.220	−0.178	0.311	−0.231	0.380
	(1.048)	(0.824)	(1.046)	(0.853)	(1.028)	(0.849)
Math st. 4: measurement	−0.210	0.258	−0.242	0.418	−0.265	0.363
	(1.102)	(0.796)	(1.009)	(0.838)	(1.044)	(0.807)
Math st. 5: statistics/probability	−0.200	0.283	−0.213	0.316	−0.227	0.368
	(1.066)	(0.815)	(1.030)	(0.871)	(1.006)	(0.894)
ELA						
ELA st. 1: information and understanding	−0.105	0.322	−0.093	0.383	−0.134	0.383
	(1.024)	(0.843)	(1.010)	(0.835)	(0.996)	(0.844)
ELA st. 2: literary response and expression	−0.138	0.374	−0.167	0.462	−0.095	0.304
	(1.015)	(0.807)	(0.976)	(0.917)	(1.019)	(0.840)
ELA st. 3: critical analysis and evaluation	−0.102	0.349	−0.102	0.350	−0.171	0.369
	(0.996)	(0.931)	(1.025)	(0.825)	(1.021)	(0.859)

(continued on next page)

Table 15 (continued)

B. Middle school

	6th Grade		7th Grade		8th Grade	
	Black	White	Black	White	Black	White
Math						
Math st. 1: number sense/operations	−0.261	0.452	−0.233	0.433	−0.225	0.366
	(0.953)	(0.890)	(0.962)	(0.877)	(0.975)	(0.915)
Math st. 2: algebra	−0.209	0.393	−0.241	0.402	−0.274	0.431
	(1.037)	(0.794)	(0.981)	(0.894)	(0.945)	(0.907)
Math st. 3: geometry	−0.249	0.397	−0.218	0.360	−0.262	0.390
	(0.970)	(0.910)	(1.003)	(0.873)	(1.000)	(0.864)
Math st. 4: measurement	−0.215	0.349	−0.286	0.497	−0.198	0.313
	(1.021)	(0.849)	(0.906)	(0.939)	(1.029)	(0.840)
Math st. 5: statistics/probability	−0.222	0.425	−0.235	0.465	—	—
	(0.994)	(0.846)	(0.984)	(0.826)		
ELA						
ELA st. 1: information and understanding	−0.111	0.322	−0.096	0.406	−0.163	0.456
	(1.008)	(0.866)	(0.967)	(0.806)	(0.945)	(0.867)
ELA st. 2: literary response and expression	−0.176	0.448	−0.126	0.438	−0.060	0.360
	(0.957)	(0.870)	(0.973)	(0.834)	(0.972)	(0.887)
ELA st. 3: critical analysis and evaluation	−0.099	0.286	−0.130	0.419	−0.036	0.224
	(1.016)	(0.815)	(0.973)	(0.852)	(1.006)	(0.935)

Entries are unadjusted mean percentage of items correct on specific areas of questions on the New York State assessments in mathematics and English Language Arts (ELA) in third through eighth grades in New York City, which are then standardized across the entire sample of test takers for each grade, so that units are standard deviations relative to the mean. Dashes indicate that Statistics/Probability was not included in the eighth grade mathematics exam. Standard deviations are located in parentheses.

Putting the pieces together, there are four insights gleaned from our analysis in this section. First, racial achievement gaps using district administrative files, which contain all students in a school district, are similar in magnitude to those estimated using national samples. Second, the evidence as to whether gaps increase over time is mixed. Washington, DC, provides the clearest evidence that black and white paths diverge in school. Patterns from other cities are less clear. Third, school fixed effects explain roughly fifty percent of the gap; adding teacher fixed effects explains about twenty-three percent more in NYC and only about two percent more in Dallas. Fourth, and perhaps most troubling, black students are behind on every aspect of the achievement tests at every grade.

6. THE RACIAL ACHIEVEMENT GAP IN HIGH SCHOOL

We conclude our descriptive analysis of the racial achievement gap with high school-aged students using the National Education Longitudinal Survey (NELS).[46] The NELS consists of a nationally representative group of students who were in eighth grade in 1988 when the baseline survey and achievement test data were collected. Students were resurveyed in 1990 at the end of their tenth grade year and again in 1992 at the anticipated end of their high school career. All three waves consist of data from a student questionnaire, achievement tests, a school principal questionnaire, and teacher questionnaires; 1990 and 1992 follow-ups also include a dropout questionnaire, the baseline and 1992 follow-up also surveyed parents, and the 1992 follow-up contains student transcript information. NELS contains 24,599 students, in 2963 schools and 5351 math, science, English, and history classrooms initially surveyed in the baseline year. Eighty-two percent of these students completed a survey in each of the first three rounds.

The primary outcomes in the NELS data are four exams: math, reading comprehension, science, and social studies (history/citizenship/government). In the base year (eighth grade), all students took the same set of tests, but in order to avoid problematic "ceiling" and "floor" effects in the follow-up testing (tenth and twelfth grades for most participants) students were given test forms tailored to their performance in the previous test administration. There were two reading test forms and three math test forms; science and social studies tests remained the same for all students. Test scores were determined using Item Response Theory (IRT) scoring, which allowed the difficulty of the test taken by each student to be taken into account in order to estimate the score a student would have achieved for any arbitrary set of test items. Table A.12 provides descriptive statistics.

---

[46] Similar results are obtained from the National Longitudinal Survey of Adolescent Health (Add Health)—a nationally representative sample of over 90,000 students in grades six through twelve. We chose NELS because it contains tests on four subject areas. Add Health only contains the results from the Peabody Picture Vocabulary Test. Results from Add Health are available from the author upon request.

Table 16 provides estimates of the racial achievement gap in high school across four subjects. For each grade, we estimate four empirical models. We begin with raw racial differences, which are displayed in the first column under each grade. Then, we add controls for race, gender, age (linear, quadratic, and cubic terms), family income, and dummies for parents' levels of education. The third empirical model includes school fixed effects and the fourth includes teacher fixed effects. The raw black-white gap in eighth grade math is 0.754 (0.025) standard deviations. Adding controls reduces the gap to 0.526 (0.021), and adding school fixed effects reduces the gap further to 0.400 (0.021), which is similar to the eighth grade disparities reported in ECLS. Including teacher fixed effects reduces the gap to 0.343 (0.031) standard deviations. In 10th and 12th grade, black-white disparities range from 0.734 (0.038) in the raw data to 0.288 (0.060) with teacher fixed effects in 10th grade, and 0.778 (0.045) to 0.581 (0.089) in 12th grade. Hispanics follow a similar trend, but the achievement gaps are nearly 40% smaller. In the raw data, Asians are the highest-performing ethnic group in eighth through twelfth grades. Including teacher fixed effects, however, complicates the story. Asians are 0.127 standard deviations ahead of whites in eighth grade. This gap diminishes over time and, by twelfth grade, Asian students trail whites when they have the same teachers.

Panels B, C, and D of Table 16, which estimate racial achievement gaps in English, history, and science, respectively, all show magnitudes and trends similar to those documented above in math. Averaging across subjects, the black-white gap in eighth grade is roughly 0.7 standard deviations. An identical calculation for Hispanics yields a gap of just under 0.6 standard deviations. Asians are ahead in math and on par with whites in all other subjects. In twelfth grade, black students significantly trail whites in science and math (0.911 (0.041) and 0.778 (0.045) standard deviations, respectively) and slightly less so in history and English. Hispanics and Asians demonstrate patterns in twelfth grade that are very similar to their patterns in eighth grade.

To close our analytic pipeline from nine months old to high school graduation, we investigate racial differences in high school graduation or GED acquisition within five years of their freshman year in high school [not shown in tabular form]. In the raw data, blacks are twice as likely as whites to not graduate from high school or receive a GED within five years of entering high school. Accounting for math and reading achievement scores in eighth grade explains all of the racial gap in graduation rates. Hispanics are 2.2 times more likely not to graduate and these differences are reduced to thirty percent more likely after including eighth grade achievement.

We learn four points from NELS. First, achievement gaps continue their slow divergence in the high school years. Second, gaps are as large in science and history as they are in subjects that are tested more often, such as math and reading. Third, similarly as in the preceding analysis, a substantial racial achievement gap exists after accounting for teacher fixed effects. Fourth, the well-documented disparities in graduation rates can be explained by eighth grade test scores. The last result is particularly striking.

Table 16 Evolution of the achievement gap over time, NELS.

	8th Grade				10th Grade				12th Grade			
A. Math												
Black	−0.754 (0.025)	−0.526 (0.021)	−0.400 (0.021)	−0.343 (0.031)	−0.734 (0.038)	−0.500 (0.034)	−0.410 (0.032)	−0.288 (0.060)	−0.778 (0.045)	−0.543 (0.042)	−0.445 (0.045)	−0.581 (0.089)
Hispanic	−0.581 (0.025)	−0.349 (0.022)	−0.236 (0.023)	−0.200 (0.034)	−0.573 (0.035)	−0.301 (0.032)	−0.220 (0.032)	−0.166 (0.064)	−0.544 (0.039)	−0.267 (0.036)	−0.212 (0.037)	−0.259 (0.105)
Asian	0.186 (0.054)	0.134 (0.045)	0.170 (0.032)	0.127 (0.048)	0.251 (0.056)	0.168 (0.051)	0.132 (0.043)	0.018 (0.082)	0.235 (0.065)	0.145 (0.057)	0.119 (0.052)	−0.118 (0.087)
Controls	N	Y	Y	Y	N	Y	Y	Y	N	Y	Y	Y
School FEs	N	N	Y	N	N	N	Y	N	N	N	Y	N
Teacher FEs	N	N	N	Y	N	N	N	Y	N	N	N	Y
Obs.	23,648	23,648	23,648	10,981	17,793	17,793	17,793	7316	14,236	14,236	14,236	5668
R^2	0.099	0.253	0.354	0.509	0.102	0.277	0.464	0.761	0.103	0.281	0.471	0.829
B. English												
Black	−0.686 (0.025)	−0.495 (0.022)	−0.399 (0.023)	−0.368 (0.034)	−0.641 (0.048)	−0.435 (0.042)	−0.377 (0.038)	−0.336 (0.056)	−0.661 (0.044)	−0.479 (0.042)	−0.430 (0.071)	
Hispanic	−0.572 (0.029)	−0.358 (0.026)	−0.242 (0.025)	−0.206 (0.037)	−0.504 (0.037)	−0.264 (0.033)	−0.211 (0.036)	−0.113 (0.061)	−0.479 (0.036)	−0.270 (0.040)	−0.250 (0.042)	
Asian	−0.082 (0.048)	−0.123 (0.040)	−0.072 (0.032)	−0.103 (0.050)	0.024 (0.057)	−0.048 (0.049)	−0.050 (0.045)	−0.134 (0.083)	0.081 (0.062)	0.003 (0.051)	0.020 (0.049)	

(continued on next page)

Table 16 (continued)

	8th Grade				10th Grade				12th Grade		
Controls	N	Y	Y	Y	N	Y	Y	Y	N	Y	Y
School FEs	N	N	Y	N	N	N	Y	N	N	N	Y
Teacher FEs	N	N	N	Y	N	N	N	Y	N	N	N
Obs.	23,643	23,643	23,643	11,158	17,832	17,832	17,832	8962	14,230	14,230	14,230
R^2	0.080	0.211	0.293	0.409	0.079	0.226	0.417	0.638	0.084	0.219	0.414

C. History

	8th Grade				10th Grade				12th Grade		
Black	−0.660	−0.453	−0.340	−0.311	−0.599	−0.390	−0.332	−0.303	−0.621	−0.429	−0.302
	(0.028)	(0.024)	(0.023)	(0.038)	(0.041)	(0.037)	(0.035)	(0.078)	(0.047)	(0.042)	(0.047)
Hispanic	−0.590	−0.369	−0.233	−0.248	−0.518	−0.275	−0.156	−0.238	−0.501	−0.266	−0.210
	(0.028)	(0.026)	(0.026)	(0.043)	(0.037)	(0.033)	(0.035)	(0.080)	(0.041)	(0.040)	(0.042)
Asian	−0.020	−0.066	0.003	−0.022	0.030	−0.049	0.018	−0.008	0.093	0.008	0.041
	(0.052)	(0.045)	(0.033)	(0.053)	(0.058)	(0.050)	(0.049)	(0.112)	(0.068)	(0.057)	(0.062)
Controls	N	Y	Y	Y	N	Y	Y	Y	N	Y	Y
School FEs	N	Y	N	N	N	Y	N	N	N	Y	N
Teacher FEs	N	N	Y	N	N	N	Y	N	N	N	Y
Obs.	23,525	23,525	23,525	10,297	17,591	17,591	17,591	4567	14,063	14,063	14,063
R^2	0.079	0.200	0.316	0.407	0.072	0.208	0.423	0.625	0.082	0.217	0.432

Table 16 (continued)

D. Science

	8th Grade				10th Grade				12th Grade			
Black	−0.792	−0.589	−0.437	−0.434	−0.848	−0.640	−0.465	−0.505	−0.911	−0.731	−0.574	−0.560
	(0.024)	(0.022)	(0.023)	(0.033)	(0.038)	(0.036)	(0.034)	(0.064)	(0.041)	(0.037)	(0.058)	(0.141)
Hispanic	−0.588	−0.377	−0.246	−0.203	−0.627	−0.382	−0.264	−0.106	−0.617	−0.389	−0.294	−0.245
	(0.026)	(0.025)	(0.025)	(0.039)	(0.034)	(0.032)	(0.033)	(0.069)	(0.038)	(0.037)	(0.040)	(0.148)
Asian	−0.045	−0.079	0.015	0.024	0.042	−0.040	0.023	−0.098	0.019	−0.056	−0.046	−0.054
	(0.053)	(0.046)	(0.033)	(0.052)	(0.061)	(0.054)	(0.044)	(0.110)	(0.056)	(0.046)	(0.050)	(0.106)
Controls	N	Y	Y	Y	N	Y	Y	Y	N	Y	Y	Y
School FEs	N	Y	Y	N	N	Y	Y	N	N	Y	Y	N
Teacher FEs	N	N	Y	N	N	N	Y	N	N	N	Y	N
Obs.	23,616	23,616	23,616	10,575	17,684	17,684	17,684	6148	14,134	14,134	14,134	3715
R^2	0.099	0.210	0.310	0.375	0.113	0.253	0.444	0.127	0.127	0.256	0.448	0.772

The dependent variable in each column is the NELS test score in the designated subject and grade. Test scores are IRT scores, normalized to have mean zero and standard deviation one in each grade. Non-Hispanic whites are the omitted race category, so all of the race coefficients are gaps relative to that group. The first specification for each grade and subject estimates the raw racial test score gap in that grade and only include race dummies and a dummy for missing race. The second specification for each grade and subject includes controls for gender, age (linear, quadratic, and cubic terms), family income, and dummies that indicate parents' level of education, as well as missing dummies for all variables with missing data. The third specification includes the same set of controls as well as school fixed effects. For grades eight through twelve of math and science, and for grades eight and ten of English and history, the fourth specification includes the same set of controls as well as teacher fixed effects. For grade twelve of English and history, teacher data were not collected in the second follow-up year of the NELS, so teacher fixed effects cannot be included. Standard errors, located in parentheses, are clustered at the school level.

7. INTERVENTIONS TO FOSTER HUMAN CAPITAL IN SCHOOL-AGED CHILDREN

In an effort to increase achievement and narrow differences between racial groups, school districts have become laboratories of innovative reforms, including smaller schools and classrooms (Nye, 1995; Krueger, 1999), mandatory summer school (Jacob and Lefgren, 2004), merit pay for principals, teachers, and students (Podgursky and Springer, 2007; Fryer, 2010), after-school programs (Lauer et al., 2006), budget, curricula, and assessment reorganization (Borman et al., 2007), policies to lower the barrier to teaching via alternative paths to accreditation (Decker et al., 2004; Kane et al., 2008), single-sex education (Shapka and Keating, 2003), data-driven instruction (Datnow et al., 2008), ending social promotion (Greene and Winters, 2006), mayoral/state control of schools (Wong and Shen, 2002, 2005; Henig and Rich, 2004), instructional coaching (Knight, 2009), local school councils (Easton et al., 1993), reallocating per-pupil spending (Marlow, 2000; Guryan, 2001), providing more culturally sensitive curricula (Protheroe and Barsdate, 1991; Thernstrom, 1992; Banks, 2001, 2006), renovated and more technologically savvy classrooms (Rouse and Krueger, 2004; Goolsbee and Guryan, 2006), professional development for teachers and other key staff (Boyd et al., 2008; Rockoff, 2008), and getting parents to be more involved (Domina, 2005).

The evidence on the efficacy of these investments is mixed. Despite their intuitive appeal, school choice, summer remediation programs, and certain mentoring programs show no effect on achievement (Krueger and Zhu, 2002; Walker and Vilella-Velez, 1992; Bernstein et al., 2009). Financial incentives for students, smaller class sizes, and bonuses for teachers in hard-to-staff schools show small to modest gains that pass a cost-benefit analysis (Fryer, 2010; Schanzenbach, 2007; Jacob and Ludwig, 2008). It is imperative to note: these programs have not been able to substantially reduce the achievement gap even in the most reform-minded school systems.

Even more aggressive strategies that place disadvantaged students in better schools through busing (Angrist and Lang, 2004) or significantly alter the neighborhoods in which they live (Jacob, 2004; Kling et al., 2007; Sanbonmatsu et al., 2006; Turney et al., 2006) have left the racial achievement gap essentially unchanged.

Table 17 describes seventeen additional interventions designed to increase achievement in public schools.[47] The first column lists the program name, the second column reports the grades treated, and the third column provides a brief description of each intervention. The final two columns provide information on the magnitude of the reported effect and a reference. The bulk of the evidence finds little to no effect of these interventions. Three programs seem to break this mold: Mastery Learning, Success for All, and self-affirmation essay writing. Mastery learning is a group-based, teacher-paced

---

[47] This list was generated by typing in "school-aged interventions" into Google Scholar, National Bureau of Economic Research, and JSTOR. From the (much larger) original list, we narrowed our focus to those programs that contained credible identification.

Table 17 School-age interventions to increase achievement.

Program	Grades treated	Treatment	Impact	Study
Career Academies	9th–12th	Small school model that combines academic and technical curricula and provides students with work-based learning opportunities	Eleven percent higher earnings per year (ages 18–27)	Kemple (2008)
Comer School Development Program	K–12th	Whole-school reform model that aims to improve intraschool relations and climate in order to improve academic achievement.	No achievement effects (7th–8th grades)	Cook et al. (1999)
Experience Corps	1st–3rd	This program trains older adults (55+) to tutor and mentor elementary school children who are at risk of academic failure.	0.13 standard deviation on reading comprehension; 0.16 standard deviation on general reading skills	Morrow-Howell et al. (2009)
Language Essentials for Teachers of Reading and Spelling (LETRS)	K–12th	Teachers received professional development during the summer and following school year focused around the LETRS model of language instruction	No significant impact (2nd grade)	Garet et al. (2008)
Learnfare	7th–12th	This conditional cash transfer program sanctions a family's welfare grant if teenagers in the family do not meet required school attendance goals.	Increased school enrollment and attendance (ages 13–19)	Dee (2009)

(continued on next page)

Table 17 (continued)

Program	Grades treated	Treatment	Impact	Study
Mastery Learning	K–12th	This group-based, teacher-paced instructional model requires that students master a particular objective before moving to a new objective. Students are evaluated on absolute scales as opposed to norm-referenced scales.	0.78 standard deviations on achievement tests (on average)	Guskey and Gates (1985)
National Guard Youth ChalleNGe Program	10th–12th	This 17-month program for high school dropouts has residential and post-residential phases. The residential phase provides students with a highly structured "quasi-military" experience and the post-residential phase provides students with mentoring.	Increased percentage earned a high school diploma or GED within 9 months	Bloom et al. (2009)
NYC Voucher Program	K–4th	This program provided low-income students in NYC with vouchers worth up to $1400 per year for three years to attend private schools.	No significant impact	Krueger and Zhu (2002)
Project CRISS	4th–12th	This teacher professional development model aims to give teachers more effective strategies for teaching reading and writing that focus on student-owned reading strategies.	No significant impact (5th grade)	James-Burdumy et al. (2009)

Table 17 (continued)

Program	Grades treated	Treatment	Impact	Study
Quantum Opportunity Program	9th–12th	This program had high school students participate in 250 hours of educational services, 250 hours of development activities, and 250 hours of community service and provided students with financial incentives.	Thirty-three percent more graduated from high school	Taggart (1995)
Seattle Social Development Project	1st–6th	Teachers received training to allow them to teach elementary school students social skills focused around problem-solving in conflict resolution.	No reported achievement outcomes	Hawkins et al. (2008)
Self-affirmation essay writing	7th–8th	Students were given structured writing assignments that required them to write about their personal values and the importance of those values.	0.24 standard deviations on GPA for black students; 0.41 standard deviations on GPA for low-achieving black students	Cohen et al. (2009)
Success for All	K–5th	This program is a school-wide program that focuses on early detection of and intervention around reading problems using a ability-level reading group instruction.	0.36 standard deviations on phonemic awareness; 0.24 standard deviations on word identification; 0.21 standard deviations on passage comprehension (2nd grade)	Borman et al. (2007)
Summer Training and Education Program (STEP)	9th–10th	This program provided summer reading and math remediation along with life skills instruction to academically struggling low-income students.	No long-term impact (ages 14–15)	Walker and Vilella-Velez (1992)

(continued on next page)

Table 17 (continued)

Program	Grades treated	Treatment	Impact	Study
Supplemental reading instruction	9th	Students who were two to five years below grade level in reading were provided with full-year supplemental literacy courses that provided an average of eleven hours per month of supplemental instruction.	0.08 standard deviations on reading comprehension	Corrin et al. (2009)
Talent Development High School	9th–12th	This comprehensive school reform model aims to establish a positive school climate and prepare all students academically for college. Two key features are the ninth-grade academy and upper grade career academies.	No significant impact on standardized tests	Kemple et al. (2005)
US Department of Education Student Mentoring Program	4th–8th	Students were matched with adult or peer mentors with whom they met weekly for six months to discuss academics, relationships, and future plans.	No significant impact	Bernstein et al. (2009)

The set of interventions included in this table were generated using a two-step search process. First, a keyword search for for "school-aged interventions" was performed in Google Scholar, JSTOR, and the National Bureau of Economic Research database. Second, we examined all of the available reports for the appropriate age groups from the What Works Clearinghouse of IES. From the original list, we narrowed our focus to those programs that contained credible identification and were large enough in scale to possibly impact achievement gaps overall.

instructional model that is based on the idea that students must attain a level of mastery on a particular objective before moving on to a new objective. Guskey and Gates (1985) perform a meta-analysis of thirty-five studies on this instructional strategy and find that the average achievement effect size from mastery learning programs was 0.78 standard deviations. The effect sizes from within individual studies, however, ranged from 0.02 to 1.70 and varied significantly depending on the age of the students and the subject tested (Guskey and Gates, 1985).

Success for All is a school-level elementary school intervention that focuses on improving literacy outcomes for all students in order to improve overall student achievement that is currently used in 1200 schools across the country (Borman et al., 2007). The program is designed to identify and address deficiencies in reading skills at a young age using a variety of instruction strategies, ranging from cooperative learning to data-driven instruction. Borman et al. (2007) use a cluster randomized trial design to evaluate the impacts of the Success for All model on student achievement. Forty-one schools from eleven states volunteered and were randomly assigned to either the treatment or control groups. Borman et al. (2007) find that Success for All increased student achievement by 0.36 standard deviations on phonemic awareness, 0.24 standard deviations on word identification, and 0.21 standard deviations on passage comprehension.

The self-affirmation essay writing intervention was intended specifically to improve the academic achievement of minorities by reducing the impact of stereotype threat. Seventh grade students were randomly assigned to either a treatment or control group. Both groups were given structured writing assignments three to five times over the course of two school years, but the treatment group was instructed to write about their personal values and why they were important, while the control group was given neutral essay topics. Cohen et al. (2009) find that for black students, this intervention increased GPA by 0.24 points and that the impact was even greater for low-achieving black students (0.41 GPA points). They also find that the program reduced the probability of being placed in remedial classes or being retained in a grade for low-achieving black students. It is unclear what the general equilibrium effects of such psychological interventions are.

Despite trillions spent, there is not one urban school district that has ever closed the racial achievement gap. Figures 5 and 6 show the achievement gap in percentage of students proficient for their grade level across eleven major US cities who participate in the National Assessment of Educational Progress (NAEP)—a nationally representative set of assessments administered every two years to fourth, eighth, and twelfth graders that covers various subject areas, including mathematics and reading.[48]

---

[48] Individual schools are first selected for participation in NAEP in order to ensure that the assessments are nationally representative, and then students are randomly selected from within those schools. Both schools and students have the option to not participate in the assessments. Tests are given in multiple subject areas in a given school in one sitting, with different students taking different assessments. Assessments are conducted between the last week of January and the first week in March every year. The same assessment is given to all students within a subject and a grade during a given administration.

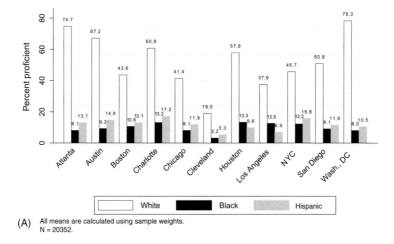

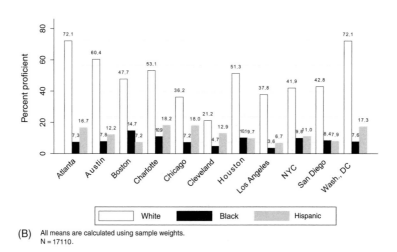

Figure 5 *(A) NAEP 2007 proficiency levels by city and race: 4th grade reading. (B) NAEP 2007 proficiency levels by city and race: 8th grade reading.*

In every city there are large racial differences. In the Trial Urban District Assessment, among fourth graders, 43.2% of whites, 12% of blacks, and 16% of Hispanics are proficient in reading. In math, these numbers are 50.9, 14, and 20.9, respectively. Similarly, among eighth graders, 40.4% of whites, 10.6% of blacks, and 13.2% of Hispanics score proficient in reading. Math scores exhibit similarly marked racial differences. Washington, DC, has the largest achievement gap of participating cities in NAEP; there is a roughly seventy percent difference between blacks and whites on both subjects and both grade levels. At the other end of the spectrum, Cleveland has the

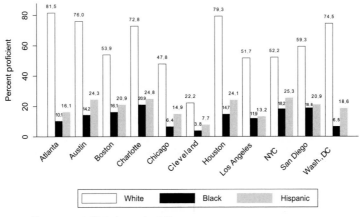

(A) All means are calculated using sample weights.
N = 21440.

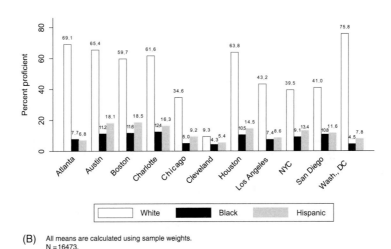

(B) All means are calculated using sample weights.
N = 16473.

Figure 6 *(A) NAEP 2007 proficiency levels by city and race: 4th grade math. (B) NAEP 2007 proficiency levels by city and race: 8th grade math.*

smallest achievement gap—less than seventeen percentage points separate racial groups. Unfortunately, Cleveland's success in closing the achievement gap is mainly due to the dismal performance of whites in the school district and not due to increased performance of black students. Remarkably, there is very little variance in the achievement of minority students across NAEP districts. There is not one school district in NAEP in which more than twenty-one percent of black students are proficient in reading or math.

The lack of progress has fed into a long-standing and rancorous debate among scholars, policymakers, and practitioners as to whether schools alone can close the achievement gap, or whether the issues children bring to school as a result of being reared in poverty are too much for even the best educators to overcome. Proponents of the school-centered approach refer to anecdotes of excellence in particular schools or examples of other countries where poor children in superior schools outperform average Americans (Chenoweth, 2007). Advocates of the community-focused approach argue that teachers and school administrators are dealing with issues that actually originate outside the classroom, citing research that shows racial and socioeconomic achievement gaps are formed before children ever enter school (Fryer and Levitt, 2004, 2006) and that one-third to one-half of the gap can be explained by family-environment indicators (Phillips et al., 1998a,b; Fryer and Levitt, 2004).[49] In this scenario, combating poverty and related social ills directly and having more constructive out-of-school time may lead to better and more focused instruction in school. Indeed, Coleman et al. (1966), in their famous report on equality of educational opportunity, argue that schools alone cannot solve the problem of chronic underachievement in urban schools.

The Harlem Children's Zone (HCZ)—a 97-block area in central Harlem, New York, that combines reform-minded charter schools with a web of community services designed to ensure the social environment outside of school is positive and supportive for children from birth to college graduation—provides an extremely rare opportunity to understand whether communities, schools, or a combination of the two are the main drivers of student achievement.

Dobbie and Fryer (2009) use two separate statistical strategies to estimate the causal impact of attending the charter schools in the HCZ. First, they exploit the fact that HCZ charter schools are required to select students by lottery when the number of applicants exceeds the number of available slots for admission. In this scenario, the treatment group is composed of students who are lottery winners and the control group consists of students who are lottery losers. The second identification strategy explored in Dobbie and Fryer (2009) uses the interaction between a student's home address and her cohort year as an instrumental variable. This approach takes advantage of two important features of the HCZ charter schools: (1) anyone is eligible to enroll in HCZ's schools, but only students living inside the Zone are actively recruited by HCZ staff; and (2) there are cohorts of children that are ineligible due to the timing of the schools' opening and their age. Both statistical approaches lead to the same result: HCZ charter schools are effective at increasing the achievement of the poorest minority children.

Figure 7A and B provide a visual representation of the basic results from Dobbie and Fryer (2009). Figure 7A plots yearly, raw, mean state math test scores, from fourth to

---

[49] The debate over communities or schools often seems to treat these approaches as mutually exclusive, evaluating policies that change one aspect of the schools or a student's learning environment. This approach is potentially informative on the various partial derivatives of the educational production function but is uninformative on the net effect of many simultaneous changes. The educational production function may, for example, exhibit either positive or negative interactions with respect to various reforms. Smaller classes and more time-on-task matter more (or less) if the student has good teachers; good teachers may matter more (or less) if the student has a good out-of-school environment, and so on.

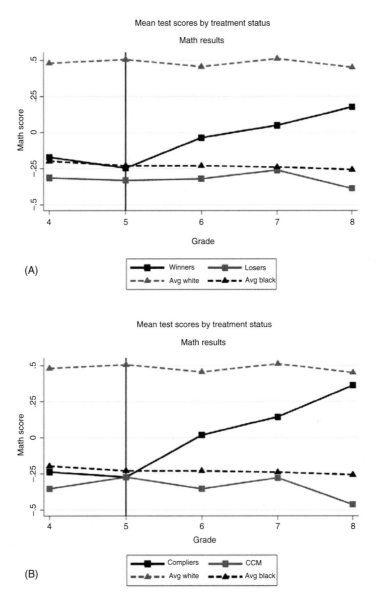

Figure 7 *Student achievement in HCZ-math. (A) Reduced Form result. (B) TOT results.* Notes: Lottery winners are students who receive a winning lottery number or who are in the top ten of the waitlist. Test scores are standardized by grade to have mean zero and standard deviation one in the entire New York City sample. The CCM is the estimated test score for those in the control group who would have complied if they had received a winning lottery number.

eighth grade, for four subgroups: lottery winners, lottery losers, white students in New York City public schools and black students in New York City public schools. Lottery winners are comprised of students who either won the lottery or who had a sibling who was already enrolled in the HCZ Promise Academy. Lottery losers are individuals who lost the lottery and did not have a sibling already enrolled. These represent reduced form estimates.

In fourth and fifth grade, before they enter the middle school, math test scores for lottery winners, losers, and the typical black student in New York City are virtually identical, and roughly 0.75 standard deviations behind the typical white student.[50] Lottery winners have a modest increase in sixth grade, followed by a more substantial increase in seventh grade and even larger gains by their eighth-grade year.

The "Treatment-on-Treated" (TOT) estimate, which is the effect of actually attending the HCZ charter school, is depicted in Panel B of Fig. 7. The TOT results follow a similar pattern, showing remarkable convergence between children in the middle school and the average white student in New York City. After three years of "treatment," HCZ Promise Academy students have nearly closed the achievement gap in math—they are behind their white counterparts by 0.121 standard deviations (p-value $= 0.113$). If one adjusts for gender and free lunch, the typical eighth grader enrolled in the HCZ middle school outscores the typical white eighth grader in New York City public schools by 0.087 standard deviations, though the difference is not statistically significant (p-value $= 0.238$).

Figure 8A plots yearly state ELA test scores, from fourth to eighth grade. Treatment and control designations are identical to those in Fig. 7A. In fourth and fifth grades, before they enter the middle school, ELA scores for lottery winners, losers, and the typical black student in NYC are not statistically different, and are roughly 0.65 standard deviations behind the typical white student.[51] Lottery winners and losers have very similar ELA scores from fourth through seventh grade. In eighth grade, HCZ charter students distance themselves from the control group. These results are statistically meaningful, but much less so than the math results. The TOT estimate, depicted in Panel B of Fig. 8, follows an identical pattern with marginally larger differences between enrolled middle-school students and the control group. Adjusting for gender and free lunch pushes the results in the expected direction.[52]

---

[50] This is similar in magnitude to the math racial achievement gap in nationally representative samples [0.082 in Fryer and Levitt (2006) and 0.763 in Campbell et al. (2000)].

[51] This is smaller than the reading racial achievement gap in some nationally representative samples [0.771 in Fryer and Levitt (2006) and 0.960 in Campbell et al. (2000)].

[52] Interventions in education often have larger impacts on math scores compared to reading or ELA scores (Decker et al., 2004; Rockoff, 2004; Jacob, 2005). This may be because it is relatively easier to teach math skills, or because reading skills are more likely to be learned outside of school. Another explanation is that language and vocabulary skills may develop early in life, making it difficult to impact reading scores in adolescence (Hart and Risley, 1995; Nelson, 2000).

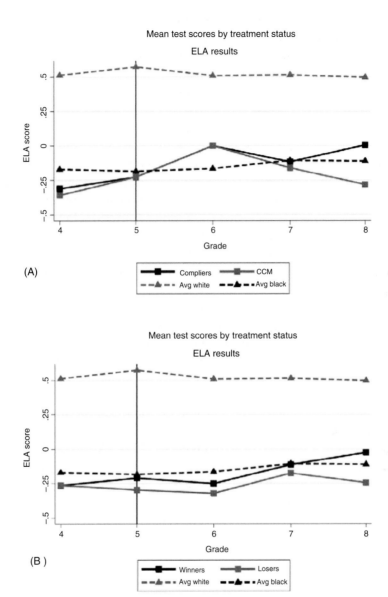

Figure 8   *Student achievement in HCZ-ELA. (A) Reduced Form Results. (B) TOT Results.* Notes: Lottery winners are students who receive a winning lottery number or who are in the top ten of the waitlist. Test scores are standardized by grade to have mean zero and standard deviation one in the entire New York City sample. The CCM is the estimated test score for those in the control group who would have complied if they had received a winning lottery number.

7.1. What do the results from HCZ tell us about interventions to close the achievement gap?

There are six pieces of evidence that, taken together, suggest schools alone can dramatically increase the achievement of the poorest minority students—other community and broader investments may not be necessary. First, Dobbie and Fryer (2009) find no correlation between participation in community programs and academic achievement. Second, the IV strategy described above compares children inside the Zone's boundaries relative to other children in the Zone who were ineligible for the lottery, so the estimates are purged of the community bundle. Recall that IV estimates are larger than the lottery estimates, however, suggesting that communities alone are not the answer. Third, Dobbie and Fryer (2009) report that children inside the Zone garnered the same benefit from the schools as those outside the Zone, suggesting that proximity to the community programs is unimportant. Fourth, siblings of HCZ students who are in regular public schools, but likely have better-than-average access and information about HCZ community programs, have marginally lower absence rates but their achievement is unchanged (Dobbie and Fryer, 2009).

The final two pieces of evidence are taken from interventions outside of HCZ. The Moving to Opportunity experiment, which relocated individuals from high-poverty to low-poverty neighborhoods while keeping the quality of schools roughly constant, showed small positive results for girls and negative results for boys (Sanbonmatsu et al., 2006; Kling et al., 2007). This suggests that a better community, as measured by poverty rate, does not significantly raise test scores if school quality remains essentially unchanged.

The last pieces of evidence stem from the rise of a new literature on the impact of charter schools on achievement. While the bulk of the evidence finds only modest success (Hanushek et al., 2005; Hoxby and Rockoff, 2004; Hoxby and Murarka, 2009), there are growing examples of success that is similar to that achieved in HCZ—without community or broader investments. The Knowledge is Power Program (KIPP) is the nation's largest network of charter schools. Anecdotally, they perform at least as well as students from HCZ on New York state assessments.[53] Angrist et al. (2010) perform the first quasi-experimental analysis of a KIPP school, finding large impacts on achievement. The magnitude of the gains are strikingly similar to those in HCZ. Figure 9 plots the reduced form effect of attending KIPP in Lynn, Massachusetts. Similar to the results of KIPP, Abdulkadiroglu et al. (2009) find that students enrolled in oversubscribed Boston charter schools with organized lottery files gain about 0.17 standard deviations per year in ELA and 0.53 standard deviations per year in math.[54]

---

[53] On the New York state assessments in the 2008-09 school year, KIPP charter schools had student pass rates that were at least as high as those at the HCZ Promise Academy. This information can be accessed through the New York State Report Cards at https://www.nystart.gov/publicweb/CharterSchool.do?year=2008.

[54] However, the typical middle school applicant in Abdulkadiroglu et al. (2009) starts 0.286 and 0.348 standard deviations higher in fourth grade math and reading than the typical Boston student, and the typical high school applicant starts 0.380 standard deviations higher on both eighth grade math and reading tests.

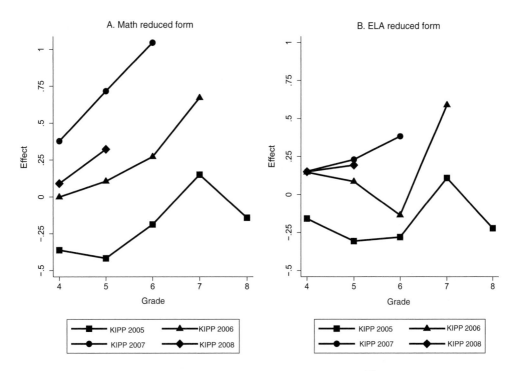

Figure 9   Student achievement in KIPP Lynn. [55]

8. CONCLUSION

In 1908, W.E.B Dubois famously noted that "the problem of the 20th century is the problem of the color line." America has undergone drastic changes in 102 years. The problem of the 21st century is the problem of the skill gap. As this chapter attempts to make clear, eliminating the racial skill gap will likely have important impacts on income inequality, unemployment, incarceration, health, and other important social and economic indices. The problem, to date, is that we do not know how to close the achievement gap.

Yet, there is room for considerable optimism. A key difference between what we know now and what we knew even two years ago lies in a series of "existence proofs" in which poor black and Hispanic students score on par with more affluent white students. That is, we now know that with some combination of investments, high achievement is possible for all students. That is an important step forward. Of course, there are many questions as to how one can use these examples to direct interventions that have the potential to close the achievement gap writ large.[56] An economist's solution might be to

---

[55] Thanks to Josh Angrist for providing his data to construct this figure.

[56] See Curto et al. (2010) for more discussion on caveats to taking strategies from charter schools to scale.

create a market for gap-closing schools with high-powered incentives for entrepreneurs to enter. The government's role would not be to facilitate the daily workings of the schools; it would simply fund those schools that close the achievement gap and withhold funds from those that do not. The non-gap-closing schools would go out of business and would be replaced by others that are more capable. In a rough sense, this is what is happening in Louisiana post-Hurricane Katrina, what cities such as Boston claim to do, and what reform-minded school leaders such as Chancellor Joel Klein in New York City have been trying accomplish within the constraints of the public system.

A second, potentially more politically expedient, way forward is to try and understand what makes some schools productive and others not. Hoxby and Murarka (2009) and Abdulkadiroglu et al. (2009) show that there is substantial variance in the treatment effect of charter schools—even though all are free from most constraints of the public system and the vast majority do not have staffs under collective bargaining agreements. Investigating this variance and its causes could reveal important clues about measures that could be taken to close the racial achievement gap.

Independent of how we get there, closing the racial achievement gap is the most important civil rights battle of the twenty-first century.

APPENDIX. DATA DESCRIPTION
A.1. National Longitudinal Survey of Youth 1979 (NLSY79)

The National Longitudinal Survey of Youth, 1979 Cohort (NLSY79) is a panel data set with data from 12,686 individuals born between 1957 and 1964 who were first surveyed in 1979 when they were between the ages of 14 and 22. The survey consists of a nationally representative cross-section sample as well as a supplemental over-sample of blacks, Hispanics, and low-income whites. In our analysis, we include only the nationally representative cross-section and the over-samples of blacks and Hispanics. We drop 2923 people from the military and low-income white oversamples and 4 more who have invalid birth years (before 1957 or after 1964). The 5386 individuals who were born before 1962 are also not included in our analysis.

AFQT score

The Armed Forces Qualification Test (AFQT) is a subset of four tests given as part of the Armed Services Vocational Aptitude Battery (ASVAB). AFQT scores as reported in the 1981 survey year are used. Scores for an individual were considered missing if problems were reported, if the procedures for the test were altered, or if no scores are reported (either valid or invalid skip) on the relevant ASVAB subtests.

The AFQT score is the sum of the arithmetic reasoning score, the mathematics knowledge score, and two times the verbal composite score. This composite score is then standardized by year of birth (in order to account for natural score differences arising because of differences in age when the test was taken) and then across the whole sample, excluding those with missing AFQT scores.

Table A.1 National Longitudinal Survey of Youth (NLSY79) summary statistics.

	Full sample	White	Black	Hispanic
White	0.495 (0.500)	—	—	—
Black	0.303 (0.460)	—	—	—
Hispanic	0.201 (0.401)	—	—	—
Female	0.488 (0.500)	0.475 (0.500)	0.492 (0.500)	0.512 (0.500)
Age	43.080 (0.802)	43.082 (0.811)	43.087 (0.803)	43.067 (0.780)
Wage (dollars per hour)	20.079 (14.267)	22.397 (15.623)	16.450 (11.117)	19.462 (13.561)
Invalid or missing wage	0.431 (0.495)	0.411 (0.492)	0.447 (0.497)	0.456 (0.498)
Unemployed	0.038 (0.191)	0.022 (0.146)	0.059 (0.235)	0.046 (0.210)
Ever incarcerated	0.075 (0.263)	0.044 (0.206)	0.115 (0.320)	0.090 (0.286)
Physical component score	−0.010 (1.014)	0.061 (0.970)	−0.134 (1.117)	0.007 (0.933)
Family income (units of $10k)	16.351 (12.300)	20.691 (13.124)	11.332 (9.377)	13.475 (10.259)
Mother: high school graduate	0.558 (0.497)	0.728 (0.445)	0.457 (0.498)	0.280 (0.449)
Mother: college graduate	0.076 (0.265)	0.109 (0.311)	0.049 (0.217)	0.033 (0.179)
Father: high school graduate	0.586 (0.493)	0.712 (0.453)	0.489 (0.500)	0.362 (0.481)
Father: college graduate	0.137 (0.343)	0.196 (0.397)	0.063 (0.243)	0.070 (0.256)
Mother: professional occupation	0.084 (0.277)	0.102 (0.303)	0.073 (0.260)	0.055 (0.228)
Father: professional occupation	0.227 (0.419)	0.311 (0.463)	0.084 (0.277)	0.122 (0.328)
Mother: works 35+ hours per week	0.405 (0.491)	0.403 (0.491)	0.444 (0.497)	0.352 (0.478)
Number of siblings	3.710 (2.580)	2.948 (1.955)	4.521 (2.923)	4.367 (2.822)
No reading materials	0.110 (0.312)	0.036 (0.186)	0.174 (0.379)	0.195 (0.396)
Numerous reading materials	0.391 (0.488)	0.544 (0.498)	0.230 (0.421)	0.254 (0.436)
Student/teacher ratio	19.729 (7.850)	19.011 (4.494)	20.161 (9.146)	21.260 (12.271)
Disadvantaged student ratio	25.000 (24.310)	16.485 (17.204)	37.192 (27.773)	32.364 (26.776)
Dropout rate	19.138 (25.557)	15.504 (24.214)	23.435 (27.284)	23.918 (25.111)
Teacher turnover rate	6.937 (8.317)	6.508 (7.584)	6.957 (8.247)	8.241 (10.261)

(continued on next page)

Table A.1 (continued)

	Full sample	White	Black	Hispanic
Private school	0.052 (0.222)	0.065 (0.247)	0.031 (0.172)	0.050 (0.218)
Percentage black in school faculty	11.902 (19.550)	4.267 (8.974)	31.625 (25.554)	5.705 (10.068)
Std. AFQT score	−0.000 (0.961)	0.456 (0.879)	−0.555 (0.769)	−0.283 (0.859)
Missing AFQT score	0.050 (0.218)	0.050 (0.218)	0.039 (0.194)	0.068 (0.252)
Missing income	0.040 (0.195)	0.051 (0.221)	0.032 (0.177)	0.022 (0.146)
Missing mother's education	0.064 (0.245)	0.048 (0.213)	0.087 (0.281)	0.072 (0.258)
Missing father's education	0.157 (0.364)	0.076 (0.266)	0.274 (0.446)	0.181 (0.385)
Missing mother's occupation	0.477 (0.500)	0.470 (0.499)	0.444 (0.497)	0.544 (0.498)
Missing father's occupation	0.338 (0.473)	0.205 (0.404)	0.533 (0.499)	0.373 (0.484)
Missing mother work hours	0.029 (0.167)	0.026 (0.159)	0.036 (0.186)	0.026 (0.158)
Missing reading materials information	0.006 (0.080)	0.004 (0.064)	0.006 (0.077)	0.013 (0.113)
Missing student/teacher ratio	0.363 (0.481)	0.296 (0.457)	0.428 (0.495)	0.430 (0.495)
Missing disadvantaged student ratio	0.429 (0.495)	0.371 (0.483)	0.492 (0.500)	0.476 (0.500)
Missing dropout rate	0.362 (0.481)	0.289 (0.453)	0.423 (0.494)	0.451 (0.498)
Missing teacher turnover rate	0.343 (0.475)	0.262 (0.440)	0.424 (0.494)	0.416 (0.493)
Missing percentage black in school faculty	0.333 (0.471)	0.261 (0.440)	0.407 (0.492)	0.397 (0.490)
Obs.	3883	1924	1178	781

The variable $AFQT^2$ is simply constructed by squaring the standardized AFQT score.

Age

In order to determine an individual's age, we use the person's year of birth. The birth year given in 1981 (the year participants took the AFQT) is used if available; otherwise the year of birth given at the beginning of the data collection in 1979 is used. Those who report birth years earlier than 1957 or later than 1964 are dropped from our sample, as these birth years do not fit into the reported age range of the survey.

Additionally, those who were born after 1961 were excluded from analyses. Those born in 1961 or earlier were at least 18 at the time of taking the AFQT and therefore were more likely to have already entered the labor force, which introduces the potential for bias in using AFQT to measure achievement. See Neal and Johnson (1996) for a full explanation.

Ever incarcerated

In order to construct this variable, we use the fact that the residence of a respondent is recorded each time they are surveyed. One of the categories for type of residence is "jail". Therefore, the variable "ever incarcerated" is equal to one if for any year of the survey the individual's type of residence was "jail". We also include in our measure those who were not incarcerated at any point during the survey but who had been sentenced to a corrective facility before the initial 1979 survey.

Family income

To construct family income, we use the total net family income variables from 1979, 1980, and 1981. We convert all incomes into 1979 dollars, and then use the most recent income available.

Numerous reading materials

We classify a person as having "numerous reading materials" if they had magazines, newspapers, and a library card present in their home environment at age 14.

Parent occupation

To construct the dummies for having a mother (father) with a professional occupation, we use the variable which gives the occupational code of the adult female (male) present in the household at age 14. We classify mothers (fathers) as professionals if they have occupational codes between 1 and 245. This corresponds to the following two occupational categories: professional, technical, and kindred; and managers, officials, and proprietors.

Physical health component score

This variable is constructed within the data set using the questions asked by the SF-12 portion of the 2006 administration of the surveys. For the analysis, the physical component score (PCS) is standardized across all individuals for whom a score is available. Those without a valid PCS are not included in the analysis.

Race

A person's race is coded using a set of mutually exclusive dummy variables from the racial/ethnic cohort of the individual from the screener. Individuals are given a value of one in one of the three dummy variables—white, black, or Hispanic. All respondents have a value for this race measure.

Sex

A person's sex was coded as a dummy variable equal to one if the person is male and zero if the person is female. Preference was given for the reported sex in 1982; if this was unavailable, the sex reported in 1979 was used.

Unemployed

The variable "unemployed" is a binary variable that is equal to one if the person's employment status states that they are unemployed. Those whose employment status states that they are not in the labor force are excluded from labor force participation analyses.

Wage

Job and wage information are given for up to five jobs per person in 2006, which was the latest year for which published survey results were available. The data contains the hourly compensation and the number of hours worked for each of these jobs, as well as an indicator variable to determine whether each particular job is a current job. The hourly wage from all current jobs is weighted by the number of hours worked at that job in order to determine an individual's overall hourly wage.

Neal and Johnson (1996) considered wage reports invalid if they were over $75. We do the same, but adjust this amount for inflation; therefore, wages over $115 (the 2006 equivalent of $75 in 1990) are considered to be invalid. Wage is also considered to be missing/invalid if the individual does not have a valid job class for any of the five possible jobs. Individuals with invalid or missing wages are not included in the wage regressions, which use the log of the wage measure as the dependent variable.

A.2. National Longitudinal Survey of Youth 1997 (NLSY97)

The National Longitudinal Survey of Youth, 1997 Cohort (NLSY97) is a panel data set with data from approximately 9000 individuals born between 1980 and 1984 who were first surveyed in 1997 when they were between the ages of 13 and 17.

AFQT score

The Armed Forces Qualification Test (AFQT) is a subset of four tests given as part of the Armed Services Vocational Aptitude Battery (ASVAB). In the NLSY97 data set, an ASVAB math-verbal percent score was constructed. The NLS staff states that the formula they used to construct this score is similar to the AFQT score created by the Department of Defense for the NLSY79, but that it is not the official AFQT score.

The AFQT percentile score created by the NLS was standardized by student age within three-month birth cohorts. We then standardized the scores across the entire sample of valid test scores.

The variable $AFQT^2$ is simply constructed by squaring the standardized AFQT score.

Age

Because wage information was collected in either 2006 or 2007 (discussed below), the age variable needed to be from the year in which the wage data was collected. The age variable was constructed first as two separate age variables—the person's age in 2006 and the person's age in 2007—using the person's birth year as reported in the baseline (1997) survey. The two age variables are then combined, with the age assigned to be the one from the year in which the wage was collected.

All age cohorts were included in the labor force analyses. Because participants were younger during the baseline year of the survey when the AFQT data were collected—all were under the age of 18—they were unlikely to have entered the labor force yet.

Ever incarcerated

In the NLSY97, during each yearly administration of the survey, individuals are asked what their sentence was for any arrests (up to 9 arrests are asked about). Individuals who reported that they were sentenced to "jail", an "adult corrections institution", or a "juvenile corrections institution" for any arrest in any of the surveys were given a value of one for this variable; otherwise this variable was coded as zero.

Race

A person's race is coded using a set of mutually exclusive dummy variables from the racial/ethnic cohort of the individual from the screener. Individuals are given a value of one in one of the four dummy variables—white, black, Hispanic, or mixed race. All respondents have a value for this race measure.

Sex

A person's sex was coded as a dummy variable equal to one if the person is male and zero if the person is female.

Unemployed

The variable "unemployed" is a binary variable that is equal to one if the person's employment status states that they are unemployed. Those whose employment status states that they are not in the labor force are excluded from labor force participation analyses.

Wage

Jobs and wage information is given for up to 9 jobs in 2007 and up to 8 jobs in 2007. We are given the hourly compensation and the number of hours worked for each of these

Table A.2 National Longitudinal Survey of Youth 1997 (NLSY97) summary statistics.

	All races	White	Black	Hispanic	Mixed race
White	0.519 (0.500)	—	—	—	—
Black	0.260 (0.439)	—	—	—	—
Hispanic	0.212 (0.408)	—	—	—	—
Mixed race	0.009 (0.096)	—	—	—	—
Male	0.512 (0.500)	0.517 (0.500)	0.501 (0.500)	0.514 (0.500)	0.482 (0.503)
Age	24.861 (1.442)	24.850 (1.437)	24.904 (1.446)	24.837 (1.447)	24.843 (1.444)
AFQT (standardized)	0.000 (1.000)	0.381 (0.947)	−0.570 (0.816)	−0.337 (0.882)	0.309 (1.009)
Missing AFQT score	0.210 (0.408)	0.173 (0.379)	0.226 (0.418)	0.285 (0.451)	0.169 (0.377)
Wage (dollars per hour)	14.994 (10.201)	15.843 (10.553)	13.306 (9.427)	14.829 (9.902)	15.461 (11.050)
Invalid or missing wage	0.278 (0.448)	0.267 (0.442)	0.316 (0.465)	0.258 (0.438)	0.337 (0.476)
Unemployed	0.066 (0.249)	0.045 (0.208)	0.111 (0.315)	0.062 (0.240)	0.084 (0.280)
Ever incarcerated	0.077 (0.266)	0.059 (0.235)	0.107 (0.310)	0.082 (0.274)	0.108 (0.313)
Obs.	8984	4665	2335	1901	83

jobs, as well as a variable to determine whether each particular job is a current job. The hourly wage from all current jobs is weighted by the number of hours worked at that job in order to determine an individual's overall hourly wage.

Once again, wages over $115 in 2006 and $119 in 2007 (the equivalent of $75 in 1990) are considered to be invalid. Wage is also considered to be missing/invalid if the individual does not have a valid job class for any of the possible jobs. Individuals with invalid or missing wages are not included in the wage regressions, which use the log of the wage measure as the dependent variable.

Wage in 2007 is converted to 2006 dollars so that the two wage measures are comparable. We use the 2007 wage measure for any individuals for whom it is available; otherwise, we use the 2006 wage measure.

A.3. College & Beyond, 1976 Cohort (C&B)

The College and Beyond Database contains data on 93,660 full-time students who entered thirty-four colleges and universities in the fall of 1951, 1976, or 1989. For this analysis, we focus on the cohort from 1976. The C&B data contain information drawn from students' applications and transcripts, SAT and ACT scores, as well as information on family demographics and socioeconomic status. The C&B database also includes responses to a survey administered in 1996 to all three cohorts that provides detailed information on post-college labor market outcomes. The response rate to the 1996 survey was approximately 80%.

Income

Income information is reported as fitting into one of a series of income ranges, but these ranges were different in the 1995 and 1996 surveys. For all the possible ranges in each survey year, the individual's income was assigned to the midpoint of the range (i.e. $40,000 for the $30,000-50,000 range); for less than $10,000, income was assigned to be $5000 (1995 survey). Income less than $1000 income was assigned to be missing because an individual could not have made this sum of money working full-time (1996 survey). For more than $200,000, income was assigned to be $250,000. If available, income reported for 1995 (the 1996 survey) was used; otherwise 1994 annual income (collected in 1995) was used. Individuals with invalid or missing wages are not included in the income regressions, which use the log of the income measure as the dependent variable.

Race

A person's race is coded using a set of mutually exclusive dummy variables from the racial/ethnic cohort of the individual from the screener. Individuals are given a value of one in one of the five dummy variables—white, black, Hispanic, other race, or missing the race variable.

Table A.3 College & Beyond, 1976 summary statistics.

	All races	White	Black	Hispanic	Other
White	0.828 (0.377)	—	—	—	—
Black	0.055 (0.229)	—	—	—	—
Hispanic	0.017 (0.128)	—	—	—	—
Other race	0.029 (0.169)	—	—	—	—
Missing race	0.070 (0.256)	—	—	—	—
Male	0.520 (0.500)	0.540 (0.498)	0.440 (0.497)	0.590 (0.492)	0.527 (0.500)
SAT	1175.890 (169.458)	1193.165 (157.052)	968.985 (181.716)	1077.122 (179.830)	1181.394 (172.493)
Annual income (units of $10K)	7.720 (6.309)	7.918 (6.442)	6.298 (4.730)	7.753 (6.368)	9.298 (6.787)
Unemployed	0.001 (0.034)	0.001 (0.035)	0.001 (0.033)	0.000 (0.000)	0.000 (0.000)
Out of labor force	0.046 (0.209)	0.050 (0.218)	0.011 (0.103)	0.041 (0.198)	0.032 (0.177)
Missing SAT score	0.080 (0.272)	0.040 (0.196)	0.042 (0.200)	0.039 (0.194)	0.062 (0.242)
Missing income	0.376 (0.484)	0.370 (0.483)	0.432 (0.495)	0.488 (0.500)	0.438 (0.496)
Obs.	33,778	27,975	1871	561	994

SAT score

The SAT score of an individual is coded as the true value of the combined math and verbal scores, with possible scores ranging between 400 (200 per section) and 1600 (800 per section). Individuals with missing scores are assigned a score of zero and are accounted for using a missing score dummy variable. The square of SAT score was also included in regressions that controlled for educational achievement.

Sex

A person's sex was coded as a dummy variable equal to one if the person is male and zero if the person is female.

Unemployed

Determining who was unemployed in this data set required a few steps. First, we had to determine who was not working at the time of the survey. This is coded within two variables, one for each survey (1995 and 1996). If an individual reports that they are not working because they are retired or for another reason, we then consider a later question, where they are asked about any times at which they were out of work for 6 months or longer. For those people who stated that they were not currently working, we considered any period of time that included the year of the survey in which they stated they were not working. We then considered the reason they gave for being out of work during that period. If the person stated that they were retired, a student, had family responsibilities, had a chronic illness, or did not need/want to work, we considered them out of the labor force. If a person was not out of the labor force but was not currently working because they were laid off or suitable work was not available, we considered that individual unemployed. Because only 39 people from the entire sample could be considered unemployed, we did not perform analyses using this variable.

A.4. Early Childhood Longitudinal Study, Birth Cohort (ECLS-B)

The Early Childhood Longitudinal Study, Birth Cohort (ECLS-B) is a nationally representative sample of over 10,000 children born in 2001. The first wave of data collection was performed when most of the children were between eight and twelve months of age. The second wave interviewed the same set of children around their second birthday; the third wave was conducted when the children were of preschool age (approximately 4 years old). The data set includes an extensive array of information from parent surveys, interviewer observation or parent-child interactions, and mental and motor proficiency tests. Further details on the study design and data collection methods are available at the ECLS website (http://nces.ed.gov/ecls).

From the total sample, 556 children had no mental ability test score in the first wave. Test scores are missing for an additional 1326 children in the second wave and 1338 children in the third wave. All subjects with missing test scores are dropped from the

Table A.4 Early Childhood Longitudinal Study—Birth cohort (ECLS-B) summary statistics.

	Full sample	White	Black	Hispanic	Asian	Other
White	0.562 (0.496)	—	—	—	—	—
Black	0.142 (0.349)	—	—	—	—	—
Hispanic	0.225 (0.418)	—	—	—	—	—
Asian	0.026 (0.159)	—	—	—	—	—
Other race	0.045 (0.208)	—	—	—	—	—
BSF-R score (9 months)	0.000 (1.000)	0.018 (0.965)	−0.058 (0.894)	−0.006 (0.885)	−0.008 (0.990)	−0.005 (1.094)
BSF-R score (2 years)	0.000 (1.000)	0.163 (0.915)	−0.230 (0.907)	−0.238 (0.866)	−0.075 (1.020)	−0.066 (1.210)
IRT literacy score (4 years)	0.000 (1.000)	0.087 (0.949)	−0.108 (0.900)	−0.206 (0.827)	0.530 (1.106)	−0.017 (1.295)
IRT math score (4 years)	0.000 (1.000)	0.120 (0.897)	−0.217 (0.939)	−0.191 (0.917)	0.417 (0.936)	−0.093 (1.374)
Age in first wave (in months)	10.430 (1.791)	10.414 (1.790)	10.393 (1.781)	10.473 (1.807)	10.507 (1.745)	10.488 (1.789)
Age in second wave (in months)	24.296 (0.809)	24.275 (0.770)	24.277 (0.857)	24.361 (0.875)	24.319 (0.794)	24.281 (0.768)
Age in third wave (in months)	52.597 (3.773)	52.301 (3.652)	52.392 (3.838)	53.445 (3.838)	53.092 (3.872)	52.409 (3.890)
Female	0.495 (0.500)	0.497 (0.500)	0.482 (0.500)	0.494 (0.500)	0.495 (0.500)	0.510 (0.500)
Northeast	0.175 (0.380)	0.183 (0.387)	0.166 (0.372)	0.164 (0.370)	0.213 (0.410)	0.133 (0.340)
Midwest	0.227 (0.419)	0.281 (0.450)	0.199 (0.399)	0.105 (0.307)	0.159 (0.366)	0.279 (0.449)
South	0.364 (0.481)	0.353 (0.478)	0.557 (0.497)	0.306 (0.461)	0.204 (0.403)	0.281 (0.450)
West	0.234 (0.424)	0.183 (0.387)	0.079 (0.269)	0.425 (0.495)	0.424 (0.462)	0.307 (0.462)

Table A.4 (continued)

	Full sample	White	Black	Hispanic	Asian	Other
Socioeconomic status quintile: 1	0.174 (0.379)	0.081 (0.273)	0.338 (0.473)	0.311 (0.463)	0.078 (0.268)	0.184 (0.388)
Socioeconomic status quintile: 2	0.201 (0.401)	0.157 (0.364)	0.239 (0.427)	0.278 (0.448)	0.124 (0.330)	0.284 (0.451)
Socioeconomic status quintile: 3	0.203 (0.402)	0.205 (0.404)	0.212 (0.409)	0.203 (0.403)	0.138 (0.345)	0.183 (0.387)
Socioeconomic status quintile: 4	0.214 (0.410)	0.269 (0.443)	0.134 (0.340)	0.138 (0.345)	0.159 (0.366)	0.201 (0.401)
Socioeconomic status quintile: 5	0.208 (0.406)	0.287 (0.453)	0.078 (0.268)	0.069 (0.254)	0.502 (0.500)	0.147 (0.354)
Number of siblings	0.982 (1.085)	0.950 (1.020)	1.120 (1.193)	1.001 (1.166)	0.778 (0.970)	0.971 (1.103)
Both biological parents	0.787 (0.409)	0.883 (0.322)	0.415 (0.493)	0.778 (0.415)	0.936 (0.245)	0.730 (0.444)
One biological parent	0.195 (0.396)	0.096 (0.294)	0.577 (0.494)	0.204 (0.403)	0.061 (0.240)	0.255 (0.436)
One biological parent & one non-biological parent	0.012 (0.111)	0.016 (0.125)	0.005 (0.073)	0.010 (0.099)	0.001 (0.032)	0.009 (0.095)
Other parental configuration	0.006 (0.075)	0.006 (0.075)	0.003 (0.050)	0.008 (0.090)	0.002 (0.044)	0.006 (0.077)
Mother's age	27.354 (6.189)	28.366 (6.016)	25.041 (6.136)	26.116 (6.081)	29.951 (5.350)	26.679 (6.141)
Parent as teacher score	34.805 (4.477)	35.423 (4.447)	33.891 (4.432)	33.795 (4.347)	34.531 (4.377)	34.647 (4.305)
Birthweight: less than 1500 grams	0.012 (0.109)	0.010 (0.097)	0.024 (0.152)	0.011 (0.105)	0.005 (0.074)	0.016 (0.126)
Birthweight: 1500–2500 grams	0.062 (0.240)	0.054 (0.227)	0.098 (0.297)	0.057 (0.232)	0.057 (0.233)	0.065 (0.247)

(continued on next page)

Table A.4 (continued)

	Full sample	White	Black	Hispanic	Asian	Other
Birthweight: 2500–3500 grams	0.542 (0.498)	0.517 (0.500)	0.601 (0.490)	0.550 (0.498)	0.702 (0.458)	0.531 (0.499)
Birthweight: more than 3500 grams	0.384 (0.486)	0.419 (0.493)	0.277 (0.448)	0.382 (0.486)	0.235 (0.424)	0.387 (0.487)
Percent premature	0.116 (0.320)	0.098 (0.297)	0.177 (0.382)	0.113 (0.317)	0.095 (0.293)	0.171 (0.377)
Days premature (if premature)	21.180 (18.193)	20.830 (17.483)	22.819 (19.901)	20.636 (17.301)	15.740 (14.046)	21.801 (20.843)
Single birth	0.968 (0.175)	0.963 (0.189)	0.970 (0.170)	0.979 (0.145)	0.985 (0.122)	0.969 (0.174)
Twin birth	0.030 (0.170)	0.034 (0.182)	0.029 (0.167)	0.021 (0.143)	0.015 (0.122)	0.031 (0.173)
Triplet or higher order birth	0.002 (0.043)	0.003 (0.053)	0.001 (0.034)	0.001 (0.023)	0.000 (0.000)	0.000 (0.019)
Missing mother's age	0.002 (0.043)	0.000 (0.016)	0.000 (0.014)	0.002 (0.040)	0.000 (0.000)	0.030 (0.169)
Missing parent as teacher score	0.141 (0.348)	0.118 (0.323)	0.155 (0.362)	0.188 (0.391)	0.193 (0.395)	0.115 (0.320)
Missing birthweight	0.002 (0.042)	0.001 (0.034)	0.005 (0.073)	0.001 (0.028)	0.000 (0.000)	0.005 (0.069)
Missing amount premature	0.013 (0.113)	0.008 (0.087)	0.005 (0.074)	0.026 (0.159)	0.020 (0.139)	0.036 (0.187)
Missing number of children in birth	0.002 (0.043)	0.000 (0.016)	0.000 (0.014)	0.002 (0.040)	0.000 (0.000)	0.030 (0.169)
Obs.	7468	3418	1160	1328	727	835

analysis. This is the only exclusion we make from the sample.[57] Throughout the analysis, the results we report are weighted to be nationally representative using sampling weights included in the data set.[58]

Bayley Short Form—Research Edition (BSF-R)

The BSF-R is an abbreviated version of the Bayley Scale of Infant Development (BSID) that was designed for use in the ECLS to measure the development of children early in life in five broad areas: exploring objects (e.g., reaching for and holding objects), exploring objects with a purpose (e.g., trying to determine what makes the ringing sound in a bell), babbling expressively, early problem solving (e.g., when a toy is out of reach, using another object as a tool to retrieve the toy), and naming objects.[59] The test is administered by a trained interviewer and takes twenty-five to thirty-five minutes to complete. A child's score is reported as a proficiency level, ranging from zero to one on each of the five sections. These five proficiency scores have also been combined into an overall measure of cognitive ability using standard scale units. Because this particular test instrument is newly designed for ECLS-B, there is little direct evidence regarding the correlation between performance on this precise test and outcomes later in life. For a discussion of the validity of this instrument, see Fryer and Levitt (2010, forthcoming). The BSF-R scores have been standardized across the population of children with available scores to have a mean of zero and a standard deviation of one.

Early reading and math scores

As the BSF-R is not developmentally appropriate for preschool-aged children, in order to measure mental proficiency in the third wave (4 years old), a combination of items were used from several assessment instruments. The test battery was developed specifically for use in the ECLS-B and included items from a number of different assessments, including the Peabody Picture Vocabulary Test (PPVT), the Preschool Comprehensive Test of Phonological and Print Processing (Pre-CTOPPP), the PreLAS 2000, and the Test of Early Mathematics Ability-3 (TEMA-3), as well as questions from other studies, including the Family and Child Experiences Study (FACES), the Head Start Impact Study, and the ECLS-K. The assessment battery was designed to test language and literacy skills (including English language skills, emergent literacy, and early reading), mathematics ability, and color knowledge. The cognitive battery was available in both English and Spanish; children who spoke another language were not assessed using the cognitive battery.

---

[57] In cases where there are missing values for another of these covariates, we set these missing observations equal to zero and add an indicator variable to the specification equal to one if the observation is missing and equal to zero otherwise. We obtain similar results for the first wave when we include all children with an initial test score, including those who subsequently are not tested.

[58] A comparison of the ECLS-B sample characteristics with known national samples, such as the US Census and the Center for Disease Control's Vital Statistics, confirms that the sample characteristics closely match the national average.

[59] See Nord et al. (2005) for further details.

The preschool cognitive scores are estimated using Item Response Theory (IRT) modeling based on the set of questions that was administered to each student. The study used IRT modeling to create skill-specific cluster scores that estimate what a student's performance within a given cluster would have been had the entire set of items been administered. Additionally, scores have been converted to a proficiency probability score that measures a child's proficiency within a given skill domain and standardized T-scores that measure a child's ability in comparison to his peers.

Age

Child's age is coded in three sets of variables, one for each wave of the survey. For the 9-month wave, dummy variables were created for each of the possible one-month age ranges between 8 months and 16 months (inclusive). Children who were younger than 8 months were included in the 8-month variable and children who were older than 16 months were included in the 16-month variable. For the 2-year wave, dummy variables were created for each of the possible one-month age ranges between 23 months and 26 months (inclusive). Children who were younger than 23 months were included in the 23-month variable, while children who were older than 26 months were included in the 26-month variable. For the preschool wave, dummy variables were created for each of the possible one-month age ranges between 47 months and 60 months (inclusive). Children who were younger than 47 months were included in the 47-month variable and children who were older then 60 months were included in the 60-month variable.

Race

Race is defined in a mutually exclusive set of dummy variables, with a child being assigned a value of one for one of white, black, Hispanic, Asian, or other race.

Region

Dummy variables were created for each of four regions of the country: Northeast, Midwest, South, and West.

Sex

The variable for a child's sex is a binary variable that is equal to one if the child is female and zero if the child is male.

Family structure

This is coded as a set of four dummy variables, each representing a different possible set of parents with whom the child lives: two biological parents, one biological parent, one biological parent and one non-biological parent, and other.

Mother's age

A continuous variable was created for the age of the child's mother. Analyses including this variable also included squared, cubic, quartic, and quintic terms. The cubic, quartic, and quintic terms were divided by 100,000 before their inclusion in the regressions.

Number of siblings

Number of siblings is coded as a set of dummy variables, each one representing a different number of siblings. All children with 6 or more siblings are coded in the same dummy variable.

Parent as teacher score

The "parent as teacher" score is coded based on interviewer observations of parent-child interactions in a structured problem-solving environment and is based on the Nursing Child Assessment Teaching Scale (NCATS). The NCATS consists of 73 binary items that are scored by trained observers. The parent component of the NCATS system has 50 items that focus on the parent's use of a "teaching loop," which consists of four components: (1) getting the child's attention and setting up expectations for what is about to be done; (2) giving instructions; (3) letting the child respond to the teaching; and (4) giving feedback on the child's attempts to complete the task. The parent score ranges from 0 to 50. Analyses including this variable also included squared, cubic, quartic, and quintic terms. The cubic, quartic, and quintic terms were divided by 100,000 before their inclusion in the regressions.

Socioeconomic status

Socioeconomic status is constructed by ECLS and includes parental income, occupation, and education. It is coded as a set of five mutually exclusive and exhaustive dummy variables, each one representing a different socioeconomic status quintile.

Birthweight

The birthweight of the child was coded in a set of four dummy variables: under 1500 grams, 1500-2500 grams, 2500-3500 grams, and over 3500 grams.

Multiple birth indicator

A set of dummy variables were created to indicate how many children were born at the same time as the child: single birth, twin birth, or triplet or higher order birth.

Premature births

Premature births are considered in two different ways. First, a dummy variable is created to classify the child as being born prematurely or not. Then a set of dummy variables were created to capture how early the child was born: less than 7 days, 8-14 days, 15-21 days, etc. in seven day increments up to 77 days premature. Any births more than 77 days premature are coded in the 71-77 days premature dummy variable.

A.5. Collaborative Perinatal Project (CPP)

The Collaborative Perinatal Project (CPP) consists of over 31,000 women who gave birth in twelve medical centers between 1959 and 1965. All medical centers were in urban areas; six in the Northeast, four in the South, one in the West, and one in the north-central region of the US. Some institutions selected all eligible women, while others took a random sample.[60] The socioeconomic and ethnic composition of the participants is representative of the population qualifying for medical care at the participating institutions. These women were re-surveyed when their children were eight months, four years, and seven years old. Follow-up rates were remarkably high: eighty-five percent at eight months, seventy-five percent at four years, and seventy-nine percent at seven years. We only include students in our analysis that had score results for all three tests.[61] Our analysis uses data on demographics, measures of home environment, and prenatal factors. In all cases, we use the values collected in the initial survey for these background characteristics.[62]

Bayley Scales of Infant Development (BSID)

The Bayley Scales of Infant Development (BSID) can be used to measure the motor, language, and cognitive development of infants and toddlers (under three years old). It is therefore used only in the first wave of the CPP. The assessment consists of 45-60 minutes of developmental play tasks administered by a trained interviewer. For use in this analysis, scores were standardized across the entire population. Individuals with scores lower than ten standard deviations below the mean are considered to have missing scores.

Stanford-Binet intelligence scales

The Stanford-Binet Intelligence Scales were used as the main measure of cognitive ability for the second wave of the CPP when the children were four years-old. The scores are standardized across the entire sample of available scores.

Wechsler Intelligence Scale for Children (WISC)

The Wechsler Intelligence Scale for Children (WISC) was used as the main measure of cognitive ability for the third wave of the CPP when the children were seven years-old. The scores are standardized across the entire sample of available scores.

Age

For the first wave of the study (8 months), age is coded as a set of dummy variables representing 5 age ranges: less than 7.5 months, 7.5-8.5 months, 8.5-9 months, 9-10 months, and over 10 months.

In the second (4 years) and third (7 years) waves of the study, age is coded as a continuous variable and given as age of the child in months at the time of the follow-up survey and testing.

---

[60] Detailed information on the selection methods and sampling frame from each institution can be found in Niswander and Gordon (1972). Over 400 publications have emanated from the CPP; for a bibliography, see http://www.niehs.nih.gov/research/atniehs/labs/epi/studies/dde/biblio.cfm. The most relevant of these papers is Bayley (1965), which, like our reanalysis, finds no racial test score gaps among infants.

[61] Analyzing each wave of the data's test scores, not requiring that a student have all three scores, yields similar results.

[62] It must be noted, however, that there are a great deal of missing data on covariates in CPP; in some cases more than half of the sample has missing values. We include indicator variables for missing values for each covariate in the analysis.

Table A.5 Collaborative Perinatal Project (CPP) summary statistics.

	Full sample	White	Black	Hispanic	Other
White	0.461 (0.498)	—	—	—	—
Black	0.504 (0.500)	—	—	—	—
Hispanic	0.029 (0.167)	—	—	—	—
Other race	0.007 (0.084)	—	—	—	—
Mental function composite score (8 months)	0.000 (1.000)	0.044 (0.925)	−0.051 (1.060)	0.227 (0.925)	−0.127 (1.292)
Mental function composite score (4 years)	0.000 (1.000)	0.424 (1.000)	−0.361 (0.843)	−0.471 (0.814)	−0.019 (1.033)
Mental function composite score (7 years)	0.000 (1.000)	0.457 (0.957)	−0.397 (0.857)	−0.389 (0.840)	0.112 (1.092)
<7.5 months	0.006 (0.080)	0.004 (0.065)	0.008 (0.091)	0.006 (0.075)	0.004 (0.067)
7.5–8.5 months	0.835 (0.371)	0.811 (0.392)	0.856 (0.351)	0.856 (0.351)	0.807 (0.395)
8.5–9 months	0.087 (0.281)	0.105 (0.306)	0.070 (0.256)	0.081 (0.273)	0.090 (0.286)
9–10 months	0.066 (0.248)	0.074 (0.262)	0.059 (0.236)	0.053 (0.224)	0.076 (0.266)
>10 months	0.006 (0.079)	0.006 (0.080)	0.006 (0.078)	0.004 (0.067)	0.022 (0.148)
Age in second wave (in months)	48.216 (1.422)	48.389 (1.302)	48.035 (1.491)	48.497 (1.578)	48.655 (1.462)
Age in third wave (in months)	84.314 (2.493)	84.335 (2.042)	84.286 (2.802)	84.446 (3.256)	84.489 (2.209)
Female	0.501 (0.500)	0.495 (0.500)	0.508 (0.500)	0.489 (0.500)	0.507 (0.501)
Father: high school dropout	0.502 (0.500)	0.396 (0.489)	0.613 (0.487)	0.781 (0.417)	0.500 (0.503)
Father: high school graduate	0.314 (0.464)	0.308 (0.462)	0.324 (0.468)	0.188 (0.393)	0.224 (0.419)
Father: some college	0.090 (0.287)	0.127 (0.333)	0.053 (0.224)	0.016 (0.125)	0.031 (0.173)
Father: at least college degree	0.094 (0.291)	0.169 (0.375)	0.011 (0.104)	0.016 (0.125)	0.245 (0.432)
Father: no occupation	0.004 (0.062)	0.001 (0.036)	0.007 (0.082)	0.000 (0.000)	0.000 (0.000)
Father: professional occupation	0.171 (0.376)	0.269 (0.444)	0.065 (0.247)	0.036 (0.189)	0.245 (0.432)
Father: non-professional occupation	0.825 (0.380)	0.730 (0.444)	0.928 (0.258)	0.964 (0.189)	0.755 (0.432)
Mother: high school dropout	0.555 (0.497)	0.423 (0.494)	0.678 (0.467)	0.918 (0.277)	0.625 (0.486)
Mother: high school graduate	0.323 (0.468)	0.371 (0.483)	0.282 (0.450)	0.055 (0.229)	0.175 (0.382)

(continued on next page)

Table A.5 (continued)

	Full sample	White	Black	Hispanic	Other
Mother: some college	0.072 (0.259)	0.111 (0.314)	0.035 (0.184)	0.014 (0.117)	0.075 (0.264)
Mother: at least college degree	0.050 (0.218)	0.095 (0.294)	0.005 (0.069)	0.014 (0.117)	0.125 (0.332)
Mother: no occupation	0.133 (0.340)	0.057 (0.232)	0.205 (0.404)	0.301 (0.462)	0.183 (0.389)
Mother: professional occupation	0.074 (0.262)	0.130 (0.336)	0.021 (0.142)	0.000 (0.000)	0.108 (0.312)
Mother: non-professional occupation	0.792 (0.406)	0.813 (0.390)	0.774 (0.418)	0.699 (0.462)	0.708 (0.456)
Income: <$500	0.157 (0.363)	0.081 (0.273)	0.230 (0.421)	0.186 (0.392)	0.196 (0.399)
Income: $500–999	0.379 (0.485)	0.262 (0.440)	0.492 (0.500)	0.600 (0.493)	0.473 (0.502)
Income: $1000–1499	0.238 (0.426)	0.292 (0.455)	0.185 (0.388)	0.157 (0.367)	0.196 (0.399)
Income: $1500–1999	0.120 (0.325)	0.183 (0.387)	0.059 (0.236)	0.029 (0.168)	0.107 (0.311)
Income: $2000–2499	0.057 (0.232)	0.094 (0.292)	0.022 (0.146)	0.014 (0.120)	0.018 (0.133)
Income: >$2500	0.049 (0.217)	0.088 (0.284)	0.012 (0.109)	0.014 (0.120)	0.009 (0.094)
Number of siblings	2.812 (2.231)	2.422 (1.783)	3.182 (2.526)	2.863 (2.742)	2.724 (2.069)
Both biological parents	0.729 (0.445)	0.851 (0.356)	0.583 (0.493)	0.875 (0.342)	0.639 (0.484)
Mother's age	30.049 (7.033)	30.836 (6.469)	29.287 (7.510)	27.625 (5.414)	31.203 (6.328)
Mother reaction: negative	0.046 (0.210)	0.060 (0.237)	0.035 (0.183)	0.012 (0.108)	0.112 (0.316)
Mother reaction: indifferent	0.256 (0.437)	0.254 (0.435)	0.265 (0.442)	0.120 (0.325)	0.293 (0.456)
Mother reaction: accepting	0.997 (0.051)	0.997 (0.059)	0.998 (0.044)	0.999 (0.034)	1.000 (0.000)
Mother reaction: attentive	0.190 (0.393)	0.205 (0.404)	0.182 (0.386)	0.106 (0.308)	0.209 (0.408)
Mother reaction: over–caring	0.032 (0.176)	0.040 (0.195)	0.026 (0.158)	0.015 (0.123)	0.065 (0.247)
Mother reaction: other	0.002 (0.049)	0.004 (0.062)	0.001 (0.034)	0.000 (0.000)	0.005 (0.068)
Birthweight: less than 1500 grams	0.007 (0.086)	0.005 (0.069)	0.010 (0.101)	0.001 (0.037)	0.000 (0.000)
Birthweight: 1500–2500 grams	0.099 (0.299)	0.070 (0.256)	0.127 (0.333)	0.087 (0.282)	0.078 (0.269)
Birthweight: 2500–3500 grams	0.657 (0.475)	0.617 (0.486)	0.693 (0.461)	0.700 (0.459)	0.620 (0.487)
Birthweight: more than 3500 grams	0.237 (0.425)	0.308 (0.462)	0.170 (0.375)	0.212 (0.409)	0.302 (0.460)

Table A.5 (continued)

	Full sample	White	Black	Hispanic	Other
Weeks premature (if premature)	5.579 (6.448)	5.894 (6.847)	5.335 (6.085)	5.128 (5.809)	8.684 (11.000)
Single birth	0.982 (0.133)	0.983 (0.130)	0.981 (0.136)	0.988 (0.111)	0.969 (0.175)
Twin birth	0.017 (0.131)	0.017 (0.128)	0.018 (0.134)	0.012 (0.111)	0.018 (0.133)
Triplet or higher order birth	0.001 (0.023)	0.000 (0.022)	0.000 (0.020)	0.000 (0.000)	0.013 (0.115)
Missing father's education	0.566 (0.496)	0.517 (0.500)	0.590 (0.492)	0.928 (0.258)	0.561 (0.497)
Missing father's occupation	0.559 (0.497)	0.510 (0.500)	0.583 (0.493)	0.938 (0.241)	0.507 (0.501)
Missing mother's education	0.521 (0.500)	0.494 (0.500)	0.524 (0.499)	0.918 (0.274)	0.462 (0.500)
Missing mother's occupation	0.519 (0.500)	0.492 (0.500)	0.522 (0.500)	0.918 (0.274)	0.462 (0.500)
Missing income	0.532 (0.499)	0.501 (0.500)	0.539 (0.498)	0.921 (0.269)	0.498 (0.501)
Missing siblings	0.708 (0.455)	0.696 (0.460)	0.706 (0.456)	0.943 (0.232)	0.659 (0.475)
Missing parental configuration	0.707 (0.455)	0.657 (0.475)	0.738 (0.440)	0.982 (0.133)	0.677 (0.469)
Missing mother's age	0.450 (0.498)	0.410 (0.492)	0.467 (0.499)	0.802 (0.398)	0.471 (0.500)
Missing mother's reaction	0.015 (0.120)	0.014 (0.118)	0.013 (0.113)	0.048 (0.214)	0.036 (0.186)
Missing birthweight	0.106 (0.308)	0.091 (0.288)	0.115 (0.319)	0.174 (0.379)	0.139 (0.347)
Missing amount premature	0.381 (0.486)	0.381 (0.486)	0.369 (0.483)	0.590 (0.492)	0.323 (0.469)
Missing birth number	0.011 (0.103)	0.003 (0.055)	0.018 (0.133)	0.003 (0.058)	0.000 (0.000)
Obs.	31,116	14,335	15,667	891	223

Race

Race is defined in a mutually exclusive set of dummy variables, with a child being assigned a value of one for one of white, black, Hispanic, or other race. Preference is given for the race reported when the child is 8 months; if no race is reported then, race is used as reported at 7 years, then at 3 years, then at 4 years.

Sex

The variable for a child's sex is a binary variable that is equal to one if the child is female and zero if the child is male. Preference is given for the sex reported when the child is 8 months; if no sex is reported then, sex is used as reported at 7 years, then at 3 years, then at 4 years.

Family structure

A dummy variable is created to indicate whether both the biological mother and biological father are present.

Income

The cumulative income of the family during the first three months of pregnancy is coded as a set of dummy variables representing a range of incomes. Each family is coded within one of the following income ranges: less than $500, $500-1000, $1000-1500, $1500-2000, $2000-2500, or more than $2500.

Mother's age

A continuous variable was created for the age of the child's mother. Analyses including this variable also included squared, cubic, quartic, and quintic terms. The quartic and quintic terms were divided by 1000 before their inclusion in the regressions.

Mother's reaction to child

A set of dummy variables for the mother's reaction to the child are included, indicating if the mother is indifferent, accepting, attentive, or over-caring toward the child, or if she behaves in another manner. These dummy variables are constructed by considering the mother's reaction to and interactions with the child, which are assessed by the interviewer. These dummy variables are not mutually exclusive, as a mother is coded as fitting into each category (negative, indifferent, accepting, attentive, caring, or other) if she fits into that category for any of the measures. Therefore, any mother who falls into different categories for the different measures will be coded with a value of one for multiple dummy variables in this set.

Number of siblings

Number of siblings is coded as a set of dummy variables, each one representing a different number of siblings from zero to six-plus siblings. All children with 6 or more siblings are coded in the same dummy variable.

Parents' education

A separate set of dummy variables are coded to represent the educational attainment of the child's mother and father. Each parent's education is coded as one of: high school dropout (less than 12 years of schooling), high school graduate (12 years of schooling), some college (more than 12 years of schooling but less than 16 years of schooling), or at least college degree (16 or more years of schooling).

Parents' occupation

A separate set of dummy variables are coded to represent the field of work done by the mother and father of the child. Each parent's occupational status is coded as one of: no occupation, professional occupation, or non-professional occupation.

Birthweight

The birthweight of the child was given as an amount in pounds and ounces. This measure was first converted to an amount in ounces and the weight in ounces was then converted to a weight in grams. The birthweight of the child was coded in a set of four dummy variables: under 1500 grams, 1500-2500 grams, 2500-3500 grams, and over 3500 grams.

Multiple birth indicator

A set of dummy variables were created to indicate how many children were born at the same time as the child: single birth, twin birth, or triplet or higher order birth.

Prematurity

Premature births are considered in two different ways. First, a dummy variable is created to classify the child as being born prematurely or not. Then a set of dummy variables were created to capture how early the child was born, in weekly increments up to 11 weeks. Any children born more than 11 weeks premature were included in the dummy variable for 11 weeks premature. The amount of time that a child was born prematurely was determined by subtracting the gestation length of the child from 37, which is the earliest gestation period at which a birth is considered full-term.

A.6. Early Childhood Longitudinal Study, Kindergarten Cohort (ECLS-K)

The Early Childhood Longitudinal Study kindergarten cohort (ECLS-K) is a nationally representative sample of 21,260 children entering kindergarten in 1998. Thus far, information on these children has been gathered at seven separate points in time. The full sample was interviewed in the fall and spring of first grade. All of our regressions and summary statistics are weighted, unless otherwise noted, and we include dummy variables for missing data. We describe below how we combined and recoded some of the ECLS variables used in our analysis.

Math and reading standardized test scores

The primary outcome variables in this data set were math and reading standardized test scores from tests developed especially for the ECLS, but based on existing instruments

Table A.6 Early Childhood Longitudinal Study—Kindergarten cohort (ECLS-K) summary statistics.

	Full sample	White	Black	Hispanic	Asian	Other
White	0.576 (0.494)	—	—	—	—	—
Black	0.172 (0.378)	—	—	—	—	—
Hispanic	0.181 (0.385)	—	—	—	—	—
Asian	0.029 (0.167)	—	—	—	—	—
Other race	0.042 (0.200)	—	—	—	—	—
Std. math score, fall kindergarten	−0.001 (0.998)	0.152 (1.086)	−0.242 (0.662)	−0.275 (0.656)	0.258 (1.123)	−0.081 (0.996)
Std. math score, spring 1st grade	0.000 (1.000)	0.141 (1.025)	−0.298 (0.832)	−0.172 (0.721)	0.158 (1.003)	−0.074 (0.899)
Std. math score, spring 3rd grade	−0.001 (1.000)	0.148 (0.979)	−0.351 (0.823)	−0.144 (0.753)	0.192 (1.107)	−0.090 (0.836)
Std. math score, spring 5th grade	0.000 (1.001)	0.145 (0.968)	−0.395 (0.825)	−0.108 (0.722)	0.285 (0.911)	−0.070 (0.904)
Std. math score, spring 8th grade	−0.001 (1.000)	0.139 (0.942)	−0.383 (0.855)	−0.101 (0.738)	0.277 (1.043)	−0.067 (0.969)
Std. reading score, fall kindergarten	−0.002 (0.993)	0.080 (1.063)	−0.166 (0.732)	−0.188 (0.694)	0.274 (1.044)	−0.096 (1.192)
Std. reading score, spring 1st grade	−0.001 (0.999)	0.070 (1.032)	−0.199 (0.817)	−0.089 (0.868)	0.269 (0.709)	−0.093 (0.933)
Std. reading score, spring 3rd grade	0.000 (0.998)	0.104 (0.977)	−0.286 (0.867)	−0.095 (0.884)	0.146 (0.724)	−0.112 (0.900)
Std. reading score, spring 5th grade	0.000 (1.000)	0.113 (0.972)	−0.341 (0.834)	−0.076 (0.828)	0.174 (0.601)	−0.075 (0.921)
Std. reading score, spring 8th grade	0.000 (0.999)	0.120 (0.939)	−0.383 (0.900)	−0.063 (0.795)	0.202 (0.684)	−0.049 (0.792)
Missing math score	0.020 (0.141)	0.012 (0.110)	0.010 (0.102)	0.024 (0.153)	0.198 (0.399)	0.031 (0.174)
Missing reading score	0.095 (0.294)	0.026 (0.160)	0.053 (0.224)	0.347 (0.476)	0.200 (0.401)	0.056 (0.230)
Male	0.518 (0.500)	0.522 (0.500)	0.536 (0.499)	0.505 (0.500)	0.420 (0.494)	0.502 (0.501)

Table A.6 (continued)

	Full sample	White	Black	Hispanic	Asian	Other
Socioeconomic status (standardized)	−0.001 (0.577)	0.174 (0.531)	−0.291 (0.546)	−0.318 (0.478)	0.292 (0.617)	−0.055 (0.607)
Socioeconomic status quintile: 1	0.180 (0.384)	0.073 (0.260)	0.300 (0.458)	0.417 (0.493)	0.158 (0.365)	0.167 (0.374)
Socioeconomic status quintile: 2	0.196 (0.397)	0.176 (0.381)	0.264 (0.441)	0.209 (0.407)	0.130 (0.337)	0.189 (0.392)
Socioeconomic status quintile: 3	0.197 (0.398)	0.197 (0.397)	0.241 (0.428)	0.154 (0.361)	0.149 (0.356)	0.246 (0.431)
Socioeconomic status quintile: 4	0.210 (0.407)	0.250 (0.433)	0.131 (0.338)	0.146 (0.353)	0.191 (0.393)	0.246 (0.431)
Socioeconomic status quintile: 5	0.217 (0.412)	0.304 (0.460)	0.064 (0.246)	0.074 (0.262)	0.373 (0.484)	0.152 (0.359)
Mother's age at child's birth	23.836 (5.525)	25.092 (5.384)	20.677 (4.555)	22.396 (5.219)	26.352 (5.394)	22.619 (5.518)
Teen mother at child's birth	0.263 (0.440)	0.180 (0.384)	0.484 (0.500)	0.328 (0.470)	0.102 (0.303)	0.416 (0.494)
Mother in her 20s at child's birth	0.567 (0.495)	0.606 (0.489)	0.455 (0.498)	0.564 (0.496)	0.602 (0.490)	0.440 (0.497)
Mother over 30 at child's birth	0.170 (0.375)	0.214 (0.410)	0.061 (0.240)	0.108 (0.311)	0.296 (0.457)	0.144 (0.352)
Two biological parents	0.677 (0.468)	0.771 (0.420)	0.322 (0.468)	0.697 (0.460)	0.836 (0.371)	0.590 (0.493)
Single mother	0.197 (0.398)	0.117 (0.322)	0.520 (0.500)	0.184 (0.388)	0.074 (0.262)	0.155 (0.363)
Northeast	0.181 (0.385)	0.219 (0.414)	0.130 (0.337)	0.112 (0.315)	0.244 (0.430)	0.110 (0.314)
Midwest	0.232 (0.422)	0.288 (0.453)	0.143 (0.351)	0.126 (0.331)	0.139 (0.347)	0.339 (0.474)
South	0.389 (0.488)	0.351 (0.477)	0.670 (0.470)	0.314 (0.464)	0.202 (0.402)	0.202 (0.402)
West	0.199 (0.399)	0.141 (0.348)	0.056 (0.230)	0.449 (0.498)	0.415 (0.493)	0.349 (0.477)
Central city	0.368 (0.482)	0.265 (0.441)	0.515 (0.500)	0.558 (0.497)	0.460 (0.499)	0.304 (0.460)

(continued on next page)

Table A.6 (continued)

	Full sample	White	Black	Hispanic	Asian	Other
Suburban	0.389 (0.488)	0.442 (0.497)	0.303 (0.460)	0.331 (0.471)	0.403 (0.491)	0.254 (0.436)
Town	0.116 (0.320)	0.142 (0.349)	0.066 (0.249)	0.065 (0.247)	0.084 (0.278)	0.190 (0.393)
Rural	0.127 (0.333)	0.151 (0.358)	0.116 (0.321)	0.046 (0.210)	0.052 (0.222)	0.253 (0.435)
Public school	0.844 (0.363)	0.803 (0.398)	0.933 (0.251)	0.919 (0.274)	0.841 (0.366)	0.734 (0.442)
Private school	0.152 (0.359)	0.197 (0.398)	0.067 (0.251)	0.081 (0.274)	0.159 (0.366)	0.184 (0.388)
Average percentage whites in school	0.565 (0.338)	0.767 (0.206)	0.262 (0.266)	0.285 (0.279)	0.358 (0.301)	0.372 (0.329)
Average percentage blacks in school	0.162 (0.262)	0.071 (0.129)	0.582 (0.313)	0.076 (0.132)	0.114 (0.201)	0.078 (0.160)
Birthweight (in ounces)	118.177 (21.071)	119.789 (20.904)	114.085 (20.648)	116.967 (21.324)	110.491 (21.332)	119.825 (20.608)
Number of children's books	75.769 (60.087)	96.451 (59.526)	39.951 (39.048)	43.983 (47.585)	53.061 (48.133)	74.275 (60.377)
WIC recipient	0.447 (0.497)	0.305 (0.460)	0.780 (0.414)	0.632 (0.482)	0.235 (0.424)	0.515 (0.500)
Missing socioeconomic status	0.028 (0.164)	0.017 (0.131)	0.035 (0.184)	0.036 (0.186)	0.137 (0.344)	0.024 (0.153)
Missing mother's age at birth	0.077 (0.266)	0.037 (0.188)	0.128 (0.335)	0.116 (0.320)	0.263 (0.441)	0.112 (0.316)
Missing family structure	0.061 (0.239)	0.033 (0.178)	0.081 (0.273)	0.104 (0.305)	0.208 (0.406)	0.083 (0.276)
Missing birthweight	0.095 (0.293)	0.047 (0.212)	0.158 (0.365)	0.156 (0.363)	0.249 (0.433)	0.123 (0.329)
Missing number of children's books	0.072 (0.259)	0.047 (0.211)	0.085 (0.279)	0.108 (0.311)	0.219 (0.414)	0.112 (0.316)
Missing WIC status	0.071 (0.257)	0.040 (0.197)	0.104 (0.305)	0.111 (0.315)	0.211 (0.408)	0.086 (0.280)
Obs.	7790	4866	774	1309	432	409

including Children's Cognitive Battery (CCB), Peabody Individual Achievement Test—Revised (PIAT-R), Peabody Picture Vocabulary Test-3 (PPVT-3), Primary Test of Cognitive Skills (PTCS), and Woodcock-Johnson Psycho-Educational Battery—Revised (WJ-R). The test questions were administered to students orally, as an ability to read is not assumed.[63] The values used in the analyses are IRT scores provided by ECLS that we have standardized to have a mean of zero and standard deviation of one for the overall sample on each of the tests and time periods.[64] In all instances sample weights provided in ECLS-K are used.[65]

Socioeconomic composite measure

The socioeconomic scale variable (SES) was computed by ECLS at the household level for the set of parents who completed the parent interview in fall kindergarten or spring kindergarten. The SES variable reflects the socioeconomic status of the household at the time of data collection for spring kindergarten. The components used for the creation of SES were: father or male guardian's education, mother or female guardian's education, father or male guardian's occupation, mother or female guardian's occupation, and household income.

Number of children's books

Parents or guardians were asked, "How many books does your child have in your home now, including library books?" Answers ranged from 0 to 200.

Child's age

We used the composite variable child's age at assessment provided by ECLS. The child's age was calculated by determining the number of days between the child assessment date and the child's date of birth. The number was then divided by 30 to calculate the age in months.

Birth weight

Parents were asked how much their child weighed when they were born. We multiplied the number of pounds by 16 and added it to the ounces to calculate birth weight in ounces.

---

[63] A "general knowledge" exam was also administered. The general knowledge test is designed to capture "children's knowledge and understanding of the social, physical, and natural world and their ability to draw inferences and comprehend implications." We limit the analysis to the math and reading scores, primarily because of the comparability of these test scores to past research in the area. In addition, there appear to be some peculiarities in the results of the general knowledge exam. See Rock and Stenner (2005) for a more detailed comparison of ECLS to previous testing instruments.

[64] For more detail on the process used to generate the IRT scores, see Chapter 3 of the ECLS-K Users Guide. Our results are not sensitive to normalizing the IRT scores to have a mean of zero and standard deviation of one.

[65] Because of the complex manner in which the ECLS-K sample is drawn, different weights are suggested by the providers of the data depending on the set of variables used (BYPW0). We utilize the weights recommended for making longitudinal comparisons. None of our findings are sensitive to other choices of weights, or not weighting at all.

Mother's age at first birth

Mothers were asked how old they were at the birth of their first child.

A.7. Children of the National Longitudinal Survey of Youth (CNLSY)

There are 11,469 children in the original sample. We drop 2413 children who do not have valid scores for an assessment. We drop 4 more children whose mothers have invalid birth years (before 1957 or after 1964), 459 more children whose mothers have invalid AFQT scores (or whose mothers had recorded problems with the test administration), and 568 more children whose mothers are from the military or low-income white oversamples, for an overall sample of 8025 children.

We define the age group with 5-year-olds as those children between 60 and 71 months old (3375 children). We define the age group with 6-10-year-olds as those children who are between 72 and 119 months old (7699 children). We define the age group with 10-14-year-olds as those children who are between 120 and 179 months old (7107 children). Note that many children have observations in multiple age groups because they participated in multiple assessments.

Income

We construct income as follows: For each child, we look at all of the incomes that the child's mother had between 1979 and 2006 which are available in the dataset. We use the income that is closest to the assessment year and convert it to 1979 dollars. If two incomes are equally close to the assessment year, then we use the earlier one.

Demographic variables

Free lunch, special education, and private school are defined as follows: The variable is 1 if the child was in the program in either the 1994 or 1995 school survey. The variable is 0 if the child was never in the program and if the child was recorded as not being in the program in the 1994 or 1995 school survey. The variable is missing otherwise.

Test scores

Test scores are standardized within the sample by age group. Mother's AFQT score is standardized within the sample.

A.8. National Assessment of Educational Progress (NAEP)

All data is derived from the 2007 NAEP data. Note that there is a different sample of students for each of the 4 tests. In the full NAEP sample, there are 191,040 children who took the 4th grade reading test, 197,703 who took the 4th grade math test, 160,674 who took the 8th grade reading test, and 153,027 who took the 8th grade math test. Within the Trial Urban District Assessment (TUDA) subsample, there are 20,352 students who took the 4th grade reading test, 17,110 who took the 8th grade reading test, 21,440 who took the 4th grade math test, and 16,473 who took the 8th grade math test.

Table A.7 Children of the National Longitudinal Survey of Youth (CNLSY) summary statistics.

	Full sample	White	Black	Hispanic
White	0.463 (0.499)	—	—	—
Black	0.330 (0.470)	—	—	—
Hispanic	0.207 (0.405)	—	—	—
Male	0.505 (0.500)	0.506 (0.500)	0.494 (0.500)	0.523 (0.500)
Female	0.495 (0.500)	0.494 (0.500)	0.506 (0.500)	0.477 (0.500)
Free lunch	0.475 (0.499)	0.262 (0.440)	0.717 (0.451)	0.617 (0.486)
Special education	0.176 (0.381)	0.151 (0.358)	0.196 (0.397)	0.213 (0.409)
Private school	0.049 (0.216)	0.062 (0.241)	0.028 (0.164)	0.057 (0.231)
Income (units of $10K)	2.074 (3.234)	2.736 (3.722)	1.284 (2.235)	1.851 (3.092)
Home environment index	46.357 (29.342)	56.904 (26.803)	33.907 (27.384)	42.278 (29.077)
Age group 1 (age 5)	0.105 (0.307)	0.112 (0.316)	0.096 (0.294)	0.104 (0.305)
Age group 2 (ages 6–9)	0.434 (0.496)	0.447 (0.497)	0.417 (0.493)	0.433 (0.496)
Age group 3 (ages 10–14)	0.443 (0.497)	0.429 (0.495)	0.460 (0.498)	0.447 (0.497)
Std. mother's AFQT score	0.000 (1.000)	0.601 (0.854)	−0.575 (0.761)	−0.429 (0.869)
Missing race	0.000 (0.000)	—	—	—
Missing sex	0.000 (0.000)	0.000 (0.000)	0.000 (0.000)	0.000 (0.000)
Missing free lunch status	0.714 (0.452)	0.697 (0.460)	0.718 (0.450)	0.748 (0.434)
Missing special education status	0.813 (0.390)	0.796 (0.403)	0.826 (0.379)	0.830 (0.376)
Missing school type	0.597 (0.491)	0.605 (0.489)	0.577 (0.494)	0.610 (0.488)
Missing income	0.000 (0.000)	0.000 (0.000)	0.000 (0.000)	0.000 (0.000)
Missing home environment index	0.024 (0.152)	0.016 (0.127)	0.029 (0.169)	0.031 (0.173)
Missing mother's AFQT score	0.000 (0.000)	0.000 (0.000)	0.000 (0.000)	0.000 (0.000)
Obs.	29,792	13,800	9833	6159

Test scores

To calculate the overall test score, we take the mean of the 5 plausible test score values. For analysis that includes the entire NAEP sample, test scores are standardized across the entire sample. For analysis that includes only the district sample, test scores are standardized across the district (TUDA) subsample.

A.9. Chicago Public Schools

We use Chicago Public Schools (CPS) ISAT test score administrative data from the 2008-09 school year. In our data file, there are 177,001 students with reading scores and 178,055 students with math scores (grades 3-8). We drop 273 students for whom we are missing race information. This leaves us with 176,767 students with non-missing reading scores and 177,787 students with non-missing math scores.

Demographic variables

We use 4 different CPS administrative files to construct demographic data. These files are the 2009-10 enrollment file, and 2008-09 enrollment file, a file from 2008-09 with records of all students in the school district, and a file from 2008-09 containing records for students in bilingual education. For the demographic variables that should not change over time (race, sex, age), we give use the variables from the 2009-10 enrollment file to construct these and then fill in missing values using the other three files in the order of precedence listed above. For the demographic variables that may vary from year to year (free lunch and ELL status), we use the same process but exclude the 2009-10 enrollment file since it is from a year that is not the same as the year in which the ISAT test score was administered. Note that we include both "free" and "reduced" lunch statuses for our construction of the free lunch variable.

School ID

In order to construct school ID, we use the school ID from the 2008-09 enrollment file but fill in missing values with the 2008-09 with records of all students in the school district. For the purposes of analysis, we assign a common school ID to the 928 students (about 0.5% of the sample) for whom we are still missing school ID information.

Test scores

Illinois Standards Achievement Test (ISAT) scores for math, reading, science, and writing were pulled from a file listing scores for all students in Chicago Public Schools. Eighth graders do not take the science portion of the test and we decided to use only math and reading scores to keep the analysis consistent across districts. ISAT test scores are standardized to have mean 0 and standard deviation 1 within each grade.

A.10. Dallas Independent School District

We pull our Dallas TAKS scores from files provided by the Dallas Independent School District (DISD). There are 33,881 students for whom we have non-missing TAKS score

Table A.8 Chicago summary statistics.

	Full sample	White	Black	Hispanic	Asian
White	0.085 (0.279)	—	—	—	—
Black	0.461 (0.498)	—	—	—	—
Hispanic	0.419 (0.493)	—	—	—	—
Asian	0.033 (0.180)	—	—	—	—
Other race	0.002 (0.041)	—	—	—	—
Male	0.506 (0.500)	0.514 (0.500)	0.503 (0.500)	0.508 (0.500)	0.515 (0.500)
Female	0.494 (0.500)	0.486 (0.500)	0.497 (0.500)	0.492 (0.500)	0.485 (0.500)
Free lunch	0.878 (0.328)	0.493 (0.500)	0.914 (0.281)	0.928 (0.258)	0.727 (0.445)
English language learner (ELL)	0.011 (0.105)	0.014 (0.116)	0.001 (0.038)	0.019 (0.136)	0.043 (0.204)
Grade 3	0.179 (0.383)	0.175 (0.380)	0.178 (0.383)	0.181 (0.385)	0.171 (0.376)
Grade 4	0.163 (0.369)	0.166 (0.372)	0.159 (0.365)	0.166 (0.372)	0.169 (0.375)
Grade 5	0.161 (0.367)	0.163 (0.370)	0.158 (0.364)	0.163 (0.370)	0.164 (0.370)
Grade 6	0.168 (0.373)	0.171 (0.376)	0.169 (0.375)	0.165 (0.371)	0.166 (0.372)
Grade 7	0.163 (0.370)	0.162 (0.369)	0.165 (0.371)	0.162 (0.369)	0.162 (0.369)
Grade 8	0.166 (0.372)	0.162 (0.369)	0.171 (0.377)	0.162 (0.368)	0.168 (0.374)
Std. ISAT math 2008-09	0.000 (1.000)	0.730 (1.131)	−0.248 (0.905)	0.043 (0.922)	0.999 (1.191)
Std. ISAT reading 2008-09	0.000 (1.000)	0.690 (1.090)	−0.156 (0.954)	−0.024 (0.941)	0.719 (1.055)
Missing race	0.000 (0.000)	0.000 (0.000)	0.000 (0.000)	0.000 (0.000)	0.000 (0.000)
Missing sex	0.000 (0.000)	0.000 (0.000)	0.000 (0.000)	0.000 (0.000)	0.000 (0.000)
Missing free lunch	0.005 (0.073)	0.012 (0.109)	0.005 (0.073)	0.003 (0.055)	0.017 (0.129)
Missing ELL status	0.023 (0.151)	0.042 (0.199)	0.023 (0.149)	0.017 (0.130)	0.061 (0.239)
Obs.	178,242	15,151	82,118	74,718	5957

data. We use two files to construct grade and school ID information for these students: the 2008-09 DISD enrollment file and the 2008-09 DISD transfers file (containing students who were either not in the school district at the time the enrollment file information was compiled or who ever transferred schools during the school year). We drop 15 students (about 0.04% of the sample) whose grade at the time of the tests cannot be definitively determined either because they skipped a grade during the school year or because their grade levels in the enrollment and transfers files conflict. This leaves us with a sample of 33,866 students in grades 3-5 with non-missing TAKS score data. Within this sample, there are no students with missing race data. This leaves us with 28,126 students in grades 3-5 with non-missing TAKS reading scores and 33,561 students in grades 3-5 with non-missing TAKS math scores.

Age

To calculate age in months, we calculate the exact number of days old each student was as of August 25, 2008 (the first day of the 2008-09 school year) and then divide by 30 and round down to the nearest integer number of months.

Demographic variables

In order to construct demographic data, we use the demographic information from the 2008-09 enrollment file. For the race, sex, and age variables, we fill in missing information using the enrollment files from 2002-03 through 2007-08, giving precedence to the most recent files first.

Income

In order to construct the income variable, we use ArcGIS software to map each student's address from the 2008-09 enrollment file to a 2000 census tract block group. Then we assign each student's income as the weighted average income of all those who were surveyed in that census tract block group in 2000.

School ID

We construct school ID as follows: For students who attended only one school during the 2008-09 school year, we assign them to that school. For students who attended more than one school according to the transfers file, we assign the school that they attended for the greatest number of days. If a student attended more than one school for equally long numbers of days, we use the school among these with the lowest school identification number.

Test scores

Students in grades three through five take the Texas Assessment of Knowledge and Skills (TAKS). TAKS has a variety of subjects. We use scores from the reading and math sections of this exam. Unlike the Iowa Test of Basic Skills (ITBS) scores, the TAKS data that we have are not grade-equivalent scores. In order to ease interpretation of these scores, we standardize them by, for every subject and year, subtracting the mean and dividing by the standard deviation.

Table A.9 Dallas summary statistics.

	Full sample	White	Black	Hispanic	Asian
White	0.045 (0.208)	—	—	—	—
Black	0.261 (0.439)	—	—	—	—
Hispanic	0.684 (0.465)	—	—	—	—
Asian	0.008 (0.090)	—	—	—	—
Other race	0.002 (0.042)	—	—	—	—
Male	0.499 (0.500)	0.512 (0.500)	0.494 (0.500)	0.501 (0.500)	0.500 (0.501)
Female	0.501 (0.500)	0.488 (0.500)	0.506 (0.500)	0.499 (0.500)	0.500 (0.501)
Free lunch	0.574 (0.494)	0.218 (0.413)	0.395 (0.489)	0.668 (0.471)	0.419 (0.494)
English language learner (ELL)	0.391 (0.488)	0.020 (0.139)	0.007 (0.082)	0.563 (0.496)	0.279 (0.450)
Special education	0.039 (0.193)	0.079 (0.270)	0.043 (0.203)	0.034 (0.182)	0.044 (0.206)
Age (in months)	117.021 (12.087)	116.707 (11.593)	117.028 (12.009)	117.050 (12.155)	116.106 (11.476)
Income (units of $10K)	4.538 (2.330)	6.729 (3.303)	4.106 (1.860)	4.549 (2.322)	5.343 (2.867)
Grade 3	0.365 (0.481)	0.351 (0.477)	0.357 (0.479)	0.369 (0.482)	0.369 (0.483)
Grade 4	0.316 (0.465)	0.337 (0.473)	0.329 (0.470)	0.310 (0.462)	0.288 (0.454)
Grade 5	0.319 (0.466)	0.311 (0.463)	0.314 (0.464)	0.321 (0.467)	0.343 (0.476)
Std. TAKS math score	−0.000 (1.000)	0.447 (1.024)	−0.243 (0.986)	0.055 (0.983)	0.663 (0.920)
Std. TAKS reading score	−0.000 (1.000)	0.670 (1.127)	−0.112 (0.997)	−0.010 (0.965)	0.475 (1.028)
Missing race	0.000 (0.000)	0.000 (0.000)	0.000 (0.000)	0.000 (0.000)	0.000 (0.000)
Missing sex	0.000 (0.000)	0.000 (0.000)	0.000 (0.000)	0.000 (0.000)	0.000 (0.000)
Missing free lunch	0.005 (0.073)	0.010 (0.102)	0.008 (0.091)	0.004 (0.062)	0.007 (0.085)
Missing ELL status	0.005 (0.073)	0.010 (0.102)	0.008 (0.091)	0.004 (0.062)	0.007 (0.085)
Missing special education status	0.005 (0.073)	0.010 (0.102)	0.008 (0.091)	0.004 (0.062)	0.007 (0.085)
Missing age	0.000 (0.000)	0.000 (0.000)	0.000 (0.000)	0.000 (0.000)	0.000 (0.000)
Missing income	0.010 (0.101)	0.014 (0.119)	0.013 (0.111)	0.009 (0.095)	0.007 (0.085)
Obs.	33,866	1532	8830	23,169	274

A.11. New York City Department of Education

We pull our NYC math and ELA scores from NYC Public Schools (NYCPS) test score administrative files. There are 427,688 students (in grades 3-8) with non-missing ELA score data and 435,560 students (in grades 3-8) with non-missing math score data. We drop 1230 students for whom we are missing race information (about 0.3% of the sample). This leaves us with a sample of 426,806 students with non-missing ELA score data and 434,593 students with non-missing math score data.

Age

To calculate age in months, we calculate the exact number of days old each student was as of September 2, 2008 (the first day of the 2008-09 school year) and then divide by 30 and round down to the nearest integer number of months.

Demographic variables

In order to construct demographic data, we use the demographic information from the 2008-09 enrollment file. For the race, sex, and age variables, we fill in missing information using the enrollment files from 2003-04 through 2007-08, giving precedence to the most recent files first.

Income

In order to construct the income variable, we use ArcGIS software to map each student's address from the 2008-09 enrollment file to a 2000 census tract block group. Then we assign each student's income as the weighted average income of all those who were surveyed in that census tract block group in 2000.

School ID

We assign school ID for each subject as the school ID recorded in the 2008-09 test score file for that subject. We use Human Resources files provided by NYCPS to link students to their teachers for ELA and math.

Test scores

The New York state math and ELA tests, developed by McGraw-Hill, are high-stakes exams conducted in the winters of third through eighth grades. Students in third, fifth, and seventh grades must score proficient or above on both tests to advance to the next grade. The math test includes questions on number sense and operations, algebra, geometry, measurement, and statistics. Tests in the earlier grades emphasize more basic content such as number sense and operations, while later tests focus on advanced topics such as algebra and geometry. The ELA test is designed to assess students on three learning standards—information and understandings, literary response and expression, and critical analysis and evaluation—and includes multiple-choice and short-response sections based on a reading and listening section, along with a brief editing task.

In our analysis ELA and math scores are standardized by subject and by grade level to have mean 0 and standard deviation 1.

Table A.10 New York City summary statistics.

	Full sample	White	Black	Hispanic	Asian
White	0.140 (0.347)	—	—	—	—
Black	0.316 (0.465)	—	—	—	—
Hispanic	0.397 (0.489)	—	—	—	—
Asian	0.143 (0.350)	—	—	—	—
Other race	0.005 (0.069)	—	—	—	—
Male	0.512 (0.500)	0.523 (0.499)	0.505 (0.500)	0.512 (0.500)	0.519 (0.500)
Female	0.488 (0.500)	0.477 (0.499)	0.495 (0.500)	0.488 (0.500)	0.481 (0.500)
Free lunch	0.651 (0.477)	0.335 (0.472)	0.723 (0.448)	0.746 (0.435)	0.531 (0.499)
English language learner (ELL)	0.138 (0.345)	0.061 (0.240)	0.025 (0.156)	0.242 (0.428)	0.175 (0.380)
Special education	0.103 (0.304)	0.079 (0.270)	0.123 (0.328)	0.120 (0.326)	0.032 (0.175)
Age (in months)	132.564 (22.728)	130.057 (21.894)	133.646 (22.907)	133.258 (22.967)	130.745 (22.114)
Income (units of $10K)	4.462 (1.847)	6.173 (2.171)	4.135 (1.661)	3.906 (1.492)	5.014 (1.584)
Math grade 3	0.168 (0.374)	0.182 (0.386)	0.161 (0.367)	0.165 (0.371)	0.176 (0.381)
Math grade 4	0.163 (0.370)	0.169 (0.375)	0.160 (0.367)	0.164 (0.371)	0.161 (0.367)
Math grade 5	0.164 (0.371)	0.165 (0.371)	0.165 (0.371)	0.165 (0.371)	0.161 (0.368)
Math grade 6	0.163 (0.369)	0.157 (0.364)	0.165 (0.371)	0.163 (0.370)	0.164 (0.370)
Math grade 7	0.165 (0.371)	0.161 (0.367)	0.167 (0.373)	0.165 (0.371)	0.167 (0.373)
Math grade 8	0.169 (0.375)	0.162 (0.368)	0.174 (0.379)	0.170 (0.376)	0.167 (0.373)
ELA grade 3	0.165 (0.371)	0.180 (0.384)	0.160 (0.367)	0.162 (0.368)	0.170 (0.376)
ELA grade 4	0.161 (0.367)	0.167 (0.373)	0.159 (0.366)	0.161 (0.367)	0.156 (0.363)

(continued on next page)

Table A.10 (continued)

	Full sample	White	Black	Hispanic	Asian
ELA grade 5	0.162 (0.368)	0.163 (0.369)	0.164 (0.370)	0.162 (0.368)	0.156 (0.363)
ELA grade 6	0.160 (0.367)	0.156 (0.362)	0.164 (0.371)	0.160 (0.366)	0.157 (0.364)
ELA grade 7	0.162 (0.369)	0.159 (0.366)	0.167 (0.373)	0.161 (0.368)	0.159 (0.365)
ELA grade 8	0.166 (0.372)	0.160 (0.366)	0.173 (0.378)	0.166 (0.372)	0.159 (0.366)
Std. math scale score	0.000 (1.000)	0.428 (0.982)	−0.268 (0.899)	−0.187 (0.909)	0.693 (1.013)
Std. ELA scale score	−0.000 (1.000)	0.469 (1.104)	−0.165 (0.861)	−0.201 (0.901)	0.476 (1.132)
Missing race	0.000 (0.000)	0.000 (0.000)	0.000 (0.000)	0.000 (0.000)	0.000 (0.000)
Missing sex	0.000 (0.000)	0.000 (0.000)	0.000 (0.000)	0.000 (0.000)	0.000 (0.000)
Missing free lunch	0.018 (0.132)	0.030 (0.170)	0.023 (0.149)	0.012 (0.107)	0.012 (0.109)
Missing ELL status	0.000 (0.000)	0.000 (0.000)	0.000 (0.000)	0.000 (0.000)	0.000 (0.000)
Missing special education status	0.000 (0.000)	0.000 (0.000)	0.000 (0.000)	0.000 (0.000)	0.000 (0.000)
Missing age	0.000 (0.000)	0.000 (0.000)	0.000 (0.000)	0.000 (0.000)	0.000 (0.000)
Income	0.072 (0.258)	0.052 (0.222)	0.075 (0.263)	0.075 (0.264)	0.076 (0.264)
Obs.	437,416	61,049	138,115	173,682	62,477

A.12. District Data: Washington, DC

We pull our DCCAS test scores from DC Public Schools (DCPS) test score administrative files from 2008-09. There are 20,249 students with non-missing reading scores and 20,337 students with non-missing math scores. We drop 6 observations because the students have two observations with conflicting test scores. This leaves us with a sample of 20,243 students with non-missing reading scores and 20,331 students with non-missing math scores, all from grades 3-8 and 10 (the full set of grades for which the DCCAS tests are administered).

Age

To calculate age in months, we calculate the exact number of days old each student was as of August 25, 2008 (the first day of the 2008-09 school year) and then divide by 30 and round down to the nearest integer number of months.

Demographic variables

In order to construct demographic data, we use the demographic information from the 2008-09 enrollment file and use the DCCAS test score file from 2008-09 to fill in missing demographic information. For the race, sex, and age variables, we fill in missing information using the enrollment files from 2005-06 through 2007-08, giving precedence to the most recent files first.

Income

In order to construct the income variable, we use ArcGIS software to map each student's address from the 2008-09 enrollment file to a 2000 census tract block group. Then we assign each student's income as the weighted average income of all those who were surveyed in that census tract block group in 2000.

School ID

We assign school ID as the school ID recorded in the 2008-09 DCCAS test score file.

Test scores

The DC CAS is the DC Comprehensive Assessment System and is administered each April to students in grades three through eight as well as tenth graders. It measures knowledge and skills in reading and math. Students in grades four, seven, and ten also take a composition test; students in grades five and eight also take a science test; and students in grades nine through twelve who take biology also take a biology test

DCCAS scores are standardized by subject and by grade level to have mean 0 and standard deviation 1.

A.13. National Education Longitudinal Study of 1988 (NELS)

We use the first three waves (1988, 1990, and 1992) of the NELS panel dataset for our analysis, when respondents were in 8th, 10th, and 12th grade, respectively. There were 19,645 students in the 8th grade cohort, 18,176 students in the 10th grade cohort, and

Table A.11 Washington, DC summary statistics.

	Full sample	White	Black	Hispanic	Asian
White	0.070 (0.255)	—	—	—	—
Black	0.795 (0.404)	—	—	—	—
Hispanic	0.115 (0.319)	—	—	—	—
Asian	0.019 (0.137)	—	—	—	—
Other race	0.001 (0.034)	—	—	—	—
Male	0.507 (0.500)	0.520 (0.500)	0.504 (0.500)	0.517 (0.500)	0.521 (0.500)
Female	0.493 (0.500)	0.480 (0.500)	0.496 (0.500)	0.483 (0.500)	0.479 (0.500)
Free lunch	0.655 (0.475)	0.039 (0.194)	0.704 (0.457)	0.738 (0.440)	0.435 (0.496)
English language learner (ELL)	0.077 (0.266)	0.045 (0.207)	0.011 (0.102)	0.511 (0.500)	0.320 (0.467)
Special education	0.168 (0.373)	0.110 (0.313)	0.184 (0.388)	0.108 (0.311)	0.044 (0.205)
Age (in months)	137.513 (29.689)	128.707 (25.736)	138.742 (29.696)	135.111 (30.899)	133.665 (28.882)
Income (units of $10K)	4.778 (2.726)	10.856 (3.379)	4.096 (1.757)	5.155 (2.270)	8.046 (4.186)
Grade 3	0.180 (0.384)	0.232 (0.422)	0.170 (0.376)	0.209 (0.407)	0.211 (0.409)
Grade 4	0.162 (0.369)	0.195 (0.396)	0.157 (0.364)	0.175 (0.380)	0.178 (0.383)
Grade 5	0.160 (0.367)	0.187 (0.390)	0.159 (0.366)	0.155 (0.362)	0.147 (0.354)
Grade 6	0.123 (0.329)	0.135 (0.342)	0.124 (0.330)	0.114 (0.318)	0.103 (0.304)
Grade 7	0.123 (0.329)	0.094 (0.292)	0.128 (0.334)	0.111 (0.314)	0.124 (0.330)
Grade 8	0.125 (0.331)	0.074 (0.262)	0.131 (0.338)	0.113 (0.316)	0.121 (0.327)
Grade 10	0.126 (0.332)	0.083 (0.275)	0.130 (0.337)	0.124 (0.330)	0.116 (0.321)
Std. DCCAS math score	0.000 (1.000)	1.013 (0.858)	−0.141 (0.957)	0.188 (0.900)	0.963 (0.910)
Std. DCCAS reading score	0.000 (1.000)	1.044 (0.824)	−0.113 (0.962)	0.044 (0.962)	0.638 (0.899)
Missing race	0.000 (0.000)	0.000 (0.000)	0.000 (0.000)	0.000 (0.000)	0.000 (0.000)
Missing sex	0.000 (0.000)	0.000 (0.000)	0.000 (0.000)	0.000 (0.000)	0.000 (0.000)
Missing free lunch	0.027 (0.162)	0.014 (0.117)	0.029 (0.167)	0.024 (0.153)	0.023 (0.151)
Missing ELL status	0.000 (0.000)	0.000 (0.000)	0.000 (0.000)	0.000 (0.000)	0.000 (0.000)
Missing special education	0.000 (0.000)	0.000 (0.000)	0.000 (0.000)	0.000 (0.000)	0.000 (0.000)
Missing age	0.013 (0.113)	0.011 (0.105)	0.012 (0.110)	0.016 (0.126)	0.023 (0.151)
Missing income	0.028 (0.166)	0.014 (0.117)	0.031 (0.172)	0.024 (0.154)	0.023 (0.151)
Obs.	20,386	1430	16,199	2346	388

Table A.12 National Education Longitudinal Study (NELS) summary statistics: baseline year.

	Full sample	White	Black	Hispanic	Asian
White	0.670 (0.470)	—	—	—	—
Black	0.124 (0.329)	—	—	—	—
Hispanic	0.130 (0.337)	—	—	—	—
Asian	0.063 (0.244)	—	—	—	—
Other race	0.013 (0.113)	—	—	—	—
Male	0.498 (0.500)	0.500 (0.500)	0.489 (0.500)	0.485 (0.500)	0.514 (0.500)
Female	0.502 (0.500)	0.500 (0.500)	0.511 (0.500)	0.515 (0.500)	0.486 (0.500)
Age	14.599 (0.608)	14.561 (0.553)	14.717 (0.734)	14.698 (0.701)	14.519 (0.601)
Income (units of $10K)	4.143 (3.781)	4.696 (3.958)	2.333 (2.333)	2.668 (2.492)	4.834 (4.379)
Parents' education: less than high school	0.106 (0.307)	0.057 (0.232)	0.157 (0.364)	0.331 (0.471)	0.083 (0.276)
Parents' education: high school graduate	0.194 (0.395)	0.199 (0.399)	0.230 (0.421)	0.176 (0.381)	0.112 (0.315)
Parents' education: some college	0.392 (0.488)	0.397 (0.489)	0.443 (0.497)	0.360 (0.480)	0.306 (0.461)
Parents' education: college graduate	0.309 (0.462)	0.348 (0.476)	0.170 (0.376)	0.132 (0.339)	0.500 (0.500)
Std. math IRT–estimated number right	0.000 (1.000)	0.175 (0.985)	−0.610 (0.761)	−0.459 (0.812)	0.431 (1.082)
Std. English IRT–estimated number right	0.000 (1.000)	0.180 (0.992)	−0.512 (0.843)	−0.424 (0.852)	0.114 (1.019)
Std. science IRT–estimated number right	0.000 (1.000)	0.197 (0.992)	−0.615 (0.743)	−0.438 (0.827)	0.169 (1.050)
Std. history IRT–estimated number right	0.000 (1.000)	0.176 (0.973)	−0.498 (0.824)	−0.449 (0.927)	0.185 (1.080)
Public	0.788 (0.408)	0.757 (0.429)	0.853 (0.355)	0.874 (0.331)	0.809 (0.393)
Private	0.212 (0.408)	0.243 (0.429)	0.147 (0.355)	0.126 (0.331)	0.191 (0.393)
Urban	0.310 (0.462)	0.233 (0.423)	0.517 (0.500)	0.454 (0.498)	0.411 (0.492)
Suburban	0.417 (0.493)	0.443 (0.497)	0.278 (0.448)	0.386 (0.487)	0.490 (0.500)
Rural	0.274 (0.446)	0.323 (0.468)	0.205 (0.403)	0.161 (0.367)	0.099 (0.299)

(continued on next page)

Table A.12 (continued)

	Full sample	White	Black	Hispanic	Asian
Enrollment: 1–99	0.342 (0.474)	0.394 (0.489)	0.258 (0.437)	0.213 (0.410)	0.221 (0.415)
Enrollment: 100–199	0.208 (0.406)	0.219 (0.413)	0.233 (0.423)	0.148 (0.355)	0.158 (0.365)
Enrollment: 200–299	0.198 (0.399)	0.192 (0.394)	0.222 (0.415)	0.206 (0.405)	0.208 (0.406)
Enrollment: 300–399	0.135 (0.341)	0.116 (0.320)	0.154 (0.361)	0.195 (0.396)	0.176 (0.381)
Enrollment: 400+	0.117 (0.322)	0.079 (0.270)	0.134 (0.340)	0.239 (0.426)	0.237 (0.425)
Missing race	0.009 (0.096)	0.000 (0.000)	0.000 (0.000)	0.000 (0.000)	0.000 (0.000)
Missing sex	0.000 (0.000)	0.000 (0.000)	0.000 (0.000)	0.000 (0.000)	0.000 (0.000)
Missing age	0.029 (0.167)	0.025 (0.157)	0.037 (0.188)	0.031 (0.174)	0.036 (0.185)
Missing income	0.122 (0.327)	0.101 (0.301)	0.139 (0.346)	0.179 (0.383)	0.146 (0.353)
Missing parents' education	0.253 (0.435)	0.222 (0.416)	0.379 (0.485)	0.271 (0.444)	0.270 (0.444)
Missing school type	0.000 (0.000)	0.000 (0.000)	0.000 (0.000)	0.000 (0.000)	0.000 (0.000)
Missing school locale	0.000 (0.000)	0.000 (0.000)	0.000 (0.000)	0.000 (0.000)	0.000 (0.000)
Missing enrollment	0.000 (0.000)	0.000 (0.000)	0.000 (0.000)	0.000 (0.000)	0.000 (0.000)
Obs.	24,599	16,321	3011	3177	1546

17,161 students in the 12th grade cohort. We use IRT-estimated number right scores for the analysis. In the base year, there are 23,648 students with non-missing math scores, 23,643 students with non-missing English scores, 23,616 students with non-missing science scores, and 23,525 students with non-missing history scores. In the first follow-up year, there are 17,793 students with non-missing math scores, 17,832 students with non-missing English scores, 17,684 students with non-missing science scores, and 17,591 students with non-missing history scores. In the second follow-up year, there are 14,236 students with non-missing math scores, 14,230 students with non-missing English scores, 14,134 students with non-missing science scores, and 14,063 students with non-missing history scores. If first follow-up and second follow-up scores are missing, we impute them from one another.

Age
We use birth year and birth month to calculate each student's age as of September 1988.

Income
The income variable is constructed using the income reported in the base year parent questionnaire. The variable in the dataset categorizes income into different ranges, and our income variable is coded as the midpoint of each range, with the exception of the lowest income category (which corresponds to no income), which we code as $0, and the highest income category (which corresponds to an income of $200,000 or more), which we code as $200,000. We divide income by $10,000.

Parent's education
Parents' education refers to the highest level of education obtained by either parent.

School ID
In order to construct the base year school ID, we use the base year school ID variable but supplement it using the student ID when it is missing. The base year school ID is embedded in the student ID as all but the last two digits of the student ID.

Socioeconomic status
We take the SES quartile variable directly from the dataset.

REFERENCES

Abdulkadiroglu, Atila, Angrist, Joshua, Dynarski, Susan, Kane, Thomas J., Pathak, Parag, 2009. Accountability and flexibility in public schools: evidence from Boston's charters and pilots. Working paper no. 15549, NBER, Cambridge, MA.

Administration for Children and Families, 2006. Preliminary Findings from the Early Head Start Prekindergarten Followup. US Department of Health and Human Services Report, Washington, DC.

Andrews, Susan Ring, Blumenthal, Janet Berstein, Johnson, Dale L., Kahn, Alfred J., Ferguson, Carol J., Lancaster, Thomas M., Malone, Paul E., Wallace, Doris B., 1982. The skills of mothering: a study of parent child development centers. Monographs of the Society for Research in Child Development 47 (6), 1–83.

Angrist, Joshua D., Lang, Kevin, 2004. Does school integration generate peer effects? Evidence from Boston's Metco program. The American Economic Review 94 (5), 1613–1634.

Angrist, Joshua D., Dynarski, Susan M., Kane, Thomas J., Pathak, Parag A., Walters, Christopher R., 2010. Who benefits from KIPP? Working paper no. 15740, NBER, Cambridge, MA.

Banks, James A., 2001. Approaches to multicultural curriculum reform. In: Banks, James A., Banks, Cherry A.M. (Eds.), Multicultural Education: Issues and Perspectives, fourth ed., John Wiley & Sons, Inc., New York.

Banks, James A., 2006. Cultural Diversity and Education: Foundations, Curriculum, and Teaching. Pearson Education, Inc., Boston, MA.

Barton, Paul E., 2003. Parsing the achievement gap: baselines for tracking progress. Policy Information Report, Educational Testing Service Policy Information Report, Princeton, NJ.

Bayley, Nancy, 1965. Comparisons of mental and motor test scores for ages 1 to 15 months by sex, birth order, race, geographical location, and education of parents. Child Development 36, 379–411.

Becker, Douglas F., Forsyth, Robert A., 1994. Gender differences in mathematics problem solving and science: a longitudinal analysis. International Journal of Educational Research 21 (4), 407–416.

Bernstein, Lawrence, Dun Rappaport, Catherine, Olsho, Lauren, Hunt, Dana, Levin, Marjorie, et al., 2009. Impact evaluation of the US Department of Education's Student Mentoring Program: final report. US Department of Education, Institute of Education Sciences, Washington, DC.

Bethel, James, Green, James L., Kalton, Graham, Nord, Christine, 2004. Early childhood longitudinal study, birth cohort (ECLS–B), sampling. Volume 2 of the ECLS-B Methodology Report for the 9-Month Data Collection, 2001–02, US Department of Education, NCES, Washington, DC.

Bloom, Dan, Gardenhire-Crooks, Alissa, Mandsager, Conrad, 2009. Reengaging high school dropouts: early results of the National Guard Youth Challenge Program evaluation, MDRC Report, New York.

Borman, Geoffrey D., Slavin, Robert E., Cheung, Alan C.K., Chamberlain, Anne M., Madden, Nancy A., Chambers, Bette, 2007. Final reading outcomes of the national randomized field trial of Success for all. American Educational Research Journal 44 (3), 701–731.

Bornstein, Marc H., Sigman, Marian D., 1986. Continuity in mental development from infancy. Child Development 57 (2), 251–274.

Boyd, Donald, Grossman, Pamela, Lankford, Hamilton, Loeb, Susanna, Wyckoff, James, 2008. Teacher preparation and student achievement. Working paper no. 14314, NBER, Cambridge, MA.

Brooks-Gunn, Jeanne, Liaw, Fong-ruey, Klebanov, Pamela Kato, 1992. Effects of early intervention on cognitive function of low birth weight preterm infants. Journal of Pediatrics 120 (3), 350–359.

Campbell, Frances A., Ramey, Craig T., 1994. Cognitive and school outcomes for high-risk African-American students at Middle Adolescence: positive effects of early intervention. American Educational Research Journal 32 (4), 743–772.

Campbell, Jay R., Hombo, Catherine M., Mazzeo, John, 2000. NAEP 1999 trends in academic progress: three decades of student performance. US Department of Education, NCES, Washington, DC.

Carneiro, Pedro, Heckman, James, 2003. Human capital policy. Working paper no. 9495, NBER, Cambridge, MA.

Chenoweth, Karin, 2007. It's Being Done: Academic Success in Unexpected Schools. Harvard University Press, Cambridge, MA.

Cohen, Geoffrey L., Garcia, Julio, Purdie-Vaughns, Valerie, Apfel, Nancy, Brzutoski, Patricia, 2009. Recursive processes in self-affirmation: intervening to close the minority achievement gap. Science 324 (5925), 400–403.

Coleman, James S., Campbell, Ernest Q., Hobson, Carol J., McPartland, James, Mood, Alexander M., Weinfeld, Frederic D., York, Robert L., 1966. Equality of educational opportunity. US Department of Health, Education, and Welfare, Office of Education, Washington, DC.

Congressional Record, No. 11, p. H417 (daily ed. Jan. 27, 2010) (statement of The President).

Cook, Thomas D., Habib, Farah-Naaz, Phillips, Meredith, Settersten, Richard A., Shagle, Shobha C., Degirmencioglu, Serdar M., 1999. Comer's School Development Program in Prince George's county, Maryland: a theory-based evaluation. American Educational Research Journal 36 (3), 543–597.

Corrin, William, Somers, Marie-Andree, Kemple, James J., Nelson, Elizabeth, Sepanik, Susan, et al., 2009. The enhanced reading opportunities study: findings from the second year of implementation. US Department of Education, Institute of Education Sciences, Washington, DC.

Currie, Janet, Thomas, Duncan, 1995. Does Head Start make a difference? American Economic Review 85 (3), 341–364.

Curto, Vilsa E., Fryer, Roland G., Howard, Meghan L., 2010. It may not take a village: increasing achievement among the poor. Unpublished paper, Harvard University.

Darity Jr., William A., Mason, Patrick L., 1998. Evidence on discrimination in employment: codes of color, codes of gender. Journal of Economic Perspectives 12 (2), 63–90.

Datnow, Amanda, Park, Vicki, Kennedy, Brianna, 2008. Acting on data: how urban high schools use data to improve instruction. Center on Educational Governance, USC Rossier School of Education, Los Angeles.

Decker, Paul, Mayer, Daniel, Glazerman, Steven, 2004. The effects of teach for America on students: findings from a national evaluation. Mathematica Policy Research, Inc., Report, Princeton, NJ.

Dee, Thomas, 2009. Conditional cash penalties in education: evidence from the learnfare experiment. Working paper no. 15126, NBER, Cambridge, MA.

Dickens, William T., Flynn, James R., 2001. Heritability estimates versus large environmental effects: the IQ paradox resolved. Psychological Review 108 (2), 346–369.

Dickens, William T., Flynn, James R., 2006. Black Americans reduce the racial IQ gap: evidence from standardization samples. Psychological Science 17 (10), 913–920.

Dobbie, Will, Fryer, Jr. Roland G., 2009. Are high quality schools enough to close the achievement gap? Evidence from a social experiment in Harlem. Working paper no. 15473, NBER, Cambridge, MA.

Domina, Thurston, 2005. Leveling the home advantage: assessing the effectiveness of parental involvement in elementary school. Sociology of Education 78 (3), 233–249.

Easton, John Q., Flinspach, Susan Leigh, O'Connor, Carla, Paul, Mark, Qualls, Jesse, Ryan, Susan P., 1993. Local school council governance: the third year of Chicago school reform. Chicago Panel on Public School Policy and Finance, Chicago, IL.

Farber, Henry S., Gibbons, Robert, 1996. Learning and wage dynamics. Quarterly Journal of Economics 111 (4), 1007–1047.

Franzini, L., Ribble, J.C., Keddie, A.M., 2001. Understanding the Hispanic paradox. Ethnicity and Disease 11, 496–518.

Fryer, Roland G., Levitt, Steven D., 2004. Understanding the black-white test score gap in the first two years of school. Review of Economics and Statistics 86 (2), 447–464.

Fryer, Roland G., Levitt, Steven D., 2006. The black-white test score gap through third grade. American Law and Economics Review 8 (2), 249–281.

Fryer, Roland G., Levitt, Steven D., 2010. An empirical analysis of the gender gap in mathematics. American Economic Journal: Applied Economics 2 (2), 210–240.

Fryer, Roland G., Levitt, Steven D., Testing for racial differences in the mental ability of young children. American Economic Review (forthcoming).

Fryer, Roland G., 2010. Financial incentives and student achievement: evidence from randomized trials. Unpublished paper, Harvard University.

Garber, Howard L., 1988. The Milwaukee Project: preventing mental retardation in children at risk. National Institute of Handicapped Research Report, Washington, DC.

Garces, Eliana, Thomas, Duncan, Currie, Janet, 2002. Longer-term effects of Head Start. American Economic Review 92 (4), 999–1012.

Garet, Michael S., Cronen, Stephanie, Eaton, Marian, Kurki, Anja, Ludwig, Meredith, Jones, Wehmah, Uekawa, Kazuaki, Falk, Audrey, Bloom, Howard, Doolittle, Fred, Zhu, Pei, Sztenjnberg, Laura, Silverberg, Marsha, 2008. The impact of two professional development interventions on early reading instruction and achievement. US Department of Education, Institute of Education Sciences, Washington, DC.

Goolsbee, Austan, Guryan, Jonathan, 2006. The impact of Internet subsidies in public schools. Review of Economics and Statistics 88 (2), 336–347.

Gormley Jr., William T., Gayer, Ted, Phillips, Deborah, Dawson, Brittany, 2005. The effects of universal Pre-K on cognitive development. Developmental Psychology 41 (6), 872–884.

Gray, Susan W., Klaus, Rupert A., 1970. The early training project: a seventh-year report. Child Development 41, 909–924.

Greene, Jay P., Winters, Marcus A., 2006. Getting ahead by staying behind: an evaluation of Florida's program to end social promotion. Education Next 6 (2), 65–69.

Guryan, Jonathan, 2001. Does money matter? Regression-discontinuity estimates from education finance reform in Massachusetts. Working paper no. 8269, NBER, Cambridge, MA.

Guskey, Thomas R., Gates, Sally L., 1985. A synthesis of research on group-based mastery learning programs. American Educational Research Association Presentation, Chicago, IL.

Hanushek, Eric A., Kain, John, Rivkin, Steven, Branch, Gregory, 2005. Charter school quality and parental decision making with school choice. Working paper no. 11252, NBER, Cambridge, MA.

Hart, Betty, Risley, Todd R., 1995. Meaningful Differences in the Everyday Experience of Young American Children. Brookes, Baltimore, MD.

Hawkins, J. David, Kosterman, Rick, Catalano, Richard F., Hill, Karl G., Abbott, Robert D., 2008. Effects of social development intervention in childhood fifteen years later. Archives of Pediatrics & Adolescent Medicine 162 (12), 1133–1141.

Heckman, James J., Moon, Seong Hyeok, Pinto, Rodrigo, Savelyev, Peter A., Yavitz, Adam, 2009. The rate of return to the High/Scope Perry Preschool program. Working paper no. 15471, NBER, Cambridge, MA.

Heckman, James J., 1998. Detecting discrimination. Journal of Economic Perspectives 12 (2), 101–116.

Heckman, James J., 1999. Policies to foster human capital. Working paper no. 7288, NBER, Cambridge, MA.

Henig, Jeffrey R., Rich, Wilbur C., 2004. Mayors in the Middle: Politics, Race, and Mayoral Control of Urban Schools. Princeton University Press, Princeton, NJ.

Hoxby, Caroline M., Murarka, Sonali, 2009. Charter schools in New York City: who enrolls and how they affect their students' achievement. Working paper no. 14852, NBER, Cambridge, MA.

Hoxby, Caroline M., Rockoff, Jonah E., 2004. The impact of charter schools on student achievement. Unpublished paper, Harvard University.

Jacob, Brian A., Lefgren, Lars, 2004. Remedial education and student achievement: a regression-discontinuity analysis. Review of Economics and Statistics 86 (1), 226–244.

Jacob, Brian A., Ludwig, Jens, 2008. Improving educational outcomes for poor children. Working paper no. 14550, NBER, Cambridge, MA.

Jacob, Brian A., 2004. Public housing, housing vouchers, and student achievement: evidence from public housing demolitions in Chicago. American Economic Review 94 (1), 233–258.

Jacob, Brian A., 2005. Accountability, incentives and behavior: the impact of high-stakes testing in the Chicago public schools. Journal of Public Economics 89, 761–796.

James-Burdumy, Susanne, Mansfield, Wendy, Deke, John, Carey, Nancy, Lugo-Gil, Julieta, Hershey, Alan, Douglas, Aaron, Gersten, Russell, Newman-Gonchar, Rebecca, Dimino, Joseph, Faddis, Bonnie, Pendleton, Audrey, 2009. Effectiveness of Selected Reading Comprehension Interventions: Impacts on a First Cohort of Fifth-Grade Students. US Department of Education, Institute of Education Sciences, Washington, DC.

Jencks, Christopher, 1998. Racial bias in testing. In: Jencks, Christopher, Phillips, Meredith (Eds.), The Black-White Test Score Gap. The Brookings Institution Press, Washington, DC, pp. 55–85.

Jensen, Arthur R., 1973. Educability and Group Differences. The Free Press, New York.

Jensen, Arthur R., 1978. Genetic and behavioral effects of nonrandom mating. In: Noble, Clyde E. (Ed.), Human Variation: Biogenetics of Age, Race, and Sex. Academic Press, New York.

Jensen, Arthur R., 1998. The G Factor: The Science of Mental Ability. Praeger, Westport, CT.

Kane, Thomas J., Rockoff, Jonah E., Staiger, Douglas O., 2008. What does certification tell us about teacher effectiveness? Evidence from New York City. Working paper no. 12155, NBER, Cambridge, MA.

Kemple, James J., 2008. Career academies: long-term impacts on labor market outcomes, educational attainment, and transitions to adulthood. MDRC Report, New York.

Kemple, James J., Herlihy, Corinne M., Smith, Thomas J., 2005. Making progress toward graduation: evidence from the talent development high school model. MDRC Report, New York.

Klebanov, Pamelo Kato, 1994. Does neighborhood and family poverty affect mothers' parenting, mental health, and social Support? Journal of Marriage and Family 56 (2), 441–455.

Kling, Jeffrey R., Liebman, Jeffrey B., Katz, Lawrence F., 2007. Experimental analysis of neighborhood effects. Econometrica 75 (1), 83–119.

Knight, Jim (Ed.), 2009. Coaching: Approaches and Perspectives. Corwin Press, Thousand Oaks, CA.

Krieger, Nancy, Sidney, Stephen, 1996. Racial discrimination and blood pressure: the CARDIA study of young black and white adults. American Journal of Public Health 86 (10), 1370–1378.

Krueger, Alan B., 1999. Experimental estimates of education production functions. Quarterly Journal of Economics 114 (2), 497–532.

Krueger, Alan B., Whitmore, Diane, 2001. Would smaller classes help close the black white achievement gap? Working paper no. 451, Industrial Relations Section, Princeton University.

Krueger, Alan B., Zhu, Pei, 2002. Another look at the New York City school voucher experiment. Working paper no. 9418, NBER, Cambridge, MA.

Lally, J. Ronald, Mangione, Peter L., Honig, Alice S., 1987. The Syracuse University Family Development Research Program: Long-Range Impact of an Early Intervention with Low-Income Children and their Families. Center for Child & Family Studies, Far West Laboratory for Educational Research & Development, San Francisco, CA.

Lang, Kevin, Manove, Michael, 2006. Education and labor-market discrimination. Working paper no. 12257, NBER, Cambridge, MA.

Lauer, Patricia A., Akiba, Motoko, Wilkerson, Stephanie B., Apthorp, Helen S., Snow, David, Martin-Glenn, Mya L., 2006. Out-of-school-time programs: a meta-analysis of effects for at-risk students. Review of Educational Research 76 (2), 275–313.

Levin, Jessica, Quinn, Meredith, 2003. Missed opportunities: how we keep high-quality teachers out of urban classrooms. Unpublished paper, The New Teacher Project.

Lewis, Michael, McGurk, Harry, 1972. Evaluation of infant intelligence. Science 178 (December 15), 1174–1177.

List, John A., 2005. The behavioralist meets the market: measuring social preferences and reputation effects in actual transactions. Working paper no. 11616, NBER, Cambridge, MA.

Lochner, Lance, Moretti, Enrico, 2004. The effect of education on crime: evidence from prison inmates, arrests, and self-reports. American Economic Review 94 (1), 155–189.

Marlow, Michael L., 2000. Spending, school structure, and public education quality: evidence from California. Economics of Education Review 19 (1), 89–106.

McCall, Robert B., Carriger, Michael S., 1993. A meta-analysis of infant habituation and recognition memory performance as predictors of later IQ. Child Development 64 (1), 57–79.

Morrow-Howell, Nancy, Jonson-Reid, Melissa, McCrary, Stacey, Lee, YungSoo, Spitznagel, Ed, 2009. Evaluation of experience corps: student reading outcomes. Unpublished paper, Center for Social Development, George Warren Brown School of Social Work, Washington University, St. Louis, MO.

Neal, Derek A., Johnson, William R., 1996. The role of premarket factors in black-white wage differences. Journal of Political Economy 104 (5), 869–895.

Neal, Derek, 2005. Why has black-white skill convergence stopped? Working paper no. 11090, NBER, Cambridge, MA.

Neisser, Ulric, Boodoo, Gwyneth, Bouchard Jr., Thomas J., Wade Boykin, A., Brody, Nathan, Ceci, Stephen J., Halpern, Diane F., Loehlin, John C., Perloff, Robert, Sternberg, Robert J., Urbina, Susana, 1996. Intelligence: knowns and unknowns. American Psychologist 51 (2), 77–101.

Nelson, Charles A., 2000. The neurobiological bases of early intervention. In: Shonkoff, Jack P., Meisels, Samuel J. (Eds.), Handbook of Early Childhood Intervention. Cambridge University Press, New York.

Nisbett, Richard E., 1998. Race, genetics, and IQ. In: Jencks, Christopher, Phillips, Meredith (Eds.), The Black-White Test Score Gap. The Brookings Institution Press, Washington, DC, pp. 86–102.

Niswander, K.R., Gordon, M., 1972. The Women and their Pregnancies: The Collaborative Perinatal Study of the National Institute of Neurological Diseases and Stroke. US Government Print Office, Washington, DC.

Nord, Christine, Andreassen, Carol, Branden, Laura, Dulaney, Rick, Edwards, Brad, Elmore, Anne, Flanagan, Kristin Denton, Fletcher, Philip, Green, Jim, Hilpert, Richard, et al., 2005. Early Childhood Longitudinal Study, Birth cohort (ECLS-B), user's manual for the ECLS-B nine-month public-use data file and electronic code book. US Department of Education, NCES, Washington, DC.

Nye, K.E., 1995. The effect of school size and the interaction of school size and class type on selective student achievement measures in Tennessee elementary schools. Unpublished doctoral dissertation, University of Tennessee, Knoxville, TN.

Olds, David, Henderson, Charles R., Cole, Robert, Eckenrode, John, Kitzman, Harriet, Luckey, Dennis, Pettitt, Lisa, Sidora, Kimberly, Morris, Pamela, Powers, Jane, 1998. Long-term effects of nurse home visitation on children's criminal and antisocial behavior. Journal of the American Medical Association 280 (14), 1238–1244.

Olds, David L., Robinson, JoAnn, O'Brien, Ruth, Luckey, Dennis W., Pettitt, Lisa M., Henderson, Charles R., Ng, Rosanna K., Sheff, Karen L., Korfmacher, Jon, Hiatt, Susan, Talmi, Ayelet, 2002. Home visiting by paraprofessionals and by nurses: a randomized, controlled trial. Pediatrics 110 (3), 486–496.

O'Neill, June, 1990. The role of human capital in earnings differences between black and white men. Journal of Economic Perspectives 4 (4), 25–45.

Pager, Devah, 2007. The use of field experiments for studies of employment discrimination: contributions, critiques, and directions for the future. Annals of the American Academy of Political and Social Science 609 (1), 104–133.

Phillips, Meredith, Brooks-Gunn, Jeanne, Duncan, Greg J., Klebanov, Pamela, Crane, Jonathan, 1998a. Family background, parenting practices, and the black-white test score gap. In: Jencks, Christopher, Phillips, Meredith (Eds.), The Black-White Test Score Gap. The Brookings Institution Press, Washington, DC, pp. 103–147.

Phillips, Meredith, Crouse, James, Ralph, John, 1998b. Does the black-white test score gap widen after children enter school? In: Jencks, Christopher, Phillips, Meredith (Eds.), The Black-White Test Score Gap. The Brookings Institution Press, Washington, DC, pp. 229–272.

Plomin, Robert, DeFries, John C., McClearn, Gerald E., McGuffin, Peter, 2000. Behavioral Genetics. Worth, New York.

Podgursky, Michael J., Springer, Matthew G., 2007. Teacher performance pay: a review. Journal of Policy Analysis and Management 26 (4), 909–949.

Protheroe, Nancy J., Barsdate, Kelly J., 1991. Culturally Sensitive Instruction and Student Learning. Educational Research Center, Arlington, VA.

Puma, Michael, Bell, Stephen, Cook, Ronna, Heid, Camilla, Lopez, Michael, et al., 2005. Head Start Impact Study: First Year Findings. US Department of Health and Human Services, Washington, DC.

Puma, Michael, Bell, Stephen, Cook, Ronna, Heid, Camilla, et al., 2010. Head Start Impact Study: Final Report. US Department of Health and Human Services, Washington, DC.

Reuter, E.B., 1945. Racial theory. American Journal of Sociology 50 (6), 452–461.

Rock, Donald A., Stenner, Jackson, 2005. Assessment issues in the testing of children at school entry. The Future of Children 15 (1), 15–34.

Rockoff, Jonah E., 2004. The impact of individual teachers on student achievement: evidence from panel data. American Economic Review 94 (2), 247–252.

Rockoff, Jonah E., 2008. Does mentoring reduce turnover and improve skills of new employees? Evidence from teachers in New York City. Working paper no. 13868, NBER, Cambridge, MA.

Rouse, Cecilia E., Krueger, Alan B., 2004. Putting computerized instruction to the test: a randomized evaluation of a 'scientifically based' reading program. Economics of Education Review 23 (4), 323–338.

Rushton, J. Philippe, Jensen, Arthur, 2005. Thirty years of research on race differences in cognitive ability. Psychology, Public Policy, and Law 11 (2), 235–294.

Rushton, J. Philippe, 1995. Race and crime: international data for 1989-1990. Psychological Reports 76 (1), 307–312.

Sanbonmatsu, Lisa, Kling, Jeffrey R., Duncan, Greg J., Brooks-Gunn, Jeanne, 2006. Neighborhoods and academic achievement: results from the moving to opportunity experiment. The Journal of Human Resources 41 (4), 649–691.

Schanzenbach, Diane Whitmore, 2007. What have researchers learned from project STAR? Brookings Papers on Education Policy 2006/07: 205–228.

Schultz, T. Paul, Strauss, John, 2008. Handbook of Development Economics, vol. 4. North-Holland, Amsterdam, New York.

Schweinhart, Lawrence J., Barnes, Helen V., Weikart, David P., 1993. Significant benefits: the High/Scope Perry Preschool study through age 27. High Scope Press, Ypsilanti, MI.

Shapka, Jennifer D., Keating, Daniel P., 2003. Effects of a girls-only curriculum during adolescence: performance, persistence, and engagement in mathematics and science. American Educational Research Journal 40 (4), 929–960.

Shonkoff, Jack P., 2006. A promising opportunity for developmental and behavioral pediatrics at the interface of neuroscience, psychology, and social policy: remarks on receiving the 2005 C. Anderson Aldrich Award. Pediatrics 118, 2187–2191.

Shukla, S., 1971. Priorities in educational policy. Economic and Political Weekly 6 (30–32), 1649–1651; 1653–1654.

Taggart, Robert, 1995. Quantum Opportunity Program Opportunities. Industrialization Center of America, Philadelphia, PA.

Thernstrom, Abigail, 1992. The drive for racially inclusive schools. Annals of the American Academy of Political and Social Science 523, 131–143.

Thompson, Ross A., 2000. The legacy of early achievements. Child Development 71 (1), 145–152.

Turney, Kristin, Edin, Kathryn, Clampet-Lundquist, Susan, Kling, Jeffrey R., Duncan, Greg J., 2006. Neighborhood effects on barriers to employment: results from a randomized housing mobility experiment in Baltimore. Brookings-Wharton Papers on Urban Affairs 2006, 137–187.

Wagner, Mary M., Clayton, Serena L., 1999. The parents as teachers program: results from two demonstrations. The Future of Children 9 (1), 91–115.

Walker, Gary, Vilella-Velez, Frances, 1992. Anatomy of a Demonstration: The Summer Training and Education Program (STEP) from Pilot through Replication and Postprogram Impacts. Public/Private Ventures, Philadelphia, PA.

Wigdor, Alexandra K., Green, Bert F., 1991. Performance Assessment for the Workplace, vol. 1. National Academies Press, Washington, DC.

Wilson, William Julius, 2010. More than Just Race: Being Black and Poor in the Inner City (Issues of Our Time). W.W. Norton & Company, New York.

Wong, Kenneth L., Shen, Francis X., 2002. Do school district takeovers work? Assessing the effectiveness of city and state takeovers as school reform strategy. State Education Standard 3 (2), 19–23.

Wong, Kenneth L., Shen, Francis X., 2005. When mayors lead urban schools: assessing the effects of takeover. In: Howell, William G. (Ed.), Beseiged: School Boards and the Future of Education Politics. The Brookings Institution Press, Washington, DC, pp. 81–101.

Yeates, Keith Owen, MacPhee, David, Campbell, Frances A., Ramey, Craig T., 1983. Maternal IQ and home environment as determinants of early childhood intellectual competence: a developmental analysis. Developmental Psychology 19 (5), 731–739.

Ziedenberg, Jason, Schiraldi, Vincent, 2002. Cellblocks or classrooms? The funding of higher education and corrections and its impact on African American men. Unpublished paper, Justice Policy Institute.

CHAPTER 11

Imperfect Competition in the Labor Market

Alan Manning[1]

Centre for Economic Performance, London School of Economics, Houghton Street, London WC2A 2AE

Contents

[1] I would like to thank the editors and conference participants for their comments. And Claudia Steinwender for her research assistance.

Abstract

It is increasingly recognized that labor markets are pervasively imperfectly competitive, that there are rents to the employment relationship for both worker and employer. This chapter considers why it is sensible to think of labor markets as imperfectly competitive, reviews estimates on the size of rents, theories of and evidence on the distribution of rents between worker and employer, and the areas of labor economics where a perspective derived from imperfect competition makes a substantial difference to thought.

JEL classification: J0; J42; J63; J64

Keywords: Imperfect competition; Labor markets; Rents; Search; Matching; Monopsony

INTRODUCTION

In recent years, it has been increasingly recognized that many aspects of labor markets are best analyzed from the perspective that there is some degree of imperfect competition. At its most general, "imperfect competition" should be taken to mean that employer or worker or both get some rents from an existing employment relationship. If an employer gets rents, then this means that the employer will be worse off if a worker leaves i.e. the marginal product is above the wage and worker replacement is costly. If a worker gets rents then this means that the loss of the current job makes the worker worse off—an identical job cannot be found at zero cost. If labor markets are perfectly competitive then an employer can find any number of equally productive workers at the prevailing market wage so that a worker who left could be costlessly replaced by an identical worker paid the same wage. And a worker who lost their job could immediately find another identical employer paying the same wage so would not suffer losses.

A good reason for thinking that there are rents in the employment relationship is that people think jobs are a "big deal". For example, when asked open-ended questions about the most important events in their life over the past year, employment-related events (got job, lost job, got promoted) come second after "family" events (births, marriages,

Table 1   Self-reported important life events in past year: UK data.

	All	Men	Women
Family	38	33	42
Employment	22	24	20
Nothing	20	22	18
Leisure	19	19	19
Education	13	11	15
Health	12	10	13
Consumption	9	9	8
Housing	8	7	9
Other	7	6	7
Financial	4	4	4

Source: British household panel study.

divorces and death)—see Table 1 for some British evidence on this. This evidence resonates with personal experience and with more formal evidence—for example, the studies of Jacobson et al. (1993) and Von Wachter, Manchester and Song (2009) all suggest substantial costs of job loss. And classic studies like Oi (1962) suggest non-trivial costs of worker replacement.

This chapter reviews some recent developments in thinking about imperfect competition in labor markets. The plan is as follows. The next section outlines the main sources of rents in the employment relationship. The second section discusses some estimates of the size of rents in the employment relationship. The third section then consider theoretical models of how the rents in the employment relationship are split between worker and employer (the question of wage determination) and the fourth section considers evidence on rent-splitting. I argue that this all adds up to a persuasive view that imperfect competition is pervasive in labor markets. But, up to this point, we have not considered the "so what" question—how does the perspective of imperfect competition alter our views on substantive labor market issues?—that is the subject of the fifth section. The sixth section then reviews a number of classic topics in labor economics—the law of one wage, the effect of regulation, the gender pay gap, human capital accumulation and economic geography—where the perspective of imperfect competition can be shown to make a difference.

This chapter is rather different in style from other excellent surveys of this area (e.g. Rogerson et al., 2005 or Mortensen and Pissarides, 1999 or Mortensen, 1986). Much work in this area is phrased in terms of canonical models—one might mention the search and matching models of Pissarides (1985, 2000) or Mortensen and Pissarides (1994) or the wage-posting model of Burdett and Mortensen (1998). New developments are often thought of as departures from these canonical models. Although the use of very particular models encourages precise thinking, that precision relates to the models and not the world and can easily become spurious precision when the models are very abstract with assumptions designed more for analytical tractability than realism. So, a model-based approach to the topic is not always helpful and this survey is based on the belief that it can be useful to think in very broad terms about general principles and that one can say useful things without having to couch them in a complete but necessarily very particular model.

1. THE SOURCES OF IMPERFECT COMPETITION

As will be discussed below there are different ways in which economists have sought to explain why there are rents in the employment relationship. This section will argue they are best understood as having a common theme—that, from the worker perspective, it takes time and/or money to find another employer who is a perfect substitute for the current one and that, from an employer perspective, it is costly to find another worker who is a perfect substitute for the current one. And, that, taken individually, these explanations of the sources of rents often do not seem particularly plausible but, taken together, they add up to a convincing description of the labor market.

1.1. Frictions and idiosyncracies

First, consider search models (for relatively recent reviews see Mortensen and Pissarides, 1999; Rogerson et al., 2005). In these models it is assumed that it takes time for employers to be matched with workers because workers' information about the labor market is imperfect (an idea first put forward by Stigler, 1961, 1962)—in some versions, the job offer arrival rate can be influenced by the expenditure of time and/or money (see Section 2.2.1 below for such a model). These models have become the workhorse model in much of macroeconomics (see Rogerson and Shimer, 2011) because one cannot otherwise explain the dynamics of unemployment. But, taken literally, this model is not very plausible. It is not hard to find an employer—I can probably see 10 from my office window. But, what is hard is to find an employer who is currently recruiting[2] who is the same as my current one i.e. a perfect substitute for my current job. This is because there is a considerable idiosyncratic component to employers across a vast multitude of dimensions that workers care about. This idiosyncratic component might come from non-monetary aspects of the job (e.g. one employer has a nice boss, another a nasty one, one has convenient hours, another does not) or from differences in commuting distances or from many other sources. A good analogy is our view of the heavens: the stars appear close together but this is an illusion caused by projecting three dimensions onto two. Neglecting the multitude of dimensions along which employers differ that matter to workers will seriously overestimate our impression of the extent to which jobs are perfect substitutes for each other from the perspective of workers.

---

[2] It is an interesting question why not all employers are recruiting all the time if the typical employment relationship has rents. Manning (2003a, chapter 10) offers an answer to this apparent conundrum—it is costly to create jobs and employers do not create jobs they do not expect to be able to fill. Vacancies, in this view, are best seen as "accidents".

One other commonly given explanation for why there may be rents in the employment relationship is "specific human capital". Although this is normally thought of as distinct from the reasons given above, it is better thought of as another way in which employers may not be perfect substitutes for each other—in this case in terms of the quality of the match or the marginal product of the worker. This comes out clearly in the discussion of specific human capital provided by Lazear (2003). He struggles with the problem of what exactly are specific skills, coming up with the answer that "it is difficult to generate convincing examples where the firm-specific component [of productivity] approaches the general component". He goes on to argue that all skills are general skills but that different employers vary in how important those skills are in their particular situation. So, a worker with a particular package of general skills will not be faced with a large number of employers requiring exactly that package. As Lazear (2003, p. 2) makes clear, this relies on employers being thin on the ground otherwise a large supply of employers demanding exactly your mix of skills would be available and the market would be perfectly competitive. Again, it is the lack of availability of employers who are perfect substitutes that can be thought of as the source of the rents.

A key and eminently sensible idea in the specific human capital literature originating in Becker (1993) is that specific human capital accumulates over time. This means that rents in the employment relationship are likely to be higher for those workers who have been in their current job for a long time—very few labor economists would dissent from this position. The very fact that we turn up to the same employer day after day strongly suggests there are some rents from that relationship. More controversial is whether, on a worker's first day in the job, there are already rents because the employer has paid something to hire them and the worker could not get another equivalent job immediately. This paper is predicated on the view that there are rents from the first day[3]— that the worker would be disappointed if they turned up for work to be told there was no longer a need for them and that the employer would be irritated if the new hire does not turn up on the first morning.

One interesting question to think about is whether the rapid decline in the costs of supplying and acquiring information associated with the Internet is going to make labor markets more like the competitive ideal in the future than the past. There is no doubt that the Internet (and earlier communication technologies) have transformed job search. In late 19th century London an unemployed worker would have trudged from employer to employer, knocking on doors and enquiring whether there were any vacancies, often spending the whole day on it and walking many miles. In contrast, a worker today can, with access to the Internet, find out about job opportunities throughout the globe. Using the Internet as a method of job search has rapidly become near-universal. For example, in

---

[3] Though, as discussed below, it may be the case that workers are not profitable from their first day because they need some training. Employers will then be most unhappy if a worker quits on the first day they become profitable, though will still be unhappy if a worker leaves on the first day if it takes time and/or money to replace them.

the UK Labour Force Survey the percentage of employed job-seekers using the Internet rose from 62% in 2005 to 82% in 2009 and the percentage of unemployed job-seekers using the Internet rose from 48% to 79% over the same period. These figures also indicate that the "digital divide", the gap in access to the internet between the rich and the poor, may also be diminishing.

But, while there is little doubt that Internet use is becoming pervasive in job search, there is more doubt about whether it is transforming the outcomes of the labor market. Autor (2001) provides a good early discussion of the issues. While the Internet has increased the quantity of information available to both workers looking for a job and employers looking for a worker has gone up, it is much less clear that the quality has also risen. If the costs of applying for a job fall then applications become particularly more attractive for those who think they have little chance of getting the job—something they know but their prospective employer may only discover at some expense. One way of assessing whether the Internet has transformed labor markets is to look at outcomes. Kuhn and Skutterud (2004) do not find a higher job-finding rate for those who report using the Internet and the Beveridge curve does not appear to have shifted inwards.

So, the conclusion would seem to be that the Internet has transformed the labor market less than one might have thought from the most common ways in which frictions are modeled. If one thinks of frictions as being caused by a lack of awareness of where vacancies are, and the cost of hiring the cost of posting a vacancy until a suitable job application is received, then one might have expected a large effect of the Internet. But if, as argued here and later in this chapter, one thinks of frictions as coming from idiosyncracies in the attractiveness of different jobs, and the costs of hiring as being primarily the costs of selection and training new workers, then one would be less surprised that the effects of the Internet seem to be more modest.

1.2. Institutions and collusion

So far, the discussion has concentrated on rents that are inevitable. But rents may also arise from man-made institutions that artificially restrict competition. This implicit or explicit collusion may be by workers or employers. Traditionally it is collusion by workers in the form of trade unions that has received the most attention. However, this chapter does not discuss the role of unions at all because it is covered in another chapter (Farber, 2011).

Employer collusion has received much less attention. This is in spite of the fact that Adam Smith (1970, p. 84) wrote: "we rarely hear... of the combinations of masters; though frequently of those of workmen. But whoever imagines, upon this account, that masters rarely combine, is as ignorant of the world as of the subject". Employer collusion where it exists is thought to be in very specific labor markets e.g. US professional sports or, more controversially, nurses (see, for example, Hirsch and Schumacher, 1995) and teachers who may have a limited number of potential employers in their areas (see Boal and Ransom, 1997, for a discussion).

There a number of more recent papers arguing that some institutions and laws in the labor market serve to aid collusion of employers to hold down wages. For example, Naidu (2010) explores the effect of legislation in the post–bellum South that punished (almost exclusively white) employers if they enticed (almost exclusively black) workers away from other employers. Although it might appear at first sight to be white employers who suffered from this legislation, Naidu (2010) presents evidence that, by reducing competition for workers, it was blacks who were made worse off by this. The legislation can be thought of as a way for employers to commit not to compete for workers, leading to a more collusive labor market outcome.

A more contemporary example would be the debate over the "National resident Matching Program" (NMRP) that matches medical residents and hospitals. In 2002 a class action suit was brought against hospitals alleging breach of anti-trust legislation, essentially that the NMRP enabled hospitals to collude to set medical resident wages at lower than competitive levels. This case was eventually resolved by Congress passing legislation that effectively exempted the NMRP from anti-trust legislation (details of this can be found at http://kuznets.fas.harvard.edu/~aroth/alroth.html#MarketDesign). There is some theoretical work (e.g. Bulow and Levin, 2006; Niederle, 2007) arguing whether, in theory, the NMRP might reduce wages. These papers look at the incentive for wage competition within the NMRP. More, recently Priest (2010) has argued that the "problems" of the labor markets for medical interns (which have led to the use of matching algorithms like the NMRP) are in fact the consequences of employer collusion on wages in a labor market with very heterogeneous labor and that a matching algorithm would not be needed if the market was allowed to be competitive. He also argues that the market for legal clerks is similar.

Another recent example is Kleiner and Won Park (2010), who examine how different state regulations on dentists and dental hygienists affect the labor market outcomes for these two occupations. They present evidence that states which allow hygienists to practice without supervision from dentists (something we would expect to strengthen the market position of hygienists and weaken that of dentists) have, on average, higher earnings for hygienists and lower earnings for dentists.

All of these examples relate to very specific labor markets that might be thought to all be highly atypical. But there remains an open question as to whether employer collusion is important in more representative labor markets. It is clear that employers do not en masse collude to set wages, but there may be more subtle but nevertheless effective ways to do it. For example, as the physical location of employers is important to workers, it is likely that, for many workers, the employers who are closest substitutes from the perspective of workers are also geographically close, making communication and interaction between them easy. Manning (2009) gives an example of a model in which employers are on a circle (as in Bhaskar and To, 1999) and collude only with the two neighboring employers in setting wages. Although there is no collusion spread over the whole market, Manning (2009) shows that a little bit of collusion can go a long way leading to labor market outcomes a long way from perfect competition. One way of putting the question is "Do managers of neighboring fast food restaurants talk to each other or think about how the other might react if wages were to change?". Ethnographic studies of labor markets may give us some clues. The classic study of the New Haven labor market in Reynolds (1951) did conclude there was a good deal of discussion among employers about economic conditions, and that there was an implicit agreement not to poach workers from each other. One might expect this to foster some degree of collusion though Reynolds (1951, p. 217) is clear that there is no explicit collusive wage-setting. In contrast, the more recent ethnographic study of the same labor market by Bewley (1999) finds that the employers source of information about their rivals comes not from direct communication but from workers or from market surveys provided by consultancies. Those institutions sound less collusive than those described by Reynolds. But, the honest answer is that we just don't know much about tacit collusion by employers because no-one has thought it worthwhile to investigate in detail.

2. HOW MUCH IMPERFECT COMPETITION? THE SIZE OF RENTS

A natural question to ask is how important is imperfect competition in the labor market? As explained in the introduction, this is really about the size of rents earned by employer and worker from an on-going employment relationship. The experiment one would like to run is to randomly and forcibly terminate employment relationships and examine how the pay-offs of employer and worker change. We do not have that experiment and, if we did, it would not be that easy to measure the pay-offs which would not just be in the current period but also into the future.

Nonetheless we can make some attempt to measure the size of rents, and this section illustrates the way in which we might attempt to do that. First, we seek to exploit the idea that the larger the size of rents, the more expenditure on rent-seeking activity we would expect to see—we use this idea from both worker and employer perspectives. Second, we consider what happens when workers lose their jobs. Before we review these estimates, one should be aware that there is almost certainly huge variation in the extent of rents in the labor market so that one has to bear in mind that the estimates that follow are not from random samples and should not automatically be regarded as representative of the labor market as a whole. And, as will become apparent, these estimates are pretty rough and ready, and should be interpreted as giving, at best, some idea of orders of magnitude.

2.1. The costs of recruitment
2.1.1. Theory
First, consider how we might attempt to measure rents from the perspective of employers. If an employer and worker are forcibly separated then a good estimate of the size of the

rents is the cost of replacing the worker with an identical one—what we will call the marginal hiring cost. Using the marginal hiring cost as a measure of employer rents is quite a general principle but let's see it worked out in a specific model, the Pissarides (1990) matching model. Denote by J the value of a filled job and J_v the value of a vacant job—the size of the rents accruing to an employer can be measured by $(J - J_v)$. The value function of a vacant job must be given by:

$$r J_v = -c + \theta \, (J - J_v) \tag{1}$$

where r is the interest rate, c is the per-period cost of a vacancy and θ is the rate at which vacancies are filled. As firms can freely create vacant jobs (it is a filled vacancy that can't be costlessly created) we will have $J_v = 0$ in equilibrium, in which case (1) can be re-arranged to give us:

$$(J - J_v) = \frac{c}{\theta} \tag{2}$$

which can be interpreted as saying that the value of a filled job to an employer is equal to the per period vacancy cost times the expected duration of a vacancy. This can be interpreted as the marginal cost of a hire. This latter principle can be thought of as much more general than the specific model used to illustrate the idea.

The specific model outlined here suggests a very particular way of measuring the rents accruing to employers—measure the cost of advertising a job and the expected duration of a vacancy. Both of these numbers are probably small, at least for most jobs (for example, the study of five low-wage British employers in Brown et al. (2001), found that the advertising costs were often zero because they used the free Public Employment Service). However, the way in which the hiring cost is modeled here is not the best. Actual studies of the costs of filling vacancies find that the bulk of the costs are not in generating applicants as this model suggests but in selecting workers from applicants and training those workers to be able to do the job[4].

Even once one has got an estimate of the marginal hiring cost, which we will denote for the moment by h, one needs to scale it in some way to get an idea of how important they are. The natural way to do that would is to relate it to the wage, w. However, salary is a recurrent cost whereas the hiring cost is a one-off cost. How large are hiring costs depends in part on how long the worker will be with the firm. Given this it is natural to multiply the hiring costs by the interest rate plus the separation rate i.e. to use the measure $(r + s)h/w$. Because separation rates are often about 20% and much bigger than real interest rates, this is approximately equal to multiplying the hiring costs by the separation rate, $(s * h/w)$ which can also be thought of as dividing the hiring cost by the expected tenure of the worker (which is $1/s$), to give the hiring cost spread over each

---

[4] It is also likely that the capital cost of having unused capital when there is an unfilled vacancy is also quite large.

period the firm expects to have the worker. Another way of looking at the same thing is the share of wage payments over the whole job tenure that is spent on recruiting and training a worker. In a steady-state this will be equal to the ratio of total hiring costs to the current wage bill as the total hires must be equal to sN with total hiring costs sNh, compared to total wage bill wN, giving the same measure.

Hiring costs play an important role in macroeconomic models based on imperfect competition in the labor market deriving from search. These studies (e.g. Silva and Toldeo, 2009; Pissarides, 2009) generally choose to parameterize hiring costs differently—as the cost of posting a vacancy (c/θ in (2)) for a period relative to the wage for the same period. This can be converted to the measure proposed above by recognizing this needs to then be scaled by the expected duration of a newly-filled job (which is $1/s$). So one can go from the measure I am reporting to the measure preferred by macroeconomists the importance of hiring costs by dividing by the expected duration of a job.

2.1.2. Evidence on hiring costs

It is hard to get direct data on hiring costs and the estimates we do have are for very different times and places and from very different data sets. In a very brief review of some estimates, Hamermesh (1993, p. 208-9) noted the paucity and diversity of estimates and argued the problem derived from the difficulty of defining and measuring hiring costs. Not much has changed since then. Some estimates are summarized in Table 2, where we report two measures of the size of hiring costs—hiring costs as a percentage of total labor costs (the measure described above) and hiring costs as a percentage of monthly earnings. The second measure can be turned into the first by dividing by the expected duration (in months) of a job—this measure of job tenure is not available in all data sets (notably, Barron et al., 1997). Not all of the estimates measure all aspects of hiring costs and not all the studies contain enough information to enable one to compute both measures. For example, the French studies of Abowd and Kramarz (2003) and Kramarz and Michaud (2010) exclude the amount of time spent by workers in the firm on the recruitment process.

Although there is a very wide range of estimates in Table 2, some general features do emerge. First, the original Oi (1962) estimates seem in the right ballpark—with hiring costs a bit below 5% of the total labor costs. The bulk of these costs are the costs associated with training newly-hired workers and raising them to the productivity of an experienced worker. The costs of recruiting activity are much smaller. We also have evidence of heterogeneity in hiring costs, both across worker characteristics (the hiring costs of more skilled workers typically being higher) and employer characteristics (the hiring costs of large employers typically being higher). But, one should recognize that we do not know enough about the hiring process—another chapter in this volume (Oyer and Schaefer, 2011) makes a similar point.

Table 2 Estimates of hiring costs.

Study	Sample	Costs included	Hiring costs as percentage of wage bill	Hiring costs as percentage of monthly pay
Oi (1962)	International Harvester, 1951	Recruitment and training costs	7.3% (all workers) 4.1% (common laborers)	
Barron et al. (1997)	US Firms, 1980, 1982, 1992, 1993	Recruitment and training costs		34%–156% (total) 5%–14% (recruitment) 34%–156% (training)[a]
Manning (2006)	British firms	Recruitment and training costs	2.4% (unskilled) 4.5% (others) 11.2% (sales)	
Brown et al. (2001)	5 low-paying British firms	Recruitment and training costs	2.3%–11%	55%–118%
Abowd and Kramarz (2003), Kramarz and Michaud (2010)	French firms, 2002	Includes training and external hiring costs; excludes internal hiring costs	2.8%	
Blatter et al. (2009)	Skilled workers with vocational degree in Swiss firms, 2000, 2004	Costs of recruitment and initial training	3.3%	
Dube, Freeman and Reich (2010)	California establishment survey, 2003, 2008	Costs of recruitment and training and separation	1.5%	72%

[a] This is an estimate derived from Table 7.1 of Barron et al. (1997), with the reported hours of those spent on the recruiting and/or training multiplied by 1.5, a crude estimate of the relative wage of recruiters/trainers to new recruits taken from Silva and Toldeo (2009). This is then divided by an assumption of a 40 hour week to derive the fraction of a month's pay spent on recruiting/training.

2.1.3. Marginal and average hiring costs

It is not entirely clear from Table 2 whether we have estimates of average or marginal hiring costs—from the theoretical point of view we would like the latter more than the former. In some surveys (e.g. Barron et al., 1997) the questions on hiring costs relate to the last hire, so the responses might be interpreted as a marginal hiring cost. In other studies (e.g. Abowd and Kramarz, 2003) the question relates to all expenditure on certain activities in the past year, so are more likely to be closer to average hiring costs. In others studies, it is not clear.

To think about the relationship between average and marginal hiring costs suppose that the total cost of R recruits is given by:

$$C = h_0 R^{\frac{1}{\beta}}. \tag{3}$$

Then there is the following relationship between marginal hiring cost and the average hiring cost:

$$\text{marginal hiring cost} = \frac{1}{\beta} * \text{average hiring cost}. \tag{4}$$

If β is below (above) 1 there are increasing (decreasing) marginal costs of recruitment, and the marginal cost will be above (below) the average cost.

We do have some little bits of evidence on the returns to scale in hiring costs. Manning (2006), Blatter et al. (2009) and Dube, Freeman and Reich (2010) all report increasing marginal costs, although the latter study finds that only in a cross-section. However, Abowd and Kramarz (2003) and Kramarz and Michaud (2010) report decreasing marginal costs, as they estimate hiring to have a fixed cost component. However, this last result may be because they exclude the costs of recruitment, where one would expect marginal costs to be highest. The finding in Barron et al. (1997) that large firms have higher hiring costs might also be interpreted as evidence of increasing marginal costs, as large firms can only get that way by lots of hiring. Our evidence on this question is not strong, and one cannot use these studies to get a reliable point estimate of β. One can also link the question of whether there are increasing marginal costs of hiring to the older literature on employment adjustment costs (e.g. Nickell, 1986; Hamermesh, 1993)—the traditional way of modeling these adjustment costs as quadratic corresponds to increasing marginal hiring costs.

Worrying about a possible distinction between marginal and average hiring costs might seem a minor issue, but Section 4.3.4 shows why it is more important than one might have thought for how one thinks about the nature of labor markets and the likely effects of labor market regulation.

2.2. The search activity of the non-employed

2.2.1. Theory

Now consider the size of rents from the perspective of workers. One cannot use a similar methodology to that used in the previous section because, while it is reasonable to assume that vacant jobs are in potentially infinite supply, one cannot make the same assumption about unemployed workers. The approach taken here is that if employment offers sizeable rents we would expect to see the unemployed making strenuous efforts to find employment and the size of those efforts can be used as a measure of the rents.

Consider an unemployed worker who faces a wage offer distribution, $F(w)$, and can influence the arrival rate of job offers, λ, by spending time on job search. Denote by γ the fraction of a working week spent on job search and $\lambda(\gamma)$ the function relating the job offer arrival rate to the time spent on job search. The value of being unemployed, V^u, can then be written as:

$$rV^u = \max_{(w^*,\gamma)} b_u + b[1 - \gamma] + \lambda(\gamma) \int_{w^*} [V(w) - V^u] dF(w) \qquad (5)$$

where r is the interest rate, b_u is the income received when unemployed, b is the value of leisure, w^* is the reservation wage (also a choice variable), and $V(w)$ is the value of a job that pays a wage w. This is a set-up first used by Barron and Mellow (1979). Taking the first order condition for the time spent on job search, γ:

$$b = \lambda'(\gamma) \int_{w^*} [V(w) - V^u] dF(w). \qquad (6)$$

This shows us that the incentive for workers to generate wage offers is related to the rents they will get from those offers. Let us rearrange (6) to give us:

$$\frac{\int_{w^*} [V(w) - V^u] dF(w)}{1 - F(w^*)} = \frac{b}{1 - F(w^*)} \cdot \frac{1}{\lambda'(\gamma)} = \frac{b}{\lambda(1 - F(w^*))} \cdot \frac{\lambda'(\gamma)}{\lambda'(\gamma)}$$

$$= \frac{bd_u\gamma}{\varepsilon_{\lambda\gamma}} \qquad (7)$$

where $\varepsilon_{\lambda\gamma}$ is the elasticity of the job offer arrival rate with respect to search effort and d_u is the expected duration of unemployment[5].

The left-hand side of (7) is the rents from employment averaged over all the jobs the unemployed worker might get. This is unobservable and what we would like to estimate. Equation (7) says that these average rents should be equated to the monetary value of leisure multiplied by the expected total time spent searching until getting a job (which is the duration of unemployment multiplied by time per week spent on job search) divided by the inverse of the elasticity of the job offer arrival rate to search effort. All of these elements are things that we might hope to be able to estimate, some more easily than others.

---

[5] Which is given by the inverse of $\lambda[1 - F(w^*)]$, the rate at which job offers arrived multiplied by the fraction of them that are acceptable to the worker.

Table 3 Estimates of time spent on job search by unemployed workers.

Study	Data set	Sample	Time spent on job search (hours per week)
Krueger and Mueller (2010)	Time Use surveys for 14 countries	Unemployed	3.5 (US) 0.5 (Nordic) 1.1 (Other Europe)
Holzer (1988)	NLSY, 1981	Young US unemployed	15 (mean)
Barron and Mellow (1979)	CPS Supplement, 1976	US unemployed	7 (mean)
Smith et al. (2000)	JSA Survey, 1996	UK UI claimants	6.8 (mean) 4 (median)
Erens and Hedges (1990)	Survey of incomes in and out of work, 1987	UK UI claimants	7.3 (mean) 5 (median)

The intuition for (7) is simple—if workers typically get rents from jobs we would expect to see them willing to expend considerable amounts of time and money to get a job. However, to convert the right-hand side of (7) to monetary units we need a monetary value for leisure when unemployed. We would like to normalize these costs to get an estimate of the "per period" rent. Appendix A works through a very simple model to sketch how one might do that and derives the following formula for the gap between the average wage, $\bar{w}$, and the reservation wage, w^*:

$$\frac{\bar{w} - w^*}{w^*} = (1 - \rho) \frac{\gamma}{\varepsilon_{\lambda\gamma}[1 - \gamma] + \gamma} \cdot \frac{u}{1 - u} \tag{8}$$

where ρ is the income when unemployed as a fraction of the reservation wage and u is the steady-state unemployment rate for the worker. The elements on the right-hand side of (8) are all elements we might hope to estimate.

2.2.2. Evidence

A crucial element in (8) is the fraction of a working week that the unemployed spend on job search. Table 3 provides a set of estimates of the time spent on job search by the unemployed, though such estimates are not as numerous as one would like. Probably the most striking fact about the job search activity of the unemployed is often how small is the amount of time they seem to spend on it. The most recent study is the cross-country comparison of Krueger and Mueller (2010), who use time-use surveys to conclude that the average unemployed person spends approximately 4 minutes a day on job search in the Nordic countries, 10 minutes in the rest of Europe, and 30 minutes in North America.

But the other US and UK studies reported in Table 3 find higher levels of job search[6]. These studies use a methodology where a direct question is asked of the unemployed about the amount of time spent searching, a very different methodology from the time-use studies. However, even these studies do not suggest a huge amount of time spent unemployed as it is essentially a part-time activity. Taking these numbers at face value they perhaps suggest a value for γ in the region of 0.1-0.2.

If one assumed that the steady-state unemployment rate for currently unemployed workers is 10%, and that the replacement rate was 0 and that $\varepsilon_{\lambda\gamma}$ was 1 so that a doubling of search effort leads to a doubling of the job offer arrival rate, one would conclude from the use of the formula in (8) that the rents for unemployed workers are small, no more than 2%. However, there are a number of reasons to be cautious about this conclusion.

First, the formula in (8) is very sensitive to the assumed value of $\varepsilon_{\lambda\gamma}$. If increases in search time lead to little improvement in job offer arrival rates, a small amount of job search is consistent with large rents. Ideally we would like to have some experimental evidence on what happens when we force individuals to increase job search activity. Although there are a large number of studies (many experimental or quasi-experimental), that seek to estimate the effect of programmes designed to assist with job search on various outcomes for the unemployment, many of these job search assistance programs combine more checking on the job search activity of the unemployed with help to make search more effective. For current purposes we would like only the former. One study that seems to come close is Klepinger et al. (2002) which investigates the effect of Maryland doubling the number of required employer contacts from 2 to 4. This doubling of required contacts significantly reduced the number of weeks of UI receipt by 0.7 weeks on a base of 11.9 so a doubling in the required number of contacts reduces unemployment durations by 6%. Assuming that the doubling of the number of contacts doubles the cost leads to a very small implied elasticity of 0.04. There are a number of reasons to be cautious—we do not have evidence about how much employer contacts were actually increased and, second, when individuals are forced to comply with increased employer contacts they would not choose for themselves, they will probably choose low-cost but ineffective contacts. These would tend to lead to lower estimates of the elasticity. On the other hand exits from UI are not the same as exits to employment and the employment outcomes are not so favorable.

There are also a number of non-experimental studies that seek to relate unemployment durations to job search intensity, with mixed results that suggest caution in interpretation. For example, Holzer (1987) reports estimates for the effect of time spent on a variety of search methods on the probability of gaining new employment (though he also controls for the number of search methods used)—many of the estimated effects are insignificant or even "wrongly-signed".

---

[6] There may well be similar studies for other countries but I have been unable to find any. Apologies to those that I missed but statistics on time spent searching are often buried in articles whose main subject is rather different.

Secondly, the formula in (8) assumes that the cost of time in job search and employment can be equated. However, the time cost of job search may be higher than one might think as Krueger and Mueller (2010) find that levels of sadness and stress are high for the unemployed while looking for a job and levels of happiness are low. If these emotional costs are high, the cost of job search will be higher than one otherwise would have thought, reducing the incentives to spend time on it.

Thirdly, while job search seems to use more time than money (something that motivated the model used here), the monetary cost is not zero. While the unemployed have a lot of time on their hands, they are short of money. Studies like Card et al. (2007) suggest that the unemployed are unable to smooth consumption across periods of employment and unemployment so that the marginal utility of income for the unemployed may be much higher than for the employed. For example, in the UK evaluation of the Job Seekers' Allowance, one-third of UI recipients reported that their job search was limited because of the costs involved, with the specific costs most commonly mentioned being travel, stationery, postage and phone. If time and money are complements in the job search production function, low expenditure will tend to be related to low time spent.

Finally, DellaVigna and Daniele Paserman (2005) investigate the effect of hyperbolic discounting in a job search model. They present evidence that, in line with theoretical predictions, the impatient engage in lower levels of job search and have longer unemployment durations. If this is the right model of behavior one would have to up-rate the costs of job search by the degree of impatience to get an estimate of the size of rents from jobs.

So, the bottom line is that although the fact that the unemployed do not seem to expand huge amounts of effort into trying to get employment might lead one to conclude that the rents are not large, there are reasons why such a conclusion might be hasty. And we do have other evidence that the unemployed are worse off than the employed in terms of well-being—see, for example, Clark and Oswald (1994), Krueger and Mueller (2010). I would be hesitant to conclude that the rents from employment are small for the unemployed because of the low levels of search activity as I suspect that if one told a room of the unemployed that their apathy showed they did not care about having a job, one would get a fairly rough reception. When asked to explain low levels of search activity, one would be much more likely to hear the answer "there is no point", i.e. they say that the marginal return to more search effort, $\varepsilon_{\lambda\gamma}$, is low.

One possible explanation for why the unemployed do not spend more time on job search is that the matching process is better characterized by stock–flow matching rather than the more familiar stock–stock matching (Coles and Smith, 1998; Ebrahimy and Shimer, 2010). In stock–flow matching newly unemployed workers quickly exhaust the stock of existing vacancies in which they might be interested and then rely on the inflow of new vacancies for potential matches. It may be that rapid exhaustion of possible jobs provides a plausible reason for why, at the margin, there is little return to extra job search.

Before we move on, it is worth mentioning some studies that have direct estimates of the left-hand side of (8). These are typically studies of the unemployed that ask them about the lowest wage they would accept (their reservation wage) and the wage they expect to get. For example Lancaster and Chesher (1983) report that expected wages are 14% above reservation wages. The author's own calculations on the British Household Panel Study, 1991-2007 suggest a mean gap of 21 log points and a median gap of 15 log points. These estimates are vulnerable to the criticism that they are subjective answers, though the answers do predict durations of unemployment and realized wages in the expected way[7]. They are perhaps best thought of as very rough orders of magnitude

The discussion has been phrased in terms of a search for *the* level of worker rents, ignoring heterogeneity. However, it should be recognized that there are a lot of people without jobs who do not spend any time looking for a job. For this group—classified in labor market statistics as the inactive—the expected rents from the employment relationship must be too small to justify job search. The fact that some without jobs search and some do not strongly suggests there is a lot of heterogeneity in the size of rents or expected rents. Once one recognizes the existence of heterogeneity one needs to worry about the population whose rents one is trying to measure. The methodology here might be useful to tell us about the rents for the unemployed but we would probably expect that the average rents for the unemployed are lower than for the employed. Estimating the rents for the employed is the subject of the next section.

2.3. The costs of job loss

To estimate rents for the employed, the experiment one would like to run is to consider what happens when workers are randomly separated from jobs. There is a literature that considers exactly that question—studies of displaced workers (Jacobson et al., 1993; Von Wachter, Manchester and Song, 2009). One concern is the difficulty of finding good control groups, e.g. the reason for displacement is presumably employer surplus falling to less than zero. But, for some not totally explained reason, it seems that wages prior to displacement are not very different for treatment and control groups—it is only post-displacement that one sees the big differences. Under this assumption one can equate these estimates to loss of worker surplus.

For a sample of men with 5 years previous employment who lost their jobs in mass lay-offs in 1982, Von Wachter, Manchester and Song (2009) estimate initial earnings losses of 33% that then fall but remain close to 20% after 20 years. Similar estimates are reported in Von Wachter, Bender and Schmeider (2009) for Germany. These samples are workers who might plausibly be expected to have accumulated significant amounts of

---

[7] Hornstein et al. (2006) use observed wages to estimate rents, finding they are enormous. However, there are a considerable number of problems with their methodology so their conclusion is probably not reliable.

specific human capital, so one would not be surprised to find large estimated rents for this group. However, Von Wachter, Manchester and Song (2009) find sizeable though smaller earnings losses for men with less stable employment histories pre-displacement and for women. At the other extreme, Von Wachter and Bender (2006) examine the effects of displacement on young apprentices in Germany. For this group, where we would expect rents to be small, they find an initial earnings loss of 10%, but this is reduced to zero after 5 years.

We also have a number of other studies looking at how the nature of displacement affects the size of earnings losses. Neal (1995), and Poletaev and Robinson (2008) show that workers who do not change industry or occupation or whose post-displacement job uses a similar mix of skills have much smaller earnings losses. This is as one would expect given what was said earlier about the reason for rents being the lack of an alternative employer who is a perfect substitute for the present one. Those displaced workers fortunate enough to find another job which is a close substitute for the one lost would be expected to have little or no earnings loss. But, the sizeable group of workers whose post-displacement job is not a perfect substitute for the one lost will suffer larger earnings losses. For example, Poletaev and Robinson (2008) estimated an average cost of displacement for all workers of 7% but the 25% of workers who switch to a job with a very different skill portfolio suffer losses of 15%. The fact that 25% of workers cannot find a new job that is a close match to their previous one suggests there are not a large number of employers offering jobs that are perfect substitutes for each other.

2.4. Conclusions

The methods discussed in this section can be used to give us ballpark estimates of the extent of imperfect competition in labor markets. They perhaps suggest total rents in the 15-30% range with, perhaps, most of the rents being on the worker side. However, one should acknowledge there is a lot of variation in rents and enormous uncertainty in these calculations. Because we have discussed estimates of the rents accruing to employers and workers, one might also think about using these estimates to give us some idea of how the rents are split between worker and employer. However, because none of the estimates come from the same employment relationship, that would be an unwise thing to do. The next section discusses models of the balance of power between employers and workers and these are reviewed in the next section.

3. MODELS OF WAGE DETERMINATION

When there are rents in the employment relationship, one has to model how these rents are split between worker and employer, i.e. one needs a model of wage determination. This is a very old problem in economics in general and labor economics in particular, going back to the discussion of Edgeworth (1932), where he argued that the terms of exchange in a bilateral monopoly were indeterminate. That problem has never been definitively resolved, and that is probably because it cannot be. In this section we describe the two main approaches found in the literature and compare and contrast them.

3.1. Bargaining and posting

The two main approaches that have been taken to modeling wage determination in recent years are what we will call ex post wage-bargaining and ex ante wage-posting (though we briefly discuss others at the end of the section). In ex post wage-bargaining the wage is split after the worker and employer have been matched, according to some sharing rule, most commonly an asymmetric Nash bargain. In ex ante wage-posting the wage is set unilaterally by the employer before the worker and employer meet.

These two traditions have been used in very different ways. The bargaining models are the preferred models in macroeconomic applications (see Rogerson and Shimer, 2011) while microeconomic applications tend to use wage-posting[8]. But, what is often not very clear to students entering this area is why these differences in tradition have emerged and what are the consequences. Are these differences based on good reasons, bad reasons or no reasons at all? Here we try to provide an overview which, while simplistic, captures the most important differences.

Although the models used are almost always dynamic, the ideas can be captured in a very simple static model and that is what we do here. The simple static model derives from Hall and Lazear (1984) who discuss a wider set of wage-setting mechanisms than we do here. Assume that there are firms, which differ in their marginal productivity of labor, p. A firm is assumed to be able to employ only one worker.

In ex post wage-bargaining models, the wage in a match between a worker with leisure value b and a firm with productivity p is chosen to maximize an asymmetric Nash bargain:

$$(p - w)^{(1-\alpha)} (w - b)^\alpha \tag{9}$$

leading to a wage equation:

$$w = \alpha p + (1 - \alpha)b \tag{10}$$

where α can be thought of as the bargaining power of the worker, which is typically thought of as exogenous to the model. The match will be consummated whenever there is some surplus to be shared, i.e. whenever $p \geq b$ so that there is ex post efficiency. There will not necessarily be ex ante efficiency if worker or employer or both have to

---

[8] Though there is some sign of cross-over (with mixed success) in recent years, e.g. Moscarini and Postel-Vinay (2008) attempt to use wage-posting models to address macroeconomic issues and wage-bargaining models have been used address issues of microeconomic concern (though more traditional labor economists often view these attempts as reinventing the wheel and not always a round one at that).

make investments ahead of a match, investments either in the probability of getting a match or in the size of rents when a match is made. For example, if $\alpha = 0$ workers get no surplus from the employment relationship so would not invest any time in trying to find a job.

Now consider a wage-posting model in which employers set the wage before being matched with a worker. To derive the optimal wage in this case we need to make some assumption about the process by which workers and employers are matched—for the moment, assume that is random though alternatives are discussed below. And assume that workers differ in their value of leisure, b—denote the distribution function of this across workers by $G(b)$.

If the firm sets a wage w, a worker will accept the offer if $w > b$, something that happens with probability $G(w)$. So expected profits will be given by:

$$\pi(w) = (p - w)G(w). \tag{11}$$

This leads to the following first-order condition for wages:

$$w(p) = \frac{\varepsilon(w(p))}{1 + \varepsilon(w(p))}p \tag{12}$$

where ε is the elasticity of the function G with respect to its argument and the notation used reflects the fact that this elasticity will typically be endogenous. Higher productivity firms offer higher wages. An important distinction from ex post wage-bargaining is that not all ex post surplus is exploited—some matches with positive surplus (i.e. with $p > b$) may not be consummated because $b > w$. In matches that are consummated the rents are split between employers and workers, so employers are unable to extract all surplus from workers even though employers can unilaterally set wages.

In this model $G(w)$ can be thought of as the labor supply curve facing the firm, in which case can think of it as a standard model of monopsony in which the labor supply to a firm is not perfectly elastic and (12) as the standard formula for the optimal wage of a monopsonist. There is a simple and familiar graphical representation of the decision-making problem for the firm—see Fig. 1. In contrast, there is no such simple representation for the outcome of the ex post wage-bargaining model[9].

One might think that the two wage Eqs (10) and (12) are very different. But they can easily be made to look more similar. Suppose that the supply of labor can be written as:

$$G(w) = (w - b_0)^{\varepsilon} \tag{13}$$

---

[9] Actually, the natural place to look for familiar models which are similar would be trade union models which typically have a bargaining model for wage determination. But the tradition in ex post wage-bargaining models of having one worker per employer tends to limit the analogy.

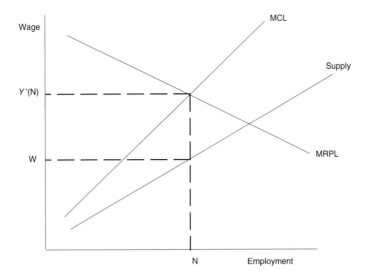

Figure 1 *The textbook model of monopsony.*

where b_0 is now to be interpreted, not as a specific worker's reservation wage, but as the lowest wage any worker will work for. Then the wage equation in (11) can be written as:

$$w = \frac{\varepsilon}{1+\varepsilon}p + \frac{1}{1+\varepsilon}b_0 \tag{14}$$

which is isomorphic to (9) with $\alpha = \frac{\varepsilon}{1+\varepsilon}$. In some sense, the bargaining power of workers in the wage-posting model is measured by the elasticity of the labor supply curve to the firm. However, note that the interpretation of the reservation wage in (10) and (14) is different—in (10) it is the individual worker's reservation wage while in (14) it is the general level of reservation wages measured by the lowest in the market.

The assumption of random matching plays an important role in the nature of the wage-posting equilibrium so it is instructive to consider other models of the matching process. The main alternative to random matching is "directed search" (see, for example, Moen, 1997). Models of directed search typically assume that there is wage-posting but that all wage offers can be observed before workers decide on their applications.

Although models of directed search make the same assumption about the availability of information on wage offers as models of perfect competition (i.e. complete information), they do not assume that an application necessarily leads to a job, so there is typically some frictional unemployment in equilibrium caused by a coordination problem. So the expected utility of a worker applying to a particular firm is not just the wage, but needs to take account of the probability of getting a job. In the simplest model this expected utility must be equalized across jobs, giving the model a quasi-competitive feel, and it is perhaps then no surprise that the outcomes are efficient. The literature has evolved with different assumptions being made about the number of applications that can be made, what happens if workers get more than one job offer, what happens if the first worker offered a job does not want it (e.g. Albrecht et al., 2006; Galenianos and Kircher, 2009; Kircher, 2009). It would be helpful to have some general principles which help us understand the exact feature of these models that do and do not deliver efficiency.

3.2. The right model?

Rogerson et al. (2005, p. 984) conclude their survey of search models by writing that one of the unanswered questions is "what is the right model of wages?", with the two models described above being the main contenders. If we wanted to choose between these two descriptions of the wage determination process, how would we do so? We might think about using theoretical or empirical arguments. As economists abhor unexploited surpluses, theory would seem to favor the ex post wage-bargaining models in which no match with positive surplus ever fails to be consummated[10]. One might expect that there would be renegotiation of the wage in a wage-posting model if $p > b > w$.

However, over a very long period of time, many economists have felt that this account is over-simplistic, that wages, for reasons that are not entirely understood, have some form of rigidity in them that prevents all surplus being extracted from the employment relationship. There are a number of possible reasons suggested for this. Hall and Lazear (1984) argue this is caused by informational imperfections while Ellingsen and Rosen (2003) argue that wage-posting represents a credible commitment not to negotiate wages with workers something that would cost resources and raise wages. There is also the feeling that workers care greatly about notions of fairness (e.g. see Mas, 2006) so that this makes it costly to vary wages for workers who see themselves as equals. There is also the point that if jobs were only ever destroyed when there was no surplus left to either side, there would be no useful distinction between quits and lay-offs, though most labor economists do think that distinction meaningful and workers losing their jobs are generally unhappy about it. The bottom line is that theory alone does not seem to resolve the argument about the "best" model of wage determination.

What about empirical evidence? In a recent paper Hall and Krueger (2008) use a survey to investigate the extent to which newly-hired workers felt the wage was a "take-it-or-leave-it" offer, as ex ante wage-posting models would suggest. All those who felt there was some scope for negotiation are regarded as being ex post wage-bargaining. They show that both institutions are common in the labor market, with negotiation being more prevalent. In low-skill labor markets wage-posting is more common than in high-skill labor markets, as perhaps intuition would suggest.

---

[10] Though this statement should not be taken to mean that markets as a whole with ex post wage-bargaining need be more efficient than those with wage-posting. The efficiency concept referred to here is an ex post notion and labor market efficiency is an ex ante notion.

This direct attempt to get to the heart of the issue is interesting, informative and novel, but the classification is not without its problems. For example, some of those who report a non-negotiable wage may never have discovered that they had more ability to negotiate over the wage than the employer (successfully) gave them the impression there was. For example, Babcock and Laschever (2003) argue that women are less likely to negotiate wages than men and more likely to simply accept the first wage they are offered.

Similarly, there are potential problems with assuming that all those without stated ex ante wages represent cases of bargaining. For example, employers with all the bargaining power would like to act as a discriminating monopsonist tailoring their wage offer to the circumstances of the individual worker, not the simple monopsonist the wage-posting model assumes. Hall and Krueger (2008) are aware of this line of argument but argue it is not relevant because wage discrimination would result in all workers in the US being held to their reservation wage, a patently ridiculous claim. But, there is a big leap from saying some monopsonistic discrimination is practiced to saying it is done perfectly, so this argument is not completely compelling.

There is also the problem that the methodology used, while undoubtedly fascinating and insightful, primarily counts types of contract without looking at the economic consequences. For example, Lewis (1989, p. 149) describes how Salomon Brothers lost their most profitable bond-trader because of their refusal to break a company policy capping the salary they would pay. Undoubtedly, this contract should be described as individualistic wage-bargaining, but there were limits placed on that which resulted in some ex post surplus being lost as suggested by the wage-posting models.

One possible way of resolving these issues would be to look at outcomes. For example, ex post individualistic wage-bargaining would suggest, as from (10), that there would be considerable variation in wages within firms between workers with different reservation wages—see (10). On the other hand, ex ante wage-posting would suggest no wage variation within firms between workers with different reservation wages. Machin and Manning (2004) examine the structure of wages in a low-skill labor market, that of care workers in retirement homes. They find that, compared to all other characteristics of the workers, a much greater share of the total wage variation is between as opposed to within firms. Reservation wages are not observed directly, but we might expect to be correlated with those characteristics, so ex post wage-bargaining would predict correlations of wages with those variables[11].

One could spend an enormous amount of time debating the "right" model of wage determination. But we will probably never be able to resolve it because the labor market is very heterogeneous, so that no one single model fits all, so the question of "what is the right model?" is ill-posed. In fact, it is the very existence of rents that gives the

---

[11] This is not inconsistent with the conclusions of studies like Lazear and Shaw (2009), who argue that most wage dispersion is within firms, as that is primarily about wage dispersion between managers and janitors who differ in their productivity and not among workers who might be expected to have similar levels of productivity.

breathing-space in the determination of wages in which the observed multiplicity of institutions can survive. In a perfectly competitive market an employer would have no choice but to pay the market wage and to deviate from that, even slightly, leads to disaster.

It is also worth reflecting that, in many regards, wage-bargaining and wage-posting models are quite similar (e.g. they both imply that rents are split between worker and employer) so that it may not make very much difference which model one uses as a modeling device. The main substantive issue in which they differ is in whether one thinks that all ex post surplus is extracted. But, because even ex post efficiency does not mean ex ante efficiency, this may not be such a big difference in practice. However, this is not to say that the choice of model has had no consequences for labor economics because too many economists see the labor market only through the prism of the labor market model with which they are most familiar.

For example, as illustrated above, a wage-posting model naturally leads one to think in terms of the elasticity of the labor supply curve to an individual firm and that one can represent the wage decision using the familiar diagram of Fig. 1. It is easy to forge links with other parts of labor economics, so it is perhaps not surprising that this has often been the model of choice for microeconomic models of imperfect competition in the labor market. It is much more difficult to forge such links with an ex post bargaining model and the literature that uses such models sometimes seems to have developed in a parallel universe to more conventional labor economics and has concentrated on macroeconomic applications.

3.3. Other perspectives on wage determination

I have described the two most commonly found models of wage determination. But just as I have emphasized that one should not be thought as obviously "better" than the other, so one should not assume that these are the only possibles. Here we simply review some of the others that can be found in the literature. We make no attempt to be exhaustive (e.g. see Hall and Lazear, 1984, for a discussion of a range of possibilities we do not discuss here).

The simple model sketched above only has workers moving into jobs from non-employment because it is a one-period model. In reality, over half of new recruits are from other jobs (Manning, 2003a; Nagypal, 2005) so that one has to think about how wages are determined when a worker has a choice between two employers.

In models with ex-post wage-bargaining, on-the-job search is a bit tricky to incorporate into standard models because it is not clear how to model the outcome of bargaining when workers have a choice of more than one employer, and different papers have taken different approaches, e.g. Pissarides (1994) assumes that the fall-back position for workers with two potential employers is unemployment while Cahuc et al. (2006) propose that the marginal product at the lower productivity firm be the outside option. Shimer (2006) points out that the value function for employed workers is typically convex in the wage when there is the possibility of moving to a higher-wage job in the future, and derives another bargaining solution, albeit one with many equilibria.

In contrast, models based on wage-posting do not find it hard to incorporate on-the-job search, as they typically simply assume that the worker accepts the higher of the two wage offers. But, they do find it difficult to explain why the employer about to lose a worker does not seek to retain them by raising wages. A number of papers look at the institution of offer-matching (Postel-Vinay and Robin, 2002) in which the two employers engage in Bertrand competition for the worker. However, many have felt that offer-matching is not very pervasive in labor markets and have offered reasons for why this might be the case (see, for example, the discussion in Hall and Lazear, 1984).

4. ESTIMATES OF RENT-SPLITTING

The previous section reviewed theoretical models of the ways in which rents are divided between workers and employers—this section reviews empirical evidence on the same subject.

Section 2 reviewed some ways in which one might get some idea of the size of rents accruing to employers and workers. Because it produced estimates of the rents accruing to employer and worker, one could use these estimates to get some idea of how the rents are shared between employer and worker. But, because these estimates are assembled from a few, disparate sources of evidence, we have no study in which we could estimate both employer and worker rents in the same labor market, so that estimating how rents are shared by using an estimate of employer rents in one labor market and worker rents in another would not deliver credible evidence. So, in this section we review some other methodologies that can be thought of as seeking to estimate the way in which rents are split between worker and employer.

The part of the literature on imperfect competition in labor markets that has used ex post wage-bargaining as the model of wage determination and, consequently, uses an equation like (10) would tend to see rents being split according to the bargaining power of the workers. The studies that attempt to estimate a rent-sharing parameter are reviewed in Section 4.1. In contrast, models that are based on wage-posting have a monopsony perspective on the labor market and view the elasticity of the labor supply curve facing the employer as the key determinant of how rents are split. We review these ideas in Sections 4.2 and 4.3. Finally, we briefly review some studies that have sought to use estimates of the extent of frictions in the labor market to estimate how rents are divided.

4.1. Estimates of rent-sharing

In a bargaining framework, we are interested in how wages respond to changes in the surplus in the employment relationship, i.e. to measure something like (10). There is a small empirical literature that seeks to estimate the responsiveness of wages to measures of rents. These studies differ in the theoretical foundation for the estimated equation, the way in which the rent-sharing equation is measured and the empirical methodology used.

The Eq. (10) was derived from a model of bargaining between a worker and employer where the bargaining relationship covers only one worker. But, there are alternative ways of deriving a similar equation from other models. For example, Abowd and Lemieux (1993) assume that the firm consists of a potentially variable number of workers with a revenue function $F(N)$, and that the firm bargains with a union with preferences $N(w - b)$ over both wages and employment, i.e. we have an efficient bargaining model (McDonald and Solow, 1981). That is, wages and employment are chosen to maximize:

$$[F(N) - wN]^{(1-\alpha)} [N(w - b)]^{\alpha} . \tag{15}$$

One way of writing the first-order condition for wages in this maximization problem is:

$$w = \alpha \frac{F(N)}{N} + (1 - \alpha) b \tag{16}$$

i.e. wages are a weighted average of revenue per worker and reservation wages with the weight on revenue per worker being α. The similarities between (16) and (10) should be apparent as $F(N)/N$ is the average productivity of labor. In this model employment will be set so that:

$$F'(N) = b. \tag{17}$$

There are other models from which one can derive a similar-looking equation to (16), though we will not go into details here. For example, if one assumes that employment is chosen by the employer given the negotiated wage (what is sometimes called the right-to-manage or labor demand curve model—see, for example, Booth, 1995) or a more general set of "union" preferences.

In all the specifications derived so far, it is a measure of revenue per worker or quasi-rents per worker put on the right-hand side. But, many studies write the wage equation in terms of profits per worker, i.e. take $-\alpha w$ from both sides of (16) and write it as:

$$w = \frac{\alpha}{1 - \alpha} \frac{F(N) - wN}{N} + b = \frac{\alpha}{1 - \alpha} \frac{\Pi}{N} + b. \tag{18}$$

In all these cases it should be apparent that the outcome of rent per worker or profit per worker is potentially endogenous to wages, so that OLS estimation of these equations is likely to lead to biased estimates. Hence, some instrument is used, and the obvious instrument is something that affects the revenue function for the individual firm but does not affect the wider labor market (here measured by b). Although revenue function shifters sound very plausible, it is not clear that they are good instruments. For example if the revenue function is Cobb–Douglas (so the elasticity of revenue with respect to employment is a constant) then the marginal revenue product of labor is proportional to the average revenue product and the employment equation in (17) makes clear the marginal revenue product will not be affected by variables that affect the revenue function. In this case shifts in the revenue function result in rises in employment such that rents per worker and wages are unchanged[12]. The discussion in Abowd and Lemieux (1993, p. 987) is very good on this point. In cases close to this, instruments based on revenue function shifters will be weak. Many of the rent-sharing studies are from before the period when researchers were aware of the weak instrument problem (see Angrist and Pischke, 2008, for a discussion) and the instruments in some studies (e.g. Abowd and Lemieux, 1993) do not appear to be strong.

Some estimates of the rent-sharing parameter are shown in Table 4. In this table we have restricted attention to those that estimate an equation that is either in the form of (16) or (18) or can be readily transformed to it[13]. Table 4 briefly summarizes the data used in each study, the measure of rents or profits used, and the method (if any) used to deal with the endogeneity problem. In some studies the instruments are lags of various variables while others use exogenous shifts to demand, e.g. as caused by exchange rate movements. There are a couple of "case studies" of the impact of de-regulation in various industries.

What one would ideally like to measure is the effect of a change in rents in a single firm on wages in that firm. It is not clear whether that is what is being estimated. For example, several studies in Table 4 use industry profits as a measure of rents. If labor has any industry-specific aspect to it then a positive shock to industry profits would be expected to raise the demand for labor in a competitive market and, hence, raise the general level of wages (represented by b in the model above)[14]. If this is important one would expect that the estimates reported in Table 4 are biased upwards. And the studies that use firm-level profits or rents but instrument by industry demand shifters are potentially vulnerable to the same criticism.

The final column in Table 4 presents estimates of the α implied by the estimates. Most of these studies do not report an estimate of α directly (e.g. the dependent variable is normally in logs whereas the theoretical idea is in levels) so a conversion has taken place based on other information provided or approximations. For example if the equation is

[12] In this case wages are a mark-up on the outside option of workers, b, and it is the size of this mark-up that contains the rent-sharing parameter.

[13] This excludes studies like Nickell and Wadhwani (1990), and Currie and McConnell (1992) that use sales per worker as the measure of rents, as I lack information on the share of value-added in sales which would be needed to go from these estimates to the parameter of rent-sharing. It also excludes some studies that model the link between measures of rents and wages but measure rents as, for example, a rate of return on capital (e.g. Bertrand, 2004).

[14] One should perhaps here mention the evidence presented in Beaudry et al. (2007) of spill-overs in wages at the city level from one sector to others.

Table 4 Estimates of rent-sharing.

Study	Sample	Rents variable	How deal with endogeneity problem?	Estimate of rent-sharing parameter
Blanchflower et al. (1996)	US workers in manufacturing, 1964-85	Industry profits per worker	Use lagged profits, energy costs as instruments	0.19[a]
Hildreth and Oswald (1997)	2 panels of UK firms in 1980s	Company profits per worker	Lagged profits	0.02[b] 0.14[c]
Van Reenen (1996)	Panel of UK firms	Company profits per worker	Use innovation as instrument	0.34
Abowd and Lemieux (1993)	Canadian collective bargaining contracts	Quasi-rents per worker	Use exchange rate shocks as instrument	0.20
Arai (2003)	Matched worker-firm Swedish data	Company Profits per worker	OLS but argues weaker endogeneity problem	0.15
Black and Strahan (2001)	US bank employees	Own "back-of-envelope" calculation	Changes in bank entry regulations	0.25
Rose (1987)	US unionized truckers	Own "back-of-envelope" calculation	Deregulation of trucking	0.65-0.76
Guiso et al. (2005)	Matcher worker-firm Italian data	Company value-added per worker		0.06
Christofides and Oswald (1992)	Canadian collective bargaining agreements, 1978-84	Industry profits per worker	Lags as instruments	0.02[a]
Card et al. (2010)	Social security data from Veneto, Italy	Firm value-added per worker	Industry value-added per worker	0.07

[a] The equation is estimated with log earnings as dependent variable and rent-sharing parameter derived using reported figures for average profits per worker and a labor share in value-added of 75%.

[b] This is computed using ratio of reported levels of earnings to profits per head in the data which is extremely low at 1.1. Using a ratio of 2 or 3 would raise these estimates considerably.

[c] This is computed using ratio of reported levels of earnings to profits per head in the data which is high at 5.3. Using a ratio of 2 or 3 would lower these estimates considerably.

specified with the log of wages on the left-hand side and the log of profits on the right-hand side so that the reported coefficient is an elasticity then one needs to multiply by the ratio of wages to profits per head to get the implied estimate of α. If, for example the share of labor in value-added is 75% then one needs to multiply the coefficient by 3, while if it is 66% one needs to multiply by 2. In addition there is a wide variation in the reported ratio of wages to profit per head in the data sets used in the studies summarized in Table 4 from a minimum of 1.1 to a maximum of 5.3. Unsurprisingly this can make a very large difference to the estimates of α and this is reflected in Table 4. In addition, the difficulty in computing the "true" measure of profits or rents may also lead to considerable variation in estimates.

There are a number of studies (Christofides and Oswald, 1992; one of the samples in Hildreth and Oswald, 1997) where α is estimate to be close to zero, but a number of other estimates are in the region 0.2-0.25. Studies from Continental European countries—the Italian and Swedish studies of Arai (2003), Guiso et al. (2005) and Card et al. (2010)—are markedly lower—this might be explained by the wage-setting institutions in those countries where one might expect the influence of firm-level factors to be less important than in the US (see the neglected Teulings and Hartog, 1998, for further elaboration of this point) though there are also some methodological differences from the other studies. And the study of Rose (1987) also looks an outlier with an estimate of α around 0.7. However, this estimate is derived using some back-of-the-envelope calculations and is for a very specific industry so may not be representative. It is worth remarking that all of these studies suggest that most rents accrue to employers, not workers while the direct estimates of the size of rents accruing to employer and workers in previous sections perhaps suggested the opposite. That is an issue that needs to be resolved.

The estimates of α discussed so far have all been derived from microeconomic studies. But the rent-splitting parameter also plays an important role in macroeconomic models of the labor market, and such studies often use a particular value. It has been common to assume the rent-splitting parameter is set to satisfy the Hosios condition for efficiency (often around 0.4), though no convincing reason for that is given, sometimes calibrated or estimated to help to explain some aspects of labor market data (and Hagedorn and Manovskii, 2008 suggest a value of 0.05 based on some of the studies reported in Table 4). A recent development (e.g. Pissarides, 2009; Elsby and Michaels, 2008) has been to argue that there is an important difference between the sensitivity of the wages of new hires and continuing workers to labor market conditions. The micro studies reviewed in Table 4 have not pursued this dimension.

Many of the studies summarized in Table 4 are of unionized firms, motivated by the idea that non-union firms are much less likely to have rent-sharing. Although a perspective that there are pervasive rents in the labor market would lead one to expect that even non-union workers get a share of the rents, one might expect unions to be institutions better-able to extract rents for workers, so that one would estimate a higher

Table 5 Quasi-experimental estimates of wage elasticity of supply to individual employer.

Study	Sample	"Experiment"	Outcome variable	Estimated elasticity
Staiger et al. (2010)	Veteran affairs hospitals	Permanent rise in wages where recruitment difficulties	Employment rise 1 year later	0.1
Falch (2010a)	Norwegian schools	Wage Premium at schools with recruitment difficulties	Contemporaneous employment	1.0-1.9
Matsudaira (2009)	Californian care homes	Increase in required minimum staffing levels	Change in wages	0

α in the union sector. But the few studies that distinguish between union and non-union sectors (e.g. Blanchflower et al., 1996, 1990[15]) often find that, if anything, the estimate of α is larger in the non-union sector. However, this is what one might expect from a wage-posting perspective, because a union setting a take-it-or-leave-it wage makes the labor supply to a firm more wage elastic (like the minimum wage) than that faced by a non-union firm. Hence, one then predicts one would find a higher rent-sharing parameter in the non-union sector. This leads on to estimates of rent-sharing based on the elasticity of the labor supply curve to employers.

4.2. The elasticity of the labor supply curve to an individual employer

As the formula in (12) makes clear, a wage-posting model would suggest that it is the elasticity of the labor supply curve facing the employer that determines how rents are split between worker and employer. This section reviews estimates of that elasticity. An ideal experiment that one would like to run to estimate the elasticity of the labor supply curve to a single firm would be to randomly vary the wage paid by the single firm and observe what happens to employment. As yet, the literature does not have a study of such an experiment.

What we do have are a number of quasi-experiments where there have been wage rises in some firms—these are summarized in Table 5. Typically those experiments have been of public sector firms where there have been perceived to be labor shortages because wages have been set below prevailing market levels. So, they sound like the type of situation where one would expect to be tracing out the elasticity of a labor supply curve.

Staiger et al. (2010) examine the impact of a legislated rise in the wages paid at Veteran Affairs hospitals. They estimate the short-run elasticity in the labor supply to the firm to

---

[15] This study uses a qualitative measure of financial performance so is not reported in Table 4.

be very low (around 0.1), implying an enormous amount of monopsony power possessed by hospitals over their nurses. Falch (2010a) investigates the impact on the supply of teachers to individual schools in northern Norway in response to a policy experiment that selectively raised wages in some schools with past recruitment difficulties. He reports an elasticity in the supply of labor to individual firms in the region 1.0-1.9—higher than the Staiger et al study, but still very low.

Looking at these studies, one clearly comes away with the impression not that it is hard to find evidence of monopsony power but that the estimates are so enormous to be an embarrassment even for those who believe this is the right approach to labor markets. The wage elasticities are too large to be credible.

This means it makes sense to reflect on possible biases. There are a number of possibilities that come to mind. First, some of these studies only look at the response of employment to wage changes over a relatively small time horizon. As one would expect supply elasticities to be smaller in the short-run, these estimates are not reliable as estimates of the long-run elasticity. There is a simple back-of-the-envelope rule that can be used to link short-run and long-run elasticities. Boal and Ransom (1997) and Manning (2003a, chapter 2) show that if the following simple model is used for the supply of labor to a firm:

$$N_t = [1 - s(w_t)]N_{t-1} + R(w_t),\tag{19}$$

where $s(w)$ is the separation rate and $R(w)$ is the recruitment rate, then there is the following relationship between the short-run and long-run elasticities:

$$\varepsilon^s \equiv s(w_t)\varepsilon.\tag{20}$$

So one needs to divide the short-run elasticity by the quit rate to get an estimate of the long-run elasticity. If, for example, labor turnover rates are about 20% then one needs to multiply the estimates of short-run elasticities by 5 to get a better estimate of the long-run elasticity.

A second issue is whether the wage premia are expected to be temporary or permanent. If they are only temporary then one would not expect to see such a large supply response. In this regard, it is reasonable to think of the wage increases studied by Staiger et al. (2010) as permanent, those studied by Falch (2010a) as temporary. It is not clear whether an argument that the wage premia were viewed as only temporary are plausible as explanations of the low labor supply elasticities found.

Here, I suggest that there is another, as yet unrecognized, problem with these estimates of labor supply elasticities. The reason for believing this comes from thinking about estimates of the labor supply elasticities from an alternative experiment—force an employer to raise its employment level and watch what happens to the wages that they pay. This is what is analyzed by Matsudaira (2009) who analyzes the effect of a 1999

California law that required all licensed nursing homes to maintain a minimum number of hours of nurses per patient. This can be thought of as a mandated increase in the level of employment.

According the simplest models of monopsony in which there is a one-to-one relationship between wages and labor supply to the firm, the wage response to the mandated employment increase should give us an estimate of the inverse of the wage elasticity. If the studies of mandated wage increases cited above are correct and the labor supply elasticity is very small, we should see very large wage increases in response to mandated employment changes. This is especially true if the short-run elasticity is very low. In fact, Matsudaira finds that firms that were particularly affected by the mandated increased in employment did not raise their wages relative to other firms who were not affected. As a result, the labor supply to the employer appears very elastic, seemingly inconsistent with studies of mandated wage increases. It is possible that, as these are studies of different labor markets there is no apparent inconsistency but I would suggest that is not the most likely explanation and that the real explanation is a problem with the simple model of monopsony.

How can we reconcile these apparently conflicting findings? The problem with the simple-minded model of monopsony is that it assumes that the only way an employer can raise employment is by raising its wage. A moment's reflection should persuade us that this is not very plausible. There are a number of possible reasons for this—I will concentrate on one in some detail and then mention others.

We have already seen that hiring costs money and used estimates of these hiring costs to shed light on the size of employer rents from the employment relationship. If employers want to hire more workers, they can spend more resources on trying to recruit workers, e.g. advertising vacancies more frequently or extensively. Hence, the supply of workers to the firm will then be a function not just of the wage but also of the expenditure on recruitment. This model is examined in Manning (2006), who terms it the "generalized model of monopsony" and it can easily explain the paradox described above.

To see how it can do this assume there are constant marginal hiring costs, $h(w)$, which might depend on the wage. If the separation rate is $s(w)$ a flow of $s(w)N$ recruits is necessary for the employer to maintain employment at N which will cost $s(w)h(w)N$. This represents the per period expenditure on recruitment necessary to keep employment at N if the wage paid is w. Note that, unlike the simple monopsony model, any level of employment is compatible with any level of the wage but that there are associated recruitment costs. If, in the interests of simplicity, we ignore discounting (the recruitment costs of a worker must be paid up-front but profits accrue in the future), the profits of the firm can be written as:

$$\pi = F(N) - wN - s(w)h(w)N. \tag{21}$$

First, consider the choices of wage and employment by an unconstrained profit-maximizing firm. The wage will be chosen to satisfy the first-order condition:

$$-1 - s'(w)h(w) - s(w)h'(w) = 0. \tag{22}$$

Denote this choice by w^*. The first-order condition for employment will then be:

$$F'(N) = w^* + s\left(w^*\right)h\left(w^*\right). \tag{23}$$

Now, consider what happens in this model when we mandate wages or mandate employment. Consider, mandated employment first, as in the Matsudaira paper. If the government requires an increase in employment, the optimal thing for the firm to do is to increase recruitment activity—the optimal wage (22) remains completely unchanged. This is, to a first approximation, what Matsudaira finds. However, it tells us nothing about the degree of imperfect competition in the labor market which is related to the elasticity of separation rates and recruitment with respect to the wage.

Now consider a mandated increase in the wage. This reduces separations and may reduce the marginal cost of recruitment. But, if it is a small increase from the optimal wage the first-order effect will be to leave employment unchanged—the employer responds by reducing recruitment expenditure. One might explain the small positive effects on employment found in the literature as being the result of mandated wage increases in public sector firms where wages had been held artificially low.

In the generalized model of monopsony, the two experiments of mandated wage or employment increases are no longer mirror images of each other. A rise in mandated wages which, ceteris paribus, leads to a rise in labor supply to the firm could be met with an off-setting fall in recruitment activity, leaving overall employment unchanged. On the other hand, a rise in mandated employment may be met with a rise in recruitment activity to generate the extra supply with no increase in wages. This can be understood with Fig. 2. Starting from an initial position the line labelled "mandated wage" rise tells us how employment will change if the firm is forced to raise wages. This suggests a low elasticity of supply. The line labelled "mandated employment" rise tells us how wages will change when the firm is forced to raise employment—this suggests a high elasticity of labor supply.

We used a very simple model to break the one-to-one link between wages and employment found in the standard model of monopsony. The change is plausible but does substantially affect how one interprets the empirical results of estimates of the effects of raising wages on employment (or vice versa). This is not the only way in which one might seek to reconcile these conflicting empirical findings. Another alternative is to assume that workers are heterogeneous in terms of quality so that employers also face an intensive margin in deciding the cut-off quality level for workers. Employers do not

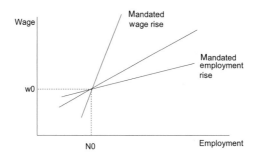

Figure 2   *Mandated wage and employment rises.*

simply accept all workers who apply—they reject those they deem of poor quality, and how poor one has to be to be rejected is clearly endogenous. An example in Appendix B shows how, if the distribution of worker ability in the applicant pool is exponential then firms respond to mandated wage increases by increasing worker quality and not employment, and to mandated employment increases by reducing worker quality and not increasing wages. It also shows how a model with non-wage aspects of work can deliver the same conclusion.

All of these quasi-experimental studies described above are studies of mandated changes to wages or employment which might be thought to force employers to move along their labor supply curves. But, another empirical strategy is to consider changes in variables which induce moves along the labor supply curve. To identify the labor supply curve (which is all we want here) a variable that shifts the MRPL curve without shifting the supply curve is needed. One can then use this as an instrument for the wage or employment (depending on which way round we are estimating the supply curve) in estimating the supply curve. But, of course, it requires us to be able to provide such an instrument.

If one is interested in estimating the elasticity of labor supply to an individual firm then the instrument needs to be something that affects the demand curve for that firm but has negligible impact on the labor market as a whole. The reason is that a pervasive labor market demand shock will raise the general level of wages, so is likely to affect the labor supply to an individual firm. So, for example, the approach of using demand shocks caused by exchange rate fluctuations (as in Abowd and Lemieux, 1993) does not seem viable here. Sullivan (1989) uses the population in the area surrounding the hospital as an instrument affecting the demand for nurses This is a serious attempt to deal with a difficult problem, but their instruments are not beyond criticism. If the main variation in the number of children or the number of patients comes from variation in population it is also likely that the supply of nurses in an area is proportional to population as well.

The studies reviewed in this section do provide us with the best estimates we have of how employers respond to mandated wage and employment changes. But, as has been made clear, they probably do not tell us about the wage elasticity of the labor supply to an individual firm, which was the original motivation. How we might estimate that elasticity is the subject of the next section.

4.3. The sensitivity of separations to wages

This section reviews estimates of the sensitivity of separations to wages. Although this might be thought a topic of interest in its own right, we include it here because such studies might shed some light on the elasticity of the labor supply curve to individual employers. Why this might be thought useful can be explained very simply. Suppose that the flow of recruits to a firm is $R(w)$, that this dependent only on the wage (an assumption we relax below where we allow for recruits to also be affected by recruitment expenditure) and the separation rate is $s(w)$ also dependent on the wage. In a steady-state, recruits must equal separations, which leads to:

$$N(w) = \frac{R(w)}{s(w)}. \tag{24}$$

As pointed out by Card and Krueger (1995), this implies that:

$$\varepsilon = \varepsilon_{Rw} - \varepsilon_{sw} \tag{25}$$

so that knowledge of the elasticities of recruitment and quits with respect to the wage can be used to estimate the elasticity of labor supply facing the firm. The elasticity of separations with respect to the wage is important here but so is the elasticity of recruits with respect to the wage. However, as discussed below there are arguments for linking the two. But, before discussing that argument, let us discuss estimates of the sensitivity of separations with respect to the wage.

There is a long tradition of being interested in the sensitivity of labor turnover to the wage, quite apart from any insight these studies might have for the extent of imperfect competition in the labor market. These studies are not confined to economics, e.g. see Griffeth et al. (2000) for a meta-analysis from the management literature. The bottom line is that, as predicted by models of imperfect competition, a robust negative correlation between the wages paid and labor turnover is generally found, so that the vast majority (though not all) of the studies reported below do find a significant link between separations and wages.

4.3.1. Experimental and quasi-experimental evidence
First, let us consider evidence on the sensitivity of separations to wages that are derived from studies where the variation in wages can be argued to be "exogenous". These estimates are summarized in Table 6.

Table 6 Quasi-experimental estimates of wage elasticity of separation.

Study	Sample	"Experiment"	Estimated elasticity
Clotfelter et al. (2008)	Maths.science, special education teachers in selected North Carolina schools	Annual bonus—meant to be permanent but perhaps perceived as temporary	3.5-4.3
Falch (2010b)	Norwegian schools	Wage premium at schools with recruitment difficulties	3.3
Reich et al. (2005)[a]	Workers at San Francisco Airport	Living wage ordinance	4 occupational groups: 0.3, 1.4, 1.4, 2.9
Howes (2005)[b]	Homecare workers in San Francisco	Living wage ordinance and other policy changes	1.4
Brenner (2005)	Boston firms	Living wage ordinance	Negative (n.s.)
Dube et al. (2007)[c]	Restaurants in Bay Area	San Francisco minimum wage	2.6 (tenure) −2.9 (separations) (n.s.)

n.s. denotes "not significant".

[a] The estimates of the responsiveness of turnover rates to wage changes come from Table 9. Note, that there is no "control" group in Table 9.

[b] Computed from Table 4 in text for non-family worker. Identification is from changes in earnings over time.

[c] Reported elasticities are derived from "full sample" estimates. Tenure and separations move in opposite directions.

Two studies, Clotfelter et al. (2008) and Falch (2010b) consider the impact on separations of policies designed to retain teachers in particular schools. The other studies reported in Table 6 analyze the effect of "living wage" ordinances (which are effectively higher minimum wages for public-sector workers or those who work for public-sector contractors), or local minimum wages. In many of these studies, separations are not the primary focus of interest and outcomes related to separations are often reported in the "other outcomes" Table.

One feature of Table 6 is the wide range of variation in the reported elasticities. Both Clotfelter et al. (2008) and Falch (2010b) report high values of the wage elasticity of separations—in the region of 3-4. A study of the wage rises at San Francisco airport (Reich et al., 2005) report a similar elasticity for one occupational group but two of the others are at 1.4 and one is at 0.25. Furthermore, Brenner (2005) reports an insignificant "wrongly-signed" elasticity, as do Dube et al. (2007) for separations—though they report a large "correctly-signed" elasticity for job tenure. Howes (2005) reports an elasticity of 1.4.

These differences may reflect the fact that the samples are very different and that there is a lot of heterogeneity across labor markets in the sensitivity of separations to the wage.

But, it may also reflect the fact that these different "quasi-experiments" are estimating different elasticities. One would ideally like to see the responsiveness of separations to a permanent change in wages in a single firm holding the wages in all neighboring firms constant. It is not clear whether any of these studies does exactly that. For example, living and minimum wage changes affect the wages paid by potentially large numbers of employers in a labor market, so even if there is the control group of a labor market unaffected by the wage change one may be estimating the elasticity of separations at the level of a market as a whole to changes in wages.

4.3.2. Non-experimental studies

In this section we review non-experimental estimates of the elasticity of separations with respect to wages. In these studies the wage variable used is simply what is available. A wide range of studies is reported in Table 7.

The earliest studies (e.g. Pencavel, 1970; Parsons, 1972, 1973) used industry data, either cross-section or time series. These estimates are probably not what good estimates of what we would like—the effect of a wage rise in a single firm—but do serve to make the point that economists have now been looking at the link between separations and wages for 40 years.

The more recent studies all use individual data but differ in a number of dimensions. First, there is the specification of the dependent variable—in some it is any separation while in others it is a "quit" defined as being a voluntary move on the part of the worker (typically self-defined). Separations that are not quits can be thought of as involuntary lay-offs—these have also been found to be sensitive to the wage, as one might expect if there is less surplus in the jobs of low-wage workers so that shocks are more likely to make employer rents negative, initiating a lay-off.

Secondly, there are differences in the way the wage variable is defined. In most studies it is simply the current hourly wage derived from the survey. A few studies use measures either of contractual wages (Ransom and Oaxaca, 2010; Ransom and Sims, 2010) or of wages workers might expect to get in the job (e.g. Meitzen, 1986; Campbell, 1993). One might expect the estimates to be sensitive to the wage measure used because we would expect the separation decision to be based not just on the current wage but future prospects as well (see Fox, 2010, for a model that explicitly models forward-looking workers). We would like to have a measure of the sensitivity of separations to a permanent change in the wage but the actual wage measures used may have a sizeable transitory component or measurement error that would be expected to attenuate elasticities. The one study that seeks to instrument the wage (Barth and Dale-Olsen, 2009)—using employer characteristics associated with higher wages—finds that this raises the elasticity (from 0.9 to 2.4 for men and 0.5 to 0.9 for women).

Thirdly, there are differences in the other variables included in the separations equations. Omitted variables, correlated with the wage, will obviously bias estimates. One potential source of problems in estimating the separation elasticity is a failure to control

Table 7 Non-experimental estimates of wage elasticity of separation.

Study	Sample (US unless otherwise stated)	Dependent variable	Wage variable	Estimated elasticity
Pencavel (1970)	Manufacturing cross-section, 1959	Industry quit rate	Median wage	0.8–1.2
Parsons (1972)[a]	Industry cross-section, 1963	Industry quit rates	Production worker wage	1.2
Parsons (1973)	Time series for 27 industries	Industry quit rate	6-month geometric average of relative wages	1.3 (average across industries)
Wickens (1978)	UK manufacturing	Industry quit rate	Average wage	1.2
Viscusi (1980)	PSID 1975/6	Quit	Hourly wage	Male: 0.8 Female: 0.8
Blau and Kahn (1981)	NLS circa 1970	Voluntary quit	Hourly wage	Male white: 0.4 Male black: 0.6 Female white: 0.4 Female black: 0.4
Meitzen (1986)	EOPP employer survey, 1980	Quit	Top wage in job	Male: 0.8 Female: 0.4
Lakhani (1988)	US Army non-graduates, aged 18–32, 1981	Quit rate	Regular military compensation	0.25
Campbell (1993)	EOPP employer survey, 1980	Quit	Top wage in job	1
Royalty (1998)[b]	NLSY, 1979–87	Separation	Hourly wage	Male < HS: 0.5 Male >= HS: 0.6 Female < HS: 0.4 Female >= HS: 0.6

Table 7 (continued)

Study	Sample (US unless otherwise stated)	Dependent variable	Wage variable	Estimated elasticity
Manning (2003a)	NLSY, PSID UK LFS, BHPS	Separation	Hourly wage	NLSY: 0.5 PSID: 1.0 BHPS: 0.7 LFS: 0.5
Martin (2003)	UK establishment survey, 1991	Turnover rate	Relative wage	0.2
Barth and Dale-Olsen (2009)[c]	Norwegian social security data, 1989/97	Separation	Daily wage	Male low educated: 0.8 Female low-educated: 0.6 Male high educated: 0.6 Female high-educated: 0.6
Booth and Katic (2009)	Australian HILDA survey	Separation	Hourly wage	Male: 0.4 Female: 0.3
Ransom and Sims (2010)	Missouri school teachers	Separation	Base salary in school district	1.8
Ransom and Oaxaca (2010)	Grocery retailer	Separation	Wage for job	Male: 1.6 Female: 1.3
Hirsch et al. (2010)	German social security data	Separation	Daily wage	Male: 1.9 Female: 1.7

[a] Only reports estimate for 1963 with average production worker wage and quit rate retrieved from original data sources.
[b] These are read off from Figures B2 and B4.
[c] Only OLS estimates are reported here. Some higher IV estimates for manufacturing are discussed in the text.

adequately for the average level of wages in the individual's labor market. Separations are likely to depend on the wage relative to this alternative wage so that a failure to control for the alternative wage is likely to lead to a downward bias on the wage elasticities. On the other hand, we would expect separations to be more sensitive to the permanent component of wages than to the part of wages that is a transitory shock or measurement error. In this case, the inclusion of controls correlated with the permanent wage is likely to reduce the estimated wage elasticity. Manning (2003a,b, chapter 4) investigates this and finds that, for a number of US and UK data sets, the inclusion of standard human capital controls does not make much difference to the estimated wage elasticities.

However, one variable whose inclusion or exclusion makes a lot of difference to the apparent estimated wage elasticity is job tenure[16]. The inclusion of job tenure always reduces the estimated coefficient on the wage, as high-tenure workers are less likely to leave the firm and are more likely to have high wages. There are arguments both for and against the inclusion of job tenure. One of the benefits of paying high wages is that tenure will be higher, so that one needs to take account of this endogeneity of tenure if one wants the overall wage elasticity when including tenure controls: in this situation, excluding tenure may give better estimates[17]. On the other hand, if there are seniority wage scales, the apparent relationship between separations and wages may be spurious. Some studies that attempt to deal with this last problem are Ransom and Sims (2010), which uses the base wage in the school district as their wage measure, or Ransom and Oaxaca (2010), which uses the contractual wage for the job.

Table 6 reports estimates of the wage elasticity of separations from a number of studies. There is considerable variation in the estimates from a low of about 0.4 to a high of about 2. There are of course an enormous number of reasons for why the estimates might vary from differences in the sample to differences in the specification and no attempt is made in Table 6 to measure all the dimensions in which the studies differ.

But, there is perhaps a suggestion that those studies which have higher quality information on contemporaneous wages (e.g. from social security data) or use measures of contractual wages find elasticities in the region 1.5-2, while those with elasticities well below 1 generally just use standard self-reported measures of wages.

The bottom line from these studies is that while wages do undoubtedly affect quit rates, worker mobility does not appear to be hugely sensitive to the wage, with the highest reported elasticity being about 4 and most being well below 2^{18}. On its own this does not imply that the wage elasticity of labor supply to an employer is low because, as (25) makes clear, we also need the recruitment elasticity. But, as the next section makes clear,

---

[16] The word "apparent" is appropriate here because the dependence of job tenure on the wage needs to be taken account of here when estimating the full wage elasticity.

[17] For the studies that report estimates both including and excluding tenure, Table 7 only reports those estimates excluding tenure.

[18] Such a conclusion is not new—the ethnographic study of Reynolds (1951) reached a similar conclusion.

we would expect the recruitment and separation elasticities to be closely related to each other.

4.3.3. The link between separation and recruitment elasticities

The studies that have used the separations elasticity to estimate the elasticity of labor supply to the individual employer have all equated the recruitment elasticity to the separation elasticity, essentially using the formula in (25) to double the separation elasticity to get an estimate of the elasticity of labor supply to an individual employer. Equating the quit and recruitment elasticities was first proposed in Manning (2003b) and attracts a certain amount of suspicion, some suspecting it something of a sleight of hand. In fact, there are good reasons to believe it a reasonable approximation for separations to other jobs and recruits from other jobs. The reason is that when a worker leaves employer A for employer B because B offers a higher wage, this is a worker who is recruited to B because it is paying a higher wage than A.

To illustrate the robustness of the idea a more general result is shown here, using the generalized model of monopsony in which employers can also influence their supply of labor by spending more resources on recruitment. Assume that job offers arrive at a rate λ and that the distribution of wages in those job offers is $g(x)$. Furthermore, assume that a worker who is currently paid w and who receives a job offer of x will leave with a probability $\phi(\frac{x}{w})$. If the wage is the only factor in job mobility decision this will be one if x is above w and zero if it is below, but it is probably more realistic to think of it as a differentiable function. The assumption that it is only the relative wage that matters is the critically important assumption for what follows, but it is not an unreasonable assumption. If this condition was not satisfied, one would expect, as average wages rise, separations to trend up or down which they do not. Define $\varepsilon_\phi(\frac{x}{w})$ to be the elasticity of $\phi(\frac{x}{w})$ with respect to its argument—we will call this the wage-specific quit elasticities.

Consider a firm that pays wage, w. The overall separation rate will be given by:

$$s(w) = \lambda \int g(x)\phi\left(\frac{x}{w}\right) dx. \tag{26}$$

Appendix C then proves the following result:

Result 1: The elasticity of the separation rate with respect to the wage is given by:

$$\varepsilon_s(w) = \frac{ws'(w)}{s(w)} = \int g_s(x; w)\, \varepsilon_\varphi\left(\frac{x}{w}\right) dx \tag{27}$$

where $g_s(x; w)$ is the share of separations in a firm that pays w that go to a firm that pays x i.e.

$$g_s(x; w) = \frac{g(x)\phi\left(\frac{x}{w}\right)}{\int g(x')\,\phi\left(\frac{x'}{w}\right) dx'}. \tag{28}$$

Proof. See Appendix C.

Equation (27) says that the overall separation elasticity can be thought of as a weighted average of the wage-specific elasticities, where the weights are the shares of quits to firms with different wages.

To derive the elasticity of recruits with respect to the wage we need to think about the distribution of wage offers, $g(w)$. This will be influenced by the distribution of wages across firms—which we will denote by $f(w)$ and, we will assume, the hiring activity of firms. If $H(w)$ is the amount of resources spent on hiring by a firm that pays w, then we will assume that the distribution of wage offers is given by:

$$g(w) = \frac{H(w)^\beta f(w)}{\int H(x)^\beta f(x)dx} = \left(\frac{H(w)}{\tilde{H}}\right)^\beta f(w) \tag{29}$$

where:

$$\tilde{H} = \left[\int H(x)^\beta f(x)dx\right]^{\frac{1}{\beta}} \tag{30}$$

is an index of aggregate hiring activity. It is natural to assume that λ, the job offer arrival rate, depends on $\tilde{H}$, the aggregate hiring activity, as well as other factors (e.g. the intensity of worker job search). The parameter β is of critical importance as it measures whether marginal costs of recruitment are increasing ($\beta < 1$) or decreasing ($\beta > 1$) in the level of recruitment.

Now, consider recruitment. The flow of recruits to a firm that pays w and recruits at intensity H can be written as:

$$R(w, h) = \left(\frac{H}{\tilde{H}}\right)^\beta \lambda \int f(x)N(x)\phi\left(\frac{w}{x}\right)dx = \left(\frac{H}{\tilde{H}}\right)^\beta R(w) \tag{31}$$

where $N(x)$ is employment in a firm that pays x. Note the multiplicative separability in (31). From this we have that:

Result 2: The elasticity of the recruitment rate with respect to the wage is given by:

$$\varepsilon_R(w) = \frac{wR'(w)}{R(w)} = \int g_R(x, w)\,\varepsilon_\phi\left(\frac{w}{x}\right)dx \tag{32}$$

where:

$$g_R(x, w) = \frac{f(x)N(x)\phi\left(\frac{w}{x}\right)}{\int f(x')N(x')\phi\left(\frac{w}{x'}\right)dx'}. \tag{33}$$

Is the density of recruits to a firm that pays w from firms that pay x.

Proof. See Appendix C.

Comparing (28) and (32) one can see the inevitable link between the quit elasticity and the recruitment elasticity—they are both averages of the wage-specific elasticities. The quit elasticity for a firm that pays w is a weighted average of the elasticity of quits to firms that pay other wages with the weights being the share of quits that go to these firms. The recruitment elasticity for a firm that pays w is a weighted average of the elasticity of quits from firms that pay other wages to firms that pay w with the weights being the share of recruits that come from these firms. If this function was iso-elastic then quit and separation elasticities have to be equal, though this is impossible as ϕ has to be between zero and one. However, a further result shows how they must be linked.

For an individual firm the quit and recruitment elasticity will not generally be the same but, averaging across the economy as a whole they must be.

Result 3: The recruit-weighted recruitment elasticity must be equal to the recruit-weighted quit elasticity i.e.:

$$\int f(w)R\,(w,\,H(w))\,\varepsilon_R(w)\mathrm{d}w = \int f(w)R\,(w,\,H(w))\,\varepsilon_s(w)\mathrm{d}w. \qquad (34)$$

Proof. See Appendix C.

The intuition for this result is simple—every quit from one employer to another is a recruit for the other employer.

Now consider what this implies about the labor supply to a firm in the long-run. For a firm that has hiring resources of H and pays a wage w, (31) implies we have that:

$$N(w,\,H) = \frac{R\,(w,\,H)}{s(w)} = \left(\frac{H}{\tilde{H}}\right)^{\beta}\frac{R(w)}{s\,(w)} = \left(\frac{H}{\tilde{H}}\right)^{\beta}n(w). \qquad (35)$$

And the elasticity of $n(w)$ with respect to the wage is—using the argument given above—approximately twice the quit elasticity.

All of this discussion has been about moves between employers. One cannot apply the same approach for the elasticity of separations to non-employment and recruits from non-employment as there is no need for one to be the mirror image of the other. However, Manning (2003a) discusses how one can deal with this problem.

However, the way in which one interprets and uses this elasticity does need to be modified. Using a simple-minded model of monopsony, one would be inclined to conclude that there is an incredible amount of monopsony power in labor markets and conclude there is a massive amount of exploitation in the labor market that could, for example, be reduced by a very large increase in the minimum wage. In a later section we make clear that this is not the correct conclusion. It is the presence of hiring costs in (35) that makes the difference.

4.3.4. Hiring costs revisited

Earlier, we discussed how important it is whether there are increasing marginal costs to hiring but also emphasized how hard it is to get good estimates of this parameter. Here, we show how an estimate can be backed-out from the model described above.

Consider a firm choosing the wage and recruitment intensity to maximize steady-state profits[19]:

$$\pi = F(N) - wN - H. \tag{36}$$

Subject to the constraint that labor supply is given by (35). In this specification we are assuming that all hiring costs are recruitment costs—the equations would need modification if one also wanted to model training costs. The first-order condition for the wage is going to be:

$$\pi = \left[F'(N) - w\right]\frac{\partial N}{\partial w} - N = 0 \tag{37}$$

which can be re-written as the condition:

$$w = \frac{\varepsilon}{1 + \varepsilon}F'(N). \tag{38}$$

So that the relationship between the wage and the marginal product is the familiar one. If, as the estimates discussed above suggest, the elasticity is low there will be a big gap between the marginal product and the wage. This then implies that employers make considerable rents from the employment relationship, so should be prepared to spend quite large amounts of money to hire workers. But, as we saw in the previous section, the estimates of the average hiring cost are, while not trivial, not enormous. What we show here is that these two facts can only be reconciled if there is a big difference between the marginal and average costs of hiring, which implies strongly diminishing returns to hiring expenditure.

To see this, consider the choice of hiring rate. From (36) and (35) this will be given by:

$$\left[F'(N) - w\right]\frac{\partial N}{\partial H} - 1 = 0 \tag{39}$$

which can be written as:

$$\left[F'(N) - w\right]\frac{\beta N}{H} = 1. \tag{40}$$

---

[19] Note that this specification assumes that the hiring resources cost the same to all firms. As hiring costs are mostly the labor of workers within the firm an alternative assumption would be to assume they are proportional to w. The evidence in Blatter et al. (2009) and Dube, Freeman and Reich (2010) suggests recruitment costs are increasing in the wage which could be argued to favor this specification.

So that the optimal hiring expenditure per worker is given by:

$$\frac{H}{N} = \beta \left[F'(N) - w \right].$$ (41)

Using (38) this can be re-arranged to give:

$$\frac{H}{wN} = \frac{\beta}{\varepsilon}.$$ (42)

The left-hand side is the ratio of total expenditure on hiring to the total wage bill. We have already discussed data on this in Section 2.1.2. We have also discussed how one can get an estimate of ε from the separation elasticities in Sections 4.3.1–4.3.3. This can then be used to give us an estimate of β, the sensitivity of recruits to hiring expenditure. The implied value is small—for example, if the elasticity is 8 (double the highest estimates of the separation elasticity) and hiring costs are 5% of the total wage bill, this implies that $\beta = 0.4$. Assume that hiring costs are less important or that labor supply to the firm is less elastic and that implies a lower value of β suggesting more strongly increasing marginal hiring costs. Our estimates of the importance of hiring costs and the wage elasticity of the labor supply curve to the firm are not sufficiently precise to be able to do anything more with (42) than some back-of-the-envelope calculations.

4.3.5. The employer size-wage effect

It is a well-documented empirical fact (Oi and Idson, 1999; Brown and Medoff, 1989; Brown et al., 1990) that large establishments pay higher wages than small establishments. A natural explanation for the ESWE is that employers face an upward-sloping supply curve of labor[20]. We might then expect the strength of the relationship to give us an estimate of the elasticity of that supply curve. However, there are problems with using a raw ESWE as an estimate of the elasticity of the labor supply curve to an employer (see Manning, 2003a, chapter 4) as, for example, there is little doubt that part of the raw ESWE is due to the fact that large employers have, on average, better-quality workers in both observed and unobserved dimensions. But, even so, one finds that workers moving from small to large employers make wage gains on average.

Here we derive the implications for the ESWE of the model of the previous section in which firms can get big by paying a high wage or spending a lot on recruiting. For a given target employment level, N, a firm will choose the least cost way of attaining it. Given the wage paid, a firm will have to spend the following amount on recruitment to

---

[20] In a dynamic monopsony model one might also expect a relationship between wages and employment growth. This has not been explored much in the literature, but a recent paper by Schmeider (2009) does find evidence that faster-growing establishments pay higher wages.

have employment in steady-state of N: Subject to the constraint that labor supply is given by the inverse of (35):

$$H = \tilde{H}\left(\frac{N}{n(w)}\right)^{\frac{1}{\beta}}. \tag{43}$$

So that an employer with a target employment level of N will choose w to minimize:

$$wN + H = wN + \tilde{H}\left(\frac{N}{n(w)}\right)^{\frac{1}{\beta}}. \tag{44}$$

Taking the first-order condition leads to the equation:

$$N = \frac{1}{\beta}\tilde{H}\left(\frac{N}{n(w)}\right)^{\frac{1}{\beta}}\frac{n'(w)}{n(w)} = \frac{1}{\beta}\tilde{H}\left(\frac{N}{n(w)}\right)^{\frac{1}{\beta}}\frac{\varepsilon}{w} \tag{45}$$

where ε is the elasticity of $n(w)$ with respect to the wage that, for simplicity, we assume to be a constant. Taking logs and re-arranging leads to the equation:

$$\log w + \frac{1}{\beta}\log n(w) = \log \tilde{H} + \log \varepsilon + \left(\frac{1}{\beta} - 1\right)\log N. \tag{46}$$

Differentiating with respect to N leads to:

$$\frac{\partial \log w}{\partial \log N} = \frac{1-\beta}{\varepsilon + \beta}. \tag{47}$$

This is what our simple model predicts about the size of the ESWE, and one can see that it depends on the elasticity of marginal hiring costs and the elasticity of $n(w)$. If marginal hiring costs are constant so that $\beta = 1$, then we would not expect to see an ESWE, as firms who want to be large would simply raise hiring efforts and not wages. So, the existence of an ESWE is another piece of evidence suggesting increasing marginal hiring costs. We can go further and use empirical estimates of the ESWE to get some idea of the value of these parameters. The best estimates we have of the ESWE are quite low though these are contaminated perhaps by the difficulty of controlling for shocks to the labor supply curve that would tend to induce a negative correlation between wages and employment. Manning, (2003a, chapter 4) reports a best estimate an elasticity of wages with respect to employer size of about 0.035. Using a high value of ε of 8 (47) would then imply a value of $\beta = 0.69$. A less elastic labor supply curve would suggest a higher value of β, e.g. $\varepsilon = 5$ implies $\beta = 0.80$, again suggesting increasing marginal costs of hiring. These back-of-the-envelope calculations do not line up with those reported at the end of Section 4.3.4 but there should be very large standard errors attached to them.

4.4. Measuring labor market frictions

We conclude this section with a discussion of a very different approach to measuring the degree of rent-splitting. A simple yet plausible idea is that the higher the degree of competition among employers for workers, the greater will be workers' share of the surplus. In the important and influential strand of work that sees rents in the labor market as deriving primarily from labor market frictions, the fact that it takes time for workers and employers to find each other, a natural way to capture this idea is to seek some measure of transition rates between employment and non-employment and from one employer to another.

One particular measure that has been used in the literature is the ratio of the arrival rate of job offers for an employed worker (denote this by λ_e) to the rate at which workers leave employment for non-employment (denote this by δ). We will denote this ratio by k. A higher value of k is more competition among employers for workers, which would be expected to raise wages. In many canonical search models e.g. Burdett and Mortensen (1998), the share of rents going to the workers can be shown to be some function of k. It can be interpreted as the expected number of job offers a worker will receive in a spell of employment (Ridder and van den Berg, 2003).

There are a lot of measures of k in the literature, with a large degree of variation. Often these estimates come from the estimation of structural models in which it is not entirely clear which features of the data play the most important role in influencing the estimates. Here, we will simply describe ways in which k can be estimated directly using data on labor market transition rates.

δ can be estimated very simply using data on the rate at which the employed leave for non-employment. λ_e is more complicated, as the theoretical concept is the rate at which job opportunities arrive to the employed. One might think about simply using the job-to-job transition rate, but as the employed only move jobs when the new offer is better than the current one, this is an under-estimate of the rate at which new job opportunities arise. However, in simple search models there is a mapping between the two. The reason is that if all workers always prefer high-wage to low-wage jobs and always move whenever they get a higher wage offer (however small the wage gain), then there is a simple expression for the fraction of workers $G(f)$ who are in jobs at or below position f in the wage offer distribution. Equating inflows and outflows we have that:

$$[\delta + \lambda_e (1 - f)] G (f) (1 - u) = f \lambda u \tag{48}$$

where u is the unemployment rate. As, in steady-state we must have that:

$$u = \frac{\delta}{\delta + \lambda}. \tag{49}$$

(48) can be written as:

$$G(f) = \frac{\delta f}{[\delta + \lambda_e (1 - f)]}. \tag{50}$$

Now the transition rate to unemployment rate is δ and the transition rate to other jobs is:

$$\lambda_e \int (1 - f) g(f) \, df = \lambda_e \int G(f) \, df = \int \frac{\lambda_e \delta f}{[\delta + \lambda_e (1 - f)]} df$$
$$= \delta \left[\frac{\delta + \lambda_e}{\lambda_e} \ln \left(\frac{\delta + \lambda_e}{\delta} \right) - 1 \right] \tag{51}$$

which means that the ratio of transition rates to employment relative to transition rates to non-employment is given by:

$$\left[\frac{1 + k}{k} \ln (1 + k) - 1 \right]. \tag{52}$$

This is monotonically increasing in k. In a steady-state this can be shown to be equal to the fraction of recruits who come from unemployment, a measure proposed by Manning (2003a).

One might wonder about the relationship between k and estimates of the labor supply elasticity discussed earlier in this section. In many search models there is a simple connection between the two because one can always write the profit-maximizing choice of the wage as being related to the elasticity of the labor supply curve to the firm so that k must be related to this. However, if, for example, one relaxed the assumption that it is only current or future wages that motivate job changes, then k would not seem to be a good measure of the market power of employers while an estimate of the wage elasticity still gets to the heart of the issue.

How do estimates of the balance of power between workers and employers based on this methodology compare to those based on the wage elasticity of the labor supply curve (or separations)? The advantage is perhaps that they are relatively easy to compute with nothing more than data on labor market transitions, but the disadvantage is that they are indirect (not requiring any data on actual wages) and may rely for their validity on assumptions that do not hold. For example, in these models perfect competition is the case where there is massive churning of workers, where the employer you work for one day (or hour?) has no bearing on who you work for the next. In some sense, that is a correct characterization of a perfectly competitive equilibrium, as that determines the market wage but not who of the large number of identical employers a worker works for, which is indeterminate. But, the inclusion of even a small fixed cost of changing jobs would change the prediction to one of very little turnover in an equilibrium close to perfect competition. Secondly, there is good reason to believe that not all turnover is for wage gains, which is what is relevant for employers deciding on the wage to pay. The one empirical application (Hirsch and Schumacher, 2005) does not find this measure works well in explaining variation in nurse pay across US cities.

4.5. Conclusions

This section has reviewed estimates we have of the distribution of rents in the typical employment relationship. These estimates do suggest the existence of non-trivial rents in the employment relationship. However, it is not completely clear that they are internally consistent. For example, the estimates of the rent-splitting parameter would suggest that most of the rents go to the employer. However the estimates from the actual size of rents probably suggest the workers getting most of the rents. Clearly, there is more work to be done here. While the importance of imperfect competition in labor markets might be regarded as intrinsically interesting, one still has to deal with the "so what?" question, what difference does this make to how one thinks about labor markets.

5. SO WHAT?

If there are clearly rents in the typical employment relationship, why is an imperfect competition perspective not pervasive in labor economics? There are two sorts of answers. First that it has little value-added above the perfectly competitive model—it adds more complication than insight[21]. This might be because perfect competition is seen as a tolerable approximation to reality so that the mistakes one makes by assuming the labor market is perfectly competitive are small. Or it might be because the comparative statics of models of imperfect and perfect competition are the same in many cases so give the same answers to many questions. For example, shifts in the demand curve and supply curve of labor will be predicted to have the same effects in perfect and imperfect competition.

The second reason why many labor economists do not adopt the perspective that the labor market is imperfectly competitive in their work is that they do not adopt any conceptual framework at all[22]. A well-designed and executed randomized experiment

---

[21] Although, there is a part of economics that sees complication as a virtue and there does seem to be a part of research on imperfect competition in labor markets that is attracted to that.

[22] Mention should be made here of one part of labor economics that has taken models of imperfect competition very seriously, perhaps too seriously. This is the small industry of structural modeling of the labor market. A full review will not be attempted here (see, for example, Eckstein and van den Berg, 2006), just a few observations about the pluses and minuses of this strategy. Structural models have the advantage that they can be used to make a prediction about anything. However, the problem is that one can estimate any model, however crazy (just write down its likelihood function and maximize it) so it is not clear that the predictions of these models are any good. The discussion of identification often leaves a lot to be desired, relying heavily on functional forms and arbitrary assumptions about the sources of heterogeneity in the labor market. Structural modelers often seem more interested in the technical details than in whether their model is the right model and rather unconcerned about how obviously poorly many of these models fare in dimensions other than that which is sought to be fitted to the data. My personal view is that we have, as yet, learned relatively little from these studies about the way in which labor markets operate. Others think very differently.

tells us about the effect of an intervention without the need for any theory or conceptual framework at all. A generation of labor economists have grown up who are not accustomed to thinking in terms of economic models at all, seeking instead good research designs. But, while estimates from randomized experiments have internal validity, their external validity is more problematic. The results tell us what happened but not why. And without at least some understanding of "why" it is difficult to draw conclusions from such studies that are of general use and enable us to make a forecast of will happen with a similar but not identical treatment in another time and place. We want to use evidence not just to understand the past but to improve the future. In practice, people do assume estimates have external validity all the time—they implicitly generalize. But perhaps it would be better if this was more explicit and we had a theory of why, and this is where an overall perspective on the workings of the labor market might help. The section that follows seeks to do just that.

6. APPLICATIONS

As argued in the previous section, labor economists will probably only be convinced of the merits of thinking about labor markets through the lens of imperfect competition if they can be convinced that it makes a difference to perspectives on certain issues. In this section we review several areas in which it has been argued to make a difference, though we make no claims that this is exhaustive and we try to list others at the end.

6.1. The law of one wage

In a perfectly competitive market, the elasticity of labor supply to a single firm is perfectly elastic at the market wage for that type of worker[23]. Any attempt to pay a lower wage will result in a complete inability to recruit any workers at all, while any higher wage simply serves to reduce profits. As a result, all employers who employ this type of worker will pay them the same wage—the law of one wage holds. And all workers of that quality will be paid the same wage, irrespective of their reservation wage.

Those who have studied actual labor markets have often observed that the law of one wage seems to be violated, that there is, to use the jargon, equilibrium wage dispersion. Such a conclusion can be found from studies dating back to the late 1940s (e.g. Reynolds, 1946; Lester, 1946; Slichter, 1950) but more recent empirical studies all come to much the same conclusion. The existence of equilibrium wage dispersion requires some degree of imperfect competition in labor markets.

In models of imperfect competition that are based on ex post wage-bargaining, it is simple to explain the existence of equilibrium wage dispersion. Refer back to the wage Eq. (10)—this has wages depending on the specific productivity of that employer and the

---

[23] Abstracting from compensating differentials.

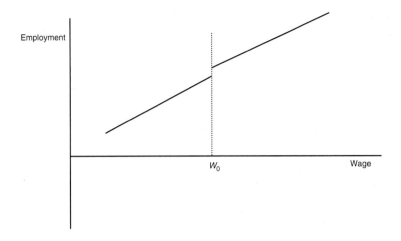

Figure 3   *The labor supply to a firm in the Burdett-Mortensen model when there is a mass point at w_0.*

specific reservation wage of the worker, something that should not happen in a perfectly competitive labor market[24].

In wage-posting models the most celebrated paper is Burdett and Mortensen (1998). They present a model with homogeneous workers and employers in which the only possible equilibrium is a wage distribution with no mass points. While that is an elegant and striking result, there is a very good reason for thinking it is deficient as an account of the origin of equilibrium wage dispersion. The reason is that one can track the result to an assumption of the model, which is very unappealing as an assumption about the real world and, if this assumption is made more realistic, the result collapses. That assumption is that all workers will move for the smallest gain in wages. How this delivers equilibrium wage dispersion as the only possible equilibrium can be explained with a simple diagram. Think about the labor supply curve facing an individual employer in which there is a mass of firms paying some wage w_0. The labor supply curve will be discontinuous at this point so looks something like that drawn in Fig. 3. No profit-maximizing employer would then want to pay the wage w_0—they would rather pay something infinitesimally higher and get a lot more workers. The mass point will unravel.

But the assumption that all workers move for the smallest gain in wages is totally implausible, so this is not a credible account of the origin of equilibrium wage dispersion. Furthermore, we do observe mass points of wages at, for example, the minimum wage and round numbers. Does this mean this type of model has no credible explanation of equilibrium wage dispersion? Far from it—the simplest and most plausible explanation is that, faced with the same labor supply curve that is always continuous in the wage,

---

[24] Though a statement like this should not be confused with the fact that the level of reservation wages and marginal products will affect the equilibrium wage in a perfectly competitive market.

heterogeneous employers will choose to locate at different points on that supply curve. As put succinctly by Mortensen (2003, p. 6) "wage dispersion is largely the consequence of search friction and cross-firm differences in factor productivity".

The failure of the law of one wage in labor markets has important consequences, some of which we will discuss below. It means that achieving a higher level of earnings is, in part, the result of working oneself into the best jobs, but that the outcome of this process will contain a considerable element of luck.

6.2. Labor market regulation

If labor markets are perfectly competitive then we know that the equilibrium will be Pareto efficient and that regulation can only be justified on distributive and not efficiency grounds. If labor markets are imperfectly competitive there is no such presumption that the market is efficient and there is at least the potential for some regulation to improve efficiency.

The labor market regulation that has received the most attention is the minimum wage. If the labor market is perfectly competitive then a minimum wage must reduce employment, as it raises the cost of labor. However, this is not necessarily the case if the labor market is imperfectly competitive. To illustrate this, we will consider the case of monopsony, though one could do the same with a matching-style model.

In the simplest model of monopsony, in which there is a single employer and the wage is the only available instrument for influencing its labor supply, there is a very simple formula relating the minimum wage to the elasticity of the labor supply to an individual employer. As we have emphasized that the labor supply to individual firms is not very sensitive to the wage, this would suggest very large potential rises in employment could be obtained from an artfully chosen minimum wage.

However, there are at least two important reasons for why such a conclusion is likely to be misleading. First, we have emphasized how the simple model of monopsony is not the best way to think about the labor market. Secondly, the model of market power we have used is a model of a single employer that ignores interactions between employers, so is only a partial equilibrium analysis.

Let's consider the first point first. Take the model of the previous section in which the labor supply curve is given by (35) and can be influenced not just by the wage paid but also by the level of recruitment activity. To keep things simple assume the marginal revenue product of labor is constant and equal to p. First, consider the optimal employment level given the wage paid. This satisfies the first-order condition:

$$(p - w) = \frac{1}{\beta N} \left[\frac{N}{n(w)} \right]^{\frac{1}{\beta}}. \tag{53}$$

Re-arranging leads to the following "labor demand curve":

$$N = n(w)^{\frac{1}{1-\beta}} [\beta(p-w)]^{\frac{\beta}{1-\beta}} . \tag{54}$$

Assume, again, that $n(w)$ is iso-elastic with elasticity ε. If the employer has a free choice of the wage we know they will choose a wage like (38). First, consider the minimum wage that will maximize employment, i.e. the wage that maximizes (54). It is easy to show that this is given by:

$$w^* = \frac{\varepsilon}{\beta + \varepsilon} p. \tag{55}$$

The important point is that this is bigger than the wage that the employer will choose for itself, which will be given by:

$$w^m = \frac{\varepsilon}{1 + \varepsilon} p \tag{56}$$

where the "m" superscript denotes the choice of a monopsonist. The log difference between the free market wage and the employment-maximizing wage is hence given by:

$$\ln w^* - \ln w^m = \ln \left(\frac{\varepsilon}{\beta + \varepsilon} \right) - \ln \left(\frac{\varepsilon}{1 + \varepsilon} \right) = \ln \left(\frac{1 + \varepsilon}{\beta + \varepsilon} \right) > 0. \tag{57}$$

Now consider the gain in employment from an artfully chosen minimum wage. Using (54) and the wage Eqs (55) and (56), one can show that this is given by:

$$\ln N^* - \ln N^m = \frac{\beta}{1 - \beta} \ln \left(\frac{\beta(1 + \varepsilon)}{\beta + \varepsilon} \right) + \frac{\varepsilon}{1 - \beta} \ln \left(\frac{1 + \varepsilon}{\beta + \varepsilon} \right). \tag{58}$$

The standard monopsony case corresponds to the case where $\beta = 0$. This leads to the prediction of very large potential employment gains from an artfully-chosen minimum wage, e.g. even a high wage elasticity of 5 leads to a predicted employment gain of 91 log points from a wage rise of 18 log points. But if $\beta = 0.8$ this is much lower—a predicted employment gain of 9 log points from a wage rise of 3.3 log points.

The important point to note is that, unlike the simple model of monopsony, the potential gains from the minimum wage are not just influenced by the wage elasticity ε but also the parameter β, which is the relationship between average and marginal costs of hiring.

This is a partial equilibrium conclusion and not a reliable guide for policy. There are two important distinctions between partial equilibrium models of monopsony and general equilibrium models of oligopsony. First, in general equilibrium there is an important distinction between the elasticity of labor supply to the market as a whole and to individual employers. While the gap between marginal product and the wage is determined by the elasticity of the labor supply curve facing an individual employer, any employment effect will be determined by the elasticity of the labor supply curve to the labor market as a whole. There is no reason why these should be the same but it is exactly that assumption that is made by the model of a single monopsonist.

Secondly, it is important to take account of heterogeneity. There is no doubt that the minimum wage is a blunt instrument, applied across whole labor markets on employers who would otherwise choose very different wages. This means that it is almost certainly the case that the minimum wage will have different effects on employment in different employers and any measure of the impact on aggregate employment must take account of this heterogeneity. Manning (2003a, chapter 12) takes account of both these effects, showing that even in a labor market in which all employers have some market power, a minimum wage, however low, may always reduce employment.

However, models of imperfect competition are different from models of perfect competition in not making a clear-cut prediction about the employment consequences of raising the minimum wage. It is empirical studies that are important and, though this is a long debate which will not be surveyed here (see Brown, 1999, for an earlier survey), recent studies with good research designs typically fail to find any negative effects on employment for the moderate levels of minimum wages set in the US (Dube, Lester and Reich, forthcoming; Giuliano, 2009).

Although the employment effect of minimum wages has become the canonical issue in wider debates about the pros and cons of regulating labor markets, one should also recognize that models of imperfect competition in the labor market often have different predictions from competitive models about many interventions. For example, one can show that regulation to restrict aspects of labor contracts like hours or holidays can improve employment (Manning, 2003a, chapter 8). However, although imperfect competition can be used as a justification for some regulation on efficiency grounds, it always predicts some limits to regulation, with quite what those limits are left to empirical research to decide.

6.3. The gender pay gap

When Joan Robinson (1933) invented the term monopsony she used it as a potential explanation of the gender pay gap. If the labor supply of women to a firm is less elastic than that of men, then a profit-maximizing employer will choose to pay lower wages to women than men even if they have the same productivity.

A recent literature essentially builds on that observation to explain at least part of the gender pay gap. The main approach has been to see whether the separation elasticity of women is lower than that of men and then apply the logic outlined in Sections 4.3.1

and 4.3.2 to argue that this can explain some of the gender pay gap. A priori this sounds a plausible idea, as women do report that non-wage attributes are more important in their choice of a job and that they are more restricted by domestic commitments in the employment they can accept. However, this conclusion does not pop out of all the estimates. Some studies that estimate distinct separation elasticities for men and women (e.g. Barth and Dale-Olsen, 2009; Hirsch et al., 2010; Ransom and Oaxaca, 2010) do report estimates suggesting that female separation elasticities are lower than the male but this is not true of all studies (e.g. it is not true for any of the four data sets examined in Manning, 2003a, chapter 6). Perhaps worryingly, Barth and Dale-Olsen (2009) report that the estimates are sensitive to the specification used, arguing that, in their data, better specifications do deliver the conclusion that the female elasticity is below the male.

It is important to realize that a difference in separation elasticity is not necessary for models of imperfect competition to be able to explain the gender pay gap. Nor is actual wage discrimination by employers. It could simply be that women are more likely to interrupt their careers with spells of non-employment, primarily to look after young children. In a labor market where the law of one wage does not hold, this will reduce the ability of women to work themselves into and remain in the best-paying jobs. Several recent studies of the gender pay gap find that career interruptions can explain a sizeable proportion (Bertrand et al., 2009). While the most common explanation for this is that those with career interruptions accumulate less human capital, the size of the pay penalty for even small interruptions seem very large. It is not surprising that career interruptions reduce wages, but is the penalty proportionate? Research in this area needs to answer this question.

Finally, mention should be made of the effects of equal pay legislation. In the US, equal pay legislation did not seem to have an immediate effect on the gender pay gap. But, in some other countries (e.g. the UK and Australia) there was a very clear fall in the gender pay gap associated with the passing of the legislation. This change in relative wages was far more dramatic than the wage changes induced by rises in the minimum wage. If the labor market was perfectly competitive, we would expect this legislated rise in the relative wage of women to result in a fall in their relative employment. Yet, this is not what seemed to happen and Manning (1996) argues this is because the labor market has monopsonistic elements.

6.4. Economic geography

Much of economic geography is about explaining the distribution of economic activity over space—in particular, why it is so uneven, the phenomenon of agglomeration. There are many theories of agglomeration which are not reviewed here. The current literature on agglomeration tends to focus on the product market more than the labor market—but there is considerable useful research that could be done on labor market explanations.

In his classic discussion of agglomeration, Alfred Marshall (1920) speculated about possible labor market explanations, e.g. "a localized industry gains a great advantage from the fact that it offers a constant market for skill. Employers are apt to resort to any place where they are likely to find a good choice of workers with the special skill which they require; while men seeking employment naturally go to places where there are many employers who need such a skill as theirs and where therefore it is likely to find a good market. The owner of an isolated factory, even if he has access to a plentiful supply of general labor, is often put to great shifts for want of some special skilled labor; and a skilled workman, when thrown out of employment in it, has no easy refuge".

The important point is these arguments make little sense if the labor market is perfectly competitive. In such a market the prevailing wage conveys all the information a firm or worker needs to know about the labor market[25]. In a perfectly competitive labor market, an employer who is small in relation to the whole market will not care about the total supply of labor to the market except insofar as it affects the prevailing level of wages. Hence, to make any sense of Marshall's arguments, one would seem to require some degree of imperfect competition in labor markets. The formalization of Marshall's "labor pools" theory in Krugman (1991) rests explicitly on there being a small number of employers in the labor market.

Once the labor market is monopsonistic, one can begin to make sense of some of Marshall's arguments for agglomeration. If the labor supply curve to an individual employer is upward-sloping it makes sense to talk about a labor supply curve being "further out" because of a generally high supply of labor. One might think that monopsony models would struggle to explain agglomeration because it might be thought that an employer would like to be the only employer in an area because they would then have enormous monopsony power over the workers in that area. But that is based on a misunderstanding. Although the degree of monopsony power over the workers in an area will be high, there will be few of them and this is not to the advantage of an employer. Fig. 4 conveys this very simply. It draws two labor markets, one (the "village") in which there are very few workers but over whom the employer has a lot of monopsony power so the labor supply curve is very inelastic. In the other (the "city'), there are more workers but less monopsony power. In which labor market will the employer choose to locate? They will choose the market where the level of employment they desire can be obtained most cheaply. So, if the desired level of employment is low, they will choose the village, while if it is high they will choose the city. Manning (forthcoming) uses this idea to explain the existence of agglomeration with employers who desire to be small locating in rural areas where they have more monopsony power and large employers locating in urban areas. And Overman and Puga (2009) investigate the implication that firms with more volatile employment will want to locate where the labor supply curve is more elastic.

---

[25] Although, it may be that, when making a relatively long-term location decision, it is not just the level but also the variability in wages that affects choices.

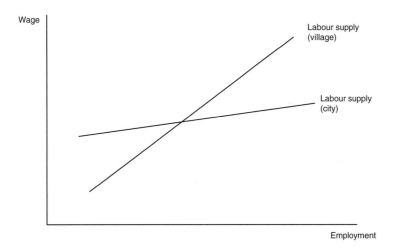

Figure 4   *City and village with a monopsonistic labor market.*

Another aspect of spatial economics that has received some attention is the estimation of commuting costs. From the perspective of a perfectly competitive labor market, one would expect workers to be fully compensated for a longer commute so that the costs of commuting can be estimated using an earnings function with the commute as an explanatory variable. But, in a labor market with frictions, we would not expect full compensation for a long commute (see Hwang et al., 1998; Manning, 2003b) so that this approach will under-estimate the cost of recruiting. An alternative approach is to use a method based on job search that worker separation rates will be based on the utility in the job and that one can get some idea of the costs of commuting by examining how wages and commute affect separations (Manning, 2003b; Van Ommeren et al., 2000). These studies often suggest a higher commuting cost, with potentially important implications for transport planning and regional development policies.

6.5. Human capital accumulation and training

Imperfection in labor markets has important implications for the incentives to acquire human capital and make investments to raise productivity. As shown by Acemoglu (1998), part of the returns to investments by workers in general human capital can be expected to accrue to future employers of the worker as the wage will be below the marginal product—this is very different from the prediction of Becker (1993) that all of the returns to general human capital will accrue to workers. The argument that workers do not fully capture the returns to investment in human capital could be used to provide a justification for the massive level of public subsidy to education that is a marked feature of all the richest economies.

Imperfect labor markets can also offer an explanation for why firms often seem to pay for the acquisition of general training by their workers—explaining this is a major problem for those who believe the labor market to be perfectly competitive. A series of papers by Acemoglu and Pischke (1998, 1999a,b) outline the theory, emphasizing the role of "wage compression" and provide some evidence in support of that theory. They conclude that "labour market imperfections have to be an ingredient of any model attempting to understand why firms pay for general training (Acemoglu and Pischke, 1999a, p. F139).

Some other papers have found evidence supportive of their ideas. For example, Booth et al. (2004) examine the effect of the UK National Minimum Wage on training, concluding that there is no evidence it reduced the training of the affected workers (as a perfectly competitive model would predict) and some evidence that training increased. Benson (2009) investigates the reason why many hospitals sponsor students to train as nurses in local nursing schools. In a perfectly competitive labor market, this behavior would not make sense, as it is a subsidy to general training. But, in a monopsonistic labor market one can explain it as a desire of a local employer to increase its supply of labor if, as seems plausible and can be verified from the data, nurses are likely to remain in the area in which they trained. But the incentives for hospitals to subsidize nurse-training are higher where the hospital represents a higher share of nurse employment. In labor markets where there are several hospitals one might expect them to subsidize joint programs, as they have a collective interest in increasing nurse supply. Benson (2009) claims to find evidence for these predictions.

6.6. Conclusion

The list of issues, where the perspective of imperfect competition might be thought to make a difference, given above is far from exhaustive. Another chapter in this Handbook (Rogerson and Shimer, 2011) discusses potential insights of interest to macroeconomists. But there are many other labor market phenomena where imperfect competition might be thought to offer plausible explanations. Examples include the growth in wages over the life-cycle as workers try to exploit the wage dispersion in the labor market, the earnings assimilation of immigrants. Brown et al. (2008) and Hotchkiss and Quispe-Agnoli (2009) argue that monopsony can be used to explain why undocumented workers earn lower wages while the firms that employ them seem to make more profits.

What this section should have made clear is that the perspective that labor markets are pervasively imperfectly competitive has important implications for "big" questions, about the desirability and impact of labor market regulation, about the gender pay gap and about decisions about human capital accumulation. It is simply not true to claim that the perspective of perfect competition tells us all we need to know.

7. CONCLUSION

There are rents in the typical job. This should not be a controversial claim—workers care when they lose or get jobs, employers care when workers leave. There is more doubt about the size and distribution of those rents. A very rough benchmark might put them in the region 15%–30% of the wage, with a best guess being that most of them go to the worker. But there is undoubtedly considerable heterogeneity across jobs, the estimates have very large standard errors, and not all the evidence is mutually consistent.

The fact that there are rents in the typical job has important consequences for our view of how labor markets work and how their performance can be improved. Many empirical observations (e.g. equilibrium wage dispersion, the gender pay gap, the effect of minimum wages on employment, employers paying for general training, costs of job loss for workers with no specific skills to list only a few) that are puzzles if one thinks the labor market is perfectly competitive are simply what one might expect if one thinks the labor market is characterized by pervasive imperfect competition. One's views of the likely effects of labor market regulation should be substantially altered once one recognizes the existence of imperfect competition. All labor economists should take imperfect competition seriously.

APPENDIX A. ESTIMATING THE SIZE OF RENTS FROM A SEARCH MODEL

In this Appendix we use a simplified version of the model in Section 2.2 outlined in section to derive an equation for the importance of rents to unemployed workers. The simplification is to assume that there is no on-the-job search. With this assumption the value of a job that pays w, $V(w)$, can be written as:

$$rV(w) = w - \delta\left[V(w) - V^u\right] \tag{59}$$

where δ is the rate of job loss and r the interest rate. Combining (5) and (59), and assuming r is small relative to δ we have that:

$$V'(w) = \frac{1}{r+\delta} \approx \frac{1}{\delta} \quad \Rightarrow \quad V(w) - V^u = \frac{1}{\delta}[w - w^*] \tag{60}$$

which implies that:

$$\frac{\int_{w^*}\left[V(w) - V^u\right]\mathrm{d}F(w)}{[1 - F(w^*)]} = \frac{1}{\delta}[\bar{w}\left(w^*\right) - w^*] \tag{61}$$

where $\bar{w}(w^*)$ is the average value of wages above the reservation wage. Now, consider the choice of the reservation wage, w^*, which must satisfy $V(w^*) = V^u$. From (5) and

(59) we must have:

$$w^* = b_u + b\,[1 - \gamma] + \lambda\,(\gamma) \int_{w^*} \left[V(w) - V^u \right] \mathrm{d}F\,(w)$$

$$= b_u + b\,[1 - \gamma] + \frac{b\lambda\,(\gamma)}{\lambda'\,(\gamma)} = b_u + b\,[1 - \gamma] + \frac{b\gamma}{\varepsilon_{\lambda\gamma}}. \tag{62}$$

If we assume that the income when unemployed is a fraction ρ of the reservation wage then this can be re-arranged to give:

$$b = \frac{(1 - \rho)\,w^*}{[1 - \gamma] + \frac{\gamma}{\varepsilon_{\lambda\gamma}}} \tag{63}$$

which forms the basis for (8) as $u/(1 - u) = \delta \mathrm{d}_u$.

APPENDIX B. A MODEL WITH HETEROGENEOUS WORKER ABILITY

Here we present a model to explain the difference in the apparent labor supply elasticity from a mandated wage increase and a mandated employment increase.

For simplicity, let us assume that the labor supply of workers of quality a (measured as efficiency units) to a firm that pays wage w, $L\,(w, a)$ is given by:

$$L\,(w, a) = L(w) f\,(a) \tag{64}$$

where we assume $f\,(a)$ is a density function. A firm has to make two decisions—the wage to pay and the minimum quality worker, a^*, to employ. Profits will be given by:

$$\pi\,(w, a) = pL(w) \int_{a^*} af\,(a)\,\mathrm{d}a - wL(w) \int_{a^*} f\,(a)\,\mathrm{d}a$$

$$= \left(p\bar{a}\,(a^*) - w \right) N\,(w, a^*) \tag{65}$$

where:

$$\bar{a}\,(a^*) = \frac{\int_{a^*} af\,(a)\,\mathrm{d}a}{\int_{a^*} f\,(a)\,\mathrm{d}a} \tag{66}$$

and:

$$N\,(w, a^*) = L(w) \int_{a^*} f\,(a)\,\mathrm{d}a = L(w) \left[1 - F\,(a^*) \right]. \tag{67}$$

Now let us consider the two types of policy intervention. First, the Matsudaira type intervention. The firm is required to increase the amount of employment it has. It needs to choose (w, a^*) to solve:

$$\max \left(p \bar{a} \left(a^* \right) - w \right) \quad s.t. \quad L(w) \left[1 - F \left(a^* \right) \right] = N. \tag{68}$$

If μ is the multiplier on the constraint, the first-order conditions for this can be written as:

$$-1 + \mu L'(w) \left[1 - F \left(a^* \right) \right] = 0 \tag{69}$$
$$p \bar{a}' \left(a^* \right) - \mu L(w) f \left(a^* \right) = 0. \tag{70}$$

Collecting these leads to:

$$w = \varepsilon p \left[\bar{a} \left(a^* \right) - a^* \right] \tag{71}$$

where ε is the elasticity of the labor supply curve, which, to keep things simple we will assume is constant. (71) gives a relationship between w and a^*—denote this by $a^*(w)$.

Now consider a change in N, we will have, from the constraint in (68):

$$\frac{L'(w)}{L(w)} \frac{\partial w}{\partial \log N} - \frac{f \left(a^* \right)}{1 - F \left(a^* \right)} \frac{\partial a^*}{\partial w} \frac{\partial w}{\partial \log N} = 1. \tag{72}$$

which can be written as:

$$\frac{\partial \log w}{\partial \log N} = \frac{1}{\varepsilon - \frac{f(a^*)}{1 - F(a^*)} \frac{w}{\varepsilon p (\bar{a}'(a^*) - 1)}} = \frac{1}{\varepsilon + \frac{\bar{a}'(a^*)}{(\bar{a}'(a^*) - 1)}}. \tag{73}$$

Note that in the case where a has an exponential distribution this implies that the wage w will not change, as is found by Matsudaira. In this case:

$$\bar{a} \left(a^* \right) = a^* + \alpha. \tag{74}$$

Now consider a forced change in the wage as examined by Staiger et al. (2010). The firm wants to maximize (65). This leads to the first-order condition for a^* of:

$$p \bar{a}' \left(a^* \right) \left[1 - F \left(a^* \right) \right] - f \left(a^* \right) \left(p \bar{a} \left(a^* \right) - w \right) = 0 \tag{75}$$

which can be written as:

$$a^* = \frac{w}{p}. \tag{76}$$

If the firm can freely choose the wage, the first-order condition for w can be written as:

$$w = \frac{\varepsilon}{1 + \varepsilon} p \bar{a} \left(a^* \right). \tag{77}$$

Now, consider a rise in the wage. We will have:

$$\frac{\partial \log N}{\partial \log w} = \varepsilon - \frac{f(a^*)}{1 - F(a^*)} \frac{\partial a^*}{\partial \log w} = \varepsilon - \frac{a^* f(a^*)}{1 - F(a^*)}. \tag{78}$$

In the case with the exponential distribution and for a just–binding wage this becomes:

$$\frac{\partial \log N}{\partial \log w} = 0. \tag{79}$$

Another alternative is an effort model, then, if a denotes the effort of workers, the profit can be written as:

$$(pa - w) N. \tag{80}$$

And $N = U(w)G(a)$, with $G'(a) < 0$ reflecting the fact that workers dislike effort. This model is isomorphic to the quality model just described.

APPENDIX C. RESULTS EQUATING SEPARATION AND RECRUITMENT ELASTICITY

Proof of Result 1. Simple differentiation of (26) leads to:

$$\varepsilon_s(w) = \frac{w s'(w)}{s(w)} = \frac{-\lambda \int g(x) \frac{x}{w} \phi'\left(\frac{x}{w}\right) dx}{\lambda \int g(x) \phi\left(\frac{x}{w}\right) dx} = \int g_s(x; w) \varepsilon_\phi\left(\frac{x}{w}\right) dx \tag{81}$$

where $g_s(x; w)$ is given by:

$$g_s(x; w) = \frac{g(x)\phi\left(\frac{x}{w}\right)}{\int g(x')\phi\left(\frac{x'}{w}\right) dx'}. \tag{82}$$

Proof of Result 2. Differentiation of (31) leads to:

$$\varepsilon_R(w) = \frac{w R'(w)}{R(w)} = \frac{\int f(x) N(x) \frac{w}{x} \phi'\left(\frac{w}{x}\right) dx}{\int f(x) N(x) \phi\left(\frac{w}{x}\right) dx} = \int g_R(x, w) \varepsilon_\phi\left(\frac{w}{x}\right) dx \tag{83}$$

where:

$$g_R(x, w) = \frac{f(x) N(x) \phi\left(\frac{w}{x}\right)}{\int f(x') N(x') \phi\left(\frac{w}{x'}\right) dx'}. \tag{84}$$

Proof of Result 3. Using (31) and the equilibrium condition that firms that pay w spend $H(w)$ on recruitment (whatever that may be), one can write (33) as:

$$g_R(x, w) = \frac{f(x)N(x)\phi\left(\frac{w}{x}\right)\lambda\left(\frac{H(w)}{H}\right)^\beta}{R(w, H(w))}.$$

(85)

Now use (28) and reverse the roles of x and w to give:

$$g_s(w; x) = \frac{g(w)\phi\left(\frac{w}{x}\right)}{\int g(x')\phi\left(\frac{x'}{x}\right)dx'} = \frac{\lambda f(w)\phi\left(\frac{w}{x}\right)\left(\frac{H(w)}{H}\right)^\beta}{s(x)}.$$

(86)

Combining (85) and (86) one obtains:

$$g_R(x, w) = \frac{f(x)N(x)g_s(w, x)}{s(x)f(w)R(w, H(w))} = \frac{f(x)R(x, H(x))}{f(w)R(w, H(w))}g_s(w, x).$$

(87)

Or:

$$f(w)R(w, H(w))g_R(x, w) = f(x)R(x, H(x))g_s(w, x).$$

(88)

Now we have that:

$$\int f(w)R(w, H(w))\varepsilon_R(w)dw = \iint f(w)R(w, H(w))g_R(x, w)\varepsilon_\phi\left(\frac{w}{x}\right)dxdw$$

$$= \iint f(x)R(x, H(x))g_s(w, x)\varepsilon_\phi\left(\frac{w}{x}\right)dxdw$$

$$= \int f(x)R(x, H(x))\varepsilon_s(x)dx.$$

(89)

So the recruit-weighted quit and recruitment elasticities must be equal.

REFERENCES

Abowd, John M., Kramarz, Francis, 2003. The costs of hiring and separations. Labour Economics 10, 499–530.

Abowd, John M., Lemieux, Thomas, 1993. The effects of product market competition on collective bargaining agreements: the case of foreign competition in Canada. Quarterly Journal of Economics 108, 983–1014.

Acemoglu, Daron, 1998. Training and innovation in an imperfect labour market. Review of Economic Studies 64, 445–464.

Acemoglu, Daron, Pischke, Jörn-Steffen, 1998. Why do firms train? Theory and evidence. Quarterly Journal of Economics 113 (1), 79–119.

Acemoglu, Daron., Pischke, Jörn-Steffen, 1999a. Beyond Becker: training in imperfect labour markets. Economic Journal 109 (453), 112–142.

Acemoglu, Daron, Pischke, Jörn-Steffen, 1999b. The structure of wages and investment in general training. Journal of Political Economy 107 (3), 539–572.

Albrecht, James, Gautier, Pieter A., Vroman, Susan, 2006. Equilibrium directed search with multiple applications. Review of Economic Studies 73, 869–891.

Angrist, Joshua D., Pischke, Jörn-Steffen, 2008. Mostly harmless econometrics: an empiricist's companion. Princeton University Press, Princeton.

Arai, Mahmood, 2003. Wages, profits, and capital intensity: evidence from matched worker-firm data. Journal of Labor Economics 21, 593–618.

Autor, David, 2001. Wiring the labor market. Journal of Economic Perspectives 15, 25–40.

Babcock, Linda, Laschever, Sara, 2003. Women Don't Ask: Negotiation and the Gender Divide. Princeton University Press, Princeton.

Barron, John M., Berger, Mark C., Black, Dan A., 1997. On the Job Training. Upjohn Institute, Kalamazoo, Michigan.

Barron, John M., Mellow, Wesley, 1979. Search effort in the labor market. Journal of Human Resources 14, 390–404.

Barth, Erling, Dale-Olsen, Harald, 2009. Monopsonistic discrimination, worker turnover and the gender wage gap. Labour Economics 16, 589–597.

Beaudry, Paul, Green, David, Sand, Benjamin, 2007. Spill-overs from good jobs. NBER Working Paper No. 13006.

Becker, Gary S., 1993. Human Capital: A Theoretical and Empirical Analysis, with Special Reference to Education, third ed., University of Chicago Press, Chicago.

Benson, Alan, 2009. Firm-sponsored general education and mobility frictions: evidence from hospital sponsorship of nursing schools and faculty. MIT Sloan School.

Bertrand, Marianne, 2004. From the invisible handshake to the invisible hand? How import competition changes the employment relationship. Journal of Labor Economics 22, 723–765.

Bertrand, Marianne, Goldin, Claudia, Katz, Lawrence F., 2009. Dynamics of the gender gap for young professionals in the financial and corporate sectors, Aug. 2009.

Bewley, Truman F., 1999. Why Wages Don't Fall During a Recession. Harvard University Press, Cambridge, Mass.

Bhaskar, V., To, Ted, 1999. Minimum wages for Ronald McDonald monopsonies: a theory of monopsonistic competition. Economic Journal 109 (455), 190–203.

Black, Sandra E., Strahan, Philip E., 2001. The division of spoils: rent-sharing and discrimination in a regulated industry. American Economic Review 91, 814–831.

Blanchflower, David G., Oswald, Andrew J., Garrett, Mario D., 1990. Insider power in wage determination. Economica 57, 143–170.

Blanchflower, David G., Oswald, Andrew J., Sanfey, Peter, 1996. Wages, profits, and rent-sharing. Quarterly Journal of Economics 111, 227–251.

Blatter, Marc, Muhlemann, Samuel, Schenker, Samuel, 2009. The costs of hiring skilled workers. University of Zurich.

Blau, Francine D., Kahn, Larry M., 1981. Race and sex differences in quits by young workers. Industrial and Labor Relations Review 34, 563–577.

Boal, William, M., Ransom, Michael R., 1997. Monopsony in the labor market. Journal of Economic Literature 35 (1), 86–112.

Booth, Alison L., 1995. The Economics of the Trade Union. Cambridge University Press, Cambridge, England.

Booth, Alison, Arulampalam, Wiji, Bryan, Mark, 2004. Training and the new minimum wage. Economic Journal 114, 87–94.

Booth, Alison, Katic, Pamela, 2009. Estimating the wage elasticity of labour supply to a firm: is there monopsony down-under? Unpublished, Australian National University.

Brenner, Mark D., 2005. The economic impact of the Boston living wage ordinance. Industrial Relations 44, 59–83.

Brown, Charles, 1999. Minimum wages, employment, and the distribution of income. In: Orley, Ashenfelter, Card, David (Eds.), Handbook of Labor Economics, vol. 3. North-Holland, Amsterdam, pp. 2101–2163.

Brown, Charles, Medoff, James, 1989. The employer size-wage effect. Journal of Political Economy 97 (5), 1027–1059.

Brown, Charles, Hamilton, James, Medoff, James, 1990. Employers Large and Small. Harvard University Press, Cambridge, Mass.

Brown, J. David, Hotchkiss, Julie L., Quispe-Agnoli, Myriam, 2008. Undocumented worker employment and firm survivability. Federal Reserve Bank of Atlanta Working Paper 2008-28 (December 2008).

Brown, Donna, Dickens, Richard, Stephen Machin, PaulGregg, Manning, Alan, 2001. Everything Under a Fiver: Recruitment and Retention in Lower Paying Labor Markets. Joseph Rowntree Foundation, London.

Bulow, Jeremy, Levin, Jonathan, 2006. Matching and price competition. American Economic Review 652–668.

Burdett, Kenneth, Mortensen, Dale T., 1998. Wage differentials, employer size, and unemployment. International Economic Review 39 (2), 257–273.

Cahuc, Pierre, Postel-Vinay, Fabien, Robin, Jean-Marc, 2006. Wage bargaining with on-the-job search: theory and evidence. Econometrica 74, 323–364.

Campbell, C., 1993. Do firms pay efficiency wages? Evidence with data at the firm level. Journal of Labor Economics 11, 442–470.

Card, David, Chetty, Raj, Weber, Andrea, 2007. Cash-on-hand and competing models of intertemporal behavior: new evidence from the labor market. Quarterly Journal of Economics 122, 1511–1560.

Card, David E., Devcienti, Francesco, Maida, Agata, 2010. Rent-sharing, holdup, and wages: evidence from matched panel data. NBER Working Paper No. 16192.

Card, David E., Krueger, Alan B., 1995. Myth and Measurement: The New Economics of the Minimum Wage. Princeton University Press, Princeton.

Christofides, Louis N., Oswald, Andrew J., 1992. Real wage determination and rent-sharing in collective bargaining agreements. Quarterly Journal of Economics 107, 985–1002.

Clark, Andrew, Oswald, Andrew, 1994. Unhappiness and unemployment. Economic Journal 104, 648–659.

Clotfelter, Charles, Glennie, Elizabeth, Ladd, Helen, Vigdor, Jacob, 2008. Would higher salaries keep teachers in high-poverty schools? Journal of Public Economics 92, 1352–1370.

Coles, Melvyn G., Smith, Eric, 1998. Marketplaces and matching. International Economic Review 39 (1), 239–254.

Currie, Janet, McConnell, S., 1992. Firm-specific determinants of the real wage. Review of Economics and Statistics 74, 297–304.

DellaVigna, Stefano, Daniele Paserman, M., 2005. Job search and impatience. Journal of Labor Economics 23, 527–588.

Dube, Arindrajit, Freeman, Eric, Reich, Michael, 2010. Employee replacement costs. University of California, Berkeley.

Dube, Arindrajit, Lester, T. William, Reich, Michael, 2010. Minimum wage effects across state borders: estimates using contiguous counties. Review of Economics and Statistics (forthcoming).

Dube, Arindrajit, Naidu, T. Suresh, Reich, Michael, 2007. The economic effects of a citywide minimum wage. Industrial and Labor Relations Review 60, 522–543.

Ebrahimy, Ehsan, Shimer, Robert, 2010. Stock-flow matching. Journal of Economic Theory 145, 1325–1353.

Eckstein, Zvi, van den Berg, Gerard, 2006. Empirical labor search: a survey. Journal of Econometrics 136, 531–564.

Edgeworth, Francis Ysidro, 1932. Mathematical Psychics: An Essay on the Application of Mathematics to the Moral Sciences. London School of Economics and Political Science, London.

Ellingsen, Tore, Rosen, Asa, 2003. Fixed or flexible? Wage setting in search equilibrium. Economica 70, 233–250.

Elsby, Michael, Michaels, Ryan, 2008. Marginal jobs, heterogeneous firms, & unemployment flows. NBER Working Paper No. 13777.

Erens, Bob, Hedges, Barry, 1990. Survey of Incomes in and Out of Work. Social and Community Planning Research, London.

Falch, Torberg, 2010a. Estimating the elasticity of labor supply utilizing a quasi-natural experiment. Journal of Labor Economics 28, 237–266.

Falch, Torberg, 2010b. Teacher mobility responses to wage changes: evidence from a quasi-natural experiment, unpublished.

Farber, Hank, 2011. Unions and their effects: a comparative perspective. In: Orley, Ashenfelter, Card, David (Eds.), Handbook of Labor Economics, vol. 5. North-Holland, Amsterdam.

Fox, Jeremy, 2010. Estimating the employer switching costs and wage responses of forward-looking engineers. Journal of Labor Economics 28, 357–412.

Galenianos, Manolis, Kircher, Philipp, 2009. Directed search with multiple job applications. Journal of Economic Theory 114, 445–471.

Giuliano, Laura, 2009. Minimum wage effects on employment, substitution, and the teenage labor supply: evidence from personnel data.

Griffeth, Rodger W., Peter W, Hom, Stefan, Gaertner, 2000. A meta-analysis of antecedents and correlates of employee turnover. Journal of Management 26, 463–488.

Guiso, Luigi, Pistaferri, Luigi, Schivardi, Fabiano, 2005. Insurance within the firm. Journal of Political Economy 113, 1054–1087.

Hagedorn, Marcus, Manovskii, Iourii, 2008. The cyclical behavior of equilibrium unemployment and vacancies revisited. American Economic Review 98, 1692–1706.

Hall, Robert E., Krueger, Alan B., 2008. Wage formation between newly hired workers and employers: survey evidence. NBER WP 14329.

Hall, Robert E., Lazear, Edward P., 1984. The excess sensitivity of layoffs and quits to demand. Journal of Labor Economics 2 (2), 233–257.

Hamermesh, Daniel.S., 1993. Labor Demand. Princeton University Press, Princeton.

Hildreth, Andrew K.G., Oswald, Andrew J., 1997. Rent-sharing and wages: evidence from company and establishment panels. Journal of Labor Economics 15, 318–337.

Hirsch, Barry T., Schumacher, Edward J., 1995. Monopsony power and relative wages in the labor market for nurses. Journal of Health Economics 14, 443–476.

Hirsch, Barry T., Schumacher, Edward J., 2005. Classic or new monopsony? Searching for evidence in nursing labor markets. Journal of Health Economics 24, 969–989.

Hirsch, Boris, Schrank, Tomas, Schnabel, Claus, 2010. Differences in labor supply to monopsonistic firms and the gender pay gap: an empirical analysis using linked employer-employee data from germany. Journal of Labor Economics 28, 291–330.

Holzer, Harry J., 1987. Job search by employed and unemployed youth. Industrial and Labor Relations Review 40, 601–611.

Holzer, Harry J., 1988. Search method use by unemployed youth. Journal of Labor Economics 6, 1–20.

Hornstein, Andreas, Krusell, Per, Violante, Giovanni L., 2006. Frictional wage dispersion in search models: a quantitative approach. CEPR Discussion Papers 5935.

Howes, Candace, 2005. Living wages and retention of homecare workers in San Francisco. Industrial Relations 44, 139–163.

Hotchkiss, Julie L., Quispe-Agnoli, Myriam, 2009. Employer monopsony power in the labor market for undocumented workers. Federal Reserve Bank of Atlanta Working Paper 2009-14a (revised June 2009).

Hwang, Hae-shin, Mortensen, Dale T., Reed, Walter R., 1998. Hedonic wages and labor market search. Journal of Labor Economics 16 (4), 815–847.

Jacobson, Louis S., LaLonde, Robert J., Sullivan, Daniel S., 1993. Earnings losses of displaced workers. American Economic Review 83 (4), 685–709.

Kircher, Philipp, 2009. Efficiency of simultaneous search. Journal of Political Economy 117, 861–913.

Kleiner, Morris, Won Park, Kyoung, 2010. Battles among licensed occupations: analysing government regulations on labor market outcomes for dentists and hygienists, University of Minnesota.

Klepinger, Daniel H., Johnson, Terry R., Joesch, Jutta M., 2002. Effects of unemployment insurance work-search requirements: the Maryland experiment. Industrial and Labor Relations Review 56, 3–22.

Kramarz, Francis, Michaud, Marie-Laure, 2010. The shape of hiring and separation costs in France. Labour Economics 17, 27–37.

Krueger, Alan B., Mueller, Andreas, 2010. Job search and unemployment insurance: new evidence from time use data. Journal of Public Economics 94, 298–307.

Krugman, Paul A, 1991. Geography and Trade. MIT Press, Cambridge, Mass.

Kuhn, Peter, Skutterud, Mikal, 2004. Internet job search and unemployment durations. American Economic Review 94, 218–232.

Lancaster, Tony, Chesher, Andrew, 1983. An econometric analysis of reservation wages. Econometrica 51, 1661–1676.

Lakhani, Hyder, 1988. The effect of pay and retention bonuses on quit rates in the US army. Industrial and Labor Relations Review 41, 430–438.

Lazear, Edward P., 2003. Firm-specific human capital: a skill-weights approach. NBER Working Paper No. W9679.

Lazear, Edward P., Shaw, Kathryn L. (Eds.), 2009. The Structure of Wages: An International Comparison. University of Chicago Press, Chicago.

Lester, Richard A., 1946. Wage diversity and its theoretical implications. The Review of Economic Statistics 28 (3), 152–159.

Lewis, Michael, 1989. Liar's Poker. Coronet Books, London.

McDonald, Ian M, Solow, Robert M., 1981. Wage bargaining and employment. American Economic Review 71, 896–908.

Machin, Stephen J., Manning, Alan, 2004. A test of competitive labor market theory: the wage structure among care assistants in the south of England. Industrial and Labor Relations Review 57, 371–385.

Manning, Alan, 1996. The equal pay act as an experiment to test theories of the labour market. Economica 63 (250), 191–212.

Manning, Alan, 2003a. Monopsony in motion: imperfect competition in labor markets. Princeton University Press, Princeton.

Manning, Alan, 2003b. The real thin theory: monopsony in modern labour markets. Labour Economics 10, 105–131.

Manning, Alan, 2006. A generalised model of monopsony. Economic Journal 116, 84–100.

Manning, Alan, 2009. A little collusion can go a long way.

Manning, Alan, 2010. The plant size-place effect: monopsony and agglomeration. Journal of Economic Geography (forthcoming).

Marshall, Alfred, 1920. Principles of Economics: an Introductory Volume, eighth ed., Macmillan, London.

Martin, Christopher, 2003. Explaining labour turnover: empirical evidence from UK establishments. Labour 17, 391–412.

Mas, Alex, 2006. Pay, reference points, and police performance. Quarterly Journal of Economics 121, 783–821.

Matsudaira, Jordan, 2009. Monopsony in the labor market for nurses: evidence from minimum staffing legislation in California, Cornell University.

Meitzen, Mark E., 1986. Differences in male and female job-quitting behavior. Journal of Labor Economics 4, 151–167.

Moen, Espen R., 1997. Competitive search equilibrium. Journal of Political Economy 105 (2), 385–411.

Moscarini, Giuseppe, Postel-Vinay, Fabien, 2008. The timing of labor market expansions: new facts and a new hypothesis. NBER Macroeconomics Annual.

Mortensen, Dale T., 1986. Job search and labor market analysis. In: Orley, Ashenfelter, Layard, Richard (Eds.), Handbook of Labor Economics, vol. 2. North-Holland, Amsterdam, pp. 849–919.

Mortensen, D.T., 2003. Wage Dispersion: Why Are Similar Workers Paid Differently? MIT Press, Cambridge Mass.

Mortensen, Dale T., Pissarides, Christopher A., 1994. Job creation and job destruction in the theory of unemployment. Review of Economic Studies 61 (3), 397–415.

Mortensen, Dale T., Pissarides, Christopher A., 1999. New developments in models of search in the labor market. In: Orley, Ashenfelter, Card, David (Eds.), Handbook of Labor Economics, vol. 3B. North-Holland, Amsterdam, pp. 2567–2627.

Nagypal, Eva, 2005. On the extent of job-to-job transitions.

Naidu, Suresh, 2010. Recruitment restrictions and labor markets: evidence from the post-Bellum US South. Journal of Labor Economics 28, 413–445.

Niederle, Muriel, 2007. Competitive wages in a match with ordered contracts. American Economic Review 97, 1957–1969.

Neal, Derek A., 1995. Industry-specific human capital: evidence from displaced workers. Journal of Labor Economics 13 (4), 653–677.

Nickell, Stephen J., 1986. Dynamic models of labor demand. In: Ashenfelter, O., Layard, R. (Eds.), Handbook of Labor Economics.

Nickell, Stephen J, Wadhwani, Sushil, 1990. Insider forces and wage determination. Economic Journal 100, 496–509.

Oi, Walter, 1962. Labor as a quasi-fixed factor. Journal of Political Economy 70, 538–555.

Oi, Walter Y., Idson, Todd L., 1999. Firm size and wages. In: Orley, Ashenfelter, Card, David (Eds.), Handbook of Labor Economics, vol. 3B. North-Holland, Amsterdam, pp. 2165–2214.

Overman, Henry G., Puga, Diego, 2009. Labor pooling as a source of agglomeration: an empirical investigation, LSE.

Oyer, Paul, Schaefer, Scott, 2011. Personnel economics: hiring and incentives. In: Ashenfelter, O., Card, D. (Eds.), Handbook of Labor Economics, vol. 4b. pp. 1769–1823.

Parsons, Donald O., 1972. Specific human capital: an application to quit rates and layoff rates. Journal of Political Economy 80 (6), 1120–1143.

Parsons, Donald O., 1973. Quit rates over time: a search and information approach. American Economic Review 63, 390–401.

Pencavel, John H., 1970. An Analysis of the Quit Rate in American Manufacturing Industry. Princeton: Industrial Relations Section. Princeton University.

Pissarides, Christopher A., 1985. Short-run equilibrium dynamics of unemployment vacancies, and real wages. American Economic Review 75 (4), 676–690.

Pissarides, Christopher A., 1994. Search unemployment with on-the-job search. Review of Economic Studies 61, 457–475.

Pissarides, Christopher A., 2000. Equilibrium Unemployment Theory. MIT Press, Cambridge, Mass.

Pissarides, Christopher A., 2009. The unemployment volatility puzzle: is wage stickiness the answer? Econometrica 77, 1339–1369.

Poletaev, Maxim, Robinson, Chris, 2008. Human capital specificity: evidence from the dictionary of occupational titles and displaced worker surveys. 1984-2000. Journal of Labor Economics 26, 387–420.

Postel-Vinay, Fabien, Robin, Jean-Marc, 2002. Wage dispersion with worker and employer heterogeneity. Econometrica 70, 2295–2350.

Priest, George, 2010. Timing "disturbances" in labor market contracting: Professor Roth and the effects of labor market monopsony. Journal of Labor Economics 28, 447–472.

Ransom, Michael, Oaxaca, Ronald, 2010. Sex differences in pay in a "new monopsony" model of the labor market. Journal of Labor Economics 28, 267–289.

Ransom, Michael, Sims, David, 2010. Estimating the firm's labor supply curve in a "new monopsony" framework: school teachers in Missouri. Journal of Labor Economics 28, 331–355.

Reich, Michael, Hall, Peter, Jacobs, Ken, 2005. Living wage policies at the San Francisco airport: impacts on workers and businesses. Industrial Relations 44, 106–138.

Reynolds, Lloyd G., 1946. Wage differences in local labor markets. American Economic Review 36 (3), 366–375.

Reynolds, Lloyd G., 1951. The Structure of Labor Markets: Wages and Labor Mobility in Theory and Practice. Harper and Brothers, New York.

Ridder, Geert, van den Berg, Gerard, 2003. Measuring labor market frictions: a cross-country comparison. Journal of the European Economic Association 1, 224–244.

Robinson, Joan, 1933. The Economics of Imperfect Competititon. Macmillan, London.

Rogerson, Richard, Shimer, Robert, 2011. Search in macroeconomic models of the labor market. In: Ashenfelter, O., Card, D. (Eds.), Handbook of Labor Economics, vol. 4a. pp. 619–700.

Rogerson, Richard, Shimer, Robert, Wright, Randall, 2005. Search-theoretic models of the labor market: a survey. Journal of Economic Literature 43, 959–988.

Rose, Nancy L, 1987. Labor rent sharing and regulation: evidence from the trucking industry. Journal of Political Economy 95, 1146–1178.

Royalty, Anne Beeson, 1998. Job-to-job and job-to-nonemployment turnover by gender and education level. Journal of Labor Economics 16 (2), 392–443.

Schmeider, Johannes F., 2009. Labor costs and the evolution of new establishments, unpublished.

Shimer, Robert, 2006. On-the-job search and strategic bargaining. European Economic Review 50, 811–830.

Silva, Jose, Toldeo, Manuel, 2009. Labor turnover costs and the cyclical behavior of vacancies and unemployment. Macroeconomic Dynamics 13, 76–96.

Slichter, Sumner H., 1950. Notes on the structure of wages. Review of Economic Statistics 32 (1), 80–91.

Smith, Adam, 1970. The Wealth of Nations. Harmondsworth, Penguin, London.

Smith, Alison, Youngs, Rachel, Ashworth, Karl, McKay, Stephen, Walker, Robert, Elias, Peter, McKnight, Abigail, 2000. Understanding the impact of Jobseeker's Allowance, Department of Social Security, Research Report No. 111.

Staiger, Douglas, Spetz, Joanne, Phibbs, Ciaran, 2010. Is there monpsony in the labor market? Evidence from a natural experiment. Journal of Labor Economics 28, 211–236.

Stigler, George J., 1961. The economics of information. The Journal of Political Economy 69 (3), 213–225.

Stigler, George J., 1962. Information in the labor market. The Journal of Political Economy 70 (5), 94–105.

Sullivan, Daniel, 1989. Monopsony power in the market for nurses. Journal of Law and Economics 32 (2), S135-78.

Teulings, Coen, Hartog, Joop, 1998. Corporatism or Competition? Labour Contracts, Institutions and Wage Structures in International Comparison. Cambridge University Press, Cambridge.

Van Ommeren, Jos, van den Berg, Gerard, Gorter, Cees, 2000. Estimating the marginal willingness to pay for commuting. Journal of Regional Science 40, 541–563.

Van Reenen, John, 1996. The creation and capture of rents: wages and innovation in a panel of UK companies. Quarterly journal of economics 96, 195–226.

Von Wachter, Till, Bender, Stefan, 2006. In the right place at the wrong time: the role of firms and luck in young workers' careers. American Economic Review 96, 1679–1705.

Von Wachter, Till, Bender, Stefan, Schmeider, Johannes, 2009. The long-term impact of job displacement in Germany during the 1982 recession on earnings, income, and employment Columbia University, Department of Economics Discussion Paper Series DP0910-07.

Von Wachter, Till, Manchester, Joyce, Song, Jae, 2009. Long-term earnings losses due to mass-layoffs during the 1982 recession: an analysis using longitudinal administrative Data from 1974 to 2004.

Viscusi, W. Kip, 1980. Sex differences in worker quitting. Review of Economics and Statistics 62 (3), 388–398.

Wickens, M.R., 1978. An econometric model of labour turnover in UK manufacturing industries, 1956-73. Review of Economic Studies 45, 469–477.

CHAPTER *12*

Skills, Tasks and Technologies: Implications for Employment and Earnings[☆]

Daron Acemoglu[*], David Autor[**]

[*] MIT, NBER and CIFAR
[**] MIT, NBER and IZA

Contents

[☆] We thank Amir Kermani for outstanding research assistance and Melanie Wasserman for persistent, meticulous and ingenious work on all aspects of the chapter. We are indebted to Arnaud Costinot for insightful comments and suggestions. Autor acknowledges support from the National Science Foundation (CAREER award SES-0239538).

Abstract

A central organizing framework of the voluminous recent literature studying changes in the returns to skills and the evolution of earnings inequality is what we refer to as the *canonical model*, which elegantly and powerfully operationalizes the supply and demand for skills by assuming two distinct skill groups that perform two different and imperfectly substitutable tasks or produce two imperfectly substitutable goods. Technology is assumed to take a *factor-augmenting* form, which, by complementing either high or low skill workers, can generate skill biased demand shifts. In this paper, we argue that despite its notable successes, the canonical model is largely silent on a number of central empirical developments of the last three decades, including: (1) significant declines in real wages of low skill workers, particularly low skill males; (2) non-monotone changes in wages at different parts of the earnings distribution during different decades; (3) broad-based increases in employment in high skill and low skill occupations relative to middle skilled occupations (i.e., job "polarization"); (4) rapid diffusion of new technologies that directly substitute capital for labor in tasks previously performed by moderately skilled workers; and (5) expanding offshoring in opportunities, enabled by technology, which allow foreign labor to substitute for domestic workers specific tasks. Motivated by these patterns, we argue that it is valuable to consider a richer framework for analyzing how recent changes in the earnings and employment distribution in the United States and other advanced economies are shaped by the interactions among worker skills, job tasks, evolving technologies, and shifting trading opportunities. We propose a tractable task-based model in which the assignment of skills to tasks is endogenous and technical change may involve the substitution of machines for certain tasks previously performed by labor. We further consider how the evolution of technology in this task-based setting may be endogenized. We show how such a framework can be used to interpret several central recent trends, and we also suggest further directions for empirical exploration.

JEL classification: J20; J23; J24; J30; J31; O31; O33

Keywords: College premium; Directed technical change; Earnings inequality; Occupations; Returns to schooling; Skill biased technical change; Skill premium; Tasks; Wage inequality

1. INTRODUCTION

The changes in the distribution of earnings and the returns to college over the last several decades in the US labor market have motivated a large literature investigating the relationship between technical change and wages. The starting point of this literature is the observation that the return to skills, for example as measured by the relative wages of college graduate workers to high school graduates, has shown a tendency to increase over multiple decades despite the large secular increase in the relative supply of college educated workers. This suggests that concurrent with the increase in the supply of skills, there has been an increase in the (relative) demand for skills. Following Tinbergen's pioneering (1974; 1975) work, the relative demand for skills is then linked to technology, and in particular to the *skill bias* of technical change. This perspective emphasizes that the return to skills (and to college) is determined by a race between the increase in the supply of skills in the labor market and technical change, which is assumed to be skill biased, in the sense that improvements in technology naturally increase the demand for more "skilled" workers, among them, college graduates (relative to non-college workers).

These ideas are elegantly and powerfully operationalized by what we refer to as the *canonical model*, which includes two skill groups performing two distinct and imperfectly substitutable occupations (or producing two imperfectly substitutable goods).[1] Technology is assumed to take a *factor-augmenting* form, and thus complements either high or low skill workers. Changes in this factor-augmenting technology then capture skill biased technical change.[2] The canonical model is not only tractable and conceptually attractive, but it has also proved to be empirically quite successful. Katz and Murphy (1992), Autor et al. (1998, 2008), and Carneiro and Lee (2009), among others, show that it successfully accounts for several salient changes in the distribution of earnings in the United States. Katz et al. (1995), Davis (1992), Murphy et al. (1998), Card and Lemieux (2001a), Fitzenberger and Kohn (2006) and Atkinson (2008) among others, show that the model also does a good job of capturing major cross-country differences among advanced nations. Goldin and Katz (2008) show that the model, with some minor modifications, provides a good account of the changes in the returns to schooling and the demand for skills throughout the entire twentieth century in the United States.

In this paper, we argue that despite the canonical model's conceptual virtues and substantial empirical applicability, a satisfactory analysis of modern labor markets and recent empirical trends necessitates a richer framework. We emphasize two shortcomings of the canonical model. First, the canonical model is made tractable in part because it does not include a meaningful role for "tasks," or equivalently, it imposes a one-to-one mapping between skills and tasks. A *task* is a unit of work activity that produces output (goods and services). In contrast, a skill is a worker's endowment of capabilities for performing various tasks. Workers apply their skill endowments to tasks in exchange for wages, and skills applied to tasks produce output. The distinction between skills and tasks becomes particularly relevant when workers of a given skill level can perform a variety of tasks and change the set of tasks that they perform in response to changes in labor market conditions and technology. We argue that a systematic understanding of recent labor market trends, and more generally of the impact of technology on employment and earnings, requires a framework that factors in such changes in the allocation of skills to tasks. In particular, we suggest, following Autor et al. (2003), that recent technological developments have enabled information and communication technologies to either directly perform or permit the offshoring of a subset of the core job tasks previously performed by middle skill workers, thus causing a substantial change in the returns to certain types of skills and a measurable shift in the assignment of skills to tasks.

---

[1] In many cases, this model is extended to more than two skill groups (see., e.g., Card and Lemieux, 2001a,b; Acemoglu et al., 2001). Atkinson (2008) refers to the Tinbergen education-race model as the Textbook Model.

[2] In addition to Tinbergen (1974, 1975), see Welch (1973), Freeman (1976), Katz and Murphy (1992) and Autor et al. (1998, 2008) on the canonical model. Acemoglu (2002a) develops several implications of the canonical model and relates these to other approaches to the relationship between technology and skill premia.

Second, the canonical model treats technology as exogenous and typically assumes that technical change is, by its *nature*, skill biased. The evidence, however, suggests that the extent of skill bias of technical change has varied over time and across countries. Autor et al. (1998), for example, suggest that there was an acceleration in skill bias in the 1980s and 1990s.[3] Goldin and Katz (2008) present evidence that manufacturing technologies were skill complementary in the early twentieth century, but may have been skill substituting prior to that time. The available evidence suggests that in the nineteenth century, technical change often replaced—rather than complemented—skilled artisans. The artisan shop was replaced by the factory and later by interchangeable parts and the assembly line, and products previously manufactured by skilled artisans started to be produced in factories by workers with relatively few skills (e.g., Hounshell, 1985; James and Skinner, 1985; Mokyr, 1992; Goldin and Katz, 2008). Acemoglu (1998, 2002a) suggested that the endogenous response of technology to labor market conditions may account for several such patterns and significantly enriches the canonical model.

To build the case for a richer model of skill demands and wage determination, we first provide an overview of key labor market developments in the United States over the last five decades, and in less detail, across European Union economies. This overview enables us to highlight both why the canonical model provides an excellent starting point for any analysis of the returns to skills, and also why it falls short of providing an entirely satisfactory framework for understanding several noteworthy patterns. In particular, in addition to the well-known evolution of the college premium and the overall earnings inequality in the United States, we show that (1) low skill (particularly low skill male) workers have experienced significant real earnings declines over the last four decades; (2) there have been notably non-monotone changes in earnings levels across the earnings distribution over the last two decades (sometimes referred to as wage "polarization"), even as the overall "return to skill" as measured by the college/high school earnings gap has monotonically increased; (3) these changes in wage levels and the distribution of wages have been accompanied by systematic, non-monotone shifts in the composition of employment across occupations, with rapid simultaneous growth of both high education, high wage occupations and low education, low wage occupations in the United States and the European Union; (4) this "polarization" of employment does not merely reflect a change in the composition of skills available in the labor market but also a change in the allocation of skill groups across occupations—and, in fact, the explanatory power of occupation in accounting for wage differences across workers has significantly increased over time; (5) recent technological developments and recent trends in offshoring and outsourcing appear to have directly replaced workers in certain occupations and tasks. We next provide a brief overview of the canonical model, demonstrate its empirical success in accounting for several major features of the evolving wage distribution, and highlight the key labor market developments about which the canonical model is either silent or at odds with the data.

---

[3] Later analyses have not confirmed this conclusion, however. See Goldin and Katz (2008).

Having argued that the canonical model is insufficiently nuanced to account for the rich relationships among skills, tasks and technologies that are the focus of this chapter, we then propose a task-based framework for analyzing the allocation of skills to tasks and for studying the effect of new technologies on the labor market and their impact on the distribution of earnings. We further show how technology can be endogenized in this framework.[4]

The framework we propose consists of a continuum of tasks, which together produce a unique final good. We assume that there are three types of skills—low, medium and high—and each worker is endowed with one of these types of skills.[5] Workers have different comparative advantages, a feature that makes our model similar to Ricardian trade models. Given the prices of (the services of) different tasks and the wages for different types of skills in the market, firms (equivalently, workers) choose the optimal allocation of skills to tasks. Technical change in this framework can change both the productivity of different types of workers in all tasks (in a manner parallel to factor-augmenting technical change in the canonical model) and also in specific tasks (thus changing their comparative advantage). Importantly, the model allows for new technologies that may directly replace workers in certain tasks. More generally, it treats skills (embodied in labor), technologies (embodied in capital), and trade or offshoring as offering competing inputs for accomplishing various tasks. Thus, which input (labor, capital, or foreign inputs supplied via trade) is applied in equilibrium to accomplish which tasks depends in a rich but intuitive manner on cost and comparative advantage.

We show that even though this framework allows for an endogenous allocation of skills to tasks and a richer interaction between technology and wages than the canonical model, it is tractable. Relative wages of high to medium and medium to low skill workers are determined by relative supplies and task allocations. The canonical model is in fact a special case of this more general task-based model, and hence the model generates similar responses to changes in relative supplies and factor-augmenting technical change. Nevertheless, there are also richer implications because of the endogenously changing allocation of skills to tasks. Notably, while factor-augmenting technical progress always increases all wages in the canonical model, it can reduce the wages of certain groups in this more general model. Moreover, other forms of technical change, in particular the introduction of new technologies replacing workers in certain tasks, have richer but still intuitive effects on the earnings distribution and employment patterns.

---

[4] Autor et al. (2003), Goos et al. (2009) and Autor and Dorn (2010) provide related task-based models. The model we propose builds most directly on Acemoglu and Zilibotti (2001) and is also closely related to Costinot and Vogel (forthcoming), who provide a more general approach to the assignment of skills tasks and derive the implications of their approach for the effect of technical change on wage inequality. Similar models have also been developed and used in the trade literature, particularly in the context of outsourcing and offshoring. See, for example, Feenstra and Hanson (1999), Grossman and Rossi-Hansberg (2008), Rodriguez-Clare and Ramondo (2010), and Acemoglu et al. (2010).

[5] We also offer an extension to the model in which workers have multiple skills and choose the allocation of their skills across tasks given a fixed time budget.

We then show how this framework can be enriched by endogenizing the supply of skills and technology. We finally show how the mechanisms proposed by this framework suggest new ways of analyzing the data and provide some preliminary empirical evidence motivated by this approach.

The rest of the paper is organized as follows. The next section, Section 2, provides an overview of labor market trends, with an emphasis on changes in the earnings distribution, in the real wages of different demographic groups, in the distribution of employment by occupation, and in the allocation of skill groups to job tasks. Section 3 provides a brief recap of the canonical model, which has become the natural starting point of most analyses of recent labor market trends, and explains why several of the patterns highlighted in Section 2 are challenging for the canonical model and suggest the need to move beyond this framework. Section 4 presents a tractable task-based model of the labor market, which we then use to reinterpret the patterns discussed in Section 2. Section 5 provides a first look at the evolution of real wages by demographic groups in the US labor market through the lens of the framework developed in Section 4. Section 6 concludes with a brief summary and with several areas for future research suggested by our paper. Two appendices contain additional details on the sources and the construction of the data used in the text and some further theoretical arguments.

2. AN OVERVIEW OF LABOR MARKET TRENDS

This section provides an overview of trends in education, wage levels, wage distribution, and occupational composition in the US labor market over the last five decades, and also offers some comparisons with labor market developments in European Union economies. Our objective is not to provide a comprehensive account of labor market developments but to highlight those that we view as most relevant for understanding the changing structure of the supply and demand for skills.[6] We focus on changes in earnings levels and earnings inequality not only because of the intrinsic importance of the topic but also because the evolution of the wage distribution provides information on how the market values of different types of skills have changed over time.

2.1. A brief overview of data sources

To summarize the basic changes in the US wage structure over the last five decades, we draw on four large and representative household data sources: the March Current Population Survey (March CPS), the combined Current Population Survey May and

---

[6] A more detailed account of several other trends related to labor market inequality and more extensive references to the literature are provided in Katz and Autor (1999). Goldin and Katz (2008) provide an authoritative account of the evolution of labor market inequality and the supply and demand for education in the United States from the dawn of the twentieth century to the mid 2000s. Card and DiNardo (2002) offer a skeptical perspective on the literature linking trends in wage inequality to the evolution of skill demands. See also the recent overview papers by Autor et al. (2008) and Lemieux (2008).

Outgoing Rotation Group samples (May/ORG CPS), the Census of Populations (Census), and the American Community Survey (ACS).[7] We describe these sources briefly here and provide additional details on the construction of samples in the Data Appendix. The March Annual Demographic Files of the Current Population Survey offer the longest high-frequency data series enumerating labor force participation and earnings in the US economy. These data provide reasonably comparable measures of the prior year's annual earnings, weeks worked, and hours worked per week for more than four decades. We use the March files from 1964 to 2009 (covering earnings from 1963 to 2008) to form a sample of real weekly earnings for workers aged 16 to 64 who participate in the labor force on a full-time, full-year (FTFY) basis, defined as working 35-plus hours per week and 40-plus weeks per year.

We complement the March FTFY series with data on hourly wages of all current labor force participants using May CPS samples for 1973 through 1978 and CPS Outgoing Rotation Group samples for 1979 through 2009 (CPS May/ORG). From these sources, we construct hourly wage data for all wage and salary workers employed during the CPS sample survey reference week. Unlike the retrospective annual earnings data in the March CPS, the May/ORG data provide point-in-time measures of usual hourly or weekly earnings. We use CPS sampling weights for all calculations.[8]

As detailed in Autor et al. (2005) and Lemieux (2006b), both the March and May/ORG CPS surveys have limitations that reduce their consistency over the fifty year period studied. The March CPS data are not ideal for analyzing the hourly wage distribution since they lack a point-in-time wage measure and thus hourly wages must be computed by dividing annual earnings by the product of weeks worked last year and usual weekly hours last year. Estimates of hours worked last year from the March CPS appear to be noisy, and moreover, data on usual weekly hours last year are not available prior to the 1976 March CPS. The May/ORG samples provide more accurate measures of the hourly wage distribution (particularly for hourly workers) but cover a shorter time period than the March CPS. Both the March and May/ORG CPS samples have undergone various changes in processing procedures over several decades that affect the top-coding of high earnings, the flagging of earning imputations, and the algorithms used for allocating earnings to individuals who do not answer earnings questions in the

---

[7] The ACS is the successor to the Census' long form questionnaire, which collected detailed demographic data from a subset of Census respondents. The long form was retired after the 2000 Census. The ACS is conducted annually and currently contains a 5 percent population sample. The ACS survey questions closely follow the Census long form.

[8] Beginning with DiNardo et al. (1996), many studies (e.g., Autor et al., 1998; Lemieux, 2006b; Autor et al., 2008) have further weighted samples by workers' hours and weeks worked when computing sample statistics. Statistics calculated using these weights therefore correspond to the average paid hour of work rather than the wage paid to the average worker. We break with this tradition here because we view the conceptual object of interest for this chapter to be the distribution of prices (or wages) that workers' skills command in the labor market rather than the interaction between these prices and workers' realized choice of hours. To the extent that we have experimented with the weighting scheme, we have found that the choice of weights—hours versus bodies—has only second-order effects on our substantive results. Thus, our use of the bodies rather than hours-weighting scheme is of notional but not substantive importance.

survey. These changes create challenges in producing consistent data series over time, and we have tried to account for them to the greatest extent possible.[9]

To analyze levels and changes in *occupational* structure within and across detailed demographic groups, we exploit the 1960, 1970, 1980, 1990 and 2000 Census of Populations and the 2008 American Community Survey (ACS). Because these data sources provide substantially larger samples than either the March or May/ORG surveys, they are better suited for a fine-grained analysis of changing occupational employment patterns within detailed demographic groups.[10] The earnings and employment questions in the Census and ACS files are similar to those in the March CPS and similarly offer retrospective measures of annual earnings and labor force participation that we use to calculate implied weekly or hourly earnings.

2.2. The college/high school wage premium

Motivated by the canonical relative supply-demand framework discussed in the Introduction and developed further in Section 3, a natural starting point for our discussion is to consider the evolution of the wage premium paid to "skills" in the labor market. A useful, though coarse, approximation is to consider a labor market consisting of two types of workers, "skilled" and "unskilled," and identify the first group with college graduates and the second with high school graduates. Under these assumptions, the *college premium*—that is, the relative wage of college versus high school educated workers—can be viewed as a summary measure of the market's valuation of skills.

Figure 1 plots the *composition-adjusted* log college/high school weekly wage premium in the US labor market for years 1963 through 2008 for full-time, full-year workers. This composition adjustment holds constant the relative employment shares of demographic group, as defined by gender, education, and potential experience, across all years of the sample. In particular, we first compute mean (predicted) log real weekly wages in each year for 40 sex-education-experience groups. Mean wages for broader groups shown in the figures are then calculated as fixed-weighted averages of the relevant sub-group means (using the average share of total hours worked for each group over 1963 to 2008 as weights). This adjustment ensures that the estimated college premium is not mechanically

---

[9] The major redesign of the earnings questions in the CPS ORG in 1994 led to a substantial rise in non-response to these questions as well as other potential consistency issues that are only imperfectly addressed by our processing of the data. For example, the earnings non-response rate in the CPS ORG increased from 15.3 percent in 1993 to 23.3 percent in the last quarter of 1995 (the first quarter in which allocation flags are available in the redesigned survey), and reached 31 percent by 2001 (Hirsch and Schumacher, 2004). The contemporaneous rise in the earnings imputation rate in the March survey was comparatively small. This redesign may be an important factor in accounting for the significant discrepancies in inequality trends in the May/ORG and March samples beginning in 1994 (see Lemieux, 2006b; Autor et al., 2008).

[10] The Census samples comprise 1 percent of the US population in 1960 and 1970, and 5 percent of the population in 1980, 1990, and 2000.

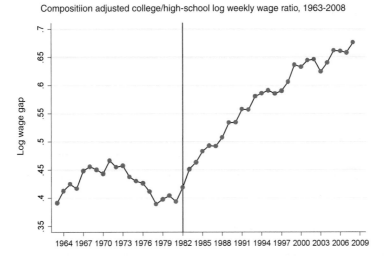

Compositiion adjusted college/high-school log weekly wage ratio, 1963-2008

Figure 1   *Source: March CPS data for earnings years 1963-2008. Log weekly wages for full-time, full-year workers are regressed separately by sex in each year on four education dummies (high school dropout, some college, college graduate, greater than college), a quartic in experience, interactions of the education dummies and experience quartic, two race categories (black, non-white other), and a full set of interactions between education, experience, and sex. The composition-adjusted mean log wage is the predicted log wage evaluated for whites at the relevant experience level (5, 15, 25, 35, 45 years) and relevant education level (high school dropout, high school graduate, some college, college graduate, greater than college). The mean log wage for college and high school is the weighted average of the relevant composition adjusted cells using a fixed set of weights equal to the average employment share of each sex by potential experience group. The ratio of mean log wages for college and high school graduates for each year is plotted. See the Data Appendix for more details on the treatment of March CPS data.*

affected by shifts in the experience, gender composition, or average level of completed schooling within the broader categories of college and high school graduates.[11]

Three features of Fig. 1 merit attention. First, following three decades of increase, the college premium stood at 68 points in 2008, a high water mark for the full sample period. A college premium of 68 log points implies that earnings of the average college graduate in 2008 exceeded those of the average high school graduate by 97 percent (i.e., $\exp(0.68) - 1 \simeq 0.974$). Taking a longer perspective, Goldin and Katz (2008) show that the college premium in 2005 was at its highest level since 1915, the earliest year for which representative data are available—and as Fig. 1 makes clear, the premium rose

---

[11] These 40 groups consist of five education categories (less than high school, high school graduate, some college, four-year college degree, post-college schooling), four potential experience levels (0 to 9 years, 10 to 19 years, 20 to 29 years, and 30 to 39 years), and two genders. Full-time, full-year workers are those who work at least 40 weeks per year and at least 35 hours per week. The construction of the relative wage series follows Katz and Murphy (1992), Katz and Autor (1999), and Autor et al. (2008). We follow closely the conventions set by these prior studies to facilitate comparisons. The Data Appendix provides further details.

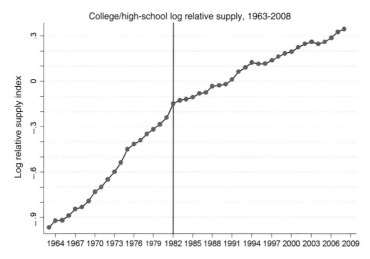

College/high-school log relative supply, 1963-2008

Figure 2   *Source: March CPS data for earnings years 1963-2008. Labor supply is calculated using all persons aged 16-64 who reported having worked at least one week in the earnings years, excluding those in the military. The data are sorted into sex-education-experience groups of two sexes (male/female), five education groups (high school dropout, high school graduate, some college, college graduate, and greater than college) and 49 experience groups (0-48 years of potential experience). The number of years of potential experience is calculated by subtracting the number six (the age at which one begins school) and the number of years of schooling from the age of the individual. This number is further adjusted using the assumption that an individual cannot begin work before age 16 and that experience is always non-negative. The labor supply for college/high school groups by experience level is calculated using efficiency units, equal to mean labor supply for broad college (including college graduates and greater than college) and high school (including high school dropouts and high school graduate) categories, weighted by fixed relative average wage weights for each cell. The labor supply of the "some college" category is allocated equally between the broad college and high school categories. The fixed set of wage weights for 1963-2008 are constructed using the average wage in each of the 490 cells (2 sexes, 5 education groups, 49 experience groups) over this time period.*

further thereafter. Second, the past three decades notwithstanding, the college premium has not always trended upward. Figure 1 shows a notable decline in the college premium between 1971 and 1978. Goldin and Margo (1992) and Goldin and Katz (2008) also document a substantial compression of the college premium during the decade of the 1940s. A third fact highlighted by the figure is that the college premium hit an inflection point at the end of the 1970s. This premium trended downward throughout the 1970s, before reversing course at the end of the decade. This reversal of the trend in the college premium is critical to our understanding of the operation of supply and demand in the determination of between-group wage inequality.

The college premium, as a summary measure of the market price of skills, is affected by, among other things, the relative supply of skills. Figure 2 depicts the evolution of the relative supply of college versus non-college educated workers. We use a standard measure of college/non-college relative supply calculated in "efficiency units" to adjust for changes in labor force composition.[12] From the end of World War II to the late 1970s, the relative supply of college workers rose robustly and steadily, with each cohort of workers entering the labor market boasting a proportionately higher rate of college education than the cohorts immediately preceding. Moreover, the increasing relative supply of college workers accelerated in the late 1960s and early 1970s. Reversing this acceleration, the rate of growth of college workers declined after 1982. The first panel of Fig. 3 shows that this slowdown is due to a sharp deceleration in the relative supply of young college graduate males—reflecting the decline in their rate of college completion—commencing in 1975, followed by a milder decline among women in the 1980s. The second panel of Fig. 3 confirms this observation by documenting that the relative supply of experienced college graduate males and females (i.e., those with 20 to 29 years of potential experience) does not show a similar decline until two decades later.

What accounts for the deceleration of college relative supply in the 1980s? As discussed by Card and Lemieux (2001b), four factors seem particularly relevant. First, the Vietnam War artificially boosted college attendance during the late 1960s and early 1970s because males could in many cases defer military service by enrolling in post-secondary schooling. This deferral motive likely contributed to the acceleration of the relative supply of skills during the 1960s seen in Fig. 2. When the Vietnam War ended in the early 1970s, college enrollment rates dropped sharply, particularly among males, leading to a decline in college completion rates half a decade later.

Second, the college premium declined sharply during the 1970s, as shown in Fig. 1. This downturn in relative college earnings likely discouraged high school graduates from enrolling in college. Indeed, Richard Freeman famously argued in his 1976 book, *The Overeducated American*, that the supply of college-educated workers in the United States had so far outstripped demand in the 1970s that the net social return to sending more high school graduates to college was negative.[13]

Third, the large baby boom cohorts that entered the labor market in the 1960s and 1970s were both more educated and more numerous than exiting cohorts, leading to a rapid increase in the average educational stock of the labor force. Cohorts born after 1964 were significantly smaller, and thus their impact on the overall educational stock of the labor force was also smaller. Had these cohorts continued the earlier trend in college-going behavior, their entry would still not have raised the college share of the workforce as rapidly as did earlier cohorts (see, e.g. Ellwood, 2002).

Finally, and most importantly, while the female college completion rate rebounded from its post-Vietnam era after 1980, the male college completion rate has never returned

---

[12] This series is also composition adjusted to correctly weight the changing gender and experience composition of college and non-college labor supply. Our construction of this figure follows Autor et al. (2008) Figure 4b, and adds three subsequent years of data. See the Data Appendix for details.

[13] One should not blame the entire rise in US earnings inequality on Richard Freeman, however. His book correctly predicted that the college glut was temporary, and that demand would subsequently surpass the growth of supply, leading to a rebound in the college premium.

College/high-school log relative supply, 1963-2008

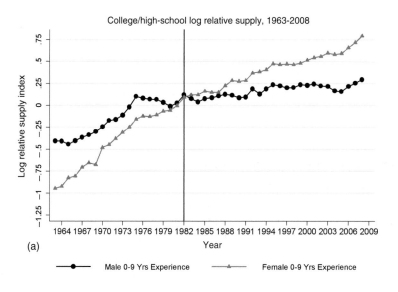

(a)

Male 0-9 Yrs Experience   Female 0-9 Yrs Experience

College/high-school log relative supply, 1963-2008

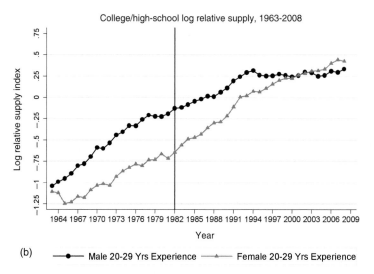

(b)   Male 20-29 Yrs Experience   Female 20-29 Yrs Experience

Figure 3 *Source: March CPS data for earnings years 1963-2008. See note to Fig. 2. Log relative supply for 0-9 and 20-29 years of potential experience is plotted for males and females.*

to its pre–1975 trajectory, as shown earlier in Fig. 3. While the data in that figure only cover the period from 1963 forward, the slow growth of college attainment is even more striking when placed against a longer historical backdrop. Between 1940 and 1980, the fraction of young adults aged 25 to 34 who had completed a four-year college degree at the start of each decade increased three-fold among both sexes, from 5 percent and 7 percent among females and males, respectively, in 1940 to 20 percent and 27 percent, respectively, in 1980. After 1980, however, this trajectory shifted differentially by sex. College completion among young adult females slowed in the 1980s but then rebounded in the subsequent two decades. Male college attainment, by contrast, peaked with the cohort that was age 25-34 in 1980. Even in 2008, it remained below its 1980 level. Cumulatively, these trends inverted the male to female gap in college completion among young adults. This gap stood at positive 7 percentage points in 1980 and *negative* 7 percentage points in 2008.

2.3. Real wage levels by skill group

A limitation of the college/high school wage premium as a measure of the market value of skill is that it necessarily omits information on *real* wage levels. Stated differently, a rising college wage premium is consistent with a rising *real* college wage, a falling real high school wage, or both. Movements in real as well as relative wages will prove crucial to our interpretation of the data. As shown formally in Section 3, canonical models used to analyze the college premium robustly predict that demand shifts favoring skilled workers will both raise the skill premium *and* boost the real earnings of all skill groups (e.g., college and high school workers). This prediction appears strikingly at odds with the data, as first reported by Katz and Murphy (1992), and shown in the two panels of Fig. 4. This figure plots the evolution of real log earnings by gender and education level for the same samples of full-time, full-year workers used above. Each series is normalized at zero in the starting year of 1963, with subsequent values corresponding to the log change in earnings for each group relative to its 1963 level. All values are deflated using the Personal Consumption Expenditure Deflator, produced by the US Bureau of Economic Analysis.

In the first decade of the sample period, years 1963 through 1973, real wages rose steeply and relatively uniformly for both genders and all education groups. Log wage growth in this ten year period averaged approximately 20 percent. Following the first oil shock in 1973, wage levels fell sharply initially, and then stagnated for the remainder of the decade. Notably, this stagnation was also relatively uniform among genders and education groups. In 1980, wage stagnation gave way to three decades of rising inequality between education groups, accompanied by low overall rates of earnings growth—particularly among males. Real wages rose for highly educated workers, particularly workers with a post-college education, and fell steeply for less educated workers, particularly less educated males. Tables 1a and 1b provide many additional details on the evolution of real wage levels by sex, education, and experience groups during this period.

Alongside these overall trends, Fig. 4 reveals three key facts about the evolution of earnings by education groups that are not evident from the earlier plots of the college/high school wage premium. First, a sizable share of the increase in college relative to non-college wages in 1980 forward is explained by the rising wages of post-college workers, i.e., those with post-baccalaureate degrees. Real earnings for this group increased steeply and nearly continuously from at least the early 1980s to present. By

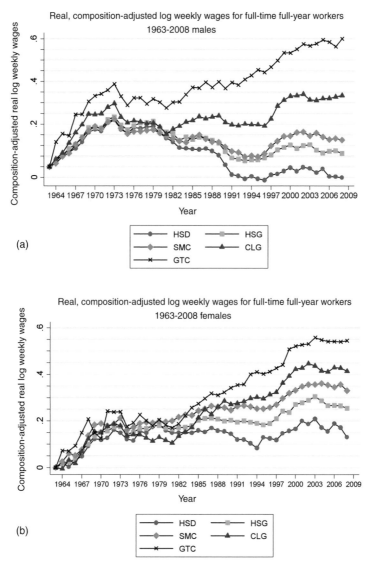

Figure 4 *Source: March CPS data for earnings years 1963-2008. See note to Fig. 1. The real log weekly wage for each education group is the weighted average of the relevant composition adjusted cells using a fixed set of weights equal to the average employment share of each group. Nominal wage values are deflated using the Personal Consumption Expenditure (PCE) deflator.*

contrast, earnings growth among those with exactly a four-year degree was much more modest. For example, real wages of males with exactly a four-year degree rose 13 log points between 1979 and 2008, substantially less than they rose in only the first decade of the sample.

Table 1a Changes in real, composition-adjusted log weekly wages for full-time, full-year workers, 1963-2008: by educational category and sex (100 × change in mean log real weekly wages).

	1963-1972	1972-1979	1979-1989	1989-1999	1999-2008	1963-2008
All	21.1	−1.7	−1.7	2.7	−0.3	20.1
Males	23.4	−2.8	−6.6	0.5	−1.2	13.3
Females	18.1	−0.2	4.9	5.8	1.0	29.6
Education (years)						
0-11						
Men	20.4	−1.5	−13.4	−7.4	−3.1	−5.1
Women	16.2	2.1	−2.7	0.2	−2.8	13.0
12						
Men	22.2	−0.7	−10.3	−2.1	−2.9	6.2
Women	17.3	0.7	1.9	3.7	1.8	25.4
13-15						
Men	20.9	−3.7	−5.8	2.8	−1.8	12.4
Women	18.7	1.0	5.8	6.4	1.0	33.0
16+						
Men	30.6	−6.3	4.9	9.5	3.6	42.2
Women	20.1	−5.0	14.6	12.8	2.5	44.9
16-17						
Men	28.0	−7.4	3.3	7.4	2.2	33.4
Women	18.7	−5.7	15.6	10.7	2.1	41.4
18+						
Men	36.0	−4.2	8.0	13.7	6.6	60.1
Women	23.7	−3.3	11.9	18.4	3.7	54.4

Source: March CPS data for earnings years 1963-2008. See note to Fig. 1.

A second fact highlighted by Fig. 4 is that a major proximate cause of the growing college/high school earnings gap is not steeply rising college wages, but rapidly declining wages for the less educated—especially less educated males. Real earnings of males with less than a four year college degree fell steeply between 1979 and 1992, by 12 log points for high school and some-college males, and by 20 log points for high school dropouts. Low skill male wages modestly rebounded between 1993 and 2003, but never reached their 1980 levels. For females, the picture is qualitatively similar, but the slopes are more favorable. While wages for low skill males were falling in the 1980s, wages for low skill females were largely stagnant; when low skill males wages increased modestly in the 1990s, low skill female wages rose approximately twice as fast.

A potential concern with the interpretation of these results is that the measured real *wage* declines of less educated workers mask an increase in their total compensation after accounting for the rising value of employer provided non-wage benefits such as healthcare, vacation and sick time. Careful analysis of representative, wage and fringe

Table 1b Changes in real, composition-adjusted log weekly wages for full-time, full-year workers, 1963-2008: by experience, educational category, and sex (100 × change in mean log real weekly wages).

	1963-1972	1972-1979	1979-1989	1989-1999	1999-2008	1963-2008
Experience						
5 years						
Men	20.8	−5.1	−10.0	4.7	−2.6	7.8
Women	18.9	−2.3	−0.6	5.6	−0.9	20.6
25-35 years						
Men	25.0	−0.9	−3.4	−2.1	−2.4	16.3
Women	17.2	2.1	8.5	5.4	1.7	34.8
Education and experience						
Education 12						
Experience 5						
Men	23.2	−3.1	−19.1	2.2	−4.4	−1.1
Women	17.3	−1.8	−6.3	3.2	0.5	12.8
Experience 25-35						
Men	20.5	1.6	−4.3	−4.2	−3.5	10.1
Women	16.9	2.7	6.4	5.2	1.8	33.0
Education 16+						
Experience 5						
Men	23.1	−11.6	8.6	10.4	0.6	31.2
Women	20.5	−5.6	14.7	9.3	−0.8	38.0
Experience 25-35						
Men	35.5	−0.1	4.4	6.8	2.9	49.6
Women	18.6	−2.3	12.7	14.5	4.2	47.6

Source: March CPS data for earnings years 1963-2008. See note to Fig. 1.

benefits data by Pierce (2001, forthcoming) casts doubt on this notion, however. Monetizing the value of these benefits does not substantially alter the conclusion that real compensation for low skilled workers fell in the 1980s. Further, Pierce shows that total compensation—that is, the sum of wages and in-kind benefits—for high skilled workers rose by more than their wages, both in absolute terms and relative to compensation for low skilled workers.[14] A complementary analysis of the distribution of non-wage benefits—including safe working conditions and daytime versus night and weekend hours—by Hamermesh (1999) also reaches similar conclusions. Hamermesh demonstrates that trends in the inequality of wages understate the growth in full earnings

[14] The estimated falls in real wages would also be overstated if the price deflator overestimated the rate of inflation and thus underestimated real wage growth. Our real wage series are deflated using the Personal Consumption Expenditure Deflator produced by the US Bureau of Economic Analysis. The PCE generally shows a lower rate of inflation than the more commonly used Consumer Price Index (CPI), which was in turn amended following the Boskin report in 1996 to provide a more conservative estimate of inflation (Boskin et al., 1996).

inequality (i.e., absent compensating differentials) and, moreover, that accounting for changes in the distribution of non-wage amenities augments rather than offsets changes in the inequality of wages. It is therefore unlikely that consideration of non-wage benefits changes the conclusion that low skill workers experienced significant declines in their *real* earnings levels during the 1980s and early 1990s.[15]

The third key fact evident from Fig. 4 is that while the earnings gaps between some-college, high school graduate, and high school dropout workers expanded sharply in the 1980s, these gaps stabilized thereafter. In particular, the wages of high school dropouts, high school graduates, and those with some college moved largely in parallel from the early 1990s forward.

The net effect of these three trends—rising college and post-college wages, stagnant and falling real wages for those without a four-year college degree, and the stabilization of the wage gaps among some-college, high school graduates, and high school dropout workers—is that the wage returns to schooling have become increasingly convex in years of education, particularly for males, as emphasized by Lemieux (2006b). Figure 5 shows this "convexification" by plotting the estimated gradient relating years of educational attainment to log hourly wages in three representative years of our sample: 1973, 1989, and 2009. To construct this figure, we regress log hourly earnings in each year on a quadratic in years of completed schooling and a quartic in potential experience. Models that pool males and females also include a female main effect and an interaction between the female dummy and a quartic in (potential) experience.[16] In each figure, the predicted log earnings of a worker with seven years of completed schooling and 25 years of potential experience in 1973 is normalized to zero. The slope of the 1973 locus then traces out the implied log earnings gain for each additional year of schooling in 1973, up to 18 years. The loci for 1989 and 2009 are constructed similarly, and they are also normalized relative to the intercept in 1973. This implies that upward or downward shifts in the intercepts of

---

[15] Moretti (2008) presents evidence that the aggregate increase in wage inequality is greater than the rise in cost-of-living-adjusted wage inequality, since the aggregate increase does not account for the fact that high-wage college workers are increasingly clustered in metropolitan areas with high and rising housing prices. These facts are surely correct, but their economic interpretation requires some care. As emphasized above, our interest in wage inequality is not as a measure of welfare inequality (for which wages are generally a poor measure), but as a measure of the relative productivities of different groups of workers and the market price of skills. What is relevant for this purpose is the *producer wage*—which does not require cost of living adjustments provided that each region produces at least some *traded* (i.e., traded within the United States) goods and wages, and regional labor market wages reflect the value of marginal products of different groups. To approximate welfare inequality, one might wish however to use the *consumer wage*—that is the producer wage adjusted for cost of living. It is unclear whether housing costs should be fully netted out of the consumer wage, however. If high housing prices reflect the amenities offered by an area, these higher prices are not a pure cost. If higher prices instead reflect congestion costs that workers must bear to gain access to high wages jobs, then they are a cost not an amenity. These alternative explanations are not mutually exclusive and are difficult to empirically distinguish since many high education cities (e.g., New York, San Francisco, Boston) feature both high housing costs and locational amenities differentially valued by high wage workers (see Black et al., 2009).

[16] Years of schooling correspond to one of eight values, ranging from 7 to 18 years. Due to the substantial revamping of the CPS educational attainment question in 1992, these eight values are the maximum consistent set available throughout the sample period.

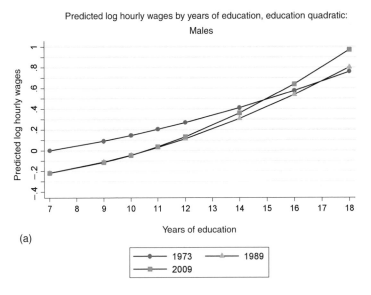

(a)

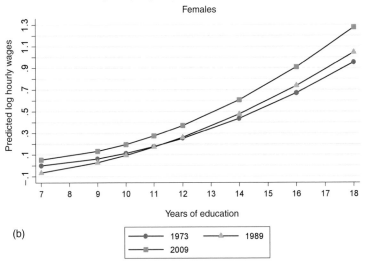

(b)

Figure 5   *Source: May/ORG CPS data for earnings years 1973-2009. For each year, log hourly wages for all workers, excluding the self-employed and those employed by the military, are regressed on a quadratic in education (eight categories), a quartic in experience, a female dummy, and interactions of the female dummy and the quartic in experience. Predicted real log hourly wages are computed in 1973, 1989 and 2009 for each of the years of schooling presented in the figure. See the Data Appendix for more details on the treatment of May/ORG CPS data.*

these loci correspond to real changes in log hourly earnings, whereas rotations of the loci indicate changes in the education-wage gradient.[17]

The first panel of Fig. 5 shows that the education-wage gradient for males was roughly log linear in years of schooling in 1973, with a slope approximately equal to 0.07 (that is, 7 log points of hourly earnings per year of schooling). Between 1973 and 1989, the slope steepened while the intercept fell by a sizable 10 log points. The crossing point of the two series at 16 years of schooling implies that earnings for workers with less than a four-year college degree fell between 1973 and 1989, consistent with the real wage plots in Fig. 4. The third locus, corresponding to 2009, suggests two further changes in wage structure in the intervening two decades: earnings rose modestly for low education workers, seen in the higher 2009 intercept (though still below the 1973 level); and the locus relating education to earnings became strikingly convex. Whereas the 1989 and 2009 loci are roughly parallel for educational levels below 12, the 2009 locus is substantially steeper above this level. Indeed at 18 years of schooling, it lies 16 log points above the 1989 locus. Thus, the return to schooling first steepened and then "convexified" between 1973 and 2009.

Panel B of Fig. 5 repeats this estimation for females. The convexification of the return to education is equally apparent for females, but the downward shift in the intercept is minimal. These differences by gender are, of course, consistent with the differential evolution of wages by education group and gender shown in Fig. 4.

As a check to ensure that these patterns are not driven by the choice of functional form, Fig. 6 repeats the estimation, in this case replacing the education quartic with a full set of education dummies. While the fitted values from this model are naturally less smooth than in the quadratic specification, the qualitative story is quite similar: between 1973 and 1989, the education-wage locus intercept falls while the slope steepens. The 1989 curve crosses the 1973 curve at 18 years of schooling. Two decades later, the education-wage curve lies atop the 1989 curve at low years of schooling, while it is both steeper and more convex for completed schooling beyond the 12th year.

2.4. Overall wage inequality

Our discussion so far summarizes the evolution of real and relative wages by education, gender and experience groups. It does not convey the full set of changes in the wage distribution, however, since there remains substantial wage dispersion within as well as between skill groups. To fill in this picture, we summarize changes throughout the entire earnings distribution. In particular, we show the trends in real wages by earnings percentile, focusing on the 5th through 95th percentiles of the wage distribution. We impose this range restriction because the CPS and Census samples are unlikely to provide accurate measures of earnings at the highest and lowest percentiles. High percentiles

---

[17] We use the CPS May/ORG series for this analysis rather than the March data so as to focus on hourly wages, as is the convention for Mincerian wage regressions.

Predicted log hourly wages by years of education, education dummies:

Males

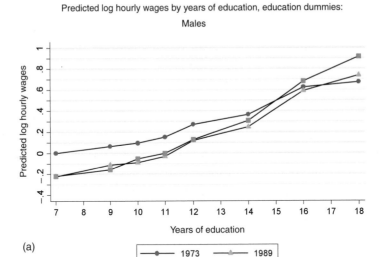

(a)

Predicted log hourly wages by years of education, education dummies:

Females

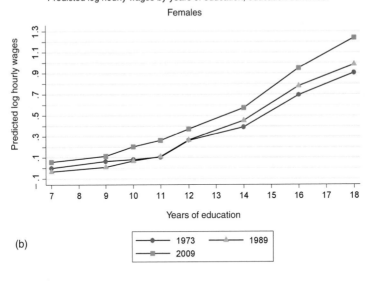

(b)

Figure 6 *Source: May/ORG CPS data for earnings years 1973-2009. For each year, log hourly wages for all workers, excluding the self-employed and those employed by the military, are regressed on eight education dummies, a quartic in experience, a female dummy, and interactions of the female dummy and the quartic in experience. Predicted real log hourly wages are computed in 1973, 1989 and 2009 for each of the years of schooling presented. See the Data Appendix for more details on the treatment of May/ORG CPS data.*

are unreliable both because high earnings values are truncated in public use samples and, more importantly, because non-response and under-reporting are particularly severe among high income households.[18] Conversely, wage earnings in the lower percentiles imply levels of consumption that lie substantially below observed levels (Meyer and Sullivan, 2008). This disparity reflects a combination of measurement error, under-reporting, and transfer income among low wage individuals.

Figure 7 plots the evolution of real log weekly wages of full-time, full-year workers at the 10th, 50th and 90th percentiles of the earnings distribution from 1963 through 2008. In each panel, the value of the 90th, 50th and 10th percentiles are normalized to zero in the start year of 1963, with subsequent data points measuring log changes from this initial level. Many features of Fig. 7 closely correspond to the education by gender real wages series depicted in Fig. 4. For both genders, the 10th, 50th and 90th percentiles of the distribution rise rapidly and relatively evenly between 1963 and 1973. After 1973, the 10th and 50th percentiles continue to stagnate relatively uniformly for the remainder of the decade. The 90th percentile of the distribution pulls away modestly from the median throughout the decade of the 1970s, echoing the rise in earnings among post-college workers in that decade.[19]

Reflecting the uneven distribution of wage gains by education group, growth in real earnings among males occurs among high earners, but is not broadly shared. This is most evident by comparing the male 90th percentile with the median. The 90th percentile rose steeply and almost monotonically between 1979 and 2007. By contrast, the male median was essentially flat from 1980 to 1994. Simultaneously, the male 10th percentile fell steeply (paralleling the trajectory of high school dropout wages). When the male median began to rise during the mid 1990s (a period of rapid productivity and earnings growth in the US economy), the male 10th percentile rose concurrently and slightly more rapidly. This partly reversed the substantial expansion of lower-tail inequality that unfolded during the 1980s.

The wage picture for females is qualitatively similar, but the steeper slopes again show that the females have fared better than males during this period. As with males, the growth of wage inequality is asymmetric above and below the median. The female 90/50 rises nearly continuously from the late 1970s forward. By contrast, the female 50/10 expands rapidly during the 1980s, plateaus through the mid-1990s, and then compresses modestly thereafter.

---

[18] Pioneering analyses of harmonized US income tax data by Piketty and Saez (2003) demonstrate that the increases in upper-tail inequality found in public use data sources and documented below are vastly more pronounced above the 90th percentile than below it, though the qualitative patterns are similar. Burkhauser et al. (2008) offer techniques for improving imputations of top incomes in public use CPS data sources.

[19] Whether the measured rise in inequality in the 1970s is reliable has been a subject of some debate because this increase is detected in the Census and CPS March series but not in the contemporaneous May CPS series (cf. Katz and Murphy, 1992; Juhn et al., 1993; Katz and Autor, 1999; Lemieux, 2006b; Autor et al., 2008). Recent evidence appears to support the veracity of the 1970s inequality increase. Using harmonized income tax data, Piketty and Saez (2003) find that inequality, measured by the top decile wage share, started to rise steeply in the early 1970s.

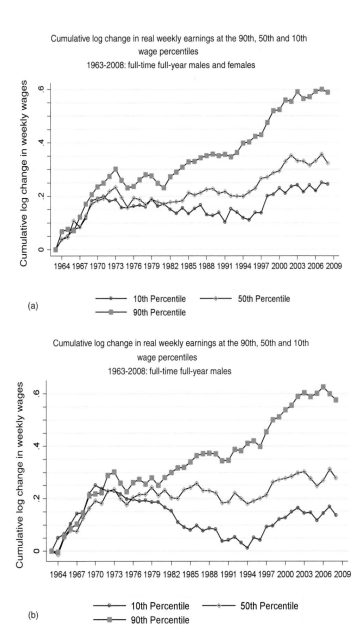

Figure 7   *Source: March CPS data for earnings years 1963-2008. For each year, the 10th, median and 90th percentiles of log weekly wages are calculated for full-time, full-year workers.*

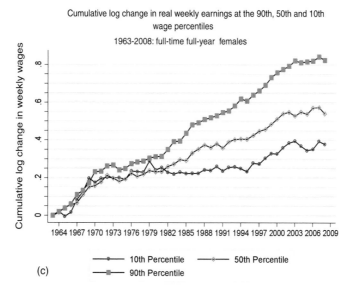

Figure 7   *(continued)*

Because Fig. 7 depicts wage trends for *full-time, full-year* workers, it tends to obscure wage developments lower in the earnings distribution, where a larger share of workers are part-time or part-year. To capture these developments, we apply the May/ORG CPS log hourly wage samples for years 1973 through 2009 (i.e., all available years) to plot in Fig. 8 the corresponding trends in real indexed hourly wages of all employed workers at the 10th, 50th, and 90th percentiles. Due to the relatively small size of the May sample, we pool three years of data at each point to increase precision (e.g., plotted year 1974 uses data from 1973, 1974 and 1975).

The additional fact revealed by Fig. 8 is that downward movements at the 10th percentile are far more pronounced in the hourly wage distribution than in the full-time weekly data. For example, the weekly data show no decline in the female 10th percentile between 1979 and 1986, whereas the hourly wage data show a fall of 10 log points in this period.[20] Similarly, the modest closing of the 50/10 earnings gap after 1995 seen in

[20] The more pronounced fall at the female tenth percentile in the distribution that includes hourly wages reflects the fact that a substantial fraction (13 percent) of all female hours worked in 1979 were paid at or below the federal minimum wage (Autor et al., 2009), the real value of which declined by 30 log points over the subsequent 9 years. It is clear that the decline in the minimum wage contributed to the expansion of the female lower tail in the 1980s, though the share of the expansion attributable to the minimum is the subject of some debate (see DiNardo et al., 1996; Lee, 1999; Teulings, 2003; Autor et al., 2009). It is noteworthy that in the decade in which the minimum wage was falling, female real wage levels (measured by the mean or median) and female upper-tail inequality (measured by the 90/50) rose more rapidly than for males. This suggests that many forces were operative on the female wage structure in this decade alongside the minimum wage.

Cumulative log change in real hourly earnings at the 90th, 50th and 10th
wage percentiles
1974-2008: males and females

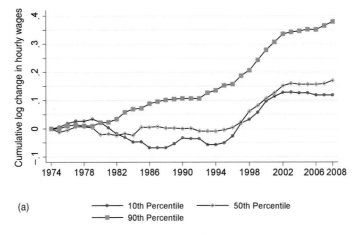

(a)
- 10th Percentile
- 50th Percentile
- 90th Percentile

Cumulative log change in real hourly earnings at the 90th, 50th and 10th
wage percentiles
1974-2008: males

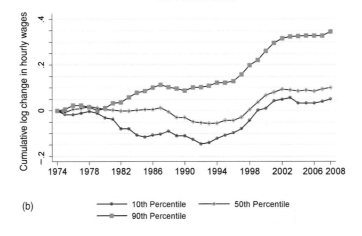

(b)
- 10th Percentile
- 50th Percentile
- 90th Percentile

Figure 8 *Source: May/ORG CPS data for earnings years 1973-2009. The data are pooled using three-year moving averages (i.e. the year 1974 includes data from years 1973, 1974 and 1975). For each year, the 10th, median and 90th percentiles of log weekly wages are calculated for all workers, excluding the self-employed and those employed in military occupations.*

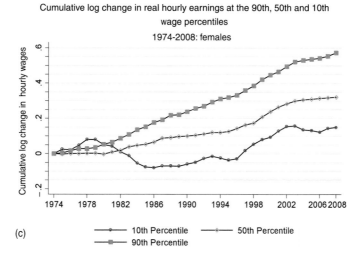

Figure 8   *(continued)*

the full-time, full-year sample is revealed as a sharp reversal of the 1980s expansion of 50/10 wage inequality in the full hourly distribution. Thus, the monotone expansion in the 1980s of wage inequality in the top and bottom halves of the distribution became notably non-monotone during the subsequent two decades.[21]

The contrast between these two periods of wage structure changes—one monotone, the other non-monotone—is shown in stark relief in Fig. 9, which plots the change at each percentile of the hourly wage distribution relative to the corresponding median during two distinct eras, 1974-1988 and 1988-2008. The monotonicity of wage structure changes during the first period, 1974-1988, is immediately evident for both genders.[22] Equally apparent is the U-shaped (or "polarized") growth of wages by percentile in the 1988-2008 period, which is particularly evident for males. The steep gradient of wage

[21] An additional discrepancy between the weekly and hourly samples is that the rise in the 90th wage percentile for males is less continuous and persistent in the hourly samples; indeed the male 90th percentile appears to plateau after 2003 in the May/ORG data but not in the March data. A potential explanation for the discrepancy is that the earnings data collected by the March CPS use a broader earnings construct, and in particular are more likely to capture bonus and performance. Lemieux et al. (2009) find that the incidence of bonus pay rose substantially during the 1990s and potentially contributed to rising dispersion of annual earnings. An alternative explanation for the March versus May/ORG discrepancy is deterioration in data quality. Lemieux (2006b) offers some limited evidence that the quality of the March CPS earnings data declined in the 1990s, which could explain why the March and May/ORG CPS diverge in this decade. Conversely, Autor et al. (2008) hypothesize that the sharp rise in earnings non-response in the May/ORG CPS following the 1994 survey redesign may have reduced the consistency of the wage series (especially given the sharp rise in earnings non-response following the redesign). This hypothesis would also explain why the onset of the discrepancy is in 1994.

[22] The larger expansion at low percentiles for females than males is likely attributable to the falling bite of the minimum wage during the 1980s (Lee, 1999; Teulings, 2003). Autor et al. (2009) report that 12 to 13 percent of females were paid the minimum wage in 1979.

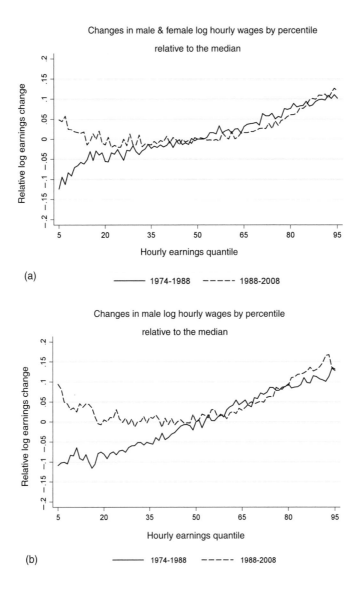

Figure 9 *Source: May/ORG CPS data for earnings years 1973-2009. The data are pooled using three-year moving averages (i.e. the year 1974 includes data from years 1973, 1974 and 1975). For each year, the 5th through 95th percentiles of log hourly wages are calculated for all workers, excluding the self-employed and those employed in military occupations. The log wage change at the median is normalized to zero in each time interval.*

Figure 9 (*continued*)

changes *above* the median is nearly parallel, however, for these two time intervals. Thus, the key difference between the two periods lies in the evolution of the lower-tail, which is falling steeply in the 1980s and rising disproportionately at lower percentiles thereafter.[23]

Though the decade of the 2000s is not separately plotted in Fig. 9, it bears note that the U-shaped growth of hourly wages is most pronounced during the period of 1988 through 1999. For the 1999 through 2007 interval, the May/ORG data show a pattern of wage growth that is roughly flat across the first seven deciles of the distribution, and then upwardly sloped in the three highest deciles, though the slope is shallower than in either of the prior two decades.

These divergent trends in upper-tail, median and lower-tail earnings are of substantial significance for our discussion, and we consider their causes carefully below. Most notable is the "polarization" of wage growth—by which we mean the simultaneous growth of high and low wages relative to the middle—which is not readily interpretable in the canonical two factor model. This polarization is made more noteworthy by the fact that the return to skill, measured by the college/high school wage premium, rose monotonically throughout this period, as did inequality above the median of the wage distribution. These discrepancies between the monotone rise of skill prices and the non-monotone evolution of inequality again underscore the potential utility of a richer model of wage determination.

---

[23] A second important difference between the two periods, visible in earlier figures, is that there is significantly greater wage growth at virtually all wage percentiles in the 1990s than in the 1980s, reflecting the sharp rise in productivity in the latter decade. This contrast is not evident in Fig. 9 since the wage change at the median is normalized to zero in both periods.

Substantial changes in wage inequality over the last several decades are not unique to the US, though neither is the US a representative case. Summarizing the literature circa ten years ago, Katz and Autor (1999) report that most industrialized economies experienced a compression of skill differentials and wage inequality during the 1970s, and a modest to large rise in differentials in the 1980s, with the greatest increase seen in the US and UK. Drawing on more recent and consistent data for 19 OECD countries, Atkinson reports that there was at least a five percent increase in either upper-tail or lower-tail inequality between 1980 and 2005 in 16 countries, and a rise of at least 5 percent in both tails in seven countries. More generally, Atkinson notes that substantial rises in upper-tail inequality are widespread across OECD countries, whereas movements in the lower-tail vary more in sign, magnitude, and timing.[24]

2.5. Job polarization

Accompanying the *wage* polarization depicted in Fig. 7 through 9 is a marked pattern of *job* polarization in the United States and across the European Union—by which we mean the simultaneous growth of the share of employment in high skill, high wage occupations and low skill, low wage occupations. We begin by depicting this broad pattern (first noted in Acemoglu, 1999) using aggregate US data. We then link the polarization of employment to the "routinization" hypothesis proposed by Autor et al., (2003 "ALM" hereafter), and we explore detailed changes in occupational structure across the US and OECD in light of that framework.

Changes in occupational structure

Figure 10 provides a starting point for the discussion of job polarization by plotting the change over each of the last three decades in the share of US employment accounted for by 318 detailed occupations encompassing all of US employment. These occupations are ranked on the *x*-axis by their skill level from lowest to highest, where an occupation's skill rank is approximated by the average wage of workers in the occupation in 1980.[25] The *y*-axis of the figure corresponds to the change in employment at each occupational percentile as a share of total US employment during the decade. Since the sum of shares must equal one in each decade, the change in these shares across decades must total zero. Thus, the height at each skill percentile measures the growth in each occupation's employment relative to the whole.[26]

---

[24] Dustmann et al. (2009) and Antonczyk et al. (2010) provide detailed analysis of wage polarization in Germany. Though Germany experienced a substantial increase in wage inequality during the 1980s and 1990s, the pattern of lower-tail movements was distinct from the US. Overturning earlier work, Boudarbat et al. (2010) present new evidence that the returns to education for Canadian men increased substantially between 1980 and 2005.

[25] Ranking occupations by mean years of completed schooling instead yields very similar results. Moreover, occupational rankings by either measure are quite stable over time. Thus, the conclusions are not highly sensitive to the skill measure or the choice of base year for skill ranking (here, 1980).

[26] These series are smoothed using a locally weighted regression to reduce jumpiness when measuring employment shifts at such a narrow level of aggregation. Due to smoothing, the sum of share changes may not integrate precisely to zero.

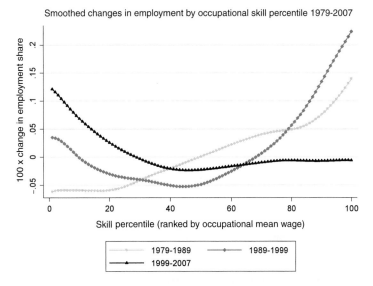

Figure 10   *Source: Census IPUMS 5 percent samples for years 1980, 1990, and 2000, and Census American Community Survey for 2008. All occupation and earnings measures in these samples refer to prior year's employment. The figure plots log changes in employment shares by 1980 occupational skill percentile rank using a locally weighted smoothing regression (bandwidth 0.8 with 100 observations), where skill percentiles are measured as the employment-weighted percentile rank of an occupation's mean log wage in the Census IPUMS 1980 5 percent extract. The mean log wage in each occupation is calculated using workers' hours of annual labor supply times the Census sampling weights.Consistent occupation codes for Census years 1980, 1990, and 2000, and 2008 are from Autor and Dorn (2009).*

The figure reveals a pronounced "twisting" of the distribution of employment across occupations over three decades, which becomes more pronounced in each period. During the 1980s (1979-1989), employment growth by occupation was nearly monotone in occupational skill; occupations below the median skill level declined as a share of employment and occupations above the median increased. In the subsequent decade, this monotone relationship gave way to a distinct pattern of polarization. Relative employment growth was most rapid at high percentiles, but it was also modestly positive at low percentiles (10th percentile and down) and modestly negative at intermediate percentiles. In contrast, during the most recent decade for which Census/ACS data are available, 1999-2007, employment growth was heavily concentrated among the lowest three deciles of occupations. In deciles four through nine, the change in employment shares was negative, while in the highest decile, almost no change is evident. Thus, the disproportionate growth of low education, low wage occupations became evident in the 1990s and accelerated thereafter.[27]

---

[27] Despite this apparent monotonicity, employment growth in one low skill job category—service occupations—was rapid in the 1980s (Autor and Dorn, 2010). This growth is hardly visible in Fig. 10, however, because these occupations were still quite small.

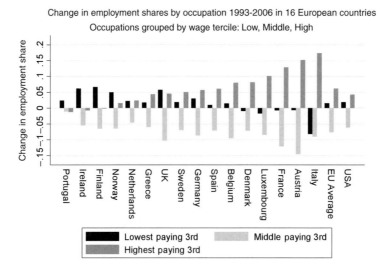

Figure 11   *Source: Data on EU employment are from Goos et al. (2009). US data are from the May/ORG CPS files for years 1993-2006. The data include all persons aged 16-64 who reported employment in the sample reference week, excluding those employed by the military and in agricultural occupations. Occupations are first assigned to 326 occupation groups that are consistent over the given time period. These occupations are then grouped into three broad categories by wage level.*

This pattern of employment polarization is not unique to the United States, as is shown in Fig. 11. This figure, based on Table 1 of Goos et al. (2009), depicts the change in the share of overall employment accounted for by three sets of occupations grouped according to average wage level—low, medium, and high—in each of 16 European Union countries during the period 1993 through 2006.[28] Employment polarization is pronounced across the EU during this period. In all 16 countries depicted, middle wage occupations decline as a share of employment. The largest declines occur in France and Austria (by 12 and 14 percentage points, respectively) and the smallest occurs in Portugal (1 percentage point). The unweighted average decline in middle skill employment across countries is 8 percentage points.

The declining share of middle wage occupations is offset by growth in high and low wage occupations. In 13 of 16 countries, high wage occupations increased their share of employment, with an average gain of 6 percentage points, while low wage occupations grew as a share of employment in 11 of 16 countries. Notably, in all 16 countries, low wage occupations increased in size relative to middle wage occupations, with a mean gain in employment in low relative to middle wage occupations of 10 percentage points.

---

[28] The choice of time period for this figure reflects the availability of consistent Harmonized European Labour Force data. The ranking of occupations by wage/skill level is assumed identical across countries, as necessitated by data limitations. Goos, Manning and Salomons report that the ranking of occupations by wage level is highly comparable across EU countries.

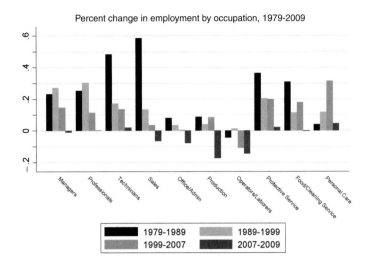

Figure 12 *Source: May/ORG CPS files for earnings years 1979-2009. The data include all persons aged 16-64 who reported employment in the sample reference week, excluding those employed by the military and in agricultural occupations. Occupations are assigned to 326 occupation groups that are consistent over the given time period. All non-military, non-agricultural occupations are assigned to one of ten broad occupations presented in the figure.*

For comparison, Fig. 11 also plots the unweighted average change in the share of national employment in high, middle, and low wage occupations in all 16 European Union economies alongside a similar set of occupational shift measures for the United States. Job polarization appears to be at least as pronounced in the European Union as in the United States.

Figure 12 studies the specific changes in occupational structure that drive job polarization in the United States. The figure plots percentage point changes in employment levels by decade for the years 1979-2009 for 10 major occupational groups encompassing all of US non-agricultural employment. We use the May/ORG data so as to include the two recession years of 2007 through 2009 (separately plotted).[29]

The 10 occupations summarized in Fig. 12 divide neatly into three groups. On the left-hand side of the figure are managerial, professional and technical occupations. These are highly educated and highly paid occupations. Between one-quarter and two-thirds of workers in these occupations had at least a four-year college degree in 1979, with the lowest college share in technical occupations and the highest in professional occupations (Table 4). Employment growth in these occupations was robust throughout the three decades plotted. Even in the deep recession of 2007 through 2009, during which the

---

[29] The patterns are very similar, however, if we instead use the Census/ACS data, which cover the period 1959 through 2007 (see Tables 3a and 3b for comparison).

number of employed US workers fell by approximately 8 million, these occupations experienced almost no absolute decline in employment.

The subsequent four columns display employment growth in "middle skill occupations," which we define as comprising sales; office and administrative support; production, craft and repair; and operator, fabricator and laborer. The first two of this group of four are middle skilled, white-collar occupations that are disproportionately held by women with a high school degree or some college. The latter two categories are a mixture of middle and low skilled blue-collar occupations that are disproportionately held by males with a high school degree or lower education. While the headcount in these occupations rose in each decadal interval between 1979-2007, their growth rate lagged the economy-wide average and, moreover, generally slowed across decades. These occupations were hit particularly hard during the 2007-2009 recession, with absolute declines in employment ranging from 7 to 17 percent.

The last three columns of Fig. 12 depict employment trends in service occupations, which are defined by the Census Bureau as jobs that involve helping, caring for or assisting others. The majority of workers in service occupations have no post-secondary education, and average hourly wages in service occupations are in most cases below the other seven occupations categories. Despite their low educational requirements and low pay, employment growth in service occupations has been relatively rapid over the past three decades. Indeed, Autor and Dorn (2010) show that rising service occupation employment accounts almost entirely for the upward twist of the lower tail of Fig. 10 during the 1990s and 2000s. All three broad categories of service occupations— protective service, food preparation and cleaning services, and personal care—expanded by double digits in both the 1990s and the pre-recession years of the past decade (1999-2007). Protective service and food preparation and cleaning occupations expanded even more rapidly during the 1980s. Notably, even during the recessionary years of 2007 through 2009, employment growth in service occupations was modestly positive—more so, in fact, than the three high skilled occupations that have also fared comparatively well (professional, managerial and technical occupations). As shown in Tables 3a and 3b, the employment share of service occupations was essentially flat between 1959 and 1979. Thus, their rapid growth since 1980 marks a sharp trend reversal.

Cumulatively, these two trends—rapid employment growth in both high and low education jobs—have substantially reduced the share of employment accounted for by "middle skill" jobs. In 1979, the four middle skill occupations—sales, office and administrative workers, production workers, and operatives—accounted for 57.3 percent of employment. In 2007, this number was 48.6 percent, and in 2009, it was 45.7 percent. One can quantify the consistency of this trend by correlating the growth rates of these occupation groups across multiple decades. The correlation between occupational growth rates in 1979-1989 and 1989-1999 is 0.53, and for the decades of 1989-1999 and 1999-2009, it is 0.74. Remarkably, the correlation between occupational growth rates during 1999–2007 and 2007–2009—that is, prior to and during the current recession—is 0.76.[30]

Sources of job polarization: The "routinization" hypothesis

Autor et al. (2003) link job polarization to rapid improvements in the productivity—and declines in the real price—of information and communications technologies and, more broadly, symbolic processing devices. ALM take these advances as exogenous, though our framework below shows how they can also be understood as partly endogenous responses to changes in the supplies of skills. ALM also emphasize that to understand the impact of these technical changes on the labor market, is necessary to study the "tasks content" of different occupations. As already mentioned in the Introduction, and as we elaborate further below, a *task* is a unit of work activity that produces output (goods and services), and we think of workers as allocating their skills to different tasks depending on labor market prices.

While the rapid technological progress in information and communications technology that motivates the ALM paper is evident to anyone who owns a television, uses a mobile phone, drives a car, or takes a photograph, its magnitude is nevertheless stunning. Nordhaus (2007) estimates that the real cost of performing a standardized set of computational tasks—where cost is expressed in constant dollars or measured relative to the labor cost of performing the same calculations—fell by at least 1.7 trillion-fold between 1850 and 2006, with the bulk of this decline occurring in the last three decades. Of course, the progress of computing was almost negligible from 1850 until the era of electromechanical computing (i.e., using relays as digital switches) at the outset of the twentieth century. Progress accelerated during World War II, when vacuum tubes replaced relays. Then, when microprocessors became widely available in the 1970s, the rate of change increased discontinuously. Nordhaus estimates that between 1980 and 2006, the real cost of performing a standardized set of computations fell by 60 to 75 percent *annually*. Processing tasks that were unthinkably expensive 30 years ago—such as searching the full text of a university's library for a single quotation—became trivially cheap.

The rapid, secular price decline in the real cost of symbolic processing creates enormous economic incentives for employers to substitute information technology for expensive labor in performing workplace tasks. Simultaneously, it creates significant advantages for workers whose skills become increasingly productive as the price of computing falls. Although computers are now ubiquitous, they do not do everything. Computers—or, more precisely, symbolic processors that execute stored instructions—have a very specific set of capabilities and limitations. Ultimately, their ability to accomplish a task is dependent upon the ability of a programmer to write a set of

---

[30] These correlations are weighted by occupations' mean employment shares during the three decade interval.

procedures or rules that appropriately direct the machine at each possible contingency. For a task to be autonomously performed by a computer, it must be sufficiently well defined (i.e., scripted) that a machine lacking flexibility or judgment can execute the task successfully by following the steps set down by the programmer. Accordingly, computers and computer-controlled equipment are highly productive and reliable at performing the tasks that programmers can script—and relatively inept at everything else. Following, ALM, we refer to these procedural, rule-based activities to which computers are currently well-suited as "routine" (or "codifiable") tasks. By routine, we do not mean mundane (e.g., washing dishes) but rather sufficiently well understood that the task can be fully specified as a series of instructions to be executed by a machine (e.g., adding a column of numbers).

Routine tasks are characteristic of many middle skilled cognitive and manual jobs, such as bookkeeping, clerical work, repetitive production, and monitoring jobs. Because the core job tasks of these occupations follow precise, well-understood procedures, they can be (and increasingly are) codified in computer software and performed by machines (or, alternatively, are sent electronically—"outsourced"—to foreign worksites). The substantial declines in clerical and administrative occupations depicted in Fig. 12 are likely a consequence of the falling price of machine substitutes for these tasks. It is important to observe, however, that computerization has not reduced the economic value or prevalence of the tasks that were performed by workers in these occupations—quite the opposite.[31] But tasks that primarily involve organizing, storing, retrieving, and manipulating information—most common in middle skilled administrative, clerical and production tasks—are increasingly codified in computer software and performed by machines.[32] Simultaneously, these technological advances have dramatically lowered the cost of offshoring information-based tasks to foreign worksites (Blinder, 2007; Jensen et al., 2005; Jensen and Kletzer, forthcoming; Blinder and Krueger, 2008; Oldenski, 2009).[33]

This process of automation and offshoring of routine tasks, in turn, raises *relative* demand for workers who can perform complementary non-routine tasks. In particular, ALM argue that non-routine tasks can be roughly subdivided into two major categories: abstract tasks and manual tasks (two categories that lie at opposite ends of the occupational-skill distribution). Abstract tasks are activities that require problem-solving, intuition, persuasion, and creativity. These tasks are characteristic of

---

[31] Of course, computerization has reduced the value of these tasks *at the margin* (reflecting their now negligible price).

[32] Bartel et al. (2007) offer firm-level econometric analysis of the process of automation of routine job tasks and attendant changes in work organization and job skill demands. Autor et al. (2002) and Levy and Murnane (2004) provide case study evidence and in-depth discussion.

[33] While many codifiable tasks are suitable for either automation or offshoring (e.g., bill processing services), not all offshorable tasks are routine in our terminology. For example, call center operations, data entry, and journeyman programming tasks are readily offshorable since they are information-based tasks that require little face-to-face interactions among suppliers and demanders. These tasks are not generally fully codifiable at present, however.

professional, managerial, technical and creative occupations, such as law, medicine, science, engineering, design, and management, among many others. Workers who are most adept in these tasks typically have high levels of education and analytical capability. ALM further argue that these analytical tasks are complementary to computer technology, because analytic, problem-solving, and creative tasks typically draw heavily on information as an input. When the price of accessing, organizing, and manipulating information falls, abstract tasks are complemented.

Non-routine manual tasks are activities that require situational adaptability, visual and language recognition, and in-person interactions. Driving a truck through city traffic, preparing a meal, installing a carpet, or mowing a lawn are all activities that are intensive in non-routine manual tasks. As these examples suggest, non-routine manual tasks demand workers who are physically adept and, in some cases, able to communicate fluently in spoken language. In general, they require little in the way of formal education relative to a labor market where most workers have completed high school.

This latter observation applies with particular force to service occupations, as stressed by Autor and Dorn (2009, 2010). Jobs such as food preparation and serving, cleaning and janitorial work, grounds cleaning and maintenance, in-person health assistance by home health aides, and numerous jobs in security and protective services, are highly intensive in non-routine manual tasks. The core tasks of these jobs demand interpersonal and environmental adaptability. These are precisely the job tasks that are challenging to automate because they require a level of adaptability and responsiveness to unscripted interactions—both with the environment and with individuals—which at present exceed the limits of machine-competency, though this will surely change in the long run. It also bears note that these same job tasks are infeasible to offshore in many cases because they must be produced and performed in person (again, for now). Yet, these jobs generally do not require formal education beyond a high school degree or, in most cases, extensive training.[34]

In summary, the displacement of jobs that are intensive in routine tasks may have contributed to the polarization of employment by reducing job opportunities in middle skilled clerical, administrative, production and operative occupations. Jobs that are intensive in either abstract or non-routine manual tasks, however, are much less susceptible to this process due to the demand for problem-solving, judgment and creativity in the former case, and flexibility and physical adaptability in the latter. Since these jobs are found at opposite ends of the occupational skill spectrum—in professional, managerial and technical occupations on the one hand, and in service

---

[34] Pissarides and Ngai (2007), Acemoglu and Guerrieri (2007), Weiss (2008) and Reshef (2009) also provide theoretical perspectives on the rise of service employment in industrialized economies, focusing on unbalanced productivity growth as in the classic analysis by Baumol (1967). The model in Autor and Dorn (2010) is similarly rooted in unbalanced growth, though Autor and Dorn focus on unbalanced productivity growth across tasks rather than sectors. See also Manning (2004) and Mazzolari and Ragusa (2008) for models of rising service demand based on substitution of market versus household provision of domestic services.

and laborer occupations on the other—the consequence may be a partial "hollowing out" or polarization of employment opportunities. We formalize these ideas in the model below.[35]

Linking occupational changes to job tasks

Drawing on this task-based conceptual framework, we now explore changes in occupational structure in greater detail. To make empirical progress on the analysis of job tasks, we must be able to characterize the "task content" of jobs. In their original study of the relationship between technological change and job tasks, ALM used the US Department of Labor's *Dictionary of Occupational Titles* (DOT) to impute to workers the task measures associated with their occupations. This imputation approach has the virtue of distilling the several hundred occupational titles found in conventional data sources into a relatively small number of task dimensions. A drawback, however, is that both the DOT, and its successor, the Occupational Information Network (O★NET), contain numerous potential task scales, and it is rarely obvious which measure (if any) best represents a given task construct. Indeed, the DOT contains 44 separate scales, and the O★NET contains 400, which exceeds the number of unique Census occupation codes found in the CPS, Census, and ACS data sets.[36]

To skirt these limitations and maximize transparency in this chapter, we proxy for job tasks here by directly working with Census and CPS occupational categories rather than imputing task data to these categories. To keep categories manageable and self-explanatory, we use broad occupational groupings, either at the level of the ten categories as in Fig. 12—ranging from Managers to Personal Care workers—or even more broadly, at the level of the four clusters that are suggested by the figure: (1) managerial, professional and technical occupations; (2) sales, clerical and administrative support occupations; (3) production, craft, repair, and operative occupations; and (4) service occupations. Though these categories are coarse, we believe they map logically into the broad task clusters identified by the conceptual framework. Broadly speaking, managerial, professional, and technical occupations are specialized in abstract, non-routine cognitive tasks; clerical, administrative and sales occupations are specialized in routine cognitive tasks; production and operative occupations are specialized in routine manual tasks; and service occupations are specialized in non-routine manual tasks.

---

[35] The literature studying the relationship between technological change, job tasks, skill demands, employment polarization, and wage structure shifts is young but expanding rapidly. In addition to the papers cited above, see especially Spitz-Oener (2006), Antonczyk et al. (2009), Dustmann et al. (2009), Firpo et al. (2009), Ikenaga (2009), Michaels et al. (2009), Black and Spitz-Oener (2010), and Ikenaga and Kambayashi (2010).

[36] By contrast, task measures collected at the level of the individual worker offer much additional insight. Such measures are available in the German IAB/BIBB survey used by DiNardo and Pischke (1997), Spitz-Oener (2006), Dustmann et al. (2009), and Gathmann and Schönberg (2010) among others. Autor and Handel (2009) also use individual task measures collected by the PDII survey instrument and demonstrate that these measures offer substantial additional explanatory power for wages relative to occupation level data from O★NET.

Before turning to the occupational analysis, we use data from both the DOT and O★NET to verify that our heuristic characterization of the major task differences across these broad occupational groups is supported. The task measures from the DOT, presented in Tables 5a and 5b, were constructed by ALM (2003) and have subsequently been widely used in the literature.[37] The companion set of O★NET task measures in the table are new to this chapter. Since the O★NET is the successor data source to the DOT, the O★NET based measures are potentially preferable. However, the O★NET's large set of loosely defined and weakly differentiated scales present challenges for researchers.[38]

Consistent with expectations, Table 5a shows that the intensity of use of non-routine cognitive ("abstract") tasks is highest in professional, technical and managerial occupations, and lowest in service and laborer occupations. To interpret the magnitudes of these differences, note that all task measures in Tables 5a and 5b are standardized to have a mean of zero and a cross-occupation standard deviation of one in 1980 across the 318 consistently coded occupations used in our classification.[39] Thus, the means of −0.67 and 1.22, respectively, for service occupations and professional, managerial and technical occupations indicate approximately a two standard deviation (−0.67 − 1.22 ≃ 2) average gap in abstract task intensity between these occupational groups. The subsequent two rows of the table present a set of O★NET-based measures of abstract task input. Our O★NET task measures also make a further distinction between non-routine cognitive analytic tasks (e.g., mathematics and formal reasoning) and non-routine cognitive interpersonal and managerial tasks. The qualitative pattern of task intensity across the occupation groups is comparable for the two measures and also similar to the DOT non-routine cognitive (abstract) task measure.

The next three rows of the table present measures of routine task intensity. Distinct from abstract tasks, routine task intensity is non-monotone in occupational "skill" level, with the highest levels of routine-intensity found in clerical/sales occupations and production/operative occupations. Using the O★NET, we make a further distinction

---

[37] The ALM DOT task measures were subsequently used by Autor et al. (2006, 2008), Goos and Manning (2007), Peri and Sparber (2008), Goos et al. (2010), and Autor and Dorn (2009, 2010). Many additional details of the construction of the DOT task measures are found in ALM (2003) and Autor et al. (2008). Borghans et al. (2008) also use task measures from the DOT, some of which overlap ALM and others of which do not.

[38] We employ a sparse set of O★NET scales that, in our view, most closely accord with the task constructs identified by the conceptual model (see the Data Appendix). Firpo et al. (2009), and Goos et al. (2009) use O★NET task measures to construct measures of routine and abstract tasks, as well as offshorability. The set of tasks used by both papers is highly inclusive, and in our view creates substantial overlap among categories. For example, several task measures used in the offshorability index created by Firpo et al. (2009) are also logical candidates for inclusion in the routine category (e.g., controlling machines or processes); and several of the items used as indices of non-offshorability are also logical candidates for the abstract/non-routine cognitive category (e.g., thinking creatively). Our offshorability measure starts from the construct created by Firpo et al. (2009), but drops nine of its 16 O★NET scales that may substantially overlap the routine and, more significantly, non-routine cognitive categories. The Data Appendix provides further details on our measures.

[39] The statistics in the table are employment-weighted means and standard deviations across the detailed occupations within each larger category. The count of detailed occupations in each category is provided in the table.

between routine cognitive and routine manual tasks. Logically, routine cognitive tasks are most intensively used in clerical and sales occupations and routine manual tasks are most prevalent in production and operative positions. Finally, non-routine manual tasks—those requiring flexibility and physical adaptability—are most intensively used in production, operative and service positions.

Blinder (2007) and Blinder and Krueger (2008) have argued that essentially any job that does not need to be done in person (i.e., face-to-face) can ultimately be outsourced, regardless of whether its primary tasks are abstract, routine, or manual. Tables 5a and 5b also provide a measure of occupational offshorability. This measure codes the degree to which occupations require face-to-face interactions, demand on-site presence (e.g., constructing a house), or involve providing in-person care to others.[40] As with routine tasks, offshorability is highest in clerical/sales occupations. Unlike the routine measure, however, offshorability is considerably higher in professional, managerial and technical occupations than in either production/operative or in service occupations, reflecting the fact that many white-collar job tasks primarily involve generating, processing, or providing information, and so can potentially be performed from any location.

Table 5b summarizes task intensity by education group and sex. Logically, both abstract and manual tasks are monotone in educational level, the former increasing in education and the latter decreasing. Routine cognitive tasks are strongly *non-monotone* in education, however. They are used most intensively by high school and some-college workers, and are substantially higher on average among women than men (reflecting female specialization in administrative and clerical occupations). Routine manual tasks, in turn, are substantially higher among males, reflecting male specialization in blue collar production and operative occupations.

Notably, the offshorability index indicates that the jobs performed by women are on average substantially more suitable to offshoring than those performed by males. Moreover, the educational pattern of offshorability also differs by sex. High school females are most concentrated in potentially offshorable tasks, while for males, college graduates are most often found in offshorable tasks. This pattern reflects the fact that among non-college workers, females are more likely than males to hold clerical, administrative and sales occupations (which are relatively offshorable), while males are far more likely than females to hold blue collar jobs (which are relatively non-offshorable).

These patterns of specialization appear broadly consistent with our characterization of the task content of broad occupational categories: professional, managerial and technical occupations are specialized in non-routine cognitive tasks; clerical and sales occupations are specialized in routine cognitive tasks; production and operative occupations are specialized in routine manual tasks; and service occupations are specialized in non-routine manual tasks. Although all occupations combine elements from each task

---

[40] Tasks with these attributes score low on our offshorability scale.

category, and moreover, task intensity varies among detailed occupations within these broad groups (and among workers in these occupations), we suspect that these categories capture the central tendencies of the data and also provide a useful mnemonic for parsing the evolution of job task structure.

The evolution of job tasks

In Figs 13 and 14, we study the evolution of employment among these four broad task/occupation categories, starting with overall shifts in employment across occupational categories between 1959 and 2007 (Fig. 13). Most evident in this figure is the secular growth of professional, managerial, and technical occupations and the secular decline of production and operative positions. Among males, blue-collar and production and operative employment fell by nearly 20 percentage points between 1959 and 1979 (from 54.0 to 36.1 percent). The two categories that absorbed this slack are professional, managerial and technical occupations and, after 1979, service occupations. Figure 14 further shows that service occupation employment rose rapidly among males with less than a four-year college degree after 1979, and most rapidly in the current decade. In net, the share of males employed in service occupations rose by 4.4 percentage points between 1979 and 2007 while the share in professional, technical and managerial occupations rose by 5.3 percentage points (Tables 3a and 3b).

This simultaneous growth of high and low-skill occupations is particularly striking in light of the substantial increases in male educational attainment in this time interval. Indeed, the fraction of employed males who had high school or lower education fell from 57 to 42 percent between 1979 and 2007, while the fraction with at least a four-year college degree rose from 20 to 28 percent.[41] Simultaneously, the fraction of males at each education level employed in the highest occupational category (professional, managerial and technical occupations) declined while the fraction of males at each educational level in the lowest occupational category (service occupations) rose. Thus, the "polarization" of male employment occurs *despite of* rather than because of changes in male educational attainment.

Arguably, some part of the movement of high education workers into traditionally low skill jobs is arguably mechanical; as the share of workers with college education rises, it is inevitable that a subset will take traditionally non-college jobs. Nevertheless, we strongly suspect that the decline of middle skill jobs—particularly blue collar occupations—has fostered a movement of male employment in both high wage, high skill and low wage, low skill occupations. Our model below provides a formal rationale for the migration of skill groups across occupational categories in response to declining comparative advantage (e.g., due to task-replacing technologies), and makes further predictions about the extent to which these occupational movements will be primarily downward or upward.

---

[41] Males with some-college make up the residual category. These statistics are calculated using our Census and ACS data.

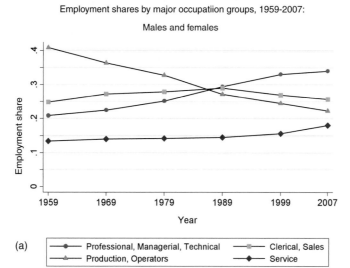

(a)

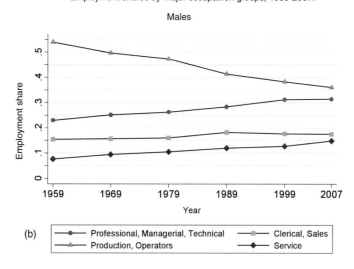

(b)

Figure 13 *Source: Census IPUMS 5 percent samples for years 1960, 1970, 1980, 1990, and 2000, and Census American Community Survey for 2008. The data include all persons aged 16-64 who reported having worked last year, excluding those employed by the military and in agricultural occupations. Occupations are first assigned to 326 occupation groups that are consistent over the given time period. All non-military, non-agricultural occupations are assigned to one of four broad occupations.*

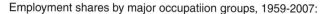

Employment shares by major occupatiion groups, 1959-2007:

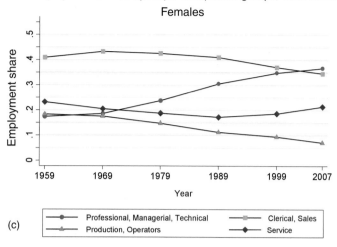

Figure 13   *(continued)*

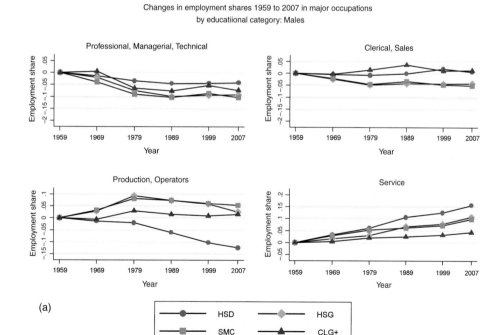

Figure 14   *Source: Census IPUMS 5 percent samples for years 1960, 1970, 1980, 1990, and 2000, and Census American Community Survey for 2008. See note to Fig. 13.*

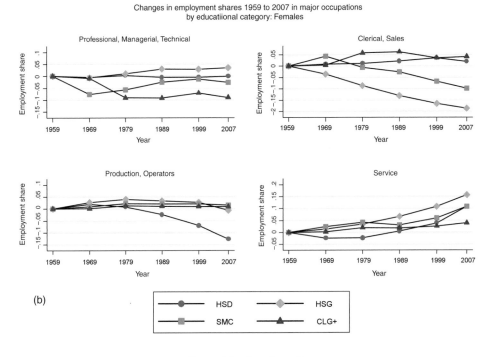

Figure 14   (continued)

The pattern of occupational polarization seen for males is equally evident for females. However, the net effect of declining middle skill employment on the female occupational distribution is distinct. Movement of females out of middle skill jobs is driven by a secular decline in female employment in production and operative positions (evident in every decade of our sample) and a sharp trend *reversal* in female employment in sales, clerical and administrative occupations—which were historically the dominant female occupational category. After hovering at 41 to 43 percent of female employment during 1959 through 1979, the share of females employed in clerical, administrative support and sales occupations fell in each of the next three decades, with a net decline of 8 percentage points.[42]

As with males, the slack at the middle was taken up by the tails. Female employment in professional, technical and managerial occupations rose in every decade of the sample, increasing by 6.4 percentage points between 1959 and 1979 and by another 13.0 percentage points between 1979 and 2007. However, female employment in low education service occupations rose rapidly starting in the 1990s. Between 1959 and 1989, the share of females employed in service occupations declined from 23.2 to 17.2 percent.

---

[42] This decline is fully accounted for by falling employment in clerical and administrative rather than sales occupations.

It then rebounded. Between 1989 and 2007, female employment in service occupations rose by 4.2 percentage points (25 percent) while female employment in clerical and administrative support occupations waned.

Thus, the polarization of employment seen in aggregate in Fig. 12 is detected for both sexes, and proximately accounted for by three factors: (1) rising employment in non-routine cognitive task-intensive professional, managerial, and technical occupations; (2) rising employment in non-routine manual task-intensive service occupations; and (3) declining employment in middle skill, routine task-intensive employment in clerical, administrative support and production occupations. Although employment in middle skill jobs has fallen by considerably more among females than males between 1979 and 2007 (15.6 versus 9.6 percentage points), the offsetting employment gains have differed sharply. For females, 85 percent of the decline in middle skill jobs was offset by a rise in professional, managerial and technical occupations. For males, this share is 55 percent, with the remaining 45 percent accruing to service occupations.

These patterns of occupational change by gender and education mirror the patterns of wage changes depicted in Fig. 4. Male wage growth was sluggish or negative after 1979 for males without at least a four-year college degree. This pattern is mirrored in the downward occupational movement of non-college males seen in Fig. 14. Conversely, real wage growth for females was modestly to strongly positive for all education groups except high school dropouts after 1979. Paralleling these wage trends, female occupational composition has shifted favorably; as middle skill occupations have contracted, females with a high school degree or greater have found employment both in low skill services and in high skill professional, managerial and technical occupations.

Cross-national evidence on employment polarization

Figures 15 and 16 explore the extent to which the contemporaneous polarization of European employment, documented in Fig. 13, has stemmed from a similar set of occupational changes. Here, we use data from Eurostat to construct non-agricultural occupational employment for ten European economies for years 1992 through 2008. The eight occupational categories provided by Eurostat are coarser than the ten broad categories used above for the US in Fig. 14, and hence we further aggregate the US data for comparison. We focus on workers under age 40, since changes in occupational composition are typically first evident among workers closer to the start of their careers (Autor and Dorn, 2009).[43]

---

[43] The Eurostat data are based on the harmonized European Labour Force survey, and are available for download at www.eurostat.org. The ten countries included in the series in the paper are Denmark, France, Germany, Greece, Ireland, Italy, the Netherlands, Portugal, Spain, and the United Kingdom. The Eurostat data include many additional EU countries, but not on a consistent basis for this full time interval. The series presented in Fig. 15 are weighted averages of occupational shares across these ten countries, where weights are proportional to the average share of EU employment in each country over the sample period. The Eurostat data for young workers include workers aged 15-39 while the US sample includes workers aged 16-39.

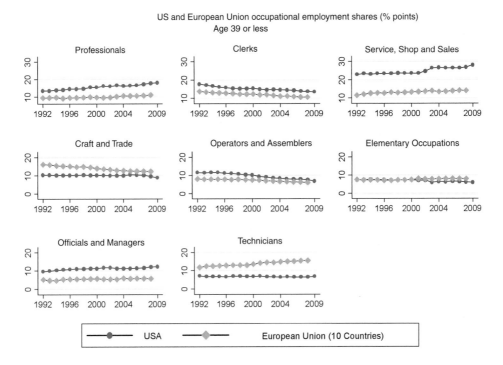

Figure 15 *Source: US data from May/ORG CPS data for earnings years 1992-2009. The data include all persons aged 16-64 who reported employment in the survey reference week, excluding those employed by the military and in agricultural occupations. Occupations are first assigned to 326 occupation groups that are consistent over the given time period. From these groups, occupations are then consolidated into the eight broad categories presented in the figure. The occupation share is the percentage of all workers employed in that occupation. European data are from Eurostat data 1992-2008. The data include all persons aged 15-59 who reported having worked in the last year, excluding family workers, those employed by the military and in agricultural occupations. Occupation shares are calculated using unweighted employment data for ten European countries: Denmark, France, Germany, Greece, Ireland, Italy, the Netherlands, Portugal, Spain, and the United Kingdom.*

Figure 15 reveals a striking commonality in employment trends in the US and EU: high education occupations (managers, professionals, and technicians) are growing; middle education occupations (clerks, crafts and trades, and operators) and assemblers are declining; and low education service occupations (which unfortunately are aggregated with sales occupations in Eurostat) are also growing. The employment-weighted correlation of US and EU changes in employment shares by occupation is 0.63.

Since the EU averages presented in Fig. 15 potentially mask considerable cross-country heterogeneity, we present in Fig. 16 individual changes in employment shares for all ten countries. We aggregate to the level of four occupational categories as in Figs 13 and 14, though there are some differences in aggregation required to accommodate

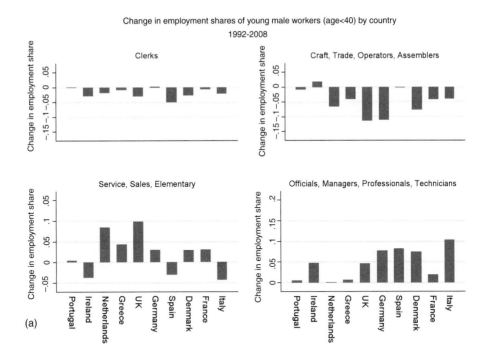

(a)

Figure 16   *Source: European data from Eurostat data 1992-2008. See note to Fig. 15. Employment shares are calculated for each of the ten European countries individually, for workers under 40 years of age.*

the categories reported by Eurostat.[44] In virtually every country, and for both sexes, we see a decline in clerical, craft, trade, and operative occupations—our two middle skill categories—and a rise in both professional, technical and managerial occupations and in service and elementary occupations. Indeed, for female workers, there are no exceptions to this pattern, while for males, only three countries (Portugal, Spain and Italy) show slight gains in skilled blue-collar employment or modest declines in service employment. Thus, the broad pattern of occupational change seen in the US appears to be pervasive among European economies, at least for the period in which comparable data are available (1992 through 2008).

Moving beyond these summary statistics, Goos et al. (2010) provide an in-depth analysis of occupational polarization in the EU and conclude that declines in routine-intensive employment (driven by technology) are by far the largest cause. Using data

[44] While our four categories above group sales occupations with clerical occupations, the Eurostat data aggregate sales with service occupations, and this aggregation carries over to our figure. Elementary occupations, as defined by Eurostat, include a mixture of service and manual labor positions. The ordering of countries in Fig. 16 follows the ordering used in Fig. 11.

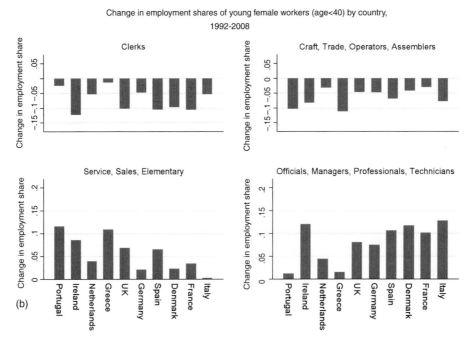

Figure 16 *(continued)*

on industry skill shares for the US, Japan, and nine EU economies between 1980 and 2004, Michaels et al. (2009) find that countries and industries (within countries) that differentially increased investment in information and communication technology raised their relative demand for high skill workers and reduced their relative demand for middle skill workers (whom the authors identify with routine-intensive occupations).

Is job polarization explained by industrial composition?

A more mundane explanation for employment polarization is not that "task demand" has changed per se, but rather that industry structure has shifted towards sectors that intrinsically use fewer "routine" occupations and more "abstract" and "manual" occupations. We test for this possibility with a standard shift-share decomposition of the form:

$$\Delta E_{jt} = \sum_{k} \Delta E_{kt}\lambda_{jk} + \sum_{j} \Delta\lambda_{jkt}E_{k}$$
$$\equiv \Delta E_{t}^{B} + \Delta E_{t}^{W}. \tag{1}$$

Here, ΔE_{jt} is the change in the overall share of employment in occupation j over time interval t, ΔE_{t}^{B} is the change in occupation j's share of employment attributable to changes in industrial composition and, conversely, ΔE_t^W is the change in occupation j's employment share attributable to within-industry shifts.[45] We implement this decomposition at the level of the 10 occupational categories used in Fig. 12 and an analogous division of industries into 11 consistent non-farm sectors.[46]

Table 6 summarizes the results. In the first set of columns, we perform the decomposition separately for each of the five decades from 1959 through 2007. In the final two columns, we compare the periods 1959-1979 and 1979-2007. This latter comparison proves particularly telling.

In both of the extended time intervals, 1959-1979 and 1979-2007, the share of employment in professional, technical and managerial occupations rose rapidly for both sexes—and particularly so for females. However, in the pre-1980 period, this rise was primarily accounted for by growth in the share of overall employment in industries that used these occupations intensively. In the latter period, three-quarters of the growth of high skill occupations reflected increased intensity of employment within rather than between industries. Similarly, the decline in clerical and sales employment was almost entirely accounted for by declining within-industry employment of workers performing these tasks. Indeed, changes in industry structure predict overall *growth* in clerical, administrative and sales occupations both before and after 1979. But in the latter period, these cross-industry shifts were more than offset by declining within-industry employment of these occupations—leading to net declines for these occupations.

The decline of blue-collar production and operative positions follows a pattern similar to clerical and administrative occupations, though here the pre/post 1979 contrast of between versus within-industry components is not quite as sharp. In the periods both before and after 1979, the share of employment in production, craft and operative occupations declined rapidly, averaging 3 to 5 percentage points per decade for males and 2 to 3 percentage points for females. Prior to 1980, approximately two-thirds of this decline was accounted for by shifts in industrial structure, with the rest explained by within-industry movements against blue-collar occupations. After 1979, the contraction of production, craft and operative occupations accelerated, but the source of this contraction moved from cross to within-sector shifts. Specifically, 70 percent of the decline among males and 35 percent of the decline among females was due to

---

[45] $\Delta E_{kt} = E_{kt_1} - E_{kt_0}$ is the change in industry k's employment share during time interval t, $E_k = \left(E_{kt_1} + E_{kt_0} \right)/2$ is the average employment share of industry k over the sample interval, $\Delta \lambda_{jkt} = \lambda_{jkt_1} - \lambda_{jkt_0}$ is the change in occupation j's share of industry k employment during time interval t, and $\lambda_{jkt} = (\lambda_{jkt_1} + \lambda_{jkt_0})/2$ is occupation j's average share of industry k employment during that time.

[46] These sectors are: extractive industries; construction; manufacturing, transportation and utilities; wholesale trade; retail trade; finance, insurance, and real estate; business services; personal services and entertainment; professional services; and public administration.

within-industry shifts, as compared to 40 percent and −15 percent for males and female respectively in the pre-1980 period.[47]

Finally, the rising share of employment in service occupations is dominated by within-industry shifts towards this occupational category. Thus, this overt manifestation of polarization is also *not* due to employment shifts towards service-occupation intensive sectors.

In net, this exercise indicates that shifts in industrial composition do not explain the observed polarization of employment across occupations. Within-industry shifts against middle skilled and favoring high and low skilled occupational categories are the primary driver, and the importance of these within-industry shifts is rising secularly.

It bears note that this exercise is performed at the level of fairly coarse industries, and it is possible that the between-industry component of occupational change would appear more pronounced if we were to disaggregate industries further. However, because our decomposition is currently performed at the level of 220 industry-occupation-gender cells, subdividing industries to a much finer degree would yield limited precision.[48]

The growing importance of occupations in wage determination

The polarization of occupational structures documented above, combined with the polarization of wage growth seen in Figs 7 through 9, jointly suggest that workers' occupational affiliations may have become a more important determinant of wages in recent decades. Intuitively, when the evolution of earnings is monotone in educational level, education itself may be a sufficient statistic for earnings. In contrast, when employment and earnings are rising more rapidly in low and high educated occupations than in middle educated occupations, it is plausible that the explanatory power of occupations for earnings may rise.

To explore this possibility, we use Census and ACS data from 1959 through 2007 to estimate a set of cross-sectional OLS regressions of log full-time, full-year weekly wages on a quartic in potential experience and four sets of control variables (included separately): (1) years of completed schooling; (2) dummy variables for highest completed educational category (less than high school, high school graduate, some college, four-year college, post-college degree); (3) dummy variables for the 10 occupational categories used above (Table 2); and (4) dummies for the 11 industry categories used in Table 6. For

---

[47] For females, this fact is partially obscured in the long change between 1979-2007 because female service employment contracted sharply in the first decade of this interval and expanded thereafter. Looking separately by decade, however, it is clear that the contraction and subsequent expansion of female employment between 1979 and 2007 are *both* due to within-industry shifts.

[48] Moreover, due to the major restructuring of the Census occupational classification scheme in 1980, we have found that it is infeasible to develop a satisfactory occupational classification scheme that is both detailed and consistent for the full 1959 through 2007 interval. Thus, while it is feasible to apply a more detailed industry scheme for the full sample, we cannot perform a parallel exercise with occupations.

Table 2 Employment and wages in ten broad occupations, 1959-2007.

	1959	1969	1979	1989	1999	2007
A. Employment shares						
Managers	8.9	8.5	9.8	11.8	14.1	14.4
Professionals	8.6	10.7	11.7	13.4	14.9	15.7
Technicians	2.2	2.6	3.1	3.6	3.6	3.5
Sales	8.3	8.3	10.0	11.9	11.3	11.4
Office and admin	15.1	18.1	17.3	16.6	15.3	14.0
Production, craft and repair	13.8	12.7	12.7	11.1	11.2	10.1
Operators, fabricators and laborers	24.7	22.6	19.2	15.6	13.0	11.9
Protective service	1.1	1.1	1.5	1.8	2.0	2.2
Food prep, buildings and grounds, cleaning	4.8	6.0	7.4	7.6	7.5	8.8
Personal care and personal services	6.7	6.6	5.0	4.9	5.9	6.8
B. 100*log weekly full-time, full-year wages relative to the 1959 mean						
Managers	47.9	67.3	60.9	67.5	80.8	88.5
Professionals	27.4	54.1	49.3	62.9	72.2	75.5
Technicians	16.5	33.5	34.3	45.6	64.3	68.5
Sales	−6.2	10.5	9.8	20.5	28.3	27.9
Office and admin	−6.5	7.6	7.1	13.8	19.3	17.5
Production, craft and repair	23.1	41.1	42.3	42.1	43.1	39.9
Operators, fabricators and laborers	−4.7	11.1	15.7	15.1	22.5	17.3
Protective service	15.3	41.4	34.3	40.6	49.1	50.3
Food prep, buildings and grounds, cleaning	−54.7	−31.5	−29.5	−23.1	−15.3	−22.0
Personal care and personal services	−76.9	−46.7	−29.2	−18.8	−5.8	−10.4

(*continued on next page*)

each set of regressors, we calculate the partial R^2 value (net of the experience quartic) in each year, and we plot these values in Fig. 17.[49]

The explanatory power of educational attainment for earnings rises sharply after 1979—approximately doubling by 2007—consistent with the rising return to skill in this period. When the linear education term is replaced with a set of five education category dummies, the dummies and linear term have comparable explanatory power for the first two decades of the sample (1959-1979). After 1979, however, the explanatory power of

---

[49] All estimates are performed using the Census/ACS data to provide the maximal time window. We use full-time, full-year log weekly earnings as our dependent variable since this variable is better measured than hourly earnings in the Census/ACS data. Models estimated using the March CPS (full-time, full-year), May/ORG CPS (all hourly earnings) and Census/ACS hourly earnings measure all produce substantively similar results.

Table 2 (continued)

	C. 100*log hourly wages (May/ORG) relative to the 1973 mean					
	1973	**1979**	**1989**	**1999**	**2007**	**2009**
Managers	36.8	33.7	39.4	49.9	58.7	60.7
Professionals	33.0	31.8	38.4	49.7	54.1	56.4
Technicians	15.3	13.7	23.9	27.7	53.6	52.5
Sales	−18.9	−17.4	−18.5	−4.2	−0.3	−1.1
Office and admin	−8.8	−9.8	−10.8	−5.8	−1.1	1.6
Production, craft and repair	21.9	21.3	14.7	19.0	18.3	21.6
Operators, fabricators and laborers	−7.5	−5.7	−16.1	−11.7	−6.1	−2.0
Protective service	8.4	5.7	3.3	13.0	25.9	23.2
Food prep, buildings and grounds, cleaning	−49.0	−49.2	−55.2	−44.8	−39.6	−38.3
Personal care and personal services	−44.1	−39.3	−43.5	−31.4	−23.7	−22.7

Source: Census IPUMS 5 percent samples for years 1960, 1970, 1980, 1990, and 2000, and Census American Community Survey for 2008. May/ORG CPS data for earnings years 1973-2009. Labor supply is calculated using all persons aged 16-64 who reported having worked at least one week in the earnings years, excluding those in the military and agriculture. Occupations are first assigned to 326 occupation groups that are consistent over the given time period.

the dummies rises substantially more (by approximately one-third) than does the linear term, reflecting the convexification of the return to education (Figs 5 and 6).[50]

Replacing the education measures with 10 occupation dummies produces a striking time pattern. The explanatory power of occupation reaches a nadir in 1979 and then, like the education measures, rises over the subsequent three decades. Distinct from the education measures, however, the explanatory power of the occupation variables rises less rapidly than education in the 1980s and *more rapidly* than education thereafter— overtaking education by 2007. Thus, as hypothesized, occupation appears to gain in importance over time. This is most pronounced starting in the 1990s, when the monotone growth of employment and earnings gives way to polarization.

One might ask whether this pattern of rising explanatory power is generally true across broad measures of job characteristics. As an alternative to occupation, we substitute the 11 industry dummies above in the wage regression. The explanatory power of industry is considerably lower than either education or occupation, and moreover has changed little over time. Thus, echoing the findings of the shift-share analysis above, occupation plays an increasingly important role in the evolution of employment and (here) earnings; it is not simply a proxy for either education or industry.

Although we have been using broad occupation categories as task proxies, it is informative to benchmark how well direct measures of job task content perform in capturing the changing wage relationships evidenced by Fig. 17. We perform this benchmark by

---

[50] A quadratic in years of schooling performs almost identically to the five education dummies.

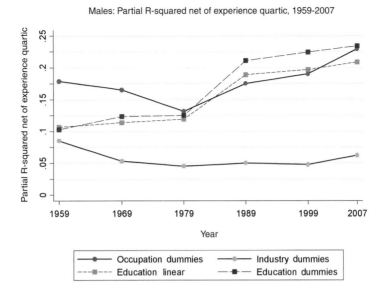

Males: Partial R-squared net of experience quartic, 1959-2007

Figure 17 *Source: Census IPUMS 5 percent samples for years 1960, 1970, 1980, 1990, and 2000, and Census American Community Survey for 2008. The data include all full-time, full-year workers aged 16-64, excluding those employed by the military and in agricultural occupations. Linear education measure is equal to years of educational attainment. For those who have not completed second grade, their years of education are imputed based on gender and ethnicity. Education dummies consist of five broad categories: high school dropouts, high school graduates, some college education, college graduates, and post-college degree. Occupations are assigned to 326 occupation groups that are consistent over the given time period. From these groups, occupations are then consolidated into ten broad categories: Managers; Professionals; Technicians; Sales; Office and administrative; Production, craft and repair; Operators, fabricators and laborers; Protective service; Food prep, buildings and grounds, cleaning; and Personal care and personal services. Industries are similarly converted from their respective scheme to a consistent set of 149 industries, as used in Autor et al. (1998). From these 149 industries, ten broad industry categories are constructed and include: Construction; Manufacturing; Transport and utilities; Wholesale trade; Retail trade; Finance, Insurance and Real Estate; Business services; Personal services and entertainment; Professional services; and Public administration. The partial R-squared values presented above are calculated as follows: Log weekly wages and each variable group above are orthogonalized using a quartic in experience and two ethnicity dummies. Using the residuals from each of these regressions, residual log weekly wages are regressed separately on the residuals from the variable groups of interest, and the R-squared value from this regression is plotted above for each year. All regressions are weighted by Census person weights.*

comparing the partial R^2 values of the task measures summarized in Tables 5a and 5b with both the education and occupation measures used above. To maintain equivalent coarseness of measurement, we assign task means at the level of the same 10 occupation categories using the three DOT and five O$\star$NET task scales from Tables 5a and 5b (excluding the offshorability index). Figure 18 plots the partial R^2 values.

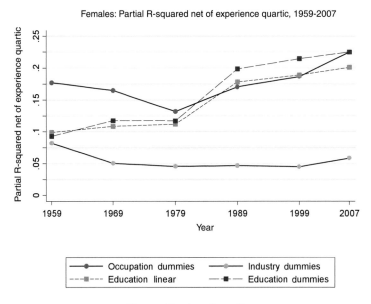

Figure 17 *(continued)*

The task measures show an even more pronounced pattern of rising explanatory power than do the occupation dummies. For males, the explanatory power of the O★NET task measures in 1979 is well below either the education or occupation dummies. But the rise in the explanatory power of the task measures is steeper than either the education or occupation measures after 1989, and it surpasses both by 2007.[51] For females, the O★NET measures also exceed the education and occupation measures in explanatory power by the end of the sample, though the nadir in 1979 is not quite as low. In all cases, the DOT task measures exhibit a similar time pattern to the O★NET measures but offer somewhat lower explanatory power.

We have excluded the offshorability measure from the prior regressions because its behavior appears distinct. In Table 7, we separately investigate the explanatory power of this measure. When entered in the wage regression with the experience quartic but no other task measures, the partial R^2 of the offshorability measure rises steeply for males after 1979 (from 0.026 in 1979 to 0.079 in 2007) but has no meaningful explanatory power or time trend for females after the first decade of the sample. What drives this difference by gender, we believe, is that the offshorability index is strongly monotone in education for males but non-monotone in education for females (Table 5b). As the return to education rose steeply between 1979 and 2007, the partial R^2 of offshorability therefore rises for males but not for females.

---

[51] Although the task measures are assigned at the level of occupation dummies, it is possible for their partial R-squared value to exceed the dummies, since the partial R-squared is calculated on the *residual* variance after the wage variable has been orthogonalized with respect to both the experience quartic and the task measures.

Males: Partial R-squared net of experience quartic, 1959-2007

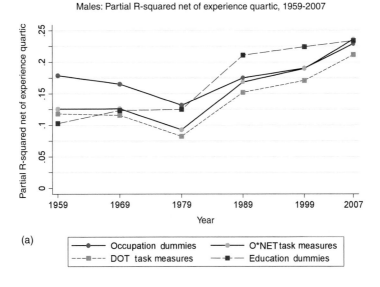

(a)

Females: Partial R-squared net of experience quartic, 1959-2007

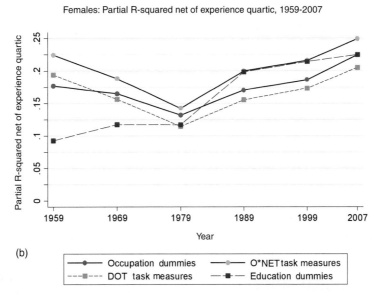

(b)

Figure 18 *Source: Census IPUMS 5 percent samples for years 1960, 1970, 1980, 1990, and 2000, and Census American Community Survey for 2008. See note to Fig. 17 for the partial R-squared calculation procedure. Five O*NET constructed task measures, constructed from a combination of O*NET activities and context scores, are utilized: routine cognitive, routine manual, non-routine cognitive analytic, non-routine manual, and non-routine interpersonal. Three DOT task measures are utilized, as in Autor et al. (2003): abstract, routine, and manual. See the Data Appendix for more information on the construction of the O*NET task measures.*

Table 3a Employment shares in four broad occupational categories (%), 1959-2007.

	1959	1969	1979	1989	1999	2007
All						
Professional, Managerial, Technical	20.9	22.4	25.1	29.4	33.0	34.0
Clerical, Sales	24.9	27.2	27.9	29.0	26.9	25.7
Production, Operators	40.8	36.3	32.8	27.1	24.5	22.3
Service	13.4	14.0	14.2	14.5	15.6	18.0
Males						
Professional, Managerial, Technical	22.9	25.2	26.2	28.4	31.3	31.5
Clerical, Sales	15.4	15.7	16.0	18.2	17.7	17.6
Production, Operators	54.0	49.7	47.3	41.4	38.3	36.1
Service	7.7	9.4	10.5	12.0	12.8	14.9
Females						
Professional, Managerial, Technical	17.4	18.6	23.8	30.5	34.9	36.8
Clerical, Sales	41.0	43.3	42.6	41.0	37.1	34.6
Production, Operators	18.4	17.6	14.8	11.2	9.4	7.1
Service	23.2	20.5	18.8	17.2	18.6	21.4

Source: Census IPUMS 5 percent samples for years 1960, 1970, 1980, 1990, and 2000, and Census American Community Survey for 2008. See note to Fig. 13.

To assess the marginal explanatory power of the offshorability measure, Table 7 reports both the partial R^2 values of the DOT and O⋆NET task measures entered separately and the partial R^2 values of the cluster of offshorability *and* task measures. The offshorability measure does not add meaningfully to the explanatory power of the task measures. This result is in line with other recent work that compares the explanatory power of offshoring versus other job task measures (e.g., most importantly, routine task content) in explaining cross-region, cross-industry and cross-national trends in employment and wage polarization (Firpo et al., 2009; Michaels et al., 2009; Autor and Dorn, 2010; Goos et al., 2010). A general finding of this set of papers is that offshorability plays a comparatively small or negligible explanatory role when considered alongside other potential causes. We caution, however, that measures of both job tasks and offshorability are highly imperfect and differ substantively across studies. The conclusions drawn at this stage of the literature should therefore be viewed as provisional.[52]

3. THE CANONICAL MODEL

Most economic analyses of changes in wage structure and skill differentials build on the ideas proposed in Tinbergen (1974, 1975) and developed in Welch (1973), Katz

[52] Firpo et al. (2009) find a significant role for offshorability in explaining wage polarization, though this effect is smaller than the estimated technology effect. Papers by Blinder (2007), Jensen et al. (2005); Jensen and Kletzer (forthcoming), and Blinder and Krueger (2008) develop innovative measures of offshorability. The efficacy of these measures relative to other task scales in predicting patterns of wage and employment polarization awaits testing.

Table 3b Mean log full-time, full-year weekly and all hourly earnings in four broad occupation categories, 1959-2007 (Census) and 1973-2009 (May/ORG).

	A. 100 × Log weekly full-time, full-year wages relative to 1959 mean					
	1959	**1969**	**1979**	**1989**	**1999**	**2007**
All						
Professional, Managerial, Technical	34.1	56.3	51.7	62.4	75.0	80.1
Clerical, Sales	−6.4	8.4	8.0	16.4	22.9	21.9
Production, Operators	5.4	22.3	25.7	25.6	31.6	27.2
Service	−58.7	−30.7	−22.2	−13.3	−3.0	−8.3
Males						
Professional, Managerial, Technical	31.4	53.4	53.1	62.8	73.4	78.1
Clerical, Sales	1.1	23.3	22.7	25.0	24.9	21.2
Production, Operators	−7.0	12.3	16.9	14.7	19.2	13.3
Service	−34.7	−13.7	−16.8	−15.0	−6.7	−13.6
Females						
Professional, Managerial, Technical	34.5	61.7	63.2	80.6	95.7	102.1
Clerical, Sales	10.8	25.9	30.5	40.4	49.3	49.0
Production, Operators	2.7	17.3	24.1	30.7	40.9	37.3
Service	−50.6	−20.2	−2.2	9.3	21.5	17.3

	B. 100*Log hourly wages relative to 1973 mean					
	1973	**1979**	**1989**	**1999**	**2007**	**2009**
All						
Professional, Managerial, Technical	32.8	30.6	37.0	47.4	56.0	57.8
Clerical, Sales	−11.6	−11.9	−13.8	−5.1	−0.8	0.5
Production, Operators	3.0	4.4	−3.8	0.7	5.4	8.9
Service	−40.5	−39.4	−43.7	−32.4	−24.9	−24.3
Males						
Professional, Managerial, Technical	16.0	12.1	12.3	17.2	26.4	28.7
Clerical, Sales	−6.8	−6.9	−12.4	−11.0	−8.6	−9.6
Production, Operators	−5.9	−0.8	−13.7	−7.9	−7.0	−8.8
Service	−28.6	−31.8	−36.3	−32.3	−22.7	−23.9
Females						
Professional, Managerial, Technical	30.2	28.4	32.7	41.4	50.9	51.5
Clerical, Sales	−3.0	2.9	3.9	13.2	17.0	16.2
Production, Operators	−4.4	2.4	−1.4	9.5	12.9	20.7
Service	−19.9	−11.4	−12.8	−6.0	7.9	6.4

Source: Census IPUMS 5 percent samples for years 1960, 1970, 1980, 1990, and 2000, and Census American Community Survey for 2008. May/ORG CPS data for earnings years 1973-2009. See note to Fig. 13.

and Murphy (1992), and Card and Lemieux (2001a,b), among many others. In this approach, the college/high school log wage ratio serves as a summary index of the premium that high skill workers command relative to low skill workers, and this premium is determined by the relative supply and relative demand for skills. The relative demand

Table 4 Education distribution by occupation and gender in 1979 (Census data).

	< High school	High school	Some college	4-year college	Post-college
A. Ten occupations					
All					
Managers	8.5	25.2	27.9	27.3	11.1
Professionals	3.1	8.5	20.7	36.6	31.1
Technicians	7.1	25.6	42.7	17.1	7.6
Sales	19.3	34.3	30.3	13.5	2.6
Office and admin	11.1	46.4	33.1	7.7	1.7
Production, craft and repair	31.2	43.5	20.1	4.2	1.0
Operators, fabricators and laborers	42.3	40.3	15.0	1.9	0.5
Protective service	17.6	34.0	37.0	9.1	2.3
Food prep, buildings and grounds, cleaning	45.0	30.5	21.2	2.5	0.7
Personal care and personal services	35.4	36.3	23.2	4.0	1.2
B. Four occupations					
All					
Professional, Managerial, Technical	5.8	17.3	26.3	30.5	20.2
Clerical, Sales	14.1	42.0	32.1	9.8	2.0
Production, Operators	37.9	41.5	17.1	2.8	0.7
Service	38.6	33.0	23.6	3.8	1.1
Males					
Professional, Managerial, Technical	5.9	15.9	24.5	29.7	24.1
Clerical, Sales	14.9	30.6	33.2	17.2	4.1
Production, Operators	36.2	41.4	18.5	3.1	0.7
Service	37.8	28.2	27.3	5.0	1.7
Females					
Professional, Managerial, Technical	5.7	19.2	28.7	31.4	14.9
Clerical, Sales	13.7	47.3	31.5	6.4	1.1
Production, Operators	44.3	42.1	11.4	1.8	0.4
Service	39.1	36.3	21.1	2.9	0.6

Source: Census IPUMS 5 percent samples for years 1960, 1970, 1980, 1990, and 2000, and Census American Community Survey for 2008. See note to Tables 3a and 3b.

for skills increases over time because changes in technology are assumed to be "skill biased," in the sense that new technologies have greater skill demands for or are more complementary to high skill workers. Since relative supply has also steadily increased over the last century and a half, both because of the greater public investments in schooling and because of greater willingness of families and individuals to acquire schooling, this leads to Tinbergen's famous race between technology and the supply of skills.

The effects of relative demand and supply on the earnings distribution is typically modeled in an environment with just two types of workers (high and low skill) and

Table 5a Means and standard deviations of DOT and O*NET task measures for four broad occupational groups in 1980 Census.

	Professional, Managerial, Technical	Clerical, Sales	Production, Operators	Service
	Males and females combined			
Non-routine cognitive				
DOT abstract (non-routine cognitive)	1.12 (0.81)	−0.27 (0.61)	−0.53 (0.68)	−0.71 (0.28)
O*NET non-routine cognitive analytic	1.19 (0.43)	−0.30 (0.69)	−0.38 (0.67)	−0.93 (0.98)
O*NET non-routine cognitive interpersonal	1.03 (0.87)	−0.34 (0.65)	−0.38 (0.82)	−0.42 (0.75)
Routine cognitive and manual				
DOT routine	−0.41 (0.91)	0.27 (1.10)	0.41 (0.84)	−0.65 (0.58)
O*NET routine cognitive	−0.23 (0.81)	0.45 (1.09)	0.19 (0.69)	−0.52 (0.91)
O*NET routine manual	−0.86 (0.57)	−0.48 (0.64)	0.98 (0.66)	0.05 (0.69)
Non-routine manual				
DOT Non-routine manual	−0.28 (0.70)	−0.77 (0.24)	0.62 (1.10)	0.40 (0.99)
O*NET Non-routine manual	−0.81 (0.55)	−0.59 (0.51)	0.95 (0.76)	0.14 (0.47)
Offshorability				
O*NET offshorability	0.24 (1.04)	0.61 (0.81)	−0.58 (0.83)	−0.35 (0.78)
# of Detailed occupations	106	51	127	34

Source: O*NET and DOT. Task measures are constructed according to the procedure in the Data Appendix.

competitive labor markets.[53] In addition, the substitution between the two types of workers is often captured using a *constant elasticity of substitution* aggregate production function. We refer to the framework with these features as the *canonical model*. In this section, we review the canonical model, explain how it provides a simple framework for interpreting several of the patterns illustrated in the previous section, and then highlight why we believe that we need to step back from or expand upon the canonical model to consider a richer framework for analyzing how the evolution of earnings and

[53] It is straightforward to extend the canonical model to include several skill groups, with each group allocated to a single occupation (or to producing a single good). Most of the features of the canonical model emphasized here continue to apply in this case, particularly when the elasticity of substitution between different groups is the same. When there are different elasticities of substitution between different factors, the implications of the canonical model become richer but also more difficult to characterize and generalize.

Table 5b Means and standard deviations of DOT and O*NET task measures by education level in 1979 Census.

	All	< High school	High school	Some college	4-year college	Post-college
A. Males						
Non-routine cognitive						
DOT abstract	0.08	−0.43	−0.18	0.15	0.84	1.01
(non-routine cognitive)	(1.05)	(0.79)	(0.91)	(1.02)	(1.02)	(0.93)
O*NET non-routine	0.09	−0.44	−0.15	0.16	0.78	1.20
cognitive analytic	(0.98)	(0.83)	(0.84)	(0.91)	(0.81)	(0.72)
O*NET non-routine	0.07	−0.34	−0.13	0.13	0.63	0.86
cognitive interpersonal	(1.03)	(0.89)	(0.96)	(1.01)	(1.00)	(0.91)
Routine cognitive and manual						
DOT routine	−0.06	0.09	0.09	−0.09	−0.36	−0.51
	(0.94)	(0.90)	(0.94)	(0.96)	(0.89)	(0.83)
O*NET routine	−0.06	0.02	0.04	−0.02	−0.22	−0.45
cognitive	(0.85)	(0.82)	(0.83)	(0.88)	(0.84)	(0.81)
O*NET routine manual	0.09	0.63	0.39	−0.06	−0.70	−0.91
	(1.03)	(0.87)	(0.95)	(0.96)	(0.77)	(0.68)
Non-routine manual						
DOT Non-routine	0.15	0.50	0.31	0.03	−0.32	−0.32
manual	(1.09)	(1.14)	(1.14)	(1.06)	(0.80)	(0.70)
O*NET Non-routine	0.21	0.72	0.52	0.09	−0.61	−0.77
manual	(1.06)	(0.92)	(0.99)	(0.99)	(0.77)	(0.69)
Offshorability						
O*NET Offshorability	−0.17	−0.40	−0.37	−0.12	0.37	0.20
	(0.99)	(0.79)	(0.94)	(1.05)	(1.00)	(0.96)
B. Females						
Non-routine cognitive						
DOT abstract	−0.19	−0.57	−0.31	−0.10	0.36	0.67
(non-routine cognitive)	(0.84)	(0.68)	(0.75)	(0.81)	(0.91)	(0.94)
O*NET non-routine	−0.12	−0.71	−0.31	0.01	0.78	1.12
cognitive analytic	(1.02)	(0.98)	(0.87)	(0.91)	(0.86)	(0.72)
O*NET non-routine	−0.06	−0.42	−0.29	0.00	0.75	1.02
cognitive interpersonal	(0.95)	(0.79)	(0.79)	(0.92)	(1.01)	(0.87)
Routine cognitive and manual						
DOT routine	0.17	0.05	0.34	0.33	−0.30	−0.64
	(1.07)	(0.96)	(1.05)	(1.09)	(1.06)	(0.87)
O*NET routine	0.25	0.11	0.42	0.41	−0.13	−0.51
cognitive	(1.02)	(0.99)	(1.01)	(0.99)	(0.99)	(0.83)

(continued on next page)

Table 5b (continued)

	All	< High school	High school	Some college	4-year college	Post-college
O★NET routine manual	−0.20	0.38	−0.12	−0.36	−0.79	−1.01
	(0.92)	(1.00)	(0.88)	(0.73)	(0.71)	(0.60)
Non-routine manual						
DOT Non-routine manual	−0.31	−0.05	−0.44	−0.40	−0.16	−0.15
	(0.76)	(0.82)	(0.71)	(0.74)	(0.77)	(0.73)
O★NET non-routine manual	−0.44	−0.03	−0.40	−0.52	−0.84	−0.98
	(0.68)	(0.63)	(0.67)	(0.60)	(0.61)	(0.58)
Offshorability						
O★NET offshorability	0.25	0.20	0.37	0.20	0.12	0.09
	(1.00)	(0.87)	(0.95)	(1.13)	(1.04)	(0.84)

Source: O★NET and DOT. Task measures are constructed according to the procedure in the Data Appendix.

employment are shaped by the interactions among worker skills, job tasks, evolving technologies, and shifting trading opportunities.

3.1. The simple theory of the canonical model

The canonical model has two skills, high and low. It draws no distinction between skills and occupations (tasks), so that high skill workers effectively work in separate occupations (perform different tasks) from low skill workers. In many empirical applications of the canonical model, it is natural to identify high skill workers with college graduates (or in different eras, with other high education groups), and low skill workers with high school graduates (or again in different eras, with those with less than high school). We will use education and skills interchangeably, but as we discuss below, the canonical model becomes more flexible if one allows heterogeneity in skills within education groups.

Critical to the two-factor model is that high and low skill workers are imperfect substitutes in production. The elasticity of substitution between these two skill types is central to understanding how changes in relative supplies affect skill premia.

Suppose that the total supply of low skill labor is L and the total supply of high skill labor is H. Naturally not all low (or high) skill workers are alike in terms of their marketable skills. As a simple way of introducing this into the canonical model, suppose that each worker is endowed with either high or low skill, but there is a distribution across workers in terms of efficiency units of these skill types. In particular, let $\mathcal{L}$ denote the set of low skill workers and $\mathcal{H}$ denote the set of high skill workers. Each low skill worker $i \in \mathcal{L}$ has l_i efficiency units of low skill labor and each high skill worker $i \in \mathcal{H}$ has h_i units of high skill labor. All workers supply their efficiency units inelastically. Thus the

Table 6 Decomposition of changes in the share of employment in four occupational categories by decade (percentage points) due to changes in industry shares and changes in occupational shares within industries, 1959-2007.

	Changes by decade					Long changes (decadal means)	
	1959-1969	1969-1979	1979-1989	1989-1999	1999-2007	1959-1979	1979-2007
A. Males							
Professional, Managerial, and Technical Occs (non-routine cognitive)							
Total Δ	2.21	1.06	2.14	2.92	0.18	1.63	2.28
Industry Δ	1.81	0.90	0.49	0.80	0.13	1.35	0.61
Occupation Δ	0.40	0.16	1.65	2.12	0.05	0.28	1.68
Clerical, Administrative, and Sales Occs (routine cognitive)							
Total Δ	0.26	0.29	2.23	−0.56	−0.07	0.28	0.95
Industry Δ	0.23	0.05	0.72	−0.16	−0.03	0.14	0.31
Occupation Δ	0.03	0.25	1.51	−0.40	−0.05	0.14	0.63
Production, Craft, Repair and Operative Occs (routine manual)							
Total Δ	−4.21	−2.41	−5.92	−3.10	−2.22	−3.31	−5.10
Industry Δ	−2.59	−1.28	−1.89	−0.70	−0.81	−1.94	−1.56
Occupation Δ	−1.62	−1.13	−4.03	−2.39	−1.41	−1.37	−3.54
Service occupations (non-routine manual)							
Total Δ	1.74	1.06	1.55	0.74	2.11	1.40	1.88
Industry Δ	0.55	0.33	0.68	0.06	0.70	0.44	0.64
Occupation Δ	1.19	0.72	0.87	0.68	1.41	0.96	1.24
B. Females							
Professional, Managerial, and Technical Occs (non-routine cognitive)							
Total Δ	1.23	5.19	6.70	4.34	1.90	3.21	5.86
Industry Δ	3.13	1.40	1.10	1.61	0.60	2.27	1.40
Occupation Δ	−1.91	3.79	5.60	2.73	1.30	0.94	4.46
Clerical, Administrative, and Sales Occs (routine cognitive)							
Total Δ	2.32	−0.73	−1.55	−3.95	−2.42	0.79	−3.18
Industry Δ	0.85	2.07	0.63	−0.55	−0.30	1.46	0.02
Occupation Δ	1.46	−2.80	−2.18	−3.40	−2.12	−0.67	−3.20
Production, Craft, Repair and Operative Occs (routine manual)							
Total Δ	−0.75	−2.79	−3.57	−1.81	−2.29	−1.77	−3.40
Industry Δ	−2.11	−1.95	−2.27	−1.36	−1.48	−2.03	−2.25
Occupation Δ	1.36	−0.83	−1.30	−0.44	−0.81	0.26	−1.15
Service occupations (non-routine manual)							
Total Δ	−2.79	−1.68	−1.59	1.41	2.81	−2.23	0.72
Industry Δ	−1.88	−1.51	0.54	0.30	1.18	−1.70	0.83
Occupation Δ	−0.91	−0.16	−2.12	1.11	1.63	−0.54	−0.11

Source: Census IPUMS 1960, 1970, 1980, 1990 and 2000, and American Community Survey 2008. Each set of three rows presents the change in the share of national employment (in percentage points) in the designated occupational category and time interval and decomposes this change into between and within-industry components. The decomposition uses 10 occupation and 11 industry groups that are harmonized for the full sample interval. See text for additional details.

Table 7 Partial R-squared values of DOT and O*NET task and offshorability measures, net of quartic in potential experience.

	Offshorability (O*NET)	O*NET Tasks (5 Vars)	O*NET Tasks + Offshorability	DOT Tasks (3 Vars)	DOT Tasks + Offshorability
A. Males					
1959	0.027	0.126	0.128	0.118	0.119
1969	0.035	0.126	0.129	0.116	0.116
1979	0.026	0.093	0.095	0.082	0.083
1989	0.055	0.168	0.172	0.152	0.152
1999	0.066	0.190	0.193	0.171	0.171
2007	0.079	0.236	0.239	0.212	0.212
B. Females					
1959	0.025	0.224	0.225	0.194	0.198
1969	0.003	0.188	0.188	0.156	0.157
1979	0.000	0.142	0.142	0.115	0.115
1989	0.001	0.200	0.202	0.155	0.162
1999	0.001	0.216	0.217	0.173	0.180
2007	0.000	0.249	0.250	0.205	0.214

Source: O*NET, DOT and Census IPUMS 5 percent samples for years 1980, 1990, and 2000, and Census American Community Survey for 2008. See note to Fig. 17.

total supply of high skill and low skill labor in the economy can be written as:

$$L = \int_{i \in \mathcal{L}} l_i \mathrm{d}i \quad \text{and} \quad H = \int_{i \in \mathcal{H}} h_i \mathrm{d}i.$$

The production function for the aggregate economy takes the following constant elasticity of substitution form

$$Y = \left[(A_L L)^{\frac{\sigma-1}{\sigma}} + (A_H H)^{\frac{\sigma-1}{\sigma}} \right]^{\frac{\sigma}{\sigma-1}}, \tag{2}$$

where $\sigma \in [0, \infty)$ is the elasticity of substitution between high skill and low skill labor, and A_L and A_H are factor-augmenting technology terms.[54]

The elasticity of substitution between high and low skill workers plays a pivotal role in interpreting the effects of different types of technological changes in this canonical model. We refer to high and low skill workers as *gross substitutes* when the elasticity of substitution $\sigma > 1$, and *gross complements* when $\sigma < 1$. Three focal cases are: (i) $\sigma \to 0$,

---

[54] This production function is typically written as $Y = [\gamma(A_L L)^{\frac{\sigma-1}{\sigma}} + (1-\gamma)(A_H H)^{\frac{\sigma-1}{\sigma}}]^{\frac{\sigma}{\sigma-1}}$, where A_L, and A_H are factor-augmenting technology terms and γ is the distribution parameter. To simplify notation, we suppress γ (i.e., set it equal to 1/2).

when high skill and low skill workers will be Leontief, and output can be produced only by using high skill and low skill workers in fixed portions; (ii) $\sigma \to \infty$ when high skill and low skill workers are perfect substitutes (and thus there is only one skill, which H and L workers possess in different quantities), and (iii) $\sigma \to 1$, when the production function tends to the Cobb–Douglas case.

In this framework, technologies are *factor-augmenting*, meaning that technological change serves to either increase the productivity of high or low skill workers (or both). This implies that there are no explicitly skill replacing technologies. Depending on the value of the elasticity of substitution, however, an increase in A_H or A_L can act either to complement or (effectively) substitute for high or low skill workers (see below). The lack of directly skill replacing technologies in the canonical model is an important reason why it does not necessarily provide an entirely satisfactory framework for understanding changes in the earnings and employment distributions over the last four decades.

The production function (2) admits three different interpretations.

1. There is only one good, and high skill and low skill workers are imperfect substitutes in the production of this good.
2. The production function (2) is also equivalent to an economy where consumers have utility function $[Y_l^{\frac{\sigma-1}{\sigma}} + Y_h^{\frac{\sigma-1}{\sigma}}]^{\frac{\sigma}{\sigma-1}}$ defined over two goods. Good Y_h is produced using only high skill workers, and Y_l is produced using only low skill workers, with production functions $Y_h = A_H H$, and $Y_l = A_L L$.
3. A mixture of the above two whereby different sectors produce goods that are imperfect substitutes, and high and low education workers are employed in both sectors.

Since labor markets are competitive, the low skill unit wage is simply given by the value of marginal product of low skill labor, which is obtained by differentiating (2) as

$$w_L = \frac{\partial Y}{\partial L} = A_L^{\frac{\sigma-1}{\sigma}} \left[A_L^{\frac{\sigma-1}{\sigma}} + A_H^{\frac{\sigma-1}{\sigma}} (H/L)^{\frac{\sigma-1}{\sigma}} \right]^{\frac{1}{\sigma-1}}. \tag{3}$$

Given this unit wage, the earnings of worker $i \in \mathcal{L}$ is simply

$$W_i = w_L l_i.$$

There are two important implications of Eq. (3):

1. $\partial w_L / \partial H/L > 0$, that is, as the fraction of high skill workers in the labor force increases, the low skill wage should increase. This is an implication of imperfect substitution between high and low skill workers. An increase in the fraction (or relative supply) of high skill workers increases the demand for the services of low skill workers, pushing up their unit wage. (Formally, high and low skill workers are q-complements.)

2. $\partial w_L / \partial A_L > 0$ and $\partial w_L / \partial A_H > 0$, that is, either kind of factor-augmenting technical change *increases* wages of low skill workers (except in the limit case where $\sigma = \infty$, the second inequality is weak). This result is intuitive but will also turn out to be important: technological improvements of any sort will lead to higher wages for both skill groups in the canonical model (also following from q-complementary). Thus unless there is "technical regress," the canonical model cannot account for declining (real) wages of a factor whose supply is not shifting outward.

Similarly, the high skill unit wage is

$$ w_H = \frac{\partial Y}{\partial H} = A_H^{\frac{\sigma-1}{\sigma}} \left[A_L^{\frac{\sigma-1}{\sigma}} (H/L)^{-\frac{\sigma-1}{\sigma}} + A_H^{\frac{\sigma-1}{\sigma}} \right]^{\frac{1}{\sigma-1}}. \tag{4} $$

We again have similar comparative statics. First, $\partial w_H / \partial H/L < 0$, so that when high skill workers become more abundant, their wages should fall. Second, $\partial w_H / \partial A_L > 0$ and $\partial w_H / \partial A_H > 0$, so that technological progress of any kind increases high skill (as well as low skill) wages. Also similarly, the earnings of worker $i \in \mathcal{H}$ is simply

$$ W_i = w_L h_i. $$

It can also be verified that an increase in either A_L or A_H (and also an increase in H/L) will raise average wages in this model (see Acemoglu, 2002a).

Combining (3) and (4), the skill premium—the unit high skill wage divided by the unit low skill wage—is

$$ \omega = \frac{w_H}{w_L} = \left(\frac{A_H}{A_L} \right)^{\frac{\sigma-1}{\sigma}} \left(\frac{H}{L} \right)^{-\frac{1}{\sigma}}. \tag{5} $$

Equation (5) can be rewritten in a more convenient form by taking logs,

$$ \ln \omega = \frac{\sigma - 1}{\sigma} \ln \left(\frac{A_H}{A_L} \right) - \frac{1}{\sigma} \ln \left(\frac{H}{L} \right). \tag{6} $$

The log skill premium, $\ln \omega$, is important in part because it is a key market outcome, reflecting the price of skills in the labor market, and it has been a central object of study in the empirical literature on the changes in the earnings distribution. Equation (6) shows that there is a simple log linear relationship between the skill premium and the relative supply of skills as measured by H/L. Equivalently, Eq. (6) implies:

$$ \frac{\partial \ln \omega}{\partial \ln H/L} = -\frac{1}{\sigma} < 0. \tag{7} $$

This relationship corresponds to the second of the two forces in Tinbergen's race (the first being technology, the second being the supply of skills): for a *given skill bias of technology,* captured here by A_H/A_L, an increase in the relative supply of skills reduces the skill premium with an elasticity of $1/\sigma$. Intuitively, an increase in H/L creates two different types of substitution. First, if high and low skill workers are producing different goods, the increase in high skill workers will raise output of the high skill intensive good, leading to a substitution towards the high skill good in consumption. This substitution hurts the relative earnings of high skill workers since it reduces the relative marginal utility of consumption, and hence the real price, of the high skill good. Second, when high and low skill workers are producing the same good but performing different functions, an increase in the number of high skill workers will necessitate a substitution of high skill workers for the functions previously performed by low skill workers.[55] The downward sloping relationship between relative supply and the skill premium implies that if technology, in particular A_H/A_L, had remained roughly constant over recent decades, the remarkable increase in the supply of skills shown in Fig. 1 would have led to a significant decline in the skill premium. The lack of such a decline is a key reason why economists believe that the first force in Tinbergen's race—changes in technology increasing the demand for skills—must have also been important throughout the 20th century (cf. Goldin and Katz (2008)).

More formally, differentiating (6) with respect to A_H/A_L yields:

$$\frac{\partial \ln \omega}{\partial \ln(A_H/A_L)} = \frac{\sigma - 1}{\sigma}. \tag{8}$$

Equation (8) implies that if $\sigma > 1$, then relative improvements in the high skill augmenting technology (i.e., in A_H/A_L) increase the skill premium. This can be seen as a shift out of the relative demand curve for skills. The converse is obtained when $\sigma < 1$: that is, when $\sigma < 1$, an improvement in the productivity of high skill workers, A_H, relative to the productivity of low skill workers, A_L, shifts the relative demand curve inward and reduces the skill premium. This case appears paradoxical at first, but is in fact quite intuitive. Consider, for example, how factor-augmenting technology change affects the wages of the augmented factor when the production function is Leontief (fixed proportions). In this case, as A_H increases, high skill workers become more productive, and hence the demand for low skill workers increases by more than the demand for high skill workers. Effectively, the increase in A_H creates "excess supply" of high skill workers given the number of low skill workers, which depresses the high skill relative wage.

---

[55] In this interpretation, we can think of some of the "tasks" previously performed by high skill workers now being performed by low skill workers. Nevertheless, this is simply an interpretation, since in this model, there are no tasks and no endogenous assignment of tasks to workers. One could alternatively say that the H and L tasks are imperfect substitutes, and hence an increase in the relative supply of H labor means that the H task is used more intensively but less productively at the margin.

This observation raises an important caveat. It is tempting to interpret improvements in technologies used by high skill workers, A_H, as "skill biased". However, when the elasticity of substitution is less than 1, it will be advances in technologies used with low skill workers, A_L, that increase the relative productivity and wages of high skill workers, and an increase in A_H relative to A_L will be "skill replacing". Nevertheless, the conventional wisdom is that the skill premium increases when high skill workers become relatively more—not relatively less—productive, which is consistent with $\sigma > 1$.[56]

While the case of $\sigma < 1$ is interesting (and potentially relevant when we think of different factors of production), in the context of the substitution between college and non-college workers, a relatively high elasticity of substitution is both plausible and consistent with several studies. Most estimates put σ in this context to be somewhere between 1.4 and 2 (Johnson, 1970; Freeman, 1986; Heckman et al., 1998). In this light, in what follows we assume that $\sigma > 1$.

3.2. Bringing Tinbergen's education race to the data

The key equation of the canonical model, (6), links the skill premium to the relative supply of skills, H/L, and to the relative technology term, A_H/A_L. This last term is not directly observed. Nevertheless, we can make considerable empirical progress by taking a specific form of Tinbergen's hypothesis, and assuming that there is a log linear increase in the demand for skills over time coming from technology, captured in the following equation:

$$\ln\left(\frac{A_{H,t}}{A_{L,t}}\right) = \gamma_0 + \gamma_1 t, \tag{9}$$

where t is calendar time and variables written with t subscript refer to these variables at time t. Substituting this equation into (6), we obtain:

$$\ln \omega_t = \frac{\sigma - 1}{\sigma}\gamma_0 + \frac{\sigma - 1}{\sigma}\gamma_1 t - \frac{1}{\sigma}\ln\left(\frac{H_t}{L_t}\right). \tag{10}$$

Equation (10) implies that "technological developments" take place at a constant rate, while the supply of skilled workers may grow at varying rates at different points in time. Therefore, changes in the skill premium will occur when the growth rate of the supply of skills differs from the pace of technological progress. In particular, when H/L grows faster than the rate of skill biased technical change, $(\sigma - 1)\gamma_1$, the skill premium will fall. And when the supply growth falls short of this rate, the skill premium will increase. In the

---

[56] Weiss (2008) considers a model in which ongoing skilled-labor augmenting (though of course not *skill biased*) technical change first raises then lowers the relative wage of skilled labor. Autor and Dorn (2010) also consider a setting where this can occur if the goods produced by high and low skill workers are gross complements.

next subsection, we will see that this simple equation provides considerable explanatory power for the evolution of the skill premium. At the same time, the limitations of the model become evident when it is confronted with a richer array of facts.

3.3. Changes in the US earnings distribution through the lens of the canonical model

We begin by replicating the seminal work of Katz and Murphy (1992), who demonstrated the power of the approach outlined above by fitting equation (10) to aggregate time-series data on college/high school relative wages and college/high school relative supplies for the years 1963 through 1987. Following their methods as closely as possible, the first column of Table 8 presents an OLS regression of the composition-adjusted college/high school log weekly wage premium (Fig. 1) on a linear time trend and our measure of college/high school log relative supply (Fig. 2) for years 1963-1987. We obtain the estimate:

$$\ln \omega_t = \text{constant} \underset{(0.005)}{+0.027 \times t} \underset{(0.128)}{-0.612 \cdot \ln\left(\frac{H_t}{L_t}\right)}.$$

As shown in Fig. 19, this simple specification performs relatively well in capturing the broad features of the evolving college premium between 1963 and 1987, most notably, the sharp reversal of the trajectory of the college premium coinciding with the deceleration in the growth of college relative supply in the late 1970s. The power of the model is underscored in Fig. 20, which plots the college premium and college relative supply measures by year, each purged of a linear time trend. The robust inverse relationship between these two series demonstrates the key role played by the decelerating supply of college workers in driving the college premium upward in recent decades.

More formally, these estimates suggest that the evolution of the college premium during the period 1963 through 1987 can be characterized by an elasticity of substitution between college graduate workers and non-college workers of about $\hat{\sigma} = 1/0.61 \approx 1.6$, and an annual increase of about 2.7 percent in the relative demand for college labor.[57]

Column 2 of Table 8 includes 21 additional years of data beyond 1987 to extend the Katz-Murphy estimate to 2008. When fit to this longer time period, the model yields a substantially higher estimate of the elasticity of substitution, $\hat{\sigma} \approx 2.9$, and a slower trend rate of demand growth (1.6 percent annually).[58] The proximate cause of this change in the model's estimated parameters can be seen in Fig. 19, which, following Autor et al. (2008), plots the out-of-sample fit of the Katz-Murphy model for the years 1987-2008. The fit of the model remains quite good through the year 1992, five years out of sample.

---

[57] Our estimates are very similar, though not identical, to those of Katz and Murphy, who find an elasticity of substitution of 1.4 and a time trend of 3.3 percent.

[58] This point is explored by Card and DiNardo (2002), Autor et al. (2008), and Goldin and Katz (2008).

Table 8 Regression models for the college/high school log wage gap, 1963-2008.

	1963-1987		1963-2008		
	(1)	(2)	(3)	(4)	(5)
CLG/HS relative supply	−0.612 (0.128)	−0.339 (0.043)	−0.644 (0.066)	−0.562 (0.112)	−0.556 (0.094)
Time	0.027 (0.005)	0.016 (0.001)	0.028 (0.002)	0.029 (0.006)	0.020 (0.006)
Time X post-1992			−0.010 (0.002)		
Time^2/100				−0.013 (0.006)	0.036 (0.012)
Time^3/1000					−0.007 (0.002)
Constant	−0.217 (0.134)	0.059 (0.039)	−0.254 (0.066)	−0.189 (0.122)	−0.145 (0.103)
Observations	25	46	46	46	46
R-squared	0.558	0.935	0.961	0.941	0.960

Source: March CPS data for earnings years 1963-2008. See notes to Figs 2 and 19.

But the model systematically deviates from the data thereafter, predicting a sharper rise in the college premium than actually occurs. While the observed college premium rose by 12 points between 1992 and 2008, the model predicts a rise of 25 log points. Without further refinements to the model, this discrepancy suggests that either the trend in relative demand decelerated after 1992 or the elasticity of substitution rose.

Subsequent columns of Table 8 explore this possibility by freeing up the linear time trend with somewhat richer specifications: a linear spline, allowing the time trend to deviate from its initial trajectory after 1992; a quadratic time trend; and a cubic time trend. When fit to the data, all three of these variants suggest a significant deceleration in trend relative demand takes place sometime during the 1990s. Conditional on the more flexible time trend, the elasticity of substitution in these estimates returns to the range of 1.6 to 1.8. Thus, taken at face value, this model suggests that relative demand for college workers decelerated in the 1990s, which does not accord with common intuitions regarding the nature or pace of technological changes occurring in this era. We return to this point below.

One can gain additional identification and explanatory power with this model by considering a slightly richer set of facts. As shown in Tables 1a and 1b, changes in the college/high school wage gap have differed substantially by age/experience groups over recent decades. This pattern may be seen through a comparison of the college premium

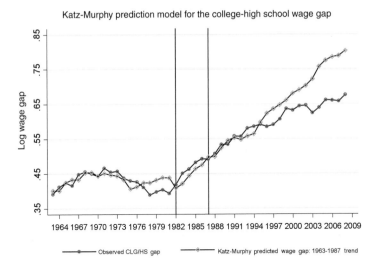

Figure 19   *Source: March CPS data for earnings years 1963-2008. Log weekly wages for full-time, full-year workers are regressed separately by sex in each year on four education dummies (high school dropout, some college, college graduate, greater than college), a quartic in experience, interactions of the education dummies and experience quartic, and two race categories (black, non-white other). The composition-adjusted mean log wage is the predicted log wage evaluated for whites at the relevant experience level (5, 15, 25, 35, 45 years) and relevant education level (high school dropout, high school graduate, some college, college graduate, greater than college). The mean log wage for college and high school is the weighted average of the relevant composition adjusted cells using a fixed set of weights equal to the average employment share of each sex by experience group. The ratio of mean log wages for college and high school graduates for each year is plotted. See the Data Appendix for more details on the treatment of March CPS data. The Katz-Murphy predicted wage gap series contains the predicted values from a regression of the college/high school wage gap on time trend term and log labor supply, as measured in efficiency units described in the note to Fig. 2, for years 1963-1987.*

for younger workers (those with 0-9 years of potential experience) and older workers (those with 20-29 years of potential experience). Figure 21 shows that the rapid rise in the college/high school gap during the 1980s was concentrated among less experienced workers. Conversely, from the mid-1990s forward, the rise in the college/high school premium was greater among experienced workers.

These facts may better accord with a simple extension to the canonical model. To the extent that workers with similar education but different ages or experience levels are imperfect substitutes in production, one would expect age-group or cohort-specific relative skill supplies—as well as aggregate relative skill supplies—to affect the evolution of the college/high school premium by age or experience, as emphasized by Card and Lemieux (2001b). Consistent with this view, Fig. 3 (presented in Section 2) shows a rapid deceleration in relative college supply among younger workers in the mid to late 1970s, several years after the end of the Vietnam war reduced male college enrollment.

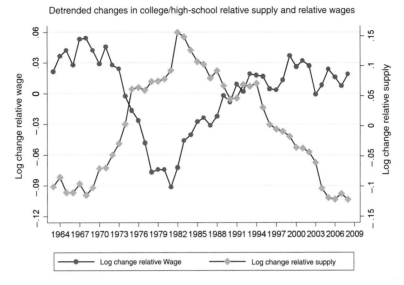

Detrended changes in college/high-school relative supply and relative wages

Figure 20 *Source: March CPS data for earnings years 1963-2008. See note to Fig. 19. The detrended supply and wage series are the residuals from separate OLS regressions of the relative supply and relative wage measures on a constant and a linear time trend.*

Two decades later (circa 1995), this kink in the relative supply schedule generates a sharp deceleration in the availability of experienced college workers. Notably, the differential rises in the college premium for young and (later) for experienced workers roughly coincide with the differential slowdown in college supply among these experience groups (though these slowdowns are 20 years apart). This pattern offers a prima facie case that the college premium for an experience group depends on its own-group relative supply as well as the overall supply of college relative to high school graduates.

We take fuller account of these differing trends by experience group in Table 9 by estimating regression models for the college wage by experience group. These extend the basic specification in Eq. (10) to include own experience group relative skill supplies. The first column of Table 10 presents a regression pooled across 4 potential experience groups (those with 0-9, 10-19, 20-29, and 30-39 years of experience), allowing for group-specific intercepts but constraining the other coefficients to be the same for all experience groups. Specifically, we estimate:

$$\ln \omega_{jt} = \beta_0 + \beta_1 \left[\ln \left(\frac{H_{jt}}{L_{jt}} \right) - \ln \left(\frac{H_t}{L_t} \right) \right] + \beta_2 \ln \left(\frac{H_t}{L_t} \right)$$
$$+ \beta_3 \times t + \beta_4 \times t^2 + \delta_j + \eta_{jt},$$

where j indexes experience groups, δ_j is a set of experience group main effects,

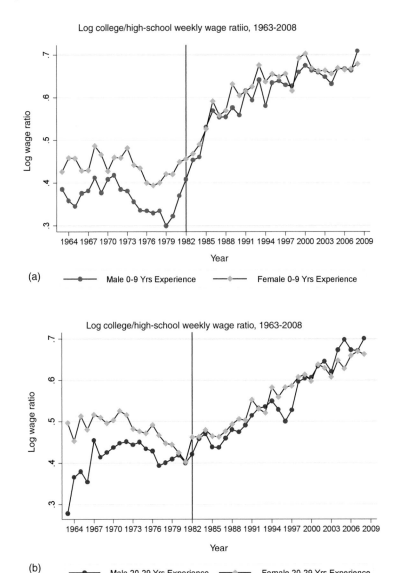

Figure 21   *Source: March CPS data for earnings years 1963-2008. See note to Fig. 19. Log college/high school weekly wage ratio for 0-9 and 20-29 years of potential experience is plotted for males and females.*

and we include a quadratic time trend. This specification arises from an aggregate constant elasticity of substitution production function in which college and high school equivalents from the aggregate inputs, similar to Eq. (2) above, where these aggregate inputs are themselves constant elasticity of substitution sub-aggregates of college and high

Table 9 Regression models for the college/high school log wage gap by potential experience group, 1963-2008.

| | Potential experience groups (years) | | | | |
	All	0-9	10-19	20-29	30-39
Own minus aggregate supply	−0.272 (0.025)	−0.441 (0.136)	−0.349 (0.095)	0.109 (0.079)	−0.085 (0.099)
Aggregate supply	−0.553 (0.082)	−0.668 (0.209)	−0.428 (0.142)	−0.343 (0.138)	−0.407 (0.141)
Time	0.027 (0.004)	0.035 (0.011)	0.016 (0.008)	0.015 (0.007)	0.020 (0.008)
Time^2/100	−0.010 (0.004)	−0.023 (0.011)	0.007 (0.008)	0.001 (0.007)	−0.008 (0.009)
Constant	−0.056 (0.085)	−0.118 (0.212)	0.120 (0.169)	0.138 (0.145)	0.018 (0.144)
Observations	184	46	46	46	46
R-squared	0.885	0.885	0.959	0.929	0.771

Source: March CPS data for earnings years 1963-2008. See notes to Figs 2 and 19.

school labor by experience group (Card and Lemieux, 2001b). Under these assumptions, $1/\beta_2$ provides an estimate of σ, the aggregate elasticity of substitution, and $1/\beta_1$ provides an estimate of σ_j, the partial elasticity of substitution between different experience groups within the same education group.

The estimates in the first column of Table 9 indicate a substantial effect of both own-group and aggregate supplies on the evolution of the college wage premium by experience group. While the implied estimate of the aggregate elasticity of substitution in this model is similar to the aggregate models in Table 8, the implied value of the partial elasticity of substitution between experience groups is around 3.7 (which is somewhat smaller than the estimates in Card and Lemieux (2001b)). This model indicates that differences in own-group relative college supply go some distance towards explaining variation across experience groups in the evolution of the college wage premium in recent decades.

The final four columns of Table 9 present regression models of the college wage premium estimated separately by experience group. These estimates show that trend demand changes and relative skill supplies play a large role in changes in educational differentials for younger and prime age workers. The college wage premium for workers with under 20 years of experience is quite responsive to both own group and aggregate relative skill supplies. However, aggregate supplies appear equally important for workers with 20-plus years of experience, while own-group supplies are not found to exert an independent effect.

3.4. Overall inequality in the canonical model

Our brief overview of the salient empirical patterns in the previous section highlights that there have been rich and complex changes in the overall earning distribution over the last four decades. While changes in the college premium (or more generally in the returns to different levels of schooling) have contributed to these changes in the earnings distribution, there have also been significant changes in inequality among workers with the same education—i.e., *within groups* as well as *between groups*.

The canonical model introduced above can also provide a first set of insights for thinking about within-group inequality and thus provides a framework for interpreting changes in the overall wage distribution. In particular, the model generates not only differing wages for high and low skill workers, but also wage variation among workers with a given level of observed skill. This follows from our assumption that the efficiency units of labor supplies vary across workers of each skill group.

Nevertheless, this type of within group inequality (i.e., due to cross-worker, within skill group heterogeneity in efficiency units) is invariant to skill prices and thus changes in overall inequality in this model will closely mimic changes in the skill premium. In particular, recall that all workers in the set $\mathcal{L}$ (respectively in the set $\mathcal{H}$) always face the same skill price. Therefore changes in the skill premium should have no direct effect on within group inequality. Mathematically, in this model the relative earnings of two workers in the same group, say $\mathcal{L}$, is given by

$$\frac{W_i}{W_{i'}} = \frac{w_L l_i}{w_L l_{i'}} = \frac{l_i}{l_{i'}} \quad \text{for } i, i' \in \mathcal{L}.$$

In this simple form, the canonical model can exhibit significant within group wage inequality, but inequality will be independent of the skill premium.[59]

Naturally, this feature can be changed by positing that there are increasing returns to efficiency units of skill, so when the relative demand for high skill labor increases, this increases the demand for "more skilled" college graduates by relatively more than for "less skilled" college graduates. One way to incorporate this idea is to extend the canonical model by drawing a distinction between observable groups (such as college vs. non-college) and skills. For example, we can remain fairly close to the spirit of the canonical model and continue to assume that there are only two skills, but now suppose that these skills are only imperfectly approximated by education (or experience).

Specifically, we can assume that the two observable groups are college and non-college, and a fraction ϕ_c of college graduates are high skill, while a fraction $\phi_n < \phi_c$ of non-college graduates are high skill (the remaining fractions in both groups being low skill as usual). Let us again denote the skill premium by $\omega = w_H/w_L$. This is no longer

---

[59] This invariance property applies when considering wage ratios or, equivalently, the variance of log wages. The variance of wage *levels* will positively covary with the skill premium in this model.

the college premium, i.e., the ratio of average college to non-college wages, however, since not all college workers have high skill and not all non-college workers have low skill. Given our assumption, we can compute the college premium simply as the ratio of (average) college wages, w_C, to (average) non-college wages, w_N, that is,

$$\omega^c = \frac{w_C}{w_N} = \frac{\phi_c w_H + (1 - \phi_c) w_L}{\phi_n w_H + (1 - \phi_n) w_L} = \frac{\phi_c \omega + (1 - \phi_c)}{\phi_n \omega + (1 - \phi_n)}.$$

It is straightforward to verify that, because $\phi_n < \phi_c$, this college premium is increasing in ω, so that when the true price of skill increases, the observed college premium will also rise. In addition, we can define within group inequality in this context as the ratio of the earnings of high wage college graduates (or non-college graduates) to that of low wage college graduates (or non-college graduates). Given our assumptions, we also have $\omega^{\text{within}} = \omega$ (since high wage workers in both groups earn w_H, while low wage workers earn w_L). As long as ϕ_c and ϕ_n remain constant, ω^c and ω^{within} will move together. Therefore in this extended version of the canonical model, an increase in the returns to observed skills—such as education—will also be associated with an increase in the returns to unobserved skills. Moreover, we can also think of large changes in relative supplies being associated with compositional changes, affecting ϕ_c and ϕ_n, so within group inequality can change differently than the skill premium, and thus overall inequality can exhibit more complex changes as supplies and technology evolve.[60]

This model thus provides a useful starting point for thinking about changes in within group inequality and the overall earnings distribution, and linking them both to the market price of skills. In light of this model, the increase in the overall earnings inequality starting in the late 1970s or early 1980s is intimately linked to the increase in the demand for skills, also reflected in the increase in the college premium. While this parsimonious framework is valuable for analyzing the evolution of distribution of earnings, it does not provide sufficient nuance for understanding why different parts of the earnings distribution move differently and, moreover, do so markedly during different time periods.

[60] Lemieux (2006a) shows that the rising share of the US labor force composed of prime age college graduates in the 1990s and 2000s contributed to the increase in residual (and, implicitly, overall) dispersion of earnings during these decades. Specifically, Lemieux observes that, education constant, earnings dispersion tends to be higher among more experienced workers, and this is particularly true for experienced college-educated workers. As the highly educated baby boom cohorts began to reach their prime years in the 1990s, this force increased the dispersion of wages and wage residuals. Lemieux concludes that a large share of the net rise in residual inequality between 1973 and 2006 can be explained by this compositional effect.

Autor et al. (2005, 2008) suggest caution in interpreting this result because the composition-based explanation for rising wage dispersion does not fit the asymmetric expansion of the upper tail and compression of the lower tail. The composition exercise implies that the rising share of prime age college employment during the 1990s and 2000s should have increased dispersion in the lower tail of the earnings distribution (overall and residual), whereas the opposite occurred (Fig. 8). Conversely, these compositional shifts are not predicted to raise dispersion in the upper-tail of the distribution, yet this is where the rise in dispersion was concentrated. This misalignment between facts and predictions underscores the limitations of this approach.

3.5. Endogenous changes in technology

The canonical model is most powerful as an empirical framework when skill biased technical change can be approximated by a steady process, such as the (log) linear trend posited in (9). However, the discussion in Autor et al. (1998) suggests that the pace of skill biased technical change was likely more rapid between 1970 and 1990 than between 1940 and 1970. The evidence discussed above, on the other hand, suggests that the pace of skill biased technical change slowed during the 1990s, at least viewed through the lens of the canonical model. As also discussed in Acemoglu (2002a), a relatively steady process of skill biased technical change is likely to be a particularly poor approximation when we consider the last 200 years instead of just the postwar period. For example, the available evidence suggests that the most important innovations of the nineteenth century may have replaced—rather than complemented—skilled workers (in particular artisans). The artisanal shop was replaced by the factory and later by interchangeable parts and the assembly line, and products previously manufactured by skilled artisans were subsequently produced in factories by workers with relatively few skills (see, e.g., Mokyr, 1992; James and Skinner, 1985; Goldin and Katz, 2008; Hounshell, 1985; Acemoglu, 2002a).

But once we recognize that skill biased technical change is not a steady process, it becomes more important to understand when we should expect it to be more rapid (and when we should expect it not to take place at all). The canonical model is silent on this question. Acemoglu (1998, 2002a) suggests that modeling the endogenous response of the skill bias of technology might generate richer insights. In particular, as we discuss further in Section 4.8, under relatively general conditions, models of endogenous (directed) technical change imply that technology should become more skill biased following increases in the supply of high skill workers (and conversely, less skill biased following increases in the supply of low skill workers). According to this perspective, steady skill biased technical change might be partly a response to the steady increase in the supply of skills during the past century (thus uniting the two parts of Tinbergen's race); the skill replacing technologies of the nineteenth century might be partly a response to the large increase in the supply of low skill workers in the cities; the acceleration in skill bias in the 1980s might, in part, be a response to the more rapid increase in the supply of college skills in the late 1960s and early 1970s noted in Section 2; and the deceleration of demand shifts favoring skilled workers in the 1990s might in part be a response to the deceleration in the supply of college skills during the 1980s (see again Section 2).

As we discussed above, computer technology is particularly well suited for automating routine tasks. This creates a natural tendency for the type of skill bias described by Autor et al. (2003). It does not, however, imply that the path of technical change and its bias are entirely exogenous. Exactly how computer technology is developed and how it is applied in the production process has much flexibility, and it is plausible that this will respond to profit opportunities created by different types of applications and uses.

3.6. Summary

To recap, the canonical model provides a parsimonious framework for thinking about the skill premium and the determinants of the earnings distribution. Its simplicity leads to several sharp results, including:

1. Changes in the wage structure are linked to changes in factor-augmenting technologies and relative supplies.
2. Overall inequality rises in tandem with the skill premium (as within group inequality is either invariant when the skill premium changes or co-moves with the skill premium).
3. The economy-wide average wage and the real wage of each skill group should increase over time as a result of technological progress, particularly if the supply of high skill labor is increasing.[61]
4. The rate and direction of technological change do not respond to the relative abundance or scarcity of skill groups.

Applied to the data, this simple supply-demand framework, emphasizing a secular increase in the relative demand for college workers combined with fluctuations in relative skill supplies, successfully accounts for some of the key patterns in the recent evolution of between-group inequality, including the contraction and expansion of the college/high school gap during the 1970s and 1980s and the differential rise in the college/high school gap by experience group in the 1980s and 1990s. However, the admirable parsimony of the canonical model also renders it a less than wholly satisfactory framework for interpreting several of the key trends we highlighted in the previous section.

1. It does not provide a natural reason for why certain groups of workers would experience real earnings declines, yet this phenomenon has been quite pronounced among less-educated workers, particularly less-educated males, during the last three decades.
2. It does not provide a framework for the analysis of "polarization" in the earnings distribution, which we documented earlier, and relatedly, it does not easily account for differential changes in inequality in different parts of the skill distribution during different periods (decades).
3. Because the model does not distinguish between skills and tasks (or occupations), it does not provide insights into the systematic changes observed in the composition of employment by occupation in the United States and in other advanced economies— in particular, the disproportionate growth of employment in both high education, high wage occupations and, simultaneously, low education, low wage service occupations (i.e., employment polarization).

---

[61] Wages for a skill group can of course fall if its supply becomes relatively more abundant. This is clearly not the explanation for declining wages of non-college workers, however.

4. The model is also silent on the question of why the allocation of skill groups across occupations has substantially shifted in the last two decades, with a rising share of middle educated workers employed in traditionally low education services, or why the importance of occupations as predictors of earnings may have increased over time.

5. Because it incorporates technical change in a factor-augmenting form, it does not provide a natural framework for the study of how new technologies, including computers and robotics, might substitute for or replace workers in certain occupations or tasks.

6. Because it treats technical change as exogenous, it is also silent on how technology might respond to changes in labor market conditions and in particular to changes in supplies.

7. Finally, the canonical model does not provide a framework for an analysis of how recent trends in offshoring and outsourcing may influence the labor market and the structure of inequality (beyond the standard results on the effect of trade on inequality through its factor content).

Recognizing the virtues of the canonical model, we propose a richer conceptual framework that nests the canonical model while allowing for a richer set of interactions among job tasks, technologies, trading opportunities, and skill supplies in determining the structure of wages.

4. A RICARDIAN MODEL OF THE LABOR MARKET

Many of the shortcomings of the canonical model can, we believe, be addressed by incorporating a clear distinction between workers' skills and job tasks and allowing the assignment of skills to tasks to be determined in equilibrium by labor supplies, technologies, and task demands, as suggested by Autor et al. (2003).[62] In this terminology, a task is a unit of work activity that produces output. A skill is a worker's *endowment* of capabilities for performing various tasks. This endowment is a stock, which may be either exogenously given or acquired through schooling and other investments. Workers apply their skill endowments to tasks in exchange for wages. Thus, the task-based approaches emphasize that skills are applied to tasks to produce output—skills do not directly produce output. Task models provide a natural framework for interpreting patterns related to occupations in the labor market, as documented above, since we can think of occupations

---

[62] The precedent of this approach is the assignment model, introduced in Tinbergen (1974), and further developed in Rosen (1974, 1981, 1982), Sattinger (1975, 1993), Heckman and Sedlacek (1985), Teulings (1995), Saint-Paul (2001) and Garicano (2000). The task-based approach has been used more recently in several papers studying the impact of technology and international trade on the labor market, including Feenstra and Hanson (1999), Acemoglu and Zilibotti (2001), Spitz-Oener (2006), Goos and Manning (2007), Grossman and Rossi-Hansberg (2008), Autor and Dorn (2009, 2010), Firpo et al. (2009), Acemoglu et al. (2010), Rodriguez-Clare and Ramondo (2010), and Costinot and Vogel (forthcoming).

as bundles of tasks. In this light, the canonical model may be seen as a special case of the general task-based model in which there is a one-to-one mapping between skills and tasks.[63]

The distinction between skills and tasks becomes relevant, in fact central, when workers of a given skill level can potentially perform a variety of tasks and, moreover, can change the set of tasks that they perform in response to changes in supplies or technology. Although a growing literature adopts the task-based approach to study technology and its role in the labor market, this literature has not yet developed a flexible and tractable task-based model for analyzing the interactions among skill supplies, technologies, and trade in sharping the earnings distribution.[64] The absence of such a framework has also meant that the power of this approach for providing a unified explanation for recent trends has not been fully exploited.

We believe that a useful task-based model should incorporate several features that are absent in the canonical model, while at the same time explicitly subsuming the canonical model as a special case. In particular,

1. Such a model should allow an explicit distinction between skills and tasks, and allow for general technologies in which tasks can be performed by different types of skills, by machines, or by workers in other countries ("offshored"). This will enable the model to allow for certain tasks to be become mechanized (as in Autor et al., 2003) or alternatively produced internationally.
2. To understand how different technologies may affect skill demands, earnings, and the assignment (or reassignment) of skills to tasks, it should allow for comparative advantage among workers in performing different tasks.
3. To enable a study of polarization and changes in different parts of the earnings distribution during different periods, it should incorporate at least three different skill groups.
4. As with the canonical model, the task-based approach should give rise to a well-defined set of skill demands, with downward sloping relative demand curves for skills (for a given set of technologies) and conventional substitutability and complementarity properties among skill groups.

The following sections present a succinct framework that enriches the canonical model in these three dimensions without sacrificing the underlying logic of the canonical model. This model is a generalization of Acemoglu and Zilibotti (2001) and is also

---

[63] Alternatively, the canonical model can be interpreted as an approximation whereby this assignment is fixed during the period of study.

[64] The assignment models mentioned in footnote 62 provide highly flexible task-based models, but are generally not tractable and do not offer a simple framework in which the interaction between technology and the allocation of tasks across different skills can be readily analyzed.

related to Costinot and Vogel (forthcoming).[65] The relationship between the framework here and these models will be discussed further below. Given the central role that the comparative advantage differences across different types of workers play in our model and the relationship of the model to Dornbusch et al. (1977), we refer to it as a *Ricardian model* of the labor market.[66]

4.1. Environment

We consider a static environment with a unique final good. For now, the economy is closed and there is no trade in tasks (a possibility we allow for later). The unique final good is produced by combining a continuum of tasks represented by the unit interval, [0, 1]. We simplify the analysis by assuming a Cobb-Douglas technology mapping the services of this range of tasks to the final good. In particular,

$$Y = \exp\left[\int_0^1 \ln y(i)\mathrm{d}i\right],\tag{11}$$

or equivalently, $\ln Y = \int_0^1 \ln y(i)\mathrm{d}i$, where Y denotes the output of a unique final good and we will refer to $y(i)$ as the "service" or production level of task i. We will also alternately refer to workers "performing" or producing a task. We assume that all markets are competitive. Throughout, we choose the price of the final good as the numeraire.

There are three factors of production, high, medium and low skilled workers. In addition, we will introduce capital or technology (embedded in machines) below. We first assume that there is a fixed, inelastic supply of the three types of workers, L, M and H. We return to the supply response of different types of skills to changes in technology later in this section.

---

[65] The assignment literature, and in particular the recent important paper by Costinot and Vogel (forthcoming), considers a similar model with a continuum of skills (as well as a continuum of tasks as in our framework). Under a comparative advantage (log supermodularity) assumption, which generalizes our comparative advantage assumption below, Costinot and Vogel (forthcoming) characterize the labor market equilibrium in terms of two ordinary differential equations, one determining the match between skills and tasks and the other determining the wage as a function of assignment. They show that a variety of changes in the patterns of comparative advantage will lead to unambiguous comparative static results. The framework of Costinot and Vogel (forthcoming) can thus also be used to study issues similar to those exposited below. As with other assignment models, one would need to impose additional structure on the pattern of comparative advantage to obtain sharp predictions.
Our framework is also related to growth models in which technical progress expands the range of tasks in which machines can be used instead of labor. See, for example, Champernowne (1963), Zeira (1998, 2006), Hellwig and Irmen (2001) and Acemoglu (2009). Finally, Saint-Paul (2008) provides a rich exposition of both conventional and unconventional models of technological change and considers their nuanced implications for wage levels and wage inequality.

[66] In particular, our model is isomorphic to a Ricardian trade model à la Dornbusch et al. (1977), with each skill group representing a country (i.e., a single factor, three-country model with a continuum of goods). Wilson (1980) provides a generalization of the Dornbusch, Fischer and Samuelson model to an arbitrary number of countries and more general preferences. Wilson's approach can be used to extend some of the results here to more than three skill groups and to more general preferences than those in Eq. (11).

Each task has the following production function

$$y(i) = A_L \alpha_L(i) l(i) + A_M \alpha_M(i) m(i) + A_H \alpha_H(i) h(i) + A_K \alpha_K(i) k(i), \quad (12)$$

where A terms represent factor-augmenting technology, and $\alpha_L(i)$, $\alpha_M(i)$ and $\alpha_H(i)$ are the task productivity schedules, designating the productivity of low, medium and high skill workers in different tasks. For example, $\alpha_L(i)$ is the productivity of low skill workers in task i, and $l(i)$ is the number of low skill workers allocated to task i. The remaining terms are defined analogously. Given this production function, we can think of A_L as (factor-augmenting) low skill biased technology, of A_M as medium skill biased technology, and of A_H as high skill biased technology. It is critical to observe that this production function for task services implies that each task can be performed by low, medium or high skill workers, but the *comparative advantage* of skill groups differ across tasks, as captured by the α terms. These differences in comparative advantage will play a central role in our model.

We impose the following assumption on the structure of comparative advantage throughout:

Assumption 1. $\alpha_L(i)/\alpha_M(i)$ and $\alpha_M(i)/\alpha_H(i)$ are continuously differentiable and strictly decreasing.

This assumption specifies the structure of comparative advantage in the model. It can be interpreted as stating that higher indices correspond to "more complex" tasks in which high skill workers are better than medium skill workers and medium skill workers are better than low skill workers. Though not very restrictive, this assumption ensures a particularly simple and tight characterization of equilibrium in this economy.

Factor market clearing requires

$$\int_0^1 l(i)\mathrm{d}i \leq L, \qquad \int_0^1 m(i)\mathrm{d}i \leq M \quad \text{and} \quad \int_0^1 h(i)\mathrm{d}i \leq H. \qquad (13)$$

When we introduce capital, we will assume that it is available at some constant price r.

4.2. Equilibrium without machines

An equilibrium is defined in the usual manner as an allocation in which (final good) producers maximize profits and labor markets clear. For now there is no labor supply decision on the part of the workers.

Let us first ignore capital (equivalently, $\alpha_K(\cdot) \equiv 0$). This implies that initially there are no machines that can substitute for labor in the production of specific tasks.

Allocation of skills to tasks

We first characterize the allocation of skills to tasks.

The characterization of equilibrium in this economy is simplified by the structure of comparative advantage differences in Assumption 1. In particular, there will exist some I_L and I_H such that all tasks $i < I_L$ will be performed by low skill workers, and all tasks $i > I_H$ will be performed by high skill workers. Intermediate tasks will be performed by medium skilled workers. We can think of these intermediate tasks as the routine tasks performed by workers in many production, clerical, and administrative support occupations. More formally, we have:

Lemma 1. *In any equilibrium there exist I_L and I_H such that $0 < I_L < I_H < 1$ and for any $i < I_L$, $m(i) = h(i) = 0$, for any $i \in (I_L, I_H)$, $l(i) = h(i) = 0$, and for any $i > I_H$, $l(i) = m(i) = 0$.*

The proof of this lemma follows a similar argument to a lemma presented in Acemoglu and Zilibotti (2001), extended to an environment in which there are three types of workers. Intuitively, if at given prices of three types of labor, w_L, w_M and w_H, the costs of producing a unit of services of task I_L using either low skill or medium skill workers are the same, then in view of the fact that $\alpha_L(i)/\alpha_M(i)$ is strictly decreasing (Assumption 1), it will cost strictly less to perform tasks $i < I_L$ using low skill rather than medium skill workers; and similarly, it will be strictly less costly to perform tasks $i > I_L$ using medium skill rather than low skill workers. The same argument applies to the comparison of medium and high skill workers below or above the threshold I_H. Note also that given Assumption 1, we do not need to compare the cost of producing a given task using low and high skill workers, since if the cost were the same with low and high skill workers, it would necessarily be strictly less with medium skill workers. Furthermore, because there is a positive supply of all three types of labor, the threshold tasks I_L and I_H must be both interior and different (i.e., $0 < I_L < I_H < 1$).

Lemma 1 shows that the set of tasks will be partitioned into three (convex) sets, one performed by low skill workers, one performed by medium skill workers and one performed by high skill workers. Crucially, the boundaries of these sets, I_L and I_H, are endogenous and will respond to changes in skill supplies and technology. This introduces the first type of substitution that will play an important role in our model: *the substitution of skills across tasks.* Given the types of skills supplied in the market, firms (equivalently workers) will optimally choose which tasks will be performed by which skill groups.

The law of one price for skills

Even though workers of the same skill level perform different tasks, in equilibrium they will receive the same wage—a simple "law of one price" that has to hold in any competitive equilibrium. We now derive these prices.

Let $p(i)$ denote the price of services of task i. Since we chose the final good as numeraire (setting its price to 1), we have

$$\exp\left[\int_0^1 \ln p(i)di\right] = 1.$$

In any equilibrium, all tasks employing low skill workers must pay them the same wage, w_L, since otherwise, given the competitive market assumption, no worker would supply their labor to tasks paying lower wages. Similarly, all tasks employing medium skill workers must pay a wage w_M, and all tasks employing high skill workers must pay a wage w_H. As a consequence, the value marginal product of all workers in a skill group must be the same in all the tasks that they are performing. In particular, in view of Lemma 1 and the production function (12), this implies:

$$w_L = p(i)A_L\alpha_L(i) \quad \text{for any } i < I_L.$$
$$w_M = p(i)A_M\alpha_M(i) \quad \text{for any } I_L < i < I_H.$$
$$w_H = p(i)A_H\alpha_H(i) \quad \text{for any } i > I_H.$$

This observation has a convenient implication. We must have that the price difference between any two tasks produced by the same type of worker must exactly offset the productivity difference of this type of worker in these two tasks. For example, for low skill workers we have

$$p(i)\alpha_L(i) = p(i')\alpha_L(i') \equiv P_L, \tag{14}$$

for any $i, i' < I_L$, where the last equality defines P_L as the price "index" of tasks performed by low skill workers. Note, however, that this price is endogenous not only because of the usual supply–demand reasons, but also because the set of tasks performed by low skill workers is endogenously determined. Similarly, for medium skill workers, i.e., for any $I_H > i, i' > I_L$, we have

$$p(i)\alpha_M(i) = p(i')\alpha_M(i') \equiv P_M, \tag{15}$$

and for high skill workers and any $i, i' > I_H$,

$$p(i)\alpha_H(i) = p(i')\alpha_H(i') \equiv P_H. \tag{16}$$

The Cobb-Douglas technology (the unitary elasticity of substitution between tasks) in (11) implies that "expenditure" across all tasks should be equalized, and given our choice of numeraire, this expenditure should be equal to the value of total output. More specifically, the first-order conditions for cost minimization in the production of the final good imply that $p(i)y(i) = p(i')y(i')$ for any i, i'. Alternatively, using our choice of the final good as the numeraire, we can write

$$p(i)y(i) = Y, \quad \text{for any } i \in [0, 1]. \tag{17}$$

(In particular, note that the ideal price index for the final good, P, is defined such that $y(i)/Y = p(i)/P$, and our choice of numeraire implies that $P = 1$, which gives (17)).

Now consider two tasks i, $i' < I_L$ (performed by low skill workers), then using the definition of the productivity of low skill workers in these tasks, we have

$$p(i)\alpha_L(i)\, l(i) = p(i')\alpha_L(i')l(i').$$

Therefore, for any i, $i' < I_L$, we conclude that $l(i) = l(i')$, and using the market clearing condition for low skilled workers, we must have

$$l(i) = \frac{L}{I_L} \quad \text{for any } i < I_L. \tag{18}$$

This is a very convenient implication of the Cobb-Douglas production structure. With a similar argument, we also have

$$m(i) = \frac{M}{I_H - I_L} \quad \text{for any } I_H > i > I_L. \tag{19}$$

$$h(i) = \frac{H}{1 - I_H} \quad \text{for any } i > I_H. \tag{20}$$

The above expressions are derived by comparing expenditures on tasks performed by the same type of worker. Now comparing two tasks performed by high and medium skill workers ($I_L < i < I_H < i'$), we obtain from Eq. (17) that $p(i)A_M\alpha_M(i)m(i) = p(i')A_H\alpha_H(i')h(i')$. Next using (14) and (15), we have

$$\frac{P_M A_M M}{I_H - I_L} = \frac{P_H A_H H}{1 - I_H},$$

or

$$\frac{P_H}{P_M} = \left(\frac{A_H H}{1 - I_H}\right)^{-1}\left(\frac{A_M M}{I_H - I_L}\right). \tag{21}$$

Similarly, comparing two tasks performed by medium and high skill workers, we obtain

$$\frac{P_M}{P_L} = \left(\frac{A_M M}{I_H - I_L}\right)^{-1} \left(\frac{A_L L}{I_L}\right). \tag{22}$$

No arbitrage across skills

The above derivations show that the key equilibrium objects of the model are the threshold tasks I_L and I_H. These will be determined by a type of "no arbitrage" condition equalizing the cost of producing these threshold tasks using different skills. We now derive these no arbitrage conditions and determine the threshold tasks.

Recall, in particular, that the threshold task I_H must be such that it can be profitably produced using either high skilled or medium skilled workers. This is equivalent to task I_H having the same equilibrium supply either when produced only with skilled or unskilled workers.[67] That is, it implies our first no arbitrage condition (between high and medium skills) is:

$$\frac{A_M \alpha_M (I_H) M}{I_H - I_L} = \frac{A_H \alpha_H (I_H) H}{1 - I_H}. \tag{23}$$

With an analogous argument, we obtain our second no arbitrage condition (between low and medium skills) as:

$$\frac{A_L \alpha_L (I_L) L}{I_L} = \frac{A_M \alpha_M (I_L) M}{I_H - I_L}. \tag{24}$$

Equilibrium wages and inequality

Once the threshold tasks, I_L and I_H, are determined, wage levels and earnings differences across skill groups can be found in a straightforward manner. In particular, wages are obtained simply as the values of the marginal products of different types of skills. For example, for low skill workers, this is:

$$w_L = P_L A_L. \tag{25}$$

Equally, or perhaps even more, important than the level of wages are their ratios, which inform us about the wage structure and inequality. For example, comparing high

---

[67] Alternatively, the unit cost of producing task I_H should be the same with medium and high skill workers, i.e., $A_M \alpha_M(I_H) w_M = A_H \alpha_H(I_H) w_H$. We then obtain (23) using (26). Similarly, (24) can be obtained from $A_M \alpha_M(I_L) w_M = A_L \alpha_L(I_L) w_L$ using (27).

and medium skill wages, we have

$$\frac{w_H}{w_M} = \frac{P_H A_H}{P_M A_M}.$$

A more convenient way of expressing these is to use (21) and write the relative wages simply in terms of relative supplies and the equilibrium allocation of tasks to skill groups, given by I_L and I_H. That is,

$$\frac{w_H}{w_M} = \left(\frac{1 - I_H}{I_H - I_L}\right)\left(\frac{H}{M}\right)^{-1}. \tag{26}$$

Similarly, the wage of medium relative to low skill workers is given by

$$\frac{w_M}{w_L} = \left(\frac{I_H - I_L}{I_L}\right)\left(\frac{M}{L}\right)^{-1}. \tag{27}$$

These expressions highlight the central role that allocation of tasks to skills plays in the model. Relative wages can be expressed simply as a function of relative supplies and equilibrium task assignments (in particular, the threshold tasks, I_L and I_H).

These equations, together with the choice of the numeraire, $\int_0^1 \ln p(i)\,\mathrm{d}i = 0$, fully characterize the equilibrium. In particular, using (14)–(16), we can write the last equilibrium condition as:

$$\int_0^{I_L} (\ln P_L - \ln \alpha_L(i))\,\mathrm{d}i + \int_{I_L}^{I_H} (\ln P_M - \ln \alpha_M(i))\,\mathrm{d}i$$
$$+ \int_{I_H}^1 (\ln P_H - \ln \alpha_H(i))\,\mathrm{d}i = 0. \tag{28}$$

Equations (26) and (27) give the relative wages of high to medium and medium to low skill workers. To obtain the wage *level* for any one of these three groups, we need to use the price normalization in (28) together with (21) and (22) to solve out for one of the price indices, for example, P_L, and then (25) will give w_L and the levels of w_M and w_H can be readily obtained from (26) and (27).

4.2.1. Summary of equilibrium
The next proposition summarizes our equilibrium characterization and highlights several important features of the equilibrium.

Proposition 1. *There exists a unique equilibrium summarized by* $(I_L, I_H, P_L, P_M, P_H, w_L, w_M, w_H)$ *given by Eqs* (21)–(28).

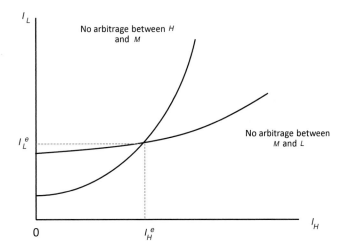

Figure 22   *Determination of equilibrium threshold tasks.*

The only part of this proposition that requires proof is the claim that equilibrium is unique (the rest of it follows from the explicit construction of the equilibrium preceding the proposition). This can be seen by noting that in fact the equilibrium is considerably easier to characterize than it first appears, because it has a block recursive structure. In particular, we can first use (23) and (24) to determine I_L and I_H. Given these we can then compute relative wages from (26) and (27). Finally, to compute wage and price levels, we can use (21), (22), (25) and (28).

Figure 22 shows a diagrammatic representation of the equilibrium, in which curves corresponding to (23) and (24) determine I_L and I_H. Both curves are upward sloping in the (I_L, I_H) space, but the first one, (23), is steeper than the second one everywhere, (24)—see below for a proof. This establishes the existence of a unique intersection between the two curves in Fig. 22, and thus there exist unique equilibrium values of I_L and I_H. Given these values, P_L, P_M, P_H, w_L, w_M and w_H are uniquely determined from (21), (22) and (25)–(28).

While Fig. 22 depicts the determination of the two thresholds, I_L and I_H, it does not illustrate the allocation of tasks to different types of skills (workers). We do this in Fig. 23, which can also be interpreted as a diagram showing "relative effective demand" and "relative effective supply". In particular, we write (23) as follows:

$$\frac{1 - I_H}{I_H - I_L} \frac{\alpha_M(I_H)}{\alpha_H(I_H)} = \frac{A_H H}{A_M M}. \tag{29}$$

The right-hand side of this equation corresponds to the relative effective supply of high to medium skills (we use the term "effective" since the supplies are multiplied by their

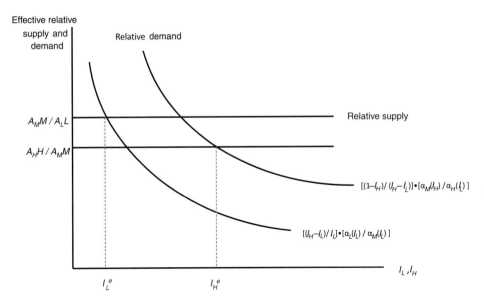

Figure 23   *Equilibrium allocation of skills to tasks.*

respective factor-augmenting technologies). The left-hand side, on the other hand, can be interpreted as the effective demand for high relative to medium skills. The left-hand side of (29) is shown as the outer curve (on the right) in Fig. 23. It is downward sloping as a function of I_H (for a given level of I_L) since $\alpha_M(I_H)/\alpha_H(I_H)$ is strictly decreasing in view of Assumption 1. Similarly, we rewrite (24) as:

$$\frac{I_H - I_L}{I_L} \frac{\alpha_L(I_H)}{\alpha_M(I_H)} = \frac{A_M M}{A_L L}$$

for given I_H, and this expression has the same relative effective demand and supply interpretation. Since $\alpha_L(I_H)/\alpha_M(I_H)$ is strictly decreasing again from Assumption 1, the left-hand side traces a downward sloping curve as a function of I_L (for given I_H) and is shown as the inner (on the left) curve in Fig. 23. Where the outer curve equals $A_H H/A_M M$, as shown on the vertical axis, gives the threshold task I_H, and where the second curve is equal to $A_M M/A_L L$ gives I_L. This picture does not determine the two thresholds simultaneously as Fig. 22 does, since the dependence of the two curves on the other threshold is left implicit. Nevertheless, Fig. 23 is helpful in visualizing the equilibrium because it shows how equilibrium tasks are partitioned between the three types of skills. We will return to this figure when conducting comparative static exercises.

4.3. Special cases

We now study some special cases that help clarify the workings of the model. Suppose first that there are no medium skill workers. Assumption 1 in this case simply implies that

$\alpha_L(i)/\alpha_H(i)$ is strictly decreasing in i. Then we are back to a two-factor world as in the canonical model.

In addition, we could assume that instead of a continuum of tasks, there are only two tasks, one in which high skill workers have a strong comparative advantage and the other one in which low skill workers have a strong comparative advantage.[68] This would be identical to the canonical model, except with a Cobb-Douglas production function (elasticity of substitution between high and low skill workers equal to one).

Another special case is found in the model studied by Acemoglu and Zilibotti (2001), who also assume that there are only two types of workers, high and low skill. In addition, Acemoglu and Zilibotti impose the following functional form on the schedule of comparative advantage schedules:

$$\alpha_L(i) = 1 - i \quad \text{and} \quad \alpha_H(i) = i. \tag{30}$$

Then an equivalent of (23) implies that all tasks below I will be performed by low skill workers and those above I will be performed by high skill workers. Moreover, exactly the same reasoning that led to the no arbitrage conditions, (23) and (24), now determines the single threshold task, I, separating tasks performed by low and high skill workers. In particular, using (30), the equivalent of (23) and (24) gives I as

$$\frac{1 - I}{I} = \left(\frac{A_H H}{A_L L}\right)^{1/2}.$$

In addition, the equivalent of (21) and (22) now gives the relative price of tasks performed by skilled compared to unskilled workers as

$$\frac{P_H}{P_L} = \left(\frac{A_H H}{A_L L}\right)^{-1/2},$$

and the equivalent of (26) and (27) gives the skill premium as

$$\frac{w_H}{w_L} = \left(\frac{A_H}{A_L}\right)^{1/2} \left(\frac{H}{L}\right)^{-1/2}.$$

Therefore, in this case the model is isomorphic to the canonical model with an elasticity of substitution equal to 2. This also shows that by choosing different forms for the comparative advantage schedules in the special case with only two types of skills,

---

[68] Or in fact, one could replicate a model with two tasks using a continuum of tasks, for example, assuming that $\alpha_L(i) = 1$ if $i \leq I$ and 0 otherwise, and $\alpha_H(i) = 0$ if $i \leq I$ and 1 otherwise (or a smooth approximation to this that would satisfy Assumption 1).

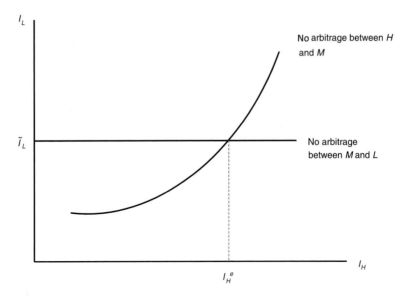

Figure 24 *Determination of threshold high skill task (I_H) with task assignment for low skilled workers fixed.*

one could obtain any elasticity of substitution, or in fact any constant returns to scale production function (with an elasticity of substitution greater than or equal to 1) as a special case of the model shown here. This is the sense in which the canonical model, and thus all of economic forces emphasized by that model, are already embedded in our more general task-based framework.

Finally, another special case is useful both to show how insights from the two–skill model continue to hold in the three–skill model and also to illustrate how technical change in this task-based model can reduce the wages of some groups. For this, let us return to our general three–skill model introduced above, but suppose that

$$\alpha_L (i) = \begin{cases} \tilde{\alpha}_L & \text{if } i \leq \tilde{I}_L \\ 0 & \text{if } i > \tilde{I}_L \end{cases} \tag{31}$$

where $\tilde{\alpha}_L$ is large and $\tilde{I}_L$ is small. While this task productivity schedule for low skill workers is neither continuous nor strictly decreasing (and thus does not satisfy Assumption 1), we can easily take a strictly decreasing continuous approximation to (31), which will lead to identical results. The implication of this task schedule is that the no arbitrage condition between low and medium skills, (24), can only be satisfied at the threshold task $I_L = \tilde{I}_L$. This fixes one of the equilibrium thresholds, while the other one, I_H, is still determined in the usual fashion from the other no arbitrage condition, (23). Figure 24 adapts Fig. 22 and shows how the determination of equilibrium task thresholds looks in this case.

This case is of interest for two reasons. First, the model is now essentially identical to the two-skill version we have just discussed, since the set of tasks performed by low skill workers is fixed by the task productivity schedule (31) (without reference to other parameters in the model). Thus the mechanics of the equilibrium are simpler. Second, in the three-skill model, as we will see further in the next subsection, a variety of changes that directly affect I_H will have an indirect impact on I_L and these tend to "soften the blow" of some of these changes on the medium skill workers. With I_L fixed at $\tilde{I}_L$, this will not be the case and thus the wage effects of certain types of technical change on medium skilled workers will be exacerbated in this case. We return to this special case again in the next subsection.

4.4. Comparative statics

The usefulness of any framework is related to the insights that it generates, which are most clearly illustrated by its comparative static results. We discuss these here.

To derive these comparative statics, we return to the general model, and take logs in Eq. (23) and (24) to obtain slightly simpler expressions, given by the following two equations:

$$\ln A_M - \ln A_H + \beta_H (I_H) + \ln M - \ln H - \ln (I_H - I_L) + \ln (1 - I_H) = 0, \quad (32)$$

and

$$\ln A_L - \ln A_M + \beta_L (I_L) + \ln L - \ln M + \ln (I_H - I_L) - \ln (I_L) = 0, \quad (33)$$

where we have defined

$$\beta_H (I) \equiv \ln \alpha_M (I) - \ln \alpha_H (I) \quad \text{and} \quad \beta_L (I) \equiv \ln \alpha_L (I) - \ln \alpha_M (I),$$

both of which are strictly decreasing in view of Assumption 1. It can be easily verified that both of these curves are upward sloping in the (I_H, I_L) space, but (32) is everywhere steeper than (33) as claimed above, which also implies that there is indeed a unique intersection between the two curves as shown in Fig. 22.

Basic comparative statics

Basic comparative statics for the allocation of tasks across different skill groups can be obtained from this figure. For example, an increase in A_H, corresponding to high skill biased technical change, shifts (32) inwards, as shown in Fig. 25, so both I_L and I_H decrease (the implications of an increase in H for task allocation, though not for wages, are identical). This is intuitive: if high skill workers become uniformly more productive because of high skill biased technical change—generating an expansion of the set of tasks in which they hold comparative advantage—then they should perform a larger range

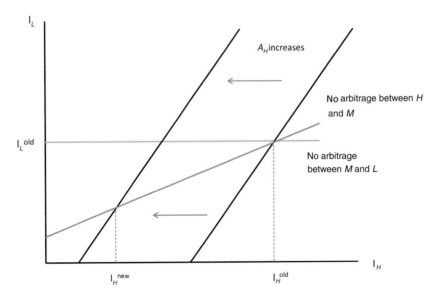

Figure 25   *Comparative statics.*

of tasks. Thus the allocation of tasks endogenously shifts away from medium to high skill workers (I_H adjusts downward). If I_L remained constant following the downward movement of I_H, this would imply from (19) an "excess" supply of medium skill workers in the remaining tasks. Therefore, the indirect effect of the increase in A_H (or H) is also to reduce I_L, thus shifting some of tasks previously performed by low skill workers to medium skill workers.

Similarly, we can analyze the implications of skill biased technical change directed towards low skill workers, i.e., an increase in A_L, (or a change in the supply of low skill workers, L), which will be to increase I_L and I_H. This has exactly the same logic (there are either more low skill workers or low skill workers are more productive, and thus they will perform more tasks, squeezing medium skill workers, who now have to shift into some of the tasks previously performed by high skill workers). The implications of an increase in A_M, i.e., medium skill biased technical change, or of an increase in M again have a similar logic, and will reduce I_L and increase I_H, thus expanding the set of tasks performed by medium skill workers at the expense of both low and high skill workers. (Formally, in this case, the curve corresponding to (32) shifts up, while that for (33) shifts down). Each of these comparative statics illustrates the substitution of skills across tasks.

It is also useful to return to Fig. 23 to visually represent changes in the task allocation resulting from an increase in A_H, and we do this in Fig. 26. Such a change shifts the outer curve in Fig. 23 downward, as shown in Fig. 26, reducing I_H. This first shift holds I_L constant. However, the inner curve in this figure also shifts, as noted above and as highlighted by Figs 22 and 24. The decline in I_H also shifts this curve down, this time

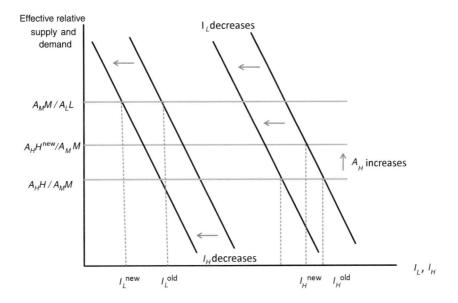

Figure 26   Changes in equilibrium allocation.

reducing I_L. Then there is a second round of adjustment as the decline in I_L shifts the outer curve further down. Ultimately, the economy reaches a new equilibrium, as shown in Fig. 26.

It is a little more difficult to visually represent the changes in the wage structure resulting from changes in technology or supplies, because these depend on how I_L changes relative to I_H. Nevertheless, obtaining these comparative static results is also straightforward. To do this, let us consider a change in A_H and let us totally differentiate (32) and (33). We thus obtain:

$$\begin{pmatrix} \beta'_H(I_H) - \dfrac{1}{I_H - I_L} - \dfrac{1}{1 - I_H} & \dfrac{1}{I_H - I_L} \\ \dfrac{1}{I_H - I_L} & \beta'_L(I_L) - \dfrac{1}{I_H - I_L} - \dfrac{1}{I_L} \end{pmatrix} \begin{pmatrix} dI_H \\ dI_L \end{pmatrix} = \begin{pmatrix} 1 \\ 0 \end{pmatrix} d\ln A_H.$$

It can be easily verified that all of the terms in the diagonals of the matrix on the left hand side are negative (again from Assumption 1). Moreover, its determinant is positive, given by

$$\Delta = \left(\beta'_H(I_H) - \frac{1}{1 - I_H} \right) \left(\beta'_L(I_L) - \frac{1}{I_L} \right)$$
$$+ \frac{1}{I_H - I_L} \left(\frac{1}{I_L} + \frac{1}{1 - I_H} - \beta'_L(I_L) - \beta'_H(I_H) \right).$$

Therefore,

$$\frac{dI_H}{d\ln A_H} = \frac{\beta_L'(I_L) - \frac{1}{I_H - I_L} - \frac{1}{I_L}}{\Delta} < 0 \quad \text{and} \quad \frac{dI_L}{d\ln A_H} = \frac{-\frac{1}{I_H - I_L}}{\Delta} < 0,$$

confirming the insights we obtained from the diagrammatic analysis. But in addition, we can also now see that

$$\frac{d(I_H - I_L)}{d\ln A_H} = \frac{\beta_L'(I_L) - \frac{1}{I_L}}{\Delta} < 0.$$

Using these expressions, we can obtain comparative statics for how relative wages by skill group change when there is high skill biased technical change. A similar exercise can be performed for low and medium skill biased technical change. The next proposition summarizes the main results.

Proposition 2. *The following comparative static results apply:*

1. *(The response of task allocation to technology and skill supplies):*

$$\frac{dI_H}{d\ln A_H} = \frac{dI_H}{d\ln H} < 0, \qquad \frac{dI_L}{d\ln A_H} = \frac{dI_L}{d\ln H} < 0$$

$$and \quad \frac{d(I_H - I_L)}{d\ln A_H} = \frac{d(I_H - I_L)}{d\ln H} < 0;$$

$$\frac{dI_H}{d\ln A_L} = \frac{dI_H}{d\ln L} > 0, \qquad \frac{dI_L}{d\ln A_L} = \frac{dI_L}{d\ln L} > 0$$

$$and \quad \frac{d(I_H - I_L)}{d\ln A_L} = \frac{d(I_H - I_L)}{d\ln L} < 0;$$

$$\frac{dI_H}{d\ln A_M} = \frac{dI_H}{d\ln M} > 0, \qquad \frac{dI_L}{d\ln A_M} = \frac{dI_L}{d\ln M} < 0$$

$$and \quad \frac{d(I_H - I_L)}{d\ln A_M} = \frac{d(I_H - I_L)}{d\ln M} > 0.$$

2. *(The response of relative wages to skill supplies):*

$$\frac{d\ln(w_H/w_L)}{d\ln H} < 0, \qquad \frac{d\ln(w_H/w_M)}{d\ln H} < 0, \qquad \frac{d\ln(w_H/w_L)}{d\ln L} > 0,$$

$$\frac{d\ln(w_M/w_L)}{d\ln L} > 0, \qquad \frac{d\ln(w_H/w_M)}{d\ln M} > 0, \quad and$$

$$\frac{d\ln(w_H/w_L)}{d\ln M} \lessgtr 0 \quad \text{if and only if} \quad |\beta_L'(I_L) I_L| \gtrless |\beta_H'(I_H)(1 - I_H)|.$$

3. *(The response of wages to factor-augmenting technologies):*

$$\frac{\mathrm{d}\ln(w_H/w_L)}{\mathrm{d}\ln A_H} > 0, \qquad \frac{\mathrm{d}\ln(w_M/w_L)}{\mathrm{d}\ln A_H} < 0, \qquad \frac{\mathrm{d}\ln(w_H/w_M)}{\mathrm{d}\ln A_H} > 0;$$

$$\frac{\mathrm{d}\ln(w_H/w_L)}{\mathrm{d}\ln A_L} < 0, \qquad \frac{\mathrm{d}\ln(w_M/w_L)}{\mathrm{d}\ln A_L} < 0, \qquad \frac{\mathrm{d}\ln(w_H/w_M)}{\mathrm{d}\ln A_L} > 0;$$

$$\frac{\mathrm{d}\ln(w_H/w_M)}{\mathrm{d}\ln A_M} < 0, \qquad \frac{\mathrm{d}\ln(w_M/w_L)}{\mathrm{d}\ln A_M} > 0, \quad and$$

$$\frac{\mathrm{d}\ln(w_H/w_L)}{\mathrm{d}\ln A_M} \lessgtr 0 \quad \text{if and only if } \left|\beta_L'(I_L)\,I_L\right| \gtrless \left|\beta_H'(I_H)(1-I_H)\right|.$$

Part 1 of this proposition follows by straightforward differentiation and manipulation of the expressions in (32) and (33) for I_L and I_H. Parts 2 and 3 then follow readily from the expressions for relative wages in (26) and (27) using the behavior of these thresholds. Here we simply give the intuition for the main results.

First, the behavior of I_L and I_H in Part 1 is intuitive as already discussed above. In particular, an increase in A_H or H expands the set of tasks performed by high skill workers and contracts the set of tasks performed by low and medium skill workers. This is equivalent to I_L decreasing and I_H increasing. An increase in A_M or M similarly expands the set of tasks performed by medium skill workers and contracts those allocated to low and high skill workers. Mathematically, this corresponds to a decline in I_L and an increase in I_H. The implications of an increase in A_L or L are analogous, and raise both I_L and I_H, expanding the set of tasks performed by low skill workers.

Second, the fact that relative demand curves are downward sloping for all factors, as claimed in Part 2, parallels the results in the canonical model (or in fact the more general results in Acemoglu (2007), for any model with constant or diminishing returns at the aggregate level). The new result here concerns the impact of an increase in M on w_H/w_L. We have seen that such an increase raises I_H and reduces I_L, expanding the set of tasks performed by medium skill workers at the expense of both low and high skill workers. This will put downward pressure on the wages of both low and high skill workers, and the impact on the relative wage, w_H/w_L, is ambiguous for reasons we will encounter again below. In particular, it will depend on the form of the comparative advantage schedules in the neighborhood of I_L and I_H. When the absolute value of $\beta_L'(I_L)$ is high (relative to $\beta_H'(I_H)$), this implies that low skill workers have a strong comparative advantage for tasks below I_L. Consequently, medium skill workers will not be displacing low skill workers much, instead having a relatively greater impact on high skill workers, and in this case w_H/w_L will decline. Conversely, when the absolute value of $\beta_L'(I_L)$ is low relative to the absolute value of $\beta_H'(I_H)$, high skill workers have a strong comparative advantage for tasks right above I_H, and medium skill tasks will expand at the expense of low skill workers relatively more, thus increasing w_H/w_L.

Third, the results summarized in Part 3 of the proposition, linking wages to technologies, are also intuitive. For example, an increase in A_H, corresponding to high skill biased technical change, increases both w_H/w_L and w_H/w_M (i.e., high skill wages rise relative to both medium skill and low skill wages) as we may have expected from the canonical model. Perhaps more interestingly, an increase in A_H also unambiguously reduces w_M/w_L despite the fact that it reduces the set of tasks performed by both medium and low skill workers. Intuitively, the first order (direct) effect of an increase in A_H is to contract the set of tasks performed by medium skill workers. The impact on low skill workers is indirect, resulting from the fact that medium skill workers become cheaper and this makes firms expand the set of tasks that these workers perform. This indirect effect never dominates the direct effect, and thus the wages of medium skill workers decrease relative to those of low skill workers when there is high skill biased technical change.

The implications of medium skill biased technical changes are distinct from the canonical case. Medium skill biased technical changes have a direct effect on both high skill and low skill workers. Consequently, the behavior of w_H/w_L is ambiguous. Similarly to how an increase in M affects w_H/w_L, the impact of a rise in A_M on w_H/w_L depends on the exact form of the comparative advantage schedules. When $\beta'_L(I_L)$ is larger in absolute value than $\beta'_H(I_H)$, w_H/w_L is more likely to decline. Intuitively, this corresponds to the case in which low skill workers have strong comparative advantage for tasks below I_L relative to the comparative advantage of high skill workers for tasks above I_H. In this case, medium skill workers will expand by more into (previously) high skill tasks than (previously) low skill tasks. The levels of I_L and $1 - I_H$ also matter for this result; the higher is I_L, the smaller is the effect on low skill wages of a given size reduction in the set of tasks performed by low skill workers (and vice versa for $1 - I_H$).

Finally, we can further parameterize the task productivity schedules, $\alpha_L(i)$, $\alpha_M(i)$ and $\alpha_H(i)$, and perform comparative statics with respect to changes in these schedules. Naturally in this case unambiguous comparative statics are not always obtainable—though, as discussed below, changes that twist or shift these schedules in specific ways lead to intuitive results.

One attractive feature of the model, highlighted by the characterization results and the comparative statics in Proposition 2, is that all equilibrium objects depend on the set of tasks performed by the three different groups of workers. Depending on which set of tasks expands (contracts) more, wages of the relevant group increase (decrease). This is useful for understanding the workings of the model and also provides a potentially tractable connection between the model and the data.

Wage effects

Given the comparative static results on the relative wages and the numeraire equation, Eq. (28), we can derive predictions on the effects of technical change on wage levels.

Although these are in general more complicated than the effects on *relative* wages, it should be intuitively clear that there is a central contrast between our framework and the canonical model: any improvement in technology in the canonical model raises the wages of all workers, whereas in our task-based framework an increase in A_H (high skill biased technical change), for example, can reduce the wages of medium skilled workers because it erodes their comparative advantage and displaces them from (some of) the tasks that they were previously performing.[69]

To see how high skill biased technical change, i.e., an increase in A_H, can reduce medium skill wages more explicitly, let us work through a simple example. Return to the special case discussed above where the task productivity schedule for the low skill workers is given by (31), implying that $I_L = \tilde{I}_L$. Suppose also that $\beta_H(i) \equiv \ln \alpha_M(i) - \ln \alpha_H(i)$ is constant, so that the no arbitrage condition between high and medium skills in Fig. 25 (or Fig. 22) is flat. Now consider an increase in A_H. This will not change I_L (since $I_L = \tilde{I}_L$ in any equilibrium), but will have a large impact on I_H (in view of the fact that the no arbitrage locus between high and medium skills is flat). Let us next turn to an investigation of the implications of this change in A_H on medium skill wages.

Recall from the same argument leading to (25) that

$$w_M = P_M A_M.$$

Since A_M is constant, the effect on medium skill wages works entirely through the price index for tasks performed by medium skill workers. To compute this price index, let us use (21) and (22) to substitute for P_L and P_H in terms of P_M in (28). This gives

$$\ln P_M = I_L \left[\ln \left(\frac{A_L L}{A_M M} \right) + \ln (I_H - I_L) - \ln I_L \right]$$
$$+ (1 - I_H) \left[\ln \left(\frac{A_H H}{A_M M} \right) + \ln (I_H - I_L) - \ln (1 - I_H) \right]$$
$$+ \int_0^{I_L} \ln \alpha_L(i) \, di + \int_{I_L}^{I_H} \ln \alpha_M(i) \, di + \int_{I_H}^1 \ln \alpha_H(i) \, di.$$

Now differentiating this expression, we obtain

$$\frac{\partial \ln P_M}{\partial \ln A_H} = \frac{1 - I_H}{A_H} + (\ln \alpha_M(I_H) - \ln \alpha_H(I_H)) \frac{dI_H}{d \ln A_H}$$

---

[69] One could, however, draw a parallel between changes in (factor-augmenting) technology in this model and changes in the distribution parameter, γ, in the canonical model (recall footnote 54). Unlike factor-augmenting technologies, shifts in the distribution parameter can reduce the wages of the skill group whose corresponding multiplier is reduced.

$$+ \left[\left(\frac{I_L}{I_H - I_L} \right) + 1 + \frac{1 - I_H}{I_H - I_L} \right.$$
$$\left. - \left(\ln \left(\frac{A_H H}{A_M M} \right) + \ln \left(I_H - I_L \right) - \ln \left(1 - I_H \right) \right) \right] \frac{dI_H}{d \ln A_H}.$$

The first term is positive and results from the indirect effect of the increase in productivity of high skill workers on the wages of medium skill workers operating through q-complementarity (i.e., an increase in productivity increases the wages of all workers because it increases the demand for all types of labor). We know from our comparative static analysis that $dI_H/d \ln A_H$ is negative, and moreover given the assumptions we have imposed here, this effect is large (meaning that there will be a large expansion of high skill workers into tasks previously performed by medium skill workers following an increase in A_H). Therefore, if $\alpha_M (I_H) \geq \alpha_H (I_H)$, $A_H H \leq A_M M$, and $1 - I_H \leq I_H - I_L$, the remaining terms in this expression are all negative and can be arbitrarily large (and in fact, some of these inequalities could be reversed and the overall expression could still be negative and arbitrarily large). This implies that an increase in A_H can significantly reduce P_M and thus w_M.

This result illustrates that in our task-based framework, in which changes in technology affect the allocation of tasks across skills, a factor-augmenting increase in productivity for one group of workers can reduce the wages of another group by shrinking the set of tasks that they are performing. This contrasts with the predictions of the canonical model and provides a useful starting point for interpreting the co-occurrence of rising supplies of high skill labor, ongoing skill biased demand shifts (stemming in part from technical change), and falling real earnings among less educated workers.

4.5. Task replacing technologies

A central virtue of our general task-based framework is that it can be used to investigate the implications of capital (embodied in machines) directly displacing workers from tasks that they previously performed. In general, we expect that tasks performed by all three skill groups are subject to machine displacement. Nevertheless, based on the patterns documented in the data above, as well as the general characterization of machine-task substitution offered by Autor et al. (2003), we believe the set of tasks most subject to machine displacement in the current era are those that are routine or codifiable. Such tasks are primarily, though not exclusively, performed by medium skill (semi-skilled) workers. For this reason, let us suppose that there now exists a range of tasks $[I', I''] \subset [I_L, I_H]$ for which $\alpha_K (i)$ increases sufficiently (with fixed cost of capital r) so that they are now more economically preformed by machines than middle skill workers. For all the remaining tasks, i.e., for all $i \notin [I', I'']$, we continue to assume that

$\alpha_K(i) = 0$. What are the implications of this type of technical change for the supply of different types of tasks and for wages?

Our analysis directly applies to this case and implies that there will now be a new equilibrium characterized by thresholds $\hat{I}_L$ and $\hat{I}_H$. Moreover, we have the following proposition generalizing Lemma 1 and Proposition 1 for this case:

Proposition 3. *Suppose we start with an equilibrium characterized by thresholds $[I_L, I_H]$ and technical change implies that the tasks in the range $[I', I''] \subset [I_L, I_H]$ are now performed by machines. Then after the introduction of machines, there exists new unique equilibrium characterized by new thresholds $\hat{I}_L$ and $\hat{I}_H$ such that $0 < \hat{I}_L < I' < I'' < \hat{I}_H < 1$ and for any $i < \hat{I}_L$, $m(i) = h(i) = 0$ and $l(i) = L/\hat{I}_L$; for any $i \in (\hat{I}_L, I') \cup (I'', \hat{I}_H)$, $l(i) = h(i) = 0$ and $m(i) = M/(\hat{I}_H - I'' + I' - \hat{I}_L)$; for any $i \in (I', I'')$, $l(i) = m(i) = h(i) = 0$; and for any $i > \hat{I}_H$, $l(i) = m(i) = 0$ and $h(i) = H/(1 - \hat{I}_H)$.*

This proposition immediately makes clear that, as a consequence of machines replacing tasks previously performed by medium skill workers, there will be a reallocation of tasks in the economy. In particular, medium skill workers will now start performing some of the tasks previously allocated to low skill workers, thus increasing the supply of these tasks (the same will happen at the top with an expansion of some of the high skill tasks). This proposition therefore gives us a way of thinking about how new technologies replacing intermediate tasks (in practice, most closely corresponding to routine, semi-skilled occupations) will directly lead to the expansion of low skill tasks (corresponding to service occupations).

We next investigate the wage inequality implications of the introduction of these new tasks. For simplicity, we focus on the case where we start with $[I', I''] = \varnothing$, and then the set of tasks expands to an interval of size ε', where ε' is small. This mathematical approach is used only for expositional simplicity because it enables us to apply differential calculus as above. None of the results depend on the set of tasks performed by machines being small.

Under the assumptions outlined here, and using the results in Proposition 3, we can write the equivalents of (32) and (33) as

$$\ln A_M - \ln A_H + \beta_H(I_H) + \ln M - \ln H - \ln(I_H - I_L - \varepsilon) + \ln(1 - I_H) = 0, \quad (34)$$

and

$$\ln A_L - \ln A_M + \beta_L(I_L) + \ln L - \ln M + \ln(I_H - I_L - \varepsilon) - \ln(I_L) = 0. \quad (35)$$

When $\varepsilon = 0$, these equations give the equilibrium before the introduction of machines replacing medium skill tasks, and when $\varepsilon = \varepsilon' > 0$, they describe the new equilibrium. Conveniently, we can obtain the relevant comparative statics by using these two equations. In particular, the implications of the introduction of these new machines on the allocation of tasks is obtained from the following system:

$$
\begin{pmatrix} \beta'_H\,(I_H) - \dfrac{1}{I_H - I_L} - \dfrac{1}{1 - I_H} & \dfrac{1}{I_H - I_L} \\[2ex] \dfrac{1}{I_H - I_L} & \beta'_L\,(I_L) - \dfrac{1}{I_H - I_L} - \dfrac{1}{I_L} \end{pmatrix} \begin{pmatrix} \mathrm{d}I_H \\[2ex] \mathrm{d}I_L \end{pmatrix} = \begin{pmatrix} -\dfrac{1}{I_H - I_L} \\[2ex] \dfrac{1}{I_H - I_L} \end{pmatrix} \mathrm{d}\varepsilon.
$$

It is then straightforward to verify that

$$
\frac{\mathrm{d}I_H}{\mathrm{d}\varepsilon} = \frac{1}{I_H - I_L}\, \frac{-\beta'_L\,(I_L) + \frac{1}{I_L}}{\Delta} > 0,
$$

$$
\frac{\mathrm{d}I_L}{\mathrm{d}\varepsilon} = \frac{1}{I_H - I_L}\, \frac{\beta'_H\,(I_H) - \frac{1}{1 - I_H}}{\Delta} < 0,
$$

$$
\frac{\mathrm{d}(I_H - I_L)}{\mathrm{d}\varepsilon} = \frac{1}{I_H - I_L}\, \frac{-\beta'_L\,(I_L) - \beta'_H\,(I_H) + \frac{1}{1 - I_H} + \frac{1}{I_L}}{\Delta} > 0,
$$

where recall that Δ is the determinant of the matrix on the left hand side. These results confirm the statements in Proposition 3 concerning the set of tasks performed by low and high skill workers expanding.

Given these results on the allocation of tasks, we can also characterize the impact on relative wages. These are stated in the next proposition. Here, we state them for the general case, rather than the case in which the range of tasks performed by machines is infinitesimal, since they can be generalized to this case in a straightforward manner (proof omitted).

Proposition 4. *Suppose we start with an equilibrium characterized by thresholds $[I_L, I_H]$ and technical change implies that the tasks in the range $[I', I''] \subset [I_L, I_H]$ are now performed by machines. Then:*

1. w_H / w_M *increases;*
2. w_M / w_L *decreases;*
3. w_H / w_L *increases if* $\left| \beta'_L\,(I_L)\, I_L \right| < \left| \beta'_H\,(I_H)\,(1 - I_H) \right|$ *and* w_H / w_L *decreases if* $\left| \beta'_L\,(I_L)\, I_L \right| > \left| \beta'_H\,(I_H)\,(1 - I_H) \right|.$

The first two parts of the proposition are intuitive. Because new machines replace the tasks previously performed by medium skill workers, their relative wages, both compared to high and low skill workers, decline. In practice, this corresponds to the wages of workers in the middle of the income distribution, previously performing relatively routine tasks, falling compared to those at the top and the bottom of the wage distribution. Thus the introduction of new machines replacing middle skilled tasks in this framework provides a possible formalization of the "routinization" hypothesis and a possible explanation for job and wage polarization discussed in Section 2.

Note that the impact of this type of technical change on the wage of high skill relative to low skill workers is ambiguous; it depends on whether medium skill workers displaced by machines are better substitutes for low or high skill workers. The condition $\left|\beta'_L(I_L)I_L\right| < \left|\beta'_H(I_H)(1-I_H)\right|$ is the same as the condition we encountered in Proposition 3, and the intuition is similar. The inequality $\left|\beta'_L(I_L)\right| < \left|\beta'_H(I_H)\right|$ implies that medium skill workers are closer substitutes for low than high skill workers in the sense that, around I_H, there is a stronger comparative advantage of high skill relative to medium skill workers than there is comparative advantage of low relative to medium skill workers around I_L. The terms I_L and $(1-I_H)$ have a similar intuition. If the set of tasks performed by high skill workers is larger than the set of tasks performed by low skill workers $((1-I_H) > I_L)$, the reallocation of a small set of tasks from high to medium skill workers will have a smaller effect on high skill wages than will an equivalent reallocation of tasks from low to medium skill workers (in this case, for low skill wages).

It appears plausible that in practice, medium skill workers previously performing routine tasks are a closer substitute for low skill workers employed in manual and service occupations than they are for high skill workers in professional, managerial and technical occupations.[70] Indeed the substantial movement of medium skill high school and some college workers out of clerical and production positions and into service occupations after 1980 (Fig. 14) may be read as *prima facie* evidence that the comparative advantage of middle skill workers (particularly middle skill males) is relatively greater in low rather than high skill tasks. If so, Part 3 of this proposition implies that we should also see an increase in w_H/w_L. Alternatively, if sufficiently many middle skill workers displaced by machines move into high skill occupations, w_H/w_L may also increase. This latter case would correspond to one in which, in relative terms, low skill workers are the main beneficiaries of the introduction of new machines into the production process.

Let us finally return to the basic comparative statics and consider a change in the task productivity schedule of high skill workers, $\alpha_H(i)$. Imagine, in particular, that this schedule is given by

$$\alpha_H(i) = \begin{cases} \theta^{\tilde{I}_H - i}\tilde{\alpha}_H(i) & \text{if } i \leq \tilde{I}_H \\ \tilde{\alpha}_H(i) & \text{if } i > \tilde{I}_H \end{cases} \tag{36}$$

where $\tilde{\alpha}_H(i)$ is a function that satisfies Assumption 1 and $\theta \geq 1$, and suppose that $\tilde{I}_H$ is in the neighborhood of the equilibrium threshold task for high skill workers, I_H. The presence of the term $\theta^{\tilde{I}_H - i}$ in (36) implies that an increase in θ creates a rotation of the task productivity schedule for high skill workers around $\tilde{I}_H$.

[70] Juhn (1994) develops a model in which middle skill workers are closer substitutes for low than high skill workers. A decline in demand for middle skill workers consequently places greater downward pressure on low than high skill wages.

Consider next the implications of an increase in θ. This will imply that high skill workers can now successfully perform tasks previously performed by medium skill workers, and hence high skill workers will replace them in tasks close to $\tilde{I}_H$ (or close to the equilibrium threshold I_H). Therefore, even absent machine–substitution for medium skill tasks, the model can generate comparative static results similar to those discussed above. This requires that the task productivity schedule for high skill (or low skill) workers twists so as to give them comparative advantage in the tasks that were previously performed by medium skill workers. The parallel roles that technology (embodied in machinery) and task productivity schedules (represented by $\alpha\,(\cdot)$) play in the model is also evident if we interpret the task productivity schedule of high skill workers more broadly as including not only their direct productivity when performing a task, but also their productivity when supervising (or operating) machinery used in those tasks. Thus the framework offers a parallel between the analytics of, on the one hand, new machinery that replaces medium skill workers and, on the other hand, changes in the task productivity schedule of high skill workers that enable them to replace medium skill workers in a subset of tasks.

4.6. Endogenous choice of skill supply

We have so far focused on one type of substitution, which we referred to as substitution of skills across tasks. A complementary force is *substitution of workers across different skills*, meaning that in response to changes in technology or factor supplies, workers may change the types of skills they supply to the market. We now briefly discuss this additional type of substitution.

Environment

To allow for substitution of workers across different types of skills, we now assume that each worker j is endowed with some amount of "low skill," "medium skill," and "high skill," respectively l^j, m^j and h^j. Workers have one unit of time, which is subject to a "skill allocation" constraint

$$t_l^j + t_m^j + t_h^j \leq 1.$$

The worker's income is

$$w_L t_l^j l^j + w_M t_m^j m^j + w_H t_h^j h^j,$$

which captures the fact that the worker with skill vector $\left(l^j, m^j, h^j\right)$ will have to allocate his time between jobs requiring different types of skills. Generally, we will see that each worker will prefer to allocate his or her time entirely to one type of skill.

The production side of the economy is identical to the framework developed so far. Our analysis then applies once we know the aggregate amount of skills of different types.

Let us denote these by

$$L = \int_{j \in E_l} l^j \, \mathrm{d}j, \qquad M = \int_{j \in E_m} m^j \, \mathrm{d}j, \quad \text{and} \quad H = \int_{j \in E_h} h^j \, \mathrm{d}j,$$

where E_l, E_m and E_h are the sets of workers choosing to supply their low, medium and high skills respectively.

Clearly, the worker will choose to be in the set E_h only if

$$\frac{l^j}{h^j} \le \frac{w_H}{w_L} \quad \text{and} \quad \frac{m^j}{h^j} \le \frac{w_H}{w_M}.$$

There are similar inequalities determining when a worker will be in the sets E_m and E_l. To keep the model tractable, we now impose a type of *single-crossing* assumption in supplies. We order workers over the interval $(0, 1)$ in such a way that lower indexed workers have a comparative advantage in supplying high relative to medium skills and in medium relative to low skills. More specifically, we impose:

Assumption 2. h^j / m^j and m^j / l^j are both strictly decreasing in j and $\lim_{j \to 0} h^j / m^j = \infty$ and $\lim_{j \to 1} m^j / l^j = 1$.

This assumption implies that lower index workers have a comparative advantage in high skill tasks and higher index workers have a comparative advantage in low skill tasks. Moreover, at the extremes these comparative advantages are strong enough that there will always be some workers choosing to supply high and low skills. An immediate implication is the following lemma:

Lemma 2. *For any ratios of wages w_H/w_M and w_M/w_L, there exist $J^*(w_H/w_M)$ and $J^{**}(w_M/w_L)$ such that $t_h^j = 1$ for all $j < J^*(w_H/w_M)$, $t_m^j = 1$ for all $j \in (J^*(w_H/w_M), J^{**}(w_M/w_L))$ and $t_l^j = 1$ for all $j > J^{**}(w_M/w_L)$. $J^*(w_H/w_M)$ and $J^{**}(w_M/w_L)$ are both strictly increasing in their arguments.*

Clearly, $J^*(w_H/w_M)$ and $J^{**}(w_M/w_L)$ are defined such that

$$\frac{m^{J^*(w_H/w_M)}}{h^{J^*(w_H/w_M)}} = \frac{w_H}{w_M} \quad \text{and} \quad \frac{l^{J^{**}(w_M/w_L)}}{m^{J^{**}(w_M/w_L)}} = \frac{w_M}{w_L}. \tag{37}$$

In light of this lemma, we can write

$$H = \int_0^{J^*(w_H/w_M)} h^j \, \mathrm{d}j, \qquad M = \int_{J^*(w_H/w_M)}^{J^{**}(w_M/w_L)} m^j \, \mathrm{d}j \quad \text{and}$$

$$L = \int_{J^{**}(w_M/w_L)}^1 l^j \, \mathrm{d}j. \tag{38}$$

Note that given Assumption 2, $J^*(w_H/w_M)$ and $J^{**}(w_M/w_L)$ are both strictly increasing in their arguments. This implies that all else equal, a higher wage premium for high relative to medium skills encourages more workers to supply high rather than medium skills to the market. The same type of comparative static applies when there is a higher premium for medium relative to low skills. In particular, rewriting (38), we have

$$\frac{H}{M} = \frac{\int_0^{J^*(w_H/w_M)} h^j \, dj}{\int_{J^*(w_H/w_M)}^{J^{**}(w_M/w_L)}} \quad \text{and} \quad \frac{M}{L} = \frac{\int_{J^*(w_H/w_M)}^{J^{**}(w_M/w_L)}}{\int_{J^{**}(w_M/w_L)}^1 l^j \, dj}. \tag{39}$$

The first expression, together with the fact that $J^*(w_H/w_M)$ is strictly increasing, implies that holding w_M/w_L constant, an increase in w_H/w_M increases H/L. Similarly, holding w_H/w_M constant, an increase in w_M/w_L increases M/L. Consequently, in addition to the comparative advantage of different types of skills across different tasks, we now have comparative advantage of workers in supplying different types of skills, which can be captured by two "upward sloping" relative supply curves.

The next proposition and the associated comparative static results exploit these insights.

Proposition 5. *In the model with endogenous supplies, there exists a unique equilibrium summarized by* $(I_L, I_H, P_L, P_M, P_H, w_L, w_M, w_H, J^*(w_H/w_M), J^{**}(w_M/w_L), L, M, H)$ *given by Eqs* (21)–(28), (37) *and* (38).

To prove the uniqueness of the equilibrium requires a little more work in this case, and the argument is thus relegated to the Theoretical Appendix.

Comparative statics and interpretation

The major change to the analysis introduced by allowing for the endogenous supply of skills is that when there is factor-augmenting technical change (or the introduction of capital that directly substitutes for workers in various tasks), the induced changes in wages will also affect supplies (even in the short run). Accordingly, there will also be substitution of workers across different types of skills. When, for example, new machines replace medium skill workers in a set of tasks, this will induce some of the workers that were previously supplying medium skills to now supply either low or high skills. If the more elastic margin is the one between medium and low skills, we would expect a significant fraction of the workers previously supplying medium skills and working in intermediate tasks to now supply low skills and perform relatively low-ranked tasks. This type of substitution therefore complements the substitution of skills across tasks. Finally, assuming that effective supplies are distributed unequally across workers, this model also generates a richer distribution of earnings inequality (and richer implications for overall inequality).

We can potentially interpret the changes in the US wage and employment structures over the last several decades through the lens of this framework. Let us take the comparative advantage schedules as given, and consider what combinations of factor-augmenting technical changes, introduction of new machines replacing tasks previously performed by different types of workers, and supply changes would be necessary to explain the patterns we observe. As we have seen, during the 1980s the US labor market experienced declining wages at the bottom of the distribution together with a relative contraction in employment in low wage occupations (though notably, a rise in employment in service occupations as underscored by Autor and Dorn (2010)), and also rising wages and employment in high skill occupations. In terms of our model, this would be a consequence of an increase in A_H/A_M and A_M/A_L, which is the analog of skill biased technical change in this three factor model. We see a different pattern commencing in the 1990s, however, where the behavior of both employment shares and wage percentiles is U-shaped, as documented above. In terms of our model, this would result from rising penetration of information technology that replaces middle skill tasks (i.e., those with a substantial routine component). This will depress both the wages of medium skill workers and reduce employment in tasks that were previously performed by these medium skill workers. In the most recent decade (2000s), employment in low wage service occupations has grown even more rapidly. In terms of our model, this could be an implication of the displacement of medium skill workers under the plausible assumption that the relative comparative advantage of middle skill workers is greater in low than high skill tasks. This would therefore be an example of substitution of skills across tasks. This process is amplified in our model if we also allow for substitution of workers across skills. In that case, some of the workers previously supplying medium skills to routine tasks switch to supplying low skills to manual and service tasks.

We stress that this interpretation of the gross patterns in the data is speculative and somewhat coarse. Our objective here is not to provide a definitive explanation for the rich set of facts offered by the data but rather to offer a set of tools that may be applied towards a more refined set of explanations.[71]

---

[71] Autor and Dorn (2010), for example, offer a closely related but distinct interpretation of the same patterns. In their model, advancing information technology displaces non-college workers performing routine tasks in production of goods, leading these workers to supply manual labor to service tasks instead. This is equivalent to substitution of skills across tasks in the current model. In Autor and Dorn (2010), this supply effect initially depresses wages in low skill services. But as the price of automating routine tasks becomes ever cheaper, the opportunity for further substitution of skills across tasks is eventually exhausted when essentially all non-college workers have exited goods production. At this point, the imperfect substitutability in consumption between goods and services outputs drives wage setting in services as in Baumol (1967). If the substitution elasticity between goods and services is less than or equal to unity, wage inequality between college workers (who supply abstract tasks to goods production) and non-college workers (who supply manual tasks to service production) either asymptotes to a constant or reverses direction—leading to wage and employment polarization. The Autor and Dorn (2010) hypothesis, as well as the framework developed here, can explain the rapid growth in service occupation employment starting in the 1980s, a period when routine-intensive occupations were in decline (see Fig. 13).

4.7. Offshoring

Alongside technological advances, a major change potentially affecting the US and other advanced market economies over the past two decades has been the change in the structure of international trade, whereby instead of simply trading finished goods and services, there has been a greater tendency to engage in trade in tasks through "outsourcing" and "offshoring" certain tasks to countries where they can now be performed at lower cost. This process particularly applies to information-based tasks, which in recent years have become nearly costless and instantaneous to transport. An advantage of our task-based model is that it provides a unified framework for the analysis of this type of offshoring (or outsourcing) in a way that parallels the impact of machines replacing tasks previously performed by certain types of workers.

To illustrate how offshoring of tasks affects the structure of wages, suppose that a set of tasks $[I', I''] \subset [I_L, I_H]$ can now be offshored to a foreign country, where wages are sufficiently low that such offshoring is cost minimizing for domestic final good producers. This assumption, of course, parallels our analysis of machines replacing tasks. In return, these firms can trade in the final good to ensure trade balance. In this case, it is straightforward to see that the equivalents of Propositions 3 and 4 will hold. In particular, the next proposition contains the relevant results summarizing the implications of offshoring for the allocation of tasks across workers and for wage inequality.

Proposition 6. *Suppose we start with an equilibrium characterized by thresholds $[I_L, I_H]$ and changes in technology allow tasks in the range $[I', I''] \subset [I_L, I_H]$ to be offshored. Then after offshoring, there exists new unique equilibrium characterized by new thresholds $\hat{I}_L < I_L$ and $\hat{I}_H > I_H$ such that $0 < \hat{I}_L < I' < I'' < \hat{I}_H < 1$ and for any $i < \hat{I}_L$, $m(i) = h(i) = 0$ and $l(i) = L/\hat{I}_L$; for any $i \in (\hat{I}_L, I') \cup (I'', \hat{I}_H), l(i) = h(i) = 0$ and $m(i) = M/(\hat{I}_H - I'' + I' - \hat{I}_L)$; for any $i \in (I', I''), l(i) = m(i) = h(i) = 0$; and for any $i > \hat{I}_H, l(i) = m(i) = 0$ and $h(i) = H/(1 - \hat{I}_H)$. The implications of offshoring on the structure of wages are as follows:*

1. w_H/w_M *increases;*

2. w_M/w_L *decreases;*

3. w_H/w_L *increases if $\left| \beta'_L (I_L) I_L \right| < \left| \beta'_H (I_H) (1 - I_H) \right|$ and w_H/w_L decreases if $\left| \beta'_L (I_L) I_L \right| > \left| \beta'_H (I_H) (1 - I_H) \right|$.*

While the extension of the model to offshoring is immediate, the substantive point is deeper. The task-based model offers an attractive means, in our view, to place labor supply, technological change, and trading opportunities on equal economic footing. In our model, each is viewed as offering a competing supply of tasks that, in equilibrium, are allocated to productive activities in accordance with comparative advantage and cost minimization. This approach is both quite general and, we believe, intuitively appealing.

4.8. Directed technical change

We have so far investigated the implications of extending and, in some senses rewriting, the canonical model by allowing for the endogenous allocation of skill groups across tasks and workers across skill groups, and considering how technology and offshoring interact with this process. A final, potentially significant aspect of the economic environment absent from the canonical model is the endogeneity of technological progress to other changes in the labor market. We now discuss how this endogenous technology aspect can be incorporated to enrich our understanding of the operation of the labor market as well as the task-based model we have so far developed.

General discussion

Acemoglu (1998, 2002a) argues that both long run and medium run changes in US labor markets can be understood, at least partly, as resulting from endogenous changes in technology that responds to changes in supplies. From this perspective, Tinbergen's race between supplies and technology is endogenously generated. Autonomous changes in skill supplies—resulting from demographic trends, evolving preferences, and shifts in public and private education—induce endogenous changes in technology, which increase the demand for skills. These demand shifts in turn lead to endogenous increases in skill supplies and, subsequently, further technological progress. While the impact of technological change on the supply of skills (responding to the skill premium) is standard, the response of technology to (relative) supplies is the more central and novel part of this explanation.

Formally, papers by Acemoglu (1998, 2002b) generalize the canonical model with two types of skills and two types of factor-augmenting technologies so as to endogenize the direction of technical change (and thus the relative levels of the two technologies). This work shows that an increase in the relative supply of skills will endogenously cause technology to become more skill biased. Moreover, this induced skill bias could be strong enough that endogenous technology (or "long-run") relative demand curves can be upward sloping rather than downward sloping. This contrasts with the necessarily downward sloping relative demand for skills in the canonical model and also in the Ricardian model studied here (which, so far, holds technology constant). If the induced response of technology is sufficiently strong to make the endogenous relative demand curves upward sloping, then the increase in the skill premium that the US and many OECD labor markets experienced during the last three decades may be, at least in part, a response to the large increase in the supply of skills that commenced in these economies some decades earlier (around the 1960s).

Acemoglu (2002b) showed that for this strong form of endogenous skill bias (in the context of the canonical model), an elasticity of substitution between high and low skill labor greater than a certain threshold (which is somewhere between one and two) is sufficient. Thus for reasonable values of the elasticity of substitution, the induced response of technology to supplies will be strong enough to make the long-run price of skills increase in response to increases in the supply of skills—a stark contrast to the neoclassical model with constant technology, which always predicts that demand curves for factors are downward sloping.

A shift in focus from the canonical model to a task-based framework significantly enriches the mechanisms by which technology can respond endogenously to changes in (relative) supplies. In particular, in the context of our Ricardian model, we can allow two types of endogenous responses of technologies to changes in supplies. First, we can assume that factor-augmenting technologies respond to skill supplies (namely the terms A_L, A_M, and A_H). This idea is analyzed by Acemoglu and Zilibotti (2001) for the special case of our model discussed in Section 4.3.[72] Second, we can also allow for the comparative advantage schedules (the $\alpha\,(\cdot)$'s) to respond endogenously to skill supplies. This case is both more novel and more relevant to our discussion of the importance of tasks to understanding major labor market developments, and we pursue it here.

While we would have to impose specific functional forms to derive exact results on how comparative advantage schedules will endogenously respond to skill supplies, we can derive more abstract (though nevertheless quite tight) predictions about the direction of change of technology by using the more general framework introduced in Acemoglu (2007). To do this, let us suppose that technologies are presented by a finite dimensional variable (vector) $\theta \in \Theta$, and all three comparative advantage schedules are functions of this vector of technology, i.e., we have $\alpha_L\,(i \mid \theta)$, $\alpha_M\,(i \mid \theta)$ and $\alpha_H\,(i \mid \theta)$. Since any changes in the factor-augmenting terms, A_L, A_M, and A_H, can be incorporated into these comparative advantage schedules, we hold the factor-augmenting terms constant.

We assume as in Acemoglu (2007) that a set of monopolistically competitive or oligopolistic firms invest in technologies θ, produce intermediate goods (or machines) embedding this technology, and sell them to final good producers. We also assume that the cost of producing technology θ is convex in θ. An equilibrium is given by a set of allocations (prices, employment levels and technology levels) such that taking technology levels as given, final good producers maximize profits, and simultaneously, taking the demands for technologies from the final good sector as given, technology monopolists (oligopolists) maximize profits. Also, following Acemoglu (2007), we will say that a change in technology is *(absolutely) biased* towards factor f (where $f \in \{L, M, H\}$) if the change in technology increases the price of that factor, w_f (where again $f \in \{L, M, H\}$) at the prevailing factor proportions (i.e., when the supplies of the three factors are given

---

[72] Acemoglu and Zilibotti (2001) showed that the response of factor-augmenting technology to supplies works exactly in the same way in this task-based model as in the canonical model studied in Acemoglu (1998, 2002b). In particular, because the special case studied in Acemoglu and Zilibotti (2001) is equivalent to a version of the canonical model with an elasticity of substitution equal to two, technology adjusts in the long run in that model to make the relative demand for skills entirely flat. It is straightforward to extend this result, again in the model with only high and low skill workers, so that technology adjusts more or less than this amount. Hence, all of the results in Acemoglu (1998, 2002b) generalize for factor-augmenting technical change in this task-based environment.

by L, M, and H).[73] Mathematically, a change in technology is biased towards factor f if $w_f(L, M, H \mid \theta)$, written as a function of the supply levels of the three factors, is nondecreasing in θ. In particular, when θ is a continuous one-dimensional variable (i.e., $\theta \in \mathbb{R}$) and the wage levels are differentiable, this is equivalent to:[74]

$$\frac{\partial w_f(L, M, H \mid \theta)}{\partial \theta} \geq 0.$$

Moreover, we say that an increase in the supply of a factor induces technical change that is *weakly biased* towards that factor (again focusing on the continuous one-dimensional variable representing technology) if

$$\frac{\partial w_f(E_{-f}, E_f \mid \theta)}{\partial \theta} \frac{\mathrm{d}\theta}{\mathrm{d}E_f} \geq 0,$$

where E_f is the supply level of factor f (for $f \in \{L, M, H\}$), $w_f(E_{-f}, E_f \mid \theta) = w_f(L, M, H \mid \theta)$, and $\mathrm{d}\theta/\mathrm{d}E_f$ is the induced change in technology resulting from a change in the supply of this factor. Using the same notation, we also say that an increase in the supply of a factor induces technical change that is *strongly biased* towards that factor if

$$\frac{\mathrm{d}w_f(E_{-f}, E_f \mid \theta)}{\mathrm{d}E_f} = \frac{\partial w_f(E_{-f}, E_f \mid \theta)}{\partial E_f} + \frac{\partial w_f(E_{-f}, E_f \mid \theta)}{\partial \theta} \frac{\mathrm{d}\theta}{\mathrm{d}E_f} > 0,$$

where the notation makes it clear that in contrast to the weak bias case, we are evaluating in this case the change in the price as the supply also changes (and thus we have the first term, which is the direct effect of a change in supply for given technology). Put differently, we are now tracing an "endogenous technology" demand curve. In the case of weak bias, however, factor supplies are held constant (as emphasized by the use of the partial derivative), so weak bias requires only that the technology-constant demand curve shifts in favor of the factor whose increased supply induced the initial change in technology (represented by $\mathrm{d}\theta/\mathrm{d}E_f$).

Without specifying either the shape of the comparative advantage schedules or how specifically they depend upon θ, the results in Acemoglu (2007) enable us to have the following two results. Here we state the results without the full mathematical details.

---

[73] The qualifier "absolutely" is introduced, since in Acemoglu (1998, 2002b), bias refers to changes in technologies affecting relative prices, whereas in this more general framework, the focus is on the price level of a factor. To obtain sharp results on relative price changes, one needs to restrict the focus to factor-augmenting changes (see Acemoglu (2007)). In what follows, all of the references to biased technical change refer to factor price levels, and thus one could insert the qualifier "absolute," though we will not do so as to simplify terminology.

[74] When θ is a continuous multidimensional variable (a vector), there is a straightforward generalization of this definition (see Acemoglu (2007)). All of the results we discuss here are valid in this general case, but to simplify the exposition, we will not introduce the necessary notation.

More rigorous statements of these propositions follow the formulation in Acemoglu (2007), where proofs for these results can be found.

Proposition 7. *Under regularity conditions (which ensure the existence of a locally isolated equilibrium), an increase in the supply of factor f (for $f \in \{L, M, H\}$) will induce technical change weakly biased towards that factor.*

This proposition thus shows that even under the richer form of technical change considered in our Ricardian model (in particular shifts in the comparative advantage schedules in response to changes in supplies), the response of the economy to any increase in the supply of a factor will be to undergo an endogenous change in technology that *weakly* increases the demand for that factor. Therefore, even in the context of the richer task-based approach developed here, this result implies that there are strong theoretical reasons to expect the increase in the supply of high skill workers, which the US and OECD economies experienced over the past three decades, to have induced the development of technologies favoring these high skill workers. This result does not, however, state that this induced response will be strong enough to increase the price of the factor that it is becoming more abundant (i.e., it does not state that long-run demand curves incorporating endogenous technological change will be upward sloping). This question is investigated in the next proposition.

Proposition 8. *Under regularity conditions (which ensure the existence of a locally isolated equilibrium), an increase in the supply of factor f (for $f \in \{L, M, H\}$) will induce technical change strongly biased towards that factor—thus increasing the wage of that factor—if and only if the aggregate production possibilities set of the economy is locally nonconvex in factor f and technology θ.*

This local nonconvexity condition implies, loosely, that if we double both the supply of factor f and the quality or quantity of technology θ, output will more than double. This form of nonconvexity is quite common in models of endogenous technical change (e.g., Romer, 1990, and see Acemoglu, 2002b), and it is *not* a very demanding condition for one primary reason: the technology is not chosen by the same set of firms that make the factor demand decisions; if it were, and if these firms were competitive, then the equilibrium could not exhibit such local nonconvexity. In our setting (as in Acemoglu, 2007), however, final good producers make factor demands decisions taking technology as given (while facing constant or diminishing returns), and technology monopolists or oligopolists make technology decisions taking the factor demands of final good producers as given (while again facing convex decision problems). In this formulation, the aggregate production possibilities set of the economy need not be locally convex (in each of the factors and the vector of technologies). For example, the result on upward sloping relative demand curves with endogenous technologies in Acemoglu (1998, 2002b) mentioned above corresponds to this type of nonconvexity, and as explained above, only relies on an elasticity of substitution greater than a certain threshold (between one and two). Therefore, strong bias of technology does not require unduly strong conditions, though of course whether it applies in practice is an empirical question on which there is limited evidence.

An example

We now provide a simple example illustrating how endogenous technology enriches the insights of our task-based model here (and conversely, how the task-based approach enriches the implications of existing models of directed technical change). Let us return to the task productivity schedule for high skill workers in (36) discussed in Section 4.5. Suppose, as we did there, that the equilibrium threshold task for high skill workers, I_H, is close to $\tilde{I}_H$. Assume, however, that θ is now an endogenous variable, taking the value θ_{low} or $\theta_{\text{high}} > \theta_{\text{low}}$. As in the general directed technical change framework described so far in this section, we continue to assume that θ is chosen by profit maximizing technology firms, which then sell machines (intermediate goods) embodying this technology to final good producers.

When will technology firms choose θ_{high} instead of θ_{low}? Recall that, as a starting point, the equilibrium threshold I_H is close to $\tilde{I}_H$. This implies that high skill workers are not performing many tasks below $\tilde{I}_H$ (or in fact, if $I_H > \tilde{I}_H$, they are not performing any tasks below $\tilde{I}_H$). As a result, the return from increasing their productivity in tasks lower than $\tilde{I}_H$ would be limited. Therefore, we can presume that to start with, $\theta = \theta_{\text{low}}$.

Now imagine that the supply of high skill workers, H, increases. The general results we have discussed so far imply that technology will adjust (if technology is indeed endogenous) in a way that is biased towards high skill workers. However, these results are silent on what the impact of this induced change in technology will be on medium skill (or low skill) workers. With the specific structure outlined here, however, this endogenous technology response will create effects that are predictable. In particular, as H increases, the equilibrium threshold task for high skill workers, I_H, will decline given the existing technology (θ_{low}). Suppose that after the change, I_H lies significantly below $\tilde{I}_H$. This generates a potentially large economic return to increasing the productivity of high skill workers in the tasks on the interval I_H to $\tilde{I}_H$. This is accomplished by raising θ from θ_{low} to θ_{high}. From our discussion in Section 4.5, however, we know that this corresponds to a change in technology that will induce high skill workers to become more productive in tasks previously performed by medium skill workers, which potentially further contracts the set of tasks performed by medium skill workers. As per our interpretation in Section 4.5, this process is analytically similar to the case in which new machines replace medium skill workers in the tasks that they were previously performing.

Hence, the endogenous technology response to an expansion in the supply of high skill workers (in this case from θ_{low} to θ_{high}) may not only bias technology in their favor (i.e., raising their productivity), but may also induce them to perform some of the tasks previously performed by medium skill workers (either directly, or by supervising the operation of new machinery). With an analysis similar to that in Section 4.4, this process of endogenous technological change can lead to a decline in the wages of medium skill workers.

Overall, this example illustrates how the endogenous response of technology to changes in relative supplies—or, similarly, to changes in trade or offshoring possibilities— may lead to a rich set of changes in both task productivities and the allocation of skills to tasks. Whether this endogenous technology response is in fact a central determinant of the changes in task allocations that have taken place over the past 30 years is an area for further research.

5. COMPARATIVE ADVANTAGE AND WAGES: AN EMPIRICAL APPROACH

We finally take a step back from the theoretical framework to consider how the broad implications of the model might be brought to the data. A key implication of the theory is that holding the schedule of comparative advantage (that is, the $\alpha\left(\cdot\right)'s$) constant, changes in the market value of tasks should affect the evolution of wages by skill group. In particular, our model makes a relatively sharp prediction: if the relative market price of the tasks in which a skill group holds comparative advantage declines, the relative wage of that skill group should also decline—*even if* the group reallocates its labor to a different set of tasks (i.e., due to the change in its comparative advantage).

Critical to this prediction is the distinction made between the wages paid to a skill group and the wages paid to a given task—a distinction that is meaningful because the assignment of skills to tasks is endogenous. To see the implications of this distinction, consider a technological change that raises the productivity of high skill workers in all tasks (e.g., an increase in A_H). The model implies that this would expand the set of tasks performed by high skill workers (i.e., lower I_H), so that some tasks formerly performed by medium skilled workers would now be performed by high skill workers instead. Thus, relative wages paid to workers performing these (formerly) "middle skill" tasks would actually increase (since they are now performed by the more productive high skill workers). But crucially, our analysis also shows that the relative wage of medium skill workers, who were formerly performing these tasks, would fall.[75]

This discussion underscores that because of the endogenous assignment of skills to tasks, it is possible for the relative wage paid to a task to move in the *opposite* direction from the relative wage paid to the skill group that initially performed the task.[76] By contrast,

---

[75] Recall in particular from Proposition 2 that $\mathrm{d}I_H/\mathrm{d}\ln A_H < 0$ and $\mathrm{d}\ln\left(w_H/w_M\right)/\mathrm{d}\ln A_H > 0$, and thus w_M/w_H will fall.

[76] Nor is this notion far-fetched. Skill levels in production and clerical occupations, as measured by the college employment or wage-bill share, have risen as employment in these occupations has declined (Autor et al., 1998). A plausible interpretation of this pattern is that educated workers have comparative advantage in the set of non-routine tasks in these occupations that remain.

the relative wage paid to a given skill group always moves in the same direction as its comparative advantage—that is, a technological change that increases the productivity of a skill group necessarily raises its relative wage. Simultaneously, it alters the set of tasks to which that skill is applied.

As a stylized example of how this insight might be brought to the data, we study the evolution of wages by skill groups, where skill groups are defined according to their initial task specialization across abstract-intensive, routine-intensive, and manual-intensive occupations. We take these patterns of occupational specialization as a rough proxy for comparative advantage. Consider the full set of demographic groups available in the data, indexed by gender, education, age, and region. At the start of the sample in 1959, we assume that these groups have self-selected into task specialities according to comparative advantage, taking as given overall skill supplies and task demands (reflecting also available technologies and trade opportunities). Specifically, let γ^A_{sejk}, γ^R_{sejk} and γ^S_{sejk} be the employment shares of a demographic group in abstract, routine and manual/service occupations in 1959, where s denotes gender, e denotes education group, j denotes age group, and k denotes region of the country.[77] By construction, we have that $\gamma^A_{sejk} + \gamma^R_{sejk} + \gamma^S_{sejk} = 1$.

Let w_{sejkt} be the mean log wage of a demographic group in year t and $\Delta w_{sejk\tau}$ be the change in w during decade τ. We then estimate the following regression model:

$$\Delta w_{sejk\tau} = \sum_t \beta^A_t \cdot \gamma^A_{sejk} \cdot 1\,[\tau = t] + \sum_t \beta^S_t \cdot \gamma^S_{sejk} \cdot 1\,[\tau = t]$$
$$+ \delta_\tau + \phi_e + \lambda_j + \pi_k + e_{sejk\tau}, \tag{40}$$

where δ, ϕ, λ, and π are vectors of time, education, age and region dummies. The β^S_t and β^A_t coefficients in this model estimate the decade specific slopes on the initial occupation shares in predicting wage changes by demographic group. The routine task category (γ^R_{sejk}) serves as the omitted reference group. Thus we are conceiving of demographic groups as skill groups, and the γ parameters as reflecting their patterns of comparative advantage in 1959.

Our working hypothesis is that the labor market price of routine tasks has declined steeply over the last three decades due to rising competition from information technology. Conversely, we conjecture that the labor market prices of abstract and manual tasks will have increased since these tasks are relatively complementary to the routine tasks (now produced at lower cost and in greater quantity by capital). This hypothesis implies that we should expect the wages of workers with comparative advantage in either abstract or manual/service tasks to rise over time while the opposite should occur for skill

---

[77] Here, abstract occupations are professional, managerial and technical occupations; routine occupations are sales, clerical, administrative support, production, and operative occupations; and service occupations include protective service, food preparation, cleaning, buildings and grounds, and personal care and personal services.

groups with comparative advantage in routine tasks. Formally, we anticipate that β_t^A and β_t^S will rise while the intercepts measuring the omitted routine task category (δ_τ) will decline. These expected effects reflect the rising earnings power of skill groups that hold comparative advantage in abstract and manual/service tasks relative to skill groups that hold comparative advantage in routine tasks.

Table 10 presents initial descriptive OLS regressions of Eq. (40) using Census wage and occupation data from years 1959 through 2008. Although this empirical exercise is highly preliminary—indeed, it is intended as an example of an empirical approach rather than a test of the theory—the pattern of results appears roughly consistent with expectations. Starting with the estimate for males in column 1, we find a rise in relative wages from the 1980s forward for male skill groups that were initially specialized in abstract tasks. Similarly, starting in the 1980s, we see a substantial increase in the relative wage of male demographic subgroups that had an initial specialization in manual/service tasks. In fact, this task specialty moved from being a strongly negative predictor of wages in the 1960s and 1970s, to a positive predictor from the 1980s forward.

Since the interactions between time dummies and each demographic group's initial routine occupation share (γ_{sejk}^R) serves as the omitted reference category in the regression model, these time intercepts estimate wage trends for demographic groups that hold comparative advantage in routine tasks. Consistent with a decline in the wages of workers with comparative advantage in routine tasks, the routine occupation intercepts fall from strongly positive in the 1960s to weakly positive in the 1970s, and then become negative from the 1980s forward.

The second column repeats the initial estimate, now adding main effects for education, age group, and region. Here, the model is identified by differences in initial comparative advantage among workers within education-age-region cells. The inclusion of these demographic group main effects does not appreciably alter the results.

Columns 3 and 4 repeat these estimates for females. As with males, the estimates indicate rising relative wages from 1980 forward for female demographic subgroups that were initially specialized in abstract tasks. The pattern for the service tasks is less clear cut for females, however. Service task specialization is surprisingly associated with strong wage gains during the 1960s and 1970s. This association becomes negative in the 1980s, which is not consistent with the hypothesis above. It then becomes positive (as predicted) in the final two decades of the sample (column 4).

Finally, the routine task specialty intercepts for females go from weakly positive in the 1960s to strongly negative in the 1970s forward. Thus, the decline in the routine task intercepts starts a decade earlier for females than males. Inclusion of main effects for education, age group and region generally strengthens these results and brings them closer in line with our hypotheses.

We stress that this initial cut of the data is intended as an example of how linking the comparative advantage of skill groups to changes over time in the demands for

Table 10 OLS stacked first-difference estimates of the relationship between demographic group occupational distributions in 1959 and subsequent changes in demographic groups' mean log wages by decade, 1959-2007.

	A. Males		B. Females	
	(1)	(2)	(1)	(2)
Abstract occupation share				
1959 share × 1959-1969 time dummy	0.021	0.033	0.146	0.159
	(0.044)	(0.104)	(0.041)	(0.081)
1959 share × 1969-1979 time dummy	−0.129	−0.123	−0.054	−0.032
	(0.044)	(0.105)	(0.036)	(0.079)
1959 share × 1979-1989 time dummy	0.409	0.407	0.143	0.174
	(0.046)	(0.106)	(0.033)	(0.079)
1959 share × 1989-1999 time dummy	0.065	0.060	0.070	0.107
	(0.049)	(0.109)	(0.033)	(0.079)
1959 share × 1999-2007 time dummy	0.198	0.194	0.075	0.113
	(0.051)	(0.11)	(0.033)	(0.08)
Service occupation share				
1959 share × 1959-1969 time dummy	−0.836	−1.014	0.359	0.404
	(0.278)	(0.303)	(0.064)	(0.09)
1959 share × 1969-1979 time dummy	−0.879	−0.991	0.304	0.363
	(0.295)	(0.316)	(0.065)	(0.091)
1959 share × 1979-1989 time dummy	1.007	0.917	−0.143	−0.060
	(0.332)	(0.349)	(0.074)	(0.096)
1959 share × 1989-1999 time dummy	0.202	0.143	0.117	0.221
	(0.378)	(0.39)	(0.086)	(0.104)
1959 share × 1999-2007 time dummy	0.229	0.212	−0.056	0.058
	(0.398)	(0.408)	(0.094)	(0.109)
Decade dummies				
1959-1969	0.274	0.274	0.120	0.046
	(0.031)	(0.037)	(0.021)	(0.032)
1969-1979	0.084	0.085	−0.083	−0.163
	(0.033)	(0.038)	(0.020)	(0.033)
1979-1989	−0.287	−0.283	−0.011	−0.099
	(0.036)	(0.041)	(0.021)	(0.034)
1989-1999	−0.002	0.002	0.061	−0.035
	(0.039)	(0.045)	(0.022)	(0.035)

(continued on next page)

their task specialties could be used to explore and interpret the evolution of wages by skill group. The evidence in Table 10 is therefore only suggestive. But we believe the premise on which this exercise is based is a sound one and has the virtue of exploring a theoretically-grounded set of empirical implications. This exercise and our discussion

Table 10 (continued)

	A. Males		B. Females	
	(1)	**(2)**	**(1)**	**(2)**
1999-2007	−0.157	−0.157	−0.073	−0.171
	(0.041)	(0.046)	(0.024)	(0.036)
Education, age group, and region main effects?	No	Yes	No	Yes
R-squared	0.789	0.821	0.793	0.844
N	400	400	400	400

Source: Census IPUMS 1960, 1970, 1980, 1990 and 2000, and American Community Survey 2008. Each column presents a separate OLS regression of stacked changes in mean log real hourly wages by demographic group and year, where demographic groups are defined by sex, education group (high school dropout, high school graduate, some college, college degree, post-college degree), age group (25-34, 35-44, 45-54, 55-64), and region of residence (Northeast, South, Midwest, West). Models are weighted by the mean start and end-year share of employment of each demographic group for each decadal change. Occupation shares are calculated for each demographic group in 1959 (using the 1960 Census) and interacted with decade dummies. Occupations are grouped into three exhaustive and mutually exclusive categories: (1) abstract—professional, managerial and technical occupations; (2) service—protective service, food service and cleaning, and personal services occupations; (3) routine—clerical, sales, administrative support, production, operative and laborer occupations. The routine group is the omitted category in the regression models.

at the beginning of this section, also emphasize that an alternative, and at first appealing, approach of regressing wages on measures of current tasks performed by workers could generate potentially misleading results.[78] In contrast, the approach here exploits the fact that task specialization in the cross section is informative about the comparative advantage of various skill groups, and it marries this source of information to a well-specified hypothesis about how the wages of skill groups that differ in their comparative advantage should respond to changes in technology, shifts in trade and offshoring opportunities, and fluctuations in skill supplies.[79]

---

[78] As above, because the allocation of workers to tasks is endogenous, the wages paid to a set of workers previously performing a given task can fall even as the wages paid to the workers now performing that task rise. Our framework therefore suggests that a regression of wages on tasks currently performed, or their change over time, would be difficult to interpret.

[79] A recent working paper by Firpo et al. (2009) also develops an innovative method for measuring the impact of changing task prices on wage structure. Using a simple statistical model of occupational wage setting, they predict that occupations that are specialized in tasks that have declining market value should see a reduction in both mean occupational wages and the *variance* of occupational wages (and vice versa for tasks with rising prices). This latter (variance) effect stems from the interaction between a falling task price and a fixed distribution of task efficiencies within an occupation; as the market value of a given task falls, the variances of wages paid to workers with differing productivities in that task compresses along with it. An issue that needs further study in their approach is that changes in task prices will presumably lead to changes in self-selection into occupations, as implied by our model (and more generally by the assumption that workers are making maximizing choices). This should also affect occupational wage means and variances. Firpo, Fortin and Lemieux's exploratory analysis finds a significant role for both routine-task displacement and, to a lesser extent, offshoring in contributing to US wage polarization between 1984 and 2001. In addition, their analysis emphasizes the contribution of declining labor union penetration and shifts in demographic composition to wage polarization.

6. CONCLUDING REMARKS

In this paper, we argue that to account for recent changes in the earnings and employment distribution in the United States and other advanced economies, and also to develop a better understanding of the impact of technology on labor market outcomes, it is necessary to substantially enrich the canonical model. Specifically, we propose relaxing the assumptions implicit in this model that: (i) the assignment of skills to tasks is fixed (or, more precisely, that skills and tasks are equivalent); and (ii) technical change takes a purely factor-augmenting form. These strictures, we believe, prevent the model from shedding light on key phenomena presented by the data and documented above. These include: (1) substantial declines in real wages of low skill workers over the last three decades; (2) marked, non-monotone changes in earnings levels in different parts of the earnings distribution during different decades; (3) the polarization in the earnings distribution, particularly associated with a "convexification" in the returns to schooling (and perhaps in the returns to other skills); (4) systematic, non-monotone changes in the distribution of employment across occupations of various skill levels; (5) the introduction of new technologies—as well as offshoring possibilities in part enabled by those technologies— that appear to directly substitute machines (capital) for a range of tasks previously performed by (moderately-skilled) workers.

Having documented these patterns and highlighted why they are particularly challenging for the canonical model, we argue that a task-based framework, in which tasks are the basic unit of production and the allocation of skills to tasks is endogenously determined, provides a fruitful alternative framework.

In the task-based framework proposed in this chapter, a unique final good is produced combining services of a continuum of tasks. Each worker has one of three types of skills, low, medium and high. We assume a pattern of comparative advantage such that tasks are ranked in order of complexity, and medium skill workers are more productive than low skill workers, and less productive than high skill workers in more complex tasks. We show that the equilibrium allocation of skills to tasks is determined by two thresholds, I_L and I_H, such that all tasks below the lower threshold (I_L) are performed by low skill workers, all tasks above the higher threshold (I_H) are performed by high skill workers, and all intermediate tasks are performed by medium skill workers. In terms of mapping this allocation to reality, we think of the lowest range of tasks as corresponding to service occupations and other manual occupations that require physical flexibility and adaptability but little training. These tasks are straightforward for the large majority of workers, but require a degree of coordination, sightedness, and physical flexibility that are not yet easily automated. The intermediate range corresponds to moderately skilled blue-collar production and white-collar administrative, clerical, accounting and sales positions that require execution of well-defined procedures (such as calculating or monitoring) that can increasingly be codified in software and performed by inexpensive machinery. Finally, the highest range corresponds to the abstract reasoning, creative, and problem-solving tasks performed by professionals, managers and some technical occupations. These tasks require a skill set that is currently challenging to automate because the procedures used to perform these tasks are poorly understood.

We show that despite the endogenous allocation of skills to tasks, the model is tractable, and that relative wages among skill groups depend only on relative supplies and the equilibrium threshold tasks. Comparative statics of relative wages then depend on how these thresholds change. For example, whenever I_L increases (for fixed supplies of low, medium and high skills in the market), there is a larger range of tasks performed by low skill workers and their relative wages increase. Similarly, when I_H decreases, the wages of high skill workers increase and when $I_H - I_L$ increases, the relative wages of medium skill workers increase. We also show that an increase in the supply of high skills, or alternatively, technical change that makes high skill workers uniformly more productive, reduces I_H (intuitively, because there is greater "effective supply" of high skills). In addition to this direct effect, such a change also has an indirect effect on I_L, because the decrease in I_H, at given I_L, creates an "excess supply" of medium skill workers in intermediate tasks and thus induces firms to substitute these workers for tasks previously performed by low skill workers.

A noteworthy implication of this framework is that technical change favoring one type of worker can reduce the real wages of another group. Therefore, the richer substitution possibilities between skill groups afforded by the endogenous allocation of skills to tasks highlights that, distinct from canonical model, technical change need not raise the wages of all workers. As importantly, this framework enables us to model the introduction of new technologies that directly substitute for tasks previously performed by workers of various skill levels. In particular, we can readily model how new machinery (for example, software that corrects spelling and identifies grammatical errors) can directly substitute for job tasks performed by various skill groups. This type of technical change provides a richer perspective for interpreting the impact of new technologies on labor market outcomes. It also makes negative effects on the real wages of the group that is being directly replaced by the machinery more likely. These same ideas can also be easily applied to the process of outsourcing and offshoring. Since some tasks are far more suitable to offshoring than others (e.g., developing web sites versus cutting hair), it is natural to model offshoring as a technology (like computers) that potentially displaces domestic workers of various skill levels performing certain tasks, thereby altering their wages by increasing their effective supply and causing a shift in the mapping between skills and tasks (represented by I_L and I_H).

We also show how the model can be extended to incorporate choices on the side of workers to allocate their labor hours between different types of activities and how technical change can be endogenized in this framework. When the direction of technical change and the types of technologies being adopted are endogenous, not only do we obtain the same types of insights that the existing literature on directed technical change generates, but we can also see how the development and the adoption of technologies substituting machines for tasks previously performed by (middle skill) workers can emerge as a response to changes in relative supplies.

We view our task-based framework and the interpretation of the salient labor market facts through the lenses of this framework as first steps towards developing a richer and more nuanced approach to the study of interactions between technology, tasks and skills in modern labor markets. Indeed, it will be a successful first step if this framework provides a foundation for researchers to generate new theoretical ideas and test them empirically. In the spirit of a first step, we suggest one means of parsing changes in real wages over time by demographic groups that is motivated by this theoretical model. Clearly, more needs to be done to derive tighter predictions from this framework and from other complementary task-based approaches for the evolution of earnings and employment distribution both in the United States and other countries. We view this as a promising area for future research.

We also believe that the study of a number of closely related topics in labor economics may be enriched when viewed through this task perspective, though we must only mention them cursorily here:

Organizational change: Acemoglu (1999), Bresnahan (1999), Bresnahan et al. (1999), Caroli and van Reenen (1999), Kremer and Maskin (1996), Garicano (2000), Autor et al. (2002), Dessein and Santos (2006), and Garicano and Rossi-Hansberg (2006) among others, have emphasized the importance of organizational changes as an autonomous factor shaping the demand for skills or, alternatively, as a phenomenon accompanying other equilibrium changes impacting earnings inequality. A task-based approach is implicit in several of these studies, and a systematic framework, like the one proposed here, may enrich the study of the interactions between organizational changes and the evolution of the distribution of earnings and employment. We also note that substitution of machines for tasks previously performed by semi-skilled workers, or outsourcing and offshoring of their tasks, may necessitate significant organizational changes. One might reinterpret the changes in equilibrium threshold tasks in our model as corresponding to a form of organizational change. One might alternatively take the perspective that organizational change will take place in a more discontinuous manner and will involve changes in several dimensions of the organization of production (managerial and job practices, the allocation of authority within the organization, the form of communication, and the nature of responsibility systems). In addition, organizational change might also create tasks, demanding both low and high skill labor inputs, that were not previously present, exerting another force towards polarization. These considerations suggest that the two-way interaction between these organizational changes and the allocation of tasks to different skill groups and technologies is an important area for theoretical and empirical study.

Labor market imperfections: The framework proposed here crucially depends on competitive labor markets, where each worker is paid the value of his or her marginal product. In reality, many frictions—some related to information and search and others resulting from collective bargaining, social norms, firing costs and minimum wage legislation—create a wedge between wages and marginal products. The allocation of skills to tasks is more complex in the presence of such labor market imperfections. Moreover, some of these imperfections might directly affect the choice of threshold tasks. The implications of different types of technical change are potentially quite different in the presence of labor market imperfections, and may in particular depend on the exact form of these frictions. Further work tractably integrating various forms of labor market imperfections within a framework that incorporates the endogenous allocation of skills to tasks appears to be another fruitful area for research.

The role of labor market institutions: Closely related to labor market imperfections, a perspective that emphasizes the importance of tasks also calls for additional study of the role of labor market institutions in the changes in employment and inequality in recent decades. Certain work practices, such as collective bargaining and unionized workplace arrangements, might have greater impact on the earnings distribution because of the way they impact the assignment of tasks to labor or capital. These institutions may restrict the substitution of machines for certain tasks previously performed by workers, particularly in the case of labor unions. Additionally, even if the substitution of machines for labor is not fully impeded, it may occur more slowly than otherwise due to the influence of these institutions. If this force raises the opportunity cost of union membership for some subset of workers (for example, by depressing the return to skill), it may undermine union coalitions, leading to an amplified impact on employment and wages (e.g., Acemoglu et al., 2001). Richer and empirically more important forms of two-way interactions between technology and unions and other workplace arrangements are another fruitful area for future research.

Cross-country trends: We have shown that changes in the occupation of distribution are surprisingly comparable across a sizable set of advanced economies. This fact not withstanding, changes in the earnings distribution have been quite different in different countries (e.g., Davis, 1992; Blau and Kahn, 1996; Card et al., 1996; Katz and Autor, 1999; Card and Lemieux, 2001a,b; Atkinson, 2008; Dustmann et al., 2009; Atkinson et al., 2010; Boudarbat et al., 2010). One interpretation of these facts is that while many advanced countries have experienced similar technological forces that have altered occupational structures, the manner in which their labor markets (in particular their wage schedules) has responded to them have been far from identical. As of yet, there is no satisfactory understanding of the root causes of these differences. One possibility is that the adoption of new technologies either replacing or complementing workers in certain tasks requires up-front fixed investments, and the incentives for adopting these technologies are not only affected by labor supply and demand, but also by existing regulations. It is then possible that firms select different technologies in different countries in accordance with these constraints, and this may affect the evolution of real wages for various skill groups. For example, Acemoglu (2003) suggests a model in which institutionally-imposed wage compression encourages the adoption of technologies that increase the productivity of low skill workers and thus slows demand shifts against these skill groups.

Changes in male-female and white-nonwhite wage differentials: Our empirical analysis highlighted the substantial differences in the evolution of employment and earnings between men and women. The framework and data both suggest that the comparatively poor labor market performance of males may in part be due to the fact that men were more heavily represented in middle skill production occupations that were undercut by automation and offshoring.[80] A similar contrast might exist between white and nonwhite workers. Juhn et al. (1991) provided an early attempt to explain the differential evolution of earnings and employment by race and gender as a result of skill biased demand shifts. A similar comprehensive exercise, with a richer conception of technology potentially rooted in a task-based approach, is a logical next step to obtain a more complete understanding of the recent changes in the distribution of employment and earnings among minority and non-minority groups.

The importance of service occupations: Our framework highlights why recent technical change might have increased employment in service occupations. The idea here is related to Baumol's classic argument, where the demand for labor from sectors experiencing slower technical advances might be greater if there is sufficient complementarity between the goods and services that they and more rapidly growing sectors produce (Baumol, 1967; see also, Acemoglu and Guerrieri, 2007; Pissarides and Ngai, 2007; Autor and Dorn, 2009, 2010). Our framework captures this phenomenon to some degree, but because of the unit elasticity of substitution across all tasks, the extent of this effect is limited. A somewhat different variant of our framework may be necessary to better capture the evolution of the demand for services during the past several decades.

DATA APPENDIX

May/Outgoing Rotation Groups Current Population Survey

Wages are calculated using May/ORG CPS data for earnings years 1973-2009 for all workers aged 16-64 who are not in the military, institutionalized or self-employed. Wages are weighted by CPS sample weights. Hourly wages are equal to the logarithm of reported hourly earnings for those paid by the hour and the logarithm of usual weekly earnings divided by hours worked last week for non-hourly workers. Top-coded earnings observations are multiplied by 1.5. Hourly earners of below $1.675/hour in 1982 dollars ($3.41/hour in 2008 dollars) are dropped, as are hourly wages exceeding

---

[80] We should caveat, however, that female workers have also been substantially displaced over the last two decades from a different set of middle skill tasks (in particular, administrative support and clerical jobs), without seemingly experiencing the adverse wage and employment consequences observed among men.

1/35th the top-coded value of weekly earnings. All earnings are deflated by the chain-weighted (implicit) price deflator for personal consumption expenditures (PCE). Allocated earnings observations are excluded in all years, except where allocation flags are unavailable (January 1994 to August 1995).

March Current Population Survey

Wages are calculated using March CPS data for earnings years 1963-2008 for full-time, full-year workers aged 16-64, excluding those who are in the military or self-employed. Full-time, full-year workers are those who usually worked 35 or more hours per week and worked forty or more weeks in the previous year. Weekly earnings are calculated as the logarithm of annual earnings divided by weeks worked. Calculations are weighted by CPS sampling weights and are deflated using the personal consumption expenditure (PCE) deflator. Earnings of below $67/week in 1982 dollars ($136/week in 2008 dollars) are dropped. Allocated earnings observations are excluded in earnings years 1967 forward using either family earnings allocation flags (1967-1974) or individual earnings allocation flags (1975 earnings year forward).

Census/American Community Survey

Census Integrated Public Use Micro Samples for years 1960, 1970, 1980, 1990, and 2000, and American Community Survey for 2008 are used in this paper. All Census samples include 5% of the population, except 1970, which includes 1% of the population. Wages are calculated for full-time, full-year workers aged 16-64, excluding those who are in the military, institutionalized or self-employed. Weekly earnings are calculated as the logarithm of annual earnings divided by weeks worked. Calculations are weighted by Census sampling weights and are deflated using the personal consumption expenditure (PCE) deflator.

Education categories used for the May/ORG and March CPS files and Census/ACS files are equivalent to those employed by Autor et al. (2003), based on the consistent classification system proposed by Jaeger (1997).

Dictionary of Occupational Titles

The US Labor Department's Dictionary of Occupational Titles (DOT) task measures used in this paper follow the construction of Autor et al. (2006), who collapse Autor et al.'s (2003) original five task measures into three categories: routine, manual and abstract. Routine corresponds to a simple average of two DOT measures: "set limits, tolerances and standards," and "finger dexterity." Manual corresponds to the DOT measure "eye-hand-foot coordination". Abstract is the simple average of two DOT measures: "direction, control and planning" and "GED math." DOT task measures are converted from their original 14,000 detailed occupations to 326 consistent occupations, which allow for merging with CPS and Census data files.

O*NET

O★NET task measures used in this paper are composite measures of O★NET Work Activities and Work Context Importance scales:

Non-routine cognitive: Analytical

> 4.A.2.a.4 Analyzing data/information
>
> 4.A.2.b.2 Thinking creatively
>
> 4.A.4.a.1 Interpreting information for others

Non-routine cognitive: Interpersonal

> 4.A.4.a.4 Establishing and maintaining personal relationships
>
> 4.A.4.b.4 Guiding, directing and motivating subordinates
>
> 4.A.4.b.5 Coaching/developing others

Routine cognitive

> 4.C.3.b.7 Importance of repeating the same tasks
>
> 4.C.3.b.4 Importance of being exact or accurate
>
> 4.C.3.b.8 Structured v. Unstructured work (reverse)

Routine manual

> 4.C.3.d.3 Pace determined by speed of equipment
>
> 4.A.3.a.3 Controlling machines and processes
>
> 4.C.2.d.1.i Spend time making repetitive motions

Non-routine manual physical

> 4.A.3.a.4 Operating vehicles, mechanized devices, or equipment
>
> 4.C.2.d.1.g Spend time using hands to handle, control or feel objects, tools or controls
>
> 1.A.2.a.2 Manual dexterity
>
> 1.A.1.f.1 Spatial orientation

Offshorability

> 4.C.1.a.2.l Face to face discussions (reverse)
>
> 4.A.4.a.5 Assisting and Caring for Others (reverse)
>
> 4.A.4.a.8 Performing for or Working Directly with the Public (reverse)
>
> 4.A.1.b.2 Inspecting Equipment, Structures, or Material (reverse)
>
> 4.A.3.a.2 Handling and Moving Objects (reverse)
>
> 4.A.3.b.4 0.5★Repairing and Maintaining Mechanical Equipment (reverse)
>
> 4.A.3.b.5 0.5★Repairing and Maintaining Electronic Equipment (reverse)

O⋆NET scales are created using the O⋆NET-SOC occupational classification scheme, which we collapse into SOC occupations. Each scale is then standardized to have mean zero and standard deviation one, using labor supply weights from the pooled 2005/6/7 Occupational Employment Statistics (OES) Survey, one of the few large surveys that uses the SOC occupational classification system. The composite task measures listed above are equal to the summation of their respective constituent scales, then standardized to mean zero and standard deviation one. In order to merge the composite task measures with the Census data, the task measures are collapsed to the Census 2000 occupational code level using the OES Survey labor supply weights and then collapsed to the 326 consistent occupations as detailed in Autor and Dorn (2010), using Census 2000 labor supply weights.

THEORETICAL APPENDIX: UNIQUENESS OF EQUILIBRIUM IN PROPOSITION 5

Let us proceed in steps. First, rewrite (23) and (24) as

$$\ln\left(\frac{w_H}{w_M}\right) = \ln\left(\frac{A_H}{A_M}\right) - \beta_H(I_H), \tag{41}$$

and

$$\ln\left(\frac{w_M}{w_L}\right) = \ln\left(\frac{A_M}{A_L}\right) - \beta_L(I_L), \tag{42}$$

where recall that $\beta_H(I) \equiv \ln \alpha_M(I) - \ln \alpha_H(I)$ and $\beta_L(I) \equiv \ln \alpha_L(I) - \ln \alpha_M(I)$ are both strictly decreasing in view of Assumption 1. Now substituting these two equations into (38), we have

$$H = \Gamma_H\left(\ln\left(\frac{A_H}{A_M}\right) - \beta_H(I_H)\right)$$

$$M = \Gamma_M\left(\ln\left(\frac{A_H}{A_M}\right) - \beta_H(I_H), \ln\left(\frac{A_M}{A_L}\right) - \beta_L(I_L)\right)$$

$$L = \Gamma_L\left(\ln\left(\frac{A_M}{A_L}\right) - \beta_L(I_L)\right),$$

where we denote derivatives of these functions by Γ'_H, Γ'_L, and Γ^1_M and Γ^2_M for the first and second derivatives of Γ_M. The arguments so far immediately imply that $\Gamma'_H > 0$, $\Gamma'_L < 0$ and $\Gamma^1_M < 0$ and $\Gamma^2_M > 0$. Now rewriting (32) and (33) substituting for these, we again have a two-equation system in I_H and I_L characterizing the equilibrium. It is given by

$$\ln A_M - \ln A_H + \beta_H (I_H) + \ln \Gamma_M \left(\ln \left(\frac{A_H}{A_M} \right) - \beta_H (I_H) , \ln \left(\frac{A_M}{A_L} \right) - \beta_L (I_L) \right)$$

$$- \ln \Gamma_H \left(\ln \left(\frac{A_H}{A_M} \right) - \beta_H (I_H) \right) - \ln (I_H - I_L) + \ln (1 - I_H) = 0, \qquad (43)$$

and

$$\ln A_L - \ln A_M + \beta_L (I_L) + \ln \Gamma_L \left(\ln \left(\frac{A_M}{A_L} \right) - \beta_L (I_L) \right)$$

$$- \ln \Gamma_M \left(\ln \left(\frac{A_H}{A_M} \right) - \beta_H (I_H) , \ln \left(\frac{A_M}{A_L} \right) - \beta_L (I_L) \right)$$

$$+ \ln (I_H - I_L) - \ln (I_L) = 0. \qquad (44)$$

Let us evaluate the Jacobian of this system at an equilibrium. Following similar steps to those we used in the comparative static analysis before, this can be written as

$$\begin{pmatrix} \beta_H' (I_H) \left[1 + \frac{\Gamma_H'}{\Gamma_H} - \frac{\Gamma_M^1}{\Gamma_M} \right] - \frac{1}{I_H - I_L} - \frac{1}{1 - I_H} & \frac{1}{I_H - I_L} - \frac{\Gamma_M^2}{\Gamma_M} \beta_L' (I_L) \\ \frac{1}{I_H - I_L} + \frac{\Gamma_M^1}{\Gamma_M} \beta_H' (I_H) & \beta_L' (I_L) \left[1 - \frac{\Gamma_L'}{\Gamma_L} + \frac{\Gamma_M^2}{\Gamma_M} \right] - \frac{1}{I_H - I_L} - \frac{1}{I_L} \end{pmatrix}.$$

Since $\Gamma_H' > 0$, $\Gamma_L' > 0$, $\Gamma_M^1 > 0$ and $\Gamma_M^2 < 0$, the diagonal elements of this matrix are always negative. In addition, we verify that the determinant of this matrix is also always positive. In particular, denoting the determinant by Δ, we have

$$\Delta = \left(\beta_H' (I_H) \left[1 + \frac{\Gamma_H'}{\Gamma_H} - \frac{\Gamma_M^1}{\Gamma_M} \right] - \frac{1}{I_H - I_L} - \frac{1}{1 - I_H} \right)$$

$$\times \left(\beta_L' (I_L) \left[1 - \frac{\Gamma_L'}{\Gamma_L} + \frac{\Gamma_M^2}{\Gamma_M} \right] - \frac{1}{I_H - I_L} - \frac{1}{I_L} \right)$$

$$- \left(\frac{1}{I_H - I_L} - \frac{\Gamma_M^2}{\Gamma_M} \beta_L' (I_L) \right) \times \left(\frac{1}{I_H - I_L} + \frac{\Gamma_M^1}{\Gamma_M} \beta_H' (I_H) \right)$$

$$= \left(\beta_H' (I_H) \left[1 + \frac{\Gamma_H'}{\Gamma_H} \right] - \frac{1}{1 - I_H} \right) \times \left(\beta_L' (I_L) \left[1 - \frac{\Gamma_L'}{\Gamma_L} \right] - \frac{1}{I_L} \right)$$

$$- \frac{1}{I_H - I_L} \times \left(\beta_H' (I_H) \left[1 + \frac{\Gamma_H'}{\Gamma_H} - \frac{\Gamma_M^1}{\Gamma_M} \right] \right)$$

$$-\frac{1}{1-I_H}+\beta_L'\left(I_L\right)\left[1-\frac{\Gamma_L'}{\Gamma_L}+\frac{\Gamma_M^2}{\Gamma_M}\right]-\frac{1}{I_L}\Bigg)$$

$$-\frac{\Gamma_M^1}{\Gamma_M}\times\left(\beta_L'\left(I_L\right)\left[1-\frac{\Gamma_L'}{\Gamma_L}s\right]-\frac{1}{I_L}\right)$$

$$+\frac{\Gamma_M^2}{\Gamma_M}\times\left(\beta_H'\left(I_H\right)\left[1+\frac{\Gamma_H'}{\Gamma_H}\right]-\frac{1}{1-I_H}\right).$$

All five lines of the last expression are positive, and thus so is Δ. This implies that the Jacobian is everywhere a P-matrix, and from Simsek et al. (2007), it follows that there exists a unique equilibrium.

Moreover, given that the determinant is everywhere positive, comparative static results are similar to those of the equilibrium with fixed supplies. For example, an increase in A_H will reduce I_H and increase w_H/w_M and w_M/w_L as before, but also it will increase H/L. Similarly, if new machines replace tasks previously performed by middle skills, this will increase w_H/w_M and reduce w_M/w_L, as workers previously performing middle skill tasks are reallocated to low and high skills. In addition, there will now be a supply response, and workers previously supplying their middle skills will shift to supplying either low or high skills. In particular, if the relevant margin of substitution in the supply side is between middle and low, many of these workers will start supplying low skills to the market, leading to an expansion of low skill tasks.

REFERENCES

Acemoglu, Daron, 1998. Why do new technologies complement skills? Directed technical change and wage inequality. Quarterly Journal of Economics 113, 1055–1090.
Acemoglu, Daron, 1999. Changes in unemployment and wage inequality: an alternative theory and some evidence. American Economic Review 89, 1259–1278.
Acemoglu, Daron, 2002a. Technology and the labor market. Journal of Economic Literature 40, 7–72.
Acemoglu, Daron, 2002b. Directed technical change. Review of Economic Studies 69, 781–810.
Acemoglu, Daron, 2003. Cross-country inequality trends. Economic Journal 113, F121-149.
Acemoglu, Daron, 2007. Equilibrium bias of technology. Econometrica 75, 1371–1410.
Acemoglu, Daron, 2009. When does labor scarcity encourage innovation? NBER working paper 14819, March.
Acemoglu, Daron, Aghion, Philippe, Violente, Gianluca, 2001. Deunionization, technical change, and inequality, Carnegie-Rochester conference series on public policy.
Acemoglu, Daron, Zilibotti, Fabrizio, 2001. Productivity differences. Quarterly Journal of Economics 116, 563–606.
Acemoglu, Daron, Guerrieri, Veronica, 2007. Capital deepening and nonbalanced economic growth. Journal of Political Economy 116 (3), 467–498.
Acemoglu, Daron, Gancia, Gino, Zilibotti, Fabrizio, 2010. Offshoring, innovation and wages. Mimeo.
Antonczyk, Dirk, DeLeire, Thomas, Fitzenberger, Bernd, 2010. Polarization and rising wage inequality: comparing the US and Germany. University of Freiburg Working Paper, March.
Antonczyk, Dirk, Fitzenberger, Bernd, Leuschner, Ute, 2009. Can a task-based approach explain the recent changes in the German wage structure? Jahrbücher für Nationalökonomie und Statistik (Journal of Economics and Statistics) 229 (2–3), 214–238.

Atkinson, Anthony B., 2008. The Changing Distribution of Earnings in OECD Countries (The Rodolfo De Benedetti Lecture Series). Oxford University Press, New York.

Atkinson, Anthony B., Piketty, Thomas, Saez, Emmanuel, 2010. Top incomes in the long run of history. UC Berkeley Working Paper, January.

Autor, David H., Dorn, David, 2009. This job is getting old: measuring changes in job opportunities using occupational age structure. American Economic Review Papers and Proceedings 99.

Autor, David H., Dorn, David, 2010. Inequality and specialization: the growth of low-skilled service employment in the United States. MIT Working Paper, April.

Autor, David H., Manning, Alan, Smith, Christopher L., 2009. The minimum wage's role in the evolution of US wage inequality over three decades: a modest reassessment. MIT Mimeograph, April.

Autor, David H., Handel, Michael, 2009. Putting tasks to the test: human capital, job tasks and wages, NBER Working Paper No. 15116, June.

Autor, David H., Levy, Frank, Murnane, Richard J., 2002. Upstairs downstairs: computers and skills on two floors of a large bank. Industrial and Labor Relations Review 55 (3), 432–447.

Autor, David H., Levy, Frank, Murnane, Richard J., 2003. The skill content of recent technological change: an empirical exploration. Quarterly Journal of Economics 116 (4).

Autor, David H., Katz, Lawrence F., Kearney, Melissa S., 2005. Rising wage inequality: the role of composition and prices. NBER Working Paper No. 11628, September.

Autor, David H., Katz, Lawrence F., Kearney, Melissa S., 2006. The polarization of the US labor market. American Economic Review Papers and Proceedings 96 (2), 189–194.

Autor, David H., Katz, Lawrence F., Kearney, Melissa S., 2008. Trends in US wage inequality: re-assessing the revisionists. Review of Economics and Statistics 90 (2), 300–323.

Autor, David, Katz, Lawrence, Krueger, Alan, 1998. Computing inequality: have computers changed the labor market? Quarterly Journal of Economics 113I, 1169–1214.

Bartel, Ann P., Ichniowski, Casey, Shaw, Kathryn L., 2007. How does information technology affect productivity? Plant-level comparisons of product innovation, process improvement and worker skills. Quarterly Journal of Economics 122 (4), 1721–1758.

Baumol, William J., 1967. Macroeconomics of unbalanced growth: anatomy of an urban crisis. American Economic Review 57 (3), 415–426.

Black, Dan, Kolesnikova, Natalia, Taylor, Lowell J., 2009. Earnings functions when wages and prices vary by location. Journal of Labor Economics 27 (1), 21–47.

Black, Sandra E., Spitz-Oener, Alexandra, 2010. Explaining women's success: technological change and the skill content of women's work. The Review of Economics and Statistics 92, 187–194.

Blau, Francine D., Kahn, Lawrence M., 1996. International differences in male wage inequality: institutions versus market forces. Journal Political Economy 104, 791–837.

Blinder, Alan, 2007. How many US jobs might be offshorable? Princeton University Center for Economic Policy Studies, Working Paper No. 142, March.

Blinder, Alan, Krueger, Alan B., 2008. Measuring offshorability: a survey approach. Princeton University Working Paper, October.

Borghans, Lex, ter Weel, Bas, Weinberg, Bruce A., 2008. Interpersonal styles and labor market outcomes. Journal of Human Resources 43 (4), 815–858.

Boskin, Michael, Dulberger, Ellen, Gordon, Robert, Griliches, Zvi, Jorgenson, Dale, 1996. Toward a more accurate measure of the cost of living, Final Report to the Senate Finance Committee.

Boudarbat, Brahim, Lemieux, Thomas, Craig Riddell, W., 2010. The evolution of the returns to human capital in Canada, 1980-2005. IZA Working Paper No. 4809, March.

Bresnahan, Timothy F., 1999. Computerisation and wage dispersion: an analytical reinterpretation. The Economic Journal 109 (456), 390–415.

Bresnahan, Timothy F., Brynjolfsson, Erik, Hitt, Lorin M., 1999. Information technology, workplace organization and the demand for skilled labor: firm-level evidence, NBER Working Paper 7136, May.

Burkhauser, Richard V., Feng, Shuaizhang, Larrimore, Jeff, 2008. Improving imputations of top incomes in the public-use current population survey by using both cell-means and variances. NBER Working Paper #14458, October.

Card, David, DiNardo, John, 2002. Skill biased technological change and rising wage inequality: some problems and puzzles. Journal of Labor Economics 20, 733–783.

Card, David, Lemieux, Thomas, 2001a. Can falling supply explain the rising return to college for younger men? A cohort-based analysis. Quarterly Journal of Economics 116, 705–746.

Card, David, Lemieux, Thomas, 2001b. Dropout and enrollment trends in the postwar period: what went wrong in the 1970s? In: Gruber, Jonathan (Ed.), Risky Behavior among Youths: An Economic Analysis. University of Chicago Press, Chicago (Chapter 9).

Card, David, Kramartz, Francis, Lemieux, Thomas, 1996. Changes in the relative structure of wages and employment: a comparison of the United States, Canada and France. Mimeo.

Carneiro, Pedro, Lee, Sokbae, 2009. Trends in quality-adjusted skill premia in the United States, 1960-2000 CEMMAP Working Paper, CWP02/09.

Caroli, Eve, van Reenen, John, 1999. Wage inequality and organizational change, Mimeo UCL.

Champernowne, David, 1963. A dynamic growth model involving a production function. In: Lutz, F.A., Hague, D.C. (Eds.), The Theory of Capital. Macmillan, New York.

Costinot, Arnaud, Vogel, Jonathan, Matching and Inequality in the World Economy. Journal of Political Economy (forthcoming).

Davis, S., 1992. Cross-country patterns of changes in relative wages. In: NBER Macroeconomic Annual. MIT Press, Cambridge, pp. 239–292.

Dessein, Wouter, Santos, Tanos, 2006. Adaptive organizations. Journal of Political Economy 114 (5), 956–995.

DiNardo, John, Fortin, Nicole, Lemieux, Thomas, 1996. Labor market institutions and the distribution of wages, 1973-1992: a semiparametric approach. Econometrica 64, 1001–1044.

DiNardo, John E., Pischke, Jörn-Steffen, 1997. The returns to computer use revisited: Have pencils changed the wage structure too? Quarterly Journal of Economics 112, 291–303.

Dornbusch, Rudiger, Fischer, Stanley, Samuelson, Paul A., 1977. Comparative advantage, trade, and payments in a Ricardian model with a continuum of goods. American Economic Review 67 (5), 823–839.

Dustmann, Christian, Ludsteck, Johannes, Schönberg, Uta, 2009. Revisiting the German wage structure. Quarterly Journal of Economics 124 (2), 809–842.

Ellwood, David, 2002. The sputtering labor force of the twenty-first century: can social policy help? In: Krueger, Alan B., Solow, Robert M. (Eds.), The Roaring Nineties: Can Full Employment be Sustained?. Russell Sage Foundation and Century Foundation Press, New York.

Feenstra, Robert, Hanson, Gordon, 1999. The impact of outsourcing and high-technology capital on wages: estimates for the United States, 1979-1990. Quarterly Journal of Economics 114 (3), 907–940.

Firpo, Sergio, Fortin, Nicole, Lemieux, Thomas, 2009. Occupational Tasks and Changes in the Wage Structure. UBC Working Paper, September.

Fitzenberger, Bernd, Kohn, Karsten, 2006. Skill wage premia, employment, and cohort effects: are workers in Germany all of the same type? University of Freiburg Working Paper, June.

Freeman, Richard, 1976. The Overeducated American. Academic Press, New York.

Freeman, Richard, 1986. Demand for education. In: Ashenfelter, Orley, Layard, Richard (Eds.), Handbook of Labor Economics, vol. I. North Holland, pp. 357–386 (Chapter 6).

Garicano, Luis, 2000. Hierarchies and the organization of knowledge in production, 108, 874-904.

Garicano, Luis, Rossi-Hansberg, Esteban, 2006. Organization and inequality in a knowledge economy. Quarterly Journal of Economics 121 (4), 1383–1435.

Gathmann, Christina, Schönberg, Uta, 2010. How general is human capital? a task-based approach. Journal of Labor Economics 28 (1), 1–49.

Goldin, Claudia, Margo, Robert, 1992. The Great compression: the wage structure in the United States at mid-century. Quarterly Journal of Economics 107, 1–34.

Goldin, Claudia, Katz, Lawrence, 2008. The Race between Education and Technology. Harvard University Press, Cambridge.

Goos, Maarten, Manning, Alan, 2007. Lousy and lovely jobs: the rising polarization of work in Britain. Review of Economics and Statistics 89 (1), 118–133.

Goos, Maarten, Manning, Alan, Salomons, Anna, 2009. The polarization of the European labor market. American Economic Review Papers and Proceedings 99 (2).

Goos, Maarten, Manning, Alan, Salomons, Anna, 2010. Recent changes in the European employment structure: the roles of technological change, Globalization and Institutions. Katholieke Universiteit Leuven. Mimeo.

Grossman, Gene, Rossi-Hansberg, Esteban, 2008. Trading tasks: a simple theory of offshoring. American Economic Review 98 (5), 1978–1997.

Hamermesh, Daniel, 1999. Changing inequality in markets for workplace amenities. Quarterly Journal of Economics 114.

Heckman, James J., Lochner, Lance, Taber, Christopher, 1998. Explaining rising wage inequality: explorations with a dynamic general equilibrium model of labor earnings with heterogeneous agents. Review of Economic Dynamics 1, 1–58.

Heckman, James J., Sedlacek, Guilherme, 1985. Heterogeneity, aggregation, and market wage functions: an empirical model of self-selection in the labor market. Journal of Political Economy 93, 1077–1125.

Hellwig, Martin, Irmen, Andreas, 2001. Endogenous technical change in a competitive economy. Journal of Economic Theory 10 (1), 1–39.

Hirsch, Barry T., Schumacher, Edward J., 2004. Match bias in wage gap estimates due to earnings imputation. Journal of Labor Economics 22 (3), 689–722.

Hounshell, David A, 1985. From the American System to Mass Production, 1800–1932: The Development of Manufacturing Technology in the United States. Johns Hopkins University Press, Baltimore.

Ikenaga, Toshie, 2009. Polarization of the Japanese labor market—adoption of ICT and changes in tasks required. Japanese Journal of Labour Studies 584, 73–90.

Ikenaga, Toshie, Kambayashi, Ryo, 2010. Long-term trends in the polarization of the Japanese labor market: the increase of non-routine task input and its valuation in the labor market. Hitotsubashi University Institute of Economic Research Working Paper, January.

Jaeger, David A., 1997. Reconciling the old and new Census Bureau education questions: recommendations for researchers. Journal of Business and Economics Statistics 15, 300–309.

James, John A., Skinner, Jonathan S., 1985. The resolution of the labor-scarcity paradox. The Journal of Economic History 45 (03), 513–540.

Jensen, J. Bradford, Kletzer, Lori G., Bernstein, Jared, Feenstra, Robert C., 2005. Tradable services: understanding the scope and impact of services offshoring. In: Brookings Trade Forum: Offshoring White-Collar Work. The Brookings Institution, Washington, DC, pp. 75–133.

Jensen, J. Bradford, Kletzer, Lori, Measuring tradable services and the task content of offshorable services jobs. In: Katharine Abraham, Mike Harper, James Spletzer (Eds.), Labor in the New Economy, University of Chicago Press, Chicago (forthcoming).

Oldenski, Lindsay, 2009. Export versus FDI: A Task-Based Framework for Comparing manufacturing and services. Georgetown University Working Paper.

Johnson, George, 1970. The demand for labor by education category. Southern Economic Journal 37, 190–204.

Juhn, Chinhui, 1994. Wage inequality and industrial change: evidence from five decades. NBER working paper no. 4684.

Juhn, Chinhui, Murphy, Kevin M., Pierce, Brooks, 1993. Wage inequality and the rise in returns to skill. Journal of Political Economy 101, 410–442.

Juhn, Chinhui, Murphy, Kevin, Topel, Robert H., 1991. Why has the natural rate of unemployment increased over time? Brookings Papers on Economic Activity 0 (2), 75–126.

Katz, Lawrence, Autor, David, 1999. Changes in the wage structure and earnings inequality. In: Ashenfelter, O. (Ed.), The Handbook of Labor Economics, vol. III. Elsevier, Amsterdam.

Katz, Lawrence, Murphy, Kevin, 1992. Changes in relative wages: supply and demand factors. Quarterly Journal of Economics CVII, 35–78.

Katz, Lawrence, Loveman, Gary W., Blanchflower, David G., 1995. A comparison of changes in the structure of wages in four OECD countries. In: Freeman, Richard, Katz, Lawrence (Eds.), Differences and Changes in Wage Structures. National Bureau of Economic Research, University of Chicago Press.

Kremer, Michael, Maskin, Eric, 1996. Wage inequality and segregation by skill. NBER Working Paper No. 5718, August.

Lee, David S., 1999. Wage inequality in the US During the 1980s: rising dispersion or falling minimum wage? Quarterly Journal of Economics 114.

Lemieux, Thomas, 2006a. Increased residual wage inequality: composition effects, noisy data, or rising demand for skill? American Economic Review 96, 461–498.

Lemieux, Thomas, 2006b. Post-secondary education and increasing wage inequality. NBER Working Paper No. 12077.

Lemieux, Thomas, 2008. The changing nature of wage inequality. Journal of Population Economics 21 (1).

Lemieux, Thomas, Bentley MacLeod, W., Parent, Daniel, 2009. Performance pay and wage inequality. Quarterly Journal of Economics 124 (1), 1–49.

Levy, Frank, Murnane, Richard J., 2004. The New Division of Labor. Princeton University Press, New Jersey.

Manning, Alan, 2004. We can work it out: the impact of technological change on the demand for low-skill workers. Scottish Journal of Political Economy 51 (5), 581–608.

Mazzolari, Francesca, Ragusa, Giuseppe, 2008. Spillovers from high-skill consumption to low-skill labor markets. University of California at Irvine Working Paper, May.

Meyer, Bruce D., Sullivan, James X., 2008. Changes in the consumption, income, and well-being of single mother headed families. American Economic Review 98 (5), 2221–2241.

Michaels, Guy, Natraj, Ashwini, Van Reenen, John, 2009. Has ICT polarized skill demand? Evidence from eleven countries over 25 years. London School of Economics Centre for Economic Performance Working Paper, December.

Mokyr, Joel, 1992. The lever of riches: technological creativity and economic progress. Oxford University Press.

Moretti, Enrico, 2008. Real wage inequality. NBER Working Paper No. 14370, September 2008.

Murphy, Kevin M., Graig Riddell, W., Romer, Paul M., 1998. Wages, skills and technology in the United States and Canada. In: Helpman, E. (Ed.), General Purpose Technologies. MIT Press, Cambridge, MA.

Nordhaus, William D., 2007. Two centuries of productivity growth in computing. Journal of Economic History 67 (1), 128–159.

Peri, Giovanni, Sparber, Chad, 2008. Task specialization, immigration and wages. CReaM Discussion Paper Series No. 02/08.

Pierce, Brooks, 2001. Compensation inequality. Quarterly Journal of Economics 116, 1493–1525.

Pierce, Brooks, Recent trends in compensation inequality. In: Katharine Abraham, Mike Harper, James Spletzer (Eds.), Labor in the New Economy, University of Chicago Press, Chicago (forthcoming).

Piketty, Thomas, Saez, Emmanuel, 2003. Income Inequality in the United States, 1913-1998. Quarterly Journal of Economics 118, 1–39.

Pissarides, Christopher A., Ngai, L. Rachel, 2007. Structural change in a multisector model of growth. American Economic Review 97, 429–443.

Reshef, Ariell, 2009. Skill biased technological change in services versus the rest: an estimate and interpretation. University of Virginia Working Paper.

Rodriguez-Clare, Andres, Ramondo, Natalia, 2010. Growth, Size and Openness: A Quantitative Approach, January.

Romer, Paul, 1990. Endogenous technological change. Journal of Political Economy 98 (S5), 71–102.

Rosen, Sherwin, 1974. Hedonic prices and implicit markets: product differentiation in pure competition. Journal of Political Economy 82, 34–55.

Rosen, Sherwin, 1981. The economics of superstars. American Economic Review 71, 845–858.

Rosen, Sherwin, 1982. Authority, control, and the distribution of earnings. Bell Journal of Economics 13, 311–323.

Saint-Paul, Gilles, 2001. On the distribution of income and workers under intrafirm spillovers with an application to ideas and networks. Journal of Political Economy 109, 1–37.

Saint-Paul, Gilles, 2008. Innovation and Inequality: How Does Technical Progress Affect Workers. Princeton University Press, Princeton.

Sattinger, Michael, 1975. Comparative advantage and the distributions of earnings and abilities. Econometrica 43, 455–468.

Sattinger, Michael, 1993. Assignment models of the distribution of earnings. Journal of Economic Literature 31, 831–880.

Simsek, Alp, Ozdaglar, Asuman E., Acemoglu, Daron, 2007. Generalized Poincaré-Hopf theorem for compact nonsmooth regions. Mathematics of Operations Research 32, 193–214.

Spitz-Oener, Alexandra, 2006. Technical change, job tasks, and rising educational demands: looking outside the wage structure. Journal of Labor Economics 24 (2), 235–270.

Teulings, Coen N., 2003. The contribution of minimum wages to increasing inequality. The Economic Journal 113, 801–833.

Teulings, Coen N., 1995. The wage distribution in a model of assignment of skills to jobs. Journal of Political Economy 103, 280–315.

Tinbergen, Jan, 1974. Substitution of graduate by other labor. Kyklos 27, 217–226.

Tinbergen, Jan, 1975. Income Difference: Recent Research. North-Holland Publishing Company, Amsterdam.

Weiss, Matthias, 2008. Skill-biased technical change: is there hope for the unskilled? Economics Letters 100 (3), 439–441.

Welch, Finis, 1973. Black-white differences in returns to schooling. American Economic Review 63, 893–907.

Wilson, Charles A., 1980. On the General Structure of Ricardian Models with a Continuum of Goods: Applications to Growth, Tariff theory, and technical change. Econometrica 48 (7), 1675–1702.

Zeira, Joseph, 1998. Workers, machines and economic growth. Quarterly Journal of Economics 113, 1091–1113.

Zeira, Joseph, 2006. Machines as engines of growth center for economic policy research, Discussion Paper 5429, 2006.

CHAPTER 13

Institutional Reforms and Dualism in European Labor Markets☆

Tito Boeri
Università Bocconi and Fondazione Rodolfo Debenedetti

Contents

☆ I thank participants to a workshop in Berkeley and Paris for useful comments on an initial draft. Massimo Anelli and Gaetano Basso provided unflagging research assistance.

Handbook of Labor Economics, Volume 4b
© 2011 Elsevier B.V.

ISSN 0169-7218, DOI 10.1016/S0169-7218(11)02411-7

Abstract

Most of the recent literature on the effects of labor market institutions on wages and employment draws on reforms used as natural experiments. This is a significant improvement with respect to the earlier literature which was based solely on cross-country variation in (highly imperfect) measures of these institutions. But this new literature lacks guidance from a body of theory acknowledging the fact that regulatory changes often create longlasting asymmetries, two-tier regimes, between a reformed and an unreformed segment of the labor market. This chapter provides new evidence on reforms in Europe, a continent with well established institutions and a very intense reform activity in the last 25 years. In light of this evidence, it extends a general equilibrium model of the labor market allowing for two-tier reforms of employment protection, unemployment benefits and employment conditional incentives. Next, it provides evidence on the scale and macroeconomic effects of the dualism induced by these reforms. Finally, it critically surveys the empirical literature drawing on institutional reforms in Europe.

JEL classification: J63; J64; J68

Keywords: Reforms; Two-tier reforms; Dualism

1. INTRODUCTION

There is a large body of academic papers and policy reports on the effects of European-type labor market *institutions* on economic performance. The early literature largely draws on cross-country (mainly Transatlantic) comparisons, and was reviewed in previous Handbook of Labor Economics (HLE) Chapters. In particular, Blau and Kahn (1999), Bertola (1999) as well as Layard and Nickell (1999) in the third HLE volume addressed various dimensions of the relationship between institutions and labor market performance. Machin and Manning (1999) also offered in that volume an extensive review of the literature on the European unemployment problem, which inspired much of the early literature on institutions.

More recent work has been identifying the effects of institutions by using differences-in-differences techniques which exploit time-series variation in these institutions as well as asymmetries in the enforcement of norms *within* each country. This most recent literature actually draws on institutional *reforms* rather than on cross-country variation in the levels of different institutions. Moreover, it widely exploits asymmetric reforms, that is, institutional changes affecting only a segment of the labor market and leaving the other segments unaffected.

The purpose of this chapter is to critically review this more recent empirical literature and motivate further research in this area. As I will argue in this chapter, further empirical work needs stronger guidance from a theory capturing the key features of these institutional *reforms*, notably their two-tier structure, the fact that they are concentrated on a subsegment of the population potentially affected by the reform. The models referred to by applied economists typically have empirical implications concerning the effects of complete reforms of these institutions, as they compare equilibrium outcomes with more or less of any given institution for everybody. However, the reforms that are actually taking place in Europe and those that are used in empirical research as "natural experiments" are mainly partial reforms, creating two-tier regimes, and longlasting asymmetries in the enforcement of these institutions.

While the pioneering work of Saint-Paul (1996) investigated the *determinants* of two-tier reforms from a political economic perspective, and there is some literature (surveyed by Roland, 2001) on dual-track liberalization in economies coming from central planning, much less is known about the *effects* on the labor market of reforms allowing for the coexistence of different institutional regimes at the equilibrium. Two-tier regimes also have an important transitional dynamics which has yet to be thoroughly investigated from a theoretical perspective.

In applied work it is very important to acknowledge that asymmetric reforms may involve relevant interactions between reformed and unreformed segments of the labor market. These interactions need to be taken into account when defining proper identification strategies. Another important issue that could be better addressed drawing on stronger theoretical guidance is endogenous sorting in treatment and control groups in the literature drawing on natural experiments.

Engineering two-tier reforms is generally a device for Governments to win political obstacles to sizeable regulatory changes. There seems to be a trade-off between the size and scope of reforms, where larger reforms are more likely to be two-tier. Thus, such reforms may generate non-negligible general equilibrium effects. Applied work on reforms would then greatly benefit also from a theory providing insights as to the effects of these reforms on the macro variables of the labor markets. Most applied work to date takes instead a partial equilibrium perspective.

The effects of two-tier reforms on aggregate labor market dynamics have been highlighted by labor market adjustment before and after the Great Recession of 2008-9. In particular, there is evidence that a higher degree of "dualism" in the enforcement of employment protection legislation contributed to an increase the elasticity of employment to output changes at unchanged regulations for permanent contracts. Dualism also in the enforcement of unemployment benefits may have reduced the coverage of income support schemes for job losers, negatively affecting the effectiveness of automatic stabilizers.

The structure of this chapter is as follows.

Section 2 defines labor market institutions, describes the key institutional clusters prevailing in Europe, and characterizes reforms, either complete or two-tier, discrete or incremental. It also provides evidence on the characteristics of institutional changes taking place in European labor markets in the last 30 years and compares them with developments in product market and financial market regulations. Section 3 extends a general equilibrium model of the labor market to allow for two-tier reforms in those institutions in which more activism has been documented. It also provides some empirical evidence on the relevance of "dualism" in labor market adjustment to shocks. Section 4 reviews the recent applied microeconomic literature on labor market institutions in light of the above characterization of reforms and theoretical predictions. Finally, Section 5 concludes.

2. INSTITUTIONS AND REFORMS

A large amount of empirical research on labor market institutions draws on cross-country comparisons of indicators of the intensity of different types of regulations. This literature was reviewed in previous handbook chapters (Bertola, 1999; Blau and Kahn, 1999; Layard and Nickell, 1999). In particular, the focus of the literature on the so-called "Eurosclerosis" (Bean, 1994; Alogoskoufis et al., 1995; Snower and de la Dehesa, 1996; Nickell, 1997) is on the role played by Transatlantic differences in the level of employment protection, unemployment benefit systems, payroll taxes and subsidies on labor as well as wage setting institutions in explaining the higher level and duration of unemployment in Europe vis-a-vis the US. Not always does this literature acknowledge the fact that unemployment had been higher in the US than in Europe in the 1960s and in the 1970s, when many of these institutions were already in place. It clearly cannot take into account that, at the time of writing this Chapter, the unemployment rate is once again higher in the US than in Europe.

Institutional comparisons between Europe and the US inspired much of the subsequent theoretical work on the aggregate implications of labor market institutions. This Transantlantic perspective misses two points: i. there are important differences in labor market institutions within Europe, and ii. institutions, notably in Europe, are undergoing important reforms. The focus of this Chapter is on what can be learned from this heterogeneity and these reforms. Thus, we begin by documenting them.

2.1. Institutional clusters in Europe

There is a high heterogeneity of labor market institutions within Europe. This heterogeneity has been extensively characterized by the political science literature on European social policy systems, the so-called "Social Europe".[1] This literature relies very much on qualitative assessments of institutions, providing at best an ordinal ranking of countries according to the different institutional features. Table 1 provides such rankings for various labor market institutions around the year 2000. In particular, we order countries according to five key institutional features, namely the strictness of employment protection legislation, the generosity of unemployment benefits, the scope of active labor market programmes, the incidence of taxes on low wages and the degree of centralization of collective bargaining institutions. The orderings are obtained from

---

[1] See Bertola et al. (2001) for a review, from an economic perspective, of this literature.

Table 1 European clusters of institutions.

	Employment protection	Unemployment benefits	Active labor market policies	Taxes on low wages	Collective bargaining	Average ranking
	Most restrictive	*Most generous*	*Highest*	*Highest*	*Most centralized*	
Belgium[c]	9	5	2	1	4	4.2
Sweden[b]	7	6	3	2	7	5
Denmark[b]	12	2	1	6	8	5.8
Netherlands[b]	10	1	4	9	6	6
France[c]	3	3	5	7	14	6.4
Finland[b]	11	8	6	5	3	6.6
Austria[c]	8	10	9	8	2	7.4
Spain[d]	4	7	7	11	9	7.6
Portugal[d]	1	4	11	12	11	7.8
Italy[d]	5	9	12	3	10	7.8
Germany[c]	6	12	8	4	12	8.4
Greece[d]	2	14	14	10	5	9
Ireland[a]	14	11	10	15	1	10.2
United Kingdom[a]	15	15	13	14	13	14
United States	16	13	16	13	16	14.8
Japan	13	16	15	16	15	15
	Less restrictive	*Less generous*	*Lowest*	*Lowest*	*Less centralized*	

Average ranking is the average of the previous columns.
 [a] Anglo–Saxon cluster.
 [b] Scandinavian cluster.
 [c] Continental European cluster.
 [d] Southern European cluster.

alternative indicators compiled by international organizations, such as the OECD, as well as by surveys of the employers and sociological studies on collective bargaining institutions (e.g., Visser, 2000). We also provide, in the sixth column on the right-hand-side of the table, a ranking of rankings, that is, a simple unweighted average of the position of the different countries along the five orderings.

As suggested by Table 1, all European countries generally have "more" of these institutions than Japan and the US. At the same time, the ranking of European countries is not uniform across the different policy domains. Some countries, for instance, rely more on employment protection to insure workers against labor market risk, while others use more unemployment benefits to attain the same objective.

The political science literature characterized this heterogeneity in terms of the following fourfold taxonomy of Social Europe(s) (Esping-Andersen, 1990).

The first group is represented by *Scandinavian* countries, featuring extensive fiscal intervention in labor markets, based on a variety of "active" policy instruments, substantial tax wedges, and reliance more on unemployment benefits than on employment protection in providing insurance against unemployment risk, along with the "flexicurity" paradigm. Union presence in the workplace and involvement in the setting and administration of unemployment benefits, if not centralized wage bargaining, generates in these countries compressed wage structures.

Anglo-Saxon countries, the second group, are characterized by weak unions and decentralized collective bargaining systems, allowing for relatively wide and increasing wage dispersion, low taxes at the bottom of the wage distribution also allowing for a relatively high incidence of low-pay employment, half-a-way between Europe and the US. Cash transfers here are primarily oriented to people in working-age. Activation measures are important as well as schemes conditioning access to benefits to regular employment.

Continental European countries rely extensively on unemployment benefits, but also maintain relatively stringent employment protection. They also tax quite heavily low wages. While union membership rates have been falling quite dramatically in the last 30 years, a strong union influence has been to a large extent preserved by regulations and practices artificially extending the coverage of collective bargaining much beyond union presence.

Finally *Mediterranean* countries rely mostly on employment protection and offer relatively low unemployment benefits, a polar case with respect to the Nordics. Collective bargaining institutions are rather centralized and, at least in the formal sector, generate highly compressed wage structures. Active policies are underdeveloped as these countries rarely developed an infrastructure, in terms of a Public Employment Service, delivering such policies.

As suggested by Table 1, the above fourfold taxonomy was still useful around the year 2000. In particular, the Nordic, Southern European and Anglo-Saxon groupings well captured institutional diversity within Europe, at least judging by the position of the countries of each group in the overall ranking. The Continental European countries group, however, looked much less homogenous than in the taxonomies provided by the political science literature a decade earlier.

The presence of different institutional clusters in Europe points to relevant complementarities across different types of institutions. These complementarities have been analyzed by the political economic literature (Saint-Paul, 2000), but rarely addressed by research on the effects of institutions on the labor market.

2.2. Institutional changes

The earlier literature on European labor market institutions did not analyze the evolution over time of these clusters. This omission is due to a lack of data. Until recently no series were available on many relevant institutional features of labor markets. Some of the institutional measures provided only ordinal measures or rankings of institutions, clearly not comparable over time. Later work, i.e., Blanchard and Wolfers (2000), Nickell et al. (2005) and Blanchard (2006), having access to cardinal measures of labor market institutions, could combine in panel estimates of aggregate employment and unemployment equations cross-sectional observations and some low-frequency time-series on institutions offering new insights, notably on the interactions between shocks and institutions. Yet, in this literature the identification comes mainly from cross-sectional variation. When fixed country effects are allowed for, many institutional variables are no longer statistically significant. Another reason for the scarce attention devoted by the literature to the evolution of European institutions is that economic models consider institutions as given, as a sort of an immanent feature of labor markets. We have theories of institutions rather than theories of institutional reforms, that is, of the effects of institutions which are being modified over time.

Labor market institutions have been subject to frequent policy changes in the last 20 years. This activism can be preliminarily characterized by moving to cardinal indicators of institutional intensity, notably some widely used indexes devised by the OECD, whose properties and shortcomings, are discussed in detail in Boeri and van Ours (2008). Figures 1 through 4 display the level of these indexes in the mid 1980s (horizontal axis) and at the most recent observation available (vertical axis). Countries located below the bisecting line through the origin have reduced over time the level of any given institution, whilst those located above the diagonal have increased it. Only countries located along the bisecting line have kept their institutions unchanged with respect to the initial year.

We consider the following four institutional indicators: the index of strictness of employment protection legislation (EPL); the summary generosity measure of unemployment benefits (UB); the active labor market policy (ALMP) expenditure to GDP ratio; and the total tax wedge on low wages. The first two measures are widely used by the literature: they draw on detailed information about

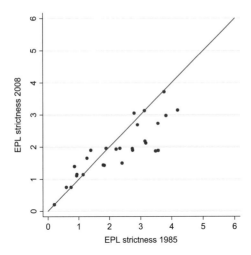

Figure 1   *OECD index of strictness of employment.*

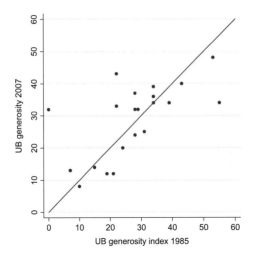

Figure 2   *OECD summary generosity measure of UB.*

national regulations and are increasing in the strictness of EPL and generosity of UB. Details on the OECD "Overall strictness of EPL" index are offered at http://stats.oecd.org/Index.aspx?DataSetCode=EPL_OV. The summary generosity measure is defined as a simple average of the de jure gross replacement rates over the first two years of an unemployment spell, still drawing on OECD data. The ALMP budget includes a variety of so-called "activation programmes" (AP) providing job counseling, placement and subsidized hiring, typically at low durations of unemployment or among youngsters, and sanctioning with benefit reductions those who did not actively seek

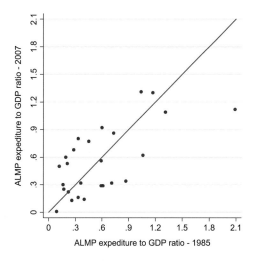

Figure 3   *ALMP expenditure to GDP ratio.*

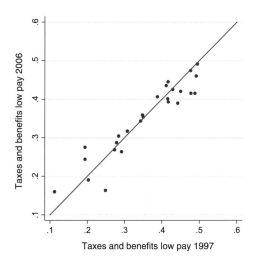

Figure 4   *Taxes and benefits on low wages.*

employment. Finally, the total tax wedge on low pay captures a wide array of employment conditional incentives (ECI) introduced to increase incentives to work at relatively low wages. It relies on detailed information on national tax and benefit systems collected in the OECD publication "Taxing wages". Reference is made to a single worker earning 2/3 of the average production (manufacturing) worker pay.

The message delivered by these figures is one of much activism. There are only 4 countries (out of 28) that did not change EPL over time, only one country (out of 21)

Table 2 Evolution of labor market institutions in OECD countries.

	EPL index				UB generosity measure			
	European		**non-European**		**European**		**non-European**	
	1985	**2008**	**1985**	**2008**	**1985**	**2007**	**1985**	**2007**
Mean	2.46	1.99	1.78	1.71	29.81	32.69	19.80	15.80
St. Dev.	1.04	0.66	1.29	1.18	14.38	9.53	8.11	6.72
Average % Variation (modulus)	23.59%		17.39%		28.87%		19.91%	

	ALMP/GDP				Tax/benefits low pay			
	European		**non-European**		**European**		**non-European**	
	1985	**2007**	**1985**	**2007**	**1997**	**2006**	**1997**	**2006**
Mean	0.64	0.68	0.42	0.27	40.02	38.55	26.92	28.28
St. Dev.	0.53	0.36	0.23	0.23	7.77	8.12	10.91	8.58
Average % Variation (modulus)	79.36%		56.38%		6.79%		16.26%	

that did not modify UB generosity, one country out of 26 that did not adjust the size of active labor market policy programmes, and one country out of 27 that did not adjust taxes and benefits for low wage earners (although the available series cover only a ten-year period in this case).

While there is not always a clear pattern in the institutional evolutions, they appear to have reduced the cross-sectional variation in the level of these institutions at least within Europe, as indicated by the beginning year and end year standard deviations of the indicators displayed in Table 2. Significantly, this "sigma convergence" has been achieved mainly *across* the four country groupings characterized in Section 2.1 than *within* each of them. Indeed, the standard deviation of EPL across groups declined over the period from 1.26 to 0.76 while the dispersion within groups has increased from 0.36 to 0.44. Similar is the case of UB (across from 14.7 to 10.9 and within from 9.7 to 11.1) and of the other institutions.

European countries are also those that have implemented the largest institutional transformations, at least judging from the average rate of change of the value of the indicators over the period (the exception is taxes on low pay), reported in Table 2 for each institution.

2.3. Some key definitions

Before we proceed any further, it is better to provide a few key definitions which will be used henceforth.

A **labor market institution** is a system of laws, norms or conventions resulting from a *collective* choice, and providing constraints or incentives which alter *individual* choices over labor and pay. Single individuals and firms consider the institutions as given

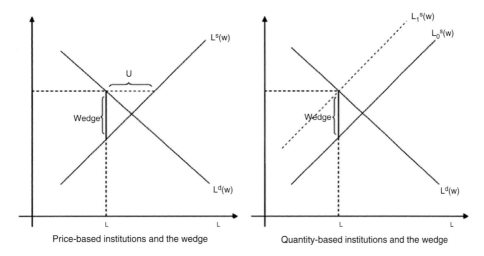

Figure 5   *Institutions and the wedge.*

when making their own, *individual*, decisions. To give an example, an individual has limited choice over the number of hours of work to be supplied when working time is determined via a collective choice mechanism. Regulations on working hours are indeed an institution aimed, inter alia, at coordinating the allocation of time to work, leisure or home activities across and within households. Due to their foundations on collective choices, institutions are the byproduct of a political process. Often, but not always, institutions are written in laws. For instance, collective bargaining institutions are most frequently regulated by social norms and conventions rather than by laws.

By affecting individual incentives, these institutions affect the structure of labor markets. For instance, they move the intensive or extensive margins of participation, they expand or reduce the size of labor markets by inducing marketization of home production or by crowding-out low productivity jobs.

It is always important to recognize that institutions fulfill a useful purpose from the point of view of at least some economic agents. Otherwise, it would hardly be possible to see why they were introduced in the first place and why reforms of these institutions are often politically difficult. The literature on the political economy of labor market institutions (e.g., summarized by Saint-Paul, 2000) is beyond the scope of this chapter, but offers insights as to the constituency behind each institution which is very useful in understanding two-tier reform strategies.

All the institutions affect directly or indirectly equilibrium take-home wages and labor costs of firms, by introducing a **wedge** between the marginal productivity of labor and its opportunity cost. As shown by Fig. 5, the wedge can be introduced either in terms of taxes on labor or markups on reservation wages (price-based institutions) or by forcing effective labor supply below potential (quantity-based institutions).

Institutional reforms are changes in the design of these institutions, potentially affecting the structure of markets. As institutions are not always written in laws, some reforms may take place also via changes in administrative rules, informal agreements between collective organizations (e.g., unions and employers' associations) and social norms.

From the standpoint of applied work it is very important to consider two characteristics of reforms.

The first is the orientation of reforms, that is, whether they *reduce* (e.g., by making employment protection less strict and/or unemployment benefits less generous or by expanding the scope of activation programmes) *or increase the wedge* (e.g., by increasing labor-supply-reducing taxes on relatively low-paid jobs) introduced by labor market institutions between supply and demand. We will accordingly classify reforms as either **decreasing or increasing the** (institutional) **wedge**.

The second characteristic relates to the phasing-in of reforms: it can be either a *complete* or a *partial* phasing-in. In the first case, the change in the regulations eventually involves everybody. In the second case, even at the steady state, the reform is confined to a subset of the population. The timing of the phasing-in is also important. Some reforms envisaging a complete phasing-in may involve a very long transitional period, so that the steady state institutional configuration is attained beyond the planning horizon of many agents potentially involved by the reform.

In the analysis below we will define an institutional change as a **two-tier reform** when it involves either a partial phasing-in or when its complete phasing-in requires more than 30 years, the average length of the working life in many countries. Two-tier reforms are typically related to the presence of strong political obstacles to reforms. Politically viable reforms must leave unaffected a significant fraction of the constituency of each institution. Clearly, the reforms themselves may alter the size of the different constituencies, creating the conditions for new reforms. For instance, reforms of employment protection legislation in the 1980s in Spain, which broadened the scope of temporary employment, created the conditions for the reforms of the mid-1990s which reduced the protection of permanent-regular employment (Dolado et al., 2002).

Notice that our definition of two-tier reform is independent of the size of reforms. Small, incremental adjustments of some institution can well be encompassing, that is, involving the entire potentially eligible population and, on those grounds, would not be considered two-tier reforms according to our definition. In the inventory of reforms that we are now going to explore, we also classify reforms depending on their size, as either **incremental** or *discrete*. In particular, incremental reforms involve a change in any given institution smaller than one-tenth of the cross-country deviation in the intensity of that regulation in the middle year of our inventory. The regulatory intensity is measured by some indicator of the characteristics of the institution in the various countries (e.g., the OECD index of strictness of employment protection, the OECD

Table 3 A taxonomy of reforms.

	Discrete	
Size	Discrete Two-tier	Structural
	Incremental Two-tier	Incremental Complete

Scope

Table 4 Number of labor market reforms by orientation in Europe (1980-2007).

Reform area	Decreasing the wedge	Increasing the wedge	Total per row	Of which decreasing
EPL	112	87	199	56%
UB	139	114	253	55%
AP	230	12	242	95%
ECI	113	11	124	91%
ER	38	27	65	58%

summary generosity measure of unemployment benefits, etc.). Discrete reforms involve changes in the indicator exceeding our arbitrary threshold.

The two latter definitions contribute to jointly identify **structural** reforms as those reforms that are either discrete and complete (not two-tier). The fourfold taxonomy is visually characterized in Table 3.

2.4. Tracking reforms in Europe

Table 4 provides information on the number and characteristics of reforms carried out in the European Union in the field of labor market and social policies in the period 1980-2007. It draws on the "Social Policy Reform Inventory", assembled by the Fondazione Rodolfo Debenedetti (recently in co-operation with IZA), which takes stock of reforms carried out in Europe in the field of employment protection legislation (EPL), unemployment benefits (UB), activation programmes (AP), employment conditional incentives (ECI), and early retirement (ER) plans. Appendix A provides information about the way in which the database was generated and is updated. The full detail on each reform is offered on the webpage of the Fondazione Rodolfo Debenedetti (www.frdb.org).

Many reforms of labor market institutions are taking place. In the observation period almost 868 reforms were counted in just 14 countries, that is, almost 2 reforms per year and country. The two policy areas more subject to reforms are UB and EPL. In these areas as well as in ER there are many reforms going in both directions, increasing and decreasing the wedge. This may be related to political opposition to reforms. There is much more consistency in AP and ECI reforms.

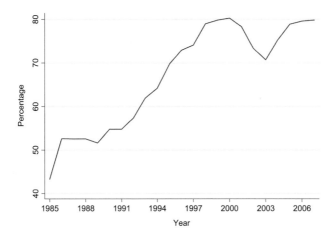

Figure 6   *Share of reforms decreasing the wedge.* Note: 5-year backward weighted moving average.

Most reforms, however, appear to reduce the wedge. This holds for each policy area. Moreover, the share of reforms reducing the wedge is increasing over time (Fig. 6). This trend can be explained as a reaction to competitive pressures arising from product market competition, which, by flattening the demand for labor, increases the employment bias of labor market institutions (Bertola et al., 2001; Bertola and Boeri, 2002). At the same time, greater competition in product markets increases the political resistance to the downscaling of the institutions protecting against labor market risk. Social norms or cultural factors supporting redistributive, typically wage compressing, institutions may become more important at times of globalization (Agell, 1999). This contributes to explain why several reforms also go opposite to the direction implied by increased product market competition. Moreover, several empirical studies (e.g., Rodrik, 1998; Wacziarg and Welch, 2008) found a positive correlation between exposure to product market competition—measured in terms of trade openness—and the presence of redistributive institutions, pointing to stronger demand for protection in competitive environments.

Reforms sometimes involve a packaging of measures covering different policy areas, e.g., EPL and UB or UB and AP along with the so-called "pathways to flexicurity". In this case they were "unbundled" in single measures and then repackaged by policy area (see Appendix B). Table 5 suggests that about 1 reform out of 5 involves some packaging. However, rarely this packaging involves more than two policy areas.

2.5. Two-tier and incremental reforms

Reforms can also be categorized considering whether they are two-tier or complete. In particular, we looked at the "target share", that is, the share of the population potentially affected by the reform which was actually targeted by the reform. If the "treatment

Table 5 Packaging of reforms (distribution of reforms by number of policy areas involved).

Number of policy areas involved	Number of reforms	Percentage on total
1 area	728	83.87
2 areas	109	12.56
3 areas	28	3.23
4 areas	3	0.35
Total	868	

Table 6 Two-tier vs. complete reforms in Europe (1980-2007).

Reform area	Two-tier	Complete	Total per row	Of which two-tier
EPL	103	96	199	52%
UB	116	137	253	46%
AP	155	87	242	64%
ECI	74	50	124	60%
ER	49	16	65	75%

group" of the reform represents less than 50% of the potentially eligible population (i.e., it is only young people out of the entire working age population, temporary workers out of total dependent employment), then the reform was classified as a two-tier reform. As shown by Table 6, two-tier reforms are predominant in all institutional areas except unemployment benefits. Not all two-tier reforms necessarily increase the dualism of regulatory regimes, as they may also reduce pre-existing asymmetries among the different regimes. However, four two-tier reforms out of five actually widen the asymmetries in regulatory regimes.

Limited to EPL and UB, we can also establish whether the reforms are incremental or discrete, according to the definitions proposed in Section 2.1. In particular, we measure the regulatory intensity of the two sets of reforms based on the recalled OECD "Overall strictness of EPL" index covering the time period 1985 to 2009 and, limited to the period 1980-85, the series of EPL strictness developed by William Nickell within a CEP-OECD project (http://cep.lse.ac.uk/_new/publications/abstract.asp?index=2424) which interpolates the OECD series with those used by Blanchard and Wolfers (2000). In the case of UB reforms, we relied on the summary generosity measure also tabulated by OECD. We classified as discrete those reforms involving a change in the value of the index larger than one-tenth of the cross country standard deviation in the index relative to the year 1995, that is, roughly in the middle of the observation period.

The results of this classification exercise are displayed in Tables 7 and 8: they show that a very few complete reforms are sizeable. The "largest" reforms are generally two-tier reforms. In other words, there seems to be a trade-off between size and scope of

Table 7 Reforms of employment protection legislation.

EPL	Two-tier	Complete	Total	Of which two-tier
Discrete	17	7	24	71%
Incremental	86	89	175	49%
Total	103	96	199	52%
Of which discrete	17%	7%	12%	

Table 8 Reforms of unemployment benefits.

UB	Two-tier	Complete	Total	Of which two-tier
Discrete	9	12	21	43%
Incremental	107	125	232	46%
Total	116	137	253	46%
Of which discrete	8%	9%	8%	

reforms. Therefore structural reforms are an exception: 7 out of 199, that is roughly the 3.5% of reforms are structural according to our definitions.

All this seems to indicate that the theoretical literature, which typically analyzes the effects of complete reforms, and the empirical literature drawing on comparisons of countries having much different levels of these institutions is of limited practical relevance. Two-tier reforms may also question some identification assumptions made by the empirical literature exploiting "natural experiments" to learn about the effects of these institutions. Before we address these issues, it is instructive to compare labor market reforms with regulatory changes occurring in other domains, such as product market and financial market regulations.

2.6. Labor market vs. financial and product market reforms

Unfortunately, there is no inventory of reforms in product market and financial market regulations to draw upon. We were forced in this case to define and measure reforms as the number of changes in the values of an index of the product market regulation devised by OECD and an index of financial regulations produced by IMF, which are tabulated at yearly frequencies. This clearly rules out the possibility of reforms moving in opposite directions within the same year, a rather frequent event in the case of labor market reforms. We can track reforms undoing other reforms only at lower frequencies.

In the case of product markets, we take an index measuring barriers to entry in seven network industries (airlines, telecoms, electricity, gas, postal services, railways and road freight). Details concerning this index are described in Conway and Nicoletti (2006) and http://www.oecd.org/eco/pmr. In the case of financial markets we drew on the IMF "Financial Reform Dataset" (see Abiad et al., 2008). We focused on the EU15 and on the same time-period (1985-2007) considered when tracking labor market reforms.

Table 9   Reforms of product, financial and labor markets (1985-2007).

	Decreasing wedge	Increasing wedge	Total	Of which decreasing
Product Mkt reforms				
Discrete	30	0	30	100%
Incremental	7	13	20	35%
Total	37	13	50	74%
Of which discrete	81%	0%	60%	
Financial Mkt reforms				
Discrete	52	0	52	100%
Incremental	42	0	42	100%
Total	94	0	94	100%
Of which discrete	55%	0%	55%	
Labor Mkt reforms				
Discrete	16	12	28	57%
Incremental	23	18	41	56%
Total	39	30	69	57%
Of which discrete	41%	40%	41%	

The results of this exercise are displayed in the top panel of Table 9. Once more, we classify reforms by orientation (increasing or decreasing the wedge, that is, the size of the market) and scope (discrete if they involve a step change of the indicator larger than one tenth of the standard deviation in the average period cross–country distribution of the indicator). The bottom panel of Table 9 displays the result of the same exercise in the case of two labor market institutions for which the same method to identify and classify reforms could be implemented, that is, EPL and UB reforms.

Three facts are relevant. First, there are more reforms in factor markets than in product markets. Second, there are more discrete reforms in product markets than in factor markets. Third, in financial markets and also in product markets there is more consistency in the orientation of the reforms than in labor markets, as there are a very few, if any, reforms increasing the wedge.

A possible explanation of these asymmetries between reforms of labor market, product market and financial market regulations is that two-tier reforms winning political obstacles to reforms can hardly take place in product markets. A two-tier reform in a specific sector would indeed result in a market with less protective rules applied to new entrants. On the one hand, incumbent firms would operate under the traditional set of regulatory protections and associated rents (i.e. government subsidies). On the other hand, new entrants would be forced to operate without these rents. This cannot work, as the incumbent firm (e.g., a former monopolist) would easily drive away from the market the new competitive fringe. In other words, two-tier reforms are a viable strategy to engineer reforms in order to make them politically viable in the labor market (Saint-Paul, 2000), but not in the product market.

Another fact highlighted by comparing Tables 9 and 4 is that many reforms occur at higher than yearly frequencies or are not, in any event, captured by the overall indicators. Indeed, by looking at changes in the value of the indicators, we identify less than one half of the reforms listed in the fRDB inventory.

2.7. How labor markets are reformed: a summary

Many reforms of labor market institutions occur every year, notably in Europe. Comparing labor market outcomes before and after these policy changes and across countries starting at similar conditions offers to researchers a great opportunity to identify the effects of these institutions on the labor market. It is very important that these analyses take into account of the nature of these reforms. The qualitative analysis of reforms and the comparisons of institutional changes across labor, product and financial markets suggest that two-tier reforms are very important in the labor market.

The next section develops a framework enabling the characterization of the macroeconomic effects of these reforms, either complete or two-tier, and the interactions between reformed and unreformed segments of the labor market. This framework is helpful in guiding empirical work because it helps defining the relevant outcomes to be considered by (ex-post) policy evaluations, identifying proper treatment and control groups, and taking into account the potential general equilibrium effects of the reforms.

3. A SIMPLE MODEL OF LABOR REALLOCATION AND REFORMS

The analysis of reforms can better develop on frameworks allowing for equilibrium unemployment, gross job and worker flows at the steady state and potential interactions between reformed and unreformed segments of the labor market. A widely used and flexible framework having these properties is the equilibrium search model developed by Dale Mortensen and Christopher Pissarides, the MP model for short, which was presented in a previous Handbook volume (Mortensen and Pissarides, 1999). We will below briefly recall and then extend the MP model in order to allow for two-tier regimes in three of the four institutions whose evolutions were characterized in Section 2, notably, employment protection, unemployment benefits and active labor market policies. We will not address early retirement rules as this would require introducing a different setup—ideally an overlapping generations model—and there has been less reform activity in the domain of pension rules for persons of working age.

We will first characterize the effects of complete reforms of EPL, UB and ALMP and subsequently consider reforms introducing two-tier regimes.

3.1. Gross job flows in the MP model

This section can be skipped by the readers who are familiar with the MP model.

Consider a market in which workers supply their services inelastically, being either unemployed (searching for a job) or employed. Symmetrically firms can either produce by employing one worker or search for one with an open vacancy. There are no restrictions in the entry of firms, but employers with open vacancies must pay, while searching for workers, a periodic recruitment cost of c per unit period.

The matching of workers to vacancies occurs via an aggregate matching function (Blanchard and Diamond, 1989; Pissarides, 1979) embodying the trading and congestion externalities of any search process. Intuitively, when there are more unemployed around per given number of vacancies it is more difficult for a jobseeker to find a job, while it is easier for a firm to fill a vacancy. Symmetrically, an increase in the number of vacancies per given unemployment pool makes life easier for the unemployed while creating congestion delays in the process by which vacancies are filled. Consistently with much of the empirical literature estimating matching functions (Petrongolo and Pissarides, 2001) we are also going to assume that matching occurs at constant returns to scale. Also from a theoretical perspective, there is no reason to believe that the size of the labor market should affect the contact probability.

In this context the job finding (or the vacancy filling rate) will depend uniquely on the ratio of the number of vacancies, v, to the number of unemployed, u, that is, on the degree of labor market tightness, $\theta \equiv v/u$. Denoting the aggregate matching function as $m = m(u, v)$, the unconditional probability of a vacancy to match with an unemployed worker is then $q = \frac{m(u,v)}{v} = m(\theta, 1)$, with $q'(\theta) < 0$, $q''(\theta) > 0$, and $\lim_{\theta \to 0} q(\theta) = \infty$, whilst the probability of an unemployed worker meeting a vacancy is $\frac{m(u,v)}{u} = \frac{\theta m(u,v)}{v} = \theta q(\theta)$.

For production to occur, a worker must be matched with a job. When matched, a firm and a worker generate periodic productivity x, where $x \in (0, 1]$. This match-specific productivity is subject to shocks, e.g., innovations or taste changes unknown at the time of match formation, occurring at a (Poisson) frequency λ. All newly-formed matches (i.e. filled jobs) begin at the highest possible value of x ($x = 1$). When a shock occurs, productivity is a random draw with a fixed, known cumulative distribution $F(x)$. These shocks are persistent: productivity remains at this level until a new shock occurs. And when productivity falls below a threshold level, R, endogenously determined in this model, it is no longer profitable to continue to produce in the existing match and the job is destroyed.

Due to the presence of search frictions, any realized job match yields a rent. Wages share this rent between workers and firms according to a Nash bargaining rule and are instantaneously renegotiated whenever a shock occurs. Insofar as R, the reservation productivity threshold, is strictly smaller than one, a non-degenerate distribution of wages is obtained at the equilibrium.

The labor market flows prevailing at the equilibrium are given by the matching of unemployed workers to vacancies (gross job creation) and by the dissolution of matches (gross job destruction) when their productivity falls below this threshold level. In this context, gross job creation coincides with unemployment outflows and gross job destruction with unemployment inflows. The evolution of unemployment is indeed governed by

$$\Delta u = \lambda F(R)(1 - u) - \theta q(\theta)u \qquad (1)$$

where the constant labor force has been conveniently normalized to one, so that $(1 - u)$ denotes employment. As the above makes clear, gross flows in the labor market occur also when unemployment is constant. Indeed, equating (1) to zero and solving for a constant (steady state) unemployment level obtains

$$u = \frac{\lambda F(R)}{\lambda F(R) + \theta q(\theta)}. \qquad (2)$$

Moreover, the two key (endogenous) variables determining the evolution of gross flows in the labor market are market tightness (affecting the job creation margin) and the threshold productivity level (affecting the job destruction margin).

3.2. Introducing institutions

In this framework it is relatively straightforward to accommodate employment protection legislation, unemployment benefits and active labor market policies, drawing also on Pissarides (2000).

First, we consider an **exogenous firing tax** T which is levied on termination of job-worker matches. The purpose of the firing tax is to reduce the probability of job loss for those having a job. It is designed as a pure deadweight loss paid to a third party or simply dissipated resources associated with government regulation. It should be distinguished from severance compensation (a lump-sum transfer from employer to employee upon severance), which can be offset by a compensating wage adjustment (Lazear, 1990) in this setup, as workers are risk-neutral and Nash bargaining allows for wage flexibility above the value of non-employment.

Second, we introduce an **unemployment benefit** $b = \rho \bar{w}$ which is offered as a replacement of earnings during an unemployment spell. To keep things simple, we consider a flat income replacement scheme providing to jobless people the fraction $0 < \rho < 1$ of average labor income, $\bar{w}$, independently of the past earning history (of the past match-specific realizations of x) of the worker. The policy parameter ρ, in particular, measures the generosity of unemployment benefits. Benefits are assumed to be open-ended and.provided conditional on unemployment status. Thus, the average duration of benefits coincides with the average duration of unemployment $\frac{1}{\lambda F(R)}$.

Third, **active labor market policies** can be accommodated in the MP model as two alternative policy instruments. On the one hand, we introduce an employment conditional incentive, e which is provided to job-holders on a flow basis, as a measure to increase rewards from participation, "making work pay". This policy instrument is isomorphic to a wage subsidy provided to employers due to the equilibrium structure of the model. The incidence of taxes (subsidies) is independent of who pays (receives) them. The second policy instrument, acts on recruitment costs, c. It reduces frictions in the vacancy filling process by activating jobseekers, providing job counseling, placement services, etc. This policy instrument (whose value is restricted to be in the range $0 < e < b$) is isomorphic to any measure increasing the job finding rate $\theta q(\theta)$ as this would also reduce the expected costs of posting a vacancy $\frac{c}{\theta q(\theta)}$. The two policy instruments, employment conditional incentives and hiring subsidies, correspond to the distinction between financial incentives and activation schemes in the design of active labor market policies.

3.3. Partial equilibrium effects of complete reforms

These institutions have both, partial equilibrium and general equilibrium effects. The partial equilibrium effects are those related to the operation of the wedge, that is, the effects on wages holding constant the macro variables. The general equilibrium effects incorporate the effects on wedges of changes in the aggregate job creation and job destruction rates. Comparisons of the two sets of results highlight what could be missed by considering only the partial equilibrium effects of reforms.

Wages are in this setup determined according to a bilateral bargaining process between each worker and each employer. It is shown in the Appendix B that the institution-free and match-specific wage obeys the Nash bargaining rule

$$w(x) = \beta(x + c\theta) \tag{3}$$

where $0 \leq \beta < 1$ measures the relative bargaining strength of workers vis-a-vis employers. Equation (3) shows that wages are increasing in match specific productivity, match frictions and market tightness at a rate which is increasing in the bargaining power of workers. The more powerful are workers, the more they appropriate of the match surplus. It is bargaining power and frictions that allow workers to obtain a markup over their reservation wage.

Introducing now the three sets of institutions described above and solving again the Nash bargaining problem we obtain (see Appendix B) a wage equation providing a weighted average of the institution-augmented reservation wage and the productivity of labor

$$w(x) = (1 - \beta)(\rho \, \bar{w} - e) + \beta[x + (c - h)\theta + rT]. \tag{4}$$

This shows that when β approaches 0, that is workers have no bargaining power, wages collapse to the unemployment benefit net of the employment conditional incentive, which is indeed a measure aimed at reducing disincentives to accept low-paid jobs associated with the provision of unemployment benefits. When instead β approaches 1, wages in (4) appropriate the entire match productivity and are augmented by recruitment cost net of the hiring subsidy and the discounted value of the firing tax (which is a lump-sum payment). Under such conditions, however, it would be unprofitable to open up a vacancy (the recruitment cost, net of the hiring subsidy, could not be covered by any ensuing flow of net revenues at match formation). Hence, the need arises to impose that β is strictly lower than 1.

By subtracting (4) from (3) at any given productivity realization, it becomes apparent that institutions, at unchanged macro variables and allocation of bargaining power, affect both the size of the wedge associated with match formation, and the way in which these rents are split between workers and firms.

$$w(x; \beta, c, \rho, e, T, h) - w(x; \beta, c) = (1 - \beta)(\rho \, \bar{w} - e) + \beta[rT - h\theta]. \qquad (5)$$

In words, wages are increasing in unemployment benefits mostly when employers have more bargaining power, and in firing taxes when it is the worker side to be more powerful. Wages (and the overall wedge) are instead decreasing in employment conditional incentives (employers succeed in extracting part of the subsidy from their workers) and in active policies improving the matching process.

Labor market institutions are, however, bound to affect wages also via changes in market tightness and the average wage (mainly via changes in the reservation productivity level below which jobs are destroyed). We will now analyze the effects of reforms having macroeconomic significance.

3.4. General equilibrium effects of complete reforms

A complete reform, even when just incremental, is bound to have effects on the labor market aggregates. We recall that our definition of a complete reform is of an institutional change in any of the above policy parameters, T, ρ, e, h affecting all potentially eligible groups, that is either all firms (in the case of T), all the unemployed (ρ), all the employees (e) or all employers having posted a vacancy (h). To investigate the comparative statics effects of incremental changes in these policy parameters, one needs to totally differentiate the two equilibrium gross job creation and gross job destruction conditions, implicitly providing the equilibrium values of market tightness and of the reservation productivity threshold, θ^* and R^* respectively. The two equations are derived in Appendix B. By applying Cramer's rule to this system of equations, it is straightforward to obtain the qualitative effects of reforms summarized in Table 10.

As shown by the table, once allowance is made for changes in the macro variables, two reforms out of four (the exception being the increase in the generosity of UB) no longer have unambiguous effects on wages.

Table 10 Comparative statics results of complete reforms.

Effect of an increase in ⟹ on⟱	ρ	T	e	h
R^*	+	−	−	+
θ^*	−	−	+	+
u^*	+	?	−	?
Probability of job loss	+	−	−	+
Job finding rate	−	−	+	+
Average wage	+	?	−	?

The economics behind these results is as follows.

Consider first an **increase in the replacement income** offered by unemployment benefits. The impact effect of this reform is to increase the reservation productivity at which matches are dissolved as the outside option of workers has improved. This means that the new equilibrium features a higher job destruction *rate* $\lambda F(R^*)$. Further effects come from wage setting. As shown above, in partial equilibrium, a rise in ρ increases wages in continuing jobs proportionally to the bargaining power of employers. In general equilibrium (of the labor market) this effect can be partly offset by the reduction in market tightness which is associated with the lower duration of jobs and the higher wages. The effect of market tightness on wages is larger in presence of significant recruitment costs and low, if any, hiring subsidies. Thus, the effects of unemployment benefits on wages interact with the size of active labor market policies. The average wage increases both because of the above effects and the higher productivity threshold that increases the average productivity in continuing jobs. As unemployment benefits are indexed to the average wage, there will be also a second-round, positive effect on the level of unemployment benefits. Insofar as gross job destruction increases, unemployment unambiguously increases, bringing down the equilibrium level of market tightness, θ^*. Overall, the new equilibrium features a higher probability of job loss, a lower job finding rate $\theta^* q(\theta^*)$, and higher unemployment and average wage.

An **increase in firing taxes** has the opposite effect of maintaining alive jobs with a lower match productivity. This reduces the gross job destruction rate. Firing taxes also positively affect wages, as in partial equilibrium. The effect on wages is partly offset by the reduction in market tightness induced by the larger firing tax and by the wage hike, which reduces the number of vacancies issued at the equilibrium. Once more, this effect of market tightness on wages is mediated by active labor market policies, notably by the relevance of activation policies reducing recruitment costs. As both job finding and job loss rates decline, the effect on equilibrium unemployment is ambiguous, consistently with the pioneering model of Bentolila and Bertola (1990). Conditional on any given realization of x, wages go up. However, the effect on average wages is also ambiguous as the new equilibrium features more low-productivity, hence low-wage, jobs. Insofar as the average wage is affected by the reform, there will be interactions with the generosity of the unemployment benefit system, which is indexed to the average wage. Overall, the new equilibrium features lower job loss and job finding probabilities, while there is ambiguity as to the effects on unemployment and the average wage.

An **increase in employment conditional incentives** makes the labor market tighter. The reduction in entry wages, hence the increase in θ^*, is larger the stronger the bargaining position of employers and the larger recruitment subsidies. As continuing jobs are subsidized, also the productivity threshold, R^* declines, increasing the duration of jobs. The new equilibrium involves a higher job finding rate and a lower job loss probability, as well as a lower unemployment and average wage. The latter declines because of both, wages are lower at any productivity realization and there are more low productivity jobs alive.

Finally, an **increase in the activation scheme** reducing recruitment costs has similar effects on the job creation margin than the other active labor market policy tool. As the costs of filling a vacancy are lower, the vacancy to unemployment ratio increases. However, lower turnover costs allow for jobs to be destroyed at a higher productivity threshold. The new equilibrium features higher job finding and job loss rates, whilst the effects on unemployment and the average wage are ambiguous.

The above occurs under the assumption that increased unemployment benefits and active policies can be funded by windfall Government revenues or, in any event, do not require increasing payroll taxes. Were we to internalize the Government budget constraint in such cases (which is rarely done in applied work as most reforms are marginal and have a negligible effect on net public expenditures), job destruction would be larger and job creation lower, involving a lower employment rate at the equilibrium. With payroll taxes funding active policies it would also be important to consider whether or not unemployment benefits are taxed (Pissarides, 1998). If they are tax-exempt, and the replacement rate is defined in terms of gross wages, then the negative effect on employment would be larger.

3.5. Two-tier reforms in the MP model

Consider now a set of two-tier reforms of the above institutions. According to our working definition, two-tier reforms affect at the equilibrium only a subset of firms, employees or unemployed workers. Alternatively, these reforms involve a very long transitional dynamics from one steady state to another.

We begin by applying the first definition as it allows for a characterization of the effects of dual track reforms by simple comparisons of steady state equilibria.

Two-tier reforms of employment protection typically expand the scope of fixed-term contracts. An example is the battery of reforms carried out in Italy in the 1997-2003 period. These reforms first (with the so-called Pacchetto Treu) expanded the scope of fixed term contracts; next they introduced Temporary Work Agency; subsequently they increased the potential duration of fixed-term contracts and finally they introduced new types of atypical contracts (e.g., job on call or staff leasing). No change was made to regulations on the dismissals of workers with open-ended contracts. Drawing on these practical examples, we can model a partial reform of employment protection in this setting as one that removes firing taxes for entry jobs, while leaving employment protection unaltered for continuing jobs and the (incumbent) workers attached to them. New jobs last until they are hit by a productivity shock, occurring, as for all types of jobs, at Poisson frequency λ. If the new productivity realization falls below a reservation productivity which is specific to entry jobs, say R_0, the match is dissolved and ends with a flow from temporary jobs into unemployment. If instead the new productivity realization is above R_0, jobs are converted into permanent contracts, covered by the standard firing taxes, T. It follows that the expected duration of a fixed-term job is $\frac{1}{\lambda}$ whilst the rate at which temporary jobs are upgraded into permanent jobs is $\lambda(1 - F(R_o))$ where R_0 is endogenously determined at the equilibrium. Due to the presence of firing taxes on continuing jobs, the reservation productivity of entry jobs is higher than the reservation productivity of continuing jobs, that is, $R_0 > R$.

In our extension of the MP model we do not allow employers (and workers) to choose the type of contract in both new and continuing matches. This restriction is less serious than it could appear at a first sight. Regulations on fixed-term contracts do constrain the number of renewals (generally no more than two renewals are allowed) of temporary contracts (Guell and Petrongolo, 2007). This means that entry jobs must be either transformed into permanent contracts at their expiration or simply not renewed, originating in the latter case a flow to unemployment. As far as entry jobs are concerned, employers will always offer temporary contracts if they are allowed to choose the contractual regime in this setup as the flow income originating from the match is higher in the case of temporary contracts (as shown below, wages, hence the share of the surplus going to the workers is lower in temporary contracts) and they can also save on the firing tax, T, at match dissolution. Evidence from countries with strict EPL on permanent contracts is also consistent with our assumption: the share of new hiring on temporary contracts can be, under labor slack, as high as 90% of total hirings in countries like Italy, Spain and Sweden.

Tracking reforms of unemployment benefits, we also found many regulatory changes reducing the generosity of transfers only for unemployment spells originated from short-tenured jobs, and leaving unaffected entitlements of workers with a relatively long seniority. An example is the 1989 reform of the British unemployment benefit system that reduced replacement rates for the short-term unemployment benefit claimants, by increasing the length of the minimum waiting period required for eligibility to benefits for this category of workers. In order to frame two-tier reforms of unemployment benefits in the MP model, we need first to allow for a tenure-related unemployment benefit system, as those existing in most OECD countries. In particular, let us introduce a lower replacement rate, $\rho_0 < \rho$ for workers flowing into unemployment from short-tenure jobs, defined here for simplicity as those dissolved after the first shock to match productivity. In other words, these flows originate from match dissolution of temporary jobs. A two-tier reform of unemployment benefits can be then framed as one increasing the difference between ρ and ρ_0.

Similarly, we allow for a two-tier structure of employment subsidies, having e_0 paid only to entry jobs. A typical example is the French 1981 reform that introduced a one-year 50% social security contribution rebate for new hires of people aged less than 26, single women, and long-term unemployed aged more than 45. Similarly the aforementioned Pacchetto Treu reduced social security contributions for temporary contracts. Activation policies involve only the job finding (or vacancy filling) process. Hence, they are by definition two-tier under the posited extensions of the MP model. Only employers issuing new vacancies benefit from h. The transformation of temporary into open-ended contracts is not affected by recruitment subsidies.

3.6. Insider and outsider wages

This characterization of two-tier reforms involves a major extension of the MP model. In particular, we now have two job destruction conditions implicitly defining the two thresholds (R and R_0), and two wage equations. The first wage equation determines workers pay in entry jobs or the wage of *outsiders*, denoted by the subscript 0.

$$w_0 = (1 - \beta) \, (\rho_0 \, \bar{w} - e_0) + \beta(1 + (c - h)\theta - \lambda T). \tag{6}$$

The second wage equation applies to continuing jobs on permanent contracts and provides *insider* wages at all productivity levels above the reservation productivity level, R

$$w(x) = (1 - \beta) \, \rho \, \bar{w} + \beta(x + (c - h)\theta + rT). \tag{7}$$

Notice that firing taxes enter negatively the outsider wage equation and positively the insider wage equation. The economics behind this result is that incumbent workers can renegotiate wages after firing taxes have been phased-in, allowing them to obtain a larger share of the match surplus while the firm is locked in by the firing tax. Such a two-tier wage structure deals with the so-called holdup problem (Williamson, 1975) arising from the improved bargaining position of the party that does not invest in the continuation of the match. In this case it is the employers who have to pay firing taxes at match dissolution and this weakens their position at the bargaining table.

The difference between insider and outsider wages at the entry productivity level is given by

$$w(1) - w_0 = (1 - \beta) \, \bar{w}(\rho - \rho_0 + e_0) + \beta(rT). \tag{8}$$

Table 11 Comparative statics results of two-tier reforms.

Effect of an increase in⟹ on⇓	ρ	T	e_0
R_o^*	0	+	+
R^*	+	−	0
θ^*	0	+	+
u^*	+	−?	−?
Job loss rate (from entry jobs)	0	+	+
Job loss rate (from continuing jobs)	+	−	0
Job finding rate	0	+	+
Premium on permanent contracts	+	+	+
Conversion temporary–permanent	0	−	−
Entry jobs as % of total employment	+	+	+

In words, insiders enjoy a surplus over outsiders (at the same match productivity levels) which is increasing in the difference in the replacement rate offered to unemployed coming from long-tenured jobs with respect to those coming from short-tenured jobs, in the employment conditional incentive and in firing taxes. The latter matter more when workers have more bargaining power. Two-tier reforms widening the institutional asymmetries are bound to increase these rents of outsiders vis-a-vis the insiders, potentially affecting also the rate of conversion of temporary into permanent jobs. To better evaluate these effects we need to consider the relationship between two-tier reforms and aggregate variables.

3.7. Job flows and two-tier reforms

Labor market equilibrium under these extensions of the MP model now features two job destruction conditions, implicitly defining the reservation productivity values R and R_0, and a job creation condition implicitly defining market tightness (see Appendix B). These equilibrium values of the aggregate variables provide also the two job loss rates (from entry and continuing jobs respectively), the premium placed on tenure by the two-tier wage structure and the rate of conversion of new (or temporary) jobs into permanent jobs.

Table 11 summarizes the comparative statics properties of two-tier reforms in the different policy areas. We analyze reforms widening the asymmetry between entry jobs and continuing jobs, by increasing ρ (at unchanged ρ_0), T or e_0. Once more we are going to neglect the effects of these reforms on payroll taxes.

A reform **increasing replacement rates to unemployed coming from continuing jobs** involves, just like in the case of complete reforms, an increase in job destruction on continuing jobs. However, due to the presence of a different regime for entry jobs, job creation is unaffected in this case. Unemployment increases and the wage tenure profile becomes steeper, allowing workers in continuing jobs to extract a larger match surplus than entrants per any given productivity level. The share of entry jobs in total employment increases because of the reduction of the average duration of continuing jobs.

A reform **increasing employment protection for incumbents** increases the wage tenure profile and the share of employment in entry (flexible) jobs. This happens because the rate of conversion of temporary into open-ended contracts is reduced, while the average duration of continuing jobs increases. As hirings in temporary contracts increases and job losses from permanent contracts decline, there is less ambiguity as to the effects of firing taxes on unemployment than in the case of complete reforms: under dualism, unemployment is more likely to decline. The model also predicts a higher churning of entry jobs.

Finally, a **reform increasing employment subsidies for entry jobs** does not affect the job destruction margin for permanent contracts, while it increases the job finding rate and job destruction among short-term contracts. There is in this case more ambiguity as to the effects on unemployment than in the case of a complete reform. This is because the reduction in unemployment associated with the increase in job finding rates is largely offset by the lower rate of conversion of fixed-term into permanent contracts, as the asymmetries between the two types of contractual conditions are magnified by the reform. Finally, just like the other two-tier reforms, there is an increase in the wage-tenure profile and in the share of entry jobs in total employment.

Overall, there are important differences in the general equilibrium effects of two-tier and complete reforms. These differences can be appreciated by comparing Tables 10 and 11. A reform increasing the generosity of unemployment benefits from continuing jobs, unlike a complete reform of UB, does not affect job creation. If accompanied by a decline of replacement rates from entry jobs, it may actually reduce unemployment. A two-tier reform of EPL increases job finding on entry jobs while a complete reform of employment protection unambiguously reduces the unemployment outflow rates. A reform increasing firing taxes only on continuing jobs may increase job turnover insofar as it induces more hirings and more separations on entry jobs, while a complete reform unambiguously reduces gross job flows. Finally, a reform increasing employment conditional incentives on entry jobs may actually increase job destruction, while a complete reform would do just the opposite. These differences between complete and two-tier reforms arise because in dual labor markets there are two destruction margins, which may move in different directions, and entry jobs insulate hiring decisions from taxes (including firing taxes) on continuing jobs.

3.8. How relevant is dualism?

What is the empirical relevance of the above theoretical predictions as to the effects of two-tier reforms? A key implication of the model is that the share of temporary contracts

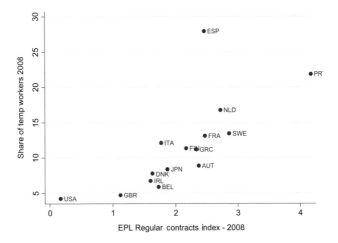

Figure 7   Strictness of EPL for permanent contracts and share of temporary contracts in total (dependent) employment.

in total (dependent) employment is increasing in the strictness of employment protection for open-ended contracts. Figure 7 displays, on the vertical axis, the share of temporary workers in total dependent employment, and, on the horizontal axis, the EPL index for regular (permanent) contracts in all OECD countries for which these data are available. The share of temporary contracts goes from a low 4.2% in the US to a high 28% in Spain, with an average of 12.4%. More importantly, there is a strong positive association between the two variables: the correlation coefficient is .73, and is significant at 99% levels.

Another key implication of the model relates to the conversion of temporary into permanent contracts. A larger asymmetry in the protection of permanent vs. temporary contracts involves lower transitions from fixed-term to permanent contracts as the reservation productivity at which jobs are upgraded is increasing in EPL on regular contracts. Fig. 8 displays, on the vertical axis, the yearly transition probability from fixed-term to permanent contracts, as can be estimated from matched records across waves of the European Union Survey of Income and Living Conditions (EU-SILC) in the 2004-7 period, and, on the horizontal axis, the index of strictness of EPL for regular contracts. According to the model, the conversion probability is declining in the asymmetries in institutional regimes across the two contractual types. The correlation coefficient is −.72, which is also significant at 95% confidence levels. Recall that from the standpoint of a worker, a permanent contract always dominates a temporary contract. Notice further that yearly transitions are relatively small (they never exceed 50% with a low 12%-13% in Portugal and France).

Two-tier reforms also involve, according to the above theoretical perspectives, two-tier wage structures, with temporary contracts being paid less than permanent contracts of the same productivity. Table 12 provides, in the first column, an estimate of the wage

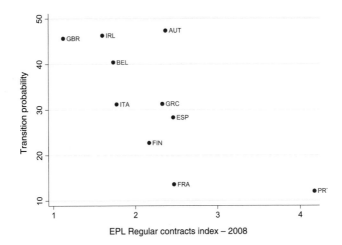

Figure 8 *Strictness of EPL for permanent contracts and transition probability from temporary to permanent contracts.*

Table 12 Wage premia on permanent contracts.

	Premium (%)	St. Err.	Obs.
Austria	20.1[c]	0.023	9867
Belgium	13.9[c]	0.017	7948
Denmark	17.7[c]	0.015	8009
Finland	19.0[c]	0.011	8940
France	28.9[c]	0.016	15260
Germany	26.6[c]	0.010	25448
Greece	20.2[c]	0.013	6978
Ireland	17.8[b]	0.069	1583
Italy	24.1[c]	0.008	30177
Luxembourg	27.6[c]	0.018	7889
Netherlands	35.4[c]	0.021	15845
Portugal	15.8[c]	0.016	7550
Spain	16.9[c]	0.007	22626
Sweden	44.7[c]	0.036	5412
United Kingdom	6.5[a]	0.037	7000

[a] Significant at 90%.
[b] Significant at 95%.
[c] Significant at 99%.

premium provided by permanent contracts vis-a-vis temporary contracts. It is estimated from micro-data (from the European Union Survey on Income and Living Condition and the European Community Household Panel) as the coefficient μ of a dummy variable capturing permanent contracts, in a (monthly) wage regression carried out over male dependent employment, controlling for education and tenure. In particular, the following equation was estimated:

$$\log w_i = \alpha + \beta_1\, EDU_i + \beta_2\, EDU_i^2 + \gamma_1\, TEN_i + \gamma_2\, TEN_i^2 + \mu\, PERM_i + \varepsilon_i$$

where w is monthly wages of individual "i", *EDU* is years of schooling, *TEN* is years of tenure and *PERM* is the dummy taking the value one in case of permanent contracts and zero otherwise. The table indicates that in all European countries workers on permanent contracts are paid, other things being equal, substantially more than workers on temporary contracts. The estimated premia are always statistically significant and range from a low 6.5% in the UK to almost 45% in Sweden.

Overall, dualism is sizeable in many European countries and its features are qualitatively in line with the predictions of the general equilibrium model of the labor market presented above.

3.9. Transitional dynamics: the "honeymoon effect"

The two-tier reforms characterized in our extensions of the MP model permanently increase the dualism of the labor market. According to the definition offered in Section 2.3, two-tier reforms can also allow for a steady state equilibrium in which only one regime survives, but involve a very long transitional dynamics. Analyzing the transitional dynamics of various types of reforms of labor market institutions goes much beyond the scope of this chapter. We will confine ourselves herein to point out that this long transitional dynamics may depart significantly from the long-term, steady state, outcomes of complete reforms. This is likely to be the case, especially when two-tier reforms are a device to engineer a discrete reform. The larger is the change in the level of the institution from one steady state to another, the larger the deviation of the transitional dynamics from the long-run equilibrium.

The example of two-tier reforms of employment protection can be particularly instructive in this respect, and can be illustrated by drawing on a simple intuition of Boeri and Garibaldi (2007). The model considered by the two authors focuses only on labor demand. In particular, it solves a dynamic and stochastic labor demand problem with attrition. They assume prohibitive firing costs in permanent contracts. In this setting, firms keep employment constant, independently of aggregate productivity (or demand) realizations, by simply replacing the workers involved in natural turnover. When temporary contracts are suddenly introduced, the firm exploits any hiring flexibility in good business conditions, but *can not* exploit downward flexibility in bad times, since it is constrained by the stock of insider workers. The profit maximizing employment dynamics is described in this dual regime by instantaneous hiring in favorable business conditions followed by optimal inertia through natural turnover in adverse business conditions. As a result, the lower the attrition, the larger is employment growth during the transition. The model therefore predicts the emergence of a *honeymoon* effect in

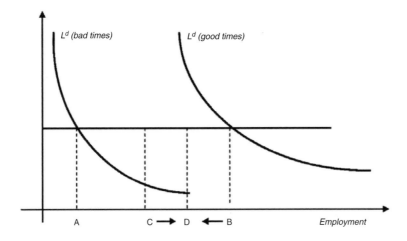

Figure 9   *The honeymoon effect.*

employment. Eventually, the employment gains are dissipated by the decline of insider workers. At the end of the transitional dynamics, all permanent workers are replaced by workers with temporary contracts end employment returns to its level before the reform.

The basic mechanism behind the honeymoon effect is described in Fig. 9, where two regimes are compared, one in which employment is at will and the second one in which firing is unboundedly expensive. When labor is perfectly flexible, the firm optimally hires labor at point A in the figure when conditions are bad and at point B when conditions are good. On average, the flexible firm hires an amount of labor around point C in the figure. If firing is unboundedly expensive, the firm sets an average employment at point C and there is zero mobility, neither hiring nor firing. In terms of average long run employment, the two regimes yield the same average employment level.

Now consider a two tier reform from a rigid regime. In particular, starting from the equilibrium in which the firm hires at point C whatever the conditions, let the firm enjoy "marginal flexibility". We assume that unexpectedly the firm can hire and fire workers on a temporary basis, but, at the same time, it cannot break the existing stock of permanent contracts. Formally, the constraint on the stock of permanent workers corresponds to an employment position at point C in Fig. 9. A firm that has suddenly the option to hire temporary workers should exploit this possibility. In good times the firm should hire temporary workers up to the optimal employment level in the frictionless regime, and dismiss such workers in bad times. In other words, the firm in the two-tier regime will have average employment at point D in the figure. This implies that a two tier regime leads to an increase in average employment.

This example suggests that a long transitional dynamics to the new steady state equilibrium may involve large effects on employment and unemployment stocks even

Table 13 Pre-reform EPL strictness and post-reform temporary employment.

Country	Time period	EPL Strictness (overall)	EPL Strictness (temporary)	Temporary Emp. Growth ΔET_t (000)	Contribution Temp. Jobs $\Delta ET_t/E_0$
Belgium	1987–1996	1.68	4.63	22.7	0.66
	1997–2005	1.71	2.63	135.3	3.54
	Δ	0.03	−2.00	112.6	2.89
Italy	1987–1997	1.77	5.38	402.9	0.02
	1998–2005	1.77	2.82	823.2	4.11
	Δ	0	−2.56	420.3	4.09
Netherlands	1987–1995	3.08	2.38	340.1	5.79
	1996–2005	3.06	1.45	288.8	3.80
	Δ	−0.02	−0.93	−51.3	−2.00
Portugal	1987–1996	4.56	3.34	−168.9	−4.10
	1997–2005	4.29	2.94	431.8	10.09
	Δ	−0.27	−0.40	600.6	14.19
Spain	1981–1984	3.83	—	0	0
	1985–1995	3.67	3.66	3377.1	28.50
	Δ	−0.16	—	3377.1	28.50
Sweden	1987–1996	2.88	3.28	−138.9	−3.22
	1997–2005	2.86	1.63	189.2	4.82
	Δ	−0.02	−1.65	328.1	8.04

Remark: for Spain, 1981-1984, the EPL index is the overall index, as calculated in Nickell (2006).

when these aggregates are unchanged across the two steady equilibria. Importantly, this occurs independently of the expectational effects, which are typically considered by the literature when explaining surprising effects of reforms (e.g., an increase in early retirement inducing a decline in the effective retirement age or a minimum wage hike resulting in higher employment). It is entirely a byproduct of the dual track design of reforms. An implication of this model is that the stricter is EPL before the reform, the larger will be the honeymoon effect. This is in line with evidence on two-tier reformers collected in Table 13. The latter documents the experience of dual reformers, countries that reduced EPL for temporary contracts while keeping unaltered (or even tightening) EPL for regular contracts (second and third column of the table). The countries having the strictest regulations before the two-tier reform experienced the largest contribution of temporary employment to job growth. Strong employment growth was observed even at times of slow output growth in several European countries having introduced fixed-term contracts from initially very strict employment protection legislations.

The downside of the honeymoon effect is that it involves a higher employment volatility than a uniform across the board reduction of EPL. Even a relatively small stock

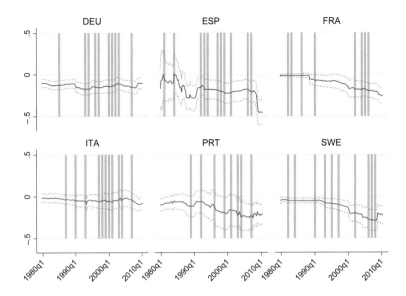

Figure 10   Okun's betas and two-tier reforms of EPL.

of temporary workers can significantly increase the responsiveness of employment and unemployment to output changes (Bentolila and Saint-Paul, 1992; Cahuc and Postel-Vinay, 2002).

Figure 10 displays Okun's betas (unemployment to output elasticities) in some of the countries having experienced more two-tier reforms of EPL. In particular the coefficient β is displayed, which is estimated over quarterly data in the following static version of Okun's law

$$\Delta u_t = \alpha + \beta \Delta y_t + \varepsilon_t$$

where u denotes the unemployment rate and Δy real output growth. The beta coefficient was allowed to vary over time by estimating rolling regressions over the previous 20 years (80 quarters) since 1960. Vertical bars denote two-tier reforms of employment protection. Figure 10 suggests that in many countries the responsiveness of unemployment to output changes increased over time, often in the aftermath of two-tier reforms of employment protection. The effect is even more visible if we consider the coefficients of a modified Okun's law where the dependent variable is the employment rate rather than unemployment (Fig. 11).

The greater volatility of unemployment over the cycle may also have a feedback effect on output volatility as automatic stabilizers, such as unemployment benefits, typically do not cover individuals with short tenures. This coverage issue is compounded by the fact that historically the countries with strictest EPL on regular contracts, hence more dualism after two-tier reforms, generally do not have a generous unemployment benefit system in

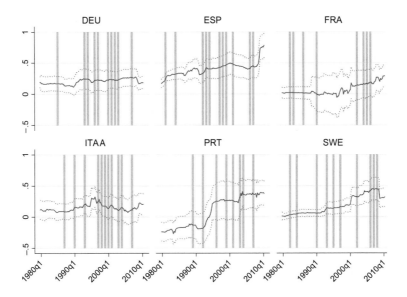

Figure 11 *The responsiveness of employment to output changes and two-tier reforms of EPL.*

place (see Section 2). This problem was highlighted by the Great Recession of 2009: job losses in dual labor markets were concentrated on temporary workers, involving in some countries very large employment/unemployment fluctuations. For example, the peak to trough employment decline for temporary workers was almost 20% in Spain (compared with 7% for total employment), almost 10% (1.5%) in Italy, 6% (0.3) in France, and 2% (compared with an increase of 0.4 in total employment) in Germany. These workers are rarely covered by unemployment insurance.

3.10. What matters in the reforms: a summary

The effects of reforms are rather intuitive when analyzed in a partial equilibrium setting. They are much harder to predict when macro variables are allowed to vary at the institutional change. In this case one should consider interactions with other institutions. For instance, we have shown above that the effects of reforms of EPL and UBs are very much affected by the design and size of activation schemes reducing the costs of recruitment for firms.

Not only the direction, but also the nature of reforms is very important. Two-tier reforms, as those documented in Section 2, involve several margins of labor market adjustment which often move in opposite directions. This does not necessarily mean that the effects of dual track reforms on labor market aggregates are ambiguous. Actually, our discussion above suggests that two-tier reforms of EPL and employment-conditional incentives can be signed in their effects on unemployment, unlike many complete reforms of the same institution.

A long phasing-in of reforms, involving a long transition in which two regulatory regime coexist, can also have different effects than those that could be predicted by comparing steady state equilibria before the reform and when the new regime is fully enacted. In particular, reforms of EPL allowing for a long transitional dynamics, may involve a temporary honeymoon effect on employment and unemployment. These effects are bound to eventually fade away together with the dualism of the labor market, but can be sizeable in the aftermath of reforms.

Given the large number of institutional changes having opposite effects on different segments of the labor markets, empirical work should allow for differential effects of these reforms within the same market for labor. Moreover, it is important to concentrate on flows as the effects of reforms can be better identified by focusing on the transitions of workers and jobs across different regimes. In the next section we will analyze to what extent the most recent empirical literature on labor market institutions has taken all this into account and which indications come from this literature as to further refinements of the theory of labor market institutions.

4. ARE WE LEARNING ENOUGH FROM THE REFORMS?

In this section we survey applied work on the effects on the labor market of institutions, which has been drawing on reforms, along with the "natural experiments" methodology. This literature is rich in interesting findings. Yet, we could have learned more in some cases, if the specific nature of reforms had been properly taken into account.

Before proceeding to the literature survey, it is useful to provide a checklist of issues to be addressed by applied work drawing on institutional reforms in light of the analysis of reforms in Section 2 and of the framework developed in Section 3.

- What are the relevant institutional interactions involved by the reform? Are the control and the treatment groups initially homogenous also in terms of the relevant institutions interacting with the reformed one?
- Is the reform packaged with other reforms? If so, how can these additional measures affect the outcomes of the reform being evaluated?
- How large is the reform with respect to the initial level of the institution?
- How tightly is the regulation enforced to start with?
- How large is the segment not involved by the reform?
- Does the reform have relevant spillovers on the unreformed segment(s)?
- How many different regimes does the reform involve? How long do these asymmetries last?
- Is the reform bound to have macro significance?

We will now pass on to analyze to what extent the applied literature on institutional reforms addresses these issues after providing more details on each institution.

4.1. The literature on reforms of employment protection

Employment Protection Legislation (EPL) refers to the set of norms and procedures to be followed in case of dismissals of redundant workers. EPL imposes legal restrictions against dismissals and on the compensations to the workers to be paid by their former employers in the case of early termination of a permanent employment contract. A number of procedures are also envisaged under EPL which have to be followed in the case of both individual and collective layoffs. The final decision on the legitimacy of a layoff generally depends on a court ruling. From the point of view of economic analysis, it is very important to note that the firing decision is not only up to the worker and/or the employer, but can involve the participation of a court, or a third party, which can be requested to assess the legal validity of the layoff. From the standpoint of economic theory, there are indeed two key components of EPL: a tax and a transfer. The *transfer component* is a monetary transfer from the employer to the worker, similar in nature to the wage. The *tax component*, instead, is more similar to a tax, because it corresponds to a payment to a third party, external to the worker-employer relationship. It is this second component which was framed in the model in Section 3. Conceptually, the transfer component of EPL corresponds to *severance payments* and the mandatory *advance notice period*, while the tax component to *trial costs* (the parcels for the lawyers, etc.) and all the other *procedural costs*. *Severance payments* refer to a monetary transfer from the firm to the worker to be paid in case of firm initiated separation. *Advance notice* refers to a specific period of time to be given to the worker before a firing can be actually implemented. Both the severance payment and advance notice that are part of EPL refer to the *legal minima*, that is, statutory payments and mandatory rules that apply to *all* employment relationships, regardless of what is established by specific labor contracts. Beyond mandatory payments, collective agreements may well specify larger severance payments for firm-initiated separations. Another important dimension of EPL consists of the *administrative procedures* that have to be followed before the layoff can actually take place. In most countries, the employer is often required to discuss the layoff decisions with workers' representatives. Further, the legislative provisions often differ depending on business characteristics such as firm (or plant) size and industry of activity.

A large body of empirical literature on employment protection is based on inferences drawing on cross-country variation in the OECD EPL strictness indicator (the time-series variation in the index is available only from 2001). Table 14 summarizes the main findings of this literature. Consistently with the theoretical predictions in Section 3, a few studies found significant effects of employment protection on employment and unemployment *stocks* while they all found that EPL negatively affects unemployment inflows and outflows: countries with the most strict EPL have more stagnant unemployment pools.

No unambiguous result is instead obtained concerning the impact of EPL on employment turnover. Many countries with strict EPL display relatively large job flows.

Table 14 The effects of employment protection on labor market: empirical results.

| | STOCKS | | FLOWS | |
Author(s)	E	U	E	U
Emerson (1988)	?	?	—	—
Lazear (1990)	—	+		
Bertola (1990)	?	?	?	—
Grubb and Wells (1993)	—			
Garibaldi et al. (1997)	?	?	?	—
Addison and Grosso (1996)	?	?		
Jackman et al. (1996)	?	?	—	—
Gregg and Manning (1997)	?	?		—
Boeri (1999)	?	?	+	—
Di Tella and MacCulloch (2005)	—	+		
OECD (1998)	?	?	+	—
Kugler and Saint-Paul (2000)			+	—
Belot and van Ours (2001)		—		
Nickell et al. (2005)	?	?		
Garibaldi and Violante (2005)	+	—		

This is at odds with the theory of complete reforms implying that the strictness of employment protection reduces job flows. Part of the discrepancy between theory and data can be related to measurement problems: there is limited cross-country comparability of gross job creation and destruction measures. However, also using the harmonized gross job flows data recently assembled at OECD (Bassanini and Marianna, 2009), the discrepancy persist: pairwise correlations of EPL and measures of worker reallocation are not statistically significant.

A possible explanation of the large job flows observed in countries with strict EPL is related to interactions with other institutions. Bertola and Rogerson (1997) argue that countries with strict dismissal regulations also have institutions compressing wage structures, preventing the work of price-driven adjustment mechanisms: if employers cannot adjust wages in response to shocks, they are forced to adjust employment. Other explanations relate to the two-tier nature of reforms (Boeri, 1999) inducing many job-to-job shifts at the expiration of fixed-term contracts that do not involve intervening unemployment spells. However, cross-country regressions—with the exception of Garibaldi and Violante (2005)—do not allow for interactions of EPL with wage setting institutions and typically do not control for the share of workers on temporary contracts.

The two-tier reforms documented in Section 2 inspired a more recent wave of studies identifying the effects of EPL via double differences (before and after the reform and between the segments affected and unaffected by the reform), in the spirit of the "natural experiments" literature. Two-tier reforms are ideal in this respect as they induce both time-series variation in institutions as well as substantial within-country variation in the actual enforcement of regulations. These studies documented that the introduction of fixed-term contracts increased the volatility of employment, by acting on both, hiring and firing margins. The earliest literature focuses on the Spanish, pioneering, case and reports quarterly job flows for temporary contracts ten times larger than for permanent contracts (García-Serrano, 1998). Most transitions are across jobs, though: García-Serrano and Jimeno (1999) estimated that an increase by one per cent of the proportion of temporary contracts in total employment raises job-to-job shifts by .34%. This effect of temporary employment on transitions across jobs is consistent with estimates provided by Boeri (1999) on job-to-job shifts in the EU15. The effects of the introduction of temporary employment on unemployment to employment transitions are less clearcut. This may also be because job-to-job shifts of temporary employees crowd-out displaced workers coming from permanent employment (Booth et al., 2002). Other studies found that marginal reforms of EPL negatively affect labor productivity (Blanchard and Landier, 2002). This is consistent with the "honeymoon" effects involved by a long transitional dynamics (Boeri and Garibaldi, 2007), which were summarized in Section 3. It can also be rationalized as due to less investment in human capital of temporary workers (Arulampalam and Booth, 1998) or by the reported self-selection into temporary positions of low-skilled and marginal groups of the labor force (Kahn, 2007).

Many studies exploit the within country asymmetry between fixed-term and permanent contracts. The second difference is obtained either by comparing pre and post reform labor market outcomes, net of any expectational effect, or by taking at least another asymmetry in the enforcement of EPL. For instance, the exemption of small units from the strictest EPL provisions can be used in conjunction with dual track reform strategies to carry out policy evaluation studies drawing on differences-in-differences (Autor et al., 2006; Boeri and Jimeno, 2005; Miles, 2000). A negative effect of EPL on dismissal rates is generally observed in these studies. Garibaldi et al. (2004) also found that the presence of firm-size thresholds (e.g., 15 employees, as in Italy) below which EPL does not hold, increases firms' persistence, that is, the probability that a firm does not change the number of employees from one year to the next, just below the threshold. These effects are generally small, but qualitatively consistent with the predictions of economic theory.

Employment and unemployment are not the only outcome variable being considered by the literature drawing on two-tier reforms. Some authors analyzed the effects of temporary employment on effort and productivity (Ichino and Riphahn, 2005; Engellandt and Riphahn, 2005). Others on job satisfaction (and self-reported job security) (Clark and Postel-Vinay, 2009), on-the-job training (Arulampalam and Booth, 1998) or work accidents (Guadalupe, 2003).

A problem with these studies is that they generally neglect general equilibrium effects of the reforms, which can be rather substantial, involving interactions between the treatment (temporary contracts) and the control (permanent contracts) groups. The relevance of these general equilibrium effects was documented both theoretically and empirically in Section 2. Bentolila and Dolado (1994) also provide evidence that flexible contracts offer a buffer stock to firms, insulating permanent workers from employment adjustment in response to exogenous shocks. Other interactions come from changes in the rate of conversion of fixed-term into permanent contracts when asymmetries between the two types of contracts are increased. Dolado et al. (2002) found that the probability of being employed with a temporary contract was significantly affected by the 1997 reform in Spain, which reduced employment protection for regular contracts. Also this effect is consistent with the predictions of the model proposed in Section 3.

Investigating the effects of EPL under dual regimes without taking into account of these interactions may induce one to overestimate the effects of EPL on the labor market. Suppose one considers a typical two-tier reform, reducing EPL limited to fixed term contracts while leaving unchanged the rules for permanent contracts. Identification of causal effects in a differences-in-differences framework requires that the two segments of the labor force taken as the "treatment" ($s = 1$) and the "control" ($s = 0$) groups respectively would have had the same trends in the outcome variable, had the reform not occurred. Assuming for simplicity that the EPL reform simply adds a constant δ to the conditional mean of some outcome variable (e.g., employment, N) in the treated segment, i.e., that:

$$N_{it} = \beta_t + \gamma_i + \delta s_i + \varepsilon_{it}$$

where i denotes the labor market segment (fixed-term vs. open-ended contracts), t is time, β is a common time trend, γ is a segment-specific fixed effect, and R is a dummy variable taking value one after the reform limited to the treatment group. In this case differences-in-differences identify δ as follows:

$$\{E[N_{it} \mid s_i = 1, t = 1] - E[N_{it} \mid s_i = 1, t = 0]\} +$$
$$- \{E[N_{it} \mid s_i = 0, t = 1] - E[N_{it} \mid s_i = 0, t = 0]\} = \delta \qquad (9)$$

as the first difference identifies $\delta + \beta + \gamma$ while the second difference identifies $\beta + \gamma$. Suppose, however, that the reform of EPL also affects the "control" group, by adding δ_2 to its conditional mean. In this case, the first difference in (9) identifies $\delta_1 + \beta + \gamma$ while the second difference $\delta_2 + \beta + \gamma$. It follows that this strategy can only identify the differential effect, $\delta_1 - \delta_2$. Thus, when reforms increase employment among fixed-term contracts and reduce employment among open-ended contracts, an identification strategy based on comparing pre–post reform employment variations across the two segments of the labor force overestimates the effects of reforms on employment.

An additional problem relates to the sorting of workers into the treatment and the control groups. This is the reason why the empirical literature looks for other differences, beyond the fixed-term/open-ended contracts divide, involving an exogenous allocation to the treatment or the control group, e.g., firm size when the worker is the unit of analysis. Most studies, however, do not go beyond controlling for observable characteristics of the treatment and control groups.

Finally, policy endogeneity is another important issue largely neglected by this literature. Some studies found EPL to become more protective during cyclical downturns or in high-unemployment regions (Bertola et al., 2000). The issues related to policy endogeneity are, however, more important with reference to the design of unemployment benefits and are therefore addressed in greater detail below.

4.2. The literature on reforms of unemployment benefits

Unemployment benefits are treated by the OECD indicators analyzed in Section 1 as a one-dimensional institution. However, there are at least three key dimensions which identify an unemployment benefit system: (i) the *eligibility* conditions (the norms determining the access to the benefit), (ii) the *entitlement* conditions (the rules concerning the duration of the payment), and (iii) the *replacement rates* (the fraction of previous income replaced by the transfer). Typically, at the beginning of the unemployment spell, the income replacement system mimics an insurance scheme: benefits are proportional to past contributions, which are themselves proportional to wages. However, the presence of benefit floors and ceilings compresses considerably the distribution of unemployment benefits with respect to the distribution of wages. Transfers to jobseekers at longer unemployment durations are generally independent of past contributions, and are offered in combination with other cash transfers to individuals who are not working, notably social assistance of the last resort. Eligibility to this second, *unemployment assistance*, component of UBs can be independent of payments (if any) made during the previous work experience. When the individual exhausts the maximum duration of benefits, they can have access to social assistance, in which case the transfer is offered for an unlimited duration, but subject to means-testing, that is, provided only to the unemployed individuals who have incomes and family assets lower than a given (poverty) threshold.

There is a huge literature on the effects of reforms of unemployment benefits on unemployment stocks, both at the macro and at the micro level.

The macro literature draws on cross-country comparisons based on aggregate indexes of UB generosity as those introduced in Section 2. Just like in the macro-EPL literature, the effects of reforms were initially identified via cross-country differences in the levels of the indicators. For instance, using cross-sectional data on 20 OECD countries, Layard et al. (2005) estimated that a 10% rise in the replacement rate involves roughly a 1.7% increase in the unemployment rate. Later studies for the same group of industrialized countries offered comparable results: Scarpetta (1996) estimated an elasticity of unemployment to UBs of the order of 1.3%, while Nickell (1997) of 1.1% and Bassanini and Duval (2006) of 1.2%. Blanchard and Wolfers (2000) found that UB replacement rates and duration are the most relevant institutions affecting unemployment, when interacted with shocks (the latter measured as deviations from country averages in TFP growth, real interest rates or a labor demand shifter). Unemployment benefits were also found to affect the composition of employment (Bertola et al., 2002) by "pricing out" women, youth and older workers.

In general it is the maximum duration of benefits, as opposed to the level of the replacement rate, which is found to have the strongest effects on unemployment rates in this macro literature. An increase of benefit levels has less effect on unemployment duration than an increase by the same percentage of the maximum duration of benefits.

The micro literature typically evaluates the effects of changes in benefit levels and in the residual entitlement to benefits on the duration of unemployment, based on longitudinal data, mostly drawn from live registers. Applied micro studies are consistent in finding positive effects of UB generosity on unemployment duration, but the effects are quantitatively small, notably when UB generosity is measured in terms of replacement rates rather than in terms of the maximum duration of benefits. Atkinson and Micklewright (1991), Devine and Kiefer (1991) and Krueger and Meyer (2002) offer excellent surveys of the earlier literature. To give a few examples as to the magnitude of the effects, Narendranathan et al. (1985) obtained a lower bound estimate of 0.08 for the effects on unemployment duration among British men of a one per cent increase in the level of benefits. van den Berg (1990) estimated that a 10% increase in the level of benefits in The Netherlands increases the duration of unemployment by one week, a result which is in line with evidence from the US (Meyer, 1989 and Katz and Meyer, 1990). The effect was found to be stronger (up to 5 weeks) when the increase in the benefit level occurs later on in the unemployment spell. Larger effects are also found when considering changes in the maximum duration of benefits (Meyer, 1990).

Spikes in the conditional probability of leaving unemployment (hazard rate) are typically observed in correspondence to the maximum duration of benefits. Although part of the spikes is attributable to measurement error (Card et al., 2007), notably exits from the unemployment register not corresponding to genuine outflows to jobs, spikes are also observed by studies tracking actual job finding rates rather than all outflows from the live register.

The stronger effects of changes in the duration of benefits vis-a-vis changes in the generosity of benefits (potentially having a larger effect on the net present value of UB entitlements) can also be explained in terms of policy endogeneity or reverse causality, thereby higher unemployment among some groups induces Governments to increase the duration of benefits (Holmlund, 1998). This is consistent with studies finding that underlying labor market conditions have important effects on UB duration. For instance, regional diversification in the maximum duration of UBs was found to be positively correlated with the duration of unemployment in US states (Card and Levine, 2000). Lalive and Zweimüller (2004) showed that estimates not correcting for policy endogeneity may significantly overstate the negative effects of the duration of UBs on the duration of unemployment in Austria. In particular, they estimated that the effects of the increase in benefit duration from 30 to 209 weeks on unemployment duration would have been 40% larger without correcting for policy endogeneity. The effects of unemployment duration on the duration of benefits were apparent also in the Great Recession of 2009, as many US states and OECD countries extended the duration of benefits in response to the spread of long-term unemployment.

The potential bias induced by policy endogeneity can be characterized by making reference to the identification strategy embedded in (9). Suppose that reforms react to stronger growth of unemployment in some group of the population (e.g., workers coming from long-tenured jobs) and that the outcome of interest is unemployment. Denote as β_{it} the group-specific time effect. As the reform is dictated by trend growth of unemployment being different in the two groups (i.e., $\beta_{00} > \beta_{10}$), a double differences approach would only identify $(\beta_{01} - \beta_{00}) - (\beta_{11} - \beta_{10}) + \delta$ potentially attributing to the reform effects which are instead related to the differential dynamics of unemployment in the absence of the reform.

Reforms of UB also involve relevant interactions with other institutions. An increasing body of literature explores interactions between UB and EPL, mainly taking a political economic perspective (Algan and Cahuc, 2009; Boeri et al., forthcoming). Other relevant interactions are those between unemployment benefits and unemployment assistance programs (Pellizzari, 2005). These interactions may reduce the elasticity of unemployment duration to changes in UB duration simply because individuals flowing from unemployment benefits to social assistance may actually experience an increase in the income transfer. This increases the reservation wage over the spell of unemployment even when the UB is provided at a flat (or mildly declining) rate (Fig. 12).

Two-tier reforms of UBs provide a second difference that can be used to control for these interactions. A number of recent studies compared hazards from unemployment across cohorts of UB recipients entitled to different durations of benefits. For instance, van Ours and Vodopivec (2006), provided a differences-in-differences analysis of reforms of the UB system in Slovenia. They considered, on the one hand, workers with 15 to 20 years of experience whose maximum duration of benefits was reduced from 18 months to 9 months of benefits and compared their experience with that of workers with more than 20 years of experience whose entitlement period was not affected by the reform. They found that spikes in the hazard rates followed very closely the change in entitlements.

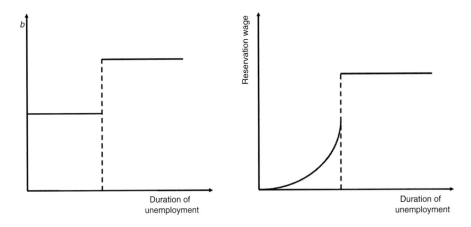

Figure 12   *Interactions between UB and social assistance.*

Lalive et al. (2004) also used differences-in-differences techniques to disentangle the effects on unemployment duration of increased replacement rates and the extension of the maximum duration of benefits, exploiting the fact that the increase in the generosity of UBs concerned only individuals aged more than 40 or with a relatively long work experience.

Interactions between treatment and control groups may be a less serious issue in this context than in the case of two-tier reforms of EPL. However, the extensions of the MP model in Section 3 suggest that also reforms of UB increasing generosity only at long tenure jobs involve a steeper-wage tenure (and wage-age) profile and a larger share of short duration jobs in total employment. Labor demand reacts to these reforms, operating substitutions of workers whose reservation wage increased as a result of the reform with workers whose reservation did not increase. Comparisons of unemployment outflow rates between cohorts whose benefits have been increased and cohorts whose benefits have not been increased (or have been reduced) may therefore induce one to overstate the responsiveness of unemployment duration to UB generosity along the lines of the argument developed when discussing the literature on EPL.

Endogenous sorting into the different regimes is less of a problem than in other institutional reforms, since typically two-tier reforms of UBs allocate individuals to treatment and control groups based on variables which are not under the control of individuals (e.g., age or past work history).

A more fundamental problem with the literature on UB reforms is that its focus is predominantly on job finding rates, while the general equilibrium framework developed in Section 3 suggests that the impact of UB reforms is likely to be perceived mainly on the job destruction margin, notably in presence of two-tier reforms.

4.3. The literature on reforms of employment conditional incentives

Empirical research on employment conditional incentives has mainly evaluated the effects on labor supply and family incomes of reforms targeting specific vulnerable groups. A narrow target is defined because reforms aim not only at encouraging participation in the labor market by conditioning state support to employment, but also at reducing poverty. For instance employment subsidies can be provided only to low-income families with children. A relatively narrow targeting of benefits also addresses the "windfall problem", thereby individuals, who are already working, opt-in the employment conditional incentive benefit ("windfall beneficiaries"): by restricting access to some classes of individuals (like the long-term welfare recipients or the unemployed) these deadweight costs are minimized. The transfers (or tax reductions) are phased in as earnings rise up to a threshold (phase-in region), are constant within an income bracket, and are gradually reduced over a set of income levels (phase-out region). Often employment subsidies impose conditions on intensive margins in order to reduce undesirable effects on hours of work. Individuals who, at the existing earnings, do not qualify for the benefits, may reduce working hours, substituting leisure for work in order to gain access to the subsidies ("opt-in beneficiaries"). In order to minimize these effects, some reforms impose a strict full-time work requirement. Adjustments of these hours of work requirements have been used to evaluate labor market adjustment to employment-conditional incentives (Blundell et al., 2008). Other institutional details which are very important in the evaluation of reforms relate to whether the benefit is provided as a tax credit or as a benefit. In the former case, reforms do not involve an increase in public expenditure, but may be less effective in encouraging participation if refunding is slow, which is frequently the case. Moreover, tax credits cannot reach those individuals who do not fill a tax form, e.g., because their incomes fall in the no-tax area.

The empirical literature evaluating these reforms is mainly focused on the US, Canada and the UK. Only limited to the US and Canada, it could draw on randomized experiments (as in the case of the *Earning Supplement Project* and the *Self-sufficiency Project* in Canada, the Minnesota *Family Investment*, the Milwaukee *New Hope*, the Vermont *Welfare Restructuring*, the Florida *Family Transition* and the Connecticut *Job First* programmes in the US). Blank (2002) offers an excellent survey of the findings of this literature. Although there has been a lot of experimentation with ECIs in Europe, regrettably there is no tradition of randomized experiments. The extensive literature on the microeconomic effects of the substitution in Britain of the *Family Credit* (FC) with the *Working Families' Tax Credit* (WFTC) had therefore to rely on quasi-experiments. This literature was reviewed by Blundell and Hoynes (2004) and Gregg and Harkness (2003) as well as in previous Handbook Chapters (Blundell and McCurdy, 1999). We offer below a short account of studies on the European experience with ECI reforms, concentrating on the results which are important from a labor force participation, rather than strictly poverty reduction, perspective.

Duncan et al. (2003) discuss the adaptation of in-work benefits in Denmark, France, UK and US. They observe that the evaluation of the employment effects points to an uneven impact across demographic groups, depending on the labor force attachment of the group and on the incentives structure of the in-work benefit program. A key issue in this respect is whether eligibility to in-work benefits is established on the basis of family income rather than individual income. In the case where eligibility is based on family income, the ECI can be better targeted to those actually in need of income support, but may have adverse effects on participation decisions of secondary earners in couples. Evidence from both the Earned Income Tax Credit (EITC) in the US (Eissa and Hoynes, 1998) and WFTC in the UK (Blundell and Hoynes, 2004; Francesconi and van der Klaauw, 2006; Brewer et al., 2006) indicates that the programs lowered the employment rate of married women with working spouses. In cases where ECI are instead conditioned on individual incomes, they may end-up rewarding high-income families. Unsurprisingly, microsimulation studies (Bargain and Orsini, 2006) suggest that individual benefits are more effective in incentivizing labor supply, notably of women, in those countries where the labor supply elasticity is larger. Pearson and Scarpetta (2000) underline that there is no single measure which of itself will have a major impact on employment. In-work benefits need to be part of a comprehensive policy and need to take into account administrative difficulties which vary from country to country. The main problems concern the take-up rate (in-work benefits need to be publicized) and the tax system used to deliver the benefit, which needs to be quick in order to make the benefit clearly linked to the current working condition. Another key factor in determining the effectiveness (and the costs) of ECIs is the dispersion of wages at the low-end of the earning distribution.

Other financial incentives aim at supporting job creation at relatively low productivity levels. Wage subsidies for low-wage employees sometimes operate also in conjunction with ECIs. They can be provided either as employment subsidies to employees or as reductions of employers' social security contributions. Wage subsidies can take several forms (e.g., subsidies or credits proportional to part or all of the annual wage, lump-sum amounts or re-employment bonuses to be redeemed by employers, etc.). As the wage level is the only qualifying condition, the reduction typically applies to both new entrants and to longstanding members of the workforce. The reduction in contributions remains in effect as long as the monthly wage is below a pre-determined ceiling. When the reduction is based only on the monthly wage and not on the number of hours worked, this measure may lead to more part-time work at what may be relatively high hourly wages. Therefore for part-time workers the cut in contributions is commensurate to the hours worked. Perhaps the most noteworthy (at least in terms of take-up rates) scheme experimented in Europe is the Dutch SPAK (see Doudeijns et al., 2000). The SPAK was introduced in 1996 and phased out in 2003 for cost-saving reasons.

It consists of a reduction of employers' contributions on low wages. The reduction in contributions declines as the wage rises and ceases at 115% of the statutory minimum wage. This may create a disincentive for firms to increase wages over this threshold. In 1997 the transitional SPAK was introduced to cushion the loss of wage subsidies and the increase in taxes for employers who raised the pay of SPAK workers over the threshold. According to the traditional SPAK, employers may apply for half of the SPAK for two years for workers who were previously on the SPAK programme but lost the benefit because they got an increase up to 130% of the minimum wage.

Evaluation of SPAK based on general equilibrium models (Bovenberg et al., 1998 and European Commission 1999) predicted a total increase in employment of 1% and 5% for the low-skilled workers. Evaluations of similar programmes in France and Belgium also report significant effects on employment. On the basis of firm-level data, Crepon and Deplatz (2001) estimate the number of jobs created in the 255,000 to 670,000 range (between 1% and 3% of total employment in the business sector). Sneessens and Shatman (2000) for Belgium estimate that a cut of 21% in employers' contributions on unskilled jobs may increase total employment of the unskilled by 6.7%. These estimates have to be judged with caution given the considerable uncertainty as to the labor demand elasticity and, to a lesser degree, the labor supply elasticity of low-wage workers. The employment effects of wage subsidies are larger the more elastic are labor demand and supply. When the labor supply elasticity is larger than the demand elasticity, the earning effect of a wage subsidy is larger than the employment effect and vice versa.

Wage subsidies, like subsidies to the employees, can generate deadweight losses in the form of windfall beneficiaries. The main criticism to this kind of policies is that they subsidize existing jobs and job creation that may have occurred anyway. The deadweight costs generated by windfall beneficiaries could be eliminated by using true marginal employment subsidies, i.e. subsidies only to job openings beyond those that would have occurred in the absence of the subsidy. But clearly the informational requirements for such subsidies are unattainable. Many countries have proxied marginal subsidies with incremental subsidies, i.e. subsidies to employment beyond a certain increment over the previous year's employment, and restrained access to firms that did not lay off workers in the previous year. However, these subsidies can generate perverse incentives for firms to implement large layoffs followed by large hirings, and may end up subsidizing high turnover sectors and firms. Furthermore these subsidies typically cover fast-expanding firms as well as those in decline.

Broad measures to reduce employers' contributions for low-paid jobs imply a big funding effort. They can also exert fiscal crowding out effects insofar as the subsidy needs to be financed by increasing tax rates (Drèze, 2002). The costs of wage subsidies are non-negligible: available estimates suggest that they may reach from 0.5% to 1% of GDP in France, Belgium, Italy and the Netherlands. Due to these high fiscal costs many ongoing experiments with ECIs provide benefits or tax credits with a limited duration. Besides the budgetary constraint, the justification for such time limits is that state support should only encourage the transition from welfare to work making a permanent break from dependency on state support. The analysis of the effects of these policies necessarily requires a dynamic analysis and observations on treatment and control groups several years after the initial treatment. Card and Hyslop (2005) analyzed one such scheme, the Canadian Self Sufficiency Project (SSP) providing a subsidy only to individuals accepting full-time jobs, and for at most 3 years. They found that SSP had a large effect in the short run: 69 months after all subsidy payments ended the welfare participation rates of the treatment and control groups were equal. Once the financial incentives for some individuals to find a full-time job were gone, these individuals no longer behaved differently from individuals that did not get the ECI. Card and Hyslop conclude that the SSP experiment offers little support for the idea that temporary wage subsidies can have a permanent effect on the labor market position of welfare benefit recipients.

According to the model developed in Section 3, two-tier reforms, subsidizing only entry jobs, may increase churning and reduce the conversion of fixed-term into permanent contracts. This hints at potential labor demand factors that could prevent employment conditional incentives to become a pathway to self-sufficiency. One way to deal with these problems is to condition employment conditional incentives to hiring on permanent contracts, as done in some countries (e.g., Italy and Spain), subsidizing the transformation of fixed-term into permanent contracts. A downside of this approach is that it may encourage employers to hire on fixed-term contracts also workers who would have been hired from the start on permanent contracts, in order to be in a position to claim the benefit. To our knowledge these demand effects have not yet been investigated by the literature on ECI reforms, which is mainly concentrated on the supply side. Nor is there work on job reallocation associated with employment conditional incentives, with the exception of the aforementioned study by Francesconi and van der Klaauw (2006).

4.4. The literature on experiments with activation programmes

Activation programmes aim at easing the job matching process, by increasing the effectiveness of job search rather than simply reducing reservation wages of jobseekers, as in the case of reductions of unemployment benefits. They rely on a public administration, offering placement and counseling services, vocational guidance and job-search courses. Participation in the programmes is compulsory for the relevant target groups. Key examples are the requirement imposed on unemployed individuals to attend intensive interviews with employment counselors, apply for job vacancies as directed by employment counselors, independently search for job vacancies and apply for jobs, accept offers of suitable work, participate in the formulation of an individual action plan, and participate in training or job-creation programs. Complying with activation requirements may be quite time consuming and cumbersome, which self-selects the most needy. In order to encourage take up, sometimes unwillingness to participate in the activation programmes is sanctioned with benefit reductions.

Kluve (2006) offers a survey of some 100 evaluation studies of active labor market policy programmes carried out in Europe since 1990. The results are not particularly encouraging. Training programmes appear to have at most a modest effect on transitions from unemployment to private employment, direct employment programmes in the public sector are rarely effective and frequently detrimental for the employment prospects of participants. Providing job search assistance and counseling and monitoring in combination with sanctions for noncompliance is more effective and less costly.

As in the case of ECIs, there have been a very few randomized experiments in Europe that could be used in learning about the effects of activation programmes. Gorter and Kalb (1996) found that intensive counseling and monitoring had positive effects on the job finding rates of unemployed workers in the Netherlands. Dolton and O'Neill (1996, 2002) evaluated the so-called Restart experiments in the UK, where unemployment benefit claimants were obliged to attend meetings with a counselor to receive advice on search behavior, finding that the interviews reduced the male unemployment rate five years later by 6% points. Black et al. (2003), studied mandatory employment and training programs for unemployed workers, finding that some unemployed workers considered the activation programmes as a sort of sanction to be avoided by leaving the live register, rather than as opportunities to enhance the effectiveness of job search. van den Berg and van der Klaauw (2006) used data from a field experiment in studying the effect of counseling and monitoring on Dutch UB recipients in 1998. The experiment consisted of randomly assigning counseling and monitoring to part of the workers. They found significant effects on job finding rates only limited to individuals with worse opportunities.

Non-experimental studies are based on cross-country comparisons or micro-oriented evaluation studies. Heckman et al. (1999) and Kluve and Schmidt (2002) provide overviews of these evaluation studies. They document that programs with a large training content are most likely to improve employment probability, while direct job creation and employment subsidies in the public sector almost always fail. The latter schemes often stimulate workers to reduce their search efforts rather than increasing them. This is due to the so-called locking-in effect (see for example van Ours, 2004). There is also considerable heterogeneity in the impact of these programs, so for some groups of workers the programs are more effective than for other groups. Heckman et al. (1999) in particular point out the presence of significant general equilibrium effects of programmes implemented on a large scale. This confirms that micro treatment effect evaluations not incorporated in a macro framework may provide poor guides to public policy. What is effective for an individual unemployed worker may not be effective in terms of the aggregate level of unemployment. One reason for this may be crowding out. If a program brings an unemployed worker back to work more quickly at the expense of another unemployed worker finding a job more slowly, the programme is not very efficient. Another reason for the differences between individual and aggregate effects is that a training program may make workers more attractive for firms, which stimulates job creation, but also job destruction of old jobs, as indicated by the framework developed in Section 3. This contributes to explain the poor record of Swedish activation programmes in improving job matching, as highlighted by Calmfors et al. (2001).

Benefit sanctions seem in general to be more effective than other active policies (Martin and Grubb, 2001). This is confirmed by more recent micro studies on the effect of benefit sanctions on outflows from unemployment to a job. Abbring et al. (2005), in particular, study the effect of financial incentives by comparing the unemployment duration of individuals who have faced a benefit reduction with similar individuals who have not been penalized. They found that benefit sanctions have a positive effect on individual transition rates from unemployment to a job. van den Berg et al. (2004) performed a similar study for welfare recipients in the city of Rotterdam, finding that benefit sanctions stimulate the transition from welfare to work. From an analysis of Swiss data on benefit sanctions Lalive et al. (2005) also concluded that by imposing a benefit sanction the unemployment duration decreases by roughly three weeks.

A key problem with the non-experimental literature on activation programs is that these schemes rely on the self-selection of the most needy, and it is often difficult to find remedies for this endogenous sorting within ex-post evaluation studies. Another problem is that they often neglect the effect of these programmes on the job destruction side, which can be non-negligible according to the theoretical perspectives offered in Section 3.

5. FINAL REMARKS

This chapter surveyed the vast applied literature drawing on reforms of labor market institutions in Europe, which offers a wealth of quasi-natural experiments. Reforms have been concentrated in four domains: employment protection legislation, unemployment benefits, employment-conditional incentives and activation programmes. Our broad conclusion from this survey is that this literature is very informative, but not sufficiently supported by a theory accounting for the particular nature of reforms that are taking place in the labor market. They are, for the most, reforms creating longlasting asymmetries, while theory typically considers complete reforms, affecting all the potentially eligible population. More theoretical work on two-tier reforms could provide better guidance to applied work suggesting refinements in the identification of the causal effects of institutions. At the same time, a more careful description of the reforms in applied work, along the checklist suggested in this Chapter, could help the development of a more realistic theory of the effects of institutional reforms on the labor market.

APPENDIX A. THE fRDB-IZA SOCIAL POLICY REFORMS DATABASE

In recent years, there has been considerable progress in the development of international comparative databases on labor market reforms and on quantitative indicators providing institutional information for many countries. However, researchers are increasingly interested not only on quantitative indicators, but also on qualitative information on labor market reforms allowing for a deeper understanding of country specific reform processes.

For this reason, fRDB (Fondazione Rodolfo Debenedetti) and IZA (Institute for the Study of Labor) are currently cooperating in constructing a comprehensive inventory of policy reforms in core areas of the EU labor market. In future, the database will cover reforms in the EU27 countries starting from 1980. The already existing "fRDB Social Reforms Database" (firstly published in 2003) is the starting point of this work.

A first version of the database has been recently released, covering seven European countries (Denmark, France, Germany, Italy, Netherlands, Spain and United Kingdom). It currently covers five main policy areas:

- employment protection legislation (EPL)
- unemployment benefits (UB)
- employment conditional incentives (ECI)
- activation programs (AP)
- early retirement (ER).

The unit of analysis in the database is the reform, i.e. a collection of policy measures referring to a unique formally approved law. Thus, collected information mainly consists of enacted national legislations. In addition, other public acts or collective agreements are recorded if they are likely to be relevant at the national level and potentially affect large sectors of the economy or a large percentage of workers. Planned reforms, proposals on future changes or bills that are not formally approved are not included. A reform is recoded only when the legislative process is formally concluded.

Reforms addressing more than one topic—or more than one policy area—are recoded several times under different categories (once per each topic addressed). This means that each measure embedded in observed reforms is individually evaluated in order to take into account of all possible characteristics of the reform process. Despite the multiple coding of measures, reforms that introduce changes in more than one policy area (or addressing more than one topic) can be easily identified through a reform-specific identification number. In other words, a reform id allows for a clear identification of all measures corresponding to a specific text law or collective agreement.

Collected information on reforms is presented in a synthetic and ready-to-use fashion, including details on the main institutional changes over time and target groups. Institutional details have been collected by fRDB and IZA researchers drawing on a variety of sources and then checked by a network of national experts. Categorical variables as well as other characteristics of reforms are also available in Stata format, ready to be used for statistical analysis (Monti and Eichhorst, "fRDB–IZA Labor Market Reforms Database. Description and User Guide", 2009).

APPENDIX B. INSTITUTIONS IN THE MP MODEL

Let us first evaluate the steady-state, equilibrium valuations of states. Given our assumptions, the continuation valuation by workers of unemployment (U), and employment $(W(x))$, and by firms of an open vacancy (V) vs. a job $(J(x))$ must solve the following four functional equations:

$$rU = \theta q(\theta)[W(1) - U] \tag{10}$$

$$rV = -c + q(\theta)[J(1) - V] \tag{11}$$

$$rW(x) = w(x) + \lambda \int_R^1 (W(z) - W(x))\mathrm{d}F(z) + \lambda F(R)(U - W(x)) \tag{12}$$

$$rJ(x) = x - w(x) + \lambda \int_R^1 (J(z) - J(x))\mathrm{d}F(z) + \lambda F(R)(V - J(x)). \tag{13}$$

Equations (10) through (13) equate normal returns on capitalized valuations of labor market states to their expected periodic payouts. In Eq. (10), the flow yield from the valuation of the state of unemployment U at interest rate r is equated to an expected "capital gain" stemming from finding new employment at $x = 1$. Eq. (11) governs the valuation of an unfilled vacancy. All filled vacancies begin at a common productivity, so all vacancies must be identical *ex-ante*. The function $W(x)$ in (12) returns the value of employment in a job-worker match with current productivity x. The implicit rate of return on the asset of working in a job at productivity x is equal to the current wage $w(x)$ plus the expected capital gain on the employment relationship. The lower bound of the definite integral, R, is the cutoff or threshold value of match productivity, determined endogenously in the model. If idiosyncratic productivity x falls below R, the match is no longer profitable and the job–worker pair is destroyed. A similar arbitrage argument determines the valuation to a firm of a filled job in (13), given the current realization of x.

Wage equation under the Nash bargaining rule should solve:

$$w(x) = \arg\max(W(x) - U)^\beta (J(x) - V)^{1-\beta}$$

yielding the first-order condition:

$$W(x) - U = \beta(J(x) + W(x) - V - U). \tag{14}$$

Use now $V = 0$ and rewrite the two asset value conditions (for jobs and employment, respectively) as follows:

$$r J(x) = x - w(x) + \lambda \int_R^1 [J(z) - J(x)] dF(z) + \lambda F(R)[V - J(x)]$$

$$r J(x) = x - w(x) + \lambda \int_R^1 J(z) dF(z) - \lambda J(x)$$

$$J(x) = \frac{x - w(x) + \lambda \int_R^1 J(z) dF(z)}{(r + \lambda)}$$

$$r W(x) = w(x) + \lambda \int_R^1 [W(z) - W(x)] dF(z) + \lambda F(R)[U - W(x)]$$

$$r W(x) = w(x) + \lambda \int_R^1 W(z) dF(z) + \lambda F(R)U$$
$$- \lambda[(W(x))(1 - F(R)) + F(R)W(x)]$$

$$W(x) = \frac{w(x) + \lambda \int_R^1 W(z) dF(z) + \lambda F(R)U}{(r + \lambda)}.$$

Now we can use the above and (14) to obtain:

$$\beta(J(x)) = (1 - \beta)(W(x) - U)$$
$$\beta[x - w(x)] = (1 - \beta)[w(x) - rU]$$
$$w(x) = (1 - \beta)rU + \beta x. \tag{15}$$

Finally obtain a closed form expression for rU as follows:

$$W(1) - U = \beta(J(1) + W(1) - U)$$
$$(1 - \beta)[W(1) - U] = \beta J(1).$$

Combining this with the free entry condition:

$$rU = \theta q(\theta)[W(1) - U]$$
$$W(1) - U = \frac{rU}{\theta q(\theta)}$$

we get:

$$(1 - \beta)\left[\frac{rU}{\theta q(\theta)}\right] = \beta \frac{c}{q(\theta)}$$

or

$$rU = \frac{\beta c\theta}{1 - \beta}. \tag{16}$$

Finally inserting this into (15), we get

$$w(x) = \beta[x + c\theta]. \tag{17}$$

Consider now the set of institutions introduced in Section 3, that is, an unemployment benefit $b = \rho w$, a firing tax T, an employment conditional incentive e and a hiring subsidy $h < c$. Let us first rewrite the steady-state, equilibrium valuations of states under these new conditions.

$$rU = b + \theta q(\theta)[W(1) - U] \tag{18}$$

$$rV = -c + h + q(\theta)[J(1) - V] \tag{19}$$

$$rW(x) = w(x) + e + \lambda \int_R^1 (W(z) - W(x))dF(z) + \lambda F(R)(U - W(x)) \tag{20}$$

$$rJ(x) = x - w(x) + \lambda \int_R^1 (J(z) - J(x))dF(z) + \lambda F(R)(V - T - J(x)). \tag{21}$$

Wages under the Nash bargaining rule will now solve:

$$w(x) = \arg\max(W(x) - U)^\beta (J(x) - V + T)^{1-\beta}$$

yielding the first-order condition:

$$(1 - \beta)[W(x) - U] = \beta(J(x) + T - V). \tag{22}$$

Use then $V = 0$ and rewrite the two asset value conditions with the institutions, following the same steps as in the institution-free model:

$$J(x) = \frac{x - w(x) + \lambda \int_R^1 J(z)dF(z) - \lambda T}{(r + \lambda)}$$

$$W(x) = \frac{w(x) + e + \lambda \int_R^1 W(z)dF(z) + \lambda F(R)U}{(r + \lambda)}.$$

Substituting these into (22) and upon some manipulation one obtains

$$w(x) = (1 - \beta)(rU - e) + \beta(x + rT). \tag{23}$$

In order to get a closed form expression for rU with institutions we use the free entry condition:

$$J(1) = \frac{c - h}{q(\theta)}$$

to obtain:

$$rU = \rho w + \frac{\beta(c - h)\theta}{1 - \beta}. \tag{24}$$

Finally inserting this into (23), we get

$$w(x) = (1 - \beta)(\rho w - e) + \beta[x + (c - h)\theta + rT]. \tag{25}$$

Job creation and destruction in the extended MP model

To obtain the job creation condition, use (24) and evaluate the asset value of a job (21) for an employer, $J(x)$, at R, where $J(R) = -T$:

$$rJ(R) = R - (1 - \beta)(\rho w - e) - \beta[(c - h)\theta + R] + \lambda \int_R^1 J(z)\mathrm{d}F(z) - \lambda J(R)$$

$$-T = (1 - \beta)(R - \rho w + e) - \beta(c - h)\theta + \lambda \int_R^1 J(z)\mathrm{d}F(z). \tag{26}$$

Solving for the last term and simplifying

$$\lambda \int_R^1 J(z)\mathrm{d}F(z) = \beta(c - h)\theta - (1 - \beta)[R - \rho w + e] - T. \tag{27}$$

Moreover, by the asset value condition of a job and the wage equation we have

$$rJ(x) - x + w(x) = \lambda \int_R^1 J(z)\mathrm{d}F(z) - \lambda J(x)$$

$$(r + \lambda)J(x) - x + (1 - \beta)(\rho w - e) + \beta[x + (c - h)\theta + rT] = \lambda \int_R^1 J(z)\mathrm{d}F(z). \tag{28}$$

Hence plugging (27) into the above and simplifying:

$$(r + \lambda)J(x) = (1 - \beta)[x - R] - T.$$

Being interested in the job creation margin, we evaluate this at the initial productivity level, and use the free entry condition:

$$(r + \lambda)\frac{c - h}{q(\theta)} = (1 - \beta)[1 - R]$$

or

$$\frac{(1 - \beta)[1 - R]}{(r + \lambda)} - T = \frac{c - h}{q(\theta)}. \tag{29}$$

This condition (*JC-curve*) is strictly downward sloping in the (R, θ) space, since $q'(\theta) < 0$. The economics behind this trade-off is that a higher R involves a shorter duration of matches, and so lower expected profits from a new job. Thus fewer vacancies are created, reducing market tightness.

Jobs are destroyed when productivity falls below its corresponding reservation or threshold level. R is implicitly defined by the condition

$$J(R) = -T. \tag{30}$$

At the same time, Nash bargaining also implies that R satisfies the zero match-surplus condition:

$$J(R) + T - V + W(R) - U = 0 \tag{31}$$

and, given the free entry condition $V = 0$, it follows that

$$W(R) = U$$

that is, separations are privately, but not necessarily socially, jointly efficient.

To obtain the *job destruction* condition implicitly providing the reservation productivity level, R, consider first that by (21)

$$rJ(x) = x - w(x) + \lambda \int_R^1 [J(z) - J(x)]dF(z)$$
$$+ \lambda F(R)[V - T - J(x)] \tag{32}$$
$$rJ(x) = x - w(x) + \lambda \int_R^1 J(z)dF(z) - \lambda J(x) - \lambda T$$
$$(r + \lambda)J(x) = x - [(1 - \beta)(rU - e) + \beta[x + (c - h)\theta + rT]]$$
$$+ \lambda \int_R^1 J(z)dF(z) - \lambda T.$$

Evaluating the above equation at $x = R$ and noting that $J(R) = -T$ by the definition of the reservation productivity

$$(r + \lambda)J(R) = R - [(1 - \beta)(rU - e) + \beta[R + (c - h)\theta + rT]]$$
$$+ \lambda \int_R^1 J(z)\mathrm{d}F(z) - \lambda T \tag{33}$$
$$-(r + \lambda)T = R - [(1 - \beta)(rU - e) + \beta[R + (c - h)\theta + rT]]$$
$$+ \lambda \int_R^1 J(z)\mathrm{d}F(z) - \lambda T.$$

Finally use (24) to obtain

$$R + \frac{\lambda}{r + \lambda} \int_R^1 (z - R)\mathrm{d}F(z) + rT = \rho w - e + \frac{\beta(c - h)\theta}{1 - \beta}. \tag{34}$$

The left-hand side is the flow benefit of a continuing match with productivity R; this is the current flow product plus the option value deriving from possible future improvements over the following time interval. The right-hand side represents the (opportunity) costs of maintaining the match at the threshold value of idiosyncratic productivity. This *job destruction* (JD) *condition* defines an upward-sloping curve in the (θ, R) space.

The intersection of (34) with the job creation condition (29) defines the aggregate labor market equilibrium. There exists a unique equilibrium reservation productivity and labor tightness pair (R^*, θ^*) given by the Poisson arrival rate λ, worker bargaining power β, the hiring subsidy h, employment conditional incentives e, firing tax T and unemployment benefits replacement rate ρ:

$$R^* = R^*(\lambda, \beta, h, e, \rho, T)$$
$$\theta^* = \theta^*(\lambda, \beta, h, e, \rho, T).$$

Given the equilibrium R^* and θ^*, the unemployment rate follows from the flow condition for constant unemployment:

$$u^* \equiv u^*(\lambda, \beta, h, e, \rho, T) = \frac{\lambda F(R^*)}{\lambda F(R^*) + \theta^* q(\theta^*)}. \tag{35}$$

Job creation and job destruction in two-tier regimes

The job creation and job destruction condition for the two-tier regimes can be derived by imposing that $V = 0$, $J(R_0) = 0$ and $J(R) = -T$ and using the Nash bargaining rule. This obtains the job creation condition

$$\frac{(1-\beta)(e_0 - R_0)}{r+\lambda} - \frac{\beta}{r+\lambda}(1-\lambda T) = \frac{c-h}{q(\theta)}. \tag{36}$$

The job destruction condition for temporary jobs

$$R_0 + \frac{\lambda}{r+\lambda}\int_{R_0}^{1}(z - R_0)dF(z) + e_0 - \lambda T = \rho_0 w + \frac{\beta(c-h)\theta}{1-\beta} \tag{37}$$

and the job destruction for permanent contracts

$$R + \frac{\lambda}{r+\lambda}\int_{R}^{1}(z - R)dF(z) + rT = \rho w + \frac{\beta(c-h)\theta}{1-\beta}. \tag{38}$$

Derivation of the outsider wage

Consider the equilibrium values for entry jobs:

$$r J_0 = 1 - w_0 + \lambda\int_{R_0}^{1}[J(z) - J_0]dF(z) + \lambda F(R_0)[V - J_0] \tag{39}$$

$$r W_0 = w_0 + e_0 + \lambda\int_{R_0}^{1}[W(z) - W_0]dF(z) + \lambda F(R_0)[U - W_0]. \tag{40}$$

Notice that:

$$-\lambda\int_{R_0}^{1}[J_0]dF(z) = -\lambda J_0 + \lambda F(R_0)J_0 \tag{41}$$

$$-\lambda\int_{R_0}^{1}[W_0]dF(z) = -\lambda W_0 + \lambda F(R_0)W_0 \tag{42}$$

hence we can rewrite (39) and (40) as follows

$$(r+\lambda)J_0 = 1 - w_0 + \lambda\int_{R_0}^{1}J(z)dF(z) \tag{38'}$$

where we have used also the free entry condition $V = 0$, and

$$(r+\lambda)W_0 = w_0 + e_0 + \lambda\int_{R_0}^{1}W(z)dF(z)\lambda F(R_0 U)$$

$$= w_0 + e_0 + \lambda\int_{R_0}^{1}[W(z) - U]dF(z) - \lambda U_0. \tag{39'}$$

Now we use the Nash bargaining rule

$$\beta J_0 = (1 - \beta)[W_0 - U]$$

$$\frac{\beta}{r + \lambda}\left[1 - w_0 + \lambda \int R_0^{\ 1} J(z)\mathrm{d}F(z)\right]$$

$$= \frac{1 - \beta}{r + \lambda}\left[w_0 + e_0 + \lambda \int_{R_0}^{1} [W(z) - U]\mathrm{d}F(z) - \lambda U_0 - (r + \lambda)U\right]$$

$$\beta(1 + w_0) + \lambda\beta \int_{R_0}^{1} J(z)\mathrm{d}F(z)$$

$$= (1 - \beta)(w_0 + e_0 - rU) + (1 - \beta)\lambda \int_{R_0}^{1} [W(z) - U]\mathrm{d}F(z)$$

$$\lambda \int_{R_0}^{1} [\beta J(z) - (1 - \beta)[W(z) - U]]\mathrm{d}F(z) = (1 - \beta)(w_0 + e_0 - rU_0) - \beta(1 - w_0)$$

and by the Nash bargaining solution, on continuing jobs:

$$\beta[J(x) + T] = (1 - \beta)[W(x) - U]$$

hence:

$$-\lambda\beta T = (1 - \beta)(w_0 + e_0 - rU_0) - \beta(1 - w_0)$$

solving for w_0:

$$(1 - \beta)w_0 + \beta w_0 = \beta(1 - \lambda T) + (1 - \beta)(rU - e_0)$$
$$w_0 = \beta(1 - \lambda T) + (1 - \beta)(rU - e_0)$$

but

$$rU = b + \theta q(\theta)[W_0 - U]$$
$$\frac{rU - b}{\theta q(\theta)} = [W_0 - U]$$

and by Nash bargaining:

$$(1 - \beta)[W_0 - U] = \beta J_0$$

while by the free entry condition:

$$\beta J_0 = \frac{(c-h)}{q(\theta)}$$

hence:

$$\frac{rU-b}{\theta q(\theta)} = \frac{\beta}{1-\beta}\frac{(c-h)}{q(\theta)}$$

$$(1-\beta)rU = (1-\beta)b + \beta\frac{(c-h)}{q(\theta)}\theta q(\theta)$$

and recalling that $b = \rho_0\bar{w}$:

$$w_0 = (1-\beta)[\rho_0\bar{w}-\rho] + \beta[(c-h)\theta + 1 - \lambda T].$$

REFERENCES

Abbring, H., van den Berg, G.J., van Ours, C., 2005. The effect of unemployment insurance sanctions on the transition rate from unemployment to employment. The Economic Journal 115, 602–630.

Abiad, A., Detragiache, E., Tressel, T., 2008. A new database of financial reforms. IMF Working Paper, IMF Institute and Research Department.

Addison, J., Grosso, J.-L., 1996. Job security provisions and employment: revised estimates. Industrial Relations 35 (4), 585–603.

Agell, J., 1999. On the benefits for rigid labour markets: norms, market failures and social insurance. The Economic Journal 109, 143–164.

Algan, Y., Cahuc, P., 2009. Civic virtue and labor market institutions. American Economic Journal: Macroeconomics, American Economic Association 1 (1), 111–145.

Alogoskoufis, G., Bean, C.R., Bertola, G., Cohen, D., Dolado, J., Saint-Paul, G., 1995. Unemployment: choices for Europe. Monitoring European integration 5. CEPR Report, London: CEPR.

Arulampalam, W., Booth, A., 1998. Training and labour market flexibility: is there a trade-off? British Journal of Industrial Relations 36 (4), 521–536.

Atkinson, A., Micklewright, J., 1991. Unemployment compensation and labor market transitions: a critical review. Journal of Economic Literature 29, 1679–1727.

Autor, D., Donohue, J., Schwab, S., 2006. The costs of wrongful discharge laws. Review of Economics and Statistics 88 (2), 211–231.

Bargain, O., Orsini, K., 2006. In-work policies in Europe: killing two birds with one stone? Labour Economics 13, 667–697.

Bassanini, A., Marianna, P., 2009. Looking inside the perpetual-motion machine: job and worker flows in OECD countries. OECD Social, Employment and Migration Working Papers 95, OECD, Directorate for Employment, Labour and Social Affairs.

Bassanini, A., Duval, R., 2006. Employment patterns in OECD countries: reassessing the role of policies and institutions. OECD Economics Department Working Papers no. 486, Paris.

Bean, C., 1994. European unemployment: a survey. Journal of Economic Literature 32 (2), 573–619.

Belot, M., van Ours, J., 2001. Unemployment and labour market institutions: an empirical analysis. Journal of the Japanese International Economies 15 (4), 403–418.

Bentolila, S., Bertola, G., 1990. Firing costs and labour demand: how bad is Eurosclerosis? Review of Economic Studies 57 (3), 381–402.

Bentolila, S., Dolado, J., 1994. Labor flexibility and wages: lessons from Spain. Economic Policy 18, 55–99.

Bentolila, S., Saint-Paul, G., 1992. The macroeconomic impact of flexible labor contracts, with an application to Spain. European Economic Review 36, 1013–1047.

Bertola, G., 1990. Job security employment and wages. European Economic Review 34 (4), 851–879.

Bertola, G., 1999. Microeconomic perspectives on aggregate labor markets. In: Ashenfelter, O., Card, D. (Eds.), Handbook of Labor Economics. Elsevier, Amsterdam, pp. 2985–3028.

Bertola, G., Blau, E., Kalm, L., 2002. Labor market institutions and demographic employment. NBER Working Paper no. 9043, Cambridge, MA.

Bertola, G., Boeri, T., Cazes, S., 2000. Employment protection in industrialized countries: the case for new indicators. International Labor Review 139 (1), 57–72.

Bertola, G., Boeri, T., Nicoletti, G., 2001. Welfare and Employment in a United Europe. MIT Press, Cambridge, MA.

Bertola, G., Rogerson, R., 1997. Institutions and labour reallocation. European Economic Review 41, 1147–1171.

Bertola, G., Boeri, T., 2002. EMU labour markets two years on: microeconomics tensions and institutional evolution. In: Buti, M., Sapir, A. (Eds.), EMU and Economic Policy in Europe. Edward Elgar.

Black, D.A., Smith, I.A., Berger, M.C., Noel, B.J., 2003. Is the threat of training more effective than training itself? Evidence from random assignments in the UI system. American Economic Review 93 (4), 1313–1327.

Blanchard, O., 2006. European unemployment: the evolution of facts and ideas. Economic Policy 22, 5–59.

Blanchard, O., Landier, A., 2002. The perverse effects of partial labor market reform: fixed-term contracts in France. The Economic Journal 112, 214–244.

Blanchard, O., Diamond, P., 1989. The Beveridge curve. In: Brookings Papers on Economic Activity. In: Economic Studies Program, vol. 20(1). The Brookings Institution, pp. 1–76.

Blanchard, O., Wolfers, J., 2000. The role of shocks and institutions in the rise of European unemployment: the aggregate evidence. The Economic Journal 110, 1–33.

Blank, R.M., 2002. Can equity and efficiency complement each other? Labour Economics 9 (4), 451–468.

Blau, Francine D., Kahn, Lawrence M., 1999. Analyzing the gender pay gap. The Quarterly Review of Economics and Finance 39 (5), 625–646.

Blundell, R., Brewer, M., Francesconi, M., 2008. Job changes and hours changes: understanding the path of labor supply adjustment. Journal of Labor Economics 26 (3), 421–453.

Blundell, R., McCurdy, T., 1999. Labor supply: a review of alternative approaches. In: Ashenfelter, O.C., Card, D. (Eds.), Handbook of Labor Economics. Elsevier, Amsterdam, pp. 1559–1695.

Blundell, R., Hoynes, H., 2004. Has in-work benefit reform helped the labor market? In: Blundell, R., Card, D., Freeman, R. (Eds.), Seeking a Premier Economy: The Economic Effect of British Economic Reforms, 1980-2000. University of Chicago Press, Chicago, pp. 411–460.

Boeri, T., 1999. Enforcement of employment security regulations, on-the-job search and unemployment duration. European Economic Review 43, 65–89.

Boeri, T., Jimeno, J., 2005. The effects of employment protection: learning from variable enforcement. European Economic Review 49 (8), 2057–2077.

Boeri, T., Garibaldi, P., 2007. Two-tier reforms of employment protection: a honeymoon effect? The Economic Journal 117 (521), 357–385.

Boeri, T., van Ours, J., 2008. The Economics of Imperfect Labor Markets. Princeton University Press, Princeton.

Boeri, T., Conde-Ruiz, I., Galasso, V., 2010. The political economy of flexicurity. Journal of the European Economic Association (forthcoming).

Booth, A., Francesconi, M., Frank, J., 2002. Temporary jobs: stepping stones or dead ends? Economic Journal 112 (480), F189–F213.

Bovenberg, A.L., de Mooij, R.A., Graafland, J.J., 1998. Tax reform and the Dutch labour market: an applied general equilibrium approach. CEPR DP 1983.

Brewer, M., Duncan, A., Shephard, A., Suarez, M.J., 2006. Did work families' tax credit work? The impact of in-work support on labour supply in Great Britain. Labour Economics 13, 699–720.

Cahuc, P., Postel-Vinay, F., 2002. Temporary jobs, employment protection and labor market performance. Labour Economics 9 (1), 63–91.

Calmfors, L., Forslund, A., Hemsvsm, M., 2001. Does active labor market policy work? Lessons from the Swedish experiences. Swedish Economic Policy Review 85, 61–124.

Card, D., Chetty, R., Weber, A., 2007. The spike at benefit exhaustion: leaving the unemployment system or starting a new job? American Economic Review 97 (2), 113–118.

Card, D., Levine, P., 2000. Extended benefits and the duration of UI spells: evidence from the New Jersey extended benefit program. Journal of Public Economics 78, 107–138.

Card, D., Hyslop, D.R., 2005. Estimating the effects of a time-limited earnings subsidy for welfare-leavers. Econometrica 73, 1723–1770.

Clark, A.E., Postel-Vinay, F., 2009. Job security and job protection. Oxford Economic Papers 61 (2), 207–239.

Conway, P., Nicoletti, G., 2006. Product market regulation of non-manufacturing sectors in OECD countries: measurement and highlights. OECD Economics Department Working Paper No. 530.

Crepon, B., Deplatz, R., 2001. Une Nouvelle Evaluation des Effets des Allegements de Charges Social sur les bas Salaries. Economie et Statistique 348 (8), 3–24.

Devine, T., Kiefer, N., 1991. Empirical Labor Economics: The Search Approach. Oxford University Press, Oxford, UK.

Di Tella, R., MacCulloch, R., 2005. The consequences of labor market flexibility: panel evidence based on survey data. European Economic Review 49 (5), 1225–1259.

Dolado, J., García-Serrano, C., Jimeno, J., 2002. Drawing lessons form the boom of temporary jobs in Spain. The Economic Journal 112, 270–295.

Dolton, P., O'Neill, D., 1996. Unemployment duration and the restart effect: some experimental evidence. Economic Journal 106, 387–400.

Dolton, P., O'Neill, D., 2002. The long-run effects of unemployment monitoring and work-search programs: experimental evidence from the United Kingdom. Journal of Labor Economics 20, 381–403.

Doudeijns, M., Einerhand, M., Van de Meerendonk, A., 2000. Financial incentives to take up low-paid work: an international comparison of the role of tax and benefit system. In: Salverda, W., Lucifora, C., Nolan, B. (Eds.), Policy Measures for Low Wage Employment in Europe. Edwar Elgar, Cheltenham, UK, pp. 43–66.

Drèze, J., 2002. Economic and social security: the role of the EU. Tinbergen Lecture, De Economist 150, 1–18.

Duncan, A., Pearson, M., Schotz, J.K., 2003. Is there an emerging consensus on making to work policies? Paper prepared for the conference "Political economy of policy transfer, learning and convergence", Tulane University, April 2003.

Eissa, N., Hoynes, H., 1998. The earned income tax credit and the labor supply of married couples. NBER Working Paper 6856.

Emerson, M., 1988. Regulation or deregulation of the labour market: policy regimes for the recruitment and dismissals of the employees in the industrialised countries. European Economic Review 32 (4), 775–817.

Engellandt, A., Riphahn, R.T., 2005. Temporary contracts and employee effort. Labour Economics 12 (3), 281–299.

Esping-Andersen, G., 1990. The Three Worlds of Welfare Capitalism. Polity Press, Cambridge, UK.

Francesconi, M., van der Klaauw, W., 2006. The socioeconomic consequences of in-work benefit reform for British lone mothers. The Journal of Human Resources XLII, 1–31.

García-Serrano, C., 1998. Worker turnover and job reallocation: the role of fixed-term contracts. Oxford Economic Papers 50 (4), 709–725.

García-Serrano, C., Jimeno, J., 1999. Labour reallocation, labour flows and labour market institutions: evidence from Spain. CEP Discussion Paper no. 414.

Garibaldi, P., Borgarello, A., Pacelli, L., 2004. Employment protection legislation and the size of firms: a close look at the Italian case. Giornale degli Economisti e Annali di Economia 63 (1), 33–68.

Garibaldi, P., Violante, G., 2005. The employment effects of severance payments with wage rigidities. Economic Journal 115 (506), 799–832.

Garibaldi, P., Koeninig, G., Pissarides, C., 1997. Gross job reallocation and labpur market policy. In: Snower, D.J., de la Dehesa, G. (Eds.), Unemployment Policy: Government Options for the Labour Market. Cambridge University Press, Cambridge, UK.

Gorter, C., Kalb, G.R.J., 1996. Estimating the effect of counselling and monitoring the unemployed using a job search model. Journal of Human Resources 31, 590–610.

Gregg, P., Harkness, S., 2003. Welfare reforms and lone parents employment in the UK. CMPO Working Paper no. 03/072.

Gregg, P., Manning, A., 1997. Skill biased change, unemployment and inequality. European Economic Review 41, 1173–1200.

Grubb, D., Wells, W., 1993. Employment regulations and patterns of work in EC countries. OECD Economic Studies 21, 7–58.

Guadalupe, M., 2003. The hidden costs of fixed term contracts: the impact of work accidents. Labour Economics 10 (3), 339–357.

Guell, M., Petrongolo, B., 2007. How binding are legal limits? Transitions from temporary to permanent work in Spain. Labour Economics 14 (2), 153–183.

Heckman, I.I., LaLonde, R.I., Smith, I.A., 1999. The economics and econometrics of active labor market programs. In: Ashenfelter, O., Card, D. (Eds.), Handbook of Labor Economics. Elsevier, Amsterdam, pp. 1865–2097.

Holmlund, B., 1998. Unemployment insurance in theory and practice. Scandinavian Journal of Economics 100 (1), 113–141.

Ichino, A., Riphahn, R.T., 2005. The effect of employment protection on worker effort: absenteeism during and after probation. Journal of the European Economic Association 3 (1), 120–143. 03.

Jackman, R., Layard, R., Nickell, S., 1996. Combatting unemployment: is flexibility enough? CEP Discussion Paper no. 0293.

Kahn, L.M., 2007. Employment protection reforms, employment and the incidence of temporary jobs in Europe: 1995-2001. IZA DP 3241.

Katz, L.F., Meyer, B.D., 1990. Unemployment insurance, recall expectations, and unemployment outcomes. Quarterly Journal of Economics 105 (4), 973–1002.

Kluve, J., 2006. The effectiveness of European active labor market policy. IZA WP 2018, IZA, Bonn.

Kluve, I., Schmidt, C.M., 2002. Can training and employment subsidies combat European unemployment? Economic Policy 35, 411–448.

Krueger, A., Meyer, B., 2002. Labor supply effects of social insurance. In: Auerbach, A., Feldstein, M. (Eds.), Handbook of Public Economics. Elsevier, Amsterdam.

Kugler, A., Saint-Paul, G., 2000. Hiring and firing costs, adverse selection and long-term unemployment. Universidad Pompeu Fabra Working Paper no. 447.

Lalive, R., Zweimüller, I., 2004. Benefit entitlement and unemployment duration: the role of policy endogeneity. Journal of Public Economics 88 (12), 2587–2616.

Lalive, R., van Ours, J.C., Zweimüller, J., 2005. The effect of benefit sanctions on the duration of unemployment. Journal of the European Economic Association 3 (6), 1386–1417.

Lazear, E.P., 1990. Job security provisions and unemployment. Quarlerly Journal of Economics 3, 699–726.

Layard, R., Nickell, S., 1999. Labor market institutions and economic performance. In: Ashenfelter, O., Card, D. (Eds.), Handbook of Labor Economics. Elsevier, Amsterdam, pp. 3029–3084.

Layard, R., Nickell, S., Jackman, R., 2005. Unemployment. Oxford University Press, New York.

Machin, S., Manning, A., 1999. The causes and consequences of longterm unemployment in Europe. In: Ashenfelter, O., Card, D. (Eds.), Handbook of Labor Economics. Elsevier, Amsterdam, pp. 3085–3139.

Martin, I.P., Grubb, D., 2001. What works and for whom: a review of OECD countries' experience with active labor market policies. OECD Economics Department Working Paper no. 14.

Meyer, B.D., 1990. Unemployment insurance and unemployment spells. Econometrica 58 (4), 757–782.

Meyer, B.D., 1989. A quasi-experimental approach to the effects of unemployment insurance. NBER WP 3159.

Miles, T., 2000. Common law exceptions to employment at will and US labor markets. Journal of Law, Economics and Organization 16 (1), 74–101.

Mortensen, D., Pissarides, C., 1999. New developments in models of search in the labor market, handbook of labor economics. In: Ashenfelter, O., Card, D. (Eds.), Handbook of Labor Economics. Elsevier, Amsterdam, pp. 2567–2627.

Narendranathan, W., Nickell, S., Stern, J., 1985. Unemployment benefit–revisited. Economic Journal 95 (378), 307–329.

Nickell, S., Nunziata, L., Ochel, W., 2005. Unemployment in the OECD since the 1960s: what do we know? Economic Journal 115, 1–27.

Nickell, S., 1997. Unemployment and labor market rigidities: Europe versus North America. Journal of Economic Perspectives 11 (3), 55–74.

OECD, 1998. Employment Outlook. OECD, Paris.

Nickell, W., 2006. The CEP-OECD institutions data set (1960-2004). CEP Discussion Paper no. 0759.

Pearson, M., Scarpetta, S., 2000. An overview, what do we know about policies to make work pay? OECD Economic Studies 31, 11–24.

Pellizzari, M., 2005. Unemployment duration and the interactions between unemployment insurance and social assistance. Labour Economics 13, 773–798.

Petrongolo, B., Pissarides, C.A., 2001. Looking into the black box: a survey of the matching function. Journal of Economic Literature, American Economic Association 39 (2), 390–431.

Pissarides, C., 1979. Job matchings with state employment agencies and random search. Economic Journal 89, 818–833.

Pissarides, C., 1998. The impact of employment tax cuts on unemployment and wages: the role of unemployment benefits and tax structure. European Economic Review 42, 155–183.

Pissarides, C., 2000. Equilibrium Unemployment Theory. MIT Press, Cambridge.

Rodrik, D., 1998. Why do more open economies have bigger governments? Journal of Political Economy 106 (5), 997–1032.

Roland, G., 2001. Ten years after. Transition and economics. IMF Staff Papers 48 (4), 3.

Saint-Paul, G., 1996. Dual Labor Markets. A Macroeconomic Perspective. MIT Press, Cambridge.

Saint-Paul, G., 2000. The Political Economy of Labor Marker Institutions. Oxford University Press, Oxford.

Scarpetta, S., 1996. Assessing the role of labor market policies and institutional factors on unemployment: a cross-country study. OECD Economic Studies 26, 43–98.

Sneessens, H., Shatman, F., 2000. Analyse macro-économique des effets de réduction ciblées des charges sociales. Revue belge de s écurité sociale 3, 613–630.

Snower, D., de la Dehesa, G. (Eds.), 1996. Unemployment Policy. CEPR and Cambridge University Press, Cambridge.

van den Berg, G.J., 1990. Search behavior, transitions to nonparticipation and the duration of unemployment. Economic Journal 100, 842–865.

van den Berg, G.J., van der Klaauw, B., 2006. Counseling and monitoring of unemployed workers: theory and evidence from a controlled social experiment. International Economic Review 47, 895–936.

van den Berg, G.J., van der Klaauw, B., van Ours, J.C., 2004. Punitive sanctions and the transition rate from welfare to work. Journal of Labor Economics 22, 211–241.

van Ours, J.C., 2004. The locking-in effect of subsidized jobs. Journal of Comparative Economics 32 (1), 37–52.

van Ours, J.C., Vodopivec, M., 2006. How shortening the potential duration of unemployment benefit's affects the duration of unemployment: evidence from a natural experiment. Journal of Labor Economics 24 (2), 351–378.

Visser, J., 2000. A combined indicator of union centralisation and coordination. Amsterdam Institute for Advanced Labour Studies, Working Paper no. 00/3.

Wacziarg, R., Welch, K.H., 2008. Trade liberalization and growth: new evidence. World Bank Economic Review 22 (2), 187–223.

Williamson, O.E., 1975. Markets and Hierarchies, Analysis and Antitrust Implication. A Study in the Economics of Internal Organization. Free Press, New York.

CHAPTER *14*

Local Labor Markets[☆]

Enrico Moretti

UC Berkeley, NBER, CEPR and IZA

Contents

[☆] This research was funded by a grant from the University of Kentucky Center on Poverty Research. I am grateful to Giacomo De Giorgi, Craig Riddell, Issi Romen, Michel Serafinelli, David Wildasin, the editors and especially Pat Kline and Gilles Duranton for useful comments on an earlier version. I thank Ana Rocca for excellent research assistance. I thank Richard Hornbeck for help with the data on total factor productivity from the Census of Manufacturers. Any opinions and conclusions expressed herein are those of the author and do not necessarily represent the views of the US Census Bureau. All results based on data from the Census of Manufacturers have been reviewed to ensure that no confidential information is disclosed.

ISSN 0169-7218, DOI 10.1016/S0169-7218(11)02412-9

Abstract

I examine the causes and the consequences of differences in labor market outcomes across local labor markets within a country. The focus is on a long-run general equilibrium setting, where workers and firms are free to move across localities and local prices adjust to maintain the spatial equilibrium. In particular, I develop a tractable general equilibrium framework of local labor markets with heterogenous labor. This framework is useful in thinking about differences in labor market outcomes of different skill groups across locations. It clarifies how, in spatial equilibrium, localized shocks to a part of the labor market propagate to the rest of the economy through changes in employment, wages and local prices and how this diffusion affects workers' welfare. Using this framework, I address three related questions. First, I analyze the welfare consequences of productivity differences across local labor markets. I seek to understand what happens to the wage, employment and utility of workers with different skill levels when a local economy experiences a shift in the productivity of a group of workers. Second, I analyze the causes of productivity differences across local labor markets. To a large extent, productivity differences within a country are unlikely to be exogenous. I review the theoretical and empirical literature on agglomeration economies, with a particular focus on studies that are relevant for labor economists. Finally, I discuss the implications for policy.

Keywords: Cities; Wage; General equilibrium; Spatial equilibrium

1. INTRODUCTION

Local labor markets in the US are characterized by enormous differences in worker earnings, factor productivity and firm innovation. The hourly wage of workers located in metropolitan areas at the top of the wage distribution is more than double the wage of observationally similar workers located in metropolitan areas at the bottom of the distribution. These differences reflect, at least in part, variation in local productivity. For example, total factor productivity of manufacturing establishments in areas at the top of the TFP distribution is three times larger than total factor productivity in areas at the bottom of the distribution. The amount of innovation is also spatially uneven. Firms in Santa Clara and San Jose generate respectively 3390 and 1906 new patents in a typical year, while the median city generates less than 1 patent per year. Notably, these differences in wages, productivity and innovation appear to be largely persistent over the last three decades.

In this chapter, I review what we know about the causes and the consequences of differences in labor market outcomes across local labor markets within a country. The focus is on a long-run general equilibrium setting, where workers and firms are free to move across localities and local prices adjust to maintain the spatial equilibrium. In particular, I develop a tractable general equilibrium framework of local labor markets with heterogenous labor. This framework—which represents the unifying theme of the chapter—is useful in thinking about differences in labor market outcomes of different skill groups across locations. It clarifies how, in spatial equilibrium, localized shocks to a part of the labor market propagate to the rest of the economy through changes in employment, wages and local prices and how this diffusion affects workers' welfare.

Using this framework, I address three related questions.

1. First, I analyze the welfare consequences of productivity differences across local labor markets. I seek to understand what happens to the wage, employment and utility of workers with different skill levels when a local economy experiences a shift in the productivity of a group of workers. I focus on welfare incidence and use the spatial equilibrium model to clarify who ultimately benefits from permanent productivity shocks.

2. Second, I analyze the causes of productivity differences across local labor markets. To a large extent, productivity differences within a country are unlikely to be exogenous. I review the theoretical and empirical literature on agglomeration economies, with a particular focus on studies that are relevant for labor economists.

3. Finally, I discuss the implications for policy, with a special focus on location-based economic development policies aimed at creating local jobs. I clarify when these policies are wasteful, when they are efficient and who the expected winners and losers are.

The topic of local labor markets should be of great interest to labor economists for two reasons. First, the issue of localization of economic activity and its effects on workers' welfare is one of the most exciting and promising research grounds in the field. This area, at the intersection of labor and urban economics, is ripe with questions that are both of fundamental importance for our understanding of how labor markets operate and have deep policy implications. Why are some cities prosperous while others are not? Given that factors of production can move freely within a country, why do firms locate in expensive labor markets? What are the ultimate effects of these differences on workers' welfare? These questions have intrigued economists for more than two centuries, but it is only in the last three decades that a body of high quality empirical evidence has begun to surface. The pace of empirical research in this area has accelerated in the last 10-15 years. It is a topic whose relative importance within the field of labor economics promises to keep growing in the next decade.

Second, and more generally, the issue of equilibrium in local labor markets should be of broader interest for all labor economists, even those who are not directly interested in economic geography per se. With notable exceptions, labor economists have traditionally approached the analysis of labor market shocks using a partial equilibrium analysis. However, a partial equilibrium analysis misses important parts of the picture, since the endogenous reaction of factor prices and quantities can significantly alter the ultimate effects of a shock. Because aggregate shocks to the labor market are rarely geographically uniform, the geographic reallocation of factors and local price adjustments are empirically important. It is difficult to fully understand *aggregate* labor market changes—like changes in relative wages or employment—if ignoring the spatial dimension of labor markets. Partial equilibrium analyses can be particularly misleading in the case where the workforce is highly mobile, like in the US. Labor flows across localities and changes in local prices have the potential to undo some of the direct effects of labor market shocks. This can profoundly alter the implications for policy. In this respect, the workings of local labor markets and their spatial equilibrium cannot be overlooked by labor economists, even those who are working on more traditional topics like wage determination, wage inequality or unemployment.

As an example, consider a nationwide increase in the productivity of skilled workers in an industry, say the software industry. Although the shock is nationwide, it affects different local labor markets differently because the software industry—like most industries—is spatially concentrated. The effect on the demand for skilled labor in a city like San Jose–in the heart of Silicon Valley—is likely to be quite different from the effect in a city like Phoenix—where the software sector is nonexistent. In a partial equilibrium setting, the only effect of this shock is an increase in the nominal wage of skilled workers in San Jose. However, in general equilibrium this shock propagates to other parts of the economy through changes in factor prices and quantities. Indeed, in general equilibrium, *all* agents in the economy are affected, irrespective of their location and their skill level. Attracted by higher demand, some skilled workers leave Phoenix and move to San Jose, thus pushing up the cost of housing and other non-tradable goods there. Unskilled workers in San Jose are affected because cost of living increases and because of imperfect substitution between skilled and unskilled labor. On net, some unskilled workers move to Phoenix, attracted by higher real wages. Skilled and unskilled workers in Phoenix also experience changes in their equilibrium wage, even if their productivity has not changed, because of changes in their local supply. Following population changes, owners of land experience changes in the value of their asset, both in San Jose and Phoenix. In this example, the direct effect of the demand shock is partially offset by general equilibrium changes due to worker relocation and local price adjustments. The ultimate change in the nominal and real wage of skilled and unskilled workers—and their policy implications— are quite different from the partial equilibrium change and crucially depends on the degree of labor mobility and the magnitude of local prices changes.

The chapter proceeds as follows. I begin by reviewing some important facts on differences in economic outcomes across local labor markets (Section 2). I focus on differences in nominal wages, real wages, productivity and innovation across US metropolitan areas.

I then present the spatial equilibrium model of the labor market (Section 3). The model is kept deliberately very simple, so that all the equilibrium outcomes have easy-to-interpret closed-form solutions. At the same time, the model is general enough to capture many key features of a realistic spatial equilibrium. While there are several versions of the spatial equilibrium model in the literature, and its basic insights are generally well understood, the focus on welfare incidence is relatively new.

In general equilibrium, a shock to a local labor market is partially capitalized into housing prices and partially reflected in worker wages. While marginal workers are always indifferent across locations, the utility of inframarginal workers can be affected by localized shocks. The model clarifies that the welfare consequences of localized productivity shifts depend on which of the two factors of production—labor or housing—is supplied more elastically at the local level.[1] A lower local elasticity of labor supply implies that a larger fraction of a shock to a city accrues to workers in that city and a smaller fraction accrues to landowners in that city. On the other hand, a more inelastic housing supply implies a larger incidence of the shock on landowners, holding constant labor supply elasticity. This makes intuitive sense: if labor is relatively less mobile, local workers are able to capture more of the economic rent generated by the shock. Additionally, a lower local elasticity of labor supply implies a smaller effect on the utility of workers in non-affected cities, since what links different local labor markers is the potential for worker mobility. The model also clarifies how the elasticity of local labor supply is ultimately governed by workers' preferences for location.

A particularly interesting case is what happens when there are two skill groups and one group experiences a localized productivity shock. This question is relevant because skill-specific shocks are common and have important consequences for nationwide inequality. The model clarifies how the relative elasticity of labor supply of different skill groups governs the ultimate effect of the shock on the utility of workers in each skill group and in each city.

Having clarified the welfare consequences of productivity differences across local labor markets, I turn to the possible causes of these differences. Because labor and land costs vary so much across local labor markets, economists have long suspected that there must exist significant productivity differences to offset the differences in factor costs, especially for industries that produce tradable goods. In the absence of significant productivity advantages, why would firms that produce tradable goods be willing to locate in places like Silicon Valley, New York or Boston, which are characterized by exorbitant labor and land costs, rather than in rural areas or in poorer cities, which are characterized by lower factor prices? Ever since at least Marshall (1890), economists have posited that these productivity advantages are not exogenous and may be explained by the existence of agglomeration economies. In Section 4, I review the existing empirical evidence on agglomeration economies, focusing on papers that are particularly relevant to labor economists. I address two related questions. First, what do we know about the magnitude of agglomeration economies? Second, what do we know about the micro mechanisms that generate agglomeration economies? The past two decades have seen a significant amount of effort devoted to answering these questions. Overall, there seems to be growing evidence that points to the fact that in many tradable goods productions, a firm's productivity is higher when it locates close to other similar firms. Notably, these productivity advantages seems to be increasing not only in geographic proximity but also in economic proximity. For example, they are larger for pairs of firms that share similar

---

[1] Capital is assumed to be supplied with infinite elasticity at a price determined by the international market.

labor pools, similar technologies, and similar intermediate inputs. The exact mechanism that generates these economies of scale remains more elusive. I discuss the most important explanations that have been proposed and the empirical evidence on each of them. I conclude that much remains to be done in terms of empirically understanding their relative importance.

Finally, in Section 5, I discuss the efficiency and equity rationales for local development policies aimed at creating local jobs. In the US, state and local governments spend $30-40 billion per year on these policies, while the federal government spends $8-12 billion. While these policies are pervasive, their economic rationale is often misunderstood by the public and economists alike. From the equity point of view, location-based policies aim at redistributing income from areas with high level of economic activity to areas with low level of economic activity. In this respect, these policies are unlikely to be effective. The spatial equilibrium model clarifies that in a world where workers are mobile, local prices adjust so that workers are unlikely to fully capture the benefits of location-based subsidies. When mobility is more limited, these policies have the potential to affect the utility of inframarginal workers', but in ways that are non transparent and difficult to know in advance, because they depend on individual idiosyncratic preferences for location. From an efficiency point of view, the main rationale for these type of subsidies is the existence of significant agglomeration externalities. If the attraction of new businesses to a locality generates localized productivity spillovers, then the provision of subsidies may be able to internalize the externality. The magnitude of the optimal subsidy depends on the exact shape of Marshallian dynamics. In this case, government intervention may be efficient from the point of view of a locality, although not necessarily from the point of view of aggregate welfare.

Ever since Adam Smith wrote his treatise on the "Nature and Causes of the Wealth of Nations" more than two centuries ago, economists have sought to understand the underlying causes of income disparities across regions of the world. While historically economists have focused on understanding the causes of differences *across countries*, the question of differences across localities *within a country* is receiving growing attention. Within county differences in productivity and wages are possibly even more remarkable than cross-country differences, since the mobility of labor and capital within a country is unconstrained and differences in institutions and regulations are small relative to cross-country differences. As a consequence, it is difficult to understand why some countries are poor and other countries are rich without first understanding why some cities within a country are poor and others are rich. The issue of local labor markets is a central one for economists, and much remains to be done to fully understand it.

2. SOME IMPORTANT FACTS ABOUT LOCAL LABOR MARKETS

Most countries in the world are characterized by significant spatial heterogeneity in economic outcomes. As an example, Fig. 1 shows the amount of income produced by square mile in the United States. The map documents enormous differences in the

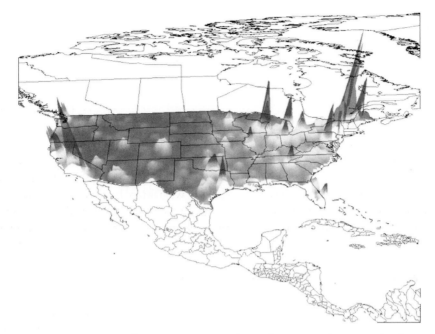

Figure 1   *Spatial distribution of economic output in the US, by square mile.* Notes: This figure reports the value of output produced in the US by square mile.

density of economic activity across different parts of the country. In the US there are a limited number of cities producing most of the country's output, surrounded by vast areas generating little output. Many other developed and developing countries show a similar pattern in the distribution of economic activity.

In this Section, I document the magnitude of the differences in labor market outcomes across local labor markets in the United States. In particular, I focus on spatial differences in nominal wages, real wages, productivity and innovation and how these differences have evolved over the last three decades.[2]

2.1. Nominal wages

The vast differences in output per mile in Fig. 1 translate into equally vast differences in workers' wages. The top panel in Fig. 2 shows the distribution of average hourly nominal wage for high school graduates by metropolitan statistical areas (MSA). Data are from the 2000 Census of Population and include all full-time US workers between the age of 25 and 60 who worked at least 48 weeks in the previous year. The figure

---

[2] Another notable feature of the spatial distribution of economic activity is represented by industry clustering, whereby firms tend to cluster near other "similar" firms (for example: firms that sell similar products). The cluster of IT firms in Silicon Valley, biomedical research in Boston, biotech in San Diego and San Francisco, financial firms in Wall Street and London are notable examples. In this section, I do not focus on this feature. However, I discuss its causes and consequences in the following sections.

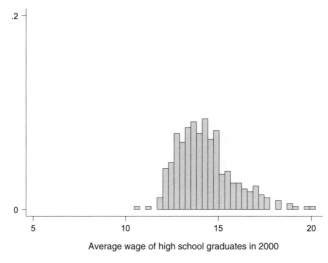

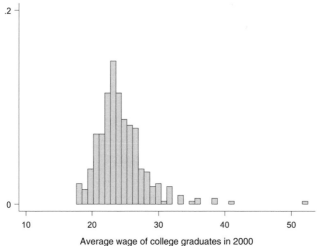

Figure 2 *Distribution of average hourly nominal wage of high school graduates and college graduates, by metropolitan area.* Notes: This figure reports the distribution of average hourly nominal wage of high school graduates and for college graduates across metropolitan areas in the 2000 Census of Population. There are 288 metropolitan areas. The sample includes all full-time US born workers between the age of 25 and 60 who worked at least 48 weeks in the previous year.

indicates that labor costs vary significantly across US metropolitan areas. The average high school graduate living in the median metropolitan area earns $14.1 for each hour worked. The 10th and 90th percentile of the distribution across metropolitan areas are $12.5 and $16.5, respectively. This amounts to a 32% difference in labor costs. The 1st and 99th percentile are $11.9 and $19.0, respectively, which amounts to a 60% difference. While some of these differences may reflect heterogeneity in skill levels within education group, differences across metropolitan areas conditional on race, experience, gender, and Hispanic origin are equally large.

Table 1 Metropolitan areas with the highest and lowest hourly wage of high school graduates in 2000.

Metropolitan area	Average hourly wage
Metropolitan areas with the highest wage	
Stamford, CT	20.21
San Jose, CA	19.70
Danbury, CT	19.13
San Francisco-Oakland-Vallejo, CA	18.97
New York-Northeastern NJ	18.86
Monmouth-Ocean, NJ	18.30
Santa Cruz, CA	18.24
Santa Rosa-Petaluma, CA	18.23
Ventura-Oxnard-Simi Valley, CA	17.72
Seattle-Everett, WA	17.71
Metropolitan areas with the lowest wage	
Ocala, FL	12.12
Dothan, AL	12.11
Amarillo, TX	12.10
Danville, VA	12.08
Jacksonville, NC	12.02
Kileen-Temple, TX	11.98
El Paso, TX	11.96
Abilene, TX	11.87
Brownsville-Harlingen-San Benito, TX	11.23
McAllen-Edinburg-Pharr-Mission, TX	10.65

The sample includes all full-time US born workers between the age of 25 and 60 with a high school degree who worked at least 48 weeks in the previous year. Data are from the 2000 Census of Population.

The bottom panel in Fig. 2 shows the distribution of average hourly nominal wage for college graduates across metropolitan areas. (Note that the scale in the two panels is different.) The distribution of the average wage of college graduates across metropolitan areas is even wider than the distribution of the average wage of high school graduates. The 10th and 90th percentile of the distribution for college graduates are $20.5 and $28.5. This amounts to a 41% difference in labor costs. The 1st and 99th percentile are $18.1 and $38.5, respectively, which amounts to a 112% difference.

Table 1 lists the 10 metropolitan areas with the highest average wage for high school graduates and the 10 metropolitan areas with the lowest average wage for high school graduates. High school graduates living in Stamford, CT or San Jose, CA earn an hourly wage that is two times as large as workers living in Brownsville, TX or McAllen, TX with the same level of schooling. This difference remains effectively unchanged after accounting for differences in workers' observable characteristics. Table 2 produces a similar list for college graduates. The difference between wages in cities at the top of the distributions and cities at the bottom of the distribution is more pronounced for

Table 2 Metropolitan areas with the highest and lowest hourly wage of college graduates in 2000.

Metropolitan area	Average hourly wage
Metropolitan areas with the highest wage	
Stamford, CT	52.46
Danbury, CT	40.81
Bridgeport, CT	38.82
San Jose, CA	38.49
New York-Northeastern NJ	36.03
Trenton, NJ	35.52
San Francisco-Oakland-Vallejo, CA	34.89
Monmouth-Ocean, NJ	33.70
Los Angeles-Long Beach, CA	33.37
Ventura-Oxnard-Simi Valley, CA	33.07
Metropolitan areas with the lowest wage	
Pueblo, CO	20.16
Goldsboro, NC	20.15
St. Joseph, MO	20.01
Wichita Falls, TX	19.74
Abilene, TX	19.70
Sumter, SC	19.57
Sharon, PA	19.52
Waterloo-Cedar Falls, IA	18.99
Altoona, PA	18.68
Jacksonville, NC	18.21

The sample includes all full-time US born workers between the age of 25 and 60 with a college degree who worked at least 48 weeks in the previous year. Data are from the 2000 Census of Population.

college graduates. The average hourly wage of college graduates in Stamford, CT is almost three times larger than the hourly wage of college graduates in Jacksonville, NC. This difference is robust to controlling for worker characteristics.

The wage differences documented in Fig. 2 are persistent over long periods of time. While in the decades after World War II regional differences in income were declining (Barro and Sala-i-Martin, 1991), convergence has slowed down significantly in more recent decades. This can be seen in Fig. 3, where I plot the average hourly wage in 1980 against the average wage in 2000 for high school graduates and college graduates, by metropolitan area. The size of the bubbles is proportional to the number of workers in the relevant metropolitan area and skill group 1980. The lines are the predicted wages in 2000 from a weighted OLS regression, where the weights are the number of workers in the relevant metropolitan area and skill group in 1980.

The figure suggests that there has been no mean reversion in wages since 1980. In fact, the opposite has happened. Wage differences across metropolitan areas have *increased* over time. The slope of the regression line is 1.82 (0.89) for high school graduates. This

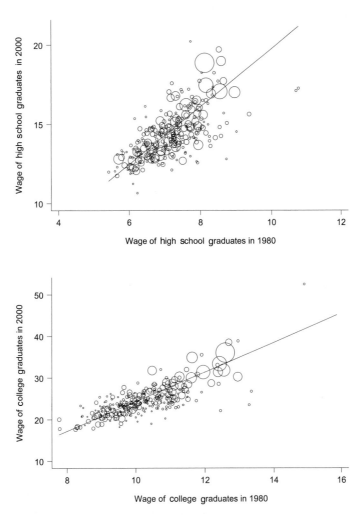

Figure 3 *Change over time in the average hourly nominal wage of high school graduates and college graduates, by metropolitan area.* Notes: Each panel plots the average nominal wage in 1980 against the average nominal wage in 2000, by metropolitan area. The top panel is for high school graduates. The bottom panel is for college graduates. The size of the bubbles is proportional to the number of workers in the relevant metropolitan area and skill group 1980. There are 288 metropolitan areas. The line is the predicted wage in 2000 from a weighted OLS regression, where the weights are the number of workers in the relevant metropolitan area and skill group in 1980. The slope is 1.82 (0.89) for high school graduates and 3.54 (0.11) for college graduates. Data are from the Census of Population. The sample includes all full-time US born workers between the age of 25 and 60 who worked at least 48 weeks in the previous year.

Table 3 Average hourly wage in 1980 and 2000, by education level and metropolitan area.

High school graduates

	Low wage in 2000	High wage in 2000
Low wage in 1980	106	40
High wage in 1980	34	108

College graduates

	Low wage in 2000	High wage in 2000
Low wage in 1980	114	32
High wage in 1980	26	116

For each skill group, metropolitan areas are classified as having a low or high wage depending on whether their average wage is below or above the average wage of the median metropolitan area in the relevant year. The sample includes all full-time US born workers between the age of 25 and 60 who worked at least 48 weeks in the previous year. Data are from the 2000 Census of Population. There are 288 metropolitan areas.

suggests that metropolitan area where high school graduates have high wages in 1980 compared to other metropolitan areas have even higher wages in 2000. The slope for college graduates is 3.54 (0.11). The fact that the slope is even higher for college graduates indicates that the increase in the spatial differences in hourly wages is larger for skilled workers.

The lack of spatial convergence is also documented in Table 3, where I classify metropolitan areas as having low or high wage depending on whether the average wage is below or above the average wage in the median metropolitan area in the relevant year. This is done separately for each year and each education group. The top panel shows that in most cases, metropolitan areas where high school graduates have high wages in 1980 also have high wages in 2000. Only a quarter of metropolitan areas change category. Consistent with the larger increase in spatial divergence uncovered in Fig. 3, this fraction is even smaller for college graduates (bottom panel).

Using data on total income instead of hourly wages, Glaeser and Gottlieb (2009) find no evidence of convergenece across metropolitan areas between 1980 and 1990, but they find some evidence of convergence between 1990 and 2000. The difference between their findings and Fig. 3 is explained by three factors. First, I am interested in labor market outcomes, so that my sample includes only workers. By contrast, the Glaeser and Gottlieb sample includes all individuals. Second, there may be differences across metropolitan areas in unearned income. Third, and most importantly, there might be differences across metropolitan areas in number of hours worked, since it is well known that, since 1980, workers with high nominal wages have experienced relatively larger increases in number of hours worked than workers with low nominal wages. The convergence in total income uncovered by Glaeser and Gottlieb (2009) in the 1990s is quantitatively limited. Consistent with my interpretation of Fig. 3, they conclude that although there has been some convergence in income, over the last three decades "rich places have stayed rich and poor places have stayed poor".

When thinking about localization of economic activity, nominal wages are more important than income because they are related to labor productivity. Since labor, capital and goods can move freely within a country, it is difficult for an economy in a long-run equilibrium to maintain significant spatial differences in nominal labor costs in the absence of equally large productivity differences. Indeed, if labor markets are perfectly competitive, nominal wage differences across local labor markets should exactly reflect differences in the marginal product of labor in industries that produce tradable goods. If this were not the case, firms in the tradable sector located in cities with nominal wages higher than labor productivity would relocate to less expensive localities. While not all workers are employed in the tradable sector, as long as there are some firms producing traded goods in every city and workers can move between the tradable and non-tradable sector, average productivity has to be higher in cities where nominal wages are higher.

Overall, if wages are related to marginal product of labor, there appears to be little evidence of convergence in labor productivity across US metropolitan areas. If anything, there is evidence of divergence: metropolitan areas that are characterized by high labor productivity in 1980 are characterized by even higher productivity in 2000. Notably, both the magnitude of geographic differences and speed of divergence appear to be more pronounced for high-skilled workers than low-skilled workers.

2.2. Real wages

The large differences in nominal wages documented above do not appear to be associated with massive migratory flows of workers across metropolitan areas.[3] The main reason for the lack of significant spatial reallocation of labor is that land prices vary significantly across locations so that differences in real wages are significantly smaller than differences in nominal wages. Figure 4 shows the distribution of average hourly real wage for high school and college graduates across metropolitan areas. Real wages are calculated as the ratio of nominal wages and a local CPI that reflects differences in the cost of housing across locations. The index is described in detail in Moretti (forthcoming). A comparison with Fig. 2 indicates that the distribution of real wages is significantly more compressed than the distribution of nominal wages. For example, the 10th and 90th percentile of the distribution for high school graduates are $10.0 and $11.7. This is only a 17% difference. The 10th and 90th percentile of the distribution for college graduates are $16.7 and $20.4, a 22% difference.

If nominal wages adjust fully to reflect cost of living differences, and if amenity differences are not too important, a regression of log nominal wage on log cost of housing should yield a coefficient approximately equal to the share of income spent on housing

---

[3] In a recent review of the evidence, Glaeser and Gottlieb (2008) conclude that "there has been little tendency for people to move to high income areas".

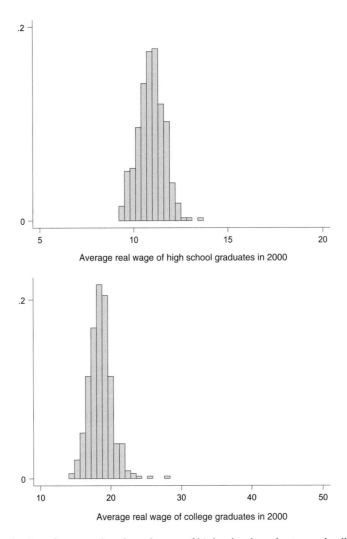

Figure 4 *Distribution of average hourly real wage of high school graduates and college graduates, by metropolitan area.* Notes: This figure reports the distribution of average hourly real wage of high school graduates and college graduates across metropolitan areas in the 2000 Census of Population. Real wage is defined as the ratio of nominal wage and a cost of living index that reflects differences across metropolitan areas in the cost of housing. The index is normalized so that it has a mean of 1. There are 288 metropolitan areas. The sample includes all full-time US born workers between the age of 25 and 60 who worked at least 48 weeks in the previous year.

(Glaeser and Gottlieb, 2008). Empirically, I find that an individual level regression of log earnings on average cost of housing in the metropolitan area of residence—measured by the log average cost of renting a two or three bedroom apartment—controlling for standard observables and clustering the standard errors by metropolitan area yields a

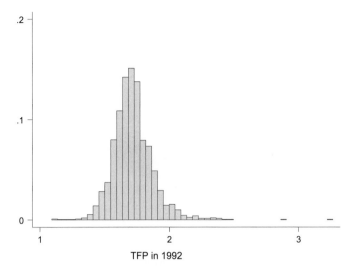

Figure 5 *Distribution of total factor productivity in manufacturing establishments, by county.*
Notes: This figure reports the distribution of average total factor productivity of manufacturing establishments in 1992, by county. County-level TFP estimates are obtained from estimates of establishment level production functions based on data from the Census of Manufacturers. Specifically, they are obtained from a regression of log output on hours worked by blue and white collar workers, book value of building capital, book value of machinery capital, materials, industry and county fixed effects. The figure shows the distribution of the coefficients on the county dummies. Regressions are weighted by plant output. The sample is restricted to counties that had 10 or more plants in either 1977 or 1992 in the 2xxx or 3xxx SIC codes. There are 2126 counties that satisfy the sample restriction. For confidentiality reasons, any data from counties whose output was too concentrated in a small number of plants are not in the figure (although they are included in the regression).

coefficient equal to 0.513 (0.024).[4] Given that the share of income spent on housing is about 41% in 2000, this regression lends credibility to the notion that nominal wages adjust to take into account differences in the cost of living across localities.

2.3. Productivity

The vast differences in nominal wages across local labor markets reflect, at least in part, differences in productivity. Productivity is notoriously difficult to measure directly. One empirical measure of productivity at the establishment level is total factor productivity (TFP), defined as output after controlling for inputs.

Figure 5 shows the distribution of average total factor productivity of manufacturing establishments in 1992 by county. County-level TFP estimates are obtained from estimates of production functions based on data from the Census of Manufacturers. Specifically, they are obtained from a regression of log output on hours worked by blue

---

[4] Data are from the 2000 Census of Population.

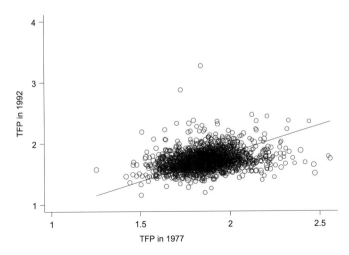

Figure 6 *Change over time in total factor productivity in manufacturing establishments, by county.*
Notes: The figure plots county-level average TFP in 1977 on the *x*-axis against TFP in 1992 on the *y*-axis.
County-level TFP estimates are obtained from estimates of establishment level production functions
based on data from the Census of Manufacturers. Specifically, they are obtained from a regression of
log output on hours worked, book value of building capital, book value of machinery capital, materials,
industry and county fixed effects. Each regression is estimated separately for 1977 and 1992. The figure
shows the coefficients on the county dummies in each year. Regressions are weighted by plant output.
The sample is restricted to counties that had 10 or more plants in either 1977 or 1992 in the 2xxx or
3xxx SIC codes. There are 2126 counties that satisfy the sample restriction. For confidentiality reasons,
any data from counties whose output was too concentrated in a small number of plants are not in the
figure (although they are included in the regression).

collar and white collar workers, building capital, machinery capital, materials, industry
fixed effects and county fixed effects.[5] The level of observation is the establishment. The
coefficients on the county dummies represent county average total factor productivity,
holding constant industry, capital and labor. The distribution of the county fixed effects
is shown in Fig. 5. The figure illustrates that there is substantial heterogeneity in
manufacturing productivity across US counties. The county at the top of the distribution
is 2.9 times more productive than the county at the bottom of the distribution. Log TFP
in the counties at the 10th percentile, median, and 90th percentile are 1.54, 1.70 and
2.20, respectively.

Figure 6 shows how TFP has changed over time. Specifically, it plots average TFP
by county in 1977 on the *x*-axis against average TFP by county in 1992 on the *y*-axis.[6]

---

[5] Regressions are weighted by plant output. The sample is restricted to counties that had 10 or more plants in either 1977
or 1992 in the 2xxx or 3xxx SIC codes. There are 2126 counties that satisfy the sample restriction. For confidentiality
reasons, any data from counties whose output was too concentrated in a small number of plants are not in the figure
(although they are included in the regression).

[6] There are 1951 counties for which data could be released by the Census. TFP estimates for each year come from separate
regressions for 1977 and 1992.

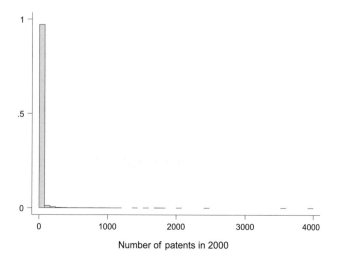

Figure 7   *Distribution in the number of patents filed by city.* Notes: The figure reports the distribution of the average yearly number of patents filed between 1998 and 2002 across cities. I use the average over 5 years to reduce small sample noise. The level of observation is the city, as reported in the patent file. This definition of city does not correspond to the definition of metropolitan statistical area.

The regression line comes from a regression of 1992 TFP on 1977 TFP weighted by the inverse of the county fixed effects' standard errors.[7] The coefficient is 0.919 (0.003), indicating a high degree of persistence of TFP over time. This coefficient is lower than the corresponding coefficient for nominal wages in Fig. 3. This difference may indicate that changes in productivity are not the only driver of changes in nominal wages across locations. Alternatively it may indicate that average productivity is measured with more error than average wages and therefore displays more mean reversion. It is plausible that measured productivity contains more measurement error than measured wages because productivity is inherently more difficult to measure and because the sample of plants available in the Economic Census is smaller than the sample of workers available in the Census of Population.

2.4. Innovation

Innovative activity is even more concentrated than overall economic activity. One measure of innovation is the number of patents filed. Figure 7 shows the distribution of the number of utility patents filed by each city per year from 1998 to 2002.[8] The level of observation here is the city, as reported in the patent file. Unlike in the rest of

---

[7] This regression does not include an intercept, because both the dependent variable and independent variable come from separate regressions that include separate constants.

[8] I include 5 years instead of one to reduce sample noise. Data are from the NBER Patent Database. Utility patents are typically granted to those who invent or discover a new and useful process or machine.

the paper, in this figure and the next figure the definition of city does not correspond to metropolitan statistical area. The figure shows that most cities generate either no patents or a limited number of patents each year. On the other hand there is a handful of cities that file a very large number of patents. Conditional on generating at least 1 patent in the five years between 1998 and 2002, the median city generates only an average of .4 patents per year, while the city at the 75% percentile has only 2 patents per year. By contrast, the two cities at the top of the distribution—Santa Clara, CA, in the heart of Silicon valley and Armonk, NY, where IBM is located—generate 3390 and 3630 patents respectively. Houston, San Jose and Palo Alto follow with 2399, 1906 and 1682 patents per year, respectively.[9] Overall, it is pretty clear that the creation of new technologies and new products is highly spatially concentrated.

Importantly, there is little evidence that the geographic concentration of innovative activity is diminishing over time. Indeed, the spatial distribution of innovation appears remarkably stable over the last 2 decades. This is shown in Fig. 8, where I plot the average yearly number of patents filed in the 1978-1982 period on the x-axis against the average yearly number of patents filed in the 1998-2002 period on the y-axis. The sample includes all cities with at least 1 patent filed in either period. For visual clarity, the figure excludes 3 cities that have more than 2000 patents per year. The regression coefficient (std error) is 1.009 (0.0311), with intercept at 15.41 (2.26). (The regression and the fitted line in the figure are both based on the full sample that includes the 3 cities with more than 2000 patents.) The regression indicates that there is no evidence of convergence in innovative activity. The number of patents per city has increased in this period, but the increase is exactly proportional to the 1980s level.

3. EQUILIBRIUM IN LOCAL LABOR MARKETS

In the previous Section I have documented large and persistent differences in productivity and wages across local labor markets within the US. In this section, I present a simple general equilibrium framework intended to address two questions. First, how can these differences persist in equilibrium? Second, what are the effects of these differences on workers in different cities?

Ever since the publication of the models by Rosen (1979) and Roback (1982), the Rosen–Roback framework has been the general equilibrium model most frequently used to model shocks to local economies. For this reason, Glaeser (2001) defines the Rosen–Roback framework "the workhorse of spatial equilibrium analysis". The main reasons for its popularity are its simplicity, tractability, and especially the fact that it captures a very intuitive notion of equilibrium across local labor markets within a country. In its most basic and most commonly used version (Roback, 1982, Section I), the model assumes that:

---

[9] The city at the 99% percentile generates 178 patents.

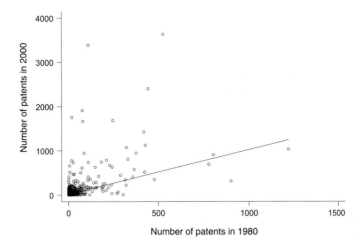

Figure 8 *Change over time in the number of patents filed by city.* Notes: The x-axis is the average yearly number of patents filed between 1978 and 1982. The y-axis is the average yearly number of patents filed between 1998 and 2002. I use the averages over 5 years to reduce sample noise. The level of observation is the city, as reported in the patent file. This definition of city does not correspond to metropolitan statistical area. For visual clarity, the figure excludes 3 cities that have more than 2000 patents per year. A regression based on the full sample (i.e. including the cities with more than 3000 patents per year) yields a coefficient (std error) equal to 1.009 (0.0311). The fitted line in the figure is based on the full sample (i.e. including the 3 cities with more than 2000 patents per year).

1. Each city is a competitive economy that produces a single internationally traded good using labor, land and a local amenity. Technology has constant returns to scale
2. Workers' indirect utility depends on nominal wages, cost of housing and local amenities
3. Labor is homogenous in skills and tastes[10] and each worker provides one unit of labor
4. Labor is perfectly mobile so that the local labor supply is infinitely elastic
5. Land is the only immobile factor and its supply is fixed.

In its simplest form, and the one that is most commonly used in the literature (Roback, 1982, Section I), the Rosen–Roback key insight is that any local shock to the demand or supply of labor in a city is, in equilibrium, *fully* capitalized in the price of land. As a consequence, shocks to a local economy do not affect worker welfare. Consider, for example, a productivity shock that makes workers in city c more productive than workers in other cities. In the Rosen–Roback framework, the increase in productivity in city c results in an increase in nominal wages in city c and a similar increase in housing costs in city c, so that in equilibrium workers are completely indifferent between city c and all the other cities. In the new equilibrium, workers are more productive but they are not better

---

[10] Roback (1988) considers the cases of heterogenous labor.

off. The owners of land in city c are better off, by an amount equal to the productivity increase. This result depends on the assumption that the local labor supply is infinitely elastic and that the elasticity of housing supply is limited.[11]

The assumptions of this model are restrictive, and rule out some interesting questions regarding the incidence of localized shocks to a local economy. In this section, I present a more general equilibrium framework that seeks to take the spatial equilibrium model a step closer to reality. The goal of the model is to clarify what happens to wages, costs of housing and worker utility when a local economy experiences a shock to labor demand or labor supply. An example of a shock to labor demand is an increase in productivity. An example of a shock to labor supply is an increase in amenities. I assume that workers and firms are mobile across cities, but worker mobility is not necessarily infinite, because workers have idiosyncratic preferences for certain locations. Moreover, housing supply is not necessarily fixed. This implies that the elasticity of local labor supply is not necessarily infinite and the elasticity of housing supply is not necessarily zero. In this context, shocks to a local economy are not necessarily fully capitalized into land prices. This is important, because it allows for interesting distributional and welfare implications. The model clarifies exactly how the welfare consequences of localized labor market shocks depend on the relative magnitude of the elasticities of local labor supply and housing supply.

In Section 3.1 I describe the case of homogenous labor. It is a useful and transparent starting point. It clarifies the role that the elasticity of labor and housing supply play in determining how shocks to a local economy affect workers' utility. In reality, however, workers are not all homogenous but they differ along many dimensions, most notably in their skill level. Moreover, shocks to local economies rarely affect all workers equally. Instead, shocks to local economies are often skill-biased in the sense that they shift the demand for some skill groups more than others. For these reasons, in Section 3.2 I describe the more general case of heterogenous labor. In Section 3.3 I allow for agglomeration economies. In Section 3.4 I discuss the case where there are multiple industries within each local economy and local multipliers. In Section 3.5 I review some of the existing empirical evidence.

---

[11] In the simplest form of the model, there is one margin of adjustment that allows to accommodate some in-migration to the more productive city. While land is assumed to be fixed, workers can adjust their consumption of housing. When housing prices increase in city c, each worker consumes a little less housing. This allows a small increase in the number of workers in the more productive city, even with fixed land. In a more general version of the model, Roback (1982, Section II) keeps the assumption that land is fixed but allows for the production of housing. Housing production is assumed to use labor, which is perfectly mobile, and land, which is fixed. In this version of the model, there are two margins of adjustment that allow to accommodate in-migration to a city. First, like before, workers can adjust their consumption of housing in response to increases in housing prices. Second, unlike before, the housing stock can increase in response to increased demand. In this version of the model, more workers change city after a city-specific productivity shock. However, the key implication for incidence of the shock does not change. Because workers are assumed to be perfectly mobile and homogenous, their utility is never affected by the shock.

Over the years, many versions of the spatial equilibrium model have been proposed. The version of model that I present is based on Moretti (forthcoming). The proposed framework is based on assumptions designed to make it very simple and transparent while at the same time not unrealistic. The model seeks to describe spatial equilibrium in the long run and is probably not well suited to describe year to year adjustments.[12] Topel (1986) and Glaeser (2008) propose alternative equilibrium frameworks that take into account the dynamics of wages and employment. Roback (1982), Glaeser (2008) and Glaeser and Gottlieb (2009) propose frameworks where housing production uses both local labor (and of course land). By contrast, in my simplified framework housing production does not use local labor. Combes et al. (2005) link the spatial equilibrium framework to some of the insights from the New Economic Geography literature.

3.1. Spatial equilibrium with homogeneous labor
3.1.1. Assumptions and equilibrium

I begin by considering the case where there is only one type of labor. As in Rosen–Roback, I assume that each city is a competitive economy that produces a single output good y which is traded on the international market, so that its price is the same everywhere and set equal to 1. Workers and firms are mobile and locate where utility and profits are maximized. Like in Roback, I abstract from labor supply decisions and I assume that each worker provides one unit of labor, so that local labor supply is only determined by workers' location decisions. The indirect utility of worker i in city c is

$$U_{ic} = w_c - r_c + A_c + e_{ic} \qquad (1)$$

where w_c is the nominal wage in city c; r_c is the cost of housing; A_c is a measure of local amenities.[13] The random term e_{ic} represents worker i idiosyncratic preferences for location c. A larger e_{ic} means that worker i is particularly attached to city c, holding constant real wage and amenities. For example, being born in city c or having family in city c may make city c more attractive to a worker irrespective of city c's real wages and amenities. Assume that there are two cities: city a and city b and that worker i's relative preference for city a over city b is

$$e_{ia} - e_{ib} \sim U[-s, s]. \qquad (2)$$

The parameter s characterizes the importance of idiosyncratic preferences for location and therefore the degree of labor mobility. If s is large, it means that preferences for location are important and therefore worker willingness to move to arbitrage away real wage differences or amenity differences is limited. On the other hand, if s is small,

---

[12] The reason is that in the short run, frictions in labor mobility and in housing supply may constrain the ability of workers and housing stock to fully adjust to shocks.

[13] In Roback's terminology, A_c is a consumption amenity.

preferences for location are not very important and therefore workers are more willing to move in response to differences in real wages or amenities. In the extreme, if $s = 0$ there are no idiosyncratic preferences for location and therefore worker mobility is perfect.

While parsimonious, the model captures the four most important factors that might drive worker mobility: wages, the cost of living, amenities, and individual preferences. A worker chooses city a if and only if $e_{ia} - e_{ib} > (w_b - r_b) - (w_a - r_a) + (A_b - A_a)$. In equilibrium, the marginal worker needs to be indifferent between cities. This equilibrium condition implies that local labor supply is upward sloping, and its slope depends on s. For example, local labor supply in city b is

$$ w_b = w_a + (r_b - r_a) + (A_a - A_b) + s \frac{(N_b - N_a)}{N} \tag{3} $$

where N_c is the endogenously determined log of number of workers in city c; and $N = N_a + N_b$ is assumed fixed. The key point of Eq. (3) is that the elasticity of local labor supply depends on worker preferences for location. If idiosyncratic preferences for location are very important (s is large), then workers are relatively less mobile and the elasticity of local labor supply is low. In this case, the local labor supply curve is relatively steep. If idiosyncratic preferences for location are not very important (s is small), then workers are relatively more mobile and the elasticity of local labor supply is high. In this case, the local labor supply curve is relatively flat. In the case of perfect mobility ($s = 0$), the elasticity of local labor supply is infinite and the local labor supply curve is perfectly flat. In that case, any difference in real wages or in amenities, however small, results in an infinitely large number of workers willing to leave one city for the other.[14] The intercept in Eq. (3) indicates that, for a given slope, if the real wage in city a increases or local amenities improve, workers leave city b and move to city a.

An important difference between the Rosen–Roback setting and this setting is that in Rosen–Roback, all workers are identical, and always indifferent across locations. In this setting, workers differ in their preferences for location. While the marginal worker is indifferent between locations, here there are inframarginal workers who enjoy economic rents. These rents are larger the smaller the elasticity of local labor supply.[15]

[14] Tabuchi and Thisse (2002) model how worker heterogeneity generates an upward sloping local labor supply and how this affects the spatial distribution of economic activity.

[15] It is not easy to obtain credible empirical estimates of the elasticity of local labor supply. First, one needs to isolate labor market shocks that are both localized and demand driven. Second, one needs to identify the effect both on wages and land prices. For example, Greenstone et al. (forthcoming) document that the exogenous opening of a large manufacturing establishment in a county is associated with a significant increase in employment and local nominal wages. The wage increase appears to persist five years after the opening of the new plant. However, this result per se does not necessarily imply that local labor supply is upward sloping. As Eq. (3) indicates, what matters in this respect is whether the demand-driven shift in employment causes wages to increase over and above land costs. The finding that an increase in the local demand for labor results in an increase in local wages does not per se imply that local labor supply is upward sloping. In principle, such finding is consistent with a spatial equilibrium where the local supply of labor is infinitely elastic but the supply of housing is inelastic.

The production function for firms in city c is Cobb–Douglas with constant returns to scale, so that

$$\ln y_c = X_c + hN_c + (1 - h)K_c \tag{4}$$

where X_c is a city-specific productivity shifter;[16] and K_c is the log of capital. I focus first on the case where X_c is given. Later, I discuss the model with agglomeration economies in which X_c is a function of density of economic activity or human capital. Firms are assumed to be perfectly mobile. If firms are price takers and labor is paid its marginal product, labor demand in city c is

$$w_c = X_c - (1 - h)N_c + (1 - h)K_c + \ln h. \tag{5}$$

I assume that there is an international capital market, and that capital is infinitely supplied at a given price i.[17] I also assume that each worker consumes one unit of housing. This implies that the (inverse of) the local demand for housing is just a re-arrangement of Eq. (3):

$$r_b = (w_b - w_a) + r_a + (A_b - A_a) - s\frac{(N_b - N_a)}{N}. \tag{6}$$

To close the model, I assume that the supply of housing is

$$r_c = z + k_c N_c \tag{7}$$

where the number of housing units in city c is assumed to be equal to the number of workers. The parameter k_c characterizes the elasticity of the supply of housing. I assume that this parameter is exogenously determined by geography and local land regulations. In cities where geography and regulations make it is easy to build new housing, k_c is small. In the extreme case where there are no constraints to building new houses, the supply curve is horizontal, and k_c is zero. In cities where geography and regulations make it difficult to build new housing, k_c is large. In the extreme case where it is impossible to build new houses, the supply curve is vertical, and k_c is infinite. A limitation of Eq. (7) is that it implicitly makes two assumptions that, while helpful in simplifying the model, are not particularly realistic. First, housing production in this model does not involve the use of any local input. Roback (1982) and Glaeser (2008), among others, discuss spatial equilibrium in the case where housing production involves the use of local labor and other local inputs. Second, Eq. (7) ignores the durability of housing. Glaeser (2008) point out that once built, the housing stock does not depreciate quickly and this introduces an

---

[16] In Roback terminology, X_c is a productive amenity.

[17] In equilibrium, the marginal product of capital has to be equal to $X_c - hK_c + hN_c + \ln(1 - h) = \ln i$.

asymmetry between positive and negative demand shocks. In particular, when demand declines, the quantity of housing cannot decline, at least in the short run. The possible implications of this asymmetry are analyzed by Notowidigdo (2010).

Equilibrium in the labor market is obtained by equating Eqs (3) and (5) for each city. Equilibrium in the housing market is obtained by equating Eqs (6) and (7).

In this framework, workers and landowners are separate agents and landowners are assumed to live abroad. While in reality most workers own their residence, keeping workers separate from landowners has the advantage of allowing me to separately identify the welfare consequences of changes in housing values from the welfare consequences of changes in labor income. This is important both for conceptual clarity and for thinking about the different implications of the results for labor and housing policies.[18]

This model differs from the model of local labor markets proposed by Topel (1986) because it ignores dynamics. This model also differs from most of the existing versions of the spatial equilibrium model in that it describes a closed economy with a fixed number of workers, so that shock to a given city affects the other city. For example, an increase in labor demand in city b affects labor supply, wages and prices in city a. By contrast, most existing versions of the spatial equilibrium model assume that local shocks to a city affect local outcomes there, but have a negligible effect on the rest of the national economy because the rest of the economy is large relative to the city. (See for example: Glaeser (2008, 2001) and Notowidigdo (2010)). In this sense most of the existing models are not truly general equilibrium models.[19]

3.1.2. Effect of a labor demand shock on wages and prices

I begin by considering the effect of an increase in labor demand in city b. This demand increase could be due to a localized technological shock that increases the productivity of firms located in city b. Alternatively, it could be due to an improvement in the product demand faced by firms in city b. Later, I consider the effect of an increase in labor supply in city b.

I assume that in period 1, the two cities are identical and in period 2, total factor productivity increases in city b. Specifically, I assume that in period 2, the productivity shifter in b is higher than in period 1: $X_{b2} = X_{b1} + \Delta$, where $\Delta > 0$ represents a

---

[18] On the other hand, this assumption has the disadvantage that it misses some important features of housing and labor markets. When workers are also property owners, a localized increase in housing values in a city implies both an increase in the value of the asset but also an increase in the user cost of housing. The only way for property owners to access the increased value of the asset is to move to a different city.

[19] In the interest of simplicity, the model completely ignores congestions costs. Equilibrium is achieved only because housing costs in a city increase when population increases. In reality, congestion costs (for example: transportation costs) are probably an another important determinant of equilibrium across cities. Allowing for congestion costs would not alter the qualitative predictions of the model, but it would result in smaller predicted increases in housing costs in cities that experience positive productivity shocks. The reason is simple. As a city becomes more productive and its workforce increases, commuting costs increase, thus reducing its relative attractiveness.

positive, localized, unexpected productivity shock.[20] I have added subscripts 1 and 2 to denote periods 1 and 2. The amenities in the two cities are assumed to be identical and to remain unchanged.

Workers are now more productive in city b than a. Attracted by this higher productivity, some workers move from a to b:

$$N_{b2} - N_{b1} = \frac{N}{N(k_a + k_b) + 2s} \Delta \geq 0. \tag{8}$$

The equation indicates that number of movers is larger the elasticity of labor supply (i.e. the smaller is s) and the larger the elasticity of housing supply in city b (i.e. the smaller is k_b). This is not surprising, because a smaller s implies that idiosyncratic preferences for location are less important, and therefore that labor is more mobile in response to real wage differentials. A smaller k_b means that it is easier for city b to add new housing units to accommodate the increased demand generated by the in-migrants.

The nominal wage in city b increases by an amount equal to the productivity increase:

$$w_{b2} - w_{b1} = \Delta. \tag{9}$$

Because of in-migration, the cost of housing in city b needs to increase. The magnitude of the increase is a fraction of Δ and depends on how elastic is housing supply in b relative to a:

$$r_{b2} - r_{b1} = \frac{k_b N}{N(k_a + k_b) + 2s} \Delta \geq 0. \tag{10}$$

This increase in housing costs is larger the smaller the elasticity of housing supply in city b (large k_b) relative to city a. Because nominal wages increase more than housing costs (compare Eqs (9) and (10)), real wages increase in b:

$$(w_{b2} - w_{b1}) - (r_{b2} - r_{b1}) = \frac{k_a N + 2s}{N(k_a + k_b) + 2s} \Delta \geq 0. \tag{11}$$

Although the original productivity shock only involves city b, in general equilibrium, prices in city a are also affected. In particular, out-migration lowers the cost of housing.[21]

---

[20] I am modeling the productivity shock as an increase in total factor productivity. Results are similar in the case where the shock only increases productivity of labor.

[21] The change in the cost of housing in a is

$$r_{a2} - r_{a1} = -\frac{k_a N}{N(k_a + k_b) + 2s} \Delta \leq 0. \tag{12}$$

Because the nominal wage in a does not change,[22] the net effect is an increase in real wages in a:

$$(w_{a2} - w_{a1}) - (r_{a2} - r_{a1}) = \frac{k_a N}{N(k_a + k_b) + 2s} \Delta \geq 0. \tag{13}$$

It is important to note that in general, real wages differ in the two cities in period 2. In particular, a comparison of Eq. (11) with Eq. (13) indicates that in period 2 real wages are higher in city b. This is not surprising, because city b is the one directly affected by the productivity shock. While labor mobility causes real wages to increase in city a as well, real wages are not fully equalized because mobility is not perfect in that only the marginal worker is indifferent between the two cities in equilibrium. With perfect mobility ($s = 0$), real wages are completely equalized because *all* workers need to be indifferent between the two cities.[23]

The marginal worker in period 2 is different from the marginal worker in period 1. Since city b offers higher real wages in period 2, the new marginal worker in period 2 has stronger preferences for city a. In particular, the change in the relative preference for city a of the marginal worker is equal to[24]

$$(e_{a2} - e_{b2}) - (e_{a1} - e_{b1}) = \frac{2s \Delta}{N(k_a + k_b) + 2s} \geq 0. \tag{14}$$

Note that firms are indifferent between cities. Because of the assumptions on technology, firms have zero profits in both cities. While labor is now more expensive in b, it is also more productive there. Because firms produce a good that is internationally traded, if skilled workers weren't more productive, employers would leave b and relocate to a.

In the production function used here, all firms in a city are assumed to share a city-specific productivity shifter. The implicit assumption is that any city-specific characteristic affects all firms equally. For example, the transportation infrastructure, the weather, local institutions, local regulations, etc. affect the productivity of all producers in the same way. It would be easy to extend this framework to allow for an additional firm–city specific productivity shifter:

$$\ln y_{jc} = (X_c + X_{jc}) + h N_{jc} + (1 - h) K_{jc} \tag{15}$$

[22] This may look surprising at first. Given that the number of workers has declined, and that the demand curve is downward sloping, one might expect an increase in wages of those workers who stay in a. Indeed, this would be true in a model without capital. But in a model that includes capital, the amount of capital used by firms declines in b and increases in a. This capital flow off-sets the changes in labor supply.

[23] To see this, compare Eq. (11) with (13), setting $s = 0$.

[24] This change is by construction equal to the change in the difference in real wages between the two cities.

where j indexes a firm, X_c is a productivity effect shared by all firms in city c, and X_{jc} is a productivity effect that is specific to firm j and city c. This formulation allows some firms to benefit more from some city characteristics than others. For example, the specific type of local infrastructure in a given city may affect the TFP of some firms more than others. This is analogous to introducing individual specific location preferences in workers' utility functions. For the same reason that preferences for location make workers less responsive to differences in real wages across locations, the term X_{jc} makes firms less mobile. Effectively, some firms enjoy economic rents generated by their location-firm specific match. Small differences in production costs may not be enough to induce these firms to relocate, in the same way that worker idiosyncratic preferences for location lower the elasticity of labor supply.

3.1.3. Incidence: who benefits from the productivity increase?
In this setting, the benefit of the increase in productivity Δ is split between workers and landowners.[25] Eqs (10)–(13) clarify that the incidence of the shock depends on which of the two factors—labor or land—is supplied more elastically at the local level. In turn, the elasticity of local labor supply and the elasticity of housing supply ultimately depend on the preference parameter s and the supply parameters k_a and k_b. For a given elasticity of housing supply, a lower local elasticity of labor supply implies that a larger fraction of the productivity shock in city b accrues to workers in city b, and a smaller fraction accrues to landowners in city b. Intuitively, when labor is relatively less mobile, it captures more of the economic rent generated by the productivity shock. A lower local elasticity of labor supply also implies a smaller increase in real wages in the non affected city (city a), since the channel that generates benefits for the non affected city is the potential for worker mobility.

On the other hand, for a given elasticity of labor supply, a lower elasticity of housing supply in city b relative to city a (k_b bigger than k_a) implies that housing quantity adjusts less in city b following the productivity shock. As a consequence, housing prices increase more and a larger fraction of the productivity gain accrues to landowners in city b and a smaller fraction accrues to workers.

The role played by the elasticity of labor and housing supply in determining the incidence of the productivity shock between workers and landowners and between city a and city b is clearly illustrated in four special cases.

1. If labor is completely immobile ($s = \infty$), Eq. (11) becomes $(w_{b2} - w_{b1}) - (r_{b2} - r_{b1}) = \Delta$, indicating that real wages in city b increase by the full amount of the productivity shock. In this case, the benefit of the shock accrues entirely to workers in city b. The intuition is that if labor is a fixed factor, workers in the city hit by the shock

---

[25] By construction: Δ = change in real wage in a + change in real wage in b + change in land price in a + change in land price in b.

capture the full economic rent generated by the shock. Nothing happens to workers in a, as their real wage is unchanged: Eq. (13) becomes $(w_{a2} - w_{a1}) - (r_{a2} - r_{a1}) = 0$. Moreover, since no worker moves in equilibrium, housing prices in both cities remain unchanged so that landowners are indifferent. For example, Eq. (10) becomes $r_{b2} - r_{b1} = 0$, indicating that housing prices in b are not affected.

2. If labor is perfectly mobile ($s = 0$), Eqs (11) and (13) become: $(w_{b2} - w_{b1}) - (r_{b2} - r_{b1}) = (w_{a2} - w_{a1}) - (r_{a2} - r_{a1}) = \frac{k_a}{k_a + k_b}\Delta$. Because of perfect labor mobility, real wages need to be identical in a and b, otherwise workers would leave one city for the other. In this case, incidence depends on the relative elasticities of housing supply in the two cities. To see this, note that the increase in real wages is a fraction $\frac{k_a}{k_a + k_b}$ of Δ. The rest of Δ accrues to landowners in b, since housing prices in b increase by $r_{b2} - r_{b1} = \frac{k_b}{k_a + k_b}\Delta$. The fraction that accrues to workers depends on which of the two cities has more elastic housing supply. For example, if the elasticity of housing supply is the same in a and b, than we have an equal split between workers and landowners, with real wages in both cities increasing by $\frac{1}{2}\Delta$, and land prices in b increasing by $\frac{1}{2}\Delta$. On the other hand, if the elasticity of housing supply is larger in city b then landowners capture less of the total economic rent, because their factor is more elastically supplied in the city originally hit by the shock.

3. If housing supply in b is fixed ($k_b = \infty$), the entire productivity increase is capitalized in land values in city b. This is the Rosen–Roback case described above. City b becomes more productive but it cannot expand its workforce because housing cannot expand. No one can move to city b, and the only effect of the productivity shock is to raise cost of housing by $r_{b2} - r_{b1} = \Delta$. All the benefit goes to landowners in b. Real wages are not affected, and workers in both cities are indifferent. This is a case where, even in the presence of a shock that makes some firms more productive, labor is prevented from accessing this increased productivity by the constraints on housing supply. Part of the increase in productivity is therefore wasted.

4. If housing supply in b is infinitely elastic ($k_b = 0$), then Eq. (10) becomes $r_{b2} - r_{b1} = 0$, indicating that housing prices in b do not change. For each additional worker who intends to move to city b, a housing unit is added so that housing prices never increase. Landowners are indifferent, and the entire benefit of the productivity increase accrues to workers. Equation (11) becomes $(w_{b2} - w_{b1}) - (r_{b2} - r_{b1}) = \Delta$, indicating that real wages in city b increase by the full amount of the productivity shock. Real wages in city a also increase, but less than in b: $(w_{a2} - w_{a1}) - (r_{a2} - r_{a1}) = \frac{k_a N}{N k_a + 2s}\Delta$.

3.1.4. Effect of a labor supply shock on wages and prices

So far, I have focused on what happens to a local economy following a shock generated by a labor demand shift. What distinguishes city b from city a, is that in city b the demand for labor is higher. I now discuss the opposite case, where a local economy experiences an increase in the supply of labor. Specifically, I consider what happens when city b becomes more desirable for workers relative to city a. I assume that in period 2, the amenity level increases in city b: $A_{b2} = A_{b1} + \Delta'$, where $\Delta' > 0$ represents the improvement in the amenity. I assume that the amenity level in a does not change, and that productivity is the same in the two cities.[26]

As in the case of a demand shift above, $\frac{N}{N(k_a+k_b)+2s}\Delta'$ workers move from a to b. As before, the cost of housing increases in b (by the amount in Eq. (10)) and declines in a (by the amount in Eq. (12)). Also, similar to before, the nominal wage in a does not change. A difference with the demand shock case is that the nominal wage in b does not increase, but it remains unchanged.[27]

As a consequence, real wages decline in city b

$$(w_{b2} - w_{b1}) - (r_{b2} - r_{b1}) = -\frac{k_b N}{N(k_a + k_b) + 2s}\Delta' \le 0 \tag{16}$$

and increase in city a:

$$(w_{a2} - w_{a1}) - (r_{a2} - r_{a1}) = \frac{k_a N}{N(k_a + k_b) + 2s}\Delta' \ge 0. \tag{17}$$

Intuitively, workers are willing to take a negative compensating differential in the form of lower real wages to live in the more desirable city. Landowners in b experience an increase in their property values, while landowners in a experience a decline.

The incidence of the shock is similar to what I discuss in Section 3.1.3. As with the case of a demand shock, the exact magnitude of workers' and landowners' gains and losses depend on the elasticity of labor supply and the elasticity of housing supply. The four special cases outlined in Section 3.1.3 apply to this case as well.

3.2. Spatial equilibrium with heterogenous labor

In Section 3.1, I have considered the case where all workers are identical in terms of productivity. In this section, I consider the case where there are 2 types of workers: skilled workers (type H) and unskilled workers (type L). I assume that skilled and unskilled workers in the same city face the same housing market. I discuss what happens in

---

[26] Here, the labor supply increase is a consequence of an increase in amenities, holding constant tastes. Results are similar if one assumes that amenities are fixed, but the taste for those amenities increases.

[27] This may seem counterintuitive at first. One might expect wage *decreases* in response to supply increases. Why do nominal wages not decline in b after it has become more attractive? After all, workers should be willing to take a negative compensating differential in the form of lower nominal wages to live in the more desirable city. Indeed, this is what a model without capital would predict. However, such a model ignores the endogenous reaction of capital. In a model with capital, nominal wages do not move in city b because capital flows to b, offsetting the changes in labor supply. The amount of capital increases in b by $K_{b2} - K_{b1} = \frac{N\Delta'}{N(k_a+k_b)+2s} \ge 0$ and decreases in a by $K_{a2} - K_{a1} = -\frac{N\Delta'}{N(k_a+k_b)+2s} \le 0$.

equilibrium when the demand for one group changes in one city, while the demand for the other group remains unchanged.

3.2.1. Assumptions and equilibrium

The indirect utilities of skilled workers and unskilled workers in city c are assumed to be, respectively

$$U_{Hic} = w_{Hc} - r_c + A_{Hc} + e_{Hic} \tag{18}$$

and

$$U_{Lic} = w_{Lc} - r_c + A_{Lc} + e_{Lic}. \tag{19}$$

In Eqs (18) and (19), skilled and unskilled workers in a city face the same price of housing so that a shock to the labor demand of one group may be transmitted to the other group through its effect on housing prices.[28] While they have access to the same local amenities, different skill groups do not need to value these amenities equally: A_{Hc} and A_{Lc} represent the skill-specific value of local amenities. Tastes for location can vary by skill group. Specifically, I assume that skilled workers' and unskilled workers' relative preferences for city a over city b are, respectively

$$e_{Hia} - e_{Hib} \sim U[-s_H, s_H] \tag{20}$$

and

$$e_{Lia} - e_{Lib} \sim U[-s_L, s_L]. \tag{21}$$

For example, the case in which skilled workers are more mobile than unskilled workers can be modeled by assuming that $s_H < s_L$.

For simplicity, I focus on the case where skilled and unskilled workers in the same city work in different firms. This amounts to assuming away imperfect substitution between skilled and unskilled workers. This assumption simplifies the analysis, and it is not crucial. The production function for firms in city c that use skilled labor is Cobb–Douglas with constant returns to scale: $\ln y_{Hc} = X_{Hc} + hN_{Hc} + (1 - h)K_{Hc}$, where K_{Hc} is the log of capital and X_{Hc} is a skill and city-specific productivity shifter. Similarly, the production

---

[28] It is easy to relax this assumption by assuming residential segregation along skill lines within a city. However, this assumption would not be particularly realistic. Although skilled and unskilled individuals may reside in different parts of a metropolitan area, there always is some overlap which ensures that shocks to a part of the metropolitan area get transmitted to the rest of the area. Empirically, changes in housing prices across neighborhoods within a city are highly correlated.

function for firms that use unskilled labor is $\ln y_{Lc} = X_{Lc} + hN_{Lc} + (1-h)K_{Lc}$. The rest of the assumptions remain unchanged.[29]

3.2.2. Effect of a labor demand shock on wages and prices

Consider the case where the relative demand for skilled labor increases in b. See Moretti (forthcoming) for the specular case where the relative supply for skilled labor increases in b.

Assume that the productivity of skilled workers increases relative to the productivity of unskilled workers in city b because the productivity shifter for skilled workers in city b is higher in period 2 than in period 1: $X_{Hb2} = X_{Hb1} + \Delta$, where $\Delta > 0$ represents a positive, localized, skill-biased productivity shock. Nothing happens to the productivity of unskilled workers in b and the productivity of skilled and unskilled workers in a. The amenities in the two cities are identical and fixed.

Attracted by higher labor demand, some skilled workers move to b from a. In particular, the number of skilled workers in b increases by

$$N_{Hb2} - N_{Hb1} = \frac{\Delta N((k_a + k_b)N + 2s_L)}{2h(k_aN(s_H + s_L) + k_bN(s_H + s_L) + 2s_H s_L)} \geq 0. \quad (23)$$

This number depends positively on the elasticity of labor supply for skilled and unskilled workers:

$$\frac{\partial(N_{Hb2} - N_{Hb1})}{\partial s_H} = -\frac{N(k_aN + 2s_L + k_bN)^2\Delta}{2h(k_aNs_H + 2s_H s_L + k_aNs_L + k_bNs_H + k_bNs_L)^2} \leq 0 \quad (24)$$

and

$$\frac{\partial(N_{Hb2} - N_{Hb1})}{\partial s_L} = -\frac{N^3\Delta(2k_ak_b + k_a^2 + k_b^2)}{2h(k_aNs_H + 2s_H s_L + k_aNs_L + k_bNs_H + k_bNs_L)^2} \leq 0. \quad (25)$$

The intuition for the first derivative is obvious: a higher elasticity of labor supply for skilled workers implies that skilled workers are more mobile. The intuition for the second

---

[29] Because skilled and unskilled workers face the same housing market within a city, to obtain the (inverse of) the aggregate demand curve for housing in a city one needs to sum the demand of skilled workers and the demand of unskilled workers. For example, in city b:

$$r_b = \frac{(2s_H s_L)}{(s_H + s_L)} - \frac{(2s_H s_L)(N_{Hb} + N_{Lb})}{N(s_H + s_L)} - \frac{s_L(w_{Ha} - w_{Hb} - r_a)}{(s_L + s_H)} - \frac{s_H(w_{La} - w_{Lb} - r_a)}{(s_L + s_H)}. \quad (22)$$

derivative is less obvious. A higher elasticity of labor supply for unskilled workers implies that a larger number of unskilled workers move out in response to the inflow of skilled workers, so that the increase in housing costs is more limited which ultimately increases the number of skilled in-migrants.

The number of movers in Eq. (23) also depends positively on the elasticity of housing supply in b:

$$\frac{\partial(N_{Hb2} - N_{Hb1})}{\partial k_b} = -\frac{N^2 \Delta s_L^2}{h(k_a N s_H + 2 s_H s_L + k_a N s_L + k_b N s_H + k_b N s_L)^2} \leq 0.$$

$$(26)$$

A higher elasticity of housing supply (lower k_b) implies that more housing units become available for the incoming skilled workers.

Because skilled workers in b have become more productive, their nominal wage increases by an amount Δ/h, proportional to the productivity increase. Following the inflow of skilled workers, the cost of housing in b increases and the increase is larger the smaller is s_H and the larger is k_b:[30]

$$r_{b2} - r_{b1} = \frac{s_L N k_b \Delta}{h(k_a N s_H + 2 s_H s_L + k_a N s_L + k_b N s_H + k_b N s_L)} \geq 0. \qquad (27)$$

Skilled workers in both cities experience increases in real wages. In b, the increase in real wages is smaller than the increase in nominal wages because of the increase in the cost of housing:

$$(w_{Hb2} - r_{b2}) - (w_{Hb1} - r_{b1})$$
$$= \frac{k_a N s_H + k_b N s_H + k_a N s_L + 2 s H s L}{h(k_a N s_H + 2 s_H s_L + k_a N s_L + k_b N s_H + k_b N s_L)} \Delta \geq 0. \qquad (28)$$

It is easy to see that this change is less than the increase in nominal wages, Δ/h. Since nominal wages don't change and housing costs decline, real wages for skilled workers in a also increase, but by less than in b:

$$(w_{Ha2} - r_{a2}) - (w_{Ha1} - r_{a1})$$
$$= \frac{s_L k_a N}{h(k_a N s_H + 2 s_H s_L + k_a N s_L + k_b N s_H + k_b N s_L)} \Delta \geq 0. \qquad (29)$$

By comparing Eq. (28) with (29), it is easy to confirm that $(w_{Hb2} - r_{b2}) - (w_{Hb1} - r_{b1}) \geq (w_{Ha2} - r_{a2}) - (w_{Ha1} - r_{a1})$.

---

[30] Because of the decline in the number of workers, the cost of housing in a declines by the same amount.

What happens to unskilled workers? In city b their productivity and nominal wages don't change, but housing costs increase. As a consequence, their real wage in b decreases by

$$(w_{Lb2} - r_{b2}) - (w_{Lb1} - r_{b1})$$
$$= -\frac{s_L N k_b}{h(k_a N s_H + 2 s_H s_L + k_a N s_L + k_b N s_H + k_b N s_L)} \Delta \leq 0. \qquad (30)$$

Effectively, unskilled workers in b compete for scarce housing with skilled workers, and the inflow of new skilled workers hurts unskilled workers through higher housing costs. (For the same reason, the real wage of unskilled workers in a increases.) Since their real wage has declined, the number of unskilled workers in b declines by

$$N_{Lb2} - N_{Lb1} = -\frac{N^2(k_a + k_b)}{2h(k_a N s_H + 2 s_H s_L + k_a N s_L + k_b N s_H + k_b N s_L)} \Delta \leq 0. \quad (31)$$

The overall population of city b increases. This is because the number of skilled workers who move to city b is larger than the number of unskilled workers who leave city b. On net

$$(N_{Hb2} + N_{Lb2}) - (N_{Hb1} + N_{Lb1})$$
$$= \frac{\Delta N s_L}{h(k_a N(s_H + s_L) + k_b N(s_H + s_L) + 2 s_H s_L)} \geq 0. \qquad (32)$$

An assumption of this model is that skilled and unskilled workers are employed by different firms, so that the labor market is segregated by skill within a city. This assumption effectively rules out imperfect substitutability between skilled and unskilled labor. In a more general setting, skilled and unskilled workers work in the same firm. Most of the results in this section generalize, but the equilibrium depends on the degree of imperfect substitution between skilled and unskilled labor.[31] Specifically, complementarity between skilled and unskilled workers implies that the marginal product of unskilled workers increases in the number of skilled workers in the same firm. Thus, the inflow of skilled workers in city b caused by the increase in their productivity endogenously raises the productivity of unskilled workers in city b. As a consequence, the real wage of unskilled workers declines less than in the case described above. This mitigates the negative effect on the welfare of unskilled workers in city b and it reduces the number of unskilled workers who leave the city.

---

[31] Given that the focus is on skill-biased productivity shocks, a CES technology is more appropriate for the case of integrated labor markets than a Cobb–Douglas technology.

3.2.3. Incidence: changes in wage and utility inequality

The model yields three conclusions regarding the incidence of the skill-biased localized shock.

First, to the extent that mobility is not perfect, a non-degenerate equilibrium is possible. After a shock that makes one group more productive, both groups are still represented in both cities. This conclusion hinges upon the assumption of a less than infinite elasticity of local labor supply. When the productivity shock attracts skilled workers to city b, housing prices increase there, and unskilled workers begin to leave, since their real wage is lower than in city a. The inflow of skilled workers to the city effectively displaces some unskilled workers. In the absence of individual preferences for location, no unskilled worker would remain in city b and the equilibrium would be characterized by complete geographic segregation of workers by skill level. This is clearly not realistic, since in reality we never observe cities that are populated by workers of only one type. In the presence of individual preferences for location, those unskilled workers who have a strong preference for city b over city a opt to stay in city b, even if their real wage is lower in b. Those who leave are those who are less attached to city b.

Therefore, the marginal unskilled worker has weaker preferences for city a after the shock than before the shock. The change in the relative preference for city a of the marginal unskilled worker is equal to

$$
\begin{aligned}
&(e_{La2} - e_{Lb2}) - (e_{La1} - e_{Lb1}) \\
&= -\frac{s_L N (k_a + k_b)}{h(k_a N (s_H + s_L) + k_b N (s_H + s_L) + 2 s_H s_L)} \Delta \le 0.
\end{aligned}
\tag{33}
$$

The opposite is true for skilled workers. Because their real wage has increased in city b more than in city a, the marginal skilled worker has stronger preferences for city a after the shock:

$$
\begin{aligned}
&(e_{Ha2} - e_{Hb2}) - (e_{Ha1} - e_{Hb1}) \\
&= \frac{s_H (k_a N + 2 s_L + k_b N)}{h(k_a N (s_H + s_L) + k_b N (s_H + s_L) + 2 s_H s_L)} \Delta \ge 0.
\end{aligned}
\tag{34}
$$

Second, skilled workers in both cities and landowners in city b benefit from the productivity increase. Inframarginal unskilled workers in city b are negatively affected, and inframarginal unskilled workers in city a are positively affected. It is important to highlight that, although inframarginal unskilled workers in city b are made worse off by the decline in their real wage, they are still better off in city b than in city a because of their idiosyncratic preferences for location.

The magnitude of these changes in utility for skilled and unskilled workers and for landowners crucially depends on the elasticities of labor supply of the two groups (which are governed by the preference parameters s_H and s_L) and the elasticities of housing supply in the two cities (which are governed by the parameters k_a and k_b). The intuition is related to the intuition provided above for the incidence in the case of homogenous labor, although it is complicated by the fact that each group's location decisions affect the other group's utility through changes in housing prices. For example, the gain in real wages experienced in equilibrium by skilled workers in city b is large if their mobility is low (s_H is large):

$$
\frac{\partial((w_{Hb2} - r_{Hb2}) - (w_{Hb1} - r_{Hb1}))}{\partial s_H}
$$
$$
= \frac{(k_a N + 2s_L + k_b N)s_L N k_b \Delta}{h(k_a N s_H + 2s_H s_L + k_a N s_L + k_b N s_H + k_b N s_L)^2} \geq 0. \tag{35}
$$

Low mobility implies that fewer skilled workers are willing to leave a and move to b, so that residents of b experience a smaller increase in the cost of housing. Similarly, the gain in real wages experienced in equilibrium by skilled workers in city b is large if the mobility of unskilled workers is high (s_L is small):

$$
\frac{\partial((w_{Hb2} - r_{Hb2}) - (w_{Hb1} - r_{Hb1}))}{\partial s_L}
$$
$$
= - \frac{k_b N^2 s_H \Delta (k_a + k_b)}{h(k_a N s_H + 2s_H s_L + k_a N s_L + k_b N s_H + k_b N s_L)^2} \leq 0. \tag{36}
$$

If unskilled workers are highly mobile, more of them leave the city in response to the increase in housing costs. The ultimate equilibrium increase in housing costs is therefore smaller, and this results in a higher real wage (and higher utility) for inframarginal skilled workers in b.

Additionally, the increase in real wages experienced by skilled workers in city b is large if the elasticity of housing supply in b is high (k_b is small), because a high elasticity of housing supply in b implies that for a given increase in city size, the increase in housing costs is small, and this translates into a larger increase into equilibrium real wages for skilled workers:

$$
\frac{\partial((w_{Hb2} - r_{Hb2}) - (w_{Hb1} - r_{Hb1}))}{\partial k_b}
$$
$$
= - \frac{N \Delta s_L (2s_H s_L + k_a N s_H + k_a N s_L)}{h(k_a N s_H + 2s_H s_L + k_a N s_L + k_b N s_H + k_b N s_L)^2} \leq 0. \tag{37}
$$

The opposite argument applies to unskilled workers. The decline in their equilibrium real wage in city b depends positively on their elasticity of labor supply:

$$
\frac{\partial((w_{Lb2} - r_{Lb2}) - (w_{Lb1} - r_{Lb1}))}{\partial s_L}
$$

$$
= -\frac{k_b N^2 s_H \Delta (k_a + k_b)}{h(k_a N s_H + 2 s_H s_L + k_a N s_L + k_b N s_H + k_b N s_L)^2} \leq 0 \qquad (38)
$$

and negatively on the elasticity of labor supply for skilled workers:

$$
\frac{\partial((w_{Lb2} - r_{Lb2}) - (w_{Lb1} - r_{Lb1}))}{\partial s_H}
$$

$$
= \frac{(k_a N + 2 s_L + k_b N) s_L N k_b \Delta}{h(k_a N s_H + 2 s_H s_L + k_a N s_L + k_b N s_H + k_b N s_L)^2} \geq 0. \qquad (39)
$$

A small elasticity of labor supply for unskilled workers implies that unskilled workers have strong idiosyncratic preferences for location, so that few move in response to the loss in real wage. With perfect mobility ($s_L = 0$), they experience no loss in real wage (See Eq. (30)). Additionally, a large s_H implies that skilled workers have low mobility so that few move in response to the increase in their wage. The ultimate increase in the price of land is therefore small, so the utility loss for inframarginal unskilled workers in b is more contained. With no mobility of skilled workers ($s_H = \infty$), unskilled workers experience no change in the real wages.

For landowners, a higher elasticity of housing supply in city b relative to city a (k_b smaller than k_a) implies that housing quantity adjusts more in city b so that a smaller fraction of the productivity gain accrues to landowners.

A third conclusion of the model is that the difference in nominal wages between skilled and unskilled workers increases nationwide more than the difference in utility between skilled and unskilled workers. To see this, note that the difference between the change in the skilled-unskilled nominal wage gap and the change in the skilled-unskilled utility gap is

$$
\frac{N k D^2 s_L (s_L + 2kN)}{2h^2 (kN s_H + s_H s_L + kN s_L)^2} \geq 0 \qquad (40)
$$

which is non-negative, indicating that the relative nominal wage of skilled workers grows more than their relative utility. The intuition is that the benefits of a higher nominal wage for skilled workers are in part eroded by the higher cost of housing they are exposed to, so that their relative utility does not increase as much as one might have thought just based on the increase in their relative nominal wage (Moretti, forthcoming).

3.3. Spatial equilibrium with agglomeration economies

In Sections 3.1 and 3.2, the productivity of firms in the two cities is determined by the city-specific productivity parameter X_c, which is taken as given. I now consider the case where there are agglomeration economies so that the productivity of firms in a locality is an endogenous function of the level of economic activity in that locality. This amounts to endogenizing the city-specific productivity shifter. For example, one can assume that productivity in a locality is a function of the number of workers in that locality, so that $X_c = f(N_c)$ with $f' > 0$. In this case, the location decisions of workers generates a positive externality. In Section 4 I discuss in detail the possible sources of agglomeration economies.

As in Sections 3.1 and 3.2, a locality that is for some reason more productive attracts more workers. But unlike Sections 3.1 and 3.2, the increase in population has the additional effect of further increasing productivity of local firms. This in turn attracts even more workers and the process continues to the point where land prices are high enough that marginal workers and firms are made indifferent between locations. Most of the results on incidence presented above remain true. The main difference with the previous analysis is that the existence of agglomeration economies has the potential to generate multiple equilibria, with some equilibria characterized by low economic activity, low cost of housing and low nominal wages, and other equilibria characterized by high economic activity, high cost of housing and high nominal wages.[32]

For concreteness, consider the case of homogenous labor and assume a specific functional form for the agglomeration externality: $X_c = x_c + \gamma N_c$, where the parameter γ governs the strength of agglomeration economies. In the version of the model without agglomeration spillovers ($\gamma = 0$), labor demand has the standard downward sloping shape (see Eq. (5)). With agglomeration spillovers, this is not necessarily the case. Eq. (5) becomes

$$w_c = x_c + (\gamma - (1 - h))N_c + (1 - h)K_c + \ln h. \qquad (41)$$

An increase in the number of workers employed in a city has two opposing effects. On the one hand, because of the standard assumptions on technology, an increase in the number of workers lowers the marginal product of labor. On the other hand, the increase in population raises labor productivity. If the agglomeration spillover is strong enough ($\gamma > (1 - h)$), the labor demand function in a city may be upward sloping.

As in Section 3.1, assume that the two cities are identical in period 1, and that in period 2 city b experiences an exogenous increase in productivity of size Δ, so that

---

[32] Glaeser (2008) proposes a comprehensive theoretical equilibrium framework with agglomeration externalities. See also Combes et al. (2005) for a useful big-picture graphical treatment of spatial equilibrium with agglomeration economies.

$x_{b2} = x_{b1} + \Delta$. This initial increase in productivity pushes nominal wages up and higher nominal wages attract more workers to city b. The arrival of new workers in city b generates productivity spillovers and, as a consequence, the initial productivity difference is magnified.

It is informative to compare the equilibrium in the case where there are agglomeration spillovers ($\gamma > 0$) with the case where there are no spillovers ($\gamma = 0$). In the presence of spillovers, a productivity shock of size Δ in city b results in an increase in the equilibrium nominal wage that is larger than Δ:

$$w_{b2} - w_{b1} = \frac{h(N(k_a + k_b) + 2s) - \gamma N}{h(N(k_a + k_b) + 2s) - 2\gamma N} \Delta \geq \Delta \geq 0. \qquad (42)$$

This is to be expected, because the agglomeration spillover magnifies the effect of the productivity shock. By contrast, in the case with no spillovers ($\gamma = 0$), the increase in nominal wage in city b is exactly equal to Δ. (See Eq. (9)). Not surprisingly, the larger is the magnitude of the agglomeration spillover—i.e. the larger the parameter γ—the larger is the ultimate increase in the equilibrium nominal wage in city b:

$$\frac{\partial(w_{b2} - w_{b1})}{\partial \gamma} = \frac{Nh(N(k_a + k_b) + 2s)\Delta}{(2\gamma N - 2hs - k_b Nh - k_a Nh)^2} \geq 0. \qquad (43)$$

Exactly as in Section 3.1, the higher productivity in city b attracts more workers there. The number of workers in city b increases by

$$N_{b2} - N_{b1} = \frac{Nh}{h(N(k_a + k_b) + 2s) - 2\gamma N} \Delta \geq 0. \qquad (44)$$

Just as in the standard case without agglomeration spillovers, if housing supply is not infinitely elastic, the increase in the population of city b ultimately results in higher housing costs:

$$r_{b2} - r_{b1} = \frac{k_b Nh}{h(N(k_a + k_b) + 2s) - 2\gamma N} \Delta \geq 0. \qquad (45)$$

It is obvious from Eqs (44) and (45) that the increase in city size and the consequent increase in housing costs are larger the larger is the spillover (i.e. the large is γ). If the spillover is zero, Eqs (44) and (45) revert to Eqs (8) and (10) in Section 3.1.

Since both nominal wages and housing costs increase in b, the ultimate effect on real wages is ambiguous and depends on whether the increase in nominal wage is larger or smaller than the increase in housing costs. In particular, the change in the equilibrium real wage is

$$(w_{b2} - w_{b1}) - (r_{b2} - r_{b1}) = \frac{(k_a N + 2s)h - \gamma N}{h(N(k_a + k_b) + 2s) - 2\gamma N}\Delta \qquad (46)$$

which is clearly smaller than the increase in nominal wage in Eq. (42). This equation indicates that the change in the real wage depends on the magnitude of the spillover relative to other parameters. To see exactly how the change in the equilibrium real wage depends on γ, note that

$$\frac{\partial((w_{b2} - w_{b1}) - (r_{b2} - r_{b1}))}{\partial \gamma} = \frac{Nh(N(k_a - k_b) + 2s)\Delta}{(2\gamma N - 2hs - k_b Nh - k_a Nh)^2} \qquad (47)$$

which can be either positive or negative depending on whether $(N(k_a - k_b) + 2s) > 0$ or $(N(k_a - k_b) + 2s) < 0$. If the elasticity of housing supply in city b is larger or equal to the elasticity of housing supply in city a, the derivative is positive, indicating that the change in the equilibrium real wage in city b is positively associated with the strength of the agglomeration spillover γ. In this case, the increase in real wages in Eq. (46) for the case of positive agglomeration spillovers is larger than the increase in real wages in Eq. (11) for the case with no spillovers.

On the other hand, if the elasticity of housing supply in b is small enough relative to the elasticity of housing supply a, the derivative is negative, and the change in the equilibrium real wage in city b is negatively associated with the strength of the spillover.[33] Intuitively, if the elasticity of housing supply in b is small (large k_b), housing prices in b increase more following the productivity shock, and this increase lowers the equilibrium real wages for a given increase in the nominal wage. In the extreme, if the elasticity of housing supply in b is zero ($k_b = \infty$), the equilibrium real wage does not change. To see why, note that if the elasticity of housing supply in b is zero nobody can move to city b because no new housing unit can be added and Eqs (42) and (45) become

$$w_{b2} - w_{b1} = \Delta \qquad (50)$$

---

[33] The change in real wages in city a is smaller than the change in b:

$$(w_{a2} - w_{a1}) - (r_{a2} - r_{a1}) = \frac{k_a Nh - \gamma N}{h(N(k_a + k_b) + 2s) - 2\gamma N}\Delta \geq 0. \qquad (48)$$

The derivative of this change with respect to γ is

$$\frac{\partial((w_{a2} - w_{a1}) - (r_{a2} - r_{a1}))}{\partial \gamma} = \frac{Nh(N(k_a - k_b) - 2s)\Delta}{(2\gamma N - 2hs - k_b Nh - k_a Nh)^2} \geq 0. \qquad (49)$$

and

$$r_{b2} - r_{b1} = \Delta. \tag{51}$$

In this case, the increase in the nominal wage is exactly equal to the productivity shock Δ even in the presence of agglomeration spillovers because the constraint on labor mobility effectively rules out endogenous changes in total factor productivity X_c. The increase in housing prices is exactly equal to the productivity shock Δ because the lack of any response in the supply of housing implies that the entire productivity shock gets capitalized into land prices. Since both nominal wages and housing cost increase by the same amount Δ, Eq. (46) becomes

$$(w_{b2} - w_{b1}) - (r_{b2} - r_{b1}) = 0. \tag{52}$$

In sum, even with agglomeration economies it is possible (although not necessary) to have a non degenerate equilibrium where both cities have positive population. Qualitatively, the incidence of the productivity shock is not very different from the case discussed above where there are no agglomeration economies.

3.4. Spatial equilibrium with tradable and non-tradable industries

In the model presented above, the only consumption good is a homogenous tradable good. In reality, however, cities produce and consume a variety of goods, both tradable and non-tradable. Here I discuss how this may affect the equilibrium. This discussion is largely based on Moretti (forthcoming).

Assume that there are K tradable industries producing goods $x_1, x_2, x_3, \ldots, x_K$ and M non-tradable industries, producing goods $z_1, z_2, \ldots, z_M$. Consider the case of a positive shock to productivity in tradable industry x_1 in city c. The direct effect of this shock is an increase in employment in industry x_1. The indirect effect is a change in employment both in the rest of the tradable sector and in the non-tradable sector.

Consider first the effect on the non-tradable sector. Following the shock to sector x_1, aggregate income in the city increases for two reasons. First, there are more local jobs; second, if local labor supply is upward sloping, as in Section 3.1, local wages are also higher. The increase in the city budget constraint results in an increase in the local demand for non-tradables $z_1, z_2, \ldots, z_M$. Employment in industries like restaurants, theaters, real estate, cleaning services, legal services, construction, medical services, retail, personal services, etc. grows both because the city has more workers and wages are higher. The magnitude of the multiplier effect depends on three factors. First, it depends on consumer preferences for tradables and non-tradables and the technology in the non-tradable sector. If preferences are such that a larger share of income is spent on locally produced non-tradables, the multiplier is larger, everything else constant. Similarly, a more labor intensive technology in the non-tradable sector results in a larger multiplier, everything else constant. Second, it depends on the type of new jobs in the tradable sector. Adding skilled jobs in x_1 should have a larger multiplier than adding unskilled jobs, because skilled jobs pay higher earnings and therefore generate a larger increase in the demand for local services.

Third, there are offsetting general equilibrium effects on wages and prices. As explained in Sections 3.1 and 3.2, the magnitude of these effects ultimately depend on the elasticities of local labor and housing supply. If those elasticities are not infinite, local wages, land prices and the price on non-tradables increase following the shock to x_1. In turn, this city-wide increase in labor and land costs causes a decline in the supply of local services. This decline partially—but not fully—undoes the effect of the increase in demand for local services. Effectively, the addition of jobs in x_1 partially crowds out jobs in other industries. If labor supply is locally very elastic, this crowding out is more limited and the increase in labor costs is small, making the multiplier larger.

The shock to industry x_1 may also affect employment in tradable industries $x_2, x_3, \ldots, x_K$, although the direction of the effect is unclear a priori. This effect is governed by three different forces. First, and most importantly, the city-wide increase in labor costs hurts employment in $x_2, x_3, \ldots, x_K$. Because these are tradable industries, the increase in production costs lowers their competitiveness. Unlike in the case of non-tradable goods, the price of tradable goods is set on the national market and cannot adjust to local economic conditions. In the long run, some of the production in these industries is likely to be shifted to different cities. Second, the increase in production of x_1 may increase the local demand for intermediate goods and services. In this case, some elements of the vector $x_2, x_3, \ldots, x_K$ are inputs to produce x_1. This effect depends on the geography of the industry supply chain. While many industries are geographically clustered, the magnitude of this effect is likely to be quantitatively limited if the market for $x_2, x_3, \ldots, x_K$ is truly national. Third, if agglomeration economies are important, the increase in production in sector x_1 may result in more local agglomeration (see Section 4).

Carrington (1996), Moretti (forthcoming) and Black et al. (2005) estimate the employment multiplier at the local level. Carrington (1996) focuses on the short-run multiplier generated by the construction of the Trans-Alaskan Pipeline System. He finds evidence that the increase in construction jobs caused by the Trans-Alaskan Pipeline System had significant multipliers for jobs in other parts of the non-tradable sector in Alaska. In contrast, Moretti (forthcoming) focuses on long-run multipliers. He quantifies the long-term change in the number of jobs in a city's tradable and non-tradable sectors generated by an exogenous increase in the number of jobs in the tradable sector, allowing for the endogenous reallocation of factors and adjustment of prices. He finds that for each additional job in manufacturing in a given city, 1.6 jobs are created in the non-tradable sector in the same city. This effect is significantly larger for skilled jobs: adding one additional skilled job in the tradable sector generates 2.5 jobs in local goods and services, while adding one additional unskilled job in the tradable sector generates 1 job in local good and services. Industry-specific multipliers indicate that high-tech industries have the largest multiplier. Using a different time horizon, and focusing on time-varying localized shocks to the coal mining sector, Black et al. (2005) uncover smaller multipliers. They find that each additional mining job generates 0.17 non-tradable jobs. Interestingly, the estimated effect is not symmetric. The loss of a mining job results in the loss of 0.34 non-tradable jobs.

Theory suggests that the local multiplier for the tradable sector should be smaller than the one for the non-tradable sector, and possibly even negative. Consistent with this hypothesis, Carrington (1996), Moretti (forthcoming) and Black et al. (2005) fail to find any significant effect of employment in the tradable sector.

The magnitude of local multipliers is important for regional economic development policies. It should be stressed, however, that the presence of large multipliers is not, in itself, a market failure, and therefore does not necessarily justify government intervention.

3.5. Some empirical evidence

The model presented in this Section appears to be general enough to capture many key features of a realistic spatial equilibrium. To get a better sense of how well the model describes the real world, I now review some of the empirical evidence on the assumptions and the predictions of the model.[34]

One type of labor The evidence in Bartik (1991), Blanchard and Katz (1992), and David et al. (1997) is broadly consistent with the predictions of the model with homogenous labor in Section 3.1. These three papers aggregate all workers into one group and find substantial evidence of large labor flows following permanent labor demand shocks to a local labor market. Using state-level variation in demand conditions, Blanchard and Katz (1992) find that the main mechanism that re-establishes the equilibrium after a demand shock appears to be labor mobility, rather than job creation or job migration. Positive demand shocks are followed by substantial in-migration, while negative demand shocks are followed by substantial out-migration, up to the point that the original equilibrium between demand and supply is restored. In other words, these shocks have permanent effects on the size of labor markets. Blanchard and Katz (1992) estimate that it takes slightly less than a decade for the affected state to return to the initial equilibrium after a localized shock. Bartik (1991) estimates suggest a somewhat slower adjustment. The difference is in part due to the fact that the type of shocks examined by Bartik and Blanchard and Katz is different. Both papers focus on permanent shocks. However, Bartik's estimates come from a model where there is a "once-and-for-all shock

---

[34] Glaeser and Gottlieb (2009) argue that the assumption and the conclusions of the spatial equilibrium model seem generally consistent with most first order facts about the US labor and housing markets. For example, geographic mobility in the US is significant, with more than 40% of households changing addresses every 5 years. Yet, Glaeser and Gottlieb note that "there has been little tendency for people to move to high income areas" even in the presence of large wage disparities across areas. However, they caution that the fact that most amenities are hard to measure makes it inherently difficult to test conclusively whether the US labor market is indeed in a spatial equilibrium.

to local job growth, with subsequent growth unchanged from what it would have been". By contrast, Blanchard and Katz's estimates come from a model where the one-time shock to local job growth is allowed to affect subsequent job growth.

Overall, the findings in Blanchard and Katz (1992) on wages and housing prices are consistent with the version of the spatial equilibrium model where both local labor supply and housing supply are quite elastic in the long run. In particular, following a negative shock, nominal wages decline in the short run, but go back to their original level in the long run. Housing prices track changes in nominal wages, so that the decline in real wages is limited.[35]

Topel (1986) generalizes the spatial equilibrium model to a dynamic setting. Consistent with Bartik (1991) and Blanchard and Katz (1992), Topel finds that positive shocks to labor demand in a local labor market increase nominal wages there. But in addition to the other two papers, Topel also finds that it is not just current shocks that matter for current wages, but also expectations of future shocks. In particular, the expectation of a future demand shock to a local labor market generates in-migration to that market and therefore ultimately results in lower current nominal wages. An implication is that wages respond more to transitory shocks to local labor markets than to permanent shocks.

More than one type of labor Topel (1986) is among the first to posit that mobility costs could be different across skill groups, with low-skilled workers having higher costs and suggest that this difference may affect the welfare incidence of demand shocks. Consistent with a version of the model with heterogenous labor in Section 3.2 where the propensity to move of unskilled workers is different from the propensity to move of skilled workers, Topel finds evidence of a larger incidence of localized labor demand shocks on low-skilled workers than on high-skilled workers. In terms of the model this implies that $s_L > s_H$. Recall that the parameter s characterizes the amount of worker preferences for location. A larger s implies a lower elasticity of local labor supply and therefore lower labor mobility in response to economic shocks.[36]

Bound and Holzer (2000) find similar results. Using data on metropolitan areas, Bound and Holzer separately quantify the effects of location-specific labor demand shocks on the labor market outcomes of skilled and unskilled workers. As in Blanchard and Katz, Bound and Holzer (2000) find that positive (negative) labor demand shocks are followed by labor in-migration (out-migration). However, unskilled workers appear to be less sensitive to possible arbitrage opportunities and therefore less mobile following good and bad shocks. This difference in labor mobility has implications for the incidence of the shock. Because of their stronger preferences for location, unskilled workers experience significantly larger declines in nominal and real wages following negative

---

[35] Additionally, David et al. (1997) document that the speed of adjustment depends on the exact source of the demand shock.

[36] Evidence in Machin et al. (2009) and in Malamud and Wozniak (2009) indicates that the difference in mobility rates between educated and less educated workers may be causal.

demand shocks than skilled workers.[37] As a consequence, it appears that low skilled workers end up suffering more from localized negative demand shocks than high-skilled workers because they see their real wages fall while high-skilled workers move to better labor markets.

Notowidigdo (2010) proposes an alternative explanation for the difference in mobility and incidence between high and low-skilled workers. He posits that low-skilled workers may be shielded from local labor demand shocks because of declining house prices and public assistance programs. Public assistance programs are naturally tilted towards low-skilled workers. Housing price declines may also benefit low-skilled workers more than high-skilled workers if low-skilled workers have higher expenditure shares on housing. In this case, local labor demand shocks have smaller incidence on low-skilled workers than high skilled workers.

Residents vs movers The spatial equilibrium model described above does a good job of characterizing the incidence of demand or supply shocks to a local labor market, when incidence is defined as the share of the gains or losses that accrues to workers and landowners, or the share that accrues to each city. However, the model is poorly equipped to deal with the question of incidence when incidence is about which workers benefit or lose: migrants or original residents. For simplicity, my assumptions completely rule out any labor supply responses by residents, thus forcing all the employment adjustment to come from mobility in and out of the city. Moreover, the model is a full-employment model where involuntary unemployment is ruled out. In reality, however, it is possible that residents may change the amount of labor that they supply following local demand shocks.

The issue of who—between residents and migrants—ends up getting the new jobs created by a positive labor demand shock is clearly important in the presence of involuntary unemployment. This issue is particularly important when thinking about policies aimed at increasing local employment, like local development policies. Implementing a local development policy that increases employment in an area and benefits only migrants from outside the area is quite different politically from implementing a local development policy that benefits residents. This is particularly true if the development policy is financed by local taxpayer money.

The literature disagrees on this point. On one hand, Renkow (2003, 2006) and Partridge et al. (2009) argue that the primary source of employment increases following localized demand shocks comes from non-residents. The evidence in these studies,

---

[37] Bound and Holzer (2000) estimate that a 10% aggregate decline in labor demand in a city causes the nominal wage of high-school and college graduates to decline in the long run by 7% and 4%, respectively. The difference is even larger for younger workers. They also find declines in real wages for both groups, although smaller than the declines in nominal wages. These findings are qualitatively consistent with the estimates in Blanchard and Katz (1992), but they require an elasticity of local labor supply that is lower than the one implied by the estimates in Blanchard and Katz. Similarly, Topel (1986) finds large wage changes following a localized shock for groups of workers with low mobility, and small wage changes for groups of workers with high mobility.

however, is not particularly convincing and is far from conclusive. A more convincing set of empirical studies is represented by Eberts and Stone (1992) and Bartik (1991, 2001). These studies find significant increases in the labor force participation of residents following localized labor demand shocks. In a authoritative review of the literature, Bartik concludes that probably 25% of the new jobs are filled by increases in the labor force participation of local residents in the long run, with the remaining 75% going to outsiders. In other words, three out of four new jobs "in a region are filled by persons who otherwise would not have lived there".

4. THE DETERMINANTS OF PRODUCTIVITY DIFFERENCES ACROSS LOCAL LABOR MARKETS

In Section 2, I documented the large and persistent differences in labor market outcomes across metropolitan areas in the US. In Section 3, I clarified how those differences can persist in equilibrium in the long run, and who the ultimate beneficiaries of those differences are. In that section, the focus is on the consequences of these differences, while the source of these differences is taken as given. City b is assumed to be more productive than city a for some exogenous reason and this higher productivity ultimately results in more population, higher wages and higher housing costs.

In reality, however, most productivity differences within a country are unlikely to be exogenous. In this section, I discuss what might determine productivity differences across locations within a country. Economists have long hypothesized that the concentration of economic activity may be explained by agglomeration economies of some kind. Agglomeration of economic activity is particularly remarkable for industries that produce tradable goods, because the areas where economic activity is concentrated are typically characterized by high costs of labor and land. The observation that firms that produce tradable goods locate in areas where economic activity is dense and labor and land costs are high is consistent with the notion that those areas enjoy agglomeration advantages that offset the higher production costs.

I review the existing empirical evidence on agglomeration economies, focusing on two related questions:

- What do we know about the magnitude of agglomeration economies? (Section 4.1)
- What do we know about the micro mechanisms that generate agglomeration economies? (Section 4.2)

The past two decades have seen significant amounts of effort devoted to answering these two questions. The key empirical challenge has been the possible existence of unobserved features of localities that affect firm productivity even in the absence of agglomeration economies. The main conclusion of this section is that the existing literature has made some progress in empirically testing for the existence and quantifying the magnitude of agglomeration economies, accounting for possible omitted variables.

However, the channels that generate these economies remain more elusive. Much remains to be done in terms of empirically understanding the exact mechanisms that generate agglomerations of economic activity.

The discussion in this section focuses on papers that might be of particular interest to labor economists. See Duranton and Puga (2004a,b), Rosenthal and Strange (2004), Glaeser and Gottlieb (2009) and Moretti (2004c) for recent surveys that are more focused on urban economics.

4.1. Empirical estimates of agglomeration economies

Two empirical approaches have been proposed to test for and quantify agglomeration economies. The first approach is based on the equilibrium location decisions of firms and seeks to infer the importance of agglomeration forces from the observed geographic distribution of employment. Empirically measuring the degree of agglomeration of different localities is not straightforward. Naive indexes of concentration are sensitive to heterogeneity in firm size and in the size of the geographic areas for which data is available. In a landmark study, Ellison and Glaeser (1997) propose a "dartboard" style methodology for comparing the degree of geographic concentration across industries, accounting for differences in firm size and in the definition of geographic units. They find that firms are spread quite unevenly across localities. Almost all industries appear to be localized to some degree, although in many industries, the degree of localization is not large. When industry is defined at the two digit level, high levels of concentration are observed in the tobacco, textile and leather industries. Low levels of concentration are observed in the paper, rubber and plastics, and fabricated metal products industries. In an important follow up, Ellison et al. (forthcoming) use data from the Longitudinal Research Database to compute pairwise coagglomeration measurements for manufacturing industries and relate these coagglomeration measurements to industry characteristics. They document that coagglomeration rates are higher between industries that are economically similar, suggesting that agglomeration advantages may depend both on physical proximity and on economic linkages between firms. In a related study, Rosenthal and Strange (2003) measure the extent of agglomeration by focusing on the localization decisions of new plants. In the presence of mobility frictions, the localization of new plants is particularly informative because it is arguably less constrained by past localization decisions. The empirical results are consistent with the notion that agglomeration economies decline rapidly over space. Duranton and Overman (2005) propose an alternative measure of agglomeration. Unlike the Ellison and Glaeser (1997) measure, the Duranton and Overman measure is based on a continuous measure of distance and therefore does not depend on arbitrary definitions of geographic units. Using data from the UK, they confirm the existence of a significant amount of spatial agglomeration.[38]

---

[38] In particular, they find that more than half of the 4-digit industries in the UK are characterized by a degree of agglomeration that is statistically significant.

While these dartboard tests are informative in quantifying agglomeration, the main challenge in interpreting these tests is that firms base their location decisions on where their profits are expected to be highest, and this could be due to spillovers, natural advantage, or other unobserved cost shifters. The mere existence of agglomeration is not conclusive evidence of agglomeration economies. A second approach to testing for agglomeration economies directly asks whether productivity is higher in areas that are economically denser. An obvious difficulty is that productivity is an elusive quantity that is hard to measure empirically. In practice, existing studies have used alternative measures of productivity, including output per worker, wages and total factor productivity.

Using data on output per worker, Sveikauskas (1975) and Ciccone and Hall (1996) show that increases in employment density in a location are correlated with significant increases in output per worker, although the lack of a solid identification strategy precludes strong conclusions about causality. In an influential paper, Glaeser and Mare (2001) use wages to measure the marginal product of labor, and ask whether wages are higher in large urban areas. Because they use a longitudinal dataset that follows workers over an extended period of time, and some workers are observed moving in and out of urban areas, the authors are able to account for permanent unobserved worker heterogeneity. Consistent with the existence of agglomeration economies, Glaeser and Mare' find a significant wage premium associated with urban areas. The wage profiles of movers indicate that a significant fraction of the urban wage premium accrues to workers over time and stays with them when they leave cities. This finding is consistent with the notion that urban areas speed the accumulation of human capital and that a significant part of the urban wage premium is due to faster productivity growth in urban areas. On the other hand, using French data, Combes et al. (2009) find evidence of significant sorting of high ability workers into urban areas. Estimates of the relationship between wages and density conditional on worker fixed effects are 50% smaller than the unconditional relationship, indicating that at least half of the wage disparity across French cities can be explained by worker quality.[39]

More recent work seeks to provide more direct evidence on the relationship between agglomeration and productivity by testing whether total factor productivity at the firm level is higher in denser areas. Studies in this group use longitudinal plant-level data to estimate firm-level production functions and test whether changes over time in plant output are systematically associated with changes in the characteristics of the area around the plant, after controlling for changes in inputs. Henderson (2003) and Moretti (2004b) are early adopters of this approach. In particular, Henderson (2003) estimates plant level production functions for machinery and high-tech industries as a function of the density of other plants in the area, both in the same industry and in different industries. Identification is based on the longitudinal nature of the data. He finds that in the high-tech sector the number of establishments in an industry is positively associated with

---

[39] See also Wheaton and Lewis (2002).

productivity, although this association is small for the machinery industry. As expected, this association is stronger for plants belonging to single-establishment firms than for plants that belong to multi-establishment firms.

More recently, Greenstone et al. (forthcoming) provide direct estimates of the magnitude of agglomeration economies by comparing the effect of attracting a new manufacturing establishment on the productivity of existing manufacturing establishments in a county. They propose a novel identification strategy that relies not just on the longitudinal nature of the data but also on reported location rankings of profit-maximizing firms to identify a valid counterfactual for what would have happened to the incumbent plants' productivity in the absence of the plant opening. Greenstone, Hornbeck and Moretti find that attracting a new manufacturing establishment to a county results in substantial increases in productivity for existing establishments in that county. Figure 9 replicates their Fig. 1 and shows that five years after the new plant opened, incumbent plants experienced a 12% relative increase in TFP. Consistent with the spatial equilibrium model in Section 3, Greenstone et al. (forthcoming) find that the increased productivity enjoyed by existing plants comes at a cost, as quality-adjusted labor costs increase. As argued in Section 3, this increase is consistent with an upward sloping local supply of labor or an upward sloping supply of housing. Since manufacturing firms produce nationally traded goods and cannot raise output prices in response to higher input prices, the ultimate increase in profits experienced by incumbents is smaller than the productivity increase.

A notable feature of the spatial distribution of economic activity is represented by industry clustering, whereby firms tend to cluster near other "similar" firms (for example: firms that sell similar products). The cluster of IT firms in Silicon Valley, biomedical research in Boston, biotech in San Diego and San Francisco, financial firms in Wall Street and London are notable examples. The findings in Greenstone, Hornbeck and Moretti have interesting implications for explaining the existence and persistence of industrial clusters. The estimated productivity spillover appears to increase with various measures of economic proximity between the new plant and the incumbent plant. Because the documented increase in labor costs applies to all firms in the affected county, while the magnitude of the documented productivity spillovers is larger for pairs of plants that are economically closer, incumbent firms that are economically further away from other firms should become less profitable over time. In the long run, this process may result in increased agglomeration of similar plants in each location.

Arzaghi and Henderson (2008) estimate the effect on the productivity of Manhattan advertising agencies of locating near other advertising agencies. Consistent with the model proposed by Lucas and Rossi Hansberg (2002), they find agglomeration economies characterized by extremely rapid spatial decay. Moreover, consistent with the spatial equilibrium model, the benefit of agglomeration appears to be at least partially offset by higher land prices. In this industry, physical proximity appears to be beneficial because it facilitates networking. Interestingly, the magnitude of the productivity spillover

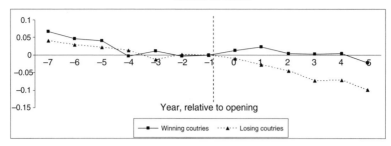

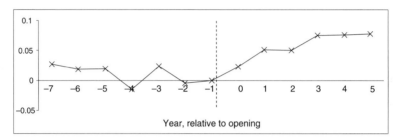

Figure 9 *Productivity of incumbent plants in counties with a new plant opening and counterfactual counties, relative to the year of plant opening.* Notes: This figure reproduces Figure 1 in Greenstone et al. (forthcoming). The solid line in the top panel shows average total factor productivity of incumbent plants in counties that successfully attract a new manufacturing plant. In Greenstone, Hornbeck and Moretti these are called winner counties. $t = 0$ represent the year of the new plant opening. The dotted line in the top panel shows average total factor productivity of incumbent plants in counties that bid for the new plant, make it into the group of finalists but ultimately fail to attract the new plant. In Greenstone, Hornbeck and Moretti these are called loser counties. The bottom panel shows the difference in average total factor productivity of incumbent plants between winner counties and loser counties.

appears to vary with firm quality, with higher quality agencies benefitting more from networking than lower quality agencies.

Of course, not every productivity spillover is necessarily a market failure that requires government intervention. Spillovers that occur within a firm, for example, can be in principle internalized. Mas and Moretti (2009) explore how the productivity of a worker varies as a function of the productivity of her co-workers and find evidence of significant within-firm productivity spillovers. The introduction of a high productivity worker in a shift significantly raises the productivity of her co-workers. In particular, substituting a worker with above average permanent productivity for a worker with below average permanent productivity is associated with a 1% increase in the effort of other workers on the same shift. While low productivity workers benefit from the presence of more capable workers, the productivity of high-skilled workers is not hurt by the presence of low-skilled co-workers. This type of spillover could be internalized by the firm by raising the salary of highly productive workers to reflect their external benefit on the productivity of less productive workers.

While significant progress has been made in estimating agglomeration economies using plausible identifying assumptions, some authors have raised the concern that the observed higher productivity in dense areas may reflect selection due to increased competition. For example, Melitz and Ottaviano (2008) develop a framework where the presence of a larger number of firms in larger markets increases competition and this ultimately causes less efficient firms to disappear. While this argument may apply to countries, it seems less obvious that it should apply to cities within a country. Within a country, firms in the tradable sector compete with firms in other cities, so it seems unlikely that local concentration offers a good measure of the relevant degree of competition. Indeed, Combes et al. (2009) provide recent convincing evidence in support this observation.[40]

4.2. Explanations of agglomeration economies

Understanding the ultimate causes of agglomeration economies is crucial to understanding persistent labor market differences across metropolitan areas. It is also very important for policy, as I discuss in Section 5. Here, I review the theory and the evidence on the three most relevant explanations that have been proposed for the agglomeration of economic activity: (1) advantages deriving from thick labor markets; (2) advantages deriving from proximity to providers of intermediate non-tradable goods and services; (3) localized knowledge spillovers.[41]

4.2.1. Thick labor markets

Thick markets have long been understood to be more attractive than thin markets when frictions of some type separate demand from supply. For example, in the influential barter model by Diamond (1982), the probability of finding a trading partner depends on the number of potential partners available, so that an increase in the thickness of the market makes trade easier. This generates multiple steady state equilibria and, in each of them, the equilibrium level of production is not efficient. In the context of local labor

---

[40] They use a generalization of the Melitz and Ottaviano (2008) model to distinguish between agglomeration economies and firm selection. Using French data on manufacturing establishments, they find that firms in large cities are more productive than firms in small cities, but find no difference in the amount of selection between small and large cities.

[41] Other explanations have been proposed for agglomeration economies, but they seem to be less relevant than the three described above. Some concentration of economic activity may be explained by the presence of natural advantages that constrain specific productions to specific locations. In practice, while natural advantages may be important in some industries, they are unlikely to be important determinants of agglomeration in most industries. In an often cited paper, Ellison and Glaeser (1999) show that natural advantages matter in some cases, but they account for only 20% of the observed degree of agglomeration. Historically, proximity of firms to consumers might also have played a role in the agglomeration of economic activity in metropolitan areas (Krugman, 1991b). In practice, however, the substantial decline in transportation costs makes this explanation less relevant for most industries at the present time. Glaeser and Kohlhase (2003) calculate that the cost of moving goods by rail or trucking has declined more than 90 percent over the last century.

markets, there are two reasons why workers and firms may find thick labor markets in large metropolitan areas attractive: better matches and lower risk.[42]

First, in the presence of worker and firm heterogeneity, a worker-firm match may be more productive in areas where there are many firms offering jobs and many workers looking for jobs. The higher quality of the worker-firm match in thicker labor markets may result in higher productivity and higher wages. This notion was first formalized twenty years ago in a model by Helsley and Strange (1990). Acemoglu (1997) and Rotemberg and Saloner (2000) propose variants of this hypothesis. In Acemoglu's model, employers in thick labor markets invest in new technologies because they know they can find specialized employees. At the same time, employees in thick markets invest in human capital because they know that when they change jobs, their human capital will be valued. Rotemberg and Saloner capture a similar idea in a model with multiple cities with identical factor endowments. In their setting, agglomeration of production is caused by the fact that having more competition between firms to hire skilled workers makes it easier for skilled workers to recoup the cost of acquiring industry-specific human capital.

Note that the relevant definition of labor market thickness is likely to depend not just on the size of a metropolitan area, but also on the skill set of a given worker. Two workers with different skills living in the same metropolitan areas may be exposed to vastly different labor market thickness. For example, a bioengineer and an architect living in the same city may face different market thickness, depending on the local agglomeration of bioengineering firms and architectural firms.

A second potential benefit of thick labor markets is the provision of insurance to workers and firms against idiosyncratic shocks. Thick labor markets reduce the probability that a worker remains unemployed following an idiosyncratic negative product demand shock to her employer. The presence of a large number of other employers implies a lower probability of not finding another job. At the same time, thick labor markets reduce the probability that a firm can't fill a vacancy, following an idiosyncratic shock to the labor supply of an employee. The presence of a large number of workers ensures a lower probability of not finding another worker. As in the case of match quality, this argument applies particularly to workers with specialized skills.

These two versions of the thick labor market hypothesis have different empirical implications. If the size of the labor market leads to better worker-firm matches, we should see that firms located in denser areas are more productive than otherwise identical firms located in less dense areas. The fact that the size of the labor market leads to a lower risk of unemployment for workers and a lower risk of unfilled vacancies for firms, does not imply differences in productivity between dense and less dense areas, but differences in wages. The sign of these wage differences is unclear a priori, because it depends on the magnitude of the compensating differential that workers are willing to pay for lower risk

---

[42] Labor market pooling externalities were first proposed by Marshall (1890).

of unemployment (generated by an increase in labor supply in denser areas) relative to the cost savings that firms experience due to lower risk of unfilled vacancies (generated by an increase in labor demand in denser areas). The former can be thought of as an increase in labor demand in thicker markets, while the latter can be thought of as an increase in labor supply in thicker markets.

Although the idea that thick labor market are beneficial is an old one, the existing empirical evidence is still limited. This is due in part to the fact that the quality of a worker-firm match has proven difficult to measure in practice.[43] Using a semi-structural model of the labor market, Petrongolo and Pissarides (2005) provide one of the earliest tests of the scale effect in job search based on the comparison of the number of job matches in labor markets of different sizes. The idea of the test is very simple. If the total number of vacancies and unemployed workers in a city is twice as large as the total number of vacancies and unemployed workers in another city, we should see that the number of matches per unit of time in the former city is more than twice as large the number of matches in the latter. Using British data, Petrongolo and Pissarides compare the offer arrival rate and the wage offer distribution in London (a thick labor market) with the rest of the country. They find significant scale effects in wage offers, but not in actual matches. However, the lack of observed scale effects in matches could in part be explained if the reservation wage endogenously adjusts to the size of the market.

A second piece of empirical evidence has to do with the relationship between frequency of job changes and size of the labor market. Wheeler (2008) and Bleakley and Lin (2006) find evidence that, although indirect, is generally consistent with localized increasing returns to scale in matching. In particular, using longitudinal data from the NLSY, Wheeler (2008) documents that the probability of changing industry is positively correlated with the size of the labor market for young workers and negatively associated with the size of the labor market for older workers. Bleakley and Lin (2006) find similar results for industry and occupation changes using cross-sectional data from the Census. They also find that this pattern remains true even in the case of involuntary separations. In other words, early in a career, when presumably workers are shopping around for a good match, industry and occupation changes occur more often in large, diverse local markets than in small, specialized ones. Later in a career, when changing industry or occupation becomes more costly because it may involve giving up specialized skills, industry and occupation changes occur less often in large markets, presumably because matches are better. The existing evidence, while generally consistent with the notion that larger labor markets facilitate matching, is still indirect. A more direct test might involve the duration of the match, as a measure of the quality of the match (Jovanovic and Rob, 1989). A testable implication is that job duration should be longer in larger labor markets than in smaller markets.

---

[43] In this respect, Puga (2009) argues that "the increasing availability of matched employer employee microdata will encourage more work on agglomeration through matching".

An additional testable implication of this hypothesis is that the productivity benefit of thick labor markets should be particularly important for industries that rely on specialized labor. Consider, for example, a digital media software engineer. If digital media firms have heterogeneous technologies, and digital media software engineers have heterogenous skills, it is likely that the match between a worker's specific skills and a firm's specific technology is more productive in a city where there are many digital media firms than in a city where there is only one digital media firm.[44] By contrast, the thickness of the labor market may not significantly improve the match quality and the productivity of less specialized workers in the same city, like manual laborers. An empirical test could involve estimating the difference in the correlation between measures of match quality (for example, wages and job duration) and market size, for workers who live in the same city but have different skill levels (specialized vs non specialized) and work in different industries (locally agglomerated vs locally non-agglomerated).

Fallick et al. (2006) posit that in high-tech industry clusters like Silicon Valley, high job mobility may facilitate the reallocation of resources towards firms with superior innovations, but it may also create human capital externalities that reduce incentives to invest in new knowledge. They argue that in the computer industry, the innovation benefits of job-hopping exceed the costs from reduced incentives to invest in human capital, while in other parts of the high-tech sector the opposite might be true. Their evidence is consistent with this notion, but it is too indirect to be definitive.[45]

The evidence in Greenstone et al. (forthcoming) also is consistent with the notion that spillovers occur between firms that share a similar worker pool. The magnitude of the productivity spillovers that they uncover depends on the economic linkages between the new plant and the incumbent plant. In their data, spillovers are larger for pairs of firms that belong to industries that share the same set of workers. This lends credibility to the notion that labor market pooling is an important source of agglomeration economies.

Costa and Kahn (2000) point out that thick labor markets are particularly important for dual career households, because thick labor markets may solve the co-location problem. The economic return of being in a large labor market relative to a small market is increasing over time and Costa and Kahn attribute at least half of the increased agglomeration of skilled workers in large cities to the growing severity of the co-location problem.

In his influential book on economic geography, Krugman (1991a,b) proposes an alternative version of the thick labor market hypothesis. He argues that an advantage

---

[44] Indirect support for this hypothesis can be found in Baumgardner (1988), who finds that doctors perform a narrower and more specialized set of activities in large metropolitan areas than in small metropolitan areas.

[45] Andersson et al. (2007) show that thicker urban labor markets are associated with more assortative matching between workers and firms and argue that production complementarity and assortative matching are important sources of the urban productivity premium. Using a matched employer–employee database for Italy, Mion and Naticchioni (2009) also find important amount of assortative matching.

of thick labor markets is that idiosyncratic demand shocks to firms are less likely to affect equilibrium wages. To see why it may matter, consider a firm experiencing an idiosyncratic positive productivity shock. If the labor market is thick, this firm faces a relatively flat supply of labor. If the labor market is thin, the firm faces an upward sloping supply of labor and the firm-specific shock may ultimately result in higher labor costs. Consistent with this hypothesis, Overman and Puga (forthcoming) show that industries characterized by more idiosyncratic volatility are more spatially concentrated.

In sum, thickness of the labor market is a potentially promising explanation for the agglomeration of economic activity in metropolitan areas. It is highly plausible that workers prefer to be in areas with thick labor markets because of an increased probability of a better match with an employer and a reduction in the probability of unemployment. At the same time, it is also highly plausible that firms prefer to be in areas with thick labor markets because of an increased probability of a better match with an employee and a reduction in the probability of unfilled vacancies. While intriguing, most of the existing empirical evidence is still quite indirect. This clearly is an area that should receive increased attention by labor economists in the years to come.

4.2.2. Thick market for intermediate inputs

A second possible explanation for agglomeration economies centers on the availability of specialized intermediate inputs. Concentration of specialized industrial production can support the production of non-tradable specialized inputs. The agglomeration economy in this case is generated by the sharing of inputs whose production is characterized by internal increasing returns to scale. This explanation is likely to be particularly relevant for firms that utilize intermediate inputs that are both highly specialized and non-tradable. Consider, for example, an industry where production crucially depends on the availability of specialized local producer services, such as specialized repair services, engineering services, venture capital financing, specialized legal support, or specialized shipping services. To the extent that these services are non-tradable—or are costly to deliver to distant clients—new entrants in this industry have an incentive to locate near other incumbents. By clustering near other similar firms, entrants can take advantage of an existing network of intermediate inputs suppliers. In equilibrium, cheaper, faster or more specialized supply of intermediate goods and services makes industrial clusters attractive to firms, further increasing the agglomeration. This concentration process will go on up to the point where the increase in land costs offsets the benefits of agglomeration.

While this idea has been around for a long time, the first to formalize it are Abdel Rahman and Fujita (1990), who propose a model where final goods are tradable, but intermediate inputs are non-tradable and are produced by a monopolistically competitive industry. In the model, firms that locate in dense areas share a larger and wider pool of intermediate inputs suppliers, while otherwise similar firms that locate in rural areas share a smaller and narrower pool of intermediate inputs suppliers. This difference generates agglomeration advantages because an increase in the number of firms in an area results in a wider local supply of inputs and therefore in an increase in productivity.

The evidence in Holmes (1999) offers direct support for the input sharing hypothesis. Using data on manufacturing plants, he documents that manufacturing establishments located in areas with many other establishments in the same industry make more intensive use of purchased intermediate inputs than otherwise similar manufacturing establishments in areas with fewer establishments in the same industry. Notably, this relationship only holds among industries that are geographically concentrated. Spatial proximity has limited impact on geographically dispersed industries.

Building on an idea first proposed by Rosenthal and Strange (2001), Overman and Puga (forthcoming) provide an alternative test of this hypothesis by relating measures of geographic concentration for each industry to industry-specific measures of the importance of input sharing. They find support for the notion that the availability of locally supplied inputs is an important empirical determinant of industrial clusters.

Ellison et al. (forthcoming) propose an alternative approach to the one taken by Rosenthal and Strange (2001) and Overman and Puga (forthcoming). They seek to understand the mechanics of the agglomeration process by focusing on how industries are coagglomerated. Different agglomeration theories have different predictions about which pairs of industries should coagglomerate. For example, if input markets are important, then firms in an industry should be observed to locate near industries that are their suppliers. On the other hand, if labor market pooling is important, then industries should locate near other industries that employ the same type of labor. Ellison, Glaeser and Kerr find evidence that input-output dependencies, labor pooling and knowledge spillovers are all significant determinants of agglomeration, but input-output dependencies appear to be empirically the most important channel.

4.2.3. Knowledge spillovers

Economists have long speculated that the agglomeration of human capital may generate positive spillovers, over and above its private effect.[46] Different explanations have been offered for such spillovers. For example, physical proximity with educated workers may lead to better sharing of ideas, faster innovation or faster technology adoption. Perhaps the most influential theoretical contribution in this area is the model by Lucas (1988). In that paper, human capital is assumed to have two effects. First, an individual's own human capital has the standard effect of increasing her own productivity. Second, the average aggregate level of human capital contributes to the productivity of all factors of production. This second effect is an externality, because "though all benefit from it, no individual human capital accumulation decision can have an appreciable effect on average human capital, so no one will take it into account" in deciding how much to invest in

---

[46] This question has important implications for education policies. The magnitude of the social return to education is important for assessing the efficiency of public investment in education.

human capital accumulation. In Lucas' view, human capital externalities may be large enough to explain long–run income differences between rich and poor countries. While in the model the externality is simply built into the production function in black-box fashion, Lucas posits that the sharing of knowledge and skills through formal and informal interaction may be the mechanism that generates the externality. More recent models build on this idea by assuming that individuals augment their human capital through pairwise meetings with more skilled neighbors at which they exchange ideas. Examples include Glaeser (1999),[47] Jovanovic and Rob (1989), Henderson and Black (1999), Jaffe et al. (1993), Duranton and Puga (2001) and Saxenian (1994).[48]

A second class of models explains positive human capital externalities as pecuniary externalities that arise because of search or endogenous skill–biased technical change. Consider for example the case proposed by Acemoglu (1996), where job search is costly, and physical and human capital are complements. The privately optimal amount of human capital depends on the amount of physical capital a worker expects to use. The privately optimal amount of physical capital depends on the supply of human capital. If a group of workers in a city increases its level of education, firms in that city, expecting to employ these workers, would invest more in physical capital. Since search is costly, some of the workers who have not increased their education would end up working with more physical capital and hence earn more than similar workers in other cities. As in Lucas, the presence of skilled workers in a city generates external benefits for other workers there. But what distinguishes Acemoglu's story from Lucas' story is that this result does not follow from assumptions on the production function, but rather is derived from market interactions. Even though all the production functions of the economy exhibit constant returns to scale in Acemoglu, the complementarity of human capital and physical capital, coupled with frictions in the job search process, generate a positive relationship between the average wage and average human capital, holding constant workers' individual human capital.[49]

---

[47] Glaeser (1999) argues that young workers move to cities because interactions with experienced workers help them increase their human capital.

[48] Of course, it is also possible that human capital externalities are negative. If education functions as a signal of productive ability, rather than enhancing productivity directly, the private return may exceed the social return. This is a case where people with higher innate ability signal their higher innate productivity by enduring extra years of schooling. If schooling is more difficult for individuals with low innate productivity than for individuals with high innate productivity, then, even if schooling itself is worthless in terms of enhancing productivity, it still may be a useful screening device for employers to identify more productive job applicants. In this case, increasing the average schooling in a city would result in an increase in aggregate earnings that is smaller than the private return to schooling.

[49] Although differences across cities in their *quantity* of physical capital play a central role in this model, differences in the *quality* of physical capital (technology) could arguably generate similar conclusions. Specifically, if skills and technology are complementary, it is plausible to assume that the privately optimal amount of human capital depends not only on the amount of physical capital a worker expects to use, but also on the technological level that characterizes such capital. Similarly, in models with endogenous skill-biased technical change, an increase in the supply of educated workers increases the size of the market for skill-complementary technologies and stimulates the R&D sector to spend more effort upgrading the productivity of skilled workers (Acemoglu, 1997).

There is growing empirical evidence that human capital spillovers and knowledge spillovers may be particularly important in certain high-tech industries, where innovation has been shown to be linked to human capital externalities. Because human capital spillovers and knowledge spillovers are invisible, most empirical studies resort to indirect evidence to test for the presence of spillovers. Jaffe et al. (1993) are an exception, in that they provide direct evidence of spillovers using a "paper trail" based on patent citations to test the extent to which knowledge spillovers are geographically localized. Because patents are publicly available, in the absence of localized spillovers, citations should not depend on the location of the inventor. The key empirical challenge of the paper is to distinguish between geographic patterns of patent citations caused by spillovers from patterns caused by other sources of agglomeration effects. To address this issue, the authors construct "control" samples of patents that have the same temporal and technological distribution as the patent citations and compare the two patterns of geographic concentration. They find that references to existing patents that inventors include in their patent applications are likely to come from the same state or metropolitan area as the originating patent application. They conclude that patent citations are geographically localized and that knowledge spillovers appear to be large.

In a related study, Zucker et al. (1998) argue that the presence of specialized human capital is the main determinant of the localization of biotechnology firms in the US. They show that the stock of human capital of scientists in certain cities—measured in terms of the number of publications reporting genetic-sequence discoveries in academic journals—is correlated with the location of new biotech firms. This effect may reflect, at least in part, human capital externalities, because it is not just a reflection of the presence of universities and government research centers in areas where outstanding scientists are located. The introduction of new products—spatially clusters more in industries where new knowledge plays a more important role, holding constant the degree of spatial clustering of economic activity.[50] In recent work, Carlino et al. (2007) use patents to measure innovation, and find that the number of patents per capita is positively correlated to the density of employment in the highly urbanized portion of metropolitan areas. A city with twice the employment density of another city has 20% more patents per capita. Local human capital appears to be the most important predictor of per capita rates of

---

[50] On the other hand, the exact magnitude of the spillovers is still debated. Audretsch and Feldman (1996) use data on the IPO's of biotech firms to link the location of the biotechnology firm with the location of the university-based scientists affiliated with the firm. They conclude that "while proximity matters in establishing formal ties between university-based scientists and companies, its influence is anything but overwhelming". In earlier work, Adams and Jaffe (1996) study the composition of the knowledge transfers within and across firms. They use manufacturing plant-level data to examine the productivity effects of R&D performed in a plant, outside a plant but inside the parent firm that owns the plant, and in external plants in the same geographic area or industry. They find that R&D of other firms in the same industry is correlated with a plant's own productivity, holding industry constant. However, identification is based on questionable assumptions and the potential for omitted variable bias makes it hard to draw firm conclusions about causality.

patenting. However, due to the absence of a credible research design, this study fails to establish causality.

These earlier studies are consistent with the notion that knowledge spillovers may be important in a limited number of high-tech or high-skill industries. More recent studies seek to provide more general—and often better identified—tests for human capital spillovers.

Using estimates of establishment-level production functions, Moretti (2004a) shows that manufacturing plants are significantly more productive in cities with higher human capital, holding constant individual plant human capital. The magnitude of spillovers between plants in the same city declines in economic distance as in Greenstone et al. (forthcoming). Much of the estimated spillover comes from high-tech plants. For non high-tech producers, the spillover appears to be limited. Consistent with the predictions of the spatial equilibrium model, the productivity gains uncovered by Moretti appear to be offset by increased labor costs. The estimated productivity differences between cities with high human capital and low human capital are similar to observed differences in wages of manufacturing workers, indicating an almost complete offset. While the documented productivity gains from human capital spillovers are statistically and economically meaningful, the implied contribution of human capital spillovers to economic growth does not appear to be large. Moretti estimates that human capital spillovers were responsible for an average of a 0.1% increase in output per year during the 1980s.[51]

A recent paper by Beaudry et al. (2006) proposes a hypothesis that may potentially explain Moretti's findings. They argue that over the past 30 years, technological change resulted in increases in the productivity of skilled workers in cities that had many educated workers. The estimates support the idea that differences in technology use across cities (measured by the adoption of computers) and its effects on wages reflect an equilibrium response to local factor supply conditions. In particular, cities initially endowed with relatively abundant and cheap skilled labor adopted computers more aggressively than cities with relatively expensive skilled labor, causing returns to skill to increase most in cities that adopted computers most intensively.

A growing number of studies focus on the effect of aggregate human capital on earnings. A simple framework indicates that increases in the aggregate level of human capital in a city have two distinct effects on wages. First, imperfect substitution between educated and uneducated workers indicates that an increase in the number of educated workers will lower the wage of the educated and raise the wage of uneducated workers. Second, human capital spillovers may raise the wage of both groups. Imperfect substitution and spillovers both increase wages of uneducated workers, while the impact of an increase in the supply of educated workers on their own wage is determined

---

[51] Glaeser et al. (1995) report that income per capita has grown faster in cities with high initial human capital in the post-war period.

by two competing forces: the first is the conventional supply effect which makes the economy move along a downward sloping demand curve; the second is the spillover that raises productivity. Using metropolitan areas as a definition of local labor markets, Rauch (1993) and Moretti (2004b), among others, document that wages are significantly higher in metropolitan areas with higher human capital, holding constant individual worker human capital. In particular, consistent with a model that includes both conventional demand and supply factors as well as human capital spillovers, Moretti finds that a one percentage point increase in the labor force share of college graduates increases the wages of high-school drop-outs, high-school graduates and college graduates by 1.9%, 1.6% and 0.4%, respectively. Using states as a definition of local labor markets, Acemoglu and Angrist (2000) fail to find significant evidence of human capital spillovers. A possible explanation of this difference is the evidence in recent work by Rosenthal and Strange (2008). They find that proximity to college graduates is associated with increases in wages but that these effects attenuate sharply with distance. If this is the case, it is possible that states are too large of geographic units to allow for the detection of human capital spillovers.[52]

The findings in Glaeser and Mare (2001) described above are consistent with a model where individuals acquire skills by interacting with one another, and dense urban areas increase the probability of interaction. In a related paper, Peri (2002) shows that young educated workers receive a lower wage premium in urban areas than their old educated workers, but in spite of this, young educated workers are overrepresented in urban areas. Peri argues that learning externalities are an important explanation. Workers learn from each other when they are young, so living in dense urban areas may raise human capital accumulation more than living in a rural area. The negative compensating differential indicates that young workers value such human capital externalities. As they grow older, the importance of knowledge spillovers diminishes, and some of them move toward non-urban areas.

Some studies have posited that areas with a more educated populace are more likely to generate new business ideas and new firms. This is not a market failure. However, if skilled people are more likely to innovate in ways that employ other skilled people, this creates an agglomeration economy where skilled people want to be around each other. Berry and Glaeser (2005) present evidence consistent with a model of urban agglomeration where the number of entrepreneurs is a function of the number of skilled people working in an area. Consistent with this hypothesis, Doms et al. (2009) use a new panel of startup firms to show that areas that possess more skilled labor also possess higher rates of self-employment and more skilled entrepreneurs. Moreover, conditional

---

[52] Additionally, Acemoglu and Angrist estimate spillovers coming from high school graduation. On the contrary, Moretti and Rosenthal and Strange identify spillovers coming from variation in college graduation. It is possible that an increase in the number of those who finish high-school has a different external effect than an increase in the number of those who go to college.

on owner's education, higher education levels in the local market are positively correlated with improved business outcomes.

5. IMPLICATIONS FOR POLICY

The empirical evidence surveyed in Section 4 points to the concrete possibility that agglomeration of economic activity generates significant economies of scale at the local level. It is therefore natural to raise the question of the desirability of government intervention. In a world with vast disparities in income levels across localities and with significant agglomeration externalities, what is the proper role of economic policy? Should national or local governments provide subsidies to firms to locate in their jurisdiction?

In this section, I discuss the economic rationales for location-based policies. I define location-based policies as government interventions aimed at reallocating resources from one location to another location. These policies are widespread both in the US and in the rest of the world. In the US, state and local governments spend $30–40 billion per year on these policies, while the federal government spends $8-12 billion (Bartik, 2002). Examples of location-based policies typically adopted by local and state governments include direct subsidies and/or tax incentives for local firms, subsidized loans, industrial parks, technology transfer programs, export assistance and export financing, the provision of infrastructure, workforce training, subsidies to higher education and area marketing. Bartik (1991) provides a comprehensive taxonomy and discussion of the different types of policies. More generally, states and cities compete based on income and corporate tax rates, labor and environmental regulations, and many other forms of intervention that affect the relative profitability for firms of locating in each jurisdiction. The US federal government also promotes several location-based policies. The Tennessee Valley Authority and the Appalachian Regional Commission are important historical examples of large federal programs that target poor rural areas for development aid. A more recent example is the Federal Empowerment Zones Program, which is a system of subsidies for businesses located in poor urban neighborhoods. Location-based policies are also widespread in Europe in the form of European Union regional transfers; and in Asia, in the form of special economic zones.[53]

In general, economists think that there are two possible rationales for government intervention in the economy: equity and efficiency. Location-based policies are no exception. I begin in Section 5.1 by discussing several aspects of the equity rationale. In Section 5.2, I turn to the efficiency rationale. Bartik (1991, 2002) and

---

[53] A prominent example of the latter is the successful program adopted by the government of Taiwan to subsidize R&D in semi-conductors and other high-tech fields.

Glaeser and Gottlieb (2009) provide authoritative discussions of the economic rationales for local subsidies with somewhat differing conclusions on their desirability.[54]

5.1. Equity considerations

5.1.1. Incidence of subsidies

It is tempting for policymakers to support policies intended to help disadvantaged areas. The main argument in favor of these policies is that by helping disadvantaged areas, the government helps disadvantaged individuals. The spatial equilibrium model outlined in Section 3 suggests that this argument is at least in part flawed, since the poor are unlikely to fully capture the benefits of location-based subsidies. In a world where workers are mobile, targeting locations instead of individuals is an ineffective way of helping disadvantaged individuals.

To see this more concretely, I consider first the case where subsidies for firms to locate in a given locality are financed by the central government, and then the case where subsidies are financed locally.

(a) Centrally financed subsidies Consider a location-based redistributive policy intended to help disadvantaged areas. Assume for example that the central government taxes residents of areas with high (nominal) income to provide subsidies to firms to locate in areas with low (nominal) income. Most countries have these types of redistributive policies. An example of this policy in the US is the Empowerment Zones Program mentioned above. Another example is represented by the ubiquitous state policies designed to attract businesses to poor parts of their jurisdiction. In Canada, an equalization program transfers income from high income provinces to low income provinces. The European Union has a similar transfer program aimed at transferring EU development funds to regions with below average income.[55]

The incidence of this policy and its redistributive implications ultimately depend on the elasticity of local labor supply and housing supply. Section 3 clarifies that if workers are highly mobile, they will arbitrage some or all of the benefits associated with this transfer by relocating to the area favored by the transfer, thus bidding up the price of housing. In the case of high elasticity of local labor supply and less than infinite elasticity of housing supply, this increase in housing prices will offset most of the welfare gains that might otherwise accrue to existing residents.[56] In the extreme case of perfect mobility,

---

[54] Boarnet and Bogart (1996), Goolsbee and Maydew (2000), Faulk (2002), Bennmarker et al. (2009), Bondonio and Engberg (2000), Peters and Fisher (2002), Greenstone and Moretti (2004), Greenstone et al. (forthcoming) provide recent estimates of the employment effects of local subsidies. The last two papers have a discussion of the policy implications of these subsidies. Work by Bartik (1991) and Papke (1993, 1994) represent important early contributions that helped to frame the policy debate on location-based policies in economic terms. See also Wasylenko (1997).

[55] Similarly, one can think of a direct subsidy to residents of poor areas. For example, the national government could tax residents of areas with high (nominal) income to provide a transfer to residents of areas with low (nominal) income. This type of redistribution has similar implications.

[56] Of course, an infinitely elastic supply of housing would prevent this price increase.

increases in the price of housing fully offset the transfer. In this setting, location-based redistributive policies intended to help areas with low nominal income have virtually no effect on the utility of workers. The only beneficiaries of this policy are landowners in the targeted areas. Effectively, this policy amounts to a transfer of wealth from landowners in the rest of the country to landowners in the targeted areas. If the theoretical model is a fair approximation of the real world, then its basic premises cast considerable doubt on the desirability of redistributing income from areas with high income to areas with low income.[57]

How does this conclusion change if labor is not highly mobile? The model in Section 3 indicates that if individuals have significant preferences over specific locations, labor is less mobile. In this case, the *marginal* worker is indifferent across locations, but the *average* worker is not and location-based redistributive policies have the potential to affect the utility of the average worker. In particular, inframarginal workers in rich areas experience an increase in taxes and a decrease in the cost of living, while inframarginal workers in poor areas experience an increase in transfers and an increase in the cost of living. Overall, the redistributive effect is complicated and unlikely to be clear ex-ante, because it crucially depends on individual preferences for location, which are unlikely to be observed by policy makers. This lack of observability makes it difficult to implement policies of this type in practice.

Busso et al. (2009) provide the first comprehensive empirical welfare analysis of a location-based policy, namely the Empowerment Zones program. Using a remarkably detailed series of data from the Census of Population, the Longitudinal Business database and the Standard Statistical Establishment List, together with an identification strategy based on areas that applied for the credits but did not receive it, they are able to credibly quantify the incidence and deadweight loss of the program. Consistent with the spatial equilibrium model outlined in Section 3, they find that both wages and housing values increase significantly in the neighborhoods that benefit from the federal subsidy relative to the counterfactual neighborhoods in rejected zones. This increase is consistent with an upward sloping local supply of labor.

In terms of incidence, Busso et al. (2009) find that the program unambiguously benefits landowners in Empowerment Zone areas. This increase in housing values is not particularly surprising. Together with the failure to find any changes in overall area population, the increase in housing values indicates that the supply of housing is inelastic, at least in the short run. More surprisingly, the program also benefits workers who reside in the area, since they experience an increase in nominal wages larger than the increase in housing costs. Based on the model in Section 3, this finding is consistent with the

---

[57] In some cases, these types of policies may even have perverse consequences for targeted localities. Since the early 1970's, the Canadian Unemployment Insurance program—a federal program—has been regionally differentiated, with more generous benefits in high unemployment areas. There is considerable evidence that this feature has had significant undesirable side effects. See Kuhn and Riddell (2010), for example.

presence of significant locational preferences on the part of residents. Workers who live in the targeted areas appear to have strong preferences for their current residence, so that their mobility is limited. This is notable, because the treated areas are neighborhoods within much larger metropolitan areas, and it is in principle possible to commute into the Empowerment Zone areas from the rest of the metropolitan area without having to change residence. Given the finding of small deadweight losses, the overall welfare assessment of the program appears encouraging.

Busso et al. (2009) also find that the provision of Empowerment Zone subsidies results in an increase in the productivity of local firms. While it is difficult to identify the exact channel for this productivity increase, three plausible candidates are: an improvement in public infrastructure or other local public goods; some form of agglomeration economy; the role of the subsidies as a coordination mechanism for private investment. Because of the nature of the subsidy and the type of production that is common in empowerment zone areas, the most plausible candidate appears to be the last one.

(b) Locally financed subsidies I consider now the case where local taxpayers bear the cost of subsidizing firms that locate in their jurisdiction. The welfare effects of this type of policy depend on how similar the locations competing to attract new firms are. In particular, in the case of homogenous locations, a locally financed subsidy has no effect on residents' welfare since all the rent associated with the subsidy is transferred to the firm. In the case of heterogenous locations, a locally financed subsidy will benefit landowners by an amount proportional to the difference in production cost between the location with the most desirable attributes and the location with the second most desirable attributes. The effect on workers depends on the importance of their preferences for location. Limited preferences for locations imply high mobility and therefore limited welfare changes. Significant preferences for locations imply low mobility and therefore significant welfare changes for inframarginal individuals.

To see this, I use the framework proposed by Greenstone and Moretti (2004). I assume that local governments bid to attract new firms to their jurisdiction by offering subsidies, and that the cost of the subsidy is financed by increases in local property taxes, and therefore is capitalized into land values. Let V_{ij} denote the benefit of the increase in the level of economic activity generated by new firm j for locality i, assumed to be known to all the other localities.[58] Unlike in the case examined in the previous subsection—where the subsidy was paid for by the central government—here a successful bid now involves a trade-off for a locality. Let C_{ij} denote the direct monetary cost of the subsidy. The partial equilibrium change in welfare for the winning county can be expressed as $V_{ij} - C_{ij}$.

---

[58] This is equal to the change in utility for local residents and landowners. If labor is mobile, workers are always indifferent, and landowners are the only set of agents whose welfare may be affected. If workers have preferences for location, however, both workers and landowners are affected. While this type of subsidy is quite common in practice, it is not always obvious what localities seek to maximize in this process. One possibility is that, in the presence of unemployment, localities seek to maximize job creation. My theoretical model in Section 3 is a full employment model that by construction rules out unemployment.

Let the value to firm j of locating in county i be Z_{ij}. Due to differences in technology, the same locality may be more or less attractive to different firms.[59] A higher Z_{ij} implies that the production costs of firm j are lower in locality i. I assume that Z is known to all localities. The total value for a firm of locating in a particular locality is the sum of the subsidy and the county-specific cost advantages. A firm will select the locality where this sum, $B_{ij} + Z_{ij}$, is maximized. In order to obtain the highest subsidy, I assume that the firms conduct an English auction in the presence of independent, or private, values. I further assume that there is no collusion in the bidding among counties.

Consider the case where counties are homogeneous in V and Z: $V_{ij} = V_0$ and $Z_{ij} = Z_0$ for all i. In this case, the firm simply chooses the location that offers the highest subsidy, B. The equilibrium bid, B^*, is $B^* = V_0$. This implies that successfully attracting the firm does not change residents' welfare: $V_0 - B^* = 0$. The reason is that each jurisdiction keeps raising its bids until it is indifferent between winning and losing, so that the equilibrium bid is such that the entire economic rent is transferred to the firm. In this case landowners are indifferent, since the benefit of the new firm is fully offset by the increase in property taxes. This result is similar to the result in the tax competition literature where local jurisdictions keep taxes on capital low because of a fear of capital flight.

Consider now the more general case where counties' valuations of attracting the plant and plants' valuations of counties are heterogenous. Assume for simplicity that there are only two locations, high V (V_H) and low V (V_L); and two levels of Z, high Z (Z_H) and low Z, (Z_L). If V and Z are positively correlated, the location with high V also has high Z. In this case, this location gains the most from attracting firm j and it is also the most attractive to firm j. The optimal bid is such that the firm is indifferent between moving to either city. Unlike the homogenous case, where all the economic rent is bid away, in this case, the H county enjoys an economic rent that comes from the fact that it has characteristics that are desirable to the firm.

If labor is highly mobile, and housing is inelastically supplied, this economic rent will be capitalized into land values. In particular, land values increase by an amount $(V_H - V_L) + (Z_H - Z_L) > 0$, proportional to the difference in V and the difference in Z. The same intuition applies to the case where V and Z are negatively correlated, and location 1 has high V and low Z, while location 2 has high Z and low V. If $V_H + Z_L > V_L + Z_H$, location 1 wins the firm by bidding an amount B^* that makes the firm indifferent: $B^* = V_L + (Z_H - Z_L)$. As in the case of positive correlation between Z and V, the winning location enjoys a rent that is capitalized in land values, although the rent is lower than the rent in the case of positive correlation: $(V_H - V_L) - (Z_H - Z_L) > 0$. A similar conclusion applies if $V_H + Z_L < V_L + Z_H$. In this case location 2 is the winner and its land prices increase by $(Z_H - Z_L) - (V_H - V_L) > 0$.

[59] For example, the presence of a harbor, an airport or a freeway may be more important for some productions than others. Similarly, the presence of stringent environmental or labor regulations may affect some firms more than others.

5.1.2. Taxes and transfers based on nominal income

An important redistributive implication of the spatial equilibrium model has to do with federal taxation and federal transfers. Federal taxes and transfers are calculated based on nominal income. By setting taxes and federal transfers in nominal terms, the federal government engages in a hidden form of location-based redistribution, because workers with the same real income pay higher federal taxes in high-cost areas than in low-cost areas. Albouy (2009) estimates that workers in cities where nominal wages are above the national average pay up to 27% more in federal taxes than similar workers in cities where nominal wages are below the national average. As a consequence, $270 billion each year are transferred from areas with high nominal wages to areas with low nominal wages.

In equilibrium, if workers are mobile, wages and land prices should adjust to compensate workers. However, the resulting geographic distribution of employment is inefficient, since it penalizes highly productive cities and favors less productive cities. In other words, this policy artificially lowers economic activity and property values in cities where labor is more productive and nominal wages are higher. At the same time it increases economic activity and property values in cities where labor is less productive and nominal wages are lower. The net result is a loss in overall welfare. Albouy calculates that the long-run employment loss in high nominal wage areas is about 13%, while the loss in land and housing values is about 21% and 5%, respectively. Albouy suggests that one solution is to make taxes independent of where workers live so that they are effectively lump sum location-wise.

A related problem arises when thinking about transfer payments. Should they be based on nominal or real income? Using a spatial equilibrium model similar to the one in Section 3, Glaeser (1998) derives the conditions under which welfare payments should be adjusted for differences in the local cost of living. He concludes that the optimal transfer depends on mobility and preferences for amenities. In the case of perfect mobility, transfer payments that correct for differences in the local cost of living are inefficient, because they end up being capitalized in the price of land, further raising land costs in expensive areas. With limited mobility, a correction for local cost of living differences is optimal under the assumption that amenities and income are complements.

5.1.3. Nominal and real differences across skill groups and regions

The spatial equilibrium model has implications for how one should measure earnings and income differences between skill groups or between regions. In most countries, there are large cost of living differences across regions. These differences are typically largely driven by differences in the price of land. When comparing earnings or income across skill groups or across regions, the question arises of whether nominal measures should be used or whether real measures should be used. This question matters because the magnitude of income differences between skill groups or between regions has implications for the desirability of redistributive policies.

Earnings differences between skill groups Consider the increase in earnings inequality in the US labor market in the past three decades. As documented by a large literature in labor economics, starting in 1980 the nominal earnings of skilled workers have grown significantly faster than the nominal earnings of unskilled workers. In the same period, there have been increasing differences in the geographic distribution of skilled and unskilled workers. Skilled workers have increasingly concentrated in cities with high costs of land, while unskilled workers have increasingly concentrated in cities with low costs of land. This geographic sorting suggests that skilled workers might have experienced higher increases in the cost of living.

Consistent with this hypothesis, Moretti (forthcoming) finds that earnings inequality measured in *real* terms has grown significantly less than earnings inequality in *nominal* terms. The model in Section 3 shows that the implications for utility inequality depend on the underlying reasons for the geographic sorting. If the sorting of skilled workers into more expensive cities is driven by increases in the relative demand of skilled labor in those cities, the increase in relative utility of skilled workers is smaller than the increase in their nominal wage. On the other hand, if the sorting of college graduates into more expensive cities is driven by an increase in the relative supply for skilled labor in those cities (i.e. an increase in the attraction of local amenities), increases in the cost of living in these cities reflect the increased attractiveness of the cities for skilled workers. In this case, there may still be a significant increase in utility inequality even if the increase in real wage inequality is limited. Moretti (forthcoming) argues that the evidence is more consistent with the notion that shifts in the relative demand for skilled labor are the main force driving changes in the number of skilled workers across metropolitan areas and that the increase in well-being inequality is smaller than the increase in nominal wage inequality. These results are related to a paper by Black et al. (2005) which, along with earlier work by Dahl (2002), criticizes the standard practice of treating the returns to education as uniform across locations. They show that, in theory, the return to schooling is constant across locations only in the special case of homothetic preferences, and argue that the returns to education are empirically lower in high-amenity locations.[60]

Regional differences in income and poverty A related question arises when measuring earnings or income differences across locations. Using data for five US regions, Slesnick (2002) shows that regional comparisons of poverty rates based on nominal figures give a different picture than regional comparisons of poverty rates based on real figures. Consistent with the spatial equilibrium model, Slesnick shows that disparities in real income across regions are smaller when cost of living differentials are accounted for, so that the prevalence of poverty across regions changes significantly. For example, rural

---

[60] In a related paper, Black et al. (2009) argue that estimates of the wage differences between blacks and whites need to account for differences in the geographic location of different racial groups. They argue that accounting for geography changes the estimates of the speed of convergence between black and white earnings. They also develop a theoretical model to understand when estimates of the black-white earnings gap can be used to infer welfare differences.

areas and Southern states have a relatively low cost of living. As a consequence, poverty rates for rural areas and for many urban areas in the South are significantly closer to the rest of the country when real income is used instead of nominal income.

While this evidence is a useful first step, it is likely that an analysis at the regional level misses important intra-regional variation in the cost of living. A geographically more detailed analysis based on city-level data may uncover an even stronger effect of cost of living differences on the geographic distribution of poverty rates.

5.1.4. Subsidies to human capital when labor is mobile

In the spatial equilibrium model, workers' mobility determines the incidence of location-based government policies through their effects on land prices. Areas that benefit from government transfers experience an increase in the price of land that offsets (at least in part) the benefit of the transfer. However, in reality, workers' mobility may affect the incidence of location-based government policies even in the absence of local price changes. A salient example is the case of subsidies to human capital accumulation. Localized human capital externalities of the type discussed in Section 4.2.3 represent an important efficiency rationale for the provision of public subsidies to investment in human capital. However, in the presence of significant worker mobility it is not clear who ultimately benefits from these subsidies. Consider for example the case of subsidies to higher education. State and local government cover a larger fraction of higher education expenditures.[61] Yet, the high mobility of educated workers across states implies that part of the investment in human capital made by one state may benefit other states. Bound et al. (2004) quantify the magnitude of this problem by relating the production of new college graduates in a state to the stock of college-educated workers in the state. They find that the elasticity of stocks to flows is approximately 0.3 for BA's. This elasticity is even lower for students with medical degrees. This implies a high degree of migration. In a simple static model of where the supply and demand for college graduates determine the stock of college graduates, increases in the stock of college graduates due to increases in supply should lead to lower relative wages for college graduates, whereas increases in the stock due to increased demand should result in higher wages. The empirical results in Bound et al. (2004) are consistent with the prediction that inelastic local demand causes the effect of flows on stocks to be smaller. Additionally, a regression of relative wages on relative stocks indicates that the elasticity of wages to stocks is negative, consistent with some areas exporting college graduates and others importing them. Using more recent data, Bartik (2009) finds lower mobility rates of skilled workers and therefore concludes that state investment in higher education is not completely dissipated by labor mobility.

---

[61] For example, the current subsidy of direct costs to students at major public universities in the US is around 80%.

5.2. Efficiency considerations

The previous subsection concluded that the equity rationale for public transfers that target locations instead of individuals is generally not very compelling. A second possible rationale for government intervention has to do with efficiency. The key question in this respect is: are there market failures that suggest that governments should use taxpayer money to provide efficiency enhancing subsidies to firms to locate in their jurisdiction? In the absence of significant market failures, it is difficult to justify the use of taxpayer money for subsidies based on efficiency grounds. Here I consider four possible market failures.

5.2.1. Internalizing agglomeration spillovers

Local economic development policies are carried out both by local governments and by national governments.[62] To draw normative implications, it is therefore important to distinguish the point of view of a locality—which maximizes its own local welfare without consideration for aggregate welfare—from the point of view of the central government, which maximizes aggregate welfare.

Local welfare From the point of view of a local government, the most important efficiency rationale for location-based incentives is the existence of significant agglomeration externalities. This rationale hinges on whether the attraction of new businesses generates some form of external benefits to other firms in the same locality. If the attraction of new business generates localized positive agglomeration externalities, then the provision of subsidies may be able to generate the efficient allocation of resources in the local economy.[63]

In a static setting, the optimal magnitude of these incentives depends on the magnitude of agglomerations externalities. The literature described in Sections 4.1 and 4.2 suggests that these externalities may be important empirically, although there is still debate on their exact magnitude and the mechanisms that generate them.

In a dynamic setting, the existence of significant agglomeration economies has the potential to generate multiple equilibria. Kline (2010) proposes a simple theoretical framework that is useful in thinking about the magnitude of the efficient subsidy in the presence of multiple equilibria. In this case, the magnitude of the optimal subsidy is more complicated to derive, because it depends on the exact shape of Marshallian

---

[62] In the case of the European Union, some location-based policies are financed by the Union itself, which is an international government.

[63] An additional, although arguably less important, rationale that has been proposed for subsidies to attract new firms—and especially headquarters—has to do with charitable contributions. Card et al. (2007) document that attracting the headquarters of a publicly traded firm yields $3-10 million per year in contributions to local non-profits. Most of the increase in charitable contributions appears to be linked to the number of highly-compensated individuals in a city, rather than through direct donations by the corporations themselves. From a normative point of view, this rationale is not unassailable. Given the magnitude of the subsidies often required to attract headquarters, if this was the only benefit of attracting headquarters, there is no reason why the municipality should not have provided subsidies directly to the non-profit sector.

dynamics. Consider for example the case where the productivity of firms in a locality is a function of the number of other similar firms in that locality so that attracting new firms to a locality raises the productivity of all the firms in that locality (as in Greenstone et al., forthcoming). If the magnitude of this agglomeration externality is large enough, it is possible that the demand for labor is locally upward sloping, since more firms in a locality imply both more workers and higher productivity (as in Eq. (41) above). As discussed in Section 3.3, this setting is inherently characterized by multiple equilibria, with some equilibria featuring low levels of economic activity, low productivity and low nominal wages and other equilibria featuring high levels of economic activity, high productivity and high nominal wages. The size of the efficient subsidy can vary enormously, depending on the exact functional form of Marshallian dynamics, and on the starting point. On the one hand, if a locality is located at an unstable tipping point, a very limited subsidy can be enough to move it to a new equilibrium with an higher level of economic activity and agglomeration. On the other hand, if a locality is trapped in a stable bad equilibrium, "Big Push" type of policies may be needed to move it to a good equilibrium (Kline, 2010).

In this context, government intervention in the form of subsidies for firms to locate in the jurisdiction has the potential to start an agglomeration process that can ultimately shift a locality from a bad equilibrium (small agglomeration, low productivity) to a good equilibrium (large agglomeration, high productivity). The provision of a subsidy can have substantial and long lasting effects on the equilibrium level of economic activity in a locality.[64] Indeed, the expectation of government intervention alone may play a role in shifting a locality from a bad to a good equilibrium. In this case, the government policy acts as a coordination mechanism that signals to workers and firms which locality among all existing localities will move to a good equilibrium in the future. If firms and workers take this signal as credible, they will move to that jurisdiction, effectively realizing the expected outcome. In practice, it is implausible to expect that announcements alone are effective enough to have substantial real-world effects on the localization of economic activity. But it is plausible to think that in the presence of multiple equilibria, expectations together with the actual provision of subsidies might play a non-trivial role in the localization of firms and workers across locations.

In the presence of multiple equilibria, the efficiency benefits for location-based policies have the potential to be quite large relative to the efficiency costs. Consider the case where the provision of location based subsidies attracts new businesses to a location and move the locality from a bad equilibrium (low density of economic activity) to a good equilibrium (high density of economic activity). In this case the short-run efficiency costs of providing location-based subsidies could be small compared to the potential long-run benefits of moving to a better equilibrium.

---

[64] Of course, the process of agglomeration in this case would continue up to the point where the productivity advantages of agglomeration are offset by the increase in land prices (Section 3.3).

Aggregate welfare The efficiency argument, however, has different implications if one takes the point of view of the national government instead of the local government. For the point of view of a national government, the main concern is that the provision of subsidies by local governments may result in a zero-sum game, where the jobs created in targeted areas come at the expense of jobs elsewhere. In this context, justifying such policies requires a rationale for moving jobs from one location to another. In their comprehensive overview of the issue, Glaeser and Gottlieb (2009) argue that the only such rationale is for local agglomeration economies to be stronger on the margin in targeted areas. In other words, aggregate efficiency would require subsidies to favor areas that are more productive and where the elasticity of productivity with respect to agglomeration is higher. To achieve this efficient allocation, policy makers need to know the exact functional form of the spillover function. In practice, this functional form is still largely unknown, because it is difficult to estimate credibly. Given the difficulty of identifying the magnitude of agglomeration economies under a linearity assumption, it is not surprising that we still do not have a good idea of possible nonlinearities. Because of this difficulty, Glaeser and Gottleib conclude that policy-makers still do not have enough information to implement location-based policies that are efficient from the aggregate point of view.

However, when the benefits of attracting a new firm are highly heterogeneous, it is in principle possible that competition among localities may result in aggregate efficiency gains. Greenstone et al. (forthcoming) document one example of significant heterogeneity in productivity spillovers. Using the methodology described in Section 4.1, they present location-specific estimates of the impact on TFP of incumbent plants of new plant openings. Their Fig 2. reveals that there is substantial heterogeneity in the estimated spillover. Importantly, the magnitude of the productivity spillover does not appear to be random, but it varies systematically with easily observable features of the new plant. In particular, Greenstone, Hornbeck and Moretti document that the productivity spillover generated by the opening of a new large manufacturing plant is larger for incumbent plants that share similar labor and technology pools with the new plant.[65] It appears plausible in this case that policy makers are able to evaluate the potential value to their locality of attracting the new plant because this value depends on the degree of proximity of the local labor and technology pools to those of the new plant. This type of heterogeneity is important because it allows for the possibility of aggregate efficiency gains. National welfare is maximized when payments are made to plants that produce the spillovers so that they internalize this externality in making their location decision. In this case the locality that has the most to gain is the one that successfully attracts the new plant. The decentralized equilibrium in the presence of significant heterogeneity in

---

[65] By contrast, using a different methodology Glaeser and Gottlieb (2009) find little evidence that agglomeration economies vary systematically based on the easily observable characteristics of metropolitan areas. For example, they find that agglomeration economies do not appear to depend on city size or on urban amenities.

productivity spillovers together with the assumption that the potential value of attracting the new plant is known to each locality is not necessarily inconsistent with aggregate efficiency. From the equity point of view, the discussion of a locally financed subsidy in Section 5.1.1 suggests that in this case some but not all of the economic rent generated by the spillover ends up being transferred to the new firm. In particular, the locality that has the most to gain should only capture the fraction of the overall benefit that reflects the difference in production costs between the location with the most desirable attributes and the location with the second most desirable attributes.

5.2.2. Unemployment, missing insurance and credit constraints

Besides the existence of agglomeration externalities, there are three additional market failures that can in principle justify location-based policies.

First, wages may not be fully responsive to local shocks. Consider the case of idiosyncratic shocks to localities, where some cities or states are hit by negative demand shocks while other are not. The theoretical model in Section 3 is a full employment model, where wages always adjust fully to local shocks. The model indicates that if workers are mobile, and wages fully adjust, counter-cyclical transfers to localities hit by negative shocks will only have a limited effect on workers' welfare. However, the model effectively assumes away unemployment. In reality, wages may not be fully responsive to local labor market conditions, at least in the short run. If wages are not fully responsive, negative demand shocks will cause socially costly involuntary unemployment. In this case, countercyclical transfers from the central government have the potential to improve aggregate welfare. Of course, this potential welfare gain should be weighed against the distortionary cost of government intervention.

Second, even with full employment, homeowners are exposed to localized demand shocks, and there is no market-provided insurance to insure against such shocks. As explained in Section 3, shocks to a local economy affect the residents' value of housing, unless the elasticity of housing supply is infinite. Since housing is the most important asset for most households, the amount of risk generated by these shocks can be large. Existing financial instruments make it difficult to diversify housing risk. In this context, redistributive countercyclical policies that are centrally financed and target localities hit by negative idiosyncratic shocks may in principle act as government-provided insurance against housing value risk that the market does not insure. This policy effectively acts as a redistributive mechanism that transfers resources from homeowners in areas affected by positive shocks to homeowners in areas affected by negative shocks, thus reducing risk.

However, it is not clear that in practice these policies improve efficiency. First, there is the general deadweight loss of government intervention. Second, and more importantly, homeowners and workers often coincide. An optimal insurance scheme should therefore take into account both housing risk and wage risk. This is very difficult to do in practice because the correlation between housing values and wages is complicated. For example, the model with heterogenous labor in Section 3 has shown that if workers have idiosyncratic preferences for location, the effect of a localized shock on a worker's welfare depends on that worker's skill level and location. If labor and housing supply elasticities are less then infinite, inframarginal skilled workers in the locality that receives a positive skill-biased productivity shock (city b) experience an increase in utility, while inframarginal unskilled workers experience a decrease. Inframarginal workers in city a, the city not directly affected by the shock, experience an increase in utility, irrespective of their skill level. In other words, in the example of the model, wages and housing values are negatively correlated for unskilled workers and for skilled workers in city a, but positively correlated for skilled workers in city b. This makes an efficient location-based insurance policy difficult to implement in practice.

Finally, the private and social costs of mobility might not be the same. When workers are mobile, and the private cost of mobility and the social cost of mobility are identical, the spatial adjustment that follows a negative shock to an area may be efficient. However, as pointed out by Blanchard and Katz (1992), credit constraints may introduce a wedge between the private and social costs of mobility. For example, following a negative shock to an area, workers without access to credit may be forced to leave even when it is optimal for them to borrow and wait for the equilibrium to be reestablished. This would lead to a socially inefficient degree of adjustment through mobility and may provide justification for efficiency-enhancing government intervention.

6. CONCLUSIONS

Understanding local labor markets is important for labor economists. The last three decades have witnessed a growing amount of empirical research on the causes and consequences of localization of workers and firms within a country. This area, at the intersection of labor and urban economics, contains important but challenging questions and is likely to generate an increasing share of high quality empirical research in the next decade.

Besides the obvious relevance for labor economists directly working on these topics, the idea of spatial equilibrium discussed in this chapter has a broader relevance for labor economists in general. It is difficult to understand the effect of nationwide labor demand changes on wages and employment without considering the role played by the spatial reallocation of labor and general equilibrium effects on local prices. Labor flows across localities and changes in local prices have the potential to undo some of the direct effects of labor market shocks.

The spatial equilibrium model presented in this chapter is a useful tool to think about the incidence of demand shocks when general equilibrium feedbacks are important. The version of the model that I propose in Section 3 is kept deliberately simple, so that all the equilibrium outcomes have transparent, closed-form solutions. Moreover, it is scalable, in the sense that it is relatively easy to relax some of the assumptions, in order to adapt it to particular circumstances. The hope is that other researchers may find the framework useful in future work.

The survey of the empirical literature in Section 4 points to a growing body of solid empirical evidence on the existence of significant agglomeration economies. Although the econometric challenges—identification in particular—have proven in many cases difficult to fully overcome, there appears to be general agreement that agglomeration economies at the city level are empirically significant for many industries. While there is still debate on the exact economic magnitude of these externalities, many studies point to externalities of an economically non-trivial magnitude.

The last decade has also witnessed increasing efforts by researchers to pinpoint the precise mechanisms that might generate agglomeration economies. This is crucial to obtaining a convincing picture of the agglomeration phenomenon. Without understanding the precise mechanisms that generate agglomeration economies it is difficult to be confident about the existence of these externalities and to draw definitive conclusions for local development policies. Moreover, the three leading explanations imply different types of market failures and therefore call for different types of policy response. While the literature has produced a number of insightful empirical studies on the three possible mechanisms, overall the literature has not been completely successful in distinguishing between their relative importance. I share the view expressed by Glaeser and Gottlieb (2008) in a recent survey of this literature, when they conclude that "the field has still not reached a consensus on the relative importance of different sources of agglomeration economies". Given the important policy implications, more work is clearly needed on this topic.

Understanding the causes and the consequences of agglomeration of economic activity is crucial to understanding the economic rationale for location-based policies and their welfare consequences. These policies are widespread, but their economic rationales are not always clear. The discussion in Section 5 indicates that in a world where workers are mobile, targeting locations instead of individuals is an ineffective means of helping disadvantaged individuals. In a world with significant agglomeration spillovers, government intervention may be efficient from the point of view of a locality, although not always from the point of view of aggregate welfare.

REFERENCES

Abdel Rahman, Hesham M., Fujita, Masahisa, 1990. Product variety, Marshallian externalities, and city sizes. Journal of Regional Science 30 (2), 165–183.

Acemoglu, Daron, 1996. A microfoundation for social increasing returns in human capital accumulation. Quarterly Journal of Economics 11 (August), 779–804.

Acemoglu, Daron, 1997. Training and innovation in imperfect labor markets. Review of Economic Studies.

Acemoglu, Daron, Angrist, Joshua, 2000. How large are human capital externalities? Evidence from compulsory schooling laws. NBER Macroeconomic Annual 15.

Adams, James D., Jaffe, Adam B., 1996. Bounding the effects of R&D: an investigation using matched establishment-firm data. RAND Journal of Economics, The RAND Corporation 27 (4), 700–721.

Albouy, David, 2009. The unequal geographic burden of federal taxation. Journal of Political Economy 117 (4), 635–667.

Andersson, Fredrik, Simon, Burgess, Lane, Julia I., 2007. Cities, matching and the productivity gains of agglomeration. Journal of Urban Economics 61 (1), 112–128.

Arzaghi, Mohammad, Henderson, J. Vernon, 2008. Networking off Madison Avenue. Review of Economic Studies 75 (4), 1011–1038.

Audretsch, David B., Feldman, Maryann P., 1996. R&D spillovers and the geography of innovation and production. American Economic Review 86 (3), 630–640.

Barro, R.J., Sala-i-Martin, X., 1991. Brookings Papers on Economic Activity.

Bartik, Tim, 1991. Who Benefits from State and Local Economic Development Policies? W.E. Upjohn Institute, Kalamazoo, MI.

Bartik, Timothy J., 2002. Evaluating the impacts of local economic development policies on local economic outcomes: what has been done and what is doable? Upjohn Working Papers 03-89, W.E. Upjohn Institute for Employment Research.

Bartik, Timothy J., 2009. What proportion of children stay in the same location as adults, and how does this vary across location and groups? Upjohn Working Papers 09-145, W.E. Upjohn Institute for Employment Research.

Baumgardner, James R., 1988. The division of labor, local markets, and worker organization. Journal of Political Economy 96 (3), 509–527.

Beaudry, Paul, Doms, Mark, Lewis, Ethan, 2006. Endogenous skill bias in technology adoption: city-level evidence from the IT revolution. NBER Working Papers 12521, National Bureau of Economic Research, Inc.

Bennmarker, Helge, Mellander, Erik, Öckert, Björn, 2009. Do Regional payroll tax reductions boost employment? Labour Economics 16, 480–489.

Berry, Christopher R., Glaeser, Edward L., 2005. The divergence of human capital levels across cities. NBER Working Papers 11617, National Bureau of Economic Research.

Black, Dan, Kolesnikova, N., Taylor, L., 2009. Earnings functions when wages and prices vary by location. Journal of Labor Economics 27 (1), 21–48.

Black, Dan, McKinnish, Terra, Sanders, Seth, 2005. The economic impact of the coal boom and bust. The Economic Journal 115 (April), 449–476.

Blanchard, Olivier, Katz, Larry, 1992. Regional evolutions. Brookings Papers on Economic Activity.

Bleakley, Hoyt, Lin, Jeffrey, 2006. Thick-market effects and churning in the labor market: evidence from US Cities, mimeo. University of Chicago.

Boarnet, Marlon, Bogart, William, 1996. Enterprise zones and employment: evidence from New Jersey. Journal of Urban Economics 40, 198–215.

Bondonio, Daniele, Engberg, John, 2000. Enterprise zones and local employment: evidence from the states' programs. Regional Science and Urban Economics 30 (5), 519–549.

Bound, John, Holzer, Harry J., 2000. Demand shifts, population adjustments, and labor market outcomes during the 1980s. Journal of Labor Economics 18 (1), 20–54.

Bound, John, Groen, Jeffrey, Kezdi, G. Gabor, Turner, Sarah, 2004. Trade in university training: cross-state variation in the production and stock of college-educated labor. Journal of Econometrics 121 (1–2), 143–173.

Busso, Matias, Gregory, Jesse, Kline, Patrick, 2009. Assessing the incidence and efficiency of a prominent place based policy, mimeo.

Card, David, Hallock, Kevin F., Moretti, Enrico, 2007. The geography of giving: the effect of corporate headquarters on local charities. University of California, Berkeley Mimeograph.

Carlino, Gerald A., Chatterjee, Satyajit, Hunt, Robert M., 2007. Urban density and the rate of invention. Journal of Urban Economics 61 (3), 389–419.

Carrington, William J., 1996. The Alaskan labor market during the pipeline era. Journal of Political Economy 104 (February).

Ciccone, Antonio, Hall, Robert E., 1996. Productivity and the density of economic activity. American Economic Review 86 (1), 54–70.

Combes, Pierre Philippe, Duranton, Gilles, Gobillon, Laurent, Puga, Diego, Roux, Sebastien, 2009. The productivity advantages of large cities: distinguishing agglomeration from firm selection. Discussion Paper 7191, Centre for Economic Policy Research.

Combes, Pierre Philippe, Duranton, Gilles, Overman, Henry G., 2005. Agglomeration and the adjustment of the spatial economy. Papers in Regional Science 84 (3), 311–349.

Costa, Dora L., Kahn, Matthew E., 2000. Power couples: changes in the locational choice of the college educated, 19401990. Quarterly Journal of Economics 115 (4), 1287–1315.

Dahl, Gordon, 2002. Mobility and the return to education: testing a Roy model with multiple markets. Econometrica 70 (6), 2367–2420.

David, Steve, Loungani, Prakash, Mahidhara, Ramamohan, 1997, Regional Labor Fluctuations: Oil Shocks, Military Spending, and other Driving Forces. Working paper, January.

Diamond, Peter A., 1982. Aggregate demand management in search equilibrium. Journal of Political Economy 90 (5), 881–894.

Doms, Mark, Lewis, Ethan, Robb, Alicia, 2009. Local labor market endowments, new business characteristics, and performance, mimeo, Federal Reserve Bank of San Francisco.

Duranton, Giles, Puga, Diego, 2004. Micro-foundations of urban agglomeration economies. In: Henderson, J. Vernon, Thisse, Jacques-François (Eds.), Handbook of Urban and Regional Economics, vol. 4. North-Holland, Amsterdam.

Duranton, Gilles, Overman, Henry G., 2005. Testing for localization using microgeographic data. Review of Economic Studies 72 (4), 1077–1106.

Duranton, Gilles, Puga, Diego, 2001. Nursery cities: urban diversity, process innovation, and the life cycle of products. American Economic Review 91 (5), 1454–1477.

Duranton, Gilles, Puga, Diego, 2004. Microfoundations of urban agglomeration economies. In: Henderson, J. Vernon, Thisse, Jacques-François (Eds.), Handbook of Regional and Urban Economics, vol. 4. NorthHolland, Amsterdam, pp. 2063–2117.

Eberts, Randall W., Stone, Joe A., 1992. Wage and Employment Adjustment in Local Labor Markets. Books from Upjohn Press, W.E. Upjohn Institute for Employment Research.

Ellison, Glenn, Glaeser, Edward L., 1997. Geographic concentration in US manufacturing industries: a dartboard approach. Journal of Political Economy 105 (5), 889–927.

Ellison, Glenn, Glaeser, Edward L., 1999. The geographic concentration of industry: does natural advantage explain agglomeration? American Economic Review Papers and Proceedings 89 (2), 311–316.

Ellison, Glenn, Glaeser, Edward L., Kerr, William, 2010. What causes industry agglomeration? Evidence from coagglomeration patterns. American Economic Review (forthcoming).

Fallick, Bruce, Fleischman, Charles A., Rebitzer, James B., 2006. Job-hopping in silicon valley: some evidence concerning the microfoundations of a high-technology cluster. The Review of Economics and Statistics 88 (3), 472–481.

Faulk, Dagney, 2002. Do state economic development incentives create jobs? An analysis of state employment tax credits? National Tax Journal 55 (June), 263–280.

Glaeser, Edward L., 1998. Should transfer payments be indexed to local price levels? Regional Science and Urban Economics 28 (1), 1–20.

Glaeser, Edward L., 1999. Learning in cities. Journal of Urban Economics 46 (2), 254–277.

Glaeser, Edward L., Mare, David C., 2001. Cities and skills. Journal of Labor Economics 19 (2), 316–342.

Glaeser, Edward, Gottlieb, Joshua, 2009. The wealth of cities: agglomeration and the spatial equilibrium in the United States. Journal of Economic Literature.

Glaeser, Edward, Gottlieb, Joshua, 2008. The economics of place-making policies. Brookings Papers on Economic Activity.

Glaeser, Edward L., 2001. The economics of location-based tax incentives. Harvard Institute of Economic Research, Discussion Paper Number 1932.

Glaeser, Edward L., Kohlhase, Janet E., 2003. Cities, regions and the decline of transport costs. Papers in Regional Science 83, 197–228.

Glaeser, Edward, 2008. Cities, Agglomeration and Spatial Equilibrium. Oxford University Press.

Glaeser, Edward L., Scheinkman, Jose A., Shleifer, Andrei, 1995. Economic growth in a cross-section of cities. Journal of Monetary Economics 36 (1), 117–143.

Goolsbee, Austan, Maydew, Edward L., 2000. Coveting thy neighbor's manufacturing: the dilemma of state income apportionment. Journal of Public Economics 75, 125–143.

Greenstone, Michael, Moretti, Enrico, 2004. Bidding for industrial plants: does winning a "Million Dollar Plant" increase Welfare? National Bureau of Economic Research Working Paper No. 9844.

Greenstone, Michael, Hornbeck, Rick, Moretti, Enrico, Identifying Agglomeration spillovers: evidence from winners and losers of large plant openings, Journal of Political Economy (forthcoming).

Helsley, Robert W., Strange, William C., 1990. Matching and agglomeration economies in a system of cities. Regional Science and Urban Economics 20 (2), 189–212.

Henderson, J. Vernon, 2003. Marshall's scale economies. Journal of Urban Economics 55 (January), 1–28.

Henderson, J. Vernon, Black, Duncan, 1999. A theory of urban growth. Journal of Political Economy 107 (April), 252–284.

Holmes, Thomas J., 1999. Localization of industry and vertical disintegration. Review of Economics and Statistics 81 (2), 314–325.

Jaffe, Adam B., Trajtenberg, Manuel, Henderson, Rebecca M., 1993. Geographic localization of knowledge spillovers as evidenced by patent citation. Quarterly Journal of Economics 108 (August), 577–598.

Jovanovic, Boyan, Rob, Rafael, 1989. The growth and diffusion of knowledge. Review of Economic Studies 56 (October), 569–582.

Kline, Patrick, 2010. Place based policies, heterogeneity, and agglomeration, American Economic Review, Papers and Proceedings.

Krugman, Paul, 1991a. Geography and Trade. MIT Press, Cambridge, MA.

Krugman, Paul, 1991b. Increasing returns and economic geography. Journal of Political Economy 99 (june), 483–499.

Kuhn, Peter, Riddell, Chris, 2010. The long-term effects of a generous income support program: unemployment insurance in New Brunswick and Maine, 1940-1991, ILLR.

Lucas Jr., Robert E., 1988. On the mechanics of economic development. Journal of Monetary Economics 22 (July), 3–42.

Lucas Jr., Robert E., Rossi Hansberg, Esteban, 2002. On the internal structure of cities. Econometrica 70 (4), 1445–1476.

Machin, Steve, Pelkonen, Panu, Salvanes, Kjell G., 2009. Education and Mobility IZA WP 3845.

Malamud, Wozniak, 2009. The impact of college graduation on geographic mobility: identifying education using multiple components of Vietnam draft risk, IZA WP 3432.

Marshall, Alfred, 1890. Principles of Economics. Macmillan and Co., London.

Mas, Alex, Moretti, Enrico, 2009. Peers at work. American Economic Review 99 (1).

Melitz, Marc, Ottaviano, Gianmarco I.P., 2008. Market size, trade and productivity. Review of Economic Studies 75 (1), 295–316.

Mion, Giordano, Naticchioni, Paolo, 2009. The spatial sorting and matching of skills and firms. Canadian Journal of Economics, Canadian Economics Association 42 (1), 28–55.

Moretti, Enrico, 2004a. Estimating the external return to higher education: evidence from cross- sectional and longitudinal data. Journal of Econometrics 120 (July–August), 175–212.

Moretti, Enrico, 2004b. Workers' education, spillovers and productivity: evidence from plant- level production functions. American Economic Review 94 (June), 656–690.

Moretti, Enrico, 2004c. Human capital externalities in cities. In: Henderson, J. Vernon, Thisse, Jacques-François (Eds.), Handbook of Urban and Regional Economics, vol. 4. North-Holland, Amsterdam.

Moretti, Enrico, 'Local Multipliers' American Economic Review, Papers and Proceedings (forthcoming).

Notowidigdo, Matthew J., 2010. The Incidence of Local Labor Demand Shocks. MIT mimeo.

Overman, Henry G., Puga, Diego, 2010. Labour pooling as a source of agglomeration: an empirical investigation. In: Glaeser Edward L. (Ed.) Agglomeration Economics. Chicago University Press, Chicago, IL (forthcoming).

Papke, Leslie E., 1993. What do we know about enterprise zone? In: Poterba, J.M. (Ed.), Tax Policy and the Economy, vol. 7. MIT Press, Cambridge, Massachusetts.

Papke, Leslie E., 1994. Tax policy and urban development: evidence from the Indiana enterprise zone program. Journal of Public Economics 54, 37–49.

Partridge, Rickman, Li, 2009. Who wins from local economic development? Economic Development Quarterly 23 (1).

Peri, Giovanni, 2002. Young workers, learning, and agglomerations. Journal of Urban Economics 52 (3), 582–607.

Peters, Alan H., Fisher, Peter S., 2002. State enterprise zone programs: have they worked? W.E. Upjohn Institute, Kalamazoo, MI.

Petrongolo, Barbara, Pissarides, Christopher A., 2005. Scale effects in markets with search. The Economic Journal 116 (January), 21–44.

Puga, Diego, 2009. The magnitude and causes of agglomeration economies. Mimeo.

Rauch, James E., 1993. Productivity gains from geographic concentration of human capital: evidence from the cities. Journal of Urban Economics 34 (November), 380–400.

Renkow, M., 2003. Employment growth, worker mobility and rural economic development. American Journal of Agricultural Economics 85 (2), 503–513.

Renkow, M., 2006. Employment growth and the allocation of new jobs. Review of Regional Studies 36 (1), 121–139.

Roback, Jennifer, 1982. Wages, rents and the quality of life. Journal of Political Economy 90 (December), 1257–1278.

Roback, Jennifer, 1988. Wages, rents and amenities: differences among workers and regions. Economic Inquiry 26 (January), 23–41.

Rosen, Sherwin, 1979. Wagebased indexes of urban quality of life. In: Miezkowski, Peter N., Straszheim, Mahlon R. (Eds.), Current Issues in Urban Economics. Johns Hopkins University Press, Baltimore, MD, pp. 74–104.

Rosenthal, Stuart S., Strange, William C., 2001. The determinants of agglomeration. Journal of Urban Economics 50 (September), 191–229.

Rosenthal, Stuart S., Strange, William C., 2004. Evidence on the nature and sources of agglomeration. In: Henderson, J. Vernon, Thisse, Jacques-François (Eds.), Handbook of Urban and Regional Economics, vol. 4. North-Holland, Amsterdam.

Rosenthal, Stuart S., Strange, William C., 2003. Geography, industrial organization, and agglomeration. Review of Economics and Statistics 85 (2), 377–393.

Rosenthal, Stuart S., Strange, William C., 2008. The attenuation of human capital spillovers. Journal of Urban Economics 64 (2), 373–389.

Rotemberg, Julio R., Saloner, Garth, 2000. Competition and human capital accumulation: a theory of interregional specialization and trade. Regional Science and Urban Economics 30 (4), 373–404. doi:10.1016/S0166-0462(99)00044-7. (ISSN: 0166-0462).

Saxenian, Anna Lee., 1994. Regional Advantage: Culture and Competition in Silicon Valley and Route 128. Harvard University Press, Cambridge, MA.

Slesnick, Daniel T., 2002. Prices and regional variation in welfare. Journal of Urban Economics 51, 446–468.

Sveikauskas, Leo, 1975. Productivity of cities. Quarterly Journal of Economics 89 (3), 393–413.

Tabuchi, Takatoshi, Thisse, Jacques-François, 2002. Taste heterogeneity, labor mobility and economic geography. Journal of Development Economics 69 (1), 155–177.

Topel, Robert H., 1986. Local labor markets. The Journal of Political Economy 94 (3).

Wasylenko, Michael, 1997. Taxation and economic development: the state of the economic literature. New England Economic Review (March/April), 37–52.

Wheaton, William C., Lewis, Mark J., 2002. Urban wages and labor market agglomeration. Journal of Urban Economics 51 (3), 542–562.

Wheeler, Christopher, 2008. Local market scale and the pattern of job changes among young men. Federal Reserve Bank of St Louis Working Paper 2005-033C. Revised.

Zucker, Lynne G., Darby, Michael R., Brewer, Marilynn B., 1998. Intellectual human capital and the birth of US biotechnology enterprises. American Economic Review 88 (March), 290–306.

CHAPTER 15

Human Capital Development before Age Five[☆]

Douglas Almond, Janet Currie
Columbia University

Contents

[☆] We thank Maya Rossin and David Munroe for excellent research assistance, participants in the Berkeley Handbook of Labor Economics Conference in November 2009 for helpful comments, and Christine Pal and Hongyan Zhao for proofreading the equations.

E-mail addresses: da2152@columbia.edu (Douglas Almond), jc2663@columbia.edu (Janet Currie).

ISSN 0169-7218, DOI 10.1016/S0169-7218(11)02413-0

Abstract

This chapter seeks to set out what economists have learned about the effects of early childhood influences on later life outcomes, and about ameliorating the effects of negative influences. We begin with a brief overview of the theory which illustrates that evidence of a causal relationship between a shock in early childhood and a future outcome says little about whether the relationship in question is biological or immutable. We then survey recent work which shows that events before five years old can have large long term impacts on adult outcomes. Child and family characteristics measured at school entry do as much to explain future outcomes as factors that labor economists have more traditionally focused on, such as years of education. Yet while children can be permanently damaged at this age, an important message is that the damage can often be remediated. We provide a brief overview of evidence regarding the effectiveness of different types of policies to provide remediation. We conclude with a list of some of the many outstanding questions for future research.

JEL classification: I12; I21; J13; J24; Q53

Keywords: Human capital; Early childhood; Health; Fetal origins

1. INTRODUCTION

The last decade has seen a blossoming of research on the long term effects of early childhood conditions across a range of disciplines. In economics, the focus is on how human capital accumulation responds to the early childhood environment. In 2000, there were no articles on this topic in the *Journal of Political Economy, Quarterly Journal of Economics,* or *the American Economic Review* (excluding the Papers and Proceedings), but there have been five or six per year in these journals since 2005. This work has been spurred by a growing realization that early life conditions can have persistent and profound impacts on later life. Table 1 summarizes several longitudinal studies which suggest that characteristics that are measured as of age 7 can explain a great deal of the variation in educational attainment, earnings as of the early 30s, and the probability of employment. For example, McLeod and Kaiser (2004) use data from the National Longitudinal Surveys and find that children's test scores and background variables measured as of ages 6 to 8 predict about 12% of the variation in the probability of high school completion and about 11% of the variation in the probability of college completion. Currie and Thomas (1999b) use data from the 1958 British Birth Cohort study and find that 4% to 5% of the variation in employment at age 33 can be predicted, and as much as 20% of the variation in wages. Cunha and Heckman (2008) and Cunha et al. (2010) estimate structural models in which initial endowments and investments feed

Table 1 How much of the differences in later outcomes (test scores, educational attainment, earnings) can be explained by early childhood factors?

Study and data	Inputs/intermediate variables	Outcomes	Results
Studies using National Longitudinal Survey of Youth-child Sample Data			
Childhood emotional and behavioral problems and educational attainment (McLeod and Kaiser, 2004) NLSY-child sample data on children 6–8 in 1986. Five waves through 2000 (when children 20–22) $n = 424$.	Emotional and behavioral problems at age 6–8 measured by BPI, mother emotional problems and delinquency, poverty status, mother's AFQT score, mother's education, mother's marital status and age, child's age, sex, and race, dummy for LBW.	Dummy for graduating high school by 2000, dummy for enrolling in college by 2000.	**R-squared for predicting HS graduation:** Only child emotional and behavioral problems: 0.046 Add child and mother demographics: 0.111 Add mother's emotional problems and delinquency: 0.124. **R-squared for predicting college enrollment:** Only child emotional and behavioral problems: 0.017 Add child and mother demographics: 0.093 Add mother's emotional problems and delinquency: 0.112.

(continued on next page)

Table 1 (continued)

Study and data	Inputs/intermediate variables	Outcomes	Results
Formulating, identifying, and estimating the technology of cognitive and noncognitive skill formation (Cunha and Heckman, 2008) NLSY-child sample data on white males. $n = 1053$.	Home environment measured by HOME score. Measures of parental investments: number of child's books, whether the child has a musical instrument, whether the family receives a daily newspaper, whether the child receives special lessons, how often the child goes to museums, and how often the child goes to the theater. Measures of child cognitive skills: PIAT test scores at various ages. Measures of child's non-cognitive skills: BPI at various ages.	Log earnings and likelihood of graduation from high school. Estimated a dynamic factor model that exploits cross-equation restrictions for identification. Estimated effects of cognitive and non-cognitive skills as well as parental investments at different stages of the child's lifecycle on log earnings and likelihood of graduation from high school.	A 10% increase in parental investments at ages 6–7 increases earnings by 24.9% (12.5% through cognitive skills, 12.4% through non-cognitive skills), and increases likelihood of graduating high school by 64.4% (54.8% through cognitive skills, 9.6% through non-cognitive skills).

Table 1 (continued)

Study and data	Inputs/intermediate variables	Outcomes	Results
Estimating the technology of cognitive and non-cognitive skill formation (Cunha et al., 2010) NLSY-child sample first-born white children. $N = 2207$.	Examples of measures of child cognitive skills: Motor-social development at birth; PIAT reading-comprehension at ages 5–6; PIAT math at ages 13–14. Examples of measures of child non-cognitive skills: BPI at various ages; "friendliness at birth". Examples of measures of parental investments: "How often child goes on outings during year of birth"; "How often mom reads to child during year of birth"; "Child has a CD player, ages 3–4"; "How often child is praised, ages 13–14".	Main outcome variable: completed years of education by age 19. Multi-stage production functions estimated in which the productivity of later investments depends on early investments and on the stock of cognitive and non-cognitive skills and investments are endogenous. Identification based on nonlinear factor models with endogenous inputs. In preferred specification, used maximum-likelihood methods to estimate the production technology.	34% of variation in educational attainment is explained by measures of cognitive and non-cognitive capabilities. 16% is due to adolescent cognitive capabilities; 12% is due to adolescent non-cognitive capabilities. Parental endowments/investments account for 15% of variation in educational attainment.

(continued on next page)

Table 1 (continued)

Studies using National Child Development Study (1958 British Birth Cohort) Data

Study and data	Inputs/intermediate variables	Outcomes	Results
Ability, family, education, and earnings in Britain (Dearden, 1998) Focus on individuals who participated in waves 4 and 5 of the survey in 1981 and 1991, who were employees in 1991. $n = 2597$ males, 2362 females.	Math and verbal ability (age 7), type of school, family characteristics—teacher's assessment of interest shown by parents in child's education at 7; type of school attended at 16 family's financial status at 11 and 16; region dummies; father's SES; parents' education levels.	Years of full-time education; Earnings at age 33.	**R-squared for education as outcome:** Including all explanatory variables: 0.33–0.34. **R-squared for earnings as outcome:** Baseline earnings equation including only years education: 0.15 (males), 0.25 (females) Add reading and math scores at age 7, school type and regional dummies: 0.26 (males), 0.31 (females) Including all explanatory variables:.029 (males), 0.41 for females.
Early test scores, socioeconomic status, and future outcomes (Currie and Thomas, 1999b)	Reading and math test scores at age 7, mother and father's SES and education, birth weight, other child background variables at age 7.	Number of O-level passes of exams by age 16; employed at age 23, 33; log wage at age 23, 33.	**R-squared for predicting age 16 exam passes:** Reading and math scores only: 0.21–0.22 Add other background variables: 0.31–0.32.

Table 1 (continued)

Study and data	Inputs/intermediate variables	Outcomes	Results
Full sample size (based on responses at 7): $n = 14, 022$.			**R-squared for predicting employment at 33:** Reading and math test scores only: 0.01 Add other background variables: 0.04–0.05. **R-squared for predicting log wage at 33:** Reading and math test scores only: 0.08–0.09 Add other background variables: 0.18–0.20.
The lasting impact of childhood health and circumstance (Case et al., 2005) $n = 14,325$ (7016 men, 7039 women)	Mother's and father's education and SES, LBW, indicators for moderate, heavy, and varied maternal smoking during pregnancy, number of chronic conditions at age 7 and 16.	Number of O-level passes of exams by age 16; adult health status at age 42; part-time or full employment at age 42.	**R-squared for predicting age 16 exam passes/adult health/employment at 42.** Mother's education and SES: 0.062/0.082/0.076 Father's education and SES: 0.241/0.189/0.173 LBW and maternal smoking: 0.024/0.086/0.052.
Explaining intergenerational income persistence: non-cognitive skills, ability, and education (Blanden et al., 2006) **A.** NCDS: 1958 cohort Focus on 2163 males. **B.** British Cohort Study: 1970 cohort Focus on 3340 males.	**A.** Family income at age 16 reading and math test scores at age 11, scores for "behavioral syndromes" at age 11, O-level exam scores at age 16. **B.** Years of preschool education, birth weight, height at 5 and 10, emotional/behavioral scores at ages 5, 10, & 16, family income at ages 10 and 16, reading and math test scores at age 10, IQ at age 10, dummy for HS degree, exam scores at age 16.	**A.** Earnings at age 33. **B.** Earnings at age 30.	**R-squared Model A.** Birth weight, childhood health, and age 11 test scores only: 0.116 Including "behavioral syndromes" at age 11: 0.151 All variables: 0.263. **R-squared Model B.** Birth weight, childhood health, and age 10 test scores only: 0.075. Including emotional/behavioral characteristics at age 10: 0.087. All variables: 0.222.

through to later outcomes; they arrive at estimates that are of a similar order of magnitude for education and wages. To put these results in context, labor economists generally feel that they are doing well if they can explain 30% of the variation in wages in a human capital earnings function.

This chapter seeks to set out what economists have learned about the importance of early childhood influences on later life outcomes, and about ameliorating the effects of negative influences. We begin with a brief overview of the theory which illustrates that evidence of a causal relationship between a shock in early childhood and a future outcome says little about whether the relationship in question is biological or immutable. Parental and social responses are likely to be extremely important in either magnifying or mitigating the effects of a shock. Given that this is the case, it can sometimes be difficult to interpret the wealth of empirical evidence that is accumulating in terms of an underlying structural framework.

The theoretical framework is laid out in Section 2 and followed by a brief discussion of methods in Section 3. We do not attempt to cover issues such as identification and instrumental variables methods, which are covered in some depth elsewhere (cf Angrist and Pischke (2009)). Instead, we focus on several issues that come up frequently in the early influences literature, including estimation using small samples and the potentially high return to better data.

Section 4 discusses the evidence for long-term effects of early life influences in greater detail, while Section 5 focuses on the evidence regarding remediation programs. The discussion of early life influences is divided into two subsections corresponding to *in utero* influences and after birth influences. The discussion of remediation programs starts from the most general sort of program, income transfers, and goes on to discuss interventions that are increasingly targeted at specific domains. In surveying the evidence we have attempted to focus on recent papers, and especially those that propose a plausible strategy for identifying causal effects. We have focused on papers that emphasize early childhood, but in instances in which only evidence regarding effects on older children is available, we have sometimes strayed from this rule. A summary of most of the papers discussed in these sections is presented in Tables 4 through 13. A list of acronyms used in the tables appears in Appendix A. We conclude with a summary and a discussion of outstanding questions for future research in Section 6.

2. CONCEPTUAL FRAMEWORK

Grossman (1972) models health as a stock variable that varies over time in response to investments and depreciation. Because some positive portion of the previous period's health stock vanishes in each period (e.g., age in years), the effect of the health stock and health investments further removed in time from the current period tends to fade out. As individuals age, the early childhood health stock and the prior health investments that it embodies become progressively less important.

In contrast, the "early influences" literature asks whether health and investments in early childhood have sustained effects on adult outcomes. The magnitude of these effects may persist or even increase as individuals age because childhood development occurs in distinct stages that are more or less influential of adult outcomes.

Defining h as health or human capital at the completion of childhood, we can retain the linearity of h in investments and the prior health stock as in Grossman (1972), but leave open whether there is indeed "fade out" (i.e. depreciation). For simplicity, we will consider a simple two-period childhood.[1] We can consider production of h:

$$h = A[\gamma I_1 + (1 - \gamma)I_2], \tag{1}$$

where:

$$\begin{cases} I_1 \cong \text{investments during childhood through age 5} \\ I_2 \cong \text{investments during childhood after age 5.} \end{cases}$$

For a given level of total investments $I_1 + I_2$, the allocation of investments between period 1 and 2 will affect h for $\gamma \neq 0.5$. If $\gamma > 0.5$, then health at the end of period 1 is more important to h than investments in the second period, and if $\gamma A > 1$, h may respond more than one-for-one with I_1. Thus, (1) admits the possibility that certain childhood periods may exert a disproportionate effect on adult outcomes that does not necessarily decline monotonically with age. This functional form says more than "early life" matters; it suggests that early-childhood events may be more influential than later childhood events.

2.1. Complementarity

The assumption that inputs at different stages of childhood have linear effects is common in economics. While it opens the door to "early origins," perfect substitutability between first and second period investments in (1) is a strong assumption. The absence of complementarity implies that all investments should be concentrated in one period (up to a discount factor) and no investments should be made during the low-return period. In addition, with basic preference assumptions, perfect substitutability "hard-wires" the optimal investment response to early-life shocks to be compensatory, as seen in Section 2.3.

As suggested by Heckman (2007), a more flexible "developmental" technology is the constant elasticity of substitution (CES) function:

$$h = A\left[\gamma I_1^\phi + (1 - \gamma)I_2^\phi\right]^{1/\phi}, \tag{2}$$

---

[1] See Zweifel et al. (2009) for a two period version of the Grossman (1972) model.

For a given total investment level $I_1 + I_2$, how the allocation between period 1 and 2 will also affect h depends on the elasticity of substitution, $1/(1 - \phi)$, and the share parameter, γ. For $\phi = 1$ (perfect substitutability of investments), (2) reduces to (1).

Heckman (2007) highlights two features of "capacity formation" beyond those captured in (2). First, there may be "dynamic complementarities" which imply that investments in period t are more productive when there is a high level of capability in period $t - 1$. For example, if the factor productivity term A in (2) were an increasing function of h_0, the health endowment immediately prior to period 1, this would raise the return to investments during childhood. Second, there may be "self-productivity" which implies that higher levels of capacity in one period create higher levels of capacity in future periods. This feature is especially noteworthy when h is multidimensional, as it would imply that "cross-effects" are positive, e.g. health in period 1 leads to higher cognitive ability in period 2. "Self-productivity" is more trivial in the unidimensional case like Grossman (1972)—even though the effect of earlier health stocks tends to fade out as the time passes, there is still memory as long as depreciation in each period is less than total (i.e., when $\delta < 1$ in Zweifel et al. (2009)).

Here, we will use the basic framework in (2) to consider the effect of exogenous shocks μ_g to health investments that occur during the first childhood period.[2] We begin with the simplest case, where investments do not respond to μ_g (and denote these investments $\bar{I}_1$ and $\bar{I}_2$). Net investments in the first period are:

$$\bar{I}_1 + \mu_g.$$

We assume that μ_g is independent of $\bar{I}_1$. While μ_g can be positive or negative, we assume $\bar{I}_1 + \mu_g > 0$. We will then relax the assumption of fixed investments, and consider endogenous responses to investments in the second period, i.e. $\delta I_2^* / \delta \mu_g$, and how this investment response may mediate the observed effect on h.

2.2. Fixed investments

Conceptually, we can trace out the effect of μ_g while holding other inputs fixed, i.e., we assume no investment response to this shock in either period. Albeit implicitly, most biomedical and epidemiological studies in the "early origins" literature aim to inform us about this *ceteris paribus*, "biological" relationship.

In this two-period CES production function adopted from Heckman (2007), the impact of an early-life shock on adult outcomes is:

$$\frac{\delta h}{\delta \mu_g} = \gamma A \left[\gamma (\bar{I}_1 + \mu_g)^\phi + (1 - \gamma) \bar{I}_2^\phi \right]^{(1-\phi)/\phi} (\bar{I}_1 + \mu_g)^{\phi-1}. \tag{3}$$

---

[2] We include the subscript here because environmental influences at some aggregated geographic level g may provide exogenous variation in early childhood investments.

The simplest production technology is the perfect substitutability case where $\phi = 1$. In this case:

$$\frac{\delta h}{\delta \mu_g} = \gamma A.$$

Damage to adult human capital is proportional to the share parameter on period 1 investments, and is unrelated to the investment level $\bar{I}_1$.

For less than perfect substitutability between periods, there is diminishing marginal productivity of the investment inputs. Thus, shocks experienced at different baseline investment levels have heterogenous effects on h. Other things equal, those with higher baseline levels of investment will experience more muted effects in h than those where baseline investment is low. A recurring empirical finding is that long-term damage due to shocks is more likely among poorer families (Currie and Hyson, 1999). This is in part due to the fact that children in poorer families are subject to more or larger early-life shocks (Case et al., 2002; Currie and Stabile, 2003). However, it is also possible that the same shock will have a greater impact among children in poorer families if these children have lower period t investment levels to begin with. This occurs because they are on a steeper portion of the production function. *Ceteris paribus*, this would tend to accentuate the effect of an equivalent-sized μ_g shock on h among poor families.[3,4]

2.2.1. Remediation

Is it possible to alter "bad" early trajectories? In other words, what is the effect of a shock $\mu'_g > 0$ experienced during the second period on h? Remediation is of interest to the extent that (3) is substantially less than zero. However, large damage to h from μ_g *per se* says little about the potential effectiveness of remediation in the second period, as both initial damage and remediation are distinct functions of the three parameters A, γ, and ϕ.

The effectiveness of remediation relative to initial damage is:

$$\frac{\delta h/\delta \mu'_g}{\delta h/\delta \mu_g} = \frac{1-\gamma}{\gamma} \left(\frac{\bar{I}_1 + \mu_g}{\bar{I}_2 + \mu'_g} \right)^{1-\phi}. \tag{4}$$

Thus, for $\bar{I}_1 > \bar{I}_2$ and a given value of γ, a unit of remediation will be more effective at low elasticities of substitution—the lack of $\bar{I}_2$ was the more critical shortfall prior to the shock. If $\bar{I}_1 < \bar{I}_2$ high elasticities of substitution increase the effectiveness of remediation—adding to the existing abundance of $\bar{I}_2$ remains effective.

---

[3] I.e. $\delta^2 h/\delta\mu_g \delta I_1 < 0$. On the other hand, $\delta^2 h/\delta\mu_g \delta I_2 > 0$ so lower period two investments would tend to reduce damage to h from μ_g. The ratio of the former effect to the latter is proportional to $\gamma/(1-\gamma)$ (Chiang, 1984). Thus, damage from a period 1 shock is more likely to be concentrated among poor families when the period-1 share parameter (γ) is high.

[4] The cross-effect $\delta^2 h/\delta\mu_g \delta I_2$ is similar to dynamic complementarity, but Heckman (2007) reserves this term for the cross-partial between the stock and flow, i.e. $\delta^2 h/\delta h_0 \delta I_t$ for $t = 1, 2$ in the example of Section 2.1.

Fortunately, it is not necessary to observe investments and estimate all three parameters in order to assess the scope for remediation. In some cases, we merely need to observe how a shock in the second period, μ'_g, affects h. Furthermore, this does not necessarily require a distinct shock in addition to μ_g. In an overlapping generations framework, the same shock, $\mu_g = \mu'_g$ could affect one cohort in the first childhood period (but not the second) and an older cohort in the second period (but not the first). For a small, "double-barreled" shock, we would have reduced form estimates of both the damage in (3) and the potential to alter trajectories in (4).[5] For example, in addition to observing how income during the prenatal period affects newborn health (Kehrer and Wolin, 1979), we might also be able to see how parental income affects the health of pre-school age children to gain a sense of what opportunities there are to remediate negative income shocks experienced during pregnancy.

2.3. Responsive investments

Most analyses of "early origins" focus on estimating the reduced form effect, $\delta h/\delta \mu_g$. Whether this empirical relationship represents a purely biological effect or also includes the effect of responsive investments is an open question. In general, to the extent that "early origins" are important, so too will be any response of childhood investments to μ_g. For expositional purposes, we will consider $\mu_g < 0$ and responses that either magnify or attenuate initial damage.

Unless the investment response is costless, damage estimates that monetize $\delta h/\delta \mu_g$ alone will tend to understate total damage. In the extreme, investment responses could fully offset the effect of early-life shocks on h, but this would not mean that such shocks were costless (Deschnes and Greenstone, 2007). More generally, the damage from early-life shocks will be understated if we focus only on long-term effects and there are compensatory investments (i.e. investments that are negatively correlated with the early-life shock ($\delta I_2^*/\delta \mu_g < 0$)). The cost of investments that help remediate damage should be included. But even when the response is reinforcing ($\delta I_2^*/\delta \mu_g > 0$), total costs can still be understated by focussing on the reduced form damage to h alone (see below).

To consider correlated investment responses more formally, we assume parents observe μ_g at the end of the first period. The direction of the investment response—whether reinforcing or compensatory—will be shaped by how substitutable period 2 investments are for those in period 1. If substitutability is high, the optimal response will tend to be compensatory, and thereby help offset damage to h.

A compensatory response is readily seen in the case of perfect substitutability. Cunha and Heckman (2007) observed that economic models commonly assume that production at different stages of childhood are perfect substitutes. When $\phi = 1$, (2) reduces to:

$$h = A\left[\gamma(I_1 + \mu_g) + (1 - \gamma)I_2\right]. \tag{5}$$

[5] How parameters of the production function might be recovered is discussed in Appendix D.

This linear production technology is akin to that used in a previous *Handbook* chapter on intergenerational mobility (Solon, 1999), which likewise considered parental investments in children's human capital. Further, Solon (1999) assumed parent's utility trades off own consumption against the child's human capital:

$$U_p = U(C, h), \tag{6}$$

where p denotes parents and C their consumption. The budget constraint is:

$$Y_p = C + I_1 + I_2/(1 + r). \tag{7}$$

With standard preferences, changes to h through μ_g will "unbalance" the marginal utilities in h versus C.[6] If μ_g is negative, the marginal utility of h becomes too high relative to that in consumption. The technology in (5) permits parents to convert some consumption into h at a constant rate. This will cause I_2^* to increase, which attenuates the effect of the μ_g damage. This attenuation comes at the cost of reduced parental utility. Similarly, if μ_g is positive parents will "spend the bounty" (at least in part), reduce I_2^* and increase consumption. Again, this will temper effects on h, leading to an understatement of biological effects in analyses that ignore investments (or parental utility). In either case, perfect substitutability hard-wires the response to be compensatory.

The polar opposite technology is perfect complementarity between childhood stages, i.e., a Leontieff production function. Here, a compensatory strategy would be completely ineffective in mitigating changes to h. As h is determined by the minimum of period 1 and period 2 investments, optimal period 2 investments should reinforce μ_g. If μ_g is negative, parents would seek to reduce I_2 and consume more. Despite higher consumption, parents' utility is reduced on net due to the shock (or this bundle of lower h and higher C would have been selected absent μ_g). Again, the full-cost of a negative μ_g shock is understated when parental utility is ignored.

The crossover between reinforcing and compensating responses of I_2^* will occur at an intermediate parameter value of substitutability. (The fixed investments case of Section 2.2 can be seen to reflect an optimized response at this point of balance between reinforcing and compensating responses). The value of ϕ at this point of balance will depend on the functional form of parental preferences in (6), as shown for CES utility in Appendix B.

To take a familiar example, assume a Cobb-Douglas utility function of the form:

$$U_p = (1 - \alpha)\log C + \alpha \log h. \tag{8}$$

---

[6] Obviously, the marginal utilities themselves will not be the same but equal subject to discount factor, preference parameters, and prices of C versus I, which have been ignored.

If the production technology is also Cobb-Douglas ($\phi = 0$), then no change to I_2^* is warranted. If instead substitution between period 1 and period 2 is relatively easy ($\phi > 0$), compensating for the shock is optimal. If substitution is relatively difficult ($\phi < 0$), then parents should "go with the flow" and reinforce. For this reason, whether conventional reduced form analyses under or over-state "biological" effects (effects with I_2 held fixed) depends on how easy it is to substitute the timing of investments across childhood. If the elasticity of substitution across periods is low, then it may be optimal for parents to reinforce the effect of a shock.

Tension between preferences and the production technology may also be relevant for within-family investment decisions. For example, Behrman et al. (1982) considered parental preferences that parameterize varying degrees of "inequality aversion" among (multiple) children. Depending on the strength of parents' inequality aversion relative to the production technology (as reflected by ϕ), parents may reinforce or compensate exogenous within-family differences in early-life health and human capital. If substitutability between periods of childhood is sufficiently difficult (low ϕ), reinforcement of sibling differences will be optimal. This reinforcement may be optimal even when the parents place a higher weight in their utility function on the accumulation of human capital by the less able sibling (see Appendix C). Thus, empirical evidence that some parents reinforce early-life shocks could reveal less about "human nature" than it would reveal about the developmental nature of the childhood production technology.

3. METHODS

As discussed above, we confine our discussion to methodological issues that seem particularly germane to the early influences literature. One of these is the question of when sibling fixed effects (or maternal fixed effects) estimation is appropriate. Fixed effects can be a powerful way to eliminate confounding from shared family background characteristics, even when these are not fully observed. This approach is particularly effective when the direction of unobserved sibling-specific confounders can be signed. For example, Currie and Thomas (1995) find that in the cross-section, children who were in Head Start do worse than children who were not. However, compared to their own siblings, Head Start children do better. Since there is little evidence that Head Start children are "favored" by parents or otherwise (on the contrary, in families where one child attends and the other does not, children who attended were more likely to have spent their preschool years in poverty), these contrasting results suggest that unobserved family characteristics are correlated both with Head Start attendance and poor child outcomes. When the effect of such characteristics is accounted for, the positive effects of Head Start are apparent.

However, fixed effects can not control for sibling-specific factors. The theory discussed above suggests that it may be optimal for parents to either reinforce or compensate for the effects of early shocks by altering their own investment behaviors. Whether parents do or do not reinforce/compensate obviously has implications for the interpretation of models estimated using family fixed effects. If on average, families compensate, then fixed effects estimates will understate the total effect of the shock (when the compensation behavior is unobserved or otherwise not accounted for). In some circumstances, such a bias might be benign in the sense that any significant coefficient could then be interpreted as a lower bound on the total effect. It is likely to be more problematic if parents systematically reinforce shocks, because then any effect that is observed results from a combination of underlying effects and parental reactions rather than the shock itself. In the extreme, if parents seized on a characteristic that was unrelated to ability and systematically favored children who had that characteristic, then researchers might wrongly conclude that the characteristic was in fact linked to success even in the absence of parental responses.

The issue of how parents allocate resources between siblings has received a good deal of attention in economics, starting with Becker and Tomes (1976) and Behrman et al. (1982). Some empirical studies from developing countries find evidence of reinforcing behavior (see Rosenzweig and Paul Schultz (1982), Rosenzweig and Wolpin (1988) and Pitt et al. (1990)). Empirical tests of these theories in developed countries such as the United States and Britain generally use adult outcomes such as completed education as a proxy for parental investments (see for example, Griliches (1979), Behrman et al. (1994) and Ashenfelter and Rouse (1998)).

Several recent studies have used birth weight as a measure of the child's endowment and asked whether explicit measures of parental investments during early childhood are related to birth weight. For example, Datar et al. (2010) use data from the National Longitudinal Survey of Youth-Child and show that low birth weight children are less likely to be breastfed, have fewer well-baby visits, are less likely to be immunized, and are less likely to attend preschool than normal birth weight siblings. However, all of these differences could be due to poorer health among the low birth weight children. For example, if a child is receiving many visits for sick care, they may receive fewer visits for well care and this will not say anything about parental investment behaviors. Hence, Datar et al. (2010) also look at how the presence of low birth weight siblings in the household affects the investments received by normal birth weight children. They find no effect of having a low birth weight sibling on breastfeeding, immunizations, or preschool. The only statistically significant interaction is for well-baby care. This could however, be due to transactions costs. It may be the case that if the low birth weight sibling is getting a lot of medical care, it is less costly to bring the normal birth weight child in for care as well, for example.

Del Bono et al. (2008) estimate a model that allows endowments of other children to affect parental investments in the index child. They find, however, that the results from this dynamic model are remarkably similar to those of mother fixed effects models in most cases. Moreover, although they find a positive effect of birth weight on breastfeeding, the effect is very small in magnitude.

We conducted our own investigation of this issue using data on twins from the Early Childhood Longitudinal Study-Birth Cohort (ECLS-B), using twin differences to control for potential confounders. At the same time, twins routinely have large differences in endowment in the form of birth weight. Table 2 presents estimates for all twins (with and without controls for gender), same sex twins, and identical twins. Overall, there are very few significant differences in the treatment of these twins: Parents seemed to be more concerned about whether the low birth weight twin was ready for school, and to delay introducing solid food (but this is only significant in the identical twin pairs). We see no evidence that parents are more likely to praise, caress, spank or otherwise treat children differently, and despite their worries about school readiness, parents have similar expectations regarding college for both twins. This table largely replicates the basic finding of Royer (2009), who also considered parental investments and birth weight differences in the ECLS-B data. In particular, Royer (2009) focussed on investments soon after birth, finding that breastfeeding, NICU admission, and other measures of neonatal medical care did not vary with within twin pair birth weight differences.

The parental investment response has also been explored in the context of natural experiments. Kelly (2009) asked whether observed parental investments (e.g., time spent reading to child) were related to flu-induced damages to test scores in the 1958 British birth cohort study but did not detect an investment response.

In an interesting contribution to this literature, Hsin (2009) looks at the relationship between children's endowments, measured using birth weight, and maternal time use using data from the Child Supplement of the Panel Study of Income Dynamics. She finds that overall, there is little relationship between low birth weight and maternal time investments. However, she argues that this masks important differences by maternal socioeconomic status. In particular, she finds that in models with maternal fixed effects, less educated women spend less time with their low birth weight children, while more educated women spend more time. This finding is based on only 65 sibling pairs who had differences in the incidence of low birth weight, and so requires some corroboration. Still, one interpretation of this result in the context of the Section 2 framework is that the elasticity of substitution between C and h varies by socioeconomic status. In particular, if $\varphi_{poor} > \varphi_{rich}$, low income parents tend to view their consumption and children's h as relatively good substitutes. This would lead low-income parents to be more likely to reinforce a negative shock than high-income parents (assuming that the developmental technology, captured by γ and ϕ, does not vary by socioeconomic status). A second possible interpretation of the finding is that parents' responses may reflect their budget constraint more than their preferences. If parents would like to invest in both children, but have only enough resources to invest adequately in one, then they may be forced

Table 2 Estimated effect of birth weight on parental investments within twin pairs, estimates from the early childhood longitudinal study.

Outcome	All twins	Same sex twins	Identical twins
9 month survey			
1 if child was ever breastfed	0.0183	0.0187	0.0031
	[0.0238]	[0.0277]	[0.0355]
	1550	1000	350
1 if child is now being breastfed	0.0038	−0.0039	−0.0007
	[0.0126]	[0.0152]	[0.001]
	1550	1000	350
How long child was breastfed in months, given breastfed	−0.0753	−0.2165	−0.343
	[0.1752]	[0.204]	[0.3182]
	800	500	150
Age solid food was introduced in months, given introduced	−0.1802	−0.2478	−0.6660★
	[0.1523]	[0.1906]	[0.2914]
	1550	1000	350
Number of well-baby visits	0.283	0.3803	0.5797
	[0.1883]	[0.2414]	[0.5253]
	1550	1000	350
Number of well-baby visits only children in excellent or very good health	0.1956	0.2329	0.2668
	[0.1624]	[0.1944]	[0.3799]
	1500	950	300
1 if caregiver praises child	−0.0015	−0.051	0.096
	[0.0941]	[0.1189]	[0.2089]
	1250	800	250
1 if caregiver avoids negative comments	−0.0051	−0.0077	0
	[0.0055]	[0.0084]	[.]
	1250	800	250
1 if somewhat difficult or difficult to raise (caregiver report)	−0.0181	−0.0772	−0.0946
	[0.0583]	[0.0712]	[0.1395]
	1550	1000	350
1 if not at all difficult or not very difficult to raise (caregiver report)	0.1065	0.153	0.2237
	[0.0707]	[0.0812]	[0.1195]
	1550	1000	350
2-year survey			
1 if caress/kiss/hug child	0.0228	0.0055	0.0021
	[0.0266]	[0.0254]	[0.0049]
	1350	850	300

(continued on next page)

Table 2 (continued)

Outcome	All twins	Same sex twins	Identical twins
1 if spank/slap child	−0.0195	−0.0095	−0.0048
	[0.0249]	[0.0192]	[0.0316]
	1350	850	300
1 if time spent calming child > 1 hr usually	0.0317	−0.024	0.0719
	[0.0646]	[0.0759]	[0.093]
	1450	950	300
1 if somewhat difficult or difficult to raise	−0.0432	−0.0901	−0.1412
(caregiver report)	[0.0555]	[0.0621]	[0.086]
	1450	950	300
1 if not at all difficult or not very difficult to raise	−0.0031	0.068	0.0527
(caregiver report)	[0.0757]	[0.0869]	[0.1258]
	1450	950	300
Age when stopped feeding formula in months	−0.1903	−0.4504	−0.5903
	[0.255]	[0.3204]	[0.7844]
	1150	750	250
Age when stopped breastfeeding in months	−0.1492	−0.0267	−0.0422
	[0.5981]	[0.044]	[0.069]
	100	50	50

Preschool survey

1 if parent expects child to enter kindergarten early	−0.0082	−0.0071	0
	[0.012]	[0.0102]	[0]
	1300	800	250
1 if parent concerned about	−0.1435**	−0.1299*	−0.1099
child's kindergarten readiness	[0.0554]	[0.0636]	[0.1253]
	1300	850	250
1 if expect child to get ≥ 4 yrs of college	−0.0073	0.0069	0.0228
	[0.0272]	[0.0327]	[0.0264]
	1350	850	300
Number of servings of milk in the past 7 days	−0.0598	−0.0577	0.0819
	[0.2074]	[0.2278]	[0.2489]
	1350	850	300
Number of servings of vegetables past 7 days	0.0632	0.2131	0.0871
	[0.2634]	[0.3027]	[0.4091]
	1350	850	300

Standard errors clustered on the mother are shown in brackets with sample sizes below. Twin pairs in which a child had a congenital anomaly are omitted. Birth weight measured in kilograms. Each entry is from a separate regression of the dependent variable on birth weight and a mother fixed effect. Models in column 1 also control for child gender. Sample sizes are rounded to the nearest multiple of 50.
Significance levels: *$p < 0.10$, **$p < 0.05$, ***$p < 0.001$.

to choose the more well endowed child.[7] Interventions that relaxed resource constraints would have quite different effects in this case than in the case in which parents preferred to maximize the welfare of a favored child. More empirical work on this question seems warranted. For example, the PSID–CDS in 1997 and 2002 has time diary data for several thousand sibling pairs which have not been analyzed for this purpose.

Parent's choices are determined in part by the technologies they face, and these technologies may change over time, with implications for the potential biases in fixed effects estimates.[8] For example, Currie and Hyson (1999) asked whether the long term effects of low birth weight differed by various measures of parental socioeconomic status in the 1958 British birth cohort. They found little evidence that they did (except that low birth weight women from higher SES backgrounds were less likely to suffer from poor health as adults). But it is possible that this is because there were few effective interventions for low birth weight infants in 1958. In contrast, Currie and Moretti (2007) looked at Californian mothers born in the late 1960s and 70s and find that women born in low income zip codes were less educated and more likely to live in a low income zipcode than sisters born in better circumstances. Moreover, women who were low birth weight were more likely to transmit low birth weight to their own children if they were born in low income zip codes, suggesting that early disadvantage compounded the initial effects of low birth weight.

To the extent that behavioral responses to early-life shocks are important empirically, they will affect estimates of long-term effects whether family fixed effects are employed or not. Our conclusion is that users of fixed effects designs should consider any evidence that may be available about individual child-level characteristics and whether parents are reinforcing or compensating for the particular early childhood event at issue. This information will inform the appropriate interpretation of the estimates. There is little evidence at present that parents in developed countries systematically reinforce or compensate for early childhood events, but more research is needed on this question.

3.1. Power

Given that there are relatively few data sets with information about early childhood influences and future outcomes, economists may be tempted to make use of relatively small data sets that happen to have the requisite variables. Power calculations can be helpful in determining *ex ante* whether analysis of a particular data set is likely to yield any interesting findings. Table 3 provides two sample calculations. The first half of the table considers the relationship between birth weight and future educational attainment

---

[7] In the siblings model of Appendix C, this can be seen in the case of a Leontief production technology, where the second period investments generate increases in h only up to the level of first period investments. If parental income $\bar{Y}$ falls below the cost of maintaining the initial investment level $2\bar{I} + \mu_g$ in the second period, it may be optimal to invest fully in child b (i.e. $I_{2b}^* = \bar{I}$), but not in child a (i.e. $I_{2a}^* < \bar{I} + \mu_g$), who experiences the negative first-period shock.

[8] For example, the effectiveness of remedial investments would change over time if γ varied with the birth cohort. Remediation would be more effective for later cohorts if $\gamma_t > \gamma_{t+1}$ in Eq. (4).

Table 3 Sample power calculations.

Given a true population effect size, what is the power of a size alpha = 0.05 test against the null hypothesis that there is no effect for different sample sizes?

Basis study	Assumptions	Sample size	Power
Black et al. (2007)	True model: Prob(HSGRAD) =	100	0.097
Key result: a 1% increase in birth weight	$0.7 + 0.1*\ln(\text{birthweight}) + \text{error}$	300	0.167
increases the probability of high school	Calculation of error variance and SD:	500	0.263
completion by 0.09 percentage points.	Let $y = \text{Prob(HSGRAD)}$, $x = \ln(\text{birthweight})$,	600	0.298
Birth weight sample summary stats (twins):	$e = \text{error}$	700	0.351
mean = 2598 g, SD = 612 g.	$\text{Var}(y) = 0.44^2 = 0.19$	800	0.376
Probability of HS grad sample summary stats:	$\text{Var}(x) = 0.26^2 = 0.07$ (where $\text{SD}(x) = 0.26$,	900	0.409
mean = 0.73, SD = 0.44.	according to the distribution of $\ln(\text{birthweight})$).	1000	0.446
	If $y = 0.7 + 0.1x + e$, and x and e are independent,	1250	0.531
	$\text{Var}(e) = \text{Var}(y) - (0.1^2)*\text{Var}(x)$	1500	0.617
	$= 0.19 - (0.1^2)*(0.07) = 0.19$.	1620	0.660
	So, $\text{SD}(e) = \text{sqrt}(\text{Var}(e)) = 0.44$	2000	0.744
	Therefore, assume: birthweight $\sim N(2598, 612)$,	2200	0.750
	and take the natural log of birthweight.	2500	0.825
	error $\sim N(0, 0.44)$.	3000	0.892
		3500	0.928
		4000	0.962
		4500	0.975
		5000	0.982
		5500	0.993
		6000	0.994
		6500	0.996
		7000	0.999

Table 3 (continued)

Given a sample size, how large would the true effect size have to be in order to be able to detect it with reliable power using a test of size alpha = 0.05?

Basis study	Assumptions	True B1	Power
Conley et al. (2007) Sibling sample from PSID ($n = 1360$)	Model: $y = B0 + B1 * x + error$ Assume: $z \sim N(2598, 612)$, $x = \ln(z)$ error $\sim N(0, 0.44)$ sample size $= 1500$	0.005	0.046
		0.01	0.047
		0.02	0.077
		0.03	0.092
		0.04	0.146
		0.05	0.198
		0.06	0.274
		0.07	0.354
		0.08	0.461
		0.09	0.525
		0.1	0.631
		0.12	0.769
		0.15	0.926
		0.17	0.975
		0.2	0.99

Power calculations are based on Monte Carlo simulations with 1000 replications.

as in Black et al. (2007). Their key result was that a 1% increase in birth weight increased high school completion by 0.09 percentage points. The example shows that under reasonable assumptions about the distribution of birth weight and schooling attainment, it requires a sample of about 4000 children to be able to detect this effect in an OLS regression. We can also turn the question around and ask, given a sample of a certain size, how large would an effect have to be before we could be reasonably certain of finding it in our data? The second half of the table shows that if we were looking for an effect of birth weight on a particular outcome in a sample of 1300 children, the coefficient on (the log of) birth weight would have to be at least 0.15 before we could detect it with reasonable confidence. If we have reason to believe that the effect is smaller, then it is not likely to be useful to estimate the model without more data.

3.2. Data constraints

The lack of large-scale longitudinal data (i.e. data that follows the same persons over time) has been a frequent obstacle to evaluating the long-term impacts of early life influences. Nevertheless, the answer may not always be to undertake collection of new longitudinal data. Drawbacks include the high costs of data collection; the fact that long term outcomes cannot be assessed for some time; and the fact that limiting sample attrition is particularly costly. Unchecked, attrition in longitudinal data can pose challenges for inference.

3.2.1. Leveraging existing datasets

In many cases, existing cross-sectional microdata can serve as a platform for constructing longitudinal datasets. First, it may be possible to add retrospective questions to ongoing data collections. Second, it may be possible to merge new group-level information to existing data sets. Third, it may be possible to merge administrative data sets by individual in order to address previously unanswerable questions. The primary obstacle to implementing each of these data strategies is frequently data security. Depending on the approach adopted, there are different demands on data security, as described below.

Smith (2009) and Garces et al. (2002) are examples of adding retrospective questions to existing data collections. Smith had retrospective questions about health in childhood added to the Panel Study of Income Dynamics (PSID). The PSID began in the 1960s with a representative national sample, and has followed the original respondents and their family members every since. Using these data, Smith (2009) is able to show that adult respondents who were in poor health during childhood have lower earnings than their own siblings who were not in poor health. Such comparisons are possible because the PSID has data on large numbers of sibling pairs. Garces et al. (2002) added retrospective questions about Head Start participation to the PSID, and were able to show that young adults who had attended Head Start had higher educational attainment, and were less likely to have been booked or charged with a crime than siblings who had not attended.

While these approaches may enable analyses of long-term impacts even in the absence of suitable "off the shelf" longitudinal data, they have their drawbacks. First, retrospective data may be reported with error, although it may be possible to assess the extent of reporting error using data from other sources. Second, only outcomes that are already in the data can be assessed, so the need for serendipity remains. Still, the method is promising enough to suggest that on-going, government funded data collections should build-in mechanisms whereby researchers can propose the addition of questions to subsequent waves of the survey.

A second way to address long-term questions is to merge new information at the group level to existing data sets. The merge generally requires the use of geocoded data. For some purposes, such as exploring variations in policies across states, only a state identifier is required. For other purposes, such as examining the effects of traffic patterns on asthma, ideally the researcher would have access to exact latitude and longitude. There are many examples in which this approach has been successfully employed. For example, Ludwig and Miller (2007) study the long term effects of Head Start, which exploits the fact that the Office of Economic Opportunity initially offered the 300 poorest counties in the country assistance in applying for Head Start. They show, using data from the National Educational Longitudinal Surveys, that children who were in counties just poor enough to be eligible for assistance were much more likely to have attended Head Start than children in counties that were just ineligible. They go on to show that child mortality rates in the relevant age ranges were lower in counties whose Head Start enrollments were higher due to the OEO assistance. Using Census data they find that education is higher for people living in areas with higher former Head Start enrollment rates. Unfortunately, however, neither the decennial Census nor the American Community Survey collect county of birth, so they cannot identify people who were born in these counties (substantial measurement error is obviously introduced by using county of residence or county where someone went to school as a proxy for county of birth). An exciting crop of new research would be enabled by the addition of Census survey questions on county of birth, as well as county of residence at key developmental ages (e.g., ages 5 and 14).[9]

In addition to the observational approaches described above, an intriguing possibility is that participants in a completed randomized trial could be followed up. For instance, Rush et al. (1980) conducted a randomized intervention of a prenatal nutrition program in Harlem during the early 1970s. Following these children over time would

---

[9] In another example, Currie and Gruber (1996a) were able to examine the effects of the Medicaid expansions on the utilization of care among children by merging state-level information on Medicaid policy to data from the National Health Interview Survey (NHIS). At the time, this was only possible because one of the authors had access to the NHIS state codes through his work at the Treasury Department. It has since become easier to access geocoded health data either by traveling to Washington to work with the data, or by using it in one of the secure data centers that Census and the National Center for Health Statistics (NCHS) support. However, it remains a source of frustration to health researchers that NCHS does not make state codes and/or codes for large counties available on its public use data sets.

allow researchers to evaluate cognitive outcomes in secondary school, and it might be possible to collect retrospective data on parental investments during childhood, and to evaluate whether parental investments were affected by the randomization.

A third approach to leveraging existing data merges administrative records from multiple sources at the individual level, which obviously requires personal identifiers such as names and birth dates or social security numbers. Access to such identifiers is especially sensitive. Nevertheless, it constitutes a powerful way to address many questions of interest. Several important studies have successfully exploited this approach outside of the US. For example, Black et al. (2005) and Black et al. (2007) use Norwegian data on all twins born over 30 years to look at long-term effects of birth weight, birth order, and family size on educational attainment. Currie et al. (2010) use Canadian data on siblings to examine the effects of health shocks in childhood on future educational attainment and welfare use. Almond et al. (2009) use Swedish data to look at the long term effects of low-level radiation exposure from the Chernobyl disaster on children's educational attainment.

In the US, Doyle (2008) uses administrative data from child protective services and the criminal justice system in Illinois to examine the effects of foster care. He shows first that there is considerable variation between foster care case workers in whether or not a child will be sent to foster care. Moreover, whether a child is assigned to a particular worker is random, depending on who is on duty at the time a call is received. Using this variation, Doyle shows that the marginal child assigned to foster care is significantly more likely to be incarcerated in future. These examples exploit large sample sizes, objective indicators of outcomes, sibling or cohort comparisons, as well as a long follow up period. Some limitations of using existing data include the fact that administrative data sets often contain relatively little background information, and that outcomes are limited to those that are collected in the data bases. Finally, the application process to obtain individual-matched data is often protracted.

Looking forward, the major challenge to research that involves either merging new information to existing data sets, or merging administrative data sets to each other, is that privacy concerns are making it increasingly difficult to obtain data just as it is becoming more feasible to link them. In some cases, access to public use data has deteriorated. For example, for many years, individual level Vital Statistics Natality data from birth certificates included the state of birth, and the county (for counties with over 100,000 population). Since 2005, however, these data elements have been suppressed and it is now necessary to get special permission to obtain US Vital Statistics data with geocodes.

3.2.2. Improvements in the production of administrative data

There are several "first best" potential solutions to these problems. First, creators of large data sets need to be sensitive to the fact that their data may well be useful for addressing questions that they have not envisaged. In order to preserve the ability to use data to answer future questions, it is essential to retain information that can be used for linkage. At a minimum, this should include geographic identifiers at the smallest level of disaggregation that is feasible (for example a Census tract). Ideally, personal identifiers would also be preserved.

Second, more effort needs to be expended in order to make sensitive data available to researchers. A range of mechanisms exist that protect privacy while enabling research:

1. Suppress small cells or merge small cells in public use data files. For example, NCHS data sets such as NHIS could be released with state identifiers for large states, and with identifiers for groups of smaller states.

2. Add small amounts of "noise" to public use data sets, or do data swapping in order to prevent identification of outliers. For example, Cornell University is coordinating the NSF-Census Bureau Synthetic Data Project which seeks to develop public-use "analytically valid synthetic data" from micro datasets customarily accessed at secure Census Research Data Centers.

3. Create model servers. In this approach, users login to estimate models using the true data, but get back output that does not allow individuals to be identified.

4. Data use agreements. The National Longitudinal Survey of Youth and the National Educational Longitudinal Survey have successfully employed data use agreements with qualified users for many years, and without any documented instances of data disclosure.

5. Creation of de-identified merged files. For example, Currie et al. (2009) asked the state of New Jersey to merge birth records with information about the location of pollution sources, and create a de-identified file. This allows them to study the effect of air pollution on infant health.

6. Secure data facilities. The Census Research Data Centers have facilitated access to much confidential data, although researchers who are not located close to the facilities may still face large costs of accessing them.

These approaches to data dissemination have been explored in the statistics literature for more than 20 years (see Dalenius and Reiss (1982)), and have been much discussed at Census (see for example, Reznek (2007)).

3.2.3. Additional issues

We conclude with two new and relatively unexplored data issues. First, how can economists make effective use of the burgeoning literature on biomarkers? These measures have recently been added to existing health surveys, such as the National Longitudinal Study of Adolescent Health data. Biomarkers include not only information about genetic variations but also hormones such as cortisol (which is often interpreted as a measure of stress). It is tempting to think of these markers as potential instrumental variables (Fletcher and Lehrer, 2009). For instance, if it was known that a particular gene was linked to alcoholism, then one might think of using the gene as an instrument for alcoholism. The potential pitfall in this approach is clear if we consider using something like skin color as an instrument in a human capital earnings function—clearly, skin color may predict educational attainment, but it may also have a direct effect on earnings. Just because a variable is "biological" does not mean that it satisfies the criteria for a valid instrument.

A second issue is the evolving nature of what constitutes a "birth cohort." Improvements in neonatal medicine have meant that stillbirths and fetal deaths that would previously have been excluded from the Census of live births may be increasingly important, e.g. MacDorman et al. (2005). Such a compositional effect on live births may have first-order implications for program evaluation and the long-term effects literature. Indeed, both the right and left tails of the birth weight distribution have elongated over time—in 1970 there were many fewer live births with birthweight either less than 1500 g or over 4000 g. To date there has been little research exploring the implications of these compositional changes.

In summary, there are many secrets currently locked in existing data that researchers do not have access to. Economists have been skillful in navigating the many data challenges inherent in the analysis of long-term (and sometimes latent) effects. Nevertheless, we need to explore ways to make more of these data available, and to more researchers. In many cases, this will be a more cost effective and timely way to answer important questions than carrying out new data collections.

4. EMPIRICAL LITERATURE: EVIDENCE OF LONG TERM CONSEQUENCES

What is of importance is the year of birth of the generation or group of individuals under consideration. Each generation **after the age of 5 years** *seems to carry along with it the same relative mortality throughout adult life, and even into extreme old age.*

Kermack et al. (1934) in The Lancet (emphasis added).

In this section, we summarize recent empirical research findings that experiences before five have persistent effects, shaping human capital in particular. A hallmark of this work is the attention paid to identification strategies that seek to isolate causal effects of the early childhood environment. An intriguing sub-current is the possibility that some of these effects may remain latent during childhood (at least from the researcher's perspective) until manifested in either adolescence or adulthood. Recently, economists have begun to ask how parents or other investors in human capital (e.g. school districts) *respond* to early-life shocks, as suggested by the conceptual framework in Section 2.3.

As the excerpt from Kermack et al. (1934) indicates, the idea that early childhood experiences may have important, persistent effects did not originate recently, nor did it first appear in economics. An extensive epidemiological literature has focussed on the early childhood environment, nutrition in particular, and its relationship to health outcomes in adulthood. For a recent survey, see Gluckman and Hanson (2006). This literature has been criticized within epidemiology for credulous empirical comparisons (see, e.g. Rasmussen (2001) or editorial in *The Lancet* [2001]). Absent clearly-articulated identification strategies, health determinants that are difficult to observe and are therefore omitted from the analysis (e.g., parental concern) are presumably correlated with the treatment and can thereby generate the semblance of "fetal origins" linkages, even when such effects do not exist.

4.1. Prenatal environment

In the 1990s, David J. Barker popularized and developed the argument that disruptions to the prenatal environment presage chronic health conditions in adulthood, including heart disease and diabetes (Barker, 1992). Growth is most rapid prenatally and in early childhood. When growth is rapid, disruptions to development caused by the adverse environmental conditions may exert life-long health effects. Barker's "fetal origins" perspective contrasted with the view that pregnant mothers functioned as an effective buffer for the fetus against environmental insults.[10]

In Table 4, we categorize prenatal environmental exposures into three groups. Specifically, we differentiate among factors affecting maternal and thereby fetal health (e.g. nutrition and infection), economic shocks (e.g. recessions), and pollution (e.g. ambient lead).

4.1.1. Maternal health

Currie and Hyson (1999) broke ground in economics by exploring whether "fetal origins" (FO) effects were confined to chronic health conditions in adulthood, or might extend to human capital measures. Using the British National Child Development Survey, low birth weight children were more than 25% less likely to pass English and math O-level tests, and were also less likely to be employed. The finding that test scores were substantially affected was surprising, as epidemiologists routinely posited fetal "brain sparing" mechanisms, whereby adverse *in utero* conditions were parried through a placental triage that prioritized neural development over the body, see, e.g., Scherjon et al. (1996). Furthermore, Stein et al. (1975)'s influential study found no effect of prenatal exposure to the Dutch Hunger Winter on IQ.

Currie and Hyson (1999) were followed by a series of papers that exploited differences in birthweight among siblings and explored their relationship to sibling differences in completed schooling. In relatively small samples (approximately 800 families), Conley and Bennett (2001) found negative but imprecise effects of low birth weight on educational attainment. Statistically significant effects of low birth weight on educational attainment were found when birth weight was interacted with being poor, but in general

---

[10] For example, it has been argued that nausea and vomiting in early pregnancy (morning sickness) is an adaptive response to prevent maternal ingestion of foods that might be noxious to the fetus.

Table 4 Prenatal effects on later child and adult outcomes.

Study and data	Study design	Results
Effects of maternal health		
Is the impact of health shocks cushioned by economic status? The case of low birth weight. Currie and Hyson (1999) NCDS 1958 cohort. $N = 11,609$ at age 20, 10,267 at age 23, 9402 at age 33.	Multivariate regression with numerous background and demographic controls (including maternal grandfather's SES, birth order, and maternal smoking during pregnancy). Key explanatory variables are indicators for LBW, SES, and the interactions. Outcomes measured are the number of O-level passes at age 16 (transcripts collected at age 20), employment, wages and health status at ages 23 and 33. SES assigned using father's social class in 1958 (or mother's SES if father is missing).	LBW children are 38–44% less likely to pass Math O-level. LBW females are 25% less likely to pass English O-level tests. LBW females are 16% less likely to be employed full-time at age 23, LBW males are 9% less likely to be employed full-time at age 33. LBW females are 54% more likely to have fair/poor health at age 23, LBW males are 43% more likely to have fair/poor health at age 33. Few significant differences by SES.
Returns to birthweight (Behrman and Rosenzweig, 2004). Monozygotic female twins born 1936–1955 from the Minnesota Twins Registry for 1994 and the birth weights of their children. $N = 804$ twins, and 608 twin-mother pairs.	Twin fixed effects estimates compared to OLS. To explore generalizability of findings from twins sample, weighted the sample using the US singleton distribution of fetal growth rates.	**Results from twins sample:** 1 oz. per week of pregnancy increase in fetal growth leads to increases of 5% in schooling attainment; 2% in height; 8% hourly wages. **Results from twins sample weighted using singleton distribution:** 1 oz. per week of pregnancy increase in fetal growth leads to increase of 5% in schooling attainment; 1.7% in height; no significant effect on wages. OLS underestimates effects of birth weight by 50%.

Table 4 (continued)

Study and data	Study design	Results
The costs of low birth weight (Almond et al., 2005). Linked birth and infant death files for US for 1983–85, 1989–91 and 1995–97. Hospital costs from healthcare cost and utilization project state inpatient database for 1995–2000 in New York and New Jersey. NCHS N = 189,036 twins, 497,139 singletons. HCUP N = 44,410.	Twin fixed effects to estimate effect of low birth weight (LBW) on hospital costs, health at birth, and infant mortality. Also estimated impact of maternal smoking during pregnancy on health among singleton births, controlling for numerous background and demographic characteristics using OLS and propensity score matching.	**Results using twin fixed effects:** 1 SD increase in birth weight leads to: 0.08 SD decrease in hospital costs for delivery and initial care 0.03 SD decrease in infant mortality rates 0.03 SD increase in Apgar scores 0.01 SD decrease in use of assisted ventilator after birth (OLS estimates w/ out twin fixed effects are 0.51 SD, 0.41 SD, 0.51 SD, 0.25 SD). **Results from OLS on effects of maternal smoking:** Maternal smoking reduces birth weight by 200 g (6%); increases likelihood that infant is LBW (<2500 g) by more than 100% (mean = 0.061). No statistically significant effects on Apgar score, infant mortality rates, or use of assisted ventilator at birth.
The 1918 influenza pandemic and subsequent health outcomes (Almond and Mazumder, 2005). Data from SIPP for 1984–1996. N = 25,169.	Compare cohorts *in utero* before, during and after Oct. 1918 flu pandemic. Regressions estimate cohort effects including survey year dummies and quadratic in age interacted with survey year.	Individuals born in 1919 are 10% more likely to be in fair or poor health, also increases of 19%, 35%, 13%, 17% in trouble hearing, speaking, lifting and walking.
Estimating the impact of large cigarette tax hikes: the case of maternal smoking and infant birth weight (Lien and Evans, 2005). 1990–1997 US Natality files. Data on cigarette taxes from the tax burden on tobacco, various years.	IV using tax hikes in four states as instruments for maternal smoking during pregnancy. Controlled for state and month of conception and background characteristics.	Maternal smoking during pregnancy reduces birth weight by 5.4% and increases likelihood of low birth weight by ~100%.

(continued on next page)

Table 4 (continued)

Study and data	Study design	Results
Long term effects of *in utero* exposure to the 1918 influenza pandemic in the post-1940 US population (Almond, 2006). 1960–1980 US Census data. 1917–1919 Vital Statistics data on mortality. For 1960 $n = 114,031$, for 1970 $n = 308,785$, for 1980 $n = 471,803$.	Estimated effects of *in utero* influenza exposure by comparing cohorts born immediately before, during, and after the 1918 pandemic and by employing the idiosyncratic geographic variation in intensity of exposure to conduct within-cohort analysis. Exposed cohort = those born in 1919. Surrounding cohorts = those born in 1918 and 1920. Used multivariate regression with dummy for birth cohort = 1919, and a quadratic cohort trend to measure departures in the 1919 birth cohort outcomes from the trend. For geographic comparison, used data on virus strength by week as well as data on epidemic timing by Census division to yield a measure of average pandemic virulence by division. Then estimated multivariate regression including the virulence measure, state and year of birth fixed effects, the infant mortality rate in state and year of birth, and the attrition of birth cohort in the Census data.	**Estimation results comparing birth cohorts:** The 1919 birth cohort, compared with the cohort trend: was 4%–5% (13%–15% among treated) less likely to complete high school received 0.6%–1.6% fewer years of education had 1%–3% less total income (for males only, 2005 dollars) had 1%–2% lower socioeconomic status index (Duncan index) was 1%–2% more likely to have a disability that limits work (for males only) had 12% higher average welfare payment (for women). Estimates are slightly larger for nonwhite subgroup. **Estimation results using geographic variation and state fixed effects:** (For the 1919 birth cohort, used average maternal infection rate = 1/3) Maternal infection: reduces schooling by 2.2% reduces probability of high school graduation by 0.05% decreases annual income by 6% reduces socioeconomic status index by 2%–3%.

Table 4 (continued)

Study and data	Study design	Results
Explaining sibling differences in achievement and behavioral outcomes: the importance of within- and between-family factors (Conley et al., 2007) Data from child development supplement of PSID. $N = 1360$.	Sibling fixed effects to examine effects of birth weight, birth order, and gender on later outcomes. Cognitive outcomes measured by the Woodcock–Johnson revised tests of achievement. Behavioral outcomes measured by the behavioral problems index (BPI). Control for family- and child-specific characteristics.	No statistically significant effects of birth weight on BPI or on cognitive assessments for whole sample. For blacks, positive effect of birth weight on cognitive assessments.
Twin differences in birth weight: the effects of genotype and prenatal environment on neonatal and postnatal mortality (Conley et al., 2006) Data on twin births from the 1995–97 matched multiple birth database. $N = 258,823$.	Twin fixed effects models of effects of birth weight on mortality for same-sex and mixed-sex pairs.	1 lb increase in birth weight leads to: 9% (10%) reduction in infant mortality for mixed-sex (same-sex) 7% (8%) reduction in neonatal mortality for mixed-sex (same-sex) 2% reduction in post-neonatal mortality for mixed-sex and same-sex. For full-term twins, mixed-sex effects much larger than same-sex effects.

(continued on next page)

Table 4 (continued)

Study and data	Study design	Results
Biology as destiny? Short- and long-run determinants of intergenerational transmission of birth weight (Currie and Moretti, 2007). California natality data for children born between 1989 and 2001 and their mothers (if born in CA) born between 1970 and 1974. Mothers who are sisters are matched using grandmother's name. $n = 638{,}497$ births.	Examine effect of mother's birth weight on child's birth weight in models with grandmother fixed effects. Examine interactions of mother's birth weight and grandmother's SES at time of mother's birth as proxied by income in zip code of mother's birth. Examine effect of maternal low birth weight on mother's SES at time she gives birth.	Mother's low birth weight increases likelihood that child is low birth weight by about 50%. The incidence of child low birth weight is 7% higher if mother was born into high poverty zip code than into low poverty zip code. Children born into poor households are 0.7% more likely to be low birth weight if their mothers were low birth weight; children born into non-poor households are 0.4% more likely to be low birth weight if their mothers were low birth weight (so, poverty raises the probability of transmission of low birth weight by 88%). Being low birth weight is associated with a loss of $110 in future income, on average, on a baseline income of $10,096 (in 1970 dollars). Being low birth weight increases the probability of living in a high-poverty neighborhood by 3% relative to the baseline. Being low birth weight reduces future educational attainment by 0.1 years.

Table 4 (continued)

Study and data	Study design	Results
From the cradle to the labor market: the effect of birth weight on adult outcomes (Black et al., 2007). Birth records from Norway for 1967–1997. Dropped congenital defects. Matched to registry data on education and labor market outcomes and to military records. $n = 33,366$ twin pairs.	Twin fixed effects, controlling for mother and birth-specific variables. Log(birth weight) is primary independent variable.	10% increase in birth weight: reduces 1-year mortality by 13% increases 5 min APGAR score by 0.3% increases probability of high school completion by 1.2% increases full-time earnings by 1%. **Male outcomes at age 18–20:** 10% increase in birth weight: increases height by 0.3% increases BMI by 0.5% increases IQ by 1.1% (scale of 1–9). **Effects of mother's birth weight on child's birth weight:** 10% increase in mother's birth weight: increases child's birth weight by 1.5%.

(continued on next page)

Table 4 (continued)

Study and data	Study design	Results
The influence of early-life events on human capital, health status and labor market outcomes over the life course (Johnson and Schoeni, 2007) PSID. Adult sample born between 1951 and 1975. $N = 5160$ people and 1655 families. Child sample 0–12 years old in 1997. $N = 1127$ mothers and 2239 children.	Sibling fixed effects to estimate impact of maternal smoking during pregnancy on birth outcomes. Also estimated model using OLS, controlling for grandparent smoking in adolescence, maternal birth weight, and paternal smoking, among other background characteristics.	Note: means are not reported, so relative effects cannot be calculated. **Effects of income and mother's birth weight on child's birth weight:** An increase in income of $10,000 raises child's birth weight by 0.12 lbs if mother was low birth weight (by 0.02 lbs if mother was not low birth weight) for a family with income of $7500 (1997 dollars). Having no health insurance increases the probability of low birth weight by 10 pp. **Effects on child health outcomes:** (health index 1–100) Low birth weight siblings have a 1.67 point lower health index. Private health insurance increases health index by 1.02 points. A $10,000 increase in income for families with $15,000–50,000 income increases health index by 0.53 pp. **Effects on adult outcomes:** Low birth weight siblings: 4.7 pp more likely to be high school dropouts, have a 3.7 point lower health index (1–100 scale). Low birth weight brothers (sample of males only): are 4.3 pp more likely to have no positive earnings (sig at 10% level) have $2966 less annual earnings (sig at 10% level).

Table 4 (continued)

Study and data	Study design	Results
Maternal smoking during pregnancy and early child outcomes (Tominey, 2007) Children of NCDS mothers born between 1973 and 2000. n = 2799 mothers and 6291 sibling children.	Sibling fixed effects to estimate impact of maternal smoking during pregnancy on birth outcomes. Also estimated model using OLS, controlling for grandparent smoking in adolescence, maternal birth weight, and paternal smoking, among other background characteristics.	Note: only reporting results from sibling fixed effects regression here. Maternal smoking during pregnancy reduces birth weight by 1.7%. No statistically significant effect of maternal smoking during pregnancy on probability of having a low birth weight child, pre-term gestation, or weeks of gestation. No statistically significant effects of maternal smoking among mothers who quit by month 5 of pregnancy. Larger effects of maternal smoking on birth weight among low educated women.
Can a pint per day affect your child's pay? The effect of prenatal alcohol exposure on adult outcomes (Nilsson, 2008). Data from Swedish LOUISE database on first-born individuals born between 1964 and 1972. n = 353,742.	Swedish natural experiment in which alcohol availability in 2 treatment regions increased sharply as regular grocery stores were allowed to market strong beer for 6 months during 1967 with the minimum age for purchase being 16 (instead of 21). Difference-in-difference-in-difference comparing under-21 mothers with older mothers in treatment and control regions pre-, during, and post-experiment. Baseline estimations focused on children conceived prior to the experiment, but exposed *in utero* to the experiment. Controlled for quarter and county of birth fixed effects.	**DDD results:** Years of schooling: decreased by 0.27 (2.1%) years for whole sample; by 0.47 years for males; no statistically significant effect for females. HS graduation: decreased by 0.4% for whole sample; by 10% for males; no stat. significant effect for females. Graduation from higher education: decreased by 16% for whole sample; by 35% for males; no stat. significant effect for females. Earnings at age 32: decreased by 24.1% for whole sample; by 22.8% for males; by 17.7% for females. Probability no income at age 32: increased by 74% whole sample. Proportion on welfare: increased by 90% for whole sample; by 5.1pp for males.

(continued on next page)

Table 4 (continued)

Study and data	Study design	Results
Short-, medium- and long-term consequences of poor infant health (Oreopoulos et al., 2008). Data from the Manitoba Center for Health Policy matching provincial health insurance claims with birth records, educational records, and social assistance records. Includes all children born in Manitoba from 1979 to 1985. $n = 54,123$ siblings and 1742 twins.	Sibling and twin fixed effects. Used three measures of infant health: birth weight, 5-min Apgar score, and gestational length in weeks; used dummies for different categories of the variables to estimate nonlinear effects. Also estimated models using OLS for the whole sample, for the siblings sample, and for the twins sample without family fixed effects.	Note: only reporting results from regressions that included family fixed effects here. BW = birth weight. Relative to Apgar score = 10, $BW > 3500$ g, gestation 40–41 weeks lower values. **Effects on infant mortality:** increase infant morality. E.g. in sibling sample (infant mortality = 0.011). Apgar score <6 increases probability of infant mortality by 31.9 pp $BW < 1000$ g increases probability of infant mortality by 87.2 pp Gestation < 36 weeks increases probability of infant mortality by 11.9 pp. **Effect on language arts score (taken in grade 12):** Apgar score < 6 decreases test score by 0.1 of SD (sig. at 10% level) BW 2501–3000 g decreases test score by 0.04 of SD **Effect on probability of reaching grade 12 by age 17:** Apgar score < 6 decreases grade 12 probability by 4.1 pp (sig. at 10%) BW 1001–1500 g decreases grade 12 probability by 14.1 pp Gestation < 36 weeks decreases grade 12 probability by 4.0 pp. **Effect on social assistance take-up during ages 18–21.25:** BW <1000 decreases probability of take-up by 21.5 pp.

Table 4 (continued)

Study and data	Study design	Results
Birth cohort and the black–white achievement gap: the role of health soon after birth (Chay et al., 2009). Data from the national assessment of educational progress long-term trends for 1971–2004. AFQT data from US military for 1976–2001 for male applicants 17–20. $n = 2,649,573$ white males and $n = 1,103,748$ black males. Hospital discharge rates from National Health Interview Survey.	Regression of test scores on year, age, and subject fixed effects (separately for blacks and whites) using NAEP-LTT and AFQT test score data. In AFQT test score data, correct for selection bias using inverse probability weighting from Natality and Census data. Estimated regressions separately for blacks and whites and for the North, the South, the Rustbelt, the deep South, and individual states within the South and North. Also estimated difference-in-difference-in-difference (DDD) models, comparing black and white test scores between cohorts born in 1960–62 and 1970–72 in the South relative to the Rustbelt, controlling for region-specific, race-specific age-by-time effects and race-by-region-by-time effects. Used post neonatal mortality rate (PNMR) as a proxy for infant health environment to assess impact of infant health on the test score gap.	**NAEP-LTT data:** The black–white test score gap declined from 1 SD to 0.6 of SD between 1971 and 2004. The convergence was primarily due to large increases in black test scores in the 1980s. Regression results indicate that the convergence was due to cohort effects, rather than time effects. **AFQT data:** The black–white gap in AFQT test scores declined by about 19% between the 1962–63 and 1972 birth cohorts. The decline in the gap is about 0.3 SDs greater in the South relative to the Rustbelt between 1960–62 and 1970–72 cohorts. Convergence in PNMR explains 52% of the variation across states in AFQT convergence. **Effects of access to hospitals:** A 30pp increase in black hospital birth rates from 1962–64 to 1968–70 increases cohort AFQT scores by 7.5 percentile points. A black child who gained admission to a hospital before age 4 had a 0.7–1 SD gain in AFQT score at age 17–18 relative to a black child who did not.

(continued on next page)

Table 4 (continued)

Study and data	Study design	Results
Separated at birth: US twin estimates of the effects of birth weight (Royer, 2009) California birth records. $n = 3028$ same-sex female twin births 1960–1982. Data from early childhood longitudinal study-birth cohort. $n = 1496$ twin births.	Twin fixed effects, allowing non-linear effects of birth weight.	**Twin fixed-effect results:** 250 g increase in birth weight leads to: 8.3% decrease in probability of infant mortality 0.82 day decrease in stay in hospital post-birth 0.02–0.04 of SD increase in mental/motor test score 0.2% increase in educ. attainment of mother at childbirth 0.5% increase in child's birth weight 11% decrease in pregnancy complications. No statistically significant effects of birth weight on adult health outcomes such as hypertension, anemia, and diabetes. No statistically significant effects of birth weight on income-related measures. 200 g increase in birth weight leads to a 0.5 pp increase in probability of being observed in adulthood—small selection bias. Found no statistically significant evidence of compensating or reinforcing parental investments when considering early medical care and breastfeeding.

Table 4 (continued)

Study and data	Study design	Results
The long-term economic impact of *in utero* and postnatal exposure to malaria (Barreca, 2010). Malaria mortality from US mortality statistics 1900–1936. $n = 1147$ state-year observations. Climate data $n = 1813$ obs. Adult outcomes from 1960 Census. All data merged at state/year of birth level.	IV using fraction of days in "malaria–ideal" temperature range as IV for malaria deaths in state and year.	Note: Only results from the IV regression are reported here. Exposure to 10 additional malaria deaths per 100,000 inhabitants causes 3.4% less years of schooling. Exposure to malaria can account for approximately 25% of the difference in years of schooling between cohorts born in high and low malaria states.
Long-run longevity effects of a nutrition shock in early life: The Dutch Famine of 1846–47 (Van Den Berg et al., in press). Historical sample of the Netherlands. Exposed cohort born 9/1/1846–6/1/1848. Non-exposed born 9/1/1848–9/1/1855 and 9/1/1837–9/1/1944.	Key independent variable is exposure to famine at birth. Instrument access to food with variations in yearly average real market prices of rye and potatoes for three different regions. Controlled for macroeconomic conditions, infant mortality rates, and individual demographic and socio-economic characteristics.	**Results from nonparametric regression:** Residual life expectancy at age 50 is 3.1 years shorter for exposed men than for men born after the famine; 1.4 years shorter than for men born before famine. Kolmogorov-Smirnov test suggests that the survival curves after age 50 differ significantly for exposed and control men. Max difference in distribution = 0.15 at age 56. **Results from parametric survival models:** Exposure to famine at birth for men reduces residual life expectancy at age 50 by 4.2 years. No statistically significant results for women.

(continued on next page)

Table 4 (continued)

Study and data	Study design	Results
Maternal stress and child well-being: evidence from siblings (Aizer et al., 2009). National Collaborative Perinatal Project. Births 1959-65 in Providence and Boston. $N = 1103$ births to 915 women. 163 siblings in sample.	Sibling fixed effects. Estimated effect of deviations from mean cortisol levels (cortisol measures maternal stress) during pregnancy on outcomes.	No significant effects on birth weight or maternal postnatal investments. Exposure to top quartile of cortisol level distribution (relative to the middle) leads to 47% of SD decrease in verbal IQ at age 7 (sign. at 10% level). 1 SD deviation in cortisol levels leads to 26% of SD decrease in educational attainment. Exposure to top quartile of cortisol level distribution (relative to the middle) leads to 51% of SD decrease in educational attainment.
The scourge of Asian flu: the physical and cognitive development of a cohort of British children *in utero* during the Asian Influenza Pandemic of 1957, from birth until age 11 (Kelly, 2009). NCDS 1958 cohort. $N = 16,765$ at birth, 14,358 at 7, 14,069 at 11.	Effect of flu on each cohort member identified using variation in incidence of epidemic by local authority of birth. Epidemic peaked when cohort members were 17-23 weeks gestation. 1/3 of women of child-bearing age were infected, hence true treatment effect can be estimated by multiplying results by 3.	No statistically significant evidence of reinforcing or compensating parental investments. 1 SD increase in epidemic intensity decreases birth weight by 0.03-0.363 SD; decreases test scores by 0.067 of SD at age 7, by 0.043 of SD at age 11; increases detrimental effect of mother preeclampsia from −0.075 to −0.11 SD on birth weight; increases detrimental effect of mother smoking by 0.03 of SD on birth weight; increases detrimental effect of mother under 8 stone weight from −0.54 to −0.61 of SD on birth weight

Table 4 (continued)

Study and data	Study design	Results
Do lower birth weight babies have lower grades? Twin fixed effect and instrumental variables evidence from Taiwan (Lin and Liu, 2009). Birth Certificate data for Taiwan. High school entrance exam results from Committee of Basic Competence Test. $N = 118,658$. Twin sample $n = 7772$.	Twin fixed effects and IV using the public health budget and number of doctors in county where child was born as instruments for child's birth weight.	**Twin FE/IV for mothers w/ <9 yrs ed & <25 yrs old** Increase in birth weight of 100 g leads to: Increase Chinese score: 0.5%/8.2% Increase English score: 0.3%/8.1%★ Increase Math score: 0.7%/12.6% Increase Natural Science score: 0.8%/11.8% Increase Social Science score: 0.4%/4.0%★ ★ means significant at 10% level IV results for other subgroups show smaller/no effects.
Poor, hungry and stupid: numeracy and the impact of high food prices in industrializing Britain, 1750–1850 (Baten et al., 2007). Data on age heaping from 1951 to 1881 British Census. Information on poor relief from Boyer (1990).	Age heaping is rounding age to nearest 5 or 10. Whipple index (WI) = number of ages that are multiples relative to expected number given uniform age distribution. Regressions use WI as dependent variable. Wheat prices and poor relief measures are independent variables.	During the Revolutionary and Napoleonic Wars, the price of wheat almost doubled—and the number of erroneously reported ages at multiples of 5 doubled from 4% to 8%. Men and women born in decades with higher WI sorted into jobs that had lower intelligence requirements. 1 SD increase in the Whipple index associated with a 2.8% increase in the earnings) decrease in earnings.

(continued on next page)

Table 4 (continued)

Study and data	Study design	Results
Impacts of economic shocks		
Birth weight and income: interactions across generations (Conley and Bennett, 2001) Data from PSID. Two samples: (1) children born 1986–1992, $n = 1654$; (2) reached 19 by 1992, $n = 1388$ individuals in 766 families.	Sibling fixed effects.	Low birth weight child who spent 6 years at poverty line is less likely to graduate high school than normal birth weight child who spent 6 years at poverty line. Low birth weight child who spent 6 years with income 5 times the poverty line is as likely to graduate high school as normal birth weight child of same income (significant at 10% level).
Economic conditions early in life and individual mortality (Van Den Berg et al., in press). Data from historical sample of the Netherlands on individuals born 1812–1903 with date of death observed by 2000. $n = 9276$. Merged with historical macro time series data.	Compared individuals born in booms with those born in the subsequent recessions. Controlled for wars and epidemics.	Comparing those born in boom of 1872–1876 with those born in recession of 1877–1881: Boom $T\|T > 2 = 66.0$ years, Recession $T\|T > 2 = 62.5$ years Boom $T\|T > 5 = 70.8$ years, Recession $T\|T > 5 = 67.5$ years **Regression results:** Boom $T\|T > 2$ is 1.58 years greater than Recession $T\|T > 2$ Notation: $T|T > 2 = $ average lifetime given survival past age 2 $T|T > 5 = $ average lifetime given survival past age 5

Table 4 (continued)

Study and data	Study design	Results
Evidence on early-life income and late-life health from America's Dustbowl era (Cutler et al., 2007). The Health and Retirement Study. $N = 8739$ people born between 1929 and 1941. Agricultural data from National Agricultural Statistics Service. Income data from Bureau of Economic Analysis.	Measured economic conditions *in utero* using income and yield from the same calendar year for those born in 3rd or 4th quarter of the year and from the previous calendar year for those born in 1st or 2nd quarter. Regressions include the *in utero* economic condition measure (log income, log yield), dummy for whether respondent's father was a farmer and interaction of the dummy with the economic conditions. Controlled for region and year of birth fixed effects, region-specific linear time trends, and region-year infant death and birth rates, and other demographic characteristics.	No statistically significant relationship between poor early-life economic conditions during the Dustbowl and late-life health outcomes such as heart conditions, stroke, diabetes, hypertension, arthritis, psychiatric conditions, etc.

(continued on next page)

Table 4 (continued)

Study and data	Study design	Results
Long-run health impacts of income shocks: wine and Phylloxera in 19th century France (Banerjee et al., forthcoming). See paper references for source of data on wine production, number of births, and infant mortality. Department level data on heights from military records 1872–1912. $n = 3485$ year-departments.	Regional variation in a large negative income shock caused by Phylloxera attacks on French vineyards between 1863 and 1890. Shock dummy equal to 0 pre Phylloxera and after 1890 (when grafting solution found). Dummy equal 1 when wine production < 80% of pre-level. Difference–in–difference comparing children born in affected and unaffected areas before and after.	Decrease in wine production was not compensated by an increase in other agricultural production (e.g. wheat), suggesting that this was truly a large negative income shock. **Main outcomes:** 3–5% decline in height at age 20 for those born in wine-growing families during the year that their region was affected by Phylloxera. Those born in Phylloxera-affected year are 0.35–0.38 pp more likely to be shorter than 1.56 cm. No statistically significant effects on other measures of health or life expectancy.

Table 4 (continued)

Study and data	Study design	Results
Impacts of environmental shocks		
Lifespan depends on the month of birth (Doblhammer and Vaupel, 2001) Data on populations of Denmark, Austria, and Australia. **Denmark:** Longitudinal data based on population registry for 1968–2000 $n = 1,371,003$. **Austria:** Data from death certificates for 1988–1996 $n = 681,677$ **Australia:** Data from death certificates from 1993–1997 $n = 219,820$ Also used data on individuals born in Britain who died in Australia: $n = 43,074$ Data on infant mortality for Denmark	Used t tests to perform pairwise comparisons between mean age at death by quarter of birth. To test whether the seasonal difference in the risk of death accounts for differences in adult life span by month of birth, calculated monthly deviations from annual death rates and used weighted least squares regression with dummies for month of birth, current month, age since last birthday in months, sex, and birth cohort. To test whether selective survival or debilitation during the 1st year of life explains differences in life expectancy at age 50, calculated monthly death rates during 1st year of life and monthly deviations from annual death rates during 1st year of life; then used a multivariate regression without controls for sex and birth cohort.	Note: Autumn-Spring = average difference in age at death between people born in Autumn (Oct–Dec) and in the Spring (Apr–Jun). **Denmark:** Mean remaining life expectancy at age 50 = 27.52 years 0.19 years shorter lifespans for those born in 2nd quarter 0.12 years longer lifespans for those born in 4th quarter Correlation between infant mortality at time of birth and adult mortality after age 50 = 0.87. **Austria:** Average age at death = 77.70 years 0.28 years shorter lifespans for those born in 2nd quarter **Austria:** average age at death = 77.70 years 0.28 years shorter lifespans for those born in 2nd quarter 0.32 years longer lifespans for those born in 4th quarter Additional results shown for specific causes of death. **Australia:** Mean age of death = 78.00 years for those born in 2nd quarter; mean age of death = 77.65 years for those born in 4th quarter British immigrants born Nov.-Jan. have age of death 0.36 years higher than natives. Those immigrants born Mar-May have age of death 0.26 years lower than Australian natives.

(continued on next page)

Table 4 (continued)

Study and data	Study design	Results
Air quality, infant mortality, and the Clean Air Act of 1970 (Chay and Greenstone, 2003a,b) County-level mortality and natality data 1969-1974. Annual monitor level data on total suspended particles (TSP) from EPA. $N = 501$ county-years.	Clean Air Act imposed regulations on polluters in counties with TSP concentrations exceeding federal ceilings. Used nonattainment status as an instrument for changes in TSP. Also used regression discontinuity methods to examine effect of TSP on infant mortality.	1% decline in TSP pollution results in 0.5% decline in infant mortality rate. Most effects driven by reduction of deaths occurring within 1 month of birth.
Air pollution and infant health: what can we learn from California's recent experience? (Currie and Neidell, 2005) Data on pollution from California EPA. Individual-level infant mortality data from California vital statistics 1989-2000. $n = 206,353$.	Estimated linear models that approximate hazard models, where the risk of death is defined over weeks of life, and length of life is controlled for with a flexible nonparametric spline. Controlled for prenatal and postnatal pollution exposure, weather, child's age, and numerous other child and family characteristics, as well as month, year, and zip code fixed effects. Examined effects of ozone (O3), carbon monoxide (CO), and particulate matter (PM110) on infant mortality.	1.1 unit reduction in postnatal exposure to CO (the actual reduction that occurred in CA in the 1990s) saved 991 infant lives, −4.6% decrease in infant mortality rate. No statistically significant effects of prenatal exposure to any of the pollutants.

Table 4 (continued)

Study and data	Study design	Results
Prenatal exposure to radioactive fallout (from Chernobyl) and school outcomes in Sweden (Almond et al., 2009). All Swedes born 1983–1988, $n = 562,637$. Data on radiation from Swedish Geological Survey at parish level.	Three empirical strategies: (1) Cohort comparisons—Compared cohorts *in utero* before, during, and after Chernobyl with particular focus on cohort 8–25 weeks post conception. (2) Within-cohort comparisons—Use geographic variation in levels of exposure. Define 4 regions, R0 (least exposure), R1, R2, R3. (3) Diff-in-diff sibling comparison—Compared those exposed to radiation *in utero* 8–25 to siblings who were not.	**Results from (1):** Probability of qualifying for high school reduced by 0.2% for cohort *in utero* during radiation; by 0.6% for cohort *in utero* 8–25. Grades reduced by 0.4% for cohort *in utero* during radiation; by 0.6% for cohort *in utero* 8–25. **Results from (2):** (R3 relative to R0) Probability of qualifying for high school reduced by 3.6% for cohort *in utero* during radiation in R3; by 4% for cohort *in utero* 8–25 in R3. Grades reduced by 3% for cohort *in utero* during radiation in R3; by 5.2% for cohort *in utero* 8–25 in R3. **Results from (3):** (R3 relative to R0) Difference in probability of qualifying for high school between siblings increased by 6% in R3. Difference in grades between siblings increased by 8% in R3.

(continued on next page)

Table 4 (continued)

Study and data	Study design	Results
Air pollution and infant health: lessons from New Jersey (Currie et al., 2009). Pollution data from EPA. Individual-level data on infant births and deaths from the New Jersey Department of Health 1989-2003. $n = 283,393$ for mother fixed effects models.	Mother fixed effects to estimate impact of exposure to pollution (during and after birth) on infant health outcomes. Air pollution measured from air quality monitors and assigned to each childbased on home address of mother. Also included interactions b/n variable for pollution exposure and maternal smoking as well as other maternal characteristics. Controlled for weather, pollution monitor locations, time trends, seasonal effects, and other background characteristics.	1 unit change in mean CO exposure during last trimester of pregnancy decreases average birth weight by 0.5%, increases likelihood of low birth weight by 8%, and decreases gestation by 0.2%. 1 unit change in mean CO exposure in first 2 weeks after birth increases likelihood of infant mortality by 2.5%. Estimated that a 1 unit decrease in mean CO exposure in first 2 weeks after birth would save 17.6 per 100,000 lives. Effects of CO exposure on infant health at birth are 2-6 times larger for smokers and mothers who are over age 35. Effects of PM10 (particulate matter) and ozone are not consistently significant across the specifications.

Table 4 (continued)

Study and data	Study design	Results
Fetal exposures to toxic releases and infant health (Currie et al., 2009) Toxic Release Inventory data at county-year level matched to county-year level natality and infant mortality data. $N = 5279$.	Multivariate regression of infant health outcomes on amount of toxic releases in each county and year, controlling for demographic and socio-economic characteristics, mother drinking or smoking during pregnancy, county employment, and county and year fixed effects. Compared effects of developmental toxins to other toxins, and "fugitive" air releases to "stack" air releases (since emissions that go up a smoke stack are more likely to be treated in some way, and hence will affect those in the vicinity less).	An additional thousand pounds per square mile of all toxic releases leads to: 0.02% decrease in length of gestation 0.04% decrease in birth weight 0.1% increase in probability of low birth weight 0.8% increase in probability of very low birth weight 1.3% increase in infant mortality Larger effects for developmental toxins and for fugitive air releases than for other toxins or for stack air releases. A 2-SD increase in lead releases decreases gestation by 0.02% and decreases birth weight by 0.05%. A 2-SD increase in cadmium releases decreases gestation by 0.03%, decreases birth weight by 0.07%, increases probability of low birth weight by 1.2%, increases probability of very low birth weight by 1.4%, and increases infant mortality by 5%. Similar results for toluene, epichlorohydrin. Reductions in releases over 1988–1999 can account for 3.9% of the reduction in infant mortality over the same time period.

(continued on next page)

Table 4 (continued)

Study and data	Study design	Results
Traffic congestion and infant health: evidence from E-ZPass (Currie and Walker, 2009) Birth records for Pennsylvania and New Jersey, 1994–2003. Data on housing prices for New Jersey. $N = 727,954$ for diff-in-diff. $N = 232,399$ for mother fixed effects.	Identification due to introduction of electronic toll collection (E-ZPass), which reduced traffic congestion and motor vehicle emissions in the vicinity of highway toll plazas. Difference-in-difference, comparing infants born to mothers living near toll plazas to infants born to mothers living near busy roadways (but away from toll plazas), before and after introduction of E-ZPass. Also estimated impacts of exposure to E-ZPass on infant health using mother fixed effects methods. Controlled for various background characteristics, year and month fixed effects, and plaza-specific time trends. Also estimated impact of E-ZPass introduction on housing prices near the toll plaza.	**Results from Difference-in-Difference Method:** Reductions in traffic congestion generated by introduction of E-ZPass reduced incidence of premature birth by 10.8% and low birth weight by 11.8% for children of mothers living w/in 2 km of a toll plaza. For those living w/in 3 km of a toll plaza, effects are 7.3% for premature births and 8.4% for low birth weight. Similar results using mother fixed effects. No effects of E-ZPass introduction on housing prices or demographic composition of mothers living near toll plazas.

Table 4 (continued)

Study and data	Study design	Results
Caution, Drivers! Children Present. Traffic, Pollution, and Infant Health (Knittel et al., 2009). Traffic data from the freeway performance measurement system. Pollution data from EPA. Birth data from California Dept. of Public Health 2002–2006. $N = 373,800$.	IV using traffic shocks (due to accidents or road closures) to instrument for air pollution. Preferred specifications include traffic flow, delays, and interactions between traffic and weather.	Note: only results from the IV regression are reported here. 1 unit decrease in exposure to particulate matter (PM10) leads to 5% decrease in infant mortality rate (saves 14 lives per 100,000 births).

Unless otherwise noted, only results significant at 5% level are reported.

sample size prevented detection of all but the largest effects (see Section 3.1). Using a comparable sample size, Behrman and Rosenzweig (2004) found the schooling of identical female twins was nearly one-third of a year longer for a pound increase in birth weight (454 grams), with relatively imprecise effects on adult BMI or wages.

In light of the above power concerns, Currie and Moretti (2007) matched mothers to their sisters in half a million birth records from California. Here, low birth weight was found to have statistically significant negative impacts on educational attainment and the likelihood of living in a wealthy neighborhood. However, the estimated magnitudes of the main effects were more modest: low birth weight increased the likelihood of living in a poor neighborhood by 3% and reduced educational attainment approximately one month on average. Like Conley and Bennett (2001), the relationship was substantially stronger for the interaction between low birth weight and being born in poor neighborhoods.

In a sample of Norwegian twins, Black et al. (2007) also found long-term effects of birth weight, but did not detect any heterogeneity in the strength of this relationship by parental socioeconomic status.[11] Oreopoulos et al. (2008) find similar results for Canada and Lin and Liu (2009) find positive long term effects of birth weight in Taiwan. Royer (2009) found long-term health and educational effects within California twin pairs, with a weaker effect of birth weight than several other studies, esp. Black et al. (2007). Responsive investments could account for this discrepancy if they differed between California and elsewhere (within twin pairs). Alternatively, there may be more homogeneity with respect to socioeconomic status in Scandinavia than in California. As described in Section 3, Royer (2009) analyzed investment measures directly with the ECLS-B data, concluding that there was no evidence of compensatory or reinforcing investments (see Section 2.2).

Following a literature in demography on seasonal health effects, Doblhammer and Vaupel (2001) and Costa and Lahey (2005) focused on the potential long-term health effects of birth season. A common finding is that in the northern hemisphere, people born in the last quarter of the year have longer life expectancies than those born in the second quarter. Both the availability of nutrients can vary seasonally (particularly historically), as does the likelihood of common infections (e.g., pneumonia). Therefore, either nutrition or infection could drive this observed pattern. Almond (2006) focused on prenatal exposure to the 1918 Influenza Pandemic, estimating that children of infected mothers were 15% less likely to graduate high school and wages were between 5 and 9% lower. Kelly (2009) found negative effects of prenatal exposure to 1957 "Asian flu" in Britain on test scores, though the estimated magnitudes were relatively modest. Interestingly, while birth weight was reduced by flu exposure, this effect appears to be independent of the test score effect. Finally, Field et al. (2009) found that prenatal iodine

---

[11] Royer (2009) notes that Black et al. (2007) find a "negligible effect of birth weight on high school completion for the 1967-1976 birth cohort, but for individuals born between 1977 and 1986, the estimate is nearly six times as large".

supplementation raised educational attainment in Tanzania by half a year of schooling, with larger impacts for girls.

4.1.2. Economic shocks

A second set of papers considers economic shocks around the time of birth. Here, health in adulthood tends to be the focus (not human capital), and findings are perhaps less consistent than in the studies of nutrition and infection described above. Van Den Berg et al. (2006)'s basic result is that adult survival in the Netherlands is reduced for those born during economic downturns. In contrast, Cutler et al. (2007) detected no long term morbidity effects in the Health and Retirement Survey data for cohorts born during the Dustbowl era of 1930s. Banerjee et al. (forthcoming) found that shocks to the productive capacity of French vineyards did not have detectable effects on life expectancy or health outcomes, but did reduce height in adulthood. Baten et al. (2007) related variations in grain prices in the decade of birth to numeracy using an ingenious measure based on "age heaping" in the British Censuses between 1851 and 1881. Persons who are more numerate are less likely to round their ages to multiples of 5 or 10. They find that children born in decades with high grain prices were less numerate by this index.

4.1.3. Air pollution

The third strand of the literature examines the effect of pollution on fetal health. Epidemiological studies have demonstrated links between very severe pollution episodes and mortality: one of the most famous focused on a "killer fog" in London, England and found dramatic increases in cardiopulmonary mortality (Logan and Glasg, 1953). Previous epidemiological research on the effects of moderate pollution levels on prenatal health suggests negative effects but have produced inconsistent results. Cross-sectional differences in ambient pollution are usually correlated with other determinants of fetal health, perhaps more systematically than with nutritional or disease exposures considered above. Many of the pollution studies have minimal (if any) controls for these potential confounders. Banzhaf and Walsh (2008) found that high-income families move out of polluted areas, while poor people in-migrate. These two groups are also likely to provide differing levels of (non-pollution) investments in their children, so that fetuses and infants exposed to lower levels of pollution may tend to receive, e.g., better quality prenatal care. If these factors are unaccounted for, this would lead to an upward bias in estimates. Alternatively, certain pollution emissions tend to be concentrated in urban areas, and individuals in urban areas may be more educated and have better access to health care, factors that may improve health. Omitting these factors would lead to a downward bias, suggesting the overall direction of bias from confounding is unclear.

Two studies by Chay and Greenstone (2003a,b) address the problem of omitted confounders by focusing on "natural experiments" provided by the implementation of the Clean Air Act of 1970 and the recession of the early 1980s. Both the Clean Air

Act and the recession induced sharper reductions in particulates in some counties than in others, and they use this exogenous variation in levels of pollution at the county-year level to identify its effects. They estimate that a one unit decline in particulates caused by the implementation of the Clean Air Act (recession) led to between five and eight (four and seven) fewer infant deaths per 100,000 live births. They also find some evidence that the decline in Total Suspended Particles (TSPs) led to reductions in the incidence of low birth weight. However, only TSPs were measured at that time, so that they could not study the effects of other pollutants. And the levels of particulates studied by Chay and Greenstone are much higher than those prevalent today; for example, PM10 (particulate matter of 10 microns or less) levels have fallen by nearly 50% from 1980 to 2000.

Several recent studies consider natural experiments at more recently-encountered pollution levels. For example, Currie et al. (2009) use data from birth certificates in New Jersey in which they know the exact location of the mothers residence, and births to the same mother can be linked. They focus on a sample of mothers who live near pollution monitors and show that variations in pollution from carbon monoxide (which comes largely from vehicle exhaust) reduces birth weight and gestation. Currie and Walker (2009) exploit a natural experiment having to do with introduction of electronic toll collection devices (E-ZPass) in New Jersey and Pennsylvania. Since much of the pollution produced by automobiles occurs when idling or accelerating back to highway speed, electronic toll collection greatly reduces auto emissions in the vicinity of a toll plaza. Currie and Walker (2009) compare mothers near toll plazas to those who live near busy roadways but further from toll plazas and find that E-ZPass increased birth weight and gestation. They show that they obtain similar estimates following mothers over time and estimating mother fixed effects models. These papers are notable in part because it has proven more difficult to demonstrate effects of pollution on fetal health than on infant health, as discussed further below. Hence, it appears that being *in utero* may be protective against at some forms of toxic exposure (such as particulates) but not others.

This literature on the effects of air pollution is closely related to that on smoking. Smoking is, after all, the most important source of indoor air pollution. Medical research has shown that nicotine constricts the oxygen supply to the fetus, so there is an obvious mechanism for smoking to affect infant health. Indeed, there is near unanimity in the medical literature that smoking is the most important preventable cause of low birth weight. Economists have focused on ways to address heterogeneity in other determinants of birth outcomes that are likely associated with smoking. Tominey (2007) found that relative to a conventional multivariate control specification, roughly one-third of the harm from smoking to birth weight is explained by unobservable traits of the mother. Moreover, the reduction in birth weight from smoking was substantially larger for low-SES mothers. In a much larger sample, Currie et al. (2009)

showed that smoking significantly reduced birth weight, even when comparisons are restricted to within-sibling differences. Moreover, Currie et al. (2009) document a significant interaction effect between exposure to carbon monoxide exposure and infant health in the production of low birth weight, which may help explain the heterogeneity in birth weight effects reported by Tominey (2007). Aizer and Stroud (2009) note that impacts of smoking on birth weight are generally much smaller in sibling comparisons than in OLS and matching-based estimates. Positing that attenuation bias is accentuated in the sibling comparisons, Aizer and Stroud (2009) use serum cotinine levels as an instrument for measurement error in smoking and find that sibling comparisons yield similar birth weight impacts (around 150 g). Lien and Evans (2005) use increases in state excise taxes as an instrument for smoking and find large effects of smoking on birth weight (182 g) as a result. Using propensity score matching, Almond et al. (2005) document a large decrease in birth weight from prenatal smoking (203 g), but argue that this weight decrease is weakly associated with alternative measures of infant health, such as prematurity, APGAR score, ventilator use, and infant mortality.

Some recently-released data will enable new research on smoking's short and long-term effects. In 2005, twelve states began using the new US Standard Certificate of Live Birth (2003 revision). Along with other new data elements (e.g., on surfactant replacement therapy), smoking behavior is reported *by trimester*. It will be useful to consider whether smoking's impact on birth weight varies by trimester, and also whether smoking is more closely tied to other measures of newborn health if it occurs early versus late in pregnancy. Second, there is relatively little research by economists on the long-term effects of prenatal exposure to smoking. Between 1990 and 2003, there were 113 increases in state excise taxes on cigarettes (Lien and Evans, 2005).[12] Since 2005, the American Community Survey records both state and quarter of birth, permitting linkage of these data to the changes in state excise taxes during pregnancy.

Almond et al. (2009) examine the effect of pollution from the Chernobyl disaster on the Swedish cohort that was *in utero* at the time of the disaster. Since the path of the radiation was very well measured, they can compare affected children to those who were not affected as well as to those born in the affected areas just prior to the disaster. They find that in the affected cohort those who suffered the greatest radiation exposure were 3% less likely to qualify for high school, and had 6% lower math grades (the measure closest to IQ). The estimated effects were much larger within families. A possible interpretation is that cognitive damage from Chernobyl was reinforced by parents.

To summarize, the recent "fetal origins" literature in economics finds substantial effects of prenatal health on subsequent human capital and health. As we discuss in

---

[12] Some states enacted earlier excise taxes: the "average state tax rate increased from 5.7 cents in 1964 to 15.5 cents in 1984" (Farrelly et al., 2003); high 1970s inflation can be an additional potential source of identification as excise taxes were set nominally.

Section 5, this suggests a positive role for policies that improve human capital by affecting the birth endowment. That is, despite being congenital (i.e. present from birth), this research indicates that the birth endowment is malleable in ways that shape human capital. This finding has potentially radical implications for public policy since it suggests that one of the more effective ways to improve children's long term outcomes might be to target women of child bearing age in addition to focusing on children after birth.

4.2. Early childhood environment

It would be surprising to find that a very severe shock in early childhood (e.g., a head injury, or emotional trauma) had no effect on an individual. Therefore, a more interesting question from the point of view of research is how developmental linkages operating at the individual level affect human capital formation in the aggregate. To answer this question, we need to know how many children are affected by negative early childhood experiences that could plausibly exert persistent effects? How big and long-lasting are the effects of less severe early childhood shocks relative to more severe shocks? Taken together, how much of the differences in adult attainments might be accounted for by things that happen to children between birth and age five? Furthermore, how are these linkages between shocks and outcomes mediated or moderated by third factors? For example, is the effect of childhood lead exposure on subsequent test scores stronger for families of lower socioeconomic status (i.e. is the interaction with SES an important one) and if so why? Alternatively, is the effect of injury mediated by health status, or is the causal pathway a direct one to cognition?

We might also wish to know how parents respond to early childhood shocks. To date, there has been less focus on this question in the early childhood period than in the prenatal period, perhaps because it seems less plausible to hope to uncover a "pure" biological effect of a childhood shock given that children are embedded in families and in society. However, this embeddedness opens the possibility that a richer set of behavioral responses—of the kind considered by economists—might be at play. Furthermore, early childhood admits a wider set of environmental influences than the prenatal period. For example, abuse in early childhood can be distinguished from malnutrition, a distinction more difficult for the *in utero* period, and these may have quite different effects.

We define early childhood as starting at birth and ending at age five. From an empirical standpoint, early childhood so defined offers advantages and disadvantages over analyses that focus on the prenatal period. Mortality is substantially lower during early childhood than *in utero*, which reduces the scope for selective attrition caused by environmental shocks to affect the composition of survivors. On the other hand, it is unlikely that environmental sensitivity during early childhood tapers discontinuously at any precise age (including age five). From a refutability perspective, we cannot make sharp temporal comparisons of a cohort "just exposed" to a shock during early childhood to a neighboring cohort "just unexposed" by virtue of its being too old to be sensitive.

Moreover, it will often be difficult to know *a priori* whether prenatal or postnatal exposure is more influential.[13] Thus, studies of early childhood exposures tend to emphasize cross-sectional sources of variation, including that at the geographic and individual level. The studies reviewed in this section focus on tracing out the relationships between events in early childhood and future outcomes, and are summarized in Table 5.

4.2.1. Infections

Insofar as specific health shocks are considered, infections are the most commonly studied. In epidemiology, long-term health effects of infections—and the inflammation response they trigger—has been explored extensively, e.g. Crimmins and Finch (2006). Outcomes analyzed by economists include height, health status, educational attainment, test scores, and labor market outcomes. The estimated impacts tend to be large. Using geographic differences in hookworm infection rates across the US South, Bleakley (2007) found that eradication after 1910 increased literacy rates but did not increase the amount of completed schooling, except for Black children. The literacy improvement was much larger among Blacks than Whites, and stronger among women then men. The return to education increased substantially, and Bleakley (2007) estimated that hookworm infection throughout childhood reduced wages in adulthood by as much as 40%. Case and Paxson (2009) focussed on reductions in US childhood mortality from typhoid, malaria, measles, influenza, and diarrhea during the first half of the 20th Century. They found that improvements in the disease environment in one's state of birth were mirrored by improved cognitive performance at older ages, but like Bleakley (2007), this effect did not seem to operate through increased years of schooling. However, the estimated cognitive impacts in Case and Paxson (2009) were not robust to the inclusion of state-specific time trends in their models.

Chay et al. (2009) found that reduced exposure to pneumonia and diarrhea in early childhood among Blacks during the late 1960s raised subsequent AFQT and NAEP scores towards those of Whites. Changes in postneonatal mortality rates (dominated by infections) explained between 50% and 80% of the (large) reduction in the Black-White AFQT gap. Finally, Bozzoli et al. (forthcoming) highlight that in developing countries, high average mortality rates cause the selection effect of early childhood mortality to overwhelm the "scarring" effect. Thus, the positive relationship between early childhood health and subsequent human capital may be absent in analyses that do not account for selective attrition in high mortality settings.

4.2.2. Health status

Many of the studies reviewed in Table 5 investigate the link between health in childhood and future cognitive or labor market outcomes. These studies can be viewed as a subset of

---

[13] For example, early postnatal exposure to Pandemic influenza apparently had a larger impact on hearing than did prenatal flu exposure (Heider, 1934).

Table 5 Impacts of early childhood shocks on later outcomes.

Study and data	Study design	Results
Childhood physical and mental health		
Mental health in childhood and human capital (Currie and Stabile, 2006). Data from NLSCY and NLSY. Canadian NLSCY: data on children aged 4–11 in 1994. Mental health screening in 1994; outcomes measured in 2002. $n = 5604$. US NLSY: data on children aged 4–11 in 1994. Mental health score averaged over 1990–1994. $n = 3758$.	Sibling fixed effects. Hyperactivity and aggression scores based on "screener" questions asked of all children. Estimated effect of hyperactivity on grade repetition, reading and math scores, special education, and delinquency. Controlled for individual background characteristics. Estimated same model omitting children with other learning disabilities besides those in the main explanatory variable.	**1 unit change in hyperactivity score:** increases probability of grade retention by 10–12% in both US and Canada decreases math scores by 0.04–0.07 SD in both US and Canada increases probability of being in special ed by 11% in US decreases reading scores by 0.05 SD in US **1 unit change in conduct disorder score (in the US only):** increases probability of grade retention by 10% decreases math scores by 0.02 SD decreases reading scores by 0.03 SD **1 unit change in aggression score (in Canada only):** decreases probability that a youth aged 16–19 is in school by 4% high depression scores increase probability of grade retention by 10% in both US and Canada no significant effects of interaction between mental health scores and income or maternal education.

Table 5 (continued)

Study and data	Study design	Results
Disease and development: Evidence from hookworm eradication in the American South (Bleakley, 2007). Data on hookworm infection rates from the Rockefeller Sanitary Commission surveys for 1910–1914. Census data from IPUMS for 1880–1990. $n = 115$ state-years.	Identification due to different pre-eradication hookworm infection rates in different states. Compare individuals born before and after eradication campaigns funded by the Rockefeller Sanitary Commission (RSC). Active years of RSC were 1910–1915. Considered contemporaneous effects on children as well as long-term effects on adult wages and educational attainment. Controlled for geographic and year fixed effects, as well as some individual characteristics. In regressions for contemporaneous effects, geographic units are state economic areas. In regressions for long-term effects, geographic units are states of birth.	**Contemporaneous effects of infections on children:** 1 SD increase in lagged hookworm infection associated with: 0.18–0.25 SD decrease in school enrollment 0.21–0.28 SD decrease in full-time school enrollment 0.1 SD decrease in literacy Results robust to inclusion of state-year fixed effects, controlling for mean-reversion in schooling, and using state-level infection rates. Larger effects for blacks than for whites. No contemporaneous effects on adults. **Long-term effects of infections in childhood on adults:** Being infected with hookworm in one's childhood leads to a reduction in wages of 43% and a decrease in returns to schooling by 5%. 80% reduction in wages due to hookworm infections explained by reduced returns to schooling. Being infected with hookworm in one's childhood leads to a reduction in occupational income score by 23% and a decrease in Duncan's Socio–Economic Index by 42%.

(continued on next page)

Table 5 (continued)

Study and data	Study design	Results
Adult health and childhood disease (Bozzoli et al., forthcoming) Data on height from the European Community Household Panel, the Health Survey of England, and the National Health Interview Survey in the US for individuals born in 1950–1980. Data on post-neonatal mortality from the World Health Organization. $n = 316$ country-years. Also used data on women's heights from the international system of Demographic and Health Surveys on women aged 15–49 in more than 40 countries in the late 1990s–2000s. Data on infant mortality from the United Nations population division. $n = 1514$ country-years.	Analyzed relationship b/n post-neonatal mortality (PNM, death after 28 days and before first birthday) and adult height. PNM is a measure of childhood health environment. OLS regression with adult height as outcome variable, controlling for country and year fixed effects and a time trend. Also controlled for neonatal mortality rates and GDP in year and country of birth. Considered mortality from pneumonia, intestinal disease, congenital anomalies, and other causes separately.	Survivors are expected to be positively selected relative to those who died, but may still be stunted by illness. In poor countries, the selection effect dominates, whereas in rich countries (with low mortality rates) the stunting effect dominates. Overall correlation b/n PNM and average adult height of the same cohort in a given country = −0.79. In the US, PNM was 3x larger than in Sweden in 1970. This diff accounts for 20–30% of the 2-cm diff in average height b/n 30-yr-old Americans and Swedes in 2000. After controlling for PNM, no relationship b/n adult height and GDP in the year and country of birth. Biggest determinant of differences in PNM rates across countries is mortality from intestinal disease, followed by mortality from pneumonia. Out of the 4 determinants of PNM, only mortality from pneumonia has a significant negative effect on adult height.

Table 5 (continued)

Study and data	Study design	Results
Stature and status: height, ability and labor market outcomes (Case and Paxson, 2008a). Data from NCDS (on cohort of individuals born in week of 3/3/1958 in Britain), BCS, NLSY (on siblings in the US), and Fragile Families and Child Well-Being Study (on young children in the US). NCDS: $n = 9155$; BCS: $n = 9003$; NLSY: $n = 13,884$ (total, not siblings); Fragile Families: $n = 2150$.	Analyzed relationship b/n adult height and cognitive ability as a potential explanation for the significant and positive relationship b/n adult height and earnings that is observed. Adult height is a proxy for early childhood health conditions. OLS regression of cognitive test scores on height-for-age (HFA) z-scores, controlling for background and demographic variables (using NCDS, BCS and fragile families data). Same regression with mother fixed effects using NLSY79 data. OLS regression of log hourly earnings on adult height, controlling for cognitive test scores at ages 7, 10, and 11, and other background and demographic variables.	**Child's height and cognitive test scores at age 3:** 1 SD increase in HFA z-score linked to a 0.05–0.1 SD increase in PPVT score. **Child's height and cognitive test scores at ages 5–10:** (reporting only mother fixed effects results) 1 SD increase in HFA z-score linked to increased PIAT math score, PIAT reading recognition score, and PIAT reading comprehension score by 0.03 SD. Height does not explain differences in test scores across racial groups. **Adult height, earnings, and cognitive test scores:** Inclusion of cognitive test scores at ages 7, 10, and 11 makes the coefficient on adult height insignificant for predicting hourly wages. Height difference b/n men and women does not account for the difference in earnings.

(continued on next page)

Table 5 (continued)

Study and data	Study design	Results
Height, health and cognitive function at older ages (Case and Paxson, 2008b). Data from HRS on men and women aged 50 and older from 1996 to 2004. $n = 72{,}258$.	OLS regression of health and cognition measures on adult height, controlling for age, survey wave, race and sex. Adult height is a proxy for early childhood health and nutrition. Also estimated models including controls for childhood health (self-reported), completed education, and a dummy for employment in a white-collar occupation.	1 in increase in height associated with: 0.9% increase in delayed word recall score 0.3% increase in probability of being able to count backwards 0.3% increase in probability of knowing the date 1.4% decrease in depression score 0.4% decrease in health status scale (1 = excellent, 5 = poor) Childhood health, completed education, and employment in a white-collar occupation all positively related to adult cognitive function and health. Inclusion of these controls makes the coefficients on adult height insignificant except for the cases of delayed word recall and depression.
The role of childhood health for the intergenerational transmission of human capital: evidence from administrative data (Salm and Schunk, 2008). Administrative data from the department of health services in the city of Osnabrueck, Germany, collected during official school entrance medical examinations on children aged 6 between 2002–2005. Sibling sample: $n = 947$. 321 children had at least one parent w/ college degree.	Sibling fixed effects to estimate impact of health conditions on cognitive and verbal ability at school entrance. Controlled for individual background characteristics. Used the Oaxaca (1973) decomposition and a nonparametric decomposition to estimate how much of the gap b/n children of college-educated parents and children of less educated parents can be explained by chronic childhood health conditions.	Mental health conditions reduce cognitive ability by 10% for the whole sample, by 9% for college-educated sample, by 11% for less-educated sample. Asthma reduces cognitive ability by 8% for less-educated sample only. Mental health conditions reduce verbal ability by 11% for the whole sample, and by 13% for the less-educated sample. Health conditions explain 18% of the gap in cognitive ability and 65% of the gap in language ability b/n children of college-educated and less-educated parents.

Table 5 (continued)

Study and data	Study design	Results
Long-term economic costs of psychological problems during childhood (Smith and Smith, 2008) Data from PSID on siblings (with a special supplement designed by the authors in the 2007 wave, asking retrospective questions about childhood health). Sample consists of sibling children of the original participants who were at least 16 in 1968. Sibling children were at least 25 in 2005.	Sibling fixed effects to estimate the impact of reporting having had childhood psychological problems (measured by depression, drug or alcohol abuse or other psychological problems before age 17) on later life socio-economic outcomes. Controlled for individual childhood physical illnesses (asthma, diabetes, allergic conditions, and many others) as well as family background characteristics.	Having had psychological problems during childhood leads to: 20% reduction in adult earnings ($10,400 less per year; $17,534 less family assets) reduction in number of weeks worked by 5.76 weeks per year 11 pp reduction in likelihood of getting married 33.5 pp reduction in educational attainment (means not reported, so can't calculate relative effect sizes) **Costs of childhood psychological problems:** Lifetime cost: $300,000 loss in family income; $3.2 trillion cost for all those affected
Early life health and cognitive function in old age (Case and Paxson, 2009) Region-level historical data on mortality from infectious diseases, as well as total infant mortality. Data for 1900–1936 from Grant Miller's data archive on NBER website. Data for 1937–1950 from vital statistics documents. Data on later life outcomes from Health and Retirement Study for 1996–2004 on men and women aged 50–90. $n = 60,000$.	Identification due to variation in mortality rates across time and regions. OLS regression of later life outcomes on log mortality rates from various infectious diseases in year of birth and in 2nd year of life in region of birth. Controlled for age, sex, race, and current Census region of residence.	Decrease in infant mortality by half during 2nd year of life associated w/ an increase in delayed word recall score by 0.1 SD. Significant negative impacts of typhoid, influenza, and diarrhea mortality in 2nd year of life on delayed word recall score. (Means not reported so can't calculate relative effect sizes). Weaker associations b/n disease mortality and ability to count backwards. No significant impacts of disease mortality and overall mortality during year of birth, once mortality in 2nd year of life is included, on either of the later life outcomes. Results not robust to adding Census region-specific time trends.

(continued on next page)

Table 5 (continued)

Study and data	Study design	Results
Child health and young adult outcomes (Currie et al., 2010) Administrative data on public health insurance records from the Canadian province of Manitoba on children born b/n 1979 and 1987, followed until 2006. $n = 50,000$.	Sibling fixed effects of the long term effects of health problems at various child ages controlling for health at birth (with birth weight and congenital anomalies). Key explanatory variables examined are: asthma, major injuries, ADHD, conduct disorders, and other major health problems at ages 0–3, 4–8, 9–13, and 14–18. Key outcome variables: achievement on standardized test on language arts in grade 12, whether child took college-preparatory math courses in high school, whether child is in grade 12 by age 17, and welfare participation after becoming eligible at 18.	**Results reported below are only those that control for health problems at all age groups:** An additional major health condition at ages 0–3/4–8/14–18 increases the probability of being on welfare by 10%/9%/31%. Effects of major health conditions at younger ages on educational outcomes not significant when controlling for health at ages 14–18. **ADHD/conduct disorders diagnosis:** at ages 0–3/4–8/9–13/14–18 decreases probability of being in grade 12 by age 17 by 4%/10%/17%/19%; at ages 4–8/9–13/14–18 increases probability of being on welfare by 38%/44%/109%; at ages 4–8/9–13/14–18 decreases probability of taking a college prep math class by 11%/25%/35%; at ages 4–8/9–13/14–18 decreases literacy score by 0.15 SD/0.23 SD/0.27 SD. Effects of asthma at younger ages not statistically significant once health at ages 14–18 is controlled for. **Major injury:** at ages 0–3/14–18 increases probability of being on welfare by 7%/9%; at ages 9–13/14–18 decreases probability of being in grade 12 by age 17 by 2%/2%; at ages 9–13/14–18 decreases probability of taking a college prep math class by 6%/8%; at ages 9–13/14–18 decreases literacy score by 0.03 SD/0.03 SD. Children who have a major physical health condition and then recover do not have significant adverse outcomes. Children with mental health conditions, children with major health conditions at ages 14–18, and those with conditions that persist for multiple age periods suffer worse outcomes.

Table 5 (continued)

Study and data	Study design	Results
The impact of childhood health on adult labor market outcomes (Smith, 2009) Data on siblings from PSID. Childhood health measured as a self-reported retrospective health index regarding health at ages younger than 17. Adult outcomes measured in 1999. $n = 2248$.	Sibling fixed effects to estimate impact of self-reported retrospective childhood health status (on a 5-point scale) before age 16 on adult earnings, employment, education, marital status, etc., controlling for demographics and family background.	Better health during childhood increases adult family income by 24%, increases adult family wealth by 200% (relative to mean = \$2000), and increases adult earnings by 25%. Better health during childhood increases probability of having worked the year before by 5.4 pp (mean not reported). About 2/3 of overall impact of poor childhood health on adult family income is present at age 25; the remaining 1/3 is due to a slower growth path after age 25 due to poor childhood health. About 1/2 of overall impact of poor childhood health on individual earnings is present at age 25; the remaining 1/2 is due to a slower growth path after age 25 due to poor childhood health. No statistically significant impacts of childhood health on educational attainment.
The effect of childhood conduct disorder on human capital (Vujic et al., 2008) Data from the Australian Twin Register on twins born between 1964 and 1971. Data collected in 1989–1990 and 1996–2000 $n = 5322$ twins; 2250 identical twins.	Twin fixed effects to estimate impact of childhood conduct disorder (measured by various indicators) based on diagnostic criteria from psychiatry on educational attainment and criminal behavior in adulthood. Controlled for birth weight, timing of the onset of conduct disorders, and other family and individual background characteristics. Conducted separate analyses for all twins and identical twins.	Childhood conduct disorders lead to: 5–16% decrease in likelihood of high school graduation 100–228% increase in likelihood of being arrested (mean =0.07) 6–68% increase in likelihood of grade retention 20–60% increase in likelihood of having 3+ job quits (not significant in identical twin sample) 50–325% increase in likelihood of telling lies (mean = 0.04) 37–526% increase in likelihood of going to jail (mean =0.019) Earlier occurrence of conduct disorder has larger negative effects than later occurrence.

(continued on next page)

Table 5 (continued)

Study and data	Study design	Results
Causes and consequences of early life health (Case and Paxson, 2010a) Data from NCDS, BCS, PSID, Whitehall II Study (longitudinal study of British civil servants b/n ages 34 and 71, collected from 1985 to 2001), HRS, and NLSY79. See Case and Paxson (2008a,b) for more info on the data sets. $n = 11,648$ (NCDS), 11,181 (BCS), 63,995 (PSID), 29,774 (Whitehall II), 66,269 (HRS), $n = 3200$–46,000 (NLSY79).	Multivariate regression of educational attainment, employment, log earnings, and self-reported health status and cognitive function on adult height in inches (proxy for early childhood health) using 5 longitudinal data sets. Controlled for age, ethnicity, sex, and survey wave. Used sibling fixed effects in NLSY79 to understand what aspects of early life health adult height captures—regressed children's test scores, grade level, self-perception in school, and childhood health outcomes on children's HAZ.	Results from NCDS, BCS, PSID, Whitehall II, and HRS: One inch of height is associated with: 0.05–0.16 more years of schooling; 0.2–0.6 pp increase in likelihood of employment; 0.012–0.028 increase in average hourly earnings for men; 0.007–0.027 increase in average hourly earnings for women. A 4-in increase in height leads to: 8% decrease in probability of long-standing illness; 40% decrease in probability of disability; 4% of SD decrease in depression score. Results from NLSY79 (reporting sibling fixed effects only) indicate that 1 pt. increase in HAZ leads to: 0.3% increase in PIAT math score; 0.1% increase in PIAT reading recognition score; 0.2% increase in PIAT reading comprehension score; 0.9% increase in digital span test score; 0.4% increase in PPVT score. 2% decrease in likelihood that child is in appropriate grade level for age (ages 6–14). 1% increase in child doing school work quickly; 1% increase in child remembering things easily; 0.9% increase in total scholastic competence score. 8% decrease in likelihood that child has limiting emotional/neurological condition; 0.105 increase in birth weight z-score (mean not reported).

Table 5 (continued)

Study and data	Study design	Results
The long reach of childhood health and circumstance: evidence from the Whitehall II Study (Case and Paxson, 2010b) Data from the Whitehall II Study (see above for description). $n = 10,308$.	Since most Whitehall II study participants belong to the highest occupational classes, estimated the selection effect using data from NCDS and BCS for comparison. OLS regressions of initial placement and promotion in Whitehall on height, family background characteristics, educational attainment, and other individual characteristics. Also estimated individual fixed effects and first-differenced regressions of future promotions on self-reported health, and of future health on grade in Whitehall.	Selectivity of Whitehall II study attenuates the impact of father's social class on various outcomes relative estimates that would be obtained in the full population. OLS regressions indicate significant correlations between family background (father's social class), initial placement and likelihood of promotion. Significant relationship between initial placement and promotion, height, and self-reported health. Although some of the effects of health on placement and promotion are mediated by educational attainment, there is an independent effect of health. Individual fixed effects estimates indicate that cohort members who report "excellent" or "very good" health are 13% more likely to be promoted (relative to lowest grade). No effect of grade in Whitehall on future health.

(continued on next page)

Table 5 (continued)

Study and data	Study design	Results
Home environment		
The impact of maternal alcohol and illicit drug use on children's behavior problems: evidence from the children of the National Longitudinal Survey of Youth (Chatterji and Markowitz, 2000) Data from the 1988, 1992, and 1994 waves of NLSY-Child surveys on children who were 4–14 yrs old during the survey years. $n = 6194$ children in total sample; $n = 2498$ mothers who have siblings in sample; $n = 7546$ obs for children who have 2 or 3 observations in sample.	Estimated impact of maternal substance abuse on children's behavior problems using OLS, IV, child-specific & maternal family fixed effects models. In IV, used alcohol and illicit drug prices as instruments for maternal substance abuse. Controlled for numerous demographic and background variables. Behavior problems measured by the Behavior Problems Index (higher BPI means more problems).	No statistically significant relationship between maternal substance abuse and child behavior in IV regressions, but 1st stage relationship is weak. Fixed effects suggest that 1 more drink consumed by mother in past month increases child BPI by 1%. Maternal marijuana use in past month increases child BPI by 7–8%. Maternal cocaine use in past month increases child BPI by 19%.

Table 5 (continued)

Study and data	Study design	Results
Parental employment and child cognitive development (Ruhm, 2004). Data from the Children of NLSY79 for 1986–1996 (mothers aged 29–38 at the end of 1995). $n = 3042$.	OLS to estimate the impact of maternal work in the year prior to child's birth, and in the first 4 years of child's life on child cognitive test scores at ages 3–4 and 5–6. Used a rich set of controls for maternal background, demographic, and socio-economic characteristics, as well as assessment year fixed effects. Maternal work measured both by hours and weeks worked during the year. Controlled for family income.	**20 more hrs. worked each week by mother during child's 1st year:** Decrease PPVT score by 0.06–0.10 SD (ages 3–4) **20 more hrs. worked each week by mother during child's age 2–3:** Decrease PIAT-Reading score by 0.06–0.08 SD (ages 5–6) Decrease PIAT-Math score by 0.05–0.06 SD (ages 5–6) Results robust to alternative specifications (measuring employment by weeks worked or part-time vs. no employment). More negative effects on PPVT and PIAT-Math scores for boys than girls. More negative effects on PIAT-Reading scores for girls than boys. More negative effects on PPVT an PIAT-Reading scores for whites than blacks. More negative effects on PIAT-Math scores for blacks than whites.
Maternity leave, early maternal employment and child health and development in the US (Berger et al., 2005) Data from the Children of NLSY79 on children born b/n 1988 and 1996. $n = 1678$.	OLS and propensity score matching to estimate impact of maternal return to work within 12 weeks of birth on child health and developmental outcomes. Models control for numerous background characteristics as well as state and year of birth fixed effects. Sample limited to mothers who worked pre-birth.	**Mother returning to work within 12 weeks of giving birth leads to:** 2.5% decrease in likelihood of well-baby visit 12.8% decrease in likelihood of any breastfeeding 40.4% decrease in number of weeks breastfed 4.3% decrease in child getting all DPT/Polio immunizations Results from OLS consistent with results from propensity score matching methods. Larger negative effects of returning to work full-time within 12 weeks of giving birth compared to any work at all.

(continued on next page)

Table 5 (continued)

Study and data	Study design	Results
Evidence from maternity leave expansions of the impact of maternal care on early child development (Baker and Milligan, 2010) Data from the NLSCY in Canada on children up to age 29 months and their mothers in 1998–2003.	Identification due to large expansions in parental leave policies in Canada on December 31, 2000 (from 25 to 50 weeks of leave). OLS regression. Key explanatory variable is a dummy for birth after December 31, 2000. Outcomes include child development indicators, maternal employment, and use of child care. Controlled for various individual and family background characteristics as well as labor market variables. Observations from Quebec omitted due to changes in childcare policies over the same time period. Observations from single-parent families omitted b/c of expansions in benefits to those families. Subsample analysis for women who returned to work within 1 year of child's birth.	Expansions in parental leave policies led to a 48-58% increase in months of maternal care during the 1st year of life and a 25-29 pp decrease in non-parental care. No statistically significant effects of parental leave expansions on child development indicators (motor/social development, behavior, physical ability, cognitive development).

Table 5 (continued)

Study and data	Study design	Results
The effect of expansions in maternity leave coverage on children's long-term outcomes (Dustmann and Schönberg, 2009) Administrative data on students in Germany attending public schools in Hesse, Bavaria, and Schleswig-Holstein (3 states in Germany) for 2002–03 to 2005-06. $n = 101,257$. Administrative data on social security records for German individuals born b/n July 1977 and June 1980. $n = 140,387$	Identification due to 3 policy reforms in Germany that expanded unpaid and paid maternity leave to estimate impact on adult wages, employment, and educational outcomes. First reform in 1979 increased paid leave from 2 to 6 months. Second reform in 1986 increased paid leave from 6 to 10 months. Third reform in 1992 increased unpaid leave from 18 to 36 months. OLS regression, comparing children born one month before and after each reform, controlling for background variables and state fixed effects. Also difference–in–difference, comparing children born before and after leave expansions with children born in the same months the year before (hence not affected by expansions).	Despite significant delays in maternal return to work due to policy reforms, there are no statistically significant impacts of expansions in maternity leave policies (paid or unpaid) on any long-run outcomes (wages, employment, selective high school attendance, grade retention and grade attendance).

(continued on next page)

Table 5 (continued)

Study and data	Study design	Results
Child protection and adult crime: using investigator assignment to estimate causal effects of foster care (Doyle, 2008) Data from computerized criminal history system from the Illinois State Police on arrests and imprisonment up to age 31 for 2000–2005, linked with child abuse investigation data on individuals who are 18–35 in 2005. $n = 23{,}254$.	IV models of the effect of foster care placement on measures of criminal activity. Identification due to the fact that child protection cases are randomized to investigators, and investigators influence whether a child is placed in foster care or remains at home. Model allows for treatment effect heterogeneity—used random coefficient model. IV where the instrument is the investigator's probability of using foster placement relative to the other investigators.	Children on the margin for placement into foster care are 1.5 times more likely to be arrested, 2.68 times more likely to have a sentence of guilty/withheld, 3.41 times more likely to be sentenced to prison if they are placed into foster care. Children on the margin are likely to include African-Americans, girls, and young adolescents.

Table 5 (continued)

Study and data	Study design	Results
Long-term consequences of child abuse and neglect on adult economic well-being (Currie and Widom, 2009). Sample of abused/neglected children based on court-substantiated cases of childhood physical and sexual abuse in 1967–1971 in one Midwestern metropolitan county. Maltreated children matched to controls on the basis of sex, race, and elementary school class/hospital of birth. Cases restricted to children 11 yrs or younger. Adult outcomes measured at mean age 41. Used info collected in 1989–95 and 2003–04 interviews. $n = 1195$ in 1989–95; $n = 807$ in 2003–04. Matched sample (both members of matched pair interviewed during the 2 waves): $n = 358$.	Multivariate regression with key explanatory variable being a dummy for having been maltreated. Controlled for demographic and family background characteristics, as well as quarter of year at time of interview. Also estimated models separately for males and females and for the subsample of participants whose families received food stamps or welfare when they were children.	**Individuals who were maltreated as children:** complete 4.3% less years of schooling (1989–95) score 5.3% lower on IQ test (1989–95) have 24% lower imputed earnings (2003–04) are 0.52 times as likely to have a skilled job (1989–95) are 0.46 times as likely to be employed (2003–04) are 0.58 times as likely to own a vehicle (2003–04) For males, the only significant effects of maltreatment are for years of schooling and having a skilled job. For females, significant negative effects of maltreatment on years of schooling, IQ test scores, imputed earnings, being employed, owning a bank account, owning a stock, owning a vehicle, and owning a home. Effects larger for females than for males.

(continued on next page)

Table 5 (continued)

Study and data	Study design	Results
Child maltreatment and crime (Currie and Tekin, 2006) Data from the National Longitudinal Study of Adolescent Health (AddHealth). First wave: 1994–95; last wave: 2001–2002. $n = 13,509$ (full sample), $n = 928$ (twins sample).	OLS, propensity score matching, and twin fixed effects methods. Estimate the impact of maltreatment on criminal activity. Controlled for numerous demographic and background characteristics as well as state fixed effects. Also controlled for parental reports of child being bad-tempered or having a learning disability.	Only results that are significant in all 3 main specifications (OLS, propensity scores, and twin fixed effects) are reported. **Children who experienced any maltreatment are:** 99–134% more likely to commit any non-drug related crime (mean = 0.109) 288–489% more likely to commit a burglary (mean = 0.009) 113–181% more likely to damage property (mean = 0.052) 106–131% more likely to commit an assault (mean = 0.049) 183–222% more likely to commit a theft > \$50 (mean = 0.018) 76–101% more likely to commit any hard-drug related crime (mean = 0.085) 96–103% more likely to be a crime victim (mean = 0.077) Probability of crime increases if a person suffers multiple forms of maltreatment. Being a victim of maltreatment doubles the probability that an individual is convicted as a juvenile. **Cost-Benefit:** Estimated costs of crime induced by abuse = \$8.8–68.6 billion/year Estimated costs of home visiting programs (that have been shown to reduce cases of maltreatment by 50%) = \$14 billion/year.

Table 5 (continued)

Study and data	Study design	Results
The effect of maternal depression and substance abuse on child human capital development (Frank and Meara, 2009) Data from children of NLSY79 on children aged 1-5 in 1987. $n = 1587$.	OLS regression of the impact of maternal depression and substance abuse on maternal inputs and children's outcomes in grades 1-5 and 6-9. Controlled for a rich set of demographic and background variables including family measures of parent and sibling behavior and health. For robustness, estimated models using mother fixed effects and propensity scores.	**Effects on maternal inputs:** Maternal depression leads to a 0.2 SD decrease in emotional stimulation sub-component of the HOME score (ages 7-10, 11-14). Maternal substance abuse leads to a 0.23 SD decrease in emotional stimulation sub-component of the HOME score (ages 11-14). **Effects on child outcomes:** Maternal depression leads to a 0.46 SD increase in behavioral problems index (ages 7-10, 11-14). Maternal alcohol abuse leads to a 0.31 SD decrease in child's PIAT math score (ages 11-14); 0.29 SD increase in behavioral problems index (ages 7-10); 377% decrease in likelihood of ever being suspended or expelled at any age (mean = 0.22).

(continued on next page)

Table 5 (continued)

Study and data	Study design	Results
Environmental shocks		
Environmental policy as social policy? The impact of childhood lead exposure on crime (Reyes, 2007). Data on lead in gasoline for 1950–1990 on a state-by-state level from Yearly Report of Gasoline Sales by State, Petroleum Marketing Annual, and Petroleum Products Survey. Data on air lead exposure from the EPA's Aerometric Information Retrieval System. Data on per capita crime rates from the Uniform Crime Reports compiled by the Federal Bureau of Investigation for 1985–2002. Data on individual blood lead levels from NHANES for 1976–1980 only.	Used state-by-year variation in the decline of lead exposure from gasoline between 1975 and 1985 due to enforcement of the Clean Air Act to identify the impacts of childhood lead exposure on violent crime in young adulthood. Also estimated the impact of lead exposure on levels of lead in blood during childhood for robustness. Primary measure of lead exposure is the grams of lead per gallon of gasoline in automobile sources. Calculated air lead exposure (measure of average concentration of lead in the air in each state and year). Calculated effective lead exposure relative to each crime in each state and year as the weighted average of lead exposure b/n ages 0 and 3 for all cohorts of arrestees. Regression of per capita crime rate on effective lead exposure, controlling for state and year fixed effects and other state-year characteristics that could affect crime rates.	Elasticity of violent crime with respect to lead exposure = 0.8. Changes in childhood lead exposure in the 1970s are responsible for a 56% decrease in violent crime in the 1990s (while abortion is responsible for a 29% drop in violent crime). Weak evidence for link b/n lead exposure and murder or property crimes. **Cost-Benefit Analysis:** Cumulative social cost of switching to unleaded gasoline: $15–65 billion. Cumulative social benefit of reduced crime from reduced lead exposure: $1.2 trillion. Note, due to data limitations, it is not possible to make a direct connection between blood lead levels, lead in gasoline, and criminal activity at the individual level.

Table 5 (continued)

Study and data	Study design	Results
The long-term effects of early childhood lead exposure: evidence from sharp changes in local air lead levels induced by the phase-out of leaded gasoline (Nilsson, 2009) Data on air lead exposure from Swedish Environmental Protection Agency that uses a nationwide grid of moss samples collected in 1000 locations evenly spread across Sweden for average lead exposure levels for 1972–74, 1977–79, and 1982–84. Individual outcome data from the Educational database at the Institute for Labor Market Policy Evaluation in Uppsala, Sweden on those born in 1972–74, 1977–79, and 1982–84. $n = 797,889$	Identification due to geographical variation in childhood lead exposure due to a policy in Sweden that induced a phase-out of leaded gasoline between 1973 and 1981. Difference-in-difference comparing children born in municipalities that experienced large reductions in lead exposure to those born in municipalities with relatively no change, before and after policy went into effect, to estimate impact of childhood lead exposure on later life outcomes. Also used mother fixed effect methods, comparing siblings who experienced different levels of lead exposure in childhood. Controlled for various background characteristics as well as year of birth and municipality of birth fixed effects.	A decrease in blood lead levels by 30 mg/kg leads to: 3% decrease in likelihood of being in the lower end of the GPA distribution 0.6 pp increase in average IQ for males 0.05 yr increase in schooling attainment 0.7 pp increase in likelihood of graduating high school 0.5 pp decrease in likelihood of receiving welfare in adulthood Effects of lead are stronger at lower end of ability/skills distribution and for children from poorer households. Effects of lead are stronger when exposure is at ages 0–2 than when exposure is at ages 5–7. No statistically significant difference in effects by gender. Nonlinear effects—significant and negative effects of lead exposure above 75th percentile (>50 mg/kg). No statistically significant effects of exposure to lead below 75th percentile levels. Estimated that there exists a blood lead threshold of 60 mg/L below which reductions in lead exposure have no effect on outcomes. Similar results using mother fixed effects. Note: means not reported, so relative effect sizes can't be calculated.

Unless otherwise noted, only results significant at the 5% level are reported. Percent changes reported relative to the mean.

a broader literature asking whether income affects health, and how health affects income. For example, using cross-sectional US data, Case et al. (2002) find a striking relationship between family income and a child's reported health status, which becomes stronger as children age. Their motivation for looking at children is that the child's health is unlikely to have a large direct effect on family income, so that the direction of causality is relatively clear. Currie and Stabile (2003) investigate this relationship using Canadian panel data and argue that one reason the relationship between income and child health increases over time is that poorer children are subject to many more negative health shocks. In fact, in Canada, this is the dominant mechanism driving the relationship (which is not surprising given that all Canadian children have public health insurance so that gaps in treatment rates are small).[14]

The question we focus on here is how much poor health in childhood, in turn, affects future outcomes. One of the chief ambiguities in answering this question is what we mean by health in childhood. While it has become conventional to measure fetal health using birth weight (though there may be better measures, see Almond, Chay and Lee, 2005) there are a wide variety of different possible measures of child health, ranging from maternal reports about the child's general health status through questions about diagnoses of specific chronic conditions, to the occurrence of "adverse events".

Case and Paxson (2008a,b, 2010a,b) do not have a direct measure of child health, but argue that adult height is a good proxy for early child health. This is a useful observation given that most surveys of adults have no direct information on child health. Height at age 5 is affected by a range of early health shocks including fetal conditions, poor nutrition, and illness. In turn, height at age 5 is strongly predictive of adult height. And like birthweight, it is predictive of many shorter and longer range outcomes.

A second problem is that it is often unclear whether the ill health dates from a particular period (e.g. an injury) or whether it might reflect a continuing, perhaps a congenital, condition. For example, Smith (2009) uses data from the Panel Study of Income Dynamics which asked young adults a retrospective question about their health status before age 16. In models with sibling fixed effects, he finds that the sib with the worse health had significantly lower earnings, although educational attainment was not significantly affected. He also finds using data from the Health and Retirement Survey that reports of general poor health in childhood do tend to be correlated in the expected way with the presence of specific health conditions. However, it is not possible to ascertain that the negative effects are due to poor health at any particular "critical" window. Salm and Schunk (2008) attempt to deal with this problem using detailed health

---

[14] Condliffe and Link (2008) argue that in the US, differential access to care also plays a role in the steepening of the relationship between income and child health with age. A number of studies have investigated this relationship, dubbed "the gradient", in other countries (cf Currie et al. (2007), Case et al. (2008), Doyle et al. (2005), Khanam et al. (2009)). Propper et al. (2007) and Khanam et al. (2009) are particularly interesting because they find that when maternal mental health is controlled, the relationship between family income and child health disappears, suggesting that it is mediated largely by factors that affect maternal mental health.

information from a medical examination of young German children entering school. In models with sibling fixed effects, they find a significant relationship between poor mental health and asthma on the one hand, and measures of cognitive functioning on the other. They control for the child's birth weight in an effort to distinguish between the effects of health at birth and health after birth (though to the extent that birth weight is an imperfect measure of health at birth, it is possible that the other health measures partly capture congenital conditions).

Currie et al. (2010) use administrative data from the Canadian province of Manitoba's public health insurance system to follow children from birth through young adulthood. Using information about all contacts with medical providers, they construct measures of whether children suffered injuries, asthma, mental health problems or other health problems at ages 0 to 3, 4 to 8, 9 to 13, and 14 to 18. It is interesting that even in a large sample, there were relatively few children with specific health problems other than injuries, asthma, or mental health problems, so that it was necessary to group the remaining problems together. They then look at the relationship between health at various ages, educational attainment, and use of social assistance as a young adult in sibling fixed effects models that also control flexibly for birth weight and for the presence of congenital anomalies. The results are perhaps surprising in view of the conceptual framework developed in Section 3. When entered by themselves, early childhood health conditions (at age 0-3 and at age 4-8) are predictive of future outcomes, conditional on health at birth. However, when early physical health conditions are entered along with later ones, generally only the later ones matter. This result suggests that physical health in early childhood affects future outcomes largely because it affects future health (i.e., subsequent health mediates the relationship), and not because there is a direct link between early physical health status and cognition. In contrast, mental health conditions at early ages seem to have significant negative effects on future outcomes even if there are no intermediate report of a mental health condition. This result suggests that common mental health problems such as Attention Deficit Hyperactivity Disorder (ADHD, also called Attention Deficit Disorder or ADD) or Conduct Disorders (i.e. disorders usually involving abnormal aggression and anti-social behavior) may impair the process of human capital accumulation even if they do not lead to diagnoses of mental health disorders in adulthood.

Several recent papers focus specifically on measures of mental health conditions. Currie and Stabile (2006) use questions similar to those on mental health "screeners" which were administered to large samples of children in the US and Canada in two national surveys. They find that children whose scores indicated mental health problems in 1994 had worse outcomes as of 2002-4 than siblings without such problems. They controlled for birth weight (among other variables) and estimated models with and without including children with diagnosed learning disabilities. In all specifications, they found negative effects of high ADHD scores on test scores on schooling attainment.

Smith and Smith (2008) report similar results using data from the PSID which includes retrospective questions about mental health problems before age 16. Like Smith (2009) and Currie et al. (2010) they estimate models with sibling fixed effects, and find significant long term effects of mental health conditions which are much larger than those of physical health conditions. Vujic et al. (2008) focus on conduct disorders using a panel of Australian twins and find that conduct disorder before age 18 has strong negative effects on the probability of high school graduation as well as positive effects on the probability of criminal activity. None of these three papers focus specifically on measures of mental health conditions before age 5 but "externalizing" mental health conditions such as ADHD and Conduct Disorder typically manifest themselves at early ages. Finally, although they are conceptually distinct, many survey measures of mental health resemble measures of "non-cognitive skills". Hence, one might interpret evidence that non-cognitive skills in childhood are important determinants of future outcomes as further evidence of the importance of early mental health conditions (Blanden et al., 2006; Heckman and Rubinstein, 2001).

4.2.3. Home environment

The home is one of the most important environments affecting a young child and there is a vast literature in related disciplines investigating the relationship between different aspects of the home environment and child outcomes. We do not attempt to summarize this literature here, but pick three aspects that may be most salient: Maternal mental health and/or substance abuse, maternal employment, and child abuse/foster care (which may be considered to be an extreme result of bad parenting). Given the importance of child mental health and non-cognitive skills, it is interesting to ask how maternal mental health affects child outcomes? Frank and Meara (2009) examine this question using data from the National Longitudinal Survey of Youth. They include a rich set of control variables (mother's cognitive test score, grandparent's substance abuse, permanent income) and estimate models with mother fixed effects and models with propensity scores. Their estimates suggest large effects (relative to the effects of income) of contemporaneous maternal depression on the quality of the home environment and on children's behavioral problems, but little effect on math and reading scores. Estimates of the effects of maternal substance abuse are mixed, which echoes the findings of Chatterji and Markowitz (2000) using the same data. Unfortunately, the authors are not able to look at the long term effects of maternal depression experienced by children aged 0 to 5 because the depression questions in the NLSY have been added only recently. As these panel data are extended in time, further investigation of this issue is warranted.

There is also a large literature, including some papers by economists, examining the effect of maternal employment at early ages on child outcomes. Much of this literature suffers from the lack of an appropriate conceptual framework. If we think of child outcomes being produced via some combination of inputs, then the important question is how maternal employment affects the inputs chosen? This will evidently depend on how much her employment income relaxes the household budget constraint, and the price and quality of the child care alternatives and other inputs that are available. Some of the literature on maternal employment seems to implicitly assume that the mother's time is such an important and unique input that no purchased input can adequately replace it. This may possibly be the case but is a strong assumption. If the mother's time is replaceable at some price, then one might expect maternal employment to have quite different effects on women with different levels of household income (moreover, mother's time may not all be of equal quality, so that it is easier to replace some mother's time than others with the market). This argument suggests that it is extremely important to consider explicitly the quality of the mother's time inputs and the availability of potential substitute inputs in models of maternal employment, something that is difficult to do in most available data sets. Studies that rely on regression methods and propensity score matching (see Berger et al. (2005) and Ruhm (2004)) often find small negative effects of maternal employment (especially in the first year) on children's cognitive development. However, two recent studies using variation in maternity leave provisions find that while more generous maternity leave policies are associated with increased maternal employment, there is little effect on children's outcomes (Baker and Milligan, 2010; Dustmann and Schönberg, 2009). Dustmann and Schönberg (2009) have data that permit cohorts affected by expansions in German maternity leave laws to be followed for many years. They see no effect of maternal employment on educational attainment or wages.

Finally, there are a few papers examining the effects of child abuse/foster care on child outcomes. This is a difficult area to investigate because it is hard to imagine that abuse (or neglect) can be divorced from other characteristics of the household. Currie and Widom (2009) use data from a prospective longitudinal study in which abused children (the treatments) were matched to controls. After following these children until their mid 40s, they found that the abused children were less likely to be employed, had lower earnings, and fewer assets, and that these patterns were particularly pronounced among women. It is possible that these results are driven by unobserved differences between the treatments and controls, although focusing on various subsets of the data (e.g. children whose mothers were on welfare; children of single mothers) produced similar results. Currie and Tekin (2006) use data from the National Longitudinal Study of Adolescent Health to examine the effect of having been abused before age 7 on the propensity to commit crime. They find strong effects which are quite similar in OLS, sibling, and twin fixed effects models. It is possible that these results reflect a characteristic of an individual child (such as difficult temperament) which makes it both more likely that they will be abused and more likely that they will commit crime. However, controlling directly for measures of temperament and genetic endowments does not alter the results. The Doyle (2008) study of the effects of foster care on the marginal child is also summarized in Table 5.

4.2.4. Toxic exposures

Epidemiological studies of postnatal pollution exposure and infant mortality have yielded mixed results and many are likely to suffer from omitted variables bias. Currie and Neidell (2005) examine the effect of more recent (lower) levels of pollution on infant health, along with the role of specific pollutants in addition to particulates (only TSPs were measured during the time periods analyzed by Chay and Greenstone (2003a,b)). Using within-zip code variation in pollution levels, they find that a one unit reduction in carbon monoxide over the 1990s in California saved 18 infant lives per 100,000 live births. However, unlike Currie et al. (2009) they were unable to find any consistent evidence of pollution effects on health at birth, probably because of the crudeness of their measure of maternal location.

Reyes (2007) found large effects of banning leaded gasoline on crime in the US, but results were not robust to state-specific time trends despite a relatively long panel of state-level lead measurements. Nilsson (2009) considered reductions in ambient lead levels in Sweden following the banning of lead in gasoline and measures possible exposures using the concentrations of lead in 1000 moss (bryophyte) collection sites that have been maintained by the Swedish environmental protection agency since the early 1970s. Nilsson (2009) found that early childhood exposure reduced human capital, as reflected by both grades and graduation rates. These effects persisted when comparisons were restricted within siblings, and were substantially larger for low-income families.

4.2.5. Summary re: long term effects of fetal and early childhood environment

The last 10 years have seen an upsurge of empirical work on the long-term effects of early childhood. As a result, much has been learned. We can state fairly definitively that at least some things that happen before age five have long-term consequences for health and human capital. Moreover, these effects are sufficiently large and general to shape outcomes at the population level. On balance, effects of fetal exposure tend to be somewhat larger than postnatal effects, but there are important exceptions. Mental health is a prime example. Mental health conditions and non-cognitive skills seem to have large, persistent effects independent of those captured by measures of child health at birth.

5. EMPIRICAL LITERATURE: POLICY RESPONSES

The evidence discussed above indicates that prenatal and early childhood often have a critical influence on later life outcomes. However, by itself this evidence says little about the effectiveness of remediation. Hence, this section discusses evidence about whether remediation in the zero to five period can be effective in shaping future outcomes. In so doing, we take a step away from explicit consideration of an early-childhood shock u_g as in Section 2. Instead, we focus on the specific public policies that may be able to alter developmental trajectories, often in disadvantaged sub-populations. We begin with programs that raise income, and then move on to programs that target specific domains.

5.1. Income enhancement

In the model sketched above, there are many ways for poverty to affect child outcomes. Even with identical preferences, poorer parents will make different investment choices than richer ones. In particular, poor families will optimize at lower investment (and consumption) levels and thereby have children with lower health and human capital, other things equal. Further, poor parents may face different input prices for certain goods, or have access to different production technologies. Providing cash transfers addresses the budgetary problems without necessarily changing the production technology. Hence, it is of interest to see whether cash transfers, in and of themselves, can improve outcomes. It is however, remarkably difficult to find examples of policies that increase incomes without potentially having a direct effect on outcomes. For example, many studies of cash welfare programs have demonstrated that children who are or have been on welfare remain worse off on average than other children. This does not necessarily mean, however, that welfare has failed them. Without welfare, their situation might have been even worse. Berger et al. (2009) explore the relationship between family income, home environments, child mental health outcomes, and cognitive test scores using data from the Fragile Families and Child Well-being Study which follows a cohort of five thousand children born in several large US cities between 1998 and 2000. They show that all of the measures of the home environment they examine (which include measures of parenting skills as well as physical aspects of the home) are highly related to income and that controlling for these measures reduces the effects of income on outcomes considerably.

Levine and Zimmerman (2000) showed that children who spent time on welfare scored lower than other children on a range of tests, but that this difference disappeared when the test scores of their mothers were controlled for, suggesting that welfare had little effect either positive or negative. Similarly, Levine and Zimmerman (2000) argue that children of welfare mothers were more likely to grow up to be welfare mothers, mainly because of other characteristics of the household they grew up in.

Currie and Cole (1993) compare siblings in families where the mother received welfare while one child was *in utero*, but not while the other child was *in utero*, and find no difference in the birth weight of the siblings. Given that research has shown little evidence of positive effects of cash welfare on children, it is not surprising that the literature evaluating welfare reform in the United States has produced similarly null findings. The National Research Council (Smolensky and Gootman, 2003) concluded that "no strong trends have emerged, either negative or positive, in indicators of parent well-being or child development across the years just preceding and following the implementation of [welfare reform]". However, US welfare reform was a complex intervention that changed many parameters of daily life by, for example, imposing work requirements on recipients.

Conditional tax credits represent an alternative approach to providing income to poor families, and hence to poor children. The early years of the Clinton administration in the

United States saw a huge expansion of the Earned Income Tax Credit (EITC), while in the UK, the Working Families Tax Credit approximately doubled in 1999. These are tax credits available to poor working families. Their essential feature is that they are "refundable"—in other words, a family whose credit exceeds its taxes receives the difference in cash. The tax credits are like welfare in that they give cash payments to poor families. But like welfare reform, the tax credits are a complex intervention in that recipients need to work and file tax returns in order to be eligible, and a great deal of research has shown that such tax credits affect maternal labor supply and marriage patterns (Eissa and Liebman, 1996; Meyer and Rosenbaum, 2001; Blundell, 2006). This is because the size of the payment increases with earnings up to a maximum level before being phased out, so that it creates an incentive to work among the poorest households but a work disincentive for households in the phase-out range. In the US, the number of recipients grew from 12.5 million families in 1990 to 19.8 million in 2003, and the maximum credit grew from $953 to $4204. The rapid expansion of this formerly obscure program run through the tax system has resulted in cash transfers to low-income families that were much larger than those that were available under welfare. Gundersen and Ziliak (2004) estimate that the EITC accounted for half of the reduction in after-tax poverty that occurred over the 1990s (the other half being mainly accounted for by strong economic growth).

Table 6 provides an overview of some of the research on the effects of income on children. Dahl and Lochner (2005) use variation in the amount of the EITC households are eligible for over time and household type to identify the effects of household income and find that each $1000 of income improves childrens' test scores by 0.02% to 0.04% of a standard deviation. An attractive feature of the changes in the EITC is that households may well have regarded them as permanent, so this experiment may approximate the effects of changes in permanent rather than transitory income. Their result implies, though, that it would take on the order of a $10,000 transfer to having an educationally meaningful effect on test scores.

Milligan and Stabile (2008) take advantage of a natural experiment resulting from changes in Canadian child benefits. These benefits vary across provinces and were reformed at different times. An advantage of their research is that the changes in income were not tied to other changes in family behavior, in contrast to programs like the EITC. They find that an extra $1000 of child benefits leads to an increase of about 0.07 of a standard deviation in the math scores and in the Peabody Picture Vocabulary Test, a standardized test of language ability for four to six year old children. If we think of a change of a third or a half a standard deviation in test scores as a meaningful educational effect, then these results suggest that an increase of as little as $5000 in family income has a meaningful effect. Milligan and Stabile (2008) go beyond Dahl and Lochner by examining effects on other indicators. They find that higher child benefits lower aggression in children and decrease depression scores for mothers. They do not find much

Table 6 Effects of income on birth and early childhood outcomes: evidence from the US and around the world.

Study and data	Study design	Results
The link between AFDC participation and birthweight (Currie and Cole, 1993). Data from NLSY merged with state and county level data. Data on children born between 1979–1988 ($n = 5000$).	IV: using parameters of AFDC, FSP and Medicaid as instruments, controlling for child characteristics and region fixed effects. Separate regressions for poor black and poor white women. Sibling FE: comparing sibs where mother on AFDC during pregnancy to others.	OLS results suggest that AFDC has negative effects. Sibling fixed effects indicate no significant effects. IV results suggest that AFDC during pregnancy causes large increases in mean birth weight among poor whites only. Hence, evidence suggests that AFDC has neutral or positive rather than negative effects. Negative estimates driven by selection.
Does money really matter? estimating impacts of family income on children's achievement with data from random-assignment experiments (Morris et al., 2004). Data from four studies that evaluated 8 welfare and anti-poverty programs with randomized designs: Connecticut's Jobs First, the Los Angeles Jobs First GAIN, the New Brunswick and British Columbia sites of the Canadian Self-Sufficiency Project, and the Atlanta, GA, Grand Rapids, MI, and Riverside, CA sites of the National Evaluation of Welfare to Work Strategies. $n = 18, 471$ children aged 2-15 at the time of random assignment.	IV models use random assignment as instruments for income, welfare receipt, and employment to estimate impact of income on children's cognitive achievement. Included dummies for sites in both stages of the regression analysis. Cognitive achievement measured with test scores and parent/teacher reports. Controlled for various baseline background family characteristics.	A $1000 increase in annual income raises cognitive achievement by 0.06 of SD for children aged 2-5. No statistically significant effects of income on children aged 6-9 or 10-15. A 3-SD increase in the proportion of quarters that welfare is received leads to a 1.5 SD decrease in cognitive achievement among 10-15 year-olds.

(continued on next page)

Table 6 (continued)

Study and data	Study design	Results
Who benefits from child benefit? (Blow et al., 2005). Data from UK Family Expenditure Survey 1980–2000. $n = 9811$ two-parent households; $n = 2920$ one-parent households.	Identification from variation in real value of Child Benefit (CB) 1980–2000 due to inflation and policy changes. Calculated anticipated and unanticipated changes in CB payments. Examine the propensity to spend CB on child goods (children's clothing) and adult goods (alcohol, tobacco and adult clothing).	**Spending out of unanticipated vs. anticipated change in CB:** 15x greater for alcohol in 2-parent households; 10x greater for adult clothing in lone-parent households. Results suggest that parents fully insure children against income shocks so that unanticipated changes only affect spending on adult goods.
Effects of EITC on birth and infant health outcomes. (Baker, 2008). US Vital Statistics Natality data file 1989–96. ($n = 781,535$). Exclude observations from 1994. Used data from 1997 March CPS to compute proportion of treatment group that is eligible for EITC.	Difference-in-Difference-in-Differences (DDD). Exploit the large expansion of EITC in 1993 (phased in 1994–96) that increased benefits to families with 2 or more children. "Treatment" group = mothers giving birth to 3rd or higher child. Control 1 = mothers giving birth to 1st or 2nd child. Control 2 = mothers giving birth to 1st child. Used mothers with less than High school as a proxy for EITC eligibility. Effect of interest is interaction between <HS*treatment*after EITC expansion.	Birth weight: Increased by 0.4% for all women Incidence of low birth weight: Decreased by 3.7% for all No statistically significant effects on # prenatal visits or maternal smoking during pregnancy.

Table 6 (continued)

Study and data	Study design	Results
The impact of family income on child achievement: evidence from the earned income tax credit (Dahl and Lochner, 2008). Data from NLSY on children and their mothers for 1988–2000. $n = 4720$ children (2527 mothers).	Identification based on EITC expansions in 1987–1993 and 1993–1997 that increased benefits for low- and middle-income. Used simulated instrumental variables (IV): IV is predicted change in EITC income. Controlled for family background and demographic variables and for time-varying state-specific policies that might affect child outcomes. Examine contemporaneous and lagged income. Also estimate OLS and child fixed effects models.	A $1000 increase in income raises combined math and reading scores by 0.06 SD. Larger gains from contemporaneous income for children aged 5 to 10 than for those aged 11–15. Larger gains for children from disadvantaged families.
Do child tax benefits affect the well-being of children? Evidence from Canadian child benefit expansions (Milligan and Stabile, 2008). Data from survey of labor and income dynamics on families with children for 1999–2004 for benefit simulation. Data from Canadian National Longitudinal Study of Children & Youth for 1994–2005 for children 10 and under ($n = 56,000$).	Instrumental variables. Used variation in child benefits across time, provinces, and number of children per family to develop a measure of benefit income as IV for child benefits in regressions of the effect of child benefits on child outcomes. Controlled for province-year fixed effects. Also reduced forms for simulated benefits' effect on child outcomes.	An increase in $ 1000 in simulated benefits leads to: 1.5% reduction in likelihood of learning disability (if mom < HS); 3.6% decline conduct disorder/aggression score 4–10; 4.3% of SD decline maternal depression; 11.6% SD decline in maternal depression (if mom < HS); 1.1% decline in child ever experiencing hunger (if mom < HS) Larger positive impacts on education and physical health for boys than girls; larger positive impacts on mental health for girls. Effects on math and vocabulary scores, behavioral outcomes, maternal depression and likelihood of ever experiencing hunger persist at least 4 years.

(continued on next page)

Table 6 (continued)

Study and data	Study design	Results
South African Child Support Grant (CSG): Unconditional cash transfer program with payments made to child's primary caregiver. Intended to cover the country's poorest 30% of children. Study of effects on child nutrition (Agüero et al., 2009). Data from KwaZulu-Natal Income Dynamics Study. Main outcome measure: Height-for-Age z-score (HAZ). T = 245, C = 886.	Exploit varying lengths of exposure to CSG among children aged 0–3 due to the timing of the rollout of CSG. Fit a quadratic OLS model to application delay (number of days between program creation and child's enrollment) using data for children born ≤ 2 years prior to survey date. Calculated an expected application delay variable for each child conditional on birth date, location and family characteristics, defined as % deviation in application delay from expected delay. Conditional on family characteristics, deviation in delay, and observables, the extent of CSG treatment should be random. Use generalized propensity scores, MLE.	No gains in HAZ for treatments covering ≤ 20% of the 0–3 window. HAZ 0.20 higher for treatment covering 2/3 of window than for a child receiving treatment covering 1% of window. **Benefit–cost ratio of CSG:** Between 1.06 and 1.48 (estimating lifetime earnings gains from gains in HAZ, using annual 5% discount rate, and assuming unemployed 33% of time). Results robust to checking for age cohort effects and location/spacial effects.

Table 6 (continued)

Study and data	Study design	Results
Conditional Cash Transfer Programs (CCT)		
Mexican "Progresa" program (now "Oportunidades"): Conditional cash transfers of 20–30% of household income every 2 months. Families must take young children to health clinics, immunizations, get adequate prenatal care, & receive nutrition supplement. (Families also to keep older children in school) (Gertler, 2004). Data from survey collected from experimental villages. Sample sizes: 7703 children under age 3 at baseline; 1501 newborns; Height analysis: T = 1049, C = 503; Anemia analysis: T = 1404, C = 608.	Program phased in to 320 treatment villages and 185 control villages randomly selected. Control villages received benefits 2 years after start of program. They did not know this would be the case. Investigate 0/1 treatment dummy as well as different lengths of program exposure.	**Treatment effects:** Newborns 25.3% less likely to be ill in past month. Children 0–3 22.3% less likely to be ill in past month. Height (12–36 mos.) 1.2% higher. Probability of being anemic (12–48 mos.) 25.5% less.

(continued on next page)

Table 6 (continued)

Study and data	Study design	Results
"Atención a Crisis" in rural Nicaragua. Conditional cash transfer ~15% average per capita expenditures. Women receive payments every 2 months if preschool children taken for regular visits to health clinics. (Older children must also be enrolled in school) (Macours et al., 2008). Sample sizes: T = 3002, C = 1019. Additional data from the 2001 Nicaragua Living Standards Measurement Study.	Randomized experimental design. 4 groups: CCT, CCT + vocational training, CCT + productive investment grant, control. Subgroup analysis by gender and age. Analyzed various transmission mechanisms by estimating expenditures on different foods (to measure nutrient intake), and differences in indicators for early childhood development.	**Treatment effects:** Developmental screener (DDST social-personal): increase by 0.13 SDs. DDST language: increase by 0.17 SDs. Receptive vocabulary (TVIP): increase by 0.22 SDs. (Children made up approx. 1.5 months of delay on TVIP.) **Effects by age:** DDST language: up 0.06 SDs 0-35 mos., up 0.20 SDs 60-83 mos. TVIP: up 0.05 SDs 36-59 mos., up 0.36 SDs 60-83 mos. (Oldest children made up 2.4 months of delay on TVIP) No statistically significant differences by gender. Transmission mechanisms: Better diet; more likely to have books, paper, pencils;more likely to be read to; more likely to have checkup, vitamins, de-worming drugs; more likely to be enrolled; more likely to see doctor when ill.

Unless otherwise noted, only results significant at 5% level are reported.
Percent changes (denoted by % instead of "pp") are reported relative to the mean, if means were reported in the paper.
"T" = Treatment group, "C" = Control group.
Outcomes written as "T > C" mean that treatment outcome greater than control outcome at 5% significance level.
Outcomes written as "T = C" mean that there is no statistically significant difference in outcomes between 2 groups at 5% level.

impact on physical health measures, though they do find a decrease in families reporting that their children went hungry. There is some evidence of gender differences, with girls showing greater responsiveness to income on the mental health and behavioral scores while boys show greater responsiveness on test scores.

These findings are extremely intriguing, but raise several questions. First, do the effects of income vary depending on the child's age? Morris et al. (2004) argue that income is more important at younger ages, though persistent poverty is worst of all. Second, are there really gender effects in the impact of income, and if so why? Third, the effects that Milligan and Stabile find are roughly twice those found by Dahl and Lochner. Is this because the former study a pure income transfer while the latter study a tied transfer? Fourth, will the effects last, or will they be subject to "fade out" as the children grow older?

Table 6 also includes examples from a growing literature analyzing "conditional cash transfer programs" (CCTs). These are programs that tie transfers to specific behavior on the part of the family. For example, the parents may be required to make sure that the children attend school or get medical care in return for the transfer. These programs have become increasingly popular in developing countries, and have also been implemented to a limited extent in rich countries (for example, there is a program in New York City which is being evaluated by Manpower Development Research Corporation). By their nature, CCTs are complex programs that cannot tell us about the pure impacts of income. Still, these programs have attracted attention because randomized controlled trials have shown at least short-term results. It is difficult however to compare across programs, given that they all tend to focus on different outcomes.

Given this positive evidence about the effects of income, it is a puzzle why so much aid to poor families is transferred in kind. Currie and Gahvari (2008) survey the many reasons for this phenomena that have been offered in the economics literature and conclude that the most likely reasons aid is offered in kind are agency problems, paternalism, and politics. In a nutshell, policy makers and the voters they represent may be more concerned with ensuring that children have medical care than with maximizing their parent's utility, even if the parent's utility is assumed to be affected by the children's access to health care. Politics come in because coherent lobby groups (such as doctors, teachers, or farmers) may have incentives to advocate for various types of in kind programs. In any case, in kind programs are an important feature of aid policies in all Organization for Economic Cooperation and Development states, accounting for over 10% of GDP if health care and educational programs are included. In what follows, we first discuss "near cash programs" and then programs whose benefits are less fungible with cash.

5.2. Near-cash programs

Programs such as the US Food Stamp Program (FSP, now renamed the Supplemental Nutrition Assistance Program, or SNAP) and housing assistance are often referred to as "near cash" programs because they typically offer households benefits that are worth less than what the household would have spent on food or housing in any case. Hence, canonical microeconomic theory suggests that households should think of them as equivalent to cash and that they should have the same impact as the equivalent cash transfer would have. In the case of food stamps, it has proven difficult to test this prediction because the program parameters are set largely at the national level, so that there is only time series variation.

Currie (2003) provides an overview of the program, and the research on its effects that had been conducted up to that point. Schanzenbach (forthcoming) uses data from a food stamp cash out experiment to examine the effect on food spending. She finds that a minority of households actually received more in food stamps than they would otherwise spend on food. In these constrained households, families did spend more on food than they would have otherwise, while in other households, food stamps had the same effect as cash. Unfortunately, there is little evidence that constrained households bought foods that were likely to have beneficial effects; they seem, for example, to have spent some of the "extra" food money on products such as soda.

Hoynes and Schanzenbach (2009) use variation from the introduction of the FSP to identify its effects on food spending. The FSP began as a small pilot program in 1961, and gradually expanded over the next 13 years: In 1971, national eligibility standards were established, and all states were required to inform eligible households about the program. In 1974, states were required to extend the program statewide if any areas of the state participated. Using data from the PSID, the introduction of the FSP was associated with an 18% increase in food expenditures in the full sample, with somewhat larger effects in the most disadvantaged households. They find that the marginal propensity to consume (MPC) food out of food stamp income was 0.16 compared to 0.09 for cash income. Thus, it does seem that many households were constrained to spend more on food than they otherwise would have (or alternatively, that the person receiving the food stamps had a stronger preference for food than the person controlling cash income in the household). From a policy maker's point of view, this means that the FSP has a bigger impact on food spending than an equivalent cash transfer. Still, it is a leaky bucket if only 16 cents of every dollar transferred goes to food.

Bingley and Walker (2007) conduct an investigation of the Welfare Milk Program in the UK. They identify the effect of the program on household milk expenditures using a large change in eligibility for the program that had differential effects by household type. They find that about 80% of a transfer of free milk is crowded out by reductions in milk purchases by the household. This estimate is quite similar to that of Hoynes and Schanzenbach, though it still suggests that the in kind transfer is having some effect on the composition of spending. Details of these two studies are shown in Table 7.

Given that these programs appear to have some effect on food expenditures, it is reasonable to ask what effect they have on child outcomes. There is a substantial older

Table 7 Impacts of Food Stamps on birth and early childhood outcomes.

Study	Study design	Results
Consumption responses to in-kind transfers: evidence from the introduction of the Food Stamp program (Hoynes and Schanzenbach, 2009). Data from PSID for 1968-78 and from the 1960, 1970, and 1980 decennial censuses. $n = 39{,}623$ person-year obs.	Difference-in-difference using variation in county-level implementation of FSP to estimate impact of FSP on food consumption and labor supply. Controlled for county and year fixed effects as well as state linear time trends. Included trends interacted w/ pre-treatment characteristics and three measures of annual per capita county transfer payments.	Introduction of FSP is associated with: 18% increase in total food expenditures (whole sample); 26-28% increase in total food expenditures for female-headed HHs; 6-13% increase in total food exp. for non-white female-headed HHs. No significant effect on meals out and cash expenditures on food at home. Elasticity of food spending with respect to income = 0.30. MPC for food out of cash income = 0.09 (for whole sample); MPC for food out of cash income = 0.111 (<\$25,000 income); MPC for food out of FSP income = 0.16 (for whole sample); MPC for food out of FSP income = 0.238 (<\$25,000 income). Decrease in whether the HH head reports any work by 21%.
There's no such thing as a free lunch: Altruistic parents and the response of household food expenditures to nutrition program reforms (Bingley and Walker, 2007). Data from UK Family Expenditure Surveys for 1981-1992. $n = 29{,}222$.	Analyzed 3 nutrition programs in the UK: free school lunch for children from poor HHs, free milk to poor HHs w/ pre-school children, and free milk at day care for pre-schoolers in attendance regardless of income. For identification, exploited 1988 reform that ended eligibility for poor HHs with working parents. Difference-in-difference (DD). Also did DD using the fact that free school lunches available only during term time, and summer holidays begin earlier in Scotland.	Free school lunch reduces food expenditure by 15% of the purchase price of the lunch. Free pint of milk reduces milk expenditure by 80%.

(continued on next page)

Table 7 (continued)

Study	Study design	Results
Impact of Food Stamp Program (FSP) on birthweight, neonatal mortality, and fertility (Almond et al., 2009). Birth and death micro data from the National Center for Health Statistics merged with county-level data for 1968–77. FSP data from USDA. County characteristics from 1960 City and County Data Book. Data on government transfers and per-capita income from REIS. Participation rates calculated using CPS. $n = 97,785$ whites; 27,274 blacks.	Difference-in-difference, using the fact that FSP was introduced to different counties at different times due to available funding and policy changes. Key policy/treatment variable is the month and year that each county implemented FSP. Estimated the impact of FSP on county-level birth outcomes, using county and time fixed effects. Main outcomes concerned with availability of FSP during 3rd trimester of pregnancy.	Introduction of FSP in 3rd trimester led to: 0.06–0.08% (0.1–0.2%) increase in birth weight for whites (blacks); a 1% (0.7–1.5%) decrease in fraction of low birth weight for whites (blacks). Insignificant impacts of exposure to FSP during earlier trimesters. Results robust to adding county & time fixed-effect and other controls, as well as various time trends to the analysis. Results robust to conducting an event study analysis.
Effects of FSP benefits on weight gained by expectant mothers (Baum, 2008). Data from the NLSY. Limited to low-income black and Hispanic women w/ pregnancy information in the surveys. $n = 1477$ pregnancy-level obs.	Random effects models using Heckman and Singer method to model unobserved heterogeneity. Dependent variable is whether women gain correct amount of weight during pregnancy based on pre-pregnancy BMI. Assume state variation in FSP eligibility rules, and program administration affects FSP takeup but not weight gain. Control for gestation, pre-pregnancy FSP, WIC.	Increasing average monthly FSP benefits from $0 to $100 decreases probability of gaining too little weight by 11.8–13.7%. No effect on probability of gaining too much weight. No statistically significant difference in effects of FSP on weight gain between first-time and non-first-time mothers.

Table 7 (continued)

Study	Study design	Results
Impact of FSP on birth outcomes in California (Currie and Moretti, 2008). Data on FSP from state records and REIS. Data from birth records in CA for 1960-74. Aggregated data into cells defined using county, race, year of birth, maternal age group, parity, and the third of the year. $n = 38,475$ cells.	Difference-in-difference using county-level variation in timing of FSP introduction. FSP measured using dummy ($= 1$ if FSP introduced), log expenditures, or log participation. FSP dummy refers to 9 months prior to birth. County fixed effects and county-specific time trends included. Examined teenage mothers and LA county separately.	FSP introduction led to a 10% increase in number of first births to white teen mothers (only in Los Angeles); a 24% increase in number of first births to black teen mothers; a 12% increase in number of first births to all blacks; a 0.1% increase in probability infant 1500-2000 g survives for whites; a 4% decrease in probability infant <3000 g survives for blacks; a 4% increase in probability of low birth weight among white teens.

Unless otherwise noted, all reported results are statistically significant at 5% level.
Percent changes (denoted by % instead of "pp") are reported relative to the mean.

literature examining this question (see Currie (2003) for a summary). The modal study compares eligible participants to eligible non-participants using a multiple regression model. The main problem with drawing inferences about the efficacy of the FSP from this exercise is that participants are likely to differ from eligible non-participants in ways that are not observed by the researcher. Thus, for example, Basiotis et al. (1998) and Butler and Raymond (1996) both find that participation in the FSP reduces consumption of some important nutrients. Since it is hard to imagine how giving people food coupons could do this, one suspects that these results are driven by negative selection into the FSP program.

Several recent papers examining the effects of the FSP on young children are summarized in Table 7. Currie and Moretti (2008) were the first to try to use variation in the timing of the introduction of the Food Stamp program to look at effects on birth outcomes. Using Vital Statistics Natality data from California, they find that the introduction of the FSP increased the number of births, particularly in Los Angeles County. They also find some evidence that the FSP increased the probability of fetal survival among the lightest white infants, but the effect is very small, and only detectable in Los Angeles. Notably, the FSP increased (rather than decreased) the probability of low birth weight but the estimated effect is small, and concentrated among teenagers giving birth for the first time. Thus, it appears that in California, the FSP increased fertility and infant survival (in some groups) with overall zero or negative effects on the distribution of birth weight.

Almond et al. (forthcoming) examine the same question using national data, and focus on receipt of the FSP during the third trimester, when the fetus typically puts on most of the weight the baby will have at birth. In contrast to Currie and Moretti, they find that the introduction of the FSP increased birth weights for whites and had even larger effects on blacks. The percentage reductions in the incidence of low birth weight were greater than the percentage increases in mean birth weight, suggesting that the FSP had its largest effects at the bottom of the birth weight distribution. Almond et al. find no effect of Food Stamp receipt in the first trimester of pregnancy and much weaker evidence for effects of receipt in the second. This suggests that one reason for the contrast between their results and those of Currie and Moretti is that the latter did not focus narrowly enough on the relevant part of pregnancy. Moreover, Almond et al. find larger effects in the South than in other regions, raising the possibility that overall effects were smaller in California than in other regions. Finally, it is possible that the effects in California are obscured by the substantial in-migration that the state experienced over this period.

Baum (2008) examines the effects of the FSP on weight gain among pregnant women, with particular attention to whether women gained either less than the recommended amount or greater than the recommended amount given their pre-pregnancy body mass index. He estimates a simultaneous equations model in which weight gain and FSP participation are jointly determined. FSP participation is assumed to be affected by various state-level rules about eligibility, outreach and so on. One difficulty is that these rules may be affected by other characteristics of states (such as overall generosity of social programs) which have direct effects on weight gain (e.g. through superior access to health care during pregnancy). Baum finds that FSP participation reduces the probability that women experienced inadequate weight gain during pregnancy, but has no effect on the probability that they gained too much weight. Since inadequate maternal weight gain is an important risk factor for low birth weight, it is likely that FSP had a positive effect on birth weights among affected mothers.

As discussed above, the other large category of "near cash" offer subsidized housing. Many OECD countries have large housing assistance programs, but their effects on families are understudied. In fact, we were able to find only one paper that examined the effects of housing programs on the outcomes of children less than five, and only a handful that examined effects on children at all. These studies are summarized in Table 8.

Since by design, families receiving housing assistance are among the poorest of the poor, it is clearly important to address the endogeneity of program receipt. Currie and Yelowitz (2000) look at the effects of living in a public housing project in families with two children. They combine information from the Census and from the Survey of Income and Program Participation in a two-sample instrumental variables framework where the instrument for receipt of housing assistance is the sex composition of the siblings (families with a boy and a girl are entitled to larger apartments, and so are more likely to take up housing benefits). They find that families living in projects are less likely to be subject to overcrowding and that the children are much less likely to have been held back in school. The latter effect is three times bigger for boys (who are more likely to be held back in any case) than for girls. Since most "holding back" occurs at younger ages (Kindergarten and grade 1), this suggests that this type of assistance is in fact beneficial for young children.

Goux and Maurin (2005) focus on the effect of overcrowding in France using a similar instrumental variables strategy: They argue that children in families in which the two eldest children are the same sex are more likely to live in crowded conditions in childhood. They also propose an alternative strategy in which crowding is instrumented with whether or not the parent was born in an urban area—parents who are from urban areas are more likely to live in crowded conditions. They find evidence consistent with Currie and Yelowitz in that crowding has a large and significant effect on the probability that a child falls behind in school and eventually drops out.

Fertig and Reingold (2007) examine the effect of receipt of public housing assistance using data from the Fragile Families Study and three instruments: the gender composition of children in the household, the supply of public housing in each location, and the length of waiting lists in each location. They find mixed estimates of effects on maternal health and little evidence of an effect on child health, though their samples are quite

Table 8 Effects of housing and neighborhoods on child outcomes.

Study and data	Study design	Results
Housing and child outcomes		
Are public housing projects good for kids? (Currie and Yelowitz, 2000). Data from SIPP for 1992–1993, March CPS for 1990–1995, and US Census for 1990 on families w/ 2 children (under 18) and income < $50,000. $n = 279{,}129$.	Two-sample instrumental variable (TSIV) of the effects of living in public housing projects on child's education, housing conditions. Outcome variables are in SIPP and Census. Endogenous regressor is in CPS. Instrument is a dummy for siblings being of different sexes since families with different sex children get larger apartments in public housing than families with same sex children. Controlled for per-capita availability of projects, vouchers, Section 8 subsidies, as well as other neighborhood and family background characteristics.	First stage results: Having siblings of different sex increases likelihood of family living in project by 24%. Second stage results: Families who live in projects are 16 pp (mean = 0.04) less likely to be overcrowded; and 12pp (mean = 0.02) less likely to live in high-density housing. Children who live in projects are 111% less likely to have been held back in school (larger effects for boys than for girls). Black children who live in projects are 19% less likely to have been held back in school. No statistically significant effect for white children.

Table 8 (continued)

Study and data	Study design	Results
The long-term effects of public housing on self-sufficiency (Newman and Harkness, 2002) Data from PSID—Assisted housing database on cohorts born b/n 1957 and 1967. Sample limited to individuals whose families were eligible for public housing b/n ages 10 and 16. $n = 1183$. Adult outcomes measured at ages 20–27.	Amemiya generalized least squares regression where the instrument was the vector of residuals from a regression of the number of public housing units per eligible family in the area on demographic characteristics of the area. Instrumented for whether child lived in public housing to estimate impact on various adult outcomes. Controlled for numerous background characteristics and state and year fixed effects.	Living in public housing as a child leads to an increase in the probability of any employment b/n ages 25 and 27 of 7.8%; an increase in annual earnings b/n ages 20 and 27 of 14.3%; an increase in the number of years not on welfare b/n ages 20 and 27 of 11.3%. No statistically significant effect on household earnings relative to the poverty line. Note: above results significant at 6% level.
Public Housing, Housing Vouchers, and Student Achievement: Evidence from Public Housing Demolitions in Chicago (Jacob, 2004) Administrative data from the Chicago Housing Authority and Chicago Public Schools for 1991–2002 on students who lived in high-rise public housing for at least one semester. $n = 10{,}556$.	Instrumental variables regression of the effect of living in a public housing project on student outcomes. Identification from variation in timing of housing demolitions in Chicago in the 1990s. Instrumented for living in public housing with a dummy for whether the student lived in a unit scheduled for demolition at the time of the closure announcement. Controls for background characteristics and project and year fixed effects.	No statistically significant effect of living in high-rise projects on student outcomes. Living in a building that was demolished leads to an 8.2% increase in probability that students> 14 yrs drop out of school within 3 years relative to those that lived in buildings scheduled for demolition that had not yet been demolished (12% more likely for girls; 4% more likely for boys).

(continued on next page)

Table 8 (continued)

Study and data	Study design	Results
Public housing, health and health behaviors: is there a connection? (Fertig and Reingold, 2007). Data from the fragile families and child well-being study on children born in 20 US cities between 1998 and 2000. Sample 1: T = 422, C = 2, 055; Sample 2: T = 323, C = 1, 999; Sample 3: T = 150, C = 919.	Instrumental variables regression. Three instruments: gender composition of household, the supply of public housing in each city, and length of waiting list. Three subsamples. "Control" group is mothers who have below 80% of median income in their area but are not in public housing. "Treatment 1" is mothers who live in public housing at time of first interview immediately after childbirth. "Treatment 2" is mothers who have moved into public housing between childbirth and second interview at child's age 1 ("move-in" subsample). "Treatment 3" is the "'move-in'" subsample limited to mothers with two or three children at second interview. Controlled for family, background, neighborhood, and other demographic and socio-economic characteristics.	Note: only reporting IV estimates with complete combination of instruments here. **Effects of moving into public housing between childbirth and one-year interview:** 1.63 point increase in mother's health index (5 point scale, mean not reported, can't calculate effect size) 55 pp decrease in likelihood that mother has limiting health condition (mean = 0.08) 41 pp decrease in likelihood that mother is underweight (mean = 0.07) 18% increase in mother's BMI Decrease in domestic violence (imprecise coefficient estimate) No statistically significant effects on child's birth weight or PPVT scores.

Neighborhood characteristics and child outcomes

The long-run consequences of living in a poor neighborhood (Oreopoulos, 2003) Data from the intergenerational income data base for 1978-1999 (taken from income tax files) on individuals living in Toronto, born b/n 1963 and 1970. *n* = 4060.	Among families who apply for housing projects, assignment to a particular project is approximately random—based on 1st available unit. Compared housing-project means of various adult outcomes across neighborhood quality (measured by density of housing, total size of project, proportion of the Census tract below the low-income cutoff, and whether the project is all high-rises).	The quality of housing project or neighborhood has no statistically significant impact on total income, annual earnings, or number of years on welfare in adulthood. Family characteristics account for up to 30% of total variation in adult outcomes.

Table 8 (continued)

Study and data	Study design	Results
Neighborhood Effects on Crime for Female and Male Youth: Evidence from a Randomized Housing Voucher Experiment (Kling et al., 2005) Data from Moving to Opportunities (MTO) experiment. Families living in public housing projects in Boston, Los Angeles, New York City, Baltimore, and Chicago were randomly chosen to stay in their current home, to receive a Section 8 housing voucher, or to receive a Section 8 housing voucher restricted to use in neighborhoods w/ poverty rate less than 10%. Surveys conducted in 2002. Data on youths aged 15-25. Data on arrest records for MTO states. $n = 4475$.	OLS regression of crime outcomes on dummy for whether family used a voucher (instrumented by whether family was assigned to treatment group) or on voucher type, and on an age-treatment interaction variable. Instrument necessary since not all families who were assigned a voucher chose to use it – some remained in their initial housing.	Assignment to a restricted voucher leads to a 31% decrease in violent crime arrests for female youths. Use of restricted voucher leads to a 76% reduction in violent crime arrests among female youths. No statistically significant effects on males for violent crime arrests. Assignment to a restricted voucher leads to a 33% decrease in property crime arrests for female youths. Use of restricted voucher leads to a 85% decrease in property crime arrests for female youths. Assignment to a restricted voucher leads to a 32% increase in property crime arrests for male youths. Use of restricted voucher leads to a 77% increase in property crime arrests for male youths.

(continued on next page)

Table 8 (continued)

Study and data	Study design	Results
Neighborhoods and Academic Achievement (Sanbonmatsu et al., 2006) Data from MTO experiment surveys for 2002 (see above) on youths aged 6–20. $n = 5074$.	Same regression as Kling et al. (2005) for educational outcomes.	Children in families assigned to a restricted voucher attend better quality schools: the mean rank of schools on state exams is 30% greater than the control group mean, and the mean proportion of school-lunch-eligible children is 8% lower. No statistically significant effects of either voucher on child educational outcomes (school attendance, whether child does homework, child's behavior in class, whether child attended class for gifted students or class for special help, and Woodcock–Johnson Revised reading and math test scores).
Close Neighborhoods Matter: Neighborhood Effects on Early Performance at School (Goux and Maurin, 2005). Data from the French Labor Force Survey for 1991–2002 on 16-year-old youths. $n = 13116$.	Authors assume that a child's birthdate will impact his/her own educational outcomes, but not the outcomes of his/her neighbors. (Proportion of 15-yr-olds held back a grade is 15 pp higher among those born at the end of the year relative to those born at the beginning of the year). IV regression, where first stages are: regression of being held back at age 15 on timing of birthday and regression of proportion of neighborhood youths held back at age 15 on their birthdays. Second stage is regression for being held back at age 16 on having been held back at age 15 and proportion of neighborhood youths held back at age 15. Controlled for year fixed effects, gender, and nationality.	1 SD increase in the proportion of neighboring youth that were held back in school at age 15 increases the probability of being held back at age 16 by 0.2 SD.

Table 8 (continued)

Study and data	Study design	Results
Experimental analysis of neighborhood effects (Kling et al., 2007). Data from MTO experiment surveys for 2002 (see above) on youths aged 15–20. $n = 1807$.	Same regression as (Kling et al., 2005) for health and behavior outcomes.	Assignment to an unrestricted voucher leads to a decrease in likelihood of experiencing anxiety symptoms by 62%/91% among females/males; a decrease in marijuana use by 44% among females; an increase in the likelihood of non-sports injury by 130% among males; an increase in incidence of smoking by 121% among males. Assignment to restricted voucher leads to a decrease in likelihood of experiencing psychological distress by 100% among females; a decrease in likelihood of experiencing anxiety by 57% among females; a decrease in marijuana use by 50% among females; an increase in likelihood of non-sports injury by 140% among males; an increase in incidence of smoking by 82% among males.

Unless otherwise noted, only results significant at 5% level are reported here.

small. Newman and Harkness (2002) use data from the PSID to examine the effect of living in public housing as a child on future earnings and employment. Living in public housing is instrumented using the residual from a regression of local housing supply on the demographic characteristics of the area. They find that public housing is associated with increases in the probability of any employment (from 88% to about 95%) and increases in annual earnings (by $1861 from a mean of $11,210). While all of these instrumental variables strategies are subject to caveats (is gender composition really uncorrelated with sibling's outcomes? Are characteristics of local housing markets associated with unobserved factors such as the quality of schools that might also affect child outcomes?) they certainly all point in a similar direction.

An important question is whether public housing assistance benefits children more than the equivalent cash transfer. It is difficult to answer this question given the available data. However, it is possible to eliminate some possible channels through which public housing programs might have different effects. One is that public housing programs may constrain the recipient's choice of neighborhoods, with either positive or negative effects. Jacob (2004) studies students displaced by demolitions of the most notorious Chicago high-rise projects. The US Congress passed a law in 1996 that required local housing authorities to destroy units if the cost of renovating and maintaining them was greater than the cost of providing a voucher for 20 years. Jacobs argues that the order in which doomed buildings were destroyed was approximately random. For example, in January 1999, the pipes froze in some buildings in the Robert Taylor Homes, which meant that those buildings were demolished before others in the same complex. By comparing children who stayed in buildings scheduled to be demolished to others who had already been displaced by demolitions, he obtains a measure of the effect of living in high-rise public housing. Despite the fact that the high rises in Jacob's study were among the most notorious public housing projects in the country, he finds very little effect of relocation on children's educational outcomes. However, this may be because for the most part, children stayed in the same neighborhoods and in the same schools.

The most exhaustive examination of the effects of giving vouchers to project residents is an ongoing experiment called "Moving to Opportunity" (MTO). MTO was inspired by the Gautreaux program in Chicago, which resulted from a consent decree designed to desegregate Chicago's public housing by relocating some black inner-city residents to white suburbs. MTO is a large-scale social experiment that is being conducted in Chicago, New York, Los Angeles, Boston and Baltimore (see Orr et al. (2003), Kling et al. (2005) and Sanbonmatsu et al. (2006)). Between 1994 and 1998, volunteers from public housing projects were assigned by lottery to one of three groups. The first group received a voucher that could only be used to rent housing in a low-poverty area (a Census tract with a poverty rate less than 10%). This group also received help locating a suitable apartment (referred to here as the "MTO group"). The second group received a voucher which they could use to rent an apartment in any neighborhood. The third group was the control and received no vouchers or assistance although they were eligible to remain in their project apartment. Families in the first group did move to lower poverty neighborhoods and the new neighborhoods of the MTO group were considerably safer. The move to new neighborhoods had positive effects on the mental health and schooling attainment of girls, and negative effects on the probability that they were ever arrested. But surprisingly, MTO either had no effect, or negative effects, on boys. Boys in the experimental group were 13% more likely than controls to have ever been arrested. This increase was due largely to increases in property crimes. These boys also report more risky behaviors such as drug and alcohol use. And boys in the MTO and voucher groups were more likely to suffer injuries. These differences between boys and girls are apparent even within families (Orr et al., 2003).

It remains to be seen how the long-term outcomes of the MTO children will differ from controls. Oreopoulos (2003) uses data from Canadian income tax records to examine the earnings of adults who lived in public housing projects in Toronto as children. There are large differences between projects in Toronto, both in terms of the density of the projects, and in terms of the poverty of the neighborhoods. Oreopoulos argues that the type of project a family lives in is approximately randomly assigned because the family is offered whatever happens to be available when they get to the top of the waiting list. Oreopoulos finds that once the characteristics of the family are controlled, the neighborhood has no effect on future earnings or on the likelihood that someone works.

The findings on near cash programs can be summarized as follows. There is credible evidence that the FSP may improve birth weight. More work remains to be done to determine whether it has positive effects on the nutrition of children after birth, whether similar programs in other countries have positive effects, and whether this particular type of in kind program has effects that are different than cash subsidies to poor households. The evidence regarding housing programs also suggests that they can be beneficial to families, but offers little guidance about the important question of whether housing programs matter primarily because they subsidize family incomes or operate through some other mechanism. It seems doubtful, given the available evidence, that housing programs benefit child outcomes primarily by improving their neighborhoods (especially since many housing projects are located in less desirable neighborhoods).

5.3. Early intervention programs

Many programs specifically seek to intervene in the lives of poor children in order to improve their outcomes. Three interventions that have been shown to be effective are nurse home visiting programs, nutritional supplementation for pregnant women, and quality early childhood education programs. Table 9 summarizes some recent evidence about home visiting programs.

Table 9 Randomized trials of home visiting programs.

Study/program name	Data, program description, and study design	Results
The Comprehensive Child Development Program (CCDP) (St. Pierre and Layzer, 1999)	Biweekly visits starting 0–1, ending at 5 years. Population served: 43% African–American, 26% Hispanic; all below poverty. Background of Home Visitors: paraprofessionals Sample sizes: T = 2, 213, C = 2, 197 Evaluation Sites: 21 sites throughout the US. Age of children at last follow-up: 5 years old	Developmental Checklist: T = 57.93, C = 57.51 Found no significant effects on wide range of outcomes including; Development and Behavior scores, medical care, mortality, HOME scores, maternal depression, welfare use, maternal income, education or employment, maternal substance use. Total cost per participant: $ 37,488. Total benefit per participant: $91. Net present value = −$37,397.
Healthy start (Duggan et al., 1999, 2004; Harding et al., 2007; DuMont et al., 2006)	Weekly visits, fading to quarterly age of participation: birth to 5 years. population served: low-income, at-risk families of newborns recruited through an HSP screening and assessment protocol. All English-speaking. Background of home visitors: paraprofessionals. Sample sizes: Alaska: T = 179, C = 185; Hawaii: T = 373, C = 270, 6 sites; Virginia: T = 422, C = 197, 2 sites. 19 additional sites discussed in (Harding et al., 2007). Age of children at last follow-up: 2 years old (3 in San Diego)	Some positive effects on parenting practices and negative effects on domestic violence in some sites. E.g. Hawaii partner violence: T = 16%, C = 24%. Less corporal/verbal punishment T < C (odds ratio 0.59). Health effects in some sites but not others, e.g. VA: birth complications T = 0.2, C = 0.48; New York: low birth weight T = 3.3%, C = 8.3%; maternal depression T = 23%, C = 38%. Increases in child Bayley Scale for Infant Development in San Diego, Arkansas. Increases in maternal education and decreases in serious child abuse only in New York (T 12.5% less than C). All sites tested for a wide range of possible effects, with generally insignificant effects on other measures of child well being and child abuse.

Table 9 (continued)

Study/program name	Data, program description, and study design	Results
The nurse-family partnership program (Olds et al., 1999)	Weekly visits, fading to monthly, prenatal to 2 yrs. Population served: disadvantaged first-time mothers less than 30 weeks pregnant (62% unmarried, 47% teenage, 23% poor, unmarried and teenage). Background of home visitors: Nurses. Sample sizes: C1 = 90, C2 = 94, T3 = 100 T4 = 116 (see below for description of groups). Evaluation site: Elmira, New York. C1 = screening; C2 = screening & transportation; T3 = screening, transportation, & prenatal home visits; T4 = screening, transportation, prenatal and postnatal home visits. Prenatal analysis: T = T3 + T4, C = C1 + C2; Postnatal analysis: T = T4, C = C1 + C2. Age of children at last follow-up: 15 years old.	Pre-term births for women who smoked more than 4 cigarettes per day: T = 2.08%, C = 9.81% (mothers also less likely to smoke during pregnancy, better nutrition during pregnancy, more likely to use WIC). For children: fewer emergency room visits at 0–12, 12–24 months. **AT 15-yr follow-up** Mother's number of months receiving AFDC: T4 = 60.4, C = 90.3; Mother's substance use impairments: T4 = 0.41, C = 0.73; Mother's arrests: T4 = 0.18, C = 0.58; Convictions: T4 = 0.06, C = 0.28; Substantiated reports of child abuse and neglect, 0 to 15 yrs: T4 = 0.29, C = 0.54; Child's incidence of arrests: T4 = 0.20, C = 0.45; Child's convictions and probation violations : T4 = 0.09, C = 0.47; Child's number of sex partners: T4 = 0.92, C = 2.48; Child's number of days drank alcohol: T4 = 1.09, C = 2.49. **Cost-benefit analysis:** Total cost per child: $10,300 ; Total benefit per child: $ 30,000. Net present value = +$19,700. Most benefits due to reduced crime on part of the child and reductions in child abuse on part of parent.

(continued on next page)

Table 9 (continued)

Study/program name	Data, program description, and study design	Results
The nurse–family partnership program (Olds et al., 2007)	Weekly visits, fading to monthly, prenatal to 2 yrs. Population served: first-time mothers less than 29 weeks pregnant and at least 2 of the following: unmarried, less than 12 yrs of education, or unemployed; 92% African-American, 98% unmarried, 64% 18 yrs of age or younger, 85% at or below poverty level. Background of home visitors: nurses. Sample sizes: C1 = 166, C2 = 515, T3 = 230, T4 = 228 (see below for description of groups). Evaluation sites: Memphis, Tennessee. C1 = transportation; C2 = screening & transportation; T3 = screening, transportation, prenatal home visits, one visit postpartum in hospital, one postpartum visit at home; T4 = T3 plus home visits through child's 2nd birthday. Prenatal analysis: T = T3 + T4, C = C1 + C2; Postnatal analysis: T = T4, C = C2. Age of children at last follow-up: 9 years old.	During first 2 years of child's life: Number of health encounters for injuries/ingestions: T = 0.43, C = 0.56 Number of outpatient visits for injuries/ingestions: T = 0.11, C = 0.20 Number of days hospitalized for injuries/ingestions: T = 0.04, C = 0.18 Mother attempted breast-feeding: T = 26%, C = 16% Subsequent live births: T = 22%, C = 31% **AT 9-yr follow-up** Child GPA (low-resource only): T = 2.68, C = 2.44 Reading and math achievement (low-resource only): T = 44.89, C = 35.72 Mother's # months with current partner: T = 51.89, C = 44.48 Number of months on AFDC/TANF per year: T = 5.21, C = 5.92 Number of months on food stamps per year: T = 6.98, C = 7.80 Maternal mastery: T = 101.03, C = 99.50 No. of months with employed partner: T = 46.04, C = 48.43 No significant effects on ER visits for injuries in first 2 years, health at birth, use of medical care, maternal health.

Table 9 (continued)

Study/program name	Data, program description, and study design	Results
Early start (Fergusson et al., 2006)	Weekly visits for 1st month, then varying age of participation: prenatal to 3 years. Population Served: families recruited through the same screening process as in Hawaii Healthy Start. Background of home visitors: "family support workers" with nursing or social work qualifications. Sample sizes: T = 220, C = 223. 1 site in New Zealand. Age of children at last follow-up: 3 years old.	Average number of doctor's visits 0–36 mo: T > C by 0.24 SD. Percentage of up-to-date well-child checks 0–36 mo: T > C by 0.25 SD. Percentage enrolled w/ dentist 0–36 mo: T > C by 0.20 SD. Percentage attended hospital for accident/injury or accidental poisoning 0–36 mo: T < C by 0.22 SD. Mean duration of early childhood education: T > C by 0.22 SD. Mean number of community service contacts: T > C by 0.31 SD. Positive parenting attitudes score: T > C by 0.26 SD. Non-punitive parenting attitudes score: T > C by 0.22 SD. Overall parenting score: T > C by 0.27 SD. Percentage of parental report of severe physical assault: T < C by 0.26 SD. Child internalizing (negative) behavior score★: T < C by 0.26 SD. Child total negative behavior score★: T < C by 0.24 SD.

(continued on next page)

Table 9 (continued)

Study/program name	Data, program description, and study design	Results
Effectiveness of home visitation by public health nurses in prevention of the recurrence of child physical abuse and neglect: a randomized controlled trial (MacMillan et al., 2005)	Weekly visits for first 6 months, then biweekly Age of participation: Entry: 0–13 yrs old, program lasted 3 years. Population served: parents who have a reported episode of physical abuse or neglect in the 3 months prior to joining program. Background of home visitors: public health nurses. Sample sizes: T = 73, C = 66. 1 site in Hamilton, Canada. Note: Control group received standard services from the child protection agency CPA). Treatment group also received the standard services in addition to the home visiting. Age of children at last follow-up: Varied (3-year follow-up).	Recurrence of physical abuse or neglect based on hospital records: T = 24%, C = 11% Also tested, but found no statistically significant effects on: Recurrence of abuse or neglect based on CPA records; HOME score; child's behavioral, anxiety, attention problems, aggression or conduct disorder scores; parenting behavior scores or CAP score.
Economic evaluation of an intensive home visiting programme for vulnerable families: A cost-effectiveness analysis of a public health intervention (McIntosh et al., 2009)	Weekly visits Age of Participation: prenatal to 18 months old. Population Served: Pregnant women identified by community midwives as being at risk for child abuse or neglect. Background of home visitors: paraprofessionals who received program training. Sample Sizes: T = 67, C = 64. 1 site in the UK. Age of Children at Last Follow-up: 1 year old	Maternal sensitivity (CARE Index): T > C by 13%. Infant cooperativeness (CARE Index): T > C by 18%. Likelihood infant placed on child protection register: T > C (1.35 times more likely). Proportion of children removed from home: T = 6%, C = 0%.

Some cost-benefit analysis from Aos et al. (2004), Technical Appendix.
"T" refers to treatment group, "C"; refers to control group. "T = C" means no discernable difference between groups at 5% significance level.

5.3.1. Home visiting

Unlike many social programs, home visiting has been subject to numerous evaluations using randomized control trials. A recent survey appears in Howard and Brooks-Gunn (2009). David Olds and collaborators have developed a particular model for home visiting and conducted randomized controlled trials in a number of settings (Olds et al., 1999, 2007) to evaluate it. Olds' programs focus on families that are at risk because the mother is young, poor, uneducated and/or unmarried, and involve home visits by trained public health nurses from the prenatal period up to two years postpartum. The evaluations have shown many positive effects on maternal behavior, and on child outcomes. As of two years of age, children in the Elmira New York were much less likely to have been seen in a hospital emergency room for unintentional injuries or ingestion of poisonous substances, although this finding was not replicated at other study sites. As of age 15, children of visited mothers were less likely to have been arrested or to have run away from home, had fewer sexual partners, and smoked and drank less. The children were also less likely to have been involved in verified incidents of child maltreatment. This finding is important given the high incidence of maltreatment among US children (and especially among poor children), and the negative outcomes of maltreated children discussed above. There was little evidence of effects on cognition at four years of age (except among children of initially heavy smokers), though one might expect the documented reduction in delinquent behavior among the teens to be associated with improvements in eventual schooling attainment.

In Olds' model, using nurses as home visitors is viewed as key to getting good results. This may be because nurse home visitors are more acceptable to parents than social workers or community workers because families may want medical services. A randomized trial of nurses versus trained paraprofessionals (Olds et al., 2002) suggests that the effects that can be obtained by paraprofessionals are smaller. Also, the Olds programs are strongly targeted at families considered to be at risk and so they do not shed light on the cost-effectiveness of the universal home visiting programs for pregnant women and/or newborns that exist in many countries.

Olds' positive results do not imply that all home visiting programs are equally effective. In fact, Table 9 suggests that the average home visiting program has relatively small effects. They often improve parenting in subtle ways and may result in some improvements in specific health outcomes. However, these may not be sufficient to justify the cost of a large scale program (Aos et al. (2004) offers a cost benefit analysis of several programs). Home visiting programs can be viewed as a type of parenting program—presumably the reason why Olds' home visitors improved outcomes is because they taught mothers to be better parents. Since parents are so important to children, programs that seek to improve parenting practices are perennially popular. Yet studies of these programs suggest that it is remarkably difficult to change parents' behavior and that many attempted interventions are unsuccessful. The most successful parenting programs are those that combine parent education with some other intervention that parents want, such as visits by nurses (as in Olds case) or child care (Brooks-Gunn and Markham, 2005).

5.3.2. US supplemental feeding program for women, infants, and children (WIC)

A second type of early intervention program that has been extensively studied is the US Supplemental Feeding Program for Women, Infants, and Children (WIC). As its name implies, WIC is a program targeted at pregnant and lactating women, infants, and children up to age 5. Participants receive vouchers that can be redeemed for particular types of food at participating retailers. Participants must generally go to the WIC office to receive the vouchers, and generally receive nutrition education services at that time. Many WIC offices are run out of clinics and may also facilitate access to medical care. Dozens of studies (many of them reviewed in Currie (2003)) have shown that participation in WIC during pregnancy is associated with longer gestations, higher birth weights, and generally healthier infants, and that the effects tend to be largest for children born to the most disadvantaged mothers. Economists have critiqued these studies, on the grounds that there may be unobservable variables that are correlated with WIC participation among eligibles and also with better birth outcomes. Moreover, it may be implausible to expect WIC to have an effect on pre-term birth. A recent Institute of Medicine report on the subject reviewed the evidence and concluded that randomized trials of many different interventions with women at risk of pre-term birth had failed to find effects (Behrman and Butler, 2007). So it might be surprising to find an effect for WIC, when more specific and intensive interventions aimed at preventing pre-term birth have generally failed.

A number of new studies have attempted to deal with various aspects of this critique, as shown in Table 10. Bitler and Currie (2005) look at data from the Pregnancy Risk Monitoring System, which contains very detailed data from new mothers obtained by combining data from birth records and survey data taken from women before and after pregnancy. They directly address the question of selection bias by examining the population of mothers eligible for Medicaid (all of whom are adjunctively eligible for WIC) and asking how participants differ from non-participants along observable dimensions. They find that the WIC women are more disadvantaged than the non-participants along all observables. This finding does not prove that WIC women are also negatively selected in terms of unobservable variables, but it does mean that women who were very negatively selected in terms of education, health, family relationships and so on would have to have other attributes that were systematically correlated with positive outcomes. Like previous studies, Bitler and Currie also find that WIC participation is associated with higher maternal weight gain, longer gestation, and higher birth weight, particularly among women on public assistance, high school dropouts, teen mothers, and single mothers.

Joyce et al. (2004) adopt a similar strategy with regard to selection, and focus on a sample of first births to women who initiated prenatal care in the first four months of

Table 10 Selected studies of special supplemental feeding program for women, infants, and children (WIC).

Study	Study design	Results
Impact on birth outcomes		
Bitler and Currie (2005). Data from Pregnancy Risk Assessment Monitoring System (PRAMS), ($n = 60,731$).	Compared WIC participants and non-participants in the sample of women whose deliveries were paid by Medicaid. Addressed selection bias by comparing a broad range of observable characteristics between eligible WIC participants and non-participants.	WIC mothers are negatively selected into the program relative to all Medicaid recipients. WIC participants are 1.4–1.5 times more likely to have had prenatal care in 1st trimester; 0.7 times as likely to give birth to low birth weight infant; 0.9 times as likely to give birth to infants who are below the 25th percentile of birth weight given gestational age; 0.9 times as likely to have their infant admitted to the Intensive Care Unit. WIC associated with increases in maternal weight gain, gestation, and birth weight. Larger impact for more disadvantaged women (such as those who received public assistance, high school drop-outs, teen mothers, single mothers).

(continued on next page)

Table 10 (continued)

Study	Study design	Results
Figlio et al. (2009). Matched data on births in Florida during 1997–2001 with school records of older siblings of the infants to identify whether the older child receives free lunch or reduced-price lunch though the NSLP (those on NSLP are WIC eligible). Marginally eligible: $n = 2530$; Marginally ineligible: $n = 1744$.	Instrumental variables comparing marginally eligible and ineligible WIC women. Marginally ineligible for WIC = families not participating in NLSP during pregnancy, but participating during either the year before or after. Marginally eligible = families that received NSLP during the pregnancy, but did not receive the lunches at least one adjacent year. A federal policy change that increased income reporting requirements for WIC eligibility in September 1999, made it more difficult for eligibles to obtain WIC. The instrument for WIC participation is an interaction between an indicator for the policy change and eligibility.	WIC participation reduces the likelihood of low birth weight by 12.9 pp (imprecise estimate). No statistically significant effect of WIC on gestational age or likelihood of prematurity.
Gueorguieva et al. (2009). Data on mother-infant pairs from birth files on all singleton births in Florida hospitals between 1996 and 2004. Merged with Medicaid eligibility and WIC participation data from the Florida Department of Health. ($n = 369,535$).	Adjusted for selection using propensity scores. "Treatment" is percent days on WIC during pregnancy. Main outcome is SGA ("small for gestational age"). Separate analyses for full-term, late pre-term, very pre-term, and extremely pre-term births.	A 10% increase in percent of time during pregnancy in WIC associated with a 2.5% decrease in probability of a full-term and SGA infant; 2.0% decrease in probability of a late pre-term and SGA infant; 3.7% decrease in probability of a very pre-term and SGA infant.

Table 10 (continued)

Study	Study design	Results
(Joyce et al., 2004). Data from birth certificate files in New York City between 1988 and 2001 on women who were on Medicaid and/or WIC during pregnancy. ($n = 35,415$ in 1988-1990; $n = 50,659$ in 1994-1996; $n = 52,608$ in 1999-2001).	Multivariate regression with dummies for WIC participation, interacted with year of birth. To address selection bias, limited analysis to women with first births who initiated prenatal care in first 4 months of pregnancy. Estimated separate models by race, ethnicity, nativity, and parity. Estimated same model comparing twin births.	Among US-born blacks, WIC participants are 2.4 pp less likely to experience a low birth weight birth than non-WIC participants in 1988-1991. No statistically significant effects of WIC participation for foreign-born Hispanic women. In twin analysis, for US-born blacks, WIC participation is associated with a 55 g increase in birth weight adjusted for gestation, and a 3.9 pp decrease in SGA rates. Effects biggest for US-born black women under age 25. (Note, means for subgroups not reported, so effect sizes can't be calculated).
Joyce et al. (2007). Pregnancy Nutrition Surveillance System (PNSS) data ($n = 2,870,031$). Included all women who were enrolled in WIC during pregnancy and re-enrolled postpartum. Comparison group is women who enrolled in WIC after delivery but were not exposed to WIC during pregnancy.	Multivariate regression with dummies for WIC in each trimester. To deal with selection bias, estimated separate models by race/ethnicity. Also analyzed subgroups whose pre-pregnancy characteristics put women at high risk for anemia, low weight gain, and intrauterine growth retardation. Finally, analyzed subgroup of first-births.	Conditional on gestational age, mean birth weight is 40 g greater among postpartum enrollees than prenatal enrollees. Rates of SGA are 1.7 pp (14%) less, and rates of term low birth weight are 0.7 pp (30%) less. Difference between 1st and 3rd trimester enrollees in mean birth weight is 13.5 g.

(continued on next page)

Table 10 (continued)

Study	Study design	Results
Kowaleski-Jones and Duncan (2002). NLSY Mother–Child data. 2000 children 1990–96. 104 sibling pairs, 71 pairs in which one child participated and one didn't.	Sibling fixed effects.	Increase of 7 ounces in mean birthweight. Positive effect on temperament score. No effect on social or motor skills test scores.
(Hoynes et al., 2009). Data on county-level WIC availability in 1971–1975 and 1978–1982 from lists of local agencies that provided WIC services. Data on birth weight from vital statistics records. Data on population of women by county-year from the CANCER–SEER population data. Data on various control variables from 1970 IPUMS. ($n = 18,517$ county-year cells)	Difference-in-difference, using variation in the timing of WIC implementation across different counties in 1972–1979, to estimate impact of WIC availability on birth weight. Controlled for three measures of per capita government transfers, an indicator for Food Stamp program availability, other demographics, and county and year fixed effects, and state-year fixed effects. Scaled estimates by WIC participation rates. Also conducted sub-group analysis in county-year-maternal education level cells.	If WIC is available in a county by the third trimester, average birth weight increases by 0.1% (estimate not scaled by participation rate). Among women with low levels of education, WIC increases average birth weight by 10% (estimate scaled by participation rate) and reduces the fraction of births classified as low birth weight by 11% (estimate scaled by participation rate). No effects of WIC on fertility—so results not driven by selection into birth.

Impact on breast feeding and infant feeding practices

Chatterji et al. (2002). NLSY Mother–Child file. 1282 children born 1991–95. 970 siblings born 1989–95.	IV with WIC state program characteristics as instruments. Sibling fixed effects.	OLS and IV indicate WIC reduces breastfeeding initiation, but no effect on duration. Fixed effect suggests reductions in length breastfeeding.

Table 10 (continued)

Study	Study design	Results
Impact on nutrition and health outcomes of children		
Black et al. (2004) Data from surveys administered by The Children's Sentinel Nutritional Assessment Program in a multi-site study at urban medical centers in 5 states and Washington, DC in 1998–2001 ($n = 5923$: 5395 received WIC assistance, 528 did not).	Compared WIC-eligible families who participated in WIC with those who did not due to self-reported access problems. Multivariate regression including a participation dummy, controlling for relevant background characteristics.	Compared to infants who received WIC assistance, those who did not receive WIC assistance were more likely to be underweight (weight-for-age z-score $= -0.23$ vs. 0.009), short (length-for-age z-score $= -0.23$ vs. -0.02), and perceived as having fair or poor health (adjusted odds ratio $= 1.92$). No statistically significant differences in rates of food insecurity.
Lee and Mackey-Bilaver (2007). Data from IL Integrated Database on Children's Services. Includes info on Medicaid, FSP, WIC enrollment. All IL children born between 1990 and 1996 who entered Medicaid within first month. Tracked to 2001. Total sample $= 252,246$. Sibling FE sample $= 36,277$.	Multivariate regression with sibling fixed-effects, using participation dummies for FSP, WIC, and FSP-WIC jointly. (Note, sibling FE only make sense for WIC, effects of FSP estimated using OLS. Also, most families on WIC also receive FSP).	Effect of WIC: Abuse or neglect rates decrease by 84% (mean $= 0.10$). Incidence of anemia decrease by 41% (mean $= 0.195$). Failure to thrive decrease by 78% (mean $= 0.128$). Nutritional deficiency decrease by 115% (mean $= 0.038$).

Unless otherwise noted, only results significant at 5% level are reported here.
Percent changes (denoted by % instead of "pp") are reported relative to the mean.

pregnancy in order to ensure that participants and non-participants were more likely to be similar in terms of unobservables. In their sample of women giving birth in New York City, they find positive effects of WIC among US born black women, but not in other groups. Joyce et al. (2007) use a national sample of women, compare women who enrolled in WIC pre and post delivery, and focus on whether infants are small for gestational age (SGA). If one does not believe that WIC can affect gestation, then focusing on SGA is appropriate because it is not affected by gestational age. They find that the incidence of SGA is lower for the prenatal enrollees than for the postpartum enrollees. Gueorguieva et al. (2009) use a large sample of births from Florida and try to deal with potential selection using propensity score matching. They side step the issue of whether WIC affects gestation by presenting separate analyses for pregnancies of different length, and focusing on SGA. They find that longer participation in WIC is associated with reductions in the incidence of SGA. Kowaleski-Jones and Duncan (2002) examine sibling pairs from the NLSY and find that WIC participation is associated with an increase of seven ounces in birth weight. However, the number of pairs in which one child participated and one did not is quite small, so it would be useful to try to replicate this finding in a larger sample of siblings.

Figlio et al. (2009) present an innovative instrumental variables strategy using a large sample of births from Florida that have been merged to school records of older siblings. While the characteristics of WIC programs vary across states, they do not show a lot of variation over time, and previous analyses have demonstrated that these characteristics are weak instruments (Bitler and Currie, 2005). Figlio et al. (2009) first try to select participant and non-participant groups who are very similar. They do this by defining "marginally ineligible" families as those who participated in the National School Lunch Program (NLSP) in the year before or after the birth, but did not participate in the birth year. Thus, the study focuses on families whose incomes hover around the eligibility threshold for NSLP, which is the same as the eligibility threshold for WIC. The instrument is a change in income reporting requirements for WIC in Sept. 1999 which made it more difficult for eligible families to receive benefits. Figlio et al. (2009) find that WIC participation reduces the probability of low birth weight, but find no significant effect on gestational age or prematurity.

There has been much less study of the effects of WIC on other outcomes, or other groups of participants. A couple of studies that make some attempt to deal with the selection issue are summarized in Table 10. One problem with WIC is that it subsidizes baby formula, which is likely to discourage breast-feeding. Chatterji and Brooks-Gunn (2004) use the NLSY Mother-Child file and estimate both sibling fixed effects models and instrumental variables models using characteristics of state programs as instruments. They find that WIC reduces breast feeding initiation and the length of breastfeeding. However, these results are subject to the caveats above (i.e. small samples and possibly weak instruments). Turning to the effects of WIC on older children, Black et al. (2004) compare WIC eligible participants and those who did not participate due to "access problems". These problems were assessed based on the families own reports about why they were not participating. They found that infants who received WIC were less likely to be underweight, short, or perceived by their parents to be in fair or poor health. Lee and Mackey-Bilaver (2007) use a large data base from Illinois that integrates administrative data from several sources. Using sibling fixed effects models, they find that siblings who received WIC were less likely to be anemic, to have exhibited failure-to-thrive, or other nutritional deficiencies, and that the infants were less likely to be abused or neglected. As discussed above, one issue in the interpretation of these findings is why one infant would receive WIC while the other did not?

In one of the most interesting recent studies, Hoynes et al. (2009) use the initial roll-out of the WIC program in the 1970s to identify its effects. They find that the implementation of WIC increased average birth weight by 10% and decreased the fraction of low birth weight births. They did not find any evidence of changes in fertility.

In summary, the latest group of studies of WIC during pregnancy largely support the findings of earlier studies which consistently found beneficial effects on infant health. The finding is remarkable because WIC benefits are relatively modest (often amounting to about $40 per month) and Americans are generally well fed (if not overfed at least in terms of total calories). Research that attempted to peer into the "black box" and shed light on why the program is effective would be extremely interesting. Another question that cries out for future research is whether WIC benefits infants and children (i.e. children who participate after birth)? While a few studies suggest that it does, the effects of WIC in this population has been subject to much less scrutiny than the effects on newborns.

5.3.3. Child care

There have been many evaluations of early intervention programs delivered through the provision of child care. One reason for focusing on early intervention through the provision of quality child care is that the majority of young children are likely to be placed in some form of care. In 2008, 64% of women with children under 3 worked for pay (US Bureau of Labor Statistics, 2009). While the US may be an outlier in this respect, labor force participation among women with children is high and rising in many other economies. Blau and Currie (2006) provide an overview of the literature on early intervention through child care. Many studies concern experimental evaluations of model programs that serve relatively small numbers of children and involve intensive services delivered by well-trained and well-supervised staff. These studies generally find that early intervention has long-lasting effects on schooling attainment and other outcomes such as teen pregnancy and crime, even if it does not result in any lasting increase in cognitive test scores. These results point to the tremendous importance of "non-cognitive skills" (cf Heckman and Rubinstein (2001)) or alternatively, to the importance of mental as well as physical health in the production of good child outcomes (Currie and Stabile, 2006).

A few of the most notable model programs are summarized in Table 11. Two studies of "model" early intervention child care programs stand out because they randomly assigned children to treatment and control group, had low dropout rates, and followed children over many years. They are the Carolina Abecedarian Project and the Perry Preschool Project. Both found positive effects on schooling. A recent cost-benefit analysis of the Abcedarian data through age 21 found that each dollar spent on Abecedarian saved tax payers four dollars. And by focusing only on cost savings, this calculation does not even include the value of higher achievement to the individual children and society (Masse and Barnett, 2002). Each dollar spent on Perry Preschool has been estimated to have saved up to seven dollars in social costs (Karoly et al., 1998), although this high benefit-cost ratio is driven largely by the effect of the intervention on crime, which in turn depends on a handful of individuals.

Anderson (2008) conducts a re-analysis of the Perry Preschool and Abcedarian data (and a third intervention called the Early Training Project) and finds that like the MTO public housing experiment, the significant effects of the intervention were largely concentrated among girls. In addition to analyzing the data by gender, Anderson pays careful attention to the idea that there may be a reporting bias in the published studies of early intervention experiments; that is, researchers who found largely null effects of the experiment might still be able to publish results focusing on one or two positive outcomes out of many outcomes investigated. Conversely, if all effects tended in the same direction, but there was insufficient power to detect significant effects on each outcome, it might be possible to detect a significant effect on an index of the outcomes. Anderson finds positive effects (for girls) on a summary index of effects, and the effects are quite large at about a half a standard deviation. This study highlights an interesting question, which is whether it is generally easier to intervene with girls than with boys, and why that might be the case?

The fact that special interventions like Perry Preschool or Abcedarian had an effect on at least some target children does not prove that the types of programs typically available to poor inner-city children will do so. Head Start is a preschool program for disadvantaged 3, 4, and 5 year olds which currently serves about 800,000 children each year. It is funded as a federal-local matching grant program and over time, federal funding has increased from $96 million when the program began in 1965 to about $7 billion in 2009 (plus additional "stimulus" funds). Head Start is not of the same quality as the model interventions, and the quality varies from center to center. But Head Start centers have historically been of higher average quality than other preschool programs available to low income people. This is because, in contrast to the private child care market, there are few very low-quality Head Start programs (see Blau and Currie (2006) for an overview of preschool quality issues).

An experimental evaluation of Head Start has recently been conducted (Puma et al., 2010). The evaluation compares Head Start children to peers who may or may not be in

Table 11 Selected recent evaluations of early childhood programs with randomized designs.

Study/program name[a]	Data, program description, and study design	Results
Carolina Abecedarian follow-up and cost-benefit analysis at 21 years of age (Barnett and Masse, 2007)	Preschoolers: full-day child care School age: parent program Sample sizes: Initial: T = 57, C = 54 Age 8: T = 48, C = 42 Age 15: T = 48, C = 44 Age 21: T = 53, C = 51 Age of participation in program: Entry: 6 weeks to 3 months old Exit: 5 to 8 years	**Follow-up at 21 years of age:** Grade retention: T = 34%, C = 65%, age 21 Special education: T = 31%, C = 49%, age 21 High school dropout: T = 33%, C = 49%, age 21 College attendance: T = 36%, C = 13%, age 21 Crime rate: T = C, age 21 Employment status: T = C at age 21 Average age first child born: T > C at age 21 **Cost-Benefit Analysis:** (using 5% discount rate, $2002) Net cost per child = $34,599 Net benefit of program = $72,591 per participant
Infant Health and Development Project Follow-up at 18 years of age (McCormick et al., 2006)	Home visits, full-day child care Sample sizes: Initial: T = 377, C = 608 Followup at age 8: T = 336, C = 538 Followup at age 18: T = 254, C = 381 (divided in 2 groups: lighter low birth weight (LLBW) and heavier low birth weight (HLBW)) Age of participation in program: Entry: birth (home visits), 1 year (care). Exit: 3 years	Math achievement: T > C by 6.8%, age 18 HLBW Reading achievement: T > C by 5.6%, age 18 HLBW Risky behaviors: T > C by 23.3%, age 18 HLBW IQ: T = C, age 18 HLBW Note: For all outcomes: T = C, age 18 LLBW

(continued on next page)

Table 11 (continued)

Study/program name[a]	Data, program description, and study design	Results
A reevaluation of early childhood intervention—Abecedarian, Perry Preschool and Early Training Project—with emphasis on gender differences and multiple inference (Anderson, 2008)	Abecedarian: T = 57, C = 54 Perry: T = 58, C = 65 ETP: T = 44, C = 21 Ages of entry: Abecedarian/Perry/ETP: 4.4 mo./3 yrs./3–4 yrs	Outcomes include: IQ, grade repetition, special ed., high school, college attendance, employment, earnings, receipt transfers, arrests, convictions, drug use, teen pregnancy, marriage. Summary index pools multiple outcomes for a single test. Separate tests by gender. Effects on summary index for girls 5–12: ABC/Perry: increase by 0.45/0.54 SDs. Effects on summary index for girls 13–19: ABC/Perry/ETP: increase by 0.42/0.61/0.46 SDs. Effects on summary index for women over 21–40: ABC/Perry: increase by 0.45/0.36 SDs. No statistically significant effects on males of any age.
High/Scope Perry Preschool project follow-up and cost-benefit analysis at 40 years of age (Barnett et al., 2006)	Home visits, Preschool program Sample sizes: Initial: T = 58, C = 65 Age 40: T = 56, C = 63 Age of participation in program: Entry: 3 to 4 years, Exit: 5 years	Arrests: T = 32%, C = 48%; In jail: T = 6%, C = 17%; Report of stopping work for health reasons: T = 43%, C = 55%; Hard drug use: T = 22%, C = 29%; Abortions: T = 17%, C = 32% **Cost–benefit analysis:** Main result: Benefit of $12.90 for each $1 cost Most benefits due to reduced crime rates for males Cost: $15,827 ($2000) per student Total Net Private Benefit = $17,730 per participant Total Net Public Benefit = $180,455 per participant

Table 11 (continued)

Study/program name[a]	Data, program description, and study design	Results
National evaluation of Early Head Start (Administration on Children, Youth and Families, 2002 & Love et al., 2005) Cost-Benefit (Aos et al., 2004).	17 Early Head Start sites selected to reflect EHS programs funded in 1995-96. Random assignment within site (possible given wait lists). Sample: T=1513, C=1488. Age of participation in program: Entry at 0–1 year, exit 3 years	Mental Development Index (MDI): T > C by 0.12 SD PPVT-III Vocabulary score: T > C by 0.13 SD Percentage with PPVT score <85 pts: T < C by 0.12 SD Aggressive behavior: T < C by 0.11 SD Supportiveness during parent-child play: T > C by 0.15 SD HOME score: T > C by 0.11 SD Index of severity of discipline: T < C by 0.11 SD No statistically significant effects on parental mental or physical health or on measures of family functioning. **Cost-benefit analysis:** Total Cost per child: $20,972 Total Benefit per child: $4768, NPV: −$16,203
Head Start impact study (US Department of Health and Human Services, 2010)	Congressionally-mandated study of Head Start. Children from wait lists randomly assigned to one of 383 randomly selected Head Start centers across 23 different states. Baseline data collected in fall 2002; annual spring follow-ups through spring 2006. Sample Sizes: T = 2783, C = 1884. Entry: 3–4 years old; Exit: 4–5 years old	Summary of effects for 4-year-old entry cohort at end of 1st grade: PPVT: T > C by 0.09 SD; Withdrawn behavior: T < C by 0.13 SD; Shy/socially reticent: T > C by 0.19 SD; Problems with teacher interaction: T > C by 0.13 SD. No statistically significant impacts at age 4, kindergarten, or 1st grade on: math scores, Spanish language tests, oral comprehension, and several parent- and teacher-reported measures of emotional and behavioral outcomes. No statistically significant impacts at kindergarten or 1st grade on: school accomplishments, promotion, language and literacy ability, math ability, and social studies and science ability. Summary of effects for 3-year-old entry cohort as of 1st grade (selected results): Oral comprehension: T > C by 0.08 SD. No significant effect on other outcomes.

(continued on next page)

Table 11 (continued)

Study/program name[a]	Data, program description, and study design	Results
The rates of return to the High/Scope Perry Preschool Program (Heckman et al., 2009)	See Barnett et al. (2006) entry for sample sizes and information about the Perry Preschool Program. Randomization was compromised because of reassignment after initial randomization. Standard errors on the rate of return estimates adjusted for failure of randomization using bootstrapping and Monte Carlo methods. Also, adjusted for the deadweight loss due to taxation (assuming 0%, 50%, and 100% deadweight losses). Used a wide variety of methods for within-sample imputation of missing earnings. Used local data on costs of education, welfare participation, and crime instead of national data, wherever possible. Used several methods to extrapolate benefits and costs beyond age 40 (after last follow-up). Used several measures of the statistical cost of life to estimate costs of murder.	Estimated social rates of return to the Perry Preschool Program are 7%–10%. Estimated benefit–cost ratio = 2.2 to 31.5 (depends on discount rate used, and the measure of cost of murder).

Throughout the table, "T" refers to treatment group and "C" refers to control or comparison group. Outcomes listed as T > C or C > T were statistically significant at the 5% level.

[a] Programs are grouped such that those enrolling children younger than three years old appear first, followed by those enrolling children after age three.

some other form of preschool (including state-funded preschools modeled in Head Start). In fact, the majority of children who did not attend Head Start did end up attending some other preschool program. Even relative to this baseline, initial results show that Head Start children make gains, particularly in terms of language ability. But children are followed only into the first grade, and so this evaluation did not address the important issue of whether Head Start has longer term effects. This example illustrates one of the limitations of experiments for the study of longer-term effects, which is that one may have to wait a long time for evidence to accumulate. There has also been a federal evaluation of Early Head Start (EHS), a version of the program geared to infants and toddlers under three years old. As Table 11 shows, EHS has small positive effects on cognitive test scores and some measures of behavior though Aos et al. (2004) conclude that it does not pass a cost-benefit test.

Table 12 summarizes notable non-experimental evaluations of Head Start and other public preschool programs. In a series of studies Currie and Thomas use national publicly-available survey data to try to measure the effect of Head Start. In most of these studies, they compare the outcomes of children who attended Head Start to siblings who did not attend. As discussed above, sibling fixed effects control for many shared characteristics of children, but are not a panacea. However, careful examination of differences between participant and non-participant children within families suggested that the Head Start sibling typically attends when the family is relatively disadvantaged. For example, a young single mother might have her first child attend Head Start. If she then marries, her next child will enjoy higher income and be ineligible for Head Start. Currie and Thomas found no within-family differences in birth weight or other individual characteristics of the children. They also investigated spillover effects, which as discussed above, can bias the estimated effect of Head Start. They found some evidence (Garces et al., 2002) that having an older sibling attend Head Start had positive effects on younger siblings. In all, it seems likely that sibling fixed effects models understate the true effect of Head Start.

Nevertheless, they found significant positive effects of Head Start on educational attainments among white youths, and reductions in the probabilities of being booked or charged with a crime among black youths (Garces et al., 2002). Test score gains for blacks and whites were initially the same, but these gains tended to fade out more quickly for black than white students, perhaps because black former Head Start students typically attend worse schools than other students (Currie and Thomas, 1995). Effects were especially large for Hispanic children (Garces et al., 2002).

More recently, Deming (2009) replicates the results of Currie and Thomas (1995) using the same cohort of NLSY children observed at older ages. Like Anderson, he focuses on an index of outcomes (although he also reports results for separate outcomes) and finds that Head Start results in an increase of 0.23 standard deviations, which is equivalent to about 1/3 of the gap between Head Start and other children. He notes

Table 12 Selected studies of large-scale public early childhood programs.

Study/program name and data	Study design	Results
Evaluations of Head Start		
Does Head Start make a difference? Does Head Start help Hispanic children? (Currie and Thomas, 1995, 1999a). NLSCM. Sample size: T = 896, C = 911 Hispanic study: T = 182, C = 568 Entry: 3 to 5 years; Exit: 5 to 6 years.	Estimate sibling fixed effects models of effects of Head Start and other preschool attendance on various outcomes. Examine differences between siblings that might potentially explain differential attendance by siblings.	**Achievement tests:** T > C (1/3 SD whites and Hispanics only) Grade retention: T < C (~50% whites and Hispanics only) Immunization rates: T > C (8%–11%) Child height-for-age: T = C
Long term effects of Head Start (Garces et al., 2002). PSID, Sample size: T = 583, C = 3502. Entry: 3 to 4 years; Exit 5 to 6 years.	Compared Head Start participants to their own siblings who did not participate. Outcomes measured between ages 18 and 31. Retrospective reports on Head Start participation.	High school graduation: T > C (~25% for whites only) Arrests T < C (~50% for African-Americans only) College T > C (~25% for Whites) Teen pregnancy T = C Welfare T = C
Effect of Head Start on health and schooling (Ludwig and Miller, 2005). Vital Statistics Compressed Mortality Files 1973–83; Individual data from NELS, where T = 649, C = 674.	Regression discontinuity around cutoff at which counties were eligible for assistance in applying for Head Start in 1965. T = 300 poorest counties in 1965, C = 301–600th poorest counties. 80% of treatment counties received funding vs. 43% of all counties nationwide.	Effects of participation in Head Start: Mortality, age 5–9: T < C by 35%–79% High school completion rates: T > C by 5.2%–8.5% Some college+: 16.2%–22.4% for oldest cohort only

Table 12 (continued)

Study/program name and data	Study design	Results
Head Start Participation and Childhood Obesity (Frisvold, 2006). PSID Child Development Supplement. Sample size = 1332.	Estimated the effect of Head Start on likelihood of a child being overweight or obese. Assume that # of spaces available in a community is a valid instrument for Head Start participation.	Head Start reduces probability of obesity at ages 5–10 among blacks. No effect in full sample of children or in children over 10. Estimates are large relative to sample means implying ~100% reductions in overweight/obesity.
Evidence from Head Start On Lifecycle Skill Development (Deming, 2009). Data from NLSY. Children for cohort enrolled in Head Start between 1984 and 1990. Children in study at least 5 years old in 1990. Sample size: 3415 total.	Sibling fixed effects estimates of benefits of Head Start.	Test scores: T > C by 0.145 SD ages 5–6, by 0.133 SD ages 7–10, by 0.055 SD ages 11–14. Noncognitive school-age outcomes index: T > C by 0.265 SD. Long-term effect on index★ of young adult outcomes: T > C by 0.228 SD. Large fade-out in test scores of African Americans, none for whites or Hispanics. No effects on criminal activity. Summary: Head Start increases index of long term outcomes by 0.23 SD (~1/3 of gap attendees and others). Projecting wages implies that benefits (~$1500 in greater earnings per year) exceed program costs of ~$6000. ★ index includes: graduate high school, complete 1 yr college idle (no job, not in school), poor health.

(continued on next page)

Table 12 (continued)

Study/program name and data	Study design	Results
Preventing behavior problems in childhood and adolescence: Evidence from Head Start (Carneiro and Ginja, 2008). NLSY Children data. Sample size = 1786 males. Behavior problems, grade rep. and obesity at 12–13. Depression, crime, and obesity at 16–17. Oldest in data—born in 1974; youngest in data—born in 1992.	Head Start eligibility rules create discontinuities in income eligibility. Compare families above and below the cutoff. Identification strategy requires that families are not able to strategically locate above or below cutoff.	**USING REDUCED FORM ESTIMATION** **Head Start participation impacts on 12–13 year-old males:** behavioral problems index decreases by 38% probability of grade retention decreases by 33.3% probability of obesity decreases by ~100% for blacks only **Head Start participation impacts on 16–17 year-old males:** Depression (CESD) decreases by 23.4% probability of obesity decreases by 57.9% probability of being sentenced decreases by >100% for blacks only **USING STRUCTURAL EQUATIONS** **Head Start participation impacts on 12–13 year-old males:** probability of grade retention decreases by >100% **Head Start participation impacts on 16–17 year-old males:** probability of being sentenced decreases by >100% probability of obesity decreases by >100% probability of being sentenced decreases by >100% for blacks only probability of obesity decreases by >100% for blacks only Note: baseline means are for sample of children with incomes between 5% and 195% of Head Start eligibility cut-off.

Table 12 (continued)

Study/program name and data	Study design	Results
Investing in health: the long-term impact of Head Start on smoking (Anderson et al., 2009). Data from the PSID. Used smoking data from 1999 and 2003 on individuals aged 21-36 in 1999. $n = 922$ in 1999; $n = 1005$ in 2003.	Compared smoking of siblings who did and did not attend Head Start or any preschool using sibling fixed effects. Controlled for family background characteristics specific to the age children were eligible for Head Start. Examined sibling differences that might be predictive of Head Start attendance. Examined spillover effects by including interactions between Head Start and birth order.	**Results from 1999 data:** Head Start participants are 58% less likely to smoke than siblings. **Results from 2003 data:** Head Start participants are 65% less likely to smoke than siblings. Including control for educational attainment makes results statistically insignificant. **Cost-Benefit:** PV reduction in smoking is $9967 per participant (using 3% discount rate, accounting for medical expenses and productivity losses) Average cost per Head Start participant in 2003 is $7092. Depending on discount rate used, the value of reduction in smoking is associated with 36–141% of program costs.
Expanding exposure: can increasing the daily exposure to Head Start reduce childhood obesity? (Frisvold and Lumeng, 2009) Administrative data from a Michigan Head Start for 2002-2006. $n = 1833$ obs. (from 1532 children, since some attend for multiple years) Full-day class sample = 424 obs. Half-day class sample = 1409 obs.	Estimated the effect of full-day vs. half-day Head Start on obesity at end of school year. Identification via elimination of a grant which led to a decrease in the # of full–day classes from 16 classrooms in 2002 to 4 classrooms in 2003. (IV = % full-day funded slots). Controls for observable family characteristics.	**First Stage Results:** 10 pp increase in percentage of full-day slots increases likelihood of full-day attendance by 85% (relative to baseline = 11% enrollment in full-day slots in 2003). **Second Stage Results:** Full-day enrollment in Head Start decreases likelihood of obesity by 143%. This implies that children who attended full-day classes would have been almost 3 lbs heavier had they attended half-day classes. Simulation results suggest that the 143% change in the likelihood of obesity can be explained by a change in caloric intake of 75 calories per day with no change in physical activity.

(continued on next page)

Table 12 (continued)

Study/program name and data	Study design	Results
Studies of public pre-K/K and child care programs		
Impact of early childhood care and education on children's preschool cognitive development: Canadian results from a large quasi-experiment (Lefebvre et al., 2006) Data from Canada's NLSCY on 4- and 5-yr old children from 5 consecutive cycles. $n = 15,546$	Identification from changes in Quebec's child care subsidies. On Sep. 1, 1997, child care facilities offered $5-per-full-day services to children who were 4 yrs old by Sep. 30th. In the following years, age cutoffs decreased and the number of spaces increased. No similar policies in other provinces of Canada in 1994–2003. Difference-in-difference (DD) and Difference-in-difference-in-difference (DDD) designs, comparing Quebec's preschool children with children of similar ages from other provinces using the fact that different cohorts of children were exposed to different numbers of treatment years.	Subsidies increase the number of hours in child care by 5.5–7.4 hours per week for children aged 4–5. Effect larger for mothers in highest educational group. No effects on 4-year-old children's PPVT scores. Decrease in PPVT scores of 0.33 SD for 5-year-old children.

Table 12 (continued)

Study/program name and data	Study design	Results
Promoting school readiness in Oklahoma: An evaluation of Tulsa's Pre-K Program (Gormley and Gayer, 2006)[a]. Data from Tulsa Public Schools (TPS) on test scores of Pre-K and Kindergarten children from test administered in Aug. 2001. T = 1112, C = 1284 (T = children who just completed Pre-K, C = children who are about to begin Pre-K). Entry: 4 years old; Exit: 5 years old.	Regression discontinuity design arising from cutoff of Sept. 1 to enroll in Pre-K in a given year. Compare kindergarten children who just completed Pre-K with slightly younger children who were ineligible to attend. Used quadratic polynomial to fit underlying age/test score relationship.	Cognitive/knowledge score: T > C by 0.39 SD Motor skills score: T > C by 0.24 SD Language score: T > C by 0.38 SD Largest impacts for Hispanics, followed by blacks, little impact for whites. Children who qualify for free school lunch have larger impacts than other children.
Does Prekindergarten Improve School Preparation and Performance? (Magnuson et al., 2007) Data from ECLS-K. n = 10, 224.	Primary method is a multivariate regression to estimate the impact of Pre-K attendance on various outcomes. Robustness checks using teacher fixed effects, propensity score matching, and instrumental variables (IV). IV is different measures of access to pre-K in a given state. Dependent variables are measured in the fall of kindergarten and in the spring of first grade to assess any lasting impacts of Pre-K.	Pre-K attendance: increases reading scores at school entry by 0.86 SD (IV); increases aggression at school entry by 0.69 SD (IV). No effect on math scores or self control in IV. Effect sizes for all outcomes are larger for Pre-K than for other forms of child care, but Pre-K children have different characteristics than other children. Among children attending Pre-K in the same public school as their kindergarten, higher reading scores are not accompanied by increased behavioral problems. For disadvantaged children, cognitive gains are more lasting than in the whole sample. Effect sizes for cognitive outcomes much lower in spring of 1st grade than at school entry. Effect sizes for behavioral outcomes are the same.

(continued on next page)

Table 12 (continued)

Study/program name and data	Study design	Results
The Effects of Oklahoma's Pre-K Program on Hispanic Children (Gormley, 2008) Tests administered by Tulsa public schools in Aug. 2006. T = 194, C = 295. (T = children who just completed Pre-K, C = children who are about to begin Pre-K). Entry: 4 years old; Exit: 5 years old.	See Gormley and Gayer (2006) entry.	Letter–Word Identification Test score: T > C by 0.846 SD Spelling score: T > C by 0.52 SD Applied Problems score: T > C by 0.38 SD Significant effects only for Hispanic students whose primary language at home is Spanish.
Universal Child Care, Maternal Labor Supply, and Family Well-Being (Baker et al., 2008). Canadian NLSCY (1994–2003) includes only married women and their children. Average of 2000 children at each age per yr. Primary sample ages 0–4, robustness checks ages 8–11.	Compare outcomes in Quebec, which began $5 per day daycare for 4 year olds in 1997, extended program to 3 year olds in 1998, 2 year olds in 1999, and all children <2 in 2000, to the rest of Canada. Difference in differences.	Increase in use of any child care/institutional care/mothers working by 35%/>100%/14.5%. Crowding out of other informal child care. Increase in emotional disorder anxiety score (physical aggression and opposition) by 12% (9%) for 2–3 yr olds. Decrease in standardized motor and social development score by 1.7%. Increase in mother depression score by 10%. 40% of the cost of the child care subsidy is offset by increased taxes on extra labor supply.

Table 12 (continued)

Study/program name and data	Study design	Results
Impacts of New Mexico Pre-K on Children's School Readiness at Kindergarten Entry: Results from the Second Year of a Growing Initiative (Hustedt et al., 2008). Data on children who participated in the 2nd year of the Pre-K program during 2006–2007 and entered kindergarten in Fall 2007. T = 405, C = 519 (T = children who just completed Pre-K, C = children who are about to begin Pre-K). Entry: 4 years old; Exit: 5 years old.	Regression discontinuity design due to a birthday eligibility cut-off of Aug. 31st to enroll in Pre-K in a given year. Compared "young" kindergarten children who just completed Pre-K with slightly younger children who are about to being Pre-K. Used linear model for vocabulary score as dependent variable, quadratic model for early literacy score as dependent variable, cubic model for math score as dependent variable.	Vocabulary (PPVT) score: T > C by 0.25 SD Math score: T > C by 0.50 SD Early literacy score: T > C by 0.59 SD No statistically significant difference in effects between Pre-K programs funded by the Public Education Department and those funded by the Children, Youth and Families Department.

(continued on next page)

Table 12 (continued)

Study/program name and data	Study design	Results
An Effectiveness-Based Evaluation of Five State Pre-Kindergarten Programs (Wong et al., 2008). Data on test scores from fall 2004 from Michigan, New Jersey, Oklahoma, South Carolina and West Virginia. Sample sizes: T = 485, C = 386 (MI); T = 1177, C = 895 (NJ); T = 431, C = 407 (OK); T = 353, C = 424 (SC); T = 379, C = 341 (WV). (T = children who just completed Pre-K, C = children who are about to begin Pre-K). Entry: 4 years old; Exit: 5 years old.	Regression discontinuity design due to a strict birthday eligibility cut-off. Looked at effect size differences due to programmatic variation between states. Used a polynomial approximation to the continuous function on the assignment variable in the regressions.	**Intent-to-Treat Results:** MI: T > C by 0.53 SD for math; 1.09 SD for Print Awareness. NJ: T > C by 0.36 SD for PPVT, 0.23 SD for math, 0.32 SD for Print Awareness. OK: T > C by 0.28 SD for PPVT, 0.78 SD for Print Awareness. WV: T > C by 0.92 SD for Print Awareness. **Treatment-on-Treated Results:** MI: T > C by 0.47 SD for math, 0.96 SD for Print Awareness. NJ: T > C by 0.36 SD for PPVT, 0.23 SD for math, 0.50 SD for Print Awareness. OK: T > C by 0.29 SD for PPVT. SC: T > C by 0.79 SD for Print Awareness. No clear relationship between state funding for Pre-K programs and effect sizes. State Pre-K programs have larger effect sizes than Head Start.

Table 12 (continued)

Study/program name and data	Study design	Results
Do Investments in Universal Early Education Pay Off? Long-term Effects of Introducing Kindergartens into Public Schools (Cascio, 2009). Data from 4 Decennial censuses for 1970, 1980, and 2000 from the Public Use Microdata Samples. $n = 840$ whites, 425 blacks. Data from PSID on Head Start enrollment: $n = 174$ whites, 126 blacks.	Analyzed effect of expansion of public kindergarten on long-term outcomes. Identification from the variation in the timing of funding initiatives among treated states. Event study model, comparing individuals aged 5 before and after the initiatives were implemented. Included dummies for cohorts interacted with dummies for 3 different groups of treated states defined on the basis of average education expenditure per pupil in the early 1960s. Also controlled for cohort-by-region-of-birth fixed effects and state fixed effects. Units of observation are cohort-state cells.	White children aged 5 after the typical state reform are 2.5% less likely to be high school drop-outs and 22% less likely to be institutionalized as adults. No significant effects on grade retention, college attendance, employment, or earnings. No significant effects for blacks, despite comparable increases in enrollment in public kindergartens post reform. Potential explanation is that state funding for public kindergartens reduced the likelihood that a black 5-year-old attended Head Start by ~100%. Reduction in Head Start attendance may account for 16% of the 1.13 pp increase in the black–white gap in high school drop-out rates. Difference in effects on educational attainment between whites and blacks are driven by females.

(continued on next page)

Table 12 (continued)

Study/program name and data	Study design	Results
No Child Left Behind: Universal Child Care and Children's Long-Run Outcomes (Havnes and Mogstad, 2009). Data from Statistics Norway on individuals from 1967 to 2006. Household information from the Central Population Register. Administrative data on child care institutions and their locations for 1972–1996. Restricted sample to individuals whose mothers were married at the end of 1975. $n = 499{,}026$ children; 318,367 families. Adult outcomes measured between ages 30 and 33.	Difference-in-differences. Exploited a child care reform in 1975 in Norway, which assigned responsibility for child care to local governments, and thus resulted in great variation in child care coverage for children aged 3–6 both between cohorts and across municipalities. T = municipalities where child care expanded a lot; C = municipalities where child care did not change much. Compared changes in outcomes for treatment and control adults who were 3–6 years old before and after the reform. Also investigated heterogeneity of effects. Controlled for various child and family-specific characteristics, as well as municipality fixed effects. Robustness checks: included a time trend, checked for placebo effect by comparing the two groups before the reform, and used sibling fixed effects comparing siblings exposed to the reform to those who were not.	**TT Effects (ITT effects in parentheses)** One more child care place: increases educational attainment by 2.7% (0.4%) decreases probability of dropping out of HS by 22.8% (3.8%) increases probability of college enrollment by 17% (2.5%) decreases probability of having little or no earnings by 23.3% (3.9%) increases probability of having average earnings by 7.4% (1.3%) decreases probability of being on welfare by 31.9% (5.6%) decreases probability of parenthood by 10.4% (1.8%) increases probability of being single with no children by 23.3% (4%) Almost all of the reduction in probability of being a low earner is driven by females. Women more likely to delay child bearing and family formation than men as a result of increased child care. Most benefits of universal child care are for children of low-educated mothers. Subsidized formal child care crowds out informal child care with almost no net increase in total child care use or maternal employment. No impact of child care reform on maternal education. **Cost–Benefit Analysis:** Cost: Annual budgetary cost per child care place = \$5400 Benefit: Increase in 0.35 yrs of education implies an increase in \$27,000 in lifetime earnings.

See Karoly et al. (2005) for more information about some of the studies described in this table. Unless otherwise noted, none of these evaluations was randomized. "T" refers to the treatment, and "C" refers to the control or comparison group. T > C means that the difference was significant at the 5% level.

[a] A very similar study by Gormley et al. (2005) evaluates the effects of Oklahoma's Universal Pre-K program on school readiness using the same regression discontinuity design, but measuring outcomes with the Woodcock–Johnson Achievement Test. They find a 0.79 SD increase in the Letter–Word Identification score, a 0.64 SD increase in the Spelling score, and a 0.38 SD increase in the Applied Problems score.

that projected gains in earnings are enough to offset the cost of the program, so that there is a positive cost/benefit ratio. Carneiro and Ginja (2008) use the same data but a different identification strategy: they focus on families around the cutoff for income eligibility for the program and compare families who are just below (and therefore eligible) to those who are just above (and therefore ineligible). A potential problem with this strategy is that it implicitly assumes that families cannot game the system by reducing their incomes in order to become eligible for the program. Consistent with other studies, they find positive effects of Head Start attendance on adolescents including reductions in behavior problems, grade repetition, depression, and obesity.

Since its inception, Head Start has aimed to improve a broad range of child outcomes (not only test scores). When the program was launched in 1965, the Office of Economic Opportunity assisted the 300 poorest counties in applying for Head Start funds, and these counties were significantly more likely than other counties to receive funds. Using a regression discontinuity design, Ludwig and Miller (2007) show that mortality from causes likely to be affected by Head Start fell among children 5 to 9 in the assisted counties relative to the others. Mortality did not fall in slightly older cohorts who would not have been affected by the introduction of the program.

Frisvold (2006) and Frisvold and Lumeng (2009) also focus on health effects by examining the effect of Head Start on obesity. The former instruments Head Start attendance using the number of Head Start places available in the community, while the later takes advantage of a cut in a Michigan Head Start program which resulted in the conversion of a number of full-day Head Start places to half day places. Both studies find large and significant effects of Head Start on the incidence of obesity. In defense of their estimates, which some might find implausibly large, Frisvold and Lumeng point out that a reduction of only 75 calories per day (i.e. less than a slice of bread or an apple) would be sufficient to yield their results. In small children, even small changes in diet may have large cumulative effects. Anderson et al. (2009) follow Garces et al. and use sibling fixed effects and data from the PSID to estimate the effect of Head Start on smoking as an adult. Again, they find large effects.

Head Start has served as a model for state preschools targeted to low-income children in states such as California, and also for new (non-compulsory) universal preschool programs in Georgia, and Oklahoma. The best available evaluations of universal preschool programs highlight the importance of providing a high quality program that is utilized by the neediest children. Baker et al. (2008) examine the introduction of a universal, $5 per day (later $7), preschool program in the Canadian province of Quebec. The authors find a strong response to the subsidy in terms of maternal labor supply and the likelihood of using care, but they find negative effects on children for a range of outcomes. Lefebvre et al. (2006) focus on the same natural experiment and examine the effects on children's vocabulary scores, which have been shown to be a good predictor of schooling attainment in early grades. They find strong evidence of negative effects.

In interpreting this study, it is important to consider who was affected by the program. Because poor children were already eligible for child care subsidies, the marginal child affected by this program was a child who probably would have stayed home with his or her middle-class, married, mother, and instead was put into child care. Moreover, the marginal child care slot made available by the program was of low quality—the sudden influx of children into care caused the province to place more emphasis on making slots available than on regulating their quality. Hence, the study should be viewed as the consequence of moving middle class children from home care to relatively poor quality care. It is not possible to draw any conclusion from this study about the effect of drawing poor children into care of good quality, which is what model preschool programs and Head Start aim to do.

Gormley and Gayer (2006) examine the effects of Oklahoma's universal pre-K program, which is run through the public schools and is thought to be of high quality. They take advantage of strict age cutoffs for the program and compare children who had just attended for a year to similar children who were ineligible to attend because they were slightly younger. They find a 52% gain in pre-reading skills, a 27% gain in pre-writing skills, and a 21% gain in pre-math skills. These results suggest that a high quality universal pre-K program might well have positive effects, though one would have to track children longer to determine whether these initial gains translate into longer term gains in schooling attainment. Several other recent studies use a similar regression discontinuity design, including Hustedt et al. (2008) and Wong et al. (2008) who examine state pre-K programs in five states. These studies find uniformly positive effects. It has been argued in fact, that the effects of quality state preschool programs are larger than those of Head Start. However, it is difficult to control for pre-existing differences between the Head Start children and children who attend other preschools. For example in Magnuson et al. (2007), the preschool children had systematically higher incomes than those who attended Head Start.

A handful of studies examine the long-term effects of public pre-school or kindergarten programs. Cascio (2009) uses data from four decennial censuses to analyze the impact of introducing kindergarten into public schools in the US, where kindergarten was phased in on a state-by-state basis. Using a cohort-based design, she finds that white children born in adopting states after the reform were less likely to dropout of high school and less likely to be institutionalized as adults. However, she finds no significant effect for blacks, which may be due to significant crowd out of blacks from other programs, such as Head Start. Like Anderson, she finds that the effects were larger for girls. Havnes and Mogstad (2009) study a 1975 policy change in Norway which increased the availability of regulated child care in some areas but not in others. They find that children "exposed" to more child care received more education and were more likely to have earnings as adults. Once again, much of the benefit was concentrated among females, and children of less educated mothers were particularly likely to benefit. In terms of mechanisms, they find that the increase in formal care largely displaced informal care, without much net effect on the mother's labor force participation.

Finally, it is worth mentioning the "Sure Start" program in England and Wales. This program aimed to provide early intervention services in disadvantaged neighborhoods but allowed a wide variety of program models, which obviously complicates an assessment of the program. An evaluation was conducted by comparing communities that were early adopters to those that adopted later. A second evaluation compared Sure Start children to children from similar neighborhoods who were drawn from the Millennium Cohort study. This second study used propensity scores to balance the samples. The first evaluation found that the most disadvantaged households were actually doing more poorly in intervention areas than in other areas (NESS, 2005), while the second found some evidence of positive effects (NESS, 2008). Following the first evaluation, there has been a move to standardize the intervention and most communities are now offering Sure Start Children's Centers. This latest incarnation of the program remains to be evaluated.

This discussion shows the value of using a framework for the production of child quality as a lens for the interpretation of the program evaluation literature. As discussed above, child human capital is produced using inputs that may come from either the family or from other sources. A program that augments the resources available to the child is likely to have positive effects (subject of course to diminishing returns), while a program that reduces the resources available to the child is likely to have negative effects. Hence, a program that causes poor quality group time to be substituted for relatively high quality maternal time can have a negative effect and vice versa. The important point is that it is possible to intervene effectively and to improve the trajectories of young children.

5.3.4. Health insurance

Health insurance is not an intervention program in the sense of the programs described above. Yet, there is a good deal of evidence that access to health insurance improves children's health at birth and afterwards. Much of the evidence comes from studies of the introduction, or expansion, of health insurance benefits. Some of this literature is summarized in Table 13. For example, Hanratty (1996) examined the introduction of public health insurance in Canada, which was phased in on a province-by-province basis. Using county-level panel data, she finds that the introduction of health insurance was associated with a decline of four percent in the infant mortality rate, and that the incidence of low birth weight also decreased by 1.3% for all parents and by 8.9% for single parents. Currie and Gruber (1996) conduct a similar exercise for the US, focusing on an expansion of public health insurance to pregnant women and infants. They find that the effects vary depending on whether the expansion covered the poorest women, or women somewhat higher in the income distribution. Narrowly targeted expansions that increased the fraction of the poorest women eligible by 30%, reduced low birth weight by 7.8%, and reduced infant mortality by 11.5%. Expansions of eligibility of a similar magnitude to women of higher incomes had very small effects on the incidence of low

Table 13 Effects of Medicaid and other public health insurance on birth and early childhood outcomes.

Study and data	Study design	Results
Effects on birth weight and health at birth		
The efficacy and cost of changes in the Medicaid eligibility of pregnant women (Currie and Gruber, 1996). Note: Authors also conduct an analysis of Medicaid take-up, which is not included in the results here. Data from CPS and Vital Statistics. Data on Medicaid expenditures from the Health Care Financing Administration. Data on the use of medical services by pregnant women from the NLSY. Simulated model for targeted changes estimated for 1979–1992. Simulated model for broad changes estimated for 1987–1992. (n = 600).	Exploited variation between states in the timing of expansions of Medicaid eligibility. Use a fixed sample to simulate the fraction eligible under different state rules. Distinguish "targeted" changes affecting very low income women from "broad" changes to women further up the income distribution. Instrument the actual fraction of women eligible in each state and year with the simulated eligibility measure. Controlled for state fixed effects and time varying state characteristics.	The percentage of 15–44 yr old women eligible for Medicaid (had they become pregnant) rose from 12.4% to 43.3% b/n 1979 and 1991. A 30% increase in eligibility leads to a 1.9% decrease in incidence of low birth weight (sig. at 10% level) and a 8.5% decrease in infant mortality rate. For targeted program changes, a 30% increase in eligibility decreases low birth weight (infant mortality) by 7.8% (11.5%). For broad program changes a 30% increase in eligibility decreases low birth weight (infant mortality) by 0.2% (2.9%).

Table 13 (continued)

Study and data	Study design	Results
Canadian National Health Insurance and Infant Health (Hanratty, 1996). County-level panel data on infant mortality from 10 provinces in 1960–1975 from the Census of Canada and from Canada's Division of Vital Statistics. ($n = 204$ counties). Data on birth weight from a sample of all birth records in Canada from 1960 to 1974.	Used variation in timing of implementation of national health insurance across provinces in Canada over 1962–72. Logit of outcomes on a dummy for having national health insurance in a particular county–year, controlling for demographic and socio-economic factors, a time trend, and year fixed effects.	Introduction of national health insurance leads to declines of 4% in infant mortality rates; 1.3% in low birth weight (whole sample); 8.9% in low birth weight (single parents). No impact on birth weight among married women.
Changes in prenatal care timing and low birth weight by race and socioeconomic status: Implications for the Medicaid expansions for pregnant women (Dubay et al., 2001). Data on births from the 1980, 1986, and 1993 Natality Files. $n = 8,100,000$ births.	Difference–in–difference, subtracting difference in obstetrical outcomes (rates of late initiation of prenatal care and rates of low birth weight) b/n 1980 and 1986 from difference in outcomes b/n 1986 and 1990, within socioeconomic (SES) groups. Also compared changes in obstetrical outcomes in 1986-93 b/n women of low and high SES (since high SES women were not affected by Medicaid expansions). SES defined by marital status and years of schooling. Medicaid expansions occurred in 1986–93. Controlled for year, age of mother, parity, and age–parity interactions.	**Results from diff-in-diff within SES:** Medicaid expansions associated with decreases of: 12%–21% prenatal care initiation after 1st trimester for white women; 3%–5% in low birth weight among white women with <12 years education; 10%–13% in prenatal care initiation after 1st trimester for black women with <12 years education; 13%–27% in prenatal care initiation after 1st trimester for black women with 12-15 years of education; 12%–35% in prenatal care initiation after 1st trimester for black women with >15 years of education. Association with a 3% increase in likelihood of low birth weight for unmarried black women with <12 years education. Similar results using diff-in-diff across SES for 1986-93.

(continued on next page)

Table 13 (continued)

Study and data	Study design	Results
Effects of Medicaid expansions and welfare contractions on prenatal care and infant health (Currie and Grogger, 2002). Data on birth outcomes from VSDN files 1990–1996. Data on fetal deaths from vital statistics fetal deaths detailed records. Data on Medicaid administrative reforms from National Governor's Association Maternal and Child Health newsletters. Data on welfare caseloads from the US Department of Health and Human Services. $n = 3,985,968$ whites; 4,014,935 blacks.	Logit regression that includes dummies for state-level Medicaid administrative reforms; income eligibility cutoffs; rates of welfare participation; unemployment rates; and maternal observable characteristics. Also estimated auxiliary regressions that examine the effect of policy variables on aggregate Medicaid caseloads.	Medicaid caseload increases by 0.233 for each 1% increase in welfare rate. Medicaid caseload increases by 0.664 for each 100% increase in income cut-off (for those not receiving cash benefits). Increase in income cutoff from 100% to 200% of poverty line increases probability of adequate prenatal care by 0.4% for whites. 2 pp increase in welfare rate associated w/ 1.1% increase in probability that prenatal care was initiated in 1st trimester; 0.7% increase in probability of adequate care for whites; 2% increase for both for blacks. Increase in income cutoff from 100% to 200% of poverty line associated w/ a decrease of 1720 fetal deaths per year among blacks. 2% increase in welfare associated w/ 10% decrease in fetal deaths per year among blacks. Most administrative reforms have no effect. But using mail-in forms (instead of in-person interviews) increases probability that prenatal care was initiated in 1st trimester by 0.7% for blacks and shorter forms increase probability that prenatal care was initiated in 1st trimester by 3% for whites. Using mail-in forms decreases probability of low birth weight by 26%; of very low birth weight by 38% for whites.

Table 13 (continued)

Study and data	Study design	Results
Using discontinuous eligibility rules to identify the effects of the federal Medicaid expansions on low-income children (Card and Shore-Sheppard, 2004). Data from SIPP for 1990–93, March CPS for 1990–96, and Health Interview Survey for 1992–1996 on children under 18 years old. $n = 10{,}268$ to $16{,}196$ across the different years in SIPP.	Two sources of identification: "The 133% expansion" (children under age 6 living in families with incomes below 133% of the poverty line became covered in 1989) and "the 100% expansion" (children born after September 30, 1983 in families with incomes below the poverty line became covered). Difference-in-difference design comparing age-6 and age-5 children in families with incomes between 100% and 133% of the poverty line for the 133% expansion, and comparing children born before and after Sep. 30, 1983 for the "100% expansion". Regression of Medicaid enrollment on dummy for being below poverty level, dummy for being born after 9/30/1983, their interaction, dummy for age <6 years old, interaction between dummy for age <6 years old and dummy for being between 100% and 133% of the poverty line, a flexible function of age and family income, and other background characteristics as well as year fixed effects.	The 100% expansion led to 7%–11% take-up rates, while the 133% expansion had <5% take-up rates. No evidence for other insurance crowd-out in SIPP data. Results from CPS data suggest that the 133% expansion led to decline in other health insurance coverage by approximately the same amount as the take-up in Medicaid. Similar results using Health Interview Survey data.

(continued on next page)

Table 13 (continued)

Study and data	Study design	Results
Effects of Medicaid managed care on prenatal care and birth outcomes (Aizer et al., 2007). Data on birth outcomes from the California Birth Statistical Master File 1990–2000 and Birth Cohort files for the same time period. Hospital-level data from Vital Statistics records. $n = 55,000$ births.	Exploited the county-by-county variation in implementation of Medicaid managed care, which resulted from a phase-in policy in California that required women enrolled in Medicaid to switch to managed care plans. Some counties switched to COHS plan, others switched to 2 or more plan system. Multivariate regression with county fixed effects, and mother fixed effects, as well as other observable characteristics. Robustness checks: Estimating same model for married women only (unlikely to be on welfare, hence unlikely to be subject to MMC); controlling for mobility b/n counties; regression discontinuity design to eliminate time trend effects; adding interaction terms b/n time trend and several dummies; "intent- to-treat" models to control for the MMC adoption being not exogenous to counties.	Probability of starting prenatal care in 1st trimester: decreased by 9%–10% in both COHS and 2-plan counties. Use of induction/stimulation of labor: increased by 43.8% in COHS counties. Use of fetal monitors: increased by 25.9% in COHS counties. Incidence of low birth weight: increased by 15% in both COHS and 2-plan counties. Incidence of short gestation: increased by 15% in both COHS and 2-plan counties. Incidence of neonatal death: increased by 50% in 2-plan counties.

Table 13 (continued)

Study and data	Study design	Results
Effects on later child outcomes		
Medicaid eligibility and the incidence of ambulatory care sensitive hospitalizations for children (Kaestner et al., 2001). Data from the Nationwide Inpatient Sample of the Healthcare Cost and Utilization Project for 1988 and 1992. $n = 36,000$.	Difference-in-difference, comparing the change in ambulatory care sensitive (ACS) hospitalizations before and after Medicaid expansions b/n poor and non-poor children. Poverty status determined by median family income in child's zip code of birth. Two treatment groups: income < $25,000 and $25,000 < income < $35,000. Control group: income >$35,000. Separate estimates for children aged 2–6, 7–9. Controlled for hospital-specific, year, and individual factors. Incidence of ACS hospitalizations calculated using both non-ACS hospitalizations and total births in the denominator.	For children aged 2–6 in families with <$25,000 income, incidence of ACS hospitalizations due to dehydration, convulsions and non-asthma illnesses declined by 10%–20%. Estimated effect sizes of 40%–80% for those affected by Medicaid expansions. For children aged 2–6 in families with $25,000 < income < $35,000, incidence of ACS hospitalizations due to non-asthma illnesses and pneumonia declined by 10%–14% (only when denominator is total births). For children aged 7–9 in families with $25,000 < income < $35,000, incidence of ACS hospitalizations due to asthma declined by 22%–30%; hospitalizations due to eye, nose and throat illnesses declined by >100%. No significant effects on children aged 2–6 in $25,000 < income < $35,000 group or on children aged 7–9 in <$ 25,000 income group.

(continued on next page)

Table 13 (continued)

Study and data	Study design	Results
Low take-up in Medicaid: does outreach matter and for whom? (Aizer, 2003). Data on monthly Medicaid enrollment for children aged 0–15 in CA from 1996 to 2000 linked with information on the number of community-based application assistants in each zip code in the month of application by age and race. $n = 324,331$ for analysis of take-up. $n = 121,806$ for analysis of hospitalizations.	Examined effects of CA outreach campaign launched in June 1998, which consisted of community-based application assistants and a media campaign to raise awareness about Medicaid, on Medicaid enrollment. Multivariate regression with key explanatory variable being the number of community-based application assistants in each zip code in the month of application by age and race. Included zip code and month fixed effects as well as controls for changes in business cycle and the demographic compositions of the state. Also examined effect of early Medicaid enrollment on ACS hospitalizations by instrumenting Medicaid enrollment with outreach measures.	Access to bilingual application assistants increases new monthly Medicaid enrollment by 4.6% among Hispanic children, and by 6% among Asian children (relative to other children in same neighborhood). A 1000-child increase in Medicaid enrollments decreases ACS hospitalizations by 3.26 hospitalizations (mean not reported, so can't calculate relative effect size).

Table 13 (continued)

Study and data	Study design	Results
Public insurance and child hospitalizations: Access and efficiency effects (Dafny and Gruber, 2005). Data from NHDS on child discharges for 1983 to 1996. Cells defined for 4 age categories (<1, 1–5, 6–10, 11–15) for each state and year. $n = 2308$ cells. Used age–state–year populations from the Census Bureau to calculate hospitalization rates for each cell.	Investigated impact of Medicaid expansions on hospitalizations using the variation in Medicaid eligibility b/n states, over time, and by age. Key explanatory variable is the eligibility rate measured by the fraction of children eligible for Medicaid in each age– state–year cell. Controlled for age, state, and year fixed effects as well as state–year interactions. Used the fraction eligible calculated using a fixed sample to instrument for actual eligibility in each state, year, and age group. Also examined effect of Medicaid eligibility on length of stay in hospital and the number of procedures performed.	A 10 pp increase in Medicaid eligibility leads to a 8.4% increase in total hospitalizations, an 8.1% increase in unavoidable hospitalizations, and no statistically significant impact on avoidable hospitalizations. Assuming access to hospital care increases the likelihood of all kinds of hospitalizations equally, these results imply that increased use of primary care engendered by Medicaid expansions mitigated the increase in total hospitalizations by reducing the increase in avoidable hospitalizations that would have otherwise occurred. A 10 pp increase in eligibility leads to a 3.1% decrease in the length of hospital stay, a 5% increase in the # of procedures performed, and a 6.6% increase in the likelihood of having any procedure performed, i.e. leads to more aggressive care.
Public health insurance, program take–up and child health (Aizer, 2007) entry for description of data.	See Aizer (2003) entry. Additional analysis: Examined heterogeneity in effects on take–up by age. Examined nonlinear effects on take–up. Examined effects of English and Spanish language advertisements on take–up.	Proximity to an additional bilingual application assistant increases new monthly Medicaid enrollment by 7%–9% among Hispanics and by 27%–36% among Asians. Smallest effects for infants who were already largely eligible; largest effects for ages 6–15. Effect is linear for Hispanics; slightly concave for Asians. English language advertisements increase Medicaid enrollment in the following month by 4.7% among all children, and Spanish language advertisements increase Medicaid enrollment in the following month by an additional 2.5% among Hispanic children. Increasing the # of children w/ Medicaid by 10% results in a 2%–3% decline in avoidable hospitalizations.

(continued on next page)

Table 13 (continued)

Study and data	Study design	Results
Has public health insurance for older children reduced disparities in access to care and health outcomes? (Currie et al., 2008). Data from the national health interview surveys for 1986-2005. $n = 474{,}164$ children <18 yrs old. Instrument data from the CPS.	Identification due to the fact that expansions in Medicaid/SCHIP eligibility for older children relative to younger children happened at different times in different states. Instrumented for individual Medicaid/SCHIP eligibility using an index of generosity of the state's public health insurance programs calculated using a fixed group of children. Then, estimated impact of public health insurance eligibility on the relationship b/n family income and child health status and on the relationship b/n family income and doctor visits in the previous year. Also tested whether the relationship b/n income and outcomes changed over time within age groups by running separate regressions for 4 age groups: 0-3, 4-8, 9-12, 13-17. Finally, estimated relationship b/n health outcomes and the fraction of children eligible in child's birth cohort in the child's current state of residence for children aged 9-17. Controlled for family background variables and year and state fixed effects.	For children aged 9-12, the coefficient on income in a model of health status declined by 20% over 2000-2005. For children aged 13-17, it declined by 18% over 1996-2000 and by 25% over 2000-05. For children 0-3/4-8/9-12 the coefficient on income in a model of doctor visits declined by 64%/62%/50% between 2000-2005. For children aged 13-17 there was no significant change in the income coefficient. Significant declines in the income coefficient over 1991-1995 and 1996-2000 for children aged 0-3 and 4-8 as well. No statistically significant impact of contemporaneous health insurance eligibility on child health status. A 100 pp increase in the fraction eligible at age 3 would reduce the probability that the average child aged 9-17 is in less than excellent health by 11%. A 100 pp increase in the fraction eligible at ages 1 and 2 would reduce the probability that the average child aged 9-17 had no doctor visit in the past year by 41%.

Table 13 (continued)

Study and data	Study design	Results
The impact of children's public health insurance expansions on educational outcomes (Levine and Schanzenbach, 2009). Data on state-level average scaled test scores from the National Assessment of Educational Progress for 1990 to 2003. ($n = 431$). Data for simulated instruments from March CPS. Data on child health from Vital Statistics for 1984–2003 ($n = 1020$).	Examine the impact of public health insurance at birth on 4th and 8th grade reading and math test scores. Difference-in-difference-in-difference using cross-state variation over time and across ages in children's health insurance eligibility due to Medicaid and SCHIP expansions. Instrumented for public health insurance eligibility using the simulated fraction eligible (as in Currie and Gruber (1996) see above). To test whether changes in educational outcomes are due to improvements in health status or to additional household income generated if the availability of public health insurance crowds out private health insurance, they estimated the direct impact of health at birth on educational outcomes. Controlled for state and year fixed effects and state-specific time trends.	A 50 pp increase in eligibility at birth increased reading test scores by 0.09 SD relative to 4th and 8th grade combined mean scaled score. No effect on math test scores. Expansions to public health insurance eligibility at birth associated w/ 1.6% reduction in low birth weight rate for whole sample and 6.7% reduction in infant mortality rates among women with at least a high school degree. A 50% increase in low birth weight (infant mortality) rate would decrease reading test scores by 0.12 SD (.07SD).

(continued on next page)

Table 13 (continued)

Study and data	Study design	Results
Public insurance, crowd-out and health care utilization (Koch, 2009). Data from the medical expenditure panel survey. Focus on subsample of children <18 yrs whose families have incomes b/n 50% and 400% of poverty line. (n = 32,609). Data on public insurance reimbursement rates from the American Academy of Pediatrics for 1998–2001.	Regression discontinuity design using family income cut-offs that determine eligibility for Medicaid and SCHIP. To distinguish b/n children who are eligible for public insurance w/out access to private insurance and those whose private insurance may be crowded-out due to expansions in public health insurance, constructed a measure of private–insurance "offer" (=1 if any of the following holds: child is privately insured at the time of the eligibility measurement or a family member is privately employed at the time and either has insurance through the job or turns down the insurance at the job). Estimated impacts of public health insurance eligibility on measures of care utilization (doctor's visits, etc.) as well as on private insurance take-up. Also estimated the differential effect of eligibility on those w/ and w/out private health insurance by interacting the eligibility variable with the "offer" variable. Controlled for background characteristics as well as state and year fixed effects. Also looked at impacts of differential reimbursement rates across states and years on access to care for the publicly insured.	Public insurance eligibility increases public insurance coverage by 21% and decreases private insurance coverage by 24%. So overall decrease in insurance coverage of about 4.8%. Eligibility decreases the number of office visits/self-reported health status/total expenditures by 12%/87%/23%. Increases the number of ER visits by 18%. Eligibility decreases the number of office visits by 18% for those with outside private health insurance. No statistically significant effects on ER visits, prescriptions, or refills. Children just eligible for public health insurance are 4% less likely to have a usual source of care and 4% more likely to go without care. No statistically significant effects on hospital or ER visits. Eligibility increases children's BMI by 2%. Parents of just eligible children are 5% less likely to be given advice about their child's eating healthfully. No significant effects on asthma diagnosis. Conditional on taking medication for asthma, eligibility increases probability of taking inhaled steroids (gold standard treatment) by 32%. A $4 increase in reimbursement for office visits leads to a 5% increase in the number of office visits.

Percent changes (denoted by % instead of "pp") are reported relative to the mean.

birth weight, but reduced infant mortality. This result suggests that among women of somewhat higher income levels, the expansions did not improve health at birth, but may have increased access to life-saving technologies after birth. Currie and Grogger (2002) focus on bureaucratic obstacles to obtaining health insurance by looking at contractions of welfare (women cut from the rolls lost automatic eligibility for Medicaid) as well as outreach measures undertaken by different states. They find that changes that reduced barriers to enrollment increased use of prenatal care and had positive effects on infant health outcomes.

Baldwin et al. (1998) use individual-level data and compare expansions in Washington, which included enhanced prenatal care services, to expansions in Colorado which did not, in a difference-in-differences design. They find reductions in low birth weight among medically high risk infants in Washington. Dubay et al. (2001) conduct a difference-in-difference investigation comparing the outcomes of high and low socioeconomic status women in the 1980-1986 period and in the 1986-1993 period. They find overall improvements in the use of prenatal care for low SES women, but find improvements in birth weight only for some groups of white women. However, this design does not really focus on health insurance *per se*, since the estimates will be affected by any other changes in health care markets between the two periods that had differential effects by SES.

Studies of the effects of health insurance expansions on children often examine preventable hospitalizations (also called ambulatory care sensitive hospitalizations). The idea is that certain conditions, such as childhood asthma, should not result in hospitalizations if they are properly treated on an outpatient basis. Hence, hospitalizations for these conditions are inefficient and indicate that children are receiving inadequate preventive care. Kaestner et al. (2001) use a difference-in-differences design comparing low income and other children before and after Medicaid expansions. They find reductions in preventable hospitalizations of 10% to 20%.

Aizer (2003) examines a California outreach program that increased child enrollments into Medicaid. She finds that an increase in enrollments of 1000 reduces hospitalizations by 3.26. Dafny and Gruber (2005) use a design similar to Currie and Gruber in which actual individual eligibility is instrumented using a "simulated eligibility measure" which is an index of the generosity of the Medicaid program in the state. The reason for adopting instrumental variables estimation is that eligibility for Medicaid is determined by endogenous variables such as parental labor supply. They find that Medicaid eligibility increased hospitalizations overall. However, there was no statistically significant increase in avoidable hospitalizations, suggesting that the increase was mainly due to children with unavoidable conditions gaining greater access to care. They also found increases in the probability of receiving a procedure and reductions in length of stay, suggesting that children who were hospitalized were receiving more aggressive care and that it may have improved their outcomes.

One difficulty with studying child health is that health today is affected by past investments, including health insurance at younger ages. Currie et al. (2008) therefore compare the health effects of contemporaneous eligibility for health insurance among older children to the effect of having been eligible since birth. They find that contemporaneous health insurance coverage has little effect on health status but that eligibility from birth is protective. Levine and Schanzenbach (2009) link health insurance eligibility at birth to 4th and 8th grade scores on the National Assessment of Educational Progress. They find that a 50% point increase in eligibility at birth is associated with a small but significant gain on reading scores at both grades, though there is no effect on math scores. A difficulty with both studies is that neither income at birth nor state of birth are directly observed in the cross sectional data sets that they use, so they must be imputed using current income and state of birth.

Another area of research focuses on the quality of care provided by public health insurance programs. Analysis of this issue is complicated by the possibility that expansions of public insurance cause people to lose private health insurance coverage, a phenomena dubbed "crowdout" (Cutler and Gruber 1996; Dubay and Kenney, 1997; Card and Shore-Shepard, 2004; Gruber and Simon, 2008). If the private insurance that is lost (or dropped) in response to expansions of public insurance is of superior quality to the private insurance, then people's health may suffer. Koch (2009) concludes that recent expansions of public health insurance to children at higher income levels have reduced access to doctor's office visits and increased reliance on emergency rooms. He also shows some evidence consistent with the idea that this is because children are being crowded out of superior (but obviously more expensive) coverage from private heath insurance plans. In fact, it is quite possible that crowding out has increased over time as the public has become familiar with public health insurance plans for children and private health insurance costs have continued to escalate.

Medicaid managed care has also been shown (in at least some cases) to reduce the quality of care. Sloan et al. (2001) conduct a difference-in-difference analysis of Tennessee and North Carolina before and after Tennessee switched its Medicaid patients to managed care. They find that use of prenatal care and birth outcomes deteriorated in Tennessee after the switch. Aizer et al. (2007) examine data from California, where Medicaid managed care was adopted on a county-by-county basis. They also find that compulsory managed care had a negative impact on use of prenatal care and birth outcomes. This may be because the California Medicaid managed care program "carved out" care for sick newborns—that is, they were covered by a state fund rather than by the managed care companies so that companies had little incentive to take actions to improve newborn health.

In summary, health insurance matters for children's outcomes. But quality of care also matters. And it is important to remember that for most children threats to health and well being come from sources such as injuries, poor nutrition, and toxins rather than only from lack of access to medical care.

6. DISCUSSION AND CONCLUSIONS

There has been an explosion of research into the early determinants of human capital development over the past 10 years. The work surveyed in this chapter conclusively shows that events before five years old can have large long term impacts on adult outcomes. It is striking that child and family characteristics measured at school entry do as much to explain future outcomes as factors that labor economists have more traditionally focused on, such as years of education. Yet evidence for long term effects of early insults should not be a cause of pessimism. While children can be permanently damaged at this age, the damage can be remediated. The picture that emerges is one of vulnerability but also of resilience.

Since early childhood is a new area of research for economists, there remain many unanswered questions. One major question implicit in the structure of this chapter is whether it will ever be possible to estimate human capital production functions. The opening sections of this chapter showed that the production function paradigm provides an extremely useful way of thinking about the problem, and in particular, that it highlights the importance of actions taken by parents and others in exacerbating or mitigating the effects of random shocks. However, to actually estimate the implied production functions would place huge demands on the data, demands that are unlikely to be met in practice.[15] Hence, the evidence we have surveyed is largely reduced form.

A second major question is whether shocks at certain key ages matter more than others? Much has been written about "critical periods". The idea is that certain functionalities must be acquired at a particular point in life, and if they are not acquired at that point, they will either not be acquired at all, or will not be acquired properly. There is to date little hard evidence of critical periods in humans. However, the evidence discussed above certainly suggests that the period while children are *in utero* is one of the most important to their later development. This has important implications for the timing of social interventions designed to mitigate harms—it may be that interventions should be targeted at pregnant women and/or women of child bearing age in addition to young children. But there is insufficient evidence at present to be able to say that insults or interventions at for example zero to one are likely to be more effective than interventions at age three or four. Moreover, the cohort designs used to establish the importance of the fetal period can tell us more about the comparison between the fetal period and the early post natal period than they do about the comparison between the fetal period and say exposures at age five.

---

[15] See however Appendix D for one thought about how a production function might be estimated.

A related question is whether some types of shocks matter more than others. This chapter surveyed many different types of shocks including exposure to disease, inadequate nutrition, exposure to pollution, injuries, maternal mental health problems, maternal smoking, and maltreatment. However, given that studies of the effects of these shocks rely on different populations, time periods, and methods, it is difficult to get any sense of whether one type of shock is more of a threat to human capital development than any other. Similarly, while it is clear that shocks to health have long-term effects on domains such as education and earnings, it is not clear whether health shocks have direct effects on cognition or learning, or whether they act mainly by affecting future health.

Several studies we reviewed suggested that both shocks and interventions can have different long-term effects on males and females. But these findings are too new for us to be able to predict when this difference will occur, and we have virtually no evidence about why it occurs. One possibility is that gender differences are biological. For example, boys may be less robust than girls so that the same health shock can "cull" boys while girls survive (e.g., see Kraemer (2000); Almond and Mazumder (2008)). In this case, average health of male survivors might be better than that of female survivors. Alternatively, gender differences could reflect differential parental or societal responses to shocks inspired by son preferences or by beliefs about biological gender differences.[16]

Finally, given all of this evidence of long-term effects of early life outcomes, what is the least costly way to intervene to improve outcomes? This is still an open question and our knowledge of the types of programs that are effective (and why) is evolving rapidly. For example, until recently, there was little evidence that income transfers had much effect, so it was easy to surmise that in-kind programs were a more effective way to improve child outcomes. Recent evidence that cash transfers are indeed effective should cause a re-evaluation of the received wisdom on this point, given the inefficiencies involved in providing transfers in-kind. Similarly, the large literature about negative effects of maternal employment in the early years is thrown into question by recent studies showing that large changes in maternity leave policies affected maternal employment without having any detectable impact on long-term child outcomes. This rapid development in our knowledge makes the study of human capital development before five an exciting frontier for research in labor economics.

APPENDIX A

The following acronyms are used in this chapter:

AFDC = Aid to Families with Dependent Children

BCS = British Birth Cohort Study of 1970.

---

[16] For example, advances in ultrasound technology could have changed the average human capital endowments of boys and girls by allowing parents who prefer sons to invest differentially prenatally (and not only by allowing them to abort female fetuses). See Lhila and Simon (2008) for recent work on this topic.

BPI = Behavioral Problems Index

BW = birth weight

CESD = Center for Epidemiological Depression scale

CCT = Conditional Cash Transfer

COHS = County Organized Health System

CPS = Current Population Survey

DDST = Denver Developmental Screening Test

ECLS-B = Early Childhood Longitudinal Study—Birth Cohort

ECLS-K = Early Childhood Longitudinal Study—Kindergarten Class of 1998-1999

EITC = Earned Income Tax Credit

EPA = US Environmental Protection Agency

FSP = Food Stamp Program

HAZ = Height for age z-score

HOME = Home Observation for Measurement of the Environment Score

IHDP = Infant Health and Development Project

IPUMS = Integrated Public-Use Microdata Samples of the US Census

IV = instrumental variables

LBW = Low Birth Weight (birth weight less than 2500 g)

MMC = Medicaid Managed Care

NBER = National Bureau of Economic Research

NCDS = National Child Development Survey (1958 British Birth Cohort)

NELS = National Education Longitudinal Study

NHANES = National Health and Nutrition Examination Survey

NHDS = National Hospital Discharge Survey

NLSY = National Longitudinal Survey of Youth, 1979 cohort

NLSY-Child = Children of the NLSY 1979 cohort

NLSCY = National Longitudinal Survey of Children and Youth (Canadian)

PIAT = Peabody Individual Achievement Test

pp = percentage points

PPVT = Peabody Picture Vocabulary Test

NSLP = National School Lunch Program

OLS = Ordinary Least Squares

PNM = Post Neonatal Mortality (death after 28 days and before 1 year)

PSID = Panel Study of Income Dynamics

RDA = Recommended Dietary Allowance

REIS = Regional Economic Information System

SCHIP = State Child Health Insurance Program

SD = Standard Deviation

SES = Socio-economic Status

SGA = Small for Gestational Age

SIPP = Survey of Income and Program Participation

SNAP = Supplemental Nutrition Assistance Program (formerly, Food Stamps)

TSIV = Two Sample Instrumental Variables

TVIP = Spanish-speaking version of the Peabody Picture Vocabulary Test

TSP = Total Suspended Particles

USDA = US Department of Agriculture

VSDN = Vital Statistics Detailed Natality files (birth certificate data for US)

WIC = Special Supplemental Nutrition Program for Women, Infants, and Children

WPPSI = Wechsler Preschool and Primary Scale of Intelligence

APPENDIX B

Human capital of a child is produced with a CES technology:

$$h = A \left[\gamma (\bar{I}_1 + \mu_g)^\phi + (1 - \gamma) I_2^\phi \right]^{1/\phi}, \tag{9}$$

where μ_g is an exogenous shock to (predetermined) period 1 investments. Parents value their consumption and the human capital of their child:

$$U_p = U(C, h) = B \left[\theta (C)^\varphi + (1 - \theta) h^\varphi \right]^{1/\varphi}, \tag{10}$$

and have the budget constraint:

$$\bar{I}_1 + I_2 + C = \bar{y}.$$

Absent discounting, the marginal utility from consuming equals the marginal utility from investing:

$$\frac{\delta U}{\delta C^*} = \frac{\delta U}{\delta h} \frac{\delta h}{\delta I_2^*}.$$

$$\theta C^{\varphi-1} = (1 - \theta) h^{\varphi-1} A [\cdots]^{\frac{1}{\phi}-1} (1 - \gamma) I_2^{*\phi-1} \tag{11}$$

$$\theta (\bar{y} - \bar{I}_1 - I_2^*)^{\varphi-1} = (1 - \theta) A^{\varphi-1} [\cdots]^{\frac{\varphi-1}{\phi}} A [\cdots]^{\frac{1}{\phi}-1} (1 - \gamma) I_2^{*\phi-1} \tag{12}$$

$$\theta (\bar{y} - \bar{I}_1 - I_2^*)^{\varphi-1} = (1 - \theta)(1 - \gamma) A^\varphi [\cdots]^{\frac{\varphi-\phi}{\phi}} I_2^{*\phi-1} \tag{13}$$

$$G(u_g, I_2^*) \equiv \theta (\bar{y} - \bar{I}_1 - I_2^*)^{\varphi-1} - (1 - \theta)(1 - \gamma) A^\varphi [\cdots]^{\frac{\varphi-\phi}{\phi}} I_2^{*\phi-1} = 0. \tag{14}$$

$$\frac{\delta I_2^*}{\delta \mu_g} = -\frac{\frac{\delta G}{\delta \mu_g}}{\frac{\delta G}{\delta I_2^*}}$$

$$= \frac{a (I_2^*)^{\phi-1} [\cdots]^{\frac{\varphi-2\phi}{\phi}} \left(\frac{\varphi-\phi}{\phi} \right) \gamma \phi (\bar{I}_1 + \mu_g)^{\phi-1}}{-(\varphi - 1)\theta (\bar{y} - \bar{I}_1 - I_2^*)^{\varphi-2} - a \left[[\cdots]^{\frac{\varphi-\phi}{\phi}} (\phi - 1) I_2^{*\phi-2} + \frac{\varphi-\phi}{\phi} [\cdots]^{\frac{\varphi-2\phi}{\phi}} \phi (1 - \gamma) I_2^{*\phi-1} I_2^{*\phi-1} \right]}, \tag{15}$$

using the implicit function theorem and defining a to be $(1 - \theta)(1 - \gamma) A^\varphi \geq 0$.

$$= \frac{(\varphi - \phi) a (I_2^*)^{\phi-1} [\cdots]^{\frac{\varphi-2\phi}{\phi}} \gamma (\bar{I}_1 + \mu_g)^{\phi-1}}{(1 - \varphi)\theta (\bar{y} - \bar{I}_1 - I_2^*)^{\varphi-2} + a [\cdots]^{\frac{\varphi-\phi}{\phi}} I_2^{*\phi-2} \left[(1 - \phi) + (\varphi - \phi)(1 - \gamma) I_2^{*\phi} / [\cdots] \right]}. \tag{16}$$

For $\varphi > \phi$, (16) is positive, so negative shocks in the first period should be reinforced. Accommodation through preferences (i.e., more consumption and less investment, which lowers h in addition to that caused by μ_g) is optimal.

APPENDIX C

Sibling a has human capital h_a, which is affected by a period 1 investment shock of μ_g:

$$h_a = A\left[\gamma(\bar{I}_{1a} + \mu_g)^\phi + (1 - \gamma)I_{2a}^\phi\right]^{1/\phi}. \tag{17}$$

Sibling b does not experience a shock to first period investments:

$$h_b = B\left[\gamma \bar{I}_{1b}^\phi + (1 - \gamma)I_{2b}^\phi\right]^{1/\phi}. \tag{18}$$

Assume further that first period investments do not distinguish between the two siblings (absent the shock experienced by sibling a):

$$\bar{I}_{1a} = \bar{I}_{1b} = \bar{I}_1.$$

Parents have Cobb-Douglas utility that cares only about the human capital of their two children:

$$U_p = U(h_a, h_b) = (1 - \alpha)\log h_a + \alpha\log h_b. \tag{19}$$

The parents exhaust their budget on investments in their children:

$$\bar{y} = 2\bar{I}_1 + I_{2a} + I_{2b}.$$

Denoting $\bar{Y} = \bar{y} - 2\bar{I}_1$ as the budget for second period investments, $I_{2b} = \bar{Y} - I_{2a}$.

To maximize utility, the marginal utilities from investing in siblings a and b should be equal:

$$\frac{\delta U_p}{\delta h_a}\frac{\delta h_a}{\delta I_{2a}} = \frac{\delta U_p}{\delta h_b}\frac{\delta h_b}{\delta I_{2b}}$$

$$\left(\frac{1 - \alpha}{h_a}\right)\frac{A}{\phi}\left[\gamma(\bar{I}_1 + \mu_g)^\phi + (1 - \gamma)I_{2a}^\phi\right]^{(1/\phi)-1}\phi(1 - \gamma)I_{2a}^{\phi-1}$$
$$= \left(\frac{\alpha}{h_b}\right)\frac{B}{\phi}\left[\gamma(\bar{I}_1)^\phi + (1 - \gamma)I_{2b}^\phi\right]^{(1/\phi)-1}\phi(1 - \gamma)I_{2b}^{\phi-1} \tag{20}$$

$$(1 - \alpha)\left[\gamma(\bar{I}_1 + \mu_g)^\phi + (1 - \gamma)I_{2a}^\phi\right]^{-1}I_{2a}^{\phi-1}$$
$$= \alpha\left[\gamma(\bar{I}_1)^\phi + (1 - \gamma)I_{2b}^\phi\right]^{-1}I_{2b}^{\phi-1} \tag{21}$$

$$G(\mu_g, I_{2a}) \equiv (1 - \alpha)\left[\gamma(\bar{I}_1 + \mu_g)^\phi + (1 - \gamma)I_{2a}^\phi\right]^{-1}I_{2a}^{\phi-1}$$
$$- \alpha\left[\gamma(\bar{I}_1)^\phi + (1 - \gamma)(\bar{Y} - I_{2a})^\phi\right]^{-1}(\bar{Y} - I_{2a})^{\phi-1} = 0 \tag{22}$$

using budget the constraint: $I_{2b} = \bar{Y} - I_{2a}$. By the implicit function theorem:

$$\frac{\delta I_{2a}^*}{\delta \mu_g} = \frac{-\frac{\delta G}{\delta \mu_g}}{\frac{\delta G}{\delta I_{2a}^*}} \tag{23}$$

$$\frac{\delta G}{\delta \mu_g} = -(1-\alpha)I_{2a}^{\phi-1}\left[\gamma(\bar{I}_1 + \mu_g)^\phi + (1-\gamma)I_{2a}^\phi\right]^{-2}\phi\gamma(\bar{I}_1 + \mu_g)^{\phi-1} \tag{24}$$

$$\Rightarrow \text{signum}\left[-\frac{\delta G}{\delta \mu_g}\right] = \text{signum}[\phi].$$

$$\frac{\delta G}{\delta I_{2a}^*} = (1-\alpha)\left[\gamma(\bar{I}_1 + \mu_g)^\phi + (1-\gamma)I_{2a}^\phi\right]^{-1}(\phi-1)I_{2a}^{\phi-2}$$

$$+ (-1)(1-\alpha)\left[\gamma(\bar{I}_1 + \mu_g)^\phi + (1-\gamma)I_{2a}^\phi\right]^{-2}\phi(1-\gamma)I_{2a}^{\phi-1}I_{2a}^{\phi-1}$$

$$- \left[\alpha\left[\gamma(\bar{I}_1)^\phi + (1-\gamma)(\bar{Y}-I_{2a})^\phi\right]^{-1}(\phi-1)(\bar{Y}-I_{2a})^{\phi-2}(-1)\right]$$

$$- \left[(-1)\alpha\left[\gamma(\bar{I}_1)^\phi + (1-\gamma)(\bar{Y}-I_{2a})^\phi\right]^{-2}\right.$$

$$\left. \times \phi(1-\gamma)(\bar{Y}-I_{2a})^{\phi-1}(-1)(\bar{Y}-I_{2a})^{\phi-1}\right] \tag{25}$$

$$= (1-\alpha)\left[\gamma(\bar{I}_1 + \mu_g)^\phi + (1-\gamma)I_{2a}^\phi\right]^{-1}(\phi-1)I_{2a}^{\phi-2}$$

$$- (1-\alpha)\left[\gamma(\bar{I}_1 + \mu_g)^\phi + (1-\gamma)I_{2a}^\phi\right]^{-2}\phi(1-\gamma)I_{2a}^{2\phi-2}$$

$$+ \left[\alpha\left[\gamma(\bar{I}_1)^\phi + (1-\gamma)(\bar{Y}-I_{2a})^\phi\right]^{-1}(\phi-1)(\bar{Y}-I_{2a})^{\phi-2}\right]$$

$$- \left[\alpha\left[\gamma(\bar{I}_1)^\phi + (1-\gamma)(\bar{Y}-I_{2a})^\phi\right]^{-2}\phi(1-\gamma)(\bar{Y}-I_{2a})^{2\phi-2}\right] \tag{26}$$

$$= (1-\alpha)\left[\gamma(\bar{I}_1 + \mu_g)^\phi + (1-\gamma)I_{2a}^\phi\right]^{-1}$$

$$\times I_{2a}^{\phi-2}\left[(\phi-1) - \frac{\phi(1-\gamma)I_{2a}^\phi}{\gamma(\bar{I}_1 + \mu_g)^\phi + (1-\gamma)I_{2a}^\phi}\right]$$

$$+ \alpha\left[\gamma(\bar{I}_1)^\phi + (1-\gamma)(\bar{Y}-I_{2a})^\phi\right]^{-1}(\bar{Y}-I_{2a})^{\phi-2}$$

$$\times \left[(\phi-1) - \frac{\phi(1-\gamma)(\bar{Y}-I_{2a})^\phi}{\gamma(\bar{I}_1)^\phi + (1-\gamma)(\bar{Y}-I_{2a})^\phi}\right] \tag{27}$$

$$= (1-\alpha)\left[\gamma(\bar{I}_1 + \mu_g)^\phi + (1-\gamma)I_{2a}^\phi\right]^{-1}I_{2a}^{\phi-2}$$

$$\times \left[\phi\left(1 - \frac{(1-\gamma)I_{2a}^\phi}{\gamma(\bar{I}_1 + \mu_g)^\phi + (1-\gamma)I_{2a}^\phi}\right) - 1\right]$$

$$+ \alpha \left[\gamma(\bar{I}_1)^\phi + (1 - \gamma)(\bar{Y} - I_{2a})^\phi \right]^{-1} (\bar{Y} - I_{2a})^{\phi - 2}$$
$$\times \left[\phi \left(1 - \frac{(1 - \gamma)(\bar{Y} - I_{2a})^\phi}{\gamma(\bar{I}_1)^\phi + (1 - \gamma)(\bar{Y} - I_{2a})^\phi} \right) - 1 \right]. \tag{28}$$

Because $\phi \le 1$ and:

$$\frac{(1 - \gamma)I_{2a}^\phi}{\gamma(\bar{I}_1 + \mu_g)^\phi + (1 - \gamma)I_{2a}^\phi} < 1 \quad \text{and} \quad \frac{(1 - \gamma)(\bar{Y} - I_{2a})^\phi}{\gamma(\bar{I}_1)^\phi + (1 - \gamma)(\bar{Y} - I_{2a})^\phi} < 1,$$

Eq. (28) is always negative. Therefore:

$$\mathtt{signum} \left[\frac{\delta I_{2a}^*}{\delta \mu_g} \right] = - \, \mathtt{signum}[\phi].$$

We consider three cases for the substitutability of period 1 and period 2 investments (as captured by ϕ):

1. **Good Substitutability Between Periods 1 and 2** When $\phi > 0$, the optimal I_{2a} moves in the opposite direction from μ_g and parents should *compensate* a negative shock to child a by reducing second period investments in child b. Intuitively, it is easier to substitute though the production function for human capital than it is through the Cobb-Douglas utility function.

2. **Cobb–Douglas Substitutability Between Periods 1 and 2** For $\phi = 0$, the elasticity of substitution between periods is the same as the elasticity of substitution in preferences between the children (both Cobb-Douglas). Here, there is no winning investment response to the shock to child a, i.e. $\frac{\delta I_{2a}^*}{\delta \mu_g} = 0$, so period 2 investments should be left unchanged.

3. **Poor Substitutability Between Periods 1 and 2** For $\phi < 0$, it is difficult to repair damage from a negative μ_g shock in the second period, so the return to period 2 investments in sibling a is below that for sibling b. Therefore, parents should *reinforce* the first period shock by allocating second period investments away from sibling a.

Importantly, the direction of these investment responses did **not** depend on α, the relative weight parents place in their utility function on the human capital of child a versus child b. Favoring the human capital formation of a particular child—even the child that experiences the negative endowment shock—does not affect the direction of the optimal investment response. Nor do differences in the "overall" productivity of the child, i.e. efficiency parameter $A \ne B$ in Eqs (17) and (18), alter the direction of the optimal investment response to μ_g. Thus, empirical evidence suggesting either reinforcing or compensating investments within the family does not reveal information on parental preferences absent additional information on the production function for human capital.

APPENDIX D

In general, we need to observe the baseline investments $\bar{I}_1$ and $\bar{I}_2$ to estimate parameters of the production function ϕ and γ. However, nearly all datasets with measures of human capital h and an observable investment shock μ_g lack measures of human capital investments $\bar{I}_1$ and $\bar{I}_2$. We can still make progress in estimating parameters of the production function despite not observing $\bar{I}_1$ and $\bar{I}_2$, so long as we expect baseline investment levels to be similar: $\bar{I}_1 \cong \bar{I}_2$. For $\mu_g = \mu'_g$,[17] Eq. (4) reduces to:

$$\frac{1-\gamma}{\gamma}. \tag{29}$$

That is, we can observe damage to h from the shock μ'_g in second period investments relative to the damage from the first period shock μ_g, which isolates γ (while remaining silent on the magnitude of ϕ).

With an estimate of γ in hand, we can then estimate ϕ by using the total derivative in investment shocks, i.e. how human capital changes as we change *both* first and second period investments (by an equal amount). In an overlapping generations framework, this would require a shock lasting two childhood periods (or longer), and "half-exposed" cohorts on either end of the shock. Damage to the fully exposed cohort relative to the cohort exposed in period 1 alone is:

$$= \frac{1}{\gamma} \left[\frac{\gamma(\bar{I}_1 + \mu_g)^\phi + (1-\gamma)(\bar{I}_1 + \mu_g)^\phi}{\gamma(\bar{I}_1 + \mu_g)^\phi + (1-\gamma)\bar{I}_1^\phi} \right]^{\frac{1-\phi}{\phi}}, \tag{30}$$

using the assumption that $\bar{I}_1 = \bar{I}_2$ and $\mu_g = \mu'_g$,

$$= \frac{1}{\gamma} \left[\frac{(\bar{I}_1 + \mu_g)^\phi}{\gamma(\bar{I}_1 + \mu_g)^\phi + (1-\gamma)\bar{I}_1^\phi} \right]^{\frac{1-\phi}{\phi}}, \tag{31}$$

$$= \frac{1}{\gamma} \left[\frac{1}{\gamma + (1-\gamma)\frac{\bar{I}_1}{\bar{I}_1 + \mu_g}^\phi} \right]^{\frac{1-\phi}{\phi}}, \tag{32}$$

$$= \frac{1}{\gamma} \left[\gamma + (1-\gamma)\left(1 + \frac{\mu_g}{\bar{I}_1}\right)^{-\phi} \right]^{\frac{\phi-1}{\phi}}. \tag{33}$$

[17] The assumption that $\mu_g = \mu'_g$ simplifies the algebra, but ϕ and γ can still be estimated for $\mu_g \neq \mu'_g$ so long as μ_g and μ'_g are observed. We thank Christine Pal for pointing this out.

Similarly, damage to the "doubly exposed" cohort relative to that experiencing a shock in just the *second* childhood period is:

$$= \frac{1}{1-\gamma} \left[(1-\gamma) + \gamma \left(1 + \frac{\mu_g}{\bar{I}_1} \right)^{-\phi} \right]^{\frac{\phi-1}{\phi}} , \tag{34}$$

Eqs (33) and (34) constitute two equations in the two unknowns $\bar{I}_1$ and ϕ, with γ known from Eq. (29).

REFERENCES

2001. An overstretched hypothesis? The Lancet 357 (9254), 405.

Agüero, Jorge M., Carter, Michael R., Woolard, Ingrd, 2009. The impact of unconditional cash transfers on nutrition: the South African child support grant. Manuscript, February.

Aizer, Anna, 2003. Low take-up in Medicaid: does outreach matter and for whom? American Economic Review Papers and Proceedings 93 (2), 238–241.

Aizer, Anna, 2007. Public health insurance, program take-up and child health. The Review of Economics and Statistics 89 (3), 400–415.

Aizer, Anna, Currie, Janet, Moretti, Enrico, 2007. Does managed care hurt health? Evidence from Medicaid mothers. The Review of Economics and Statistics 89 (3), 385–399.

Aizer, Anna, Stroud, Laura, 2009. Education, medical knowledge and the evolution of disparities in health. manuscript, Brown University, September.

Aizer, Anna, Stroud, Laura, Buka, Stephen, 2009. Maternal stress and child well-being: evidence from siblings. manuscript. Brown University, February.

Almond, Douglas, 2006. Is the 1918 Influenza Pandemic over? Long-term effects of *in utero* influenza exposure in the post-1940 US population. Journal of Political Economy 114 (4), 672–712.

Almond, Douglas, Chay, Kenneth Y., Lee, David S., 2005. The costs of low birth weight. The Quarterly Journal of Economics 120 (3), 1031–1084.

Almond, Douglas, Edlund, Lena, Palme, Mårten, 2009. Chernobyl's subclinical legacy: prenatal exposure to radioactive fallout and school outcomes in sweden. Quarterly Journal of Economics 124 (4), 1729–1772. URL http://www.mitpressjournals.org/doi/abs/10.1162/qjec.2009.124.4.1729.

Almond, Douglas, Hoynes, Hilary W., Schanzenbach, Diane Whitmore, 2010. Inside the war on poverty: the impact of food stamps on birth outcomes. The Review of Economics and Statistics (forthcoming).

Almond, Douglas, Mazumder, Bhashkar, 2005. The 1918 influenza pandemic and subsequent health outcomes: an analysis of SIPP data. American Ecnomic Review, Papers and Proceedings 95 (2).

Almond, Douglas, Mazumder, Bhashkar, 2008. Health capital and the prenatal environment: the effect of maternal fasting during pregnancy. Working Paper 14428, National Bureau of Economic Research, October, URL http://www.nber.org/papers/w14428.

Anderson, Kathryn H., Foster, James E., Frisvold, David E., 2009. Investing in health: the long-term impact of Head Start on smoking. Working Paper 1465-7295, Western Economic Association International.

Anderson, Michael, 2008. Multiple inference and gender differences in the effects of early intervention: a reevaluation of the Abecedarian, Perry Preschool, and Early Training projects. Journal of the American Statistical Association 103 (484), 1481–1495.

Angrist, Joshua D., Pischke, Jörn-Steffen, 2009. Mostly Harmless Econometrics: an Empiricist's Companion. Princeton University Press, Princeton, New Jersey.

Aos, Steve, Lieb, Roxanne, Mayfield, Jim, Miller, Marna, Pennucci, Annie, 2004. Benefits and costs of prevention and early intervention programs for youth. Technical appendix, Washington State Institute for Public Policy, September.

Ashenfelter, Orley, Rouse, Cecilia, 1998. Income, schooling, and ability: evidence from a new sample of identical twins. Quarterly Journal of Economics 113 (1), 253–284.
URL http://www.mitpressjournals.org/doi/abs/10.1162/003355398555577.

Baker, Kevin, 2008. Do cash transfer programs improve infant health: evidence from the 1993 expansion of the earned income tax credit. Manuscript, University of Notre Dame.

Baker, Michael, Gruber, Jonathan, Milligan, Kevin, 2008. Universal child care, maternal labor supply, and family well-being. Journal of Political Economy 116 (4), 709–745.
URL http://www.journals.uchicago.edu/doi/abs/10.1086/591908.

Baker, Michael, Milligan, Kevin, 2010. Evidence from maternity leave expansions of the impact of maternal care on early child development. Journal of Human Resources 45 (1), 1–32.

Baldwin, Laura-Mae, Larson, Eric H., Connell, Frederick A., Nordlund, Daniel, Cain, Kevin C., Cawthon, Mary L., Byrns, Patricia, Rosenblatt, Roger A., 1998. The effect of expanding Medicaid prenatal services on birth outcomes. American Journal of Public Health 88 (11), 1623–1629.

Banerjee, Abhijit, Duflo, Esther, Postel-Vinay, Gilles, Watts, Timothy, 2010. Long run health impacts of income shocks: wine and phylloxera in 19th century France. The Review of Economics and Statistics (forthcoming).

Banzhaf, Spencer, Walsh, Randall P., 2008. Do people vote with their feet? an empirical test of tiebout. American Economic Review 98 (3), 843–863.

Barker, D.J.P. (Ed.), 1992. Fetal and infant origins of adult disease. British Medical Journal.

Barnett, W.S., Masse, Leonard N., 2007. Comparative cost-benefit analysis of the Abecedarian program and its policy implications. Economics of Education Review 26, 113–125.

Barnett, Steven, Belfield, Clive R., Nores, Milagros, Schweinhart, Lawrence, 2006. The High/Scope Perry Preschool program: cost-benefit analysis using data from the age-40 follow-up. The Journal of Human Resources 41 (1), 162–190.

Barreca, Alan, 2010. The long-term economic impact of *in utero* and postnatal exposure to malaria. Journal of Human Resources 45 (4), 865–892.

Basiotis, Peter, Kramer-LeBlanc, Carol S., Kennedy, Eileen T., 1998. Maintaining nutrition security and diet quality: the role of the Food Stamp program and WIC. Family Economics 11 (1-2), 4–16.

Baten, Jörg, Crayen, Dorothee, Voth, Joachim, 2007. Poor, hungry and stupid: numeracy and the impact of high food prices in industrializing Britain, 1780-1850. Economics Working Papers 1120, Department of Economics and Business, Universitat Pompeu Fabra, October.
URL http://ideas.repec.org/p/upf/upfgen/1120.html.

Baum, Charles L., 2008. The effects of food stamp benefits on weight gained by expectant mothers. Discussion Paper 1343-08, Institute for Research on Poverty, September.

Becker, Gary S., Tomes, Nigel, 1976. Child endowments and the quantity and quality of children. The Journal of Political Economy 84 (4), S143–S162.

Behrman, Richard E., Butler, Adrienne S. (Eds.), 2007. Preterm Birth: Causes, Consequences, and Prevention. Institute of Medicine Report. National Academies Press.

Behrman, Jere R., Pollak, Robert A., Taubman, Paul, 1982. Parental preferences and provision for progeny. Journal of Political Economy 90 (1), 52–73.

Behrman, Jere R., Rosenzweig, Mark R., 2004. Returns to birthweight. The Review of Economics and Statistics 86 (2), 586–601.

Behrman, Jere R., Rosenzweig, Mark R., Taubman, Paul, 1994. Endowments and the allocation of schooling in the family and in the marriage market: the twins experiment. Journal of Political Economy 102 (6), 1131–1174.

Van Den Berg, Gerard J., Lindeboom, Maarten, Portrait, France, 2006. Economic conditions early in life and individual mortality. American Economic Review 96 (1), 290–302.

Van Den Berg, Gerard J., Lindeboom, Maarten, Portrait, France, 2010. Long-run longevity effects of a nutritional shock early in life: the Dutch potato famine of 1846-1847. Journal of Health Economics (in press).

Berger, Lawrence M., Hill, Jennifer, Waldfogel, Jane, 2005. Maternity leave, early maternal employment, and child health and development in the us. The Economic Journal 115, F29–F47.

Berger, Lawrence M., Paxson, Christina, Waldfogel, Jane, 2009. Income and child development. Children and Youth Services Review 31 (9), 978–989.

Bingley, Paul, Walker, Ian, 2007. There's no such thing as a free lunch: altruistic parents and the response of household food expenditures to nutrition program reforms. Discussion Paper 2007-19, University College Dublin Geary Institute, June.

Bitler, Marianne, Currie, Janet, 2005. Does WIC work? the effect of WIC on pregnancy and birth outcomes. Journal of Policy Analysis and Management 24 (1), 73–91.

Black, Maureen M., Cutts, Diana B., Frank, Deborah A., Geppert, Joni, Skalicky, Anne, Levenson, Suzette, Casey, Patrick H., Berkowitz, Carol, Zaldivar, Nievves, Cook, John T., Meyers, Alan F., Herren, Tim, 2004. Special supplemental nutrition program for women, infants, and children participation and infants' growth and health: a multi-site surveillance study. Pediatrics 114 (1), 169–176.

Black, Sandra E., Devereux, Paul J., Salvanes, Kjell G., 2005. The more the merrier? The effect of family size and birth order on children's education. Quarterly Journal of Economics 120 (2), 669–700.

Black, Sandra E., Devereux, Paul J., Salvanes, Kjell G., 2007. From the cradle to the labor market? The effect of birth weight on adult outcomes. Quarterly Journal of Economics 122 (1), 409–439.

Blanden, Jo, Gregg, Paul, MacMillan, Lindsey, 2006. Explaining intergenerational income persistence: non-cognitive skills, ability and education. CMPO Working Paper Series 06/146, University of Bristol, The Centre for Market and Public Organisation, April. URL www.bris.ac.uk/Depts/CMPO/.

Blau, David, Currie, Janet, 2006. Pre-school, day care, and after-school care: Who's minding the kids? 2: 1163–1278.

Bleakley, Hoyt, 2007. Disease amd development: evidence from hookworm eradication in the south. The Quarterly Journal of Economics 122 (1), 73.

Blow, Laura, Walker, Ian, Zhu, Yu, 2005. Who benefits from child benefit. manuscript, February.

Blundell, Richard, 2006. Earned income tax credit policies: impact and optimality: the Adam Smith lecture, 2005. Labour Economics (ISSN: 0927-5371) 13 (4), 423–443. European Association of Labour Economists, 2nd World Conference SOLE/EALE, Fairmont Hotel San Francisco, USA, 2-5 June 2005.

Boyer, George R., 1990. An Economic History of the English Poor Law. CUP, Cambridge, 1750–1850.

Bozzoli, Carlos, Deaton, Angus S., Quintana-Domeque, Climent, 2010. Child mortality, income and adult height. NBER Working Paper No. 12966, March. Demography (forthcoming).

Brooks-Gunn, Jeanne, Markham, Lisa B., 2005. The contribution of parenting to ethnic and racial gaps in school readiness. The Future of Children 15 (1), 139–168.

Butler, J.S., Raymond, Jennie E., 1996. The effect of the Food Stamp program on nutrient intake. Economic Inquiry 34, 781–798.

Card, David, Shore-Sheppard, Laura, 2004. Using discontinuous eligibility rules to identify the effects of the federal Medicaid expansions on low-income children. Review of Economics and Statistics 86 (3), 752–766.

Carneiro, Pedro, Ginja, Rita, 2008. Preventing behavior problems in childhood and adolescence: evidence from Head Start. manuscript, March.

Cascio, Elizabeth U., 2009. Do investments in universal early education pay off? long-term effects of introducing kindergartens into public schools. Working Paper 14951, National Bureau of Economic Research, May.

Case, Anne, Fertig, Angela, Paxson, Christina, 2005. The lasting impact of childhood health and circumstance. Journal of Health Economics 24, 365–389.

Case, Anne, Lee, Diana, Paxson, Christina, 2008. The income gradient in children's health: a comment on Currie, Shields, and Wheatley price. Journal of Health Economics 27 (3), 801–807.

Case, Anne, Lubotsky, Darren, Paxson, Christina, 2002. Economic status and health in childhood: the origins of the gradient. American Economic Review 92 (5), 1308–1334.

Case, Anne, Paxson, Christina, 2008a. Height, health, and cognitive function in old age. American Economic Review: Papers & Proceedings 98 (2), 463–467.

Case, Anne, Paxson, Christina, 2008b. Stature and status: height, ability, and labor market outcomes. Journal of Political Economy 116 (3), 499–532.

Case, Anne, Paxson, Christina, 2009. Early life health and cognitive function in old age. American Economic Review Papers and Proceedings 99 (2), 104–109.

Case, Anne, Paxson, Christina, 2010a. Causes and consequences of early life health. Working Paper 15637, National Bureau of Economic Research, January. URL http://www.nber.org/papers/w15637.

Case, Anne, Paxson, Christina, 2010b. The long reach of childhood health and circumstance: evidence from the Whitehall II study. Working Paper 15640, National Bureau of Economic Research, January. URL http://www.nber.org/papers/w15640.

Chatterji, Pinka, Brooks-Gunn, Jeanne, 2004. Wic participation, breastfeeding practices, and well-child care among unmarried, low-income mothers. American Journal of Public Health 94 (8), 1324–1327.

Chatterji, Pinka, Markowitz, Sarah, 2000. The impact of maternal alcohol and illicit drug use on children's behavior problems: evidence from the children of the national longitudinal survey of youth. Working Paper 7692, National Bureau of Economic Research.

Chatterji, Pinka, Bonuck, Karen, Dhawan, Simi, Deb, Nandini, 2002. WIC participation and the initiation and duration of breastfeeding. Discussion Paper No. 1246-02. Madison, WI: Institute for Research on Poverty.

Chay, Kenneth Y., Greenstone, Michael, 2003a. Air quality, infant mortality, and the Clean Air Act of 1970. Working Paper 10053, National Bureau of Economic Research, October. URL http://www.nber.org/papers/w10053.

Chay, Kenneth Y., Greenstone, Michael, 2003b. The impact of air pollution on infant mortality: evidence from the geographic variation in pollution shocks induced by a recession. Quarterly Journal of Economics 118 (3), 1121–1167.

Chay, Kenneth Y., Guryan, Jonathan, Mazumder, Bhashkar, 2009. Birth cohort and the black-white achievement gap: the roles of access and health soon after birth. Working Paper 15078, National Bureau of Economic Research, June. URL http://www.nber.org/papers/w15078.

Chiang, Alpha C., 1984. Fundamental Methods of Mathematical Economics, third edition, McGraw-Hill, New York.

Condliffe, Simon, Link, Charles R., 2008. The relationship between economic status and child health: evidence from the United States. American Economic Review 98 (4), 1605–1618.

Conley, Dalton, Bennett, Neil G., 2001. Birth weight and income: interactions across generations. Journal of Health and Social Behavior (ISSN: 00221465) 42 (4), 450–465. URL http://www.jstor.org/stable/3090189.

Conley, Dalton, Pfeiffer, Katherine M., Velez, Melissa, 2007. Explaining sibling differences in achievement and behavioral outcomes: the importance of within- and between-family factors. Social Science Research 36 (3), 1087–1104.

Conley, Dalton, Strully, Kate W., Bennett, Neil G., 2006. Twin differences in birth weight: the effects of genotype and prenatal environment on neonatal and post-natal mortality. Economics and Human Biology 4 (2), 151–183.

Costa, Dora L., Lahey, Joanna N., 2005. Predicting older age mortality trends. Journal of the European Economic Association 3 (2–3), 487–493.

Crimmins, Eileen M., Finch, Caleb E., 2006. Infection, inflammation, height, and longevity. Proceedings of the National Academy of Sciences 103 (2), 498–503.

Cunha, Flavio, Heckman, James, 2007. The technolgy of skill formation. American Economic Review 97 (2), 31–47.

Cunha, Flavio, Heckman, James J., 2008. Formulating, identifying and estimating the technology of cognitive and noncognitive skill formation. Journal of Human Resources 43 (4), 738–782. URL http://jhr.uwpress.org/cgi/content/abstract/43/4/738.

Cunha, Flavio, Heckman, James, Schennach, Susanne, 2010. Estimating the technology of cognitive and noncognitive skill formation. Econometrica 78 (3), 883–931.

Currie, Alison, Shields, Michael, Price, Stephen W., 2007. Is the child health/family income gradient universal? Evidence from England. Journal of Health Economics 26 (2), 213–232.

Currie, Janet, 2003. US food and nutrition programs. In: Moffitt, Robert (Ed.), Means-tested Transfer Programs in the United States. University of Chicago Press for NBER, Chicago, IL, pp. 199–290.

Currie, Janet, Cole, Nancy, 1993. Welfare and child health: the link between AFDC participation and birth weight. The American Economic Review 83 (4), 971–985.

Currie, Janet, Gahvari, Firouz, 2008. Transfers in cash and in-kind; theory meets the data. Journal of Economic Literature 46 (2), 333–383.

Currie, Janet, Grogger, Jeffrey, 2002. Medicaid expansions and welfare contractions: offsetting effects on prenatal care and infant health. Journal of Health Economics 21 (2), 313–335.

Currie, Janet, Gruber, Jonathan, 1996a. Health insurance eligibility, utilization of medical care, and child health. The Quarterly Journal of Economics 111 (2), 431–466.

Currie, Janet, Gruber, Jonathan, 1996. Saving babies: the efficacy and cost of recent changes in the Medicaid eligibility of pregnant women. Journal of Political Economy 104 (6), 1263. URL http://www.journals.uchicago.edu/doi/abs/10.1086/262059.

Currie, Janet, Hyson, Rosemary, 1999. Is the impact of shocks cusioned by socioeconomic status? The case of low birth weight. American Economic Review 89 (2), 245–250.

Currie, Janet, Moretti, Enrico, 2007. Biology as destiny? short- and long-run determinants of intergenerational transmission of birth weight. Journal of Labor Economics 25 (2), 231–264. URL http://www.journals.uchicago.edu/doi/abs/10.1086/511377.

Currie, Janet, Moretti, Enrico, 2008. Short and long-run effects of the introduction of food stamps on birth outcomes in California. In: Schoeni, R.F., House, J., Kaplan, G., Pollack, H. (Eds.), Making Americans Healthier: Social and Economic Policy as Health Policy. Russell Sage, New York.

Currie, Janet, Neidell, Matthew, 2005. Air pollution and infant health: what can we learn from California's recent experience? Quarterly Journal of Economics 120 (3), 1003–1030. URL http://www.mitpressjournals.org/doi/abs/10.1162/003355305774268219.

Currie, Janet, Stabile, Mark, 2003. Socioeconomic status and child health: why is the relationship stronger for older children? American Economic Review 93 (5), 1813–1823.

Currie, Janet, Stabile, Mark, 2006. Child mental health and human capital accumulation: the case of ADHD. Journal of Health Economics 25 (6), 1094–1118.

Currie, Janet, Tekin, Erdal, 2006. Does child abuse cause crime? Working Paper 12171, National Bureau of Economic Research, April. URL http://www.nber.org/papers/w12171.

Currie, Janet, Thomas, Duncan, 1995. Does Head Start make a difference? American Economic Review 85 (3), 341–364.

Currie, Janet, Thomas, Duncan, 1999a. Does Head Start help Hispanic children? Journal of Public Economics (ISSN: 0047-2727) 74 (2), 235–262.

Currie, Janet, Thomas, Duncan, 1999b. Early test scores, socioeconomic status and future outcomes. Working Paper 6943, National Bureau of Economic Research, February. URL http://www.nber.org/papers/w6943.

Currie, Janet, Walker, Reed, 2009. Traffic congestion and infant health: evidence from E-Zpass. Working Paper 15413, National Bureau of Economic Research, October. URL http://www.nber.org/papers/w15413.

Currie, Janet, Widom, Cathy S., 2009. Long-term consequences of child abuse and neglect on adult economic well-being. Manuscript, September.

Currie, Janet, Yelowitz, Aaron, 2000. Are public housing projects good for kids? Journal of Public Economics (ISSN: 0047-2727) 75 (1), 99–124.

Currie, Janet, Decker, Sandra, Lin, Wanchuan, 2008. Has public health insurance for older children reduced disparities in access to care and health outcomes? Journal of Health Economics 27 (6), 1567–1581.

Currie, Janet, Neidell, Matthew, Schmieder, Johannes F., 2009. Air pollution and infant health: lessons from New Jersey. Journal of Health Economics 28 (3), 688–703.

Currie, Janet, Stabile, Mark, Manivong, Phongsack, Roos, Leslie L., 2010. Child health and young adult outcomes. The Journal of Human Resources 45 (3), 517–548.

Cutler, David M., Miller, Grant, Norton, Douglas M., 2007. Evidence on early-life income and late-life health from America's Dust Bowl era. Proceedings of the National Academy of Sciences 104 (33), 13244–13249. URL http://www.pnas.org/content/104/33/13244.abstract.

Dafny, Leemore, Gruber, Jonathan, 2005. Public insurance and child hospitalizations: access and efficiency effects. Journal of Public Economics 89 (1), 109–129. URL http://ideas.repec.org/a/eee/pubeco/v89y2005i1p109-129.html.

Dahl, Gordon, Lochner, Lance, 2008. The impact of family income on child achievement: evidence from the earned income tax credit. Working Paper 14599. National Bureau of Economic Research, December. URL http://www.nber.org/papers/w14599.

Dahl, Gordon B., Lochner, Lance, 2005. The impact of family income on child achievement. Working Paper 11279, National Bureau of Economic Research, April. URL http://www.nber.org/papers/w11279.

Dalenius, Tore, Reiss, Steven P., 1982. Data swapping: a technique for disclosure control. Journal of Statistical Planning and Inference 6 (1), 73–85.

Datar, Ashlesha, Kilburn, Rebecca, Loughran, David S., 2010. Endowments and parental investments in infancy and early childhood. Demography 47 (1), 145–162.

Dearden, Lorraine, 1998. Ability, family, education, and earnings in Britain. Working Paper 98/114, Institute for Fiscal Studies, July.

Del Bono, Emilia, Ermisch, John, Francesconi, Marco, 2008. Intrafamily resource allocations: a dynamic model of birth weight. IZA Discussion Papers 3704, Institute for the Study of Labor (IZA), September. URL http://ideas.repec.org/p/iza/izadps/dp3704.html.

Deming, David, 2009. Early childhood intervention and life-cycle skill development. American Economic Journal: Applied Economics 1 (3), 111–134.

Deschnes, Olivier, Greenstone, Michael, 2007. Climate change, mortality, and adaptation: evidence from annual fluctuations in weather in the US. NBER Working Paper No. 13178, June.

Doblhammer, Gabriele, Vaupel, James W., 2001. Lifespan depends on month of birth. Proceedings of the National Academy of Sciences 98 (5), 2934–2939.

Doyle Jr., Joseph J., 2008. Child protection and adult crime: using investigator assignment to estimate causal effects of foster care. Journal of Political Economy 116 (4), 746–770. URL http://www.journals.uchicago.edu/doi/abs/10.1086/590216.

Doyle, Orla, Walker, Ian, Harmon, Colm P., 2005. The impact of parental income and education on the health of their children. Discussion Paper 5359, Centre for Economic Policy Research, December.

Dubay, Lisa, Joyce, Ted, Kaestner, Robert, Kenney, Genevieve M., 2001. Changes in prenatal care timing and low birth weight by race and socioeconomic status: implications for the medicaid expansions for pregnant women. Health Services Research 36 (2), 373–398.

Duggan, Anne K., McFarlane, Elizabeth, Fuddy, Loretta, Burrell, Lori, Higman, Susan M., Windham, Amy, Sia, Calvin, 2004. Randomized trial of a statewide home visiting program: impact on preventing child abuse and neglect. Child Abuse and Neglect 28 (6), 597–622.

Duggan, A.K., McFarlane, E.C., Windham, A.M., Rohde, C., Salkever, D.S., Fuddy, L., Rosenberg, L.A., Buchbinder, S.B., Sia, C.C.J., 1999. Evaluation of Hawaii's Healthy Start Program. The Future of Children 9 (1), 66–90.

DuMont, Kimberly, Mitchell-Herzfeld, Susan, Greene, Rose, Lee, Eunju, Lowenfels, Ann, Rodriguez, Monica, 2006. Healthy families New York (hfny) randomized trial: impacts on parenting after the first two years. Working Paper Series: evaluating Healthy Families New York 1, New York State Office of Children & Family Services, June.

Dustmann, Christian, Schönberg, Uta, 2009. The effect of expansions in maternity leave coverage on children's long-term outcomes. SSRN eLibrary.

Eissa, Nada, Liebman, Jeffrey B., 1996. Labor supply response to the earned income tax credit. The Quarterly Journal of Economics 113 (3), 653–691.

Farrelly, Matthew C., Nimsch, Christian T., James, Joshua, 2003. State cigarette excise taxes: Implications for revenue and tax evasion. Report 08742.000, RTI International, Research Triangle Park, NC, May.

Fergusson, David M., Grant, Hildegard, Horwood, L. John, Ridder, Elizabeth M., 2006. Randomized trial of Early Start program of home visitation. Pediatrics 117 (3), 803–809.

Fertig, Angela R., Reingold, David A., 2007. Public housing, health, and health behaviors: Is there a connection? Journal of Policy Analysis and Management 26 (4), 831–859.

Field, Erica, Robles, Omar, Torero, Maximo, 2009. Iodine deficiency and schooling attainment in Tanzania. American Economic Journal: Applied Economics 1 (4), 140–169.

Figlio, David, Hamersma, Sarah, Roth, Jeffrey, 2009. Does prenatal WIC participation improve birth outcomes? new evidence from Florida. Journal of Public Economics 93 (1–2), 235–245.

Fletcher, Jason M., Lehrer, Steven F., 2009. Using genetic lotteries within families to examine the causal impact of poor health on academic achievement. Working Paper 15148, National Bureau of Economic Research, July. URL http://www.nber.org/papers/w15148.

Frank, Richard G., Meara, Ellen, 2009. The effect of maternal depression and substance abuse on child human capital development. Working Paper 15314, National Bureau of Economic Research, September.

Frisvold, David E., 2006. Head Start participation and childhood obesity. Working Paper 06-WG01, Vanderbilt University, February.

Frisvold, David E., Lumeng, Julie C., 2009. Expanding exposure: can increasing the daily duration of Head Start reduce childhood obesity? manuscript, April.

Garces, Eliana, Thomas, Duncan, Currie, Janet, 2002. Longer-term effects of Head Start. American Economic Review 92 (4), 999–1012.

Gertler, Paul J., 2004. Do conditional cash transfers improve child health? Evidence from Progresa's control randomized experiment. Health, Health Care, and Economic Development 94 (2), 336–341.

Gluckman, Peter D., Hanson, Mark A., 2006. Adult disease: echoes of the past. European Journal of Endocrinology 155 (Suppl. 1), S47–S50.

Gormley Jr., William, 2008. The effects of Oklahoma's pre-K program on Hispanic children. Social Science Quarterly 89 (4), 916–936.

Gormley Jr., William, Gayer, Ted, 2006. Promoting school readiness in Oklahoma: an evaluation of Tulsa's pre-K program. The Journal of Human Resources 40 (3), 533–558.

Gormley Jr., William, Gayer, Ted, Phillips, Deborah, Dawson, Brittany, 2005. The effects of universal pre-K on cognitive development. Developmental Psychology 41 (6), 872–884.

Goux, Dominique, Maurin, Eric, 2005. The effects of overcrowded housing on children's performance at school. Journal of Public Economics 89 (5-6), 797–819.

Griliches, Zvi, 1979. Sibling models and data in economics: beginnings of a survey. Journal of Political Economy 87 (s5), S37. URL http://www.journals.uchicago.edu/doi/abs/10.1086/260822.

Grossman, Michael, 1972. On the concept of health capital and the demand for health. Journal of Political Economy 223–255.

Gueorguieva, Ralitza, Morse, Steven B., Roth, Jeffrey, 2009. Length of prenatal participation in WIC and risk of delivering a small for gestational age infant: Flordida, 1996-2004. Journal of Maternal and Child Health 13 (4), 479–488.

Gundersen, Craig, Ziliak, James, 2004. Poverty and macroeconomic performance across space, race, and family structure. Demography 41 (1), 61–86.

Hanratty, Maria J., 1996. Canadian national health insurance and infant health. American Economic Review (ISSN: 00028282) 86 (1), 276–284. URL http://www.jstor.org/stable/2118267.

Harding, Kathryn, Galano, Joseph, Martin, Joanne, Huntington, Lee, Schellenbach, Cynthia J., 2007. Healthy Families America effectiveness: a comprehensive review of outcomes. Journal of Prevention and Intervention in the Community 34 (1-2), 149–179.

Havnes, Tarjei, Mogstad, Magne, 2009. No child left behind: universal child care and children's long-run outcomes. Discussion Paper 582, Statistics Norway, Research Department, May.

Heckman, James, 2007. The economics, technology, and neuroscience of human capability formation. PNAS 104 (33), 13250–13255.

Heckman, James, Moon, Seong H., Pinto, Rodrigo, Savelyev, Peter A., Yavitz, Adam, 2009. The rate of return to the High/Scope Perry preschool program. Working Paper 15471, National Bureau of Economic Research, November.

Heckman, James J., Rubinstein, Yona, 2001. The importance of noncognitive skills: lessons from the GED testing program. American Economic Review: Papers & Proceedings 91 (2), 145–149.

Heider, Fritz, 1934. The influence of the epidemic of 1918 on deafness: a study of birth dates of pupils registered in schools for the deaf. American Journal of Epidemiology 19, 756–765.

Howard, Kimberly S., Brooks-Gunn, Jeanne, 2009. The role of home visiting programs in preventing child abuse and neglect. The Future of Children 19 (2), 119–146.

Hoynes, Hilary W., Page, Marianne, Stevens, Ann H., 2009. Is a WIC start a better start? evaluating WIC's impact on infant health using program introduction. Working Paper 15589, National Bureau of Economic Research, December.

Hoynes, Hilary W., Schanzenbach, Diane, 2009. Consumption responses to in-kind transfers: evidence from the introduction of the Food Stamp program. American Economic Journal: Applied Economics 1 (4), 109–139.

Hsin, Amy, 2009. Is biology destiny? Birth weight and differential parental treatment. Manuscript, Population Studies Center, University of Michigan.

Hustedt, Jason T., Barnett, W. Steven, Jung, Kwanghee, Figueras, Alexandra, 2008. Impacts of new Mexico pre-K on children's school readiness at kindergarten entry: Results from the second year of a growing initiative. Research report, National Institute for Early Education, Rutgers University, June.

Jacob, Brian, 2004. Public housing, housing vouchers, and student achievement: evidence from public housing demolitions in Chicago. American Economic Review 94 (1), 233–258.

Johnson, Rucker C., Schoeni, Robert F., 2007. The influence of early-life events on human capital, health status, and labor market outcomes over the life course. Working Paper 07-05, National Poverty Center, February.

Joyce, Theodore, Gibson, Diane, Colman, Sylvie, 2004. The changing association between prenatal participation in WIC and birth outcomes in New York city. Working Paper 10796, National Bureau of Economic Research, September.

Joyce, Theodore, Racine, Andrew D., Yunzal-Butler, Cristina, 2007. Reassessing the WIC effect: evidence from the pregnancy nutrition surveillance system. Journal of Policy Analysis and Management 87 (2), 277–303.

Kaestner, Robert, Joyce, Ted, Racine, Andrew, 2001. Medicaid eligibility and the incidence of ambulatory care sensitive hospitalizations for children. Social Science and Medicine 52 (2), 305–313.

Karoly, Lynn A., Kilburn, Rebecca M., Cannon, Jill S., 2005. Early Childhood Interventions: Proven Results, Future Promise. RAND Corporation.

Karoly, Lynn A., Greenwood, Peter W., Everingham, Susan S., Hoube, Jill, Kilburn, M. Rebecca, Rydell, C. Peter, Sanders, Matthew, Chiesa, James, 1998. Investing in our children: what we know and don't know about the costs and benefits of early childhood interventions. Consensus report, Rand, July.

Kehrer, Barbara H., Wolin, Charles M., 1979. Impact of income maintenance on low birth weight: evidence from the Gary experiment. The Journal of Human Resources 14 (4), 434–462. autumn.

Kelly, Elaine, 2009. The scourge of Asian flu: *in utero* exposure to pandemic influenza and the development of a cohort of British children. Institute for Fiscal Studies, Working Paper 09/17, September. University College London.

Kermack, W.O., McKendrick, A.G, McKinlay, P.L., 1934. Death-Rates in Great Britain and Sweden. The Lancet 698–703.

Khanam, Rasheda, Nghiem, Hong S., Connelly, Luke B., 2009. Child health and the income gradient: evidence from Australia. Journal of Health Economics 28 (4), 805–817.

Kling, Jeffrey R., Liebman, Jeffrey B., Katz, Lawrence F., 2007. Experimental analysis of neighborhood effects. Econometrica 75 (1), 83–119.

Kling, Jeffrey R., Ludwig, Jeffrey, Katz, Lawrence F., 2005. Neighborhood effects on crime for female and male youth: evidence from a randomized housing voucher experiment. The Quarterly Journal of Economics 120 (1), 87–130.

Knittel, Christopher R., Miller, Douglas L., Sanders, Nicholas J., 2009. Caution drivers! children present: Traffic, pollution and infant health. Manuscript, UC Davis.

Koch, Thomas G., 2009. Public insurance, crowd-out, and health care utilization. Manuscript, August.

Kowaleski-Jones, Lori, Duncan, Greg J., 2002. Effects of participation in the WIC program on birthweight: evidence from the National Longitudinal Survey of Youth. Am J Public Health 92 (5), 799–804. URL http://ajph.aphapublications.org/cgi/content/abstract/92/5/799.

Kraemer, Sebastian, 2000. The fragile male. BMJ 321 (7276), 1609–1612. URL http://www.bmj.com.

Lee, Bong J., Mackey-Bilaver, Lee, 2007. Effects of WIC and Food Stamp program participation on child outcomes. Children and Youth Services Review 29 (4), 501–517.

Lefebvre, Pierre, Merrigan, Philip, Verstraete, Matthieu, 2006. Impact of early childhood care and education on children's preschool cognitive development: Canadian results from a large quasi-experiment. Working Paper 06-36, Centre interuniversitaire sur le risque, les politiques conomiques et lemploi (CIRPEE), October.

Levine, Philip B., Schanzenbach, Diane W., 2009. The impact of children's public health insurance expansions on educational outcomes. Forum for Health Economics and Policy 12 (1), Article 1.

Levine, Phillip B., Zimmerman, David J., 2000. Children's welfare exposure and subsequent development. Working Paper 7522, National Bureau of Economic Research, February. URL http://www.nber.org/papers/w7522.

Lhila, Aparna, Simon, Kosali I., 2008. Prenatal health investment decisions: does the childs sex matter? Demography 45 (4), 885–905.

Lien, Diana S., Evans, William N., 2005. Estimating the Impact of large cigarette tax hikes: the case of maternal smoking and infant birth weight. J. Human Resources XL (2), 373–392. URL http://jhr.uwpress.org/cgi/content/abstract/XL/2/373.

Lin, Ming-Jen, Liu, Jin-Tan, 2009. Do lower birth weight babies have lower grades? twin fixed effect and instrumental variable evidence from Taiwan. Social Science & Medicine 68 (10), 1780–1787.

Logan, W.P.D., Glasg, M.D., 1953. Mortality in London fog incident, 1952. Lancet 1 (1), 336–338.

Love, John M., Kisker, Ellen E., Ross, Christine, Constantine, Jill, Boller, Kimberly, Chazan-Cohen, Rachel, Brady-Smith, Christy, Fuligni, Allison S., Raikes, Helen, Brooks-Gunn, Jeanne, Tarullo, Louisa B., Schochet, Peter Z., Paulsell, Diane, Vogel, Cheri, 2005. The effectiveness of Early Head Start for 3-year-old children and their parents: lessons for policy and programs. Developmental Psychology 41 (6), 885–901.

Ludwig, Jens, Miller, Douglas L., 2005. Does Head Start improve children's life chances? evidence from a regression discontinuity design. Discussion Paper 1311-05, Institute for Research on Poverty, November.

Ludwig, Jens, Miller, Douglas L., 2007. Does Head Start improve children's life chances? evidence from a regression discontinuity design. Quarterly Journal of Economics 488 (1), 159–208.

MacDorman, Marian F., Martin, Joyce A., Mathews, T.J., Hoyert, Donna L., Ventura, Stephanie J., 2005. Explaining the 2001-2002 infant mortality increase in the United States: data from the linked birth/infant death data set. International Journal of Health Services 35 (3), 415–442.

MacMillan, Harriet L., Thomas, B. Helen, Jamieson, Ellen, Walsh, Christine A., Boyle, Michael H., Shannon, Harry S., Gafni, Amiram, 2005. Effectiveness of home visitation by public health nurses in prevention of the recurrence of child physical abuse: a randomized controlled trial. Lancet 365 (9473), 1786–1793.

Macours, Karen, Schady, Norbert, Vakis, Renos, 2008. Cash transfers, behavioral changes, and cognitive development in early childhood: evidence from a randomized experiment. Working Paper 4759, The World Bank: Development Research Group, Human Development and Public Services Team, October.

Magnuson, Katherine A., Ruhm, Christopher, Waldfogel, Jane, 2007. Does pre-kindergarten improve school preparation and performance? Economics of Education Review 26 (1), 33–51.

Masse, Leonard, Barnett, W. Steven, 2002. A Benefit-cost Analysis of the Abecedarian Early Childhood Intervention. National Institute for Early Education Research, Rutgers, NJ.

McCormick, Marie C., Brooks-Gunn, Jeanne, Buka, Stephen L., Goldman, Julie, Yu, Jennifer, Salganik, Mikhail, Scott, David T., Bennett, Forrest C., Kay, Libby L., Bernbaum, Judy C., Bauer, Charles R., Martin, Camilia, Woods, Elizabeth R., Martin, Anne, Casey, Patrick H., 2006. Early intervention in low birth weight premature infants: results at 18 years of age for the infant health and development. Pediatrics 117 (3), 771–780.

McIntosh, Emma, Barlow, Jane, Davis, Hilton, Stewart-Brown, Sarah, 2009. Economic evaluation of an intensive home visiting programme for vulnerable families: a cost-effectiveness analysis of public health intervention. Journal of Public Health 31 (3), 423–433.

McLeod, Jane, Kaiser, Karen, 2004. Childhood emotional and behavioral problems and educational attainment. American Sociological Review 69 (5), 636–658.

Meyer, Bruce D., Rosenbaum, Dan T., 2001. Welfare, the earned income tax credit, and the labor supply of single mothers. Quarterly Journal of Economics 116 (3), 1063–1114. URL http://www.mitpressjournals.org/doi/abs/10.1162/00335530152466313.

Milligan, Kevin, Stabile, Mark, 2008. Do child tax benefits affect the wellbeing of children? evidence from Canadian child benefit expansions. Working Paper 14624, National Bureau of Economic Research, December. URL http://www.nber.org/papers/w14624.

Morris, Pamela, Duncan, Greg J., Rodrigues, Christopher, 2004. Does money really matter? estimating impacts of family income on children's achievement with data from random-assignment experiments. Manuscript.

Newman, Sandra J., Harkness, Joseph M., 2002. The long-term effects of public housing on self-sufficiency. Journal of Policy Analysis and Management 21 (1), 21–43.

Nilsson, Peter, 2008. Does a pint a day affect your child's pay? the effect of prenatal alcohol exposure on adult outcomes. Centre for Microdata Methods and Practice Working Paper CWP22/08, The Institute for Fiscal Studies, August.

Nilsson, Peter, 2009. e long-term effects of early childhood lead expsoure: evidence from sharp changes in local air lead levels induced by the phase-out of leaded gasoline. manuscript, Uppsala University, September.

Oaxaca, Ronald L., 1973. Male-female wage differentials in urban labor markets. International Economic Review 14, 693–709.

Olds, David L., Henderson, Charles R., Kitzman, Harriet J., Eckenrode, John J., Cole, Robert E., Tatelbaum, Robert C., 1999. Prenatal and infancy home visitation by nurses: recent findings. The Future of Children 9 (1), 44–65. Spring-Summer.

Olds, David L., Kitzman, Harriet, Hanks, Carole, Cole, Robert, Anson, Elizabeth, Sidora-Arcoleo, Kimberly, Luckey, Dennis W., Henderson Jr., Charles R., Holmberg, John, Tutt, Robin A., Stevenson, Amanda J., Bondy, Jessica, 2007. Effects of nurse home visiting on maternal and child functioning: age-9 follow-up of a randomized trial. Pediatrics 120 (4), 832–845.

Olds, David L., Robinson, JoAnn, O'Brien, Ruth, Luckey, Dennis W., Pettitt, Lisa M., Henderson Jr., Charles R., Ng, Rosanna K., Sheff, Karen L., Korfmacher, Jon, Hiatt, Susan, Talmi, Ayelet, 2002. Home visiting by paraprofessionals and by nurses: a randomized controlled trial. Pediatrics 110 (3), 486–496. URL http://pediatrics.aappublications.org/cgi/content/abstract/110/3/486.

Oreopoulos, Phil, Stabile, Mark, Walld, Randy, Roos, Leslie, 2008. Short, medium, and long-term consequences of poor infant health: an anlysis using siblings and twins. Journal of Human Resources 43 (1), Winter.

Oreopoulos, Philip, 2003. The long-run consequences of living in a poor neighborhood. Quarterly Journal of Economics 118 (4), 1533–1575. URL http://www.mitpressjournals.org/doi/abs/10.1162/003355303322552865.

Orr, Larry, Feins, Judith D., Jacob, Robin, Beecroft, Erik, Sanbonmatsu, Lisa, Katz, Lawrence F., Liebman, Jeffrey B., Kling, Jeffrey R., 2003. Moving to opportunity: interim impacts evaluation. Final report, US Department of Housing and Urban Development, Office of Policy Development and Research, June.

Pitt, Mark, Rosenzweig, Mark, Hassan, Nazmul, 1990. Productivity, health, and inequality in the intrahousehold distribution of food in low-income countries. American Economic Review 80 (5), 1139–1156.

Propper, Carol, Rigg, John, Burgess, Simon, 2007. Child health: evidence on the roles of family income and maternal mental health from a UK birth cohort. Health Economics 16 (11), 1245–1269.

Puma, Michael, Bell, Stephen, Cook, Ronna, Heid, Camilla, Shapiro, Gary, Broene, Pam, Jenkins, Frank, Fletcher, Philip, Quinn, Liz, Friedman, Janet, Ciarico, Janet, Rohacek, Monica, Adams, Gina, Spier, Elizabeth, 2010. Head start impact study: Final report; executive summary. Technical report, Administration for Children and Families. US Department of Health and Human Services, January.

Rasmussen, Kathleen Maher, 2001. The "fetal origins" hypothesis: challenges and opportunities for maternal and child nutrition. Annual Review of Nutrition 21, 73–95.

Reyes, Jessica Wolpaw, 2007. Environmental policy as social policy? the impact of childhood lead exposure on crime. Working Paper 13097, National Bureau of Economic Research, May. URL http://www.nber.org/papers/w13097.

Reznek, Arnold, 2007. Methods of confidential data protection. VirtualRDC powerpoint presentation, Cornell University, April. URL http://www.vrdc.cornell.edu/news/.

Rosenzweig, Mark R., Paul Schultz, T., 1982. Market opportunities, genetic endowments, and intrafamily resource distribution: child survival in rural India. American Economic Review 72 (4), 803–815.

Rosenzweig, Mark R., Wolpin, Kenneth I., 1988. Heterogeneity, intrafamily distribution, and child health. Journal of Human Resources 23 (4), 437–461.

Royer, Heather, 2009. Separated at girth: US twin estimates of the effects of birth weight. American Economic Journal: Applied Economics 1 (1), 49–85.

Ruhm, Christopher J., 2004. Parental employment and child cognitive development. The Journal of Human Resources 39 (1), 155–192.

Rush, David, Stein, Zena, Susser, Mervyn, 1980. Diet in Pregnancy: a Randomized Controlled Trial of Nutritional Supplements. Alan R. Liss, Inc., New York.

Salm, Martin, Schunk, Daniel, 2008. The role of childhood health for the intergenerational transmission of human capital: evidence from administrative data. Discussion Paper 3646, The Institute for the Study of Labor (IZA), August.

Sanbonmatsu, Lisa, Kling, Jeffrey R., Duncan, Greg J., Brooks-Gunn, Jeanne, 2006. Neighborhoods and academic achievement. Journal of Human Resources 41 (4), 649–690.

Schanzenbach, Diane W., What are food stamps worth. American Economic Journal - Economic Policy (forthcoming).

Scherjon, Sicco A., Oosting, Hans, Ongerboer de Visser, Bram W., deWilded, Ton, Zondervan, Hans A., Kok, Joke H., 1996. Fetal brain sparing is associated with accelerated shortening of visual evoked potential latencies during early infancy. American Journal of Obstetrics and Gynecology 175 (6), 1569–1575.

Sloan, Frank A., Conover, Christopher J., Rankin, Peter J., 2001. Effects of Tennessee Medicaid managed care on obstetrical care and birth outcomes. Journal of Health Politics, Policy, and Law 26 (6), 1291–1324.

Smith, James P., 2009. The impact of childhood health on adult labor market outcomes. The Review of Economics and Statistics 91 (3), 478–489.

Smith, James P., Smith, Gillian C., 2008. Long-term economic costs of psychological problems during childhood. Manuscript, October.

Smolensky, E., Gootman, J. Appleton, 2003. Working Families and Growing Kids: Caring for Children and Adolescents. The National Academies Press, Washington, DC.

Solon, Gary, 1999. Chapter Intergenerational mobility and the labor market. In: Ashenfelter, Orley, Card, David (Eds.), Handbook of Labor Economics, vol. 3. Elsevier, pp. 1761–1800.

St. Pierre, Robert G., Layzer, Jean I., 1999. Using home visits for multiple purposes: the comprehensive child development program. The Future of Children 9 (1), 134–151.

Stein, Zena, Susser, Mervyn, Saenger, Gerhart, Marolla, Francis, 1975. Famine and Human Development: the Dutch Hunger Winter of 1944-1945. Oxford University Press, New York.

Tominey, Emma, 2007. Maternal smoking during pregnancy and early child outcomes. CEP Discussion Papers dp0828, Centre for Economic Performance, LSE, October.
    URL http://ideas.repec.org/p/cep/cepdps/dp0828.html.

Vujic, Suncica, Konig, Pierre, Webbinnk, Dinand, Martin, Nick, 2008. The effect of childhood conduct disorder on human capital. Discussion Paper 3646, CPB Netherlands Bureau for Economic Policy Analysis, November.

Wong, Vivian C., Cook, Thomas D., Barnett, W. Steven, Jung, Kwanghee, 2008. An effectiveness-based evaluation of five state pre-kindergarten programs. Journal of Policy Analysis and Management 27 (1), 122–154.

Zweifel, Peter, Breyer, Friedrich H.J., Kifmann, Mathias, 2009. Health Economics, second edition, Oxford University Press.

CHAPTER 16

Recent Developments in Intergenerational Mobility ☆

Sandra E. Black [*], Paul J. Devereux [**]

[*] Department of Economics, University of Texas at Austin, IZA and NBER
[**] School of Economics and Geary Institute, University College Dublin, CEPR and IZA

Contents

Abstract

Economists and social scientists have long been interested in intergenerational mobility, and documenting the persistence between parents and children's outcomes has been an active area of

☆ We would like to thank Anders Bjorklund, Dan Hamermesh, Helena Holmlund, Kanika Kapur, Gary Solon, Alexandra Spitz-Oener, and Steve Trejo for helpful comments. Prudence Kwenda provided excellent research assistance. Devereux thanks the Irish Research Council for the Humanities and Social Sciences (IRCHSS) for financial support. This chapter was completed while Black was on leave from the economics department at UCLA.

E-mail addresses: sblack@austin.utexas.edu (Sandra E. Black), devereux@ucd.ie (Paul J. Devereux).

Handbook of Labor Economics, Volume 4b
© 2011 Elsevier B.V.

ISSN 0169-7218, DOI 10.1016/S0169-7218(11)02414-2

research. However, since Gary Solon's 1999 Chapter in the Handbook of Labor Economics, the literature has taken an interesting turn. In addition to focusing on obtaining precise estimates of correlations and elasticities, the literature has placed increased emphasis on the causal mechanisms that underlie this relationship. This chapter describes the developments in the intergenerational transmission literature since the 1999 Handbook Chapter. While there have been some important contributions in terms of measurement of elasticities and correlations, we focus primarily on advances in our understanding of the forces driving the relationship and less on the precision of the correlations themselves.

JEL classification: D1; D3; J3; J6

Keywords: Intergenerational transmission; Education; Income mobility; Inequality of income; Intergenerational income mobility

INTRODUCTION

Economists and social scientists have long been interested in intergenerational mobility, and documenting the persistence between parents and children's outcomes has been an active area of research. However, since Gary Solon's 1999 Chapter in the Handbook of Labor Economics, the literature has taken an interesting turn. In addition to focusing on obtaining precise estimates of correlations and elasticities, the literature has placed increased emphasis on the causal mechanisms that underlie this relationship.

This chapter describes the developments in the intergenerational transmission literature since the 1999 Handbook Chapter. While there have been some important contributions in terms of measurement of elasticities and correlations, we will focus primarily on advances in our understanding of the forces driving the relationship and less on the precision of the correlations themselves. Also, since intergenerational research has mostly used data from Europe and North America, our summary is largely restricted to these countries.

Which brings us to the motivation for all of this research: What is the "optimal" amount of intergenerational mobility? Many people favor equality of opportunity as an underlying goal of society—the idea that poor children should have the same opportunities for success as rich children. Those who work hard should be able to succeed, regardless of family background. However, zero intergenerational correlation is not necessarily the optimum.

In order to determine a socially optimal level of mobility, it is important to understand the underlying causes or determinants of the intergenerational correlation in earnings or education. As noted in Solon (2004), children of wealthy parents earn higher incomes in part because they invest more in human capital and have more education. As a result, observing zero intergenerational correlation would suggest no return to human capital investment, and it would be a strange market economy if higher human capital was not rewarded with higher earnings. This does, however, highlight the importance of understanding the mechanisms underlying the observed intergenerational correlations; if they are in fact due to differential human capital investment, this suggests a role for public provision or financing of education to equalize opportunities.

In a similar manner, there may be genetic differences in ability that are transmitted from parent to child and that lead to intergenerational persistence in income or education. To the extent that this is the underlying cause of the intergenerational correlation in income or education, it may suggest a more limited role for policy.[1]

Overall, differences in ability and human capital will tend to lead to an intergenerational correlation of greater than zero in any well-functioning market economy. Policies that compel employers to favor less qualified applicants in terms of employment or pay may reduce the intergenerational correlation but at a high cost to society in terms of efficiency and incentives for human capital accumulation. As such, they are not necessarily desirable. On the other hand, the use of connections to get jobs by the children of the wealthy when other candidates are better qualified is manifestly inefficient, and the component of the intergenerational correlation due to nepotism would be considered by most to best be eradicated.

The structure of the chapter is as follows: In the first section, we describe recent advances in the methodology for estimating intergenerational earnings and education persistence and provide an overview of the empirical findings. As noted above, throughout the handbook chapter, we focus explicitly on more recent advances in the literature, particularly since the publication of Solon's 1999 handbook chapter. Section 2 describes and critically evaluates the main methods that have been used to identify causal effects of parental earnings and education. In Section 3, we move away from earnings and education and discuss the literature on the intergenerational correlations of other family background factors. Finally, Section 4 concludes.

1. INTERGENERATIONAL CORRELATIONS OF EARNINGS AND EDUCATION

Perhaps the most basic empirical relationship in this literature relates the earnings of parents to those of their children. Given that this equation is usually estimated using log earnings for both parents and children, the resultant estimate is the intergenerational earnings elasticity. We will consider the benchmark regression:

$$\log(Y_1) = \alpha + \beta \log(Y_0) + \varepsilon. \tag{1}$$

Using lowercase for logs, and taking deviations from population means to remove the intercept, we can write this as

$$y_1 = \beta y_0 + e. \tag{2}$$

[1] Of course, the policy implications of the genetic/environmental distinction are not so clear cut, as genetic differences can be influenced by policy—a famous example is that genetic deficiencies in eye sight can be ameliorated by the provision of spectacles (Goldberger, 1979). Similarly, minimum wages can increase the earnings of low-skill workers.

Here the subscript 1 refers to the child, 0 refers to the parent, and y is a measure of permanent earnings. The parameter β is the intergenerational elasticity (henceforth, IGE) and $(1 - \beta)$ is a measure of intergenerational mobility.

The intergenerational correlation (ρ) is an alternative to the elasticity that has also been widely used in the literature. The correlation between the log earnings of parent and child equals the elasticity provided that the standard deviation of log earnings is the same for both generations. To see this, note that the intergenerational correlation

$$\rho = (\sigma_0/\sigma_1)\beta \tag{3}$$

where σ is the standard deviation of log earnings. The correlation therefore factors out the cross-sectional dispersion of log earnings in the two generations. In contrast, the elasticity can be higher in one society than in another simply because the variance of log earnings in the child's generation is higher in that society. This is related to the fact that the correlation is bounded between 0 and 1 while the elasticity, in principle, could be greater than one and would, for example, equal 2 if people from families who were 10% apart in generation 0, were 20% apart in generation 1. We don't believe one measure should be seen as dominating the other but it is important to be aware of their differing properties, particularly when making comparisons across time or place. One practical advantage of the elasticity is that, unlike the correlation, it is not biased by classical measurement error in y_1 and so is often easier to estimate with real-world data.

1.1. Issues in estimating the intergenerational elasticity of earnings

There are a number of recent developments in terms of the estimation of intergenerational income elasticities. Once again, we consider the benchmark regression in Eq. (2):

$$y_1 = \beta y_0 + \varepsilon.$$

The important issue for measurement is that y should be a measure of permanent earnings. The data requirements are obviously challenging as few datasets have information that allows the calculation of lifetime earnings for both fathers and sons. For now, we will consider the regression of son's permanent earnings on father's permanent earnings.[2] As is well known, the estimate of β will be biased if father's permanent earnings are measured with error, but not if son's earnings are subject to classical measurement error.[3]

---

[2] The literature has mostly focused on sons so, in this section, we will report only on father/son correlations and elasticities. We describe results for both sons and daughters in Section 1.2.

[3] We use the term measurement error to describe deviations between permanent earnings and whatever measure of earnings is used to proxy for it. This remains an issue even if annual earnings are reported accurately.

Early estimates of the intergenerational elasticity tended to use earnings in one year for both fathers and sons; however, pioneering work by Solon (1992) and Zimmerman (1992) demonstrated that sizeable biases arose from this approach and improved measurement of father's earnings by averaging over 4 or 5 years. Recent research has focused on obtaining better estimates of permanent earnings by (1) averaging over even more years of data to allow for persistent transitory shocks and (2) paying careful attention to the ages of both fathers and sons at the time earnings are measured.

Persistent transitory shocks

Assume $y_{0a} = y_0 + v_a$ where a is the age of the father when earnings are measured and v (assumed uncorrelated with y_0) is the deviation between measured earnings at age a and permanent earnings. If v is a purely transitory shock, the attenuation factor in the intergenerational elasticity when one year of data is used equals $\frac{\text{var}(y_0)}{\text{var}(y_0)+\text{var}(v)}$, i.e. $p \lim \hat{\beta} = (\frac{\text{var}(y_0)}{\text{var}(y_0)+\text{var}(v)})\beta$.

If we instead average earnings over T years for each father, the attenuation factor becomes $\frac{\text{var}(y_0)}{\text{var}(y_0)+\text{var}(v)/T}$ and so the bias rapidly declines with T. Solon (1992) demonstrates the impact of allowing first-order persistence in v using MA(1) and AR(1) processes and Mazumder (2005) emphasizes the importance of such persistence using an AR(1) process. Suppose $v_a = \delta v_{a-1} + \omega_a$ and ω_a is iid. The attenuation factor now becomes $\frac{\text{var}(y_0)}{\text{var}(y_0)+\gamma\text{var}(v)/T}$ where $\gamma = 1 + 2\delta(\frac{T-(1-\delta^T)/(1-\delta)}{T(1-\delta)})$.

Clearly if $\delta > 0$, the attenuation bias is larger than in the purely transitory case for any value of $T > 1$. Mazumder (2005) illustrates this point using simulations for different values of δ and T and benchmark values for the variances of y_0 and v. He finds that, if $\delta = 0.5$, the attenuation factor is 0.69 when earnings are averaged over 5 years; this contrasts with an attenuation factor of 0.83 in the same circumstances with $\delta = 0$. He suggests that intergenerational elasticity estimates from the US of about 0.4 using 5-year averages should be scaled up to about 0.4/0.69, close to 0.6. Also, the simulations show that averaging over 20 to 30 years may be necessary to obtain attenuation factors that are about 0.9 or higher.

Mazumder (2005) also uses the 1984 SIPP data matched to the Social Security Administration's Summary Earnings Records (SER) to provide empirical estimates in which T is allowed to vary up to 16 years. He finds that the IGE estimate rises from about 0.25 when $T = 2$, to 0.45 when $T = 7$, and up to 0.61 when $T = 16$. Overall, these estimates suggest that, at least in the US, a high value of T is required in order to accurately estimate the IGE.[4]

---

[4] Using Norwegian register data, Nilsen et al. (2008) find that averaging extra years of father's earnings has smaller effects on the estimated IGE. These smaller effects may be the result of lower transitory variation in earnings in Norway compared to the US, and they suggest that Mazumder's findings may be US-specific.

Ages of fathers and sons

To get a sense of how the ages of father and son matter, consider the following simple model based on Haider and Solon (2006).[5] Assume earnings for fathers and sons are measured at a particular age, a.[6]

$$y_{0a} = \mu_a y_0 + v \tag{4}$$

$$y_{1a} = \lambda_a y_1 + u. \tag{5}$$

This parameterization of the model allows for the fact that one-period earnings may be a better proxy for life-time earnings at some ages than at others. Assuming that the error terms are uncorrelated with each other and with lifetime earnings (which may be a strong assumption as fathers and sons may have similar career paths), the probability limit of the estimate of the intergenerational elasticity is

$$\beta \left[\frac{\lambda_a \mu_a \text{var}(y_0)}{\mu_a^2 \text{var}(y_0) + \text{var}(v)} \right] = \beta \lambda_a \theta_a$$

where $\theta_a = p[\frac{\mu_a \text{var}(y_0)}{\mu_a^2 \text{var}(y_0) + \text{var}(v)}]$.

This simple model has several implications. First, if $\lambda_a = \mu_a = 1$, then this is the standard errors-in-variables model and the intergenerational elasticity suffers from attenuation bias. Second, even when $\lambda_a = \mu_a = 1$, the extent of the attenuation bias may depend on father's age, as $\text{var}(v)$ may itself depend on age.[7] Baker and Solon (2003) and Mazumder (2005) provide evidence that $\text{var}(v)$ varies over the life-cycle and is at its minimum at around age 40. Third, θ_a can exceed 1 and is increasingly likely to as μ_a becomes smaller. Therefore, in general the bias to the intergenerational elasticity need not be an attenuation bias. Fourth, measurement error in the dependent variable (y_1) causes bias so long as μ_a does not equal one, and the size of the bias potentially depends on the age of the son.

Lifecycle bias

Lifecycle bias occurs when λ_a or μ_a take different values at different ages. This is an important issue in practice, as data limitations make it likely that fathers' earnings are measured relatively late in the lifecycle while sons' earnings are typically measured at quite young ages. With complete information on earnings over a full career, it is possible to estimate λ_a and θ_a at each age.

---

[5] For earlier work on this topic, see Jenkins (1987).

[6] Note that the analysis does not rely on the age of fathers and sons being the same.

[7] In the literature, this is not referred to as life-cycle bias; this phrase is reserved for the case where λ_a or μ_a take different values at different ages.

Haider and Solon (2006) show that λ_a can be estimated by simply regressing log earnings at age a on the log of the present value of lifetime earnings (which can be calculated if earnings over the entire career are observed). Similarly, θ_a can be estimated as the slope coefficient in the reverse regression of the log of the present value of earnings on the log of earnings at age a. They use social security earnings of persons sampled in the US Health and Retirement Survey (HRS) who agreed to allow access to their earnings histories. The analysis uses earnings from 1951 to 1991 and so covers most of the careers of the 821 men studied. Because the SSA earnings data are censored at the taxable limit, they use a multi-step procedure in estimation and require distributional assumptions. Böhlmark and Lindquist (2006) use Swedish register data to carry out a similar exercise to that of Haider and Solon. Because their earnings data are not censored, they estimate λ_a and θ_a using the simple regressions described above.

Both papers come to quite similar conclusions: Estimates of λ_a are low when men are in their twenties (as low as 0.2 in the US before age 25). The main reason for this is that men who will have high lifetime earnings typically have faster earnings growth and, so, the early-career earnings gap between low and high lifetime earners tends to underestimate the gap in lifetime earnings. Estimates of λ_a rise to be close to 1 once men reach their thirties and remain high until their late forties. However, by the late fifties, estimates of λ_a have declined to about 0.6. Remember that λ_a represents the attenuation bias that arises because the son's earnings at age a may not be representative of his life-time earnings. These estimates suggest that there could be large attenuation biases if earnings of sons aged younger than 30 are included in the analysis.

The estimates of θ_a are also similar in the two studies: the estimate starts at about 0.2 at age 20 and rises to about 0.6-0.7 by age 30. It stays about that value until the late 40s and then declines slowly to about 0.4-0.5 in the late 50s. Given that θ_a represents the bias component that results from mis-measurement of father's earnings, we see that, as with sons, it is optimal to measure earnings in the middle of the life cycle. However, even when earnings are measured then, the attenuation factor still rises to only about 0.7 and so there remains significant attenuation bias.[8]

Consistent with the analyses by Haider and Solon (2006) and Böhlmark and Lindquist (2006), Grawe (2006) provides two distinct sources of evidence of life-cycle bias. First, he uses estimates from 20 studies that use a variety of datasets from a number of different countries and shows that there is a negative correlation between age of father at measurement and size of the estimated IGE. Importantly, he finds that father's age at measurement accounts for 20% of the variance of estimates across the studies. Second, he uses four different datasets (the National Longitudinal Survey, PSID, German Socieconomic Panel (GSOEP), and the Canadian Intergenerational Income Data (IID)) to estimate the IGE while varying the father's age at measurement. Once again, in each dataset, he finds that

---

[8] Brenner (2010) examines life-cycle bias using German data and finds estimates for men that are similar to those of Böhlmark and Lindquist (2006).

the estimated IGE tends to fall as father's age increases. Finally, building on earlier work by Reville (1995), he shows that, for any given father's age, the IGE tends to increase as son's age increases.

Most recently, Nilsen et al. (2008) use Norwegian register data to investigate life-cycle bias. Consistent with earlier work, they find that estimated IGEs in father–son regressions decrease by about 1.1% for each extra year of father's age. These results are interesting as they show that, despite the large differences between the US and Norwegian labor markets, lifecycle bias is a problem of similar magnitude in each.

Transition matrices

While much of the literature has focused on estimating the IGE, this summary measure may conceal interesting detail about intergenerational mobility at different points of the joint distribution of parental and child earnings. An alternative strategy is to study mobility matrices and examine the quantile of the child's earnings conditional on the parent's earnings quantile. In addition to providing greater information across the distribution, transition matrices allow one to compare mobility rates of population subgroups across the full earnings distribution rather than just across the earnings distribution for that group. This is impossible with IGE estimation, as splitting the sample by group shows the degree of regression to the subgroup mean not the mean of the whole population.

In practice, researchers often group quantiles. For example, Jäntti et al. (2006) split the earnings distributions into quintiles and study mobility across quintiles. Bhattacharya and Mazumder (2007) criticize this standard transition matrices approach for relying on arbitrary discretizations of the distribution (for example, quintiles or quartiles). They propose a new measure of upward mobility—the probability that a son's percentile rank in the earnings distribution of sons exceeds the father's percentile rank in the earnings distribution of fathers. In effect, this implies more weight is placed on small moves, as mobility is noted even if it does not involve the son's quintile (or other discrete measure) being different from the quintile of the father.[9] Using data from the National Longitudinal Survey of Youth (NLSY), they show that the distinction can matter in practice as the degree of upward mobility of blacks is found to be more similar to that of whites when the new measure is used. This highlights the fact that results can vary based on the exact metric used and suggests the value of showing the robustness of estimates to different approaches.

The same issues with imperfect measures of lifetime earnings that arise in estimating the IGE manifest themselves when using mobility approaches. As in the IGE literature, researchers have tended to deal with this by averaging earnings over several years.[10] O'Neill et al. (2007) directly study the effect of measurement error on transition

---

[9] This method also relies on an arguably arbitrary discretization; for a parent in the 20th percentile, a child who moves to the 21st percentile is counted the same as a child who moves to the 95th percentile.

[10] For example, Bhattacharya and Mazumder (2007) average sons' earnings over 3 years and fathers' earnings over 4 years.

matrices. They allow for measurement error in both fathers' and sons' earnings and carry out simulations that vary both the variance of the measurement error and the correlation of the error between father and son. They find that classical measurement error in sons' earnings leads to an overestimate of mobility, with the largest bias in the bottom tail. Interestingly, when both fathers' and sons' earnings are measured with error, the impact depends on the correlation between the measurement errors. With low correlation, the measurement error leads to an overstatement of mobility; high correlations can lead to an understatement. As a result, they caution that measured mobility differences across countries or across the earnings distribution may result from data measurement issues rather than true differences.

1.2. Recent estimates of the IGE by country and over time

By now, there is a large set of estimates of intergenerational mobility from a range of different countries. The availability of large register-based samples has led to a particularly credible set of estimates for Nordic countries that have generally confirmed a higher level of mobility than in the US and UK. However, as described below, careful study of nonlinearities has shown that these differences are not uniform across the earnings distribution.

Given the large number of studies and the fact that estimation methods, variable definitions, and sample selection rules differ widely, we begin by describing results from Jäntti et al. (2006) who estimate elasticities and correlations for 6 countries in a comparable fashion.[11] They use the National Longitudinal Survey of Youth (NLSY) for the US, the National Child Development Study (NCDS) for the UK, and register data for the Nordic countries. To minimize lifecycle bias, they use fathers aged about 45 and sons and daughters aged between 30 and 42. Because they need to use a similar approach across all countries, they use only one year of earnings data for fathers. As such, these estimates should not be considered as definitive for any particular country; they are useful because they allow a comparison of the relative magnitude of the IGE across countries when similar data and sampling rules are used.

Estimates for son earnings

The top panel of Table 1 provides a summary of IGE estimates and estimated correlations for sons by country (Denmark, Finland, Norway, Sweden, the UK, and the US) from Jäntti et al. (2006).[12] Both the elasticities and correlations suggest an ordering with the lowest persistence in the Nordic countries, higher persistence in the UK, and the highest persistence in the US. These findings are generally consistent with others in the literature. Based on Table 1 and Mazumder (2005), a reasonable guess is an IGE in the

---

[11] In the last decade there have been several papers that survey international IGE estimates at length. These include Björklund and Jäntti (2009), Blanden (2009), Corak (2006), Grawe (2004), and Solon (2002).

[12] The differences between the elasticities and correlations reflect differences in the variances of earnings in the fathers' and sons' generations. For example, the elasticity is higher than the correlation for the US due to the increase in earnings inequality in recent decades.

Table 1 Elasticity and correlations from Jäntti et al. (2006).

Country	Elasticity	Correlation
Men		
Denmark	0.071	0.089
	[0.064, 0.079]	[0.079, 0.099]
Finland	0.173	0.157
	[0.135, 0.211]	[0.128, 0.186]
Norway	0.155	0.138
	[0.137, 0.174]	[0.123, 0.152]
Sweden	0.258	0.141
	[0.234, 0.281]	[0.129, 0.152]
UK	0.306	0.198
	[0.242, 0.370]	[0.156, 0.240]
US	0.517	0.357
	[0.444, 0.590]	[0.306, 0.409]
Women		
Denmark	0.034	0.045
	[0.027, 0.041]	[0.036, 0.054]
Finland	0.080	0.074
	[0.042, 0.118]	[0.045, 0.103]
Norway	0.114	0.084
	[0.090, 0.137]	[0.070, 0.099]
Sweden	0.191	0.102
	[0.166, 0.216]	[0.090, 0.113]
UK	0.331	0.141
	[0.223, 0.440]	[0.099, 0.183]
US	0.283	0.160
	[0.181, 0.385]	[0.105, 0.215]

Numbers in brackets below the point estimates show the bias corrected 95% bootstrap confidence interval.
Source: This reproduces much of Table 2 from Jäntti et al. (2006).

US of about 0.5 to 0.6. A reasonable guess for the UK is about 0.3 (see also Nicoletti and Ermisch (2007) and Blanden et al. (2004)). Elasticities for the Nordic countries are almost always found to be lower than 0.3.[13]

Jäntti et al. (2006) also use transition matrices to estimate mobility by quintile in these countries. They find that more than 40% of sons in the US who are born to fathers in the lowest quintile are in the lowest quintile themselves. Mobility from the lowest quintile is found to be much higher in Norway and Denmark. Interestingly, they find that the

[13] There are also estimates for many other countries. Examples include the following: Italy has been estimated to have an IGE of about 0.5 (Piraino, 2007; Mocetti, 2007); Lefranc and Trannoy (2005) estimate the IGE for France at about 0.4. In contrast, much lower estimates have been found for Australia (Leigh, 2007), Canada (Corak and Heisz, 1999), and Germany (Vogel, 2008).

much larger estimated IGE in the US and UK compared to the Nordic countries is almost entirely due to differences in the tails. In addition to much higher mobility from the bottom quintile in the Nordic countries, there is much higher mobility from the top quintile in these countries as well. On the other hand, mobility between the middle three quintiles is fairly similar across all countries.[14]

Bratsberg et al. (2007) use data from the US, UK, Denmark, Finland, and Norway to test for nonlinearities in the IGE. They show that while the IGE is close to linear in father's income in the US and UK, the pattern is convex in the three Nordic countries.[15] For example, in Denmark, the IGE is 0.06 at the 10th percentile but 0.31 at the 90th percentile. They suspect that the convexity in the Nordic countries is related to the strong public education systems that exist in these countries.

Estimates for daughter earnings

Until lately, most of the literature focused on the intergenerational correlation between fathers and sons, and there were few IGE estimates for daughters. However this situation has changed in recent years.[16] The bottom half of Table 1 contains the Jäntti et al. (2006) estimates for father–daughter elasticities and correlations. We can see that these are smaller than the equivalent father–son ones.[17] The pattern across countries is similar to that for sons, with smaller IGEs in the Nordic countries and larger ones in the US and UK.

Raaum et al. (2007) provide a framework to understand why IGEs may differ between women and men. The primary mechanisms are assortative mating and labor supply responses. Assortative mating implies that women from high income families are likely to marry high-earning men, and negative cross-wage or income elasticities of labor supply imply that they then choose fewer hours of work and, as a result, end up with lower labor earnings.[18] On the other hand, it is generally found that women have higher own-wage labor supply elasticities than men, and this factor tends to raise the female IGE relative to that of men.

Interestingly, Raaum et al. (2007) find that men and women have very similar inter-generational persistence of earnings capacity (as measured by returns-adjusted education)

---

[14] Using Canadian data, Corak and Heisz (1999) show using transition matrices that there is much more mobility in the middle of the distribution than in the tails.

[15] In contrast, Couch and Lillard (2004) find using the PSID that the IGE declines with father's income in the US. Bratsberg et al. (2007) use NLSY data for the US and it is not clear why their result differs.

[16] When studying daughters, the focus is sometimes on the effects of father's earnings and sometimes on joint earnings of father and mother.

[17] For the US, Mazumder (2005) finds estimates are similar for daughters and sons. However, Scandinavian evidence generally suggests that intergenerational earnings persistence is lower for women than for men when measured by individual earnings. See Österberg (2000), Österbacka (2001), Bratberg et al. (2005, 2007), Raaum et al. (2007), Holmlund (2008), Hirvonen (2008), and Nilsen et al. (2008).

[18] Single women do not experience this cross-wage effect and so should be expected to have higher IGEs than married women.

in the US, UK, and Nordic countries. This is consistent with labor supply playing a large role in reducing women's IGE relative to men. Also, they show that, among married women, US estimates of the relationship between parental income and own earnings are quite similar to those from the Nordic countries and lower than those from the UK. This surprising finding can be explained by assortative mating, with the cross-wage effects dominating in the US while own-wage labor supply elasticities are more important in the Nordic countries.

Estimates for family earnings

Given the prevalence of two-adult households, total family earnings are, in addition to individual earnings, an important subject of study. Chadwick and Solon (2002) find that, in the US, the elasticity of daughters' family earnings with respect to their parents' income is about 0.4. Here, assortative mating can have a very strong influence. Strikingly, they also show that individual earnings of husbands and wives are as highly correlated with the incomes of their in-laws as with the incomes of their own parents. Ermisch et al. (2006) conclude that about 40% of family income persistence in the UK and Germany results from assortative mating.

We have seen that there are large differences in IGEs across countries for both sons and daughters. Despite differences in the degree of assortative mating and the size of own and cross-wage labor supply elasticities across countries, Raaum et al. (2007) find that the cross-country patterns of intergenerational transmission of family earnings are quite similar to the cross-country patterns of IGEs for sons and daughters.

Changes in IGEs over time

The recent literature has also started to focus on how intergenerational persistence has changed over time. US studies have had to deal with the problems of small sample sizes for specific cohorts and have found little evidence of statistically significant trends over time (Lee and Solon, 2009). In the UK, the available evidence suggests an increase in the IGE for cohorts born between the late 1950s and the 1970s (Blanden et al., 2004; Nicoletti and Ermisch, 2007). Lefranc and Trannoy (2005) find no evidence of a trend for France. Bratberg et al. (2005) find some evidence of a decrease in persistence over time in Norway and Pekkala and Lucas (2007) similarly find declines in the IGE in Finland. Overall, the available evidence suggests no broad trends in persistence across Europe and North America but, possibly, an increase in mobility in Nordic countries coincident with the formation of strong welfare states.

Why the IGE may differ across countries and over time

Solon (1999) outlines a simple theoretical model, based on Becker and Tomes (1979), that provides an interpretation of the intergenerational earnings correlation. Intergenerational transmission occurs both because higher-earning parents invest more in their children's human capital, and because children of such parents also tend to have higher endowments arising from genetics or from environmental influences in childhood.

More recently, Solon (2004) expands this model to allow for governmental investment in the child's human capital that may be progressive in the sense that the ratio of government investment to parental income decreases with parental income. This model implies that the intergenerational elasticity is increasing in the heritability of earnings-related endowments and the earnings return to human capital investment, but is decreasing in the progressivity of government investments.[19] A significant contribution of this model is that it describes a simple optimizing framework that underlies the standard empirical approach of estimating the IGE.

The Solon (2004) model has four fundamental equations. First, the budget constraint assumes families must allocate all after-tax lifetime income to either parental consumption (C_0) or investment in the child (I_0):

$$(1 - \tau)Y_0 = C_0 + I_0. \tag{6}$$

Human capital of the child is produced by a semi-log production function:

$$h_1 = \theta \log(I_0 + G_0) + e_1. \tag{7}$$

Here e_1 is the initial endowment of the child and G_0 is governmental investment in the child's human capital. Child endowments are assumed to follow an AR(1) process;

$$e_1 = \delta + \lambda e_0 + v_1, \tag{8}$$

where λ is between 0 and 1 and v is white noise. The earnings equation is

$$\log(Y_1) = \mu + ph_1 \tag{9}$$

where p is the return to a unit of human capital.

The family maximizes utility which equals $U = (1 - \alpha) \log(C_0) + \alpha \log(Y_1)$, where α measures the degree of altruism towards the child. Solon (2004) makes an additional parameterization that $G_0/[(1 - \tau)Y_0] = \varphi - \gamma \log(Y_0)$. A positive value of γ signifies that the ratio of government investment to after-tax income is decreasing in income, so γ can be interpreted as a measure of the progressivity of government spending on children. By maximizing the utility function with respect to parental investment and collecting terms, one arrives at

$$\log Y_1 = \mu^* + [(1 - \gamma)\theta p] \log Y_0 + pe_0 \tag{10}$$

---

[19] Ichino et al. (2009) endogenize governmental human capital investments and show that the intergenerational elasticity in any society may be influenced by political economy concerns. Societies where better off families have more influence on the political process will tend to have lower redistributive human capital investments and hence higher intergenerational persistence.

which takes the exact form of the standard IGE regression. Note that Eq. (8) implies that $\log Y_0$ is correlated with the error term in Eq. (10). Solon (2004) shows that, in steady state where the variance of log earnings is the same in both generations, the probability limit of the OLS estimator of the coefficient on log fathers' earnings in (10) is

$$\frac{(1 - \gamma)\theta p + \lambda}{1 + (1 - \gamma)\theta p \lambda}.$$

Thus, the estimated IGE (and intergenerational correlation) will be greater if (1) the heritability coefficient λ is higher so ability is more highly correlated across generations, (2) θ is higher so that the human capital accumulation process is more efficient, (3) earnings returns to human capital are higher so p is larger, or (4) governmental investment in human capital is less progressive so γ is smaller.

Given that the heritability of endowments is unlikely to differ significantly across developed countries or over time (and differences in the efficiency of the education system are hard to measure), explanations for differences across countries tend to focus on differences in the returns to skills (primarily education) and differences in government investments. For example, the low IGEs for Nordic countries could be explained either by their compressed earnings distributions (low returns to skills) or by social and educational policies regarding childcare and education that tend to equalize educational opportunities for children.[20] We focus here on the second type of explanations.[21]

It is widely believed that countries with better public education systems should have lower IGEs.[22] Ichino et al. (2009) correlate the estimated IGE in 10 countries (Denmark, Finland, Canada, Sweden, Germany, France, US, UK, Spain, and Australia) with public expenditure on education and find it equals −0.54; they report that the correlation is even stronger when they focus on public expenditure on primary education.[23] They also find a large positive cross-country correlation between the rich-poor gap in political participation (as measured by membership of a political party) and the IGE. These results suggest that political economy considerations are important in determining policy and thus influencing the IGE. However, given the evidence is purely cross-sectional for only 12 countries, more work in this area is warranted.

Mayer and Lopoo (2008) use the PSID and find that intergenerational earnings elasticities are higher in low per-child spending US states compared to higher-spending

---

[20] For example, Norway has free public education up to and including University-level as well as a universal subsidized public childcare system.

[21] There is some work that calculates cross-country correlations of returns to education and/or measures of cross-sectional inequality with intergenerational persistence (for example, Blanden, 2009). Unfortunately, given small sample sizes and the fact that countries differ in many ways, this evidence is only suggestive of important labor market factors.

[22] See Davies et al. (2005) for one theoretical exposition.

[23] Blanden (2009) finds a similar relationship across countries.

ones.[24] These estimates are robust to including fixed effects for the state the child resided in at age 15 (identification then comes from changes over time in state-level spending). A nice feature of this study is that, because they include state dummies, they are not reliant on cross-sectional variation across states. Future research using more narrowly defined measures of expenditures on children and exogenous sources of variation in these expenditures would be valuable. Also, further work on the differential effects of state investments at various child ages on intergenerational transmission would be useful.

Pekkarinen et al. (2009) test the influence of the education system by examining the effects on the IGE of shifting from an early-tracking schooling system to a comprehensive system. They use the fact that, during the 1970s, a Finnish educational reform was implemented in different regions at different times over a 6-year period. They allow the IGE to depend on which system the child experienced while controlling for cohort and regional effects.

Pre-reform, all students entered primary school at age 7. After four years in the primary school, the students could apply to the general secondary school or continue in the primary school for two more years and, in some schools, continue classes for two further years. Critically, however, students who followed this second education track were not eligible for senior secondary schools or for university-level studies and so either did some vocational training or dropped out. The reform replaced this system with a nine-year comprehensive school that all children attended until age 16. Students then chose whether to apply to upper secondary schools or to vocational schools, and admission to both tracks was based solely on comprehensive school grades. Thus, tracking began much later after the reform. Pekkarinen et al. find that the IGE for sons fell from 0.3 to 0.23 as a result of the reform, suggesting that early school tracking reduces intergenerational mobility. The reform also involved curricula changes and increased educational attainment, so the exact interpretation is a bit clouded. However, it does provide evidence that the school system matters for the IGE.[25]

Machin (2007) shows that the expansion of higher education in the UK in the 1980s and 1990s led to a large increase in the proportion of children of high income families who have college degrees but a much smaller change for children of low income families. At the same time, he also shows that earnings mobility was higher for cohorts born in 1958 than for those born in subsequent decades, suggesting a link between access to higher education and intergenerational mobility.

---

[24] They divide the expenditures by the state population aged 0 to 17 to calculate per-child state expenditures in each year. They then average these per-child state expenditures over the 3 years when the child was aged 15 to 17.

[25] Holmlund (2008) also finds a reduction in the IGE arising from a similar school reform in Sweden. Consistent with this, Meghir and Palme (2005) find that the Swedish reform had a larger impact on the earnings of children of low-educated fathers.

1.3. Credit constraints and the IGE

In the Solon (2004) model of the previous section, families are credit constrained and must reduce current consumption to invest in child human capital. Some recent research has aimed to directly explore the effect of credit constraints on the IGE. Recent work on the theoretical background is provided by Han and Mulligan (2001), Grawe and Mulligan (2002), and Grawe (2004).[26] If there are no credit constraints, and thus parents can borrow from their children's future earnings, each family will optimally invest in the human capital of their children. If ability raises the marginal productivity of human capital accumulation, it will be optimal to invest more in high ability children. In this case, the IGE will be positive only if child ability and parental earnings are correlated and will depend on the strength of intergenerational ability correlations. If there are credit constraints, however, low income families may not be able to optimally invest in their children's human capital. As a result, extra income will lead to increased human capital investment. Therefore, we would expect that the IGE would be greater for credit constrained families, suggesting the presence of nonlinearities.

Testing this hypothesis is troublesome because it is difficult to identify which families are credit constrained. One approach is to assume that credit constraints are most severe for low income parents. However, Han and Mulligan (2001) point out that this effect may be mitigated because higher earning families are more likely to have high ability children and so may be credit constrained if returns to human capital rise with ability and education is costly. Also, educational policies are often designed so that access to lower levels of human capital formation is essentially free, while higher-level education can be expensive in some countries.

Indeed, Grawe (2004) shows that earnings-ability correlations could lead to varying types of nonlinearities, depending on the exact assumptions used. He also shows that, in the absence of credit constraints, there is no reason to believe that the relationship between y_1 and y_0 would be linear. Thus, he argues, searching for evidence of credit constraints from nonlinearities may be a fruitless exercise.[27]

A possibly more direct approach to testing for credit constraints is to try to identify groups who are more likely to be credit constrained. The model suggests that, for any given parental earnings, high ability children are more likely to be credit constrained. Grawe (2004) proxies ability with child earnings and tests his theory using quantile regression.[28] Credit constraints should imply that, particularly for sons of low-earning fathers, the IGE is higher at higher conditional quantiles. In fact, he finds the opposite

---

[26] They themselves build on earlier work by Becker and Tomes (1979) and Mulligan (1997).

[27] Björklund et al. (2008) use very large Swedish register samples to show that the IGE becomes large in the top percentile of the father's earnings distribution. This particular nonlinearity is hard to square with credit constraints as these are people with extremely high incomes.

[28] He acknowledges that this is a weak test as heteroskedasticity could lead to nonlinearities across the conditional quantiles.

and concludes that there is no evidence for credit constraints in his Canadian data. A disadvantage of this approach is that earnings depend on investments as well as abilities and so are endogenous to the presence of credit constraints.

In another effort to test for evidence of credit constraints, Mulligan (1997) uses PSID data and splits the sample by bequest behavior to create an "unconstrained" group of children who have received or expect to receive bequests of at least $25,000 (1989 dollars). He finds this group does not have significantly greater intergenerational mobility, suggesting credit constraints are unimportant. As one possible explanation, Mazumder (2005) notes that it is entirely possible that members of the "unconstrained" group were actually financially constrained when the child was young and this could mitigate the effect. He instead separates families by net worth (under or over the median) using the SIPP data. While he finds larger IGEs for low net worth families, the differences are generally not statistically significant.[29] Clearly there is a potential payoff to carrying out these exercises with larger datasets so that more precision can be obtained. However, even if the precision issue is dealt with, a more general problem is that any two groups (for example, the high net worth and low net worth groups) will differ along multiple dimensions, and it would dangerous to conclude that differences in IGEs come from credit constraints rather than some other set of factors.

1.4. Intergenerational transmission of education

In addition to earnings, educational attainment provides an important source of information about the lives of individuals; as a result, there has been extensive study of intergenerational transmission of education. As a practical matter, education has advantages over earnings in terms of estimation; with education, measurement issues are much less difficult. People tend to complete education by their mid twenties so, unlike with lifetime earnings, analysis can successfully take place when children are relatively early in the life-cycle. Also, non-employment causes no difficulties, and measurement error is likely to be much less of a problem as people tend to know their own educational attainment. Furthermore, there is now an extensive literature that shows that higher education is associated with many other beneficial characteristics such as higher earnings, better health and longer lifespans.[30]

Conceptually, we can think of the educational choice of children as depending on the cost of education, the return to education, and, in the case where families are credit-constrained, on family income. It is commonly assumed that the return to education is higher for high ability children and also for children of highly educated parents. These assumptions imply that children of highly educated parents will tend to choose higher

---

[29] Gaviria (2002), in the PSID, splits the sample using both bequests and family net worth but also generally finds no statistically significant differences.

[30] The extent to which these are causal effects is a subject of ongoing research.

education due both to the direct effect of having more educated parents (which could be interpreted as the causal channel), and the indirect effect of having higher ability. With credit constraints, the higher average income of highly educated parents is yet another reason for a positive relationship between parent and child education.

There are many possible underlying mechanisms that would lead to a direct effect of parental education on child education. First, as mentioned above, higher educated parents generally have higher incomes and income may impact educational attainment. Second, parental education may affect parental time allocation and the productivity of the parent in child-enhancing activities.[31] Third, education may change bargaining power in the household. More educated mothers may be more successful in directing expenditures towards child-friendly activities and investments. The focus of current research is on establishing a link between parent and child education; understanding the underlying mechanisms is a clear direction for future research.

Estimation issues

As mentioned above, compared to earnings, there are fewer difficult estimation issues when studying intergenerational correlations of education. However, there are still choices to be made regarding the measure of intergenerational persistence used. One strategy is to treat educational attainment as a continuous variable and calculate the parent–child correlation. Like the earnings correlation, this has the effect of factoring out the cross-sectional dispersion of education in the two generations. In contrast, the regression coefficient is affected by the relative variance of education across generations. If the standard deviation of education is lower in the parent's generation than in the child's, then the regression coefficient exceeds the correlation. This issue is of practical importance, as there have been large increases in educational attainment in recent decades and these have tended to cause a secular increase in the variance of education. Additionally, Hertz et al. (2007) show that, in recent decades, this secular increase has tended to occur at a decreasing rate, so changes over time in the correlation tend to be more positive (or less negative) than changes in the regression coefficient. Reporting both measures seems a sensible solution.

Of course, education is generally measured as a discrete variable and, as such, it is also natural to use methods that explicitly acknowledge that fact. Intergenerational mobility can be measured using transition matrices, where parental education is on one axis and child education on the other. For example, Chevalier et al. (2009) use two different indices that measure different types of mobility from one generation to the next. Unfortunately, these indices do not correlate very highly across countries, suggesting one should be cautious about relying too heavily on any one particular index.

---

[31] Guryan et al. (2008) show, using the American Time Use Survey, that more educated parents spend more time on average with their children.

Estimates by country and over time

Compared to earnings, there have been fewer advances in the estimation of intergenerational education correlations and elasticities since 1999, in part because there are fewer difficulties associated with timing and measurement. However, the evidence base has improved enormously. Hertz et al. (2007) provide an impressive survey of correlations and regression coefficients for a sample of 42 countries using comparable sample and variable definitions. In Table 2, we have taken Table 2 from their paper. They find that the correlations are highest in South America at about 0.6. They are typically about 0.4 in Western Europe, with the lowest estimates being for the Nordic countries. The US estimate is 0.46.

Chevalier et al. (2009) find generally similar results in their more limited sample of European countries and the US.[32] Consistent with theory, they find that intergenerational educational persistence is higher in countries with higher returns to education and lower in countries that spend more public funds on education. Other studies have found that particular features of the schooling system matter. Consistent with findings for earnings mobility, Bauer and Riphahn (2006) find that earlier school tracking increases intergenerational educational persistence using cross-sectional variation in school tracking across cantons in Switzerland. Bauer and Riphahn (2009) also use Swiss data to examine the role of school starting age on the intergenerational transmission of education; they find that early enrolment increases intergenerational educational mobility. This may arise because inequalities in family background have less impact on children once they are in school.

An interesting question is whether intergenerational persistence has changed as educational attainment has increased over time. The evidence here is fairly mixed. Hertz et al. (2007) show that, for their 42 countries, regression coefficients have tended to fall over time, but the correlation coefficients show no time trend. Using Italian data, Checchi et al. (2008) find that the intergenerational educational correlation declined from 0.58 for the oldest cohorts considered (born 1910-14), to 0.47 for the youngest cohorts (born 1970 or after). Blanden and Machin (2004) do not explicitly calculate intergenerational persistence but show that, in the UK, the recent higher education expansion has disproportionately benefited children from higher income (and presumably, higher education) families. Heineck and Riphahn (2007) find no significant change in the intergenerational persistence in education in Germany over half a century.

Güell et al. (2007) take a particularly creative approach to investigating changes in intergenerational education mobility in Spain. Because many people with the same surname belong to the same family, there are correlations in education by surname.

---

[32] The Hertz et al. (2007) and Chevalier et al. (2009) findings are generally consistent with others in the literature. Their finding of higher persistence in South America corroborates Behrman et al. (2001) who found much higher persistence in Brazil and Colombia than in the US.

Table 2 Countries ranked by average parent–child schooling correlation from Hertz et al. (2007) individuals Aged 20-69.

Country	Coefficient	Rank	Correlation	Rank
Peru	0.88	6	0.66	1
Ecuador	0.72	12	0.61	2
Panama	0.73	11	0.61	3
Chile	0.64	18	0.60	4
Brazil	0.95	4	0.59	5
Colombia	0.80	8	0.59	6
Nicaragua	0.82	7	0.55	7
Indonesia	0.78	9	0.55	8
Italy[a]	0.67	17	0.54	9
Slovenia[a]	0.54	27	0.52	10
Egypt	1.03	2	0.50	11
Hungary[a]	0.61	20	0.49	12
Sri Lanka	0.61	19	0.48	13
Pakistan	1.00	3	0.46	14
USA	0.46	33	0.46	15
Switzerland[a]	0.49	30	0.46	16
Ireland[a]	0.70	15	0.46	17
South Africa (KwaZulu-Natal)	0.69	16	0.44	18
Poland[a]	0.48	31	0.43	19
Vietnam	0.58	23	0.40	20
Philippines	0.41	36	0.40	21
Belgium (Flanders)	0.41	35	0.40	22
Estonia	0.54	28	0.40	23
Sweden	0.58	26	0.40	24
Ghana	0.71	13	0.39	25
Ukraine	0.37	40	0.39	26
East Timor	1.27	1	0.39	27
Bangladesh (Matlab)	0.58	25	0.38	28
Slovakia	0.61	21	0.37	29
Czech Republic[a]	0.44	34	0.37	30
The Netherlands	0.58	24	0.36	31
Norway	0.40	38	0.35	32
Nepal	0.94	5	0.35	33
New Zealand[a]	0.40	37	0.33	34
Finland	0.48	32	0.33	35
Northern Ireland	0.59	22	0.32	36
Great Britain[a]	0.71	14	0.31	37
Malaysia	0.38	39	0.31	38
Denmark	0.49	29	0.30	39

Table 2 (continued)

Country	Coefficient	Rank	Correlation	Rank
Kyrgyzstan	0.20	42	0.28	40
China(Rural)	0.34	41	0.20	41
Ethiopia(Rural)	0.75	10	0.10	42

Surveyed between 1994 and 2004, except Peru (1985), Malaysia (1988) and Pakistan (1991).

  [a] Ages 20 to 64 or 65 only.

Source: This reproduces most of Hertz et al. (2007, Table 2).

They find that the information content of surnames has increased over time in Spain, suggesting that there has been an increase in educational persistence despite a large increase in educational attainment. We believe that more work relating the expansion of educational opportunities to intergenerational mobility is warranted.

2. IDENTIFYING THE CAUSAL EFFECTS OF PARENTAL EDUCATION AND EARNINGS

While researchers have been studying the correlations between parents' and children's income and education for many years, much of the recent research has aimed to better understand the causal mechanisms that underlie these correlations. The earliest literature on this tried to disentangle the component due to genetics, which is predetermined, and the component due to an individual's childhood environment. While the prevailing wisdom is that at least part of the observed intergenerational correlation we observe is due to inherited genetic differences across families, quantifying how much is nature versus nurture is still an open question.[33]

More recently, economists have moved beyond the nature/nurture debate and have actually started trying to establish the effect of individual parental attributes on the outcomes of their children. As discussed earlier, understanding the determinants of intergenerational correlations is crucial for the development of appropriate public policy; without knowing the mechanisms, it is impossible to understand how to promote change. This is, of course, a much more difficult task, as it is often the case that any particular parental attribute is correlated with a variety of parental characteristics, many of which cannot be observed in the data.

Researchers have taken several different methodological approaches to shed light on the mechanisms and causes that underlie the parent–child correlations we observe. We will consider each of these approaches in turn and discuss what new information they provide. As with our earlier discussion of intergenerational correlations, our focus is on studies that looked at the impact of parental income and education.

---

[33] See Sacerdote (forthcoming) for an alternative and lengthier overview of the nature/nurture literature.

2.1. Method 1: sibling and neighborhood correlations

Sibling correlations

Sibling correlations in earnings provide an alternative measure of intergenerational influences. Positive correlations imply that shared genetic and environmental factors cause siblings to be more similar than two random members of society. Recent research has dealt with the same set of measurement issues that were discussed earlier with respect to the IGE—transitory shocks and life-cycle bias. For example, Björklund et al. (2009) average over about 8 earnings observations per person (to reduce the role of transitory variation) and center these at age 34 (to minimize life-cycle bias).

The consensus value of the correlation of log earnings between brothers in the US of about 0.4 does not seem to have changed much since Solon (1999). Mazumder (2008) finds brother correlations of almost 0.5 in the NLSY and about 0.4 in the PSID. Björklund et al. (2002) compare sibling correlations across several countries and find estimates of just over 0.4 for the US and, consistent with the findings for intergenerational elasticities, much lower estimates for Nordic countries. Using a large Norwegian sample, Raaum et al. (2006) find sibling correlations in log earnings of about 0.2 for brothers and 0.15 for sisters.[34] These sibling correlations provide further evidence that family background factors are more important in the US than in the Nordic countries.

One can then use these estimates to try to identify different components, including the IGE. The sibling correlation in earnings can be shown to equal $\rho = \beta^2 + s$ where β is the IGE and s is a measure of all variables shared by siblings that are unrelated to parental earnings (Solon, 1999). If we assume an IGE of about 0.5 for the US and a sibling correlation of 0.4, the formula implies that about five eights of the sibling correlation can be attributed to father's earnings, leaving a sizeable role for other shared variables.[35] One component of s that has been studied is neighborhood.

Neighborhood correlations

Page and Solon (2003a) explore how much of the brother correlation in earnings can be attributed to the fact that brothers grow up in the same neighborhood. They use the PSID and exploit the cluster-based sampling procedure that implies that several households in the same small area are included in the data. They use 5-year averages of log earnings and adjust for point in the life-cycle. They estimate a correlation in adult earnings of 0.16 for unrelated boys in the same neighborhood—this is about half their estimate of the brother correlation. Interestingly, a large proportion of the neighborhood correlation is accounted for by the fact that boys born in urban areas tend to stay in urban areas and urban earnings are higher. Thus, it appears that coming from an urban area is

---

[34] For education, Raaum et al. (2006) find sibling correlations of about 0.4 for brothers and close to 0.5 for sisters. These are somewhat smaller than analogous correlations for the US (Solon, 1999).

[35] This does not imply that father's earnings have a causal effect on son's earnings, as it may be other family background characteristics that are correlated with earnings that are relevant.

significant but exactly what neighborhood one is from is less relevant. It is important to remember that neighborhood correlations are an upper bound on true neighborhood effects, as other family traits are likely correlated within neighborhoods.

Raaum et al. (2006) carry out a similar exercise using much larger samples from Norwegian register data. They find that neighborhood correlations in log earnings are much lower in Norway, at about 0.05 for boys, and so are not a primary determinant of brother correlations in earnings.[36] Similarly, studying the Canadian city of Toronto, Oreopoulos (2003) finds neighborhood correlations that are very close to zero.

The findings for neighborhood correlations in education also show small effects. Solon et al. (2000) find neighborhood correlations in educational attainment of only about 0.1 in the PSID. Raaum et al. (2006) find even smaller neighborhood correlations in Norway. Overall, the literature suggests that neighborhood characteristics are not a predominant factor for explaining sibling similarities in adult earnings or education.

It is important to note that none of the sibling or neighborhood correlation studies attempts to distinguish a causal relationship. Given that sibling correlations can arise from common genetic or environmental factors (or interactions between the two), they are not very helpful for pinning down causal mechanisms. The findings of very low neighborhood correlations have the advantage of ruling out the predominance of geographic factors but leave open the question of why outcomes within families are highly correlated.

2.2. Method 2: structural analysis of different types of siblings

In and of themselves, sibling and neighborhood correlations are not useful for distinguishing between nature and nurture. A major advance in understanding the nature/nurture distinction is research by Björklund et al. (2005); using extremely rich Swedish data, they make use of correlations across a wide range of sibling types, including identical (also called monozygotic) and fraternal (dizygotic) twins, full siblings, half siblings, and adopted siblings, both raised together and raised apart, in order to distinguish nature from nurture.[37]

To get a sense of the approach, consider the following simple additive model

$$y_i = g G_i + s S_i + u U_i$$

where G represents the genetic factor, S is an environmental factor that is at least partly shared by siblings, and U is an environmental factor that is completely idiosyncratic to the individual (i.e. not at all shared by siblings). Each of these variables, along with y, is standardized to have mean 0 and variance 1. The three factors are unobserved, as are

---

[36] It has also been found that neighborhood correlations have very limited explanatory power for sister correlations in family income (Page and Solon, 2003b) or earnings (Raaum et al., 2006).

[37] The authors build on some older work done by economists during the 1970s. See, for example, Behrman et al. (1977).

the parameters g, s, u that determine the relative importance of each of the factors. The model assumes that the three factors affect log earnings linearly and additively.

In their most basic model they make the following strong assumptions:

1. G, S, and U are independent of each other for each individual and, within sibling pairs, all the cross covariances are zero. This assumption implies that having a better genetic endowment does not make it more likely that one has a better environment or one's sibling has a better environment.
2. Identical twins are genetically identical and fraternal twins, like all genetic siblings, share half of their genes. Half-siblings share 1/4 of the same genes, and adopted children have no genetic link.
3. Sibling pairs raised together share the same S, while sibling pairs raised apart have uncorrelated environments.

Using these assumptions, it is easy to calculate the following covariances: $\text{cov}(y_i, y_j)$ equals $g^2 + s^2$ for monozygotic twins raised together, $0.5g^2 + s^2$ for dizygotic twins and non-twin full siblings raised together, $0.25g^2 + s^2$ for half-siblings raised together, s^2 for sibling pairs in which one is adopted, g^2 for monozygotic twins raised apart, $0.5g^2$ for dizygotic twins and non-twin full siblings raised apart, and $0.25g^2$ for half-siblings raised apart. Also, note that the variance of earnings in the sample equals $g^2 + s^2 + u^2$.

Given the empirical correlations, one can calculate the values of g, s, and u from these equations. Indeed, there are several different ways in which they can be calculated, so the authors use minimum distance estimation and weight by the number of observations to efficiently solve this overidentified set of equations. They estimate $g^2 = 0.28$ (0.08) and $s^2 = 0.04$ (0.04) for brothers, implying that genes are more important than shared environment.

The model fits surprisingly well given the strong assumptions. For example, Assumption 1 is violated if people with good genetic endowments are also more likely to have privileged environments and Assumption 2 is violated by assortative mating (people tend to marry people with similar characteristics and so likely share genetic characteristics).[38]

Given this, the authors estimate several less restrictive models. Model 2 estimates the correlation between genes and shared environment rather than assuming it to be zero. Model 3 estimates the genetic correlations between dizygotic twins and non-twin full siblings, half-siblings, and adoptive siblings rather than assuming them to be 0.5, 0.25, and 0 respectively. Model 4 relaxes the assumption that $\text{cov}(S_i, S_j) = 1$ for all sibling pairs that are raised together and zero for all sibling pairs raised apart and instead estimates separate parameters for different sibling types. They find that Model 4 is the only one to

---

[38] Other violations occur if twins are treated more similarly than non-twins or monozygotic twins are treated more similarly than dizygotic twins, if adoptive children are not randomly placed in new homes, or if twins raised apart have been reared together after birth for some time (in the data, twins are deemed to have been raised apart if they were split before age 10).

provide substantially different estimates from Model 1 with estimates of $g^2 = 0.20$ (0.16) and $s^2 = 0.16$ (0.16) for brothers.[39] However, these parameters are rather imprecisely estimated.

The authors find that, while there is a significant role for genetic and shared environmental factors, the biggest role by far is played by non-shared environmental factors (remember that $u^2 = 1 - g^2 - s^2$ and even the monozygotic twin correlation is only 0.36). However, they only have information on 3 years of data, so downward biases in the correlations resulting from transitory measurement error may be partly contributing to this result.

This approach to separating out genetic and environmental effects relies on strong assumptions. Also, as stressed by Sacerdote (forthcoming), this type of methodology is limited to decomposing the variances that exist in the sample and the results may not extrapolate to policy changes that are outside this range. In this particular case, environmental variation in Sweden may be quite limited compared to, say, a sample that also includes persons from other countries. The evidence so far suggests that both nature and nurture are important in determining earnings and the relative role of these factors may become more precisely estimated as better datasets become available.

2.3. Method 3: decompositions of intergenerational persistence

Various studies have carried out decompositions of the IGE to assess the role of intermediate variables. The basic idea is to see how much of the IGE can be explained by the effect of parental earnings on an intermediate outcome, and the effect of the intermediate outcome on child earnings. Bowles and Gintis (2002) note that the intergenerational income correlation can be decomposed into additive direct and indirect effects. The direct effect is the effect that parents' income has directly on the income of their children, while the indirect effect is the effect of parents' income on intermediate variables that ultimately affect children's income. Bowles and Gintis treat both IQ test scores and education as intermediate variables, among other variables.

Consider a regression of log earnings of sons (y_1) on log earnings of fathers (y_0), education of sons (s_1), and cognitive achievement of sons (c_1). Assume all these variables have been normalized to have mean zero and variance of 1 so that we can write

$$y_1 = \beta_{y_1 y_0} y_0 + \beta_{y_1 s_1} s_1 + \beta_{y_1 c_1} c_1 + \varepsilon_{y_1}. \tag{11}$$

From this, we can decompose the intergenerational correlation of log earnings into

$$\rho_y = \beta_{y_1 y_0} + r_{s_1 y_0} \beta_{y_1 s_1} + r_{c_1 y_0} \beta_{y_1 c_1} \tag{12}$$

---

[39] It is perhaps surprising that allowing gene-environment correlations in model 2 makes little difference. Dickens and Flynn (2001) and Lizzeri and Siniscalchi (2008) develop models that suggest that genetic endowments endogenously affect environmental influences.

where $r_{s_1 y_0}$ is the correlation between the log earnings of the father and the schooling of the son, and $r_{c_1 y_0}$ is the correlation between the log earnings of the father and the cognitive ability of the son.

Using this simplified decomposition combined with estimates of the relevant standardized parameters and correlations obtained from existing studies, Bowles and Gintis (2002) conclude that IQ and educational attainment can explain at most three-fifths of the intergenerational transmission of earnings. Further, by making assumptions about the heritability of IQ scores, they show that genetic transmission of IQ can only explain a small proportion of the IGE because IQ scores do not have strong explanatory power for earnings.[40] However, this does not imply that other genetic factors are unimportant.

Even more recently, work by Blanden et al. (2007) examines the role of non-cognitive skills and ability for intergenerational income persistence in Britain. In their work, they demonstrate that covariates can account for approximately half of the estimated intergenerational income elasticity (of 0.32), with a sizeable portion attributable to cognitive and non-cognitive skills that work through educational attainment.[41]

It is difficult to interpret these decompositions, as the intermediate variables have both genetic and environmental underpinnings and the approach provides no way of getting at causal effects. There is no reason to believe that the OLS regressions that underpin the methodology provide consistent estimates, as there are likely to be many omitted variables. As such, we find the evidence from these approaches to be suggestive but not a compelling source of evidence on causal mechanisms.

2.4. Method 4: sibling and twin differences

A concern with using simple regression techniques to identify the sources of the intergenerational correlations we observe is omitted variable bias; to the extent that the estimated model is missing variables that are correlated with included variables, estimates will be inconsistent. One solution is to control for a sufficiently large number of covariates, leaving only one or a few identifiable sources of variation.

In an effort to approximate this, the literature has moved to looking within sibling pairs, thereby eliminating bias due to the omission of fixed family characteristics. The perceived "gold standard" in this area uses arguably exogenous variation in education within monozygotic twin pairs to examine the role of mothers' education on the education of their children.[42] By using data on pairs of identical twin mothers, one can

[40] Much of the behavioral genetics literature has attempted to estimate the genetic and environmental component of IQ scores. Sacerdote (forthcoming) reports a range of estimates from the literature in which the genetic component of IQ is generally found to be in the 50%-60% range with shared environmental influences being somewhere between 5% and 30%. These suggest IQ is strongly genetically determined but the models rely on strong assumptions.

[41] Other decompositions of the IGE have utilized health (Eriksson et al., 2005) and personality (Groves, 2005) as intermediate variables.

[42] There is very little literature that uses this approach to study the effect of parental earnings on child outcomes. Therefore, we restrict our attention to parental education in this section.

effectively "difference out" not just fixed family characteristics but also any differences due to genetics of the mother.

A very simple model takes the form:

$$S_{1ij} = \delta S_{0ij} + \Gamma h_{0j} + \varepsilon_{1ij} \tag{13}$$

for a child whose mother i comes from identical twin pair j, where S_{0ij} is the schooling of the mother, h_{0j} reflects other endowments of the mother that are correlated with child schooling (some observed, some unobserved) and assumed constant within identical twin pairs, and ε represents child-specific characteristics. To the extent that the unobserved endowment of the mother is correlated with her schooling outcome, OLS estimates of δ will be biased. Comparing identical twin mothers, in this case, would enable one to difference out the Γh_{0j} term, obtaining a consistent estimate of δ (assuming S_{0ij} is uncorrelated with the error term conditional on the twin mother fixed effects).

However, this leaves out the role of the father's education and earnings. If there is assortative matching, then estimates of δ will represent the effect on child's outcomes of increasing mother's education, inclusive of the effects on who she marries. To net out the effect of assortative mating, one can control for father's education and other characteristics of the father. Note that, in the context of the twin mother fixed effects, identification of the effects of father's education is based on the difference in education between the husbands of the twin mothers.

Behrman and Rosenzweig (2002) implement this methodology using monozygotic twins from the Minnesota Twins Register. Their simple OLS estimates, controlling for father's schooling and father's log earnings, suggest a positive and significant relationship between parents' and children's schooling (with a coefficient of 0.33 on mother's schooling and coefficient of 0.47 on father's schooling, both significant, when run separately). However, once they add twin mother fixed effects to look within female monozygotic twin pairs, thereby differencing out any genetic factors that influence children's schooling, the coefficient on mother's schooling turns negative and almost significant. The analogous fixed effects exercise using male monozygotic twin pairs gives coefficients for father's education that are about the same size as the OLS estimates. One interpretation of these estimates is that more educated women are more likely to participate in the labor market and this has a negative impact on their children. However, recent work by Antonovics and Goldberger (2005) calls into question these results and suggests that the findings (particularly the negative effect of mother's education) are quite sensitive to the coding of the data.

Most recently, Bingley et al. (2009) use Danish registry data with information on twin type (identical versus fraternal) to examine both the short- and long-run effects of parents education on children's outcomes. They find a shift in the relationship between parents' education and children's education over time; for parents born before 1945, they find results consistent with those of Antonovics and Goldberger that fathers' education has a positive effect on children's outcomes but mother's education has no effect. However, for more recent cohorts, they find that mothers' schooling has a positive effect but there is no effect of fathers' schooling. Table 3, Panel A presents a summary of the findings from the twins/sibling studies of educational transmission.[43]

While the twins research is quite innovative, it is important to note that it is reliant on strong assumptions. For example, it may be unrealistic to assume that twins differ in terms of education but not in terms of any other characteristic or experience that may influence the education of their offspring. Even monozygotic twins may differ in terms of personality and their degree of family-orientation. Certainly there can be large birth weight differences between identical twins, and these have been shown to be correlated with their schooling attainment and earnings.[44] It is also plausible that one twin is treated differently from the other based on their endowments, with parents making either compensatory or reinforcing investments. All these issues have been highlighted in the returns to education literature. (See Griliches (1979) and Bound and Solon (1999) for demonstrations that biases using sibling and twin fixed effects may be as big or bigger than OLS biases.)[45]

In the intergenerational case, there are further complications. One additional issue is that the offspring's outcomes are affected by both the twin and his or her mate and it is impossible to fully control for all characteristics of the mate. Given assortative mating, unobserved characteristics of the mate are likely correlated with education of both parents, leading to bias even with twin fixed effects. Another issue is that children of twin sisters (who are first cousins) may interact frequently and be influenced by each other and their aunt. If, for example, twin sisters are closer than twin brothers, this could bias downwards the effect of mother's education relative to that of father's. This provides a possible explanation for findings of weak effects of mother's education in this literature.

2.5. Method 5: regression analysis using adoptees

Another strand of literature aimed at understanding causal processes incorporates data on adoptees. If we assume that (1) adopted children are randomly assigned to families as infants and (2) adopted children are treated exactly the same as biological children, then adoption can be considered an experimental intervention that randomly assigns children to families. This type of intervention is very large compared to other experiments; for example the Moving to Opportunity (MTO) experiment shifted children from one neighborhood to another but generally began in adolescence and did not change their family members. Other interventions affect children's peer groups in school but do not

---

[43] Note that this table is adapted from Holmlund et al. (forthcoming), with their estimates added as the last entry of each panel.

[44] See work by Behrman and Rosenzweig (2004), Black et al. (2007), and Royer (2009).

[45] Twin fixed effects exacerbate problems with measurement error in parental education. There are also issues of external validity as twins are, on average, different in some respects from the rest of the population. For example, they tend to have much lower birth weight.

Table 3 Causal estimates of intergenerational effects of schooling—Summary of previous literature from Holmlund et al. (forthcoming), Table 1.

Author	Sample characteristics	Child's outcome	Assort. mating[c]	OLS estimates		Difference estimates	
				Father (1)	Mother (2)	Father (3)	Mother (4)
A. Twin/Sibling studies							
Behrman and Rosenzweig (2002)	MTR[a], 1994: 244 twin fathers and 424 twin mothers; average birth year parent 1947; sample 1947 and 1971.	Years of schooling	(no)	0.47[b],** 0.05	0.33** 0.05	0.36** 0.16	−0.25 0.15
			(yes)	0.33** 0.07	0.14** 0.05	0.34** 0.16	−0.27 0.15
Antonovics and Goldberger (2005)	MTR, 1994: 92 twin fathers and 180 twin mothers; sample restricted to children of 18 and older, not in school.	Years of schooling	(no)	0.49** 0.09	0.28** 0.09	0.48** 0.16	0.03 0.27
			(yes)	0.50 NA	0.10 NA	0.48 NA	−0.003 NA
Bingley et al. (2009)	DAR, 2004: 2713 twin fathers and 2975 twin mothers, children born 1956-1979, children aged 25 or older in 2004.	Years of schooling	(no)	0.18** (0.01)	0.18** (0.01)	0.08** (0.03)	0.05 (0.03)
			(yes)	0.12** (0.01)	0.14** (0.01)	0.07** (0.03)	0.03 (0.02)
Pronzato (2009)	NAR, 2001, 1606 twin fathers and 1609 twin mothers, children aged 23 or older in 2001.	Years of schooling	(no)				
			(yes)	0.21** (0.02)	0.24** (0.02)	0.16** (0.03)	0.10* (0.04)
Holmlund et al. (forthcoming)	SAR, parents born 1943-55, 5866 twin mothers and 4061 twin fathers.	Years of schooling	(no)	0.21** (0.01)	0.25** (0.01)	0.12** (0.03)	0.06* (0.03)
			(yes)	0.15** (0.01)	0.18** (0.01)	0.11** (0.03)	0.04 (0.03)

(continued on next page)

Table 3 (continued)

Author	Sample characteristics	Child's outcome	Assort. mating[c]	OLS estimates using own-birth children		OLS estimates using adopted children	
B. Adoption studies							
Sacerdote (2000)	NLSY, 1979: 5614 own birth and 170 adopted children. Average birth year child: 1961.	Years of schooling	(no)	0.28**		0.16**	
				0.01		0.04	
						0.11*	
						0.04	
			(yes)	0.35**		0.22**	
				0.01		0.06	
						0.11	
						0.07	
Plug (2004)	WLS, 1992: 15871 own birth and 610 adopted children. Birth year mother: 1940, average birth year adopted and birth child: 1969 and 1965.	Years of schooling	(no)	0.39**		0.27**	
				0.01		0.04	
				0.30**		0.23**	
				0.01		0.04	
			(yes)	0.54**		0.28**	
				0.02		0.10	
				0.30**		0.10**	
				0.02		0.08	
Sacerdote (2007)	HICS, 2003: 1051 own birth and 1256 adopted children from Korea. Average birth year adopted and birth child: 1975 and 1969.	Years of schooling	(no)	0.32**		0.09**	
				0.04		0.03	
Björklund et al. (2006)	SAR, 1999: 94079 own birth and 2125 adopted children all born in Sweden; average birth year mother: 1932; average birth year child: 1964.	Years of schooling	(no)	0.24**		0.11**	
				0.00		0.01	
				0.17**		0.09**	
				0.00		0.01	
			(yes)	0.24**		0.07**	
				0.00		0.01	
				0.16**		0.02**	
				0.00		0.01	
Holmlund et al. (forthcoming)	SAR, parents born 1943-55,	Years of schooling	(no)	0.23**		0.04**	
				0.00		0.01	
				0.15**		0.03*	
				0.00		0.01	
			(yes)	0.28**		0.04**	
				0.00		0.01	
				0.20**		0.03**	
				0.00		0.01	

Table 3 (continued)

Author	Sample characteristics	Child's outcome	Assort. mating[c]	OLS estimates		IV estimates	
C. IV studies							
Black et al. (2005)	NAR, 2000: 239854/172671 children 1965–75; birth year parent: 1947–58; instrument MSLA reform in 1960–1972.	Years of schooling	(no) (no)[e]	0.22** *0.003* 0.21** *0.02*	0.24** *0.003* 0.21** *0.02*	0.03 *0.13* 0.04 *0.06*	0.08 *0.14*** 0.12** *0.04*
Chevalier (2004)	BFRS 1994–2002: 12593 children aged 16–18 living at home; birth year parent: 1938–67; instrument MSLA reform in 1972.	Post-compuls. school attend.	(yes)	0.04[c,d]** *0.00*	0.04[c,d]** *0.00*	−0.01[c,d]** *0.06*	0.11[c,d]** *0.04*
Oreopoulos (2003); Oreopoulos et al. (2006)	IPUMS 1960–80: 711072 children aged 7–15 living at home; average birth year father and child: 1920–40 and 1950–70; instrument: MSLA reforms between 1915–70.	Grade repetition (actual–normal)	(no) (no)[e]	−0.03** *0.00* −0.04** *0.00*	−0.04** *0.00*	−0.06** *0.01* −0.07** *0.01*	−0.05** *0.01* −0.06** *0.01*
Maurin and McNally (2008)	FLFS 1990–2001: 5087 children aged 15 and living at home; birth year father 1946–52; instrument: university reform in 1968.	Grade repetition (actual–normal)	(no)	−0.08** *0.00*		−0.33** *0.12*	

(continued on next page)

Table 3 (continued)

Author	Sample characteristics	Child's outcome	Assort. mating[c]		
Carneiro et al. (2007)	NLSY, 1979: 1958 white children aged 12–14; instruments: local tuition fees, unemployment rates and wages.	Grade repetition (actual–normal)	(no)	−0.023** *0.005*	−0.028* *0.011*
Holmlund et al. (forthcoming)	SAR, parents born 1943–55, 5866 twin mothers and 4061 twin fathers.	Years of schooling	(no) (yes)	0.22** *0.01*	0.28** *0.01* −0.07 *0.10* 0.11 *0.06*

[a] Abbreviations: MTR—Minnesota Twin Registry; DAR—Danish Administrative Records, SAR—Swedish Administrative Records; NLSY—National Longitudinal Survey of Youth; WLS—Wisconsin Longitudinal Study; HICS—Holt International Children's Service; NAR—Norwegian Administrative Records; BFRS—British Family Resources Survey; IPUMS—Integrated Public Microdata Series; FLFS—French Labor Force Survey; MSLA – Minimum School Leaving Age.

[b] Standard errors in italics. Each coefficient is from a separate regression of the child's outcome on parent's years of schooling. Most regressions include individual controls for the child's age and gender and parent's age.

[c] When yes, these coefficients come from regressions that include the years of schooling of both parents simultaneously. Resulting estimates take into account the intergenerational effect of the marriage partner.

[d] These coefficients come from probit regressions.

[e] These coefficients come from a restricted sample of parents with less than 10 (12) years of schooling in Norway (The United States).

* significant at 5% level.

** significant at 1% level.

Source: This is an updated version of Table 1 from Holmlund et al. (forthcoming). Many thanks to the authors for their generosity in providing us with the table.

affect the school attended, the neighborhood lived in, or the family unit. Adoption takes a child in infancy and assigns them to a family, and in the process largely determines what type of area they will live in, what type of friends they will have, and what type of schools they will attend.

Bivariate regression approach

There are several variations of the regression approach. One is to estimate the following bivariate regression separately for adopted children and their non-adopted siblings:

$$y_1 = \alpha + \lambda y_0 + \varepsilon \tag{14}$$

where y_1 is some outcome variable for the child (for example, log earnings), and y_0 is the analogous variable for the adoptive parent. The comparison is then made between the value of λ for adoptees and non-adoptees. If nurture is unimportant, we would expect λ to be zero for adoptees and positive for non-adoptees (because of the genetic correlation between parent and child). If genetics and endowments in infancy are unimportant, we would expect λ to be positive and equal for adoptees and non-adoptees. Therefore, the relative value of λ for the two groups gives an indication of the importance of nature versus nurture. A nice feature of Eq. (14) when earnings are studied is that it is precisely the equation used to estimate the IGE and so the estimate of λ for adoptees is an estimate of what the IGE would be if all genetic influences were absent.

However, for the most part, adoptees are not randomly placed with families. Sacerdote (2007) uses data from a rare case with plausibly random assignment; the adoptees in the study are Korean-Americans who were placed with American families between 1970 and 1980. The adoption agency used a first-come first-served policy to assign adoptees to families. Thus, children are randomly assigned to families, conditional on the family being deemed suitable by the agency. When child's years of education is regressed on mother's years of education, the coefficient for non-adoptees is 0.32, while it is 0.09 for adoptees, suggesting genetics and infant endowments are more important than nurture in determining educational attainment.[46] One point worth noting is that to be allowed adopt, families are screened by the adoption agency. Therefore, it is likely that differences in observables between families overstate true differences between families; families with poor observables who are allowed adopt are likely to have higher than average unobserved characteristics. This factor would tend to move all the estimates towards zero.[47]

---

[46] Earlier studies by Sacerdote (2000, 2002) carry out similar analysis using small datasets but the coefficients tend to be imprecisely estimated. Using the NLSY, he finds larger effects of mother's education for adoptees of 0.22; this compares with a coefficient of 0.35 for non-adoptees. However, there is no reason to expect random assignment in these data.

[47] Similar in spirit to the adoptions analysis, Björklund and Chadwick (2003) use Swedish data to analyze income elasticities of both intact and separated families. They find that sons who have always lived with their biological fathers have an IGE of 0.25, sons who sometimes lived with their biological fathers have an elasticity of about 0.20, and sons who never lived with their biological fathers have a very low elasticity not significantly different from zero. These estimates are consistent with the idea that nurture is very important in determining the IGE. A caveat, of course, is that the group of sons who live apart from their father is non-random.

Plug (2004) finds larger coefficients of about 0.28 on adoptive mother's education using a sample of adopted children who graduated from high schools in Wisconsin in 1957 from the Wisconsin Longitudinal Survey (WLS); given assignment is not random, these larger coefficients may result from positive selection of better endowed children into more educated families.[48]

There are mixed findings for parental income using this approach. Björklund et al. (2006) find estimates for Sweden that suggest strong effects of adoptive parent's income on log income while Liu and Zeng (2009) find little evidence in the PSID that adoptive parent income matters. These could reflect true transmission differences across the two countries or, given neither study has random assignment, could relate to differences in the adoption selection process.[49]

Multivariate regression approach

Researchers also estimate multivariate regressions using adoptees in an attempt to determine which *particular* parental characteristics matter most. The equation tends to look like

$$y_1 = \alpha + \lambda_1 S_0^m + \lambda_2 S_0^f + \lambda_3 Z + \varepsilon \tag{15}$$

where S_0^m and S_0^f refer to education of mother and father respectively, and Z refers to other characteristics such as family income and family size. However, it is important to note that the adoption experiment cannot generally be used to identify the causal effects of specific environmental factors on child outcomes. Suppose we are interested in knowing whether maternal education matters. While some infants are assigned to highly educated mothers and others to mothers with low education, the difference in outcomes cannot be used to infer the effects of maternal education because highly educated parents will also typically have higher incomes, live in better areas, etc. Given it is impossible to control for all the possible parental characteristics that are correlated with education, one cannot in general identify the causal effect of education.

Table 3, Panel B presents a summary of the studies in this area. Using multiple regression, Sacerdote (2007) finds that the adoptive family characteristics that matter most for child education are mother's education (1 extra year of maternal education increase child education by 0.09) and family size (1 extra child reduces education by 0.12 of a year). He finds no effect of family income. Plug and Vijverberg (2005) find a positive effect of family income on education using the WLS, but it is imprecisely estimated and is consistent with very small effects. Using the same dataset, Plug (2004) finds, using multiple regression, that the education of adoptive fathers influences child education but the education of adoptive mothers has no statistically significant impact.

---

[48] He finds similar sized effects for father's education and, when both father and mother's education are included together, the effect of father's education dominates.

[49] In his US study, Sacerdote (2007), who plausibly does have random assignment, finds a log household income elasticity for adoptive children of 0.19, but it is statistically insignificant.

While this method may not convincingly pin down the effect of any one particular parental characteristic, the adoption approach is very useful for estimating the general importance of being placed in a high socio-economic status family. If one carefully defines the treatment in this way, one can estimate causal effects. For example, Sacerdote (2007) defines the treatment as being assigned to a family with three or fewer children and high parental education and can estimate the causal effect of being assigned to a family of that type. He finds that being assigned to the high educated, low family size type family increases the likelihood of graduating from college by 16% compared to being assigned to a large family in which neither parent has a college degree. We can be confident that family type matters a lot; however, one cannot be sure which components matter most.

Using information on biological and adoptive parents

A third type of analysis uses information on both biological and adoptive parents to run regressions such as the following on adopted children:

$$y_1 = \alpha + \lambda_a y_{0a} + \lambda_b y_{0b} + \varepsilon \tag{16}$$

where a references adoptive parents and b references biological parents. This model allows a direct comparison of the influence of the characteristics of biological and adoptive parents. Björklund et al. (2006) estimate separate models for years of schooling, whether or not the child obtains a university degree, earnings, and income using a population dataset of Swedish adoptees. This is an important study, as it is rare to have data on both biological and adoptive parents for each child. We present their estimates in Table 4. They find similar size effects for biological fathers and adoptive fathers when the dependent variable studied is years of education or university degree. Biological mothers have bigger effects than adoptive mothers on education. However, adoptive fathers have a larger impact than biological fathers on earnings and income. These positive effects of adoptive parents suggest that environmental factors are important.

An intriguing result is that the sum of the effects for biological and adoptive parents is generally similar to the effect of parents on non-adopted children. This is consistent with the absence of significant interactions between characteristics of biological and adoptive parents. However, when the authors include these interactions in the regressions, they generally are positive and statistically significant and indicate the presence of nature-nurture interactions. This is an important result, as it implies that additive models of genetic and environment factors (such as twin fixed effects methods) are misspecified. In contrast, Björklund et al. (2007), also using Swedish data, find evidence that the linear additive model fits well.[50] Further research is definitely warranted. Overall, the findings of these studies, and from the adoption literature more generally, suggest that both environmental and genetic factors are important.

---

[50] Note, however, that neither study has random assignment of children to parents and this could potentially bias results.

Table 4 Transmission coefficients from Björklund et al. (2006).

	(1) Years of schooling	(2) Years of schooling	(3) University (4 years)	(4) University (4 years)	(5) Earnings	(6) Income
Non adoptees						
Biological father	0.240** (0.002)		0.339** (0.004)		0.235** (0.005)	0.241** (0.004)
Biological mother		0.243** (0.002)		0.337** (0.004)		
Adoptees						
Biological father	0.113** (0.016)		0.184** (0.036)		0.047 (0.034)	0.059* (0.028)
Biological mother		0.132** (0.017)		0.261** (0.034)		
Adoptive father	0.114** (0.013)		0.165** (0.024)		0.098** (0.038)	0.172** (0.031)
Adoptive mother		0.074** (0.014)		0.145** (0.024)		
Sum of estimates for Biological and adoptive fathers	0.227** (0.019)		0.349** (0.040)		0.145** (0.049)	0.231** (0.040)
Sum of estimates for biological and adoptive mothers		0.207** (0.021)		0.406** (0.039)		

Each coefficient is from a separate regression of child's outcome on parents outcomes. Standard errors are shown in parentheses. Data are from the Swedish National Registry. All specifications include controls for the child's gender, 4 birth cohort dummies for the child, 8 birth cohort dummies for biological/adoptive father/mother, and 25 region dummies for where the biological/adoptive family lived in 1965. The numbers of observations in the second panel for own-birth and adopted children are 94,079/2125 in columns (1)–(4), 87,079/1780 in column (5) and 91,932/1976 in column (6).

 * significance at 5% level.
 ** significance at 1% level.
Source: This reproduces Björklund et al. (2006, Table II).

2.6. Method 6: natural experiments/instrumental variable estimates

Another method used to identify causation involves finding variation in parents' education and income that is arguably unrelated to other parental characteristics and using this variation to identify the effect of income/education on the outcomes of children.

Income

Despite the extensive literature on the correlation between parents and children's income, there is still little compelling work on the direct causal role of parents' income on children's outcomes. This is undoubtedly because it is difficult to isolate "random" shocks to family income. While there are a number of shocks to family income induced by divorce, job layoffs, and death, these are also likely to have direct affects on children's outcomes.

The literature has gone in two directions in trying to identify the causal role of parent's income on children's income and children's outcomes more generally. The first is to look at the effect of income provided through welfare programs on children's outcomes. The second has focused instead on the overall effect of events that shock income (among other things) on the outcomes of children.

The effect of welfare income and other forms of public support on children's outcomes is discussed in more detail in the chapter by Almond and Currie (2011). There are a number of recent papers using US data that find evidence that income provided through welfare or Earned Income Tax Credit (EITC) benefits does influence the outcomes of children. These include work by Dahl and Lochner (2005), who look at the EITC, and work by Morris et al. (2004), who use pooled microdata from four studies that evaluated eight welfare and antipoverty programs.[51]

The second literature has focused on the role of income shocks induced by the labor market status of a parent. Using US data, Shea (2000) attempts to isolate the role of income on the human capital of children by using variation induced by what he argues to be "luck"—union status, industry, and job loss. He concludes that variation in parents' income due to luck has little to no effect on children's human capital, although there is some effect for children of low-educated fathers.

Oreopoulos et al. (2008) use a Canadian administrative panel to examine the effect of father's displacement from work on the outcomes of their children. They are careful to note that this incorporates not only the shock to income the family experiences but any associated psychological costs in terms of discouragement, etc. They find that sons whose fathers were displaced have annual earnings that are about 9% lower than similar children whose fathers did not experience an employment shock; they are also more likely to receive unemployment insurance. These estimates are driven by the experiences of children whose family income was at the bottom of the income distribution.[52]

Rege et al. (2007) use Norwegian data to estimate the effect of parental job loss due to plant closure on the outcomes of children. They find that father's job loss leads to a decline in the children's graduation GPA; however, they suggest that it is not due to income loss, divorce, or relocation.[53] They also find that mothers' job loss leads to improved school performance, suggesting that time inputs may be more important than financial ones.

Overall, the results suggest that the long-term consequences of unexpected job loss extend beyond the effect on one's own income to the eventual labor market outcomes of one's children. However, given that job loss has many impacts other than its effect on

---

[51] See Almond and Currie (2011) for more detailed descriptions and references.

[52] In contrast, using Norwegian data, Bratberg et al. (2008) find that, although job displacement reduces the earnings of fathers, it does not affect the later earnings of their children.

[53] Consistent with this, Loken (2010) finds that children from families whose incomes were increased as a result of the Norwegian oil boom in the 1970s did not subsequently achieve higher educational attainment.

income, these results do not conclusively indicate a causal effect of family income on child outcomes.

Education

The instrumental variables approach has been much more widely used to look at the causal relationship between parents' and child's education. In this case, the education of the parents is "shocked" by some exogenous force (such as a policy change) and one can see the later effects on the children. Table 3, Panel C provides a summary of the studies in this area.

In Black et al. (2005), we apply this approach using register data from Norway. During the 1960s, there was a change in the compulsory schooling laws affecting primary and middle schools. Pre-reform, the Norwegian education system required children to attend school through the seventh grade; after the reform, this was extended to the ninth grade, adding two years of required schooling. Additionally, implementation of the reform occurred in different municipalities at different times, starting in 1960 and continuing through 1972, allowing for regional as well as time series variation. As a result, the reform provides variation in parental education that is exogenous to parental ability and enables us to determine the impact of increasing parental education on children's schooling decisions.

The empirical model is summarized by the following two equations:

$$S_1 = \beta_0 + \beta_1 S_0 + \beta_2 AGE_1 + \beta_3 AGE_0 + \beta_4 MUNICIPALITY_0 + \varepsilon \qquad (17)$$
$$S_0 = \alpha_0 + \alpha_1 REFORM_0 + \alpha_2 AGE_1 + \alpha_3 AGE_0 + \alpha_4 MUNICIPALITY_0 + \upsilon. \qquad (18)$$

In Eqs (17) and (18), S is number of years of education, AGE refers to a full set of years of age indicators, MUNICIPALITY refers to a full set of municipality indicators, and REFORM equals 1 if the individual was affected by the education reform, and 0 otherwise. In all cases, the subscript 0 denotes parent and the subscript 1 denotes the child. We estimate the model by parent gender and child gender using Two Stage Least Squares (2SLS), so that Eq. (18) is the first stage and $REFORM_0$ serves as an instrumental variable for S_0. Despite strong OLS relationships, we find little evidence of a causal relationship between parent education and child education.[54]

Oreopoulos et al. (2006) use a similar methodology to examine the influence of parental compulsory schooling on grade retention status for children aged 7 to 15 using the 1960, 1970 and 1980 US Censuses. They study US law changes (that occurred in different states at different times) to identify the effect of parents' educational attainment on children's school performance (as proxied by grade-for-age). They find that an

---

[54] However, there is evidence in some specifications of a positive causal impact of mother's education on son's education.

increase in parental education attainment of 1 year reduces the probability that a child repeats a grade by between 2 and 7 percentage points and their IV estimates are more negative than the OLS ones.

Chevalier (2004) uses a change in the compulsory schooling laws in Britain that occurred in 1972. Because the legislation was implemented nationwide, there is no cross-sectional variation in the British compulsory schooling law and the identifying variation in parental education arises both from secular trends in education and the once-off change in the law. He finds a large positive effect of mother's education on her child's education but no significant effect of paternal education.[55]

Other work has used different types of arguably exogenous variation in parental education to identify intergenerational mobility in education. Maurin and McNally (2008) use variation in college attendance induced by the student riots in May 1968 in Paris; because of student protests, students and authorities negotiated for more lenient exam standards for the baccalaureat exam (which, if successfully completed, guarantees access to university) for that year alone. As a result, the pass rate increased significantly for that year and more students were able to attend college. This led to significantly higher wages for the students who were then able to attend college, with an increase of about 14%. In addition, these returns were passed on to the next generation; grade repetition declined significantly for the children of the affected cohort.

Carneiro et al. (2007) use the NLSY79 and variation in maternal education induced by variation in schooling costs at the time the mother was growing up to identify the effect of maternal education on a variety of children's outcomes, including behavioral problems, achievement, grade repetition, and obesity. They find that, among children aged 7-8, an increase in mother's education by one year increases math standardized test performance by 0.1 of a standard deviation and reduces the incidence of behavioral problems.

Magnuson (2007) uses random assignment into a "human capital development" program for welfare mothers as an instrument for mother's educational attainment and finds evidence of an effect of mother's education on children's academic school readiness.

Finally, recent work by Page (2009) uses cohort level variation in schooling levels induced by the G.I. Bill in order to identify the intergenerational transmission of education. She argues that this variation was due to the timing of the draft and not unobservable individual characteristics or underlying trends. She finds that a one year increase in father's schooling reduces the probability that his child repeats a grade by 2-4 percentage points. This is quite consistent with her earlier work with Oreopoulos and Stevens, suggesting that the timing of the additional year—either in high school due to increased compulsory schooling or in college through GI benefits—does not affect the estimates.

---

[55] Work by Chevalier et al. (2005) combines the instrument for parental education used in Chevalier (2004) and union status of the father as an instrument for father's income (as used in Shea (2000)) and concludes that income matters more than education for children's outcomes.

Parental education and infant health

There are also studies of the effect of parental education on infant health. While they only study outcomes of children when they are infants, they can still be relevant to intergenerational transmission; as noted above, it has been fairly well established that better infant health has a positive causal effect on later adult outcomes. McCrary and Royer (2006) use a regression discontinuity design with data from California and Texas and compare women born just before and just after school entry dates—the latter group start school a year later and subsequently end up with lower education on average. Using this as the basis for an instrumental variable strategy, they find no effect of education on fertility or age-at-first-birth and very small and statistically insignificant effects of education on infant health as measured by birth weight. This particular instrument largely relies on educational variation for low educated women.[56]

In contrast, Currie and Moretti (2003) also use US data and find that higher maternal education reduces the number of children mothers have had at any particular age and the probability their child has low birth weight. They also use an instrumental variables strategy but are more focused on the top end of the education distribution, as their instrument is whether there is a college in the woman's county when she is aged 17. Given they use county fixed effects, identification comes from college openings. It is plausible that the differences between the findings of the two studies reflect nonlinear effects of maternal education on child health. Thus, the evidence suggests that increasing education by making compulsory schooling laws stricter is unlikely to have much impact on later child outcomes through the infant health channel. However, an expansion of college opportunity may indeed benefit long-run outcomes of children.

Limitations of the IV approach

There are a number of limitations to the instrumental variables approach, but two stand out as being the most important. The first is the credibility of the instrument; while it is not difficult to determine whether the instrument has a strong first stage, the excludability of the instrument is inherently untestable. For example, changes in compulsory education laws tend to accompany curriculum changes, new buildings, and the hiring of new teachers. Any of these could have direct effects. Also, college openings may respond to educational demand in the local area. As a result, despite the often significant efforts of the researcher, the credibility of the estimates can always be called into question.

Even if the instrument is valid, the generalizability of the estimates is also an issue. Under monotonicity, among other assumptions, IV estimates provide the LATE (local average treatment effects); that is, the causal effect for those whose behavior is actually influenced by the instrument. For example, in the case of compulsory schooling laws, the estimated effects are for people whose behavior is influenced by the change in

---

[56] Consistently, the available evidence from the UK that uses compulsory schooling laws to estimate the effect of parental education on child health has not found significant effects (Lindeboom et al., 2009; Doyle et al., 2007).

compulsory schooling legislation; i.e., those with low educational attainment. To the extent that the causal effect is different for this subgroup relative to the population as a whole, the results would not generalize.

2.7. Reconciling findings of twins/adoptees/IV literatures

It is troubling to note that, across methodologies (twins, adoptees, IV), estimates vary substantially. In recent work, Holmlund et al. (forthcoming) set out to reconcile the findings, using all three methodologies and applying them to a single dataset from Sweden. In this way, they can disentangle whether differing estimates in the literature result from the different methodologies that have been used or from the different countries that have been studied. Importantly, they are able to replicate many of the results obtained by other researchers (for example, using twins they find father's education matters more than mother's; using a change in compulsory schooling as an instrument, they find the opposite), suggesting that the differing results are, at least in part, due to methodological differences rather than differences across countries. Regardless of methodology, however, they find that OLS significantly overstates the causal intergenerational relationship. A key point stressed by these authors is that the three different methods tend to shock different parts of the education distribution. While twins are fairly evenly distributed across the parental education distribution, adoptive families generally come from the higher end of the distribution. In contrast, changes in compulsory schooling laws mostly affect people with low educational levels. Therefore, in addition to other differences, results should be expected to vary across method if there are nonlinearities in the intergenerational relationship.

Pronzato (2009) directly examines this issue using a twin fixed effects model. She uses a sample of Norwegian twins and evaluates the robustness of the estimates to restricting the sample to different parts of the parental education distribution. She finds that there is a strong positive effect of father's education on child education at the top end of the distribution but, at the bottom end, mother's education appears to matter more. These results are consistent with the idea that, by obtaining identification from different parts of the distribution, different methods should be expected to produce varying results.

In principle, the IV approach is preferable to twin/adoptee strategies as it isolates the effect of an exogenous change in education of parents. Under the IV assumptions, parental education is as good as randomly assigned conditional on the covariates. The twins fixed effects approach can be seen as an IV approach that uses the within-pair difference in mother's education as the instrument for maternal education. It thus relies very heavily on the assumption that twin differences in education are random and uncorrelated with any other differences between the twins. The adoption approach differs in that it cannot isolate the effects of parental education from that of other correlated but unobserved parental characteristics. Despite the limitations associated with all three methods, however, we can still learn from their results.

Unfortunately, as can be seen in Table 3, taken as a whole the findings in the literature are very inconsistent. Some studies find OLS estimates that are larger than the causal effects but many find the opposite. Some studies find the effects of fathers' education to be greater; others find the effects of mothers to be more important. Clearly, there is a need for further work in this area.

3. OTHER FAMILY BACKGROUND CHARACTERISTICS

Recent research has moved beyond earnings and education to study a broad range of intergenerational relationships between other child and adult outcomes. We have chosen just a few to discuss below:[57]

3.1. IQ/ability

There is a small but growing literature in economics on the intergenerational transmission of IQ.[58] Recent data innovations, particularly in the Scandinavian countries, have enabled researchers to examine the correlations in IQ scores over time. Work by Black et al. (2009) uses Norwegian military data to examine the relationship between the IQ scores of fathers and sons, both measured at the age of 18. Using fathers who enrolled for conscription in the military in 1952 and 1953 and sons who enrolled between 1984 and 2005, we find that there is substantial intergenerational transmission of IQ scores; an increase in father's IQ of 10% is associated with a 3.2% increase in son's IQ score.

Björklund et al. (2010) use similar data from Sweden to extend this work, looking at both intergenerational and sibling correlations in IQ. They find a similar estimate of intergenerational correlation to that of Black et al. However, when they examine correlations between brothers, they find that close to half of the variation in IQ is accounted for by family and community background factors common to brothers, suggesting a more substantial role for families than might be suggested by the intergenerational correlation.

Anger and Heineck (2009) use data from the German Socio-Economic Panel Study to look at intergenerational correlations in cognitive skills for both men and women. They find estimates of intergenerational transmission that are larger than those found in the Scandinavian data. When they include mother's and father's IQ separately, they find slightly stronger effects of mother's IQ than father's. When they examine sons and daughters separately, they find evidence of an own-gender effect, with mothers influencing daughters more and fathers influencing sons.

Finally, Gronqvist et al. (2009) examine both cognitive and non-cognitive intergenerational transmission using population-wide draft data in Sweden. Because the draft data are available only for men, they are limited to using predicted cognitive and

---

[57] There are large literatures in some of these areas and, by necessity, we have had to omit many interesting papers in this brief overview.

[58] Bouchard and McGue (1981) survey much of the non-economics literature.

non-cognitive ability measures for both mothers and fathers based on the enlistment evaluations of their brothers. They find a strong relationship between parents' ability and education and labor market outcomes of their children; parents' cognitive abilities matter more for educational outcomes while non-cognitive abilities matter more for earnings. Clearly, this is an area that will benefit from future research as more data become available.

This literature on IQ scores and cognitive skills is interesting as it moves us closer to understanding what exactly is handed down by parents to their children. However, given that cognitive skills are influenced by both genetic and environmental factors and are correlated with many other family background characteristics, no clear causal mechanisms have been uncovered by this literature.

3.2. Jobs and occupations

Several studies examine intergenerational mobility in occupation and find strong correlations between fathers and sons. Hellerstein and Morrill (2008) show that, in recent cohorts, about 30% of sons and 20% of daughters work in the same occupation as their father. However, these percentages are sensitive to how finely occupation is defined.[59] For this reason, many studies create some metric of occupational rank or prestige and correlate this more continuous measure of parent and child occupation. Using this type of approach, Ermish and Francesconi (2002) find intergenerational correlations that range from 0.4 to 0.75 for father-child pairs and from 0.30 to 0.50 for mother-child pairs in the British Household Panel Survey. They find that the effects are nonlinear, with a higher elasticity for higher socio-economic status parents. They also find that more recent cohorts are more mobile than their earlier counterparts. Using slightly different methods, Carmichael (2000), using the BHPS, and Di Pietro and Urwin (2003), using Italian data, find strong relationships between father and son occupations.[60] Ferrie (2005) demonstrates that occupational mobility in the US was much greater in the late 19th century than in the 20th century.

A few recent studies have moved beyond occupation to see if children get jobs in the same firms as their parents. Using Canadian data, Corak and Piraino (2010) show that, by their early 30s, about 40% of men have worked with an employer that had also employed their father at some point in time. Interestingly, they find that this occurs more frequently when fathers are higher earners. This finding is consistent with other research showing that family based succession is common in large companies—incoming CEOs are often the sons or daughters of departing CEOs or large shareholders. See Pérez-González (2006) for evidence from the United States, and Bennedsen et al. (2007) for Danish evidence.

---

[59] The focus of this paper is on disentangling the reasons for the increase over time in the proportion of daughters in the same occupation as their father.

[60] It is also well established that children are more likely to become self-employed if a parent is self-employed. See, for example, Dunn and Holtz-Eakin (2000).

Using Swedish register data, Kramarz and Skans (2007) show that boys are much more likely than their classmates to get their first stable job in the plant in which their father works. The corollary is that plants are more likely to hire a boy if his father works there. They show that while this applies most to low-educated children, fathers tend to provide access to relatively high wage plants. Symmetrically, they find that girls are more likely than their classmates to get jobs in plants in which their mother works. These findings suggest that there may be a causal effect of the jobs parents hold on their children's labor market outcomes. Further work in this area might be useful to sort out the relative roles of discrimination, preference transmission, and information.

3.3. Welfare receipt

There is also a literature focusing on the intergenerational transmission of welfare receipt. A preponderance of the evidence suggests a strong intergenerational correlation in welfare participation.[61] However, there is little evidence on the causal relationship. As Levine and Zimmerman (1996) describe, it is important, from a policy perspective, to distinguish between a poverty trap and a welfare trap. A poverty trap arises from the intergenerational correlation of income; because welfare receipt is means-tested, families with low-income parents, who are thus more likely to be welfare recipients, are more likely to have low-income children, who will also be more likely to qualify for welfare. Note that, in this case, the higher incidence of welfare receipt among the children of welfare recipients is due solely to the means-tested nature of welfare combined with the intergenerational correlation in income.

Of more concern from a policy perspective may be the notion of the welfare trap; in this case, it is not the mechanical nature of the means-tested policy that leads to the correlation between parents and children but instead some feature of the program itself. An example of this would be that children who grew up on welfare believe it is more socially acceptable to be on welfare and, as a result, for a given level of earnings as an adult, may be more likely to enroll in welfare.

It is quite difficult to distinguish between these two types of intergenerational persistence. Despite this, Levine and Zimmerman (1996) apply a number of different approaches to distinguish the poverty trap from the welfare trap, including 1. comparing actual participation of children to that predicted based on parents' income and 2. using variation in welfare generosity across states. They conclude that most of the persistence in welfare use across generations is because of the poverty trap; at least three quarters (and possibly all) of the correlation can be attributed to the expected intergenerational correlation in income and other family characteristics, leaving little if any room for a welfare trap argument.[62]

---

[61] See work by Page (2004).

[62] Pepper (2000) considers the incidence and intensity of welfare enrollment. Using data from the PSID and a nonparametric bounding method to examine the effect, he finds evidence that being on welfare as a child increases both the probability and expected duration of future welfare use.

A number of other studies focus on the intensity of exposure among children who were all exposed to welfare as a child to examine whether or not variation in the intensity of exposure leads to variation in later welfare receipt as adults. Among these are papers by Beaulieu et al. (2005) using Canadian administrative data and Mitnik (2008) using administrative data from California. The two papers use different econometric approaches and come to very different conclusions; using a structural approach, Beaulieu et al. find that increased welfare use by parents leads to increased use by children, while Mitnik, using sibling differences in exposure, finds no effect of length of exposure on future welfare dependency. Overall, while the intergenerational correlations in welfare receipt are clear, there is much less evidence that a causal relationship exists.

3.4. Health

Intergenerational transmission of health has also been a focus of recent research. A number of papers have established a positive intergenerational correlation in a variety of health outcomes. A recent study by Coneus and Spieß (2008) uses the German Socio-Economic Panel and various anthropometric (i.e. weight, height, BMI) and self-reported health measures and finds intergenerational transmission of health between parents and children younger than four years old. Akbulut and Kugler (2007) use the NLSY79 to examine correlations in height, weight, BMI, depression, and asthma in the US. They find that children inherit a substantial proportion of their health (anthropometric and emotional) from their mothers. Loureiro et al. (2006) examine intergenerational transmission of smoking habits using the BHPS (1994-2002) and find 18 year olds are about twice as likely to smoke if both parents smoke than if neither parent smokes.[63]

Fewer papers have actually tried to identify a causal link, and those that have focus on intergenerational transmission of birth weight. As with all the work in this literature, a key issue with establishing causation is whether other family characteristics (such as poverty) affect the birth weight of both the parent and the child. If this is the case, despite an observed correlation between parent and child birth weight, there may be no causal relationship. Currie and Moretti (2007) address this issue by comparing mothers who are siblings, thereby differencing out fixed family characteristics. Using data from individual birth records from California, they find that the probability that a child is low birth weight is almost 50% higher if the mother herself had low birth weight, even after controlling for a family fixed effect. They estimate an intergenerational low birth weight elasticity of 0.2, suggesting strong intergenerational correlations between mothers' and children's birth weight.[64]

Other work has looked within twin pairs of mothers. Differences in birth weight within twin pairs are unrelated to family characteristics (as both twins have the same

---

[63] Intergenerational transmission of health is an important issue in developing countries. See Bhalotra and Rawlings (2009) for a recent analysis.

[64] They also show that this effect is stronger for women living in poorer neighborhoods.

environment) and, among identical twins, there are no genetic differences either. Black et al. (2007) use data from Norway and find elasticity estimates of approximately 0.18 for a sample of twin mothers; these estimates are relatively insensitive to the inclusion of twin fixed effects.[65] We also find an elasticity of 0.18 using twin fixed effects when the sample is restricted to monozygotic twin mothers. Royer (2009), using data from California, also finds positive but smaller effects using twin fixed effects.[66]

3.5. Attitudes and social behavior

There is also a recent literature examining the intergenerational transmission of attitudes and social behaviors. It is very difficult to estimate causal effects with these types of variables, so the literature is predominantly based on correlations. Altonji and Dunn (2000) use panel data from the NLS to study intergenerational persistence in wages and work preferences and argue positive intergenerational correlations in work hours are primarily due to preferences. Mayer et al. (2004) use the NLSY and find strong correlations between mothers' and daughters' traits, behavior and attitudes; only a small fraction of this correlation is explained by family socioeconomic status, suggesting that it may be the attitudes themselves that matter. Wilhelm et al. (2008) use the PSID to examine intergenerational transmission in charitable donations and separately study secular giving and religious giving. They find that the religious elasticity is larger than the secular elasticity, with estimates ranging from 0.26 to 0.31 for religious giving and from 0.08 to 0.14 for secular giving. Using the German Socio-Economic Panel (SOEP), Dohmen et al. (2008) show that willingness to take risks and levels of trust are correlated across generations.

Almond et al. (2009) argue that there is persistence of culture across generations. To test this, they study Asian immigrants to Canada. Because these immigrants are neither poor nor in a society that tolerates sex selection, the fact that they observe son preferences (boy-girl ratios that rise with parity if there is no previous son) suggests that these preferences for sons are transmitted intergenerationally. To further validate these results, they also show significant differences across religious affiliations that coincide with historical differences in beliefs about infanticide.[67]

The preponderance of research in this area has focused on correlations across generations. The exception to this, however, is work by Fernandez et al. (2004), who argue that the behavior of the mother has a causal influence on the preferences of the son in terms of the marriage market. Using geographic variation in the importance of World War II as a shock to women's labor force participation, they find that if a mother works this has

---

[65] Note that we estimate an OLS elasticity of .25 on the sample of all siblings in the data; this estimate declines to 0.13 when we include sibling fixed effects.

[66] Currie and Hyson (1999) show that, while socioeconomic status does not mitigate the effects of low birth weight on economic outcomes of children, it does offset the effect of low birth weight on female health status.

[67] For example, Sikhs have the highest sex ratios, while Christian or Muslim Asians have the lowest, suggesting that explicit prohibition of post-birth sex selection may also be protecting unborn girls against prenatal sex selection.

a positive causal effect on the probability that the son's wife works. This suggests that the increasing number of men brought up in a family in which the mother worked may have been a significant factor in the increase in female labor force participation over time. Given the growing focus on culture and political economy in research more generally, this is clearly an interesting area for future research.

3.6. Consumption and wealth

There are other papers that attempt to determine intergenerational persistence of economic outcomes by looking at consumption or wealth instead of income. An example of this is work by Waldkirch et al. (2004), which looks at consumption using information about parents and their children from the Panel Study of Income Dynamics (PSID). Raw estimates suggest intergenerational correlations in food consumed away from home (one measure of consumption) in the range of 0.14-0.20. The authors then attempt to distinguish how much of this is due to differences in income relative to differences in taste and conclude that both parental income and tastes have statistically significant effects on consumption of their children.

In addition, work by Charles and Hurst (2003) uses data on wealth from the Panel Study of Income Dynamics to estimate the intergenerational wealth elasticity. When they regress log of child's wealth on the log of parent's wealth, controlling for child and parental age, they find an intergenerational wealth elasticity of 0.37, higher than that suggested by previous studies. They also show that twenty percent of parents in the lowest quintile of the parent's wealth distribution have children who move to the top two quintiles of the child's wealth distribution. Similarly, one-quarter of the parents in the highest wealth quintile also have children who end up in the lowest two quintiles of the child's wealth distribution.[68] It is interesting that the intergenerational wealth elasticity appears to be lower than the IGE and further work on the relationships between them may be valuable.

4. CONCLUSION

The literature on intergenerational mobility has witnessed great progress over the last decade. To understand the advances we have made, we went back to Solon's (1999) chapter to see whether his suggestions for future research actually came to fruition, and, indeed, a number of his suggestions have developed into active areas of research.

Solon suggested that we "study how the sibling resemblance in earnings varies across different sibling types known to vary in the extent to which they share genes and environments." (page 1776). Thanks to registry data from the Nordic countries, we have made significant progress in this direction. Creative use of adoptees and different sibling types has provided compelling evidence that both nature and nurture are important for

---

[68] Using data from France, Arrondel (2009) reports an elasticity of children's wealth with respect to that of their parents of around 0.22.

child outcomes. The work by Björklund et al. (2005) is at the forefront of this literature, and it is clear that we will continue to make progress as better data, including data on the underlying genetic structure of individuals, become available. An important avenue for future research is further work on gene-environment interactions and how they mediate the effects of policy interventions.

Solon also noted, "Now that we know parental income is a fairly strong predictor of offspring's earnings, it becomes that much more important to find out which of the causal processes...are mainly responsible for the empirically observed intergenerational associations of earnings." (page 1789). This, too, proved to be portentous; perhaps the most significant recent progress in the literature has been on causal processes. Work using adoptees, twins, and instrumental variables strategies has allowed us to make significant advances in our understanding of why we observe these correlations.

We have also learned something about what types of policy changes can lead to reductions in intergenerational persistence. Some of the Nordic evidence suggests that intergenerational persistence can be heavily influenced by education policy reforms that extend the length of compulsory education and delay tracking. Interestingly, work on these reforms also suggests that the positive impacts on people from less-educated backgrounds spillover to the next generation to only a limited extent. We hope there will be further work linking policy changes directly to changes in intergenerational relationships.

While intergenerational mobility has been an active area of research, there is still a lot that we cannot currently explain, and there is much room for research in this area in the future. Recent high quality estimates of IGEs and sibling correlations suggest that family background is very important in the US but much less so in the Nordic countries. Research in both the US and Norway suggests that neighborhood is not the prime determinant. However, there is still much work to do to pin down which family background factors are most important.

Additionally, despite a decade of progress, we have a wide range of findings about whether it is mother's or father's education that matters more for offspring and quite limited evidence on the causal effect of family income. There is scope for much more research on these core topics. And, clearly, as we continue to study topics such as the intergenerational transmission of health, weight, behavior, and preferences, the reach of this literature will continue to grow.

REFERENCES

Akbulut, Mevlude, Kugler, Adriana D., 2007. Inter-generational transmission of health status in the US among natives and immigrants. Mimeo, University of Houston.
Almond, Douglas, Edlund, Lena, Milligan, Kevin, 2009 Son preference and the persistence of culture: evidence from Asian immigrants to Canada. Working paper no. 15391, NBER, Cambridge, MA.
Almond, Douglas, Currie, Janet, 2011. Human capital development before age five. In: Ashenfelter, O., Card, D. (Eds.), Handbook of Labour Economics, vol. 4b. Elsevier, pp. 1315–1486 (Chapter 15).
Altonji, Joseph G., Dunn, Thomas A., 2000. An intergenerational model of wages, hours, and earnings. Journal of Human Resources 35, 221–258.

Anger, Silke, Heineck, Guido, 2009. Do smart parents raise smart children? The intergenerational transmission of cognitive abilities. Working paper no. 156, SOEP, DIW, Berlin.

Antonovics, Kate, Goldberger, Arthur S., 2005. Does increasing women's schooling raise the schooling of the next generation? Comment. American Economic Review 95, 1738–1744.

Arrondel, Luc, 2009. My father was right: the transmission of values between generations. PSE Working papers 2009-12.

Baker, Michael, Solon, Gary, 2003. Earnings dynamics and inequality among Canadian men, 1976-1992. Journal of Labor Economics 21, 289–321.

Bauer, Philipp C., Riphahn, Regina T., 2006. Timing of school tracking as a determinant of intergenerational transmission of education. Economics Letters 91, 90–97.

Bauer, Philipp C., Riphahn, Regina T., 2009. Kindergarten enrollment and the intergenerational transmission of education. Discussion paper no. 4466, Institute for the Study of Labor (IZA), Bonn.

Beaulieu, Nicolas, Jean-Yves, Duclos, Bernard, Fortin, Rouleau, Manon, 2005. Intergenerational reliance on social assistance: evidence from Canada. Journal of Population Economics 18, 539–562.

Becker, Gary S., Tomes, Nigel, 1979. An equilibrium theory of the distribution of income and intergenerational mobility. Journal of Political Economy 87, 1153–1189.

Behrman, Jere R., Gaviria, Alejandro, Székely, Miguel, Birdsall, Nancy, Galiani, Sebastián, 2001. Intergenerational mobility in Latin America. Economía 2, 1–44.

Behrman, Jere R., Rosenzweig, Mark, 2004. Returns to birthweight. Review of Economics and Statistics 86, 586–601.

Behrman, Jere R., Rosenzweig, Mark R., 2002. Does increasing women's schooling raise the schooling of the next generation? American Economic Review 92, 323–334.

Behrman, Jere R., Taubman, Paul, Wales, Terence, 1977. Controlling for and measuring the effects of genetics and family environment in equations for schooling and labor market success. In: Taubman, Paul (Ed.), Kinometrics: Determinants of Socioeconomic Success within and between Families. North-Holland, Amsterdam.

Bennedsen, Morton, Nielsen, Kasper M., Pérez-González, Francisco, Wolfenzon, Daniel, 2007. Inside the family firm: the role of families in succession decisions and performance. Quarterly Journal of Economics 122, 647–691.

Bhalotra, Sonia, Rawlings, Samantha, 2009. Gradients of the intergenerational transmission of health in developing countries. Unpublished Working Paper.

Bhattacharya, Debopam, Mazumder, Bhashkar, 2007. Nonparametric analysis of intergenerational income mobility with application to the United States, Federal Reserve Bank of Chicago WP 2007-12.

Bingley, Paul, Christensen, Kaare, Jensen, Vibeke M., 2009. Parental schooling and child development: learning from twin parents. Working paper no. 07:2009, SFI.

Björklund, Anders, Chadwick, Laura, 2003. Intergenerational income mobility in permanent and separated families. Economic Letters 80, 239–246.

Björklund, Anders, Jäntti, Markus, 2009. Intergenerational income mobility and the role of family background. In: Salverda, Wiemer, Nolan, Brian, Smeeding, Tim (Eds.), Handbook of Economic Inequality. Oxford University Press, Oxford.

Björklund, Anders, Roine, Jesper, Waldenström, Daniel, 2008. Intergenerational top income mobility in Sweden: a combination of equal opportunity and capitalistic dynasties. Discussion paper no. 3801, Institute for the Study of Labor (IZA).

Björklund, Anders, Hederos Eriksson, Karin, Jäntti, Markus, 2010. IQ and family background: are associations strong or weak? The B.E. Journal of Economic Analysis and Policy (Contributions) 10 (1).

Björklund, Anders, Jäntti, Markus, Solon, Gary, 2007. Nature and nurture in the intergenerational transmission of socioeconomic status: evidence from Swedish children and their biological and rearing parents. The B.E. Journal of Economic Analysis and Policy 7, Article 4.

Björklund, Anders, Jäntti, Markus, Solon, Gary, 2005. Influences of nature and nurture on earnings variation: a report on a study of various sibling types in Sweden. In: Bowles, Samuel, Gintis, Herbert, Osborne Groves, Melissa (Eds.), Unequal Chances: Family Background and Economic Success. Princeton University Press, Princeton, pp. 145–164.

Björklund, Anders, Jäntti, Markus, Lindquist, Matthew J., 2009. Family background and income during the rise of the welfare state: brother correlations in income for Swedish men born 1932-1968. Journal of Public Economics 93, 671–680.

Björklund, Anders, Lindahl, Mikael, Plug, Erik, 2006. The origins of intergenerational associations: lessons from Swedish adoption data. Quarterly Journal of Economics 121, 999–1028.

Björklund, Anders, Eriksson, Tor, Jäntti, Markus, Raaum, Oddbjorn, Österbacka, Eva, 2002. Brother correlations in earnings in Denmark, Finland, Norway and Sweden compared to the United States. Journal of Population Economics 15, 757–772.

Black, Sandra, Devereux, Paul, Salvanes, Kjell, 2009. Like father, like son? A note on the intergenerational transmission of IQ scores. Economics Letters 105, 138–140.

Black, Sandra E., Devereux, Paul J., Salvanes, Kjell G., 2007. From the cradle to the labor market? The effect of birth weight on adult outcomes. Quarterly Journal of Economics 122, 409–439.

Black, Sandra E., Devereux, Paul J., Salvanes, Kjell G., 2005. Why the apple doesn't fall far: understanding intergenerational transmission of human capital. American Economic Review 95, 437–449.

Blanden, Jo, 2009. How much can we learn from international comparisons of intergenerational mobility? paper no. CEEDP0111, Centre for the Economics of Education, LSE.

Blanden, Jo, Goodman, Alissa, Gregg, Paul, Machin, Stephen, 2004. Changes in intergenerational mobility in Britain. In: Corak, M. (Ed.), Generational Income Mobility in North America and Europe. Cambridge University Press.

Blanden, Jo, Machin, Stephen, 2004. Educational inequality and the expansion of UK higher education. Scottish Journal of Political Economy 51, 230–249.

Blanden, Jo, Gregg, Paul, Macmillan, Lindsey, 2007. Accounting for intergenerational persistence. Economic Journal 117, C43-C60.

Böhlmark, Anders, Lindquist, Matthew J., 2006. Life-cycle variations in the association between current and lifetime income: replication and extension for Sweden. Journal of Labor Economics 24, 879–896.

Bound, John, Solon, Gary, 1999. Double trouble: on the value of twins-based estimation of the return to schooling. Economics of Education Review 18, 169–182.

Bouchard Jr., Thomas, McGue, Matthew, 1981. Familial studies of intelligence: a review. Science 212, 1055–1059.

Bowles, Samuel, Gintis, Herbert, 2002. The inheritance of inequality. Journal of Economic Perspectives 16, 3–30.

Bratberg, Espen, Nilsen, Oivind A., Vaage, Kjell, 2008. Job losses and child outcomes. Labour Economics 15, 591–603.

Bratberg, Espen, Nielsen, Oivind A., Vaage, Kjell, 2007. Trends in intergenerational mobility across offspring's earnings distribution in Norway. Industrial Relations 46, 112–129.

Bratberg, Espen, Nielsen, Oivind A., Vaage, Kjell, 2005. Intergenerational earnings mobility in Norway: levels and trends. Scandinavian Journal of Economics 107, 419–435.

Bratsberg, Bernt, Røed, Knut, Raaum, Oddbjorn, Naylor, Robin A., Markus, Jäntti, Eriksson, Tor, Österbacka, Eva, 2007. Nonlinearities in intergenerational earnings mobility: consequences for cross-country comparisons. Economic Journal 117, C72-92.

Brenner, Jan, 2010. Life-cycle variations in the association between current and lifetime earnings: evidence for German natives and guest workers. Labour Economics 17, 392–406.

Carmichael, Fiona, 2000. Intergenerational mobility and occupational status in Britain. Applied Economics Letters 7, 391–396.

Carneiro, Pedro, Meghir, Costas, Parey, Matthias, 2007. Maternal education, home environments and the development of children and adolescents. Discussion paper no. 3072, Institute for the Study of Labor (IZA), Bonn.

Chadwick, Laura, Solon, Gary, 2002. Intergenerational income mobility among daughters. American Economic Review 92, 335–344.

Charles, Kerwin K., Hurst, Erik, 2003. The correlation of wealth across generations. The Journal of Political Economy 111, 1155–1182.

Checchi, Daniele, Fiorio, Carlo, Leonardi, Marco, 2008. Intergenerational persistence in educational attainment in Italy. Discussion paper no. 3622, Institute for the Study of Labor (IZA), Bonn.

Chevalier, Arnaud, 2004. Parental education and child's education: a natural experiment. Discussion paper no. 1153, Institute for the Study of Labor (IZA), Bonn.

Chevalier, Arnaud, Harmon, Colm, O'Sullivan, Vincent, Walker, Ian, 2005. The Impact of parental income and education on the schooling of their children. Discussion paper no. 1496, Institute for the Study of Labor (IZA), Bonn.

Chevalier, Arnaud, Denny, Kevin, McMahon, Dorren, 2009. A Multi-country study of inter-generational educational mobility. In: Dolton, Peter, Asplundh, Rita, Barth, Erling (Eds.), Education and inequality Across Europe. Edward Elgar, London.

Coneus, Katja, Spieß, Katharina C., 2008. The Intergenerational transmission of health in early childhood, SOEP papers 126, DIW Berlin, The German Socio-Economic Panel.

Corak, Miles, 2006. Do poor children become poor adults? Lessons from a cross country comparison of generational earnings mobility. In: John Creedy and Guyonne Kalb (Ed.) Research on Economic Inequality, vol. XIII, Amsterdam, pp. 143–188.

Corak, Miles, Heisz, Andrew, 1999. The intergenerational earnings and income mobility of Canadian Men. Journal of Human Resources 34, 504–533.

Corak, Miles, Piraino, Patrizio, 2010. Intergenerational earnings mobility and the inheritance of employers (unpublished).

Couch, Kenneth A., Lillard, Dean R., 2004. Nonlinear patterns of intergenerational mobility in Germany and the United States. In: Corak, M. (Ed.), Generational income mobility in North America and Europe. Cambridge University Press, Cambridge, pp. 190–206.

Currie, Janet, Moretti, Enrico, 2007. Biology as destiny? Short and long-run determinants of intergenerational transmission of birth weight. Journal of Labor Economics 25, 231–264.

Currie, Janet, Moretti, Enrico, 2003. Mother's education and the intergenerational transmission of human capital: evidence from college openings. Quarterly Journal of Economics 118, 1495–1532.

Currie, Janet, Hyson, Rosemary, 1999. Is the impact of health shocks cushioned by socioeconomic status? The case of low birthweight. American Economic Review 89, 245–250.

Dahl, Gordon B., Lochner, Lance, 2005. The impact of family income on child achievement. Working paper no. 11279, NBER, Cambridge, MA.

Davies, James, Zhang, Jie, Zeng, Jinli, 2005. Intergenerational mobility under private vs. public education. Scandinavian Journal of Economics 107, 399–417.

Dickens, William, Flynn, James R., 2001. Heritability estimates versus large environmental effects the IQ paradox resolved. Psychological Review 108, 346–369.

Di Pietro, Giorgio, Urwin, Peter, 2003. Intergenerational mobility and occupational status in Italy. Applied Economics Letters 10, 793–797.

Dohmen, Thomas J., Falk, Armin, Huffman, David, Sunde, Uwe, 2008. The intergenerational transmission of risk and trust attitudes, Working paper no. 2307, CESifo Group, Munich.

Doyle, Orla, Harmon, Colm, Walker, Ian, 2007. The impact of parental income and education on child health: further evidence for England, Working paper no. 788, University of Warwick, England.

Dunn, Thomas, Holtz-Eakin, Douglas, 2000. Financial capital, human capital and the transition to self-employment: evidence from intergenerational Links. Journal of Labor Economics 18, 282–305.

Eriksson, Tor, Bratsberg, Bernt, Raaum, Oddbjorn, 2005. Earnings persistence across generations: transmission through health? Memorandum 35/2005, University of Oslo, Norway.

Ermish, John, Francesconi, Marco, 2002. Intergenerational mobility in Britain: new evidence from BHPS. In: Corak, Miles (Ed.), Generational income mobility in North America and Europe. Cambridge University Press, Cambridge.

Ermisch, John, Francesconi, Marco, Siedler, Thomas, 2006. Intergenerational mobility and marital sorting. Economic Journal 116, 659–679.

Fernandez, Raquel, Fogli, Alessandra, Olivetti, Claudia, 2004. Mothers and sons: preference formation and female labor force dynamics. Quarterly Journal of Economics 119, 1249–1299.

Ferrie, Joseph P., 2005. History lessons: the end of American exceptionalism? Mobility in the United States since 1850. The Journal of Economic Perspectives 19, 199–215.

Gaviria, Alejandro, 2002. Intergenerational mobility, sibling inequality and borrowing constraints. Economics of Education Review 2, 331–340.

Goldberger, Arthur S., 1979. Heritability. Economica 46 (184), 327–347.

Grawe, Nathan D., 2006. The extent of lifecycle bias in estimates of intergenerational earnings persistence. Labour Economics 13, 551–570.

Grawe, Nathan D., 2004. Reconsidering the use of nonlinearities in intergenerational earnings mobility as a test for credit constraints. Journal of Human Resources 39, 813–827.

Grawe, Nathan D., Mulligan, Casey, 2002. Economic interpretations of intergenerational correlations. Journal of Economic Perspectives. 6, 45–58.

Griliches, Zvi, 1979. Sibling models and data in economics: beginnings of a survey. Journal of Political Economy 87 (5), S37-64.

Gronqvist, Erik, Ockert, Bjorn, Vlachos, Jonas, 2009. The intergenerational transmission of cognitive and non-cognitive abilities. Mimeo.

Groves, Melissa O., 2005. Personality and the intergenerational transmission of economic status. In: Bowles, Samuel, Gintis, Herbert, Groves, Melissa O. (Eds.), Unequal Chances: Family background and economic success. Princeton University Press, Princeton, pp. 145–164.

Güell, Maia, Rodríguez-Mora, Sevi, Telmer, Chris, 2007. Intergenerational mobility and the informative content of surnames. Discussion paper no. 6316, C.E.P.R., London.

Guryan, Jonathan, Hurst, Erik, Kearney, Melissa, 2008. Parental education and parental time with children. Journal of Economic Perspectives 22 (3), 23–46.

Haider, Steven J., Solon, Gary, 2006. Life-cycle variation in the association between current and lifetime earnings. American Economic Review 96, 1308–1320.

Han, Song, Mulligan, Casey, 2001. Human capital, heterogeneity, and estimated degrees of intergenerational mobility. Economic Journal 111, 207–243.

Heineck, Guido, Riphahn, Regina T., 2007. Intergenerational transmission of educational attainment in Germany: the last five decades. Discussion paper no. 2985, Institute for the Study of Labor (IZA), Bonn.

Hellerstein, Judith, Morrill, Melinda, 2008. Dads and daughters: the changing impact of fathers on women's occupational choices. Mimeo.

Hertz, Tom, Jayasundera, Tamara, Piraino, Patrizio, Selcuk, Sibel, Smith, Nicole, Verashchagina, Alina, 2007. The inheritance of educational inequality: international comparisons and fifty-year trends. The B.E. Journal of Economic Analysis & Policy 7, Article 10.

Hirvonen, Lalaina, 2008. Intergenerational earnings mobility among daughters and sons: evidence from Sweden and a comparison with the United States. The American Journal of Economics and Sociology 67 (5), 777–826.

Holmlund, Helena, 2008. Intergenerational mobility and assortative mating: effects of an educational reform. Discussion paper 0091, Centre for Economics of Education, LSE.

Holmlund, Helena, Lindahl, Mikael, Plug, Erik. The causal effect of parent's schooling on children's schooling: a comparison of estimation methods (with Mikael Lindahl and Erik Plug). Journal of Economic Literature (forthcoming).

Ichino, Andrea, Karabarbounis, Loukas, Moretti, Enrico, 2009. The political economy of intergenerational income mobility. Discussion paper no. 4767, Institute for the Study of Labor (IZA), Bonn.

Jäntti, Markus, Bratsberg, Bernt, Røed, Knut, Raaum, Oddbjørn, Naylor, Robin, Eva, Österbacka, Anders, Björklund, Eriksson, Tor, 2006. American exceptionalism in a new Light: a comparison of intergenerational earnings mobility in the Nordic countries, the United Kingdom and the United States. Discussion paper no. 1938, Institute for the Study of Labor (IZA), Bonn.

Jenkins, Stephen, 1987. Snapshots versus movies: lifecycle biases and the estimation of intergenerational earnings inheritance. European Economic Review 31, 1149–1158.

Kramarz, Francis, Skans, Oskar N., 2007. With a little help from my... parents? Family networks and youth labor market entry, CREST, mimeo.

Lee, Chul-In, Solon, Gary, 2009. Trends in intergenerational income mobility. Review of Economics and Statistics 91, 766–772.

Lefranc, Arnaud, Trannoy, Alain, 2005. Intergenerational earnings mobility in France: is France more mobile than the US? Annales d'Economie et de Statistique 78, 57–77.

Leigh, Andrew, 2007. Intergenerational mobility in Australia. B.E. Journal of Economic Analysis and Policy 7, Article 6.

Levine, Phillip B., Zimmerman, David J., 1996. The intergenerational correlation in AFDC participation: welfare trap or poverty trap? IRP Discussion paper No. 1100-96.

Lindeboom, Maarten, Llena Nozal, Ana, van der Klaauw, Bas, 2009. Parental education and child health: evidence from a schooling reform. Journal of Health Economics 28, 109–131.

Liu, Haoming, Zeng, Jinli, 2009. Genetic ability and intergenerational earnings mobility. Journal of Population Economics 22, 75–95.

Lizzeri, Alessandro, Siniscalchi, Marciano, 2008. Parental guidance and supervised learning. Quarterly Journal of Economics 123, 1161–1195.

Loken, Katrine V., 2010. Family income and children's education: using the Norwegian oil boom as a natural experiment. Labour Economics 17, 118–129.

Loureiro, Maria L., Sanz-de-Galdeano, Anna, Daniela, Vuri, 2006. Smoking habits: like father, like son, like mother, like daughter. Discussion paper no. 2279, Institute for the Study of Labor (IZA), Bonn.

Machin, Steven, 2007. Education expansion and intergenerational mobility in Britain. In: Woessman, Ludger, Peterson, Paul (Eds.), Schools and the Equal Opportunity Problem. MIT Press.

Magnuson, Katherine., 2007. Maternal education and children's academic achievement during middle childhood. Developmental Psychology 43, 1497–1512.

Maurin, Eric, McNally, Sandra, 2008. Vive la revolution! Long-term education returns of 1968 to the angry students. Journal of Labor Economics 26, 1–33.

Mayer, Susan E., Duncan, Greg, Kalil, Ariel, 2004. Like mother, like daughter? SES and the intergenerational correlation of traits, behaviors and attitudes. Working paper no. 0415, Harris School of Public Policy Studies, University of Chicago.

Mayer, Susan E., Lopoo, Leonard M., 2008. Government spending and intergenerational mobility. Journal of Public Economics 92, 139–158.

Mazumder, Bhashkar, 2008. Sibling similarities and economic inequality in the US. Journal of Population Economics 21, 685–701.

Mazumder, Bhashkar, 2005. Fortunate sons: new estimates of intergenerational mobility in the US using social security earnings data. Review of Economics and Statistics 87, 235–255.

McCrary, Justin, Royer, Heather, 2006. The effect of female education on fertility and infant health: evidence from school entry policies using exact date of birth. Working paper no. 12329, NBER, Cambridge, MA.

Meghir, Costas, Palme, Marten, 2005. Educational reform, ability and family background. American Economic Review 95, 414–424.

Mitnik, Oscar A., 2008. Intergenerational Transmission of Welfare Dependency: the Effects of Length of Exposure. Mimeo, March 2.

Mocetti, Sauro, 2007. Intergenerational earnings mobility in Italy. The B.E. Journal of Economic Analysis and Policy 7, Article 5.

Morris, Pamela, Duncan, Greg J., Rodrigues, Christopher, 2004. Does money really matter? Estimating impacts of family income on children's achievement with data from random-assignment experiments (unpublished).

Mulligan, Casey B, 1997. Parental Priorities and Economic Inequality. University of Chicago Press, Chicago.

Nicoletti, Cheti, Ermisch, John, 2007. Intergenerational earnings mobility: changes across cohorts in Britain. The B.E. Journal of Economic Analysis and Policy 7, Article 9.

Nilsen, Oivind A., Vaage, Kjell, Arkvik, Arild, Jacobsen, Karl, 2008. Estimates of intergenerational elasticities based on lifetime earnings. Discussion paper no. 3709, Institute for the Study of Labor (IZA), Bonn.

O'Neill, Donal, Sweetman, Olive, van de Gaer, Dirk, 2007. The effects of measurement error and omitted variables when using transition matrices to measure intergenerational mobility. Journal of Economic Inequality 5, 159–178.

Oreopoulos, Philip, 2003. The long-run consequences of growing up in a poor neighbourhood. Quarterly Journal of Economics 118, 1533–1575.

Oreopoulos, Philip, Page, Marianne E., Stevens, Anne H., 2008. The intergenerational effects of worker displacement. Journal of Labor Economics 26, 455–483.

Oreopoulos, Philip, Page, Marianne E., Stevens, Anne H., 2006. The intergenerational effects of compulsory schooling. Journal of Labor Economics 24, 729–760.

Österbacka, Eva, 2001. Family background and economic status in Finland. Scandinavian Journal of Economics 103, 467–484.

Österberg, Torun, 2000. Intergenerational income mobility in Sweden: what do tax-data show? Review of Income and Wealth 46, 421–436.

Page, Marianne E., 2009. Fathers' education and children's human capital: evidence from the World War II G.I. Bill. Mimeo.

Page, Marianne E, 2004. New evidence on intergenerational correlations in welfare participation. In: Corak, Miles (Ed.), Generational income mobility in North America and Europe. Cambridge University Press, Cambridge.

Page, Marianne E., Solon, Gary, 2003a. Correlations between brothers and neighboring boys in their adult earnings: the importance of being urban. Journal of Labor Economics 21, 831–855.

Page, Marianne E., Solon, Gary, 2003b. Correlations between sisters and neighboring girls in their subsequent income as adults. Journal of Applied Econometrics 18, 545–562.

Pekkala, Sari, Lucas, Robert E.B., 2007. Differences across cohorts in Finnish intergenerational income mobility. Industrial Relations 46, 81–111.

Pekkarinen, Tuomas, Uusitalo, Roope, Kerr, Sari, 2009. School tracking and intergenerational income mobility: evidence from the Finnish comprehensive school reform. Journal of Public Economics 93, 965–973.

Pepper, John V., 2000. The intergenerational transmission of welfare receipt: a nonparametric bounds analysis. Review of Economics and Statistics 82, 472–488.

Pérez-González, Francisco, 2006. Inherited control and firm performance. American Economic Review 96, 1559–1588.

Piraino, Patrizio, 2007. Comparable estimates of intergenerational income mobility in Italy. The B.E. Journal of Economic Analysis and Policy 7 Article 1.

Plug, Erik, 2004. Estimating the effect of mother's schooling on children's schooling using a sample of adoptees. American Economic Review 94, 358–368.

Plug, Erik, Vijverberg, Wim, 2005. Does family income matter for schooling outcomes? Using adoptees as a natural experiment. Economic Journal 115, 879–906.

Pronzato, Chiara, 2009. An examination of paternal and maternal intergenerational transmission of schooling. CHILD working paper no. wp20_09, CHILD—Centre for Household, Income, Labour and Demographic economics, Italy.

Raaum, Oddbjørn, Bratsberg, Bernt, Røed, Knut, Österbacka, Eva, Eriksson, Tor, Jäntti, Markus, Naylor, Robin A., 2007. Marital sorting, household labor supply and intergenerational earnings mobility across countries. The B.E. Journal of Economic Analysis and Policy Article 7.

Raaum, Oddbjørn, Salvanes, Kjell G., Sorensen, Erik O., 2006. The neighborhood is not what it used to be. Economic Journal 116, 200–222.

Rege, Mari, Telle, Kjetil, Votruba, Mark, 2007. Parental job loss and children's school performance. Discussion paper no. 517, Research Department, Statistics Norway.

Reville, Robert T., 1995. Intertemporal and life cycle variation in measured intergenerational earnings mobility. RAND working paper, Santa Monica, CA: RAND Corporation.

Royer, Heather, 2009. Separated at girth: estimating the long-run and intergenerational effects of birthweight using twins. American Economic Journal—Applied Economics.

Sacerdote, Bruce, 2008. Nature and nurture effects on children's outcomes: What have we have learned from studies of twins and adoptees? Handbook of Social Economics, Amsterdam, North Holland (forthcoming).

Sacerdote, Bruce, 2007. How large are the effects from changes in family environment? A study of Korean American adoptees. Quarterly Journal of Economics 122, 119–157.

Sacerdote, Bruce, 2002. The nature and nurture of economic outcomes. American Economic Review 92, 344–348.

Sacerdote, Bruce, 2000. The nature and nurture of economic outcomes. Working paper No. 7949, NBER, Cambridge, MA.

Shea, John, 2000. Does Parents' Money Matter? Journal of Public Economics 77, 155–184.

Solon, Gary, 2004. A model of intergenerational mobility variation over time and place. In: Corak, Miles (Ed.), Generational income mobility in North America and Europe. Cambridge University Press, Cambridge, pp. 38–47.

Solon, Gary, 2002. Cross-country differences in intergenerational earnings mobility. Journal of Economic Perspectives 16, 59–66.

Solon, Gary, 1999. Intergenerational mobility in the labor market. In: Ashenfelter, Orley, Card, David (Eds.), Handbook of Labor Economics, Vol. III. North-Holland, Amsterdam, pp. 1761–1800.

Solon, Gary, 1992. Intergenerational income mobility in the United States. American Economic Review 82, 393–408.

Solon, Gary, Page, Marianne, Duncan, Greg, 2000. Correlations between neighboring children in their subsequent educational attainment. Review of Economics and Statistics 82/3, 383–392.

Vogel, Thorsten, 2008. Reassessing intergenerational mobility in Germany and the United States: the impact of differences in lifecycle earnings patterns. Discussion paper No. SFB649DP2006-055, Sonderforschungsbereich 649, Berlin.

Waldkirch, Andreas, Ng, Serena, Cox, Donald, 2004. Intergenerational linkages in consumption behaviour. Journal of Human Resources 39, 355–381.

Wilhelm, Mark O., Brown, Eleanor, Rooney, Patrick M., Steinberg, Richard S., 2008. The intergenerational transmission of generosity. Journal of Public Economics 92, 2146–2156.

Zimmerman, David J., 1992. Regression toward mediocrity in economic stature. American Economic Review 82, 409–429.

CHAPTER 17

New Perspectives on Gender

Marianne Bertrand

Booth School of Business, University of Chicago, NBER, CEPR and IZA

Contents

Abstract

Psychological and socio-psychological factors are now more commonly discussed as possible explanations for gender differences in labor market outcomes. We first describe the (mainly) laboratory-based evidence regarding gender differences in risk preferences, in attitudes towards competition, in the strength of other-regarding preferences, and in attitudes towards negotiation. We then review the research that has tried to quantify the relevance of these factors in explaining gender differences in labor market outcomes outside of the laboratory setting. We also describe recent research on the relationship between social and gender identity norms and women's labor market choices and outcomes, as well as on the role of child-rearing practices in explaining gender identity norms. Finally, we report on some recent work documenting puzzling trends in women's well-being and discuss possible explanations for these trends, including identity considerations. We conclude with suggestions for future research.

JEL classification: J16; A12; A14

Keywords: Gender; Psychology; Identity; Well-being

Handbook of Labor Economics, Volume 4b
ISSN 0169-7218, DOI 10.1016/S0169-7218(11)02415-4

1. INTRODUCTION

At the time Altonji and Blank completed their influential Handbook chapter in 1999, the two main factors being discussed as sources of the gender gap in earnings were differences in human capital accumulation and discrimination (taste-based or statistical). Patterns of occupational segregation by gender (which have been shown to "explain" much of the gender gap in earnings) were essentially attributed either to discrimination being more pronounced in some occupations than others, or to differences in human capital accumulation pre labor market entry (such as differences in the type of education women receive) or post labor market entry (such as differences in accumulated experience).

While researchers have certainly not abandoned studying these two factors nor given up on their first order relevance, a major development over the last ten years has been the rising popularity of new classes of explanations for gender differences in labor market outcomes.[1] First and foremost is the possibility that there are important differences in psychological attributes and preferences between men and women that may make some occupations more attractive to women and others more attractive to men. While Altonji and Blank (1999) already discuss this possibility, they also point to the difficulty in pushing it further without better foundations for the source and nature of these gender differences. Thanks to advances in the psychology and experimental literatures, and a growing influence of these literatures on economics research, we now have a much more concrete sense of the psychological factors that appear to systematically differ between men and women. In particular, we review the evidence regarding gender differences in risk preferences (Section 2.1), in attitudes towards competition (Section 2.2), in the strength of other-regarding preferences (Section 2.3) and in attitudes towards negotiation (Section 2.4). While there is an abundance of laboratory studies regarding each of these psychological factors, there has been to date, as we discuss in Sections 2.5 and 2.6, only a very limited amount of research able to establish the relevance of these factors for labor market outcomes. In this regard, whether this body of psychological research will be more than just a decade-long fad and have a long-lasting impact on how labor economists think about gender differences will crucially depend on further demonstration of its economic significance in real markets. Assuming such economic significance can be established, policymakers will want to better understand the sources of

---

[1] See for example Black and Brainerd (2004) and Black and Strahan (2001) for studies of how globalization and deregulation trends may have reduced discrimination against women in various occupations. Recent research has also focused on how technological progress has affected women's educational choices and labor market experience. See for example Goldin and Katz (2002) for how the availability of the pill increased women's willingness to invest in long-duration professional degrees, or Greenwood et al. (2005) for how improvements in household technologies may have contributed to women's greater attachment to the labor force. Finally, there has been more rigorous discussion of how the shift toward a service and skill-intensive economy has increased the proportion of jobs suitable for women; see for example Weinberg (2000) and Black and Juhn (2000). Blau and Kahn (2006) provide a careful discussion of the extent to which gender differences in human capital may account for the fast convergence of male and female wages in the 1980s and the slowing convergence in the 1990s.

these gender differences in psychological attributes and traits: are evolution and biology dictating that women are more risk averse than men? Or is the gender gap in risk aversion an outcome of child-rearing practices? The review we perform in Section 2.7 suggest at least some environmental influences on top of pure biological foundations, and hence the promise of a broader set of policy tools to try to undo some of the psychological influences that might be the most damaging to women's labor market success.

Another increasingly discussed explanation for why women and men experience different labor markets is the existence of social norms about what is appropriate for men to do and what is appropriate for women to do. Influential papers by Akerlof and Kranton (2000, 2002, 2005) have helped the import into economics of earlier insights from the social psychology literature regarding an individual's social identity and how it can influence behaviors and choices in markets. One of the richest applications of the social identity model has been to gender identity and its implications for not only occupational sorting, but also labor force participation and the allocation of work within the household. We review the (gender) identity model in Section 3.1. Unfortunately, it has been difficult to design a credible causal testing of the impact of gender identity norms for women's labor market choices; we review the evidence that has been produced so far in Section 3.2. Here again, we feel that much more validating empirical work will be needed in the near future for gender identity insights to have a long-lasting impact on how labor economists approach gender issues. The review we perform in Section 3.3 shows that socialization and child-rearing practices have been singled out (in the economics literature at least) as the key drivers of social norms regarding gender roles; in fact, as we discuss in Section 3.4, a nurture explanation for why men and women exhibit different attitudes with respect to risk (or competition, or negotiation, or altruism) might be that such gendered traits are components of one's gender identity (e.g. being a woman implies displaying more risk-aversion; being a man implies behaving more aggressively).

Section 4 continues on the theme of bringing a more psychological perspective into the labor economics of gender. In that section, we review some recent work on gender differences in well-being. We are particularly motivated by a recent paper by Stevenson and Wolfers (2009) who find that, despite decades of educational gains and an unambiguous enlargement of their set of labor market opportunities, women's self-reported levels of life satisfaction appear to have declined over time, both in absolute terms and relative to men's. We discuss various explanations for this finding. More generally, we stress in this section that additional measures of women's well-being exist beyond those typically used by labor economists (see for example Blau, 1998), and that a creative use of those measures could lead to a richer perspective on women's progress.

We conclude in Section 5 with additional suggestions for future research.

2. GENDER DIFFERENCES IN PSYCHOLOGICAL ATTRIBUTES

2.1. Risk attitudes

Bonin et al. (2007) empirically demonstrate that individuals that are less willing to take risk tend to sort into occupations with more stable earnings; these occupations, due to compensating wage differentials in environments with risk-averse agents, also tend to pay less on average.[2] Hence, risk preferences may be an important determinant of earnings, in addition to the more traditional factors typically included in a Mincerian wage equation.[3]

A large experimental literature has tested whether systematic differences in risk preferences exist between men and women. This literature has been recently reviewed in two articles: Croson and Gneezy (2009) and Eckel and Grossman (2008a).[4] Most of the experimental work reviewed in these articles consists in comparing how men and women value risky gambles or choose between gambles. Some of the experiments exclusively rely on hypothetical choices; others involve real (albeit most often small) stakes. In most cases, the subject pool consists of college students.

Both Croson and Gneezy (2009) and Eckel and Grossman (2008a) come to the conclusion that the published experimental findings are broadly consistent with women being more risk averse than men. Summaries of the most important papers are presented in Table 1 of Eckel and Grossman (2008a), as well Table 1 of Croson and Gneezy (2009). For example, Levin et al. (1988) ask college students whether or not they are willing to take each of 18 different gambles; they find significantly higher reported take-up rates among men than among women. Also, Hartog et al. (2002) elicit hypothetical certainty equivalents for a series of lotteries and use those to compute risk aversion parameters; they find those risk aversion parameters to be 10 to 30 percent larger for women than for men. Eckel and Grossman (2002) ask subjects to choose among five alternative gambles that differ in expected return and variance, and pay subjects according to the outcome of the gamble that they choose; they find that men choose on average riskier gambles with higher expected payoffs. Motivated by the work of Kahneman and Tversky (1979), Eckel and Grossman (2002) also show that women's higher average level of risk aversion hold both in the loss domain (where the gambles include negative payoff amounts) and in the gain domain (where all the possible payoff amounts are non-negative).[5] Holt and Laury (2002) ask a sample of about 200 college students to make choices between 10 paired

---

[2] See also Grund and Sliwka (2006).

[3] The predictive power of risk preferences to explain important economic and social choices has been demonstrated in many other domains. For example, Anderson and Mellor (2008) show that individual-level risk aversion is negatively associated with smoking, heavy drinking, being obese, and not using a seat belt, even after controlling for demographic and socio-economic characteristics.

[4] Croson and Gneezy (2009) extend their literature review to a broader set of gender differences in preferences, including attitudes towards competition and social preferences; Eckel and Grossman (2008a) focus exclusively on risk attitudes.

[5] The evidence regarding a gender gap in risk attitudes in the loss domain appears less robust. For example, in an abstract lottery choice experiment, Schubert et al. (1999) find women to be significantly more risk averse than men in the gain domain but find the opposite (e.g. men being more risk-averse than women) in the loss domain.

lotteries, with each pair featuring a lower risk lottery (e.g. a lottery where the potential payoffs differed only slightly) and a higher risk lottery (e.g. a lottery where the potential payoffs differed more widely); they infer a subject's level of risk aversion from the point in the 10-pair suite at which they switched from the low-risk to the high-risk lottery. They also vary the level of pay (e.g. subjects make choices for both low-payoff and high-payoff lottery treatments). They find a small but a significant gender gap in risk aversion in the low-payoff treatment, with women being more risk averse. However, this gender gap disappears in the high-payoff treatment.

While the subject pool in most existing lab studies is restricted to the college population, Dohmen et al. (forthcoming-a) show evidence of higher risk aversion among women in the general population. Their study relies both on a large representative survey of the German population and a complementary experiment carried on a representative subsample. In the survey data, a global assessment of individual risk aversion is obtained by asking individuals to self-assess their willingness to take risk ("How willing are you to take risks, in general?"), on a scale from 0 to 10. This contrasts with the more traditional lottery-type elicitation of risk attitudes, and the complementary experiment is then used to validate the individual self-assessment of risk attitudes as measured in the survey data. Specifically, an additional representative sample of 450 subjects is asked both to answer the subjective self-assessment question and also to make choices in real-stakes lotteries. The subjective survey question is deemed a reliable measure of risk attitude in that it predicts actual risk-taking behavior in the experiment, even after controlling for many observable characteristics. In their large representative sample of the German population, Dohmen et al. (forthcoming-a, 2010) find that gender (but also age, height and parental education) has a quantitatively significant effect on one's self-assessed willingness to take risk: the gender effect corresponds to about a quarter of a standard deviation reduction in the willingness to take risk.

Their larger research sample also allows Dohmen et al. (forthcoming-a, 2010) to study how the gender gap in risk-taking varies over the life cycle. While the willingness to take risk goes down steadily with age among men, Dohmen et al. (forthcoming-a, 2010) find a richer dynamic among women, with the most rapid decline from the late teens to age thirty, a flattening between age thirty and the mid-fifties, and a further decline after that.

Moving beyond the lab and survey evidence, a few field studies also point at systematic differences in risk aversion between genders, even though omitted variable concerns are typically quite pronounced in these studies. For example, studying the defined contribution pension allocation decision among employees of a large US firm, Bajtelsmit and VanDerhei (1997) find that women invest a relatively greater share in low-risk assets; however, this gender gap could reflect on systematic differences in socio-economic status, income, wealth, or financial knowledge between the genders, which the authors cannot control for. Using various years from the Survey of Consumer Finances, both Jianakoplos and Bernasek (1998) and Sunden and Surette (1998) find that single women typically hold lower proportions of risky assets. While better socio-economic and wealth controls are available in those studies, there remains a concern that men and women cannot be perfectly matched on all the dimensions that are relevant for financial investment decisions. Illustrating the relevance of this concern, Dwyer et al. (2002) show that gender differences in risk taking among mutual fund investors are in part driven by systematic differences in financial knowledge between men and women. Specifically, using data from a 1995 national survey of close to 2000 mutual fund investors, they find that women exhibit less risk-taking than men in their most recent, largest, and riskiest investment decisions; however, controlling for knowledge of financial markets and investment (which is possible because the survey includes a series of questions in order to determine the respondents' understanding of basic financial concepts) greatly reduces, but does not eliminate, the estimated gender gap in risk-taking. While the lab and field evidence surveyed so far has mainly focused on decision making in the financial domain (a domain that is admittedly very relevant to labor market outcomes), researchers have also been interested in whether the observed gender differences in risk aversion hold across other tasks or domains of decision-making: are women also more risk-averse than men when it comes to, say, health-related choices? This is a relevant question because psychologists have argued that a given subject's risk preferences may vary quite a lot across domains (Slovic, 1972). Dohmen et al. (forthcoming-a, 2010) address this question by exploiting domain-specific risk attitudes questions in the German survey data. In particular, the survey includes five similarly worded questions as the general risk question, where subjects are asked to assess on a scale from 0 to 10 their willingness to take risk when it comes to: driving, financial matters, sports and leisure, health and career. They find a lower average willingness to take risk among women compared to men in each of these five domains; the gender gap in risk attitudes is greatest in the driving and financial matters domains, and smallest in the career domain.

A discussion of gender differences in risk attitudes is often accompanied by a discussion of gender differences in overconfidence. And indeed, a gender gap in overconfidence is often offered as an explanation for the gender gap in risk attitudes.[6] While both genders have been shown to display overconfidence, men appear particularly overconfident in their relative ability, especially when it comes to tasks that are perceived to be in the masculine domain (see Lundeberg et al., 1994; Beyer, 1990; Beyer and Bowden, 1997). This larger relative overconfidence may make men more likely to enter riskier situations. An interesting illustration of gender differences in overconfidence in the field can be found in Barber and Odean (2001). Barber and Odean (2001) start from the theoretical prediction that overconfident financial investors will trade stocks too much; they then show, using data from a large discount brokerage, that men trade 45 percent

---

[6] Other personality traits have been proposed as drivers of risk attitudes, and potential explanation for the gender gap in risk attitudes. See Section 2.7.

more than women and that this greater relative trading negatively impacts the relative return of their portfolio.[7]

2.2. Attitudes towards competition

Many high-profile, high-earning occupations often take place in highly competitive settings where winners and losers are singled out and winners are disproportionately rewarded. A few recent experimental papers have proposed a new explanation for why women may be relatively under-represented in those occupations. These papers suggest that women may systematically under-perform relative to men in competitive environments and that many women, even among the most able, may simply prefer to stay away from such environments.

Gneezy et al. (2003) bring students to the lab in groups of six: 3 women and 3 men. Each student is asked to solve mazes for a period of 15 minutes under one of two possible compensation schemes: a piece rate scheme, or a tournament scheme. Under the piece rate scheme, students are paid a fixed prize for each maze that they solve; under the tournament scheme, only the student in the group that solves the highest number of mazes receives some compensation. While there is no gender difference in performance under the piece rate scheme, men strongly increase their performance in the tournament setting but women do not. The gender gap in performance in the tournament setting is large, with men solving about 40 percent more mazes than women.

Because the tournament payment is more uncertain than the piece rate payment, it is possible that the gender difference in performance in the tournament setting is simply a reflection of the gender differences in risk aversion we already discussed in Section 2.1. Gneezy et al. (2003) rule out this possibility by implementing a third payment scheme under which the tournament "winner" is chosen at random; under this scheme, both men and women perform at their piece rate level, and there is no gender gap in performance.

A final important result in Gneezy et al. (2003) is that women do as well as men in the tournament setting if the groups are single-sex; hence, the authors attribute the gender gap in the tournament setting to women's relative failure to perform at a high level when competing against men, but not when competing in general. In this regard, it is interesting that the female (and male) subjects in this experiment are all students at the most competitive technology university in Israel (Technion), and hence, compared to the general population, quite used to performing in a male-dominated environment.

Niederle and Vesterlund (2007) push this research agenda further by studying the compensation choices men and women make in a mixed-sex environment (groups of 2 men and 2 women). As in the previously discussed paper, the compensation schemes under consideration are a piece rate scheme and a tournament-like winner-take-all

---

[7] While this is consistent with men being relatively more overconfident than women, one cannot rule out as an alternative explanation the possibility than men simply derive more entertainment value from trading.

scheme. The task in this case consists in solving a series of additions. The experiment is designed not only to highlight gender differences in compensation choices, but also investigate the possible explanations for these gender differences. At the end of each round, the participants are informed about their own performance but provided no information about their relative performance. The first two rounds are used to assess gender differences in performance in this task under either a piece rate setting or a tournament scheme; in neither case do the authors observe gender differences in performance.[8] The third round is when participants get to choose which compensation scheme they would prefer for their performance in that round. Despite the lack of gender differences in performance in the first two rounds, Niederle and Vesterlund (2007) find that close to three quarters of men, but only one third of women, choose the tournament scheme; most strikingly, even the women that perform in the top performance quartile in the first rounds of the experiment are less likely to choose tournament compensation than the men that performed in the lowest quartile. From a payoff maximization perspective, there are too few (high ability) women and too many (low ability) men entering the tournament.

In the remaining sections of the paper, Niederle and Vesterlund (2007) provide a careful investigation of the potential explanations for why women are so much more likely to "shy away" from the winner-take-all environment. Consistent with prior work on overconfidence, Niederle and Vesterlund (2007) find that both men and women overestimate their performance rank in their group but that men overestimate it by a greater extent than women; this gender gap in overconfidence explains some but not all of the gender difference in compensation choice. However, further accounting for the gender differences in risk attitudes, as well as women's greater aversion to negative feedback does little to further reduce the gender gap in the decision to compete.[9] The residual gender gap, Niederle and Vesterlund (2007) conclude, is best interpreted as women having less of a taste for competition.

In a complementary paper, Niederle and Vesterlund (2008) propose to re-examine the costs and benefits of affirmative action in light of an environment such as the one described above, where too few women but too many men enter competitive environments. In particular, they experimentally demonstrate a substantial increase in the share of women willing to participate in tournaments under a quota-like affirmative action policy that requires at least as many women as men to be tournament winners. The reason for this, they argue, is that the affirmative action policy essentially makes the competition more gender-specific, and that women's taste for competing is higher when

---

[8] This second round result is in contrast with Gneezy et al. (2003).

[9] By entering the winner-take-all scheme, an individual will automatically learn whether or not he or she was the highest performer on the task. If, as argued by Roberts and Nolen-Hoeksema (1989), women respond more poorly to information about how well they did compared to others, they may decide against the winner-take-all scheme to avoid being exposed to this information.

the competition is more gender-specific. Because of this entry response to the affirmative action policy, which includes entry by high ability women, the cost of affirmative action (in terms of the average ability of the tournament winners) is not as high as one might have predicted absent the change in entry.

While Gneezy et al. (2003) and Niederle and Vesterlund (2007) offer a truly original explanation for the gender gap in labor market achievement, some questions remain open for future research regarding both the robustness and interpretation of the findings in these two influential papers. One remaining source of confusion is with regard to the importance of the gender composition of the group a given individual is made to compete against, e.g. same-sex versus mixed-gender groups. For example, Gneezy and Rustichini (2004) study how fourth-graders (75 boys and 65 girls) perform on a short distance race. They first let each child run by himself or herself to establish some individual speed benchmark and then get the children to compete in pairs, where the children in a pair have been matched on their speed, independently of their gender. While there is no gender gap in performance when the children run alone, boys outpaced girls in the competitive setting, with boys running faster and girls running slower. While this in itself is consistent with the lab findings described above, it appears that the gender gap in performance is more pronounced in the single-sex races: boys' speed increases in the competitive setting by about the same amount whether they are paired with boys or girls; but girls' speed only decreases when they are paired with other girls, and they in fact run a bit faster when paired with boys. This is unlike the maze task in Gneezy et al. (2003), where women did better when competing against other women than when compensated with the piece rate. Also raising questions about the importance of the gender composition of the environment for the gender competition effects is a paper by Gupta et al. (2005). While this paper is quite similar to Niederle and Vesterlund (2007), subjects in this case choose between a piece rate or tournament pay scheme after being told whether they are matched to a man or a woman. As in Niederle and Vesterlund (2007), men are much more likely than women to select the tournament pay scheme. However, women's decision of whether or not to compete seems unrelated to whether they are paired with a man or with a woman.

Future research in this area should also aim to confirm that the gender differences in performance in competitive setting and willingness to enter competitive settings are more than just a reflection of already identified gender differences, such as attitudes towards risk and overconfidence. Indeed, in contrast with Niederle and Vesterlund (2007), Gupta et al. (2005) find that risk aversion appears to matter substantially in explaining women's compensation choices. Dohmen and Falk (forthcoming) also perform a laboratory experiment where subjects are asked to perform a task and can choose how they want to get compensated for this task. The subjects in this case can choose between a fixed pay scheme (where subject receive a fixed fee just for showing up in the laboratory, independently on how well they perform on the task) and one of three different variable pay schemes: piece rate, tournament and revenue sharing. Like Niederle and Vesterlund (2007), they find that women are relatively less likely to select into the variable pay schemes, even after controlling for gender differences in baseline productivity levels on the task. However, and in contrast with the findings in Niederle and Vesterlund (2007), they also show that the gender gap in selecting into the variable pay schemes (including the tournament pay scheme) becomes small and statistically weak after controlling for gender differences in risk attitudes.

Finally, future research in this area should investigate how robust the results are to higher stakes, as well as to repetition and learning. In a study combining field and laboratory evidence, Antonovics et al. (2009) illustrate the importance of increasing stakes. The field data comes from The Weakest Link, a television game show where groups of individuals compete for large sums of money. In contrast with Gneezy et al. (2003), they find no evidence that the gender of one's opponent matters for the performance of female participants in the game show. Yet, when replicating the game show in the laboratory with the kind of stakes that are typically used in the laboratory (around $20 for the winner), they do replicate Gneezy et al. (2003). They further manage to replicate the game show behavior in the laboratory by raising the stakes ($50 or higher) and establishing a better match between the age profile of the game show participants and that of the laboratory's subject pool. Specifically, when the stakes are low in the laboratory, women perform worse when they compete against men than when they compete against women; when the stakes are $50 or more, women perform better when they face men than when they face women.[10] Vandegrift and Yavas (2009) assess the robustness of the gender gap in tournament entry in an environment that allows for learning about absolute and relative performance. Their results suggest that gender might not be such a strong predictor of tournament entry when, as is common in many real world applications, individuals repeatedly face the same task and compensation choices, and are able to learn about their actual relative ability.[11]

2.3. Social preferences

Another "psychological" perspective on why women are not performing as well as men in the labor market has been linked to possibly systematic differences between

---

[10] One should note though that even the basic (e.g. low stake) laboratory results here are not perfectly in line with Gneezy et al. (2003) in that both men and women under-perform in this case when competing against someone of the opposite sex.

[11] The task under consideration in Vandegrift and Yavas (2009) is a forecasting task, with participants being rewarded based on the quality of their forecast. Women are disproportionately weaker at this task than men. In early rounds, male entrants into the tournament show significantly lower forecast errors than female entrants; however, the difference disappears over time and in the final rounds, there is no significant difference between the forecast errors of male and female tournament entrants. Some of the convergence in the gender gap for tournament entrants is the result of reductions in performance by male tournament entrants, but most of the convergence is caused by a large improvement in the ability of the average female tournament entrant. Weaker forecasters tend to avoid the tournament and, after controlling for forecasting skill, gender does not predict tournament entry.

genders in their level of social preferences. In particular, it has been argued that women are more socially minded than men. One can easily see how stronger redistributive preferences might interfere with women's financial success in the labor market. Stronger redistributive preferences could also be in part responsible for women being less willing to compete (Section 2.2), or less willing to negotiate (Section 2.4). A large body of experimental research on gender differences in social preferences is summarized in Croson and Gneezy (2009) and Eckel and Grossman (2008b).

Three main types of experiments have been used to study gender differences in social preferences: public good experiments, ultimatum experiments and dictator experiments. Eckel and Grossman (2008b) point towards a difficulty in interpreting and comparing the results of many of the public good and ultimatum experiments. Indeed, some of these experiments include financial risk (for example, the selfless choice in a public game typically involves some risk of financial loss) while others do not; this is problematic in that, as has been discussed before, there are systematic gender differences in risk aversion between women and men. Also, some experimental designs expose the subjects and their decisions to the judgment of others, while others do not; yet, women and men may differentially care about how others judge their behavior. As an illustration of these difficulties, Eckel and Grossman (2008b) review 7 recent public good experiments (typically, these are n-person simultaneous move games where an individual's contribution to the public good generate positive externalities but where non-contributing is a dominant strategy), and confirm the lack of uniformity across these studies. Three of those studies (Brown-Kruse and Hummels, 1993; Sell and Wilson, 1991; Sell et al., 1993) find that women contribute less to the public good than men do; two (Nowell and Tinkler, 1994; Seguino et al., 1996) find higher contribution by women; and another two (Cadsby and Maynes, 1998; Sell, 1997) find mixed results. Eckel and Grossman (2008b) argue that the experimental evidence in favor of women being more socially oriented is much stronger if one restricts oneself to those experimental designs where the researchers have managed to abstract away from risk and have provided more anonymity to the subjects. In this regard, the evidence on dictator experiments typically is subject to less confounding factors. Overall, the dictator experiments (see for example, Bolton and Katok, 1995; Eckel and Grossman, 1998, or Andreoni and Vesterlund, 2001) find evidence that is broadly consistent with women giving away more than men.[12]

There is a quite a lot of field evidence consistent with higher level of altruism and stronger preferences for redistribution among women. Some of this evidence is indirect, coming from observed gender differences in political orientation. Some papers have

---

[12] To be precise, the findings in Andreoni and Vesterlund (2001) are a bit more nuanced. When altruism is expensive, women are found to be kinder; but the opposite holds when altruism is cheap. Andreoni and Vesterlund (2001) also find that while men are more likely to be extreme types in terms of giving (e.g. either perfectly selfish or perfectly selfless), women are more likely to share evenly.

demonstrated that women are today more left-leaning than men (see for example, Edlund and Pande, 2002; Edlund et al., 2005 or Box-Steffensmeier et al., 2004).[13] However, the fact that this political gender gap has been changing over time (women were consistently more conservative than men until the mid-1960s) and that this trend can be related to an increase in divorce risk and decline in marriage (Edlund and Pande, 2002; Edlund et al., 2005) suggests a more economic, rather than pure psychological, explanation for women being more left-leaning: women may prefer more redistributive policies because they are more likely to be the beneficiaries of those policies, due to their lower average earnings.

A few recent papers provide more direct evidence on the gender gap in policy preferences between men and women (rather than just the partisan gender gap). Funk and Gathmann (2009) use time-variation in the adoption of women's suffrage across Swiss cantons and study voting behavior on a broad range of policies that were subject to direct voting through referendums and initiatives. They find that female voting has a substantial impact on the composition of spending, but a negligible effect on the total size of government spending.[14] In particular, they find that female voting is associated with stronger support for redistributive policies and public health spending.[15] While there might again be an economic explanation for this finding, Funk and Gathmann (2009) further establish that the gender gap in policy preferences remains even after controlling for socio-economic characteristics. This suggests there might be true psychological differences between men and women in the strength of their social preferences. Similar patterns are found in subjective self-reports: for example, Alesina and Giuliano (2009) examine survey data for a variety of countries and conclude that, even after controlling for a large vector of individual socio-economic characteristics, women are more pro-redistribution than men; this appears to be true holding political ideology constant.

2.4. Attitudes towards negotiation

Because a negotiation can be viewed as a competition over resource distribution, the research on gender differences in competition and gender differences in social preferences has been linked to an earlier literature on gender differences in negotiation. While earlier meta-analyses (Rubin and Brown, 1975) pointed towards a lack of consistent patterns, with many null and contradictory findings, more recent meta-analyses (Stuhlmacher and Walters, 1999; Walters et al., 1998) started highlighting the importance of situational or contextual factors for gender differences in negotiation. Building on this, a recurring

---

[13] Interestingly, Washington (2008) and Oswald and Powdthavee (2010) show that having a daughter (rather than a son) make fathers favor more liberal policies.

[14] The effect on total spending is in contrast with the results in Lott and Kenny (1999) who find increases in state-level spending after the adoption of women's suffrage in the US.

[15] Similarly, Miller (2008) finds that the suffrage rights for women in US states were associated with large increases in public health spending, and a subsequent decline in child mortality. Papers such as Thomas (1990, 1994), or Duflo (2003) also confirm that women place greater weights on the provision of public goods and child welfare.

theme in the more recent wave of research on gender differences in negotiation is that those differences are not static but highly dependent on the context, with gender effects occurring under some situational cues but disappearing (or sometimes even reversing) under other situational cues. In this regard, this work is quite different from the previously discussed research on risk attitudes, or preference for competition, or selflessness, which has been less concerned so far about the importance of situational factors.

Bowles et al. (2005) show that whether subjects are told that they are negotiating for themselves or negotiating for others matters for the resulting gender gap in negotiation outcomes. In particular, women's performance in negotiation improves significantly when negotiating for someone else as opposed to for themselves; whether men negotiate for themselves or for others has little effect on their negotiation performance. Bowles et al. (2005) relate this result to an entitlement literature that suggests that women may feel relatively less deserving (see Major, 1987). It is also possible that women expect (rightly or wrongly so) more of a backlash if they negotiate for themselves (Rudman, 1998; Rudman and Glick, 1999). Finally, women may feel more obligated towards others than men do or may care more about others (Section 2.3), which make them feel especially motivated to do well when responsible for the interests of others.

Bowles et al. (2005) also investigate the moderating role of what they call "situational ambiguity" in explaining gender difference in negotiation. In particular, Bowles and al. create a low ambiguity situation in a laboratory-based price negotiation experiment by providing buyers with specific information about what would be a good agreement price in the negotiation; in contrast, no such information was provided to buyers in the high ambiguity situation. They show that women's performance is especially low when information is poor.

Small et al. (2007) measure the gender gap in the likelihood to initiate negotiations. Subjects in their controlled laboratory experiment are paid what is presented to them as the lowest amount possible after playing a word game; the research's objective is then to analyze whether participants ask for higher payment from the experimenter. Women ask much less often than men. Offering stronger cues about the negotiability of payment does not reduce the gender gap; in contrast though, the gender gap disappears when the situation is framed as an opportunity to "ask," rather than an opportunity to "negotiate." Small et al. (2007) attribute this difference to women being more intimidated by the "negotiation" language than by the "asking" language. Building on work in politeness theory (Brown and Levinson, 1987), Small et al. (2007) suggest that the "negotiation" language might be viewed as inconsistent with the norms of politeness that socially less powerful individuals (e.g. women more than men) are more likely to abide by; in contrast, the "asking" language is more in line with what a low-power person would say (e.g., "may I borrow a dollar?" rather than "give me a dollar").

Bowles et al. (2007) also investigate gender differences in the propensity to initiate negotiations. They propose and test the view that a differential treatment of men and women that attempt to negotiate is a key driver of the gender gap in initiating negotiation for higher compensation. As a first step in their study, they first investigate how subjects evaluate accounts of male and female candidates that did or did not negotiate for their compensation. Women that initiate negotiation receive systematically worse evaluation from male evaluators than men that initiate negotiations. In particular, in both written and video-based evaluations, male evaluators report being significantly more willing to work with women who accepted their compensation offers than with those who attempted to negotiate for higher compensation, even though they perceive both groups of women as equally able. Female evaluators did not display such systematic patterns across the written and video-based evaluations. This is reminiscent of studies such as Rudman (1998) and Rudman and Fairchild (2004), who show that women who self-promote in a stereotypically masculine way are perceived to be socially less competent.[16]

In a next step, when asked to take the candidates' perspective, female subjects are shown to be less inclined to negotiate in the presence of a male evaluator; but no such difference occurred in the presence of a female evaluator. Hence, the gender of the evaluator is a key driver of the gender gap in the propensity to initiate compensation negotiations. Bowles et al. (2007) also investigate possible mediators for these effects; they conclude that neither nervousness, nor the anticipation of backlash, nor the strength of the participants' gender identity can fully explain the gender differences in the propensity to initiate compensation negotiation in the presence of a male evaluator. Bowles et al. (2007) conclude that "... women's greater hesitation (as compared to men) about attempting to negotiate for higher compensation may be informed more by emotional intuition than a conscious cost-benefit calculus based upon the anticipated social consequences of initiating negotiations."

2.5. Empirical implications for labor market outcomes

Most of the studies described above take place in controlled experimental settings. While these studies often document economically large gender differences in risk attitudes, attitudes towards competition and negotiation, or willingness to share with others, the real test for these new psychological perspectives on gender is whether they have any bite in explaining actual gender differences in labor market (or labor-market relevant) outcomes. The existing research in this area, which we describe below, is clearly just in its infancy and far from conclusive, with many contradictory findings. Trying to better establish the relevance of the psychological research for real outcomes should be a first-order priority for future research.

Manning and Saidi (2010) study data from the 1998 and 2004 British Workplace Employees Relations Survey, which contains information on the use of performance

---

[16] Similar results have been found in the leadership literature. See for example Eagly et al. (1992).

(or variable) pay at the occupation-level within establishments. Based on both the experimental literature on gender differences in attitudes towards risk and preferences for competition, they predict that there should be fewer women in those occupations and establishments that use variable pay instead of fixed pay contracts. While this is indeed what they find, the difference is quantitatively small, especially in contrast with the large gap in attitudes towards risk and competition observed in the laboratory. They also find very modest effect of performance pay on hourly wages and no significant effect of the gender mix in a job on the responsiveness to performance pay.[17]

A few recent papers have looked for field evidence on the impact of competitive pressures on male and female performance. In search of settings that are closer to the winner-take-all environments used in the laboratory, these papers have focused on narrower subgroups of the population. Paserman (2007) study how male and female tennis players react to competitive pressures in Grand Slam tournaments. By the nature of the sport, there is no variation in gender composition here: female tennis players never play against male tennis players. Paserman (2007) can therefore only look for behavioral responses to competitive pressures in single-sex environments (which, as we discussed earlier, have not been consistently found in the lab). Using a point-by-point analysis, Paserman (2007) finds that women are much more likely than men to commit unforced errors at critical points in the game; there is also some evidence that women's first serves become more conservative at critical points in the game (e.g. women have a higher first serve percentage at critical points).

In a recent working paper, Lavy (2008b) finds a real world setting that is even closer to the controlled environment designed by Gneezy et al. (2003). Specifically, Lavy studies how high school teachers' performance is affected when they are forced to participate in an academic subject-specific rank-order tournament where they are rewarded according to the relative performance of their classes on a test compared to the performance of other teachers' classes at the same school. In contrast with the laboratory evidence, Lavy finds no statistical evidence that female teachers do worse under the tournament scheme. In addition, female teachers' performance in the tournament scheme does not appear to be statistically related to the gender mix of the comparison group (e.g. other teachers at the same school in the same academic subject). One should note though that a first-order difference between the teacher environment studied here and the laboratory setting is the time frame under which the task has to be performed (15 minutes of maze solving versus months of teaching). Another first-order difference is that teachers have clearly a lot of experience with the task at hand, unlike the maze-solving students. Other possible explanations for why the Lavy results differ from the experimental results might be that

---

[17] Note that the lack of strong differential response to performance pay by gender has been documented in multiple other papers. For example, Paarsch and Shearer (2007) show how productivity responds to piece-rate incentives among employees of a Canadian tree-planting firm. They find no evidence of differential response to incentives by gender and attribute the gender gap in productivity to gender differences in tree-planting ability.

the type of men that become teachers might be a very selected group, and the fact that it is the kids' performance, rather than the teacher's input in that performance, that is being directly measured.

In contrast, Örs et al. (2008) find results that are more consistent with the competition hypothesis. They study the performance of men and women in the very competitive entry exam to the Haute Ecole de Commerce (HEC) in France, where only a little more than 1 out 10 applying students is admitted. They compare how men and women perform on the entry exam to their performance in the national high school exam (with is admittedly somewhat less competitive and less stressful), as well as, for the admitted students, to their performance in the first year of courses at HEC. They find that women perform more poorly than men on the stressful and competitive entry exam, with the performance distribution for men displaying much fatter tails. Yet, and consistent with the competition hypothesis, they find, when looking at the same set of students, that the performance of women first-order-stochastically dominates that of men in the two less competitive settings with similar academic content (national high school exam and first year at HEC).[18,19]

A few descriptive field studies have confirmed that women appear less likely to initiate negotiations. In a study of graduating professional school students, Babcock and Laschever (2003) find that only 7% of female students attempted to negotiate their initial compensation offers, as compared to 57% of men. In a survey of about 200 working adults, Babcock et al. (2006) find that men had initiated negotiations two to four times as frequently as women. Among MBA students, Babcock et al. (2006) find that more than half of the male students negotiated their job offer, compared to only about 10 percent of the female students. As in the laboratory setting, they find sharp contrasts between low-ambiguity industries, where compensation standards for starting salaries are relatively transparent and high-ambiguity industries, where compensation standards are less transparent. While there is no gender difference in negotiated starting salaries in low-ambiguity industries, there is about a $10,000 gender gap in high-ambiguity industries after controlling for a long vector of salary predictors.

Other descriptive studies have tried to link gender differences in negotiation to the under-representation of women at senior levels. Greig (2008) surveys about 300

---

[18] Rothstein (2004) observes a related pattern in US data: after controlling for SAT scores, girls have higher GPAs than men in both high school and college.

[19] Niederle and Vesterlund (2010) argue that a similar logic might be used to explain why women under-perform in math tests. Specifically, they argue that the difference between test score performance and actual ability might be particularly large for women when it comes to taking math tests (where women under-perform compared to men) because the math tests might be perceived as particularly competitive and/or stressful for women. Relying on the stereotype threat literature (Steele, 1997), they posit that women may view the math test taking task as particularly anxiety-inducing. It is also possible that compared to, say, English tests, math tests are typically taken in environments where more males tend to be present (as more of them select into math-intensive majors) and women respond particularly poorly to competitive pressures when surrounded by males. As we discuss below (Section 2.7), this last point is in line with a growing body of work discussing the benefits of single-sex education for women.

investment bankers at a major US investment bank. She finds that female employees report a lower propensity to negotiate on behalf of themselves and further shows that a correlation exists between one's propensity to negotiate and one's rate of advancement and seniority at the bank. While correlated with gender, the propensity to negotiate is not correlated with performance, suggesting that the gender gap in negotiation may bias personnel decisions and lead to an inefficient allocation of leadership positions.

Blackaby et al. (2005) examine promotion and pay patterns by gender in the UK academic labor market for economists. They find a significant gender gap in promotions, as well as a significant gender gap in the number of outside offers, holding productivity constant. Moreover, there is a stronger correlation between number of outside offers and earnings for men, but not for women. One (of admittedly many) possible interpretation for these findings is gender difference in one's ability or willingness to bargain.

Säve-Söderbergh (2009) uses a unique survey data set on a population of recent social science graduates in Sweden. In the survey, participants are asked to report if they were asked to state an explicit wage bid to their prospective employer, and if yes, what that bid level was; they are also asked to report the wage they were offered. Controlling for individual- and job-level characteristics, Säve-Söderbergh (2009) finds that women submit lower wage bids than men and are also offered lower wages; women also receive lower counter-offers than men. Säve-Söderbergh (2009) also studies the extent of self-promoting strategies by gender, by looking at how much each applicant overbids a similar applicant. Women do not appear to use self-promoting strategies less than equally qualified men in similar jobs, but they typically overbid by less than men do. Employers reward (in terms of offered wages) both men and women for self-promoting, but the rewards are slightly larger for men.

Fortin (2008) investigates the role of greed and altruism in explaining the gender wage gap. She relies on longitudinal data which allows her to capture those psychological characteristics in a pre-market environment and therefore minimize ex-post rationalization concerns. Fortin (2008) finds individual attitudes towards greed and altruism, but also ambition and leadership, to have the expected effects on a set of labor-market related behaviors and outcomes: in particular, individuals that display more greed and less altruism earn more). Moreover, women tend to score higher on most of those factors that are predictive of financially less attractive labor market outcomes; for example, women hold more altruistic values than men and rank opportunities to "help others or be useful in society" higher in their career selection. Fortin also finds evidence of gender convergence across cohorts in many of those soft factors, with the gender gap in ambition and leadership having particularly shrank a lot among the younger cohorts in her data. The psychological factor that remains an important predictor of the gender gap in earnings in the later cohorts are expectations about future income, which are themselves tightly linked to greed.

Manning and Swaffield (2008) take a stab at quantifying the importance of the previously discussed psychological factors in explaining the gender gap in early-career wage growth in the UK. They consider a comprehensive set of psychological factors, including risk attitudes, attitudes towards competition, self-esteem and overconfidence, and the strength other regarding preferences. One advantage of their data, as in Fortin (2008)'s study, is that they can define proxies for these psychological attributes prior to labor market entry. They conclude that the whole set of psychological factors can explain at most 4.5 log points of the about 25 log points gap in earnings that has built up between men and women 10 years after labor market entry; in contrast, human capital factors account for about 11 of these 25 log points.

2.6. Other personality traits

A recent literature has been interested in studying how a broader set of personality traits and characteristics affect behaviors and labor market outcomes (see Bowles et al., 2001; Borghans et al., 2008a,b). Personality traits may affect labor market earnings through different channels.[20] The most obvious model is that personality traits are part of an individuals' set of productive traits (just like cognitive skills) and these traits are directly valued in the market. In this case, any systematic difference in personality traits between men and men will translate in earnings differences, maybe in part due to occupational segregation. Personality traits may also impact pay by affecting one's preferences, such as one's willingness to take risk, or one's taste for competition.

The most commonly used inventory of personality traits is the Big Five model (see Digman, 1989, 1990; McCrae et al., 1999 or McCrae and John, 1992). The Big Five personality traits are extroversion, agreeableness, conscientiousness, neuroticism and openness to experience.[21] Psychologists have documented over the years gender differences in these five personality traits. A review by Bouchard and Loehlin (2001) suggests that agreeableness and neuroticism are the two traits that are most consistently associated with gender differences: women are consistently found to be both more agreeable and more neurotic than men.

Mueller and Plug (2006) rely on the Big Five model for an early exploration of the effects of personality traits on earnings by gender in the Wisconsin Longitudinal Study.[22] Like the earlier psychology literature, they confirm in this data the presence

[20] A well-known demonstration of the importance of personality traits for labor market success has been demonstrated in early childhood intervention programs such as the Perry Preschool Program (Heckman et al., 2007): while originally designed to improve the cognitive skills of children, this program did little to raise IQ levels among treated adults; however it did raise personality skills as well as a variety of economic outcomes among treated adults.

[21] An active debate surrounds the personality literature. One key aspect of this debate centers on the question of whether personality traits are stable across situations or whether they are essentially situation-specific. Also, the Big Five model is often criticized for its lack of theoretical foundations.

[22] Related studies by organizational and industrial psychologists have examined how the Big Five personality dimensions relate to job performance, occupational attainment and career success. See for example Judge et al. (1999).

of some gender differences in the Big Five personality traits. They find that women score significantly higher than men along the agreeableness, neuroticism, extroversion and openness dimensions, with the gender gap in agreeableness and neuroticism being the largest. Their second main finding is that while personality traits matter significantly for labor market earnings, the correlations differ quite a lot by gender. While there are positive returns to being open to experience for both men and women, men earn a premium for being antagonistic (that is, not agreeable) while women earn a premium for being conscientious. Overall, only 3 to 4 percent of the gender gap in earnings is explained by gender differences in mean personality traits and gender differences in the returns to those personality traits. A Oaxaca-type decomposition indicates that antagonism is the key trait in driving this gender gap (with men scoring higher on this trait and experiencing higher returns when displaying this personality trait). Overall, they find in this data that personality traits account for about as much earnings heterogeneity as cognitive ability does, but matter much less than a factor such as education.

A few other papers have been interested in the contribution of more specific personality traits for the gender gap in labor market achievements. Niederle and Yestrumskas (2008) test for the possibility that women's under-representation in high profile occupations might be related to their lower desire to seek challenges. Their experimental design confirms that women avoid higher difficulty levels on a task, even though there are neither gender differences in ability on that task nor gender differences in beliefs about ability on that task. Further experimental probing however suggest that those gender differences in the willingness to select more difficult tasks can be fully explained by (previously documented) gender differences in risk aversion and confidence.

Borghans et al. (2005) focus on the importance of interpersonal skills, or "people" skills. Borghans et al. (2005) argue that technological and organizational changes have induced an increase in the demand for interpersonal (or "people") skills. One explanation for this pattern is that new technologies may have led to more emphasis being placed on those skills that cannot be easily automated, which would naturally include people skills. They show that the importance of people tasks increased particularly rapidly between the late 1970s and the early 1990s. This shift in demand, the authors argue, has been particularly beneficial to women: indeed, they show that occupations in which people tasks are more important employ relatively more women, suggesting that women are relatively more endowed in those increasingly valuable interpersonal skills.[23] The authors conclude that the large increase in the importance of people tasks at work from the late

---

[23] Borghans et al. (2008a,b) present empirical evidence in both UK and German data that one's sociability level in youth affects one's job allocation in adulthood. More caring individuals are assigned to jobs in which caring is more important (e.g. teaching or nursing careers).

1970s to the early 1990s has contributed to the decline in the gender wage gap over that time period.[24,25]

In a similar spirit, a few studies highlight how other personality differences between men and women may work in women's, not men's, advantage. The focus so far has been on education. Specifically, gender differences in behavioral problems have been brought forward to explain why women are now surpassing men in terms of educational achievement.[26] The medical literature has documented the much higher rate of attention deficit hyperactivity disorder (ADHD) among boys (see for example Szatmari et al., 1989). Goldin et al. (2006) also report on the higher incidence of arrest rates and school suspension among teenage boys compared to teenage girls in the NLSY data.

The sources of the gender differences in the incidence of behavioral problems between boys and girls remain unclear. One hypothesis (Bjorklund and Kipp, 1996) is that women are better than men at delaying gratification; a meta-analysis of the relevant empirical research by Silverman (2003) suggest that there is indeed a small female advantage in the ability to delay gratification. Another explanation for boys' higher incidence of behavioral problems in high school is related to their later puberty and later maturation. In a study of the Finnish education system, Pekkarinen (2008) shows how postponing when students have to choose between vocational and academic tracks (from age 10-11 to age 15-16) led to a relative increase of the share of girls choosing the (more challenging) academic track, as well as a relative increase in the share of girls continuing into tertiary education. This differential response, Pekkarinen (2008) argues, is related to the fact that while boys and girls are at about the same stage of cognitive and psychological development by age 10-11, most girls are beyond puberty by age 14, while boys are still going through important physical and psychological changes that have adverse effects on their behavior and aspirations. Yet another hypothesis (see Sax, 2007) is that the demands that are placed on children in kindergarten have increased a lot over time (in the US at least), moving away from experiential knowledge and towards didactic knowledge; this change might have been detrimental to boys given the slower speed of development of relevant areas of their brain (such as the language area). A consequence of all this, Sax (2007) would argue, has been the increase in ADHD diagnosis, especially among very young boys, and the increase usage of ADHD drugs, which have been linked to personality changes (laziness, motivation, violence) even after short period of usage. An empirical implication of this hypothesis would be that starting kindergarten at an early

---

[24] The paper also documents that the same increase in demand for people skills may have slowed down the black–white convergence as blacks are relatively under-represented in occupations where people tasks are important.

[25] There is also been a related discussion of how modern business practices have increased the relative demand for more participative type of leadership, and hence been relatively favorable to women (see Eagly and Carli, 2007).

[26] Another explanation that has received attention for the reversal of the gender gap in college attendance is that the returns to college might be higher for women than for men (Dougherty, 2005). There has also been some discussion of increasing reverse discrimination against boys (see for example Lavy, 2008a,b).

age would be especially detrimental to boys. There is not much evidence for this so far (see for example Elder and Lubotsky, 2009).

While the literature is still unclear about the source of this gender gap in behavioral problems, it has already been established that they matter for the (reverse) gender gap in college attendance. Using NELS data on a nationally representative cohort of eight graders in 1988, Jacob (2002) shows that boys have a much higher incidence of school disciplinary and behavior problems, and that they spend fewer hours doing homework. Controlling for these non-cognitive behavioral factors, as well as the higher college premium for women, can explain most of the female advantage in college enrollment; importantly, non-cognitive factors continue to matter even after controlling for high school achievement (Jacob, 2002). Hence, as Goldin et al. (2006) put it, one can view the reversal of the gender gap in college attendance as the outcome of a "...more level playing field allowed girls to blossom and take advantage of higher expected returns of attending college. At the same time, slower social development and greater behavioral problems of boys remained and allowed girls to leap frog them."

Finally, besides papers trying to directly relate, in a reduced form way, personality traits to educational and labor market outcomes, a few studies have been interested in how personality traits predict preference parameters, such as risk preferences. For example, Croson and Gneezy (2009) offer an interesting discussion of what might explain gender differences in risk aversion. They point at systematic gender differences in emotional or affective reaction to risk, which may affect the utility one gets from making riskier choices. Indeed, women appear to experience more stress, fear or dread in situations that involve the risk of a negative outcome. (Brody, 1993; Fujita et al., 1991). Also, Fehr-Duda et al. (2006) show that women's higher relative risk aversion can be linked to women underestimating large probabilities of gains more strongly than do men; this, they argue, could be viewed as consistent with Loewenstein et al. (2001)'s "risk as feelings hypothesis," with women's stronger emotional reaction at the time of making a risky decision manifesting itself as pessimism.[27] The same pessimism may also cause women to overestimate the probability of negative outcomes, as suggested by Silverman and Kumka (1987), Flynn et al. (1994), or Spigner et al. (1993).

Borghans et al. (2009) experimentally measure risk aversion (as well as ambiguity aversion) among a sample of Dutch high school students. They then link those individual-level risk attitudes to both cognitive and non-cognitive personality traits, including the Big Five (openness, conscientiousness, extraversion, agreeableness, neuroticism) and a measure of ambition. Like much of this literature, they also find women to be more risk averse. They then try to assess how much of this can be due to differences in cognitive and non-cognitive traits between the gender. They do find personality traits to be predictive of risk aversion: in particular, being less agreeable, more

---

[27] See also Loewenstein and Lerner (2003).

neurotic and more ambitious is associated with lower levels of risk aversion. However, controlling for these psychological traits explains little of the gender gap in risk aversion.

2.7. Where do gender differences in preferences and personality traits come from?

It is obvious that there are important biological differences between men and women that have direct implications for how each sex is faring in the labor market. For example, men have a comparative advantage when it comes to occupations that require physical strength.[28] Also, as suggested in Ichino and Moretti (2009), it is likely that the menstrual cycle puts women of child-bearing age at a relative disadvantage because of it may cause them to be regularly sick and absent from work.[29] More importantly, many of the disruptions associated with child birth mechanically hurt women's chances of labor market success. In this regard, a few papers have shown how various sources of medical progress, by minimizing the influence of these biological differences, have contributed to a reduction in the gender gap in education and labor force participation. Goldin and Katz (2002) argue, and empirically demonstrate, that the availability of oral contraceptives (the pill) increased the likelihood that college-educated women choose to further invest in long-duration professional education (such as by entering medical school or law school). Similarly, Bailey (2006) shows that legal access to the pill for young unmarried women significantly increased their labor force participation later in their life cycle, as well as their number of hours worked. Also, Albanesi and Olivetti (2009) discuss how medical improvements in maternal health and the introduction of infant formula increased the labor force participation of married women of child-bearing age.[30]

Besides these obvious biological differences between the sexes lies the question of whether more subtle gender differences, such as the gender differences in preferences and personality traits discussed in the prior sections, also have biological roots (a "nature" explanation) or whether, in contrast, they mainly are the outcomes of environmental influences (a "nurture" explanation). As we discuss earlier, some of the research summarized above already highlights the importance of situational cues for the measurement of gender gap in attitudes (see in particular the work on gender differences in negotiation in Section 2.4), strongly suggesting a non-trivial role for environmental

---

[28] Welch (2000) presents in a two-skill (brain and brawn) model that can explain both the reduction in the gender gap in earnings, and the increase in income inequality. The model assumes that women are relatively well endowed in brains, and that brains are less equally distributed than brawn. With these two assumptions, an increase in the price of brain (such as likely occurred in the 1970s and 1980s) can at the same time reduce the gender gap in earnings and increase wage inequality.

[29] While Ichino and Moretti (2009) find evidence of 28-day cycles in absence for women working in a large Italian bank, Rockoff and Herrmann (2009) fail to detect any such cycles among female teachers in the New York City public schools. They argue that the different explicit financial incentives surrounding sick days in the US and Italy, and different levels of intrinsic motivation, can account for the lack of consistent results.

[30] See also Buckles (2007), who examines how easier access to infertility treatments affects women's labor force participation and wages.

factors. In general though, either nurture or nature factors could explain why men and women differ in their attitudes towards risk, or competition, or their willingness to share with others.

Proponents of a nurture explanation emphasize that parents, teachers and peers tend to treat boys and girls differently from a very young age, maybe being more tolerant of more aggressive or competitive behavior for boys, or having higher expectations them. Proponents of a nature explanation have emphasized arguments from evolutionary biology and evolutionary psychology. For example, an evolutionary explanation for gender differences in attitudes towards competition relies on the view that competitiveness may be a positive factor in the reproductive success of men, but a negative factor for the reproductive success of women. Because men can have many more children than women, they have more to gain from a reproductive perspective from winning competition against other men (Daly and Wilson, 1988); in contrast, more competitive tendencies among women may be destructive as their death may also imply the death of their offspring (Campbell, 2002).

Sorting out the relative importance of nature versus nurture has important policy implications. Finding a large role of environmental factors in explaining why women are, for example, more risk averse than men (and hence under-represented in riskier higher-earnings jobs) would imply that well thought-out educational reforms might be effective in undoing at least some of the gender gap. In contrast, affirmative action policies to increase women's representation in competitive sectors, or a push for further medical and pharmaceutical advances, might be the only effective policy tools if differences between the genders in the willingness to operate in a competitive environment are biological rather than environmental. Of course, it is also possible that both nature and nurture are at play, with these two explanations complementing one another rather than competing with one another. This last possibility is broadly supported by the body of research we review below.

2.7.1. Nurture

Gneezy et al. (2008) present a case study that appears to rule out a pure nature-based explanation for gender differences in attitudes towards competition. The idea behind this research consists in measuring gender differences in behavior across two distinct societies with as close as possible to opposite cultures when it comes to women's position in the society. Finding evidence that women behave differently across such two distinct societies would run against the view that the behavioral differences between the genders are purely determined by biology. The two societies selected by Gneezy et al. (2008) are the Maasai in Tanzania and the Khasi in Northeast India. The Maasai are a classic example of a patriarchal society where "women are said to be less important than cattle." The Khasi are matrilineal with inheritance and clan membership following a female lineage; Khasi women are the head of their household and make all important economic decisions. After these two societies have been identified, the study then consists in asking participants to perform a simple task and ask them to choose, ahead of performing the task, how they want to get compensated for the task. The task in this case, chosen for its simplicity and gender neutrality, consists in tossing a small ball 10 times in a bucket. The participants are further informed that they will be paired with someone else performing the same task in another location in the village, and can choose between being compensated a fixed amount for each successful throw or three times that fixed amount per successful throw if they outperform the other participant (and nothing if they are outperformed). Gneezy et al. (2008) find that while the patriarchal society follows the same gender patterns as found in the West (with 50 percent of the Maasai men choosing to compete compared to only 26 percent of Maasai women), the exact opposite pattern holds in the matriarchal society (with 54 percent of Khasi women choosing to compete compared to only 39 percent of Khasi men). While this result runs against the view that gender differences in the willingness to compete are purely driven by biology, it remains possible that different socialization processes between these two societies resulted in a large evolutionary distance between them.

Two other recent papers also pointing towards a role of socialization and environmental factors in explaining gender differences in preferences (risk attitudes and attitudes towards competition) are Booth and Nolen (2009a,b). Booth and Nolen (2009a) show that gender differences in risk attitudes in a sample of English 15-year-olds depend on whether the girls have attended a single-sex school or mixed-gender school. Girls from single-sex schools display risk attitudes that are no different from the average boy; in contrast, girls from mixed-gender schools are significantly more risk averse. Clearly, an advantage of this study compared to Gneezy et al. (2008) is that one is less concerned about evolutionary distance between students in single-sex schools and those in mixed-gender schools. There is however a clear concern about differential selection into these two types of school, and in particular that the more able students attend the single-sex grammar schools.[31] Booth and Nolen (2009a) try as much as possible to address this concern by restricting their analysis to the top students in both types of schools, by showing the robustness of the results to propensity score matching of students, and by instrumenting for school type with relative distance between the child's residence and the closest mixed-gender or single-sex school.

Booth and Nolen (2009b) use another part of the same experiment to study how the educational environment might relate to the gender differences in the willingness to compete. Specifically, the boys and girls in the experiment are also asked to solve mazes first under a piece-rate scheme, then under a tournament scheme where their performance is compared to others in a group they were randomly assigned to. Finally, they are asked to choose whether they want their performance in a last round to get compensated under the piece rate scheme or under the tournament scheme. Consistent

---

[31] Prior research has established a negative correlation between cognitive skills and risk aversion, even after controlling for socio-economic background and educational attainment. See for example Dohmen et al. (forthcoming-a, 2010).

with the findings on risk attitudes in Booth and Nolen (2009a), they find that girls from single-sex schools behave more like boys in that they are 42 percentage points more likely to choose the tournament compensation compared to girls from the mixed-gender schools; in contrast, boys from mixed-gender schools are statistically as likely to enter the tournament as boys from single-sex schools. These findings are robust to controlling for ability on the task (as measured in the first rounds of play), as well as to performing the same set of robustness checks as in Booth and Nolen (2009a).[32]

While our focus has been on the role of environmental factors for the gender gap in non-cognitive skills, we also discuss for the sake of completeness recent work on how nurture may affect the gender gap in some key cognitive skills. Hoffman et al. (2010) focus on spatial abilities, a skill that has been shown to correlate with success in engineering courses as well as the decision to major in physical sciences (Humphreys et al., 1993), and a skill at which men significantly outperform women (Voyer et al., 1995). Hoffman et al. (2010) use a research approach similar to Gneezy et al. (2008) to assess the role of nurture in the gender gap in spatial reasoning, which they measure by the time needed to solve a puzzle. They show that women's relative disadvantage on this task disappears when they move from a patrilineal society (the Karbi) to a geographically and ethnically close matrilineal society in Northeast India (the Khasi).

Much of the remaining research on how environmental factors influence the gender gap in cognitive skills has put the emphasis on the possible role model effects associated with teacher gender. While a lot of the earlier research on this topic has delivered mixed results (most likely because of an inability to deal well with obvious omitted variable and selection issues), a few recent papers have come to more consistent evidence of non-trivial role model effects. In a sample of eighth graders in the US, Dee (2005, 2007) studies how within-children cross-subject assignment to a same-sex rather than opposite-sex gender teacher affects both the children's performance in the subject and the teacher's perception of the student's performance.

Assignment to a same-gender teacher improves performance for both girls and boys; it also improves the teacher's perceptions of the student's performance. Hoffmann and Oreopoulos (2009) exploit both within student and within instructor variation and find qualitatively similar effects among first-year college students, even though the economic magnitude of these effects is rather small (at most 5 percent of a standard deviation improvement in grade). Another study of college students (Carrell et al., 2009) focuses on how same-sex teachers in introductory university courses affect a student's majoring choices. The experimental design here is particularly appealing in that the focus is on an educational institution where students are randomly assigned to professors for those

---

[32] Note that there is also some evidence that girls that are randomly assigned by the experimenter to all-girls groups are less likely to shy from competition than girls assigned to mixed-gender or all-boys groups; however, this does not cancel out the direct effect of being female on one's willingness to compete. Similarly, Booth and Nolen (2009a) find that girls assigned to all-girls groups display a higher risk tolerance than girls assigned to mixed-gender or all-boys groups.

introductory courses. The results suggest that female students that are assigned to female professors for their introductory math and science classes not only perform better in those classes but are also much more likely to major in science, math, or engineering; professor gender does not appear to matter much for male students. This is qualitatively consistent with Bettinger and Long (2005) who use within course and student variation (e.g. no random assignment in this case) and find small but positive effects of same-sex instructors on course credits and major choices for female students.

A recent study by Fryer and Levitt (2010) fails to find such role model effects to mothers' influences on their daughter's math skills. Fryer and Levitt (2010) relies on ECLS-K, a data set that covers a sample of more than 20,000 children entering kindergarten in the fall of 1998 and interviews them in the spring of kindergarten, first grade, third grade, and fifth grade. They find that girls with highly-educated mothers, or mothers working in math-related occupations, lose as much ground in math compared to girls whose mothers are less educated or do not work in math-related occupations. The data further shows that parents report spending equal amounts of time with boys and girls doing math-related activities. More generally, a set of variables capturing parental behavior or parental expectations do little to explain the gender gap in math scores among these young children.

A few recent papers have debated whether socialization or environmental forces can account for some of the cross-country variation in the gender gap in math test scores. Guiso et al. (2008) focus on whether the degree of sexism in 40 countries relates to how well 15-year-old girls are doing in math and reading compared to 15-year-old boys. The proposed measure of sexism include the World Economic Forum's Gender Gap Index, as well an index of attitudes towards women built from the World Values Surveys. The findings suggest that the gender gap in math disappears in more gender-equal societies and the reading gender gap (which always favors women) becomes even larger in those societies. However, Fryer and Levitt (2010) show that this correlation between the gender gap in math and the gender equality indicators no longer holds when the list of countries is extended to include more middle-eastern countries (countries that generally score low on the gender equality indices but where girls do relatively well in math). Reminiscent of the work of Booth and Nolen (2009a,b), Fryer and Levitt (2010) note that one of the (many) distinctive features of these middle-eastern countries is their disproportionate reliance on single-sex schools.

2.7.2. Nature
While the evidence discussed so far is suggestive of at least some environmental influences, there has also been quite a lot work suggesting biological influences. Scientists have argued that differences in male and female brain structures, and in the exposure to sex hormones influence gender specific skills (see for example Kimura, 1999). In particular, a lot of research has focused on establishing that testosterone levels, which of course differs on average between men and women but also differ within gender, are

predictive of important behavioral outcomes. Studies have related higher testosterone levels to more positive attitudes towards competition and dominance (Archer, 2006), lower fear levels (Hermans et al., 2006) and more gambling and alcohol consumption (Dabbs and Morris, 1990; Mazur, 1995; Blanco et al., 2001). Also, Baron-Cohen (2003) argues that lower prenatal exposure to testosterone is related to how social a child is, and his or her ability to empathize with others.

A few recent studies have tried to directly establish a link between testosterone levels and the willingness to take financial risk. Dreber and Hoffman (2007) study the correlation between risk preferences and prenatal exposure to testosterone in a sample of Swedish university students. To proxy for prenatal exposure to testosterone, they use the ratio of the length of their second finger (index) to the length of their fourth finger (ring finger), a measure also known as the "2D:4D" ratio. There is suggestive but not conclusive evidence that the 2D:4D ratio is a marker for the permanent effects of prenatal hormones on the organizational structure of the brain: the 2D:4D ratio has been shown to be negatively correlated with prenatal testosterone exposure and to be fixed very early in life (see Manning et al., 1998). Dreber and Hoffman (2007) find that, both across and within-gender, a higher 2D:4D ratio predicts more risk aversion. In men, a similar correlation has been observed between levels of circulating testosterone and their risk attitudes (Apicella et al., 2008). Also, women's willingness to take financial risk has been shown to vary over the menstrual cycle (Broder and Hohmann, 2003).

A couple of recent papers show that testosterone levels are related to career choices and professional success. Maestripieri et al. (2009) focus on a sample of about 500 MBA students and first investigate how between- and across-gender variation in risk aversion in that sample relates to variation in both circulating testosterone (as measured in the saliva) and testosterone exposure in utero (proxied for with the 2D:4D ratio). Among female MBAs, those with higher circulating testosterone, and (but somewhat more weakly) higher levels of prenatal exposure testosterone, display lower levels of risk aversion; however, in contrast to Dreber and Hoffman (2007) and Apicella et al. (2008), testosterone levels (either prenatal or circulating) do not appear predictive of risk aversion among male MBAs. In the low testosterone range though (where most women are), there appears to be no gender differences in risk aversion between men and women. When it comes to occupational choices, Maestripieri et al. (2009) find that female MBAs are much less likely to enter a financial career than male MBAs; this gap becomes smaller and statically less precise in a regression that controls for both circulating and prenatal testosterone levels (with both testosterone level variables having the expected effect on career choices—e.g higher testosterone levels increase the chance of pursuing a career in finance). Also, Coates et al. (2009) focus on prenatal exposure to testosterone among male financial traders in the City of London, also using the 2D:4D ratio as a proxy. They find a relationship between an individual trader's 2D:4D ratio and his long-term profitability as a trader, as well as the number of years he remains active as a trader.

Studies such as these are certainly suggestive of a role for nature in explaining at least some of the underlying gender differences in both preferences and labor market outcomes. Yet, in the end, none of this evidence implies causality. This is clearly obvious when it comes to circulating testosterone levels, which could be strongly affected by environmental factors, or be an outcome, rather than a cause, of behavioral choices. This is also true, even though in a less obvious way, when it comes to prenatal exposure measures. Indeed, it remains unclear what drives the variation in the levels of testosterone in utero. One could imagine this variation to be related to mother's socio-economic characteristics or behaviors, and those could directly feed into different child-rearing practices.

3. GENDER IDENTITY

Another explanation that has gained in popularity over the last decade for the persistence of a gender gap in labor market outcomes is that this gap is an outcome of prevailing social norms about what is appropriate for men to do and what is appropriate for women to do. Such social norms may induce differential sorting of men and women across occupations; they may also drive women's decisions to participate in the workforce. While Altonji and Blank (1999) already mention the potential role of social norms in their review article, new research has emerged since their article, both theoretical and empirical, that helped refine our understanding of what those social norms are and how they might matter for labor market outcomes. On the theoretical front, a key development has been the import into economics, from social psychology, of the concept of identity, and the recognition that one's identity, which includes but goes far beyond one's "gender identity," could be an important factor in driving economic decisions. A 2000 paper by Akerlof and Kranton has anchored much of this recent literature. We first review this paper, as well as a few related theoretical pieces. We then discuss the empirical research aiming to test the link between gender identity and women's labor market outcomes, as well as the empirical research that has been interested in explaining the origin of gender identity norms. Finally, in an attempt to close the loop between this and the prior section of this article, we review some research that has proposed to link gender differences in preferences to gender identity; indeed, under a nurture view of gendered preferences, one could argue that women display more risk aversion (or a stronger dislike for competitive situations, or more altruistic tendencies) because this is what is expected from them under the prevailing gender identity norms.

3.1. Theoretical foundations

Akerlof and Kranton (2000) define identity as one's sense of self, or one's sense of belonging to one or multiple social categories. One's identity encompasses a clear view about how people that belong to that category should behave.[33] Akerlof and Kranton (2000) propose a model where one's identity directly enters the utility function: under this model, one's identity can influence economic outcomes because deviating from the behavior that is expected for one's social category is assumed to decrease utility. Hence, people's economic actions can in part be explained by a desire to conform with one's sense of self.

Most relevant to this review is the lengthy application Akerlof and Kranton (2000) propose of the identity model to the concept of gender identity. In this case, the two relevant social categories are those of "man" and "woman," and these two categories are associated with specific behavioral prescriptions which, if violated, will decrease utility. One obvious application is labor force participation: as long as there is a strong behavioral prescription indicating that "men work in the labor force and women work in the home", norms regarding gender identity could explain why women have been slow at increasing their labor force participation.

Another application Akerlof and Kranton (2000) consider is that of occupational segregation by gender. How could gender identity explain why such segregation has been slow to disappear? Akerlof and Kranton (2000) ask that we put ourselves in the shoes of a woman Marine. Because Marines are essentially all viewed as men, a woman in this occupation may feel discomfort as her decision to become a Marine is in conflict with the behavioral prescription for her gender category (only men, not women are Marines). This could explain why women have been slow at entering male professions, despite financial incentives to do so.

Moreover, male Marines may feel the need to tease or mistreat the woman Marine, as accepting her as a co-worker threatens their own gender identity, which reinforces women's reticence to enter this male profession. Note that in this last implication, the identity model can be regarded as a micro-foundation for reduced form discrimination models, such as Becker's, which assumes that people from one group have a dislike for working with people from another group (Becker, 1971). While such a dislike for being around people of the other group may capture quite well the feeling that many whites may still experience against non-whites, it does not fit so well when the groups are men and women. In contrast, the identity model provides a reasonable explanation for why men may be averse to being surrounded by women at work. This is related to Goldin (2002)'s pollution theory of discrimination, who also assumes that men derive utility from their work not just due to the wage they earn but also from how their image is affected by where they work and who they work with. Under Goldin (2002)'s model, men want to keep women away from certain jobs because broad female participation in those jobs would reduce the prestige men get from working in those jobs. The driver of the reduction in prestige in Goldin (2002)'s case is more about the signals that might

---

[33] See also Akerlof and Kranton (2002, 2005). Akerlof and Kranton's approach to identity is most directly related to social psychology research by Tajfel (1981) and Turner (1985). For a survey of recent research on identity, see Hill (2006).

be send to outsiders about the qualifications that are required to perform these jobs if too many women enter, as their productivity is not directly observable and verifiable by those outsiders whose opinion drives occupational prestige. In other words, Goldin's model is much closer to a statistical discrimination model while Akerlof and Kranton's is more directly reminiscent of the taste-based discrimination model. While Akerlof and Kranton's model can only explain big shifts in occupational segregation through changes in societal norms regarding gender, Goldin's model puts the focus on the credentialization process (such as the one induced by women entering professional schools in the late 60s and early 70s) as an important driver of the "declining significance of gender" and of occupational de-segregation.

Akerlof and Kranton (2000) also apply their gender identity model to the allocation of housework tasks between spouses. They discuss how gender identity considerations may explain why even those women that are employed full-time in the labor market still do a disproportionate share of the housework. If behavioral prescriptions dictate that "men work in the labor force and women work in the home", men's gender identity is threatened if their wives work in the labor market, and especially if they do well (better than their husband). One way to rebalance utility in the household would be for those "threatening" women to engage in a larger share of the housework tasks. The prediction of the gender identity model here clearly runs counter to the prediction of the bargaining model, which would call for a monotonic negative relationship between women's relative labor market earnings and their relative contribution to housework activities.

3.2. Does gender identity influence women's labor market decisions?

A couple of recent papers can be regarded as direct attempts to test the relevance of the gender identity model to explain female labor market outcomes both across countries and within-country over time. Fortin (2005) uses data from the World Values Surveys to assess how women's sense of selves relate to their labor force participation and relative earnings in a sample of 25 OECD countries over a 10-year period. She shows that the social representation of women as homemakers and men as breadwinners (as captured by a statement such as "being a housewife is just as fulfilling as working for pay") appears quite stable across cohorts and over time and is very predictive of women's labor market outcomes. There is also evidence that holding less egalitarian attitudes (as captured by a statement such as "when jobs are scarce, men should have more right to a job than women") is another powerful predictor of female employment and earnings; agreement with this statement has been declining both across cohorts and over time, which Fortin (2005) views as consistent with a decline in traditional forms of discrimination. Finally, there is evidence that what Fortin referred to as "mother's guilt" (as captured by disagreeing with a statement such as "a working mother can establish just as warm and secure a relationship with her child as a mother who does not work") is also closely related to a woman's labor force participation.

Fortin (2009) re-examines a similar question in a single country (the US) over a much longer time period (1977 to 2006). A more central motivation to this particular paper is to provide an explanation for the slowdown in the closing of the gender gap since the mid-1990s, which has occurred despite women's continued progress in terms of educational attainment (Blau and Kahn, 2006). Fortin shows that the evolution of gender role attitudes over time appears to map very well with the evolution of female labor force participation over time. Indeed, while women's gender role attitudes steadily became less traditional (e.g. more and more women disagreeing with the notion that husbands should be the breadwinners and wives should be the homemakers) and more egalitarian (e.g. more and more women agreeing with the notion that they are as capable as men in the workforce) until the mid-1990s, these trends reversed in the mid-1990s. Fortin (2009) further argues that the HIV/AIDS crisis might have been one of the factors responsible for the shift towards more conservative gender role attitudes.[34]

Important to an identity interpretation of the findings in Fortin's 2005 and 2009 papers is that the evolution of women's own sense of self, not just men's views about what women should do, drive the observed variation in labor force participation. This fact has been recently put into question by a paper by Charles et al. (2009). Charles et al. (2009) construct a measure of male sexism across US states, which they define based on men's responses to the gender role questions similar to those used by Fortin. They find a strong relationship between men's views on these questions in a given labor market and how women fare relative to men in that market (measured in terms of the gender wage gap and relative employment gap). Moreover, after controlling for men's views regarding gender roles, they fail to find that women's own views are predictive of their labor market outcomes. Charles et al. (2009)'s analysis further shows that it is the attitudes of the median man, but not the attitudes of the men at the tails of the distribution, that matters for women's relative labor market outcomes in a state. This, they argue, is consistent with the prediction of Becker's taste-based discrimination model.[35]

Another indirect test of the gender identity model is provided by Booth and van Ours (2009), who investigate the relationship between part-time work and well-being for Australian couples. They use three measures of satisfaction: hours satisfaction, job satisfaction, and life satisfaction. Controlling for family income, they find that part-time women are more satisfied with working hours than full-time women, and that women's life satisfaction is increased if their partners work full-time but decreased if they themselves work full-time. Male partners' life satisfaction is unaffected by their partners' market hours but is greater if they themselves are working full-time. This difference in

---

[34] Fortin (2009) writes: "The effect of the AIDS scare on egalitarian gender role attitudes would operate through preoccupations about reducing risk; it would make the lifestyle of the single, but not celibate, "career woman" less attractive. With the Pill, some women could become as sexually promiscuous as some men without facing the gender specific consequences; with the AIDS epidemic this equality of "opportunities" was severely tested."

[35] See also Pan (2010) for an empirical analysis of the link between men's sexism in a state and the dynamics of occupational segregation in that state.

the impact of part-time or full-time work on male and female partners' hours and life satisfaction is suggestive of Australian households having traditional gender role divides. In addition, when they use time use data to explore the relationship between male shares of market work and housework, they find that patterns more consistent with Akerlof and Kranton (2000)'s gender identity hypothesis than with the more standard household specialization model.

3.3. Empirical determinants of gender identity norms

Assuming that the gender identity model is relevant to women's labor market outcomes, one is left with the question of what drives gender identity. Under an identity model, the changes in women's labor market outcomes over the last decades could only have occurred in conjunction with deep societal changes in the strength and meaning of the male and female social categories.

Innovations in contraception, and the introduction of the Pill in particular, may have contributed to altering women's identity in the 1960s and 1970s. As Goldin and Katz (2002) show, the introduction of the Pill led to both an increase in women's investment in schooling and an increase in the age at first marriage. This, Goldin (2006) argues, meant that women's adult identities were less influenced by traditional gender roles (as these identities were now more likely to be formed before marriage) and more influenced by career considerations.[36] Also, as we just discussed, Fortin (2009) singles out the AIDS crisis as an exogenous shock that may have undone some of the "liberating" effects of the Pill and contributed to a return to more conservative gender identity norms in the 1990s.

Other papers have discussed the influence of nurture in the formation of gender identities. Many believe that gender role attitudes are largely determined early in childhood, and several papers have documented something akin to an intergenerational transmission of gender identity norms. In an early paper, Vella (1994) establishes a relationship between a young female's attitudes towards working women and her background characteristics, including her religious affiliation, and the educational background and labor market behavior of her parents.[37]

Fernandez et al. (2004) provide a related explanation for why men may differ in how traditional their views are with respect to whether women belong at home or in the office. They argue that a significant factor in the steady increase in women's involvement in the labor force has been the growing number of men growing up in families with working mothers. These men may have developed less stereotypical gender role attitudes, with weaker association between their masculinity and them being the only or main breadwinner in their household. In particular, they show that men whose

---

[36] Goldin (2006) also discusses the possible influence of the rise in divorce rate in the 1960s. See Stevenson and Wolfers (2007) for a discussion of historical trends in marriage and divorce.

[37] Guiso et al. (2003) also show that religious people are less favorable of working women.

mothers worked are more likely to have working wives. The paper follows Acemoglu et al. (2004) and uses variation in the male draft across US states as an exogenous source of variation in mothers' labor force participation. This finding suggests a virtuous cycle: with more of these "new" men around, women should rationally invest more in labor market skills work and thereby expose their sons to this less traditional family structure.[38]

Farre and Vella (2007) directly test for the intergenerational transmission of gender role attitudes. Using the NLSY1979, they find that a woman's view regarding the role of females in the labor market and family affects her children's views towards working women. Farre and Vella (2007) also show the impact of those attitudes in labor market participation: mothers with less traditional views about the role of women are more likely to have working daughters and (reminiscent of Fernandez et al. (2004)) more likely to have working daughters-in-law.

A broader take on the importance of intergenerational transmission for gender role attitudes is to demonstrate the relevance of one's cultural background in shaping identities, attitudes and behavior. In a recent paper, Fernandez and Fogli (2009) study the labor force participation and fertility choices of second-generation American women.[39] They use past values of female labor force participation and fertility rate in these women's country of ancestry as cultural proxies. The underlying logic for isolating cultural effects this way is that while these women live in the economic and formal institutional environments of the US, conditions in the country of origin might have been transmitted to them by their parents. Controlling for individual and spousal socio-economic backgrounds, they find that American women whose ancestry is from higher labor force participation countries work more; similarly, American women whose ancestry is from higher fertility countries have more children. Interestingly, spousal culture appears to also matter in explaining these women's labor force participation.

The schooling environment, which was earlier singled out as a driver of gender differences in preferences, has also been linked to gender identity. Specifically, adolescent girls in a coed environment could see their traditional female identity reinforced as they are trying to be attractive to the surrounding boys and are competing with other girls to get boys' attention. Studies by Maccoby (1990, 1998) suggest that the pressure might be greater on girls to develop stereotypical gender identities when they are surrounded by boys, than they are on boys when they are surrounded by girls. Also, Lee and Marks (1990) discuss how girls that attend single-sex schools were less likely to hold stereotypical views of gender roles even after they no longer attended these schools.

Dasgupta and Asgari (2004) study gender stereotypes (as measured by performance on a gender-stereotype Implicit Association Test), among college-age women both before

---

[38] An alternative, non-identity based, interpretation for the findings in this paper is that men with working mothers were more exposed in childhood to household tasks and became relatively more productive at those tasks, hence making them better partners for working women.

[39] See also Fernandez and Fogli (2006). A few older papers linking culture to female labor supply include Reimers (1985) and Pencavel (1998).

and after their first year at either a coeducational or a women's college. While the two groups of women do not differ in their level of gender stereotyping at college entry, differences start emerging one year later: students in the women's college display no gender stereotyping, while the female students at the coeducational college show higher levels of gender stereotyping than in the previous year. Interestingly, Dasgupta and Asgari (2004) argue that their finding is mediated through female students' exposure to female professors: being exposed to more women in counter-stereotypical positions appears to undermine the automatic stereotypical associations women hold about themselves.[40]

3.4. Does gender identity drive psychological attributes?

A reasonable question one could ask in light of all the work we have reviewed so far is whether gender identity norms are responsible for gender differences in psychological attributes, such as attitudes towards risk, competition, and negotiation, or altruism. Psychologists have shown that people expect women to be docile and generous, while they expect men to be confident and self-assertive (see Eagly, 1987). Some have argued that a higher degree of risk aversion is viewed as the norm for females while part of the male identity is to be risk-takers: for example, Eckel and Grossman (2002) show that men expect women to be even more risk averse than they truly are. These expectations could be part of the socially constructed gender norms, rather than a reflection on innate differences; behaving according to these expectations may reflect a willingness to conform with what is expected from one's social category.

Earlier studies in psychology have investigated how gender triggers matter for performance in negotiation. For example, Kray et al. (2001, 2002) demonstrate that a subtle priming of gender identity in a negotiation task, which they achieve by telling the students engaged in the task that their performance will be regarded as highly predictive of their actual negotiation skills, makes women less effective in that task.

A couple of very recent studies have tried to establish even more directly a causal link between gender identity and preferences, with mixed results. Benjamin et al. (forthcoming) study in a laboratory setting how making salient a specific aspect of one's social identity (they consider gender but also racial identities) affects a subjects' likelihood to make riskier choices, or more patient choices. From a methodological perspective, the study consists in generating temporal exogenous variation in identity effects by temporarily making more salient ("priming") a certain social category and seeing how the subjects' choices are affected. The gender identity salience manipulation is done through a questionnaire included in the beginning of the experiment and where subjects are asked to identify their gender and whether they are living on a coed versus single-sex dormitory floor.[41] While the study uncovers some rich patterns with respect to racial

---

[40] See also Beaman et al. (2009) for a study of how exposure to women in leadership position affects gender stereotypes (in this case among men).

[41] In the control condition, the first section asked about living on or off campus.

identity (for example, priming a subject's Asian-American identity makes the subject more patient), making gender salient appears to have no significant effects on either men's or women's patience, or their level of risk aversion. Of course, it is possible that the priming performed in this experiment was too weak to temporarily affect preferences.

Another recent study aimed at assessing how preferences are affected by gender identity is by Boschini et al. (2009). The question under study here is whether gender identity priming affects subjects' level of altruism. The experiment consists in comparing behavior in a dictator game for subjects whose gender identity has been primed versus not. The results indicate that the priming does affect behavior (with women being more generous) but only when the subjects are assigned to mixed-gender groups. Moreover, the effect is driven by males: men are sensitive to priming and become less generous in a mixed-gender setting when primed with their male identity. Women do not appear to respond to the treatment.

4. WOMEN'S WELL-BEING

Probably the most striking labor market change over the last 30 to 40 years has been the enormous gains women have experienced along several objective outcome dimensions, including their educational achievement, their labor force participation, and their earnings. These revolutionary changes have been witnessed in the US but also in most other economically advanced countries. For example, Goldin et al. (2006) document how, starting in the 1970s, US girls started narrowing the gender gap in high school in terms of science and math courses; while men born in the late 1940s had about a 10 percentage point lead in terms of college graduation rates compared to women born in the late 1940s, that gap had been eliminated by 1980; women are now the majority among graduates of four-year colleges. Blau and Kahn (2008) document the rise in women's labor force participation (both absolutely and relative to women) and the decline in the male to female pay ratio between 1980 and 2000 across ten economically advanced countries.

In a recent paper, Stevenson and Wolfers (2009) ask the obvious complementary question, which is: how have those changes in objective outcomes mapped into changes in well-being for women? The core of their evidence for the US is based on data from the General Social Survey going back to the early 1970s and up to the present. The subjective well-being question available in this dataset is the one that has been most commonly used by happiness researchers: "Taken all together, how would you say things are these days, would you say that you are very happy, pretty happy, or not too happy?" Surprisingly, Stevenson and Wolfers (2009) find that women appear to have become somewhat less happy over time, both absolutely and relative to men. A similar pattern of relative decline in women's happiness exists across a variety of European countries (with West Germany being an interesting exception).

What explains these trends? One possibility Stevenson and Wolfers (2009) investigate is that the trends reflect on the changes in family structure over that time period, which include a rising share of single mothers, especially among the less educated (see Elwood and Jencks, 2004). Stevenson and Wolfers (2009) however argue against this view, in that the trends are not concentrated among less educated women, or those that are single parents.

Another possibility, closely related to our previous discussion of the gender identity literature, is that the decline in women's well-being reflects on the difficulty women face in attempting to balance the multiple and competing expectations associated with being a woman: women may now, more than before, feel a need to both be a good wife, a good mother, and have a career in order to be fulfilled, and these multiple behavioral prescriptions are competing for the women's time and resources (Benabou and Tirole, 2007). In contrast with this possibility, Stevenson and Wolfers (2009) report similar well-being trends for women with and without children as well as for employed and non-employed mothers. However, more consistent with the view that today's women might be emotionally struggling in that they have to juggle more complicated lives and many more objectives in their life, they do find that young women are increasingly attaching importance to multiple domains of their life, beyond the domestic domain.

Lalive and Stutzer (2010) present more evidence consistent with the view that increasingly complicated gender identities explain the decline in women's well-being. They study how women are faring both in terms of labor market outcomes and subjective well-being across various communities in Switzerland that differed in how they voted in a national referendum on an equal rights amendment to the Constitution. They argue that the communities more people agreed with the proposition that "women and men shall have the right to equal pay for work of equal value" capture environments where traditional gender role models are being challenged. They find that the gender gap in pay is smaller in those communities where a larger fraction of people supported the equal rights amendment. But they also find that women report lower level of overall life satisfaction in those communities. Hence, women appear to be particularly unhappy when and where they are expected to (and succeeding at) break(ing) away from traditional gender identity norms.

Another possible explanation for the trends uncovered by Stevenson and Wolfers (2009) is that women, as they progressively close the gender gap in labor market achievements, are shifting who they use as a standard of reference when answering an otherwise unchanged subjective well-being question. In particular, one could imagine that women are now, more than in the past, deriving their well-being from how well they are doing compared to men, while they used to mainly compare themselves to other women in the past. If such an adaptation to improving circumstances is indeed explaining the central results in Stevenson and Wolfers (2009), it would have unclear implications for how women's true level of utility has been changing over time (see for example Kahneman et al., 2004). Indeed, such a change in reference group may indicate that women's preferences have adapted and that their utility is truly dependent on their relative income or consumption compared to men, and not higher than in the past despite the material gains. Alternatively, it is possible that women are in fact experiencing higher utility today than in the past but that they now have higher standards for what their life should be like, with the lower self-reports on the well-being question just being a reflection of the higher aspirations women now have for themselves.

While this discussion highlights the difficulty in interpreting the observed trends in women's self-reported life satisfaction, alternative sources of data have been used to provide a complementary perspective on how women's life experiences have been changing over time. In particular, a more objective measure of women's relative gain or loss in well-being might be obtained by looking at time use data. As summarized in a book such as "the Second Shift" (Hochschild and Machung, 1989), some female activists would argue that the results in Stevenson and Wolfers are indicative of the fact that women have not been able to fully enjoy their improved position in the labor market because they have taken on this additional labor market work without a compensating break in their responsibilities in household production. So, while women are making objective gains in the labor market, the addition of labor market to home production work may have just have translated into too much work. Time trends in time use data, such as studied by Aguiar and Hurst (2007), offer a direct way to test the relevance of such a view. Aguiar and Hurst (2007) study how the allocation of time has changed for various demographic groups in the US between 1965 and 2003. Most relevant for us is a comparison of time trends in total work (which is defined as market work plus non-market work) between men and women over that period. The main finding is that both men and women have experienced a decline in total work over that period. While the decline is slightly larger for men than women, the difference is not large in light of the colossal changes in women's labor force attachment over the same time period (7.6 hours per week for men compared to 6.4 hours per week for women). Compositionally, though, and not surprisingly, the sources of the decline in total work are different for men and women. Over that period, men have decreased their market work by about 11.5 hours per week and increased their non-market work by nearly 3.9 hours; in contrast, women have seen their market work increase by about 6.2 hours per week but have experienced a very sharp decline in their non-market work (12.6 hours per week). So, while men may have taken up a huge share of home production tasks, it seems pretty clear that new home production technologies have protected working women from the reality of a "second shift."

Of course, translating these trends in time use into information about experienced well-being implies making important assumptions about how much men and women value their time at work, be it market work or non-market work, and how much they value their time out of work.[42] Krueger (2007) exactly performs such a translation by

---

[42] This is well illustrated in the exchange between Aguiar and Hurst (2007) and Ramey (2007).

combining Aguiar and Hurst's time use data with information on how individuals affectively experience various activities they engage in. This measurement of "experienced utility" is at the core of the Day Reconstruction Method (DRM) research agenda, as presented in Kahneman and Krueger (2006). Under this method, survey participants are asked to report what activities they engaged in during the prior day (very similar to the time diary surveys that are used for the collection of time use data); the survey participants are then further probed, typically for a random subset of the reported activities about the extent to which they experienced various feelings (such as happiness, stress or sadness) while engaged in each of these activities. Based on this data, it is possible to compute how pleasant or unpleasant various activities are on average. This can be done across all individuals, but this also can be by subgroups (e.g. percent of time men find taking care of children pleasant versus percent of time women find taking care of children pleasant).[43]

Combining DRM data with the trends in time allocation data uncovered in Aguiar and Hurst therefore allows one to build a more precise picture of how men and women experience their daily life and how that has changed over time.[44] Using this finer approach, Krueger (2007) finds that there has been among men a gradual decline in the proportion of time spent in unpleasant activities; among women, despite the colossal changes in time allocation, there has been no detectable trend in the proportion of time spent in unpleasant activities. While these differences and changes are small (men went from spending about 20.8 percent of their time in unpleasant activities in 1965 down to 19.8 percent in 2005; women spent about 19.4 percent of their time in unpleasant activities in 1965 and 2005), they do coincide with Stevenson and Wolfers (2009)' evidence of a relative decline in female well-being over time compared to men.

5. CONCLUSION

Compared to ten years ago, labor economists now have a much larger set of potential explanations to draw from when trying to explain gender differences in labor market outcomes. While education, experience and discrimination might have been the primary factors considered in the past to account for, say, the lack of women in investment banking, most labor economists would now also discuss why investment banking jobs might be particularly unattractive to women because of the cut-throat competition that exists between bankers, or because of the heavy reliance on incentive pay in this

---

[43] There have been various demonstrations that subjective well-being and hedonic experiences are clearly different concepts. For example, Krueger et al. (2007) study overall life satisfaction and recalled affective experience in random samples of women in France and the US. Based on the standard subjective well-being question, they find American women to report higher levels of satisfaction with their life than French women. Based on the DRM data, though, they find the opposite ranking: French women are on average in a more positive mood during the course of a day; moreover, they spend a higher share of their time in more pleasant activities.

[44] Note that one important additional assumption that needs to be made given that the lack of historical data is that how pleasant or unpleasant a given activity is has not changed over time.

profession, or because women do not view succeeding in their investment banking career as something as crucial to their sense of selves as men do. These new perspectives on gender reflect growing influences of psychology and social-psychology literatures on economics research; in many cases, they provide micro-foundations for why women may choose different educational paths than men, or why they may not be as committed to their career as men are.

While there is a wealth of laboratory evidence suggesting that women differ from men on some of these key, theoretically relevant, psychological attributes, there is to this date a striking lack of research establishing the empirical relevance of these factors for actual outcomes. While the laboratory evidence shows in many cases large gender differences (say, in attitudes towards risk, or attitudes towards competition), most of the existing attempts to measure the impact of these factors on actual outcomes fail to find large effects. This is undoubtedly the reflection of a rather new research agenda, as well as of the difficulty of finding databases that combines good measures of psychological attributes with real outcomes. More direct demonstrations of field relevance will be crucial for these new perspectives to have a lasting impact on how labor economists approach their study of gender gaps.

Future work will also need to tackle the question of how these psychological factors fit within the time series of women's improving educational and professional achievements. While we have discussed some historical factors that may have shocked women's social identities away from the traditional stereotypes, is it also the case that women's attitudes towards, say, risk or other-regarding preferences, have been converging over time towards men's? This would certainly fit with the view that the gender differences in preferences are not hard-wired but rather a reflection of environmental influences, and warrant more research on the specific changes in the home or schooling environments that might have triggered the convergence in attitudes. It is also possible to reconcile women's progress in the labor market with stable gender preferences. For example, some of the work we discussed above raises the possibility that institutional changes (such as more strictly enforced affirmative action or quota policies that reduce women's need to directly compete with men) or technological changes (such as an increase in the demand for those interpersonal skills in which women are relatively more endowed) may have reduced, and even maybe reversed, the disadvantage associated with women's psychological profile.

Building on this, we expect that much more research will be devoted over the next decade to understanding why women are now surpassing men in terms of educational attainment. It is interesting that the research that already exists on this topic centers on those behavioral and psychological factors that give girls an advantage over boys while at school. It is possible that the same factors that are giving women an edge at school may start giving them an edge at work as other forces that have previously constrained women slowly disappear.

We devoted the last section of this chapter to alternative approaches to measuring women's well-being. Researchers have not found that the dramatic gains that women have made in terms of labor force participation and earnings translated in more satisfying lives, whether measured globally or based on the detailed tracking of their daily activities and emotions. While acknowledging all the caveats associated with the interpretation of well-being data, future research may try to better understand how differentially women and men evaluate the quality of their life in relation to their objective achievements (both professional and family-related), as well as how those evaluations have changed over time, maybe as a reflection of shifting gender identities. A more detailed look at how men and women emotionally experience various activities in their daily life (such as time spent in labor market work versus time spent taking care of children, or time spent in routine labor market work versus time spent in more challenging labor market work) may offer some clues on the trade-offs men and women are making when opting for the career job, the "quiet" job, or opting out.

REFERENCES

Acemoglu, Daron, Autor, David, Lyle, David, 2004. Women war and wages: the impact of female labor supply on the wage structure at mid-century. Journal of Political Economy 112 (3), 497–551.

Aguiar, Mark, Hurst, Erik, 2007. Measuring trends in leisure: the allocation of time over five decades. Quarterly Journal of Economics 122 (3), 969–1006.

Akerlof, George A., Kranton, Rachel E., 2002. Identity and schooling: some lessons for the economics of education. Journal of Economic Literature 40 (4), 1167–1201.

Akerlof, George A., Kranton, Rachel E., 2005. Identity and the economics of organizations. Journal of Economic Perspectives 19, 9–32.

Akerlof, George A., Kranton, Rachel E., 2000. Economics and identity. Quarterly Journal of Economics 115, 715–753.

Albanesi, Stefania, Olivetti, Claudia, 2009. Gender roles and medical progress. NBER Working Paper 14873.

Alesina, Alberto F., Giuliano, Paola, 2009. Preferences for redistribution. Harvard Institute of Economic Research Discussion Paper No. 2170.

Altonji, Joseph G., Blank, Rebecca M., 1999. Race and gender in the labor market. In: Ashenfelter, Orley C., Card, David (Eds.), Handbook of Labor Economics, vol. 3. Elsevier.

Anderson, Lisa R., Mellor, Jennifer M., 2008. Predicting health behaviors with an experimental measure of risk preference. Journal of Health Economics 27 (5), 1260–1274.

Andreoni, James, Vesterlund, Lise, 2001. Which is the fair sex? Gender differences in altruism. Quarterly Journal of Economics 116 (1), 293–312.

Antonovics, Kate, Arcidiacono, Peter, Walsh, Randall, 2009. The effects of gender interactions in the lab and in the field. Review of Economics and Statistics 91 (1), 152–163.

Apicella, C.L., Dreber, A., Campbell, B., Gray, P., Hoffman, M., Little, A.C., 2008. Testosterone and financial risk-taking. Evolution and Human Behavior 29, 385–390.

Archer, J., 2006. Testosterone and human behavior: an evaluation of the challenge hypothesis. Neuroscience and Biobehavioral Reviews 30, 319–345.

Babcock, Linda, Gelfand, Michele, Small, Deborah, Stayn, Heidi, 2006. Gender differences in the propensity to initiate negotiations. In: De Cremer, D., Zeelenberg, M., Murnighan, J.K. (Eds.), Social Psychology and Economics. Erlbaum, Mahwah, NJ.

Babcock, Linda, Laschever, Sarah, 2003. Women Don't Ask: Negotiation and the Gender Divide. Princeton University Press, Princeton, Oxford.

Bailey, Martha J., 2006. More power to the pill: the impact of contraceptive freedom on women's lifecycle labor supply. Quarterly Journal of Economics 121, 289–320.

Bajtelsmit, Vickie L., VanDerhei, Jack L., 1997. Risk aversion and pension investment choices. In: Gordon, Michael S., Mitchell, Olivia S., Twinney, Marc M. (Eds.), Positioning Pensions for the Twenty-First Century. University of Pennsylvania Press, Philadelphia, pp. 45–66.

Barber, Brad M., Odean, Terrance, 2001. Boys will be boys: gender, overconfidence, and common stock investment. Quarterly Journal of Economics 116, 261–292.

Baron-Cohen, Simon, 2003. The Essential Difference. Men, Women, and the Extreme Male Brain. Allan Lane, London.

Beaman, Lori, Chattopadhyay, Raghabendra, Duflo, Esther, Pande, Rohini, Topalova, Petia, 2009. Powerful women: female leadership and gender bias. Quarterly Journal of Economics 124 (4), 1497–1540.

Becker, Gary S., 1971. The Economics of Discrimination, second ed., University of Chicago Press, Chicago.

Benabou, Roland, Tirole, Jean, 2007. Identity, dignity and taboos: beliefs as assets. IZA Discussion Paper No. 2583.

Benjamin, Daniel J., Choi, James J., Strickland, Joshua A., Social Identity and Preferences. American Economic Review (forthcoming).

Bettinger, Eric, Long, Bridget T., 2005. Do faculty members serve as role models? The impact of faculty gender on female students. American Economic Review 95 (2), 152–157.

Beyer, Sylvia, Bowden, Edward M., 1997. Gender differences in self-perceptions: convergent evidence from three measures of accuracy and bias. Personality and Social Psychology Bulletin 23, 157–172.

Beyer, Sylvia, 1990. Gender differences in the accuracy of self-evaluations of performance. Journal of Personality and Social Psychology 59, 960–970.

Bjorklund, D.F., Kipp, K., 1996. Parental investment theory and sex differences in the evolution of inhibition mechanisms. Psychological Bulletin 120, 163–188.

Black, Sandra E., Brainerd, Elizabeth, 2004. The impact of globalization on gender discrimination. Industrial and Labor Relations Review 57, 540–559.

Black, Sandra E., Strahan, Philip E., 2001. The division of spoils: rent-sharing and discrimination in a regulated industry. American Economic Review 91, 814–831.

Black, Sandra E., Juhn, Chinhui, 2000. The rise of female professionals: women's response to rising skill demand. American Economic Review 90 (2), 450–455.

Blackaby, D., Booth, A.L., Frank, J., 2005. Outside offers and the gender pay gap: empirical evidence from the UK academic labor market. Economic Journal 115, F81–F107.

Blanco, C., Ibanez, A., Blanco-Jerez, C.R., Baca-Garcia, E., Saiz-Ruiz, J., 2001. Plasma testosterone and pathological gambling. Psychiatry Research 105, 117–121.

Blau, Francine D., Kahn, Lawrence M., 2006. The US gender pay gap in the 1990s: slowing convergence. Industrial and Labor Relations Review 60, 45–66.

Blau, Francine D., 1998. Trends in the well-being of American women, 1970–1995. Journal of Economic Literature 36 (1), 112–165.

Blau, Francine D., Kahn, Lawrence M., 2008. Women's work and wages. In: Durlauf, Steven N., Blume, Lawrence E. (Eds.), The New Palgrave Dictionary of Economics, second ed., Palgrave Macmillan.

Bolton, Gary E., Katok, Elena, 1995. An experimental test for gender differences in beneficent behavior. Economics Letters 48 (3–4), 287–292.

Bonin, Holger, Dohmen, Thomas, Falk, Armin, Huffman, David, Sunde, Uwe, 2007. Cross sectional earnings risk and occupational sorting: the role of risk attitudes. Labour Economics 14 (6), 926–937.

Booth, Alison L., Nolen, Patrick, 2009a. Gender differences in risk behaviour: does nurture matter? CEPR Discussion Paper 7198.

Booth, Alison L., Nolen, Patrick, 2009b. Gender differences in competition: the role of single-sex education. CEPR Discussion Paper 7214.

Booth, Alison L., van Ours, Jan, 2009. Hours of work and gender identity: does part-time work make the family happier? Economica 76 (301), 176–196.

Borghans, Lex, Golsteyn, Bart, Heckman, James, Meijers, Huub, 2009. Gender differences in risk aversion and ambiguity aversion. Journal of the European Economic Association 7 (2–3), 649–658.

Borghans, Lex, Duckworth, Angela Lee, Heckman, James, ter Weel, Bas, 2008a. The economics and psychology of personality traits. Journal of Human Resources 43 (4), 972–1059.

Borghans, Lex, ter Weel, Bas, Weinberg, Bruce A., 2005. People people: social capital and the labor-market outcomes of underrepresented groups. IZA Discussion Paper No. 1494.

Borghans, Lex, ter Weel, Bas, Weinberg, Bruce A., 2008b. Interpersonal styles and labor market outcomes. Journal of Human Resources 43 (4), 815–858.

Boschini, Anne, Muren, Astri, Persson, Matz, 2009. Constructing gender in the economics lab. Department of Economics, Stockholm University. Research Papers in Economics, 15.

Bouchard Jr., Thomas, Loehlin, John C., 2001. Genes, evolution, and personality. Behavioral Genetics 31 (3), 243–273.

Bowles, Hannah R., Babcock, Linda, Lai, Lei, 2007. Social incentives for sex differences in the propensity to initiate negotiation: sometimes it does hurt to ask. Organizational Behavior and Human Decision Processes 103, 84–103.

Bowles, Hannah R., Babcock, Linda, McGinn, Kathleen L., 2005. Constraints and triggers: situational mechanics of gender in negotiation. Journal of Personality and Social Psychology 89, 951–965.

Bowles, Samuel, Gintis, Herbert, Osborne, Melissa, 2001. The determinants of earnings: a behavior approach. Journal of Economic Literature 39 (4), 1137–1176.

Box-Steffensmeier, J.M., de Boef, S., Lin, T., 2004. The dynamics of the partisan gender gap. American Political Science Review 98, 515–528.

Broder, A., Hohmann, N., 2003. Variations in risk taking behavior over the menstrual cycle: an improved replication. Evolution and Human Behavior 24, 391–398.

Brody, Leslie R., 1993. On understanding gender differences in the expression of emotion. In: Ablon, Steven L., Brown, Daniel, Khantzian, Edward J., Mack, John E. (Eds.), Human Feelings: Explorations in Affect Development and Meaning. Analytic Press, Hillsdale, NJ, pp. 87–121.

Brown, P., Levinson, S.C., 1987. Politeness: Some Universals in Language Usage. Cambridge University Press, New York.

Brown-Kruse, J., Hummels, D., 1993. Gender effects in laboratory public goods contributions: do individuals put their money where their mouth is? Journal of Economic Behavior and Organization 22, 255–268.

Buckles, Kasey, 2007. Stopping the biological clock: infertility treatments and the career-family tradeoff. Working paper, University of Notre Dame.

Cadsby, C.B., Maynes, E., 1998. Gender and free riding in a threshold public goods game: experimental evidence. Journal of Economic Behavior and Organization 34, 603–620.

Campbell, Anne, 2002. A Mind of Her Own: the Evolutionary Psychology of Women. Oxford University Press, Oxford, UK.

Carrell, Scott E., Page, Marianne E., West, James E., 2009. Sex and science: how professor gender perpetuates the gender gap. NBER Working Paper No.14959.

Charles, Kerwin, Guryan, Jonathan, Pan, Jessica, 2009. Sexism and women's labor market outcomes. Working Paper, University of Chicago.

Coates, J.M., Gurnell, M., Rustichini, A., 2009. Second-to-fourth digit ratio predicts success among high-frequency financial traders. Proceedings of the National Academy of Sciences 106, 623–628.

Croson, Rachel, Gneezy, Uri, 2009. Gender differences in preferences. Journal of Economic Literature 47 (2), 1–27.

Dabbs, J.M., Morris, R., 1990. Testosterone, social class, and antisocial behavior in a sample of 4462 men. Psychological Science 1, 209–211.

Daly, M., Wilson, M., 1988. Homicide. Aldine de Gruyter, New York.

Dasgupta, N., Asgari, S., 2004. Seeing is believing: exposure to counterstereotypic women leaders and its effect on the malleability of automatic gender stereotyping. Journal of Experimental Social Psychology 40, 642–658.

Dee, Thomas S., 2005. A teacher like me: does race, ethnicity or gender matter? American Economic Review 95 (2), 158–165.

Dee, Thomas S., 2007. Teachers and the gender gaps in student achievement. Journal of Human Resources 42 (3), 528–554.

Digman, John M., 1989. Five robust trait dimensions: development, stability, and utility. Journal of Personality 57 (2), 195–214.

Digman, John M., 1990. Personality structure: emergence of the five-factor model. Annual Review of Psychology 41, 417–440.

Dohmen, Thomas J., Falk, Armin, Performance pay and multi-dimensional sorting: productivity, preferences and gender. American Economic Review (forthcoming).

Dohmen, Thomas J., Falk, Armin, Huffman, David, Schupp, Juergen, Sunde, Uwe, Wagner, Gert G., Individual risk attitudes: measurement, determinants and behavioral consequences. Journal of the European Economic Association (forthcoming-a).

Dohmen, Thomas J., Falk, Armin, Huffman, David, Sunde, Uwe, 2010. Are risk aversion and impatience related to cognitive ability? American Economic Review 100 (3), 1238–1260.

Dougherty, Christopher, 2005. Why are the returns to schooling higher for women than for men? Journal of Human Resources 40 (4), 969–988.

Dreber, Anna, Hoffman, Moshe, 2007. Portfolio selection in utero. Working Paper, University of Chicago.

Duflo, Esther, 2003. Grandmothers and granddaughters: old age pension and intrahousehold allocation in South Africa. World Bank Economic Review 17, 1–25.

Dwyer, Peggy D., Gilkeson, James H., List, John A., 2002. Gender differences in revealed risk taking: evidence from mutual fund investors. Economics Letters 76 (2), 151–158.

Eagly, A.H., 1987. Sex Differences in Social Behavior: A Social-role Interpretation. Erlbaum, Hillsdale, NJ.

Eagly, A.H., Carli, L.L., 2007. Through the Labyrinth: The Truth about How Women Become Leaders. Harvard University Press, Boston, MA.

Eagly, A.H., Makhijani, M.G., Klonsky, B.G., 1992. Gender and the evaluation of leaders: a meta-analysis. Psychological Bulletin 111, 3–22.

Eckel, Catherine C., Grossman, Philip J., 1998. Are women less selfish than men? Evidence from dictator experiments. Economic Journal 108 (448), 726–735.

Eckel, Catherine C., Grossman, Philip J., 2002. Sex differences and statistical stereotyping in attitudes toward financial risk. Evolution and Human Behavior 23 (4), 281–295.

Eckel, Catherine C., Grossman, Philip J., 2008a. Sex and risk: experimental evidence. In: Plott, Charles, Smith, Vernon (Eds.), Handbook of Experimental Economics Results, vol. 1. Elsevier, New York.

Eckel, Catherine C., Grossman, Philip J., 2008b. Differences in the economic decisions of men and women: experimental evidence. In: Plott, Charles, Smith, Vernon (Eds.), Handbook of Experimental Economics Results, vol. 1. Elsevier, New York.

Edlund, Lena, Pande, Rohini, 2002. Why have women become left-wing? The political gap and the decline in marriage. Quarterly Journal of Economics 117, 917–961.

Edlund, Lena, Haider, Laila, Pande, Rohini, 2005. Unmarried parenthood and redistributive politics. Journal of the European Economic Association 3 (1), 95–119.

Elder, Todd, Lubotsky, Darren, 2009. Kindergarten entrance age and children's achievement: impacts of state policies, family background, and peers. Journal of Human Resources 44 (3), 641–683.

Elwood, David T., Jencks, Christopher, 2004. The spread of single-parent families in the empirical analysis of a sample of new hires. Industrial Relations 46, 511–550.

Farre, Lidia, Vella, Francis, 2007. The intergenerational transmission of gender role attitudes and its implications for female labor force participation. IZA Discussion Paper No. 2802.

Fehr-Duda, Helga, de Gennaro, Manuele, Schubert, Renate, 2006. Gender, financial risk, and probability weights. Theory and Decision 60, 283–313.

Fernandez, Raquel, Fogli, Alessandra, 2006. Fertility: the role of culture and family experience. Journal of the European Economic Association 4 (2–3), 552–561.

Fernandez, Raquel, Fogli, Alessandra, 2009. Culture: an empirical investigation of beliefs, work, and fertility. American Economic Journal: Macroeconomics 1 (1), 146–177.

Fernandez, Raquel, Fogli, Alessandra, Olivetti, Claudia, 2004. Mothers and sons: preference development and female labor force dynamics. Quarterly Journal of Economics 119 (4), 1249–1299.

Flynn, James, Slovic, Paul, Mertz, C.K., 1994. Gender, race, and perception of environmental health risks. Risk Analysis 14, 1101–1108.

Fortin, Nicole, 2008. The gender wage gap among young adults in the United States: the importance of money vs. people. Journal of Human Resources 43 (4), 886–920.

Fortin, Nicole, 2005. Gender role attitudes and women's labour market outcomes across OECD countries. Oxford Review of Economic Policy 21 (3), 416–438.

Fortin, Nicole, 2009. Gender role attitudes and women's labor market participation: opting out, AIDS, and the persistent appeal of housewifery. Working paper, University of British Columbia.

Fryer, Roland G., Levitt, Steve, 2010. An empirical analysis of the gender gap in mathematics. American Economic Journal: Applied Economics 2 (2), 210–240.

Fujita, Frank, Diener, Ed, Sandvik, Ed, 1991. Gender differences in negative affect and well-being: the case for emotional intensity. Journal of Personality and Social Psychology 61 (3), 427–434.

Funk, Patricia, Gathmann, Christina, 2009. Gender gaps in policy-making: evidence from direct democracy in Switzerland. Working Paper, Universitat Pompeu Fabra.

Gneezy, Uri, Rustichini, Aldo, 2004. Gender and competition at a young age. American Economic Review 94 (2), 377–381.

Gneezy, Uri, Leonard, Kenneth L., List, John A., 2008. Gender differences in competition: evidence from a matrilineal and a patriarchal society. Econometrica 77 (3), 909–931.

Gneezy, Uri, Niederle, Muriel, Rustichini, Aldo, 2003. Performance in competitive environments: gender differences. Quarterly Journal of Economics. 118, 1049–1074.

Goldin, Claudia, Katz, Lawrence F., 2002. The power of the pill: oral contraceptives and women's career and marriage decisions. Journal of Political Economy 110 (4), 730–770.

Goldin, Claudia, Katz, Lawrence F., Kuziemko, Ilyana., 2006. The homecoming of American college women: the reversal of the college gender gap. Journal of Economic Perspectives 20 (4), 133–156.

Goldin, Claudia, 2002. A pollution theory of discrimination: male and female differences in occupations and earnings. NBER Working Paper No. 8985.

Goldin, Claudia, 2006. The quiet revolution that transformed women's employment, education, and family. American Economic Review 96 (2), 1–21.

Greenwood, Jeremy, Seshadri, Ananth, Yorukoglu, Mehmet, 2005. Engines of liberalization. Review of Economic Studies 72, 109–133.

Greig, Fiona, 2008. Propensity to negotiate and career advancement: evidence from an investment bank that women are on a "Slow Elevator". Negotiation Journal 24 (4), 495–508.

Grund, Christian, Sliwka, Dirk, 2006. Performance pay and risk aversion. IZA Discussion Paper No. 2012.

Guiso, Luigi, Monte, Ferdinando, Sapienza, Paolo, Zingales, Luigi, 2008. Culture, gender and math. Science 320, 1164–1165.

Guiso, Luigi, Sapienza, Paola, Zingales, Luigi, 2003. People's opium? Religion and economic attitudes. Journal of Monetary Economics 50 (1), 225–282.

Gupta, Nabanita Datta, Poulsen, Anders, Villeval, Marie-Claire, 2005. Male and female competitive behavior—experimental evidence. IZA Working Paper No. 1833.

Hartog, J., Ferrer-i-Carbonell, A., Jonker, N., 2002. Linking measured risk aversion to individual characteristics. Kyklos 55 (1), 3–26.

Heckman, James J., Malofeeva, Lena, Pinto, Rodrigo R., Savelyev, Peter, 2007. The effect of the Perry Preschool Program on the cognitive and noncognitive skills of its participants. Working Paper, University of Chicago.

Hermans, E., Putman, P., Baas, J., Koppeschaar, H., van Honk, J., 2006. A single administration of testosterone reduces fear-potentiated startle in humans. Biological Psychiatry 59, 872–874.

Hill, C., 2006. What the new economics of identity has to say to legal scholarship. University of Minnesota Legal Studies Research Paper No. 05-46.

Hochschild, Arlie, Machung, Anne, 1989. The Second Shift. Viking, New York.

Hoffman, Moshe, Gneezy, Uri, List, John, 2010. Nurture affects gender differences in cognition. Working Paper, University of Chicago.

Hoffmann, Florian, Oreopoulos, Philip., 2009. A professor like me: the influence of instructor gender on college achievement. Journal of Human Resources 44 (2), 479–494.

Holt, Charles A., Laury, Susan K., 2002. Risk aversion and incentive effects. American Economic Review 92 (5), 1644–1655.

Humphreys, L.F., Lubinski, D., Yao, G., 1993. Utility of predicting group membership and the role of spatial visualization in becoming an engineer, physical scientist, or artist. Journal of Applied Psychology 78, 250–261.

Ichino, Andrea, Moretti, Enrico, 2009. Biological gender differences, absenteeism and the earnings gap. American Economic Journal: Applied Economics 1 (1), 183–218.

Jacob, Brian A., 2002. Where the boys aren't: non-cognitive skills, returns to school and the gender gap in higher education. Economics of Education Review 21 (6), 589–598.

Jianakoplos, Nancy Ammon, Bernasek, Alexandra, 1998. Are women more risk averse? Economic Inquiry 36 (4), 620–630.

Judge, Timothy A., Higgins, Chad A., Thoresen, Carl J., Barrick, Murray R., 1999. The big five personality traits, general mental ability, and career success across the life span. Personnel Psychology 52 (3), 621–652.

Kahneman, Daniel, Krueger, Alan B., 2006. Developments in the measurement of subjective well-being. Journal of Economic Perspectives 20 (1), 3–24.

Kahneman, Daniel, Tversky, Amos, 1979. Prospect theory: an analysis of decision under risk. Econometrica 47 (2), 263–292.

Kahneman, Daniel, Krueger, Alan B., Schkade, David, Schwarz, Norbert, Stone, Arthur A., 2004. A survey method for characterizing daily life experience: the day reconstruction method. Science 306, 1776–1780.

Kimura, D., 1999. Sex and Cognition. Cambridge, MA, MIT Press.

Kray, Laura J., Galinsky, Adam D., Thompson, Leigh, 2002. Reversing the gender gap in negotiations: an exploration of stereotype regeneration. Organizational Behavior and Human Decision Processes 87 (2), 386–410.

Kray, Laura J., Thompson, Leigh, Galinsky, Adam D., 2001. Battle of the sexes: gender stereotype confirmation and reactance in negotiations. Journal of Personality and Social Psychology 80 (6), 942–958.

Krueger, Alan B, Kahneman, Daniel, Schkade, David, Schwarz, Norbert, Stone, Arthur A., 2007. National time accounting: the currency of life. In: Measuring the Subjective Well-Being of Nations: National Accounts of Time Use and Well-Being. National Bureau of Economic Research, Inc.

Krueger, Alan B., 2007. Are we having more fun yet? Categorizing and evaluating changes in time allocation. Brookings Papers on Economic Activity (2), 193–215.

Lalive, Rafael, Stutzer, Alois, 2010. Approval of equal rights and gender differences in well-being. Journal of Population Economics 23 (3), 933–962.

Lavy, Victor, 2008a. Do gender stereotypes reduce girls' or boys' human capital Outcomes? Evidence from a natural experiment. Journal of Public Economics 92 (10–11), 2083–2105.

Lavy, Victor, 2008b. Gender differences in market competitiveness in a real workplace: evidence from performance-based pay tournaments among teachers. NBER Working Paper No. 14338.

Lee, Valerie E., Marks, Helen M., 1990. Sustained effects of the single-sex secondary school experience on attitudes, behaviors and value on college. Journal of Educational Psychology 81, 578–592.

Levin, I.P., Snyder, M.A., Chapman, D.P., 1988. The interaction of experiential and situational factors and gender in a simulated risky decision-making task. The Journal of Psychology 122, 173–181.

Loewenstein, George F., Lerner, Jennifer S., 2003. The role of affect in decision making. In: Davidson, Richard J., Scherer, Klaus R., Goldsmith, H. Hill. (Eds.), Handbook of Affective Sciences. Oxford University Press.

Loewenstein, George F., Weber, Elke U., Hsee, Christopher K., Welch, Ned, 2001. Risk as feelings. Psychological Bulletin 127 (2), 267–286.

Lott, John R., Kenny, Lawrence W., 1999. Did women's suffrage change the size and scope of government? Journal of Political Economy 107 (6), 1163–1198.

Lundeberg, Mary A., Fox, Paul W., Punccohar, Judith, 1994. Highly confident but wrong: gender differences and similarities in confidence judgments. Journal of Educational Psychology 86 (1), 114–121.

Maccoby, E.E., 1990. Gender and relationships: a developmental account. American Psychologist 45 (4), 513–520.

Maccoby, E.E., 1998. The Two Sexes: Growing up Apart, Coming Together. Harvard University Press, Cambridge, Ma.

Maestripieri, Dario, Sapienza, Paola, Zingales, Luigi, 2009. Gender differences in financial risk aversion and career choices are affected by testosterone. Proceedings of the National Academy of Science 106 (36), 15268–15273.

Major, Brenda, 1987. Gender, justice, and the psychology of entitlement. In: Shaver, P., Hendricks, C. (Eds.), Sex and Gender: Review of Personality and Social Psychology. Sage, Newbury Park, CA.

Manning, Alan, Saidi, Farzad, 2010. Understanding the gender pay gap: what's competition got to do with it? Industrial and Labor Relations Review 63 (4), 681–698.

Manning, Alan, Swaffield, Joanna, 2008. The gender gap in early-career wage growth. Economic Journal 118 (530), 983–1024.

Manning, John T., Scutt, Diane, Wilson, James, Lewis-Jones, D. Iwan, 1998. The ratio of 2nd to 4th digit length: a predictor of sperm numbers and concentrations of testosterone luteinizing hormones and oestrogen. Human Reproduction 13 (11), 3000–3004.

Mazur, Allan, 1995. Biosocial models of deviant behavior among male army veterans. Biological Psychology 41, 271–293.

McCrae, Robert R., John, Oliver P., 1992. An introduction to the five-factor model and its applications. Journal of Personality 60 (2), 175–215.

McCrae, Robert R., Costa, Paul T., 1999. A five-factor theory of personality. In: Pervin, Lawrence A., John, Oliver P. (Eds.), Handbook of Personality: Theory and Research. Guilford, New York.

Miller, Grant., 2008. Women's suffrage, political responsiveness, and child survival in American history. The Quarterly Journal of Economics 123 (3), 1287–1327.

Mueller, Gerrit, Plug, Eric, 2006. Estimating the effect of personality on male and female earnings. Industrial and Labor Relations Review 60 (1), 3–22.

Niederle, Muriel, Vesterlund, Lise, 2007. Do women shy away from competition? Do men compete too much? Quarterly Journal of Economics 122 (3), 1067–1101.

Niederle, Muriel, Vesterlund, Lise, 2008. Gender differences in competition. Negotiation Journal 24 (4), 447–463.

Niederle, Muriel, Vesterlund, Lise, 2010. Explaining the gender gap in math test scores: the role of competition. Journal of Economic Perspectives 24 (2), 129–144.

Niederle, Muriel, Yestrumskas, Alexandra H., 2008. Gender differences in seeking challenges: the role of institutions. NBER Working Paper No. 13922.

Nowell, Clifford, Tinkler, Sarah, 1994. The influence of gender on the provision of a public good. Journal of Economic Behavior and Organization 25, 25–36.

Örs, Evren, Palomino, Frederic, Peyrache, Eloic, 2008. Performance gender-gap: does competition matter? CEPR Working Paper No. 6891.

Oswald, Andrew, Powdthavee, Nattavudh, 2010. Daughters and left wing voting. Review of Economics and Statistics 92 (2), 213–227.

Paarsch, Harry J., Shearer, Bruce, 2007. Do women react differently to incentives? Evidence from experimental data and payroll records. European Economic Review 51, 1682–1707.

Pan, Jessica, 2010. Gender segregation in occupations: the role of tipping and social interactions. Working Paper, University of Chicago.

Paserman, Daniele, 2007. Gender differences in performance in competitive environments: evidence from professional tennis players. IZA Working Paper No. 2834.

Pekkarinen, Tuomas, 2008. Gender differences in educational attainment: evidence on the role of tracking from a Finnish quasi-experiment. Scandinavian Journal of Economics 110 (4), 807–825.

Pencavel, John, 1998. The market work behavior and wages of women, 1975-94. Journal of Human Resources 38 (4), 771–804.

Ramey, Valerie, 2007. How much has leisure really increase since 1965? Working Paper, University of Califormia, San Diego.

Reimers, Cordelia W., 1985. Cultural differences in labor force participation among married women. American Economic Review 75 (2), 251–255.

Roberts, Tomi-Ann, Nolen-Hoeksema, Susan, 1989. Sex differences in reactions to evaluative feedback. Sex Roles 21, 725–747.

Rockoff, Jonah, Herrmann, Mariesa, 2009. Biological gender differences, absenteeism, and the earnings gap: comment. Working Paper, Columbia University.

Rothstein, Jesse, 2004. College performance predictions and the SAT. Journal of Econometrics 121 (1–2), 297–317.

Rubin, Jeffrey Z., Brown, Bert R., 1975. Bargainers as individuals. In: The Social Psychology of Bargaining and Negotiation. Academic Press, New York.

Rudman, Laurie A., 1998. Self-promotion as a risk factor for women: the costs and benefits of counterstereotypical impression management. Journal of Personality and Social Psychology 74, 629–645.

Rudman, Laurie A., Fairchild, Kimberly, 2004. Reactions to counterstereotypic behavior: the role of backlash in cultural stereotype maintenance. Journal of Personality and Social Psychology 87, 157–176.

Rudman, Laurie A., Glick, Peter, 1999. Feminized management and backlash toward agentic women: the hidden costs to women of a kinder, gentler image of middle managers. Journal of Personality and Social Psychology 77 (5), 1004–1010.

Säve-Söderbergh, Jenny, 2009. Are women asking for low wages? Gender differences in competitive bargaining strategies and ensuing bargaining success, mimeo, Stockholm University.

Sax, Leonard, 2007. Boys Adrift: The Five Factors Driving The Growing Epidemic of Unmotivated Boys and Underachieving Young Men. Basic Books, New York.

Schubert, Renate, Brown, Martin, Gysler, Matthias, Brachinger, Hans W., 1999. Financial decision-making: are women really more risk-averse? American Economic Review 89 (2), 381–385.

Seguino, Stephanis, Stevens, Thomas, Lutz, Mark, 1996. Gender and cooperative behaviour: economic man rides alone. Feminist Economics 2, 1–21.

Sell, Jane, 1997. Gender, strategies, and contributions to public goods. Social Psychology Quarterly 60, 252–265.

Sell, Jane, Wilson, Rick K., 1991. Levels of information and contributions to public goods. Social Forces 70, 107–124.

Sell, Jane, Griffith, W.I., Wilson, Rick K., 1993. Are women more cooperative than men in social dilemmas? Social Psychology Quarterly 56, 211–222.

Silverman, Irwin W., 2003. Gender differences in delay of gratification: a meta-analysis. Sex Roles 49 (9–10), 451–463.

Silverman, Jane M., Kumka, Donald S., 1987. Gender differences in attitudes toward nuclear war and disarmament. Sex Roles 16, 189–203.

Slovic, Paul, 1972. Information procession, situation specificity, and the generality of risk taking behavior. Journal of Personality and Social Psychology 22, 128–134.

Small, Deborah A., Gelfand, Michele, Babcock, Linda, Gettman, Hilary, 2007. Who goes to the bargaining table? The influence of gender and framing on the initiation of negotiation. Journal of Personality and Social Psychology 93 (4), 600–613.

Spigner, C., Hawkins, W., Lorens, W., 1993. Gender differences in perception of risk associated with alcohol and drug use among college students. Women and Health 20, 87–97.

Steele, Claude M., 1997. A threat in the air: how stereotypes shape intellectual identity and performance. American Psychologist 52 (6), 613–629.

Stevenson, Betsey, Wolfers, Justin, 2007. Marriage and divorce: changes and their driving forces. Journal of Economic Perspectives 21 (2), 27–52.

Stevenson, Betsey, Wolfers, Justin, 2009. The paradox of declining female happiness. American Economic Journal: Economic Policy 1 (2), 190–225.

Stuhlmacher, Alice F., Walters, Amy E., 1999. Gender differences in negotiation outcome: a metaanalysis. Personnel Psychology 52 (3), 653–677.

Sunden, Annika E., Surette, Brian J., 1998. Gender differences in the allocation of assets in retirement savings plans. American Economic Review 88 (2), 207–211.

Szatmari, Peter, Offord, David R., Boyle, Michael H., 1989. Ontario child health study: prevalence of attention deficit disorder with hyperactivity. Journal of Child Psychology and Psychiatry 30 (2), 219–230.

Tajfel, H., 1981. Social Identity and Intergroup Relations. Cambridge University Press, Cambridge, UK.

Thomas, Duncan, 1990. Intra-household resource allocation: an inferential approach. Journal of Human Resources 25, 635–664.

Thomas, Duncan, 1994. Like father, like son or like mother, like daughter: parental education and child health. Journal of Human Resources 29, 950–989.

Turner, J., 1985. Social categorization and the self-concept: a social cognitive theory of group behavior. In: Lawler, E. (Ed.), Advances in Group Processes: theory and Research, vol. 2. Greenwich, CT.

Vandegrift, Donald, Yavas, Abdullah, 2009. Men, women, and competition: an experimental test of behavior. Journal of Economic Behavior and Organization 72, 554–570.

Vella, Francis, 1994. Gender roles and human capital investment: the relationship between traditional attitudes and female labour market performance. Economica 61 (242), 191–211.

Voyer, D., Voyer, S., Bryden, Mark P., 1995. Magnitude of sex differences in spatial abilities: a meta-analysis and consideration of critical variables. Psychological Bulletin 117, 250–270.

Walters, Amy E., Stuhlmacher, Alice F., Meyer, Lia L., 1998. Gender and negotiator competitiveness: a meta-analysis. Organizational Behavior and Human Decision Processes 76 (1), 1–29.

Washington, Ebonya, 2008. Female socialization: how daughters affect their legislator fathers' voting on women's issues. American Economic Review 98 (1), 311–332.

Weinberg, Bruce A., 2000. Computer use and the demand for female workers. Industrial and Labor Relations Review 53, 290–308.

Welch, Finis R., 2000. Growth in women's relative wages and in inequality among men: one phenomenon or two? American Economic Review 90 (2), 444–449.

CHAPTER 18

Great Expectations: Law, Employment Contracts, and Labor Market Performance

W. Bentley MacLeod[1]

Columbia University, Department of Economics, 420 West 118th, MC 3308, New York, NY 10027-7296, USA

Contents

Abstract

This chapter reviews the literature on employment and labor law. The goal of the review is to understand why every jurisdiction in the world has extensive employment law, particularly

[1] I am grateful to Janet Currie, Harold Demsetz, Victor Goldberg, Lance Liebman, and seminar participants at the Columbia Law School Faculty seminar and the American Law and Economics Association meetings for helpful discussions and comments. I am also grateful to Elliott Ash, Wil Lim, and Uliana Logina for invaluable research assistance. *E-mail address:* bentley.macleod@columbia.edu.

Handbook of Labor Economics, Volume 4b

ISSN 0169-7218, DOI 10.1016/S0169-7218(11)02416-6

employment protection law, while most economic analysis of the law suggests that less employment protection would enhance welfare. The review has three parts. The first part discusses the structure of the common law and the evolution of employment protection law. The second part discusses the economic theory of contract. Finally, the empirical literature on employment and labor law is reviewed. I conclude that many aspects of employment law are consistent with the economic theory of contract—namely, that contracts are written and enforced to enhance *ex ante* match efficiency in the presence of asymmetric information and relationship specific investments. In contrast, empirical labor market research focuses upon *ex post* match efficiency in the face of an exogenous productivity shock. Hence, in order to understand the form and structure of existing employment law we need better empirical tools to assess the *ex ante* benefits of employment contracts.

JEL classification: J08; J33; J41; J5; K31

Keywords: Employment law; Labor law; Employment contract; Employment contract Law and economics

> *"Now, I return to this young fellow. And the communication I have got to make is, that he has great expectations."*
>
> **Charles Dickens, Great Expectations**

> *"Take nothing on its looks; take everything on evidence. There's no better rule."*
>
> **Charles Dickens, Great Expectations**

1. INTRODUCTION

New jobs and relationships are often founded with great expectations. Yet, despite one's best efforts, jobs and relationships may end prematurely. These transitions might be the result of an involved search for better opportunities elsewhere, or in the less happy cases they may stem from problems in the existing relationship. These endings can be difficult, especially when parties have made significant relationship-specific investments. The purpose of this chapter is to review the role that employment and labor law play in regulating such transitions. This body of law seeks a balance between the need to enforce promises made under great expectations and the need to modify those promises in the face of changed circumstances.

The chapter's scope complements the earlier chapter on labor-market institutions in Volume 3 of this handbook by Blau and Kahn (1999). That chapter focused on policies affecting wage-setting institutions. Like much of modern empirical labor economics, Blau and Kahn (1999) use the competitive model of wage determination as the central organizing framework. Economists begin with the competitive model because it provides an excellent first-order model of wage and employment determination. The competitive model assumes that wages reflect the abilities of workers as observed by the market; this information, combined with information about a worker's training, provides sufficient information for the efficient allocation of labor.

Even if a labor market achieves production efficiency, it may nevertheless result in an inequitable distribution of income, as well as inadequate insurance for workers against unforeseen labor shocks. A number of institutions—such as a minimum wage, unions, mandated severance pay, unemployment insurance, and centralized bargaining—are viewed as ways to address these inequities and risks. Given that a competitive market achieves allocative efficiency, then these interventions necessarily result in allocative inefficiency. Hence, the appropriate policy entails a trade-off between equity and efficiency. For example, Lazear (1990) views employment law as the imposition of a separation cost upon firms wishing to terminate or replace workers. From this perspective, the policy issue is whether or not the equity gains from employment law are worth the efficiency costs. Many policymakers, such as the OECD and the World Bank, have taken the view that these employment regulations have for the most part gone too far—that they restrict the ability of countries to effectively adjust to economic changes and make workers worse off in the long run.[2]

Notwithstanding the mainstream skepticism toward efforts to regulate the employment relationship, it remains true that some form of employment law has operated in every complex market society for at least the last 4000 years—for example, the first minimum wage laws on record date back to Hammurabi's code in 2000 BC. This chapter therefore takes a somewhat different perspective, drawing upon the literature in transaction-cost economics pioneered by Coase (1937), Simon (1957) and Williamson (1975), as well as the work on law and institutions by Posner (1974) and Aoki (2001). This research on the economics of institutions, like empirical labor economics, begins with the hypothesis that long-lived institutions are successful precisely because they are solving some potential market failure. Accordingly, this chapter is organized around the following question: How can labor-market institutions be viewed as an *efficient* response to some market failure? Just as the competitive-equilibrium model supposes that wages are the market's best estimate of workers' abilities, the institutional-economics program views successful institutions as solving a resource-allocation problem.

This approach does not assume that these institutions are perfect. On the contrary, just as the competitive model yields predictions regarding how wages and employment respond to shock, the hypothesis that institutions efficiently solve a resource-allocation problem generates predictions regarding the rise and fall of these institutions. Important precursors to this approach are found in labor economics. In a classic paper, Ashenfelter and Johnson (1969) suggest that we should be able to understand union behavior, including the strike decision, as the outcome of the interaction between several interested parties. The work of Card (1986) demonstrates that observed contracts cannot be viewed as achieving the first best, and hence transaction costs are a necessary ingredient for understanding the observed structure of negotiated employment contracts. Despite this

[2] See the influential Jobs Study by the OECD (1994) and the recent work by the World Bank economists Djankov and Ramalho (2009).

early progress, the literature I review is still undeveloped. We do not have a good understanding of how the law works, nor do we understand the impact of legal rules on economic performance. In an effort to summarize what *is* known, this review is divided into three sections that correspond to coherent bodies of research.

Section 2 briefly reviews the structure of employment law and discusses some exemplary cases. A full review of employment law is not provided—for an excellent review, see Jolls (2007). My more modest goal is to provide some relevant insights into what law is and how it works. This sort of targeted inquiry is desirable because the standard assumption in economics is that the law enforces contracts as written. In practice, private law imposes *no* restrictions on behavior. It is mainly an adjudication system that can, after a careful review of the evidence, exact monetary penalties upon parties who have breached a duty. Hence, private law is a complex system of incentive mechanisms that affects the payoffs of individuals but does not typically constrain their choices. The distinction is important for economics because it is convenient to model legal rules as hard constraints on behavior—that is, as structuring the *available moves* in a game rather than just altering some of the expected payoffs. This approach also implies, wrongly, that rules apply equally to all individuals. Treating private law as an incentive system, instead, implies that the impact of the law is heterogeneous—an individual's response to a legal rule will vary with an individual's characteristics, such as wealth, attitudes toward risk, and the evidence that one can present in court.

Heterogeneity and information also play key roles in the theory of employment contracts reviewed in Section 3. The past forty years have witnessed tremendous progress in the economic theory of contract, especially in terms of teasing out how a particular set of parties should design a contract given the transaction costs characterizing the employment relationship. The influential principal-agent model, for example, was developed in the context of the insurance contract, which specifies state-contingent payments.[3] The modern theory of contract, building on the work of Grossman and Hart (1986), recognizes that an important function of economic institutions and contracts is the efficient allocation of authority and decision rights within a relationship.

Most economists agree that unions and employment law affect the relative bargaining power of individuals. These institutions are usually interpreted as mere re-distribution of rents, and so any allocation of bargaining power that results in prices diverging from competitive levels is inherently inefficient. The modern literature on contract views authority as an instrument for mitigating transaction costs due to asymmetric information and holdup. This perspective also naturally admits a role for fairness in decision-making, and hence can provide an economic rationale for why fairness concerns are important in the adjudication of a dispute.[4]

---

[3] See Pauly (1968).
[4] See Kornhauser and MacLeod (2010) for a fuller discussion of this point.

Section 3 also discusses the empirical content of these models. The modern empirical literature is concerned with identifying a causal link between various labor-market interventions and performance. Unfortunately, much of the economic theory of contract is not amenable to this approach. These models typically describe how matches with certain observable features (X variables) result in an employment-compensation package (Y variables). As Holland (1986) makes clear, these are not causal relationships, but merely associations. For example, the predicted relation between the sex of a worker and the form of his/her employment contract is not causal, since the sex of a worker is not a treatment variable.

This distinction is useful because it helps explain the gulf between much of the theory discussed in Section 3 and the empirical evidence discussed in Section 4. It is also worthwhile to keep in mind that *all economic models are false*. This does not imply that these models are not useful. As Wolfgang Pauli quipped regarding a paper by a young colleague — "it's not even wrong!"[5] Rather, economic models are decision aids that guide further data collection and help in selecting between different policy interventions. The upshot for empirical researchers is that one typically tests the associations that the theory predicts, rather than the theory itself. Empirical determinations of the validity of these associations can help us decide whether and to what extent we can rely on the model as a decision aid.

The theory section discusses how contract theory can be used to understand employment law, and the conditions under which it may be desirable. We begin with a discussion of how contract design is affected by the interplay between risk, asymmetric information and the holdup that arises from the need for parties to make relationship specific investments. These models can be used to explain the role of the courts in enforcing the employment contract. The recent property rights theory of the firm developed by Grossman and Hart (1986) illustrates the importance of governance and the associated allocation of decision rights in order to achieve an efficient allocation.[6] A contract is an instrument that explicitly allocates certain decision rights between the contract parties. This can also be achieved with unions. This section discusses how the appropriate allocation of power and decision rights can enhance productive efficiency. Thus, these theories provide conditions under which union power may enhance productive efficiency, as suggested by Freeman and Medoff (1984).

Section 4 reviews the empirical evidence on employment and labor law. Here we are concerned with explicitly causal statements such as the question of whether or not a reduction in dismissal barriers will reduce unemployment. This is a causal inquiry because it compares the outcomes from two different choices: having more or less employment protection law. Section 4.2 discusses the literature on unions that addresses

---

[5] See Peierls (1960). It is also worthwhile to point out that even though Newtonian physics is false, it is all that one needs for most practical applications.

[6] See Hart (1995) for a full discussion of this approach.

two questions. First, does unionization of a workforce increase productive efficiency? Second, does unionization increase or decrease firm profits? Even if a union increases productive efficiency, if the increase in rents extracted by the unions is greater than the increase in productive efficiency, then profits would fall as a consequence, which in turn may lead to a decrease in unionization. The chapter concludes with an assessment of the evidence and a discussion of future directions for research.

2. THE LAW

"The law embodies the story of a nation's development through many centuries, and it cannot be dealt with as if it contained only the axioms and corollaries of a book of mathematics. In order to know what it is, we must know what it has been, and what it tends to become."

Oliver Wendell Holmes, The Common Law, 1881

The purpose of this section is not to provide a comprehensive review of employment law. Rather, the goal is to provide a sense of how employment law has developed so that one might better understand its impact on the employment relationship.[7] In the United States, employment law is primarily the domain of the states. Section 4 reviews several empirical studies that have exploited the natural experiments resulting from variations in state laws to measure the impact of various laws on economic performance. Overlaying the state laws are a number of federal statutes affecting the employment relationship, including the National Labor Relations Act of 1935 (allowing workers to organize collective bargaining units), Fair Standards Act of 1938 (establishing minimum employment standards), Employee Retirement Income Security Act of 1973 (ERISA) (ensuring that employee benefits meet national standards), Occupational Safety and Health Act of 1970 (OSHA) (establishing minimum health and safety standards in the workplace), and Family and Medical Leave Act (establishing protections for leave related to personal sickness or family emergencies). These laws are enumerated in Table 1.

While the primary concern of the present chapter is the United States, studies of employment law in other countries are also discussed. Blanpain (2003), for example, provides a comprehensive review of European law. As in the United States, European law is complicated by the fact that both individual countries and the European Parliament create rules that affect the employment relationship. More generally, all countries in the world have some system of employment laws, created and adapted to the circumstances of each jurisdiction.

One chapter cannot do justice to the dizzying complexity of the law across jurisdictions, even if attention were restricted to a narrow area such as employee-dismissal law. As the quote from Holmes (1881) illustrates, legal systems are complex

[7] See Jolls (2007) for a survey of employment law, and Rothstein and Liebman (2003) for a more comprehensive review of US law. Gould (2004) provides an accessible discussion of American labor law, and how it differs from European labor law.

Table 1 United States employment laws.

Racial discrimination	Civil Rights Acts of 1866, 1964	1866	Bars racial discrimination by employers.
Social security	Social Security Act	1935	Distributes social security benefits to those of retirement age.
Minimum wage	Fair Labor Standards Act	1938	Establishes a minimum hourly wage.
Overtime rights	Fair Labor Standards Act	1938	Requires that employers pay a higher wage for work exceeding 40 hours a week.
Child labor	Fair Labor Standards Act	1938	Places limits on many forms of child labor.
Gender discrimination	Civil Rights Act of 1964	1964	Prohibits gender-based discrimination.
Religious discrimination	Civil Rights Act of 1964	1964	Prohibits discrimination against employees on the basis of religion.
Age discrimination	Age Discrimination in Employment Act	1967	Prohibits discrimination against workers above the age of 40.
Workplace safety	Occupational Safety and Health Act	1970	Establishes minimum standards for workplace safety.
Good faith exception	*Fortune v. National Cash Register Co.*, 373 Mass. 96	1977	Provides for a wrongful discharge claim against employers violating the common-law contract duty of good faith and fair dealing.
Public policy exception	*Tameny v. Atlantic Richfield Co.*, 27 Cal.3rd 167	1980	Provides for a wrongful discharge claim against employers when the discharge would be a violation of public policy, for example, when the employee is fired for refusing to commit a crime.
Implied contract exception	*Wooley v. Hoffmann-La Roch*, 99 NJ 284	1985	Provides for a wrongful discharge claim against employers when an employment contract is implied.

(*continued on next page*)

Table 1 (continued)

Sexual harassment	*Meritor savings bank v. Vinson*, 477 US 57	1986	Recognizes sexual harassment as a violation of the Civil Rights Act of 1964.
Layoff notice	Worker Adjustment and Retraining Notification Act	1988	Companies must give 60 days' notice before large-scale layoffs.
Whistleblower protection	Whistleblower Protection Act of 1989	1989	Prohibits retaliation against employees for reporting illegal acts against the federal government.
Disability discrimination	Americans with Disabilities Act	1990	Prohibits discrimination based on disability.
Pregnancy discrimination	Civil Rights Act of 1991	1991	Probits discrimination against employees because they are pregnant.
Medical leave protection	Family and Medical Leave Act	1993	Requires employers to allow workers 12 weeks of unpaid medical leave for certain medical conditions of themselves or close relatives.

systems that evolve over time to resolve the variegated disputes faced by parties of commercial transactions. To make sense of this complexity, I follow the lead of the law-and-economics movement as epitomized in the work of Richard Posner, who argues that the law, especially the common law, has evolved over time to address the needs of individuals trading in a market economy.[8] Posner (2003) explicitly poses the rhetorical question: "How is it possible, the reader may ask, for the common law—an ancient body of legal doctrine, which has changed only incrementally in the last century—to make as much economic sense as it seems to?"[9]

The claim is not that the entire body of rules and norms governing economic activity can be viewed as the solution to the problem of efficiently organizing economic activity. Rather, the claim is that individual rules have evolved to solve particular problems that appeared repeatedly before the courts. From this perspective flow some observations that may help explain the theoretical and rhetorical gaps between legal rule making, economic models of the labor market, and economic policy making. The advantage of the economic approach is that it allows one to explore the empirical implications of a simplified representation of the law. The disadvantage, particularly for purposes of

---

[8] See Ehrlich and Posner (1974), and also Posner's classic work, *Economic Analysis of Law*, now in its seventh edition.

[9] See p. 252.

economic policy analysis, is that the simplifying assumptions may miss key characteristics of the law that are important in practice.

This gap between law and economics is particularly salient in laws protecting employees from discharge, wrongful or otherwise. In economics, employment protections are typically modeled as a form of turnover costs, leading to the view that such laws probably interfere with an economy's efficient response to shocks. As a consequence, organizations such as the OECD (see OECD (1994)) have advocated reducing or abandoning employment protections. Recent work by Blanchard and Tirole (2008) addressing how France and other countries should design unemployment insurance and employment protection concludes that there is no role for the law beyond enforcing employment contracts.

Nonetheless, as a matter of law, there are no jurisdictions where courts enforce all privately agreed-upon contracts. Labor contracts with young children, for example, are almost universally prohibited. Generally speaking, there is a substantial gap between the law in practice and the law as represented in many economic models of employment. One reason for this gap is that legal practitioners rarely have any reason to use an explicitly economic approach to understand the form of a particular contract. Lawyers typically represent clients in cases after the fact; the question of why a legal rule exists is not important to them. The real issue is to predict how a judge will rule and then present the case so that their client will do as well as possible in what is essentially a negative-sum game between the plaintiff and defendant. In this game, the details of the law are crucial, but the reasons why they have a particular form are not usually relevant.[10]

In consequence, the concerns of the legal scholar are quite different from those of the economist, which in turn creates a gap between the law as it exists and the law as modeled in economics.[11] The goal of the next two sections is to narrow that gap ever so slightly, at least in the context of employment regulation. The next subsection discusses the generic structure of the law. Even though legal rules vary greatly from jurisdiction to jurisdiction, the notion of law and how it works has some universal features. More specifically, Section 2.1 examines three well-known employment-law cases in the United States and the United Kingdom. These cases illustrate the complex problem faced by a judge in an employment dispute. Moreover, as these cases demonstrate, the courts are not passive agents; they play an active role in resource allocation. Consistent with the "Posnerian" perspective, the decisions in some cases can be viewed as enhancing economic performance.

2.1. What is law?

The notion of a legal rule dates back at least as far as 2000 BC, with the Babylonians following Hammurabi's code and the Mesopotamians following the code of Urukagina.

---

[10] Furthermore, judges are often economically illiterate—and are often suspicious of statistical evidence—so economic arguments might even be counterproductive. See the discussion by Posner (2008) and Breyer (2009).

[11] See discussion in MacLeod (2007b).

While some of these ancient edicts imply curious beliefs about causality,[12] it is clear that the purpose of many of these rules is to modify or constrain human behavior. For as long as law has existed, its purpose has been to facilitate the efficient functioning of civil society.

The aforementioned codes even had room for what we would now call labor law. Hammurabi's code includes, for example:

- Minimum wage rules: "If any one hire a day laborer, he shall pay him from the New Year until the fifth month (April to August, when days are long and the work hard) six gerahs in money per day; from the sixth month to the end of the year he shall give him five gerahs per day".
- Liability rule: "If a herdsman, to whom cattle or sheep have been entrusted for watching over, and who has received his wages as agreed upon, and is satisfied, diminish the number of the cattle or sheep, or make the increase by birth less, he shall make good the increase or profit that was lost in the terms of settlement".

These are remarkable examples of how legal rules are created to regulate the employment relationship. That minimum wage rules persist to this day suggests that there are robust reasons for the existence of such rules. Recognizing this possibility, the law-and-economics approach seeks to explain the rules as solutions to well-defined market imperfections. Ostrom (2000), for example, has shown that many societies have developed efficient systems of rules and adjudication for regulating the use of common-pool resources, thereby avoiding the tragedy of the commons (Hardin, 1968). Ostrom observes that all successful commons-governance regimes consist of a set of rules that have the following features:

1. The rules are commonly known;
2. There are penalties for breaking rules that increase in intensity with the severity and frequency of violation;
3. There is an organization or an individual who is responsible for imposing penalties when informed; and
4. There is a process of adjudication when there are disagreements regarding whether an offense has occurred and what penalty should be imposed.

All organizations, including firms and families, have rule systems with these features. The economic analysis of such rule systems typically entails asking what set of rules would achieve an efficient allocation.[13] In the common-pool-resource problem, for

---

[12] Hammurabi's code, Paragraph 2, decrees: "If any one bring an accusation against a man, and the accused go to the river and leap into the river, if he sink in the river his accuser shall take possession of his house. But if the river prove that the accused is not guilty, and he escape unhurt, then he who had brought the accusation shall be put to death, while he who leaped into the river shall take possession of the house that had belonged to his accuser".

[13] Determining the optimal system for selecting a course of action given the preferences of individuals, the technology of the environment, and the information available is the subject of mechanism design theory. See Jackson (2001).

example, one seeks a set of rules ensuring that each person with access does not overuse the resource. Organizational economics tries to determine which systems of rules and compensation in firms or public entities ensure that agents reveal useful information and choose efficient levels of effort.

What distinguishes the law's rule system from a family's or organization's is not the existence of binding rules, but the sources of enforcement and adjudication. When we speak of a legal system, we mean the set of rules and associated penalties that are enforced by the state.[14] As discussed above, however, the jurisdiction associated with a dispute is often poorly defined. Even when the jurisdiction is well-defined, disputes can often be decided by multiple judicial bodies (including private mediation and arbitration). Many countries, such as Italy and the United Kingdom, maintain a separate system of courts for ruling on employment disputes. In the United States, disputes regarding a collective-bargaining agreement may be brought before the National Labor Relations Board, employment disputes before a state court, and Title VII discrimination suits before a federal court.

To illustrate what we mean by a legal system (and employment law in particular), let us consider the proverbial worker-firm relationship. In the standard neoclassical model of employment, the worker agrees to supply L hours of labor for a wage w. This can be viewed as a supply contract where the hours are, say, consulting time. In that case, the relationship would be governed by contract law. The worker must supply L hours, and the employer must pay wL dollars.

Should the worker supply less than L hours, the worker has *breached* the contract. Suppose that the firm has paid P_0 in advance, a common practice if the worker is, for example, a lawyer. Some sort of binding agreement is needed; otherwise, the worker would simply take the P_0 and try to find employment elsewhere. The question, then, is: What incentives does the worker have *not* to breach the agreement?

One possibility is the use of an informal enforcement mechanism. This would include firms' telling each other that the individual has breached, and hence should not be dealt with.[15] Another alternative is to use physical violence against the individual, a common technique in the illegal drug trade and other black markets.[16] While both enforcement systems are still widely used, societies have evolved more legalistic systems of adjudication for the simple reason that parties sometimes fail to perform even if they act in good faith.

---

[14] It is worth highlighting the fact that a set of written rules is not a requirement, nor even a defining feature of a legal system. In the Middle Ages, the subjects of a feudal lord faced a number of rules regulating their life on the manor, most of which were not written (Bloch, 1961); nonetheless, the set of rules was widely understood. Written rules do have good social consequences, however, by assisting with evidentiary issues and facilitating agreement among parties regarding the applicable rule. Inter-subjective agreement on the law is an important issue in modern labor law, as we shall see in the case of employee handbooks.

[15] Greif (1989) has some nice examples from the Maghrebi traders, who did write letters to each other in this regard.

[16] Naidu and Yuchtman (2009) document that criminal law, with punitive sanctions, was widely used to enforce employment contracts in 19th century England.

Enforcement systems that trigger punishment regardless of the *reason* for breach, such as violence among drug dealers, are simply not always efficient.[17]

In contrast, if the contract is viewed as a *legally binding* agreement, then the breach of contract by the worker gives the firm the *right* to seek damages in court. If the firm prevails, the court can order the worker to pay damages to the firm; if the worker refuses to pay, the court can still enforce the decision by ordering the seizure of the worker's assets.

The fact that contract breach leads to the right to file suit—as opposed to an automatic penalty—is a feature that distinguishes legal enforcement from other forms of rule systems, such as rewards within a firm. In the economics literature, it is common to view any agreement between parties that links future rewards to actions as a "contract". Jensen and Meckling (1976), for example, famously proposed that one should conceptualize a firm as a "nexus of contracts". If all contracts are enforceable at negligible cost, a reward system that promotes an employee for good performance and an agreement with an outside supplier to pay a bonus for sufficient quality are assumed to be equally enforceable. If employment contracts are enforceable at no cost, subject only to information constraints, then explaining the contract form requires only that one carefully specify the environment and then use principal-agent theory to work out the optimal contract.

The difficulty, as Williamson (1991) observes, is that the law uses forbearance for transactions within a firm. Even if a firm promises a promotion, that does not confer a right upon the worker to sue the firm should the promotion not be offered. All dispute resolutions of this sort occur strictly within the firm, with no appeal to an outside legal authority available. A full discussion of the role of courts in such disputes must wait until the next subsection, but for now the relevant point is that for any contract between two legal persons (in our example, firm and consultant), both parties *always* have the right to seek damages in court should there be a breach of contract.[18]

That the decision to sue is discretionary implies that the same rule may have different effects depending on the characteristics of the parties of the contract. The characteristics of the parties might even be the most important factor in whether a lawsuit is filed. For example, suppose that a company has illegal discriminatory hiring practices. If the market is thick, with plenty of employment alternatives, potential employees may not find it worthwhile to bring suit against the company. In a less friendly employment market, if an individual believes he has been the victim of illegal discrimination and cannot find another job, he may bring suit. This point is illustrative of the fact that we will always find differences between a legal rule on paper and the same rule in practice.[19]

---

[17] See MacLeod (2007a) for discussion and proof of this point.

[18] See Kornhauser and MacLeod (2010) for a discussion of the concept of a legal person.

[19] Dunford and Devin (1998) have a nice discussion of how employee perceptions affect the decision whether to file suit. For a review of the literature on the decision to file a suit see Kessler and Rubinfeld (2007).

A second source of uncertainty is how the court will decide a case. In the case of the breaching consultant, the court has to make two decisions, each of which is prone to statistical error: (1) deciding whether a breach has occurred, and (2) if so, the damages to be paid. For damages, the general rule is that courts order expectations damages—namely, the losses associated with the worker's breach. An example of a formula that the court might use is:

$$\text{damages} = P_0 + w_1 L - wL,$$

$$= \text{prepayment} + \text{cost of replacement} - \text{promised wages not paid}.$$

Here w_1 is the wage for the replacement worker. The worker has to pay the costs associated with finding a replacement worker rather than the value of the work done, due to contract law's requirement that injured parties make every effort to mitigate losses arising from breach. The mitigation rule is mandatory, meaning that parties cannot contract around it. Employment law has many other mandatory rules; slavery is prohibited, for example, as is discrimination on the basis of race, age, or sex.

Expectation is not the only way to calculate damages from contract breach. In a famous paper on contract damages, Fuller and Perdue (1936) identified restitution and reliance as other possible measures of damages.[20] *Restitution* damages, for one, are intended to put the firm into the same financial position—as if the contract had never been signed. In our consultant example, restitution damages would only require the worker to repay P_0. Matters are less clear if P_0 is paid to the worker so that he can buy passage to the job site and secure accommodation. Suppose upon arriving, the worker is injured and cannot perform his duties; the firm sues for breach. If the contract does not specify what happens in this contingency, a court may be asked to fill in the gaps in the agreement. Some other issues that might not be described in the contract (and which the court must adjudicate) include whether the injured worker may be fired or whether he must take out a loan to repay P_0.

Alternatively, the firm, in the expectation of being able to rely upon performance, may have paid for passage and accommodation. In that case, if the worker does not perform, then she may be asked to compensate the firm for these *reliance* expenditures.

Finally, the contract could have provided that a non-performing worker pay a fine P_0. In this case, non-performance would *not* be a breach of contract, and a breach would occur only if the worker failed to pay back P_0. Notice that in this case, the damages would simply be P_0, even under the expectation-damages rule. This example illustrates that for the same exchange relationship there is no unique notion of contract breach. Rather, the

---

[20] This work has been influential in law and economics. Economists have used the three damages measures—expectations, restitution, and reliance—as alternative legal rules that can be analyzed using the standard tools of economics. See, in particular, Shavell (1984) and Rogerson (1984).

contract *defines* what constitutes breach, and then the courts must decide whether or not to enforce the terms set out in the agreement.[21]

Defining the conditions for breach is not a clear-cut exercise. For example, the contract could have specified *liquidated damages* in the amount P_0. In this case, breach would occur for non-performance, but then the contract would direct the court to set damages at P_0. This contract seems to be equivalent to the previous one (indeed, most economic theories of contract would see them as equivalent), but there is an important distinction. In the previous case, if the worker pays P_0, no breach has occurred, and the firm has no right to bring suit against the worker. In the liquidated-damages case, even if the worker offers to pay P_0, the firm still has a right to sue the worker because technically a breach has still occurred. Admittedly, the firm would face an uphill battle in court if the worker had offered to pay—and normally would have no reason not to accept the offer as part of a settlement agreement—but the right exists nonetheless. The firm might believe, for example, that the worker abused the liquidated-damages clause, accepting the consulting job only as a contingency in case another opportunity did not work out. If the firm's belief is true, the worker has arguably violated the requirement of good faith and fair dealing—another mandatory rule in the common law of contracts. Arguing that the liquidated-damages clause no longer applies, the firm might ask for expectation damages larger than P_0.

Conversely, assume that the firm sets liquidated damages at three times P_0. Breach occurs, and the worker declares these damages to be unconscionably high. The worker may have a valid claim under contract law's prohibition against penalty clauses. This doctrine—another mandatory rule—provides that liquidated damages far exceeding the losses to the injured party will not be enforced by courts.

The prohibition on penalty clauses, along with the other examples of mandatory rules discussed above, illustrate that the law allows for a significant degree of judicial intervention into private contracts. Among other things, a court can fill in missing terms and refuse to enforce unreasonable terms. The decision whether to intervene is often at the court's discretion, but courts usually turn to the Uniform Commercial Code and other statutes, as well as previous court decisions, to justify these interventions. Thus the legal system is an adjudication process that modifies contracts in the face of a breach as a function of past experience and practice.

The extent to which courts should intervene into freely entered agreements has proven to be controversial. Early scholars, such as MacNeil (1974), proposed that courts rely on many sources of information, including industry custom and the history of the relationship between the plaintiff and the defendant, when making a decision. If parties have a longstanding relationship, Macneil argued, contract terms should be enforced

---

[21] See MacLeod (2007a) for a discussion of whose reputational concerns interact with the breach decision. In particular, the theory predicts that the party whose reputation is the most valuable should be the one who is responsible for initiating breach.

within the context of the relationship. Macneil and many others believed that this sort of context-sensitive adjudication could help repair the parties' relationship and facilitate the continuation of mutually beneficial exchange. Most economic theories of contract, in contrast, work from the assumption that parties have well-defined interests and can draft agreements efficiently, implying that contracts should be enforced as written. This presumption has led to a law-and-economics scholarship that mostly argues for the curtailment of judicial discretion, and for a more systematic dependence upon basic economic reasoning when ruling on a case (see Goetz and Scott (1980) and more recently Schwartz and Scott (2003)).

Regardless of one's theoretical commitments, it remains the case that the law does not simply enforce a set of well-defined rules. The law does include a set of rules, but along with a system of adjudication that results in a context-sensitive application of these rules to individual cases. This context sensitivity includes, among other things, consideration for the idiosyncratic features of the parties. The basic principles of contract law apply to all agreements between two parties, but more specialized bodies of law have evolved to regulate specific classes of contracts. The insurance industry is regulated by a specialized area of contract rules (see for example Baker (2003)) as is employment law. It is to this latter body of law that we now turn.

2.2. Employment law

Employment law evolved from contract law and master-servant law to deal with the unique problems characterizing the modern employment relationship. The first task is to determine the difference between (1) a firm's relationship with an outside contractor selling services, and (2) its relationship with an employee. The difference not only affects the area of law that regulates the relationship, but it also affects the relevant tax law. In the United States, the Internal Revenue Service will find that an employment relationships exists when "the person for whom services are performed has the right to control and direct the individual who performs the services, not only as to the result to be accomplished by the work but also as to the details and means by which that result is accomplished".[22]

As this tax regulation exemplifies, the obligation of the employee is to follow his employer's directions, not to produce a specific service with particular characteristics. Simon (1951)'s model nicely captures this distinction between sales and employment. In a *sales contract*, says Simon, the seller agrees to supply a particular good or service x from the set of all possible goods and services X, and in exchange the buyer agrees to pay a sum P. An *employment relationship*, in contrast, is characterized by a subset of all possible goods and services, $A \subset X$, that represents the set of duties that the employer might ask the employee to carry out. A might include the service x defined in the aforementioned

---

[22] Treas. Reg. Sections 31.3121(d)-1(c)(2).

sales contract, but that single task would normally be just one component in a broad complex of obligations defining an employment relationship. In exchange for a promise to carry out these duties, the employer agrees to pay a wage w.

Simon's simple model highlights an essential feature of the employment relationship, namely, the admissible scope of a person's job as represented by the set A. The admissible set of tasks $S \subset X$—that is, the set of acts that an employer is allowed by law to command—has been subject to a plethora of regulation and litigation. For example, is it conscionable for a firm to require 50 hours a week? Can a manager ask her assistant to commit crimes?

An employment relationship often begins with little formal agreement about the tasks the employee will be asked to carry out. The longer the potential duration of the employment, the more incomplete the initial employment agreement. Given the informal nature of such agreements, when disputes do arise the courts will have little to rely upon when constructing the obligations of each party. With poorly defined obligations, determining whether a breach occurred presents a difficult task, as does choosing an appropriate remedy.

The combination of extreme contract incompleteness and daunting litigation costs have convinced many legal scholars that the appropriate default rule is at-will employment. The courts have converged to this default rule partly because they now view employment law as an extension of contract law. That view diverges significantly from the early case law on employment disputes, which was mostly governed by "master-servant law".[23] That old body of law consisted of a set of legal default rules developed in England and the United States to deal with cases involving domestic servants. In the master-servant relationship, the customary period of employment lasted one year; courts held that neither party should sever the relationship before then.

In a widely cited work, Wood (1877) argued for replacing this law with the rule of at-will employment, where both parties can sever the relationship whenever they wish and face no liability beyond the requirement that the employer pay her employee the agreed-upon wage for work already completed. Wood's argument was a pragmatic one, based on the bad experiences of many employers and employees with the inflexibility of master-servant law. As detailed in Feinman (1978), the new rule was quickly adopted by the New York courts and remains the default rule today. In California, the legislature adopted what is now Section 2922 of the California Labor code, which provides that "employment, having no specified term, may be terminated at the will of either party on notice to the other".

The at-will-employment rule figures prominently in most economic models of the labor market. As these models have it, workers and firms enter into relationships that are preferred to the alternatives in the marketplace. Should a firm mistreat a worker, or

---

[23] See Feinman (1978) for a review of the development of this law.

have high standards for performance or number of hours worked, the firm will have to pay relatively high wages or else the worker will leave. Similarly, if a worker demands a higher wage or better working conditions, the firm is free to search for another worker who will abide by the current arrangements. In equilibrium, all firms and workers are satisfied with their lot relative to the alternatives.

The hypothesis of a perfectly competitive market can explain many broad features of wages and employment over time, but it cannot explain the emergence of the at-will-employment rule. This is an example of the model's inability to explain the emergence of laws that seem to constitute reasonable responses to real economic issues. That failure indicates flaws in popular economic models—but not in economic reasoning generally. Consider the case of child labor. As societies have become more wealthy, they have gradually imposed stricter legal constraints on the minimum age and maximum hours for minors in the workplace. By the perfectly-competitive-market hypothesis, these restrictions would be unjustified because only those families for which child labor is efficient would put their children to work rather than in school. On the other hand, a more realistic economic inquiry recognizes the market imperfection imposed by liquidity constraints: children (and parents) cannot borrow against future income arising from education, so many families send their children to work for a short-term gain in income rather than invest in a long-term gain from education. Investing in education results in superior overall welfare, so the choice to put children to work is inefficient. Laws that regulate child labor, like the Fair Labor Standards Act, are justified because, by increasing the cost of child labor, they motivate families to substitute education for labor. By increasing investments in education, these laws increase social welfare.

The analysis in the previous paragraph indicates the potential insight to be gained from an evolutionary perspective when investigating the law and economics of employment law. Applying this perspective to our law's historical origins, we observe that employment law adapts to the changing macroeconomic environment. One of the earliest labor statutes on record, the Ordinance of Labourers, addressed the problems of unharvested crops, rising wages, and poaching of workers faced by English landowners at the height of the Black Death. Similarly, in 1630, the Massachusetts General Court placed a wage cap of 2 shillings a day on skilled craftsmen, who were at that time taking advantage of limited supply. More recently, the Fair Labor Standards Act became law in the midst of the Great Depression, when workers lacked market power to ensure good working conditions. Mandatory overtime pay, meanwhile, incentivized firms to hire more workers at fewer hours each, thereby serving as an income- and risk-sharing function.

These legal adaptations to changes in the labor-market environment can all be conceived as forms of insurance, whether against the waste of unharvested crops, gouging by craftsmen, or unemployment. In the next subsection, we discuss recent work based on the hypothesis that workers are risk-averse, which might help explain some of the features of these laws. Certainly, both minimum-wage laws and unemployment insurance can be viewed as forms of imperfect insurance.[24]

Once the issue of risk is put aside, the law-and-economics movement has tended to take the view that employment at will is the optimal default rule (see, e.g., Epstein (1984)). Within economics, a tradition including Friedman (1962) and Alchian and Demsetz (1972) has viewed labor services from the perspective of the buyer-seller contract—with *no* remedies for contract breach. Specifically, Friedman argued that a competitive market with free entry and exit is the most efficient market form, even when contracts cannot clearly specify quality. In his vision of the world, workers and firms trade freely within the context of the sales contract (quality x in exchange for price p); should performance be inadequate, the worker would gain a poor reputation and thereafter be excluded from the market.

There are two difficulties with this argument. The first, as MacLeod (2007a) discusses, is that the literature on relational contracts shows that reputational concerns are neither necessary nor sufficient to ensure efficient exchange. Second, the common law has developed many doctrines that limit the freedom of contract in the context of the simple buyer-seller model. Posner (2003) suggests that these developments tend to enhance contract performance. Chakravarty and MacLeod (2009) present evidence that this is indeed the case for a large class of contracts that are common in the construction industry.

As the Simon model highlights, the employment relationship is different because a performance obligation is created *ex post*. If the worker accepts a contract with scope $A \subset X$, then the performance obligation is created when the employer asks the employee to carry out $x^* \in A$. If the relationship were governed by standard contract law, then if the employee chooses $x^b \neq x^*$ the employer-cum-buyer could sue for damages $B(x^*) - B(x^b)$, where $B(x)$ is the benefit to the employer of action x. Under employment at will the general rule would be that the employer has no right to sue, but she can freely dismiss the employee, even if performance is satisfactory.

Correspondingly, the employee has the right to leave whenever he wishes. For example, if the employer asks the employee to carry out an action outside the scope of his duties, then under at-will employment the employee has the right to refuse to carry out the task and find another job. In contrast, in the case of a construction contract, if the buyer were to ask for a modification to the building plan, then under US law the contractor would have an *obligation* to carry out the modification, but he would also have the right to sue for the additional cost of the change if the buyer/builder does not adequately compensate him for the changes.

The defining feature of at-will employment is that in each period parties are free to renegotiate the contract, with the outside options defined by each parties'

---

[24] The reader is referred to Blau and Kahn (1999) and Rogerson et al. (2005) for excellent reviews of this literature.

market opportunities. Consistent with the Coase theorem, we should expect at-will employment to give rise to arrangements that are *ex post* efficient. This observation has led some legal scholars (e.g., Epstein (1984)) to suggest that exceptions to employment at will are inefficient. Yet today in the United States, as in most other jurisdictions worldwide, the law of wrongful discharge is alive and well. Indeed, there are clear exceptions to the rule of employment at will. In the next section, we discuss three of the most important exceptions figuring in recent empirical work on employment law.

2.3. Exceptions to employment at will

This section discusses three exceptions to employment at will that have found broad support in US courts. These exceptions are judge-made laws, created in response to difficult cases; hence, they are good examples of how the common law evolves in response to the disputes that arise in practice. The three exceptions we consider are (1) the public policy exception, protecting from employer retaliation those workers that act in a way consistent with accepted state policy, (2) the implied contract exception, protecting workers who can show that the implicit contract with the employer entails just-cause dismissal, and (3) the good-faith exception, requiring employers and employers to behave in ways consistent with fair dealing.

US courts rarely order specific performance—that is, the losing employer typically still has the right to discharge the employee—and hence the issue is usually one of damages: How much should she have to pay for this right? In other jurisdictions, however, reinstatement is sometimes considered an acceptable remedy. One of the few US cases in which specific performance was granted in an employment dispute was *Silva v. University of New Hampshire*.[25]

The question of damage awards is not straightforward, but economics can assist in organizing our thinking. If markets are perfectly competitive—and a worker's compensation is equal to his best market alternative—dismissal does not entail any harm. However, as Mincer (1962) has shown, the second assumption can break down when the worker's training costs were significant. If the worker paid for some of the training costs, he will be compensated for them through increased future compensation, and therefore his income may be in excess of the best market alternatives. More often, dismissal entails a costly job search and possibly relocation. When an employee has been wrongfully discharged, the court will award damages that reflect these costs.

An additional complication is whether the wrongful-discharge action comes under tort or contract law. The first exception to the at-will employment rule, a claim for wrongful discharge as violation of public policy, is considered a tort claim.[26] A tort claim, put briefly, is distinguished from contract disputes by there being no requirement

---

[25] 888 F.Supp. 293 (D.N.H. 1994) (granting a preliminary injunction preventing a tenured professor's suspension for comments that offended some students).

[26] See Rothstein and Liebman (2003), Chapter 10.B.

for a prior contractual relationship. Standard examples include traffic accidents and medical malpractice. The practical implication of this distinction is that tort law allows for the recovery of both consequential damages and punitive damages, which may far exceed the direct economic harm suffered by the discharged employee. In contract law, consequential damages and punitive damages are in general not recoverable.

2.3.1. Public policy exception

Under the public-policy exception, an employee may sue for wrongful discharge if he is dismissed for conduct that is protected by law. Miles (2000) summarizes the four types of terminations that fit under this class of exception.[27] They are (1) "an employee's refusal to commit an illegal act, such as perjury or price-fixing"; (2) "an employee's missing work to perform a legal duty, such as jury duty or military service"; (3) "an employee's exercise of a legal right, such as filing a workman's compensation claim"; and (4) "an employee's 'blowing the whistle,' or disclosing wrongdoing by the employer or fellow employees".

A well-known example of the first type of public-policy exception is the 1980 case *Tameny v. Atlantic Richfield Co.*[28] Plaintiff Tameny, the dismissed employee, claimed that his discharge resulted from a refusal to participate in the company's unlawful price-fixing scheme. Defendant Atlantic Richfield argued that since there was no employment contract, Tameny's employment was at-will and could be terminated at any time. The California Supreme Court ruled for Tameny, holding that an employer cannot discharge an employee for refusing to perform an illegal act. The court further held that the employee can recover under tort law, thereby allowing for potentially higher damages. On this last point, the moral distinction between tort and contract—specifically, that a breach is blameless, but a tort is wrongful—is relevant. Atlantic Richfield did not just breach a contract, it retaliated against an employee for refusing to do its criminal dirty work. Consistent with our moral intuitions, the court considered the company's conduct to be morally wrong—not just business as usual—and therefore established a legal mechanism for increased punishment of such conduct.

Economic models of employment mostly ignore illegal activity on the part of employees, yet *Tameny* and other cases involving the public-policy exception clearly demonstrate that some employers do ask employees to commit crimes. The economic implications of this rule are difficult to tease out. In *Tameny*, at least, the employee was asked to engage in anti-competitive activity, so in this case the public-policy exception probably enhanced economic efficiency. But economic evaluations of public-policy cases are generally more difficult. If the illegal activity entails consumer goods, such as drugs or gambling, then the public-policy exception likely decreases output, albeit in a direction that arguably enhances social welfare. The prohibition against discharge for military

---

[27] See page 78.
[28] 27 Cal.3rd 167 (Calif, 1980).

service, meanwhile, reduces economic efficiency because it prevents the employer from finding a more productive replacement. As with the illegal-consumer-goods exception, the military-service exception to at-will employment arguably serves other social-welfare goals.

2.3.2. Implied contract exception

When a worker can verify that a permanent employment relationship is promised by his employer, such employment can no longer be regarded as at-will and can be terminated only under just cause.[29] Under reigning court precedent in some states, if a personnel manual given to employees specifies that termination is only with cause, a binding contract exists. *Woolley v. Hoffmann-La Roch* was the first opinion to hold that employee handbooks can be part of a legally binding employment contract.[30]

The facts of *Woolley* are as follows. Plaintiff Richard Woolley was hired by defendant Hoffmann-La Roche, Inc. in 1969 as section head in one of defendant's engineering departments. The parties did not sign a written employment contract, but the plaintiff received a personnel manual which read, in part, that "[i]t is the policy of Hoffmann-La Roche to retain to the extent consistent with company requirements, the services of all employees who perform their duties efficiently and effectively". In 1978, after Woolley's submission of a report on piping problems at one of defendant's buildings, defendant requested that he resign. Plaintiff refused, and he was fired.

The trial court judge held for the defendant on summary judgment. On Woolley's appeal, the New Jersey Supreme Court reversed and remanded the case for trial, holding that an employee's handbook could be evidence of a binding contract. The court couched its ruling in notions of fairness:

> All that this opinion requires of an employer is that it be fair. It would be unfair to allow an employer to distribute a policy manual that makes the workforce believe that certain promises have been made and then to allow the employer to renege on those promises. What is sought here is basic honesty: if the employer, for whatever reason, does not want the manual to be capable of being construed by the court as a binding contract, there are simple ways to attain that goal. All that need be done is the inclusion in a very prominent position of an appropriate statement that there is no promise of any kind by the employer contained in the manual...

In this case, as in many others, one party is not completely truthful with the other party. This possibility is ignored by most economic models of contract. Economists typically assume that both parties do what they say they will do, and if they do not, any malfeasance is anticipated by the other party. The *Woolley* opinion can be seen as requiring employers

---

[29] See, e.g., Toussaint v. Blue Cross & Blue Shield, 292 N.W.2d 880 (Mich. 1980) ("When a prospective employee inquires about job security and the employer agrees that the employee shall be employed as long as he does his job, a fair construction is that the employer has agreed to give up his right to discharge at will...and may only discharge for cause").

[30] Woolley v. Hoffmann-La Roch, Inc., 499 A.2d 515 (N.J. 1985).

to comply with previous agreements not to engage in malfeasance. The judgment does not prohibit dismissal without cause; it simply requires that employers honor promises not to dismiss without cause.

Employee handbooks are not the only example of an implied contract. For example, *Pugh v. See's Candies* held that a long employment with regular promotion can establish a long-term contract.[31] In this case, the plaintiff-worker Pugh reported to company higher-ups that his current supervisor was a convicted embezzler, for which the supervisor subsequently fired him. Pugh filed suit, but the trial court dismissed the case at summary judgment. On appeal from the dismissal, the appellate court agreed that Pugh's reporting his supervisor's past conviction was not "whistle-blowing" under the public policy exception, but the long duration of Pugh's good service was sufficient to establish an implied contract. The court therefore reversed and remanded the case for trial.[32]

This example illustrates a concrete case in which an employee is dismissed not because of an objective failing (otherwise one could provide cause for dismissal) but because, essentially, he did not get along with his new supervisor. If the contract were at-will, then dismissal would be immediate. This rule prohibits the dismissal of long-term employees who may not fit in, or, if delinquent in their performance, the employers are unable to provide sufficient evidence of this poor performance.

2.3.3. Good faith exception

The requirement of good faith and fair dealing is a mandatory rule in contract law, and consequently in employment law. The employment cases involving this exception typically turn on the use of at-will employment by the employer to deprive the employee of compensation. In *Mitford v. Lasala*,[33] the discharged employee, who was a party of a profit-sharing agreement with the defendant, was fired to ensure that he would not share profits. The court held that "good faith and fair dealing. . . would prohibit firing [an employee] for the purpose of preventing him from sharing in future profits".

Currently, courts typically find a rather narrow application of this rule to the timing of dismissal and payment of compensation, rather than to other forms of bad behavior by employers.[34] Typical examples of wrongful terminations that fit under this class are: (1) a salesman being fired right before his commissions should be paid to him, and (2) an employee being dismissed in order to avoid paying retirement benefits.

As we can see from Fig. 1 there are many fewer states adopting this law than in the case of the implied contract rule. Given the more narrow applicability of the rule,

---

[31] Pugh v. See's Candies, 171 Cal. Rptr. 917 (Cal. Ct. App. 1981).

[32] At trial, the jury rendered a verdict in favor of the company notwithstanding the appellate court's holding on implied contracts. Pugh v. See's Candies, 250 Cal. Rptr. 195 (Cal. Ct. App. 1988).

[33] 666 P.2d 1000 (Alaska 1963).

[34] See Section 10.2 of Rothstein and Liebman (2003).

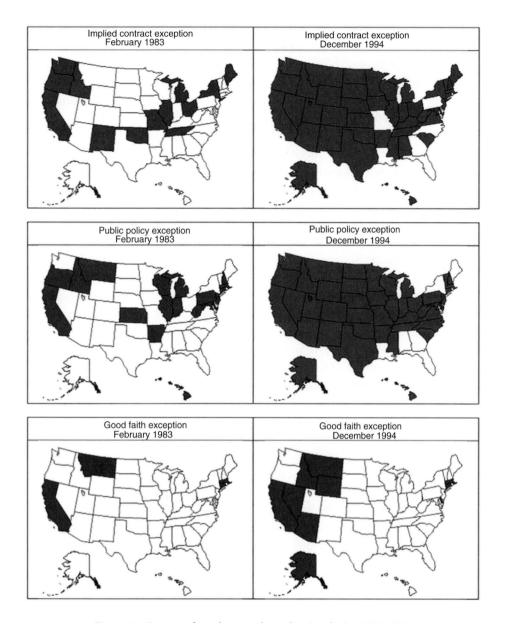

Figure 1   *Pattern of employment law adoption during 1983-1994.*

this may simply reflect the fact that courts in these states have adhered more closely to the common-law principle of at-will employment, and hence there was a need for statutory intervention to deal with cases where employers avoid paying compensation by a preemptive dismissal. If so, then we might expect this rule to have a substantial impact.

This impact is not due to the effect upon firing costs, but rather because it corrects poorly drafted contracts. In the case of *Mitford v. Lasala*, the contract was quite clear, and it implied that the firm had no obligation to pay the bonus. Most employees would expect to be paid in such a case, but at the time of writing the agreement they simply would not expect the deception to occur. In such cases, the courts can enhance productive efficiency by essentially completing an incomplete contract.

Consider now the case of *Fortune v. National Cash Register Co.*[35] Plaintiff Orville E. Fortune, a former salesman of National Cash Register Company (NCR), brought a suit to recover certain commissions allegedly due from a sale of cash registers to First National Stores. Inc. Fortune had been employed by NCR under a written contract that provided for at-will mutual terminable with notice. The contract also specified that Fortune would receive an annual bonus computed as a percentage of sales that he performed or supervised. In November 1968, Fortune was involved in a supervisory capacity in a sale of 2008 cash registers to First National, for which the bonus credit was recorded as $92,079.99. The next month, Fortune was given notice of termination. NCR ended up keeping Fortune on staff in a demoted capacity, and paid him three-fourths of the First National bonus during the summer of 1969. Fortune requested the other 25% of the bonus, but his manager told him "to forget about it". Fortune was finally asked to retire in June 1970, and then fired upon his refusal.

At trial, the jury was asked to render two special verdicts: "1. Did the Defendant act in bad faith ... when it decided to terminate the Plaintiff's contract as a salesman by letter dated December 2, 1968, delivered on January 6, 1969? 2. Did the Defendant act in bad faith ... when the Defendant let the Plaintiff go on June 5, 1970?" The jury answered both questions in the affirmative, and the judge ordered damages of $45,649.92. The state supreme court affirmed the judgment.

What is interesting about this case is that NCR did not breach the written terms of the agreement, but the court nevertheless allowed a jury to find that they had acted in bad faith in depriving Fortune of bonuses from the transactions he helped procure. *Fortune* can be seen as an efficient outcome in that it reduces employee uncertainty about whether they will be rewarded for their efforts and thereby incentivizes optimal investment in the employment relationship.

2.4. Discussion

The economic model of contract tends to view legal rules as constraints upon individual decision-making, either in terms of increasing transaction costs or imposing constraints upon the wages, hours, and other conditions of employment. In practice, the law is a complex adjudication system that is difficult to describe with an elegant model. Some of the distinctive features of a legal system that are not captured in the economic model of the employment contract include:

---

[35] 373 Mass. 96 (Mass. 1977).

1. Contract terms are not self-enforcing. Enforcement is a privately motivated activity that occurs when a plaintiff brings a case before a court. Even rules that have bureaus dedicated to their enforcement—such as the minimum wage and overtime requirements—rely on information provided by private parties—as well as the volition of agency officials. This demonstrates that enforcement is heterogeneous and a function of employer, employee, and regulator characteristics.

2. When a case is brought to a court, parties cannot rely upon the courts to enforce the agreement as written. Excessive penalties for non-performance are not enforced, for example. Although employment at will is the default rule in the United States, there are several exceptions.

3. Judges do not restrict themselves to contract terms, explicit or otherwise, as relevant legal factors. Courts may collect a large body of evidence regarding the communications and actions of both parties before reaching a decision. Thus, information regarding events not mentioned in the employment contract may nevertheless play a role in adjudicating the dispute.

The fact that courts may overrule contract terms is well-recognized in the legal literature. One of the central issues of this literature is the question of whether or not there is anything we can reasonably call "the law" that allows one to consistently anticipate how courts will rule on a given dispute. There is a related debate regarding how best to think about judicial behavior.[36]

Within economics, there is a small but growing literature that explores the role of the law in ensuring performance. Johnson et al. (2002) find that even if enforcement is imperfect, the existence of courts can help entrepreneurs enter into new supply contracts. Djankov et al. (2003) construct a database consisting of how costly it is to evict a tenant and collect on a bounced check across a large sample of countries, finding that the cost of collection in civil-law countries is significantly higher than in common-law countries. This result is consistent with subsequent work reported in Djankov et al. (2008) for the problem of debt collection. See La Porta et al. (2008) for a more comprehensive discussion of this literature.

For the most part, this work focuses on the costs of the legal system and assumes that variations in these costs across jurisdictions affect economic performance. Botero et al. (2004), and more recently Djankov and Ramalho (2009), explore the extent to which employment law and regulation affect labor market performance. This work uses cross-country variation in measures of employment-law flexibility to identify the effects of the law upon labor-market performance. These papers suggest that the historical origin of the country's legal regime—whether common-law or civil-law—is often the decisive factor in the evolution of the country's employment rules. However, these papers do not *explain* this observation. One possible interpretation, perhaps in need of further

---

[36] See Stephenson (2009) for a nice summary of this debate.

research, is that laws, like organisms, are adapted not just to the environment but to other laws. The various laws in a legal system—of which employment law is a small part—persist at a steady-state equilibrium unless an overwhelming shock—whether political or economic—suffices to move enough laws to another equilibrium to pull the rest of the legal regime along with them. The rarity of such events—Russia's transition to capitalism is a plausible example—might explain the durable influence of common-law and civil-law institutions on employment laws.

Regardless of this latter conjecture, what is clear from the analysis above is that the law is adaptive, yet existing work does not adequately explain why there is variation in the law. The plausible view taken here is that the law evolves in response to cases brought before the courts. New types of disputes breed new types of law. To understand why these cases arise, we need to understand what exactly is the role of the law in an employment contract. In the next section, we review the literature on the economics of the employment relationship, placing legal rules in the context of the full relationship.

3. THE ECONOMICS OF THE EMPLOYMENT RELATIONSHIP

Economic theories of employment begin with a model of human behavior and choice. The standard assumption in economics models of employment is that the worker is a risk-averse individual who wishes to maximize expected utility adjusted for the utility from doing specific tasks and the work environment.[37] One of the lessons of contract theory is that the optimal contract is often a complex function of the technology of production, the characteristics of the prospective employer and employee, and the information available. In order to highlight the empirical implications of the theory, we begin with a discussion of causality. We then discuss economic models of the employment relationship, highlighting their empirical implications.

3.1. Why do we need models?

The purpose of this section is to review the role that economic theory plays in understanding the significance of the law. As discussed in Section 2, even though economic concerns shape the development of the law, economic analysis as developed by the economics profession has played a relatively minor role in explicitly guiding court decisions.[38] While there may be no explicit accounting of economic effects, it is safe to say that employment rules established by courts have measurable effects on the economy. Accordingly, the goal of the theory discussed here is to structure empirical tests of the impact of employment policy on economic performance.

---

[37] See Rebitzer and Taylor (2011) for a discussion of recent research in behavioral economics as applied to labor economics.

[38] For example, see Justice Breyer (2009)'s observation that economics plays a small role in US Supreme Court decision-making.

The recent empirical work in labor economics has been greatly influenced by the potential-outcomes framework, as beautifully exposited by Holland (1986).[39] I shall briefly review this approach when using economic theory to understand the effects of the law on labor-market performance. First, the framework provides guidance on how to best organize and *represent* data. Second, it provides guidance on how to estimate a causal effect. Holland emphasizes that it is *impossible* to establish a causal relationship without some additional hypotheses that themselves can rarely be tested; they must rely on a *model* of how the world works.

Formally, the model proceeds by supposing that we have a universe of units to be treated, denoted by $u \in U$. For the purposes of our discussion, let U denote all potential workers in the economy. In addition, we might also be interested in outcomes at a state or country level. In that case we let $u^s \subset U$ be the subset of individuals living in state $s \in S$, where s could denote a US state among all states or one country among all countries.

This chapter's main concern is labor-market performance, so we restrict our attention to the question of how policy might affect wages and employment. For individual u, let $y^E \in Y^E = \{0, 1\}$ be employment status (with 1 meaning employed), and let her wage per period be given by $y^w \in Y^W = [0, \infty)$. Suppose that these outcomes will be observed in the next period (t). Employment and wages are likely to be affected by employment policies in the next period, denoted by l_t.

Rubin's model was developed in the context of a medical treatment where one asks if a particular drug has an effect. This question is typically answered by randomly dividing a group of individuals into a treatment and a control group. The causal effect of the drug is measured by comparing the outcomes in the two groups. The problem is that this procedure does not identify the effect of the treatment on a particular individual. In some illnesses, individuals become well in the absence of treatment. For others, the illness may be fatal regardless of the treatment. By chance, it is possible that all the former individuals (the false positives) would be assigned to the treatment group, while the latter individuals (the false negatives) would be assigned to the control group. In that case, the experiment would show that the drug had an effect, even though it did not.

The first issue is how to define a causal effect. In the context of our simple model, let $y(u, l^0, t)$ be the outcome under the status-quo law in the next period, and let $y(u, l^1, t)$ be the outcome under the new rule, say an increase in the minimum wage. Let $\Delta = l^1 - l^0$ denote the policy change. Following Holland (1986), we say that the policy change Δ at date t *causes the effect*:

$$D(u, \Delta, t) = y(u, l^1, t) - y(u, l^0, t).$$

This definition is concrete: It is the difference in potential outcomes. In order to measure this "effect", we would have to *observe* the same outcome for two different policies at the

---

[39] See also Angrist et al. (1996) and particularly Imbens and Wooldridge (2009) for an up-to-date discussion.

same time, something that is clearly impossible without time travel. Holland (1986) calls the impossibility of observing a causal effect the *Fundamental Problem of Causal Inference*. His analysis emphasizes the fact that measuring the causal impact of a treatment entails additional hypotheses.

Most solutions to the problem of causal inference rely upon versions of *unit homogeneity* or *time homogeneity*. By unit homogeneity we mean that there is a set of units $U' \subset U$ with the feature that the effect of the change Δ is the same for all $u \in U'$, in which case the effect can be estimated by policy change to unit $u^1 \in U'$ but not to unit $u^0 \in U'$, in which case for $u \in U'$ we have:

$$D(u, \Delta, t) = y(u^1, l^1, t) - y(u^0, l^0, t).$$

By time homogeneity, we mean that the effect of the treatment in different periods is the same. Hence, if we can estimate the effect of a treatment on a unit u by comparing the effect over time:

$$D(u, \Delta, t) = y(u, l^1, t+1) - y(u, l^0, t).$$

The challenge then becomes finding the homogeneous group. Regression discontinuity is an example of a recent popular technique that provides a way to create homogeneous groups that allow for the estimate of the effect of a treatment.[40] For example, DiNardo and Lee (2004) argue that firms in closely contested unionization drives are almost identical in most respects. Because the outcomes of union certification votes are very close, one can assume that for these firms union status is randomly assigned. Consequently, we can compare the change in firm value for those firms that were unionized to the change for those that were not, and thereby procure a robust measure of the effects of unionization on a firm's productivity.

Lee and McCrary (2005) provide an example of *time homogeneity*. Specifically, they look at the effect on behavior of sanctions against crime. Their study exploits the fact that when a person turns 18, they suddenly become eligible to be tried in adult courts, where they will face more severe sanctions than a juvenile court would impose. On the supposition that a person's characteristics just before and after they turn 18 are the same, observed changes in crime-related behavior can be ascribed to changes in criminal sanctions.

Notice that all the work is being done by the assumption of continuity over time with the same union, or across units with very similar characteristics. The great benefit of this approach is that, beyond the continuity assumption (which *is* a strong assumption), this approach is relatively model-free. The problem is that while it may provide a credible

---

[40] See Imbens and Lemieux (2008) and Lee and Lemieux (2009) for a discussion of the technique.

measure of the effect of a policy change, the approach says little if one moves away from the point at which the policy change or treatment is applied.

A formal model in this framework has two distinct goals. The first is that it may provide a concise *representation* of a set of facts about the world. It describes the set of measured characteristics that one needs to know in order to capture the effect of a treatment. For unit $u \in U$, let $X(u, t) \in \Theta$ be a set of characteristics. In practice, one may not be able to measure all dimensions of Θ, but let us suppose for the moment that we can. Suppose u is a worker and we are interested in explaining worker wages. Then, we would say that a model that specifies a wage $f(X, l, t)$ for a worker with characteristics X is an *unbiased representation* of the data at date t if for all $u \in U$,

$$\phi_{ut} = y(u, l_u, t) - f(X(u, t), l_u, t)$$

is an iid set of random variables with zero mean.

If our model is linear, we can let $\beta(t, l) = \partial f / \partial X$, in which case we can write our model in the familiar regression form:

$$y_{ut} = \beta(t, l_{ut})^\top X_{ut} + \phi_{ut}.$$

If our model is unbiased, then this is a well-specified model that can be estimated by ordinary least squares. However, even if the model is well-specified, as Holland (1986) emphasizes, the coefficients of the model *cannot* be assumed to represent a *causal* relationship. For example, one of the parameters might be the gender of a worker, say 0 is male and 1 is female. If y_{ut} is the wage, and the coefficient on gender is negative, we cannot say that gender *causes* a wage drop. This is because gender is not a treatment or something that one normally assumes can be varied within a person.

We can use the coefficient on gender to test various theories. For example, human capital theory predicts that a person's wage is a function only of their productive characteristics, such as schooling, ability, and experience. One reason women might be paid less is that they spend more time out of the labor force in child rearing. This reasoning implies that once the full set of characteristics reflecting productivity is included in X, then the coefficient on gender should be zero. If it is not, then we can say there is discrimination in the labor force.

A good theory specifies the set of parameters X that provide all the information necessary to describe wages while preserving *time independence*:

$$y_{ut} = \beta(l_{ut})^\top X_{ut} + \phi_{ut}.$$

Any variation in wages that occurs over time is explained via either changes in the parameters X_{ut} or by changes in the environment l_{ut}. In practice, the econometrician may not have access to all the relevant information X_{ut}, which leads to the well-known omitted variable bias problem in econometrics. For the present discussion, let us suppose that the relevant data are available and ask how the model can help in measuring the causal impact of a change in law l.

In general, economic theories do not provide precise point predictions; more typically, they make predictions about the sign of an effect. In the context of measuring the effect of the law on outcomes, the variation in treatment typically occurs either across jurisdictions—namely, the experiment assumes that all individuals in a particular jurisdiction $u \in U_s$ face the same legal environment $l_{st,}$, and it is the legal environment that varies across jurisdictions. For example, many countries can be characterized as civil-law or common-law legal systems. We can let U_1 be individuals in common-law countries and U_0 be individuals in civil-law countries, and set $l_s = s$.

In the example of civil- and common-law countries, one could estimate $\beta_s = \beta(l_s)$ for each jurisdiction. In this case, the causal impact of the legal system depends on the distribution of characteristics of individuals in the economy. We would estimate the causal effect of changing from a civil-law system to a common-law system for regions that are currently under civil law in period t by:

$$\text{Effect of common law} = \frac{1}{n_0} \sum_{u \in U_0} (\beta_1 - \beta_0)^\top X_{ut}.$$

In order to estimate the causal effect of a change in the legal system, one needs to use the characteristics of the jurisdiction where the change is to occur. This adjustment is a version of the well-known Oaxaca decomposition, which is widely used in studies of income inequality (see Altonji and Blank (1999)) and union wage differentials. As we discuss in more detail in Section 4, this is not the literature's usual technique. The more common assumption is that the effect of a policy is linearly separable, where for $u \in U_s$ we have:

$$y_{ut} = \beta^\top X_{ut} + \beta_l^\top l_s + \phi_{ut}. \tag{1}$$

Using data for a single period t, then, we can estimate the average effect of the legal system on the wages and employment of individuals by:

$$\beta_l = \frac{1}{n_1} \sum_{u \in U_1} \left(y_{ut} - \beta^\top X_{ut} \right) - \frac{1}{n_0} \sum_{u \in U_0} \left(y_{ut} - \beta^\top X_{ut} \right).$$

The goal of the theory discussed in this section can be summarized as follows. The theory makes predictions regarding the characteristics X that are needed to represent individual outsources. In particular, it will provide predictions regarding how variations in individual characteristics relate to variations in outcomes. Theory has predictive power if we can safely assume that the relationship between the Xs and the ys is stable over time.

A theory has more predictive power if one can represent outcomes using a smaller set of Xs. Given the difficulty of obtaining good measures of individual characteristics, theories with fewer Xs are inherently easier to test. On a related note, there is a line of inquiry in statistics that attempts to be model free. This is achieved by supposing that one has a rich set of X variables and that the environment is inherently continuous; as a result, good representations of the data can be used to make predictions on how changes in an individual's Xs will affect outcomes. Breiman (2001) suggests that such an approach is sometimes more feasible given present computing resources and the large data sets we have in some domains.

However, representation is not causation. Many individual characteristics are not amenable to experimental treatment. Making causal statements requires that we assume we have a valid representation of the data that allows one to compare outcomes either: (1) across units with similar characteristics but in different treatments, or (2) the same units faced with different treatments over time. In these cases, the theory—in addition to specifying the relevant X variables—also specifies an explicit mechanism by which the law affects the actions of individuals, and hence how one can obtain a valid measure of the causal impact of a change.

3.2. Economics of the employment contract

This section discusses the literature that seeks to explain the form and function of employment contracts. Fundamentally, parties who enter into a contract have agreed to have their behavior constrained in the future. The most basic reason for a contract is to support inter-temporal exchange, something that cannot be avoided in the context of labor services. For example, a day laborer agrees to work eight hours in exchange for a wage at the end of the day. When it comes to paying, the employer may have an incentive to renege or attempt to reduce the agreed-upon wage. One role of the law is to enforce such agreements.

In economics, such simple exchanges are typically assumed to be enforceable. The literature has focused on explaining the form of observed contracts that address one of three more subtle issues:

1. *Risk.* Demand for a worker's services, and hence wages, is likely to change from period to period. Risk-averse workers would like to enter into long-term contracts that would shield them from such shocks.
2. *Authority and Asymmetric Information.* Decision-making and bargaining are costly under asymmetric information. In this case, contract form can affect performance.
3. *Reliance.* Once a worker-firm match has been formed, a contract is needed to ensure that each party makes the appropriate investments into the relationship.

What makes the study of employment contracts difficult is that every relationship has elements of these three ingredients. In particular, teasing out the empirical implications of these models has proven difficult. Nonetheless, much of the structure of the legal rules governing employment can be understood as an attempt to address risk, information asymmetries, or hold-up.

3.2.1. Insurance

We shall illustrate these ideas using a simple three-period employment model. Suppose that in period 0 the firm offers the worker a long-term employment contract C, which the worker can either accept or reject. If the worker does not accept the contract, then in period 1 she will earn w_1^0 and in period 2 she will earn ω_2^0, which is a random variable with mean m_2^0 and variance σ^2. We will let the realized value of ω_2^0 be w_2^0. The utility of the worker in this outside market is given by:

$$U^0 = u(w_1^0) + \delta E\{u(\omega_2^0)\}.$$

The expected lifetime income of the worker is:

$$W^0 = w_1^0 + \delta m_2^0.$$

Given that the worker is risk-averse, a risk-neutral firm who wished to hire this worker for two periods could do so by paying a fixed wage w^* per period at an expect cost of $W^0 - \delta \frac{r}{2} \sigma^2$, where $r = -u''(m)/u'(m)$ is the coefficient of absolute risk aversion for the worker.[41] Let us consider the case in which the owner of the firm is assumed to be able to fully diversify market risk, and hence is able to offer the worker a perfect risk-sharing contract. The firm would be willing to do this because she can offer a wage contract to a risk-averse worker that has a lower expected cost than the worker's market alternative.

Azariadis (1975) introduced the term *implicit contract* to describe the idea that firms voluntarily smooth workers' income over time in order to lower expected labor costs. Azariadis (1975) and Baily (1974) both observe that the enforceability of these contracts depends upon the existence of turnover costs, otherwise under at-will employment wages would necessarily equal the market alternative. Recently, Blanchard and Tirole (2008) have revisited this issue and suggested that mandated severance pay may enhance the risk-sharing properties of labor contracts. They explore the question of how to optimally design minimum wages and severance pay to insure risk-averse workers. There is little role for the law in their model beyond enforcing the agreed-upon severance payments.

---

[41] The wage is $w^* = \frac{1}{1+\delta}\left(W^0 - \delta r\sigma^2/2\right)$.

We consider a two-period extension of their model that will allow for a substantive role for the courts. Rather than supposing that the employment contract is implicit, I follow Blanchard and Tirole (2008) and consider the problem of implementing the optimal allocation. Suppose that in period 0 it is efficient for the worker to contract with a firm with the following profit function:

$$\Pi = y_1 - w_1 + E\{\psi_2 - \omega_2\},$$

where y_1 and ψ_2 is firm output in periods 1 and 2, while w_1 and ω_2 is the wage paid to the worker in each period. Again, Greek letters refer to random variables.

We begin with a case that entails no enforcement problems, and characterize the empirical implications of the optimal allocation. In this case, we do not have any explicit treatments—rather, we wish to describe the wage and employment profile of the worker (the y's of the model) in relation to the worker's outside options, the worker's risk preferences, and the firm's productivity in each period (the explanatory X variables of the model).

The optimal allocation is the solution to:

$$\max_{w_1,\omega_2,e_2} y_1 - w_1 + \delta E\{e_2\psi_2 - \omega_2\}, \tag{2}$$

subject to:

$$u(w_1^0) + \delta E\{u(e_2\omega_2 + (1 - e_2)\omega_2^0)\} \geq u(w_1^0) + \delta E\{u(\omega_2^0)\}. \tag{3}$$

In addition to wage payment each period, the optimal allocation must also determine the worker's employment status in period 2, where $e_2 = 1$ if employed at the firm and 0 otherwise. If the worker is not employed, the she earns ω_2^0 in the market, which is assumed to be paid to the worker. The next proposition characterizes the first best:

Proposition 1. *The optimal risk sharing allocation has the following properties:*

1. *Employment is ex-post efficient: $e_2^* = 1$ if and only if $\psi_1 \geq \omega_2^0$ (and zero otherwise).*
2. *The worker is fully insured: $w_1^* = w_2^* = w^*$.*
3. *Expected labor cost is equal to the worker's expected future income less a risk premium that increases with worker's aversion to risk (r): $(1 + \delta)w^* \simeq W^* - \delta\frac{r}{2}\sigma^2$.*

Observe that this result provides an *institution-free* description of the optimal allocation that links the characteristics of the optimal contract with potentially observable features of the worker, firm, and labor-market alternatives. In practice, there are a large number of institutions that have been created to insure workers, including workman's compensations, unemployment insurance, transfers within the household, and so on.

Rather than delve into the details of these institutions, one may ask the question whether or not institutions are sufficiently rich that something approaching efficient risk-sharing occurs in practice.

Cochrane (1991) works out the implications of the complete risk-sharing model for consumption growth. In our simple model, notice that the wage of a worker (here consumption is assumed equal to wage for simplicity) is independent of whether she works for the current firm or takes up a market alternative (which might mean unemployment). More generally, Cochrane (1991) observes that consumption growth should be independent of idiosyncratic shocks. He finds that full insurance is not rejected for spells of unemployment, loss of work due to strikes, and involuntary moves. However, insurance appears to be incomplete for long illnesses and involuntary job loss. In recent work, von Wachter (2007) finds with German data that the effect of job loss is temporary, with workers returning to their previous earnings in 5 years. Taking a similar approach with data from India, Townsend (1994) rejects the perfect insurance model but does find evidence of significant, albeit imperfect, risk sharing.

This work illustrates the usefulness of the insurance model in organizing consumption data. The work does not test a *causal* relationship, nor does it describe a mechanism that would generate a relationship between wages and risk attitudes. That mechanism could involve, for example, firms setting wage contracts in advance and workers selecting into contracts that are most appropriate for their risk preferences. Alternatively, firms might negotiate contracts directly with the workers and use worker-specific information, such as marital status, to set the wage contract. In addition, the implicit contract model does not explain wage rigidity per se—and certainly not nominal wage rigidity (see Card and Hyslop (1997))—only consumption smoothing. If a worker has access to other insurance opportunities, say via their family, then their actions might appear less risk-averse, implying that there may not be a stable relationship between an individual's risk preference and the wage contract.

Consider the question that Blanchard and Tirole (2008) ask, namely: How can one *implement* the efficient allocation using available legal instruments? The answer to this question can generate some predictions about the effects of changes in the law or in the parameters of social programs such as unemployment insurance. These predictions are causal statements because the choice of law is a treatment; we can ask explicitly what the *causal impact* of a policy change will be.

Insurance contracts require some form of enforcement when employment with the firm in period 2 is efficient. Whenever $\psi_2 < w^*$ the firm would like to dismiss the worker, while the worker would like to quit whenever $\omega_2^0 > w^*$. Given that it is always efficient to perform, the parties would never voluntarily renegotiate the contract price. If the contract were between commercial parties for services, termination of the relationship by either party could be followed by a suit for damages. Under the rule of common law the standard remedy is *expectation damages*—harm caused by the contract breach. Let us suppose that there is a cost k in pursuing a court case. If the employment contract is adjudicated under standard common-law rules, we would have the following outcomes for contract termination[42]:

State of the world	Breach decision	Remedy
$\psi_2 < w^* - k$	Firm lays off worker	Worker paid $D = w^* - \omega_2^0$
$\omega_2^0 - k > w^*$	Worker quits	Firm paid $D = \psi_2 - w^*$

Observe that under this rule, if it is efficient for parties to stay together (it is always the case that $\psi_2 - \omega_2^0 > 0$), then there would never be breach. For example, suppose that the worker's outside option is so great that it is worthwhile to quit even while paying legal fees, namely $\omega_2^0 - k > w^*$. Once she pays the damages to the firm, her income would be:

$$w^* - k - (\psi_2 - \omega_2^0) < w^*.$$

Hence, under the standard legal rule of expectation damages, an employment contract that fully insures workers would be enforceable and would implement the efficient contract when turnover is not efficient. In practice, however, these rules are rarely used in employment cases. The common-law rule is employment at will, not expectation damages.

Parties might try to achieve a binding contract by stipulating that each party would pay a large fine F if there is breach. In practice, requiring workers to pay large penalties to leave employment are not enforceable in most legal jurisdictions—this would be akin to a slavery contract. One exception is requiring a worker to pay for training she has received. In the case of professional sports, this goal is achieved by requiring teams to pay a fee to acquire a player. This rule has become controversial, though, and was recently overturned by the European Court of Justice.[43]

The case of sports teams is the exception. For most employment contracts, employees can leave at will. There is literature, beginning with Harris and Holmström (1982), that explores the optimal wage contract under the assumption that the firm cannot fire the worker, but the worker can leave at will. Under such a rule, the optimal contract is downward rigid. It is fixed in real terms and readjusted upwards each time a worker gets an outside offer. Beaudry and DiNardo (1991) suggest that this model can explain why individuals who are hired during recessions are worse off in the long run than workers

---

[42] I assume that the terms of the wage payment are enforceable, so it is only the decision to quit or layoff that is liable to legal recourse. There is a well-known UK case, Rigby v. Ferodo [1988] ICR 29, House of Lords, that establishes the enforceability of the wage payment.

[43] This is the so-called Boseman case. See Feess and Muehlheusser (2002) for a discussion.

hired in boom periods. Chiappori et al. (1999) point out that there may be other reasons for this result, including holdup (which we discuss below).

3.2.2. Asymmetric information and the employment relationship

Consider the following extension of Simon (1951)'s employment model, allowing for task allocation *ex post* in the presence of asymmetric information. Suppose that in period 2 the worker can be assigned to one of two tasks, $x \in \{a, b\}$, and that the productivity of task x is ψ_2^x, which is assumed to be observed only by the firm. In addition, there is a private cost of carrying out task x to the worker given by $c_2^x > 0$, and which is observed only by the worker. If we let $x = 0$ denote the outside option, with $\psi_2^0 = 0$ and $c_2^0 = -\omega$, then the respective payoffs to the firm and worker under task x are:

$$\Pi^x = y_1 - w_1 + \delta I_x \left\{ \psi_2^x - \omega_2^x \right\},$$
$$U^x = u(w_1) + \delta u(\omega_2^x - c_2^x),$$

where $I_x = 1$ if $x \in \{a, b\}$ and 0 otherwise.

Note that regardless of the contract, the optimal task allocation is given by:

$$x^*(\theta_2) = \arg\max_{x \in \{0,a,b\}} \{\omega_2^0, \psi_2^a - c_2^a, \psi_2^b - c_2^b\}.$$

Let us first suppose that it is efficient for the worker and the firm to stay together both periods. Also suppose that there is no variation in task productivity, but that the worker's cost, c_2^x, can vary. In this case, the efficient solution is to allocate the choice of task to the worker, who will always choose the efficient allocation. More generally, as Milgrom (1988) argues, this effect leads to an organizational structure that limits the authority of the firm, so that within certain task groups individuals are given autonomy.

Given that the worker is risk-averse, the optimal solution entails a fixed wage and an allocation of decision rights to the worker. If $w^* > \psi_2^a$, $\psi_2^b > \omega_2^0 + c_2^{a,b}$, it is efficient for the worker to stay matched with the firm, but the firm would prefer to lay the worker off rather than pay wage w^*. Enforcing the efficient contract requires a stipulated severance pay that is sufficiently large but conditional upon worker's performance. Similarly, the efficient contract should ensure that the worker does not threaten to renegotiate the wage contract in period 2. These points are summarized in the following proposition:

Proposition 2. *If the firm is indifferent over task assignment ($\psi_2^a = \psi_2^b$), then the optimal contract has the following conditions:*

1. *The worker has the right to choose her preferred task.*
2. *The contract wage each period is decreasing with the worker's risk aversion, increasing with minimum cost of effort and expected lifetime market income ($w_1^* = w_2^* - \min\{c_2^a, c_2^b\} \simeq (W^0 - \delta \frac{r}{2}\sigma^2 - \delta \min\{c_2^a, c_2^b\})/(1 + \delta)$).*

3. *If the worker leaves in period* 2, *then she pays a penalty* $P > \omega_2^0 - w_2^* + c$. *If the firm dismisses the worker, it pays* $f > \max\{\psi_2^a, \psi_2^b\} - w_2^*$ *in severance.*

This contract is very much like the contract for a tenured academic. The contract asks the professor to carry out teaching duties but typically allows a great deal of discretion over how she teaches and the material she will use. Second, the demand for the services of an academic is stable, and hence there is little benefit from turnover. As a consequence, the academic cannot be fired. The optimal contract also precludes the worker from leaving without paying a penalty, but this sort of provision is not typically observed (aside from the sports contracts mentioned earlier). For academics, the resignation penalty is implicit, consisting in large moving costs, lowering the incentives to leave. Note that a consequence of removing the penalty clause for leaving is that the period 2 wage would be more responsive to the outside market, and as a consequence the first-period wage would *fall*. Conversely, sometimes it is suggested that tenure be abolished. The consequence of abolition would be to lower expected income in period 2, which in turn would *raise* period 1 wages.

In terms of empirical predictions, this result merely links X variables—the risk aversion of the worker and job characteristics—to predicted contract choice. Hence, this proposition does not make any causal claims, but predicts that there should be an association between measured risk aversion of the worker, job characteristics, and turnover. It predicts that certain jobs, such as academic jobs, combine substantial job protection with the freedom to control activities on the job.

In order to introduce a notion of just cause for dismissal, there needs to be a substantive role for the firm in task allocation. The next case supposes that effort costs do not vary with the task, $c_2 = c_2^a = c_2^b$, but the productivity of the tasks vary, $\psi_2^a \neq \psi_2^b$. Let us continue to suppose that it is always efficient to be employed at the same firm for two periods. In this case, it is efficient to provide the worker with a fixed wage contract, $w_1^* = w_2^* - c_2$. It is crucial that the worker and firm *not* negotiate the task allocation. If the wage paid for each task is the same, and the firm has the right to make the task allocation $x \in \{a, b\}$, then it will choose the most productive task. Hence, this contract is *incentive-compatible* in the sense that the firm will make the most efficient choice even though she holds private information. In order to provide the firm with authority over the worker, there must be a penalty associated with not following the firm's instructions. More formally, we have:

Proposition 3. *Suppose that employment with the firm is always efficient. Then the optimal contract consists of a fixed wage each period along with the following conditions:*

1. *The contract wage each period is decreasing with her risk aversion and increasing with cost of effort* $(w_1^* = w_2^* - c_2 \simeq (W^0 - \delta\frac{r}{2}\sigma^2 - \delta c_2)/(1 + \delta))$.

2. *Should the firm dismiss the worker without cause, the worker is paid* $f > \max\{\psi_2^a, \psi_2^b\} - w_2^*$ *in severance.*

3. *If the worker is indifferent over task assignment ($c_2 = c_2^a = c_2^b$), then she agrees to carry out the task assigned by the firm; otherwise she is dismissed and pays a penalty.*

This proposition describes the features of an optimal contract when the worker is risk-averse and separation is not efficient. It is useful because it captures some features of observed default rules in employment law. Notice that the firm has authority because it has the information regarding the best task to carry out. More generally, Aghion and Tirole (1997) have shown that authority should be allocated to the best-informed individual.[44] Dessein (2002) extends this point to look at the trade-off between communication and delegation, finding that delegation can be more efficient than communication when there is little conflict between the preferences of the worker and firm.

The provision of insurance via wages does create potential conflict. The firm must have the right to penalize workers who do not carry out their assigned tasks. But this power cannot be unchecked. For example, the firm might try to renege upon the wage contract by assigning a worker very unpleasant tasks—formally, those with a high cost of effort c_2—that would effectively cause the worker to quit. Such a case might lead to litigation where the worker would claim *constructive dismissal*.[45] Hence, in practice, such a contract may still face significant litigation.

The results above suggest that if labor contracts are incomplete, with parties relying upon the courts to set the default terms, then both propositions predict that a change from at-will to just-cause dismissal will lead to lower wages and higher employment. Higher employment occurs because just-cause dismissal is more efficient in these cases, and hence should increase employment.[46] Wages are lower because the worker faces less risk.

Note that the employment result does not fundamentally depend on worker's risk aversion. The employment law we have discussed builds upon contract law, where the key issue is ensuring that parties deliver the promised quality. Disputes arise when firms feel that workers have not performed as promised, or workers believe they have performed as promised but the firm has not compensated or continued employment as promised. This set of issues is legally distinct from the body of law that has developed to enforce insurance contracts, and accordingly the doctrines regarding damages in employment law rarely entail an explicit discussion of risk.

Finally, there is literature, beginning with Shapiro and Stiglitz (1984), that views the right of dismissal as a necessary ingredient for effort provision. In their model, the

[44] See also Chakravarty and MacLeod (2009), who discuss the allocation of authority in the context of contract law. They show that construction contracts carefully allocate authority between the buyer and seller to ensure efficient production.

[45] This is a legal term of art in English law defined by the UK Employment Rights Act of 1996, Sections 95(1)(c). Even if an employee resigned from her post, she can claim that she was forced to quit due to the employer's action.

[46] See MacLeod (2005) and MacLeod and Nakavachara (2007) for more details on how employment law may enhance efficiency.

firm offers a high wage and threatens to dismiss the worker should she shirk. In this model, this results in an inefficient allocation due to the high wages offered by the firm. However, as MacLeod and Malcomson (1989) show, the threat of firing is not necessary for effort provision. The firm can use bonus pay, in which enforcement depends upon the firm facing a cost should it renege upon a promised payment. MacLeod (2003) extends this result to the case of a risk-averse worker employed with an imperfect performance measure.[47] He shows that a necessary condition for the implementation of an efficient contract is the ability to impose a cost upon firms that renege on bonus pay. The good-faith exception to employment at will is one mechanism that may achieve this condition.

3.2.3. The reliance interest

In a famous paper, Fuller and Perdue (1936) introduced a conceptual framework that has formed the basis of the modern law-and-economics treatment of contract law. The goal of their paper was to provide a framework for the setting of damages for contract breach. They introduced three ways to measure damages. The first of these, as discussed earlier, is expectation damages. This is the rule that one would use if one wished to enforce an insurance contract because it ensures that each party obtains the desired outcome while ensuring that matching is efficient.

The notion of expectations is not always well defined, particularly in the case where the value of the worker's performance is private information. Another way of measuring damages is the notion of restitution. This damages rule strives to restore the harmed party to the state she was in before the contract was agreed upon. For example, suppose a worker sells her house and moves to a new city in order to take up employment. If the potential employer reneges on the contract, restitution damages would entail paying the harmed worker the costs of relocation so that she may return to her previous state.

A third measure of damages is the *reliance interest*. Take, for example, an employer that spends a significant amount of money training a worker, as in the military providing pilot training. In that case, if the worker were to leave employment early, the employer may ask the worker to repay part of the training expenses.

The early literature on the economics of contract law, notably Rogerson (1984) and Shavell (1984), consider the case in which parties make a sunk investment into a relationship, and then ask, which of this damage rules leads to the most efficient level of investment. This work illustrates an important third motivation for an employment contract: namely, to provide incentives for efficient relationship-specific investments. The early literature assumed that the investment was observable by the courts, and hence could be used to set damages. In an influential paper, Grout (1984) showed that if parties could not write a binding contract, then there would be inefficient investment into the relationship. This model has become the paradigm for the *holdup problem*, a term coined

---

[47] See Levin (2003) and Fuchs (2006) for a more detailed analysis of the risk-neutral case in a repeated-game setting.

by Goldberg (1976) to describe situations in which the buyer or seller attempts to change the terms of an agreement after have there been significant sunk investments. Williamson et al. (1975) similarly make the point that relationship-specific investments imply that the employment relationship must be carefully governed to avoid opportunistic behavior by the worker.

These points can be formally illustrated in our model by supposing that the employer makes an investment into capital k in period 1, while the risk-neutral worker makes a similar investment i. In this case, the worker's investment can be any activity that lowers the cost of supplying labor, which might include making friends, investing in a new home, or acquiring skills on the job. Formally, the payoffs of the firm and the worker would be:

$$\Pi = y_1 - w_1 - k + \delta E \left\{ e_2(\psi_2 + y(k)) - \omega_2 \right\},$$
$$U = w_1 - i + \delta E \{ \omega_2 + e_2 v(i) + (1 - e_2)\omega_2^0 \},$$

where the notation is as above, except now worker productivity depends on investment k via $y(k)$, and worker utility depends upon her investment i via the $v(i)$. It is assumed that $y(0) = v(0) = 0$, $y', v' > 0$, and $y'', v'' < 0$, and that the efficient levels of investment are characterized by:

$$v'(i^*) = y'(k^*) = 1/\delta \rho_2^*$$

where ρ_2^* is the probability that the worker and firm trade in period 2 under efficient matching (namely $\rho_2^* = \Pr[\psi_2 \geq \omega_2^0]$).

Observe that the level of investment into a relationship depends upon both the discount rate and the expectation that the relationship will continue. This implies that if a worker, for example, overestimates the likelihood that an employment relationship will continue in period 2, this can lead to over-investment, and an increased incentive to litigate discharge should she believe it to be unjustified.

The holdup problem arises when the worker and firm have no binding labor contract but instead negotiate the wage in period 2 *after* the value of their outside options have been realized. Grout (1984) supposes that period 2 wage is given by the Nash bargaining solution, which entails parties dividing evenly the gains from trade to yield a wage:

$$w_2(\psi_2, \omega_2, k, i) = (\psi_2 + y(k) - v(i) - \omega_2^0)/2.$$

When this wage is negative, parties will choose the outside option rather than trade. This rule ensures efficient matching in period 2, but the returns from the specific investments are divided equally between the worker and the firm. In consequence, we have *underinvestment*:

Proposition 4. *In the absence of a binding employment contract, the worker and the firm choose investments to satisfy:*

$$y'(k^{nc}) = v'(i^{nc}) = 1/\delta\rho_2^{nc},$$

where the probability of employment in period 2, $\rho_2^{nc} < \rho_2^*$, is less than the efficient level, and hence investments are less than the first best ($k^{nc} < k^*$ and $i^{nc} < i^*$).

The motivation for Grout's model is the legal rule in the United Kingdom that makes it impossible for unions to enter into binding contracts with employers. The substance of the Trade Disputes Act of 1906 made it impossible for employers to sue unions, and hence to recover damages should a union strike.

To predict the causal impact of such a policy, one needs to work out what would happen if contracts were enforceable. The holdup model supposes that investments are observable by the two parties but cannot be used to set contract terms. Under this assumption, Hart and Moore (1988) show that parties would agree to a contract with a stipulated wage w_2 and severance payment s_2 that would improve upon no contract. In general, however, the contract will not implement the first best. This can only occur in this model if it is always efficient to trade, and there is a contract that, with probability 1:

$$\psi_2 + y(k^*) - w_2 \geq -s_2,$$
$$w_2 + v(i^*) \geq \omega_2^0 + s_2.$$

For this contract to work, one does need legal enforcement. If either the worker or the firm attempts to modify the contract terms, the other party should be able to seek relief in court. This is not to say that parties cannot, if they wish, renegotiate the contract by mutual consent. Given that both parties are better off under the contract than on the outside market, however, the threat not to trade is not credible. Hence, the wage would not be renegotiated in period 2, and both parties receive the full return from any specific investment.

Hart and Moore (1988)'s result that contracts can always improve matters holds only for the case of specific *self-investments*: the investments that affect one's own payoff but not the other party's payoff. Che and Hausch (1999) show that in the case of cooperative investments—that is, when one party's investments affect the payoffs of both parties—and when contract renegotiation cannot be precluded, then there is no benefit from writing any contract. This result depends on the hypothesis that the courts cannot observe the investments. Given the level of litigation in employment, one must conclude that parties do indeed find it useful to write contracts. The issue is how the courts should enforce these contracts.

An interesting feature of the holdup model is that the efficiency of the relationship can be enhanced in some cases with the appropriate allocation of bargaining power. This idea begins with the so-called property-rights approach of Grossman and Hart (1986). They observe that even though contract may not be explicitly conditioned upon certain events, the law can allocate residual decision rights. The example they explore in detail is property, which in effect is a contract that gives the owner of property the right to carry out any action that is not constrained by other contracts.

We have a similar issue in employment law. That is, under what conditions does the worker or the firm have the right to leave a relationship based on information that may not be observable by the courts? Aghion et al. (1994) show that if one can design contracts to allocate the bargaining power of parties, then one can achieve an efficient allocation in the models of Grout (1984) and Hart and Moore (1988).[48]

These are useful abstract results that delineate conditions under which efficient allocations can be achieved, but they do not specify the legal institutions that would achieve these allocations. MacLeod and Malcomson (1993) explicitly explore the implications of the holdup model on wages over time when the market alternatives are viewed as an outside option in the sense of Shaked and Sutton (1984). The outside option principle has two parts.

First, if at the current, *enforceable* wage both parties are better off than at their next best alternative, then threats to leave/layoff are not credible and hence the wage is *insensitive* to current market conditions. As Howitt (2002) observes, this observation has the potential to provide a theory of rigid wages. Second, when the current wage is worse than, say, the worker's best alternative, then either the wage will be renegotiated to be equal to this alternative, or the worker will leave.

Given these rules, MacLeod and Malcomson (1993) show the following:

1. When investments are *general* and there is a fixed cost to changing jobs or employees, then a fixed wage contract that is renegotiated to match outside offers implements the first best.

2. In the case of two-sided self-investments, if it is possible to index wages so that the outside options are binding only when separation is efficient, then such an indexed wage contract implements the first best.

3. In the case of cooperative relationship-specific investments by the firm, an efficient allocation is implemented with a contract that leaves the worker indifferent between employment and taking up the outside option. Conversely, if the worker is making the investment, then the efficient rule leaves the firm indifferent between hiring the worker and taking up the outside option.

These three cases are not comprehensive, however. For example, Rogerson (1992) shows in a more general, asymmetric-information setup that there is a wide variety of situations where there exist efficient contracts when both parties are risk-neutral. The holdup

---

[48] These results build upon the implementation results of Moore and Repullo (1988).

model is attractive because it provides some predictions on contract form when parties approximately satisfy these contracts.

What is particularly interesting about these results is that they are broadly consistent with the doctrine of employment at will. The first case merely requires that the worker and the firm agree to some wage contract that can be periodically renegotiated. In particular, the wage can be in real or nominal terms, and hence, as Howitt (2002) points out, can explain nominal wage rigidity. Though the model also predicts that nominal wages may be renegotiated up or down by arbitrary amounts, depending upon the outside market, a behavior that is consistent with the evidence of Blinder and Choi (1990), McLaughlin (1994) and Card and Hyslop (1997), but not consistent either with menu-cost models or the model with risk-averse agents.

These models do rely upon the legal enforcement of a contract wage that cannot be unilaterally changed by one party, a principle that was affirmed in the United Kingdom by *Rigby v. Ferodo* (1987).[49] We also observe the use of indexed contracts, particularly union contracts: Cousineau et al. (1983) document the use of indexed contracts by Canadian unions. Notice that the risk-sharing model would predict fixed real wages, with corresponding penalty clauses to enforce the risk-sharing agreement. The fact that penalty clauses are typically not enforceable, especially in the case of employment contracts, leads to the prediction that if parties are going to index, then the indexed contract should approximately follow the market wage, which is what we observe in Canada (and also in the case of long-term supply contracts, as documented by Joskow (1988)).

Crawford (1988) shows that the holdup problem can also be solved when parties sign a series of short-term contracts. Essentially, parties anticipate the future holdup and mitigate its effect by agreeing in the current period to lower wages combined with higher investment. Card et al. (2010) find some evidence in support of this prediction using Italian data. Given that these are unionized firms, this suggests that the firms are able to reach efficient bargains.

The final case is implemented in the absence of any contract, and can help explain the puzzling fact that contracts do not consistently have index terms. As Cousineau et al. (1983) have shown, about 50% of unionized firms in Canada did not index their employment contracts during a period of high inflation. This would imply that unions would have to constantly renegotiate their contracts to match market conditions. Result 3 implies that this contract form provides first-best incentives for the firm to invest in capital and into relationship-specific worker training. Acemoglu and Pischke (1998) also show that if there are significant turnover costs, then firms may also invest into general human capital.

---

[49] [1988] ICR 29, [1987] IRLR 516.

3.3. Implementing the efficient employment contract in a market

The literature on the employment contract has identified three broad economic motivations for an employment contract: insuring risk-averse employees, ensuring the revelation of relevant information for decision-making, and encouraging relationship-specific investments. Given these transaction costs, the next issue is: What sort of labor-market institutions ensure efficient matching and trade?

In principle, one could construct a model that includes all the ingredients that have been identified as relevant for understanding employment. At a purely abstract level, Rogerson (1992) and Aghion et al. (1994) have shown that under the appropriate conditions, one can construct an abstract mechanism that implements the efficient allocation in a variety of cases, some of which combine risk aversion and asymmetric information. However, as Tirole (1999) discusses, we still do not know how to relate these abstract results to observed institutions and contract forms. The literature on employment typically explores the implications of regulation for a simple model that has one or at most two transaction costs. The literature on employment protection has for the most part followed the lead of Bentolila and Bertola (1990) and Lazear (1990) in supposing that an increase in labor protection is parsimoniously modeled as an increase in turnover costs.

Lazear (1990) observes that if complete contracts are possible, mandated severance payments can always be undone via the labor contract. In that case, a law mandating severance payments would have no effect on employment but would lower starting wages. Lazear carries out a study of 22 countries over a 29-year period and concludes that increasing severance pay to 3 months' salary for workers with 10 years' experience leads to a 1-percent reduction of the employment-to-population ratio. This is a reduced-form analysis that does not take into account the complex inter-temporal optimization problem faced by firms. This is the goal of Bentolila and Bertola (1990). They find that firing costs create complex inter-temporal incentives that depend upon the state of the business cycle. Specifically, firing costs reduce labor demand in good times but *increase* demand in bad times. Lower starting wages translate into lower firing costs, and hence firms have greater incentives to hire workers during downturns.

The literature has mostly followed the lead of this work and modeled employment protection as a turnover cost. The theoretical contributions have begun with one of the transaction costs (risk, asymmetric information, or holdup) and then explored the implications of employment protection modeled as a turnover cost. This allows one to explore the implications of treating a relationship with a particular policy choice. If we suppose that in different relationships one of the three transaction costs is more important, then this approach generates testable predictions of the effect of a law change for different relationships, which hopefully can be measured and hence form right-hand-side X variables.

I complete the section with a brief discussion of unions. From the perspective of transaction costs, one can view unions as an alternative to employment law. This provides a system for the implementation, enforcement, and arbitration of employment disputes between the firm and unionized employees.

Risk

Since the work of Azariadis (1975) and Baily (1974), the assumption of risk-averse workers has played an important role in the development of labor policy. I showed above that if the main role of the labor contract is to insure workers, then such a contract can be enforced with the use of expectation damages. Moreover, the contract will have the feature that if a relationship is no longer efficient, then the firm has the obligation to "sell" the worker's contract to another firm. In the absence of bankruptcy constraints and asymmetric information, such an institution would implement the first best.[50]

In practice, we observe contracts with features similar to this in the area of sports, but rarely elsewhere. In the case of athletes, the quality of the player and hence the value of a trade is information that is easily available to the teams in a league. Such conditions are not likely to be satisfied in general, however. There is an active literature in macro-economics that explores the role of turnover taxes and mandated severance pay when complete contracts are not possible. A seminal contribution in this literature is Hopenhayn and Rogerson (1993). They assume that workers have access to complete financial markets and hence can diversify firm risk. Under these assumptions they show that a turnover tax (or severance pay) is equal to one year of wages leads to a 2.5% reduction in employment.

Their model assumes away market incompleteness. Hopenhayn and Nicolini (1997) consider the case in which the firm provides the insurance services for the worker, but the worker is responsible for finding a new job. The point is that the matching process is both costly, and is an important element in labor market performance. They show that there should be a mandated unemployment insurance that is financed out of a re-employment tax. Moreover, the level of insurance (or replacement rate, that is, the fraction of one's wages that are paid when unemployed) should fall with time. They show that this rule can result in a significant increase in market performance. The result also illustrates one role for government intervention that arises when there is a combination of risk aversion and moral hazard (worker's search effort is not observed).

Notice that in the presence of fixed unemployment insurance payments, mandated severance pay provides an approximation to such a rule because it provides a high income to the worker early in her unemployment that is lost once the severance pay is spent. In the event of an employment dispute, even if the worker wins the case, in most jurisdictions there is a mandatory rule that parties should mitigate their losses from

---

[50] See Dye (1985), who uses this point to build a theory of contract length.

contract breach. In the case of an employee, this means that the employee should make a reasonable effort to find alternative employment. Any damages due to the worker would be based upon lost income given the new job.

Acemoglu and Shimer (1999) introduce a careful model of the matching process that generalizes many of the previous matching process, and then derive the optimal unemployment insurance. If the agent is risk-neutral, then there should be no unemployment insurance. This is equivalent to saying that employment at will is efficient when workers are risk-neutral. However, when workers are risk-averse, the provision of unemployment insurance increases wages, employment, and the capital-labor ratio. Pissarides (2001) explicitly discusses the role of employment protection. He also shows that with search frictions it is optimal to have unemployment insurance, and observes that employment legislation is an (imperfect) substitute for employment protection.

Finally, the recent paper Blanchard and Tirole (2008) builds upon these themes to explore the implementation of an efficient severance pay—unemployment insurance system in the face of a variety of market imperfections. There are cases in which there are limits on insurance and layoff taxes, *ex post* wage bargaining, and *ex ante* heterogeneity of firms or workers. The key insight is that not only do these various cases affect the design of insurance system, but that a third party such as the government is needed in order to implement the second-best optimum. In particular, if the state merely provided a set of courts that enforce private agreements, this would not achieve the first best.

This body of work is carried out using relatively conventional assumptions regarding the operation of the labor market. Together they suggest that arguments by legal scholars—such as Epstein (1984) or Morriss (1995–1996)—that the efficiency of free markets implies that there is no role for government intervention into labor markets are not correct as rhetorical statements. However, there are many issues that this literature does not address.

First, these results depend upon workers having stable risk-averse preferences. There is a large body of work that finds that the fine-grained predictions from a model with risk-averse preferences are not consistent with the data. See Rosen (1985) and Hart and Holmström (1987) for important early evaluations of the literature. More recently, Gibbons (1997) has argued that the standard agency model does not adequately explain many features of observed contracts.

Some recent exciting research on the preferences of individuals may provide a way forward. Andreoni and Sprenger (2010a) show that previous research measuring risk and time preferences do not adequately control for the risk inherent in future rewards. In a follow-up paper, Andreoni and Sprenger (2010b) explicitly measure risk and time preferences. They find that individuals cognitively view choices as risky or not, but among risky choices they have relatively flat attitudes toward risk. This is consistent with the fact that individuals want to avoid risk but that there is no stable empirical relationship between attitudes toward risk and the form of the optimal contract. This research is very new, and this latter point is yet a conjecture. If these results hold, they may allow for much better models of contract and optimal unemployment insurance.

Asymmetric information

Asymmetric information is ubiquitous in the employment relationship, which leads naturally to the question of how employment law and other labor market-institutions should be designed to handle this problem. Section 3.2.2 provided some examples of situations where asymmetric information can help explain both contract form and the allocation of authority within a relationship. The difficulty is how best to mediate the information problems that arise both within the relationship and between different potential matches.

The early literature focuses on the question of how contracts should be designed to ensure optimal matching when the firm has private information on worker productivity and the worker has private information on alternative opportunities. In a classic paper, Diamond and Maskin (1979) compare expectation damages (they call them compensatory damages) to privately negotiated liquidated damages in a buyer-search model. When parties match, they obtain a gain from trade that is split evenly. The issue is how much they should pay should they find a better match—this will affect the incentives to search and whether or not separations are efficient. They find whether or not one damage rule is better than another depends upon the technology of search; hence, in general, it illustrates that in a world with costly search it is difficult to obtain a clear general prediction on the optimal default rule.

In the employment context, workers are rarely asked to pay for damages should they find a better match. Hall and Lazear (1984) begins with this observation and compares three contract forms:

1. *Fixed wage w is set in advance.* Trade occurs only if both parties prefer trade to no trade at this price. This contract leads to inefficient quits and layoffs.
2. *Firm sets wage knowing worker's productivity.* This is essentially the monopsony solution: The firm has an incentive to set wages above the marginal product of labor, so there are inefficient separations whenever the worker's outside option is between the wage and the worker's marginal product.
3. *Workers set wages (monopoly union model).* In this case, the worker sets his wage above his outside option, resulting in the firm inefficiently not employing the worker when marginal product of the worker is greater than his outside option, but below the wage demanded.

If information is symmetric, then in case 1 we should observe renegotiation and efficient trade. However, as Myerson and Satterthwaite (1983) have shown in a general mechanism-design framework, when there is two-sided asymmetric information, efficient trade is impossible. Hence, as Hall and Lazear (1984) observe, there is no simple contract that implements efficient trade *ex post.* Even in the absence of risk aversion or relation-specific investments, there are limits to efficient trade that no legal rule or contract can overcome.

There are, however, situations under which efficient trade is possible. If a worker's outside option is known, then giving the firm all the bargaining power results in efficient separations, just as it resulted in efficient task assignment in Section 3.2. This is a reasonable assumption when the labor market is thick, as would be the case for, say, casual day labor. In that case, at-will employment is an efficient rule. If variations in outside options are due to variations in worker's ability, then efficiency can still be achieved with the use of piece-rate contracts, as Kanemoto and MacLeod (1992) show. Such a result is consistent with the good-faith exception to employment at will that requires firms to follow through upon promised performance pay.

If it is possible to measure firm productivity, then the efficient rule is to give the worker all the bargaining power. In that case, the worker would offer a wage contract that would make the firm indifferent between acceptance and rejection, with the result that trade would occur if and only if it is efficient. Gibbons (1987), in a paper that complements Kanemoto and MacLeod (1992), shows that if the firm has bargaining power and the workers have information regarding the difficulty of the job, then the resulting contract is inefficient. If the workers were given all the bargaining power in this case, then the first best would be restored.

Though this point follows naturally from the question of how to implement efficient exchange under asymmetric information, it is oddly missing from the literature on unions. Freeman and Medoff (1984) made the point that unions can enhance efficiency via the "voice" mechanism, which can be interpreted as solving the problem of asymmetric information. Beginning with McDonald and Solow (1981), there is a literature that wonders why unions cannot bargain over both wages and employment to achieve an efficient outcome.

One reason is that, in practice, we are typically in a situation with two-sided asymmetric information. In that case, one cannot in general achieve the first best. However, if there are choices whose marginal costs vary with the hidden information, then optimal contracts should incorporate this information. This observation has lead to several contributions that explain observed contracts as a solution to this problem. The early work of Grossman and Hart (1981) shows that the employment-wage policies of a firm are designed to reveal underlying productivity, which can result in observed wages that are different from the true marginal product of labor. Moore (1985) has refined this analysis, to show that when there is two-sided asymmetric information with risk-averse workers, the extent to which the optimal employment contract exhibits over- or under-employment depends upon the preferences of the workers, as well as the nature of uncertainty.

Aghion and Hermalin (1990) introduce a contracting model with asymmetric information and signaling. They show that laws mandating employer-provided benefits can enhance efficiency. There are also papers illustrating that several features of union contracts can be viewed as solving an information problem. Kuhn and Robert (1989) show that seniority rules are a form of efficient price discrimination against the firm. Laing (1994) provides a more general analysis of employment contracts with asymmetrically informed agents, finding that a seniority layoff rule may improve efficiency. Levine (1991) suggests that requiring just cause for dismissal risks attracting low-quality workers. Hence, it is argued that mandated just cause rules may enhance efficiency. Kuhn (1992) observes that requiring mandatory notice of plant closings enhances labor-market performance by ensuring that the firms inform workers in a timely fashion and allow them to make more efficient separation decisions.

There is a recent literature that takes a reduced-form approach to employment protection based on the idea that employment protection acts as a turnover tax that interacts with asymmetric information. Kugler (2004b) observes that in the presence of turnover costs, firms favor more skilled employees, and hence try to fill vacancies from currently employed workers. Hence, she finds that increases in employment protection reduces the flow from unemployment. Pries and Rogerson (2005) introduce more structure to the process regarding worker quality. They suppose that the formation of a match is both an inspection and experience good. The former requires firms and workers to engage in explicit search to form matches, while the latter implies that the signal of match quality becomes more precise with tenure. They explore several labor-market policies, including unemployment insurance, a minimum wage, and dismissal costs. They find that dismissal costs lead to higher unemployment, lower turnover, and higher-quality matches. In contrast, Burguet and Caminal (2008) show that if there is contract renegotiation and uncertainty regarding match, then turnover costs can enhance market performance. Guerrieri (2008) introduces a dynamic general equilibrium model with asymmetric information regarding match quality. She shows that in a dynamic economy the first best cannot be achieved without government intervention in the form of a lump sum tax upon all workers. Finally, Matouschek et al. (2009) formally consider the implications of contract renegotiation when there is asymmetric information regarding outside options.

The extent to which asymmetric information might "explain" observed contracts, and justify the existence of unions or additional taxation, depends upon the magnitude of the asymmetric information. Using evidence from layoffs, Gibbons and Katz (1991) find that workers who lose jobs from a plant closing have higher subsequent wages than those who are laid off. This is consistent with later work by Gibbons et al. (2005), where high-skilled workers earn greater returns to their skill. This evidence supports the hypothesis that labor market wages are a first-best approximation for worker ability. If it is true, then this would suggest that *ex post* efficiency is best achieved with as little market intervention as possible.

This policy choice is no longer ideal if the labor contract must also ensure *ex ante* efficient investment. We turn to this issue next.

Holdup

When worker's productivity is common knowledge, but the cost of labor supply is private to the worker, then it is optimal to allocate all *ex post* bargaining power to the worker. However, this is not in general *ex ante* efficient. When unions and firms are in a long-term relationship, the firm will make investment decisions a function of their expected return from these investments. Grout (1984) has shown that if the union (or worker) has *ex post* bargaining power during contract renegotiation, then there is underinvestment.

Becker (1962), Mincer (1962) and Williamson et al. (1975) have emphasized that the employment relationship typically entails relationship-specific investments. This raises two issues. First, can the employment relationship be governed in such a way that one has efficient investment combined with efficient matching? Second, what are the implications for wages over time? Hashimoto (1981) introduces a model of incomplete wage contracting with relationship-specific investment into worker skill. He shows that if parties cannot condition the wage contract upon the worker's or the firm's alternative opportunities, then there will be inefficient quits (as in Hall and Lazear (1984) discussed above). The result is a wage contract at which the worker and the firm share the rents from firm-specific investments, as hypothesized by Becker (1962) and Mincer (1962).

This result assumes that the worker and the firm can commit to a fixed wage contract. If that is not possible, then the current wage is always set by *ex post* renegotiation, which can be expected to lead to an *ex post* efficient allocation when information is symmetric. Grout (1984) has shown that this leads to the worker's capturing a positive fraction of the rent created by the firm's investments, which in turn leads to lower investment by the firm and slower employment growth. Grout's goal is to model the implications of a UK law making it impossible to enforce wage agreements between a union and a firm. Even when such commitment is possible, Hart and Moore (1988) show that the fact that the worker and the firm can voluntarily renegotiate a contract in the face of new information implies that in general the first best cannot be achieved with a binding agreement.

However, Carmichael and MacLeod (2003) show that if parties can agree upon a *fair division rule* that divides the gains to trade in proportion to the investments made by each party, then the first best can be achieved even in the absence of a binding complete contract. Such a rule requires one party to penalize the other should the agreement be perceived as unfair. In the context of union-firm bargaining, there is some recent evidence that unions do retaliate when it is perceived that the wage bargain is unfair. Krueger and Mas (2004) show that a dispute between Firestone and their union led to lower-quality tires. Mas (2006) finds that the resale value of Caterpillar products fell for equipment built during a labor dispute, suggesting again that labor unrest resulted in lower product quality. Finally, Mas (2008) finds that when police unions in New Jersey got adverse rulings in arbitration that led to lower wages, the police reduced their effort as measured by arrest rates.

These results fit in with an extensive literature, beginning with Akerlof (1982), that the extent to which a worker believes that treatment is fair affects productivity (see in particular the work by Bewley (1999) and Fehr and Schmidt (1999)). The holdup model provides an elegant explanation of why fairness is so important. The economic model predicts that investment into a relationship is a function of the return from such an investment. Note that after an investment has been made, however, it is a sunk cost, and hence rational choice theory would predict that any agreement made *after* investments have been made should be independent of these investments. Consequently, the only way compensation can be linked to investments *ex post* is for parties to follow a social norm that links them—in other words, parties should believe and enforce a norm of fairness that results in parties who invest more receiving more compensation. Carmichael and MacLeod (2003) provide a general proof of the existence of such norms. See also the work of Hart and Moore (2004), who argue that contracts can act as efficiency-enhancing focal points.

Such models have a potential to provide an efficiency-based explanation of why unions with bargaining power can enhance firm productivity. The next section discusses some of the empirical evidence in this regard. This perspective may also provide some insights into the decline in unionization that has occurred in the private sector in the United States (see Farber and Western (2001)). The issue is whether or not there exist alternatives to unions that enhance the productivity of the employment relationship. First, there is the possibility that employment law is a substitute for union protection. At the moment, we simply do not have any studies that explore this idea. Acemoglu and Pischke (1998) show that firm-sponsored investment into training can be enhanced by the fact that firms have superior knowledge regarding worker productivity. In Acemoglu and Pischke (1999), they also argue that increased employment protection enhances firm-sponsored training. They suggest that firm-sponsored training is higher in Europe than in the United States due to higher employment protection in Europe. We do know if the increase in employment protection in the US has lead to more training. MacLeod and Nakavachara (2007) introduce a model with investment and asymmetric information, and show that increased employment regulation in the US would lead to a more productive relationship for highly skilled workers.

For lower-skilled workers, Autor (2003) has documented the fact that there has been an increase in temporary help agencies in the United States. He finds that this is in part explained by the increase in employment protection. However, Autor (2001) also documents that as an organizational form, temporary help agencies play a significant role in screening and training of workers.

3.4. Summary

In this section, we have reviewed the literature on the theory of the employment relationship from the perspective of transaction-costs economics and contract theory. From this research, we learn that an optimal employment contract is shaped by many factors in addition to the demand and supply of factors of production. The need to provide insurance to workers underlies many of the contributions, in part because this model is quite elegant and can in many situations deliver clear predictions. One prediction that it does not deliver is a theory of why employment relations can entail conflict, and why the allocation of bargaining power has important efficiency consequences.

Models of asymmetric information naturally deliver a theory of conflict, and can explain why parties for whom trade is efficient may fail to reach an agreement (see Crawford (1982)). The vast majority of work on employment focuses on the case in which the asymmetric information concerns the outside options for the worker and firm. Many of the employment disputes discussed in the previous section deal with disagreements concerning what happened within the relationship. The model in Simon (1951) is a useful starting point for thinking about these issues, but currently there is little work on the role of the courts in finding facts in employment cases.[51] The main message here, consistent with the work of Milgrom (1988), is that the efficient contract for task assignments is to give the informed party decision rights. Chakravarty and MacLeod (2009) discuss how the law can achieve this goal in the context of construction contracts. The way the law achieves the formal allocation of authority within an employment relationship has not been explored in detail, however. Williamson (1991) makes the point that for the most part courts do not intervene in the day-to-day management of employees. The question of how various employment law doctrines affect this authority relationship is still an open question.

The provision of incentives to make relationship-specific investments gives the third motivation for entering into a binding contract. What is interesting is that the contractual instruments here—specifically, the allocation of authority and bargaining power—also play a central role in achieving efficient investment. There is a need for work that helps us understand which, if any, of these theories provide the most useful way to think about the employment contract. The theories by themselves are not typically framed in terms of making causal inferences. Rather, they make predictions regarding how variations in match characteristics (X variables) are related to observed features of the relationship (wages, employment, bonus or severance pay).

There is some recent work by Cahuc et al. (2006) and Postel-Vinay and Robin (2002) that uses the holdup model of wage determination developed in MacLeod and Malcomson (1993) to empirically estimate models of wage and employment

---

[51] See MacLeod and Nakavachara (2007) and Stahler (2008) for a start.

determination. Cahuc et al. (2006) find that only highly skilled workers have significant bargaining power, while low-skilled workers have none. Postel-Vinay and Robin (2002) find in a panel with French data that personal characteristics tend to be more important for highly skilled workers. These are not causal exercises, but they do suggest that employment law is more likely to be important for highly skilled workers.

4. THE EVIDENCE

The theory of transaction costs provides an economic rationale for intervention into labor markets. Each of the models we have discussed capture some features of the employment relationship that seem empirically plausible. The next step is to see whether changes in employment law do improve matters. We discuss two sets of empirical results that illustrate a range of approaches. First, we review the literature on the employment contract suggesting that there are likely to be mechanisms by which employment law and unions affect the efficiency of labor markets. Second, we review the literature that asks to what extent unions enhance productivity.

4.1. Employment law

In terms of Rubin's model, the unit of analysis for employment laws are typically governments. The most common outcome variables are employment per unit of population, wages, the unemployment rate, and GDP growth. The issue then is how does a change in employment law change these outcome variables? This is a very difficult question because many events occur along with changes in the law that make it difficult to identify a causal effect. Surprisingly, the results tend to be relatively consistent. The majority of studies find either no effect or a negative effect of increasing employment protection. The results of this work are summarized in Table 2. We do not discuss all of these papers, but note that they can be divided into three broad classes: cross-sectional country studies, cross-sectional country studies with time, and the studies from the United States and India that use within-country state variation.

A good starting point are the cross-country studies. Botero et al. (2004) gather data from a several sources to construct measures of various types of employment regulation, including hours restrictions and dismissal procedures. They find that stricter employment protection is associated with countries whose law originated in the civil law tradition. For these countries, it is found that labor force participation is lower and unemployment is higher. Of course, these statements are not causal, but rather say that there is a co-variation between legal origins and employment performance. Djankov et al. (2003) show that civil codes make it more costly to use the courts for contract enforcement, but even this evidence is not necessarily causal. For example, if judges in civil law countries are more corrupt, then the more bureaucratic rules may be a response to this corruption. These basic results have recently been replicated by Djankov and Ramalho (2009), and hence there appears to be a relationship. The question is, why?

Table 2 Employment law summary.

Author, year and journal	Title	Sample	EP measure	Finding on employment
Addison and Grosso (2000)	The effect of dismissals protection on employment: more on a vexed theme	As Lazear (1990)	As Lazear (1990).	Employment protection is statistically insignificant.
Aghion (2008)	The unequal effects of liberalization: evidence from dismantling the License Raj in India	Indian states	Following, Besley and Burgess (2004), indicator of whether state amendment to Industrial Disputes Act of 1947 is neutral, pro-worker, or pro-employer.	Pro-worker states experience less employment growth relative to pro-employer states following delicensing.
Ahsan and Pages (2009)	Are all labor regulations equal? Evidence from Indian manufacturing	Indian states	Employment Protection Legislation according to Besley and Burgess (2004) methodology.	6.5% reduction in employment.
Amin (2009)	Labor regulation and employment in India's retail stores	Retail stores in India	Regulation index from Besley and Burgess (2004) and Regulation index based on stores' perceptions about severity of labor laws.	Flexible labor regulations increase employment by 22% for the average stores.

Table 2 (continued)

Author, year and journal	Title	Sample	EP measure	Finding on employment
Autor et al. (2006)	The costs of wrongful-discharge laws	United States	Implied-contract, public-policy, and good-faith exceptions.	Implied-contract: 0.8%–1.7% reduction in state employment rates. No effect for public-policy and good-faith.
Autor et al. (2007)	Does employment protection reduce productivity? Evidence from US states	United States, establishment-level data from the Census Bureau	Adoption of wrongful-discharge protection by state courts in the US from 1970 to 1999.	Wrongful-discharge protection reduces employment flows and firm entry rates. Moreover, plants engage in capital deepening and experience a decline in total factor productivity, indicative of altered production techniques. Evidence of strong contemporaneous growth in employment, however, leads us to view the findings as suggestive but tentative.
de Barros and Corseuil (2004)	The impact of regulations on Brazilian labor market performance	Brazilian establishment-level data; 1985–1998	New constitution of 1988, which caused many changes in labor codes, including increasing compensation for dismissals without just cause fourfold.	Effect of 1988 constitutional change on lagged employment is statistically insignificant.

(continued on next page)

Table 2 (continued)

Author, year and journal	Title	Sample	EP measure	Finding on employment
Besley and Burgess (2004)	Can labor regulation hinder economic performance? Evidence from India	Indian states	Indicator of whether amendment is neutral, pro-worker, or pro-employer.	States that amended in a pro-worker direction experienced lowered employment. 7.2% decrease in registered manufacturing employment; 28.5% decrease in daily employment in registered manufacturing.
Bird and Knopf (2009)	Do wrongful-discharge laws impair firm performance?	US data from approximately 18,000 commercial banks	Wrongful-discharge protections	The authors estimate the effects of wrongful-discharge protections adopted by US state courts during 1977–99. After controlling for local state economic conditions, the authors find evidence of a relationship between the adoption of the implied contract exception and the increase in labor expenses. In addition, adoption of the implied contract exception is found to have a significant and negative effect on overall profitability. The study corroborates previous findings that wrongful-discharge laws place increased costs on employers.

Table 2 (continued)

Author, year and journal	Title	Sample	EP measure	Finding on employment
Blanchard and Wolfers (2000)	The role of shocks and institutions in the rise of European unemployment: the aggregate evidence	20 OECD countries; 1960–1999; 8 five-year averages of data	Static and time-varying measures taken from Nickell (1997); time-varying measure taken from Lazear (1990) and updated.	Looking at unemployment, they find that shock–EP interaction terms point to amplification of the effects of adverse shocks. Essentially the same is true for the remaining institutional variables with two exceptions. The exceptions are coordination of collective bargaining and active labor market policies, which ameliorate the effects of adverse shocks. In general, much weaker interaction effects and poorer fit when static EP (and UI) measures are replaced by their time-varying counterparts.
Botero et al. (2004)	The regulation of labor	85 countries	Employment laws index composed measuring alternative employment contracts, cost of increasing hours worked, cost of firing workers, and dismissal procedures.	No significant effect on employment in the unofficial economy, negative effect on male LFP, positive effect on UE rate.

(continued on next page)

Table 2 (continued)

Author, year and journal	Title	Sample	EP measure	Finding on employment
Caballero et al. (2004)	Effective labor regulation and microeconomic flexibility	New sectoral panel for 60 countries	Job security regulation.	The job security regulation clearly hampers the creative–destruction process, especially in countries where regulations are likely to be enforced. Moving from the 20th to the 80th percentile in job security, in countries with strong rule of law, cuts the annual speed of adjustment to shocks by a third while shaving off about one percent from annual productivity growth. The same movement has negligible effects in countries with weak rule of law.
Di Tella and MacCulloch (2005)	The consequences of labor market flexibility: panel evidence based on survey data	21 OECD countries: 1984–1990	World Competitiveness Report data; indicator of flexibility (see text); Time-varying measure with five data points.	Statistically significant positive association between flexibility indicator and overall employment population ratio across all specifications. By demographic group this effect is much stronger for females than for males. Parallel results are obtained for the participation rate. Some evidence that flexibility increases average hours worked. The association between flexibility and the unemployment rate is negative throughout but not always statistically significant. The results for long-term unemployment are less precisely estimated.

Table 2 (continued)

Author, year and journal	Title	Sample	EP measure	Finding on employment
Djankov and Ramalho (2009)	Employment laws in developing countries	The Doing Business database, the World Development Indicators, informality data from the Global Competitiveness Report	Rigidity of employment index published by Doing Business.	Developing countries with rigid employment laws tend to have larger informal sectors and higher unemployment, especially among young workers. A number of countries, especially in Eastern Europe and West Africa, have recently undergone significant reforms to make employment laws more flexible. Conversely, several countries in Latin America have made employment laws more rigid. These reforms are larger in magnitude than any reforms in developed countries and their study can produce new insights on the benefits of labor regulation.
Downes (2004)	Labor market regulation and employment in the Caribbean	Barbados, Trinidad, and Jamaica aggregate data	Categorical measure of severance payment regime.	Statistically insignificant effect.
Elmeskov (1998)	Key lessons from labor market reforms: evidence from OECD countries' experience	19 OECD countries; 1983–1995	OECD (1994, Table 6.7, panel B, col. 2) ranking, but modified to take account of changes since late 1980s; two observations, time-varying indicator.	Employment protection raises structural unemployment but interaction effects are important. Employment protection not statistically significant in either highly centralized/coordinated or decentralized bargaining regimes.

(continued on next page)

Table 2 (continued)

Author, year and journal	Title	Sample	EP measure	Finding on employment
Eslava (2004)	The effects of structural reforms on productivity and profitability enhancing reallocation: evidence from Colombia	Plant-level longitudinal dataset for Colombia for the period 1982–1998	Market reforms in 1990s	Market reforms are associated with rising overall productivity that is largely driven by reallocation away from low- and towards high-productivity businesses. In addition, the allocation of activity across businesses is less driven by demand factors after reforms. The increase in aggregate productivity post-reform is entirely accounted for by the improved allocation of activity.
Feldmann (2008)	Business regulation and labor market performance around the world	74 countries; 2000–2003	Labor market regulations ratings from Economic Freedom of the World index.	Labor market regulations increase unemployment and reduce employment.
Feldmann (2009)	The unemployment effects of labor regulation around the world	73 countries; 2000–2003	Labor market regulations from the EFW index as well as the component indicators.	Stricter regulation generally appears to increase unemployment.

Table 2 (continued)

Author, year and journal	Title	Sample	EP measure	Finding on employment
Freeman (2002)	Institutional differences and economic performance among OECD countries	23 + countries; 1970–1990	Fraser Institute index of economic freedom (see text); time-varying measure with 6 data points.	Countries with a high degree of economic freedom have high employment-population rates and low unemployment—at least in terms of levels. Only for unemployment do the results survive the inclusion of country fixed effects.
Garibaldi (1999)	Deconstructing job creation	21 OECD countries; 1980–1998	OECD (1994, Table 6.5 panel B, col. 5) ranking; Moment-in-time measure.	There is a strong negative association between EP measure and employment growth in cross section (for 24 out of 27 cases), but in panel regressions the association is less precisely estimated and is statistically significant in one of five specifications only.
Grubb and Wells (1993)	Employment regulation and patterns of work in EC countries	11 EU countries; 1989	Authors' own indicators of restrictions on overall employee work (ORDW), dismissal of regular workers (RDSM), fixed-term contracts (RFTC), and temporary work agencies (RTWA).	ORDW reduces employment, increases self-employment, and reduces part-time work. RDSM (RFTC) increases (decreases) temporary work. RTWA but not RDSM reduces temporary agency work.

(continued on next page)

Table 2 (continued)

Author, year and journal	Title	Sample	EP measure	Finding on employment
Heckman and Pagés (2000)	The cost of job security regulation: evidence from Latin American labor markets	41 countries from LAC and OECD; 1980–1997 (max)	Authors' own cardinal measure based on severance pay, notice interval, and compensation for unfair dismissal (see text). Two period time-varying measure.	EP effect is negative and statistically significant for total employment for each estimating procedure. Similar results obtained for males and youth, but not females, the impact of EP on male employment being half the total employment effect and the youth effect is almost double the average effect. EP effects for females and self employment vary widely across estimating procedure. The results for unemployment depend on methodology and there is no statistically significant effect of EP on longer-term unemployment. Disaggregation by broad national grouping reveals that the employment effects of EP by demographic group are negative and mostly statistically significant. The exception is females in the Latin–American grouping. The effects of EP on unemployment are nearly always positive and stronger for the OECD grouping.

Table 2 (continued)

Author, year and journal	Title	Sample	EP measure	Finding on employment
Kahn (2010)	Employment protection reforms, employment and the incidence of temporary jobs in Europe: 1996–2001	Belgium, Finland, France, German, Italy, Netherlands, Portugal, Spain, United Kingdom, 1996–2001.	European Community Household Panel (ECHP)	A robust finding is that policies making it easier to create temporary jobs on average raise the likelihood that wage and salary workers will be in temporary jobs. This effect is felt primarily when the regional unemployment rate is relatively high. However, there is no evidence that such reforms raise employment. Thus, these reforms, while touted as a way of jump-starting individuals' careers in the job market, appear rather to encourage a substitution of temporary for permanent work.
Kaplan (2009)	Job creation and labor reform in Latin America	Firm level data from 14 Latin American countries	Index from the Economic Freedom of the World report as indicator of labor market rigidity.	More flexible labor regulations would lead to an average net increase of 2.08% in total employment. Firms with fewer than 20 employees would benefit the most, with average gains in net employment of 4.27%.
Kugler (1999)	The impact of firing costs on turnover and unemployment: evidence from the Colombian labor market reform	Repeated cross-sections from the Colombian National Household Survey (NHS)	Colombian Labor Market Reform of 1990, which substantially reduced dismissal costs.	The exit hazard rates into and out of unemployment increased after the reform by over 1% for formal workers (covered by the legislation) relative to informal workers (uncovered). The increase of the hazards implies a net decrease in unemployment of a third of a percentage point, which accounts for about one quarter of the fall in unemployment during the period of study.

(continued on next page)

Table 2 (continued)

Author, year and journal	Title	Sample	EP measure	Finding on employment
Kugler (2004a)	The Effect of job security regulations on labor market flexibility: evidence from the Colombian labor market reform	Colombian household data on employment; 1988, 1992, 1996	Colombia labor market reform of 1990 reduced severance payments, widened the definition of "just" dismissals, extended the use of temporary contracts, and sped up the process of mass dismissals.	Reform contributed to about 10% of the reduction in the unemployment rate between the pre and post reform periods.
Kugler (2004b)	How do firing costs affect worker flows in a world with adverse selection?	National Longitudinal Survey of Youth	Unjust-dismissal provisions in US states.	As firing costs increase, firms increasingly prefer hiring employed workers, who are less likely to be lemons. Unjust-dismissal provisions in US states reduce the re-employment probabilities of unemployed workers relative to employed workers. The relative effects of unjust-dismissal provisions on the unemployed are generally smaller for union workers and those who lost their previous jobs due to the end of a contract.
Lazear (1990)	Job security provisions and employment	20 countries; 1956–1984	Severance pay due blue-collar workers with 10 years of service; time-varying measure.	Employment protection raises unemployment and reduces employment participation and hours.

Table 2 (continued)

Author, year and journal	Title	Sample	EP measure	Finding on employment
MacLeod and Nakavachara (2007)	Can wrongful discharge law enhance employment?	United States	Implied-contract exception.	Implied-contract: 3.6% reduction in employment of medium-investment group under school training criteria; 3.0% reduction in employment of medium-investment group under informal training criteria; other results are insignificant, but can reject null hypothesis that all adoption variables are insignificant for any training (11.7% level) and school training (0.0% level). Public-policy: No effect on employment of low and high investment groups across all criteria of investment. Good-faith: 7.1%–9.6% reduction in employment of low-investment group, 0%–3.4% increase in employment of medium-investment group, and 6.5%–14.5% increase in employment of high-investment group under any training, school training, and formal training criteria. No significant effects under informal-training criterion.
Miles (2000)	Common law exceptions to employment at will and US labor markets	US panel of state labor market aggregates from 1965 to 1994	The exceptions to employment at will that limit the circumstances of worker dismissal.	The exceptions to employment are seen to have no effect on aggregate employment nor unemployment. However, temporary employment is observed to increase by a statistically significant 15% following the adoption of an exception. The implied contract exception, in particular, appears to be responsible for this increase.

(continued on next page)

Table 2 (continued)

Author, year and journal	Title	Sample	EP measure	Finding on employment
Mondino and Montoya (2004)	The effects of labor market regulations on employment decisions by firms: empirical evidence for Argentina	Argentinian panel of manufacturing firms	Measure of regulation, composed of taxes and expected severance payment.	Negative effect of rigid labor regulation on employment.
Montenegro and Pagés (2004)	Who benefits from labor market regulations? Chile, 1960–1998	Chilean household survey data; 1960–1998	Job security measure derived in Pagés and Montenegro (2007) which captures the expected cost, at the time a worker is hired, of dismissing the worker in the future.	Job security is associated with lower employment rates for young workers, female and unskilled workers, and higher employment for older and skilled workers.
Nickell (1997)	Unemployment and labor market rigidities: Europe versus North America	20 OECD countries; 1983–1988 and 1989–1994	OECD (1996, Table 6.7, panel B, col. 5) ranking; also use of labor standards measure covering in addition to employment protection working time, minimum wages, and employee representation rights (OECD, 1994, Table 4.8, col. 6).	Employment protection reduces overall employment rate but not that of prime-age males. For unemployment, employment protection effect is negative but statistically insignificant. Employment protection reduces short-term unemployment and increases long-term unemployment. Coefficient estimate for worker labor standards variable is statistically insignificant in unemployment regression.

Table 2 (continued)

Author, year and journal	Title	Sample	EP measure	Finding on employment
Nicoletti et al. (2003)	Interactions between product and labor market regulations: do they affect unemployment?	20 OECD countries; 1982–1998	Two indicators of the stringency of the regulatory apparatus. The first is EP per se, and is based on the time varying OECD (1999, Table 2.5) measure. The second is a measure of the degree of product model regulation and is both static (based on Nicoletti et al., 1999) and time varying (based on the authors' evaluation of regulation and market conditions in 7 energy and service industries, 1970–1998).	In initial fixed effects specification, EP is associated with a statistically significant reduction in employment. When EP enters in interaction with the coordination of collective bargaining dummies, its effects are negative and statistically significant for both intermediate and high coordination. The same results obtain for the random effects and second stage regressions. In each case, the negative effect on employment is stronger in countries with an intermediate degree of coordination. The effect of the static product market regulation variable is statistically significant and negative. Finally, for the fixed effect panel regressions, EP is negative and statistically significant in the basic specification. In interactive form, however, the negative coefficient estimate for EP is only statistically significant for the intermediate coordination measure. In interaction with the coordination measure, the product market regulation variable is negative throughout, but is statistically significant for low and intermediate coordination.
OECD (1993)		19 OECD countries; 1979–1991	Severance pay and notice periods combined across blue– and white–collar workers; moment-in-time indicator.	Employment protection has positive effects on jobless duration, especially in southern Europe.

(continued on next page)

Table 2 (continued)

Author, year and journal	Title	Sample	EP measure	Finding on employment
OECD (1999)	Economic protection and labor market performance	19 OECD countries; 1985–1990, 1992–1997	OECD (1999, Table 2.5) measures for late 1980s and late 1990s; single overall indicator and also separate indicators for regular employment, temporary employment and collective dismissals; in some specifications further disaggregations for regular and temporary employment.	Irrespective of the form of the indicator, EP coefficient estimate is statistically insignificant for overall unemployment. It is positive and statistically significant for prime-age male unemployment (overall indicator only). For all other demographic groups EP is statistically insignificant. Further, changes in EP do not affect changes in unemployment for other than prime-age females, where the effect is negative and statistically significant (strictness of EP with respect to regular employment). For employment, the coefficient estimates for EP are negative but statistically insignificant for overall, prime-age female, youth, and temporary employment. Otherwise they are positive and in the case of self-employment statistically significant (overall EP measure and its regular employment variant). Further, changes in EP have statistically insignificant effects for overall employment and for all demographic groups. For self-employment, some statistically negative effects are observed.

Table 2 (continued)

Author, year and journal	Title	Sample	EP measure	Finding on employment
Pagés and Montenegro (2007)	Job security and the age-composition of employment: evidence from Chile	Chilean annual household surveys; 1960–1998	Index combining information on notice periods, compensation for dismissal, the likelihood that a firms' difficulties be considered as justified cause of dismissal, and severance pay due to that event. This index measures the expected cost, at the time the worker is hired, of dismissing a worker in the future.	Job security is associated with a substantial decline in the wage employment-to-population rate of young workers. No decline in young self-employment rates or in the wage employment rates of older workers. Adverse effect of job security on youth employment is driven by the link between severance payments and tenure. Job security does not have a significant impact on overall aggregate employment, participation or unemployment rates.
Saavedra and Torero (2004)	Labor market reforms and their impact over formal labor demand and job market turnover: the case of Peru	Peruvian firm and sector level data; 1986–1997.	Expected severance payment	Reduction in firing costs (as measured by expected severance payment) has positive effect on employment level.
Scarpetta (1996)	Assessing the role of labor market policies and institutional settings on unemployment: a cross-country study	17 OECD countries; 1983–1993	OECD strictness ranking for regulation of dismissal averaged over regular and fixed-term contracts (OECD, 1994, Table 6.7, panel B, col. 2).	Employment protection raises structural unemployment, with stronger effects for youth and long-term unemployment. Employment protection increases nonemployment rate.

Table 3 Employment law for a selected set of countries.

Country	Min. work age	Holidays	OT Prem.	Sev. Pay	Ret. Ben. Yrs.	Unemp. Wait	Matern. Leave
Switzerland	15	9	1.25	0.0	1	5	4.5
United States	16	0	1.5	0.0	20	3	1.35
Singapore	12	11	1.5	12.9	5	n.a.	3.0
Finland	16	11	2.0	0.0	0	7	4.2
Italy	15	11	1.1	0.0	19	7	1.35
New Zealand	16	11	1.0	0.0	0	70	1.5
Portugal	16	12	1.5	12.9	15	0	2.0
Uruguay	15	5	2.0	12.9	35	0	4.1
Malaysia	14	10	1.5	2.14	20	n.a.	4.05
Mexico	14	7	2.0	18.04	10	n.a.	3.0
Lebanon	13	13	1.5	12.9	20	n.a.	3.5
Russia	16	9	2.0	8.6	25	0	12.0
Lithuania	14	11	1.0	8.6	30	8	2.0
Jordan	16	12	1.25	12.9	10	7	2.0
Morocco	12	11	1.25	0.0	9	n.a.	3.0
Indonesia	12	12	1.5	25.8	20	n.a.	2.25
Zimbabwe	17	11	1.0	0.0	10	n.a.	3.0
Armenia	16	13	1.5	6.45	25	0	6.0
India	14	5	2.0	6.43	10	n.a.	4.0
Vietnam	18	5	1.5	12.9	20	n.a.	3.0
Madagascar	14	2	1.3	4.2	15	n.a.	3.0
Mozambique	18	9	1.5	25.8	10	n.a.	0.0

Employment Rules in Sample of OECD Countries. The 85 countries studied in Botero et al. (2004) were ranked by per capita income, and every fourth country was selected. The table presents measurements for the following employment rules. *Min. Work Age.* The minimum legal age for attaining full-time employment. *Holidays.* Number of legally mandated paid holidays per year. *OT Prem.* The premium for working overtime, as a multiple of normal-time wages. *Sev. Pay.* Legally mandated severance payment for terminated workers, in week's pay. *Ret. Ben. Yrs.* Years of work required before a worker is eligible for retirement benefits through the country's social security program. Obtained by multiplying the relevant index by 45 (the maximum observation in years) and subtracting that number from 45. *Unemp. Wait.* Waiting period in days before a worker becomes eligible for unemployment benefits. Obtained by multiplying the relevant index by 70 (the maximum observation in days), and subtracting that number from 70. "n.a." indicates that the country does not offer unemployment benefits. *Matern. Leave.* Number of months of legally mandated maternity leave.

A natural way to control for cross-country variations is to use variation over time in laws. Early studies along these lines include the influential work of the OECD (1993). They found that employment protection increased jobless duration. In subsequent work, the OECD (2003) finds that employment protection is often insignificant, but is associated with increased unemployment for prime-age males. These, like the cross-section studies, must construct measures of employment protection that are meaningful in different countries. The difficulty, as we see in Table 3, is that there are a large number of possible laws, each of which get implemented in an idiosyncratic fashion. One way to deal with this complexity is to have a more narrow study of a law change. A series of studies by Kugler (1999, 2004a, 2005) uses the 1990 market-based reforms in Columbia.

Kugler finds that these reforms generally lead to more flexible labor markets and lower unemployment.

Given that these changes occurred at a single point in time, this implies a true causal effect under the hypothesis that other secular changes would not have produced this effect. One way to satisfy this assumption is to narrow the analysis to a set of units that are more similar, but face changes at different times. Besley and Burgess (2004) pioneered this approach using variations in employment law across states in India. Given that all the units (states) are in the same country, this controls for legal origin. Using data from 1958-1992 on employment law legislation, Besley and Burgess (2004) find that pro-worker legislation lowers economic growth. Similar results have been replicated by Aghion (2008) and Ahsan and Pages (2009). However, given the large cultural diversity in India, one might question the extent to which the law is exogenous to other events in society.

Possibly, the most convincing studies on the effect of the law exploit the fact that in the United States employment law is under state jurisdiction. One can then estimate the effect that state level changes in exceptions to employment at will have on the labor market. These law changes for the 1983-95 period are illustrated in Fig. 1. As we can see, a large number of states adopted the implied-contract and public-policy exceptions during this time period. In this case, the identifying assumption is that US states are sufficiently similar that one can assume that the impact of the law in each state is similar. One then uses a generalization of model (1):

$$y_{ut} = \beta^\top X_{ut} + \beta_l^\top l_{st} + \phi_{ut},$$

where u denotes state. In most papers, the Current Population Survey (CPS) is used to measure employment and wages by state. Bertrand et al. (2004) show that one cannot assume that the error term ϕ_{ut} is iid, and one must allow for correlation over time. In practice this is achieved by adding state-specific time trends and computing standard errors with clustering of the errors at the state level (in effect allowing arbitrary covariance over time within states, but assuming independent errors across states).

Miles (2000) is an early study by a legal scholar who carefully ensured that employment law is correctly coded. This can be difficult in the United States because law is created by both the courts and the states. He finds very little effect on employment from any of the law variables, but finds that the implied contract exception leads to an increase in temporary employment, consistent with the later work of Autor (2003). Autor et al. (2004, 2006) further refine the law variables used by Miles (2000), finding that the implied-contract exception leads to a robust reduction in state employment, but that the public-policy and good-faith exceptions have no effect.

The theory discussed above predicts that the effect of the law depends upon the characteristics of the employment relationship. In particular, if hold-up is the transaction cost most responsible for the creation of employment law, then we would expect the law to have more effect on matches with higher levels of relationship-specific investment. This idea motivates the work of MacLeod and Nakavachara (2007). They match the CPS job training supplement that measures the amount of skill in a job with an occupation code to divide occupations in the low, middle, and high skill. They then use the data created by Autor et al. (2004) to explore the effect of relating skill requirement with the law. They find that the negative effects of the implied contract and good faith exceptions tend to be concentrated in low-skill (high-turnover) jobs. In fact, the good faith exception has a *positive* effect on employment for high-skill workers.

Though this appears to be at odds with the previous literature, it should be noted that the earlier literature focuses on the average effects, which obscures the effect on different subgroups. One of the messages from the recent research on contract theory is that optimal contract form *should* be sensitive to the characteristics of the job, particularly for high-performance jobs. Consequently, we cannot obtain a complete understanding of how the law works without taking into account its impact on different types of relationships. Both the theory and the early work of Freeman and Medoff (1984) predict that if transaction costs are a significant source of inefficiency in employment relationships, then there is a role for unions to enhance performance.

4.2. The effect of unions

Table 4 provides a list of studies that explore the effect of unions upon firm productivity. The early studies by Brown and Medoff (1978) and Clark (1980b) explicitly recognize that unions may enhance performance by increasing investments in firm-specific human capital, improving worker morale and other organizational parameters. Clark (1980b) also observes that union contracts have many terms that address issues in the workplace other than compensation. Brown and Medoff (1978) estimate a Cobb-Douglas production function using data from the May CPS merged with the 1972 Census of Manufacturers (COM). They find that labor productivity is consistently higher at unionized firms. They are careful to point out that this result can be explained by several factors, and while consistent with the hypothesis that unions enhance productivity, they do not establish a causal link.

Clark (1980b) refines this approach by using a time series on US cement plants, which allows one to explore the effect of unions upon plants in the same industry, with precise control on capital equipment. Like Brown and Medoff (1978), Clark finds that unions enhance productivity. One of the interesting findings is that if one compares only new plants, then unionized firms have 3.6% higher productivity, but a lower capital/labor ratio. This is consistent with the holdup model of Grout (1984), which predicts that firms will invest less in physical capital in response to union bargaining power. Abowd (1989) uses stock market data to conclude that unions and firms maximize total wealth.

Table 4 Unions and productivity.

Author, year and journal	Title	Sample	Main dependent variables	Main independent variables	Finding on productivity
Abowd (1989)	The effect of wage bargains on the stock market value of the firm	Contract settlements, 1976–1982	Change in value of common stock	Unexpected change in collectively bargained labor costs	The change in the value of common stock resulting from an unexpected change in collectively bargained labor costs is estimated. Using bargaining unit wage data and NYSE stock returns, it is shown that there is a dollar-for-dollar tradeoff between these variables. This result is consistent with stock valuations based on present value maximizing managerial decisions (Hotelling's lemma). The analysis provides support for the hypothesis that collective bargains maximize the sum of shareholders' and union members' wealth.
Allen (1984)	Unionized construction workers are more productive	US manufacturing industries, 1972	Value added	Fraction unionized	This paper presents evidence on the effect of unionism on productivity in construction. The linkages are distinct from those studied previously in industrial settings. Apprenticeship training and hiring halls probably raise union productivity, while jurisdictional disputes and restrictive work rules lower it. Using Brown and Medoff's methodology, union productivity, measured by value added per employee, is 45% to 52% higher than nonunion. The estimate declines to 17% to 22% when estimates of inter-area construction price differences are used to deflate value added. Occupational mix differences and, possibly, apprenticeship training account for 15% to 27% of this difference.

(continued on next page)

Table 4 (continued)

Author, year and journal	Title	Sample	Main dependent variables	Main independent variables	Finding on productivity
Allen (1986)	The effect of unionism on productivity in privately and publicly owned hospitals and nursing–homes	Publicly and privately owned hospitals and nursing homes, 1976	Value added, square feet	Union dummy, union dummy *public ownership	This paper examines the effect of unions on productivity within a sample of publicly and privately owned hospitals and nursing homes to determine whether public ownership influences union behavior. The results show that the productivity of union contractors is much greater in private than in public projects. Within the sample of private projects, the estimates of the union–nonunion productivity difference are generally positive but very imprecise.
Allen (1986)	Unionization and productivity in office building and school construction	Commercial office buildings completed in 1973–74, elementary schools completed in 1972	Value added, square feet	Union dummy	This study examines the difference in productivity between union and nonunion contractors in the construction industry within two samples, one of 83 commercial office buildings completed in 1973–74 and the other of 68 elementary and secondary schools completed in 1972. An analysis that includes controls for differences in capital-labor ratios, observable labor quality, region, and building characteristics shows that union productivity in the office building projects was at least 30% higher than nonunion productivity, measured in terms of square feet of floor space completed per hour worked; and from zero to 20% higher in school projects, measured in physical units and value added, respectively.

Table 4 (continued)

Author, year and journal	Title	Sample	Main dependent variables	Main independent variables	Finding on productivity
Becker and Olson (1990)	The effects of the NLRA on stockholder wealth in the 1930s	Firms at risk of being unionized in the 1930s	Cumulative average excess return	NLRA and related events	Whereas most recent research examining the effects of the NLRA on labor–management relations has focused on the impact of specific provisions of the law, this study provides an estimate of the impact of the passage of the NLRA on 75 firms that were at great risk of being unionized in the 1930s. Taking changes in shareholder wealth as a measure of the shift in the balance of power caused by the NLRA, the authors find that the passage of the NLRA caused a statistically and economically significant decline in shareholder wealth for the sampled firms. Specifically, by April 1937, stockholder wealth in the firms was 15.9% lower than would have been expected had the NLRA not been enacted.
Becker and Olson (1992)	Unions and firm profits	US manufacturing firms, 1977	Excess value, price–cost margin	Fraction unionized	This study examines the effect of unionization on manufacturing firm profits, extending earlier research by combining industry-level and firm-level measures of unionization. Using several profit measures, we find that quasi-rents from firm investments in intangible assets are a relatively greater source of union profit effects than product market concentration and that union profit effects occur largely in the first 10% of firm coverage, suggesting spillover effects on nonunion employees.

(continued on next page)

Table 4 (continued)

Author, year and journal	Title	Sample	Main dependent variables	Main independent variables	Finding on productivity
Bemmels (1987)	How unions affect productivity in manufacturing plant	Manufacturing plants, 1982	Value added	Fraction unionized, fraction unionized squared, fraction unionized *participative management, fraction unionized *performance appraisal, fraction unionized *incentive pay	This study investigates several hypotheses as to how unions may affect productivity. Analysis of data from 46 manufacturing plants for 1982 indicates a negative union impact on productivity. The author finds evidence suggesting that unions reduce the effectiveness of some managerial practices undertaken to increase productivity, and that poor labor–management relations climate also reduce productivity. These two factors account for almost 50% of the negative union impact.

Table 4 (continued)

Author, year and journal	Title	Sample	Main dependent variables	Main independent variables	Finding on productivity
Black and Lynch (2001)	How to compete: the impact of workplace practices and information technology on productivity	Manufacturing establishments, 1987–1993	Sales	Union dummy, union dummy * TQM (total quality management system), union dummy * profit sharing for non-managerial workers	Using data from a unique, nationally representative, sample of businesses, the authors examine the impact of workplace practices, information technology, and human capital investments on productivity. The authors estimate an augmented Cobb–Douglas production function with both cross section and panel data covering the period of 1987–1993, using both within and GMM estimators. It is found that it is not whether an employer adopts a particular work practice but rather how that work practice is actually implemented within the establishment that is associated with higher productivity. Unionized establishments that have adopted human resource practices that promote joint decision making coupled with incentive-based compensation have higher productivity than other similar nonunion plants, whereas unionized businesses that maintain more traditional labor management relations have lower productivity. Finally, plant productivity is higher in businesses with more-educated workers or greater computer usage by non-managerial employees.

(continued on next page)

Table 4 (continued)

Author, year and journal	Title	Sample	Main dependent variables	Main independent variables	Finding on productivity
Bronars and Deere (1990)	Union representation elections and firm profitability	US union elections, 1962–1980	Petition date excess return; certification date excess return	Firm and industry characteristics	Union representation elections are associated with significant declines in firm profitability. In addition to the significant mean effect of union elections on the equity value of firms, there exists substantial variation in the magnitude of equity losses across individual election events. Cross-sectional variation in shareholder equity losses can be explained by the labor intensity of the firm, the size of the union wage premium and fraction of workers organized in the firm's industry, the presence or absence of right-to-work laws in the state where the election is held, the number of workers covered in the representation election, and the number of previous union representation elections in the firm. The empirical results indicate that equity losses are the greatest in industries where union wage gains are the largest, and in the most labor-intensive firms, independent of the size of the bargaining unit involved in the election. The latter result indicates the presence of union spillover effects.

Table 4 (continued)

Author, year and journal	Title	Sample	Main dependent variables	Main independent variables	Finding on productivity
Bronars and Deere (1994)	Unionization and profitability— evidence of spillover effects	US union elections, 1962–1980	Excess return	Petition date	Ruback and Zimmerman's (1984) event study, which showed that formal union-organizing activity significantly lowers a firm's market value, provides compelling evidence that unionization reduces a firm's profitability. Union-organizing activity may also have sizable cross-firm or spillover effects on the performance of neighboring firms. Thus the total impact of union organizing on the wealth of firm owners may be substantially understated by focusing only on the firm in which the union-organizing activity occurs. This paper presents an alternative approach for estimating union spillover effects on profitability using a data set and methodology similar to Ruback and Zimmerman's. Analysis of the impact of petitions for NLRB representation elections at one firm on the share prices of other firms in the same narrowly defined industry suggests that the total negative effects of unionization on profits, after cross-firm or spillover effects are included, are nearly three times as large as the own-firm effects reported by Ruback and Zimmerman.

(continued on next page)

Table 4 (continued)

Author, year and journal	Title	Sample	Main dependent variables	Main independent variables	Finding on productivity
Brown and Medoff (1978)	Trade unions in the production process	US manufacturing industries, 1972	Value added	Fraction unionized	In order to estimate the effects of unions on worker productivity, a Cobb-Douglas production function is modified so that unionization is included as a variable. The resulting functional form is similar to that used to isolate the effect of worker quality in previous studies. Using state by two-digit SIC observations for US manufacturing, unionization is found to have a substantial positive effect on output per worker. However, this result depends on two important assumptions which we cannot verify directly; attempts to relax these assumptions are not conclusive.

Table 4 (continued)

Author, year and journal	Title	Sample	Main dependent variables	Main independent variables	Finding on productivity
Clark (1980a)	The impact of unionization on productivity: a case study	Six establishments in US cement industry, 1953–1976	Tons per man–hour	Union dummy	This study examines the effect of unionization on productivity through the use of time-series data on selected establishments in the US cement industry. The analysis combines statistical estimation of the union impact and interviews with union and management officials to forge a link between econometric estimation and the traditional institutional analysis of union policy and management practice. The econometric analysis deals primarily with the problem of controlling for interfirm differences in variables such as the quality of management and also for the possible union impact on labor quality. The case studies are designed to show the specific ways in which unionization affects productivity. The empirical results indicate that unionization leads to productivity gains, deriving in large part from a series of extensive changes in management personnel and procedures.

(continued on next page)

Table 4 (continued)

Author, year and journal	Title	Sample	Main dependent variables	Main independent variables	Finding on productivity
Clark (1980b)	Unionization and productivity: micro-econometric evidence	US cement industry, 1973–1976	Tons per man–hour	Union dummy	It is widely agreed that unionization affects the rules and procedures governing the employment relation in organized establishments. The effect of these changes on establishment productivity, however, is unclear. This issue is examined using establishment level data from the US cement industry. A positive union effect on the order of 6%–8% is found in both cross-section and time series data. Although some caution is in order in interpreting the results, the evidence suggests that unionization can lead to productive changes in the operation of the enterprise.

Table 4 (continued)

Author, year and journal	Title	Sample	Main dependent variables	Main independent variables	Finding on productivity
Clark (1984)	Unionization and firm performance: the impact on profits, growth, and productivity	Product-line businesses, 1970–1980	Sales, value added, return on capital, return on sales, rate of growth of deflated sales	Union dummy	The history of collective bargaining in the US has been marked by dramatic episodes of confrontation that underscore the change unionization brings to the operation of an enterprise. In spite of the diffusion of many practices associated with collective bargaining recent research has revealed the continuing existence of important differences between union and nonunion establishments in policies governing compensation, exit and entry, dispute resolution and internal promotion. Unionization works through more than one mediating factor and the impact of the union on a given measure of firm performance depends on the particular context in which bargaining and production take place. This article uses microeconomic data on over 900 product-line businesses to gauge the impact of the union on economic performance. A clear implication of the theoretical analysis is the need to examine several indicators of firm behavior in order to draw inferences about the operation and consequences of collective bargaining.

(continued on next page)

Table 4 (continued)

Author, year and journal	Title	Sample	Main dependent variables	Main independent variables	Finding on productivity
Cooke (1994)	Employee participation programs, group-based incentives, and company performance: a union–nonunion comparison	Michigan manufacturing firms, 1989	Value added	Union dummy interacted with work teams and profit/gain sharing plan	This analysis examines whether union representation positively or negatively influences the effectiveness of employee participation programs and group-based incentives in improving firm performance. Examined at the firm level, a model of the independent and interaction effects of participation, profit and gain sharing, and union representation is estimated against data on 841 manufacturing firms in Michigan in 1989. The evidence indicates that employee participation programs contributed substantially more to performance in unionized firms than in nonunion firms, whereas profit and gain sharing programs contributed substantially more to performance in nonunion firms than in unionized firms.

Table 4 (continued)

Author, year and journal	Title	Sample	Main dependent variables	Main independent variables	Finding on productivity
DiNardo and Lee (2004)	Economic impacts of new unionization on private sector employers: 1984–2001	US union elections, 1984–1999	Total value of shipments	Vote share	Economic impacts of unionization on employers are difficult to estimate in the absence of large, representative data on establishments with union status information. Estimates are also confounded by selection bias, because unions could organize at highly profitable enterprises that are more likely to grow and pay higher wages. Using multiple establishment-level data sets that represent establishments that faced organizing drives in the United States during 1984–1999, this paper uses a regression discontinuity design to estimate the impact of unionization on business survival, employment, output, productivity, and wages. Essentially, outcomes for employers where unions barely won the election (e.g., by one vote) are compared with those where the unions barely lost. The analysis finds small impacts on all outcomes that we examine; estimates for wages are close to zero. The evidence suggests that—at least in recent decades—the legal mandate that requires the employer to bargain with a certified union has had little economic impact on employers, because unions have been somewhat unsuccessful at securing significant wage gains.

(continued on next page)

Table 4 (continued)

Author, year and journal	Title	Sample	Main dependent variables	Main independent variables	Finding on productivity
Eberts and Stone (1987)	Teacher unions and the productivity of public schools	Educational programs, late 1970s	Standardized test scores	Union dummy	Do teacher unions affect the productivity of public schools? The authors examine this question using individual student data from the Sustaining Effects Survey sponsored by the US Department of Education. Holding resources constant and using achievement gains on standardized tests as the measure of output, they find that union districts are seven percent more productive for average students. For the minority of students who are significantly above or below average, however, nonunion districts are more productive by about the same margin, apparently because teacher unions reduce the use of specialized instructional techniques. This result is consistent with the view that unions tend to standardize the workplace. Across all students, the average union productivity advantage is three percent.
Ehrenberg et al. (1983)	Unions and productivity in the public sector: a study of municipal libraries	Municipal libraries, 1977	Number of information requests, number of borrowers, number of interlibrary loans, total circulation, book and periodical circulation	Union dummy	This paper develops and illustrates the use of two methodologies to analyze the effect of unions on productivity in the public sector. Although the methodologies are applicable to a wide variety of public sector functions, the focus of the paper is on municipal libraries because of the availability of relevant data. The empirical analysis, which uses 1977 cross-section data on 260 libraries, suggests that collective bargaining coverage has not significantly affected productivity in municipal libraries.

Table 4 (continued)

Author, year and journal	Title	Sample	Main dependent variables	Main independent variables	Finding on productivity
Hirsch (1991)	Union coverage and profitability among United States firms	US manufacturing firms, 1972–1980	Tobin's q, rate of return on capital	Fraction unionized	This paper utilizes unique survey data on labor union coverage at the firm level to examine union effects on the profitability of 705 US companies during the 1970s. Market value and earnings are estimated to be about 10%–15% lower in an average unionized company than in a nonunion company, following extensive control for firm and industry characteristics. Deleterious union effects on firm profitability are sizable throughout the 1972–80 period, but vary considerably across industries. The relatively poor profit performance of unionized companies may help explain the recent decline in US union membership.
Hirsch and Connolly (1987)	Do unions capture monopoly profits?	US manufacturing firms, 1977	Tobin's q, rate of return on sales	Fraction unionized	This paper challenges the conclusion reached in recent studies that unions reduce profits exclusively in highly concentrated industries. From their review of previous studies and their analysis of 1977 data on 367 Fortune 500 firms, the authors conclude that there is no convincing evidence that concentration produces monopoly profits for unions to capture. Moreover, they find that the union wage effect is not greater in concentrated industries, as suggested by the hypothesis that unions capture concentration-related profits. Evidence is found suggesting that a firm's market share, its expenditures on research and development, and its protection from foreign competition provide more likely sources for union rents than does industry concentration.

(continued on next page)

Table 4 (continued)

Author, year and journal	Title	Sample	Main dependent variables	Main independent variables	Finding on productivity
Lee and Mas (2009)	Long-run impacts of unions on firms: new evidence from financial markets, 1961–1999	US union elections, 1961–1999	Abnormal return	Election	The authors estimate the effect of new unionization on firms' equity value over the 1961–1999 period using a newly assembled sample of National Labor Relations Board (NLRB) representation elections matched to stock market data. Event-study estimates show an average union effect on the equity value of the firm equivalent to a cost of at least $40,500 per unionized worker. At the same time, point estimates from a regression-discontinuity design—comparing the stock market impact of close union election wins to close losses—are considerably smaller and close to zero. The analysis indicates a negative relationship between the cumulative abnormal returns and the vote share in support of the union, which allows to reconcile these seemingly contradictory findings. Using the magnitudes from the analysis, the authors calibrate a structural "median voter" model of endogenous union determination in order to conduct counterfactual policy simulations of policies that would marginally increase the ease of unionization.

Table 4 (continued)

Author, year and journal	Title	Sample	Main dependent variables	Main independent variables	Finding on productivity
Lovell et al. (1988)	The effect of unionization on labor productivity: some additional evidence	US Economy, 1948–1973	GDP	Fraction unionized	Following Brown and Medoff (1978), a number of studies have investigated the effect of unionization on labor productivity using a log-linear, Cobb–Douglas model of technology. To derive this model, a first-order Taylor-series approximation to the intrinsically nonlinear unionization variable is made; the resulting linear equation is estimated with generalized least-squares (GLS) techniques. The authors demonstrate that this approximation introduces a bias that necessarily results in an overstatement of the absolute value of the exact union productivity effect. The authors illustrate the magnitude of this bias by comparing GLS estimates of the linear Brown–Medoff model with GLS estimates of the exact, nonlinear relationship, using aggregate time-series data from the private domestic sector of the US economy.
Machin (1991)	The productivity effects of unionization and firm size in British engineering firms	52 British engineering firms over the period 1978–82	Value-added	Several indicators of union presence	Average union–nonunion effects on labor productivity estimated using this measure, or using a dummy variable indicating the presence of closed-shop arrangements, are found to be statistically insignificant. However, there is some variation around this average, and the union impact on value added per employee is found to depend significantly on firm size, the estimated effects being more negative in larger firms.

(continued on next page)

Table 4 (continued)

Author, year and journal	Title	Sample	Main dependent variables	Main independent variables	Finding on productivity
Mitchell and Stone (1992)	Union effects on productivity: evidence from western US sawmills	Western US sawmills, 1986	Lumber (million board feet)	Union dummy	The authors conjecture that previous studies have tended to overestimate the productivity of union firms relative to nonunion firms due to inadequate controls for output quality and input usage–important omissions if the higher cost of unionized labor leads to less labor-intensive products and techniques. To avoid those problems, this study examines a fairly standardized commodity, lumber, and controls for detailed product attributes and inputs. An analysis of data from a survey administered by the authors shows that unionized sawmills were between 12% and 21% less productive than nonunionized mills in fiscal year 1986. As predicted, when product quality and raw material usage are not included in the analysis, the estimate of union productivity is biased upward.
Ruback and Zimmerman (1984)	Unionization and profitability: evidence from the capital market	US union elections, 1962–1980	Abnormal return	Petition and certification dates	This paper examines the effect of unionization on the profitability of firms. Abnormal monthly common stock returns for a sample of 253 NYSE-listed firms are estimated for the month in which the union petitions for an election and for the month in which the National Labor Relations Board certifies the election outcome. The results suggest that unionization, on average, is associated with a reduction in equity value. When unions win an election, the average loss associated with the unionization drive is 3.8% of equity value. When unions lose an election, there is an average net reduction of 1.3% in the equity value of the firm.

Table 4 (continued)

Author, year and journal	Title	Sample	Main dependent variables	Main independent variables	Finding on productivity
Salinger (1984)	Tobin's q, unionization, and the concentration-profits relationship	Manufacturing firms, 1979	Tobin's q, profit rate	Fraction unionized	This article uses Tobin's q, the ratio of the market value of a firm to the replacement value of its physical assets, to measure monopoly power and to examine the relationship between market structure and profitability. Tobin's q is a better measure of monopoly profits than indices of single-period profitability because it measures long-run monopoly power. In additions, it is subject to less measurement error and it contains an adjustment for risk. The relationship between q and long-run monopoly power is established. Provided that all inputs are supplied competitively, q should be highly sensitive to even small amounts of monopoly power. Since the level of q is generally not high in the American economy, the result suggests either that monopoly power is absent or that unions manage to capture monopoly rents. Empirical tests of the relationship between Tobin's q and measures of market structure and unionization provide evidence that unions do capture most monopoly rents.

(continued on next page)

Table 4 (continued)

Author, year and journal	Title	Sample	Main dependent variables	Main independent variables	Finding on productivity
Voos and Mishel (1986)	The union impact on profits: evidence from industry price–cost margin data	US manufacturing firms, 1968–1972	Price–cost margin	Fraction unionized	This paper uses industry price–cost margin data to estimate the extent to which unions reduce profits. Estimates allowing for the endogeneity of union status are contrasted with estimates that assume union status is exogenous and not determined in part by either profitability or industry structure. Endogeneity is found to be an important consideration in estimating the union impact on profits: two-stage estimates are considerably larger than OLS estimates. The final section explores the total estimated redistribution from capital to labor in the manufacturing sector. An important conclusion is that unions raise prices less than was previously believed.

Recently, developments have begun to focus on workplace organization.[52] Black and Lynch (2001) find that there is an interaction between workplace practice and unionization. When firms have more consensual decision-making in the workplace, then unionization is associated with higher productivity. Conversely, unions are associated with lower productivity in firms that use "traditional" management practices. Doucouliagos and Laroche (2003) carry out a meta-analysis of a large number of studies on the productivity impact of unions. They find that the evidence is broadly consistent with a positive-productivity effect in the United States and a negative effect in the United Kingdom. This is an interesting observation given that the law is quite different in the two jurisdictions. In the United Kingdom, unions cannot commit to a binding agreement, whereas this is possible in the United States. This difference in productivities is consistent with the evidence, though we are far from having convincing causal evidence.

Even if unions enhance firm productivity, this does not necessarily translate into an increase in profits. This depends on the bargaining power of unions, and the extent to which firms earn rents.[53] A common strategy is to merge National Labor Relations Data on union certification with firm stock-market data to look at the impact of certification on profits. Ruback and Zimmerman (1984) find that unionization causes a 3.8% fall in equity value. Abowd (1989) finds that unionization can also reduce profits, but that this is an efficient redistribution from firms to workers. These and similar studies must deal with the fact that unionization is endogenous, and hence it is very difficult to estimate the causal impact of a union, independent from other factors. DiNardo and Lee (2004) use a regression discontinuity design in which they compare the outcomes in firms where the unions barely won certification, to ones where there was a close lost. Under the hypothesis that the groups have similar characteristics, then differences can be attributed to union status. Their finding is that the effect is essentially zero.

Lee and Mas (2009) use a similar approach, but obtain a better measure of abnormal stock-market returns. They find that unionization causes a 10% decline in abnormal returns. What is particularly interesting (especially in the light of the efficient-markets hypothesis) is that the negative effect is largest a year after the vote for unionization. This result is consistent with the body of research that looks at the impact of unions on firm productivity (see Doucouliagos and Laroche (2009)). Even if unions truly enhance productivity, if they lower profitability then we should expect firms to reallocate resources to jurisdictions with less union penetration. Kuhn (1998) suggests that there seems to be little evidence of this in Canada, while Machin (2000) finds that new firms in the United Kingdom tend not be unionized.

---

[52] See Ichinowski and Shaw (2003), and the Handbook chapters by Bloom and Van Reenen (2011) and Oyer and Schaefer (2011).

[53] See Ashenfelter and Johnson (1969) for a classic discussion of union-firm bargaining and associated empirical implications.

As Farber and Western (2001) documents for the United States, and Machin (2000) for the United Kingdom, there has a been a large decline in unionization that is consistent with the hypothesis of excessive rent extract by unions in the face of alternative, nonunion, investment opportunities for firms. Yet, there are still some areas with significant union presence. For example, workers in the entertainment industry are unionized. This is an industry where highly skilled actors, writers, and musicians must move from job to job, and where for each job there is a large number of potential candidates. In the absence of a union contract, the wage would be set at the talent's opportunity cost, which is likely to be far below the return necessary to make it profitable to invest in his or her particular skill. In this case, a union has the potential to increase the talent pool, though this is a hypothesis that has not been carefully tested.

The other area with significant union presence is the public sector. Ehrenberg et al. (1983) find that unions do not significantly affect productivity for municipal librarians. Byrne et al. (1996) find that unionized police are less effective in dealing with crime. Eberts and Stone (1987) explore the effect of unions upon teacher productivity, finding that on average unionized teachers increase test scores by about 3%. However, their impact is more homogeneous, and they do not do as well with students with above- or below-average ability. In a recent study, Lovenheim (2009) finds that teacher unions raise costs by about 15% while having no impact on school performance.[54]

In summary, the evidence on unions is consistent with the hypothesis that they do have some bargaining power with respect to the firm. As we discussed in the previous section, bargaining power may allow parties to implement more efficient arrangements. The extent to which this is possible in practice is controversial. It is clear that over the past century we have witnessed a large rise and fall in unionization rates in the United States. The transaction-cost perspective suggests that unions can be viewed as substitutes for legal enforcement of contracts and other forms of labor-market regulation. The fact that employment law in the United States has become stronger in the last 30 years—in the sense of providing more protection for disadvantaged groups[55] and stronger employment protection—suggests that private law may be providing a substitute for unionization.

In the case of the public sector, the skills acquired by workers are likely to be job-specific, and moreover the demand for these skills are stable. This suggests that the optimal contract is of a long duration, which may explain why public-sector unions are so prevalent. However, it is extremely difficult to measure public-sector productivity, and hence to evaluate properly the available labor institutions for these relationships. Moreover, it is difficult to argue that public-sector unions are purely rent-seeking organizations. As Blank (1994) documents, the public/private sector wage ratio has been

[54] See Eberts (2007) for a general discussion of the role of teacher unions in education.

[55] See Chay (1998), Oyer and Schaefer (2002), and Jolls and Prescott (2004) for studies of the labor-market impact of legislation to protect civil rights and disabled individuals.

falling in the United States, even while private-sector unionization has been falling. If unions were the main source of wage growth for workers, then we should observe the opposite. We do not have definite answers to any of these questions, and hence there is much room for further research.

5. DISCUSSION

There is a remarkable consensus that increased employment protection law tends to reduce employment for individuals with less attachment to the labor market. Increases in employment protection law tend to adversely affect matches at the margin. That being said, the economics research uses a relatively crude representation of the law. We know virtually nothing about how specific legal rules interact with different types of worker-firm matches.

At a policy level, employment protection entails changes to specific rules, such as the number of days' notice for a dismissal, mandatory dismissal payments, and specification of the conditions under which a protected employee may be dismissed. At the moment, policymakers have little guidance on how to set these parameters, aside from the blanket recommendation to reduce them all.

Our discussion of the law illustrates that rules evolve in response to specific issues that need to be addressed in the labor market. In the case of common law rules, as in the United States or United Kingdom, a judge may create law in response to a specific set of facts, yet this new law affects all matches. This process is not well understood. The benefit of common-law rule making is that it usually restricts itself to the bounds of particular cases, and therefore is not speculative. However, though judges are aware and are certainly concerned with the broad impact that a decision may have, there is no systematic feedback mechanism for evaluating the consequences of these rule changes.[56]

In a global context, we see a great deal of competition between different legal systems. Firms may opt out of the courts completely by relying upon mandatory arbitration. However, arbitration courts are increasingly looking like public courts, where there is a long process of deposing witnesses and presentation of volumes of evidence before a decision is reached. More generally, all adjudication systems consist of evidence-collection and decision-making that complement the employment practices used by a firm. We need to better understand the substantive role that these courts play in the complex problem of managing human resources.[57] The literature on employment law has focused on turnover costs. Yet, the discussions of both the law and the literature on transaction costs suggest that information costs are key to understanding the role that the courts play in handling disputes.

---

[56] See Krueger (1991), who suggests that the most important feature of the law for private parties is predictability.

[57] See the chapters by Rebitzer and Taylor (2011) and Van Reenen (2010) on human resource management.

In addition, the focus on turnover costs fails to deal with the selective nature of court decisions. The courts are a venue of last resort for a party who feels that another party has breached a duty. This implies that the law is not applied equally to all individuals. All contracts in the United States are subject to the rule of good faith and fair dealing, which is meant to protect individuals from others, such as managers who blatantly breach their obligations. An issue that is rarely addressed in the economics literature is the extent to which we need courts to protect individuals who face poor treatment from bad managers.[58] The law, and employment law in particular, exists to deal with specific extreme cases, and not the average employment relationship. In contrast, empirical research on employment law is focused on the average effect.

In this chapter, unions and labor law are discussed as alternative governance structures that may enhance the management of the employment relationship. In theory, allocating more power to workers can be efficiency-enhancing when they have private information that can impact match quality. The difficulty is that such power also results in more rent extraction by workers. The existing evidence is consistent with the hypothesis that union power leads to lower profits for firms. There is also mixed evidence regarding whether or not unions enhance match quality. Unions, like managers, are likely to vary in their ability to strike efficient agreements. Hence, we should not be surprised that there is mixed evidence regarding their effects on match quality. The theory suggests that the rise and fall of unions in the private sector can be explained by the extent to which unions enhance the productive efficiency of firms. At the moment we simply do not have any evidence that explains the observed pattern.[59]

Finally, I have characterized elsewhere the literature on employment law as consisting of *three solitudes* (see MacLeod (2007b)), namely, that the law, the economic theory of contract, and empirical labor economics each has its own aesthetic and group of scholars that have developed for the most part independently of each other. One reason for this is that the law evolved to deal with the pragmatic issue of how to govern the exchange relationship before the analytic tools were in place to study these phenomena. We can view the existing structure of the law as evidence that the central ingredients of contract theory—the insurance motive, asymmetric information and incomplete contracts—are empirically relevant concepts, though we do not know to what extent they provide the best unifying framework.

Ensuring that the economic theory of contract is empirically relevant is not helped by the fact that the theory evolved out of the need to extend the reach of general equilibrium theory, which itself developed from the mathematically sophisticated models of Arrow (1951) and Debreu (1959). The important work of Hart (1975) illustrates a fundamental shortcoming of this approach and shows that when markets are incomplete we cannot

---

[58] For example, Sullivan and von Wachter (2009) show that job loss leads to measurable declines in health; hence, there are real costs for workers who invest in a long-term match with a poor employer.

[59] See Farber and Western (2001) for an explanation for the decline.

expect competitive equilibria to achieve an efficient outcome. This work illustrates that simply extending the model of general equilibrium to deal with incomplete markets is not likely to be a fruitful path.

As discussed in Section 3, the subsequent literature on game theory and mechanism design developed a theory that is much more specific to the nature of individual transactions, and allows one to link transactions costs to the observed structure of employment contracts.[60] The fact that the law has a long and rich history with its own mode of thought and language has made it difficult to link these abstract models of contract theory to legal practice. The work of Williamson (1975) appeared before much of modern contract theory was developed, and hence his analysis has roots in the legal tradition. As a consequence, his work develops a language that has been influential in introducing the notion of a transaction cost to law and economics, though at the cost of making it very difficult for the scholar schooled in modern theory to tease out the empirical implications of the theory.

In contrast, the third solitude of empirical labor economics uses the model of a competitive market as developed by Marshall (1948) and Samuelson (1947) to successfully organize vast quantities of data on employment and wages, as we can see in the first three volumes of the *Handbook of Labor Economics*. The goal of the empirical literature reviewed in Section 4 is to establish a causal link between changes in law and the union status of workers and the change in employment and wages. Such identification is more credible the closer it is to approximating the treatment-control paradigm that is widely used in science. Hence, there is a bias in this literature towards studying changes that occur over fairly short time periods.[61] Yet the economic theory of contract highlights the fact that individuals enter into agreements because they expect that these relationships will be rewarding in the future, sometimes the distant future. The temporal distance between cause and effect makes it very difficult to explore the implications of these models.

The essence of a contract is that we voluntarily give up freedom of action in the expectation that this reduction will make us better off. It is a fact of life that these great expectations are often dashed, requiring changes to our plans. The history of employment and labor law can be viewed as a sequence of changes that were brought about in the expectation of improving the lives of workers in the long run. We certainly need better ways to measure and evaluate these expectations, so that we may find the optimal trade-off between opportunities of the moment and those that require durable investment and commitment. There is a growing literature that is beginning to explore these issues and the interplay between law and long term outcomes. Harrison and Scorse (2010) explore the effect of anti-sweatshop campaigns and find that they lead to higher

---

[60] See in particular the recent books by Laffont and Maritmort (2002) and Bolton and Dewatripont (2005).

[61] See Lemieux and MacLeod (2000) for a study where we show that previous studies could not properly identify the effect of unemployment insurance parameters because they ignore learning effects that take many years to work their way through the system.

wages, with little employment lost. Fiess et al. (2010) explore the impact of informal labor markets upon growth.

Finally, Sullivan and von Wachter (2009) show that job loss leads to higher worker mortality. This research is very important because it illustrates why the pecuniary costs and benefits of job loss cannot fully capture the effect of job loss upon individual well being. This can help explain why employment and labor law have for centuries played such an important role in civil society, and why we need more research on the interplay between law, employment contracts, and labor market performance.

REFERENCES

Abowd, J.M., 1989. The effect of wage bargains on the stock-market value of the firm. American Economic Review 79, 774–800.

Acemoglu, D., Pischke, J.-S., 1998. Why do firms train? Theory and evidence. Quarterly Journal of Economics 113, 79–119.

Acemoglu, D., Pischke, J.-S., 1999. The structure of wages and investment in general training. Journal of Political Economy 107, 539–572.

Acemoglu, D., Shimer, R., 1999. Efficient unemployment insurance. Journal of Political Economy 107, 893–928.

Addison, Teixeira, Grosso, 2000. The effect of dismissals protection on employment: more on a vexed theme. Southern Economic Journal 67, 105–122.

Aghion, E.A., 2008. The unequal effects of liberalization: evidence from dismantling the license Raj in India. American Economic Review 98, 1397–1412.

Aghion, P., Dewatripont, M., Rey, P., 1994. Renegotiation design with unverifiable information. Econometrica 62, 257–282.

Aghion, P., Hermalin, B., 1990. Legal restrictions on private contracts can enhance efficiency. Journal of Law, Economics, and Organization 6, 381–409.

Aghion, P., Tirole, J., 1997. Formal and real authority in organizations. Journal of Political Economy 105, 1–29.

Ahsan, Pages, 2009. Are all labor regulations equal? Evidence from Indian manufacturing. Journal of Comparative Economics 37, 62–75.

Akerlof, G.A., 1982. Labor exchange as partial gift exchange. Quarterly Journal of Economics 97, 543–569.

Alchian, A., Demsetz, H., 1972. Production, information costs, and economic organization. American Economic Review 62, 777–795.

Allen, 1984. Unionized construction workers are more productive. Quarterly Journal of Economics 99, 251–274.

Allen, S.G., 1986. The effect of unionism on productivity in privately and publicly owned hospitals and nursing-homes. Journal of Labor Research 7, 59–68.

Altonji, J.G., Blank, R.M., 1999. Race and gender in the labor market. In: Ashenfelter, O., Card, D. (Eds.), Handbook of Labor Economics, vol. 3C. North-Holland, Amsterdam, pp. 3143–3260.

Amin, 2009. Labor regulation and employment in India's retail stores. Journal of Comparative Economics 37, 47–61.

Andreoni, J., Sprenger, C., 2010a. Estimating time preferences from convex budgets. Tech. Rep. University of California, San Diego.

Andreoni, J., Sprenger, C., 2010b. Risk preferences are not time preferences. Tech. Rep. University of California, San Diego.

Angrist, J.D., Imbens, G.W., Rubin, D.B., 1996. Identification of causal effects using instrumental variables. Journal of the American Statistical Association 91, 444–455.

Aoki, M., 2001. Towards a Comparative Institutional Analysis. MIT Press, Cambridge, MA.

Arrow, K.J., 1951. An extension of the basic welfare theorems of classical welfare economics. In: Neyman, J. (Ed.), Proceedings of the Second Berkeley Symposium on Mathematical Statistics and Probability. University of California Press, Berkeley, California, pp. 507–532.

Ashenfelter, O., Johnson, G.E., 1969. Bargaining theory, trade unions, and industrial strike activity. American Economic Review 59, 35–49.

Autor, D.H., 2001. Why do temporary help firms provide free general skills training? Quarterly Journal of Economics 116, 1409–1448.

Autor, D.H., 2003. Outsourcing at will: the contribution of unjust dismissal doctrine to the growth of employment outsourcing. Journal of Labor Economics 21, 1–42.

Autor, D.H., Donohue, J.J., Schwab, S.J., 2004. The employment consequences of wrongful-discharge laws: large, small, or none at all? American Economic Review 94, 440–446.

Autor, D.H., Donohue, J.J., Schwab, S.J., 2006. The costs of wrongful-discharge laws. Forthcoming Review of Economics and Statistcs 88, 211–231.

Autor, D.H., Kerr, W.R., Kugler, A.D., 2007. Does employment protection reduce productivity? Evidence from US States. The Economic Journal 117, F189–F213.

Azariadis, C., 1975. Implicit contracts and underemployment equilibria. Journal of Political Economy 83, 1183–1202.

Baily, M.N., 1974. Wages and employment under uncertain demand. Review of Economic Studies 41, 37–50.

Baker, T., 2003. Insurance Law and Policy. Aspen Publishers.

Beaudry, P., DiNardo, J., 1991. The effect of implicit contracts on the movement of wages over the business cycle: evidence from micro data. Journal of Political Economy 99, 665–688.

Becker, Olson, 1990. The effects of the NLRA on stockholder wealth in the 1930s. Industrial & Labor Relations Review 44, 116–129.

Becker, Olson, 1992. Unions and firm profits. Industrial Relations 31, 395–416.

Becker, G., 1962. Investment in human capital: a theoretical analysis. Journal of Political Economy 70, 9–49.

Bemmels, B., 1987. How unions affect productivity in manufacturing plant. Industrial & Labor Relations Review 40, 241–253.

Bentolila, S., Bertola, G., 1990. Firing costs and labour demand: how bad is eurosclerosis? Review of Economic Studies 57, 381–402.

Bertrand, M., Duflo, E., Mullainathan, S., 2004. How much should we trust differences-in-differences estimates? Quarterly Journal of Economics 119, 249–275.

Besley, T., Burgess, R., 2004. Can labor regulation hinder economic performance? Evidence from India. Quarterly Journal of Economics 119, 91–134.

Bewley, T.F., 1999. Why Wages don't Fall during a Recession. Harvard University Press, Cambridge and London.

Bird, R.C., Knopf, J.D., 2009. Do wrongful-discharge laws impair firm performance? Journal of Law & Economics 52, 197–222.

Black, S.E., Lynch, L.M., 2001. How to compete: the impact of workplace practices and information technology on productivity. Review of Economics and Statistics 83, 434–445.

Blanchard, Wolfers, 2000. The role of shocks and institutions in the rise of European unemployment: the aggregate evidence. Economic Journal 119, 1339–1382.

Blanchard, O.J., Tirole, J., 2008. The joint design of unemployment insurance and employment protection: a first pass. Journal of the European Economic Association 6, 45–77.

Blank, R.M., 1994. Public sector growth and labor market flexibility: the United States vs. the United Kingdom. In: Social Protection Versus Economic Flexibiolity: Is there a Trade-off? University of Chicago Press.

Blanpain, R., 2003. European Labour Law, 9th and rev. ed., Kluwer Law International, The Hague, Boston.

Blau, F., Kahn, L., 1999. Institutions and laws in the labor market. In: Ashenfelter, O., Card, D. (Eds.), Handbook of Labor Economics, vol. 3A. North-Holland, Amsterdam, pp. 1399–1461.

Blinder, A.S., Choi, D.H., 1990. A shred of evidence on theories of wage stickiness. Quarterly Journal of Economics 105, 1003–1015.

Bloch, M., 1961. Feudal Society, Routledge & Kegan Paul.

Bloom, Nicholas, Van Reenen, John, 2011. Human resource management and productivity. In: Ashenfelter, Orley, Card, David (Eds.), Handbook of Labor Economics, vol. 4b. Elsevier, pp. 1697–1767.

Bolton, P., Dewatripont, M., 2005. Contract Theory. MIT Press, Cambridge, MA.

Botero, J.C., Djankov, S., La Porta, R., Lopez-de Silanes, F., Shleifer, A., 2004. The regulation of labor. Quarterly Journal of Economics 119, 1339–1382.

Breiman, L., 2001. Statistical modeling: the two cultures. Statistical Science 16, 199–215.

Breyer, S., 2009. Economic reasoning and judicial review. Economic Journal 119, F135–F215.

Bronars, S., Deere, D., 1994. Unionization and profitability — evidence of spillover effects. Journal of Political Economy 102, 1281–1287.

Bronars, S.G., Deere, D.R., 1990. Union representation elections and firm profitability. Industrial Relations 29, 15–37.

Brown, C., Medoff, J.L., 1978. Trade unions in the production process. Journal of Political Economy 86, 355–378.

Burguet, R., Caminal, R., 2008. Does the market provide sufficient employment protection? Labour Economics 15, 406–422.

Byrne, D., Dezhbakhsh, H., King, R., 1996. Unions and police productivity: an econometric investigation. Industrial Relations 35, 566–584.

Caballero, R.J., Cowan, K.N., Engel, E.M., Micco, A., 2004. Effective Labor Regulation and Microeconomic Flexibility. NBER Working Paper No. 10744.

Cahuc, P., Postel-Vinay, F., Robin, J., 2006. Wage bargaining with on-the-job search: theory and evidence. Econometrica 74, 323–364.

Card, D., 1986. Efficient contracts with costly adjustment: short-run employment determination for airline mechanics. American Economic Review 76, 1045–1071.

Card, D., Hyslop, D., 1997. Does inflation 'grease the wheels of the labor market'? In: Romer, C.D., Romer, D.H. (Eds.), Reducing Inflation: Motivation and Strategy. University of Chicago Press, Chicago, IL.

Card, D., Devicienti, F., Maida, A., 2010. Rent-sharing, holdup, and wages: evidence from matched panel data. NBER Working Paper 16192.

Carmichael, H.L., MacLeod, W.B., 2003. Caring about sunk costs: a behavioral solution to hold-up problems with small stakes. Journal of Law, Economics and Organization 19, 106–118.

Chakravarty, S., MacLeod, W.B., 2009. Contracting in the shadow of the law. Rand Journal of Economics 40, 533–557.

Chay, K.Y., 1998. The impact of federal civil rights policy on black economic progress: evidence from the equal employment opportunity act of 1972. Industrial and Labor Relations Review 51, 608–632.

Che, Y.-K., Hausch, D.B., 1999. Cooperative investments and the value of contracting. American Economic Review 89, 125–147.

Chiappori, P.-A., Salanié, B., Valentin, J., 1999. Early starters versus late beginners. Journal of Political Economy 107, 731–760.

Clark, K.B., 1980a. The impact of unionization on productivity — a case-study. Industrial & Labor Relations Review 33, 451–469.

Clark, K.B., 1980b. Unionization and productivity — micro-econometric evidence. Quarterly Journal of Economics 95, 613–639.

Clark, K.B., 1984. Unionization and firm performance — the impact on profits, growth, and productivity. American Economic Review 74, 893–919.

Coase, R., 1937. The nature of the firm. Economica 4, 386–405.

Cochrane, J.H., 1991. A simple test of consumption insurance. The Journal of Political Economy 99, 957–976.

Cooke, W.N., 1994. Employee participation programs, group-based incentives, company performance — a union-nonunion comparison. Industrial & Labor Relations Review 47, 594–609.

Cousineau, J.-M., Lacroix, R., Bilodeau, D., 1983. The determination of escalator clauses in collective agreements. Review of Economics and Statistics 65, 196–202.

Crawford, V.P., 1982. A theory of disagreement in bargaining. Econometrica 50, 607–637.

Crawford, V.P., 1988. Long-term relationships governed by short-term contracts. The American Economic Review 78 (3), 485–499.

de Barros, P., Corseuil, 2004. The impact of regulations on Brazilian labor market performance. In: Law and Employment: Lessons from Latin America and the Caribbean. The University of Chicago Press.

Debreu, G., 1959. Theory of Value. Yale University Press, New Haven, CT.

Dessein, W., 2002. Authority and communication in organizations. Review of Economic Studies 69, 811–838.

Di Tella, R., MacCulloch, R., 2005. The consequences of labor market flexibility: panel evidence based on survey data. European Economic Review 49, 1225–1259.

Diamond, P.A., Maskin, E., 1979. An equilibrium analysis of search and breach of contract, I: steady states. Bell Journal of Economics 10, 282–316.

DiNardo, J., Lee, D.S., 2004. Economic impacts of new unionization on private sector employers: 1984–2001. Quarterly Journal of Economics 119, 1383–1441.

Djankov, S., Hart, O., McLiesh, C., Shleifer, A., 2008. Debt enforcement around the world. Journal of Political Economy 116, 1105–1150.

Djankov, S., La Porta, R., Lopez-de Silanes, F., Shleifer, A., 2003. Courts. Quarterly Journal of Economics 118, 453–517.

Djankov, S., Ramalho, R., 2009. Employment laws in developing countries. Journal of Comparative Economics 37, 3–13.

Doucouliagos, C., Laroche, P., 2003. What do Unions do to productivity? A meta-analysis. Industrial Relations 42, 650–691.

Doucouliagos, H., Laroche, P., 2009. Unions and profits: a meta-regression analysis. Industrial Relations 48, 146–184.

Downes, E.A., 2004. Labor market regulation and employment in the Caribbean. In: Law and Employment: Lessons from Latin America and the Caribbean. The University of Chicago Press.

Dunford, B.B., Devin, D.J., 1998. Employment at-will and employee discharge: a justive perspective on legal action following termination. Personnel Psychology 51, 903–934.

Dye, R.A., 1985. Optimal length of labor contracts. International Economic Review 26, 251–270.

Eberts, R., Stone, J.A., 1987. Teacher unions and the productivity of public schools. Industrial & Labor Relations Review 40, 354–363.

Eberts, R.W., 2007. Teachers unions and student performance: help or hindrance? Future of Children 17, 175–200.

Ehrenberg, R.G., Sherman, D., Schwartz, J., 1983. Unions and productivity in the public sector: a study of municipal libraries. Industrial & Labor Relations Review 36, 199–213.

Ehrlich, I., Posner, R.A., 1974. An economic analysis of legal rulemaking. The Journal of Legal Studies 3, 257–286.

Elmeskov, Martin S., 1998. Key lessons for labour market reforms: evidence from OECD countries' experience. Swedish Economic Policy Review 5.

Epstein, R.A., 1984. In defense of the contract at will. The University of Chicago Law Review 51, 947–982.

Eslava, E.A., 2004. The effects of structural reforms on productivity- and profitability-enhancing reallocation: evidence from Colombia. Journal of Development Economics 75, 333–371.

Farber, H.S., Western, B., 2001. Accounting for the decline of unions in the private sector, 1973–98. Journal of Labor Research 22, 459–485.

Feess, E., Muehlheusser, G., 2002. Economic consequences of transfer fee regulations in European football. European Journal of Law and Economics 13, 221–237.

Fehr, E., Schmidt, K.M., 1999. A theory of fairness, competition, and cooperation. Quarterly Journal of Economics 114, 817–868.

Feinman, J.M., 1978. The development of the employment at will rule. American Journal of Legal History 20, 118–135.

Feldmann, H., 2008. Business regulation and labor market performance around the world. Journal of Regulatory Economics 33, 201–235.

Feldmann, H., 2009. The unemployment effects of labor regulation around the world. Journal of Comparative Economics 37, 76–90.

Fiess, N.M., Fugazza, M., Maloney, W.F., 2010. Informal self-employment and macroeconomic fluctuations. Journal of Development Economics 91, 211–226.

Freeman,, 2002. Institutional Differences and Economic Performance Among OECD Countries. CEP Discussion Papers.

Freeman, R.D., Medoff, J.L., 1984. What do Unions do? Basic Books, New York, NY.

Friedman, M., 1962. Capitalism and Freedom. University of Chicago Press, Chicago, with the assistance of Rose D. Friedman. 23 cm.

Fuchs, W., 2006. Contracting with repeated moral hazard and private evaluations. Tech. Rep. University of Chicago, Chicago.

Fuller, L.L., Perdue Jr., William R., 1936. The reliance interest in contract damages: 1. The Yale Law Journal 46, 52–96.

Garibaldi, M., 1999. Deconstructing job creation. IMF Working Paper No. 99/109.

Gibbons, R., 1987. Piece rate incentive schemes. Journal of Labor Economics 5, 413–429.

Gibbons, R., 1997. Incentives and careers in organizations. In: Kreps, D.M., Wallis, K.F. (Eds.), Advances in Economics and Econometrics: Theory and Applications. Cambridge University Press, Cambridge, UK, pp. 1–37.

Gibbons, R., Katz, L.F., 1991. Layoffs and lemons. Journal of Labor Economics 9, 351–380.

Gibbons, R., Katz, L.F., Lemieux, T., Parent, D., 2005. Comparative advantage, learning, and sectoral wage determination. Journal of Labor Economics 23, 681–723.

Goetz, C.J., Scott, R.E., 1980. Enforcing promises: an examination of the basis of contract. Yale Law Journal 89, 1261–1322.

Goldberg, V.P., 1976. Regulation and administered contracts. Bell Journal of Economics 7, 426–448.

Gould IV, W.B., 2004. A Primer on American Labor Law. MIT Press.

Greif, A., 1989. Reputation and coalitions in medieval trade — evidence on the Maghribi traders. Journal of Economic History 49, 857–882. times Cited: 79.

Grossman, S.J., Hart, O.D., 1981. Implicit contracts, moral hazard, unemployment. American Economic Review 71, 301–307.

Grossman, S.J., Hart, O.D., 1986. The costs and benefits of ownership: a theory of vertical and lateral integration. Journal of Political Economy 94, 691–719.

Grout, P., 1984. Investment and wages in the absence of binding contracts: a Nash bargaining approach. Econometrica 52, 449–460.

Grubb, Wells, 1993. Employment regulation and patterns of work in EC countries. OECD Economic Studies 21.

Guerrieri, V., 2008. Inefficient unemployment dynamics under asymmetric information. Journal of Political Economy 116, 667–708.

Hall, R.E., Lazear, E.P., 1984. The excess sensitivity of layoffs and quits to demand. Journal of Labor Economics 2, 233–257.

Hardin, G., 1968. Tragedy of commons. Science 162, 1243–1248.

Harris, M., Holmström, B., 1982. A theory of wage dynamics. Review of Economic Studies 49, 315–333.

Harrison, A., Scorse, J., 2010. Multinationals and anti-sweatshop activism. American Economic Review.

Hart, O., 1975. On the optimality of equilibrium when the market structure is incomplete. Journal of Economics Theory 11, 418–443.

Hart, O.D., 1995. Firms, Contracts and Financial Structure. Oxford University Press, Oxford, UK.

Hart, O.D., Holmström, B., 1987. The theory of contracts. In: Bewley, T. (Ed.), Advances in Economic Theory: Fifth World Congress. Cambridge University Press, Cambridge, UK, pp. 71–155.

Hart, O.D., Moore, J., 1988. Incomplete contracts and renegotiation. Econometrica 56, 755–785.

Hart, O.D., Moore, J., 2004. Agreeing now to agree later: contracts that rule out but do not rule in. Tech. Rep. 10397. NBER, Cambridge, MA.

Hashimoto, M., 1981. Firm specific capital as a shared investment. American Economic Review 71, 475–482.

Heckman, J.J., Pagés, C., 2000. The cost of job security regulation: evidence from Latin American labor markets. Economia 1, 109–154.

Hirsch, B.T., 1991. Union coverage and profitability among US firms. Review of Economics and Statistics 73, 69–77.

Hirsch, B.T., Connolly, R., 1987. Do unions capture monopoly profits? Industrial & Labor Relations Review 41, 118–136.

Holland, P.W., 1986. Statistics and causal inference. Journal of the American Statistical Association 81, 945–960.

Holmes Jr., O.W., 1881. The Common Law. Little, Brown, Boston, MA.

Hopenhayn, H., Nicolini, J., 1997. Optimal unemployment insurance. Journal of Political Economy 105, 412–438.

Hopenhayn, H., Rogerson, R., 1993. Job turnover and policy evaluation: a general equilibrium analysis. Journal of Political Economy 101, 915–938.

Howitt, P., 2002. Looking inside the labor market: a review article. Journal of Economic Literature 40, 125–138. tY - JOUR Accession Number: 0603937. Geographic Descriptors: US. Publication Type: Journal Article. Update Code: 200205.

Ichinowski, C., Shaw, K., 2003. Beyond incentive pay: insiders' estimates of the value of complementary human resource management practices. Journal of Economic Perspectives 17, 155–180.

Imbens, G.W., Lemieux, T., 2008. Regression discontinuity designs: a guide to practice. Journal of Econometrics 142, 615–635.

Imbens, G.W., Wooldridge, J.M., 2009. Recent developments in the econometrics of program evaluation. Journal of Economic Literature 47, 5–86.

Jackson, M.O., 2001. Mechanism theory. In: The Encyclopedia of Life Support Systems.

Jensen, M., Meckling, W., 1976. Theory of the firm: managerial behavior, agency costs and ownership structure. Journal of Financial Economics 3, 305–360.

Johnson, S., McMillan, J., Woodruff, C., 2002. Courts and relational contracts. Journal of Law, Economics, and Organization 18, 221–277.

Jolls, C., 2007. Employment law. In: Polinsky, A.M., Shavell, S. (Eds.), Handbook of Law and Economics, vol. 2. Elsevier, Amsterdam, The Netherlands (chapter 17).

Jolls, C., Prescott, J.J., 2004. Disaggregating employment protection: the case of disability discrimination. Tech. Rep. National Bureau of Economic Research, Cambridge, MA.

Joskow, P.L., 1988. Price adjustment in long-term-contracts—the case of coal. Journal of Law & Economics 31, 47–83.

Kahn, L.M., 2010. Employment protection reforms, employment and the incidence of temporary jobs in Europe: 1996–2001. Labour Economics 17, 1–15.

Kanemoto, Y., MacLeod, W.B., 1992. The ratchet effect and the market for second hand workers. Journal of Labor Economics 10, 85–92.

Kaplan, D., 2009. Job creation and labor reform in Latin America. Journal of Comparative Economics 37, 91–105.

Kessler, D.P., Rubinfeld, D.L., 2007. Empirical study of the civil justice system. In: Polinsky, A.M., Shavell, S. (Eds.), Handbook of Law and Economics, vol. I. Elsevier B. V, Oxford, UK.

Kornhauser, L., MacLeod, W.B., 2010. Contracts between legal persons. In: Gibbons, R., Roberts, J. (Eds.), Handbook of Organizational Economics. Princeton University Press.

Krueger, A., Mas, A., 2004. Strikes, scabs, and tread separations: labor strife and the production of defective Bridgestone/Firestone tires. Journal of Political Economy 112, 253–289.

Krueger, A.B., 1991. The evolution of unjust-dismissal legislation in the United States. Industrial and Labor Relations Review 44, 644–660.

Kugler, A., 2004a. The effect of job security regulations on labor market flexibility: evidence from the Colombian labor market reform. In: Heckman, J.J., Pags, C. (Eds.), Law and Employment: Lessons from Latin American and the Caribbean. The University of Chicago Press, Chicago.

Kugler, A., 2005. Wage-shifting effects of severance payments savings accounts in Colombia. Journal of Public Economics 89, 487–500.

Kugler, A.D., 1999. The impact of firing costs on turnover and unemployment: evidence from the Colombian labour market reform. International Tax and Public Finance 6, 389–410.

Kugler, A.D., 2004b. How do firing costs affect worker flows in a world with adverse selection? Journal of Labor Economics 22, 553–584.

Kuhn, P., 1992. Mandatory notice. Journal of Labor Economics 10, 117–137.

Kuhn, P., 1998. Unions and the economy: what we know; what we should know. Canadian Journal of Economics-Revue Canadienne D'Economique 31, 1033–1056.

Kuhn, P., Robert, J., 1989. Seniority and distribution in a 2-worker trade union. Quarterly Journal of Economics 104, 485–505.

La Porta, R., Lopez-de Silanes, F., Shleifer, A., 2008. The economic consequences of legal origins. Journal of Economics Literature 46, 285–332.

Laffont, J.-J., Maritmort, D., 2002. The Theory of Incentives. Princeton University Press, Pinceton, NJ.

Laing, D., 1994. Involuntary layoffs in a model with asymmetric information concerning worker ability. Review of Economic Studies 61, 375–392.

Lazear, E.P., 1990. Job security provisions and employment. Quarterly Journal of Economics 105, 699–726.

Lee, D.S., Lemieux, T., 2009. Regression discontinuity designs in economics. Tech. Rep. 14723. NBER, Cambridge, MA.

Lee, D.S., Mas, A., 2009. Long-run impacts of unions on firms: new evidence from financial markets, 1961-19991. Tech. Rep. 14709. Princeton University, Cambridge, MA.

Lee, D.S., McCrary, J., 2005. Crime, punishment, and myopia. Tech. Rep. 11491. NBER, Cambridge, MA.

Lemieux, T., MacLeod, W.B., 2000. Supply side hysteresis: the case of the Canadian unemployment insurance system. Journal of Public Economics 78, 139–170.

Levin, J., 2003. Relational incentive contacts. American Economic Review 93, 835–857.

Levine, D.I., 1991. Just-cause employment policies in the presence of worker adverse selection. Journal of Labor Economics 9, 294–305.

Lovell, Sickles, Warren, 1988. The effect of unionization on labor productivity: some additional evidence. Journal of Labor Research 9, 55–63.

Lovenheim, M.F., 2009. The effect of teachers' unions on education production: evidence from union election certifications in three midwestern states. Journal of Labor Economics 27, 525–587.

Machin, S., 1991. The productivity effects of unionization and firm size in British engineering firms. Economica 58, 479–490.

Machin, S., 2000. Union decline in Britain. British Journal of Industrial Relations 38, 631–645.

MacLeod, W.B., 2003. Optimal contracting with subjective evaluation. American Economic Review 93, 216–240.

MacLeod, W.B., 2005. Regulation or markets? The case of employment contracts. Cesifo Economic Studies 51, 1–46.

MacLeod, W.B., 2007a. Reputations, relationships and contract enforcement. Journal of Economics Literature XLV, 597–630.

MacLeod, W.B., 2007b. Three solitudes in contract: law, data, and theory. Scottish Journal of Political Economy 54, 606–616.

MacLeod, W.B., Malcomson, J.M., 1989. Implicit contracts, incentive compatibility, and involuntary unemployment. Econometrica 57, 447–480.

MacLeod, W.B., Malcomson, J.M., 1993. Investments, holdup, and the form of market contracts. American Economic Review 83, 811–837.

MacLeod, W.B., Nakavachara, V., 2007. Legal default rules: the case of wrongful discharge laws. Economic Journal 117, F1–F62.

MacNeil, I.R., 1974. The many futures of contracts. Southern California Law Review 47, 691–816.

Marshall, A., 1948. The Principles of Economics. Macmillan, New York, NY.

Mas, A., 2006. Pay, reference points, and police performance. Quarterly Journal of Economics 121, 783–821.

Mas, A., 2008. Labour unrest and the quality of production: evidence from the construction equipment resale market. Review of Economic Studies 75, 229–258.

Matouschek, N., Ramezzana, P., Robert-Nicoud, F., 2009. Labor market reforms, job instability, and the flexibility of the employment relationship. European Economic Review 53, 19–36.

McDonald, I.M., Solow, R.M., 1981. Wage bargaining and employment. American Economic Review 71, 896–908.

McLaughlin, K., 1994. Rigid wages. Journal of Monetary Economics 34, 383–414.

Miles, T.J., 2000. Common law exceptions to employment at will and US labor markets. Journal of Law Economics & Organization 16, 74–101.

Milgrom, P., 1988. Employment contracts, influence actitivities, and efficient organizational design. Journal of Political Economy 96, 42–60.

Mincer, J., 1962. On-the-job training: cost, returns and some implications. Journal of Political Economy 70, 50–79.

Mitchell, M.W., Stone, J.A., 1992. Union effects on productivity — evidence from western United States sawmills. Industrial & Labor Relations Review 46, 135–145.

Mondino, Montoya, 2004. The effects of labor market regulations on employment decisions by firms: empirical evidence for Argentina. In: Law and Employment: Lessons from Latin America and the Caribbean. The University of Chicago Press.

Montenegro, C.E., Pagés, C., 2004. Who benefits from labor market regulations? Chile 1960-1998. In: Heckman, James J., Pagés, Carmen (Eds.), Law and Employment: Lessons from Latin America and the Caribbean. The University of Chicago Press, Chicago, IL, pp. 401–434.

Moore, J., Repullo, R., 1988. Subgame perfect implementation. Econometrica 56, 1191–1220.

Moore, J.H., 1985. Optimal labour contracts when workers have a variety of privately observed reservation wages. Review of Economic Studies 52, 37–67.

Morriss, A.P., 1995–1996. Bad data, bad economics, and bad policy: time to fire wrongful discharge law. University of Texas Law Review 74, 1901.

Myerson, R.B., Satterthwaite, M.A., 1983. Efficient mechanisms for bilateral trading. Journal of Economic Theory 29, 265–281.

Naidu, S., Yuchtman, N., 2009. How Green was my Valley? Coercive contract enforcement in 19th century industrial Britain. Tech. Rep. Havard University.

Nickell, S., 1997. Unemployment and labor market rigidities: Europe versus North America. Journal of Economic Perspectives 11 (3), 55–74.

Nicoletti, G., Scarpetta, S., Lane, P., 2003. Regulation, productivity and growth—OECD evidence. Economic Policy.

OECD, 1993. Employment Outlook. OECD.

OECD, 1994. The Jobs Study: Evidence and Explanations. OECD, Paris, France.

OECD, 1996. Employment Outlook. OECD, Paris, France.

OECD, 1999. Employment Outlook. OECD, Paris, France.

OECD, 2003. Employment Outlook. OECD, Paris, France.

Ostrom, E., 2000. Collective action and the evolution of social norms. Journal of Economic Perspectives 14, 137–158.

Oyer, P., Schaefer, S., 2002. Litigation costs and returns to experience. American Economic Review 92, 683–705.

Oyer, P., Schaefer, S., 2011. Personnel economics: hiring and incentives. In: Ashenfelter, Orley, Card, David (Eds.), Handbook of Labor Economics, vol. 4b. Elsevier, pp. 1769–1823.

Pagés, C., Montenegro, C.E., 2007. Job security and the age-composition of employment: evidence from Chile. Estudios de Economia 34 (2), 109–139.

Pauly, M.V., 1968. The economics of moral hazard. American Economics Review 58, 531–537.

Peierls, R.E., 1960. Wolfgang Ernst Pauli. 1900–1958. Biographical Memoirs of Fellows of the Royal Society 5, 175–192.

Pissarides, C.A., 2001. Employment protection. Labour Economics 8, 131–159.

Posner, R., 2008. How Judges Think. Harvard University Press.

Posner, R.A., 1974. Theories of economic regulation. The Bell Journal of Economics and Management Science 5, 335–358. fLA 00058556 American Telephone and Telegraph Company Copyright 1970 American Telephone and Telegraph Company.

Posner, R.A., 2003. Economic Analysis of Law, 6th ed., Little, Brown and Company, Boston, USA.

Postel-Vinay, F., Robin, J., 2002. Equilibrium wage dispersion with worker and employer heterogeneity. Econometrica 70, 2295–2350.

Pries, M., Rogerson, R., 2005. Hiring policies, labor market institutions, and labor market flows. Journal of Political Economy 113, 811–839.

Rebitzer, J.B., Taylor, L.J., 2011. Extrinsic rewards and intrinsic motives: standard and behavioral approaches to agency and labor markets. In: Ashenfelter, Orley, Card, David (Eds.), Handbook of Labor Economics, vol. 4a. Elsevier, pp. 701–772.

Rogerson, R., Shimer, R., Wright, R., 2005. Search-theoretic models of the labor market: a survey. Journal of Economic Literature 43, 959–988.

Rogerson, W.P., 1984. Efficient reliance and damage measures for breach of contract. RAND Journal of Economics 15, 39–53.

Rogerson, W.P., 1992. Contractual solutions to the hold-up problem. Review of Economic Studies 59, 777–793.

Rosen, S., 1985. Implicit contracts: a survey. Journal of Economic Literature 23, 1144–1175.

Rothstein, M.A., Liebman, L., 2003. Employment Law. Thomson West, New York, NY.

Ruback, R.S., Zimmerman, M.B., 1984. Unionization and profitability: evidence from the capital market. Journal of Political Economy 92, 1134–1157.

Saavedra, J., Torero, M., 2004. Labor market reforms and their impact on formal labor demand and job market turnover: the case of Peru. In: Law and Employment: Lessons from Latin America and the Caribbean. The University of Chicago Press.

Salinger, 1984. Tobin's q, unionization, and the concentration-profits relationship. The RAND Journal of Economics 15, 159–170.

Samuelson, P., 1947. Foundations of Economic Analysis. Harvard University Press.

Scarpetta, S., 1996. Assessing the role of labour market policies and institutional settings on unemployment: a cross-country study. OECD Economic Studies.

Schwartz, A., Scott, R.E., 2003. Contract theory and the limits of contract law. The Yale Law Journal 113, 541–619.

Shaked, A., Sutton, J., 1984. Involuntary unemployment as a perfect equilibrium in a bargaining model. Econometrica 52, 1351–1364.

Shapiro, C., Stiglitz, J.E., 1984. Equilibrium unemployment as a worker discipline device. American Economic Review 74, 433–444.

Shavell, S., 1984. The design of contracts and remedies for breach. Quarterly Journal of Economics 99, 121–148.

Simon, H., 1957. Administrative Behavior. The MacMillan Company, New York.

Simon, H.A., 1951. A formal theory of the employment relationship. Econometrica 19, 293–305.

Stahler, N., 2008. Firing costs, severance payments, judicial mistakes and unemployment. Labour Economics 15, 1162–1178.

Stephenson, M.C., 2009. Legal realism for economists. Journal of Economic Perspectives 23, 191–211.

Sullivan, D., von Wachter, T., 2009. Job displacement and mortality: an analysis using administrative data. Quarterly Journal Of Economics 124, 1265–1306.

Tirole, J., 1999. Incomplete contracts: where do we stand? Econometrica 67, 741–782.

Townsend, R.M., 1994. Risk and insurance in village India. Econometrica 62, 539–591.

von Wachter, T., 2007. In the right place at the wrong time: the role of firms and luck in young workers' careers. American Economic Review.

Voos, Mishel, 1986. The union impact on profits: evidence from industry price-cost margin data. Journal of Labor Economics 4, 105–133.

Williamson, O.E., 1975. Markets and Hierarchies: Analysis and Antitrust Implications. The Free Press, New York.

Williamson, O.E., 1991. Comparative economic organization: the analysis of discrete structural alternatives. Administrative Science Quarterly 36, 269–296.

Williamson, O.E., Wachter, M.L., Harris, J.E., 1975. Understanding the employment relation: the analysis of idiosyncratic exchange. Bell Journal of Economics 6, 250–278.

Wood, H.G., 1877. A Treatise on the Law of Master and Servant. J.D. Parsons, Albany, NY.

CHAPTER *19*

Human Resource Management and Productivity

Nicholas Bloom[*], John Van Reenen[**]

[*] Stanford, Centre for Economic Performance and NBER
[**] London School of Economics, Centre for Economic Performance, NBER and CEPR

Contents

E-mail addresses: n.bloom@stanford.edu (Nicholas Bloom), j.vanreenen@lse.ac.uk (John Van Reenen).

Handbook of Labor Economics, Volume 4b
© 2011 Elsevier B.V.

ISSN 0169-7218, DOI 10.1016/S0169-7218(11)02417-8

Abstract

In this chapter we examine the relationship between Human Resource Management (HRM) and productivity. HRM includes incentive pay (individual and group) as well as many non-pay aspects of the employment relationship such as matching (hiring and firing) and work organization (e.g. teams, autonomy). We place HRM more generally within the literature on management practices and productivity. We start with some facts on levels and trends of both HRM and productivity and the main economic theories of HRM. We look at some of the determinants of HRM—risk, competition, ownership and regulation. The largest section analyzes the impact of HRM on productivity emphasizing issues of methodology, data and results (from micro-econometric studies). We conclude briefly with suggestions of avenues for future frontier work.

JEL classification: L2; M2; O32; O33

Keywords: Human resource management; Productivity; Personnel Economics

1. INTRODUCTION

Traditionally, labor economics focused on the labor market rather than looking inside the "black box" of firms. Industrial sociologists and psychologists made the running in Human Resource Management (HRM). This has changed dramatically in last two decades. Human Resource Management (HRM) is now a major field in labor economics. The hallmark of this work is to use standard economic tools applied to the special circumstances of managing employees within companies. HRM economics has a major effect on the world through teaching in business schools and universities, and ultimately what gets practiced in many organizations.

HRM covers a wide range of activities. The main area we will focus on will be incentives and work organization. Incentives include remuneration systems (e.g. individuals or group incentive/contingent pay) and also the system of appraisal, promotion and career advancement. By work organization we mean the distribution of decision rights (autonomy/decentralization) between managers and workers, job design (e.g. flexibility of working, job rotation), team-working (e.g. who works with whom) and information provision.

Space limitations mean we do not cover matching (see Oyer and Schaefer, 2010) or skill development/training. Second, we will only devote a small amount of space to employee representation such as labor unions. Third, we should also mention that we focus on empirical work rather than theory (for recent theory surveys see Gibbons and Roberts, forthcoming, and in particular Lazear and Oyer, forthcoming) and micro-econometric work rather than macro or qualitative studies. Fourth, we focus on HRM over employees rather than CEOs, which is the subject of a vast literature (see Murphy, 1999, or Edmans et al., 2008, for surveys).

Where we depart from several of the existing surveys is to put HRM more broadly in the context of the economics of management. To do this we also look in detail at the literature on productivity dispersion.

The structure of the chapter is as follows. In Section 2 we detail some facts about HRM and productivity both in the cross sectional and time series dimension. In Section 3 we look at the impact of HRM on productivity with an emphasis on methodologies and mechanisms. In Section 4 we discuss some theoretical perspectives, contrasting the usual "Design" approach to our concept of HRM as one example of "management as a technology". In Section 5 we discuss some of the factors determining HRM, focusing on risk, competition, ownership, trade and regulation. Section 6 concludes.

2. SOME FACTS ON HRM AND PRODUCTIVITY

2.1. HRM practices

In the 1970s the general assumption was that incentive pay would continue to decline in importance. This opinion was based on the fact that traditional unskilled jobs with piece-rate incentives were declining, and white collar jobs with stable salaries and promotion based incentives were increasing. Surprisingly, however, it appears that over the last three decades a greater proportion of jobs have become rewarded with contingent pay, and this is in fact particularly true for salaried workers.

There are two broad methods of assessing the importance of incentive pay: Direct and Indirect methods. Direct methods use data on the incidence of HRM, often drawn from specialist surveys. Indirect methods use various forms of statistical inference, ideally from matched worker-firm data, to assess the extent to which pay is contingent on performance. We deal mainly with the direct evidence and then discuss more briefly the indirect evidence.

2.1.1. HRM measured using direct methods

Incentive Pay

Individual incentive pay information is available from a variety of sources. Using the Panel Study of Income Dynamic (PSID) Lemieux et al. (2009) estimate that about 14% of US prime age men in 1998 received performance pay (see Fig. 2.1). They define a worker as receiving performance pay if any part of compensation includes bonus, commission or piece rate[1] (data on stock options and shares is not included). They find a much higher incidence of performance pay jobs (37% on average between 1976-1998) defined as a job where a worker ever received some kind of performance pay[2].

---

[1] Overtime is removed, but the question is imperfect pre-1993 which could lead to undercounting performance pay.

[2] The difference is somewhat surprising as it suggests that performance pay jobs only pay out infrequently, which does not comply with casual observation (e.g. piece rates will almost always pay something). This may be because of measurement error where an individual has received an in-year bonus but does not state this. By looking over a longer period on the same "performance pay job", a more accurate figure is recorded.

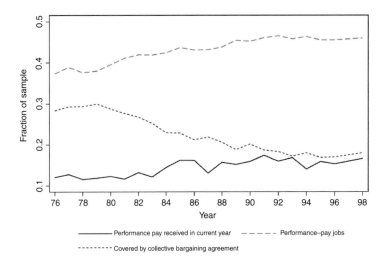

Figure 2.1   *Incidence of performance pay, US men in PSID, 1976-1998.* Notes: Male heads of household earning between $1 and $100 per hour. Self employed and public sector excluded. 30,424 observations on 3181 workers. Performance pay in current year $= 1$ if any part of compensation includes bonus, commission or piece rate. Stock options and shares are not included. A performance pay job is one where the worker *ever* receives some performance pay over the life of the job-match. *(Source: Lemieux et al. (2009))*

Other papers deliver similar estimates of around 40% to 50% of US employees being covered by some form of performance pay. For example, using the US General Social Survey Kruse et al. (2009) estimate that 47% of American workers were covered by some group incentive scheme in 2006. Of this 38% of employees were covered by profit sharing, 27% by gain-sharing, 18% by stock ownership (9% by stock options) and 4.6% by all three types. Lawler and Mohrman (2003) surveyed Fortune 1000 corporations between 1987 and 2002 asking detailed questions on their HRM[3]. Using midpoints of their results (which are in bands) Lemieux et al. (2009) calculate that 44% of workers were covered by incentive pay in 2002.

It is also interesting to look at the trends in incentive pay over time. In US data, Lemieux et al. (2009) find that for the wider definition of performance pay (if the worker was eligible for any performance related pay) the incidence rises from 38% in the 1970s to 45% in the 1990s (see Fig. 2.1). Interestingly, this rise in performance pay was mostly driven by increases in performance pay for salaried workers, for whom this rose from 45% in the 1970s to 60% in the 1990s. In contrast hourly paid workers have both lower levels and growth rates in performance pay. Lawler and Mohrman (2003) show similar rises

[3] The problem with the Lawler surveys is that the sampling frame is only larger companies compared to the more representative individual level PSID. Furthermore, the response rate to the survey has declined rapidly from over 50% in 1987 to only 15% by 1999. This poses a serious concern that the time series trends are not representative even of larger firms.

Table 2.1   Increases in incentive pay in large publicly listed US firms.

Year of survey	More than 20% of employees have Individual incentives (e.g. performance bonuses) (1)	More than 20% of employees have gainsharing (e.g. team bonuses) (2)	More than 20% of employees in teams (3)
1987	38	7	37
1990	45	11	51
1993	50	16	65
1996	57	19	66
1999	67	24	61

Source: Lawler et al. (1995, 2001), Lawler and Mohrman (2003).

in performance pay, increasing from 21% (1987) to 27% (1990) to 35% (1996) to 45% (2002). Lazear and Shaw (2008) also show some trends reproduced in Table 2.1, showing again that performance pay increased over time in the US.

In the UK the British Workplace Employment Relations Surveys (WERS) contains a cross section of all establishments with 25 or more employees in the UK (over 2000 observations in each year). There are consistent questions in 1984, 1990 and 2004 on whether the firm used any form of performance/contingent pay for workers both individually and collectively (e.g. team bonuses, Profit-related pay or Employee Share Ownership Schemes). Figure 2.2 shows that 41% of UK establishments had contingent pay in 1984, and this rose to 55% twenty years later. Two other points are noteworthy. First, this time series change is driven by the private sector: not only was the incidence of incentive pay very low in the public sector 10% or less, it actually fell over time (Lemieux et al., 2009 exclude the public sector in their US analysis). Second, the growth of incentive pay in the UK is primarily in the 1980s with no growth in the 1990s, similar to the US results shown in Fig. 2.1.

So in summary, the evidence is that overall performance pay related covers about 40% to 50% of US workers by the 2000s, has been increasing over the last three decades, particularly over the 1970s and 1980s and particularly in the private sector salaried jobs. A number of reasons have been suggested for the increase in performance related pay which we will examine in detail in Section 5 below.

Other HRM practices

Turning to more general forms of HRM than pay, like self-managed teams, performance feedback, job rotation, regular meetings, and training it becomes rather harder to summarize the existing information. In the cross section there are a number of surveys, with different sampling bases, response rates and questions making them hard to compare. Perhaps the most representative example for the US is Black and Lynch (2001, 2004) who collected information from a survey backed by the US Department of Labor (used also by Capelli and Neumark, 2001). In 1996, for example, about 17% of US establishments

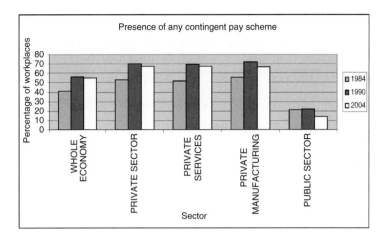

Figure 2.2 *Trends in performance Pay 1984-2004, UK.* Notes: This data is derived from the UK Workplace Employment Relations Surveys (WERS) in 1984, 1990 and 2004. This is a representative sample of all UK establishments with over 25 employees. Although there were other WERS in 1980 and 1998 the questions are not consistent. The consistent question relates to the incidence of any form of contingent pay for workers (Individual, Collective—such as team bonuses, Profit-related pay or Employee Share Ownership Schemes). The incidence of contingent pay grew from 41% to 56% by 1990, but fell to 55% in 2004. The data relates to whether there was any incidence of this type of pay—we do not know how many workers were covered or what proportion of their remuneration was contingent. *(Source: Pendleton et al. (2009))*

had self-managed teams, 49% in formal meetings and 25% in job rotation. Lawler and Mohrman (2003)'s data of larger firms unsurprisingly shows a greater incidence of "innovative" HRM practices. In their data for 1996, 78% of firms had self-managed teams and this covered at least 20% of the workforce for just under a third of all corporations.

Bryson and Wood (2009) present an analysis of "high involvement" HRM using the UK WERS data (see Table 2.2). About half of all UK establishments had "team-working" in 1998. More interestingly, the WERS data allows an analysis of changes over time. The incidence of teamwork (as indicated by "team briefings") has grown from 31% in 1984 to 70% in 2004 and "suggestion schemes" has grown from 22% in 1984 to 36% 20 years later. Most other forms of innovative HRM look stable, however, with the exception of incentive pay that has already been discussed.

Wider international comparisons

To compare a wider basket of countries beyond the UK and US the best source of information is probably the Bloom and Van Reenen (2007) surveys on general management practices. These have some specific questions on HRM or "people management", which have been collected from 17 countries. Since we will refer to this work at several points we describe the methodology in a little detail as it is somewhat

Table 2.2 Trends in general HRM using British WERS survey.

	1980	1984	1990	1998	2004	P value for change
High involvement practices						
Work organization						
Team working				49	54	0.11
Functional flexibility				71	75	0.21
Quality circles			30	39	28	0.45
Suggestion schemes		22	26	30	36	0.00
Skill and knowledge acquisition						
Team briefings		31	42	49	70	0.00
Induction training				76	90	0.00
Training in human relations skills				38	52	0.00
Information disclosure about investment plans		32	44	49	46	0.00
Information disclosure about financial position		56	56	60	58	0.47
Information disclosure about staffing plans		57	52	52	61	0.01
Appraisals				49	67	0.00
Work enrichment						
Job variety				40	39	0.65
Method discretion				21	19	0.59
Time control				20	21	0.77
Motivational practices						
Motivation a major selection criterion				84	80	0.11
Internal recruitment				32	26	0.04
Job security guarantees				6	10	0.01
Single status				63	61	0.57
Profit-related pay			42	46	45	0.31
Share-ownership scheme	14	23	31	24	28	0.00
Total quality management						
Self-inspection				53	44	0.01
Records on faults and complaints				64	62	0.52
Customer surveys				47	53	0.05
Quality targets				39	55	0.00
Training in problem solving				23	23	0.90
Just-in-time production				35	32	0.47

The following variables relate to practices as they pertain to the core non-managerial occupation at the workplace; team-working (equals 1 if 80%+ core employees in teams); functional flexibility; appraisals (equals 1 if all core employees appraised); work enrichment. Single status is if core workers are treated the same as managers in terms of benefits such as pensions.
Source: Bryson and Wood (2009) based on UK WIRS/WERS data.

different than the standard HRM surveys described above. The essential method was to start with a grid of "best practices" in HR and non-HR management and then score firms along each of the eighteen dimensions of this grid following an in-depth telephone interview with the plant manager. These eighteen dimensions covered three broad areas: monitoring, target setting and people management (see Bloom and Van Reenen, 2007, Appendix Table A1 for details). The people management section covers a range of HR practices including whether companies are promoting and rewarding employees based on worker ability and effort; whether firms have systems to hire and retain their most productive employees; and whether they deal with underperformers through retraining and effective sanctions. For example, we examine whether employees that perform well, work hard and display high ability are promoted faster than others.

To obtain accurate responses from firms the survey targeted production plant managers using a "double-blind" technique. One part of this double-blind technique is that managers are not told they are being scored or shown the scoring grid. They are only told they are being "interviewed about management practices for a piece of work". To run this blind scoring we used "open" questions since these do not tend to lead respondents to a particular answer. For example, the first people management question starts by asking respondents "tell me how does your promotion system work" rather than a closed question such as "do you promote on ability (yes/no)". Interviewers also probed for examples to support assertions, for example asking "tell me about your most recent promotion round". The other side of the double-blind technique is interviewers are not told in advance anything about the firm's performance to avoid prejudice. They are only provided with the company name, telephone number and industry. Since the survey covers medium-sized firms (defined as those employing between 100 and 5000 workers) these would not be usually known *ex ante* by the interviewers.

These management practices were strongly correlated with firm's performance data from their company accounts (total factor productivity, profitability, growth rates, and Tobin's Q and survival rates). These correlations are not causal but do suggest that HR practices that reward effort and performance are associated with better firm performance, implying that these "good" management practice measures do contain some useful information and are not just arbitrary noise. Other research shows that these practices are also associated with better patient outcomes in hospitals (Bloom et al., 2010c) and improved work-life balance indicators (Bloom et al., 2009c).

Figure 2.3 shows the distribution of these people management practices across countries. The US clearly has the highest average scores for people management. Bloom et al. (2009b) show that this appears to be due to a combination of the US being absolutely good at managing firms across all 18 questions on average, and also having a particular advantage in people (HR) management. Other countries with light labor regulation like Canada, Great Britain and Northern Ireland also display relatively strong

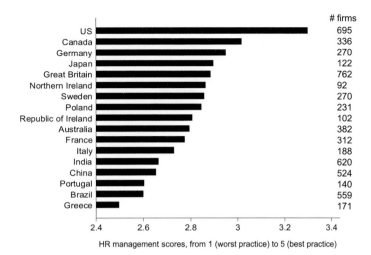

Figure 2.3 *HR management practices across countries.* Notes: Averages taken across a random sample of the population of medium sized (100 to 5000 employees) manufacturing firms within each country. 5850 observations in total. Firms per country in the right column. Scores firms on seven practices around pay, promotions, retention and hiring, where high scores denote stronger association with employee performance. *(Source: Authors' calculations from Bloom et al. (2009b) data)*

HR management practices. Interestingly Germany and Japan also fare well, in large part reflecting the fact that these countries have generally well managed manufacturing firms.

Figure 2.4 breaks out the people management score into three of the key areas in the overall people management score, which are promotions, fixing/firing underperformers and rewards. What is clear is that US firms have the globally highest scored practices across all three dimensions, but are particularly strong on "fixing/firing" practices. That is, in the US employees who underperform are most likely to be rapidly "fixed" (dealt with through re-training or rotated to another part of the firm where they can succeed), or if this fails fired. In contrast in countries like Greece and Brazil underperforming employees are typically left in post for several months or even years before any action is taken to address them. In Section 4.1 we discuss reasons for these patterns. Broadly speaking, the high levels of competition and low incidence of family firms are the main contributing factors to the leading position of the US in overall management. On top of this, high levels of education and weaker labor regulations give American firms a particular advantage in the HR aspect of management.

Figure 2.5 displays the firm level distributions within each country for these management practices, showing there is a wide dispersion of practices within every country. The US average score is the highest because it has almost no firms with weak HR management practices, while Brazil and Greece has a large tail of firms with poor HR management practices. This wide variation within each country is what most of the

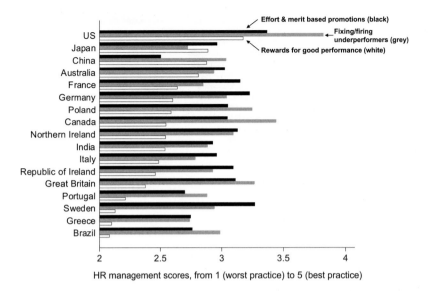

Figure 2.4 **Promotions, fixing/firing, and rewards practices by country.** Note: Averages taken across a random sample of medium (100 to 5000 employees) manufacturing firms within each country. 5850 observations in total. *(Source: Bloom et al. (2009b))*

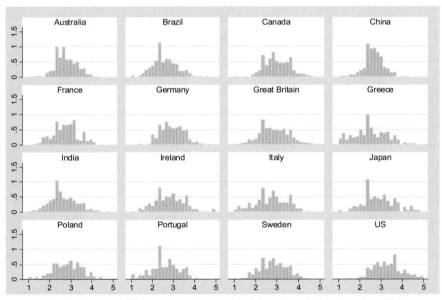

Firm level average HR management scores, from 1 (worst practice) to 5 (best practice)

Figure 2.5 **Firm level distribution of HR management by country.** Notes: Bars are the histogram of the density at the firm level on a country by country basis. Randomly sampled from all medium sized (100 to 5000 employee) manufacturing firms in each country. *(Source: Bloom et al. (2009b))*

prior micro literature has focused on, with Fig. 2.5 showing this variation is common across every country we have investigated.

2.1.2. Measuring incentive pay through indirect methods

The indirect method has been common in labor economics mainly due to data constraints. Essentially this method examines the correlation of workers' remuneration with firm-specific characteristics that should be important if pay is contingent on performance such as profitability, market value, etc. For example, if there are profit-related pay schemes, increases in firm profits should cause increases in worker pay. If pay was set solely on the external labor market, it should be unrelated to idiosyncratic changes in the firm's financial position. An advantage of this approach over the direct approach is that many of the incentive schemes may not be explicitly written down as contracts. A disadvantage is that the correlations between firm performance and pay we observe may be unrelated to incentive schemes for econometric reasons—e.g. a positive demand shock may simultaneously raise a firm's profitability and mean it hires workers of an unobservably higher skill level. Further, to the extent we do credibly identify a causal effect of firm performance on worker pay we cannot discern easily whether this is due to explicit contracts, implicit contracts, union bargaining[4] or some other model.

Having said this, there is substantial evidence that firm performance does matter a lot for worker remuneration. This is clearest in the many studies of matched worker firm data, which generally shows an important role for firm characteristics in determining worker wages (e.g. Abowd et al., 1999). Simple OLS regressions of changes of wages on changes of firm's profitability tend to find a positive effect (e.g. Blanchflower et al., 1996), but these are likely to be downward biased as shocks to wages will tend to reduce profitability. Using trade-based (Abowd and Lemieux, 1993) or technology-based (Van Reenen, 1996) instrumental variables tends to significantly increase the effect of firm performance on wages as we would expect. Matched worker-firm data is now commonly available in a large number of countries (see the collection of papers in Lazear and Shaw, 2008, for example). In the US, for example, Abowd et al. (2008) use the LEHD (Longitudinal Employer- Household Dynamics Program) covering about 80% of all employees. They show that about one half of all individual wage variance is associated with individual characteristics and about a half due to firm effects.

Although the focus of the literature has mainly been on explaining the distribution of wages at a point in time Dunne et al. (2004) show that between firm effects are important in understanding the growing inequality of wages over time in the US. Faggio et al. (2007) also find this for the UK and furthermore, offer evidence that the association of firm performance with wages has grown stronger over time. This is consistent with the more direct evidence discussed above that performance pay (explicit or implicit) may be more prevalent in recent years.

---

[4] Abowd (1989) looks at unexpected changes to wages and finds that shareholders wealth falls by an equal and opposite amount. He interprets this as consistent with strongly efficient bargaining over the rents between unions and firms.

2.2. Productivity dispersion

Research on firm heterogeneity has a long history in social science. Systematic empirical analysis first focused on the firm size distribution measured by employment, sales or assets. Most famously, Gibrat (1931), characterized the size distribution as approximately log normal and sought to explain this with reference to simple statistical models of growth (i.e. Gibrat's Law that firm growth is independent of size). In the 1970s as data became available by firm and line of business, attention focused on profitability as an indicator of performance (e.g. Kwoka and Ravenscraft, 1986). Accounting profitability can differ substantially from economic profitability, however, and may rise due to market power rather than efficiency.

In recent decades the development of larger databases has enabled researchers to look more directly at productivity. The growing availability of plant-level data from the Census Bureau in the US and other nations, combined with rapid increases in computer power has facilitated this development. Bartelsman et al. (2008) offer many examples of the cross country micro-datasets now being used for productivity analysis.

One of the robust facts emerging from these analyses is the very high degree of heterogeneity between business units (see Bartelsman and Doms, 2000). For example, Syverson (2004a) analyzes labor productivity (output per worker) in US manufacturing establishments in the 1997 Economic Census and shows that on average, a plant at the 90th percentile of the labor productivity distribution is over four times as productive as a plant at the 10th percentile in the same four digit sector. Similarly, Criscuolo et al. (2003) show that in the UK in 2000 there is a fivefold difference in productivity between these deciles.

What could explain these differences in productivity, and how can they persist in a competitive industry? One explanation is that if we accounted properly for the different inputs in the production function there would be little residual productivity differences[5]. It is certainly true that moving from labor productivity to total factor productivity (TFP) reduces the scale of the difference. For example, in Syverson (2004a) the 90-10 productivity difference falls from a factor of 4 to a factor of 1.9, but it does not disappear.

These differences show up clearly even for quite homogeneous goods. An early example is Salter (1960) who studied the British pig iron industry between 1911 and 1926. He showed that the best practice factory produced nearly twice as many tons per hour as the average factory. More recently, Syverson (2004b) shows TFP (and size) is very dispersed in the US ready mix concrete industry. Interestingly, the mean level of productivity was higher in more competitive markets (as indicated by a measure of spatial demand density) and this seemed to be mainly due to a lower mass in the left

---

[5] This is analogous to the historical debate in the macro time series of productivity between Solow, who claimed that TFP was a large component of aggregate growth and various critics who claimed that there was little role for TFP when all inputs were properly measured (see Griliches, 1996). A similar debate is active in "levels accounting" of cross-country TFP (e.g. Caselli, 2005).

tail in the more competitive sector consistent with the thin tail of bad management in Fig. 2.5 for US firms compared to those of other countries. Studies of large changes in product market competition such as trade liberalization (e.g. Pavcnik, 2002), foreign entry into domestic markets (Schmitz, 2005) or deregulation (e.g. Olley and Pakes, 1996) suggest that the subsequent increase in aggregate productivity has a substantial reallocation element[6].

A major problem in measuring productivity is the fact that researchers rarely observe plant level prices so an industry price deflator is usually used. Consequently, measured TFP typically includes an element of the firm-specific price-cost margin (e.g. Klette and Griliches, 1996). Foster et al. (2009) study 11 seven-digit homogeneous goods (including block ice, white pan bread, cardboard boxes and carbon black) where they have access to plant specific output (and input) prices. They find that conventionally measured revenue based TFP ("TFPR") numbers actually *understate* the degree of true productivity dispersion ("TFPQ"), especially for newer firms as the more productive firms typically have lower prices and are relatively larger[7].

Higher TFP is positively related to firm size, growth and survival probabilities. Bartelsman and Dhrymes, (1998, Table A.7) show that over a five year period around one third of plants stay in their productivity quintile. This suggests that productivity differences are not purely transitory, but partially persist.

Analysis of changes in aggregate productivity over time has shown that this productivity dispersion is also important in explaining economic growth. For example, Baily et al. (1992) find that half of the change in US industry-level productivity is due to the reallocation of output from lower productivity plants to those with higher productivity. This reallocation effect is partly due to the shift in market share between incumbents and partly due to the effects of exit and entry. Bartelsman et al. (2008) show that the speed of reallocation is much stronger in some countries (like the US) than others. There is also significant sectoral variation. For example, Foster et al. (2006), show that reallocation between stores accounts for almost all aggregate productivity growth in the US retail sector.

In summary, there is a substantial body of evidence of persistent firm-level heterogeneity in firm productivity (and other dimensions of performance) in narrow industries in many countries and time periods. Differential observable inputs, heterogeneous prices and idiosyncratic stochastic shocks are not able to adequately account for the remarkable dispersion of productivity. So what could account for this? One long suggested factor

---

[6] There is also a significant effect of such policy changes on the productivity of incumbent firms. Modeling the changing incentives to invest in productivity enhancing activities, such as R&D, is more difficult in heterogeneous firm models, but some recent progress has been made (e.g. Aw et al., 2008).

[7] Foster et al. (2009) show that measured revenue TFP will in general be correlated with true TFP but also with the firm specific price shocks. Hsieh and Klenow (2007) detail a model where heterogeneous TFPQ produces no difference in TFPR because the more productive firms grow larger and have lower prices, thus equalizing TFPR. In their model intra-industry variation in TFPR is due to distortions as firms face different input prices.

is management practices, with authors going back at least to Walker (1887) suggesting that management practices play an essential role in explaining differences in performance across firms[8].

3. THE EFFECTS OF HRM ON PRODUCTIVITY

Do variations in variations in HRM practices play a role in driving differences in productivity? We find that the answer is "probably, yes", although the empirical basis for this is surprisingly weak given the importance of the topic. In fact, as Syverson (forthcoming) notes in discussing management as a driver of productivity "*no potential driving factor of productivity has seen a higher ratio of speculation to empirical study*".

We should also state in advance that in this section we focus on productivity as the key outcome. Many studies look at other outcomes such as worker turnover, absenteeism, worker perceptions, etc. These are useful, but if they have no effect on productivity then in our view they are second order—generally studies use them because they have no direct evidence on productivity (e.g. Blasi et al., 2009:4). We do not focus on measures of worker wellbeing such as job satisfaction or wages. Lazear and Shaw (2008) suggest that some of the dramatic increase in wage inequality in the US, UK and other country since the late 1970s is due to HRM practices. Lemieux et al. (2009) and Guadalupe and Cunat (forthcoming) also take this position, although the current state of the evidence is still limited. These are interesting outcomes in their own right, and may also feed through into productivity, but we are space constrained and refer the reader to the wider literature where relevant.

An important issue is the correct way to econometrically estimate production functions and TFP. Ackerberg et al. (2007) have surveyed such methods in a recent Handbook chapter, and this is a lively (but still unsettled) area of research. Many of the issues on econometric identification of the parameters of conventional factors of production (such as labor or capital) are the same as those that will be discussed in Section 3.2 below. There is also a growing literature on examining the impact of worker characteristics (or "human resources" such as skills, gender, race, seniority and age) on productivity through direct estimation in production functions rather than the traditional approach of looking at these indirectly through including them in wage equations. Interested readers are referred to recent examples of this approach in Moretti (2004), Hellerstein et al. (1999) and Dearden et al. (2006).

3.1. Why should we expect to see an impact of HRM on productivity?

Before discussing issues of identification and the results from these studies, it is worth asking some basic questions: (a) why is this an interesting empirical question? and (b) why

---

[8] Walker was an important character in the early years of the economics discipline as the founding president of the American Economics Association, the second president of MIT, and the Director of the 1870 Economic Census.

would we expect to see any positive average effect of HRM practices on productivity? Note that the answer to this question is not specific to human resources, but any endogenously chosen organizational feature of the firm.

One response is that we should *not* expect to see any effects. The design perspective on HRM (discussed more fully in Section 4 below) assumes that all firms are continuously optimizing their HRM practices. This may vary between firms because of different environments—for example, variations in technologies across industries—but each firm is still optimizing. Externally manipulating the firm to "force" it to do something sub-optimal (e.g. adopt incentive pay schemes) can only harm the firm's performance. By contrast, using actual changes in the firm's choices of HRM (such as Lazear's (2000) Safelite Glass example discussed below) will show that firms improve productivity as they will be optimizing so we expect any change to produce a positive outcome on average.

An important rejoinder to this is that firms maximize discounted profits, not productivity. It may increase productivity to introduce a given HRM practice, but this may still reduce profits, which is why firms have chosen not to adopt. One example is (Freeman and Kleiner, 2005), who found that the abolition of piece rates reduced productivity but increased profits as quality rose in the absence of piece rates. This is analogous to any factor input such as capital—increasing capital per hour will increase output per hour, but the firm already takes this into account in its maximization program. Thus, just as we are interested in estimating the parameters of a conventional production function for capital and labor, we may be interested in the parameters associated with an HRM augmented production function even if all management practices are chosen optimally.

A second reason for studying the effect of HRM on productivity is that if we do see any effect, we are interested in the *mechanisms* through which this effect is working. For example, we expect the introduction of incentive pay to affect the type of workers who want to join and leave the firm. How important are these sorting and selections effect relatively to the pure incentive effect? Moreover, even if we expect a positive effect, we may not be so interested in the average effect but rather how this varies with observable characteristics of sub-groups of workers, or of the firm or of its environment. Theory suggests that changing HRM will have heterogeneous effects in this way, so this places some more testable restrictions on the data.

Finally, we describe below in Section 4, theories that regard some management practices partially as a technology. In this case the investigation of the productivity effects of HRM is analogous to examining the effects of the diffusion of any "hard" technology such as computers or hybrid corn. With a new technology we generally expect to see slow and staggered diffusion across firms. Some of this is due to firms optimizing given heterogeneous costs and benefits in a full information world. But slow diffusion may also be due to the differential arrival rate of information about the new technology. More subtly, the optimal HRM type may have changed over time. For example, performance pay may now be optimal in many sectors where previously it was unprofitable due to rapid falls in the cost of Electronic Resource Planning systems (such as SAP) that measure worker output (but not effort) more accurately and rapidly. If the "management as technology" perspective is correct, we would expect to see positive productivity effects from the adoption of these new HRM practices.

3.2. HRM and productivity: the identification problem

The typical study in the HRM and productivity literature in Personnel Economics examines the change in HR policy (typically an incentive pay reform) in a single firm, and a key concern is the effect on worker productivity. As Shaw (2009) points out, this set-up looks extremely similar to the literature on policy evaluation and its concern with correctly identifying treatment effects. Of course, in standard policy evaluation the arena is usually larger than a single firm—a country or state; and the policy maker the government rather than the CEO. Nevertheless, all the many issues germane to identifying treatment effects are present and we discuss these links in this sub-section. For a longer discussion on different treatment effects (Local Average Treatment Effects, Marginal Treatment Effects, etc.) and estimation strategies (IV, control function, regression discontinuity design, matching, etc.) see DiNardo and Lee (2011) or Blundell and Costa-Diaz (2009).

To be precise, let d_{it} represent the treatment status of individual i at time t. Potential outcomes (productivity) are y_{it}^1 and y_{it}^0 under the treated and non-treated scenarios. These are specified as $y_{it}^1 = c + \alpha_i + u_{it}$ for the treated and $y_{it}^0 = c + u_{it}$ for the non-treated, where α_i is the effect of the policy on individual i, c the common intercept and u_{it} the unobservable error. We assume that the policy effects are heterogeneous over individuals. This allows us to write the potential outcome equation as:

$$y_{it} = c + \alpha_i d_{it} + u_{it}.$$

There are a variety of treatment effects that we may be interested in. The traditional one in the homogenous treatment case is the average treatment effect (ATE), defined as the average outcome if an individual was assigned at random to the treatment group, $E(\alpha_i)$. More commonly, we can only identify the Average Treatment on the Treated effect (ATT), which is the average effect for the individuals who went through the program at some point, $E(\alpha_i | d_i = 1)$, where d_i indicates an individual who is assigned to treatment, even if they are not currently being treated.

Consider the model where each individual i is observed before and after the policy change at times $t_o < k$ and $t_1 > k$ respectively. The popular Difference in Differences (DD) estimator makes the assumption that the error term, u_{it}, takes a variance components form: $u_{it} = \eta_i + \tau_t + \varepsilon_{it}$, where η_i is correlated with d_i, τ_t is a common time effect, but ε_{it} is orthogonal to the other right hand side variables.

$$y_{it} = c + \alpha_i d_{it} + \eta_i + \tau_t + \varepsilon_{it}. \tag{1}$$

Sequential differencing eliminates the fixed effect and the time effect so that

$$\alpha^{DID} \equiv (\bar{y}_{t_1}^1 - \bar{y}_{t_0}^1) - (\bar{y}_{t_1}^0 - \bar{y}_{t_0}^0) = E(\alpha_i | d_i = 1) = ATT$$

where $\bar{y}_t^d$ is the average outcome in group d at time t. Under the difference in difference assumptions we recover the average effect of treatment on the treated. This is equivalent to adding in time dummies and individual fixed effects in estimating Eq. (1).

Most of the HR studies have longitudinal data so they are able to do the first difference $(\bar{y}_{t_1}^1 - \bar{y}_{t_0}^1)$. However, many studies do not have a control group in the firm who are not treated, thus there is no second difference. This is a drawback because the second difference controls for unobservable time shocks that are common to the two groups but unobserved to the econometrician. In other words, a major concern is that the supposed effect of the HRM policy is actually just some other event simultaneously dated with the introduction of the program.

In fact, many of the studies discussed below do have some more variance than just before and after for a single organization. First, the object of study may be a few firms in a narrowly defined industry (which is the usual strategy in Industrial Organization). Second, there may be variation in the introduction of the policy across different sub-units within the firm (e.g. different plants, different geographical regions[9], different production lines, different teams, etc.). Exploiting this form of variation, however, highlights the classical assignment problem—even if the macro time shock is common between the two groups, the decision to adopt the policy for plant A and not to adopt it for plant B is unlikely to be exogenous.

To see this, consider an assignment rule which is $d_{it} = 1$ if $d_{it}^* > 0$ and $d_{it} = 0$ otherwise, where d_{it}^* is a latent index defined by the linear rule:

$$d_{it}^* = 1(\gamma Z_{it} + \upsilon_{it} \geq 0). \tag{2}$$

In other words, plants that introduce the HRM policy may also be those that the CEO thinks are most likely to benefit from it. If this could all be captured by observables then we would be able to control for this bias. But we are unlikely in most datasets to have such a rich set of controls.

The credibility of the identification of treatment effects from cross-plant variation will hinge on the assignment rule of Eq. (2), which is of course a selection equation.

---

[9] Examining the branches of a multinational firm across different countries is an attractive strategy—e.g. Lafontaine and Srinivasan (2009).

Lazear (2000), for example, argues that the rollout of the policy across regions within Safelite Glass was essentially unrelated to differential potential benefits being determined by geography. Bandiera et al. (2007) examine whether similar productivity increases occurred at the same time in the season in a previous year when the policy experiment was not in place (a placebo test).

Having information on productivity prior to the policy is clearly helpful in considering selection. Lazear (2000) and Bandiera et al. (2007) can show that workers who *ex ante* had lower productivity were less likely to be selected into employment *ex post*. Since the selection mechanism in both papers means the more able workers are more likely to be employed, the ATT effect will be an upper bound of the effect on the compliers.

What is the advantage of single firm studies? Single firm studies are now the dominant form of methodology in Personnel Economics, but given the problem of the absence of an obvious control group, one might wonder whether this is such a good idea. Usually it is thought that focusing on a single firm enables researchers to control for many aspects that would be impossible to deal with in a larger cross-firm study. But what does this exactly mean?

Consider the possibility that we have multiple firms $j = 1, \ldots, J$ as well as multiple workers, $i = 1, \ldots, I$, and the difference in difference assumptions hold. Further, let us assume that there is some exogenous within firm variation that enables us to identify the ATT from a single firm estimation strategy.

$$y_{ijt} = c + \alpha_{ij}d_{ijt} + \eta_{ij} + \tau_{jt} + \varepsilon_{ijt}. \qquad (3)$$

If each firm j is "different" in the sense it has different time shocks (τ_{jt}), then estimating Eq. (3) by including a common time shock τ_t, as is typically done in the cross firm literature (e.g. Black and Lynch, 2004), will generally produce inconsistent estimates of the ATT effect. However, one could include firm dummies interacted with time dummies in Eq. (3) and recover the ATT in each firm j if the treatment randomly varied by worker within each firm. This would clearly be more informative than just recovering the ATT for one firm alone.

As second possible advantage of single firm strategies is that we may simply not have comparable policies across firms, in the sense that the policy changes d_{ijt} are not measured in the same units. To some extent this is true, but there are ways in which different policies can be made comparable. In the work on tax policies for example, we need to calculate what effect a tax reform has on the incentives facing individuals. If policies are incomparable then the generalizability of such studies is severely limited.

A third possible advantage of single firm studies is sheer institutional detail. Knowing a single firm well may make it possible to collect more detailed information and rule out many of the alternative explanations that might explain the results.

All three possible advantages of confining attention to a single firm strike us as differences in degree rather than in kind. The future of the field may be to move away from purely single firm studies to consider larger numbers of firms who are subject to HRM policy interventions where we have better ways of measuring the relevant management policy in a comparable way. One way to do this is to explicitly run experiments on firms, for example Karlan and Valdivia (2009) randomize the provision of training for the owners of micro-enterprises in Peru, including some HRM training, and find some significant positive impact of sales and growth. Bruhn et al. (2010) provide management training for small firms in Mexico, and again find some evidence for significant improvements on a range of performance metrics. Bloom et al. (2009a) run experiments on large Indian firms to introduce a modern management practices, including modern HR practices around piece-rate pay for workers and pay for performance for managers, and find large effects on productivity and profitability. While this literature is at an early stage, the broad results are that introducing modern HRM practice into firms in developing countries leads to significant improvements in performance. It would clearly be helpful to have more such studies, and particularly in developed countries.

3.3. Econometric studies of the productivity impact of HRM

Having discussed the caveats in the previous sub-section, we now turn to the huge number of empirical studies on HRM and productivity which we attempt to summarize in Table 3.1. Before discussing these in detail, here is our four point summary.

1. First, high quality studies generally show that there is a positive effect on productivity of incentive pay, both individual bonuses and (more surprisingly) group bonuses. This seems true across many sectors, including the public sector (see, for example, the Prentice et al., 2007 survey).

2. Second, in addition to a pure incentives effect, there is usually also an important selection effect generating higher productivity—productivity increases because high ability workers are attracted to organizations offering higher powered incentives.

3. Third, the introduction of new forms of incentive pay is generally more effective when combined with other "complementary" factors. There are complements within the bundles of HRM practices (e.g. team work and group bonuses), and between some HRM practices and other firm characteristics (e.g. decentralization and information technology).

4. Fourth, there are many examples of perverse incentives, for example, when rewards are tied to specific periods of time (such as quarters) so that workers manipulate commissions to hit quarterly targets.

5. Fifth, incentive pay schemes tend to be associated with greater dispersion of productivity, as the effects are stronger on the more able workers, and this is stronger than the selection effect (which pushes towards reduced dispersion).

Table 3.1 Studies of the "effects" of HRM on productivity.

Study	Data	HRM measures	Method	Results
Panel A: general HRM practices				
Bartel et al. (2007)	US Valve manufacturing, panel data on one plant and survey data on 212 plants.	Teams, incentive pay and basic and technical training.	Site visits plus a telephone survey matched to US Census data (the LRD).	Modern HRM practices associated with the adoption of new IT technologies.
Black and Lynch (2001)	1993 EQW-NES Educational Quality of the Workforce National employer Survey. An establishment level surveys of US plants (in all private sector with over 20 employees) matched to Census manufacturing data 1987–1993.	Large variety including self-managed teams, profit sharing, job rotation, unions, Total Quality Management (TQM), benchmarking, communication, meetings, training, etc.	Cross sectional OLS. Using Census panel use GMM-DIF to estimate plant productivity and relate this to HRM practices.	Profit sharing for non-managers significantly related to productivity (stronger in union firms).
Black and Lynch (2004)	1993 and 1996 EQW-NES matched to Census data. 72% response rate in 1993 and 78% in 1996. In 1996 1493 observations in cross section, 284 in panel.	See Black and Lynch (2001)	OLS in cross section and long-differenced, regressions.	Profit sharing significantly related to productivity in cross section, but insignificant in changes.

Table 3.1 (continued)

Study	Data	HRM measures	Method	Results
Bloom et al. (2010a)	1633 firms in 7 European countries. Cross section of management data in 2006 combined with panel of firm-level accounting data and IT data from Harte-Hanks.	People management score (see Section 2) over careful hiring, performance pay, merit-based promotion, fixing/firing, etc.	OLS production functions with and without fixed effects.	Complementarity between IT and people management. Higher coefficient on IT in production functions for subsidiaries of US multinationals (compared to other multinationals) accounted for higher IT productivity.
Capelli and Neumark (2001)	EQW-NES (see Black and Lynch, 2004). Manufacturing only—match in plants from 1977. $N = 433$ (1993–77); $N = 666$ (1996–1977).	Large variety including teamwork, profit sharing, job rotation, etc.	Estimate cross sectional OLS and 2 long-differenced equations: 1993–1977 and 1996–1977. Assumption is that workplace practices all zero in 1977 so level in later period can be treated as a difference.	Almost all variables insignificant in cross section and panel in productivity equations (a few more in wage equations). Profit sharing★self managed team interactions significantly positive.
Caroli and Van Reenen (2001)	UK (re-organization) and French (delayering) establishment level data.	3 equations with dependent variables as (i) growth of skill shares; (ii) organizational form (delayering in France, general organizational change in UK); (iii) productivity.	OLS cross section and long-differences.	Evidence for "Skill-biased organizational change". Organizational changes appear to (i) increase demand for more skilled workers; (ii) have larger positive effect on productivity when combined with more skilled workers. (iii) Regions with lower costs of skills are more likely to introduce organizational change.

(continued on next page)

Table 3.1 (continued)

Study	Data	HRM measures	Method	Results
Cooke (1994)	Manufacturing firms in Michigan.	Employee participation and group incentives.	OLS	Value added increases. Wages also increase (but by less than value added).
Cristiner et al. (2001)	100 Italian manufacturing firms.	Adoption of HRM practices around job-rotation, team work and selective hiring and performance pay.	Cross-sectional survey and panel performance data.	Find HRM practices clustered within firms, and associated with improved firm level performance.
Easton and Jarrell (1998)	Publicly quoted firms.	TQM	Matching techniques	Positive effect of TQM on financial performance.
Griffith and Neely (2009)	Introduction of "Balanced Scorecard" in single UK retail firm.	Scorecard a mix of several factors. Individual and group performance taken into account.	Look at monthly data for 3 years before and after the roll-out of the program.	No effect at the mean. Productivity dispersion rises—more able managers increase effort by more than less able managers.
Huselid (1995)	Survey of senior HR executives (28% response rate). 826 large (100+ employees) publicly quoted US firms in 1991.	Uses Principal Components to get 2 factors analysis from multiple questions. (1) employee skills and organization (8 items); (2) employee motivation (3 items).	OLS regressions with dependent variables: sales per employee, profitability and Tobin's q.	One or both variables significant in each of 3 performance equations.

Table 3.1 (continued)

Study	Data	HRM measures	Method	Results
Huselid and Becker (1996)	Repeat Huselid (1995) survey to get cross section and panel data in 1993. 740 responses (20% rate) and 218 firms in panel.	As Huselid (1995)	OLS and FE regressions with dependent variables as profitability and Tobin's q.	Sum is significant in cross section, but insignificant in panel dimension.
Ichniowski (1990)	65 business units in manufacturing, 7% response rate.		OLS	Clusters of practices (including enriched job design) associated with better financial performance.
Ichniowski et al. (1997)	Integrated steel mills. Steel finishing lines. Monthly productivity is downtime due to defects rates. 36 mills and 17 companies over 5 years.	Introduction of an HRM system of 7 dimensions—incentive pay; careful hiring; teams; training; information sharing; broad job design and job security.	OLS regressions with fixed effects.	Large increases in productivity from adopting innovative HRM system (scores highly on all dimensions). Adopting one or two practices do not help. Find practices tend to be clustered suggesting complementarities.
MacDuffie (1995)	A 1989–1990 survey of human resource practices in 62 automotive assembly plants.			Finds bundles of practices clustered across plants, and that these bundles are correlated with performance.

(continued on next page)

Table 3.1 (continued)

Study	Data	HRM measures	Method	Results
Mas and Moretti (2008)	Supermarket checkout clerks; all supermarket transactions in 6 stores.		Within a 10 min work interval, personal productivity rises by 1.7% when working in front of a peer who is 10% more productive than average.	High productivity clerks increase the productivity of low productivity clerks, but only if the high productivity clerk can observe the low productivity clerk.
Osterman (2006)	National Establishment Survey (NES). Uses panel of around 800 US private sector establishments (see Black and Lynch, 2004)	High-performance workplace organization, defined as employee involvement in self-managing teams, job-rotation and quality circles.	OLS	Increased wages from adoption of high-performance workplace organization, appears due to increased productivity.

Table 3.1 (continued)

Study	Data	HRM measures	Method	Results
Panel B: individual incentive pay				
Bandiera et al. (2005)	Workers on a UK soft fruit picking farm. Daily field productivity data of workers, and the peer groups they interact with.	Piece-rate pay (bonus for amount of fruit picked) and relative performance pay (bonus for amount of fruit picked relative to rest of the picking group).	Mid-season change in bonus system from relative pay to piece-rate pay.	Relative bonus led to lower picking rates, particularly if the rest of the comparison group were friends, especially if they could mutually monitor performance. Suggests workers internalize impact of their performance on their colleagues.
Bandiera et al. (2007)	Managers on UK soft fruit picking farm. Daily field productivity data on workers under manager.	Performance bonus to manager depending on average worker (fruit picker) productivity in the day. Previously flat hourly wage.	Mid-season change in payment system by company (designed by researchers) in 2003. Include manager and field fixed effects.	Pickers' productivity increases by 21% (at least half is selection). Variance of productivity (and earnings) increases because managers target their effort towards more able workers. Selection effect arises because managers drop the less able workers from their teams.
Bandiera et al. (2009a)	As in Bandiera et al. (2007). Also use 3 measures of social connectedness: same nationality; live in close proximity to each other on farm; arrived at similar time on farm.	Individual (from flat hourly wage)	Mid-season change in payment system by company (designed by researchers) in 2003.	Under flat pay productivity of a worker 9% higher when socially connected to manger, but under incentive pay this difference is zero. After incentive pay, productivity of highly able increases and less able decreases. Average productivity lower because of favoritism.

(continued on next page)

Table 3.1 (continued)

Study	Data	HRM measures	Method	Results
Bandiera et al. (2009b)	As in Bandiera et al. (2007) but this time a change in 2005. Survey of friends.	Change in the type of team incentive—feedback vs. tournament.	Fruit pickers are in teams of c.5. Engineer a change from team piece rates to (i) give feedback, then (ii) give tournament prize.	Both interventions increase sorting: high ability want to work with each other). Productivity increases by 24% with tournament (strong incentive effect) but decreases by 14% with public ranking feedback (because sorting reduces social ties). Note cannot look at causal effect of group vs. individual pay.
Fernie and Metcalf (1999)	413 British jockeys (184 in balanced panel)	Some employed on fixed retainers and others offered prizes for winning races. Different prizes across races.	(i) Random effects controlling for bookie's estimates of horse and race likely success.; (ii) control for jockey fixed effects for small sample where incentives reduced due to new owner.	Large incentive effects—those facing prizes supply much more effort. Switching to lower powered incentives reduces effort.
Foster and Rosenzweig (1996)	Agricultural workers in Philippines. Body weight changes for those on different types of pay. Weight changes a proxy for effort.	Piece rate workers vs. flat rate workers.		Conditional on calorie intake piece rate workers lose more weight. But calories for piece rate higher overall due to higher wages.

Table 3.1 (continued)

Study	Data	HRM measures	Method	Results
Freeman and Kleiner (2005)	US Shoe manufacturer. Monthly data on shoes produced (And scheduled production) 1991–1994 in 2 plants.	Switch away from individual piece rates to hourly pay. Also coincided with other changes to management—continuous production.	OLS regressions with dummies for pay regimes. Monthly trend and other controls.	Worker productivity 6% higher under piece rate pay. But profits increased with abolition due to lower inventory, higher quality, and more frequent product changes.
Kahn et al. (2001)	Brazilian tax collection authority. Productivity measured by number of inspections and amount of fines collected from tax evaders.	Individual and group incentives introduced in 1989. Objective and subjective performance.	Look 3 years before and after scheme introduced.	75% increase in rate of growth of fines per inspection. Problem that extortion may also increase.
Lavy (2009)	Israeli teachers. Policy introduced in 50 schools in December 2000.	Policy introduced of awarding bonuses to teachers based on pupils' pass rates and scores in matriculation exams in English and math. Rank order tournament. Only about a third of eligible teachers won awards (ranged from 6–25% of salary).	Schools treated based on a policy rule—threshold based on 1999 matriculation results with error. Consider 18 schools in treatment and 18 in control.	Significant improvement in teacher performance. Appears to be through changes in teaching methods. No evidence of distortions.

(continued on next page)

Table 3.1 (continued)

Study	Data	HRM measures	Method	Results
Lazear (2000)	Safelite Glass Company (windshield installers). 2755 workers over 19 month period. 29,837 person months.	Individual (change from flat hourly wage to per windshield piece rate pay)	Change in payment system by company. OLS regressions with and without fixed effects.	44% increase in productivity (22% incentive, 22% selection from new hires, not from leavers)
Shearer (2004)	One firm of tree planters in British Columbia (Feb–July).	9 male workers randomized in and out of piece rate and hourly rate (so same worker observed under both systems). Up to 16 days per worker.	Random assignment (design doesn't allow him to look at selection)	20% increase in productivity (22% in structural model)
Panel C: group incentive pay				
Baiker and Jacobson (2007)	US Police Departments	1984 Comprehensive Crime Control act provided police departments opportunity to share in proceeds of drug-related asset seizures.	OLS	10% increase in fraction returned to police department associated with a $0.19 increase in values of seizures. Police work strategically putting greater emphasis on possession (high cash component) rather than drugs sales.
Blasi et al. (2009)	Survey of 100+ studies on group incentives ("shared capitalism").		OLS	Average increase in productivity by 4.5%.

Table 3.1 (continued)

Study	Data	HRM measures	Method	Results
Boning et al. (2007)	One product line in US steel mini mills (bars from recycled steel). 36 mills (20 firms) over 5 years.	Proportion of mills with problem solving teams rises by 10% to 50%.	OLS regressions with fixed effects.	Productivity rises 6% with team-working and effect strongest when products are complex; incentive pay also associated with higher productivity.
Burgess et al. (2007)	UK HM Customs and Excise (tax collection department) April-Dec 2002. Weekly data. Look at yield and time (mainly on "trader audit").	Office managers given incentive on team bonus. 2 treatment teams ($N = 154$ in 3 offices bonus equal across all workers), another $N = 158$ in 6 offices bonus varied according to grade). One blind control ($N = 281$).	OLS difference in differences.	Team productivity increased. Main effect through selection where most efficient workers were allocated to the more incentivized task.
Hamilton et al. (2003)	US unionized garment manufacturer (Koret in Napa), 1995–1997. Weekly production data on sewing function for women's skirts, pants, etc. 288 employees (20,627 person-weeks).	Change from individual piece rate to teams with group based incentives pay. Production from Taylorist to "modular" in response to demands for more flexible batches from retailers Workers have some discretion over when they switch.	OLS with person effects and time effects. Dummy for team membership. Puzzle of more able switching first (some lost income) and having the same exit rate as least able. Assumes due to non-pecuniary benefits of team work.	No evidence of free-riding. On average productivity rose 18%. Increased use of collaborative skills. Gains greater for more heterogeneous teams. More productive workers switched earlier, so 4% is selection, 14% effect on same workers.

(continued on next page)

Table 3.1 (continued)

Study	Data	HRM measures	Method	Results
Jones and Kato (1995)	109 large unionized manufacturing firms in Japan 1973–1980.	ESOPs (presence) and Bonuses (amount of bonus per worker)	OLS estimation of production functions with fixed effects. No IV for incentive pay introduction.	Introduction of ESOP increases productivity 4%–5%, takes 3–4 years of this effect. A 10% increase in bonus per employee leads to a 1% increase in productivity the following year.
Knez and Simester (2001)	Continental Airlines Personnel data. Productivity measured by on-time departure rate. 648 airports over 22 months.	Continental airlines in 1995. Promised $65 monthly bonus to all employees if firm-wide goals met. Used outsourced airports (Continental's operations managed by outside workers who were not covered by scheme) as a control group.	Regress change in on-time departures on full outsourced and partially outsourced. Control for lagged performance.	Significant increase in productivity. Mutual monitoring in team based production.
Lavy (2002)	Israeli teachers. February 1995 competition announced for monetary bonus to secondary school teachers.	Compares introduction of group bonuses (based on pupil performance) with more schools resources. Awards tied to average student credit, matriculation diplomas and dropout rates. 62 schools eligible, one third won. $1.5 m disbursed, about 75% went to teacher pay (Bonuses only 1%–3% of average salary).	Compared results in treatment and control group by 1997.	Significant improvement in teacher performance. Incentive pay more cost effective than general increase in resources. Stronger effects for weaker students.

Table 3.1 (continued)

Study	Data	HRM measures	Method	Results
Panel D: distortions associated with incentive pay schemes				
Asch (1990)	US Navy recruiters	Individual (Recruiters paid & measured) based on enlisted sailors.	Non-linear incentives	If Navy recruiters near their targets they worked harder, especially nearer the end of the year.
Chevalier and Ellison (1997)	Mutual fund managers	At end of year managers have an incentive to change level of risk.		Distortion present for many years
Courty and Marschke (2004)	Managers of Federal job training centers (JTPA). 16 agencies.	Group (budget of training office) and nonlinear scheme. Bonuses augment operating budget of agencies by 7% on average.	Choice of termination date (up to 90 days after end of training)	Managers act to increase payouts near end of each measurement period. Quality of overall training fell. Strategic behavior lowers program graduates wages and therefore welfare.
Glewwe et al. (2003)	Kenyan schools (50 schools in treatment group)	2 year program offering school wide bonuses to teachers. Awards given if schools improved test scores and reduced dropout rates.	Randomized control trial	Test scores improved significantly for treatment group the 2 years when the program ran. But after finished no lasting gain. No improvement in drop-out rates. Teacher attendance and methods did not change. Teachers put on extra exam preparation classes to "cram" for tests.

(continued on next page)

Table 3.1 (continued)

Study	Data	HRM measures	Method	Results
Larkin (2007)	Salespeople in a Software Firm	Bonuses given when sales people hit their targets.		Costs firm 6%–8% in potential revenue. Distortions induced from salespeople substituting sales across periods, and giving discounts if they are going to just miss their targets.
Oyer (1998)	Quarterly accounting data from US manufacturing firms (Compustat) 1985–1993. Over 19,000 observations.	None — use indirect methods, assuming that many managers and salespersons have contracts with bonuses depending on end of year performance	OLS regression of sales and profit growth on quarterly dummies over fiscal year (differs by firm). Many controls for other effects.	Effort high at end of fiscal year and low at beginning as indicated by sales growth and other proxies.

We divide this sub-section into general HRM studies (Panel A), individual incentive pay (Panel B), group incentive pay (Panel C) and distortions (Panel D).

3.3.1. General HRM studies

There are a huge number of studies that have correlated various aspects of the firm's performance on various aspects of its HRM (recall Table 3.1 for some of the measures used). There is generally a strong and positive correlation between HRM and productivity.

The better studies use micro data and pay careful attention to the measurement issues and need to control for many covariates. Black and Lynch (2001) examine various aspects of "high performance" workplaces including profit related pay, but also Total Quality Management, benchmarking, self managed teams, recruitment strategies, etc. This was from a rich cross sectional survey that they helped design (the EQW-NES) that could be matched to plant-level panel data from the Census Bureau. They estimated production functions controlling for conventional inputs such as labor, capital and materials, but also included a large number of these HRM practices. They found relatively few practices were significantly related to total factor productivity—profit sharing for non-managers and benchmarking were two of the stronger ones. The Bloom and Van Reenen (2007) management scores also show high correlations of HR management scores with labor productivity, as illustrated in the regressions in Table 3.2. A significant correlation is also apparent when other controls are added (columns (2) and (3)) or alternative measures of performance are used such as profitability, sales growth and firm survival (columns (4) through (6)). Of course none of these results are causal in the sense that cross-sectional correlations between HR and productivity may be driven by reverse causality, or correlations with other omitted factors as discussed above.

Some studies have tried to get a better handle on causation by using panel data on management practices to try and control for fixed cross-sectional differences between firms. In Black and Lynch (2004) the authors analyzed a second wave of the EQW-NES data so they could examine changes between 1996 and 1993. Again, some practices (such as profit related pay) showed up as informative in the cross section, but HRM practices were usually insignificant after controlling for fixed effects (only "re-engineering was significant). Capelli and Neumark (2001) come to a similar conclusion also examining the same data.

Since many of these practices appear to be highly correlated some researchers have aggregated them into a smaller number of summary measures. Huselid (1995) and Huselid and Becker (1996) did this in combining questions of his survey of HR managers into two principal components—"employee skills and organization" and "employee motivation". They found that in the cross section one or other of these factors was positively and significantly related to productivity, profitability and Tobin's Q. However, like Black and Lynch (2004), once fixed effects were included these factors were not significant.

Table 3.2 Performance and people management practices.

Dependent variable	(1) Ln (Sales/employee)	(2) Ln (Sales/employee)	(3) Ln (Sales/employee)	(4) Profitability (ROCE)	(5) Sales growth	(6) Survival
People management	0.299 (0.028)	0.178 (0.021)	0.142 (0.024)	1.417 (0.701)	0.041 (0.013)	0.49[a] (0.26)[a]
Ln (Capital/Employee)			0.115 (0.014)			
% College degree			0.078 (0.014)			
Country & industry dummies	No	Yes	Yes	Yes	Yes	Yes
General controls	No	No	Yes	Yes	Yes	Yes
Noise controls	No	No	Yes	Yes	Yes	Yes
Firms	3380	3380	3380	2369	2298	3627

All columns estimated by OLS with standard errors are in parentheses under coefficient estimates clustered by firm, except for column (6) which is estimated by Probit (we report marginal effects at the sample mean). Survival is defined as firms who are still in operation in Spring 2009 (including if they have been taken over by another firm). Sample of all firms with available accounts data at some point between 2000 and 2008. Management score has a mean of 2.973 and a standard-deviation of 0.664. "**Country and industry dummies**" includes a full set of 17 country and 162 SIC 3-digit dummies. "**General controls**" comprise of firm-level controls for ln (average hours worked) and ln (firm age). "**Noise controls**" are 78 interviewer dummies, the seniority and tenure of the manager who responded, the day of the week the interview was conducted, the time of the day the interview was conducted, the duration of the interviews and an indicator of the reliability of the information as coded by the interviewer. All regressions include a full set of time dummies. "**People Management**" is the firm-level people management score covering pay, promotion, hiring, firing, retaining employees, consequence management and human capital targets. "% College Degree" is the share of employees with a college degree (collected from the survey). "Profitability" is ROCE which is "Return on Capital Employed" and "**Sales growth**" is the 5-year growth of sales. **Survival** is equal to zero if a firm exited due to bankruptcy/liquidation by the end of 2008 and one otherwise. The sample mean of non-survival is 2.1% so the marginal effect of −0.49 implies one management point is associated with 23.5% (=0.49/2.1) lower exit rate.

[a] marginal effect and standard error multiplied by 100.

Source: Authors' calculations using Bloom et al. (2009b) data.

The disappointing results for the absence of any "effect" in the time series dimension could be due to the fact that there genuinely is no relationship between productivity and HRM practices. Under this interpretation the cross sectional results are due to a spurious correlation with a time-invariant unobservable. Alternatively, there may be a downward endogeneity bias in the time-series, for example, because negative productivity shocks are positively correlated with the introduction of new practices. Nickell et al. (2001) argue that firms organizationally innovate when they are doing badly and this would cause such a downward bias. Another factor is measurement error, which if it is of the classical form can cause attenuation bias towards zero. This is likely to be particularly problematic for HRM practices if they do not change much over time and are measured with substantial error.

3.3.2. Individual incentive pay

A pioneering study is Lazear (2000) who looked at the replacement of a flat rate hourly pay system by a piece rate pay system for windshield installers in the Safelite Glass Company. In this firm each employee has a truck and drives to the homes of people who have broken car windshields and installs a new one. Looking 19 months before and after the introduction of the incentive pay plan, Lazear found that productivity increased by around 44% after the policy change, with about half of this due to selection effects and half from the same individuals changing their behavior. The selection effects are because less productive workers left the company and more productive workers joined, presumably attracted by the higher powered incentives.

More recently, Bandiera et al. (2007) engineered a change in the incentive pay system for managers in a UK fruit farm. All the workers (fruit pickers) were on piece rate pay, but prior to the policy change the managers were paid a flat rate, whereas afterwards there was a strong element of pay tied to the performance of the workers they managed. The average picker's productivity rose by 21% after the introduction of performance related pay and at least half of this was due to improved selection. The remainder of the effect is due to managers focusing their efforts more on the workers where it had the greatest marginal effect. Examining the mechanism through which this happened, Bandiera et al. (2009a) gathered information on social connections from their survey. They found that prior to the introduction of incentive pay managers favored workers to whom they were socially connected, irrespective of the workers' ability. After the introduction of performance bonuses they targeted their efforts towards high ability workers, regardless of whether they were socially connected or not. This had the effect of increasing the dispersion of productivity (as well as the level).

Freeman and Kleiner (2005) examine the elimination of piece rates for a US shoe manufacturer. They focused on two plants of the same firm who switched at different times and focused on what happened to productivity (monthly shoes produced per worker) and profits before and after the change in the pay scheme. Consistent with the other "insider" studies, productivity fell after the workers were put on a flat hourly rate.

Interestingly, the authors show that profits rose after the change, which they attribute in part to improved quality with flat pay, plus a variety of other managerial changes complementary to flat rate pay.

A criticism of these studies is that the workers who are treated are not random. The firm who introduced the policy presumably believed there would be some benefits from doing so, thus it is hard to rule out the idea that there may have been some other contemporaneous change that affected worker productivity. Shearer (2004) addresses this problem in his study of tree planters in British Columbia. He worked with the company employing the planters and designed an experiment where all workers were randomly assigned to the incentive pay group for some days and flat hourly time rates for others (so the same worker is observed under both systems). He cannot look at selection effects, but found that the pure incentive effect was to increase productivity by around 22%, very similar to Lazear (2000).

Another example of cleaner identification is Lavy (2009), who exploits a quasi-experiment in Israeli schools where teachers were offered individual bonuses based on their relative performance as indicated by pupil scores in math and English exams. School assignment was based on a rule determined by past matriculation results, and this gives several identification methods including a regression discontinuity design around the threshold. He finds significant improvements in teacher performance and no evidence of distortions. Interestingly, the improvement in performance appeared to be due to changes in teaching methods and management. Not all evaluations of performance pay for teachers are so positive, although Lavy's (2007) survey does suggest that the weight of evidence is in favor, and more so for individual incentive pay than for group incentives, which we turn to in the next sub-section.

In summary, these studies do suggest that individual incentive pay increases productivity. Other studies also show evidence that incentives affect employee behavior, but the precise "incentive effect" on productivity is not so easy to interpret[10].

3.3.3. Group incentive pay

In Section 2 we saw that collective payment by results (such as team bonuses) has become much more important over the last 30 years or so. In the US almost half of employees participate in such schemes (see Section 2). There has been a recent review of the effects of such schemes in Blasi et al. (2009), who consider over 100 studies. In general a positive association is revealed between group incentive schemes and company performance, but with substantial diversity in results. The average estimated increase in productivity associated with employee ownership and profit sharing is 4.5%[11]. A survey of UK schemes by the UK Treasury (Oxera, 2007) found a mean effect across studies of 2.5% and larger

---

[10] For example see Gaynor et al. (2004), Groves et al. (1994) and Fernie and Metcalf (1999).

[11] On employee ownership see Kruse and Blasi (1997). On profit-sharing and gain-sharing see Weitzman and Kruse (1990).

effects for share ownership schemes[12]. Combinations of such schemes with other HRM practices were found to be particularly effective—e.g. employee involvement in teams.

A recent example of this literature would be Bryson and Freeman (2009), who use the 2004 UK WERS survey discussed in Section 2 to relate various measures of company performance to the presence of incentive pay. They find that employee share ownership schemes are associated with 3.3% high value added per worker compared to no other form of incentive pay, but other forms of group incentive pay are insignificant. As with most of the other studies, the problem is that there are many potential omitted variables that are not controlled for, so we are concerned whether this is a causal effect or simply an association with an unobservable[13]. Jones and Kato (1995) go one step further as they have panel data on ESOPs and bonuses in Japanese firms. Switches to ESOPS were associated with 4%-5% higher productivity after 3-4 years. Although panel data is an improvement, there is still the problem that the adopting firms are non-random, as discussed in Section 3.2.

Boning et al. (2007) examine the introduction of team-based systems (including group incentive pay) in a distinct product line across 36 mini-mills. These mini-mills take scrap metal and recycle it into steel bars used, for example, in freeways. They find team-based work (including team bonuses) are associated with 6% higher productivity, especially in more complex products, which indicates the importance of the complementarity between HRM and the wider strategy of the firm (see Section 3.4).

Hamilton et al. (2003) study the shift by a US garments manufacturer from individual pay towards group pay ("gain-sharing"). This coincided with a more general change in the firm's production strategy to produce smaller more custom-made batches (reflecting demand from their major customer—retail clothing stores). This "modular" approach required more team work, so group bonuses were more appropriate incentives. Productivity rose by about 18%, and this increase was stronger for more heterogeneous teams. The authors suggest that this came from exploiting unused collaborative skills of workers. Surprisingly given the free rider problem, the more productive workers were earlier to switch. This suggests some non-pecuniary benefits and also positive peer effects (see below)[14].

Boning et al. (2007) and Hamilton et al. (2003) have the advantage that some of the unobservable shocks are controlled for by focusing on a narrower group of individuals (working in a single industry or a single firm). Although they still face the issue of endogeneity, as there is no random assignment, their intimate knowledge of the change enables them to examine the mechanisms through which group pay influences productivity in a richer manner. Bloom et al. (2009a) do randomly assign

---

[12] 10 of the 13 studies of profit related pay were positive and 7 out of the 10 studies of share ownership.

[13] The study does not control for capital inputs or fixed effects, although some of the other studies do.

[14] Knez and Simester (2001) also found productivity increases following the promise of a company-wide bonus for improvements in on-time takeoffs in Continental Airways.

firms to interventions including the introducing performance related pay and find a 10% improvement in productivity.

Burgess et al. (2007) obtain something that is closer to random assignment by examining the introduction of a group incentive system in the UK tax collection agency. The preliminary results from this work suggest that group bonuses were effective in significantly raising productivity. Also in the public sector, Lavy (2002) finds that group bonuses for Israeli school teachers were highly effective in raising performance (compared to simply increasing school resources). Schools were given awards for improvements in dropout rates, matriculation rates and credits. The effects were stronger for weak students. Finally, Baiker and Jacobson (2007) find that group incentives in the form of keeping a greater share of the value of seized assets caused police productivity to rise in catching drug offences.

In summary, there does then, appear to be evidence that group incentive schemes also raise productivity, which is surprising given the free rider problem. Overall, in our opinion, however the evidence is weaker here than that for individual incentive pay.

3.3.4. Distortions due to incentive pay

The studies in the previous sub-sections suggested that individuals do respond to pay incentives and generally in a way that usually increases productivity. The theoretical literature has emphasized many ways in which incentive pay can cause distortions which could reduce productivity. First, employees are more risk averse than firms and incentive pay increases the risks faced by workers. Thus it may discourage some high ability (but risk averse) workers from joining the firm and encourage excessive risk taking[15]. Second, firms cannot always credibly commit to reward performance *ex post*. For example, Gibbons (1987) details a model where only the worker knows the difficulty of job and the true action. He shows how this generates a "ratchet effect" where workers will restrict output unless the employer can commit not to use the information it obtains from learning the difficulty of the task. Third, measures of the worker's productivity are imperfectly related to inputs (worker effort). Baker (1992) shows how incentive pay tied to a measurable output will cause workers to increase effort to improve the measured output and reduce effort on the unmeasured output (e.g. quantity instead of quality in Lazear, 1986)[16].

Given the difficulty with tying incentives to objective measures what about the common practice of using supervisors' subjective measures of performance? Several

---

[15] Much of the remuneration of many financial workers, such as traders is based on an annual bonus. Since this can never be less than zero it may encourage excessively risky positions.

[16] Holmstrom and Milgrom (1991) have a similar finding in the context of a multi-tasking model where incentive contracts can cause agents to under or over invest sub-optimally in different tasks. This could explain the well-known phenomenon of "teaching to the test". This what led performance related pay to increase productivity but reduce productivity in Freeman and Kleiner (2005), as workers measured increased output of shoes but at the expense of unmeasured quality.

papers have modeled the optimal mix of incentives based on imperfect objective measures and perfect (but unverifiable) subjective measures[17]. The problem with subjective measures is that, although they provide stronger incentives, workers have to trust that the firm does not renege *ex post*, which is a particular danger with unverifiable information. Furthermore, there will still be the problem of the gap between actual and measured effort. This can mean (i) employees engage in "influence activity" to alter supervisors' decisions in their favor (e.g. Milgrom and Roberts, 1988)[18]; (ii) there may be favoritism on the behalf of supervisors for particular workers (Prendergast and Topel, 1996)[19]; (iii) the supervisor and employee may hold different opinions about employee's performance (MacLeod, 2003).

Empirical work has tended to focus on the potential distortions in explicit incentive schemes. One key distortion that occurs is the measurement *period*. Asch (1990) examines US Navy recruiters who were incentivized based on their ability to enlist sailors (partly through measurement and some also through explicit payments). This was based on annual quotas, so only affected those who were close to missing their quota. In addition, the effect was extremely strong near year end, but weak afterwards, causing inconsistent efforts over time. Courty and Marschke (2004) analyze managers of job training centers and show that managers work very hard at the end of the measurement period, but generated some costs in the form of lower training quality. Glewwe et al. (2003) examined a school-wide incentives program in Kenya. The program randomly assigned fifty elementary schools to a treatment group eligible for monetary incentives (21%-43% of monthly salary). All teachers in winning schools received rewards based on average test score performance and dropout rates. Student scores improved significantly in the treatment schools for the two years the program was in place. But this appeared to be due solely to teachers conducting test preparation outside of regular class and there were no long-run effects on pupil performance. This appeared to be a classic case of incentives simply causing "teaching to the test".

One might think that since these are examples from the public sector it is no surprise that incentives are poorly designed. Yet there are also many private sector examples. Oyer (1998) shows that firms typically build incentives around fiscal years. Consequently, firms sell more (at lower margins) near the end of the fiscal year compared to the middle of the year, and even less just at the start of the accounting year. Larkin (2007) looks at a large software company and shows that salesmen acted on their incentives to shift effort towards the end of their measurement period. Compared to the counterfactual of no incentive contracts it is unclear whether these imperfect incentive contracts reduce

---

[17] For example see Baker et al. (1994), Bull (1987) and MacLeod and Malcomson (1989).

[18] This may be a reason why some firms commit to promoting based on seniority rather than subjective assessments of performance.

[19] MacLeod (2003) shows how this will act as a multiplier effect on discrimination, making the discriminated group suffer further from lower effort.

overall productivity (although Larkin argues that there is a 6%-8% cost in potential revenue)[20].

A more subtle form of distortion can occur between types of individual incentive pay systems when workers have social preferences. Many economists (e.g. Lazear, 1989) have puzzled over why relative performance benchmarks are not used more commonly in pay systems given their desirable properties (i.e. common time specific shocks outside the employees' control are removed). Bandiera et al. (2005) examined a change of incentive pay among workers in their firm from a system based on relative performance to piece rates based on absolute performance. They found that productivity increased by 50% as a result of the experiment and attributed this to the fact that workers have social preferences (using their measures of friendship networks). Under a relative performance system a worker who increases his effort puts a negative externality on other workers under a relative system, but has no such affect under a piece rate system.

Overall, there is clear evidence that distortions often occur in response to incentive pay schemes, especially when badly designed. Nevertheless, the evidence that many performance pay schemes—whether individual or group—can raise productivity suggests that these distortions are not generally overwhelming.

3.3.5. Labor unions

A related literature is on the productivity impact of labor unions, an important human resource policy choice (see Freeman and Medoff, 1984). One recent attempt at an identification strategy here is DiNardo and Lee (2004), who exploit a regression discontinuity design. In the US a union must win a National Labor Relations Board election to obtain representation, so one can compare plants just above the 50% cut-off to plants just below the 50% cut-off to identify the causal effects of unions. In contrast to the rest of the literature, DiNardo and Lee (2004) find no effect of unions on productivity, wages and most other outcomes. The problem, of course, is that union effects may only "bite" when the union has more solid support from the workforce.

More generally, there is the question of whether unions inhibit incentive pay. Arguments can be made both ways. Although Fig. 2.1 is suggestive of the rise in incentive pay moving in the opposite way to the fall in union power, and unions are certainly associated with lower pay dispersion within firms, Brown (1990) found no relationship with performance pay.

---

[20] Chevalier and Ellison (1997) show that calendar year non-linearities lead to persistent distortions for mutual fund managers risk profiles. These are not chosen by the firm, however. We have even personally exploited year end incentives to buy cheap data in the past by agreeing with a salesman that he can choose each year which quarter we buy data from him (so he can use this to hit a quarterly target he would otherwise narrowly miss) in return for a 50% reduction in price.

3.4. Complementarities

One of the key reasons why firms may find it difficult to adjust their organizational form is that there are important complementarities between sets of organizational practices. Milgrom and Roberts (1990) build a theoretical structure where such complementarities (or more precisely, super-additivities) mean that firms optimally choose clusters of practices that "fit together". When the environment change so that an entrant firm would use this group of optimal practices, incumbent firms will find it harder—they will either switch a large number together or none at all.

This has important implications for productivity analysis. The effects of introducing a single practice will be heterogeneous between firms and depend on what practices they currently use. This implies linear regressions of the form of Eq. (1) may be misleading. To see this, consider that rather than a single HRM practice (d_{it}) there are two management practices, m^1 and m^2 and their relationship with productivity is such that TFP (the y_{it} considered here) increases by more when they are used together.

$$y_{it} = c + \beta_1 m_{it}^1 + \beta_2 m_{it}^2 + \beta_{12}(m_{it}^1 * m_{it}^2) + \eta_i + \tau_t + \varepsilon_{it}. \tag{4}$$

A simple version of the complementary hypothesis is $\beta_{12} > 0$. A stronger form is that the disruption caused by just using one practice alone actually reduced productivity, $\beta_1 < 0, \beta_2 < 0$. In this case a regression which omits the interaction term may actually only find only a zero coefficient on the linear terms.

The case study literature emphasizes the importance of complementarities. Econometrically, testing for their existence poses some challenges, however, as pointed out most clearly by Athey and Stern (1998). A common approach is a regression of practice 1 on practice 2 (and more) with a positive covariance (conditional on other factors) indicating complementarity. It is true that complements will tend to co-vary positively, but this is a very weak test. There could be many other unobservables causing the two practices to move together. Essentially, we need instrumental variables for at least one of the practices (e.g. Van Biesebroeck, 2007), but this is hard to obtain as it is unclear what such an instrument would be—how could it be legitimately excluded from the second stage equation? In classical factor demand analysis we would examine the cross price effects to gauge the existence of Hicks-Allen complements versus substitutes, i.e. does demand for practice 1 fall when the price of practice 2 rises (all else equal). Analogously, we would like to observe some cost shock to the adoption of practice 1 that is uncorrelated with the error term in the practice 2 adoption equation. Unfortunately, such tests are particularly hard to implement because there are generally no market prices for the organizational factors we are considering.

An alternative strategy is to work straight from the production function (or performance equation more generally). In an influential paper Ichniowski et al. (1997) estimate a version of Eq. (4) using very disaggregate panel data on finishing lines in integrated US steel mills using eleven human resource practices (including incentive pay, recruitment, teamwork, job flexibility and rotation). Their measure of productivity is based on downtime—the less productive lines were idle for longer. They find that introducing one or two practices has no effect, but introducing a large number together significantly raises productivity. Although the endogeneity problem is not eliminated, the controls for fixed effects, looking at very disaggregated data and a performance measure suited to the sector (downtime) helps reduce some of the more obvious sources of bias. Gant et al. (2002) show that the productivity benefits of team working in steel plants appear to be due to faster problem solving because of tighter horizontal interactions and networks between workers. They use detailed surveys of who is talking to who to show that plants involved with innovative HRM systems have this feature.

In addition to endogeneity concerns, there is a further problem with interpreting a positive estimate of β_{12} in Eq. (1) as evidence of complementarities. The true model may be one where there is a single latent factor for "good HRM management" and the many individual HRM measures may be (noisy) signals of this latent factor. This will generate positive covariance between the practices and could also cause the interaction to be positive. Thus, some care is required in the interpretation of the production function coefficients.

We have focused on complementarities between types of HR practices. New technology is often discussed in this context and we turn to this next (see also Section 5).

3.5. The role of information and communication technologies (ICT)

One of the key productivity puzzles of recent years has been why the returns to the use of information and communication technologies appear to be so high and so heterogeneous between firms and between countries. For example, Brynjolfsson and Hitt (2003) find that the elasticity of output with respect to ICT capital is far higher than its share in gross output (see also Stiroh, 2004). This reversed the well known Solow Paradox that one could find computers everywhere except the productivity figures. Not only was there evidence for large and significant returns at the micro-level, US productivity growth accelerated at the macro level from 1995 onwards. A substantial fraction of this appears to be linked to the production and use of ICT (e.g. Jorgenson et al., 2008), and the greater pay-off to ICT usage seems to be a reason why European productivity growth was much slower than that in the US since the mid 1990s (ending the catching up process).

One explanation for these phenomena was that effective use of ICT also requires significant changes in firm organization. Changing the notation of (5) slightly we could write

$$y_{it} = \beta_c c_{it} + \beta_m m_{it} + \beta_{cm}(c * m)_{it} + u_{it} \tag{5}$$

where c is ln(ICT capital) and m is an HRM practice. The hypothesis that $\beta_{cm} > 0$ would be consistent with complementarity between some HRM practices and ICT.

Bresnahan et al. (2002) try to test this directly by surveying the organizations of large US firms on decentralization and team work (for a cross section) and combining this with data on ICT (from a private company Harte-Hanks) and productivity from Compustat. They find evidence that $\beta_{cm} > 0$. Bloom et al. (2010a) broaden the sample to cover firms in seven European countries and find evidence of complementarity of ICT with the Bloom-Van Reenen measure of HR management discussed in Section 2. They also show that their results are robust to controlling for firm fixed effects. Careful econometric case studies (e.g. Baker and Hubbard, 2004; Bartel et al., 2007) also identify differential productivity effects of ICT depending on organization form. We will return to the issues of complementarity between HRM, technology and human capital in Section 5.

4. TWO PERSPECTIVES ON HRM AND PRODUCTIVITY: DESIGN AND TECHNOLOGY

In thinking about the reasons for variations in HRM and productivity a contrast can be drawn between two possible approaches. The first is the now classic approach of Personnel Economics, which we label the "design" approach. The view here is that the HRM practices we observe are chosen and continuously optimized by a profit maximizing firm: they are explicit strategic choices of the firm, and observable variations in HRM reflect variations in the firm's environment.

A second approach is becoming more common, but has not been closely linked to labor economics. We label this the "managerial technology" approach because of the recent stress in diverse fields of economics, such as trade, public and macro, but above all Industrial Organization, that there are large and persistent differences in firm productivity (see Section 2.2 above). In this view some aspects of HRM could be considered as a technology or "best practice" in the jargon. Adopting these forms of HRM would improve productivity in a typical firm. This leads on naturally to the question of why all firms have not adopted such practices. We discuss this below, but one immediate explanation is that all technologies have some diffusion curve whereby not all firms immediately adopt them. For example, it took American car manufacturers decades to accept and then implement Japanese style "lean manufacturing" techniques pioneered by Toyota. Informational constraints (and other factors we discuss below) could be an explanation for the slow diffusion of major managerial innovations.

The firm heterogeneity inherent in the managerial technology perspective mirrors the traditional labor economist's emphasis on heterogeneity amongst workers. Interestingly, the many recent contributions in labor economics have found that fundamental features of the labor market such as the persistent dispersion in equilibrium wage distribution for similar workers cannot be easily understood without appealing to some sort of firm heterogeneity (e.g. Postel-Vinay and Robin, 2002; Cahuc et al., 2006). Such models are generally silent on how this firm heterogeneity comes about, but their existence seems important in quantitatively matching features of wage dispersion in real labor markets.

The Design and Technology perspectives are not mutually exclusive, of course. As economists, we believe that there is always some element of maximization. The managerial technology perspective highlights, however, that some firms are constrained by being less productive than others. We believe that this is an important empirical phenomenon which can explain many puzzling facts and requires integration into the dominant design paradigm. We overview both perspectives and refer readers who want more depth to the surveys in Gibbons and Waldman (1999), Malcomson (1999), Prendergast (1999), Lazear (1999) and especially Lazear and Oyer (forthcoming) which summarizes the most recent theory and some more recent empirical evidence.

4.1. The design perspective

The economics of contracts (see Bolton and Dewatripont, 2005, for an overview) and the economics of organizations (see Gibbons and Roberts, forthcoming) have made huge strides in recent decades. HRM or Personnel Economics is a sub-class of this broader field with a focus on explaining the type of institutions we observe in real employment contracts and organization.

Prior to the emergence of Personnel Economics, the study of HRM was dominated by industrial psychologists and sociologists, who emphasized institutions and culture as determining the internal organization of firms. Generalizations were eschewed. Traditionally labor economists focused on labor demand and supply, unemployment and investment in education, issues that saw the firm as a single unit rather than a complex organization and so had little to directly say on the structure of pay, promotions and design of work within firms. This started changing in the 1970s, partly as new techniques of agency and contract theory allowed a more systematic treatment of activity inside companies.

The design perspective borrows three key principles from economics. First, firms and workers are rational maximizing agents (profits and utility respectively). Secondly, it is assumed that labor and product markets must reach some sort of price-quantity equilibrium, which provides some discipline for the models. Finally, the stress is very much on private efficiency, with an emphasis on why some employment practices which may look to be perplexing and inefficient on the surface (e.g. mandatory retirement and huge pay disparities for CEOs) may actually be (at least privately) optimal.

The key feature of the design approach is that the HRM practices we observe are chosen by firms to maximize profits in an environment that departs from perfectly competitive spot markets. Unlike the standard Personnel Management texts, Personnel Economics leads to sharper predictions and generalizations: it is not the case that "every workplace is fundamentally different". However, the design approach puts the reason for heterogeneity in the adoption of different practices as mainly due to the different environments firms face—say in the industry's technology, rather than inefficiencies. The managerial technology view, described next, sees a large role for inefficiencies.

4.2. The managerial technology perspective

4.2.1. What are HRM best practices?

The large dispersion in firm productivity discussed in Section 2.2 motivates an alternative perspective that some types of HRM (or bundles of HRM practices) are better than others for firms in the same environment. There are three types of these best practices. First, there are some practices that have always been better throughout time and space (e.g. not promoting gross incompetents to senior positions) or collecting some information before making decisions. Second, there may be genuine managerial innovations (Taylor's Scientific Management; Toyota's Lean Manufacturing System; Demming's Quality movement, etc.) in the same way there are technological innovations. There are likely to be arguments over the extent to which an innovation is real technical progress or just a fad or fashion. It is worth recalling that this debate historically occurred for many of the "hard" technological innovations which we take for granted now such as computers and the Internet. Thirdly, many practices may have become optimal due to changes in the economic environment over time, as the design perspective highlights. Incentive pay may be an example of this: piece rates declined in the late 19th Century, but incentive pay appears to be making somewhat of a comeback (see Section 2.1.1). Lemieux et al. (2009) suggest that this may be due to advances in ICT—companies like SAP make it much easier to measure output in a timely and robust fashion, making effective incentive pay schemes easier to design[21]. In these circumstances, some firms may be faster than others in switching to the new best practice. The differential speed of adjustment to the new equilibrium can be due to information differences, complementarities (see sub-section 3.4) and agency issues.

Notice that there is nothing in what we have said that is specifically tied to HR in this description. If productivity dispersion is due (at least in part) to differential managerial quality then this applies both to the HR and non-HR aspects of management. We next examine some of the theories of management that could help account for productivity dispersion (of which HRM is a subset).

4.2.2. Theories of management quality

The large-scale productivity dispersion described in Section 2 poses serious challenges to the representative firm approach. It has always been germane to Industrial Organization, but there has been a wholesale re-evaluation of theoretical approaches in several fields. For example, in international trade the dominant paradigm has already started to shift towards heterogeneous firm models. This is due to the increasing weight of empirical

---

[21] Hard technological advances have also facilitated managerial innovations such as Just in Time. Keane and Feinberg (2008) stress the importance of these improved logistics for the growth of intra-firm trade between the US and Canada

evidence documenting the persistent heterogeneity in firm export patterns (exporters tend to be larger and more productive). Melitz (2003) follows Hopenhayn (1992) in assuming that firms do not know their productivity before they pay a sunk cost to enter an industry, but when they enter they receive a draw from a known distribution. Productivity does not change over time and firms optimize subject to their constraint of having high or low productivity. Firms who draw a very low level of productivity will immediately exit, as there is some fixed cost of production they cannot profitably cover. Those who produce will have a mixture of productivity levels, however. A natural interpretation of this set-up is that entrepreneurs found firms with a distinct managerial culture which is imprinted on them until they exit, so some firms are permanently "better" or "worse" managed. Over time, the low productivity firms are selected out and the better ones survive and prosper. There is some stochastic element to this, however, so in the steady state there will always be some dispersion of productivity.

Identifying the permanent productivity advantage in this model as "managerial quality" is consistent with the tradition in the panel data econometric literature. Indeed, Mundlak's (1961) introduction of the original fixed effects panel data model was designed to control for this unmeasured managerial ability (the title of his paper was "Empirical Production Function Free of Management Bias"). Rather than just treat this as a nuisance parameter, however, more recent attempts have tried to measure management directly.

Imperfect competition is one obvious ingredient for these models. With imperfect competition firms can have differential efficiency and still survive in equilibrium. With perfect competition inefficient firms should be rapidly driven out of the market as the more efficient firms undercut them on price. In Syverson (2004b), for example, there is horizontal product differentiation based on transport costs so firms have local market power. He shows theoretically and empirically that increases in competition will increase average productivity by reducing the mass of less productive plants in an area.

Another important element is "frictions". Costs of adjustment are ubiquitous in capital investment and have usually been found for labor, especially skilled labor (see Bond and Van Reenen, 2007 and Bloom, 2009, for surveys). Thus, firms facing asymmetric shocks will adjust differentially to their new conditions only slowly over time even if they all have identical adjustment cost technologies. In such an environment, low TFP firms will not immediately vanish as there is an option value to remaining active in the sector. The Melitz model could be regarded as a limiting case of introducing frictions where the TFP draw cannot be altered over time by say investing in improving management. The managerial factor is "trapped" as there is no direct market for it as it cannot be transferred between firms. When the firm exits, so does the productivity advantage—entrepreneurs take a new draw if they enter again. In reality, adjustment costs can take more general forms and are likely to be important as management practices and organizational forms can adjust.

The management quality measures in Bloom and Van Reenen (2007) can be interpreted as the permanent draw from the productivity distribution when firms are born. Alternatively, it may reflect that some individuals have superior managerial skill and can maintain a larger span of control as in Lucas (1978). A drawback of the Lucas and Melitz approaches is the assumption that management capacities are static and non-transferable. More generally management practices can be allowed to evolve over time through investments in training, consultancy etc. The "organizational capital" approach allows for this (see Prescott and Visscher, 1980; Atkeson and Kehoe, 2005; Corrado et al., 2006).

A common feature of these models is that management is partially like a technology, so there are distinctly good (and bad) practices that would raise (or lower) productivity. We believe that this is an important element in management quality, and the traditional models that seek to understand technological diffusion (e.g. Hall, 2003) are relevant for understanding the spread of managerial techniques.

4.2.3. "Behavioral" explanations of management

None of the exposition of the Managerial Technology perspective has relied on any "Behavioral economics", in the sense of non-optimizing agents. Of course, one potential explanation for the non adoption of seemingly profitable HRM practices could be behaviorally based. One line of the literature focuses on managerial over-confidence, in which managers are excessively optimistic about their own abilities and the investment returns of their firms. In the case of HRM they may believe their current policies are optimal and so no changes are needed. The other focuses on managerial faults like procrastination towards undertaking profitable activities, so they may believe they need to adopt more modern HRM practices but repeatedly defer actually doing this.

Managerial overconfidence

This builds on the well known result from the psychology literature showing routine overconfidence in individuals over their abilities. For example, Svenson (1981) showed that 82% of students placed their driving ability in the top 30%. Exacerbating this is attribution bias, whereby managers attribute good performance to their own ability, despite this often being due to luck, leading to more senior managers to become increasing overconfident. Since senior managers often have few peers to correct them, this type of over-confidence can persist. Malmendier and Tate (2005) show that overconfident managers—defined as those who hold excessively high portfolios of their company's shares (failing to diversify)—undertake excessively high investments that are less profitable on average, less well regarded by stock-markets and more internally financed[22].

---

[22] Likewise the Bloom and Van Reenen (2007) survey asked managers the question "Excluding yourself, please score your firms management practices on a scale of 1 to 10, where 1 is worst practice, 10 is best practice and 5 is average". The average response from managers was 7.1, and was correlated at only 0.035 with each firm's actual labor productivity. This suggests that to the extent that managers are reporting their self assessment accurately, they are substantially over rating their managerial ability, and also struggling to benchmark this against their actual management ability.

Procrastination

Another literature has pointed out the procrastination—or failure to take known optimal actions—by individuals and managers. For example, Duflo et al. (2009) show how Kenyan maize farmers do not use fertilizer despite returns of over 100% to the investment, unless they are provided with some form of commitment mechanism like advanced buying of the fertilizer. Similarly, Conley and Udry (2010) show how pineapple farmers in Ghana also under-use fertilizer in their farms, again despite having the resources to purchase this and without any superior savings mechanism. This type of behavior is certainly not limited to developing countries—for example, Choi et al. (2008) show that many employees of US firms are directly losing money from not making investments in 401K plans which have matching top-ups by employers and permit instant withdrawal.

In all cases the behavior is irrational from a standard optimizing framework in that agents are aware of utility maximizing actions but do not take them. One framework for explaining these actions goes back to O'Donoghue and Rabin (1999), who propose a model in which agents are present-biased and as least partially naïve, systematically underestimating the odds they will be impatient in the future. Hence, agents defer taking improving actions today under the belief they will take them in future, but never do. As a result agents repeatedly procrastinate on taking profitable actions, like introducing modern HRM practices into their firms.

4.3. The two perspectives: summary

In the Design approach firms at every point are choosing their optimal set of management practices and no firm is more efficient than another based on these. In management science, "contingency theory" (e.g. Woodward, 1958) is akin to this. Any coherent theory of management has firms choosing different practices in different environments, so there will always be some element of contingency. For example, Bloom and Van Reenen (2007) show that firms appear to specialize more in investing in "people management" (practices over promotion, rewards, hiring and firing) when they operate in a more skill-intensive industry. If we examine the relative scores by country for monitoring and target setting practices compared to people management, the US, India and China have the largest *relative* advantage in people management, and Japan, Sweden and Germany the largest *relative* advantage in monitoring and target setting management. The systematic difference in the relative scores of different types of management across countries also suggests that there may be some specialization in areas of comparative advantage, perhaps due to labor market regulation. Figure 4.1 shows some evidence for this. The cross country differences in people management are related to the degree of labor market regulation (lightly regulated countries such as the US and Canada do better than heavily regulated countries such as France, Brazil and Greece).

The interesting question is whether there really are any "universals", i.e. some practices that would be unambiguously better for the majority of firms? If this is so, why

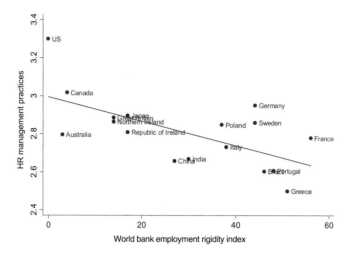

Figure 4.1　*Labor market regulation and HR management practices.* Notes: World Bank index from the Doing Business database, http://www.doingbusiness.org/ExploreTopics/EmployingWorkers/. *(Source: Bloom et al. (2009b))*

are these firms not adopting them? The answer to this question is identical to that of the adoption of any new technology—there are costs to adoption in the form of information, incentives, regulatory constraints, externalities, etc. These will vary somewhat by time and place and we turn to some of these factors next.

5. SOME DETERMINANTS OF HRM PRACTICES

Given the dispersion in HRM practices and productivity outlined in Section 2 we naturally turn to the question of why such variations exist. The large span of theories and empirical work makes it impossible to discuss all areas of the determinants of HRM, so we focus on some key themes: insurance, competition, ownership and work organization.

5.1. Insurance and incentive pay

One of the most basic features of performance pay from the design perspective is the incentive vs. insurance trade-off. A first best contract could be written on effort, but the essence of the principal agent problem is that the agent's effort is not perfectly observable. An obvious way to solve the principal agent problem is for the principal to sell the firm to the agent whose incentives would then be aligned with value maximization. This does sometimes happen in market stalls and some other contexts, but it is the exception in the modern economy.

A fundamental reason for this is that individuals are more risk averse than firms. A flat salary provides insurance to an employee because when the firm experiences a negative shock his wage will remain constant (assuming that he is not laid off). Consider a contract that is partially base salary and partially tied to a measure of employee output (a signal of effort). The observable measure of worker output is a function of effort and stochastic factors: these might be measurement error in the signal or truly exogenous shocks to output. The greater the variance of the noise relative to the signal, the greater is the risk that the employee is forced to bear. Thus, in order to attract the employee to supply his labor to the firm (the participation constraint), the lower will be the weight attached to the employee's measured output in the optimal contract. Thus, there is a trade-off between insurance and incentives.

Prendergast (1999) analyzed this in detail and lamented that the evidence here did not really give great support to the basic insurance-incentive trade off. For example, Garen (1994) examines the degree to which CEO compensation is linked to performance (the "β" in a linear contract). The relationship between β and the noisiness of performance measures should be negative, but appeared to be statistically zero in his data. Brown (1990), examining a wider range of occupations, also finds little relationship between incentive pay and the riskiness of the environment.

Prendergast (2000, 2002a,b) looks at this evidence in more detail and offers several possible explanations. In Prendergast (2002a) risky environments will be ones where the manager's private information is more valuable. This is because the uncertainty in this environment will make it much more likely that the agent knows what the "right" thing is to do rather than the principal. In such circumstances delegating decisions to the agent become more attractive. In other words, the increased cost of incentive pay in terms of lower insurance to an employee in a risky environment has also to be set against the higher value of employee's information. Thus, uncertain environments increase the value of giving more decision rights to employees, which will increase the probability of incentive pay even though the insurance mechanism leans in the opposite way. Prendergast (2002a) hypothesizes that because the degree of delegation is hard to control for at the same time as environmental uncertainty, this is why the effects of uncertainty on incentive pay have been empirically ambiguous.

Prendergast's point is a specific example of a more general principle in terms of the incentives to decentralize when it is hard for the principal to learn about the "right action" in a noisy environment. We describe this model in more detail in Section 5.4 below and show that there is string of empirical evidence that more uncertain/heterogeneous environments do cause greater decentralization as Prendergast suggests (Acemoglu et al., 2007). Whether this resolves the empirical problem of insurance vs. incentive pay is still unclear, however[23].

[23] There have been attempts to combine information on delegation and incentive pay (e.g. Adams, 2005 and DeVaro and Kurtulus, 2007, but both incentive pay and delegation are exogenous variables so some additional exogenous variation is needed to be conclusive. Wulf (2007) finds that, for managers at the same level, incentive pay is less prevalent when there is more volatility. More recent work has found some support for the incentives-risk trade off by gathering more direct measures of risk aversion (Bandiera et al., 2010) or modeling the matching process between principals and agents (Ackerberg and Botticini, 2002).

5.2. Product market competition

From the "management technology" perspective, it is clearer why competition has a positive effect on best practice HRM. Adam Smith, for example, wrote that "Monopoly...is a great enemy to good management."[24] Higher product market competition, as indexed by say an increase in consumer price sensitivity, will tend to drive the less productive firms out of the market. Firms that have failed to adopt better HR management practices will tend to exit, so this should improve the HR management quality and productivity in the average firm. To the extent that incentive pay and some of the other Bloom and Van Reenen HR practices really do increase productivity, the time series trends identified in Section 2 might be due to increases in global competition caused by deregulation and globalization.

Effort to improve managerial practices may also increase through incentive effects on incumbent firms. Schmidt (1997) formalizes the intuition that tougher competition will bring the interests of the managerial agent more into line with the firm's owners. In his model, managers have borrowing constraints, so lose wealth when their firm goes bankrupt. High levels of competition increase bankruptcy risk and increase managerial effort.

Theoretically, however, the effects of competition on the form of incentive pay is ambiguous from the design perspective. The analysis in Vives (2008) is very useful, as he shows that higher powered incentives can be considered in some respects as an investment in non-tournament R&D. The firm invests in an HR system that has a fixed cost but lowers marginal costs as the improved management increases productivity of all factors. Consider again an increase in consumer price sensitivity as an index of product market competition. The "stakes" are now higher: through greater managerial effort a firm can reduce marginal costs and this will have a larger effect on relative market share or relative profitability than when competition is lower. On the other hand, higher competition means that profits are lower in the industry, so any given performance contract will generate lower expected benefits because for a given effort level the profit related part of pay will be lower. This is the standard Schumpeterian reason for expecting lower innovative effort in high competition industries.

Vives (2008) shows that there are other forces at play when we allow endogenous entry and exit even for symmetric firms. In general, the average firm will be larger in equilibrium as the more intense competition induces exit, and the larger firms will have a greater incentive to introduce productivity increasing HR practices, with the fixed costs of introducing them over a large sales base. Thus, allowing for entry will tend to strengthen the positive effect of competition, as firms will in equilibrium be larger and so have higher sales to spread fixed costs.

What about the empirical evidence? The evidence from Fig. 2.4 suggested that HR management practices were better in the US, where competitive selection forces are likely

[24] *The Wealth of Nations*, Book I Chapter XI Part I, p. 148.

to be very strong. More formally, we can look at the conditional correlation between the HR management score and indicators of competitive intensity. Whether measured by trade openness, the industry inverse Lerner Index or simply the number of perceived rivals, competition is robustly and positively associated with higher management practice scores both with and without firm fixed effects (see Bloom et al., 2009b). Note that the obvious endogeneity bias here is to underestimate the importance of competition, as better managed firms are likely to have higher profit margins, lower import penetration ratios and drive out their rivals[25]. Bloom et al. (2010c) use political competition as an instrumental variable to account for unusually high numbers of hospitals in some areas of the country in the UK public healthcare system (hospitals are rarely closed down in politically marginal constituencies). They find that the positive effects of competition grow stronger when endogeneity is taken explicitly into account.

Consistent with these general results on the positive association of competition on explicit measures of HR management, there is other evidence which also gets closer to causal effects when focusing explicitly on incentive pay. Guadalupe and Cunat (forthcoming) show that the pay-performance sensitivity for US CEOs is stronger when import competition is stronger (as measured by tariffs). Guadalupe and Cunat (2009) they show a similar result using US banking deregulation as an exogenous shift to competition. And in Guadalupe and Cunat (2005) they also find that the correlation between pay and firm performance (for UK workers and executives) strengthens with competition, using the exchange rate appreciation in 1996 which differentially affected traded and non-traded sectors.

5.3. Ownership and governance

The managerial technology perspective suggests that organizations with poor governance are less likely to use appropriate HR management techniques. In particular, there has been a lively debate on the performance effects of family firms (e.g. Bertrand and Schoar, 2006). Firms which are both family owned and family run (typically by the eldest son—*primogeniture*) are very common, especially in developing countries. Figure 5.1 plots the averages of the Bloom-Van Reenen HR management scores by ownership category. Firms that are family owned and family managed ("Family, family CEO") tend to be badly managed on average, while the family owned but externally managed ("Family, external CEO") look very similar to dispersed shareholders. Government-owned firms also have low management scores, while firms owned by Private Equity score well.

This finding is robust to more systematic controls for other covariates (see Bloom and Van Reenen (2007)). Family ownership *per se* is not correlated with worse HR management practices, it is when family ownership is combined with the CEO being

---

[25] There is a literature examining how incentive pay contracts can be used as commitment devices to tougher competition (e.g. Aggarwal and Samwick, 1999). They find evidence of lower pay-performance sensitivity in firms with more volatile stock prices.

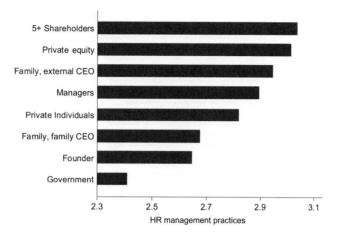

Figure 5.1 *Ownership, governance and HR management.* Note: Averages taken across a random sample of medium (100 to 5000 employee) manufacturing firms within each country. 5850 observations in total. *(Source: Bloom et al. (2009b))*

chosen as the eldest son that the quality of management appears to be very poor. This is consistent with the idea that limiting the talent pool to a single individual is not the optimal form of CEO selection. It is also consistent with Pérez-Gonzáles (2006) and Bennesden et al. (2007), who find that inherited family control appears to cause worse performance. This result is strengthened by using the gender of the eldest child as an instrumental variable for family management, as families usually only relinquish control and bring in external managers when faced with a severe crisis.

Another dimension of ownership is whether the firm is domestic or multinational. Bloom et al. (2009b) found that there is a "pecking order" in management scores, with purely domestic firms at the bottom, firms that export but do not produce overseas next and multinational firms at the top[26]. This is broadly consistent with Helpman et al. (2004). In fact, multinational subsidiaries tend to have better HR management in every country (see Fig. 5.2), consistent with the idea that they can "transplant" some of their HR practices overseas. This is important, as it suggests that a mechanism for management practices to diffuse internationally is through the investments of overseas firms.

Some direct evidence on the importance of this mechanism is presented in Bloom et al. (2010a). As noted in Section 3.5 they found that US firms appear to be much more effective in using IT to improve their productivity, and this in turn is related to American firms' greater use of modern HRM practices (incentive pay, careful hiring, rigorous appraisals and promotions, etc.). They show that the subsidiaries of US multinationals in Europe have higher IT productivity than comparable multinational affiliates, use more

---

[26] Osterman (1994) also finds that firms who sell in international markets are more likely to have adopted an "innovative work practice (teams, job rotation, TQM or Quality Circles).

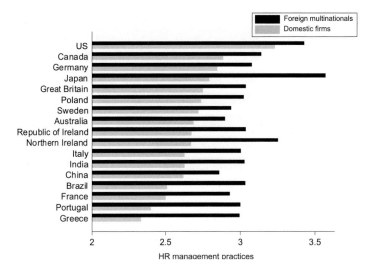

Figure 5.2 *Multinationals take good HR management practices abroad.* Note: Averages taken across a random sample of medium (100 to 5000 employee) manufacturing firms within each country. 5850 observations in total. *(Source: Bloom et al. (2009b))*

of these HRM practices and have higher productivity, primarily from their superior use of IT. The authors argue that the US advantage in HRM practices could account for about half of the faster productivity growth in the US (over Europe) post 1995.

5.4. Work organization: the example of decentralization

An important aspect of HRM is work design—how are roles ascribed to different jobs? In this sub-section we focus on one aspect of design which we label "decentralization". For example, how many decision rights are delegated from the CEO to the plant manager? How much control over the pace of work is delegated from the plant manager to the production worker? This is perhaps the most widely studied theoretical aspect of the workplace after pay incentives and there is a smaller, but growing empirical literature.

Note that decentralization is different from managerial spans of control. These are distinct concepts as the span and depth (number of levels) of a hierarchy are compatible with different power relationships between the levels. Nevertheless there is some evidence that the move towards delayering over the last twenty years has been associated with decentralization (see Rajan and Wulf, 2006), and we will touch on this below.

5.4.1. Measurement of decentralization

A key factor in any organization is who makes the decisions? A centralized firm is one where these are all taken at the top of the hierarchy and a decentralized firm is where decision-making is more evenly dispersed throughout the hierarchy. An extreme case of decentralized organization is a market economy where atomistic individuals make all the decisions and spot contract with each other. The origin of many of the debates on decentralization has their origins in the 1930s over the relative merits of a market economy relative to a centrally planned one.

How can this concept be operationalized empirically? One way is to look at the organization charts of firms ("organogram") as graphical representations of the formal authority structure. One of the best studies in this area is Rajan and Wulf (2006) who use the charts of over 300 large US corporations 1987-1998 to examine the evolution of organizations (e.g. how many people directly report to the CEO as a measure of the span of control). They find that the number of people reporting to the CEO has been rising over the period because intermediate managers—particularly the COO (Chief Operations Offices)—have been removed. Whether the lower levels have obtained more power because their immediate bosses (the COOs) have gone, or less power because they are now dealing directly with the CEOs is not so clear. What is clear is that these large US corporations have been delayering systematically over time by removing senior managerial layers, leading to more junior managers reporting directly in to the CEO. Hence, this highlights the differences between measuring organizational shape (the number of layers in an organization) and real power (where the actual decisions are made).

Observing whether a firm is decentralized into profit centers is useful, as this is a formal delegation of power—the head of such a business unit will be performance managed on profitability. If the firm is composed of cost (or revenue) centers this indicates less decentralization. If the firm does not even delegate responsibility at all, this is more centralized. Acemoglu et al. (2007, henceforth AALVZ) use this distinction.

Unfortunately, as Max Weber and (more recently) Aghion and Tirole (1997) stressed, formal authority is not the same as real authority as the company organogram may not reflect where real power lies. A criticism of AALVZ is that just using profit centers as an indicator is rather crude and a better way is directly survey the firms themselves. Bloom et al. (2009d) measure decentralization from the central headquarters (CHQ) to the plant manager over investment, hiring, marketing and product introduction, and combine these four indictors into one (mean-zero) decentralization index. As with management quality, decentralization displays considerable variation across firms. There is also a large difference across countries as shown in Fig. 5.3. Interestingly, the US, UK and Northern European countries are the most decentralized and Southern Europe and the Asian countries the most centralized.

5.4.2. Theories of decentralization

The basic trade off in the decentralization decisions is between the efficient use of local information (see Radner, 1993) favoring delegation and the principal-agent problem where the agent has weaker incentives to maximize the value of the firm than the principal (on the trade-off see Aghion and Tirole, 1997).

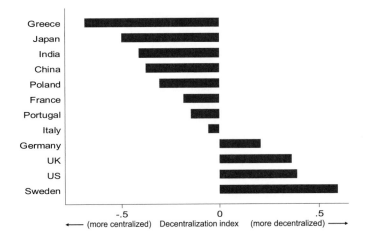

Figure 5.3 *Decentralization of firm decision making by country.* Note: High (positive) scores means plant managers have more autonomy of plant level investment, hiring, new products and marketing from the corporate head-quarters. Low (negative) scores means plant managers have little autonomy and mainly follow instructions from their corporate head-quarters. Averages taken across a random sample of medium (100 to 5000 employee) manufacturing firms within each country. 5850 observations in total. *(Source: Bloom et al. (2009a))*

The benefits from decentralization arise from at least three sources. First, decentralizing decision-making reduces the costs of information transfer and communication. In a hierarchical organization, information that has been processed at lower levels of the hierarchy has to be transferred upstream. This induces a cost due to the need that information be codified and then received and analyzed at various levels (Bolton and Dewatripont, 1994). When decision-making is decentralized, information is processed at the level where it is used so that the cost of communication is lower. Second, decentralization increases firms' speed of response to market changes (Thesmar and Thoenig, 1999). One reason for this is that hierarchical organizations are characterized by a high degree of specialization of workers. Any response to market changes involves the coordination of a great number of activities so that overall firm's reaction speed is low. When responsibility is transferred downstream, it is most often delegated to teams of workers, generally involved in multi-tasking. This allows a swifter reaction to market changes given that coordination involves a limited number of multi-skilled workers. Finally, decentralization of decision-making may increase productivity through rising job satisfaction. Delegation of responsibility goes along with more employee involvement, greater information sharing and a greater participation of lower level staff.

Turning to the costs of decentralization, we highlight four of them. First, costs arise from the risk of duplication of information in the absence of centralized management. Workers are now in charge of analyzing new pieces of information. With decentralization the risk of replication in information processing increases, both across individuals and across teams. A related risk is that of an increase in the occurrence of "mistakes" as there is less co-ordination. A second standard cost is the loss of co-ordination efficiencies as externalities between units are not internalized (e.g. plants producing substitutable products will tend to price too low)—see Alonso et al. (2008) for a general discussion. A third cost is that decentralization makes it more difficult to exploit returns to scale (Thesmar and Thoenig, 2000). The reason for this is that as multi-tasking develops returns to specialization decreases so that large-scale production becomes less beneficial. Finally, decentralization may reduce workers' efficiency if the increase in responsibility that it implies induces rising stress (Askenazy, 2001). In this case, productivity may be directly affected and/or reduced through lower job satisfaction.

5.4.3. What influences decentralization?

We divide our analysis into the examination of three groups of factors that influence decentralization: technological (complexity, ICT and heterogeneity), economic (human capital and competition) and cultural.

Complexity

Some basic factors determine decentralization. All else equal a larger firm will require more decentralization than a small firm. A sole entrepreneur does not need to delegate because he is his own boss, but as more workers are added, doing everything by himself is no longer feasible. Penrose (1959) and Chandler (1962) stressed that decentralization was a necessary feature of larger firms, because CEOs do not have the time to take every decision in large firms. Similarly as firms expand in their scope both geographically and in product space, local information will become more costly to transmit so this will also favor decentralization. Bloom et al. (2009d) find that larger firms and plants owned by foreign multinationals are significantly more likely to be decentralized. This is likely to be because of increased complexity[27].

Information and communication technology

Garicano (2000) formalizes the idea of the firm as a cognitive hierarchy. There are a number of problems to be solved and the task is how to solve them in the most efficient manner. The simplest tasks are performed by those at the lowest level of the hierarchy and the "exceptional" problems are passed upwards to an expert. The cost of passing problems upwards is that communication costs are non-trivial. The benefit of passing the problem upwards is that it economizes on the cognitive burden of lower level employees.

This framework was designed to address the impacts of ICT. Interestingly, information technologies have different implications for decentralization than communication technologies. Consider again the decentralization decision between the

---

[27] Colombo and Delmastro (2004) also find that complexity related variables are associated with decentralization in their Italian firms.

central headquarters and plant manager. When communication costs fall through (for example) the introduction of a company intranet, it is cheaper for the plant manager to refer more decisions to the corporate officers. So communication technologies should cause centralization. By contrast, technologies that make it easier for the plant manager to acquire information (e.g. Enterprise Resource Planning software, ERP like SAP) means that decentralization should increase. An example in law firms would be Lexus Nexus that enables junior lawyers to quickly find relevant cases without consulting a more senior associate or partner.

Bloom et al. (2009e) test this theory and find considerable empirical support. Computer networks (reducing communication costs) significantly increase centralization, whereas tools to help managers access more information significantly increase decentralization. The magnitude of the effect is substantial. An increase in the use of Enterprise Resource Planning usage by 60% (the average difference in ICT between Europe and the US) is associated with an increase of the index of their plant manager's autonomy index by 0.025, which is equivalent to a large increase in the supply of human capital (roughly the same as the increase in US college graduates between 1990 and 2000). The finding that information technology is a complement with a particular form of HRM (decentralization) is consistent the productivity evidence discussed in Section 3.5.

Heterogeneity

AALVZ present a model of decentralization in which firms learn about how to implement a new technology from other firms in their industry. The new technology on average improves productivity, but there is heterogeneity in the benefits from introducing it, so not all firms should do things in the same way. The set-up is of a principal (central headquarters) deciding whether or not to delegate to a local agent (plant manager) who is better informed about the technology but has imperfectly aligned incentives. As more firms experiment with the technology in the same industry the principal has a better public history of information about the right way to implement the new technology, so has less need to decentralize to the agent.

One key result follows: the greater the heterogeneity of the industry the more decentralized will be the average firm. Heterogeneity here means that "right" way to implement the technology has a larger variance, so the opportunity to learn from other firms is circumscribed because what is good for my neighbor is less likely to be what is good for me. As discussed earlier, this is akin to Prendergast (2002a)—the more uncertain the environment the greater the relative value of local knowledge. Two other implications are that, first, the more innovative the technology (i.e. closer to the frontier), the less will be known about how to use it so the greater will be the likelihood of decentralization. Second, if a firm can learn from its past experience, older firms will be less likely to delegate than younger firms.

AALVZ measure decentralization using both formal measures of whether firms are organized into profit centers and "real" survey measures of the power managers have over hiring decisions. Their results are illustrated in Fig. 5.4, where Panel A shows there is a positive relationship between decentralization and heterogeneity[28], Panel B shows decentralization is higher among firms closer to the technological frontier, and Panel C shows older firms appear more centralized than younger firms. These are all consistent with the theory.

Human capital

One of the reasons for the renewed interest in organizational change by labor economists was the attempt to understand why technology seemed to increase the demand for human capital, and thus contribute to the rise in wage inequality experiences by the US, UK and other countries since the late 1970s (e.g. Machin and Van Reenen, 1998, 2008). Many theories have been proposed (see Autor et al., 2003, for a review), but one hypothesis is that lower IT prices increased decentralization incentives for the reasons outlined in Garicano (2000)'s model discussed above. Further, decentralization could be complementary with skills because more educated workers are better able to analyze and synthesize new pieces of knowledge so that the benefits of the local processing of information are enhanced. Second, the cost of training them for multi-tasking is lower and they are more autonomous and less likely to make mistakes.

This has three main implications: (i) Decentralization leads to skill upgrading within firms. This is due to the fact that the return to new work practices is greater when the skill level of the workforce is higher; (ii) a lower price of skilled labor relative to unskilled labor will accelerate decentralization; (iii) skill intensive firms will experience greater productivity growth when decentralizing.

Caroli and Van Reenen (2001) find support for all three predictions. They estimate production functions (with the relevant interactions), skill share equations and organizational design equations. A novel feature of this approach is that because labor is traded in a market, it is possible to use local skill price variation to examine the complementarity issues. They find that higher skill prices make decentralization less likely, consistent with "skill biased organizational change"[29].

Product Market Competition

If competition has made swift decisions more important then this will have increased the salience of local knowledge, leading to greater decentralization under the framework discussed above. Similarly if competition reduces the agency problem then decentralization is more likely. There are countervailing forces however. For example, a larger number of firms help learning, which in the AALVZ framework will *reduce* the need to decentralize.

---

[28] The authors show that the anomalous first decile is due to the disproportionate number of older and less productive firms in this decile (this is controlled for in the regressions). Kastl et al. (2008) also find more innovative firms (as measured by R&D intensity) are more decentralized.

[29] Bloom et al. (2009d) also find robust empirical evidence that firms with more skilled employees are more decentralized. Bartel et al. (2007) also find human capital complementary with "innovative" HR practices.

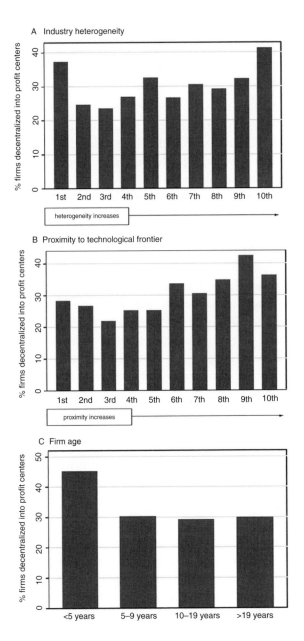

Figure 5.4 *Factors associated with decentralization.* Notes: Decentralization defined in terms of percentage of firms that are profit centers (rather than cost centers). Data from 3570 firms in French COI national survey. *(Source: Acemoglu et al. (2007))*

The empirical evidence is clearer cut. Bloom et al. (2010b) find a robust positive association between competition and decentralization. A similar positive correlation was reported in AALVZ and Marin and Verdier (2008). All of these are cross sectional studies. Guadalupe and Wulf (forthcoming) use the Rajan and Wulf (2006) panel data on the changing organizational structure of firms over time. They argue that the Canadian-US Free Trade Agreement in 1989 constitutes an exogenous increase in competition for US firms in the industries where tariffs were removed. Exploiting this policy experiment they find that competition is associated with delayering (increasing span for CEO) and that this is likely to also reflect increased delegation.

Culture

In recent years, economists have started to take cultural factors more seriously in determining economic outcomes (e.g. Guiso et al., 2006; Greif, 1994). Part of this is due to the influence of Putnam (1993) on the importance of social capital and the finding that trust is important in a number of economic dimensions (e.g. see Knack and Keefer, 1997, on economic growth or Guiso et al., 2009, on foreign trade).

Trust is an obvious candidate from improving delegation incentives as it will relieve the agency problem that the delegated agent will steal from the principal. Bloom et al. (2009d) observe more delegation in countries where rule of law is strong. However, contracts are never perfectly enforceable and this leaves a role for trust to help generate more delegation. And indeed trust also appears important—they also find a higher level of trust in the region where a firm is located is associated with a significantly greater degree of decentralization. They also exploit the fact that they have many subsidiaries of multinational firms so they can construct measures of trust in the country of origin (the multinational's headquarters) and location (country were affiliate is set up), and find that both of these seem to matter for decentralization. Further, using the bilateral trust between countries they find that when trust between pairs of countries is high, decentralization is more likely (even after controlling for region of location and country of origin fixed effects). This suggests that trust can affect the structures of global firms and that some aspects of organization are transplanted abroad, as suggested by recent theories of international trade.

6. CONCLUSIONS

Human Resource Management (HRM) has changed dramatically in the last two decades, with Personnel Economics now a major field in labor economics. The mark of this work is to use standard economic tools applied to the special circumstances of managing labor within companies. In surveying the literature we have detected several broad themes:

First, although there have been significant improvements in measuring management in general and HRM in particular, we are struck by the scarcity of high quality data. This is especially true in the time series dimension, where our basic understanding of trends, even in the more easily measured dimensions of HRM such as incentive pay, is remarkably poor. This reflects a general paucity of data on the internal structures of firms which needs to be addressed by researchers and statistical agencies.

Second, data concerns notwithstanding, there do appear to be some facts emerging. There is a discernible trend towards the incidence of more incentive pay in recent decades (at least in the US and the UK). More aggressive use of high powered-incentives on pay, promotions, hiring and firing is more prevalent in the US and Northern Europe than Southern Europe and Asia. The data on productivity is much better: we have shown wide distributions of productivity within and between countries and HRM appears to mirror these patterns.

Third, there is suggestive evidence that certain types of HRM raise productivity. There is certainly a robust positive cross sectional association between bundles of "modern" HRM practices and productivity, but with some exceptions (e.g. Ichniowski et al., 1997) these are not robust in the time series dimension. Studies of single or small groups of firms have been more successful in identifying a positive association of changes in HRM policies (in particular individual and group incentive pay) and productivity. But hard causal evidence of the type common in program evaluation elsewhere in labor economics is rare, and a major future research challenge is to generate better designs to test the causal relationship.

Fourth, causality issue apart, there is suggestive evidence of widespread complementarities both between different types of HRM practices and between HRM and other aspects of firm organization (Milgrom and Roberts, 1990). Information and Communication Technology appears particularly important, with several pieces of evidence that combining ICT with the right fit of HRM practices makes a large difference for productivity.

Fifth, although the "Design" perspective of Personal Economics has led to powerful insights, we have argued that some types of HRM (and management in general) has technological aspects in the sense that they are likely to raise profitability in a firm, on average, are likely to be the right ones for all firms to adopt. Under this view, the productivity dispersion we observe is partially linked to the fact that some firms that been slower to adopt these than others. Weak competition and poor governance in family run firms are both associated with sub-optimal HRM practices, consistent with this "Managerial Technology" perspective.

Finally, we have made substantial theoretical and empirical progress in one aspect of work organization—the decentralization of decisions. Technological complexity, ICT, skill supply and social capital all seem to foster more decentralization (although causality remains an issue again). It would be good to see more efforts to drill down on other forms of work organization.

HRM and productivity is an exciting and lively field and has made great strides in the last two decades. We see its future as being integrated in the general research programs of the economics of organization and management, which are becoming a major part of modern labor economics.

ACKNOWLEDGEMENTS

We would like to thank the Economic and Social Research Council for their financial support through the Center for Economic Performance. This survey draws substantially on joint work with Daron Acemoglu, Philippe Aghion, Eve Caroli, Luis Garicano, Christos Genakos, Claire Lelarge, Ralf Martin, Raffaella Sadun and Fabrizio Zilibotti. We would like to thank Orley Ashenfelter, Oriana Bandiera, Alex Bryson, David Card, Edward Lazear, Paul Oyer, John Roberts, Kathy Shaw and participants in conferences in Berkeley and the LSE for helpful comments.

REFERENCES

Abowd, John M., 1989. The effect of wage bargains on the stock market value of the firm. American Economic Review 79 (4), 774–800.

Abowd, John M., Kramarz, Francis, Margolis, David, 1999. High wage workers and high wage firms. Econometrica 67 (2), 251–333.

Abowd, John M., Lemieux, Thomas, 1993. The effects of product market competition on collective bargaining agreements: the case of foreign competition in Canada. Quarterly Journal of Economics 108 (4), 983–1014.

Abowd, John H., Haltiwanger, John, Lane, Julia, 2008. Wage structure and labor mobility in the United States. In: Lazear, Edward, Shaw, Kathryn (Eds.), An International Comparison of the Structure of Wages within and Across Firms. University of Chicago, Chicago.

Acemoglu, Daron, Aghion, Philippe, Lelarge, Claire, Van Reenen, John, Zilibotti, Fabrizio, 2007. Technology, information and the decentralization of the firm. Quarterly Journal of Economics 122 (4), 1759–1799.

Ackerberg, Daniel, Benkard, Lanier, Berry, Steven, Pakes, Ariel, 2007. Econometric tools for analyzing market outcomes. In: Heckman, James, Leamer, Edward (Eds.), Handbook of Econometrics, vol. 6A. North-Holland, Amsterdam.

Ackerberg, Daniel, Botticini, Maristella, 2002. Endogenous matching and the empirical determinants of contract form. Journal of Political Economy 110, 564–591.

Adams, Christopher, 2005. Agent discretion, adverse selection and the risk-incentive trade-off. Working Paper, Federal Trade Commission.

Aggarwal, Rajesh K., Samwick, Andrew A., 1999. The other side of the trade-off: the impact of risk on executive compensation. Journal of Political Economy 107 (1), 65–105.

Aghion, Philippe, Tirole, Jean, 1997. Formal and real authority in organizations. Journal of Political Economy 105 (1), 1–29.

Alonso, Ricardo, Dessein, Wouter, Matouschek, Niko, 2008. When does coordination require centralization? American Economic Review 98 (1), 145–179.

Asch, Beth, 1990. Do incentives matter? the case of navy recruiters. Industrial and Labor Relations Review 43 (3), 89–107.

Askenazy, Philippe, 2001. Innovative workplace practices and occupational injuries and illnesses in the United States. Economic and Industrial Democracy 22 (4), 485–516.

Athey, Susan, Stern, Scott, 1998. An empirical framework for testing theories about complementarity in organizational design. NBER Working Paper 6600.

Atkeson, Andrew, Kehoe, Patrick J., 2005. Modeling and measuring organization capital. Journal of Political Economy 113 (5), 1026–1053.

Autor, David, Levy, Frank, Murnane, Richard, 2003. The skill content of recent technological change: an empirical exploration. Quarterly Journal of Economics 118 (4), 1279–1334.

Aw, Bee Yan, Roberts, Mark J., Xu, Daniel, 2008. R&D Investments, exporting, and the evolution of firm productivity. American Economic Review 98 (2), 451–456.

Baily, Martin, Hulten, Charles, Campbell, David, 1992. Productivity dynamics in manufacturing plants. Brookings Papers on Economic Activity, Microeconomics 187–249.

Baiker, Katherine, Jacobson, Mireille, 2007. Finders keepers: forfeiture laws, policing, and local budgets. Journal of Public Economics 91 (11–12), 2113–2136.

Baker, George, 1992. Incentive measures and performance measurement. Journal of Political Economy 100, 598–614.

Baker, George, Gibbons, Robert, Murphy, Kevin, 1994. Subjective performance measures in optimal incentive contracts. Quarterly Journal of Economics 109, 1125–1156.

Baker, George, Hubbard, Thomas, 2004. Contractibility and asset ownership: on board computers and governance in US trucking. Quarterly Journal of Economics 119 (4), 1443–1479.

Bandiera, Oriana, Barankay, Iwan, Rasul, Imran, 2005. Social preferences and the response to incentives: evidence from personnel data. Quarterly Journal of Economics 120 (3), 917–962.

Bandiera, Oriana, Barankay, Iwan, Rasul, Imran, 2007. Incentives for managers and inequality among workers: evidence from a firm-level experiment. Quarterly Journal of Economics.

Bandiera, Oriana, Barankay, Iwan, Rasul, Imran, 2009a. Social connections and incentives in the workplace: evidence from personnel data. Econometrica 77, 1047–1094.

Bandiera, Oriana, Barankay, Iwan, Rasul, Imran, 2009b. Team incentives: evidence from a field experiment, LSE mimeo.

Bandiera, Oriana, Guiso, Luigi, Prat, Andrea, Sadun, Raffaella, 2010. Matching firms, managers and incentives, LSE mimeo.

Bartel, Ann, Ichniowski, Casey, Shaw, Kathryn, 2007. How does information technology really affect productivity? Plant-level comparisons of product innovation, process improvement and worker skills. Quarterly Journal of Economics 122 (4), 1721–1758.

Bartelsman, Eric, Dhrymes, Phoebus, 1998. Productivity dynamics US manufacturing plants 1972-1986. Journal of Productivity Analysis 9 (1), 5–33.

Bartelsman, Eric, Doms, Mark, 2000. Understanding productivity: lessons from longitudinal microdata. Journal of Economic Literature 38 (3), 569–594.

Bartelsman, Eric, Haltiwanger, John, Scarpetta, Stefano, 2008. Cross country differences in productivity: the role of allocative efficiency. University of Maryland mimeo.

Bennesden, Morten, Nielsen, Kasper, Pérez-Gonzáles, Francisco, Wolfenzon, Daniel, 2007. Inside the family firm: the role of families in succession decisions and performance. Quarterly Journal of Economics 122 (2), 647–691.

Bertrand, Marianne, Schoar, Antoinette, 2006. The role of family in family firms. Journal of Economic Perspectives 20 (2), 73–96.

Black, Sandra, Lynch, Lisa, 2004. What's driving the new economy? The benefits of workplace innovation. Economic Journal 114 (493), 97–116.

Black, Sandra, Lynch, Lisa, 2001. How to compete: the impact of workplace practices and information technology on productivity. Review of Economics and Statistics 83 (3), 434–445.

Blanchflower, David, Oswald, Andrew, Sanfrey, Peter, 1996. Wages, profits and rent sharing. Quarterly Journal of Economics 111 (1), 227–251.

Blasi, Joseph, Freeman, Richard, Mackin, Christopher, Kruse, Douglas, 2009. Creating a bigger pie? The effects of employee ownership, profit sharing, and stock options on workplace performance. In: Kruse, Douglas, Blasi, Joseph, Freeman, Richard (Eds.), Shared Capitalism at Work: Employee Ownership, Profit and Gain Sharing, and Broad-based Stock Options. University of Chicago Press.

Bloom, N., 2009. The impact of uncertainty shocks. Econometrica 77 (3), 623–685.

Bloom, Nick, Van Reenen, John, 2007. Measuring and explaining management practices across firms and countries. Quarterly Journal of Economics 122 (4), 1341–1408.

Bloom, N., Eifert, B., Mahajan, A., McKenzie, D., Roberts, J., 2009a. Does management matter: evidence from India. Stanford mimeo.

Bloom, Nick, Genakos, Christos, Sadun, Raffaella, Van Reenen, John, 2009b. Does Management Matter? New empirics and old theory. LSE/Stanford mimeo.

Bloom, Nick, Kretschmer, Tobias, Van Reenen, John, 2009c. Work-life balance, management practices and productivity. In: Freeman, Richard, Shaw, Kathy (Eds.), International Differences in the Business Practice and Productivity of Firms. University of Chicago Press, Chicago.

Bloom, Nick, Sadun, Raffaella, Van Reenen, John, 2009d. The organization of firms across countries. Centre for Economic Performance Discussion Paper No 937.

Bloom, Nick, Garicano, Luis, Sadun, Raffaella, Van Reenen, John, 2009e. The distinct effects of information technology and communication technology on firm organization. Centre for Economic Performance Discussion Paper No. 927.

Bloom, Nick, Sadun, Raffaella, Van Reenen, John, 2010a. Americans do IT better: American multinationals and the productivity miracle. LSE/Stanford mimeo (revision of NBER Working Paper 13085). American Economic Review (forthcoming).

Bloom, Nick, Sadun, Raffaella, Van Reenen, John, 2010b. Does product market competition lead firms to decentralize? American Economic Review Papers and Proceedings 100, 434–438.

Bloom, Nick, Propper, Carol, Seiler, Stephan, Van Reenen, John, 2010c. The impact of competition on management quality: evidence from public hospitals. Centre for Economic Performance Discussion Paper 983.

Bolton, Patrick, Dewatripont, Mathias, 1994. The firm as a communication network. Quarterly Journal of Economics 109 (4), 809–839.

Bolton, Patrick, Dewatripont, Mathias, 2005. Contract Theory. MIT Press, Cambridge.

Boning, Brent, Ichniowski, Casey, Shaw, Kathryn, 2007. Opportunity counts: teams and the effectiveness of production incentives. Journal of Labor Economics 25 (4), 613–650.

Blundell, Richard, Costa-Diaz, Monica, 2009. Alternative approaches to evaluation in empirical micro-economics. Journal of Human Resources 44 (3), 565–640.

Bond, Steve, Van Reenen, John, 2007. Micro-econometric models of investment and employment. In: Heckman, James, Leamer, Edward (Eds.), Handbook of Econometrics, vol. 6A. pp. 4417–4498 (Chapter 65).

Bresnahan, Timothy, Brynjolfsson, Erik, Hitt, Lorin, 2002. Information technology, workplace organization and the demand for skilled labor: firm-level evidence. Quarterly Journal of Economics 117 (1), 339–376.

Brown, Charles, 1990. Firms' choice of method of pay. Industrial and Labor Relations Review 43, 165–182.

Bruhn, M., Karlan, D., Schoar, A., 2010. The effect of mentorship on SME growth in Mexico. University of Chicago, mimeo.

Brynjolfsson, Erik, Hitt, Lorin, 2003. Computing productivity: firm-level evidence. Review of Economics and Statistics 85 (4), 793–808.

Bryson, Alex, Freeman, Richard, 2009. Work and wellbeing. National Institute Economic Review 209, 70–71.

Bryson, Alex, Wood, Stephen, 2009. High involvement management. In: Brown, W., Bryson, Alex, Forth, John, Whitfield, K. (Eds.), The Evolution of the Modern Workplace. Cambridge University Press, Cambridge.

Bull, Clive, 1987. The existence of self-enforcing implicit contracts. Quarterly Journal of Economics 102 (1), 147–159.

Burgess, Simon, Propper, Carol, Ratto, Marisa, von Hinke, Vanessa, Scholder, Kessler, Tominey, Emma, 2007. Smarter task assignment or greater effort: the impact of incentives on team performance. Economic Journal.

Capelli, Peter, Neumark, David, 2001. Do 'high-performance' work practices improve establishment-level outcomes? Industrial and Labor Relations Review 54 (4), 737–775.

Caroli, Eve, Van Reenen, John, 2001. Skill biased organizational change. Quarterly Journal of Economics 116 (4), 1449–1492.

Caselli, Francesco, 2005. Accounting for cross country income differences. In: Aghion, Philppe, Durlauf, S. (Eds.), Handbook of Economic Growth. Elsevier, North-Holland.

Cahuc, Pierre, Postel-Vinay, Fabienne, Robin, Jean-Marc, 2006. Wage bargaining and on-the-job search. Econometrica 323–364.

Chandler, Alfred, 1962. Strategy and Structure: Chapters in the History of the Industrial Enterprise. MIT Press, Cambridge.

Chevalier, Judith, Ellison, Glenn, 1997. Risk taking by mutual funds as a response to incentives. Journal of Political Economy 105 (6), 1167–1200.

Choi, James, Laibson, David, Madrian, Brigitte, 2008. $100 Bills on the sidewalk: suboptimal investment in 401 (k) Plans. NBER Working Paper #11554.

Cristiner, Annalisa, Leoni, Riccardo, Sandrine, Labory, Gai, Alessandro, 2001. New work practices in Italy. Adoption and performance effects. University of Bergamo, mimeo.

Colombo, Massimo, Delmastro, Marco, 2004. Delegation of authority in business organizations: an empirical test. Journal of Industrial Economics 52 (1), 53–80.

Conley, Timothy G., Udry, Christophe, 2010. Learning about a new technology: pineapple in Ghana. American Economic Review 100 (1), 35–69.

Cooke, William, 1994. Employee participation programs, group-based incentives, and company performance: a union-nonunion comparison. Industrial and Labor Relations Review 47 (4), 594–609.

Corrado, C., Hulten, C., Sichel, D., 2006. Intangible capital and economic growth. NBER Working Paper No. 11948.

Courty, Pascal, Marschke, Gerald, 2004. An empirical investigation of gaming responses to performance incentives. Journal of Labor Economics 22 (1), 23–56.

Criscuolo, Chiara, Haskel, Jonathan, Martin, Ralf, 2003. Building the evidence base for productivity policy using business data linking. Economic Trends 600, 39–51.

Duflo, Esther, Kremer, Michael, Robinson, Jonathan, 2009. Nudging farmers to use fertilizer: theory and experimental evidence from Kenya. Harvard mimeo.

Dearden, Lorraine, Reed, Howard, Van Reenen, John, 2006. Training and corporate productivity: evidence from a panel of UK industries. Oxford Bulletin of Economic and Social Research 68 (4), 397–421.

DeVaro, Jed, Kurtulus, Fidan A., 2007. An empirical analysis of risk, incentives, and the delegation of worker authority. Working Paper, University of Massachusetts at Amherst.

DiNardo, John, Lee, David, 2004. Economic impacts of new unionization on private sector employers: 1984–2001. Quarterly Journal of Economics 119, 1383–1441.

DiNardo, John, Lee, David, 2011. Program evaluation and research designs. In: Card, David (Ed.), Handbook of Labor Economics, vol. 4a. Elsevier, pp. 463–536.

Dunne, Timothy, Foster, Lucia, Haltiwanger, John, Troske, Kenneth, 2004. Wage and productivity dispersion in US manufacturing: the role of computer investments. Journal of Labour Economics 22 (2), 397–429.

Easton, George, Jarrell, Sherry, 1998. The effects of total quality management on corporate performance: an empirical investigation. Journal of Business 71 (2), 253–307.

Edmans, Alex, Gabaix, Xavier, Landier, Augustin, 2008. A multiplicative model of optimal CEO incentives in market equilibrium. Review of Financial Studies.

Faggio, Giulia, Salvanes, Kjell, Van Reenen, John, 2007. The evolution of inequality in productivity and wages: panel data evidence. Centre for Economic Performance Discussion Paper No. 821.

Fernie, Sue, Metcalf, David, 1999. It's not what you pay it's the way that you pay it and that's what gets results: jockeys' pay and performance. Labour 13 (2), 385–411.

Foster, Lucia, Krizan, C.J., Haltiwanger, John, 2006. Market selection, reallocation and restructuring in the US retail trade sector in the 1990s. Review of Economics and Statistics 88 (4), 748–758.

Foster, Lucia, Haltiwanger, John, Syverson, Chad, 2009. Reallocation, firm turnover and efficiency: selection on productivity or profitability. American Economic Review 98 (1), 394–425.

Foster, Andrew, Rosenzweig, Mark, 1996. Comparative advantage, information and the allocation of workers to tasks: evidence from an agricultural labor market. Review of Economic Studies 63 (3), 347–374.

Freeman, Richard, Kleiner, Morris, 2005. The last American shoe manufacturers: decreasing productivity and increasing profits in the shift from piece rates to continuous flow production. Journal of Industrial Relations 44 (2), 307–330.

Freeman, Richard, Medoff, James, 1984. What Do Unions Do? Basic Books, New York.

Gant, Jon, Ichniowski, Casey, Shaw, Kathryn, 2002. Social capital and organizational change in high-involvement and traditional work organizations. Journal of Economics & Management Strategy 11 (2), 289–328.

Garicano, Luis, 2000. Hierarchies and the organization of knowledge in production. Journal of Political Economy 108 (5), 874–904.

Gibbons, Robert, 1987. Piece-rate incentive schemes. Journal of Labor Economics 5 (4), 413–429.

Gibbons, Robert, Roberts, J., 2009. The Handbook of Organizational Economics. Princeton University Press, Princeton (forthcoming).

Gibbons, Robert, Waldman, Michael, 1999. Careers in organizations: theory and evidence. In: Ashenfelter, Orley C., Card, David (Eds.), Handbook of Labor Economics, vol. III. North Holland, Amsterdam.

Gibrat, Robert, 1931. Les Inegalites Economiques, Sirey, Paris.

Garen, John, 1994. Executive compensation and principal-agent theory. Journal of Political Economy 102 (6), 1175–1199.

Gaynor, Martin, Rebitzer, James, Taylor, Lowell, 2004. Physician incentives in health maintenance organizations. Journal of Political Economy 112, 915–931.

Glewwe, Paul, Ilias, Nauman, Kremer, Michael, 2003. Teacher incentives. NBER Working Paper 9671.

Greif, Avner, 1994. Cultural beliefs and the organization of society: a historical and theoretical reflection on collectivist and individualistic societies. Journal of Political Economy 102 (5), 912–950.

Griffith, Rachel, Neely, Andrew, 2009. Incentives and managerial experience in multi-task teams: evidence from within a firm. Journal of Labor Economics 27 (1), 49–82.

Griliches, Zvi, 1996. The discovery of the residual: a historical note. Journal of Economic Literature 34 (3), 1324–1330.

Groves, Theodore, Hong, Yongmiao, McMillan, John, Naughton, Barry, 1994. Autonomy and incentives in Chinese state enterprises. Quarterly Journal of Economics 109, 183–209.

Guadalupe, Maria, Cunat, Vicente, 2005. How does product market competition shape incentive contracts? Journal of the European Economic Association MIT Press 3 (5), 1058–1082.

Guadalupe, Maria, Cunat, Vicente, 2009. Globalization and the provision of incentives inside the firm. Journal of Labor Economics (forthcoming).

Guadalupe, Maria, Cunat, Vicente, 2009. Executive compensation and competition in the banking and financial sectors. Journal of Banking and Finance 33, 439–474.

Guadalupe, Maria, Wulf, Julie, 2007. The flattening firm and product market competition: the effects of trade costs and liberalization. American Economic Journal: Applied (forthcoming).

Guiso, Luigi, Sapienza, Paola, Zingales, Luigi, 2006. Does culture affect economic outcomes? The Journal of Economic Perspectives 20 (2), 23–48.

Guiso, Luigi, Sapienza, Paola, Zingales, Luigi, 2009. Cultural biases in economic exchange. Quarterly Journal of Economics 124 (3), 1095–1131.

Hall, Bronwyn, 2003. Innovation and diffusion. In: Fagerberg, Jan, Mowery, Davis, Nelson, Richard (Eds.), Handbook of Innovation. Oxford University Press, Oxford.

Hamilton, Barton H., Nickerson, Jack A., Owan, Hideo, 2003. Team incentives and worker heterogeneity: an empirical analysis of the impact of teams on productivity and participation. Journal of Political Economy 111 (3), 465–497.

Hellerstein, Judith, Neumark, David, Troske, Ken, 1999. Wages, productivity and worker characteristics: evidence from plant level production functions and wage equations. Journal of Labor Economics 17, 409–446.

Helpman, Elhanhan, Melitz, Marc, Yeaple, Stephen, 2004. Export versus FDI with heterogeneous firms. American Economic Review 94 (1), 300–316.

Holmstrom, Bengt, Milgrom, Paul, 1991. Multitask principal-agent analyses: incentive contracts, asset ownership, and job design. Journal of Law, Economics, and Organization 7, 24–52.

Hopenhayn, Hugo, 1992. Entry, exit, and firm dynamics in long run equilibrium. Econometrica 60, 1127–1150.

Hsieh, Chang-Tai, Klenow, Peter, 2007. Misallocation and manufacturing TFP in China and India. NBER Working Paper 13290.

Huselid, Mark, 1995. The impact of human resource management practices on turnover, productivity and corporate financial performance. Academy of Management Journal 38, 635–672.

Huselid, Mark, Becker, Brian, 1996. Methodological issues in cross-sectional and panel estimates of the human resource-firm performance link. Industrial Relations 35, 400–422.

Ichniowski, Casey, 1990. Human resource management systems and the performance of US manufacturing businesses. NBER Working Paper 3449.

Ichniowski, Casey, Shaw, Kathryn, Prennushi, Giovanna, 1997. The effects of human resource management practices on productivity: a study of steel finishing lines. American Economic Review 87 (3), 291–313.

Jones, Derek, Kato, Takao, 1995. The productivity effects of employee stock ownership plans and bonuses: evidence from Japanese panel data. American Economic Review 85 (3), 391–414.

Jorgenson, Dale, Ho, Mun, Stiroh, Kevin, 2008. A retrospective look at the US productivity growth resurgence. Journal of Economic Perspectives 22 (1), 3–24.

Karlan, Dean, Valdivia, Martin, 2009. Teaching entrepreneurship: impact of business training on microfinance clients and institutions. Yale mimeo.

Kastl, Jacob, Martimort, David, Piccolo, Salvatore, 2008. Delegation and R&D incentives: theory and evidence from Italy. Stanford mimeo.

Kahn, Charles, Silva, Emilson, Ziliak, James, 2001. Performance-based wages in tax collection: the Brazilian tax collection reform and its effects. Economic Journal 111 (468), 188–205.

Keane, Michael, Feinberg, Susan, 2008. Advances in logistics and the growth of intra-firm trade: the case of Canadian affiliates of US multinationals. Journal of Industrial Economics LV (4), 571–632.

Klette, Tor, Griliches, Zvi, 1996. The inconsistency of common scale estimators when output prices are unobserved and endogenous. Journal of Applied Econometrics 11, 343–361.

Knack, Stephen, Keefer, Philip, 1997. Does social capital have an economy payoff? A cross-country investigation. Quarterly Journal of Economics 12 (4), 1251–1288.

Knez, Marc, Simester, Duncan, 2001. Firm-wide incentives and mutual monitoring at Continental Airlines. Journal of Labor Economics 19 (4), 743–772.

Kruse, Douglas, Blasi, Joseph, 1997. Employee ownership, employee attitudes, and firm performance. In: Mitchell, Daniel J.B., Lewin, David, Zaidi, Mahumdad (Eds.), Handbook of Resource Management. JAI, Greenwich, CT.

Kruse, Douglas, Blasi, Joseph, Park, Rhokuen, 2009. Shared capitalism in the US economy: prevalence, characteristics, and employee views of financial participation in enterprises. In: Kruse, Douglas, Blasi, Joseph, Freeman, Richard (Eds.), Shared Capitalism at Work: Employee Ownership, Profit and Gain Sharing, and Broad-based Stock Options. University of Chicago Press.

Kwoka, John, Ravenscraft, David, 1986. Cooperation versus rivalry: price-cost margins by line of business. Economica 53, 351–364.

Lafontaine, Francine, Srinivasan, Jagadeesh, 2009. Within firm labor productivity across countries: a case study. In: Freeman, Richard, Shaw, Katheryn (Eds.), International Differences in Business Practices and Productivity of Multinational Firms: A Case Based Approach. University of Chicago Press.

Larkin, Ian, 2007. The cost of high-powered incentives: employee gaming in enterprise software sales. Working Paper, Harvard University.

Lavy, Victor, 2002. Evaluating the effect of teachers' performance incentives on pupils' achievement. Journal of Political Economy 110 (6), 1283–1317.

Lavy, Victor, 2007. Using performance-based pay to improve the quality of teachers. The Future of Children 7 (1), 87–109.

Lavy, Victor, 2009. Performance pay and teachers' effort, productivity and grading ethics. American Economic Review 99 (5), 1979–2011.

Lawler, Edward, Mohrman, Susan, Ledford Jr., Gerald E., 1995. Creating High Performance Organizations: Practices and Results of Employee Involvement and TQM in Fortune 1000 Companies. Jossey-Bass, San Francisco.

Lawler, Edward, Mohrman, Susan, Benson, George, 2001. Organizing for High Performance: Employee Involvement, TQM, Reengineering, and Knowledge Management in the Fortune 1000. Jossey-Bass, San Francisco.

Lawler, Edward, Mohrman, Susan, 2003. Creating a Strategic Human Resources Organization: An Assessment of Trends and New Directions. Stanford University Press.

Lazear, E., 1986. Salaries and piece rates. Journal of Business 9 (3), 405–431.

Lazear, Edward, 1989. Pay equality and industrial politics. Journal of Political Economy 97, 561–580.

Lazear, Edward, 1999. Personnel economics: past lessons and future directions. Journal of Labor Economics 17 (2), 199–236.

Lazear, Edward, 2000. Performance pay and productivity. American Economic Review 90 (5), 1346–1361.

Lazear, Edward, Oyer, Paul, 2009. Personnel economics. In: Gibbons, E., Roberts, D.J. (Eds.), Handbook of Organizational Economics. Princeton University Press, Princeton (forthcoming).

Lazear, Edward, Shaw, Kathryn, 2008. An International Comparison of the Structure of Wages within and across Firms. University of Chicago.

Lemieux, Thomas, MacLeod, W. Bentley, Parent, Daniel, 2009. Performance pay and wage inequality-super. Quarterly Journal of Economics 124 (1), 1–49.

Lucas, Robert, 1978. On the size distribution of business firms. Bell Journal of Economics 9, 508–523.

Machin, Stephen, Van Reenen, John, 1998. Technology and changes in the skill structure: evidence from seven OECD countries. Quarterly Journal of Economics CXI 4 (113), 1215–1244.

Machin, Stephen, Van Reenen, John, 2008. Changes in wage inequality. In: Weinberg, Bruce, Taber, Chris (Eds.), New Palgrave Dictionary of Economics.

MacLeod, W. Bentley, 2003. On optimal contracting with subjective evaluation. American Economic Review 93 (1), 216–240.

MacLeod, W. Bentley, Malcomson, James M., 1989. Implicit contracts, inventive compatibility, and involuntary unemployment. Econometrica 57 (2), 447–480.

Malcomson, James, 1999. Individual employment contracts. In: Ashenfelter, Orley C., Card, David (Eds.), Handbook of Labor Economics, vol. III. North Holland, Amsterdam.

Marin, Dalia, Verdier, Thierry, 2008. Corporate hierarchies and the size of nations: theory and evidence. Paris School of Economics mimeo.

Mas, Alexandre, Moretti, Enrico, 2008. Peers at work. American Economic Review 99 (1), 112–145.

MacDuffie, John, 1995. Human resource bundles and manufacturing performance: organizational logic and flexible production systems in the world auto industry. Industrial and Labor Relations Review 48 (2), 197–221.

Malmendier, Ulrike, Tate, Geoffrey, 2005. Does overconfidence affect corporate investment? CEO overconfidence measures revisited (with G. Tate). European Financial Management 11 (5), 649–659.

Melitz, Mark, 2003. The impact of trade on intra-industry reallocations and aggregate industry productivity. Econometrica 71 (6), 1695–1725.

Milgrom, Paul, Roberts, John, 1988. An economic approach to influence activities in organizations. American Journal of Sociology 94 (Suppl.), S154-S179.

Milgrom, Paul, Roberts, John, 1990. The economics of modern manufacturing: technology, strategy, and organization. American Economic Review 80 (3), 511–528.

Moretti, Enrico, 2004. Workers' education, spillovers and productivity: evidence from plant level production functions. American Economic Review 94, 656–690.

Mundlak, Yair, 1961. Empirical production function free of management bias. Journal of Farm Economics 43, 44–56.

Murphy, Kevin, 1999. Executive compensation. In: Ashenfelter, Orley C., Card, David (Eds.), Handbook of Labor Economics, vol. III. North Holland, Amsterdam.

Nickell, Steve, Nicolistsas, D., Patterson, M., 2001. Does doing badly encourage innovation? Oxford Bulletin of Economics and Statistics 63 (1), 5–28.

O'Donoghue, Ted, Rabin, Matthew, 1999. Doing it now or doing it later. American Economic Review 89 (1), 103–124.

Olley, Steven, Pakes, Ariel, 1996. The dynamics of productivity in the telecommunications equipment industry. Econometrica 64 (6), 1263–1298.

Osterman, Paul, 1994. How common is workplace transformation and who adopts it? Industrial and Labor Relations Review 47 (2), 173–188.

Osterman, Paul, 2006. The wage effects of high performance work organizations in manufacturing. Industrial and Labor Relations Review 59 (2), 187–204.

Oxera,, 2007. Tax-advantaged employee share schemes: analysis of productivity effects. HM Revenue and Customs Research Report No. 33.

Oyer, Paul, 1998. Fiscal year ends and nonlinear incentive contracts: the effect on business seasonality. Quarterly Journal of Economics 113 (1), 149–185.

Oyer, Paul, Schaefer, Scott, 2010. Personal economics: hiring and incentives. Stanford mimeo.

Pavcnik, Nina, 2002. Trade liberalization, exit, and productivity improvement: evidence from Chilean plants. Review of Economic Studies 69, 245–276.

Pendleton, Andrew, Whitfield, Keith, Bryson, Alex, 2009. The changing use of contingent pay in the modern British workplace. In: Brown, William, Bryson, Alex, Forth, John, Whitfield., Keith (Eds.), The Evolution of the Modern Workplace. Cambridge University Press.

Penrose, Edith, 1959. Theory of the Growth of the Firm. J. Wiley & Sons, New York.

Pérez-Gonzáles, Francisco, 2006. Inherited control and firm performance. American Economic Review 96 (5), 1559–1588.

Postel-Vinay, Fabienne, Robin, Jean-Marc, 2002. Equilibrium search with heterogeneous workers and firms. Econometrica 70, 1295–1350.

Prendergast, Canice, 1999. What happens within firms? A survey of empirical evidence on compensation policies. Journal of Economic Literature 37, 7–63.

Prendergast, Canice, 2000. What trade-off of risk and incentives? American Economic Review 90 (2), 421–425.

Prendergast, Canice, 2002a. The tenuous trade-off between risk and incentives. Journal of Political Economy 110 (5), 1071–1102.

Prendergast, Canice, 2002b. Uncertainty and incentives. Journal of Labor Economics 20 (2), S115-S137.

Prendergast, Canice, Topel, Robert, 1996. Favoritism in organizations. Journal of Political Economy 104 (5), 958–978.

Prentice, Graham, Burgess, Simon, Propper, Carol, 2007. Performance-pay in the public sector: a review of the issues and evidence. Office of Manpower Economics.

Prescott, Edward, Visscher, Michael, 1980. Organization capital. Journal of Political Economy 88 (3), 446–461.

Putnam, Robert, 1993. Making Democracy Work: Civic Traditions in Modern Italy. Princeton University Press, Princeton, NJ.

Radner, Roy, 1993. The organization of decentralized information processing. Econometrica 61 (5), 1109–1146.

Rajan, Raghuram, Wulf, Julie, 2006. The flattening firm: evidence from panel data on the changing nature of corporate hierarchies. Review of Economics and Statistics 88 (4), 759–773.

Salter, W.G., 1960. Productivity and Technical Change. Cambridge University Press, Cambridge.

Schmidt, K., 1997. Managerial incentives and product market competition. Review of Economic Studies 64 (2), 191–213.

Schmitz, James, 2005. What determines productivity? Lessons from the dramatic recovery of the US and Canadian iron ore industries following their early 1980s crisis. Journal of Political Economy 113 (3), 582–625.

Shaw, K., 2009. Insider econometrics: a roadmap with stops along the way. Labor Economics.

Shearer, Bruce, 2004. Piece rates, fixed wages and incentives: evidence from a field experiment. Review of Economic Studies 71 (2), 513–534.

Stiroh, Kevin, 2004. Reassessing the role of IT in the production function: a meta analysis. Federal Reserve Bank of New York mimeo.

Svenson, Ola, 1981. Are we all less risky and more skillful than our fellow drivers? Acta Psychologica 47, 143–148.

Syverson, Chad, 2004a. Product substitutability and productivity dispersion. Review of Economics and Statistics 86 (2), 534–550.

Syverson, Chad, 2004b. Market structure and productivity: a concrete example. Journal of Political Economy 112 (6), 1181–1222.

Syverson, 2010. What determines productivity. Journal of Economic Literature (forthcoming).

Thesmar, David, Thoenig, Mathias, 1999. From flexibility to insecurity: how vertical separation amplifies firm-level uncertainty. Journal of the European Economic Association 5 (6), 1161–1202.

Thesmar, David, Thoenig, Mathias, 2000. Creative destruction and organization change. The Quarterly Journal of Economics 115 (4), 1201–1237.

Van Biesebroeck, Johannes, 2007. Complementarities in automobile production. Journal of Applied Econometrics 22, 1315–1345.

Van Reenen, John, 1996. The creation and capture of economic rents: wages and innovation in a panel of UK companies. Quarterly Journal of Economics CXI (443), 195–226.

Vives, Xavier, 2008. Innovation and competitive pressure. Journal of Industrial Economics 56 (3), 419–469.

Walker, Francis A., 1887. The source of business profits. Quarterly Journal of Economics 1 (3), 265–288.

Weitzman, Martin, Kruse, Douglas, 1990. Profit sharing and productivity. In: Blinder, A. (Ed.), Paying for Productivity: A Look at the Evidence. The Brookings Institution, Washington, DC.

Wulf, Julie, 2007. Authority, risk and performance incentives: evidence from division manager positions insider firms. Journal of Industrial Economics LV (1), 169–186.

Woodward, J., 1958. Management and Technology. Cambridge University Press, Cambridge.

CHAPTER *20*

Personnel Economics: Hiring and Incentives☆

Paul Oyer[*], Scott Schaefer[**]

[*] Stanford GSB and NBER
[**] David Eccles School of Business and Institute for Public and International Affairs, University of Utah

Contents

Abstract

We survey the Personnel Economics literature, focusing on how firms establish, maintain, and end employment relationships and on how firms provide incentives to employees. This literature has been very successful in generating models and empirical work about incentive systems. Some of

---

☆ This survey has benefitted from conversations with colleagues too numerous to mention. We thank the editors, Orley Ashenfelter and David Card, for detailed comments.

E-mail addresses: oyer_paul@gsb.stanford.edu (Paul Oyer), scott.schaefer@utah.edu (Scott Schaefer).

ISSN 0169-7218, DOI 10.1016/S0169-7218(11)02418-X

the unanswered questions in this area—for example, the empirical relevance of the risk/incentive tradeoff and the question of whether CEO pay arrangements reflect competitive markets and efficient contracting—are likely to be very difficult to answer due to measurement problems. The literature has been less successful at explaining how firms can find the right employees in the first place. Economists understand the broad economic forces—matching with costly search and bilateral asymmetric information—that firms face in trying to hire. But the main models in this area treat firms as simple black-box production functions. Less work has been done to understand how different firms approach the hiring problem, what determines the firm-level heterogeneity in hiring strategies, and whether these patterns conform to theory. We survey some literature in this area and suggest areas for further research.

JEL classification: J23; J33; J63

Keywords: Human resource management; Incentives; Hiring

1. INTRODUCTION

Personnel Economics is the study of the employment relationship. It is unlike most other fields of labor economics for two reasons. First, Personnel Economics has grown up largely within leading business schools, not economics departments. This has given the field a more normative orientation than what is typically found in economics. Because many researchers in this field must take their insights into MBA classrooms and offer advice to future managers, Personnel Economists are typically interested in how firms can solve human resource management problems and how the solutions to HR problems are related to firms' broader strategic contexts. Second, Personnel Economics is notable in that it is shared between the fields of Labor Economics and Organizational Economics. Because of this, Personnel Economists typically do not treat a firm as a mere "black box" production function. The field is instead interested in understanding and explaining the wide array of human resource management choices made by firms.

Personnel Economics has made great progress in the past few decades, especially in the area of incentives. Personnel Economists, often applying key insights from advances in information economics, have developed theoretical models that capture both the broad issues and many of the details facing firms as they set up incentive systems. Rigorous and clever empirical work has confirmed the relevance of these models and, in some cases, found some potential holes as well. We highlight the success of both empirical and theoretical studies of incentives relative to the literature on hiring. As the labor market continues to get more skilled and employer human resource strategies continue to get more sophisticated, the opportunities to create economic surplus through efficient matching of employees and firms have likely grown and probably will continue to grow. We argue that hiring models developed to date are too far removed from the strategic issues firms face and the empirical work is simply too limited. The relative weakness of the hiring literature is a function of several things, including idiosyncrasies in how firms approach the issues and data limitations. But we are hopeful that new data and new approaches will make research advances possible in this area and we suggest some avenues for future research.

More specifically, we believe that, in developing the literature on incentives in firms, economists have got it right (mostly). Agency-theoretic models—which explain the risk/incentive tradeoff, multitasking, gaming, subjective performance evaluation, career concerns, tournaments, and the like—are probably right (again, mostly). Empirical work has either confirmed the relevance of these theories or researchers have reached a point where limits on measurement preclude sharp tests of the theory. Further, this research provides a good sense for what factors explain across-firm and within-firm variation in the use of various incentive tools. Scholars who teach MBAs at leading (and some not-so-leading) business schools have used these ideas—specifically ideas about firm-level factors that influence the efficiency of various incentive mechanisms—to integrate the economics of incentives into broader discussions of organizational and product-market strategy.

While economists have a lot to say about how a firm can motivate an employee, we have far less to say about how the firm should go about finding the right employee in the first place. We do think there are models that help identify the main economic problem—matching in the presence of search costs and bilateral asymmetric information—in hiring. And there is empirical research consistent with the hypotheses that matching, search costs, and asymmetric information all affect firms' hiring choices, as well as scattered research on specific strategies that firms might pursue to hire employees.[1]

But as business economists, our critique of this hiring literature is that for the most part the firm is treated as a black box. What is lacking is (a) documentation of across-firm variation in hiring strategies, (b) linkage of this across-firm variation in strategy to firm-level characteristics, and (c) a tie from these facts back to theory. For example, as we shall discuss, Lazear (1998) offers conditions under which hiring risky workers can be a profit-maximizing strategy for firms. But there are notably few studies that examine across-firm variation in propensity to hire risky workers, and then whether the observed variation fits with Lazear's theory. As another example, Montgomery (1991) suggests that firms can mitigate asymmetric information problems by accessing workers' social networks in making hiring decisions. But how much across-firm variation is there in network-based hiring? And what exactly does theory lead us to expect about this across-firm variation?

We have two primary goals in writing this survey. First, we hope to encourage Personnel Economists to redirect their efforts (at least partially) away from explaining firms' choices with regard to incentive compensation and toward firms' choices with regard to recruitment strategies. We believe such a shift will benefit organizational economics generally, but may also have important spillover effects on other fields of economics. Macroeconomists have, for example, long focused on frictions in labor

---

[1] We are certainly not the first to make the point that the demand side of the labor market—and hiring, in particular—is understudied. See Devine and Kiefer (1991), for example.

markets as an important source of business cycles (see Oi, 1962). Second, we offer a catalog of research on firm-level recruitment strategies, in the hope that economists will work to improve this literature.

This isn't to say that the marginal social return to research on incentives in organizations is zero. Many unanswered questions remain in that area—especially, we think, surrounding the use of relational incentive contracts and subjective assessments of employee performance—and we look forward to reading that research in the future. But we believe the social return to research on hiring is much larger, both because we know less about hiring, and because hiring the right employee is potentially as important or more so than motivating the employee to take the right action after the employee has been hired (at least for some firms).

We organize this survey as follows. First, we offer a short review of the literature on incentives in organizations. Our aim here is not to be exhaustive or complete (see Lazear and Oyer (2010) for a fuller discussion); instead, we hope to point out some successes and attribute some of the failures to measurement problems that will be hard to solve in future research. Our two broad conclusions here are: (a) we have good answers to many of the big questions, and (b) some of the unanswered questions are likely to be very hard to answer well.

Then, we turn our attention to the question of how firms hire. We outline the basic models of matching, search, and asymmetric information. We discuss the empirical evidence that speaks to the importance of each of these factors. Then we review the somewhat scattered literature on firms' actual hiring practices. Specific hiring practices we discuss include hiring risky workers, use of labor-market intermediaries, raiding other employers, hiring CEOs, use of various screening techniques, accessing employees' social networks, and the influence of firing costs on hiring choices. We conclude with a call for new research.

2. INCENTIVES IN ORGANIZATIONS

The broad economic question surrounding incentives involves distributed benefits and costs in the presence of asymmetric information. Most employees take actions that lead to direct benefits to the firm but not to the employee; that is, employees do not directly capture the full marginal benefit of their actions. Efficiency requires that employees' actions be the ones that maximize total benefit less total cost, but the distributed nature of benefit and cost plus the potential asymmetry of information regarding these benefits and costs makes the problem of motivating efficient actions quite complex.

Over the past 40 years, the huge "Contract Theory" literature has developed around this set of issues. While contract theory is far broader than the narrow study of incentives in employment relationships, the insights developed there have been very useful in understanding pay-for-performance relationships in employment. We review this literature while making three main points. First, we argue that it is well established that financial incentives do change behavior in organizations. Second, we argue that Personnel Economists understand the broad outlines of how incentives in organizations work. Firms provide incentives through a great variety of means, and empirical research suggests that our models of incentive pay are (mostly) right. Third, we argue that two of the large unanswered questions in this literature—the risk/incentive tradeoff and whether CEO pay packages are structured correctly—are unlikely to be easily answered. We do not intend for our discussion below to be a complete survey of the field; see, for example, Gibbons and Roberts (2010) for a more detailed summary.

2.1. Financial incentives do change behavior

One does still hear the claim that financial incentives do not change behavior (see, for example, Ariely, 2008). If true, this claim would be very problematic for Personnel and Organizational Economics. The agency-theoretic view of behavior—which is foundational to these fields—is that an agent selects from a set of actions with the objective of maximizing his or her expected utility. In a basic agency model, the agent bears 100% of the disutility or cost of effort, but the principal captures 100% of the benefit. In the absence of some means for aligning the two parties' interests, the agent will not select the efficient effort level. A solution to this problem is to tie the agent's utility to the principal's benefit, usually by varying the monetary payment made to the agent in response to variation in some measure that's related to the principal's benefit. By changing the mapping from actions to utility, the principal changes the set of utility-maximizing actions, and this means that financial incentives can change the agent's action. If financial incentives do not change behavior, then economists err in writing down incentive constraints in principal/agent models.

This point is so fundamental to both Personnel and Organizational Economics that it bears repeating. Empirical research shows that financial incentives do change behavior in organizations. This has been shown repeatedly by economists using controlled field experimental methods in real firms using real incentives. The most convincing of these studies examine simple jobs where researchers are allowed by the firm's management to vary the firm's incentive pay plans using an experimental design. Simple jobs are preferred because employees' actions can easily be measured, and the experimental design eliminates issues surrounding the endogenous choice of compensation plans.

Lazear (2000) studies the implementation of a pay-for-performance plan for automobile windshield installers at Safelite Glass. He reports four main results. First, a switch from hourly to piece rate pay led to a 44% increase in per-worker output. Second, about half of this gain came from an increase in individual-level productivity as a result of the stronger incentives. The remainder is attributable to changes in the composition of the firm's workforce after the implementation of the pay plan. Third, it appears the firm is compensating the employees for higher effort costs as a result of the switch. Per-worker pay increased about 10% after the implementation of the piece rate plan. Fourth, piece rates increased the across-worker variance of output, as better workers faced a stronger incentive to differentiate from others.

Shearer (2004) examines data from a field experiment involving tree planters in British Columbia. In his experiment nine men were randomly selected from the firm, and then randomly assigned to be paid using piece rates or a fixed wage. Each worker was observed under piece rates for 60 days, and also under fixed wages for 60 days. Piece rates led to a 20% increase in individual-level productivity, a figure that is on par with that observed by Lazear (2000). Shearer goes on to estimate a structural model of the worker's response to incentives.

Bandiera et al. (2009) study a change in managerial incentives in an English fruit-picking operation. When managers are paid using fixed wages, they tend to favor those with whom they are "socially connected," as measured by shared country-of-origin, shared living quarters, or whether the manager and worker arrived at the farm at the same time. Socially connected workers benefit from managerial favoritism in the form of higher output—by 9%—which leads to higher pay since workers are paid piece rates throughout this experiment. However, when managerial pay is switched from a fixed wage to bonuses based on the overall output, managers change their behavior. They instead begin favoring the most able workers regardless of the social connections.

So, do pay-for-performance incentives work? As Besanko et al. (2009) point out, the answer to this question likely depends on what we mean by the word "work." Pay-for-performance incentives surely change behavior in organizations, as the studies cited above make clear. But this is different from saying that pay-for-performance incentives improve organizational performance in all contexts. Pay-for-performance appears to induce employees to take actions that improve *measured* performance, but (as the multi-tasking literature discussed below emphasizes) there may be important-but-harder-to-measure aspects of performance that are ignored as employees work to hit measured-performance benchmarks. The studies cited above could omit such effects, as they focus on simple-to-measure aspects of employee performance. Further, it is easy to find cases where pay-for-performance does not improve performance (and see Freeman and Kleiner (2005) for one such example in the context of shoe manufacturing). Broadly speaking, however, the available empirical evidence suggests that pay-for-performance incentives are associated with improvements in organizational performance; see Bloom and Van Reenen (2011) for a thorough review of this literature.

2.2. How do firms provide incentives?

Firms provide incentives in an astonishing variety of ways. In some jobs, pay is tied to a specific performance measure using a specific functional form. In others, supervisors make subjective judgments about the quality of an employee's performance. Promotions are important in other cases, and in still other cases access to future labor-market opportunities seems to drive choices.

Important early insights were offered by Holmstrom (1979). In his model, a risk-averse agent selects a level of costly effort e to maximize his expected utility. A risk-averse principal does not observe the agent's effort choice, but does observe "output" x which is affected both by the agent's effort choice and by a random state of nature. It is important to recognize the specific (and narrow) agency problem considered in this paper. The agent's choice is simply how much effort to exert—not what kind of effort to exert—and the marginal return to effort is known. This turns the principal's problem into one of statistical inference. Holmstrom shows that the optimal sharing rule—$s(x)$, the share of output x that the principal pays to the agent—is characterized by

$$\frac{G'(x - s(x))}{U'(s(x))} = \lambda + \mu \frac{f_e(x; e)}{f(x; e)}. \tag{1}$$

Condition (1) is intuitive. The left-hand side is the ratio of the marginal utilities for the principal (G) and agent (U). The right-hand side is a Lagrange multiplier for the agent's participation constraint (λ) and a multiplier for the incentive constraint (μ) times the marginal effect of effort on the likelihood of obtaining that x, scaled by the likelihood of obtaining that x. Efficient risk-sharing requires the ratio of the principal and agent marginal utilities to be equated across all output levels. Motivating effort, however, requires the agent to be paid more—yielding lower agent marginal utility—when the output is indicative of high effort. The x for which f_e/f is large are those indicative of high effort, and so the agent is paid more for these states. The optimal contract is monotone in x if f satisfies the monotone likelihood ratio property (that is, f_e/f is increasing in x). This model also offers guidance on what information (in addition to output x) should be used in an optimal contract. Holmstrom's Informativeness Principle states that any information that is incrementally informative about e should be used. That is, if x is not a sufficient statistic for y with respect to effort e, then y is part of the second-best contract. The Informativeness Principle suggests, for example, that relative performance evaluation can improve contracts when two employees' outputs are positively correlated.

It is difficult to identify specific employment contracts that are well described by Holmstrom's model. The model suggests that optimal sharing rules should be quite sensitive to the shape of the underlying probability distribution f. Monotonicity and even linearity of sharing rules are common in organizations, but are predicted by this model only in very special cases. Further, firms commonly appear to violate the Informativeness Principle by ignoring some performance-related information in determining pay.

Models by Holmstrom and Milgrom (1991) and Baker (1992) connect agency theory more closely to observed employment relationships. Holmstrom and Milgrom (1991) build on the linear-contracting model in Holmstrom and Milgrom (1987) to examine "multi-task" principal/agent models. In their model, the agent privately makes a vector of effort choices, where we can interpret the elements of the vector as efforts toward various tasks. The principal is concerned not just with the overall level of effort (as in Holmstrom, 1979), but also with how the agent allocates effort across the various tasks. When the components of the effort vector are substitutes in the agent's cost function, the principal needs to take account of how offering stronger incentives toward one task will affect the agent's choices toward other tasks. To see how this works, consider a simple two-task version of their model in which effort e toward task $i \in \{1, 2\}$ influences output x according to

$$x_i = e_i + \tilde{\epsilon}_i,$$

where $\tilde{\epsilon}_i$ is a normal, mean-zero random variable. If the agent's pay varies with x_1 and x_2 according to

$$\beta_1 x_1 + \beta_2 x_2,$$

then first-order conditions for effort are

$$\beta_1 = \frac{\partial c(e_1, e_2)}{\partial e_1}$$

$$\beta_2 = \frac{\partial c(e_1, e_2)}{\partial e_2}.$$

Assuming $\frac{\partial^2 c(e_1, e_2)}{\partial e_2 \partial e_1} < 0$, higher β_1 implies that the agent will exert less effort toward task 2. The principal balances concerns for overall effort levels, allocation of effort across tasks, and optimal risk sharing in designing the optimal compensation contract. One important comparative static in their model is that the strength of incentives for task 1 (β_1) can be decreasing in the noise in the measurement of task 2 ($\tilde{\epsilon}_2$). When there is more risk associated with rewarding task 2, the firm optimally shifts toward weaker pay-for-performance incentives on that task. As task 2 incentives weaken, the employee will, according to the first order conditions above, shift effort away from task 2 and toward task 1. If the firm values task 2 sufficiently, it may find it optimal to weaken incentives toward task 1. This weakens overall effort incentives, but improves balance. This notion can be applied to, for example, the question of whether to pay school teachers for test results. "Teaching to the test" is easily measurable, but other tasks—such as fostering student maturity and higher-order thinking skills—are not. Poor measurement of "student maturity" means that rewarding testing will lead teachers to shift effort excessively in this direction. School administrators may, in this case, prefer not to use test scores to determine teacher pay. This finding illustrates that the Informativeness Principle need not apply when firms need to motivate the right kind of effort rather than simply motivating the level of effort.

Baker (1992) makes a similar point using a single-task model in which a risk–neutral agent is privately informed about how a performance measure reflects effort. In this model, the marginal return to agent effort is constant, but the employee's output cannot be measured directly. Instead, the principal observes an imperfect performance measure. The marginal effect of effort on the performance measure is random, and is privately observed by the employee. This randomness in the measurement of performance means the employee sometimes exerts more effort than the first best, and sometimes less. Convexity of the agent's cost function means the agent's expected effort cost is higher when the performance measure is worse. Because the principal must compensate the agent for expected effort costs, the principal ties pay less closely to performance when performance is less well measured.

Broadly speaking, the Holmstrom (1979), Holmstrom and Milgrom (1991), and Baker (1992) models suggest two main costs of using pay-for-performance incentives when performance measurement is imperfect. First, tying pay to badly measured performance shifts risk onto agents, and the firm must compensate agents for bearing risk. Second, tying pay to badly measured performance can lead agents to choose the wrong actions. We discuss the empirical research on the risk/incentive tradeoff below. There is ample evidence that problems with performance measurement can lead agents to "game" the measures by selecting inefficient actions. Oyer (1998), for example, examines the relation between firms' fiscal-year ends, non-linear incentive pay, and seasonality in revenues. He finds that fiscal-year ends influence business seasonality in most manufacturing industries. Revenues are higher toward the end of a fiscal year and lower at the beginning, compared to the middle. This is consistent with the notion that salespeople facing year-end quotas work to pull sales from the beginning of fiscal year t to the end of fiscal year $t - 1$. Larkin (2007) offers more direct evidence on this point in his study of proprietary sales data from a large enterprise software firm. He finds the firm's non-linear incentive plan induces salespeople to shift a number of deals into a single quarter and avoid making deals in other quarters. Salespeople also use their (limited) discretion over pricing to entice customers into buying during periods that yield greater returns to the salespeople.

Firms commonly attempt to combat the problems with "objective" performance measures—numerical quotas and targets—with "subjective" assessments of employee performance. Subjective measures can include things like supervisors' assessments or 360-degree peer reviews. Academic economists are subject to subjective performance evaluation at the tenure decision. In most universities, tenure isn't based on a formula combining publication counts and citations; instead, senior faculty subjectively assess the quality of a junior professor's work. Baker et al. (1994a) examine the interplay between objective and subjective assessments of employee performance. An important distinction between objective and subjective measures is that the latter are non-verifiable. Thus, contracts based on subjective assessments cannot be enforced by courts, and instead must be self-enforcing. Building on a repeated-game model of implicit contracts by Bull (1987), Baker et al. (1994a) first show that bonuses based on subjective evaluations are limited due to the firm's reneging constraint. A firm that pays a promised bonus today maintains the employee's trust and, as a result, is able to make credible promises to pay bonuses based on subjective measures in the future. The firm therefore compares the cost of paying the bonus to the value of future cooperation. Firms that value the future more heavily than the present are better able to pay bonuses based on subjective measures of employee performance. Baker et al. (1994a) then consider how the presence of an objective measure of firm performance affects the subjective bonus. They find that objective and subjective measures are substitutes; as the objective measure of performance becomes a better alternative for the subjective measure, the firm places less value on its reputation for paying bonuses based on subjective measures.

We believe there is a great need for more empirical research on the use of implicit contracts and subjective performance evaluation in employment relationships. Hayes and Schaefer (2000) offer evidence consistent with the use of implicit contracts and subjective performance evaluation. They argue that if boards of directors base pay for CEOs partially on information that is not publicly available, then current pay for CEOs should predict future firm performance. Following the reasoning in Baker et al. (1994a), they argue that this link should be stronger when the available objective performance measures are weaker. Their empirical analysis is consistent with these hypotheses, but this is at best indirect support for the Baker et al. (1994a) model.

Promotion tournaments—which can be based either on objective or subjective measures of performance—are a common feature within many firms. Lazear and Rosen (1981) model a firm that will promote one of two employees to a new position. Each employee takes an action that translates into noisy output and the firm commits in advance to promote the individual with the higher output. For an employee participating in a promotion tournament, the first order condition for effort is given by

$$\frac{\partial p(e_1, e_2)}{\partial e_1} \Delta W = c'(e_1).$$

Effort increases the probability (p) of winning the promotion tournament. The employee gets an increase in compensation of amount ΔW if she wins, so the marginal benefit of effort is the marginal effect of effort on the probability of winning times ΔW. Employees equate this to the marginal cost. Note that employee 1's probability of winning depends also on employee 2's effort choice, so equilibrium effort levels e_1 and e_2 are where this first-order condition holds for both employees simultaneously. Lazear and Rosen (1981) document a number of features of tournaments. First, appropriate choice of ΔW can lead the employees to select the first-best effort level. Second, holding ΔW constant, more noise in performance measurement will reduce effort. This effect occurs because luck, rather than skill, becomes relatively more important in determining the tournament winner. This reduces $\frac{\partial p(e_1,e_2)}{\partial e_1}$. Third, tournaments are a form of relative performance evaluation, so any common shocks to employee performance are netted out. Fourth, when more employees compete for a promotion, $\frac{\partial p(e_1,e_2)}{\partial e_1}$ falls and the firm may need to raise the prize ΔW to compensate.

Empirical evidence suggests that promotions are an important determinant of wage changes. In their study of 20 years of wage data from a large firm, Baker et al. (1994b) find that promotions and wage growth are highly correlated. This appears, however, to operate in a somewhat different manner to that suggested by Lazear and Rosen (1981). Individuals who are promoted receive small wage premiums in the year of the promotion but tend to be those individuals who receive large wage increases even in years when they are not promoted. Further, wage levels in this firm are not tied directly to job levels, as there is substantial variation in wages even among individuals at the same job level. DeVaro (2006) shows that promotions seem to be determined by relative performance for workers in a cross-section of establishments. He also estimates a structural model of tournaments, finding support for the assertions that employers set wage spreads to induce effort and that workers are motivated by larger promotion wage spreads.

Employees may also be motivated by the possibility of receiving outside offers. Fama (1980) introduced this notion of "career concerns," which was then studied in detail by Holmstrom (1982). Holmstrom develops a model of symmetric uncertainty regarding worker ability. An employee's output today depends both on his ability and his hidden effort. The employee's wage next period depends on the market's posterior belief regarding his ability, given observed output today. From this setting, Holmstrom derives a "rat-race" equilibrium. Employees exert effort in a futile (at least in equilibrium) attempt to boost the market's assessments of ability. Effort incentives in the model are strongest when the market's prior about employee ability is more diffuse. Chevalier and Ellison (1999) study data on mutual fund managers, and show that portfolio choices seem to be influenced by career concerns. They show first that termination is more sensitive to performance for younger managers. Younger managers appear to respond to the market's updating regarding ability by selecting portfolios with less unsystematic risk and more conventional sector weights.

2.3. Some important but hard-to-answer questions
2.3.1. The risk/incentive tradeoff
One of the oldest theoretical predictions in the agency literature has proved to be one of the most difficult for empirical researchers. The tradeoff between risk and incentives arises if (a) employees have convex disutility for both risk and effort, and (b) performance measures are subject to random variation. In this case, the marginal benefit of using incentives comes from the fact that the employee's effort choice is closer to the first-best when incentives are stronger, while the marginal cost is the increase in the employee's risk premium. Because greater risk increases the marginal cost of incentives without affecting

the marginal benefit, we get a clear comparative statics prediction: greater risk should be associated with weaker pay-for-performance incentives.

As Prendergast (1999, 2002a,b) has pointed out, however, empirical research on this topic offers weak support at best. This challenge has led many empirical researchers to look for new evidence in support of the tradeoff between risk and incentives and has also led to the development of models that lead to the prediction that incentives and risk will be positively related. This literature has been useful but not fully satisfying. The central problem is that almost any moral hazard model suggests that a large number of unobservables will influence the strength of the pay-for-performance relationship. To identify these, we examine a simple linear-exponential-normal agency model (of the type studied by Holmstrom and Milgrom, 1991, and applied to CEOs by Schaefer, 1998). Let an agent have CARA utility with coefficient ρ, and convex disutility of effort with monetary equivalent given by $\frac{c}{2}e^2$, where e is a real-valued effort choice and c is a constant cost of effort parameter. Suppose further that effort translates into value V to the principal as follows:

$$V = ve + \tilde{\epsilon},$$

where $v > 0$ and $\tilde{\epsilon}$ is a mean-zero normal random variable with variance σ^2. Assuming a wage contract that is linear in V,

$$\text{Wage} = \alpha + \beta V,$$

it is easy to show that the optimal wage contract maximizes the total certainty equivalent of the two parties, subject to the agent's incentive constraint. The problem is

$$\max_{\beta} \, ve - \frac{c}{2}e^2 - \frac{1}{2}\rho\beta^2\sigma^2$$

subject to

$$e \in \arg\max_{e} \, \beta ve - \frac{c}{2}e^2.$$

The solution is

$$\beta^* = \frac{1}{1 + \frac{c}{v^2}\rho\sigma^2},$$

and note that β^*—the optimal slope of the pay-performance relation—is strictly decreasing in σ^2, consistent with the prediction of a risk-incentive tradeoff.

We now consider the measurement challenges in devising a test of this relation. First is the simple problem of measuring "risk." The σ^2 parameter in the theory is the conditional variance of the output measure V. If effort e and the marginal productivity of effort v could somehow be held constant, then the conditional variance would be equal to the unconditional variance, and a test could examine whether var(V) affects the slope of the pay-for-performance relation. In most tests of the risk/incentives tradeoff (see Aggarwal and Samwick, 1999), some measure of the unconditional variance of a performance measure is used to assess risk. But, of course, the marginal return to effort v and the agent's effort choice e are typically not observed by the econometrician. It remains unclear whether var(V) truly reflects the conditional variance of output.

Second, note that there are three parameters besides σ^2 in our expression for β^*. Incentives are stronger when the marginal return to effort is higher (higher v), when the agent is more risk tolerant (lower ρ), and when the agent is more responsive to strong incentives (lower c). Notably none of these parameters are easily observable by the econometrician, and any correlation between these unobservables and σ^2 can confound tests of the risk/incentive tradeoff. Suppose, for example, that the marginal return to effort tends to be high in exactly the cases where σ^2 is high. Then we may observe stronger incentives in exactly the cases where risk is greatest. Such a finding would not imply that the theory of the risk/incentive tradeoff is necessarily wrong, but instead could indicate that we are unable to make a ceteris paribus comparison. Prendergast (2002a) argues that such a pattern might arise if firms delegate more decision-making authority to agents—leading to a higher marginal productivity of effort—in exactly those cases where more risk is present. Following Prendergast, Adams (2005) and DeVaro and Kurtulus (2010) attempt to control for the degree of delegation in framing a risk/incentives test, but find both measuring delegation and identifying exogenous variation in delegation to be significant challenges. Further, delegation is just one of many potential avenues that could lead to a positive association between v and σ^2.

We think it is not clear how to solve these measurement problems surrounding the risk/incentive tradeoff. An empirical design with agent fixed effects can likely control for variation in ρ. But the marginal return to effort v and the second-derivative of the agent's cost function c are presumably match specific, and this means it will be difficult to control for these with agent or firm fixed effects. Match-specific fixed effects could help, but only if we could identify sources of exogenous variation in the within-match σ^2 *and* be confident that this variation in risk is not also leading to variation in the marginal productivity of effort. We think this is likely to be a very tough nut to crack and, absent some novel measurement technique that we cannot currently envision, we do not see this as a fruitful research area.

2.3.2. The structure of CEO pay

Another persistent question in the broad incentives literature surrounds the structure of CEO pay packages. US CEO paychecks have risen ten times as fast as those of average workers since the 1970s (The Economist, 2006). Further, the tie between CEO pay and firm performance has strengthened, as more and more of CEO pay has come in the form of equity-based instruments. Literally hundreds of studies—in economics, finance, accounting, and management—have studied the question of whether CEO pay packages are efficient. Our fear is that despite all this research—some of it conducted by the authors of this survey—social scientists really have very little conclusive evidence on whether CEO pay is structured correctly.

As with the risk/incentive tradeoff, we think the problems boil down to one of measurement. Our agency-theoretic models of pay suggest that the efficient sensitivity of pay to performance and the efficient level of pay depend on many unobservables. To illustrate our concerns, we return to the linear contracting model we developed above. To add in a discussion of the level of pay, we assume that the agent's reservation utility is given by $\bar{u}$ and that the firm's reservation profit level is $\bar{\pi}$. Again assuming a linear wage contract

$$\text{Wage} = \alpha + \beta V,$$

we ask what this model can tell us about α and β. As above, the efficient pay-for-performance term β maximizes the total certainty equivalent subject to the agent's incentive constraint. We again have

$$e^* = \frac{\beta^* v}{c}$$

$$\beta^* = \frac{1}{1 + \frac{c}{v^2}\rho\sigma^2}.$$

The term α—which can be interpreted as the employee's level of pay when $V = 0$—must be large enough to satisfy the agent's participation constraint, which is given by

$$\alpha + \beta^* E(V \mid e^*) - \frac{c}{2}e^{*2} - \frac{1}{2}\rho\beta^{*2}\sigma^2 \geq \bar{u}. \tag{2}$$

The α term must not be so large as to leave the employer worse off than its reservation profit level. This implies

$$(1 - \beta^*)E(V \mid e^*) - \alpha \geq \bar{\pi}. \tag{3}$$

If this employment match is efficient, we must have

$$E(V \mid e^*) - \frac{c}{2}e^{*2} - \frac{1}{2}\rho\beta^{*2}\sigma^2 \geq \bar{u} + \bar{\pi}. \tag{4}$$

Note that if the inequality in (4) is strict, then there are rents. For CEOs in particular, matching and specificity of human capital would seem to make it likely that rents are present. Combining the inequalities in (2) and (3), we have

$$E(V \mid e^*) - \pi \geq \alpha + \beta^* E(V \mid e^*) \geq \frac{c}{2} e^{*2} + \frac{1}{2} \rho \beta^{*2} \sigma^2 + \bar{u}.$$

In words, our basic contracting model suggests that the employee's expected level of pay $\alpha + \beta^* E(V \mid e^*)$ must insure participation of both parties, but beyond that the level of pay simply splits any match surplus.[2] We assume this surplus is split according to Nash Bargaining where the employee gets share γ. Given this, the CEO's expected level of pay is given by

$$\gamma (E(V \mid e^*) - \pi) + (1 - \gamma) \left(\frac{c}{2} e^{*2} + \frac{1}{2} \rho \beta^{*2} \sigma^2 + \bar{u} \right).$$

This model suggests that CEO pay should depend on

1. The marginal return to managerial effort v,
2. The second derivative of the manager's cost-of-effort function c,
3. The manager's degree of risk aversion ρ,
4. The conditional variance of output σ^2,
5. The manager's reservation utility $\bar{u}$,
6. The firm's reservation profit level $\bar{\pi}$,
7. The manager's bargaining power γ.

Not one of these seven factors can be easily measured by empirical researchers. On top of that, several features of this market make it difficult to control for these factors using manager or firm fixed effects. First, firms employ just a single CEO at a time, and CEO tenure is typically a number of years. This means firm fixed effects are useful only to the extent that we believe firm characteristics do not change very quickly over time. Second, managers change jobs infrequently and not for exogenous reasons. Third, as we noted in our discussion of the risk/incentive tradeoff, factors like the marginal return to effort and the shape of the manager's cost-of-effort function are likely to be match specific, which means they cannot be conditioned out easily.

Given this, we think it is very difficult to draw conclusions over whether CEO pay practices are well explained by our basic models of contracting and labor markets. It seems that practically any broad pattern appearing in CEO pay data can be rationalized by a clever theorist who reverse-engineers the unobservables in such a way as to fit the data (see Edmans and Gabaix, 2009). This literature has, as a result, followed a bit of a he-said,

---

[2] Note, however, that many papers on efficient CEO pay contracts assume that the CEO is on his/her participation constraint and the firm captures all the rents. See, for example, Aggarwal and Samwick (1999). Kuhnen and Zwiebel (2009) take a different approach, by modeling pay as being set by the CEO himself, subject to limits on his entrenchment.

she-said spiral, with few conclusions drawn. As examples, Bertrand and Mullainathan (2001) point out that CEOs are paid for "luck," which seems to be inconsistent with the agency-theoretic Informativeness Principle from Holmstrom (1979). Oyer (2004) replies that if the employee's outside option ($\overline{u}$, in our model above) is correlated with industry-wide share prices, then arrangements that look like pay-for-luck can be part of an optimal employment contract. Bebchuk and Fried (2003) are the most vocal current academic critics of CEO pay arrangements; broadly, their argument is that the patterns in CEO pay are hard to reconcile with any model of efficient contracting or competitive labor markets. Tervio (2008), Gabaix and Landier (2008), and Gayle and Miller (2009) reply that changes in firm scale may have affected the marginal return to managerial ability, which in turn changes the reservation utilities of all managers through labor market competition, which leads to a system of interrelated changes in firms' pay plans that broadly seems to fit the pattern of changes in CEO pay over the past 30 years. Hayes and Schaefer (2009) further complicate the picture by offering a model in which CEO pay signals rents in the CEO-firm employment relationship. If firms care about short-run share prices, they may inflate CEO pay (above full-information levels) in a futile (in equilibrium) attempt to boost market value.

Having read (and written some of) this literature, we feel simply stuck. Theory suggests a long list of unobservables that should matter for CEO pay arrangements. It is not clear how empirical researchers can control for all of these factors well enough to draw firm conclusions about the degree to which CEO pay arrangements are or are not in line with theory. We know that CEO pay is not fully efficient at all firms, given the problems at firms such as MCI and Tyco. We also know that CEO pay contracts typically have features that economists predict to be part of an optimal contract (pay-for-performance that varies with regulation, age, and governance in the ways we might expect). But it seems unlikely that economic research will ever tell us exactly where the typical CEO pay arrangement lies on the spectrum from completely inefficient to completely optimal.

3. HIRING

In this section, we argue that while the fundamental economic problem in hiring is well understood, the methods that firms use to solve hiring problems still need a lot more research.

The fundamental economic problem in hiring is one of matching with costly search and bilateral asymmetric information. Job seekers have varying levels of aptitude, skill, and motivation, and firms have varying needs for these attributes. Economic efficiency requires that the labor market identify the best matches of workers to firms. The matching problem is complicated by the fact that firms and workers cannot costlessly observe all relevant aspects of potential trading partners. This means search is a common feature of hiring. A further complication is that firms and job seekers may each be able to misrepresent their quality as a trading partner. Potential employees are known to polish resumes or fabricate credentials, and firms at times may choose to downplay or conceal unpleasant aspects of the job. Labor markets are, of course, heterogeneous, so the extent to which matching, search, and asymmetric information are prevalent is likely to vary across labor markets.

To review this literature, we first outline the basic structure of our models of matching, search, and asymmetric information in labor markets. We then critique these basic models by pointing out that firms are, for the most part, treated as mere production functions. The objective function given to firms in these models is to maximize the difference between an employee's productivity and his wage. Because firms, in these models, are completely homogeneous, these models are by and large not useful for understanding firm-level heterogeneity in hiring strategies. We then discuss the literature on specific hiring practices and issues. This literature lacks focus, to a certain degree, and so our treatment here reads a bit like a laundry list of unconnected issues. We discuss hiring risky workers, use of labor-market intermediaries, raiding other employers, hiring CEOs, firms' use of various screening techniques, accessing employees' social networks, and the influence of firing costs on hiring choices.

3.1. Black-box models of hiring

As noted above, labor economists have long recognized that hiring involves matching with costly search and bilateral asymmetric information. Jovanovic (1979b) draws out the implications of matching for labor markets. In his model, the productivity of a given worker/firm match is unknown at the time of hiring. Once on the job, the worker/firm match quality becomes known over time as the firm gains observations about worker productivity. Employment matches persist as long as the expected surplus in the current employment relationship exceeds the parties' outside options. Matches that are revealed, over time, to be poor are terminated. Good matches persist, which implies that the hazard rate of worker/firm separations decreases with job tenure. This empirical implication is strongly borne out by the data (see Farber, 1999). The implications of job matching are, however, difficult to distinguish from those of firm-specific human capital (Jovanovic, 1979a). Under the hypothesis of firm-specific human capital formation, job matches improve over time as workers invest in skills that are specific to the firm. The question of whether the decreasing hazard rate of job loss is due to matching or firm-specific human capital remains open.

A large literature examines the effects of costly search on labor markets (see Mortensen and Pissarides, 1999). In the basic search model, workers sequentially sample wages from a known distribution. An unemployed worker's strategy is characterized by an optimal stopping rule. Job offers that pay wages above an endogenous reservation wage are accepted, while others are declined. The basic employee search model has been applied to study unemployment durations, which are a function of the exogenous wage distribution and the exogenous rate at which wage offers arrive. Equilibrium search models explicitly consider search on both sides of the labor market, and endogenize wage distributions, job offer arrival rates, and firm-level vacancy durations. Search models that explicitly model heterogeneity in worker/firm match quality have been applied to understand both job flows and unemployment, and equilibrium wage dispersion.

The canonical Spence (1973) signaling model begins with the presumption that workers are privately informed about their productivity, and may take costly actions that credibly convey information about productivity. Greenwald (1986) notes that an employee's incumbent employer is likely to hold a significant informational advantage (over potential rival employers) with regard to a given employee's productivity. If employers focus their efforts on retaining those workers they privately observe to be able, then the stream of job changes will be adversely selected. Employers hiring from the pool of the unemployed will hire at low wages only. Asymmetric information can therefore impede the efficient matching of workers to firms.

3.2. Firm-level hiring strategies

Despite the obvious success and empirical relevance of the models above, we think there is much work yet to be done to understand firm-level hiring choices. The work to date does not provide a good picture of where employers spend their resources and efforts when hiring workers and which hiring investments have proven most successful in various circumstances. They have also not generated a good sense for how to advise managers on developing a comprehensive recruitment strategy for their organizations. We review the work to date and discuss opportunities for future research (while noting the considerable impediments to doing the research we propose).

3.2.1. Sources of match-specific productivity

Discussions of hiring often begin with a desire to hire the right worker. But what makes a worker "right?" To put this in Jovanovic's terms, what are the sources of match-specific productivity?

Complementarities

Firm-level heterogeneity can lead to match-specificity in productivity if there is a complementarity between firm attributes and attributes of the employee. The assumption of such a complementarity underlies the large literature on assortive matching in labor markets (see Rosen, 1982, and Sattinger, 1993), but most of this literature simply assumes a complementarity between, say, firm size and employee ability, and goes on to derive implications for equilibrium matching. But what specific attributes are complementary? And what sources of firm-level heterogeneity give rise to these complementarities?

One answer is that employee attributes may complement certain production technologies. Information technology, for example, may be most productively utilized by employees with high skill levels. Such a complementarity lies at the root of the large literature on skill-biased technical change.[3] Real prices for computing power have fallen dramatically since the 1970s, and this period has also seen dramatic changes in skill differentials in wages, as skilled workers saw much faster wage increases than unskilled. A complementarity between skilled labor and information technology can explain these facts, if falling IT prices caused firms to shift labor demand toward skilled workers.

To cite some examples from this literature, Berman et al. (1994) use the US Annual Survey of Manufactures to examine skill upgrading in the 1980s. They show first that employment of production workers in US manufacturing dropped 15% in the 1980s, while employment of nonproduction workers rose 3%. This occurred despite the fact that relative wages for skilled labor rose over this period. The shift in employment toward nonproduction workers was driven primarily by changes within industry rather than between industries, and was larger in industries that made larger investments in computer technology. Autor et al. (1998) show that within-industry skill-upgrading (where skill is measured by educational attainment) accelerated from the 1970s to the 1980s and 1990s, and that various measures of computer usage were higher in the industries where skill-upgrading was highest.

Falling prices for information technology cannot, however, serve as an explanation for firm-level match-specificity in employee productivity. Changes in relative prices hit all firms equally, and hence in the absence of other firm-specific factors, all firms would shift their demand toward skilled workers equally. Bresnahan et al. (2002) argue that investments in IT require coinvention on the part of individual firms. That is, firms cannot benefit fully from investments in IT without also reorganizing work practices and rethinking product offerings, a process that requires experimentation. Using detailed firm-level survey data, Bresnahan et al. (2002) show that conditional on investments in computerization, firms that do workplace reorganizations are more likely to also adopt high-investment human resource policies, such as screening for education in hiring, training, and cross training. The authors also report evidence of a complementarity in production between skilled labor, workplace reorganization and IT, as there are positive interaction effects in a regression of log value added on these variables. Ichniowski et al. (1997) report similar findings in their study of steel-finishing lines. Selection and training of skilled workers are complementary to adoption and installation of IT investments. Taken together, these results suggest that worker characteristics can be part of a constellation of complementary firm-level attributes, as suggested by Milgrom and Roberts (1990, 1995).

Potential employees, of course, can vary on a large number of dimensions, and most of the literature on skill-biased technical change focuses simply on a single dimension of skill as measured by educational attainment or a production/nonproduction worker

---

[3] Katz and Autor (1999) review much of the work on skill-biased technical change as part of a review of the literature on changing wage inequality. Autor et al. (2006) update that review in light of critiques such as Card and DiNardo (2002).

distinction. Using detailed firm-level data, Abowd et al. (2007) consider how various components of skill are related to firms' technological inputs. As with the skill-biased technical change literature, the authors report a strong relationship between technology and skill. Different dimensions of skill interact with technology in different ways, however. Using methods from Abowd et al. (1999), the authors decompose worker skill into a time-invariant worker effect ("basic ability") and an experience effect that varies in proportion to labor-market experience. Interestingly, firms that use advanced production technologies are more likely to use high-ability workers, but less likely to use workers with extensive labor-market experience.

Complementarities between potential employee characteristics and firm characteristics can extend beyond firms' technology choices. Andersson et al. (2009) use matched employee–employer data in the software industry to study links between product-market segment and hiring strategies. They develop a simple theoretical model in which firms' relative demand for successful innovation depends on characteristics of the product-market segment. Firms operating in market segments where payoff distributions are highly variable—video games, where having a blockbuster game can be worth hundreds of millions of dollars, are one example—will place a greater value on innovative employees. Empirical analysis supports this assertion. Firms operating in market segments with highly variable payoffs pay higher starting salaries than other firms. These firms also offer greater rewards for employee loyalty or experience.

Specific weights on general skills

Lazear (2009) proposes a model in which all skills are general, but firms place different weights on various combinations of skills. As an example, Lazear offers the case of a Silicon Valley startup that does tax optimization. A managerial employee in this firm may need to know about tax law, economics, and Java programming. These skills are all general, in the sense that there are other firms that would value each of these skills. But there may be no other firm that values an employee who holds *all* of these skills. An accounting firm may, for example, value knowledge of tax law and economics, but not Java programming. An employee with all three skills who suffered job loss may, depending on market thickness and search costs, be unable to find another job demanding his full basket of skills, and may therefore receive lower wages. This observation reconciles the difficulty one often has with describing skills that are truly firm-specific with the empirical facts of wage reductions on job loss and positive tenure coefficients.

While Lazear's model focuses largely on a number of questions related to human capital theory—such as employees' incentives to invest in skill and who pays for such investments—he also interprets the model as generating a match-specific productivity as in Jovanovic (1979a,b). Suppose there are two dimensions of skills, A and B, and let potential employee i's endowment of skill A (B) be given by A_i (B_i). Suppose skill endowments are heterogeneous in the population of potential workers. Let potential employers be heterogeneous in their demands for skills, with the output generated by employee i working at firm j given by

$$\alpha_j A_i + \beta_j B_i.$$

The right employee for firm j is one whose skill endowment (A_i, B_i) matches with the firm's skill-weights (α_j, β_j). A firm with a high α_j and low β_j (relative to the population of firms) will hire employees with large A_i and small B_i. Such a firm would still find skill B to be of value, but its willingness-to-pay for this skill would be smaller than that of other firms in the market.

Lazear does not address the question of what gives rise to firm-level heterogeneity in skill-weights. Presumably these derive from firm-level differences in endowments of other factors of production or product-market strategy, but connections between, say, product-market differentiation and skill-weight-driven labor-market differentiation have yet to be drawn out. It may be fruitful to connect Lazear's skill-weights approach to the different dimensions of worker skill as measured by Abowd et al. (2007). A natural story for the lower relative demand for experienced workers by firms with large technology investments is that experienced workers have invested in specific skills that are made obsolete by the investments in new technologies. Drawing such connections would require detailed firm- and employee-level data on specific skills required in jobs and held by employees.

Some of the main empirical predictions of Lazear's model—on market thickness and firm size effects in tenure coefficients in wage regressions—have yet to be examined by empiricists. Geel et al. (2009) use data from the German BIBB/IAB Qualification and Career Surveys to test some implications of the model for occupational training. They argue first that when the skill requirements of an occupation are more specific, firms should bear a higher share of training costs. Second, they argue that more specificity in occupational skill-weights should be associated with a smaller likelihood of changing occupations. The Qualification Survey studied by Geel et al. (2009) offers detailed survey evidence on skills possessed by individuals in different occupations, which allows the authors to construct an index of occupational skill-specificity. Greater skill-specificity is associated with both a larger investment by firms in training, and lower across-occupation mobility after skills have been acquired.

Risky workers

Lazear (1998) argues that potential employees may vary not just in their skill (that is, the first moment of the distribution of their productivity) but also in the degree to which the employee is risky (that is, the second moment of the employee's productivity distribution). He develops an equilibrium model where potential employees vary in terms of their riskiness, and derives predictions about which firms are good matches for risky workers. If firms can easily terminate risky workers whose productivity is revealed to be low and earn rents on those with high realized productivity, then hiring a risky worker has option value. Some barriers to mobility—either from direct turnover costs or employer private information about worker ability—must be in place in order to give risky employees option value. Given these ingredients, risky workers will be preferred to safe workers at a given wage. In equilibrium, wages adjust so that the marginal firm is indifferent between hiring risky and safe workers. Firms that expect to be in business for a long period of time value risky workers more, since they will be in position to earn the full stream of possible rents. Firms facing high turnover costs or low information barriers to raids will find it more attractive to hire safe workers. Lazear's theory suggests that good matches for a given employer can depend on the second moment of employee productivity and firm-level characteristics such as firing costs, expected firm lifespan, and the degree of private information.

Burgess et al. (1998) examine one prediction of this model, specifically that firms with short expected time horizons will hire safe workers and therefore have low turnover. The authors use establishment-level data to relate firm-level churning flows—that is, changes in a firms' workforce that are not accounted for by growth or contraction of the firm itself—to industry growth rate and mean firm age. Results suggest that firms in growing industries (as measured by industry growth rate) do indeed have higher churning flows. Firms in industries with older firms have lower churning. It is not clear from the analysis whether industries with older firms should have longer or shorter expected *future* life; one can imagine that effect going in either direction.

Lazear also suggests that younger workers—who have less history in the labor market and therefore greater uncertainty about future productivity—might have greater option value. If so, then increases in termination costs will reduce this option value, and cause employers to shift demand away from younger workers. This argument is developed further by Oyer and Schaefer (2002), who extend it by connecting termination costs to data on how propensity-to-litigate varies with age for members of protected classes. Their empirical analysis studies how the Civil Rights Act of 1991 (CRA91)—which increased termination costs for members of certain protected classes—affected returns to experience. Unlike some prior affirmative action legislation, CRA91 had small aggregate wage and employment effects. However, CRA91 does seem to have changed the wage/experience profile for members of some protected groups.

Both Burgess et al. (1998) and Oyer and Schaefer (2002) are somewhat indirect as tests of Lazear's hypothesis, because neither study is directly able to measure across-worker variation in "risk." Indeed, it is difficult to imagine how one might do this in a standard employment setting. Two papers, Bollinger and Hotchkiss (2003) and Hendricks et al. (2003), use sports as a laboratory to examine the impact of uncertainty on hiring. These measurement benefits do come with a cost, however, since sports leagues often restrict within-league competition for players. Bollinger and Hotchkiss (2003) study baseball, where detailed statistics on player performance permit the explicit calculation of both the level and variability of expected performance. They show that players who have not yet become free agents earn a premium for riskiness—players with performance variability that is higher by one standard deviation earn 7% more, holding all else constant. It is not clear to us what the source of this premium is, however. In their sample, reserve clause players (those in the early years of their career) were governed by strict monopsony rules that limited bidding for players. In Lazear's model it is competition that drives wages up for riskier workers, and this effect is necessarily absent for young baseball players. It is possible that their results are driven by some feature of the salary arbitration process, rather than the effects in Lazear's model.

Hendricks et al. (2003) study the US National Football League (NFL), which has a number of features that make it a useful setting in which to test Lazear's model. First, the NFL features a "draft" in which teams select, in a predetermined order, players who have completed their college football careers. Second, players vary in terms of the quality of their college teams; Hendricks et al. (2003) use this variation to proxy for risk under the hypothesis that a player from a minor college team will not have faced strong competition during his college career, and therefore professional teams will have less information regarding productivity. Third, players are bound to teams for a fixed period of time after the draft and players can be terminated costlessly. The authors find that conditional on being selected in an early round of the draft, players from less prominent colleges tend to have better careers. In later rounds of the draft, the reverse is true, which suggests that teams might place a higher value on uncertainty in later rounds. The authors conclude that there is support both for Lazear's model and for various forms of statistical discrimination.

Employee preferences or beliefs

The right employee might also be one who has the right beliefs or preferences. Under a standard agency model, all employers would prefer to have employees who are tolerant of risk and effort. It is also straightforward to show that employers will benefit from selecting employees who are intrinsically motivated to perform the task required for the job. But organization theorists have recently begun to develop models in which firms might heterogeneously demand employees with certain beliefs or preferences that *differ* from those of the firm's owners.

Van den Steen (2005) starts by eliminating the common priors assumption that is standard in much of economic theory. He considers a firm that must first identify a project and decide whether to invest, when the state of the world is unknown. There are two potential states of the world, and the firm's project will succeed only if it matches the actual state. An employee must choose one of the potential states, and then exert costly effort that increases the probability that the employee will identify a project. Direct pay-for-performance effort incentives are ruled out. If a project is identified, then a manager sees the (random) cost of implementing the project and decides whether to implement. If the project is implemented, then it succeeds if the employee's initial choice of state was correct, and fails otherwise. Both manager and employee receive a deterministic benefit for project success.

Van den Steen (2005) shows that expected profits (relative to a reference belief) are higher when the firm hires a manager who is a "visionary," in the sense that the manager has a much stronger prior about the true state of the world than does the firm. As an example, if a firm thinks the states A and B are equally likely, it can still profit by hiring a manager whose prior is that state A obtains with probability 1. There are two reasons for this. First, hiring a visionary manager induces a beneficial sorting in the labor market. Firms with visionary managers will hire workers who agree with the manager's vision. Second, agreement within the organization about the correct course of action is valuable because it encourages the employee to exert high effort in searching for a project. An employee who knows his manager agrees with him about the likely state will exert more effort looking for a project, because conditional on finding a project the likelihood of implementation is higher. Thus, the right employee for a firm to have is one who agrees with the vision laid out by the firm's top management.

One implication of the Van den Steen model is that turnover of manager and subordinate should be temporally linked; a manager with a strong vision will attract a subordinate with similar beliefs, and these subordinates will not be the efficient matches for a successor manager who holds different beliefs. This implication is supported by the results of Hayes et al. (2006), who study top executive teams for evidence of complementarities among co-workers. Their main results are that the probability of non-CEO turnover increases markedly around times of CEO turnover, and that this effect depends on how long the CEO and non-CEO managers have worked together. Their evidence, however, is consistent with any source of complementarity among co-workers. Employees who have complementary skills, or invest in co-worker-specific human capital, or who simply enjoy working together will exhibit a similar pattern in turnover.

Prendergast (2007) begins from the premise that providing monetary incentives for "bureaucrats" is difficult. He observes that incentives for effort must then be provided through selecting the preferences of the bureaucrat, but that bureaucracies seem to differ in their selection. While some bureaucrats—teachers, firemen, and social workers—appear to be selected for preferences that are biased toward their clients, others—police and tax agents—appear to be biased against. Prendergast develops a model in which a social planner hires a bureaucrat to generate information used to assign a treatment to a client. As in Van den Steen's model (where the agent's incentives to develop a project are shaped entirely by his belief congruence with the manager), here the bureaucrat's effort incentives are driven by his preferences regarding the client. Social surplus is highest when the bureaucrat puts more effort into acquiring information, so the key effect in the model is how bias influences effort choice. When client and social interests are aligned (as in the case where the bureaucrat's job is to assess whether cardiac surgery is warranted), a bureaucrat who is altruistic—that is, biased in favor of the client—exerts greatest effort. If client and social interests are not aligned, as in the case where the "treatment" is a prison sentence, then clients benefit from a less informed bureaucrat and hence an altruistic bureaucrat would exert too little effort. In this case, a bureaucrat who is actively hostile to the client's interest can yield higher social surplus. Prendergast then shows that selecting the appropriate employees into a bureaucracy is likely to be difficult when potential employee preferences are not publicly observed. One possible outcome is bifurcated selection, where bureaucrats are either those most preferred by the principal or those *least preferred* by the principal.

Prendergast (2009) develops another model in which the inability to contract on output holds implications for the selection of workers. An institution carries out two tasks and employs two agents to do so. Each of the two workers is primarily responsible for one of the tasks, but contributes to the institution's success with regard to both. An example is a university's faculty and its administration. The university aims to both serve students and alumni and conduct research, and each party (faculty and administration) impact both. Incentives in the model come both from direct monetary payments from the institution to the agents and from career concern incentives. Notably, however, incentives from career concerns are biased toward one of the tasks. As the institution's ability to contract on output falls, it substitutes toward the biased career-concern-based incentives. This yields a benefit in the form of higher effort, but generates costs in that the two agents will frequently fail to cooperate.

3.2.2. Inducing self-selection

The problem of hiring the "right" employee is further complicated by the possibility that employees may be privately informed about relevant personal attributes. Employees may have an incentive to misrepresent qualifications and overplay experience. Since Salop and Salop (1976), labor economists have thought about how firms might solve informational problems by inducing employees to reveal information prior to the hiring decision. Salop and Salop point out that compensation policy is one tool firms can use to induce self-selection. In their model, potential employees are privately informed about their exogenous short-run probability of quitting the job. Firms incur training expenses, so quits are costly and firms prefer to hire only workers with lower quit probabilities. Firms can induce self-selection by asking employees to post a bond up front, and then making a payment to the employee that is conditioned on the employee remaining with the firm. See, also, Lazear (1979) on the role of mandatory retirement in settings where firms overpay relative to productivity late in an employee's career. In general, firms will want to offer forms of compensation that are most valuable to the type of employee the firm wishes to attract.

Inducing self-selection is one of the leading explanations for the use of performance-based pay in organizations. As Lazear (1986, 2004) notes, employees who believe themselves to be productive will expect to earn larger payments in a pay-for-performance scheme. It is straightforward for firms to structure "incentive" compensation such that the participation constraint is met for a high-ability worker, but not for a low-ability worker. Such pay plans can be profit-maximizing even if there is no hidden-action problem. In his Safelite study (discussed earlier), Lazear (2000) shows that the implementation of a piece-rate incentive system was associated with an increase in the quality of newly hired workers. Janssen (2002) shows how compensation policy can be used to encourage employees to signal. He shows that firms may want to raise wages when job openings attract an excess supply of applicants. Raising the posted wage offer increases the return associated with being hired, and thus encourages the best of the potential applicants to engage in costly signaling.

More recent research has focused on how firms can induce self-selection on dimensions other than simple ability. Oyer and Schaefer (2005) argue that inducing self-selection is one of the leading potential explanations for the recent rise in stock-based pay for lower-level employees. Because lower-level employees have little, if any, impact on a firm's share price, a grant of stock options to a lower-level employee cannot induce selection on ability. But if potential employees' valuations of option grants are heterogeneous, the requirement that employees accept options as part of pay will tend to select those individuals who value the option grant most highly. Thus, option grants will tend to select employees who are (a) less risk averse and (b) more optimistic regarding the firm's prospects. Firms can benefit from attracting such employees in a variety of ways; for example, employees who are optimistic about the firm's prospects will tend to be those who agree with the "vision" proposed by top management (as in Van den Steen, 2005), and hence will be more willing to make investments that are specific to that vision.

Using survey data on actual option grants made by US firms, Oyer and Schaefer (2005) show that the magnitudes of and risk-premia generated by these grants are consistent with this sorting explanation. For example, they show that a somewhat risk-averse employee who believes the firm's stock will appreciate by 25% annually would prefer the observed option-plus-salary package to a cash-only compensation plan that yields the same net cost to the employer. Magnitudes of the option grants they observe are also consistent with a retention story of stock option use (see Oyer, 2004), but are hard to reconcile with an incentives-based explanation of stock option use. Oyer and Schaefer (2006) derive conditions under which options perform better than stock grants at inducing this selection. Bergman and Jenter (2007) note that optimistic employees can purchase equity-based instruments on their own accounts, and derive conditions under which the firm can extract some rents by making direct grants of options. They show that firms extract rents if employees prefer equity that has been granted by the firm to that sold in the market, or if the firm's equity is overvalued in the market. Their empirical analysis suggests that firms may use options when boundedly rational employees are excessively optimistic about future share prices. Given the changes to the accounting treatment of stock options (in 2005) and the stock market crash of 2008, we think it possible that firms may change their stock-option-granting behavior going forward, and we encourage further research in that direction.

Delfgaauw and Dur (2007) study a model in which workers are heterogeneous in their intrinsic motivation to work for a firm. Offering higher wages increases the pool of potential applicants, but results in lower profits for the firm. When the firm can observe worker motivation, it faces a time-inconsistency problem. The firm wants to offer high wages to ensure a large pool of applicants, but then will be tempted to renege on this commitment (to grab rents) once it identifies a worker with high intrinsic motivation. A solution is to commit to a high minimum wage *ex ante*. When the firm cannot observe worker motivation, paying a high minimum wage would induce workers with low intrinsic motivation to apply. In this case, the firm ensures a good match by offering a lower wage, but this leads to a higher likelihood of having the vacancy go unfilled.

3.2.3. Labor-market intermediaries

Autor (2009) summarizes a recent volume of collected papers on labor market intermediation, and argues that intermediation arises primarily to solve problems of costly search, asymmetric information, or collective action. (We discuss some of the papers in this volume when discussing recruiting on the Internet, below.) We think the field could benefit from continued research in this area, specifically in the area of how employers interface with intermediaries.

One stream of literature focuses on the role of temporary help firms as an intermediary. Autor (2001a) notes that temp agencies often provide free training in general skills such as computer software packages, in apparent violation of standard human capital theory. He argues that this training both induces worker self-selection and allows these firms to privately screen on worker ability. Temp agencies can then exploit this short-run information advantage about unobserved worker ability to recoup the costs of training. Notably, Autor reports that firms are increasingly using temp agencies to identify candidates for permanent employment. Thus, a firm hiring through a temp agency essentially outsources the screening function to a specialist intermediary. Despite this, Autor and Houseman (2005) report that low-skilled workers in Michigan did not find better permanent employment matches when placed initially with temp agencies.

One intermediary about which very little is known (at least by labor economists) is the executive search firm.[4] While search firms surely account for a very small fraction of overall hiring, they are commonly used to fill important positions at the top of large organizations, both for-profit and non-profit. Bull et al. (1987) offer a theoretical model of executive search firms, in which employers must undertake costly screening to determine whether a prospective employee is a good fit. In their model, executive search

---

[4] Kaplan et al. (forthcoming) study a related labor market intermediary—a firm that assesses the talent of candidates for top management positions. They show that certain skills are particularly valuable to Private Equity and Venture Capital firms choosing managers for their portfolio companies.

firms incur the same costs as employers when screening potential employees. Search firms have two advantages in this model: (1) they can diversify sampling risk, and (2) they can screen potential employees in advance, and therefore fill vacancies more quickly than the employer could do on its own.

It has now been more than twenty years since the preliminary step of Bull et al. (1987), and there has been essentially no follow-on literature in economics on executive search.[5] While some economists have succeeded in getting data from prominent search firms about their businesses, there has been little progress toward understanding the economic role of the search firm itself. Cappelli and Hamori (2006), for example, use detailed records from a search firm—including whether target executives contacted by the search firm have declined or pursued offers of employment—to assess factors that affect employee loyalty.

While it is certainly possible that search economies of the type considered by Bull et al. (1987) are valuable, our sense is that other factors play a more important role in explaining executive search. There are small literatures in management and sociology examining executive search. Khurana (2002), for example, conducts a series of interviews with search firm employees, CEOs who had been recruited by search firms, and directors who had participated in CEO selections. He argues that the CEO labor market is characterized by "few buyers and sellers, high risk, and institutionalized gaps between buyers and sellers," and that these factors together give rise to intermediation. Buyers and sellers in this market, he argues, are often well aware of each other's availability as a trading partner. That is, an aspiring CEO or business school dean may well know which jobs are open or likely to come open, and a board of directors or university provost may well know which candidates are looking. But Khurana argues direct communication between the parties is difficult, and the search firm plays an important role in legitimating the relationship. Finlay and Coverdill (1998) describe a number of "soft" dimensions on which search firms attempt to assess fit with client firm needs, while Beaverstock et al. (forthcoming) stress legitimization of potential trading relationships in their study of European search firms. A richer understanding of this process would help provide some nuance and realism to basic models of search and matching.

3.2.4. Firms accessing social networks

For decades, social scientists have studied the role of informal social connections on labor markets (Granovetter, 1974). While it is by now well documented that social networks matter in labor markets, it is somewhat less clear *why* they matter. Do networks simply facilitate the search for job openings by potential employees? To what extent do network connections play a role in screening? To what extent does firm-level decision-making influence the process of matching through employees' social networks?

---

[5] There is some discussion of search firms in Simon and Warner (1992), which we discuss below, but they treat search firms as simply another source of employee referrals.

To illustrate this question, consider the recent study by Bayer et al. (2008), which uses detailed Census data on individuals' precise Boston-area residence and employment locations. They report that a pair of individuals who live on the same block are a third more likely to work together than individuals who live close to each other, but not on the same block. Thinness of local housing markets means it is hard to imagine this result is driven by a correlation in unobservables at the block level, so this study is a convincing identification of a local network effect on labor market matches. The study is unfortunately silent on the precise mechanism through which the neighborhood effects operate. Do neighbors simply mention job openings to each other when waiting at the bus stop? Or are the social connections between neighbors sufficiently strong that employers can rely on a current employee's recommendation to hire a neighbor? If so, under what circumstances should an employer trust a current employee's recommendation?

Many of the models of how social networks impact labor markets are of the "black box" variety, and focus solely on the role of the network in transmitting information about job openings. Calvo-Armengol and Jackson (2004), for example, use a network model of job search to offer an explanation for persistent race-based differences in labor market participation. Individuals randomly receive information about job openings, and can either act on those opportunities themselves or pass information to contacts. This mechanism gives rise to a positive correlation in employment status among individuals who are connected to each other. If there are costs associated with remaining in the labor force, those connected to a good network will be more willing to bear these costs than those who are not. See Ionnides and Loury (2004) for a recent survey of research on job networks and inequality.

We focus our attention on the part of the literature that features an active role for employers in accessing social networks. Saloner (1985) offers a model of a firm that uses an "old boy" network as a screening mechanism. Job seekers have heterogeneous ability, and are assumed to be unable to signal. Each employee has access to one of two "referees," who privately observes a signal that is related to the job seeker's productivity. Referees then communicate a hire/don't hire recommendation to the employer. Saloner shows that despite the difference in objective between the employer and the reference— employers are profit-maximizers, while referees care about both placement rates and the quality of their contacts who are placed—the equilibrium features truth-telling and first-best hiring choices.

Montgomery (1991) offers a model in which a firm can screen by hiring the social contacts of its current employees. Current employees are randomly endowed with social ties to potential future employees, and future employees are exogenously assumed to be likely to have the same type (productive or not) as the current employee. In the first period of this model, employers hire with no knowledge of worker productivity, so the market clears at a single wage. Employers then learn the productivity of their current employees and can make wage offers to potential employees who are tied to current employees. Firms with good-type first period employees make high wage offers to the ties of those employees, and earn profits due to some informational monopsony power.

Casella and Hanaki (2006, 2008) move this literature—in what we think is a very productive direction—by explicitly considering two channels through which firms can hire, and modeling job seekers incentives to reach employers through each channel. They begin with the Montgomery (1991) model, and endogenize the formation of networks. At cost λ_N, a young worker can establish a connection with an older worker. As in Montgomery, young workers are disproportionately likely to establish links to older workers of the same type: conditional on forming a link, the probability that the two connected workers have the same type is $\alpha_N > \frac{1}{2}$. Unlike Montgomery's analysis, however, employees who don't form a network link still have options. At cost λ_S, workers can attempt to signal—by, perhaps, acquiring a credential such as schooling. High (low) types succeed at acquiring the signal with probability α_S $(1 - \alpha_S)$. Importantly, both networks and signals have the potential to assist the employer in screening worker types.

Casella and Hanaki then ask where employers will prefer to look for workers. For the case where networking is free $(\lambda_N = 0)$, they find that referral-based hiring is almost always preferred by employers, even when, in equilibrium, certification is more informative. The key intuition here is simply that referrals allow the firm to privately screen, while certification is, by nature, public. Certified job seekers are known by all employers to be disproportionately likely to be high ability, and therefore their wages are bid up and all rents flow to the worker. Referred job seekers are somewhat less likely to be high ability than certified in this case, but because of the firm's informational monopsony it is able to capture rents.

When both forms of information transmission by workers are costly, the workers will compare the expected informational rent from pursuing referral or certification to the up-front cost. Networking always necessitates rent-sharing with the firm, so workers only pursue it if it is either less costly or if it is more precise as an indicator of ability. We see, in the work of Casella and Hanaki, the seeds of a theory of firm-level hiring strategy. Models of hiring to date have tended to focus on a single hiring practice and examine its efficacy. But real firms face a portfolio of choices over how to recruit. If we are to understand firm-level variation in hiring strategy, we need more models in which firms must choose how to access the labor market. We believe that future work along these lines can proceed in a number of directions. It would be useful, first, to expand the range of hiring venues available to firms. Second, researchers will need to introduce various forms of firm-level heterogeneity (both observable and unobservable). Third, ability is completely general in the Casella and Hanaki model, and it would be useful to know how match-specificity of ability impacts hiring channel choice. Fourth, search is missing from this model. Finally, it would be useful to understand to what extent rents associated with good employment matches can be captured by the referring employee.

The empirical literature on firm-level choices when accessing employees' social networks is still in its infancy. Most large, nationally representative datasets contain little information that could be used to do within-firm comparisons of employees hired via different means. This makes it difficult to rule out unobserved firm effects as an explanation for differences in wages across hiring method. And studies of firms' personnel records—often performed by sociologists—suffer from potential limits on generalizability. Much work remains to be done in this area, but we next survey the extant research.

Simon and Warner (1992) develop a search model of referrals from various sources (employees among them). Their model assumes the role of referrals is to reduce the employer's *ex ante* uncertainty about worker productivity. Workers exogenously receive an offer either through a referral or through non-referral means. Because the better information results in better *ex ante* matches, Simon and Warner predict that referred workers will receive higher up-front wages, have lower wage growth (conditional on continued employment), and lower turnover probabilities. Support for all three assertions is found in data from the 1972 Survey of Natural and Social Scientists and Engineers. However, the data does not permit any within-firm analysis of different hiring practices, so it is difficult to rule out the hypothesis that differences in the firms hiring via referrals (rather than the referral method itself) is driving the results.

Kugler (2003) builds efficiency wages into a model of referrals, and derives an equilibrium in which industries that pay efficiency wages prefer to hire through referral, both because connected workers can engage in peer monitoring and because markets where referrals are important are likely to be thin. Empirical evidence suggests that high-wage sectors do tend to engage in more referral-based hiring, and individuals hired by employee referral earn higher wages. Again, however, it is difficult to rule out various forms of firm-level heterogeneity as an alternative to the efficiency wage explanation.

Mosca and Pastore (2009) study the personnel records of organizations—public, private for-profit, and private non-profit—that provide social services in Italy. Unusual in this literature, they find that being hired through informal networks brings a substantial wage penalty (6.5%) for employees hired to public agencies. Interestingly, those hired through "public competitions"—which, presumably, could play the same role as signal in the Casella and Hanaki model—earn a 7% to 32% wage premium. Differences in hiring method account for a large fraction of the overall variation in wages across organization types.

Antoninis (2006) studies the personnel records of 209 employees of an Egyptian manufacturing firm. Conditional on observables such as experience and education, workers hired on the recommendation of someone holding direct knowledge of the new employee's productivity (an old work colleague) earned higher wages, on average, and this effect was larger for employees hired into higher skilled jobs. New workers hired on the recommendation of friends or family received no wage premium, and may have taken a wage discount in lesser skilled occupations.

Organizational sociologists have conducted some excellent single-firm studies of social networks in hiring practices. Fernandez and Weinberg (1997) study hiring processes used for four entry-level jobs at a retail bank in the early 1990s. Because the firm rewarded current employees for referring new hires, the source of initial contact between the firm and each job candidate was carefully tracked. Fernandez and Weinberg (1997) document several ways in which referred candidates differ from non-referred. First, referred candidates were more likely to fit the skill profile desired by the firm. Second, referred candidates disproportionately applied for jobs where there were fewer applicants, which suggests the firm was relying on its employees' networks more heavily when it was having trouble drawing applicants through other means. Third, referred candidates are both more likely to get interviewed and more likely to receive a job offer, even conditional on observables. Thus, it appears that this firm is using employee referrals in matching, search, and screening. It would be interesting to know whether the firm still uses referrals extensively when it is not having trouble finding applicants; presumably search costs have been affected by the possibility of Internet recruiting for entry level positions like these.

Fernandez et al. (2000) study similar data from a phone center. Strikingly, they find that new hires identified through a referral are no less likely to turn over than hires identified through other means, suggesting that better job matches are not uncovered through referrals. Employees hired through referrals are, however, more likely to turn over when the referrer turns over, suggesting that social connections matter both pre- and post-hiring. Fernandez et al. (2000) close with a call for a greater dialogue between economic theory and case-study-based empirical work, which we endorse.

3.2.5. Employer-to-employer transitions and "raids"

To what extent do firms look to other firms' employees—rather than the pool of unemployed job seekers or those just entering the labor market—to fill vacancies? And what factors facilitate and impede employer-to-employer job transitions?

Employer-to-employer job transitions appear to be fairly common. Fallick and Fleischman (2004) use the Current Population Survey's (CPS) dependent interviewing techniques to measure the extent of employer-to-employer job transitions in the United States. They report that 2.6% of employed persons change jobs each month. This figure is comparable in magnitude to the number of people moving from employment out of the labor force, and is twice as large as the number of people who move from employment to unemployment. Fallick and Fleischman further report that almost 40% of new jobs started between 1994 and 2003 were employer-to-employer transitions, a figure that supports the importance of on-the-job search.

The efficacy of "raids" as a source of new employees depends on two main factors. First, to what extent is employee productivity firm-specific? In settings where firm-specific matching or skill acquisition are important, we would expect to see less employer-to-employer movement of employees. Second, how does the labor market learn about the productivity of employees? If learning is symmetric—in that the current employer and potential future employers observe the same information regarding worker productivity—then raiders can bid for other employers' workers without fear of a winner's curse. If learning is asymmetric, then informational problems can impede employer-to-employer worker flows (Greenwald, 1986).

Models of symmetric employer learning have been used to explain a number of facts about wage growth over time. Farber and Gibbons (1996) develop a model in which education or other employee characteristics observable to labor market participants convey information about worker productivity. Employers also learn about productivity over time by observing output, and update accordingly. Consistent with the model, they show that time-invariant unobservables (the Armed Forces Qualification Test, for example) explain more of the variability in wages as workers gain labor market experience. Altonji and Pierret (2001) enrich this framework by showing that if firms statistically discriminate using education, then education should hold less explanatory power for wages as workers gain experience. This assertion is supported in NLSY data.

Lazear (1986) considers a model of raids under symmetric learning. An incumbent firm hires a worker with *ex ante* unknown ability to a job with a downward rigid wage. The worker's productivity at the incumbent firm is revealed. The worker's productivity at a potential raider is given by his productivity at the incumbent plus a random positive or negative shock. The main result is that it is the good workers who are raided. This is because raids happen under two conditions: (1) the worker's productivity is higher at the raider than at the incumbent, and (2) the worker's productivity at the raider is higher than the worker's *wage* at the incumbent.

Tranaes (2001) allows firms to endogenously select whether to attempt to hire a currently employed worker or hire from the pool of unemployed. He assumes symmetric learning—all potential employers can observe the abilities of all employees—but assumes that it is not possible for firms to observe abilities of workers who are not currently employed. Hiring an employed worker is costly because the firm must offer a higher wage than the incumbent, but hiring from the pool of unemployed is likely to yield a worker of low quality. Equilibrium in the model features unemployment even for good workers (separations happen exogenously). As raiding becomes more difficult (proxied by an exogenous friction), unemployment falls as hiring from the pool of unemployed becomes more attractive. Because raids impose a negative externality on unemployed job searchers, social welfare is strictly improved if raids are prohibited. Note the model does not included any gains from matching.

The literature on asymmetric learning has focused to a large extent on how incumbent employers might exploit their informational advantage. Waldman (1984) considers how the desire of an incumbent firm to preserve its informational advantage can distort job assignments and promotions within a firm. In Waldman's model, rival employers cannot observe a worker's productivity directly, and instead make inferences about productivity from job assignment. The main findings are that the information asymmetry causes the incumbent firm to tie wages to jobs rather than productivity and also to distort job assignments away from first-best.

The basic insight that asymmetric learning can distort choices inside organizations has been applied in a variety of theoretical models. Milgrom and Oster (1987) show that asymmetric learning can distort incentives for human capital investments for workers with high unobserved ability. Bernhardt (1995) applies Waldman's idea to promotion decisions, and compares the cost (from inefficient job assignment) and benefit (from reduced labor market competition) of delaying promotions. This cost is higher for more able workers, which may explain fast-track promotion paths in organizations. Scoones and Bernhardt (1998) show that if wages are attached to promotions (due to asymmetric learning), then employee human capital investment incentives may be distorted toward skills that will lead to promotions. If a general skill investment is efficient, employees may prefer to make a firm-specific investment if doing so is the surest path to promotion.

Of greater interest here is how asymmetric learning affects strategies pursued by raiding firms, and research on this question is somewhat more limited. Waldman (1990) shows how up-or-out promotion decisions—where a retention decision signals high productivity—can provide incentives for general-purpose human capital investments even if such investments are not directly observable to raiders. In Waldman's model, a crucial role of the retention decision is to spur labor-market competition from raiders, as this improves *ex ante* incentives. Bernhardt and Scoones (1993) consider a raider who must make a decision about whether to invest in learning whether an incumbent firm's employee is a good match. The incumbent can deter such an investment (and hence deter wage competition in the event the raider determines the employee is a good match with the raider) by making preemptive wage offers.

Empirical evidence on symmetric vs. asymmetric learning is, perhaps not surprisingly, broadly in support of the notion that both models hold some explanatory power, depending on context. As noted above, Farber and Gibbons (1996) and Altonji and Pierret (2001) offer evidence consistent with symmetric learning. DeVaro and Waldman (2009) show that promotion decisions in the Baker et al. (1994b) data appear to conform to signaling theories stemming from asymmetric learning; specifically, they show that wage increases associated with promotions are smaller when worker education levels are higher. Schonberg (2007) develops a learning model with endogenous mobility that allows for both forms of employer learning. She argues that under symmetric learning, job movers and stayers should have the same average ability (as proxied by AFQT), while movers should be lower ability under asymmetric learning. Further, asymmetric learning suggests that education should better explain wages for movers than stayers (because the raider lacks the incumbent's direct observations of productivity). She estimates the model using the NLSY data studied by Farber and Gibbons (1996) and Altonji and Pierret (2001) and finds support primarily for symmetric learning, with some support for asymmetric learning for more educated workers. Kahn (2009) also uses the NLSY but identifies the relative importance of symmetric and asymmetric learning using layoffs, economic conditions at the time of starting a job, and differences across occupations. Like Schonberg (2007), Kahn (2009) finds evidence of both types of learning. However, in contrast to Schonberg (2007), she concludes that asymmetric learning is economically and statistically more important than symmetric learning. Pinkston (2009) offers a model in which raiders receive noisy private evaluations of potential hires. Because raiders receive a signal the incumbent employer does not, the raider can profitably bid for the employee even in the absence of matching. The key empirical prediction of the model is that as experience increases wages reflect evidence of public learning, while as job tenure increases wages reflect private learning. Analysis of the NLSY supports both forms of learning.

Our view is that this literature needs industry studies, of the type commonly seen in industrial organization economics. While important progress has been made on understanding employer learning using aggregate data sets like the NLSY, it is likely the case that different markets vary dramatically in the extent to which asymmetric learning and matching are important. It is not hard to imagine that hiring another firm's CEO would present a markedly different set of issues from hiring another firm's retail clerk. We think the broad outlines of the raiding problem are well understood, but what is needed is an understanding of how matching and learning play out in specific labor markets. There are studies of a few such markets—which we review next—but much more is needed.

Fallick et al. (2006) use the CPS to examine how employer-to-employer flows vary by industry and geographic region. Specifically, they examine interfirm mobility of college educated men working in the computer industry, and find the rate of such flows to be significantly higher in California than elsewhere. Employer-to-employer transitions among this group average 1.95% monthly nationwide, but are around 3% in California. The authors note that rates of employer-to-employer job changes are no higher in Silicon Valley than in the rest of California, which suggests that California law (which does not permit the enforcement of noncompete clauses) may play a role in explaining this effect. Notably, employer-to-employer transitions *outside* of the computer industry are no higher in California than elsewhere in the US. Thus, it appears that it is the interaction of California law with specific features of the computer industry that drives this higher mobility.

There is a reasonably large literature on across-firm mobility of Chief Executive Officers. One advantage of using this setting as a laboratory is that in the US both pay and performance for these employees are publicly observed, albeit noisily. Murphy and Zabojnik (2006) document a striking trend in employer-to-employer flows in this market. For firms appearing in *Forbes* compensation surveys, between 1970 and 1979, just 14.9% of newly appointed CEOs were hired from outside the firm. This figure rose to 17.2% in the 1980s, and 26.5% in the 1990s. Murphy and Zabojnik develop a model in which managerial technology became more general over this period. That is, due to standardization of various accounting, management and IT practices in the US economy, it became easier for outsiders to manage large US firms. An associated increase in wage competition for the most able managers is offered as an explanation for the large increases in CEO pay over the same period.

Fee and Hadlock (2003) study a sample of managers who were hired from outside to either the CEO position or a senior non-CEO managerial role. They report that the prior employers of outside CEOs tended to have above-average stock price performance prior to the manager's departure, as measured by stock returns. This pattern does not hold for outsiders hired to non-CEO positions. They also report that the existence of an "heir-apparent" manager at the incumbent firm—a non-CEO manager who has been tagged as the likely next CEO—increases the likelihood that other managers at that firm will depart for better employment opportunities elsewhere. Huson et al. (2004) document that outsider CEOs are associated with larger subsequent improvements in operating performance.

Hiring from outside can also have implications for the incentives of current employees. Chan (1996) considers the effects of this choice in the context of promotion tournaments. External recruitment reduces the likelihood that an insider will win the promotion tournament, and hence weakens incentives. A firm can restore incentives by increasing the promotion-based wage differential, but this may lead to increased rent-seeking efforts on the part of insiders. Alternatively, the firm can commit to hire from outside only if the external candidate is substantially better than the insider. Thus, there is a tradeoff between attracting good candidates from outside and *ex ante* effort incentives for insiders. Agrawal et al. (2006) provide empirical evidence consistent with the hypothesis that firms hire external CEOs only when the external candidates are considerably superior to internal candidates on observable dimensions. The findings of Hassink and Russo (2008) run counter to this, however. Using matched employee–employer data from the Netherlands, they find that candidates hired internally into open jobs earn a 15% wage premium (conditional on observables) compared to those hired from outside.

Securities analysts—stock market observers who offer forecasts of corporate earnings—offer another market where employer-to-employer job mobility can be easily tracked. This setting has both advantages and disadvantages relative to the CEO context: analysts wages are not commonly disclosed, but it is relatively easy to devise measures of employee performance that can be compared pre- and post-mobility. Groysberg et al. (2008) find that star analysts who change jobs show a long-lasting reduction in job performance. This suggests that, despite claims of industry observers, there may be substantial firm-specificity in analyst skills that is lost upon job mobility. It is also possible that this is evidence of a winner's curse stemming from asymmetric learning. It is not clear how this set of facts is consistent with equilibrium behavior by market participants, unless there is some gain that offsets the losses due to reduced performance.

3.2.6. Employer search

While there is an enormous literature on employee job search, the literature on search by employers is less developed. An early contribution by Rees (1966) focuses attention on two channels of search. Employers can expand search on the extensive margin, by gathering more applications. On the intensive margin, employers can expand search by gathering more information on each potential applicant. More recently, researchers have examined choices over the range of search activities a firm may engage in.

Barron et al. (1985) study the 1980 Employer Opportunity Pilot Project (EOPP) survey, for which employers who had recently hired were asked about staff hours spent on recruiting, the number of applications received and interviews conducted, and wages for the new hire. The paper is perhaps best known for a simple but striking fact: 90% of the job offers made by firms in this sample were accepted. The authors then relate these search choices to firm and job characteristics. A primary result is that firms spend more time on the search process when the job requires larger training expenditures by the firm. Human capital theory suggests firm-specific training generates rents, so firms will want to insure a good match prior to making such investments. Firms also spend more time recruiting when the educational requirements for the job are greater. Jobs that feature higher training expenditures by the firm are associated with more hours spent interviewing. Finally, firm size appears to be correlated with recruiting expenditures; a doubling in firm size increases the number of applicants per offer by 10%.

Another early contribution is Holzer (1987). Again using the EOPP data (this time from the 1982 wave), he shows that advertising openings to current employees is the most commonly used recruitment method.[6] Interviews and reference checks are overwhelmingly popular as screening mechanisms. There is some evidence that employees hired through personal referrals have higher productivity, lower turnover, and lower screening costs.

There is a fairly sizable empirical literature on vacancies. The approach taken here is from search theory. Employers sequentially sample from a pool of potential employees with a known ability distribution. A vacancy duration is simply the amount of time until the vacancy is filled. Typical empirical design involves estimation of a hazard rate of vacancy filling, and examining how this rate varies with characteristics of the job or firm. Data sources are mostly from one-off surveys, which makes it difficult to examine how the mechanism by which the vacancy is filled is related to job tenure, wage growth, turnover and other measures of match success one would like to examine.

---

[6] It is not clear in this entire literature whether the new hires are all external hires. If a firm advertises to its current employees, the firm may want them to refer friends or apply for the job themselves.

In a series of papers, van Ours and Ridder (1991, 1992, 1993) examine a pair of Dutch surveys on vacancies. van Ours and Ridder (1991) examine data from the Dutch Bureau of Statistics and study how vacancy durations and vacancy flows—defined as the rate at which new vacancies are created—varies over the business cycle. The authors estimate the vacancy duration hazard rate and find that vacancies fill more slowly when the vacancy flow rate is higher. Jobs that require more education also fill more slowly. Further, vacancy flow is more sensitive to the business cycle for low-education openings.

Using data from the Organization for Strategic Labor Market Research, van Ours and Ridder (1992) again find that higher educational requirements are associated with longer vacancy durations. Vacancies also exhibit positive duration dependence. The main contribution here, however, is to examine the timing of applications. van Ours and Ridder (1992) show that the acceptance probability (that is, the probability a candidate accepts a job offer) is zero for the first two weeks after the vacancy's posting. The probability rises after the first two weeks, and stays high for another ten weeks. The arrival rate of applicants is very high for the first two weeks, essentially zero for the next two weeks, before rising again. The evidence points to a non-sequential search strategy, where firms cast a net, draw in a pool of applicants, simultaneously screen, then make an offer or draw again. Thus, while employee search appears to be sequential, employer search is not. van Ours and Ridder (1993) find that employers spend far more time on selection than on search. Mean application period—estimated off of the hazard rate of applications—is 3.1 weeks, while the mean selection period is 14.6 weeks (21.1 weeks when university education is required). Thus, vacancy durations should be thought of not as the duration of search but rather as a combination of search duration and screening duration. This raises the question of whether the Internet has affected screening times; presumably the process of screening on observables is considerably faster now than it was in 1992. Abbring and van Ours (1994) also partition vacancy durations into search and selection periods, and find that the ratio of unemployed to vacancies affects search durations—longer when the ratio is smaller—but not selection periods.

Barron et al. (1997) develop new theory on employer search when screening expenditures (intensive search) are endogenous. They predict that vacancies for jobs requiring more training will see both more applications before an offer is made, and greater screening expenditures per application. Analysis of four data sets from the US supports this contention. Barron et al. (1997) also show that job offers are rarely rejected, and that there seems to be no pattern in the data on rejected offers.

Burdett and Cunningham (1998), studying the 1982 EOPP data, echo many of the findings of Barron et al. (1985). Firms undertake longer searches when the training expenditures associated with the job are higher. Larger firms fill vacancies faster, presumably because of easier access to pools of employees. There is some evidence that jobs with high skill and/or education requirements take longer to fill. The primary distinction between the results in Burdett and Cunningham (1998) and Barron et al. (1985) is that the later study examines vacancy duration as its measure of selectivity in recruiting, while the earlier study used surveys of staff hours. Burnett and Cunningham go on to report evidence of a non-monotonic hazard function for filling vacancies. When a vacancy is "young," the hazard function is increasing, but as the vacancy gets old the likelihood of filling it drops. Finally, the authors report that vacancy durations are longer when the employer has advance notice that the vacancy will occur. Brencic (2009c) confirms this advance notice finding using detailed data on all employment vacancies in Slovenia, and Brencic (2009a) finds (using Slovenian and US data) that firms also adjust hiring standards when advance notice periods are expiring.

Another series of papers examines the Dutch "How Do Firms Recruit?" survey (conducted for the Dutch Ministry of Social Affairs). Gorter et al. (1996) study the relation between recruitment strategy and vacancy duration. They first estimate a multinomial logit model of first recruitment method choice—advertisements, informal channels, labor office, or other—and then estimate vacancy duration. Advertisements are used more heavily when the vacancy stipulates work experience, and the labor office is commonly used for low-education jobs. Hazard rates for vacancy duration show that when informal recruitment is the first choice, the vacancy tends to fill immediately or not at all. Further, advertised vacancies fill more slowly when education is required. Russo et al. (2000) use the same data set to examine recruitment method choice and the rate of applicant arrival. They report that the flow of applicants is, not surprisingly, related to overall labor market conditions. Further, when conditions are tight, employers adjust recruitment methods to use additional advertisements. This method of recruitment is shown to have the largest impact on the flow of applicants. Russo et al. (2001) build on this work to show that firms are less likely to hire currently unemployed workers when conditions are tight. Finally, Van Ommeren and Russo (2008) argue that sequential search implies that the number of rejected applicants should be proportional to the number of vacancies. As an example, suppose a firm searches sequentially to fill a single vacancy, and must perform a costly screen on each candidate. If one-third of sampled applicants pass the screen, then on average the firm will reject two applicants for each one it hires. This reasoning implies the elasticity of the number of rejected applicants to vacancies should be one. If, on the other hand, search is not sequential, then there is no requirement that this elasticity be unity. This observation forms the basis of a test. Sequential search is not rejected for informal methods (social networks, school recruiting, and temp agencies), but is rejected when firms access employment agencies and run advertisements.

Manning (2000) studies proprietary data from a small set of firms employing low-wage workers, and reports three main facts. First, most vacancies generate few applicants (less than three, on average). Second, wage and non-wage aspects of the job influence the number of applicants. Third, firms are more likely to grant an interview to workers who are currently employed, but conditional on making it to the interview stage, currently unemployed workers are no less likely to receive a job offer. A small literature examines the duration of vacancies.

Andrews et al. (2008) note that while employees infrequently reject job offers, employers often allow vacancies to go unfilled, simply by withdrawing the vacancy from the market. Using detailed data on vacancies from the UK's Lancashire Career Services Agency, they show that the hazard rate of filling a vacancy exhibits positive duration dependence, while the hazard for withdrawal exhibits negative duration dependence.

Brencic (2009b) interacts the vacancies literature with that on Employment Protection Legislation. She reasons first that firms facing costly search—measured by the immediacy with which a vacancy needs to be filled—may respond by relaxing hiring standards. Doing so, however, can result in poor matches and hence greater likelihood of termination. This implies a complementarity between relaxed hiring standards and temporary employment, especially in cases where firing is costly. Brencic examines this relation using very detailed data on vacancies in Slovenia. During her sample period, there is no variation in firing costs—although she reports that changes in these costs occurred just after her sample period—so the test simply examines the cross-sectional association between costly search, relaxation of hiring standards, and temporary employment. She finds that employers facing costly search tend to relax hiring standards, but only when the position being hired for is temporary. She does not find evidence that employers switch permanent positions to temporary when reducing hiring standards, as theory might suggest.

DeVaro (2005) adds both a new data source and an emphasis on starting wages. He studies the Multi-City Study of Urban Inequality (MCSUI), a large cross-sectional survey of employers in four metropolitan areas of the United States. He first documents that recruitment strategies vary with firm and job characteristics. As prior literature finds, firms rely more heavily on referrals when hiring for professional occupations. Next, he includes recruitment method in a standard wage regression. While Casella and Hanaki (2006, 2008) would suggest that personal referrals should be paid less conditional on human capital observables, there is little evidence to suggest this is the case. In his richest specification (personal, firm, and industry controls), DeVaro finds that referrals from friends and current employees are associated with small wage premiums relative to those recruited via help-wanted signs, but there is essentially no statistical difference between personal referrals and newspaper ads or school referrals. Clearly there is work to be done to reconcile screening-based theories of network hiring with the facts.

DeVaro and Fields (2005) use the MCSUI as well, and regress worker performance (on a 100-point scale, employer-reported) on indicators for recruitment and screening method, and firm characteristics. Data show very little support for the assertion that recruiting and screening methods are related to performance. Conditional on firm, worker and job characteristics, method of recruitment bears little relationship to subjectively assessed performance. The approach—using employer-evaluated performance as a dependent variable—is subject to some criticism. Presumably employers would be pleased to hire a less able worker at a sufficiently discounted wage. It is not clear how one might combine wages with this numerical performance score to get the net impact on the firm's bottom line.

DeVaro (2008) uses the same data to estimate a dynamic, discrete-choice structural model of recruitment. The firm is modeled as choosing recruitment strategies and wage offers over time to try to fill a vacancy. The primary advantage of this structural approach is that it permits the study of the effects of various counterfactuals on firms' recruitment policies. It does come at a cost of some generality, however. Here a firm is modeled as choosing either formal or informal recruiting methods at the beginning of the recruiting period, but Holzer (1987) and others show that firms tend to use multiple recruiting methods simultaneously. The analysis suggests that, due to higher offer-acceptance probabilities, the firm will tend to offer lower wages when engaged in informal recruiting. Note that this is a different rationale for the informal-recruitment/lower-wages channel than that offered by Casella and Hanaki (2006, 2008). Counterfactual simulations suggest that wage subsidies, "information policies" that improve match qualities through formal methods, and changes in the degree of employee heterogeneity can have important effects on firms' recruitment decisions and wages. Wage subsidies shift firms toward informal means, in part because the subsidy makes employment more attractive and employees identified through informal means are (assumed to be) more likely to accept. Information policies, modeled on the Workforce Investment Act of 1991, push recruitment toward formal channels to take advantage of improved matching. Increases in employee heterogeneity shift recruiting to formal methods through an order-statistic effect. Formal methods allow quicker sampling and reviewing many applications quickly, and selecting the best is most valuable when the variance of match quality is high.

Finally, some papers consider a potential complementarity between various recruitment and screening strategies. Under the complementarity hypothesis, one might expect positive interaction effects between screening and recruitment methods. In the MCSUI data, DeVaro and Fields (2008) find very little support for the complementarity hypothesis. Interaction terms in performance regressions are typically negative.

Bartling et al. (2009) argue that choice of recruitment method—screening, in particular—can have complementarities with discretion, rent-sharing, and wages. In an experimental setting, they document the endogenous emergence of two markedly different organizational design strategies. One focuses on control, with little discretion, no rent sharing, low wages, and no screening, and one focuses on trust, with discretion, high wages, rent sharing, and screening. A key driver of this choice is the information available to employers about potential employees pre-hiring. When employers can observe a signal about employee past performance, many employers conditioned wages on this signal; this gives employees a reputational incentive to reciprocate employer trust, which facilitates discretion. When no such signal is available, employers cannot condition wages on past performance—so no career concerns operate—and employers tend not to trust.

3.2.7. Recruiting on the Internet

As rates of Internet adoption rose in the 1990s, participants in labor markets began to experiment with ways to use this tool in economic activity. Early attempts in this direction are summarized by Autor (2001b), who hypothesizes a number of ways that the Internet might affect labor markets, including the processes through which employers and employees match. He points out that the Internet may improve aggregate match efficiency by reducing search costs, thus allowing both firms and workers to consider many potential trading partners much more quickly than before. This effect may be offset by concerns about adverse selection. Because electronic communication makes it easy for workers to apply for many jobs—even jobs they (privately) know themselves to be poorly suited for—recruiting on the Internet may lead to sharply increased screening costs for employers. Thought of another way, applying for a job imposes some match-specific costs on the applicant. As the Internet has lowered this application cost, the signal generated by the application process (as in the Spence (1973) model) has become less meaningful and the application process is less good at inducing applicants to self-select efficiently.

The years since 2001 have seen a trickle rather than a flood of research about online job matching. Much of the existing research focuses on search by potential employees, rather than on recruiting by employers. Kuhn and Skuterud (2004), for example, use the CPS Computer and Internet Supplements to examine selection into Internet job search and unemployment durations among online job searchers. They find that Internet search is associated with lower unemployment durations, but that this effect is entirely explained by worker observables such as education and occupation. Once these observables are controlled for, Internet job search is associated with similar, or in some specifications, longer unemployment durations. Kuhn and Skuterud conclude that either Internet job search is ineffective at reducing unemployment durations, or that the pool of Internet job searchers is adversely selected.

Stevenson (2009) points out that 22% of workers who began a new job in mid-2002 cited the Internet as the primary means through which they found the job. She further reports that state-level Internet penetration is associated with a reallocation of job search activity, and an increase in the overall level of job search. Finally, Stevenson documents that most Internet job searchers are employed, and that employed workers who search online are more likely to experience an employer-to-employer job transition than those who do not search online.

Bagues and Labini (2009) analyze the impact of the Italian *AlmaLaurea* online job board, and exploit the fact that different universities joined the board at different times to construct a difference-in-differences estimator of the impact of the online board on labor market outcomes. Notably the *AlmaLaurea* is unlike the US-based Internet job boards studied by Stevenson (2009) in that it provides employers with detailed records—supplied by the colleges not the students—on students' academic careers. This compulsory disclosure may serve to mitigate adverse selection in the labor market. Bagues and Labini find that the *AlmaLaurea* reduces the likelihood of unemployment by 1.6 percentage points, increased wages by three percentage points, and also increased the likelihood of regional mobility for university graduates. The study is silent, however, about whether the job board improves employers' ability to find high ability workers or those with high idiosyncratic match values. Understanding this distinction has important implications for the effects of Internet hiring on inequality and whether some potential employees will be made worse off.

Some researchers have studied the question of how firms incorporate the Internet into recruiting strategies. Hadass (2004) uses proprietary data from a US-based multinational firm to examine the impact of Internet recruiting on various aspects of job match. Online recruiting at the firm accounted for just 0.2% of the firm's hires in 1996, but grew to 20% by 2002. A Cox duration model shows that Internet recruiting leads to job durations that are statistically identical to that found for print advertising, but durations that are significantly (both statistically and economically) shorter than those for employee referral and college recruiting. Employee referrals and college recruiting lead to job durations that are 1.7 times as long as those found for Internet and print.

Nakamura et al. (2009) offer a descriptive discussion of modern e-recruiting services, and give a list of five key facts. First, they point out that the main commercial job sites are not standalone corporate entities. Monster, CareerBuilder, and HotJobs are all parts of larger firms that engage in multiple activities. Second, online recruiting allows firms to search more widely and consider a larger variety of applicants. Third, there are substantial returns to scale in online recruiting. The costs to a large employer of advertising to find ten employees of a given type is not substantially larger than the cost of advertising to find one. This fact would seem to explain why large US retailers account for such a large fraction of overall Internet job search traffic. (Target's career site by itself accounted for more Internet traffic in early 2007 than the site that hosts all US federal government jobs.) Fourth, in line with the results in Stevenson (2009), online methods allow firms to access currently employed workers who are only passive job seekers. Fifth, US-based firms currently dominate online job search worldwide.

Brencic and Norris (2009) focus on some specific choices facing employers when posting job openings online. They collect a sample of job postings made to Monster.com and compare job openings that the employer reports must be filled immediately to openings where employers do not make this statement. When employers report greater impatience, they also tend to list more information about the job application process and less information about hiring requirements. Further, openings for jobs that need to be filled immediately tend to be withdrawn from the job board more quickly.

Finally, Kuhn and Shen (2009) use online job postings in China to provide direct evidence on employer preferences for gender, age, height, and beauty. Labor-market discrimination based on such characteristics is illegal in much of the world, but, strikingly, remains legal in the world's largest labor market. Surprisingly, online job postings in China often contain explicit requirements on such "US-prohibited" characteristics: 90% of firms posting 50 or more ads in the Kuhn and Shen sample expressed at least one such preference. Notably, firms are less likely to express such a preference when educational requirements for the job are more stringent.

3.2.8. Organizational demography

A developing literature in economics examines organizational demography; that is, factors that influence the demographic characteristics of those hired by the firm. Giuliano et al. (2009) use personnel data from a large US retail chain to show that the race or ethnicity of the hiring manager appears to be an important determinant of the racial composition of new hires. While store fixed effects—which capture both store characteristics and characteristics of the store's local labor market—are the largest determinant of a store's racial mix of hiring, Giuliano et al. (2009) find that the race of the hiring manager matters as well. Specifically, they report that non-black managers hire more whites and fewer blacks than black managers. Estimates suggest that the race of the store manager shifts the black employee share by around four percentage points. On average, black managers hire workforces that are 21% black, while non-black managers hire just 17% black. Similar effects are found for Hispanic vs. white managers, when restricting attention to stores where Hispanics make up 30% or more of the local population.

It is not clear what accounts for this propensity for racial match of hiring. It is possible that hiring managers are accessing their social networks (which may be partially segregated by race) to identify promising employees. Another hypothesis is that there are direct productivity effects, if, for example, black managers communicate better with black subordinates. This pattern could also be accounted for by preferences of managers or employees. It is difficult to disentangle these effects, but Giuliano et al. (2009) show that store-level sales do not appear to be significantly impacted by the racial match of the manager and employees.

Oyer and Schaefer (2010) examine the organizational demography of large US law firms. Using lawyer biographies posted to firms' web sites, they document substantial across-firm variation in hiring strategies. Law firms are found to be somewhat concentrated with regard to the law schools where they hire. Oyer and Schaefer find that for the average firm, the probability that two lawyers selected at random attended the same law school is about six percent higher than this probability for two attorneys selected at random from the sample. Some firms pursue a fairly unconcentrated hiring strategy, and the distribution of law schools attended by their attorneys is comparable to the overall sample distribution of law schools. Other firms appear to hire from a narrow set of law schools located in close geographic proximity to the firm offices. Still others hire nationally, but only from the very top law schools.

Oyer and Schaefer find that about a third of the observed variation in office-level law-school shares can be accounted for by simple geographic proximity. Law offices, by and large, disproportionately tend to hire from close law schools. Higher ranked law firms also tend to hire from high-ranked law schools, and this effect explains a small additional amount of variation in hiring practices. Even conditional on geography and reputation match, they report a strong association between associate-level law-school shares and partner-level shares. They estimate that when a firm's partner law-school share is higher by one percentage point, the firm's associate law-school share is higher by around 0.6 percentage points. As with the study by Giuliano et al. (2009), it is difficult to say whether social networks, production complementarities, or employee preferences are driving this relation. Wage and/or productivity measures are required to more specifically identify the causes and effects of these relationships.

3.2.9. Hiring, agglomeration, and firm location

The optimal matching and searching processes that firms engage in will vary across local labor markets. Larger and more concentrated populations typically lead to thicker labor markets which may reduce search costs and can also lead to better average matches between firms and workers. While this will tend to increase surplus, thicker labor markets also lead to greater competition in the labor market. So, while total surplus may be greater in thicker labor markets, firms may have to settle for a smaller share of that surplus because it is more difficult to generate monopsony power.

There is a large literature on firm location and, more specifically, agglomeration economies, that studies the relationship between firm co-location and other variables. One of the factors that often lead similar employers to locate near each other is a source of certain types of worker (such as skilled workers near university towns).[7] However, firm location decisions and the supply of labor in a given labor market will clearly affect one another, so it is difficult to generate credible causal statements about the effect of either one of these.

Several recent studies have analyzed the relationship between labor market thickness, firm location, and worker/firm matching. Wheeler (2001) develops a model where capital and worker skill are complements. In this model, thicker labor markets lead to higher productivity, greater wage inequality, and higher returns to skill. He cites and generates empirical evidence that is consistent with all these ideas. Andersson et al. (2007) put this same basic idea to somewhat more rigorous scrutiny. They use matched employer/employee data from California and Florida to show that there is more

---

[7] Local labor markets are just one of several important reasons firms agglomerate. See Ellison and Glaeser (1997) and Ellison and Glaeser (1999) who look at other sources of "natural advantage" and "spillovers" that drive co-location of similar firms.

assortative matching between "high quality" workers and "high quality" firms in thicker labor markets. They show that establishment-level productivity is related to match quality and argue that the relationship between better matching and thick labor markets can explain a substantial portion of the urban productivity premium. Freedman (2009) looks at similar issues, with a focus on the software industry in a single (unnamed) state. He first derives a model where firm/worker match quality is based on differences in the Human Resources packages offered by firms and variation in employee preferences. Empirically, he finds that agglomeration of software firms is associated with higher wages, bigger firms, and less wage dispersion, as his model would suggest.

Garicano and Hubbard (2007) and Garicano and Hubbard (2009) analyze how market thickness affects the organization of law firms and the kind of work lawyers perform. In Garicano and Hubbard (2007), they show that bigger markets allow lawyers to specialize more, to be more likely to work in a hierarchy, and to have more leveraged hierarchies. That is, labor market thickness affects the matching process in that more senior attorneys can better leverage their unique skills. Garicano and Hubbard (2009) find that lawyers become more specialized as market size increases. The analysis drops the largest legal markets, so that they can be sure they are isolating the effect of the way work is organized (rather than the type of work). But they also show that some of the most skill-intensive and expensive work gets done in a few big cities, indicating that firms and lawyers locate there to do certain types of work.

3.3. Post-hiring matching—retention and displacement

This section is titled "Hiring" because no labor market matching can take place without an initial employment contract being formed. But labor market matching is constantly going on as firms decide who to retain and workers decide whether to engage in on-the-job search. While there is a large literature on the effects of job loss, there is relatively little on firms' choices about retention and worker displacement. We have already touched on the post-hiring matching issues in our discussions of firing "risky" workers that turn out to have low productivity, raids, and up-or-out systems. We now add a short discussion of the literature on firms' strategies regarding retaining and displacing workers.

Gibbons and Katz (1991) extended basic adverse selection models of hiring to the firing context. They derive a model where firms, when faced with a negative shock to productivity, lay off their less productive workers. Other firms draw inferences about workers' ability when a prior employer selectively chooses who to lay off, while no such inference is possible for workers who lose their job because their firm shuts down altogether. Consistent with the model, they find that workers who are laid off from a continuing operation suffer more from job loss than workers who lose their jobs when their establishment shuts down. Though others have called the empirical results of Gibbons and Katz (1991) into question (see, for example, Krashinsky, 2002), the important conceptual distinction between "layoffs" and "plant closings" has been widely accepted in the literature.[8]

When the match-specific component of productivity is important and firms pay workers something close to the marginal product of their effort, firms can (at least in principle) let employees efficiently separate from the firm when they need to reduce staff. That is, under the right conditions, there should not be a substantial adverse selection problem in offering voluntary severance packages and doing so may enhance the firm's reputation and/or be necessary to honor written or implicit labor contracts. Pencavel (2001) studies this issue by looking at which University of California employees accepted buyouts in the early 1990s. As one might expect, larger severance benefits increase the probability of a worker accepting a buyout. But Pencavel also shows that it is otherwise very difficult to predict who will accept buyouts. Kim (2003) shows that the University of California got positive selection in one set of layoffs, because faculty whose productivity had been on the decline were more likely to accept buyouts.

There is one group that has been closely studied (over-studied?) in terms of job dismissal—CEOs of large American corporations. As with incentives, CEOs present an unusually public group in terms of observability of dismissal and performance.[9] However, CEOs are also not very representative of employees more generally because of the large cost of not replacing a bad CEO, the fact that they may earn substantial rents, and the inability to move them to a new job within the firm if they are not working out as CEO.

Two recent papers have taken a careful look at the drivers of CEO dismissal. Both Jenter and Kanaan (forthcoming) and Kaplan and Minton (2009) find that CEO turnover is sensitive to firm performance and that the effects of industry and total stock market performance are not completely filtered out of the relationship between performance and forced turnover. Kaplan and Minton (2009) also show that forced turnover have become more responsive to performance over time and question whether turnover decisions made by boards of directors are generally efficient. While these results are very useful for corporate governance scholars, it is hard to draw broad conclusions about displacement from these workers.

The availability of large employer/employee matched datasets has the potential to generate insights into displacement strategies of firms, though these data do not generally distinguish between layoffs, firings, and quits. Matching to the next job or to unemployment records may help narrow down the potential reasons for leaving, however. In the absence of being able to make such distinctions, even these rich datasets have little to add relative to the factors we already know to be associated with job loss (see, for example, Kletzer, 1998).

---

[8] Oyer and Schaefer (2000) further break down layoffs into those that are driven by economic issues and those driven by an individual's poor performance ("firings"). They show that firms appear to choose which of these ways to displace workers at least partially based on the firing costs associated with each.

[9] One minor complication is determining whether a departing CEO is leaving voluntarily, but researchers have developed credible methods for separating voluntary and involuntary departures. See, for example, Parrino (1997).

3.4. Do hiring practices matter?

We conclude this section by asking a big question that has received far too little attention: Do hiring practices matter for the performance of an organization or a business unit?

There is limited evidence on this question, mostly coming from the growing literature on productivity effects of firm-level human resource management choices (and see Bloom and Van Reenen (2011) in this Volume for a thorough review of this literature). As we noted above, the Ichniowski et al. (1997) study of steel finishing lines considers "extensive selection procedures" as one of a set of complementary HR practices that appear to have boosted productivity. Bresnahan et al. (2002) show that one hiring practice—screening for education—appears to be part of a bundle of organizational practices that complement investments in information technology. Adoption of this set of complementary practices is associated with higher organizational value added. Bloom and Van Reenen (2007) conduct a survey of management practices and show that a variety of performance metrics—productivity, profitability, and sales growth, among others—are associated with advanced management practices. Their survey questions address a broad range of management practices, and among them is a series of questions about the firm's attitude toward attracting human capital.

We think highly of these papers, but also believe this literature can be moved forward in a couple of ways. First, these papers are not, primarily, about hiring. Rather, they are about how a much broader set of human resource management choices are related to organizational performance. As a result, these papers do not generally make careful distinctions between, say, hiring practice A and hiring practice B. In some sense, the level of detail with regard to hiring choices is limited to simple questions about whether the firm thinks hiring is important, as opposed to gathering information about firm-level differences in specific hiring strategies. Second, this literature is subject to questions about causality. Firms in these studies are clearly choosing one set of organizational practices over another, and it remains unclear whether hiring choices are driving good performance, or whether there is some third factor that explains both.

We think this literature needs a series of carefully constructed hiring-related field experiments. Personnel Economics now has a very solid tradition of incentives-related field experiments, and we are eager to see this toolkit applied to hiring decisions. The lack of hiring-related experiments is, we think, evidence of the great importance of hiring in modern firms. What manager, after all, would allow an academic economist to experiment with the firm's screening, interviewing, or hiring decisions? We hope this concern will not prevent economists from performing Safelite-style experiments on hiring practices in the future.

4. CONCLUSION

We can summarize our view of the last few decades of Personnel Economics research as, "Incentives matter. Getting them right is important for firms. Measurement limitations and other challenges to employers' ability to implement incentive programs are well explained by recent agency models." The primary drivers of this success in studying incentives have been theorists' ability to use advances in information economics to generate realistic and detailed models of employment relationships and the availability of new firm-level and matched employer/employee datasets.

We hope that the authors of the review of Personnel Economics in the next volume of this Handbook are able to conclude, "Recent research has generated important and practical insights into the ways firms and workers generate economic surplus by matching appropriately. Firms' strategic decisions about how to source appropriate workers and how to craft attractive job packages have advanced significantly in the last few years. This is primarily driven by the development of more nuanced models of hiring and the creative use of firm-level and employer–employee datasets." We recognize, however, that is more easily hoped for than done. There are significant challenges to the matching research we call for. While data limitations are the most obvious challenge (it is very rare to have a data source with information both on people that a firm hires and those that the firm does not hire, for example), there may well be others such as the possibility that the heterogeneity of optimal hiring strategies may simply be much greater than the heterogeneity of optimal incentives. We hope that, on balance, these potentially higher costs of doing research on matching and hiring do not discourage researchers from undertaking work in this area and we hope that at least a few others will join us in trying to advance this research area.

REFERENCES

Abbring, J., van Ours, J.C., 1994. Sequential or non-sequential employers' search? Economics Letters 44, 323–328.

Abowd, J.M., Haltiwanger, J., Lane, J., McKinsey, K.L., Sandusky, K., 2007. Technology and the demand for skill: an analysis of within and between firm differences. NBER Working Paper 13043.

Abowd, J.M., Kramarz, F., Margolis, D.N., 1999. High wage workers and high wage firms. Econometrica 67, 251–333.

Adams, C., 2005. Agent discretion, adverse selection and the risk-incentive tradeoff. Federal Trade Commission.

Aggarwal, R., Samwick, A.A., 1999. The other side of the tradeoff: the impact of risk on executive compensation. Journal of Political Economy 108, 65–105.

Agrawal, A., Knoeber, C.R., Tsoulouhas, T., 2006. Are outsiders handicapped in CEO successions? Journal of Corporate Finance 12, 619–644.

Altonji, J.G., Pierret, C.R., 2001. Employer learning and statistical discrimination. Quarterly Journal of Economics 116, 313–350.

Andersson, F., Burgess, S., Lane, J.I., 2007. Cities, matching and the productivity gains of agglomeration. Journal of Urban Economics 61, 112–128.

Andersson, F., Freedman, M., Haltiwanger, J., Lane, J., Shaw, K., 2009. Reaching for the stars: who pays for talent in innovative industries? The Economic Journal 119, F308–F332.

Andrews, M.J., Bradley, S., Stott, D., Upward, R., 2008. Successful employer search? An empirical analysis of vacancy duration using micro data. Economica 75, 455–480.

Antoninis, M., 2006. The wage effects from the use of personal contacts as hiring channels. Journal of Economic Behavior and Organization 59, 133–146.

Ariely, D., 2008. What's the value of a big bonus? New York Times November 20, A43.

Autor, D.H., 2001a. Why do temporary help firms provide free general skills training? Quarterly Journal of Economics 116, 1409–1448.

Autor, D.H., 2001b. Wiring the labor market. Journal of Economic Perspectives 15, 25–40.

Autor, D.H., 2009. Studies of labor market intermediation: introduction. In: Autor, D.H. (Ed.), Studies of Labor Market Intermediation. University of Chicago Press.

Autor, D.H., Katz, L.F., Kearney, M.S., 2006. The polarization of the US labor market. American Economic Review 96, 189–194.

Autor, D.H., Katz, L.F., Krueger, A.B., 1998. Computing inequality: have computers changed the labor market? Quarterly Journal of Economics 113, 1169–1213.

Autor, D., Houseman, S., 2005. Do temporary help jobs improve labor market outcomes for low-skilled workers? Evidence from random assignments. NBER Working Paper 11743.

Bagues, M.F., Labini, M.S., 2009. Do on-line labor market intermediaries matter? The impact of AlmaLaurea on the university-to-work transition. In: Autor, D.H. (Ed.), Studies of Labor Market Intermediation. University of Chicago Press.

Baker, G., 1992. Incentive contracts and performance measurement. Journal of Political Economy 100, 598–614.

Baker, G., Gibbons, R., Murphy, K.J., 1994a. Subjective performance measures in optimal incentive contracts. Quarterly Journal of Economics 109, 1125–1156.

Baker, G., Gibbs, M., Holmstrom, B., 1994b. The internal economics of the firm: evidence from personnel data. Quarterly Journal of Economics 109, 881–919.

Bandiera, O., Barankay, I., Rasul, I., 2009. Social connections and incentives in the workplace: evidence from personnel data. Econometrica 77, 1047–1094.

Barron, J.M., Berger, M.C., Black, D.A., 1997. Employer search, training, and vacancy duration. Economic Inquiry 35, 167–192.

Barron, J.M., Bishop, J., Dunkelberg, W.C., 1985. Employer search: the interviewing and hiring of new employees. Review of Economics and Statistics 67, 43–52.

Bartling, B., Fehr, E., Schmidt, K.M., 2009. Screening, competition, and job design: economic origins of good jobs. Working Paper, University of Munich.

Bayer, P., Topa, G., Ross, S., 2008. Place of work and place of residence: informal hiring networks and labor market outcomes. Journal of Political Economy 116, 1150–1196.

Beaverstock, J.V., Faulconbridge, J.R., Hall, S.J.E., 2010. Professionalization, legitimization and the creation of executive search markets in Europe. Journal of Economic Geography 10 (forthcoming).

Bebchuk, L.A., Fried, J.M., 2003. Executive compensation as an agency problem. Journal of Economic Perspectives 17, 71–92.

Bergman, N.K., Jenter, D., 2007. Employee sentiment and stock option compensation. Journal of Financial Economics 84, 667–712.

Berman, E., Bound, J., Griliches, Z., 1994. Changes in the demand for skilled labor within US manufacturing: evidence from the annual survey of manufacturers. Quarterly Journal of Economics 109, 367–397.

Bernhardt, D., 1995. Strategic promotion and compensation. Review of Economic Studies 62, 315–339.

Bernhardt, D., Scoones, D., 1993. Promotion, turnover, and preemptive wage offers. American Economic Review 83, 771–791.

Bertrand, M., Mullainathan, S., 2001. Are CEOs rewarded for luck? The ones without principals are. Quarterly Journal of Economics 116, 901–932.

Besanko, D., Dranove, D., Shanley, M., Schaefer, S., 2009. Economics of Strategy, 5th ed., Wiley.

Bloom, N., Van Reenen, J., 2007. Measuring and explaining management practices across firms and countries. Quarterly Journal of Economics 122, 1351–1408.

Bloom, N., Van Reenen, J., 2011. Human resource management and productivity. In: Ashenfelter, O., Card, D. (Eds.), Handbook of Labor Economics, vol. 4b. Elsevier, pp. 1697–1767.

Bollinger, C.R., Hotchkiss, J.L., 2003. The upside potential of hiring risky workers: evidence from the baseball industry. Journal of Labor Economics 21, 923–944.

Brencic, V., 2009a. Do employers respond to the costs of continued search? Oxford Bulletin of Economics and Statistics 71, 1–25.

Brencic, V., 2009b. Employers' hiring practices, employment protection, and costly search: a vacancy-level analysis. Labour Economics 16, 461–479.

Brencic, V., 2009c. Employers' search prior to exhaustion of advance notice period. Economics Letters 94, 266–270.

Brencic, V., Norris, J.B., 2009. Employers' online search: an empirical analysis. Industrial Relations 48, 684–709.

Bresnahan, T.F., Brynjolfsson, E., Hitt, L.M., 2002. Information technology, workplace organization, and the demand for skilled labor: firm-level evidence. Quarterly Journal of Economics 117, 339–376.

Bull, C., 1987. The existence of self-enforcing implicit contracts. Quarterly Journal of Economics 102, 147–160.

Bull, C., Ornati, O., Tedeschi, P., 1987. Search, hiring strategies, and labor market intermediaries. Journal of Labor Economics 5, S1–S17.

Burdett, K., Cunningham, E.J., 1998. Toward a theory of vacancies. Journal of Labor Economics 16, 445–478.

Burgess, S., Lane, J., Stevens, D., 1998. Hiring risky workers: some evidence. Journal of Economics and Management Strategy 7, 669–676.

Calvo-Armengol, A., Jackson, M.O., 2004. The effects of social networks on employment and inequality. American Economic Review 94, 426–454.

Cappelli, P., Hamori, M., 2006. Executive loyalty and employer attributes. IE Working Paper 06-10.

Card, D., DiNardo, J.E., 2002. Skill-biased technological change and rising wage inequality: some problems and puzzles. Journal of Labor Economics 20, 733–783.

Casella, A., Hanaki, N., 2006. Why personal ties cannot be bought. American Economic Review 96, 261–264.

Casella, A., Hanaki, N., 2008. Information channels in labor markets: on the resilience of referral hiring. Journal of Economic Behavior and Organization 66, 492–513.

Chan, W., 1996. External recruitment versus internal promotion. Journal of Labor Economics 14, 555–570.

Chevalier, J., Ellison, G., 1999. Career concerns of mutual fund managers. Quarterly Journal of Economics 114, 389–432.

Delfgaauw, J., Dur, R., 2007. Signaling and screening of workers' motivation. Journal of Economic Behavior and Organization 62, 605–624.

DeVaro, J., 2005. Employer recruitment strategies and the labor market outcomes of new hires. Economic Inquiry 43, 263–282.

DeVaro, J., 2006. Internal promotion competitions in firms. RAND Journal of Economics 37, 521–542.

DeVaro, J., 2008. The labor market effects of employer recruitment choice. European Economic Review 52, 283–314.

DeVaro, J., Fields, G., 2005. Waging the war for talent: do recruitment and screening strategies raise employee performance? Cornell ILR Working Paper 74.

DeVaro, J., Fields, G., 2008. Employer strategies for recruitment and screening: high-performance systems or diminishing returns? Cornell ILR Working Paper 73.

DeVaro, J., Kurtulus, F., 2010. An empirical analysis of risk, incentives, and the delegation of worker authority. Industrial and Labor Relations Review 63, 637–657.

DeVaro, J., Waldman, M., 2009. The signaling role of promotions: further theory and empirical evidence. Working Paper, Cornell University.

Devine, T.J., Kiefer, N.M., 1991. Empirical Labor Economics: The Search Approach. Oxford University Press, Oxford.

Edmans, A., Gabaix, X., 2009. Is CEO pay really inefficient? A survey of new optimal contracting theories. European Financial Management 15, 486–496.

Ellison, G., Glaeser, E.L., 1997. Geographic concentration in manufacturing industries: a dartboard approach. Journal of Political Economy 102, 889–927.

Ellison, G., Glaeser, E.L., 1999. The geographic concentration of industry: does natural advantage explain agglomeration? American Economic Review 89, 311–316.

Fallick, B., Fleischman, C.A., 2004. Employer-to-employer flows in the US labor market: the complete picture of gross worker flows. Federal Reserve Board Working Paper.

Fallick, B., Fleischman, C.A., Rebitzer, J.B., 2006. Job-hopping in Silicon Valley: some evidence concerning the microfoundations of a high-technology cluster. Review of Economics and Statistics 88, 472–481.

Fama, E., 1980. Agency problems and the theory of the firm. Journal of Political Economy 88, 288–307.

Farber, H.S., 1999. Mobility and stability: the dynamics of job change in labor markets. In: Ashenfelter, O., Card, D. (Eds.), Handbook of Labor Economics, vol. 3. North-Holland, Amsterdam.

Farber, H.S., Gibbons, R., 1996. Learning and wage dynamics. Quarterly Journal of Economics 111, 1007–1047.

Fee, C.E., Hadlock, C.J., 2003. Raids, rewards and reputations in the market for managerial talent. Review of Financial Studies 16, 1315–1357.

Fernandez, R.M., Castilla, E.J., Moore, P., 2000. Social capital at work: networks and employment at a phone center. American Journal of Sociology 105, 1288–1356.

Fernandez, R.M., Weinberg, N., 1997. Sifting and sorting: personal contacts and hiring in a retail bank. American Sociological Review 62, 883–902.

Finlay, W., Coverdill, J.E., 1998. Fit and skill in employee selection: insights from a study of headhunters. Qualitative Sociology 21, 105–127.

Freedman, M.L., 2009. Preference-based Sorting and Matching in Industrial Clusters. Cornell University.

Freeman, R.B., Kleiner, M.M., 2005. The last American shoe manufacturers: changing the method of pay to survive foreign competition. Industrial Relations 44, 307–330.

Gabaix, X., Landier, A., 2008. Why has CEO pay increased so much? Quarterly Journal of Economics 123, 49–100.

Garicano, L., Hubbard, T.N., 2007. Managerial leverage is limited by the extent of the market: hierarchies, specialization, and the utilization of lawyers' human capital. Journal of Law and Economics 50, 1–43.

Garicano, L., Hubbard, T.N., 2009. Specialization, firms, and markets: the division of labor within and between law firms. Journal of Law, Economics and Organization 25, 339–371.

Gayle, G.-L., Miller, R.A., 2009. Has moral hazard become a more important factor in managerial compensation? American Economic Review 99, 1740–1769.

Geel, R., Mure, J., Backes-Gellner, U., 2009. Specificity of occupational training and occupational mobility: an empirical study based on Lazear's skill-weights approach. Working Paper, University of Zurich.

Gibbons, R., Katz, L.F., 1991. Layoffs and lemons. Journal of Labor Economics 9, 351–380.

Gibbons, R., Roberts, J., 2010. Incentives in organizations. In: Gibbons, R., Roberts, J. (Eds.), Handbook of Organizational Economics, North-Holland, Amsterdam.

Giuliano, L., Levine, D.I., Leonard, J., 2009. Manager race and the race of new hires. Journal of Labor Economics 27, 589–632.

Gorter, C., Nijkamp, P., Rietveld, P., 1996. Employers recruitment behaviour and vacancy duration: an empirical analysis for the dutch labour market. Applied Economics 28, 1463–1474.

Granovetter, M.S., 1974. Getting a Job: A Study of Contracts and Careers. Harvard University Press, Cambridge, MA.

Greenwald, B.C., 1986. Adverse selection in the labour market. Review of Economic Studies 53, 325–347.

Groysberg, B., Lee, L.-E., Nanda, A., 2008. Can they take it with them? The portability of star knowledge workers' performance. Management Science 54, 1213–1230.

Hadass, Y.S., 2004. The effect of internet recruiting on the matching of workers and employers. Working Paper, Harvard University.

Hassink, W., Russo, G., 2008. Wage differences between internal and external candidates. International Journal of Manpower 29, 715–730.

Hayes, R.M., Oyer, P., Schaefer, S., 2006. Co-worker complementarity and the stability of top management teams. Journal of Law, Economics and Organization 14, 182–212.

Hayes, R.M., Schaefer, S., 2000. Implicit contracts and the explanatory power of top executive compensation for future performance. RAND Journal of Economics 31, 273–293.

Hayes, R.M., Schaefer, S., 2009. CEO pay and the Lake Wobegon effect. Journal of Financial Economics 94, 280–290.

Hendricks, W., DeBrock, L., Koenker, R., 2003. Uncertainty, hiring and subsequent performance: The NFL draft. Journal of Labor Economics 21, 857–886.

Holmstrom, B., 1979. Moral hazard and observability. Bell Journal of Economics 10, 74–91.

Holmstrom, B., 1982. Moral hazard in teams. Bell Journal of Economics 13, 324–340.

Holmstrom, B., Milgrom, P.R., 1987. Aggregation and linearity in the provision of intertemporal incentives. Econometrica 55, 308–328.

Holmstrom, B., Milgrom, P.R., 1991. Multi-task principal-agent analyses: incentive contracts, asset ownership and job design. Journal of Law, Economics and Organization 7, 524–552.

Holzer, H.J., 1987. Hiring procedures in the firm: their economic determinants and outcomes. NBER Working Paper 2185.

Huson, M.R., Malatesta, P.H., Parrino, R., 2004. Managerial succession and firm performance. Journal of Financial Economics 74, 237–275.

Ichniowski, C., Shaw, K., Prennushi, G., 1997. The effects of human resource management practices on productivity. American Economic Review 86, 291–313.

Ionnides, Y.M., Loury, L.D., 2004. Job information networks, neighborhood effects, and inequality. Journal of Economic Literature 42, 1056–1093.

Janssen, M.C.W., 2002. Catching hipos: screening, wages, and competing for a job. Oxford Economic Papers 54, 321–333.

Jenter, D., Kanaan, F., 2011. CEO turnover and relative performance evaluation. Journal of Finance (forthcoming).

Jovanovic, B., 1979a. Firm specific capital and turnover. Journal of Political Economy 87, 1246–1260.

Jovanovic, B., 1979b. Job matching and the theory of turnover. Journal of Political Economy 87, 972–990.

Kahn, L.B., 2009. Asymmetric Information Between Employers. Yale University.

Kaplan, S.N., Klebanov, M.M., Sorensen, M., 2011. Which CEO characteristics and abilities matter. Journal of Finance (forthcoming).

Kaplan, S.N., Minton, B.A., 2009. How has CEO Turnover Changed? University of Chicago and Ohio State University.

Katz, L.F., Autor, D.H., 1999. Changes in the wage structure and earnings inequality. In: Ashenfelter, O., Card, D. (Eds.), Handbook of Labor Economics, vol. 3. North-Holland, Amsterdam.

Khurana, R., 2002. Market triads: a theoretical and empirical analysis of market intermediation. Journal for the Theory of Social Behaviour 32, 239–262.

Kim, S., 2003. The impact of research productivity on early retirement of university professors. Industrial Relations 42, 106–125.

Kletzer, L.G., 1998. Job displacement. Journal of Economic Perspectives 12, 115–136.

Krashinsky, H., 2002. Evidence on adverse selection and establishment size in the labor market. Industrial and Labor Relations Review 56, 84–96.

Kugler, A.D., 2003. Employee referrals and efficiency wages. Labour Economics 10, 531–556.

Kuhn, P., Shen, K., 2009. Employers' preferences for gender, age, height and beauty: direct evidence. Working Paper, University of California Santa Barbara.

Kuhn, P., Skuterud, M., 2004. Internet job search and unemployment durations. American Economic Review 94, 218–232.

Kuhnen, C.M., Zwiebel, J., 2009. Executive Pay, Hidden Compensation and Managerial Entrenchment. Northwestern and Stanford Universities.

Larkin, I., 2007. The Cost of High-Powered Incentives: Employee Gaming in Enterprise Software Sales. Harvard Business School.

Lazear, E.P., 1979. Why is there mandatory retirement? Journal of Political Economy 87, 1261–1284.

Lazear, E.P., 1986. Raids and offer matching. Research in Labor Economics 8, 141–165.

Lazear, E.P., 1998. Hiring risky workers. In: Ohashi, I., Tachibanaki, T. (Eds.), Internal Labor Market, Incentives and Employment. St. Martin's, New York.

Lazear, E.P., 2000. Performance pay and productivity. American Economic Review 90, 1346–1361.

Lazear, E.P., 2004. Output-based pay: incentives, retention or sorting? Research in Labor Economics 23, 1–25.

Lazear, E.P., 2009. Firm-specific human capital: a skill-weights approach. Journal of Political Economy 117, 914–940.

Lazear, E.P., Oyer, P., 2010. Personnel economics. In: Gibbons, R., Roberts, J. (Eds.), Handbook of Organizational Economics, North-Holland, Amsterdam.

Lazear, E.P., Rosen, S., 1981. Rank-order tournaments as optimum labor contracts. Journal of Political Economy 89, 841–864.

Manning, A., 2000. Pretty vacant: recruitment in low-wage labor markets. Oxford Bulletin of Economics and Statistics 62, 747–770.

Milgrom, P., Oster, S., 1987. Job discrimination, market forces, and the invisibility hypothesis. Quarterly Journal of Economics 102, 453–476.

Milgrom, P.R., Roberts, J., 1990. The economics of modern manufacturing: technology, strategy and organization. American Economic Review 80, 511–528.

Milgrom, P.R., Roberts, J., 1995. Complementarities and fit: strategy, structure, and organizational change in manufacturing. Journal of Accounting and Economics 19, 179–208.

Montgomery, J.D., 1991. Social networks and labor-market outcomes: toward an economic analysis. American Economic Review 81, 1408–1418.

Mortensen, D.T., Pissarides, C.A., 1999. New developments in models of search in the labor market. In: Ashenfelter, O., Card, D. (Eds.), Handbook of Labor Economics, vol. 3. North-Holland, Amsterdam.

Mosca, M., Pastore, F., 2009. Wage effects of recruitment methods: The case of the Italian social service sector. In: Destefanis, S., Musella, M. (Eds.), Paid and Unpaid Labour in Social Utility Services. Physica-Verlag, Heidelberg.

Murphy, K.J., Zabojnik, J., 2006. Managerial capital and the market for CEOs. Working Paper, USC Marshall School of Business.

Nakamura, A.O., Shaw, K., Freedman, R.B., Nakamura, E., Pyman, A., 2009. Jobs online. In: Autor, D.H. (Ed.), Studies of Labor Market Intermediation. University of Chicago Press.

Oi, W.Y., 1962. Labor as a quasi-fixed factor. Journal of Political Economy 70, 538–555.

Oyer, P., 1998. Fiscal year ends and nonlinear incentive contracts: the effect on business seasonality. Quarterly Journal of Economics 113, 149–185.

Oyer, P., 2004. Why do firms use incentives that have no incentive effects? Journal of Finance 59, 1619–1640.

Oyer, P., Schaefer, S., 2000. Layoffs and litigation. RAND Journal of Economics 31, 345–358.

Oyer, P., Schaefer, S., 2002. Litigation costs and returns to experience. American Economic Review 92, 683–705.

Oyer, P., Schaefer, S., 2005. Why do some firms give stock options to all employees? An empirical examination of alternative theories. Journal of Financial Economics 76, 99–133.

Oyer, P., Schaefer, S., 2006. Costs of broad-based stock option plans. Journal of Financial Intermediation 15, 511–534.

Oyer, P., Schaefer, S., 2010, Firm/employee matching: an industry study of American lawyers. Working Paper, University of Utah.

Parrino, R., 1997. CEO turnover and outside succession: a cross-sectional analysis. Journal of Financial Economics 46, 165–197.

Pencavel, J., 2001. The response of employees to severance incentives: the University of California's faculty, 1991-94. Journal of Human Resources 36, 58–84.

Pinkston, J., 2009. A model of asymmetric employer learning with testable implications. Review of Economic Studies 76, 367–394.

Prendergast, C., 1999. The provision of incentives in firms. Journal of Economic Literature 37, 7–63.

Prendergast, C., 2002a. The tenuous trade-off between risk and incentives. Journal of Political Economy 110, 1071–1102.

Prendergast, C., 2002b. Uncertainty and incentives. Journal of Labor Economics 110, 1071–1102.

Prendergast, C., 2007. The motivation and bias of bureaucrats. American Economic Review 97, 180–196.

Prendergast, C., 2009. Contracts and conflict in organizations. Working Paper, University of Chicago.

Rees, A., 1966. Information channels in labor markets: on the resilience of referral hiring. American Economic Review 56, 559–566.

Rosen, S., 1982. Authority, control and the distribution of earnings. Bell Journal of Economics 13, 311–323.

Russo, G., Gorter, C., Schettkat, R., 2001. Searching, hiring and labour market conditions. Labour Economics 8, 553–571.

Russo, G., Rietveld, P., Nijkamp, P., Gorter, C., 2000. Recruitment channel use and applicant arrival: an empirical analysis. Empirical Economics 25, 673–697.

Saloner, G., 1985. Old boy networks as screening mechanisms. Journal of Labor Economics 3, 255–267.

Salop, J., Salop, S., 1976. Self-selection and turnover in the labor market. Quarterly Journal of Economics 90, 619–627.

Sattinger, M., 1993. Assignment models of the distribution of earnings. Journal of Economic Literature 31, 831–880.

Schaefer, S., 1998. The dependence of pay-performance sensitivity on the size of the firm. Review of Economics and Statistics 80, 436–443.

Schonberg, U., 2007. Testing for asymmetric employer learning. Journal of Labor Economics 25, 651–692.

Scoones, D., Bernhardt, D., 1998. Promotion, turnover, and discretionary human capital acquisition. Journal of Labor Economics 16, 122–141.

Shearer, B., 2004. Piece rates, fixed wages and incentives: evidence from a field experiment. Review of Economic Studies 71, 513–534.

Simon, C.J., Warner, J.T., 1992. Matchmaker, matchmaker: the effect of old boy networks on job match quality, earnings, and tenure. Journal of Labor Economics 10, 306–330.

Spence, M., 1973. Job market signaling. Quarterly Journal of Economics 87, 355–374.

Stevenson, B., 2009. The internet and job search. In: Autor, D.H. (Ed.), Studies of Labor Market Intermediation. University of Chicago Press.

Tervio, M., 2008. The difference that CEOs make: an assignment model approach. American Economic Review 98, 642–668.

The Economist, 2006. The rich, the poor and the growing gap between them. June 17.

Tranaes, T., 2001. Raiding opportunities and unemployment. Journal of Labor Economics 19, 773–798.

Van den Steen, E., 2005. Organizational beliefs and managerial vision. Journal of Law, Economics and Organization 21, 256–283.

Van Ommeren, J., Russo, G., 2008. Firm recruitment behaviour: sequential or non-sequential search? IZA Discussion Paper 4008.

van Ours, J., Ridder, G., 1991. Cyclical variation in vacancy durations and vacancy flows. European Economic Review 35, 1143–1155.

van Ours, J., Ridder, G., 1992. Vacancies and the recruitment of new employees. Journal of Labor Economics 10, 138–155.

van Ours, J., Ridder, G., 1993. Vacancy duration: search or selection? Oxford Bulletin of Economics and Statistics 55, 187–198.

Waldman, M., 1984. Job assignments, signaling and efficiency. RAND Journal of Economics 15, 255–267.

Waldman, M., 1990. Up-or-out contracts: a signaling perspective. Journal of Labor Economics 8, 230–250.

Wheeler, C., 2001. Search, sorting, and urban agglomeration. Journal of Labor Economics 19, 879–899.

A

M